1987
EDITION OF
J. K. LASSER'S
YOUR
INCOME TAX

Prepared by the J. K. LASSER TAX INSTITUTE

Editor: BERNARD GREISMAN, *Member of the New York Bar*

PRENTICE HALL PRESS — NEW YORK

PUBLISHER'S NOTE: YOUR INCOME TAX *is published in recognition of the great need for a clarification of the income tax laws for the millions of men and women who must make out returns. We believe the research and interpretation by the* J. K. LASSER TAX INSTITUTE *to be authoritative and of service to taxpayers. We acknowledge the editorial contribution of Elliott Eiss, member of the New York Bar, and the assistance of Katherine Torak and Elizabeth McKenna.*

Guide to New Tax Law

Since 1980, Congress has passed four major tax acts including the latest 1986 Tax Act. The new act repeals tax-saving provisions of the recent tax acts as well as those passed decades ago. In return, the general public is promised tax simplification and lower taxes within a two-bracket rate framework which will not take effect until 1988. *Overall* the new law generally favors the Treasury as evidenced by—

Repeal of long-term capital gain deduction, dividend exclusion, exclusion for prizes and awards for scientific or artistic accomplishments, investment credit, political contributions credit, income averaging, two-earner married couple deduction, charitable deduction for non-itemizers, exclusion for unemployment compensation, exclusion for cancellation of debt on depreciable business property and the reserve method of writing off bad debts.

Restrictions on investment and tax shelter loss deductions, family income splitting, IRA deductions, scholarship benefits, salary reduction (401(k)) plans, business fiscal years, business meal deductions, itemized miscellaneous (nonbusiness-investment) expenses,

Increasing tax penalties and the estimated tax percentage to 90%.

Allowing the IRS to pay 1% lower interest on refunds than charged on tax deficiencies.

Reducing the foreign earned income exclusion from $80,000 to $70,000 after 1986.

Important. Most new law provisions do not affect the law applying to the preparation of your 1986 tax return except in the following cases.

Changes Effective in 1986

Investment credit repeal. The credit is generally repealed for investments after 1985, but transition rules allow the credit for certain property contracted for by the end of 1985. Credits on transition property and credit carryovers are subject to a 17.5% reduction in 1987, 35% in 1988. *See* the Supplement for details of the transition rule.

General business credit. Starting in 1986, the overall limit for the general business credit is reduced to $25,000 plus 75% of tax liability in excess of $25,000 instead of 85% of the excess as under prior law. The limit applies to the sum of the investment credit, if available for 1986, the targeted

jobs credit, alcohol fuels credit and employee stock ownership (ESOP) credit. The ESOP credit is generally repealed for compensation paid after 1986. Further, the credit for increasing research and development expenses is made subject to the general business credit limit starting in 1986, with the research credit rate reduced from 25% to 20%; after 1986, more favorable credit rules will apply to expenditures for basic research.

The targeted jobs credit is reduced for workers hired after 1985. The 1986 credit is 40% instead of 50% of the first $6,000 of wages paid in the first year. The 25% credit for second-year wages is repealed.

Spousal IRAs. If only one spouse works, the maximum IRA contribution deduction on a joint return may be up $2,250. Under the new law, the $2,250 limit also applies in 1986 where a spouse has earned income of less than $250 and elects to be treated as if he or she had no compensation.

Three-year cost recovery rule for retirement benefits. Under prior law, retired employees who in the first three years receive annuity payments at least equal to their contributions did not have to pay tax until all the contributions were recovered. *See* ¶ 7.101. This three-year recovery rule is repealed for annuities starting after July 1, 1986. Under the new law, income is reported according to regular annuity rules. *See* the Supplement.

Fringe benefits. The exclusions for educational assistance and group legal services, both of which expired at the end of 1985, are extended through 1987. Further, the cap on annual excludable educational assistance is increased from $5,000 to $5,260.

Effective for tax years after 1986, a $5,000 ceiling ($2,500 for married individuals filing separately) is placed on the exclusion for dependent care assistance provided under a qualified employer plan. Under prior law, the exclusion could not exceed the employee's earned income, and there was no dollar limitation.

Lost savings accounts. A new election allows a casualty loss deduction instead of a bad debt deduction. Election is available for taxable years after 1982, *see* discussion on itemized deductions.

Interest exclusion on insurance installments. The $1,000 interest exclusion for surviving spouses will not be allowed where the insured dies after the date of the enactment of the new law.

Allocation of purchase price on sale of business. Buyers and sellers of a business are required to allocate the sale proceeds among the sold assets using the Treasury's "residual method." The new rule generally applies to transactions after May 6, 1986.

Amortization of bond premium. If you amortize bond premiums on bonds issued after September 27, 1985, you may have to use a constant yield method of writeoff, *see* Supplement for further details.

New Tax Rates

The new law sets two bracket rates of 15% and 28% which become effective in 1988. In 1987, an interim five-bracket rate structure applies. The lower 15% bracket in 1988 may not benefit middle and high income taxpayers. To eliminate the 15% tax benefit built into the tax schedule, a 5% surcharge will be imposed on taxable income within a specific range. Further, an additional 5% surcharge will also eliminate the benefit of personal exemptions. On income subject to these surcharges, you will in effect be subject to a tax rate of 33% instead of 28%. Tax schedules are on page VII.

Whether or not the new tax rates will give you a tax savings depends on the effect of the new law on the amount of your taxable income. You may wind up with a larger tax if your taxable income is increased by the loss of prior tax benefits. A worksheet for tax liability comparisons is on page VIII.

Dependency Exemptions Increased

In	Each exemption will be
1987	$1,900
1988	1,950
1989	2,000

Anyone who is claimed as an exemption by another taxpayer is not allowed a personal exemption. The extra exemption for the elderly and the blind is also not allowed.

Example—
You claim your child as an exemption. In 1987, he files a tax return to report income. He may not claim a personal exemption on his tax return.

Exemption phaseout. In 1988, exemptions will be phased out for single individuals with taxable incomes of $89,560 or more; for married couples filing jointly, the phaseout begins at taxable income of $149,250. For every $10,920 of taxable income in 1988 above $89,560 or $149,250, one personal exemption is totally phased out. Thus, if a married couple claims four exemptions on a 1988 joint return, the four $1,950 personal exemptions will be completely phased out at taxable income of $192,930. Beginning in 1989, the income range subject to the phaseout rule will be adjusted for inflation and the $10,920 phaseout amount per exemption will be increased to $11,200.

Tax-free Scholarship Restrictions

Starting in 1987, scholarships and fellowships granted after August 16, 1986 are tax free only for degree candidates, and only to the extent the grant pays for tuition and course-related fees, books, supplies and equipment. Amounts for room, board and incidental expenses are taxable. Further, no tax-free exclusion is allowed for grants or tuition reductions that pay for teaching or other services. No exclusion is allowed for Federal grants where the recipient agrees to future work with the Federal government.

Standard Deduction Reinstated

The new law replaces the zero bracket amount with the following standard deduction amounts:

In	Married (joint)	Single	Head of Household
1987*	$3,760	$2,540	$2,540
1988	5,000	3,000	4,400

*If you are 65 or over or blind in 1987, take the standard deduction amounts listed for 1988.

For each married spouse, an extra $600 may be added to the standard deduction for being 65 or over or blind. If you are single, an extra $750 may be added for being 65 or over or blind. If both elderly and blind, the extra deduction is $1,200 for married persons and $1,500 for unmarried persons. Thus, in 1987, a single taxpayer over age 65 will be allowed a $3,750 deduction ($3,000 plus $750). Starting in 1989, the 1988 deduction amounts and the extra $600 and $750 deduction for the aged or blind will be adjusted for inflation.

You will claim the standard deduction only if your itemized deductions for charitable donations, certain local taxes, interest, allowable casualty loss, miscellaneous expenses, and medical expenses are less than the standard deduction.

Example—
You are single and your adjusted gross income is $15,000. Your itemized deductions total $2,000. In 1986, your zero bracket amount is $2,480; thus you do not claim excess itemized deductions. You figure your tax after deducting a personal exemption of $1,080 from your adjusted income.

Adjusted gross income	$15,000
Less exemption	1,080
Taxable income	$13,920

The zero bracket amount is built into tax tables from which you take the tax applied to taxable incomes of $13,920.

In 1987, you deduct the standard deduction from adjusted gross income.

Adjusted gross income	$15,000
Less standard deduction	2,540
	$12,460
Less exemption	1,900
Taxable income	$10,560

A special standard deduction rule applies to dependents. Under pre-1987 law, a dependent may use the zero bracket amount to offset earned income but not unearned income. In 1987, a dependent may use up to $500 of the standard deduction to offset unearned income such as interest or dividends.

Alternative Minimum Tax Increased

Starting in 1987, the AMT rate is increased from 20% to 21%. The AMT exemption amounts of $40,000 on joint returns, $30,000 for unmarried individuals and $20,000 for married persons filing separately, will be reduced by 25 cents for each $1 that alternative minimum taxable income exceeds these amounts: $150,000 for joint filers, $112,500 for individuals and $75,000 for married couples filing separately. The effect of the exemption phaseout is to apply roughly a 26% tax for those with incomes in the phaseout range.

Passive losses from tax shelters and other investments plus certain passive farming losses may not be used to reduce alternative minimum taxable income. The full passive loss is denied for AMT purposes although for purposes of the regular income tax, the limits on passive losses will be phased in over five years.

After 1986, the untaxed appreciation on charitable contributions of property and interest paid on tax-exempt bonds for non-essential private functions issued after August 7, 1986 will be AMT preference items.

Long-Term Capital Gain Taxed As Ordinary Income

The 60% exclusion for long-term capital gain is repealed for years beginning after December 31, 1986. Profit on the sale of a capital asset will be taxed at the same rate as other income, with this exception: In 1987, the maximum rate on long-term gains will be 28%, even though the maximum rate for other income will be 38.5%.

Capital losses will be deductible first against capital gains and then against up to $3,000 of other income. Net long-term losses will no longer have to be reduced by 50% before being deducted against other income.

Homeowners age 55 or over will still be allowed to elect the $125,000 gain exclusion. For other homeowners, gain will still be deferred on a home sale if a reinvestment in another residence is made within two years.

Incentive stock options. Options granted after 1986 will no longer have to be exercised in the order granted. After 1986, an employer may not grant incentive options that are first exercisable during a single year to the extent the value of the stock (when the options are granted) exceeds $100,000.

Year-end stock sales may not be deferred to next year. Under pre-1987 law, it is possible under the installment sale rule to execute a sale of stock on the public exchange at the end of the year and defer the reporting of gain until the next year. Starting in 1987, gains are recognized on the day the trade is executed, even though cash is not received until the next year. Under both prior and new law, losses are deductible in the year of sale.

Itemized Deductions Reduced

Starting in 1987, the new law restricts itemized deductions as follows:

Medical expenses. The ceiling is increased from 5% to 7.5% of adjusted gross income. Thus in 1987, only medical expenses exceeding 7.5% of adjusted gross income are deductible. Handicapped individuals may treat as deductible medical expenses the cost of making structural changes to their residence such as adding exit ramps, modifying doorways, and installing railings and support bars. Such improvements are treated for deduction purposes as not increasing the value of the house.

Interest deduction. Restrictions limit deductions for interest on consumer and investment loans and are explained in the paragraph Interest Deduction Cutback.

Sales tax. A deduction for sales taxes is barred. Sales tax incurred in a business or investment activity is treated as part of the cost of the asset for depreciation purposes. State and local income taxes and real and personal property taxes remain deductible.

Miscellaneous deductions. Starting in 1987, a 2% floor applies to deductions for *unreimbursed* travel costs, meals and entertainment expenses and educational and home office expenses, union or professional association dues, work clothes, costs of looking for a new job, tax preparation fees, appraisal fees related to casualty losses and charitable property contributions, and investment expenses such as sale deposit rentals and fees to investment counselors. The 2% floor will not apply to miscellaneous expenses such as gambling losses up to gambling income, estate tax attributable to income in respect of a decedent, the deduction for repayment of amounts held under a claim of right, impairment-related work expenses for handicapped employees, amortizable bond premium, certain costs of cooperative housing corporations, interest expenses of short-sales, and certain terminated annuity payments. Further details on deducting travel and entertainment expenses are covered in the section Restrictions on Business Travel and Entertainment Expenses.

Casualty losses. Starting in 1987, a nonbusiness casualty loss deduction may not be claimed for insured property unless you file a timely insurance claim. Only the uninsured loss is deductible.

Moving expenses. Under pre-1987 law, moving expenses to a new job location are deductible whether or not you itemize deductions. Starting in 1987, moving expenses are treated as itemized deductions but are not subject to the 2% ceiling.

Performing artists with low income may report their performing art income and expenses as independent contractors if he or she has (1) two or more employers in the performing arts during the tax year, (2) performing art expenses exceed 10% of gross income and (3) adjusted gross income (before deducting these expenses) does not exceed $16,000. Independent contractor status will allow a deduction of such expenses before claiming itemized deductions or the standard deduction.

Adoption expenses. Starting in 1987, the itemized deduction for adoption expenses will not be allowed.

Casualty loss deduction for deposits lost in bank failures. You may claim a bad debt deduction for a loss of a bank deposit in the year there is no reasonable prospect of recovery from an insolvent or bankrupt bank. The loss is claimed as a short-term capital loss unless the deposit was made in your business. Under a new law, you have another choice for taxable years after 1982. You may elect to take a casualty loss deduction for the year in which the loss can be reasonably estimated. The loss is subject to the 10% adjusted gross income floor for casualty losses. Choose the election that gives the greater tax reduction. The election is generally not allowed to stockholders or officers of the bank.

Interest Deduction Cutbacks

Mortgage interest. Interest on debt secured by a first and/or second home is generally deductible. However, if a loan made after August 16, 1986 exceeds the purchase price of the home plus improvement costs, the loan proceeds must be used for educational or medical purposes in order to claim an interest deduction after 1986.

Example—
The cost of your house is $100,000 subject to a mortgage of $25,000. You may make a new mortgage loan up to $75,000. Interest is deductible regardless of how the proceeds are used. However, assume the value of the home is $125,000 and you borrow an additional $25,000. Interest on the additional loan is deductible if used for home improvements, medical or educational costs.

Consumer interest. Deductions for consumer interest, such as credit card charges and installment interest charges, will be reduced and phased out over five years. In 1987, you may deduct 65% of consumer interest payments; in 1988, 40%; in 1989, 20%; in 1990, 10%. After 1990, no consumer interest will be deductible. The term consumer interest covers a broad range of interest expense such as interest on tax deficiencies and educational loans. The phase-out applies to consumer interest paid after 1986 even if the debt was incurred before 1987.

Investment interest will be deductible only to the extent of net investment income after 1990. Before then, the first $10,000 of investment interest exceeding investment income is partially deductible: 65% in 1987, 40% in 1988, 20% in 1989, 10% in 1990. Disallowed interest may be carried forward if there is investment income in excess of net investment interest in the later year. In calculating net investment income, interest expenses and income attributable to tax shelters and other passive activities subject to the loss limitation rules will be disregarded. However, if a loss is allowed under the five-year phaseout rule for passive losses, the loss will reduce investment income for purposes of figuring the investment interest deduction.

Restrictions On Business Travel And Entertainment Expenses

The new law cuts back on deductions for business entertainment and travel expenses and the way such expenses, if deductible, are claimed on your tax return.

Restrictive tests for business meals. Under 1986 law, deductions for business meals are not subject to the requirements that business discussions take place. Starting in 1987, meal costs are deductible only if bona fide business discussion occurs during or directly preceding or following the meal. This discussion requirement does not apply when you are away from home on a business trip and eating alone. No deduction is allowed for meals during which investment rather than business interests are discussed.

80% deduction limit. Only 80% of the cost of deductible expenses for meals and entertainment are deductible. This 80% rule also applies to meal costs on business trips away from home. It does not apply to certain convention and business banquets, company summer outings or holiday parties, promotion events to the general public and costs of attending a sporting event where the proceeds of the event go to a charity.

Tax return restrictions. Under 1986 law, job expenses (travel and entertainment) are deductible as follows:

From gross income. Expenses deductible before claiming itemized deductions are sometimes described as "above the line" deductions, including travel expenses away from home, local transportation expenses, and reimbursed job expenses.

From adjusted gross income. Expenses deductible as miscellaneous expenses included unreimbursed entertainment expenses as well as out-of-pocket costs for work clothes, and job education costs.

Starting in 1987, *unreimbursed* travel expenses are no longer deductible by employees above the line from gross income. They are treated as miscellaneous deductions and subject to the 2% floor.

Deductions for business travel on ocean liners or cruise ships are limited to double the highest Federal per diem amount allowed to government employees traveling away from home in the U.S.

Family Income Shifting

Shifting income to children under 14 will no longer accomplish substantial income tax savings. Starting in 1987, investment income of a child under age 14 in excess of $1,000 is taxed to the child at the parent's top marginal rate. Children who have reached age 14 by the close of a taxable year are not subject to this rule. In a last minute change, Congress dropped the distinction between income from property transferred by a parent and income from property transferred by another person mentioned in ¶33.00. Under earlier House and Senate versions, income from property transferred from persons other than a parent would *not* have been subject to the tax at the parent's marginal rate.

A child claimed as a dependent by a parent or other taxpayer may not claim a personal exemption after 1986.

With the reduction of tax rates, the spread between the high and low tax rates is narrowed. As a result, the overall after tax saving of income splitting is reduced. In the 28% bracket, $1,000 after taxes leaves $720; in the 15% bracket, $850. Under prior law where the top tax bracket may have been as high as 50%, the overall saving was substantially greater.

Tax-Savings For 10-Year Trusts Curtailed

10-year (Clifford) trusts have been widely used to shift income to relatives in lower tax brackets. Where a trust met the 10-year exception, trust income was taxed to the beneficiary, usually a minor child. Another type of trust used for income splitting was the spousal remainder trust set up for less than 10 years. It allowed income shifting to a child beneficiary when the trust property went to the grantor's spouse after the trust period ends.

Under the new law, both types of trust may no longer be used to shift income to the income beneficiary. The 10-year exception for grantor trusts is repealed. The grantor of a grantor trust is taxed on income of the trust. A trust is treated as a grantor trust where the grantor has a reversionary interest (at the time of the transfer) of more than 5% of the value of the property transferred to the trust. Spousal remainder trusts are neutralized as tax saving techniques by a new law treating the grantor as holding a reversionary interest held by his spouse if the spouse is living with the grantor.

The new rules apply to trust transfers made after March 1, 1986. An exception applies to the 10-year trusts created pursuant to a binding property settlement entered into before March 2, 1986 which required the taxpayer to establish a grantor trust.

Status of prior 10-year trusts. Trusts created before the effective date continue to shift income to the income beneficiary. However, tax savings are nullified for trust beneficiaries under the age of 14. Unearned income over $1,000 of a child under 14 is taxed to the child at the top marginal rate of the parents.

Pre-March 1, 1986 10-year trusts will continue to shift income and provide tax savings to trust beneficiaries 14 or over.

Tax rates for trusts and estates. For taxable years beginning after December 31, 1987, the first $5,000 of retained income of a trust or estate will be taxed at a 15% rate, with excess income taxed at a 28% rate. The benefit of the 15% bracket will be phased out between $13,000 and $26,000 of taxable income.

Earned Income Credit Increased

For 1986, the maximum credit is $550. In 1987, the credit is 14% of the first $5,714 of earned income, for a maximum credit of $800. These amounts may be increased by an inflation factor. The credit starts to phase out at adjusted gross income of $6,500 and is eliminated at $14,500. In 1988, the phase-out begins at $9,000 and ends at $17,000.

Tax Shelter Losses Restricted

Starting in 1987, investors may not generally deduct from other income losses from tax shelters and businesses in which they do not "materially" participate. Such deductions may only offset income from shelters and other passive business interests. Similarly, tax credits from passive activities will be limited to the tax allocable to such activities. Disallowed losses and credits are suspended and carried forward to the next taxable year, where they may be used only against passive income. Any remaining suspended loss may be deducted when the investor's interest is sold. A phase-in for loss deductions is allowed where the investment and activity started by the enactment date of the new law or there was a binding contract as of August 16, 1986 to acquire assets for the activity. For other interests, the limitation on losses will take full effect starting in 1987. Under the phase-in, 35% of passive losses in excess of passive income will be disallowed in 1987, 60% in 1988, 80% in 1989, 90% in 1990 and in 1991 and later years, no passive losses may be claimed against other income.

The above restrictive rule does not apply to owners of "working" interests in oil or gas property who must forego limited liability. Further, owners of rental property may deduct up to $25,000 in losses (and credits under a deduction equivalent formula) if they are actively involved in management decisions. However, the $25,000 loss allowance is phased out by 50% of adjusted gross income above $100,000 so that this rental exception may not be claimed by owners with adjusted gross incomes of $150,000 or more.

IRA Cutbacks and Other Retirement Benefit Changes

Deductions for IRA contributions after 1986 will be cut back or eliminated for many taxpayers and the rules made more complicated.

No plan coverage. For taxable years after 1986, if you are not an active participant in an employer plan, you may deduct IRA contributions of up to $2,000, as under current law. If you are married, the current deduction rules apply if neither spouse is an active participant in an employer plan. The maximum contribution remains $2,000 per working spouse, $2,250 if there is only one working spouse.

Employer plan coverage. As an unmarried person covered by an employer plan, you may claim a full IRA deduction after 1986 if your adjusted gross income is below $25,000. If you are married filing jointly where either spouse is covered by an employer plan, you may deduct IRA contributions if joint adjusted gross income is below $40,000. The deduction is phased out for singles with adjusted gross income of more than

$25,000 but less than $35,000, and for couples filing jointly with adjusted gross income of more than $40,000 but less than $50,000. No deduction is allowed for taxpayers with adjusted gross incomes exceeding these ceilings unless they are not participants in an employer plan.

To the extent deductible IRA contributions are not allowed, a nondeductible contribution may be made. Even though you may not deduct an IRA contribution, there is this advantage. Income earned on an IRA account accumulates tax free until withdrawn. You may be able to withdraw the nondeductible contribution without tax at any time.

Starting in 1987, IRA investments may be made in gold or silver coins issued by the U.S. government. Under current law, IRA investments may not be made in metals or other collectibles such as coins or stamps.

IRA distributions after 1986 made before age 59½, disability or death will generally remain subject to a 10% penalty. However, withdrawals of nondeductible contributions will not be subject to the penalty. Further, no penalty will be imposed for payments before age 59½ that are part of an annuity for life or the joint lives of the taxpayer and a beneficiary.

Lump-sum retirement distributions. A lump-sum distribution in 1986 qualifies for 10-year averaging under prior law rules. The new law repeals 10-year averaging after 1986 for taxpayers who were under the age of 50 as of January 1, 1986. They may elect five-year averaging after they reach age 59½. This means that if a person who was under age 50 as of January 1, 1986 separates from service in 1987 or a later year, five-year averaging will not be allowed if he or she is under age 59½ when the distribution is made. Only one lifetime election is allowed. Under pre-1987 law, averaging was allowed to those under 59½ upon separation from service.

Those age 50 or older as of January 1, 1986 have one life-time election after 1986 to use 10-year averaging based on 1986 rates or five-year averaging under rates effective in the year of distribution. They may make the election for a lump-sum distribution even if they are under 59½.

For 1986 distributions, capital gain treatment is still available for the portion of a lump sum attributable to pre-1974 contributions; an election may be made to report the entire distribution as ordinary income subject to 10-year averaging.

For distributions after 1986, capital gain treatment will be phased out between 1987 and 1991 for those who were under age 50 as of January 1, 1986. Under this phaseout rule, 100% of the pre-1974 portion of a 1987 distribution will qualify as capital gain subject to a 20% tax rate. In 1988, 95% of the pre-1974 portion will qualify, 75% in 1989, 50% in 1990, and 25% in 1991; after 1991 no part of the lump-sum will qualify for the 20% capital gain rate.

Those age 50 or older as of January 1, 1986 will be allowed a one-time election to have the pre-1974 portion of a lump sum treated as capital gain, to be taxed at a 20% rate. This election will not be subject to the phaseout.

Penalties for early or excessive withdrawals from qualified retirement plans. A 10% penalty for withdrawals before age 59½, disability or death may apply to distributions after 1986 from qualified employer plans and annuity plans. The penalty will not apply to distributions in the form of an annuity over the life of the taxpayer or joint lives of the taxpayer and a beneficiary. Further, the following exceptions to the penalty will be allowed: (1) Withdrawals upon early retirement after age 55; (2) withdrawals used to pay deductible medical expenses (subject to 7.5% income floor); (3) withdrawals paid to an alternate payee pursuant to a qualified domestic relations court order; (4) withdrawals received before March 15, 1987, if you separated from service in 1986 and you pay 1986 tax on the distributions.

In years beginning after 1986, distributions exceeding $112,500 in any year from all qualified plans plus IRAs will generally be subject to a 15% penalty. Only the excess above $112,500 is subject to the penalty. However, under an exception, the penalty does not apply to excess benefits accrued before August 1, 1986.

Cash or deferred 401(k) plans. In taxable years beginning after 1986, the maximum amount that an employee will be able to defer for any year under all 401(k) plans is $7,000 subject to indexing. Nondiscrimination tests for 401(k) plans are tightened.

Withdrawals for hardship reasons will be limited to an employee's elective deferrals and may not include the employer's contributions or income on any contributions.

Distributions will be subject to the same 10% premature withdrawal penalty rules as distributions from IRAs and qualified plans.

Contributions over the $7,000 limit together with income earned on such contributions is taxable to an employee for the year to which the contributions relate. Income earned on excess contributions is determined on a pro-rata basis. Excess contributions and income not returned to an employee by April 15 of the year following contribution is not treated as after-tax employee contributions. The return of excess contributions and related income to the employee is not subject to the additional income tax on early withdrawals and may be made despite plan provisions to the contrary until the plan is amended.

New Depreciation and Other Property Writeoff Rules

Assets placed in service after 1986 other than real estate are depreciable over three, five, seven, ten, 15 or 20 years. Automobiles and light trucks are in the five-year class. Property in the three, five, seven and 10-year classes are depreciable using the double declining balance method, switching to the straight line method so as to maximize the deduction. The new rates may be elected for assets placed in service after July 31, 1986.

Annual depreciation ceilings for business autos placed in service after 1986: first year, $2,560; second, $4,100; third, $2,450; $1,475 for later years.

Transition rules apply current law depreciation rules for assets constructed or acquired under contracts binding in 1986 and placed in service by a specified future date. *See* the Supplement for transition date.

The first-year expensing deduction for property placed in service after 1986 increases to $10,000 from the current $5,000. However, the annual $10,000 limit will be reduced for every $1 of qualifying investment in excess of $200,000. Further, the expensing deduction may not exceed the taxable income from the business in which the property was used; amounts in excess of taxable income are carried forward and added to the amount eligible for expensing in the later year.

Real Estate: Depreciation, At Risk, and Credit Changes

The depreciation period for real estate is extended from 19 years to 27.5 years for residential buildings and 31.5 years for non-residential buildings. Writeoffs must be based on the straight-line method. The longer depreciation periods generally apply to buildings placed in service after 1986. Transition rules providing exemptions for buildings constructed or acquired under a written contract binding during 1986 are in the Supplement.

Accounting conventions. For personal property, both the first and last depreciation allowances for an asset would reflect the half-year convention. The present law mid-month convention would apply to real property, and a mid-quarter convention would be applied to taxpayers who place more than 40% of their property in service during the last quarter of the tax year.

At risk. Starting in 1987, at risk rules limiting losses to cash and recourse loan obligations apply to real estate acquired after 1986, but an exception is allowed for nonrecourse financing secured by the real property. The loan must be from a government agency, bank or other lender but not including the seller. Real estate joint ventures may obtain financing from an otherwise qualified lender who has an equity interest in the venture provided that the financing terms are commercially reasonable and substantially similar to loans offered to unrelated borrowers.

Low-income rental housing credit. A new tax credit will replace the current tax incentives for low-income housing after 1986. Separate credits will apply for new construction and rehabilitation of low income housing and for costs of acquiring existing low-income housing units. The credits will be claimed over a 10-year period. For property placed in service in 1987, a credit rate of 9% will apply for new construction, 4% for acquisition cost of existing low income housing.

Housing will generally qualify for the credit only if at least 20% of the units are occupid by tenants whose income is less than 50% of the median area income.

The credit will apply to property placed in service after 1986 and before 1990, with an exception for certain projects begun before 1989 and placed in service before 1991.

Business Changes

Profit presumption period for hobby losses extended. Under pre-1987 law, if you show a profit in an activity in two or more years during a period of five consecutive years, the law presumes that you are in the activity in order to make a profit. In the case of horse breeding, training, racing or showing, the profit presumption rule applies if you show profits in two of seven consecutive years. The IRS may rebut the presumption in case you claim loss deductions in the other year. The new law increases the presumption test to three or more years for regular businesses.

Health insurance deduction for self-employed. A deduction will be allowed in 1987, 1988 and 1989 for 25% of the amounts paid for health insurance on behalf of a self-employed individual and his or her spouse and dependents. The deduction may not exceed net earnings from self employ-

ment. No deduction is allowed for a year in which the self-employed individual or his or her spouse is covered by an employer's health plan.

Fiscal year restrictions. For taxable years beginning after 1986, partnerships, S corporations and personal service corporations will generally have to use the same taxable year as their owners, usually calendar years, unless a business purpose is shown. Deferring income to partners or shareholders will not be considered a business purpose. Partners or S corporation shareholders required by the new rules to include more than 12 months of income during a year may be allowed to report the excess over a four-year period.

Bad debt reserve method repealed. The reserve method of deducting business bad debts for all taxpayers other than financial institutions is repealed for taxable years beginning after 1986. Bad debts will be deductible only when the debt becomes worthless. The balance of any existing reserve must be taken into account as income ratably over a four-year period. Further, partners or S corporation shareholders who are required to report more than 12 months of income in a single year as a result of the repeal may report the excess income ratably over four years.

Corporate taxes. A 15%, 25%, 34% rate structure takes effect for taxable years beginning on or after July 1, 1987. For taxable years including July 1, 1987, blended rates apply.

The 15% rate for years after July 1, 1987 will apply to the first $50,000 of taxable income. The 25% rate will apply to taxable income over $50,000 but not over $75,000. The top rate of 34% will generally apply to taxable income over $75,000. However, the benefit of the 15% and 25% brackets will be phased out by imposing a 5% surtax on taxable income between $100,000 and $335,000. Corporations with more than $335,000 of taxable income will be subject to a flat 34% rate.

For taxable years beginning on or after July 1, 1987, the alternative tax rate on corporate net long-term capital gain (currently 28%) will not apply. For gains included in income after 1986 but in taxable years beginning before July 1, 1987, the alternative tax rate will be 34%. As under present law, capital losses will be deductible only against capital gains.

Cash method of accounting limited. For taxable years starting after 1986, the following entities may not use the cash method: a regular C corporation, a partnership with a C corporation as a partner, a tax shelter or a tax-exempt trust with unrelated business income. Exceptions: the cash method may be used by professional corporations, entities other than tax shelters with average annual gross receipts of $5 million or less, and farming and timber businesses.

Businesses required to switch to the accrual method will be allowed a four-year phase-in period for income reporting.

Alimony Changes

In a technical amendment, the alimony rules for post-1985 agreements have been changed. Under this amendment, an agreement does not have to specifically state that alimony must end at death of payee-spouse and the minimum payout and recapture period is reduced from six to three years. The Supplement will provide further details to the rules that generally take effect for agreements made after 1986.

Penalties, Reporting Requirements, Legal Awards

Penalties. Taxes not paid by the due date are subject to a monthly penalty of 0.5% with a maximum penalty of 25%. The new law allows the IRS to double the monthly penalty to 1% after repeated IRS requests and a notice of levy. The higher penalty can be assessed after December 31, 1986.

Under current law, failure to include interest or dividend income from an information return (Form 1099) on your tax return is presumed to be negligence subject to a 5% penalty unless you prove you were not negligent. On returns due after 1986, this rule is extended to amounts shown on other types of information returns, such as proceeds from a stock sale reported on Form 1099-B. The new rule applies to returns due after 1986; thus, the penalty applies to 1986 returns.

Under current law, a 50% penalty applies to the total tax underpayment if any portion of the underpayment is due to fraud. The new law increases the fraud penalty to 75% for returns due after 1986, but the penalty will apply only to the underpayment which is attributable to fraud.

You are subject to a penalty where you understate tax liability on a return by the greater of $5,000 or 10% of the proper tax (¶38.07). The penalty is 10% of the underpayment for returns due before 1987, 20% for returns originally due (without extensions) after 1986.

Tax-exempt interest reporting. Starting with your 1987 return, you will have to list amount of tax-exempt interest. Under current law, only taxpayers with taxable Social Security benefits were required to indicate their tax-exempt interest, although the IRS form instructions also asked for listing in Schedule B.

Real estate sales. Under the new law, all real estate transactions will have to be reported to the IRS if the closing on the contract occurs on or after January 1, 1987. The attorney or other person who is responsible for closing the transaction will file the report on Form 1099, with a copy sent to the seller.

Identification number of dependent child. If you claim dependency exemptions for a dependent child age five or older, you will have to obtain a Social Security number for the child and report the number on your 1987 tax return. An exception is allowed to members of religious groups except from Social Security taxes.

Federal contracts. If you have a contract with a Federal executive agency after 1986, that agency will file a report with the IRS. All contracts signed after 1986 are subject to reporting, as are contracts signed before January 1, 1987 if still in effect on that date.

Royalties. Under current Treasury regulations, royalty payments of $600 or more are subject to information reporting. The new law requires payers of $10 or more in royalties to file an information return, starting in 1987.

Legal fee awards. The rules for recovery of attorney's fees and other litigation costs have been changed for cases begun after 1985 (¶38.08). Generally, prevailing taxpayers who have exhausted all administrative remedies within the IRS may recover up to $75 an hour for litigation costs if they prove that the IRS acted unreasonably. Further details are in the Supplement.

Planning Tips

In 1986, consider—

Realizing long-term capital gains to take advantage of lower 1986 capital gain rates. *See* ¶ 30.00. However, before selling consider further profit potential and after-tax cost of sales in 1987. Consider deferring (1) long-term capital losses to 1987 when the loss will not be reduced by 50% before deduction from other income and (2) short-term gains if subject to lower 1987 tax rates.

Buying high-priced consumer items such as a personal automobile in 1986 to take a 1986 sales tax deduction and get a full first-year consumer interest deduction before the phaseout of consumer interest deduction starts in 1987.

Paying year-end medical bills in 1986 instead of 1987 to avoid higher 7.5% floor in 1987.

Paying nonbusiness expenses such as investment expenses, safe deposit box fees, professional union dues, subscriptions, tax advice expenses that may not be deductible in 1987 because of the 2% floor applied to your income in 1987.

Prepaying in 1986 donations you would make in 1987 if you do not itemize. No deduction for charitable contributions will be allowed after 1986 unless you itemize.

Making gifts of appreciated securities to avoid reporting the untaxed appreciation as tax preference item for 1987 AMT purposes.

Paying interest on tax deficiencies in 1986 to get full deduction of interest in 1986 rather than subject the interest to consumer interest restrictions in 1987.

Contribute maximum amount allowed in 1986 for 401(K) plan.

Defer income that will be subject to lower 1987 rates.

For 1987, consider—

Investing in profitable investment ventures, such as rental property, if you have tax shelter losses which are not deductible because of the passive loss restrictions. You may deduct the losses from the income.

Review your travel and entertainment arrangement with your company if you incur such expenses. Provide for full reimbursement to avoid the 2% AGI floor on miscellaneous expense deductions.

Gifts to minors within the new income splitting limits. Tax at parent's bracket does not apply to income on gift property to children 14 or over. A child under 14 years of age may earn up to $500 of investment income without tax. Giving tax-exempt bonds to children under 14 may also provide a build-up of tax-free funds.

Deferring income to 1988 when tax rates will be lower than the tax rates of 1987. Consider accelerating payment of deductible expenses in 1987.

Consider investments in tax-exempt bonds. However, check prospectus for issue dates. The new law treats interest on certain nongovernmental purpose bonds issued after August 7, 1986 as an AMT preference item; further interest on bonds issued after August 31, 1986 for nongovernmental purposes may be taxable.

You may also want to consider taking an additional mortgage on your residence to carry consumer debt if the mortgage loan comes within the new deduction limit rules discussed on page IV.

Please mail the card in front of this book for the free Supplement which will give further developments and perspectives of the 1986 Tax Act.

1987 TAX RATES

| If taxable income is | | | Plus | |
Over	but not over	Tax is	Following percent	of amount over
JOINT RETURN				
	$3,000		11%	0
$3,000	$28,000	$330	15	$3,000
28,000	45,000	4,080	28	28,000
45,000	90,000	8,840	35	45,000
90,000		24,590	38.5	90,000
SINGLE				
	$1,800		11%	0
$1,800	16,800	$198	15	$1,800
16,800	27,000	2,448	28	16,800
27,000	54,000	5,304	35	27,000
54,000		14,754	38.5	54,000
HEAD OF HOUSEHOLD				
	$2,500		11%	0
$2,500	23,000	$275	15	$2,500
23,000	38,000	3,350	28	23,000
38,000	80,000	7,550	35	38,000
80,000		22,250	38.5	80,000

1988 TAX RATES

| If taxable income is | | | Plus | |
Over	but not over	Tax is	Following percent	of amount over
JOINT RETURN				
$ 0	$ 29,750		15%	0
29,750	71,900	$4,462.50	28	$29,750
71,900	149,250	16,264.50	33 *	71,900
149,250			28 **	0
SINGLE				
$ 0	$17,850		15%	0
17,850	43,150	$2,677.50	28	$17,850
43,150	89,560	9,761.50	33 *	43,150
89,560			28 **	0
HEAD OF HOUSEHOLD				
	$23,900		15%	0
23,900	61,650	$ 3,585	28	$23,900
61,650	123,790	14,155	33 *	61,650
123,790			28 **	0

*Reflects 5% surtax phasing out 15% rate benefit on part of your taxable income.

**Flat tax of 28% on all taxable income. Further, add 5% surtax phasing out tax benefit of personal and dependent exemptions. The surtax is the lower of (a) $546 times number of exemptions or (b) 5% of (taxable income—$149,250) on joint return; 5% of (taxable income—$89,560) on single return; 5% of (taxable income—$123,790) on head of household return.

TAX COMPARISON WORK SHEETS

Income	1986	1987	1988
(Include spouse's income if filing jointly)			
Compensation	$____	$____	$____
Interest	____	____	____
Dividends			
(no $100/$200 exclusion after 1986)	____	____	____
Capital gain			
(less 60% of long-term capital gain in 1986, fully taxable afterwards)	____	____	____
Unemployment compensation			
(fully taxable after 1986)	____	____	____
Rent and royalties			
(passive losses are not applied against other income after 1986)	____	____	____
Partnership loss			
(passive losses are not applied against other income after 1986)	____	____	____
Scholarship and grants			
(may be taxable after 1986)	____	____	____
All other income	____	____	____
Total Step 1	$____	$____	$____
Adjustments			
Employee expenses			
(unreimbursed travel costs deductible after 1986 as itemized deduction subject to 2% AGI ceiling)	$____	$____	$____
IRA deduction			
(may not be deductible in 1987 depending on income and company coverage)	____	____	____
Married couple earner deduction			
(not after 1986)	____		
Other adjustments			
(moving expenses deductible here in 1986; itemized after 1986)	____	____	____
Total Step 2	$____	$____	$____

Itemized deductions	1986	1987	1988
Medical and dental			
(5% AGI floor in 1986; 7.5% after 1986)	$____	$____	$____
Contributions	____	____	____
State and local income tax	____	____	____
Property tax	____	____	____
Sales tax			
(not deductible after 1986)	____		
Consumer interest			
(65% deductible in 1987, 40% in 1988)	____	____	____
Investment interest			
(65% deductible in 1987)	____	____	____
Mortgage interest			
(restrictions after 1986)	____	____	____
Casualty and theft losses			
(exceeding 10% AGI)	____	____	____
Miscellaneous nonbusiness expenses (less 2% AGI floor after 1986)	____	____	____
Minus zero bracket amount in 1986 (see ¶13.00)	____		
Other deductions			
Nonitemized charitable donation deduction (not deductible after 1986)	____		
Standard deduction (if you do not itemize after 1986)		____	____
Total Step 3	$____	$____	$____

Summary	1986	1987	1988
Income Step 1	$____	$____	$____
Less Step 2 Adjustments	(____)	(____)	(____)
Step 3 Itemized Deductions	(____)	(____)	(____)
Less Exemptions			
____ x $1,080 (1986; age/blind extra)	(____)		
____ x $1,900 (1987)		(____)	
____ x $1,950 (1988)			(____)
Taxable Income	$____	$____	$____

Apply applicable rates: 1986 rates are at ¶22.00; 1987 and 1988 rates are on page VII.

Itemized deductions	1986	1987	1988
Charitable donation	1,000	1,000	1,000
Real estate taxes	2,000	2,000	2,000
Mortgage interest	3,000	3,000	3,000
Consumer interest	300	195	120
Sales tax	700		
Miscellaneous job and investment expense	300	*	*
	$ 7,300		
Less 1986 ZBA	3,670		
Step 3 Deductions	$ 3,630	$ 6,195	$ 6,120

Summary	1986	1987	1988
Step 1	$84,000	$95,200	$95,200
Less Step 2	(7,000)		
Step 3	(3,630)	(6,195)	(6,120)
Step 4	(2,160)	(3,800)	(3,900)
Taxable Income	$71,210	$85,205	$85,180
Tax	$19,082	22,912**	20,646

*Does not exceed 2% ceiling of adjusted gross income.

**Tax will be about $700 less than $22,912 after taking into account the 1987 capital gain adjustment for 28% rate.

Example—

You and your spouse work and file a joint return. Your salary in 1986 is $50,000; your spouse earns $32,000. You have interest income of $2,000, dividend income of $1,200 and net long-term capital gains of $10,000. You and your spouse contribute $2,000 each to an IRA. You are both covered by company retirement plans. You make charitable donations of $1,000, pay $2,000 in real estate taxes, $3,000 interest on your home mortgage, $300 interest on consumer loans and $700 in state and local sales taxes. You also had $300 of investment and unreimbursed job related expenses.

Here is a comparison of your tax liability in 1986, 1987 and 1988 taking into account the new law changes and assuming the same income and expenses for each of the three years. Under the new law, no IRA, married couple earner, sales tax, and capital gain deductions are allowed, the consumer interest deduction is reduced, and miscellaneous deductions are not deductible because of the 2% AGI floor.

Income	1986	1987	1988
Salary	$82,000	$82,000	$82,000
Dividends	1,000	1,200	1,200
Interest	2,000	2,000	2,000
Capital gain	4,000	10,000	10,000
Loss	(5,000)		
Step 1 Income	$84,000	$95,200	$95,200
Less IRA deduction	(4,000)		
Married couple earner deduction	(3,000)		
Step 2 Adjustments	(7,000)		

Contents

Who Must File a Return?

Your personal tax status and age determines the income limits that require you to file a tax return. In the charts below, find your personal status in the first column and in the second column, you will find the income limit.

IF YOU ARE—	YOU MUST FILE IF GROSS INCOME* IS AT LEAST—
Single (not a dependent of another taxpayer)	
—under 65	$3,560
—65 or over	4,640
Married filing jointly	
—under 65	5,830
—one spouse 65 or over	6,910
—both spouses 65 or over	7,990
Surviving spouse with dependent child (deceased spouse died in 1984 or 1985)	
—under 65	4,750
—65 or over	5,830

IF YOU ARE—	YOU MUST FILE IF GROSS INCOME* IS AT LEAST—
Head of household	
—under 65	$3,560
—65 or over	4,640
Married filing separately	1,080
Married living apart at end of 1986	1,080
Nonresident alien	1,080
U.S. citizen with most of income from U.S. possession	1,080
Individual with tax year of less than 12 months	1,080

* These filing floors for joint returns apply only if the spouses live together at the end of 1986 and neither spouse is claimed as a dependent on another taxpayer's return.

You must also file a return in these cases:
Your net self-employment earnings are $400 or more, or
You are a dependent and you have investment income of at least $1,080, or
You are entitled to a refund of taxes withheld from your wages or a refund based on the earned income credit for low income householders (¶24.50), or

You received any earned income credit payments in advance from your employers (¶24.53), or
You owe any tax (such as alternative minimum tax (¶23.10); IRA penalty (¶7.19); FICA on tips (¶25.06)).

THIS IS GROSS INCOME

Salary, wages, bonuses, commissions
Professional fees
Interest
Dividends
Rents
Royalties
Gains from property sales
Pension income
Annuity income
Alimony meeting the rules of ¶1.70
Business gross income
Gambling winnings
Lottery winnings
Jury fees
Director fees
Sick vacation or severance pay
Employer contributions to SEP
Foreign earned income even though tax free
Gain from home sale qualifying for $125,000 exclusion
Social Security benefits tax free under the rules of ¶34.11

THIS IS NOT TAXABLE INCOME

Gifts from relatives and friends
Inheritances
Scholarship and fellowships, meeting rules of ¶12.10 and ¶12.11
Employee educational assistance payments
Certain medical benefits paid by employers, *see* ¶2.19
Rental value of parsonage
Fringe benefits meeting rules of ¶2.20
Meals and lodging furnished for the employer's convenience
Benefits under qualified group legal services plans, cafeteria plans, qualified transportation, dependent care assistance programs, group term life insurance up to $50,000.
Child support payments, *see* ¶20.04.
Social Security benefits that are tax free under the rules of ¶34.11
Life insurance proceeds meeting rules of ¶12.30

WHEN TO FILE

April 15 is the general filing due date. However, you may qualify for a later date by filing for an extension or if you are abroad.

IF YOU ARE—	YOU FILE BY	IF YOU ARE—	YOU FILE BY
Citizen or resident of the U.S.	April 15	Executor, administrator, or trustee of estate or trust	April 15
If abroad on April 15	June 15	Resident alien about to leave U.S.	Within 10 days before departure
Filing the last return of a person who died during the year	April 15	Committee for a person unable to manage his own affairs	April 15
Resident of Canada or Mexico and U.S. taxes were withheld from your wages	April 15	Reporting for a fiscal year	15th day of the 4th month after close of fiscal year.
Nonresident alien if no taxes were withheld from wages	June 15		

For a timely filing, be sure your return is postmarked by midnight of the due date. The return is considered to have been filed on the postmark date, even though received by the IRS afterwards. Where a filing date falls on a Saturday, Sunday, or legal holiday, the filing date is extended to the next business day.

Apply for an extension if you cannot file on time. You may get an automatic four-month extension without waiting for the IRS to act on your request by filing Form 4868 and paying the full amount of tax you estimate that you owe, *see* ¶27.05.

Outside the U.S. on April 15. You are entitled to an automatic extension to June 15 without filing Form 4868. Attach a statement to your return saying that you were outside the U.S. or Puerto Rico on April 15 and include interest on any unpaid tax from due date.

A general extension of time to file outside of the automatic extension rules above may be granted by showing undue hardship.

WHERE TO FILE

IF YOU ARE FILING—	DO THIS—	IF YOU ARE FILING—	DO THIS—
Personal return	File with Service Center listed for your place of legal residence. Use the envelope included in the IRS packet of forms if the envelope address is the same as the Center listed for your residence. *See* ¶27.09 for Service Center addresses.	As a U.S. citizen abroad who claims exclusion benefits of ¶36.00	File with the Service Center at Philadelphia, Pa. 19255. If you do not claim tax free benefits abroad, file with the Service Center listed for your legal residence. If you have no legal residence or business in the U.S. file with the Service Center, Philadelphia, Pa. 19255.
Business return	File with Service Center where your principal place of business is located.	As a nonresident alien	File with the Service Center, Philadelphia, Pa. 19255.
		As a Serviceman	File with the Service Center listed for your civilian legal residence.

Do not allow your inability to pay the tax stop you from filing a return. Inability to pay the tax is not a reason for which an extention is granted. If you cannot pay your tax, file your return and apply for an extension of time to pay your tax on Form 1127, *see* ¶27.06.

Filing an amended return. If, after filing your return, you find that an error has been made, you should file an amended return, Form 1040X, which may be used to correct a return filed in 1985 or an earlier year, *see* ¶27.07.

FILING POINTERS FOR MARRIED PERSONS

FILING JOINTLY

Married couples pay less tax by filing jointly. Filing jointly allows the use of joint return rates.

You may file a joint return if you are legally married on the last day of 1986.

You need not live together provided you are legally married. A couple legally separated under a final decree of divorce or separate maintenance may *not* file a joint return.

You may file jointly if your spouse died during 1986. See ¶1.02.

If one spouse is a nonresident alien, you may file jointly *only* if you make a special election to be taxed on your world-wide income. *See* ¶1.03.

You *must* file jointly to claim the deduction for two-earner married couples (¶1.01), to make an IRA deduction on behalf of a non-working spouse (¶7.171), to claim the credit for the elderly (¶34.02), dependent care credit (¶24.20), or earned income credit (¶24.50).

On a joint return, each spouse is liable for the entire tax. If one spouse does not pay, the other spouse may be liable even though all of the income was earned by the spouse who failed to pay the tax. A spouse who files a joint return may be relieved of fraud penalties and tax liability in certain circumstances. *See* ¶1.011.

For community property rules, *see* ¶1.04.

FILING SEPARATELY

You may not file a joint return and must use tax rates for married persons filing separately in these cases:

1. You and your spouse have different tax reporting years. If you report on the calendar year but your spouse reports on a fiscal year, you must file separately unless you get permission from the IRS to change your reporting year (Form 1128). This bar to joint filing does not apply when your tax year begins on the same day, but ends because of the death of either or both spouses. A spouse who has never filed a tax return may elect to use the other spouse's tax year as his first tax year. Then they can file a joint return. That a husband and wife had different tax years before their marriage is no bar to a joint return.

2. You or your spouse is a nonresident alien and you do not make an election to be taxed on your world-wide income. *See* ¶1.03.

3. Your spouse files a separate return. If you are experiencing marital discord, you may be forced to file separately unless your spouse consents to a joint return.

4. You or your spouse is claimed by someone else as a dependent. *See* ¶1.58.

LIVING APART FROM SPOUSE: FILING AS UNMARRIED HEAD OF HOUSEHOLD

If you live apart from your spouse, you may qualify for tax purposes as "unmarried" and use head of household rates which are less than single person rates.

You qualify if:

1. You file a separate return.

2. Your spouse was not a member of your household during the last six months of 1986.

3. You maintained your home as a household which was the principal place of abode for your child, adopted child, foster child, or stepchild, for more than half of 1986. However, a foster child must be a member of your household for the entire year.

4. You are entitled to claim the child as a dependent. Ignore this test if the noncustodial spouse claims the exemption for the child under the rules of ¶1.554.

5. You provide over half of the cost of supporting the household.

FILING POINTERS FOR SINGLE PERSONS

SINGLE PERSON

If you are not married at the end of 1986, use the rate for "unmarried" single individuals, unless you qualify as a surviving spouse or a head of household.

If you are widowed, you are "unmarried" and use rates for single individuals regardless of the number of years you were married. There is an exception for recent widows or widowers supporting children, as explained in the column "surviving spouse."

HEAD OF HOUSEHOLD

You may use special head of household rates if you meet these tests:

1. You are not married at the end of the year.

2. You maintain a household for more than half of 1986 for your child or a dependent relative. The household must be your home and the main residence of your dependent relative except that a dependent parent need not live with you. However, you must maintain a dependent parent's separate household for the entire year to claim head of household status based on that support.

3. You pay more than one-half the cost of the household.

4. You are a U.S. citizen or resident alien during the entire tax year.

These rules are explained in detail in ¶1.05.

SURVIVING SPOUSE

If you are a widow or widower and your spouse died in 1984 or 1985, you may use 1986 joint return tax rates if you meet these four tests:

1. You maintain your home as the main home of your child for the entire year and you furnish over half the cost of maintaining the household.

2. You are entitled to claim the child as a dependent. *See* ¶1.50.

3. In the year your spouse died, you could have filed a joint return.

4. You did not remarry before January 1, 1987.

Tax rate schedules are at ¶22.00.

Exemptions

EACH EXEMPTION you claim on your 1986 return is the equivalent of a deduction of $1,080.

You claim exemptions for:

Yourself. Every taxpayer is allowed one exemption.

Your spouse. You claim your spouse as an exemption when you file a joint return. If you file a separate return, you claim your spouse as an exemption if he or she has no income and is not a dependent of another person. *See* ¶1.51.

Being 65 or over. When you are 65 or over, you get an extra exemption for your age. If your spouse is also 65 or over, he or she gets an extra exemption as well. This extra exemption may not be claimed by a person claiming an aged dependent as an exemption. For example, a son claiming his over-65 father as a dependent gets one $1,080 exemption for him, not the $2,160 the father could claim had he sufficient income to file his own return.

Blindness. A blind taxpayer takes an extra exemption for his disability. Similarly, you may claim an extra exemption for a spouse who is blind.

Parents, other relatives and dependents. As long as you satisfy four tests for each dependent, there is no limit to the number of dependents you may claim.

Test 1. Relative or member of household. A qualifying relative may be your:

Child, grandchild, great grandchild, or stepchild;

Brother, sister, half-brother, half-sister, stepbrother or stepsister;

Parent, grandparent, great grandparent or stepparent;

Brother or sister of your father or mother;

Son or daughter of your brother or sister;

Father-in-law, mother-in-law, son-in-law, daughter-in-law, brother-in-law, or sister-in-law.

A qualifying member of your household may be any person, whether or not related, who for the entire year made your home his or her principal home and is a member of your household (except if the relationship between you and such person violates state law).

Test 2. Your support. You either contribute more than half the dependent's support, or contribute more than 10% and together with others contribute more than half (*see* ¶1.553).

Test 3. Dependent's gross income. Your dependent must have less than $1,080 of gross income for the year. This test does not apply if the dependent is your child who is under 19 or a full-time student, in which case the amount of his or her gross income may be $1,080 or more.

Test 4. Dependent's citizenship or resident status. Your dependent must be a United States citizen or national, or a resident of the United States, Canada, or Mexico.

Generally, you may not claim an exemption for a dependent who files a joint return with another unless the joint return is used merely to get a refund of withheld taxes and the income of each spouse is under the income limits required for filing a return. If one or both spouses have income over the filing limits, then their filing of a joint return prevents you from claiming an exemption. For example, you meet all of the four tests entitling you to an exemption for your married daughter who has no income. She files a joint return with her husband whose income is slightly over the filing income limit. You may not claim her as your dependent on your tax return. The loss of the exemption may cost you more than the joint return saves the couple. In such a case, it may be advisable for the couple to file separate returns so that you can benefit from the larger tax savings allowed by claiming your daughter as a dependent.

For further details on claiming exemptions, *see* ¶1.50 and ¶1.54.

Reporting Pay and Social Security Benefits

PRACTICALLY EVERYTHING you receive for your work or services is taxed, whether it is paid in cash, property, or services. Taxed pay includes: Salaries, wages, expense allowances, honoraria, commissions, tips, bonuses, jury fees, director fees, employee prizes or awards, severance pay, dismissal pay, back pay, sick pay, and vacation pay. Also included in income are employer contributions under Simplified Employee Pension plans (SEP), although an offsetting deduction may be claimed.

The amount of your pay is shown on Form W-2. Report the full pay listed on the form. Do not decrease the amount by the amount your employer withholds for income taxes, Social Security taxes, disability insurance payments, hospitalization insurance premiums, U.S. Savings Bonds, pension funds, union dues, or payments to a creditor who has attached your salary.

If you are self-employed, do not report your fees on Form 1040 as salary or wages, even if you consider your drawings as salary. Report your business or professional income on Schedule C.

Tax-free pay benefits. Fringe benefits provided you by your employer may be tax free. The most common tax-free benefit is employer-paid premiums for health and accident plans and certain group-term life insurance plans for coverage up to $50,000. Other tax-free fringes are discussed in the section beginning at ¶2.00.

Unemployment benefits may be taxable. Unemployment benefits paid under state or federal law are taxable if your income and benefits exceed certain limits. The benefits are taxable if the total of your adjusted gross income and the benefits exceeds:

$12,000 if you are single, or
$18,000 if you are married and file a joint return.

If adjusted gross income increased by the amount of the benefits exceeds $12,000 or $18,000 (whichever applies), you report as taxable income the *lesser* of either: The unemployment benefits or 50% of the excess of adjusted gross income and the benefits over $12,000 or over $18,000 (whichever applies).

If you are married and file a separate return, you may not use the base of $18,000. The taxable amount is the lower of either the benefits or 50% of the total of adjusted gross income and the benefits. This restrictive rule does not apply to a separate return if you lived apart from your spouse at all times during 1986. In such a case, you may use the $12,000 floor on the separate return.

Do not include in the above computation supplemental unemployment benefits paid by company or union funds or Workmen's Compensation.

Disability pensions. The exclusion for disability pensions received by disabled persons under age 65 is no longer allowed. However, those under age 65 who retired on permanent and total disability may be eligible for a tax credit. *See* ¶34.02.

Social Security benefits. Part of your Social Security benefits may be taxable if your income exceeds a base amount of $25,000 if you are single or $32,000 if you are married filing jointly. To determine if your income exceeds the $25,000 or $32,000 base, you add to adjusted gross income 50% of your Social Security benefits, tax-free interest income, the marriage penalty deduction, and tax-free foreign earned income. Social Security benefits include your monthly retirement, survivor, or disability benefits. Monthly Tier 1 Railroad Retirement benefits are treated as Social Security benefits; Tier 2 Railroad Retirement benefits are not treated as Social Security benefits. For further details, *see* ¶34.11.

Deducting Travel, Entertainment and Other Job Expenses

Y OU MAY DEDUCT expenses that are necessary to earn your salary. Typical expenses are those incurred for traveling to see customers or clients, food and lodging on business trips away from home, entertaining business customers, work clothes, and union and business association dues.

Job expenses are deducted on different schedules. One class of expenses is deductible from income before you itemize; others are deductible only if you claim excess itemized deductions. This difference in treatment is fixed by law.

Job expenses deductible from gross income on Form 1040 whether or not you itemize deductions are:

Travel expenses away from home
Transportation expenses
Reimbursed expenses
Moving expenses

On your Form 1040, these deductions are taken in the section titled "Adjustments to Income." Travel expenses away from home, transportation expenses, and expenses reimbursed by your employer are referred to as "employee business expenses."

Job expenses deductible as itemized deductions only if you claim excess itemized deductions are:

Entertainment expenses
Business gifts
Union dues
Uniform and work clothes costs

Exception for outside salespersons. The above expenses are deductible from gross income if you are an outside salesperson.

Recordkeeping. By law, you must prove the cost and business purpose of expenses with records or similar evidence. Starting at ¶2.35, you will find a discussion of the evidence you must have to support your deduction if your return is examined.

Travel expenses incurred to look after investments are deducted as itemized deductions. Travel costs incurred to look after rental or royalty-producing property are deducted in Schedule E.

When you deduct travel expenses away from home and transportation expenses, you attach to your tax return Form 2106. A sample Form 2106 may be found in the Supplement to this book.

Travel and entertainment expense restrictions. Restrictive rules apply to the deduction of travel and entertainment expenses. To support your deductions, you must keep a diary or similar record of the background and details of your travel and entertainment expenses. Keep receipts, itemized paid bills and similar statements for expense items exceeding $25. In determining which receipts to keep, note these exceptions: A receipt for travel expenses exceeding $25 is required only when it is readily obtainable, as, for example, for air travel. A receipt for lodging is required regardless of the amount unless its cost is covered by a per diem allowance, generally $44 or less. See ¶2.35. It is advisable to keep a log of business mileage to claim auto expense deductions. See ¶3.05.

If you do not have records for meal costs on overnight business trips, you may claim a flat IRS meal allowance. See ¶2.221.

Deduct moving expenses to a new job location. You may deduct the cost of moving to a new place of work or doing business if:

1. The distance between your new place of work and your old home exceeds by at least 35 miles the distance between the former place of work and your old home; and

2. You have been or will be working at the new location for at least 39 weeks as a full-time employee, or 78 weeks on a full-time self-employed basis.

The move should take place within one year from the time you first start to work at the new location. If not, the deduction for moving costs may be disallowed. However, the IRS may allow a deduction if you delayed your family's move so that your children could finish a school year.

You explain and list the expenses on Form 3903, which you attach to your return. Your employer reports moving expense payments and reimbursements on Form 4782. Do not file this form with your tax return. See ¶2.40 for further details.

Reporting Dividend Income

IVIDENDS PAID OUT of current or accumulated earnings of a corporation are subject to tax. Most dividends fall into this class. However, stock dividends and stock rights on common are generally not taxed. See ¶4.56.

Up to $100 ($200 on a joint return) of dividends qualifying for the dividend exclusion are not taxed. See ¶4.501.

Dividends paid to you during 1986 are reported by the company on an information return to the IRS. The IRS uses this information as a check on your reporting of dividends. You receive a copy of this information return, but do not attach it to your tax return.

Publicly-held corporations generally inform their stockholders of the tax consequences of stock dividends and other distributions. Keep such letters with your tax records. You may also want to consult investment publications such as Moody's or Standard and Poor's annual dividend record books for details of dividend distributions and their tax treatment.

Mutual fund dividends. Mutual funds (open-end regulated investment companies) may pay five kinds of dividends: (1) Ordinary dividends which are attributed to income from the fund's investments. These qualify for the dividend exclusion. (2) Capital gain dividends which are attributed to proceeds from the fund's profits on its sale of securities. These are reported as long-term capital gain even if you held the fund shares for a year or less. (3) Return of capital dividends which are attributed to proceeds from the receipt by the mutual fund of corporation distributions which were not out of earnings. These are not generally subject to tax. (4) Tax-exempt interest which is not subject to tax. (5) Dividends from foreign corporations. See ¶4.53.

Money market fund dividends do not qualify for the exclusion where the income is derived from interest. The fund will inform you of the nature of its payments.

Reporting Interest Income

LMOST ALL interest received or earned is subject to tax. This includes interest paid on notes, bonds (except state and municipal bonds), loans, and savings accounts. Banks and other payors of interest report to the IRS on information returns their payments made to you; a copy is sent to you. The IRS checks its copies against the items reported on your return. If there are any discrepancies, you will receive a computerized statement asking for an explanation and for payment of any deficiencies.

The following checklist summarizes the tax treatment of usual receipts of interest income:

Interest on deposits in savings account. Report interest credited to your savings account for 1986, even though you do not present your passbook to have the amount entered. Dividends on deposits or accounts in the following institutions are reported as interest income: Mutual savings banks, cooperative banks, domestic building and loan associations, domestic and federal savings and loan associations.

Interest and any principal forfeited on a premature withdrawal of principal of a time savings account is deductible. See ¶4.01.

Savings certificates, deferred interest or bonus plans. The deferred interest element is generally treated as original issue discount and is taxable on an annual basis. The bank, in an information return, will notify you of the amount to be reported as taxable interest for 1986. If you discontinue the savings plan before maturity, you may have a loss deduction. See ¶4.00.

U.S. Savings Bonds, Series "E" and "EE." The increase in redemption value is interest income. You do not have to report the annual increase in value until the year in which you cash the bond or the year in which the bond finally matures, whichever is earlier. See ¶4.08.

U.S. Savings Bonds, Series "H" and "HH." Semi-annual interest is taxable when received. See ¶4.08.

U.S. Treasury bills. You report as interest the difference between the cost and amount received on a sale or redemption of the bills at maturity for 1986. It is possible to sustain a loss on the sale of Treasury bills before maturity. *See* ¶4.07.

Bearer or coupon bonds. Interest coupons due and payable in 1986 are taxable on your 1986 return, regardless of when they were presented for collection. For example, a coupon due January 1986 and presented for payment in 1985 is taxable in 1986. Similarly, a coupon due December 1986, but presented for payment in 1987, is taxable in 1986.

Corporate obligations in registered form. You report interest when received or made available to you. *See* ¶4.03 which explains how to treat interest when you buy or sell bonds between interest dates.

State and local government obligations. For federal tax purposes, you do not report interest received on obligations issued by a state or local government or its agencies, such as Toll Road Commissions, Port Au-thorities, and Utility Service Authorities. However, the interest may be subject to state income tax. The investment value of tax-exempt bonds is discussed at ¶30.06.

Insurance proceeds. You report interest paid on insurance proceeds left with an insurance company or included in installment payments (under optional modes of payment). Exception: Up to $1,000 a year of interest in the year the anniversary date of the policy (or the other specified date).

Unwithdrawn life insurance dividends. If you can withdraw the interest annually, you report the interest in the year it is credited to your account. However, if, under the terms of the insurance policy, the interest can be withdrawn only on the anniversary date of the policy (or some other specified date), then you report the interest in the year in which the anniversary date of the policy (or the other specified date), falls.

Interest on GI insurance dividends on deposit with the VA is taxable, although the dividends were not taxable. *See* ¶4.61.

Reporting Business or Professional Income

Filing Schedule C. You file a separate Schedule C along with Form 1040 if you are a:

Sole proprietor of a business (whether a manufacturing, construction, retail, wholesale or service enterprise).

Professional in your own practice (lawyer, accountant, doctor, dentist, osteopath, engineer, etc.) or an independent contractor.

Even if you do not fit into the above classes, report on Schedule C any self-employment income and expenses incurred in earning it.

Do not file Schedule C if your business is operated through a partnership or corporation. If you are in farming, use Schedule F (not discussed in this book) instead of Schedule C. If you made an S corporation election, *see* ¶10.05.

Business profit (or loss) figured on Schedule C is entered on Form 1040 and the net profit (or loss) is added to (or subtracted from) nonbusiness income on Form 1040. This procedure allows you to deduct your business expenses, whether or not you claim excess itemized deductions for your nonbusiness expenses.

Did you suffer a business loss? You may get a refund of taxes paid in three prior tax years if current business losses exceed current income. If the loss is not fully eliminated by income of the three prior years, the balance of the loss may be used to reduce income of 15 following years. You may elect to forego the three-year carryback and just carry forward the loss for 15 years. *See* ¶5.23.

Accounting basis to report business income. You may report your business income on either the accrual or cash basis. If you have inventories, you must use the accrual basis in your business. On the cash basis, you report income items in the taxable year in which they are received; you deduct all expenses in the taxable year in which they are paid. On the accrual basis, you report income that has been earned whether or not received, unless a substantial contingency affects your right to collect the income. You deduct costs and expenses that have been incurred, whether or not paid, provided certain tests explained at ¶5.01 are met. Accrued interest, salaries, and other expenses to members of your family and other controlled relationships are deducted when paid.

Tax reporting year. Tax reporting years must be the same for both your business and nonbusiness income. If you report your business income on a fiscal year basis, you must also report your nonbusiness income on a fiscal year basis. Generally, you report the tax consequences of transactions that have occurred during a 12-month period. If the period ends on December 31, it is called a calendar year. If it ends on the last day of any month other than December, it is called a fiscal year. A reporting period may be less than 12 months whenever you start or end your business in the middle of your regular taxable year, or change your taxable year. *See* ¶5.02.

Reporting receipts or sales on Schedule C. Your total receipts can be found in your sales journal, deposit slips, or whatever record you use for listing your sales. If you report on an accrual basis, include all of the charges that you have billed in the taxable year. If on the cash basis, include only your actual or constructive receipts during the taxable year. Do not include consigned goods, sales on approval, or memorandum sales. These items are still part of your inventory of unsold goods.

If you do not produce, purchase or sell merchandise, that is, if your business or professional income is earned from personal services performed as a doctor, lawyer, accountant, engineer, barber, painter, plumber, real estate or insurance broker, etc., you are not concerned with detailing cost of goods. You report only your receipts from services.

Do not report as receipts on Schedule C gains or losses on the sales of property used in your business or profession. These transactions are reported on Schedule D and Form 4797. *See* ¶5.45. You also do not report on Schedule C dividends from stock held in the ordinary course of your business. These are reported on Schedule B as dividends from stocks held for investment.

Deductions from business income. You deduct from business income ordinary and necessary expenses incurred in your business. A checklist of expenses that are generally deductible on Schedule C is at ¶5.03.

Sideline business expenses. As long as you show a profit, you may deduct the expenses of the activity. But when expenses exceed income and your return is examined, an agent may allow expenses only up to the amount of your income and disallow the remaining expenses that make up your loss. To claim the loss deduction, you may be able to take advantage of a "presumption" explained at ¶5.06.

Claiming depreciation. Depreciation is an annual expense deduction through which you write off your investment in equipment, machinery, automobiles, buildings, and other property used in your business, rental or other income-producing activities. Depreciation is explained in ¶5.30.

You may not claim depreciation on property used for only personal use, such as a personal residence or pleasure car. But, if the property is used both for business and pleasure, the business portion may be depreciated. *See* ¶5.47.

You may elect to deduct up to $5,000 of the cost of business equipment in lieu of depreciation. *See* ¶5.38.

Self-employment tax. You are liable for self-employment tax if you have income of $400 or more from operating a business or profession as sole proprietor, in partnership with others, or as an independent contractor.

For 1986, you pay a tax of 12.3% on net self-employment income of up to $42,000 ($5,166 maximum) when you pay your income tax. The self-employment tax provides funds for Social Security and Medicare benefits. You compute the tax on Schedule SE.

You continue to pay self-employment tax on self-employment income even if you receive Social Security benefits.

Retirement plans. You may set up a Keogh plan if you earn self-employment income through your performance of personal services. For purposes of a Keogh plan, this income is called earned income and is your net profit (gross business or professional income less allowable business deductions). Contribution and deduction limits are explained at ¶7.30.

Capital Gains and Losses

CAPITAL GAINS AND LOSSES are generally realized on the sale of property, such as securities, real estate, and personal belongings.

There are two classes of capital gains and losses, short term and long term. Short-term or long-term gain or loss is generally determined by how long you held the property before its sale. For long-term capital gain, you must hold the property for more than six months before the sale. Only 40% of long-term capital gain is treated as taxable income. Short-term capital gains are fully taxable. Long-term capital losses are reduced by 50% before they are deducted from other income. Whether long- or short-term, only up to $3,000 of net capital losses may be deducted from other income, although capital losses are deductible without limit against capital gains. If capital losses in excess of capital gains exceed $3,000, the balance may be deductible against gains and income of later years.

Schedule D. The steps of calculating capital gains and losses are incorporated in Schedule D. An explanation of the principles of capital gain treatment may be found in ¶6.00. Illustrations of capital gain transactions are shown at ¶6.32 and in the Supplement.

If you are in a business or other income-producing activity, the tax treatment of sales of property used in your business is determined by special rules discussed at ¶5.45. Profits from the sales of inventory or stock-in-trade are taxed at ordinary income rates; losses are generally fully deductible. *See* ¶5.03.

Figuring gain or loss. In most cases, you know if you have realized a profit or loss on the sale or exchange of property. The difference between your cost and the selling price is your profit or loss. The tax computation of gain or loss is figured the same way, except that the tax rules may require you to increase or decrease your cost or selling price. As a result, your gain or loss for tax purposes may differ from your initial calculation. These adjustments are discussed at ¶6.07–¶6.11

Reporting a sale of your house. If you sold your home at a profit, you may be able to avoid tax if you are age 55 or over, or you may defer the tax on the profit if you buy or build another house at a cost at least equal to the sales price less selling costs and certain fix-up costs. To defer tax you must buy or build and use your new house within two years before or after you sell your old house. If you go on active military duty for more than 90 days, the two-year period is suspended while you are in the Service. *See* ¶29.10.

If you sold your house at a loss, you may not deduct your loss. Losses on the sale of property devoted to personal use are not deductible.

If you are 55 years of age or over and sell or exchange your home at a profit, you may avoid the tax on profits up to $125,000. To claim this exclusion, you must: (1) elect to avoid tax; (2) be 55 or over before the date of sale; and (3) have owned and occupied the house as your principal residence for at least three of the five years preceding the day of sale. *See* ¶29.30.

Installment sale reporting. If you arrange to receive one or more payments from a sale of property after the year of sale, installment sale rules automatically apply unless you elect otherwise. Under the installment method, your gain from the sale is reported over the period of payment, thereby deferring tax payments over several years. If you do not want the installment method, you make an election to report your entire gain in the year of sale. You might want to report the entire gain in the year of sale if you have losses to offset the gain. *See* ¶6.16.

Tax-free exchanges. Gain may not be taxed immediately where an exchange of property falls within the tax-free exchange rules explained at ¶6.20. Gain may be taxed at a future time when you dispose of the exchanged property. This is because the basis in your new property will reflect the gain not taxed on the exchange.

Loss realized on a nontaxable exchange is generally not deductible.

Alternative minimum tax. Long-term capital gains may be subject to the alternative minimum tax. *See* ¶23.10.

Reporting Pension Income

THE WAY YOU RECEIVE your retirement pension determines tax treatment. You may receive a lump-sum distribution or an annuity type payment.

Special tax advantages are available for a lump-sum distribution of all your benefits made within one taxable year. If you want to defer current tax on a lumpsum distribution, you may make a rollover to an IRA. On the other hand, if you can take advantage of the special averaging method, you may want to incur a current low tax on the distribution rather than make a rollover. Ten-year averaging available in 1986 generally results in a low effective rate of tax. You use Form 4972 to compute ten-year averaging. *See* ¶7.02 for sample effective tax rates of ten-year averaging. If your Form 1099-R allocates capital gain to part of your distribution, you may report that amount as long-term capital gain. However, it is generally preferable to forego capital gain treatment and apply ten-year averaging to the entire distribution.

Instead of paying current tax on the distribution, you may make a complete or partial rollover of the lump sum into an IRA or a qualified pension plan of a new employer. A rollover may be advisable if you anticipate your future tax bracket to be substantially lower when you plan to withdraw benefits. You must complete the rollover within 60 days of receiving the distribution.

Annuity payments. Part of your annuity payments may not be subject to tax if you contributed to your retirement account. Where you made contributions and you will recover your cost within 36 months after the date you receive the first payment, you do not report any amounts as income until you recover your cost. Thereafter, benefits are fully taxed as ordinary income.

Where you will not recover cost within 36 months, part of each payment will be taxable as ordinary income and part will be a tax-free return of your cost. To determine the annuity exclusion attributable to your contributions, *see* ¶7.10. Your employer will inform you of the extent of your contributions. If you did not contribute, you report all the payments as ordinary income.

Retired federal, state, county, and municipal employees usually recover their cost within 36 months.

Employees of tax-exempt religious or educational organizations may be covered by a special annuity contract generally funded by a salary reduction. *See* ¶7.11. Benefits are taxable under the annuity rules discussed above. Where benefits are paid in a lump sum, you may roll over the distribution to an IRA; you may not use ten-year averaging to report the lump-sum distribution.

Beneficiaries of deceased employees. Where you receive a lump sum or an annuity on account of an employee's death, you report the benefits according to the rules described above. However, you may be entitled to a $5,000 death benefit exclusion. The exclusion is added to the employee's cost and thus reduces the amount of benefits subject to tax. *See* ¶7.103.

Individual retirement accounts (IRAs). You may contribute to your 1986 retirement plan up to $2,000. If earnings are less than $2,000, your contribution is limited to earnings. *See* ¶7.16. A contribution of up to $2,000 may be based on alimony received. *See* ¶7.182. If you contribute to an IRA, you may also make deductible contributions on behalf of your nonworking spouse. The maximum deductible contribution is $2,250. *See* ¶7.181.

Income earned on your contributions is not taxed until you begin to receive benefits. When benefits are received, whether as an annuity or in a lump sum, they are taxed as ordinary income.

In 1986, you may not receive benefits before age 59½ (unless disabled) without incurring a penalty tax. You must begin receiving some benefits by age 70½ to avoid a penalty tax.

If your employer has a Simplified Employee Pension (SEP) plan, you report the company contribution to your account and claim an offsetting deduction. Benefits are fully taxable. *See* ¶7.22.

Withholding. Pension, IRA, and annuity payments are subject to withholding unless you elect otherwise. *See* ¶25.09.

Reporting Rent Income

IN SCHEDULE E, you report the gross amount of rent received from which you deduct rental expenses, such as mortgage interest, property taxes, maintenance costs, and depreciation. The net profit is added to your other taxable income. If you incur a loss, the loss reduces the amount of your other taxable income. However, if you rent out a vacation home which you also use yourself for part of the year, an expense deduction may be limited to rental income. *See* ¶29.40 and ¶5.06.

A most important rental expense deduction is depreciation through which you write off the cost of the building and improvements. Depreciation is discussed in detail in ¶5.30.

If you own a multiple-family dwelling and live in one of the units, you allocate expenses between rental and personal use. For example, if you own a three-family house and use one apartment for yourself, you allocate one-third of your expenses to personal use and two-thirds to business use. You deduct depreciation and expenses allocated to the rental use. You may not claim depreciation and maintenance expenses allocated to personal purposes. However, mortgage interest and taxes allocated to personal use are deductible if you itemize deductions.

For further rental income details, *see* ¶9.00.

Partnerships, S Corporations, Trusts and Estates

Partnership income. A partnership lists on Schedule K-1, Form 1065, the proportional share of profits, gains, losses, deductions, and credits of each partner. As a partner, you report your share of these items on your income tax return. Your share of capital gains and losses from the sale of partnership assets is reported on Schedule D. *See* ¶10.01.

If you invest in a syndicate, joint venture, or pool, you are treated as a partner.

S corporation income. Where a corporation has an S election in effect, the stockholders report each item of corporate income, loss, gain, deduction, or credit directly on their tax returns. The corporation does not pay corporate tax but is a corporation for all other purposes. The corporation informs the IRS of the stockholders' share of each item. You report your share on your income tax return. Your share of corporate capital gains and losses is reported on Schedule D. For a discussion on how to figure your reportable share, *see* ¶10.05.

You do not pay self-employment tax on your share of corporate income.

Trust and estate income. If you are a beneficiary of a trust or estate that is required to distribute all its income currently, you report your share of the distributable net income on Schedule E, whether or not you actually receive it. If the fiduciary has the discretion to distribute all or a part of the current income, you report all income required to be distributed to you, whether or not actually distributed. You also report all other amounts actually paid or credited to you to the extent of your share of distributable net income. *See* ¶11.01.

You report your share of income in the year the estate or trust distributes, credits, or is required to distribute the income to you if you have the same taxable year as the trust or estate. If your tax year is different, you report income of the trust's or estate's taxable year ending in your taxable year.

Nontaxable Income

Life insurance proceeds. Life insurance proceeds are generally tax free. Interest paid on proceeds left with the insurer is taxable except in this case: A surviving spouse who elects to receive installments rather than a lump sum does not pay tax on the first $1,000 of interest received each year. You are still treated as a spouse if separated from the insured at the date of death, but not if divorced. *See* ¶12.30.

Gifts and inheritances. The receipt of a gift or inheritance, regardless of size, is not taxable. Income earned on the gift or inheritance is taxable. *See* ¶12.01.

Prizes and awards. A prize or award is not taxable if (1) it is in recognition of past accomplishments in religious, charitable, scientific, educational, artistic, literary, or civic fields, (2) you did not enter the contest, *and* (3) you are not required to perform substantial future services. All other prizes and awards not meeting these conditions are taxable. *See* ¶12.03.

Scholarships and fellowships. If you are a candidate for a degree, amounts paid under a grant for tuition, fees, room, board, laundry and other services, and family allowances are tax free. If you are not working for a degree, part of your grant may be tax free. *See* ¶12.10.

Damages received in court actions. Amounts received in suits for personal injuries, defamation of personal reputation, or for child support, whether by verdict or settlement, are tax free. All other awards are taxable. *See* ¶12.22.

Alimony

COMMON RULES DETERMINE whether alimony is deductible by one spouse and taxable to the other. If a husband claims the deduction, the wife must report the alimony as income. If a wife pays alimony, the same rules apply. The rules for determining the tax status of alimony depend on the date of the decree. Different rules apply to alimony agreements and decrees made before 1985 and after 1984 and they are discussed in ¶1.70.

Payments specifically designated for child support are not deductible.

Itemized Deductions

YOU MAY REALIZE a substantial tax reduction by claiming itemized deductions for state and local sales taxes, income and real estate taxes, charitable contributions, medical expenses, interest, casualty and theft losses, and certain job and investment expenses. When itemized deductions exceed the following amounts, you may deduct the excess: $3,670 if you are married and file a joint return; $2,480 if you are single; $1,835 if you are married and file a separate return.

If your itemized deductions do not exceed these amounts, you still benefit from an income reduction, called the zero bracket amount. The zero bracket amount is $3,670 if you are married filing jointly ($1,835 if filing separately), and $2,480 if you are single. The zero bracket amount is built into the tax rate schedules and tax table so that you automatically receive the benefit when you compute your tax.

Deducting Medical Costs

THE UNREIMBURSED EXPENSES you paid for the medical care of you, your family, and your dependents in 1986 are deductible if they exceed 5% of your adjusted gross income. To determine if your expenses exceed the 5% floor, total the amounts paid in 1986 to or for:

Doctors, dentists, optometrists, chiropractors, chiropodists, podiatrists, osteopaths, psychiatrists, psychoanalysts, psychologists, authorized Christian Science practitioners, acupuncturists, nurses (but not for domestic services), physiotherapists, hospitals, medical laboratories, and convalescent homes (but only for medical treatment).

Costs of *prescribed* medicines and drugs, wheelchairs, ambulance hire, medical supplies and appliances (artificial teeth and limbs, eyeglasses, hearing aids, crutches, etc.).

Cost of transportation on a trip prescribed for the relief of a specific ailment. You may not deduct the cost of meals and lodgings on such a trip or the cost of a trip for the general improvement of your health. You may also deduct the cost of transportation to and from a doctor's office. If you accompany your minor child, you may deduct transportation expenses for both of you. *See* ¶17.08. Daily lodging costs of up to $50 on a trip to obtain medical care may also be deductible. *See* ¶17.08.

Dependents' medical costs. Even though you cannot claim your dependent as an exemption because he has income of $1,080 or more, you may still deduct your payments of his medical expenses if you prove you contributed more than half of his support. If you claim a dependent as an exemption under a multiple support agreement, you may deduct your payment of the dependent's medical costs, even though you contribute less than half of his support. Where divorced or separated parents provide more than half of their child's support and one or both parents have custody for more than half the year, both parents may deduct medical payments for the child.

Cost of equipment. You may deduct the cost of maintaining and operating equipment installed in your home for a medical reason. You may also deduct the cost of the equipment if it does not increase the value of your property, for example, the cost of a detachable window air conditioner. Where equipment increases the value of your house, you may generally take a medical deduction to the extent that the cost of the equipment exceeds the increase in the value of the property.

Schooling costs for the handicapped. You may deduct as medical expenses the cost of sending a mentally or physically handicapped person to a special school or institution to overcome or alleviate his handicap. Such costs may cover teaching braille or lip reading; training, caring for, supervising, and treating a mentally retarded person; cost of meals and lodgings, if boarding is required at the school; cost of regular education courses also taught at the school provided they are incidental to the special courses and services furnished by the school.

The parent of a problem child may deduct only that part of a private school fee directly related to psychological aid given to the child.

Premiums of medical care policies. You may deduct as a medical expense the cost of premiums paid for medical care policies covering you, your spouse, or dependents.

The premiums are included with other medical expenses subject to the 5% of income limit. There is no longer a separate deduction for premiums.

Typical medical care policies are Blue Cross, Blue Shield, federal voluntary Medicare (Part B), and Medicare (Part A) paid by persons 65 or over who are not covered by Social Security. (A payroll deduction to provide coverage under Part A is not deductible.) A deduction may be claimed for membership payments in associations furnishing cooperative or free-choice medical services, group hospitalization or clinical care policies, or health insurance policies which provide reimbursement for hospital, surgical, and other medical expenses.

No deduction may be claimed for premiums paid for a policy which compensates you for loss of earnings while ill or injured or for loss of life, limb, or sight. If your policy covers both medical care and loss of income or loss of life, limb, or sight, no part of the premium is deductible unless (1) the contract or a separate statement from the insurance company states what part of the premiums is allocated to medical care, and (2) the premium allocated to medical care is reasonable in relation to the total premium. If such an allocation is made, part of the premium allocated to medical care is deductible.

Important: You may not deduct medical expenses that have been reimbursed by insurance or other awards. Furthermore, reimbursement of previously deducted medical expenses may give you taxable income. *See* ¶17.04.

Deducting State and Local Taxes

YOU MAY DEDUCT as itemized deductions your 1986 payments of:

Real property taxes
State, local, and foreign income taxes
State and local personal property taxes
State and local general sales and use taxes

Sales tax tables. The Treasury sales tax table lists sales tax deductions according to size of income and family. It may be found in the Supplement. You may add to the tax listed in the table: sales taxes incurred on the purchase of a car, boat, airplane, mobile home, or materials you bought to build a new home where you are your own contractor. You may also add the sales tax paid on the purchase of a car, unless you bought it in Vermont or West Virginia. Since local sales taxes may not be included in the Treasury table, you may add the local tax according to Treasury table instructions.

The table does not limit the amount you may deduct. You may deduct more than the Treasury figure if your actual sales tax payments are more, but be prepared to support your deduction with records if your return is questioned.

When you deduct state or local income taxes, include the amount of state or local income tax withheld or estimated tax you have paid in 1986. You may also deduct as a personal property tax that part of the cost of your automobile tags that is based on the value of your car. Although most state motor vehicle registration fees are not deductible, several states and localities impose personal property taxes on motor vehicles that may qualify for the deduction. *See* ¶16.09.

You may not deduct cigarette and tobacco taxes, alcoholic beverage taxes, poll taxes, admission and occupancy taxes, gasoline taxes for personal driving, and taxes assessed for local improvements that tend to increase the value of your property.

See ¶16.00 for further details.

Deducting Casualty or Theft Losses

YOU MAY DEDUCT personal casualty and theft losses that exceed 10% of adjusted gross income.

Deductible losses must arise from uncompensated property losses from thefts, automobile accidents, fire, storm, flood, earthquake, and other natural catastrophes. You may not deduct for damage caused by a natural action such as erosion or termite infestation occurring over a period of time. Nor may you deduct for accidental loss of money or other personal property.

Each uncompensated loss is also reduced by $100 before total losses are subject to the 10% limitation.

The amount of your loss is generally the difference between the value of the damaged property before and after the casualty. If you cannot get these values, you may be able to deduct the cost of repairs if it is not excessive and does nothing more than restore your property to its condition immediately before the casualty. A casualty loss deduction may not exceed the cost of the property.

Generally, you deduct a casualty loss in the year the casualty occurs. However, if you reasonably expect reimbursement in a later year, deduct in the year of the casualty only that part of your loss for which you do not expect reimbursement. *See* ¶18.05.

Your insurance contract may reimburse you for excess living costs when a casualty or threat of casualty forces you to vacate your home. The living expenses paid by the insurance company are generally not taxable.

Deducting Education Costs

YOU DEDUCT the cost of courses you take to maintain or improve your job, business, or professional skills in 1986. To support the deduction, you have to show: (1) You are employed or self-employed; (2) you meet the minimum requirements of your job, business, or profession; and (3) the course maintains or improves skills required for your job, or you are required by your employer or by law to take the course to keep your present salary or position.

You may not deduct the cost of courses to satisfy your desire for learning or to meet the minimum educational requirements of your occupation. Also, you may not deduct the cost of courses qualifying you to practice a new profession.

Provided the above tests are met, the fact that a course leads to a degree will not bar a deduction for educational expenses. Also, if the courses lead to a change of position or promotion within the same occupation, the deduction for their costs will be allowed if your new duties involve the same general type of work.

If your courses meet the tests, you may deduct: (1) Cost of the courses, such as tuition, textbooks, fees, equipment and other aids required by the courses. (2) Travel to and from a school away from home. (3) Living expenses (food and lodging) while at the school away from home. (4) Cost of transportation from your job to your courses, plus parking and tolls. If the school is beyond your general area of employment you may deduct round trip transportation costs.

For further details, *see* ¶21.00.

Deducting Charitable Contributions

YOU MAY DEDUCT your donations to religious, charitable, scientific, literary and educational organizations, and donations to or for the use of local and federal government bodies. But note that your donation is deductible only when the organization has been approved by the IRS. Ask the organization to which you contribute if it has been approved, or check the IRS's published list of approved organizations. Also, note the ceiling placed on the maximum deduction. It is generally 50% of your adjusted gross income where you itemize deductions.

If you donated property, such as furniture, clothing, real estate, securities or works of art to an approved charity, attach to the return a statement showing date of gift, description of the property, and how you valued it, if it is not securities.

You must have a written appraisal for property (except publicly traded securities) valued at more than $5,000, and a summary of the appraisal must be attached to your return.

If you use your automobile for volunteer charity work, you may claim a deduction based on a flat IRS mileage rate of 12¢ per mile.

Even if you do not itemize deductions in 1986, you may deduct 100% of your contributions. For further details, *see* ¶14.00.

Deducting Interest

YOU DEDUCT INTEREST in 1986 even though it is paid on money borrowed for personal expenses. Include interest on your personal note to a bank, credit union, or individual for money you borrowed. The debt need not be evidenced by a note, lien, judgment, or mortgage. But it must be your debt or obligation; otherwise you may not deduct the interest even though you paid it.

Mortgage interest is deductible. If you make one monthly payment on your mortgage, covering interest, taxes, and amortization, a breakdown of deductible interest and taxes is usually provided in the annual statement sent by the bank. A portion of payment on a zero interest mortgage may be treated as interest. *See* ¶15.011.

You deduct interest paid on delinquent tax payments and judgments. On a discounted note, you deduct interest when you make payments on the note, not when the loan is made, even though interest is taken in advance.

If you borrow against your life insurance, deduct interest when you pay off the loan, not when the insurance company adds the interest to your debt.

Interest on credit purchases. If you buy on credit using a bank credit card, oil company credit card, or a revolving credit account at a retail store, you may deduct the finance charge. Finance charges paid on an installment contract may also be deductible where the charge is based on a percentage of the unpaid balance. If a fixed finance fee is charged on an installment contract to purchase personal property or educational services, only the part of the fee allocable to interest may be deductible.

Cooperative apartments. If you are a tenant-stockholder in a cooperative apartment, you may deduct your portion of (1) interest paid by the cooperative on its debts and (2) taxes paid by the cooperative. (However, if the cooperative leases the land and building and under the lease is required to pay real estate taxes, you may not deduct your share of the tax payment.)

If you own a condominium, you may deduct your payments of real estate taxes and mortgage interest.

Excess investment interest. In 1986 interest in excess of net investment income plus $10,000 ($5,000 if married and filing a separate return) paid on loans to carry investments may be partially disallowed. For the details, see Form 4952.

See ¶15.00 for further details.

Other Itemized Expenses

HERE ARE the kinds of expenses you may deduct as "miscellaneous deductions" in 1986.

Union dues and assessments

Safety equipment, small tools and supplies for your job

Costs of producing or collecting income

Uniform and special work clothing costs and their upkeep (the clothing must be required to keep your job and not adaptable to general use as clothing after work hours)

Dues to professional societies

Fees paid to a tax advisor to prepare your tax return or to represent you at a tax audit

Safe deposit box fees

Investment counselor fees and investment service costs

You may deduct the expenses of looking for a new job in the same line of work, whether or not a new job is found. If you are unemployed when seeking a job, the IRS may disallow the deduction if it finds a substantial lack of continuity of time between the past job and the current job search. It provides no specific guidelines for what it considers a continuity of time.

If you travel to find a new job in the same line of work, such as to an interview in a distant city, you may deduct travel expenses, including living costs. If, during the trip, you also do personal visiting, you may deduct the transportation expenses if the trip was primarily related to your job search. Time spent on personal activity is compared with time spent looking for a job to determine the primary purpose of the trip. If the transportation expenses to and from the destination are not deductible under this test, you may still deduct expenses allocated to seeking the new job.

If an employer pays the fee under an agreement with an agency, you may disregard the payment for tax purposes. However, if you pay the fee and are afterwards reimbursed by the employer, you must report the reimbursement as taxable income. This additional income may be offset by deducting the fee as an itemized deduction.

Expenses of seeking a job for the first time are not deductible, even if a job is obtained. This rule prevents a person seeking his first job from deducting job-hunt expenses.

See ¶19.05 for details.

Figuring Your Tax

SPECIFIC TAX LIABILITIES are listed in the tax table according to amounts of taxable income and filing status. You use the tax table if your taxable income is less than $50,000, regardless of your filing status or number of exemptions.

If your taxable income is not within the tax table, you must compute your tax using a tax rate schedule. You must also use a tax rate schedule if you income average, claim the foreign income exclusion, or file for a short period due to change of accounting period. For further details. *See* ¶22.00.

Can you average your income? If there was a substantial rise in your income in 1986, it may be to your advantage to figure your tax by averaging your income. Income averaging will generally benefit you when you receive in one taxable year a large increase in income. You may even be able to average when your income has steadily increased over the years. You may average if your taxable income in 1986 exceeds by more than $3,000 140% of average taxable income for the three preceding years (1983–1985).

Averaging is available to citizens and residents of the United States. But if you have recently graduated from school, you may not qualify. *See* ¶23.00.

Alternative minimum tax (AMT). If your regular income tax is less than the 20% alternative minimum tax, you pay the difference. You may be subject to the AMT if you have substantial long-term capital gains and certain tax preference items and credits.

Deduction for two-earner married couples. A special deduction of up to $3,000 is allowed in 1986 to married couples where both spouses are working. The deduction is figured on the earnings of the spouse who earns less. The deduction is 10% of lower net earnings up to $30,000 (maximum deduction of $3,000).

Self-employment income qualifies as earned income for purposes of the deduction. Earned income does not include pension income, deferred pay, distributions from IRA or Keogh plans, and unemployment compensation paid under a government program.

You may not figure the deduction on wages you earn by working for your spouse if the wages are exempt from certain Social Security taxes. Similarly, no deduction may be claimed if you or your spouse elects the foreign earned income exclusion or the exclusion for income from sources within U.S. possessions.

Before applying the 10% rate, you reduce earned income by deductible job expenses (business expenses of self-employed persons, reimbursed expenses, travel expenses away from home, transportation expenses of employees and outside salespersons' expenses) and by contributions to an IRA, Keogh plan, or retirement plan of an S corporation, and any repaid supplemental unemployment compensation.

To claim the deduction you must file a joint return. The deduction may be claimed whether or not you itemize deductions.

For further details, *see* ¶1.01.

Claiming Tax Credits

THE FOLLOWING tax credits reduce your tax liability dollar for dollar. Check if you qualify for:

Credit for dependent care expenses. You may claim a credit for a percentage of dependent care expenses that you paid for the care of a child under 15 or a disabled dependent to allow you to work or to seek employment and earn income. The amount of the credit varies with your income. Details of computing the credit are at ¶24.20.

Tax credit for disability pensions and for the elderly. The full benefit of the credit is available mainly to retired people who do not receive Social Security. The maximum amount of the credit may be as high as $750 (15% × $5,000) or $1,125 (15% × $7,500) on a joint return where both spouses qualify for the credit. *See* ¶34.02.

If you are under age 65, the credit applies only if you are permanently and totally disabled.

Earned income credit. A special tax credit for low income workers with families may provide a refund or subsidy of up to $500. An "earned income credit" is available only to low income workers who have children and maintain a household. *See* ¶24.50.

Political campaign contributions. If you make contributions to a political campaign, you may claim a 1986 tax credit; the credit is one-half the contribution, up to $100 on a joint return ($50 on a separate return).

For a list of other tax credits *see* ¶24.00.

Keep Tax Records

TAX SAVING requires keeping records which will help you to figure your income and deductions. Do not trust to memory. With bills accumulating during the year, you are bound to overlook items. But more importantly, you will have no record to present to the IRS if your return is audited.

Establish record-keeping methods to insure completeness and to ease your burden at tax time: Use only one room to record your data and store receipts. Keep receipts in a handy place. You may find it convenient to store receipts in an envelope or even a shoe box until you need to organize the information to prepare your return. Also, after you have balanced your monthly checking account statement, segregate all tax-related canceled checks and retain them with your other receipts. Be sure to keep receipts from one year separate from another. If your work involves travel or entertaining business clients, you should keep a day-by-day record of expenses. A diary devoted exclusively to this purpose should be used and information recorded as expenses are incurred. *See* ¶2.35. If you own a home and make improvements, records must be kept to help you minimize gain in the event of sale. *See* ¶29.24. If you invest in stock, keep detailed records of purchases so that you can plan your investment strategy. *See* ¶30.00.

Be sure to retain past tax returns, not only in the event of IRS questions, but to see if you are eligible to income average. *See* ¶23.00. Also save information returns sent to you, such as interest and dividend statements, in the event your return is questioned.

How long should you keep your records? Your records should be kept for a minimum of three years after the year to which they are applicable. Some authorities advise keeping them for six years, since in some cases the IRS may go back as far as six years to question a tax return. In cases of suspected tax fraud, there is no time limitation at all. Certain records, such as home improvements and stock information, should be kept until you use the information, as in the event of sale, and then for at least three years thereafter.

File the Right Tax Form

For 1986, there are three income tax forms: Form 1040, which may be used to report any type of income, deduction or credit, and two short forms, Form 1040EZ and Form 1040A. Use the form that permits you to report all of your income and take all of your deductions and credits.

Filled-in samples of Forms 1040, 1040EZ and 1040A may be found in the *Supplement* which you may obtain free by mailing the card at the front of this book.

Form 1040EZ. Form 1040EZ may be used only if (1) you are single; (2) you claim only one exemption (no exemptions are allowed on Form 1040EZ for being age 65 or over or blind or for dependents); (3) your taxable income is less than $50,000; (4) your income besides wages and tips consists solely of interest of $400 or less (and you had no dividend income); and (5) you do not itemize deductions or claim any credits.

You may claim the nonitemized charitable deduction on Form 1040EZ provided you did not give over $3,000 to any one charity or make any noncash donation.

Form 1040A. Form 1040A may be used if (1) your income consists solely of wages (including tips) subject to withholding, taxable unemployment compensation, ordinary dividends and interest income; (2) your taxable income is *less* than $50,000; (3) your itemized deductions do not exceed the zero bracket amount of $3,670 if you are married filing jointly, or $2,480 if you are single or head of household. If you are married, filing separately, you may use Form 1040A if your itemized deductions are $1,835 or less, provided your spouse does not claim excess itemized deductions. If your itemized deductions exceed the zero bracket amount, or you are otherwise required to itemize deductions, you must file Form 1040.

Form 1040. Use Form 1040 and its supplemental schedules if your income, deductions, or credits may not be reported on either Form 1040EZ or Form 1040A. For example, you must use Form 1040 if your taxable income is at least $50,000 or to claim itemized deductions in excess of the zero bracket amount.

Use Form 1040 to:

Report capital gains, gain from the sale of your home, taxable alimony, taxable Social Security benefits, self-employment income, interest received as a nominee for someone else, taxable unemployment compensation, rent and royalty income, and foreign earned income.

Claim alimony deductions, itemized deductions, employee job expenses, moving expenses, Keogh plan contributions, deduction of penalty for premature savings withdrawal, tax credit for elderly and disabled, business tax credits, mortgage interest credit, diesel vehicle credit, and foreign tax credit.

Check your return. Avoid common errors that may delay a refund or result in a tax deficiency and interest costs. Before filing, check that:

- Your arithmetic is correct.
- Your Social Security number is correctly recorded on each form and schedule and remittance, if any.
- You have used the tax table or schedule applicable to your tax status.
- You have filled in the proper boxes which state your filing status and exemption claims.
- You have put the tax payable or refund due you on the correct line.
- You have signed your return; if you file a joint return, both you and your spouse must sign.

Photocopy your return. Keep it along with receipts, canceled checks and other items used to support your deductions.

Tax saving techniques. Tax saving is a year round, almost daily, activity. It involves being aware of tax-saving techniques such as those discussed in the following sections for:

	See ¶
Homeowners	29.00
Investors in securities	30.00
Investors in realty	31.00
Business executives	32.00
Family income planners	33.00
Senior citizens	34.00

¶ 1.00

How Your Personal and Family Status Affects Your Taxes

Your family and personal status directly affects the tax you pay.

For each qualified dependent, you claim a deduction of $1,080. The tax-saving rules for claiming exemptions for yourself, your spouse and dependents are discussed at ¶1.50.

For paying care costs of dependent children while you work you may claim a tax credit as explained in ¶1.60.

For paying qualifying alimony, you may claim a deduction. If you receive such alimony, you report income. Pay special attention to the rules at ¶1.70 in planning alimony agreements so that you achieve favorable tax consequences.

Your tax rates depend on your personal status. There are four tax rate classes: Rates for married persons filing jointly, unmarried person rates, head of household rates, rates for married persons filing separate returns. The lowest tax rates are provided to married persons filing jointly; the next lowest to unmarried persons filing as head of household; the highest rates apply to married persons filing separate returns. Joint return rates favor married couples where only one spouse earns income. When both spouses have income, the joint return rates usually result in a higher tax than if the two were reporting as single persons and applying single person rates. The difference in tax is called the "marriage penalty." In 1986, this "penalty" is eased by a special deduction of up to $3,000. If you are married your best tax-saving choice is almost surely to file jointly; filing separately almost always results in a higher combined tax because of the tax rates applied to separate returns of married couples, as explained in ¶1.012. In special cases, a recently widowed individual may use joint return rates, which is an advantage to a single person; and certain separated married persons may use head of household rates under ¶1.05 rather than the higher rates applied to married persons filing separately. Tax rate schedules are at ¶22.00.

Filing Joint Returns

	See ¶
Deduction for two-earner married couples	1.001
Signing the joint return	1.01
Innocent spouse rules	1.011
Married persons may choose to file separately	1.012
Death of spouse during the year	1.02
Effect of divorce or separation decree	1.021

	See ¶
Joint return if spouse is a nonresident alien	1.03
Community property rules	1.04
Unmarried head of household	1.05
Tax returns for your children	1.12
Filing income tax returns for a decedent	1.14
Return for an incompetent person	1.16

¶1.001 • TWO-EARNER MARRIED COUPLES MAY DEDUCT UP TO $3,000 IN 1986

Do you and your spouse both work? If so, you may claim a deduction based on the earnings of the spouse who earns less. The deduction is 10% of lower net earnings up to $30,000. This gives a maximum deduction of $3,000 ($30,000 × 10%). You must file a joint return to claim the deduction. The deduction is allowed even if you do not itemize deductions on your return. The deduction is figured on Schedule W.

WORK SHEET FOR FIGURING LOWER NET EARNINGS AND DEDUCTION

1. Your wages $_____
2. Less: Job expenses*
3. Your net wages $_____
4. Your spouse's wages $_____
5. Less: Job expenses*
6. Your spouse's net wages $_____
7. Choose the lower of line 3 or 6   _____
8. Take 10% of line 7—This is your deduction $_____

* Job expenses are: Business expenses of self-employed persons, reimbursed expenses, travel expenses away from home, transportation expenses of employees, outside salesmen expenses, contributions to an IRA, Keogh plan, or retirement plan of an S

corporation and repaid supplemental unemployment compensation.

Example—

You earn $35,000 and have deducted travel expenses of $5,000 and an IRA contribution of $2,000. Your spouse has a salary of $32,000 and deducts $2,000 for an IRA contribution.

1. Your salary	$35,000
2. Less expenses and IRA deduction	7,000
3. Your net wages	28,000
4. Your spouse's salary	$32,000
5. Less IRA deduction	2,000
6. Your spouse's net wages	30,000
7. Lower net wages	28,000
8. 10% deduction	$2,800

Self-employment income qualifies as earned income for purposes of the deduction. Before applying the 10% rate, you reduce salary or wage or self-employment income by deductible job expenses and contributions to an IRA or Keogh plan.

You may not figure the deduction:

On wages you earn by working for your spouse if the wages are exempt from certain Social Security taxes;

On pension income, deferred pay, and distributions from an IRA or Keogh plan and unemployment compensation paid under a government program;

If either spouse elects the foreign earned income exclusion or the exclusion for income from sources within U.S. possessions;

If you file a separate return.

¶1.01 • SIGNING THE JOINT RETURN

Both you and your spouse must sign the return. Under the following rules, if your spouse is unable to sign, you may sign for him or her.

You may sign your spouse's name as agent by adding these words: by _____ Husband (or Wife), and attaching to the return your authorization.

If, because of illness, your spouse is physically unable to sign the joint return, you may, with the oral consent of your spouse, sign his or her name on the return followed by the words "By _____, Husband (or Wife)." You then sign the return again in your own right and attach a signed and dated statement with the following information: (1) The return or declaration being filed, (2) the tax year, (3) the reason for the inability of the sick spouse to sign, and (4) that the sick spouse has consented to your signing.

You might be able to prove you filed a joint return even if your spouse did not sign and you did not sign as your spouse's agent where:

You intended it to be a joint return—your spouse's income was included (or the spouse had no income).

Your spouse agreed to have you handle tax matters and you filed a joint return.

Your answers to the questions on the tax return indicate you intend to file a joint return.

Your spouse's failure to sign can be explained.

Example—
The Hills generally filed joint returns. In one year, Hill claimed joint return filing status and reported his wife's income as well as his own; in place of her signature on the return, he indicated that she was out of town caring for her sick mother. She did not file a separate return. The IRS refused to treat the return as joint. The Tax Court disagreed. Since Mrs. Hill testified that she would have signed had she been available, her failure to do so does not bar joint return status. The couple intended to make a joint return at the time of filing.

If a third party signs as agent for your spouse, power-of-attorney, Form 2848, must accompany the return.

Joint liability. When you sign a joint return, you and your spouse may be held individually liable for the entire tax due, plus interest and any penalties. You may be held liable if your spouse does not pay the tax, even if he or she earned all the income.

If you divorce, you remain jointly liable for joint returns filed before the divorce.

In limited cases, an innocent spouse may avoid liability, as discussed below.

¶1.011 • INNOCENT SPOUSE RULES

To a limited extent, a spouse who files a joint return may be relieved of tax liability based on omitted income or invalid tax deductions or credits. These conditions must be met: (1) There is a tax underpayment exceeding $500 due to the omission of gross income attributable to the other spouse or inflated deductions or credits claimed by the other spouse, provided the "innocent" spouse's tax liability exceeds certain limits discussed below. In determining gross income, community property rules are disregarded, except for income from property. (2) In signing the joint return, the innocent spouse did not know of and had no reason to know of the omission of income or inflated deductions or credits. (3) Taking into account all the circumstances, it would be inequitable to hold the innocent spouse liable for the tax. The IRS will consider the extent to which the "innocent" spouse benefited from the tax underpayment in deciding the "equity" issue.

Innocent spouse's tax liability must exceed percentage of income. Where relief is based on the other spouse's claiming of invalid deductions or credits, the innocent spouse's tax liability must exceed $500 and a specific percentage of adjusted gross income for the taxable year preceding the year in which the IRS mails a deficiency notice. If the innocent spouse's adjusted gross income

in the year preceding the mailing of a deficiency notice was $20,000 or less, the tax liability attributable to the other spouse's improper deductions must exceed 10% of the preceding year's adjusted gross income. If adjusted gross income was more than $20,000, the tax liability for which relief is sought must exceed 25% of the preceding year's adjusted gross income. If the innocent spouse has remarried as of the end of the preceding year, the new spouse's income must be included to determine the innocent spouse's adjusted gross income for purposes of the 10%/25% tests.

Important: The above innocent spouse rules apply to all preceding taxable years which are not closed by the statute of limitations; it also applies to pending court cases in which a final decision has not been made.

¶1.012 • MARRIED PERSONS MAY CHOOSE TO FILE SEPARATELY

It is generally advisable to file jointly even though your spouse may have earned a small sum and could get a refund by filing separately. If your spouse files separately, you must file separately and your tax may be substantially higher than if you had filed jointly.

In the following limited situations, filing separately may reduce the overall taxes for a husband and wife: (1) Each spouse has capital losses from pre-1970 taxable years (*see* ¶6.003), (2) both husband and wife have separate incomes and one pays substantial medical expenses, and (3) one spouse in a low tax bracket in 1986 has long-term capital gains and the other spouse is in a high tax bracket and has capital losses. To determine if there is a saving, figure the tax on both types of returns.

Effect of filing separate returns. If you and your spouse file separate returns, you have three years from the due date to change to a joint return. If a joint return is filed and the due date has passed, you may not elect to file separate returns. The choice of a joint return is irrevocable once the due date is passed.

The filing of separate or joint estimated tax does not commit you to a similar tax return.

You must file jointly to claim the following tax benefits: The deduction for two-earner married couples, IRA deduction for a nonworking spouse, and the credit for the elderly, dependent care credit, and the earned income credit. Further, if you receive Social Security benefits, one half of your benefits are generally subject to tax on a separate return because on a separate return you are not allowed a base amount exemption, see ¶34.11.

¶1.02 • DEATH OF A SPOUSE DURING THE YEAR

You do not lose the right to file a joint return when your spouse dies during the year. Generally, a joint return is filed by you and the executor or administrator. But you alone may file a joint return if you are otherwise entitled to file jointly and:

1. The deceased has not filed a separate return, and
2. No executor or administrator has been appointed when the joint return is made, or no executor or administrator was appointed before the last day required to file the return of the surviving spouse.

As a surviving spouse, you may not file a joint return if:

1. You remarry before the end of the year of your spouse's death (but you may file a joint return with your new spouse).
2. You or your deceased spouse has a short year because of a change in the accounting period.
3. Either spouse was a nonresident alien at any time during the tax year. But *see* ¶1.03.
4. The executor or administrator disaffirms. When the executor or administrator is later appointed, he may disaffirm the joint return by filing a separate return for the decedent. The executor or administrator is the person who is actually appointed to that office. It is not the person who may be in charge of the property of the decedent. Even if a surviving spouse has properly filed a joint return for himself and the deceased spouse (*see* above)—the executor or administrator is given the right to disaffirm the joint return. But in one case, a state court held that a co-executrix

could not refuse to sign a joint return where it would save the estate money.

The executor may disaffirm within one year after the time required to file the return of the surviving spouse by filing a separate return. The executor's separate return is treated as a late return. He has to pay interest and a penalty for a late filing. The return of the surviving spouse is deemed to be his or her separate return. Tax on that return is computed by excluding all items belonging to the deceased spouse.

Signing the return. A joint return reporting a decedent's income should list the names of the surviving spouse and the deceased. Where there is an executor or administrator, the return is signed by the surviving spouse and the executor or administrator in his official capacity. If the surviving spouse is the executor or administrator, he signs once as surviving spouse and again as the executor or administrator. Where there is no executor or administrator, the surviving spouse signs, followed by the words, "Taxpayer and surviving spouse."

If a joint return is filed and the estate cannot pay its share of the joint income tax liability, the surviving spouse may be liable for the full amount. Once the return is filed and the time for filing passes, the survivor can no longer change the joint return election and file a separate return unless an administrator or executor is appointed after the due date of the return. In that case, as explained above, the executor may disaffirm the joint return.

If a surviving spouse who will be appointed executor or administrator is concerned about insolvency, it may be advisable to hedge as follows: (1) File separate returns and if it is later seen that a joint return is preferable, the surviving spouse has three years to change to a joint return. (2) File jointly but postpone being appointed executor or administrator until after the due date of the joint return. In this way, the joint return may be disaffirmed if the estate cannot cover its share of the taxes.

Death of spouse in 1984 or 1985. You may use joint return rates for 1986 if you did not remarry before 1987 and in 1986 a dependent child lived with you and you paid over half the cost of maintaining your home. Further, you must have been able to file jointly in the year of your spouse's death.

¶1.021 • EFFECT OF DIVORCE OR SEPARATION DECREE ON JOINT RETURN

A decree of divorce or separate maintenance before the end of the year. A decree entered before the end of 1986 prevents you from filing a joint return. Unless you qualify as head of household (¶1.05), you must use the rates for single individuals. You may not claim an exemption for a divorced or legally separated spouse, even if you contribute all support.

If you are married but live apart from your spouse and care for a child, you may be able to qualify as a head of household, see ¶1.05.

You may file a joint return after an interlocutory decree of divorce. Once the decree is made final, the privilege to file jointly ends. Alimony paid during the period covered by the interlocutory decree is deducted by the husband and reported by the wife as income if separate returns are filed.

If a divorce decree is interlocutory but another state waives the waiting period and permits a spouse to remarry, the IRS will recognize the new marriage and allow the filing of joint returns by the newly married couple. But a court has refused to allow a joint return where a new marriage took place in Mexico during the interlocutory period in violation of California law.

The IRS and an appeals court conflict over whether a joint return with a new spouse is permissible if a prior divorce decree has been declared invalid by a state court. The appeals court allows the joint return; the IRS does not.

Year-end foreign divorce may not be recognized. A married couple with two incomes may pay more tax on a joint return than unmarried couples who file separately using single person rates. To avoid it, some married couples made quick year-end divorces to file as unmarried persons and then remarried the next year. The Tax Court has ruled two Caribbean divorces obtained by a Mary-

land couple during a two-year period were ineffective for tax purposes; the couple remained married and could not use unmarried person rates.

¶1.03 • JOINT RETURN IF SPOUSE IS A NONRESIDENT ALIEN

You may not be able to file a joint return if either you or your spouse was a nonresident alien during any part of the year. Thus, a joint return may be barred if the alien spouse enters the United States in the middle of the taxable year or departs before it ends. Nevertheless, you may be able to claim your nonresident alien spouse as an exemption on a return filed as married filing separately if the spouse had no income and could not be claimed as a dependent by another taxpayer (see ¶1.51). If the alien spouse becomes a resident before the beginning of the next tax year, you may file jointly thereafter.

Election to file a joint return. Where a U.S. citizen or resident is married to a nonresident alien, the couple may file a joint return if both elect to be taxed on their world-wide income. The requirement that one spouse be a U.S. citizen or resident need be met only at the close of the year. Joint returns may be filed in the year of the election and all later years until the election is terminated.

A couple that makes the election must keep books and records of their world-wide income and give the IRS access to such books and records. If either spouse does not provide the necessary information to the IRS, the election is terminated. Further, the election is terminated if either spouse revokes or dies. Revocation before the due date of return is effective for that return. The election automatically terminates for the year of death of either spouse. However, if the survivor is a U.S. citizen or resident, he or she may claim the benefits of being a surviving spouse (see ¶1.00). The election to file jointly also terminates if the couple is legally separated under a decree of divorce or separate maintenance. Termination is effective as of the beginning of the taxable year of the legal separation. If neither spouse is a citizen or resident for any part of the taxable year, an election may not be made and an existing election is revoked. Once the election is terminated, neither spouse may ever again make the election.

Electing to file a joint return does not terminate the special withholding on the nonresident alien's income. See ¶37.07.

Special election where one spouse is a U.S. citizen or resident and the other is a nonresident alien who becomes a resident during the tax year. The couple may file a joint return for that year if both elect to be taxed on their world-wide income. This is a one-time election; neither spouse may make the election again even if married to a new spouse.

If a couple does not make the election to file jointly, certain community property rules do not apply. See ¶1.04.

¶1.04 • COMMUNITY PROPERTY RULES

If you live in Arizona, California, Idaho, Louisiana, Nevada, New Mexico, Texas, or Washington, and beginning in 1986, Wisconsin, the income and property you and your spouse acquire during the marriage is generally regarded as "community property." But note that there are some instances in which community property rules are disregarded for tax purposes; these instances are clearly highlighted in the pertinent sections of this book.

Community property means that each of you owns half of the community income and community property, even if legal title is held by only one spouse.

Separate property may be owned. Property owned before marriage generally remains "separate property"; it does not become community property when you marry. Property received during the marriage by one spouse as a gift or inheritance from a third party is generally separate property. In some states, if the nature of ownership cannot be fixed, the property is presumed to be community property.

In some states, income from "separate property" may be treated as community property income. In other states, income from "separate property" remains the separate property of the individual owner.

Divorce or separation. If you and your spouse divorce, your community property automatically becomes separate property. For the division of community property pursuant to a divorce, *see* ¶20.06.

A wife, while separated from her husband, does not generally report temporary alimony payments. She reports her share of community income until the date of the interlocutory divorce decree.

When community income rules do not apply to separated couples. If a husband and wife in a community property state file separate returns, each spouse must generally report one-half of the community income. However, a spouse may be able to avoid reporting income earned by his or her spouse if they live apart during the entire calendar year and do not file a joint return. To qualify, one or both spouses must have earned income for the year and none of that earned income may be transferred, directly or indirectly, between the spouses during the year. One spouse's payment to the other spouse solely to support the couple's dependent children is not a disqualifying transfer. If the separated couple qualifies under these tests, community income is allocated as follows: Earned income (excluding business or partnership income) is taxed to the spouse who performed the personal services. Business income (other than partnership income) is treated as the husband's income, unless the wife exercises substantially all of the management and control of the business. However, a similar rule for self-employment income was held unconstitutional on the basis of sex, and the IRS agreed to follow the court rule that the spouse actually carrying on the business is the spouse subject to self-employment tax. Partnership income is taxed to the spouse entitled to a distributive share of partnership profits.

Innocent spouse rules applied to community property. As discussed above, community property rules may not apply to earned income where spouses live apart for the entire year and file separate returns. In addition, a spouse who files a separate return may be relieved of tax liability on community income which is attributable to the other spouse if he or she does not know (or have reason to know) about the income and if it would be inequitable under the circumstances for him or her to be taxed on such income.

This rule applies to all tax years not closed by the statute of limitations and to court cases in which a final decision has not been made.

The IRS may disregard community property rules and tax income to a spouse who treats such income as if it were solely his or hers and who fails to notify the other spouse of the income before the due date of the return (including extensions).

Death of spouse. The death of a spouse dissolves the community property relationship, but income earned and accrued from community property before death is community income.

Moving from a community property to a common law (separate property) state. Most common law states (those which do not have community property laws) recognize that both spouses have an interest in property accumulated while residents of a community property state. If the property is not sold or reinvested, it may continue to be treated as community property. If you and your spouse sell community property after moving to a common law state and reinvest the proceeds, the reinvested proceeds are generally separate property, which may be held as joint tenants, or in another form of ownership recognized by common law states.

Moving from a common law state to a community property state. Separate property brought into a community property state generally retains its character as separately owned property. Property acquired by a couple after moving to a community property state is generally owned as community property. In at least one state (California), personal property which qualifies as community property is treated as such, even though it was acquired when the couple lived in a common law state.

Claiming dependents on separate returns. Married parents in community property states who plan to file separate returns should be aware that neither parent may be able to claim an exemption for a dependent child. Where all of the couple's income is considered community income, each parent on a separate return is treated as having provided exactly one-half of the child's support, regardless of who actually paid the support. Since neither parent has provided more than one-half of the support, neither can claim the child as a dependent.

To avoid this result, parents whose sole income is community income and who want to file separately should consider signing a multiple support agreement, Form 2120, designating which parent may claim the exemption. Filing Form 2120 is not necessary where either parent can prove that he or she has income which is considered separate income rather than community income; that parent may be able to satisfy the more than 50% support test. In certain community property states, the law may provide that income of a husband and wife living apart is considered separate income rather than community income.

Filing as Head of Household

¶1.05 • UNMARRIED "HEAD OF HOUSEHOLD"

If you are an unmarried head of a household, you may compute your tax at a rate lower than that imposed on unmarried persons who do not qualify as heads of households. Tax rates are at ¶22.00. If you live apart from your spouse, you may also qualify for head of household rates that are lower than rates for married persons filing separately; *see* rule 1 below.

You have to meet the following five tests to qualify as head of household:

1. You are not married at the end of the year. You are any one of the following:

Single.

A widow or widower and your spouse died before the beginning of 1986. (*Also see* ¶1.02 if you may use joint return rates.)

Separated or divorced under a final court decree. A custody and support order does not qualify as a legal separation. An interlocutory decree, such as a support order pendente lite, has no effect for tax purposes until the decree is made final.

Married but living apart from your spouse. You are considered unmarried for 1986 if your spouse was not a member of your household during the last six months of 1986, you file separate returns, and you maintain a household for more than half the year for a dependent child, stepchild or adopted child. A foster child qualifies if a member of your household for the whole year. You must be able to claim the child as a dependent unless your spouse (the noncustodial parent) has the right to the exemption under rules of ¶1.554.

Your spouse was a nonresident alien during any part of 1986, and you do not qualify to file a joint return.

2. You maintain a household for your child or a dependent relative.

Your parent must qualify as an exemption on your return and live in a home maintained by you, although not necessarily the home in which you live. Supporting a parent in a separate household or a home for the aged qualifies. Support in an outside household must be for the whole year.

Example—

Your mother lived with your sister in your sister's apartment, which cost $4,000 to maintain. Of this amount, you contributed $2,500, your sister $1,500. Your mother has no income and did not contribute any funds to the household. You qualify as head of household: For 1986, you paid over half the cost of maintaining the home for your mother who also qualifies as an exemption on your return.

Your child, stepchild, adopted child, foster child, or grandchild must live with you in your *principal residence for more than half* of 1986 (*see* 3 below). An unmarried child, stepchild, adopted child or grandchild must be your dependent; a foster child does not have to be your dependent. If the child is married, he must qualify as an exemption for you to claim head of household status unless you are divorced or separated and you have waived the exemption for your married child or the child's other parent may claim the exemption under a pre-1985 agreement. *See* ¶1.554. A person married on the last day of the year is considered married for the whole year.

If you are married and living apart from your spouse, you must be able to claim your child, married or unmarried, as an exemption unless you waive the exemption or your spouse (the noncustodial parent) may claim the exemption under a pre-1986 instrument, as explained at ¶1.554.

Any other relative must live with you (*see* 3 below) in your principal residence for more than half of 1986 and qualify as an exemption. Dependent relatives, other than children or parents, who may qualify you for head-of-household status are: Sons- or daughters-in-law, father- or mother-in-law, brothers- or sisters-in-law, brothers, sisters, grandparents, stepparents, stepbrothers or sisters, half-brothers or sisters, and uncles, aunts, nieces or nephews by blood.

If a child or other relative qualifies as an exemption on the basis of a multiple support agreement (*see* ¶1.553), you do not qualify as head of household.

A spouse who is a nonresident alien during any part of the year is not a dependent who can qualify you for head of household status, even though you maintain a home for him or her.

The support of an unrelated family, such as a mother and her children, does not qualify you as head of household, even if you are entitled to dependency exemptions for the children. See ¶1.541.

3. The household must be your home and the main residence of a dependent relative (described in 2 above). The home maintained for your dependent relative must be his or her principal residence for more than half of 1986, or for all of 1986 in the case of a dependent parent's separate household. That same home must also be *your* principal residence unless the dependent is your parent. For example, an IRS ruling held that a serviceman who supports his illegitimate child may not be a head of a household unless the child lives in the same house with him. However, an appeals court disagreed in one case; it allowed a mother to claim head of household status where she maintained a home for a child in one state and had her principal residence in another state.

The household relationship is not disqualified by your or your dependent's temporary absences, such as for illness, education, business, vacation, military service or child custody agreement. You must continue to maintain the household during the temporary absence.

' You may claim head of household status when your dependent is confined to a hospital or sanitarium and his absence is temporary and you continue to maintain a household in expectation of his return.

A dependent who was born or died during the year is considered as having lived with you the entire year.

Custody decree does not determine child's residence for head of household purposes. A divorce decree will generally specify the parent who has custody of the children. In one case, a decree gave custody to the mother, but the child attended boarding school and lived with his father during vacations. The IRS held that the father could not claim head of household status. The child's principal place of abode could not be with his father because the mother had legal custody. The child's principal place of abode was the boarding school because the child lived there. The Tax Court disagreed, allowing the father to use head of household rates. Legal custody of a child does not determine the child's principal place of abode. The school was not the child's home; he lived there only temporarily. The father maintained a home with a room for him where his clothes and other belongings were kept. He furnished all his support, including tuition. The son could not live with his mother because of extreme hostility between them.

4. You pay more than one-half the cost of the household you maintain. The costs of maintaining a household include: Property taxes, mortgage interest, rent, utility charges, upkeep and repairs, domestic help, property insurance, and food eaten in the household. You do not, as in the case of figuring support for a dependency exemption, consider the rental value of the lodgings provided

the dependent. Also not included in the cost of maintaining a household are: Clothing, education costs, medical expenses, vacation costs, life insurance premiums, transportation costs, and you include the value of your work around the house.

> You may be head of household although not head of the family.
> **Example—**
> A son who earns more than his father and contributes more than half of the cost of maintaining the family may be a head of a household. That his father, not he, "exercises family control" does not matter. The important factor is a dollar test—whether he contributed more than half the cost of maintaining the household which is his home and the principal home of his qualifying dependents.

5. You are a U.S. citizen or resident alien during the entire tax year.

Two-family house. A mother was allowed head of household status by the Tax Court in the following case. She and her unmarried daughter rented one floor of a multi-level home. A married daughter lived on a different floor with her family. Parts of the home were shared. According to the court, the mother was a head of household, based on support of her unmarried daughter. Although she did not pay more than half of the total household expenses, she paid more than half the expenses attributable to her and her unmarried daughter.

Filing Returns for Children, Decedents, and Incompetent Persons

¶1.12 • TAX RETURNS FOR YOUR CHILDREN

The income of your minor child is not included in your return. A minor is considered a taxpayer in his own right. If the child is required to file a return (*see* below) but is unable to do so because of age or for any other reason, his parent or guardian is responsible for filing the return. If the child is unable to sign the return, the parent or guardian should sign the child's name in the proper place, followed by the words "By (signature), Parent (or guardian) for minor child." A parent is liable for tax due on pay earned by the child for services, but not on investment income.

A parent or guardian must obtain a Social Security number for a child before filing the child's first income tax return. The child's Social Security number must also be provided to banks, brokers and other payers of interest and dividends to avoid penalties and backup withholding (¶25.10). To obtain a Social Security number, file Form SS-5 with your local Social Security office. If you have applied for a Social Security number but not yet received it by the filing due date, write "Applied for" on the tax return.

Filing tests for children. A return must be filed for a child who has *any* of the following:
Unearned income (such as interest, dividends, capital gains, trust income, rents and royalties) of $1,080 or more,
Self-employment income of $400 or more, or,
Gross income of $3,560 or more.
A child must pay estimated tax if he meets the tests at ¶26.00.
A child who may be claimed as a dependent may have to compute the unused zero bracket amount if his unearned income is $1,080 or more (*see* ¶13.032).
A child who is not required to file a return should still do so for a refund of taxes withheld, if any.
In figuring 1986 gross income, long-term capital gains are included in full—at 100%. For example, if your dependent child has no income except a long-term capital gain of $1,080 he must file a return, but he would owe no tax.

> You may deduct wages paid to your children in your business. Keep records showing that their activities are of a business rather than household nature.

If your child pays you for board and lodging, the payments probably are not income to you. The amount contributed by the child is usually less than the cost of his board. If the child works for you, you may not take a deduction for board and lodging you provide—unless the child has been freed from your parental control.

Children with small wages, such as from summer jobs, should file Form W-4 with their employer and claim exemption from withholding.

¶1.14 • TAX RETURN FOR A DECEASED PERSON

When a person dies, another taxpaying entity is created—the decedent's estate. Until the estate is fully distributed, it will generally earn income for which a return must be filed. For example, decedent had a savings account. Decedent dies on June 30. Income earned on the account through June 30 is reported on decedent's final income tax return, Form 1040. Income earned on the account from July 1 is reported in the estate's income tax return, fiduciary Form 1041. See ¶11.01.

What income tax returns must be filed? If decedent died after close of taxable year, but before income tax return was filed, the following must be filed:

1. Income tax return for prior year
2. Final income tax return, covering earnings in period from beginning of taxable year to date of death, and
3. Estate income tax return, covering earnings in period after decedent's death.

If decedent died after filing a return for prior tax year, then only (2) and (3) are filed.
Example—
Jones died on March 31, 1987, before he could file his 1986 tax return due April 15, 1987. A regular income tax return must be filed by April 15, 1987. A final income tax return to report earnings from January 1, 1987 through March 31, 1987 will have to be filed on April 15, 1988. Similarly, an estate income tax return to report earnings on or after April 1, 1987 will have to be filed. The due date for the estate income tax return depends on the tax year of the estate. If the estate adopts a fiscal year beginning April 1, the first return is due July 15, 1988.

For purposes of determining whether a final income tax return is due, the annual gross income test in ¶1.00 is considered in full. You do not prorate it to the part of the year decedent lived.
An income tax return for the estate must be filed if the estate has gross income of $600 or more.

Who is responsible for filing? The executor, administrator, or other legal representative is responsible for filing all returns. A surviving spouse may assume responsibility for filing a joint return for the year of death if no executor or administrator has been appointed and other tests are met (¶1.02). However, if a legal representative has been appointed, he or she must consent to the filing of a joint return for the year of decedent's death.

How do you report the decedent's income and deductions? You follow the method used by the decedent during his life to account for the income up to his death. The income does *not* have to be put on an annual basis. Each item is taxed in the same manner as it would have been taxed had he lived for the entire year.
If the deceased owned U.S. savings bonds. See ¶4.08.

Do not report on the decedent's final return income that is received after his death or accrues after or because of his death. It is taxed to the estate or beneficiary receiving the income in the year of the receipt. On the decedent's final return, only deductible expenses paid up to and including the date of death may be claimed. If the decedent reported on the accrual basis, those deductions accruable up to and including the date of death are deductible. If a check for payment of a deductible item was delivered or mailed before the date of the decedent's death, a deduction is allowable on the decedent's last return, even though the check was not cashed or deposited until after the decedent's death. If the check was not honored by the bank, the item is not deductible.

The payment of medical expenses of the decedent by his estate within one year after his death is treated as having been paid by the decedent when incurred. Consequently, the expenses are deductible on the decedent's last return. However, the expenses are not deductible for income tax purposes if they are deducted for estate tax purposes. To deduct such medical expenses on the decedent's last return, a statement must be filed affirming that no estate tax deduction has been taken and waiving the rights to the deduction.

Partnership income. The final return includes partnership income or loss only from a partnership year that ends within the decedent's tax year. Thus, if a partner dies in July 1986 and the partnership's calendar year ends December 31, 1986, no partnership income or loss is included on the partner's final 1986 return. It is reported by the partner's executor or other successor in interest on the estate's income tax return.

May you use the full zero bracket amount on a final return? Yes, the full zero bracket amount is allowed even though the period covered is less than 12 months. If the zero bracket amount is used for the deceased, it must be used by the surviving spouse. If the surviving spouse files a separate return and itemizes deductions, the zero bracket amount may not be claimed on the decedent's final return. It may be necessary to compute the unused zero bracket amount for the decedent (see ¶13.031).

What exemptions are allowed on a final return? Generally, the same exemptions the decedent would have had if he had not died. You do not reduce them because of a shorter taxable year. If the deceased had contributed more than one-half of a dependent's annual support, a dependency exemption is claimed on his final return. If the deceased died in his 65th year, but more than one day before his 65th birthday, an extra exemption may not be claimed for him because of age.

Income in respect of a decedent is discussed at ¶11.03.

Does estimated tax have to be paid? No estimated tax need be paid after the death of an unmarried individual by the executor;

the entire tax is paid when filing the final tax return. But where the deceased and a surviving spouse paid estimated tax jointly, the rule is different. The surviving spouse is still liable for the balance of the estimated tax unless an amended estimated tax voucher is filed. Further, if the surviving spouse plans to file a joint return (¶1.02) which includes the decedent's income, estimated tax payments may be required. *See* ¶26.00.

What if a refund is due? The decedent's return may also be used as a claim for a refund of an overpayment of withheld or estimated taxes. But to get the refund, Form 1310 must be filed with the final return with an attached certificate of death. Form 1310 is available from your local District Director.

When one spouse dies in a community property state (*see* ¶1.04), how should the income from the community property be reported during the administration of the estate? The IRS says that half the income is the estate's and the other half belongs to the surviving spouse.

Signing the return. An executor or administrator of the estate signs the return. If it is a joint return, *see* ¶1.02.

To expedite the closing of the decedent's estate, an executor or other personal representative of the decedent may file a written request for a prompt assessment. Once filed, the IRS has 18 months to assess additional taxes. Without the request, the IRS has three years from the due date of the return to make assessments. In making a request, state that it is being made under Section 6501(d) of the Code. The request must be filed *separately* from the return but should be sent to the District Director for the district in which the return is filed.

¶1.16 • RETURN FOR AN INCOMPETENT PERSON

A legal guardian of an incompetent person files Form 1040 for him if the incompetent's gross income meets the filing tests at page 1. For example, a return must generally be filed for an unmarried incompetent whose gross income is $3,560 or more ($4,640 if 65 years or older). Where a spouse becomes incompetent, the IRS says the other spouse may file a return for the incompetent without a power of attorney, if no legal guardian has been appointed. For example, during the period an individual was in a mental hospital, and before he was adjudged legally incompetent, his wife continued to operate his business. She filed an income tax return for him and signed it for him although she had no power of attorney. The IRS accepted the return as properly filed. Until a legal guardian was appointed, she was charged with the care of her husband and his property.

The IRS had accepted a joint return filed by a wife and in her capacity as legal guardian for her missing husband. However, the Tax Court has held that where one spouse is mentally incompetent, a joint return may not be filed because the incompetent spouse was unable to consent to a joint return; an appeals court agreed.

¶1.50

Claim All Your Exemptions

Illustrations listing exemptions may be found in the Supplement to YOUR IN-COME TAX. Mail the card at the front of this book for your FREE Supplement which includes filled-in returns and last-minute information.

Every person who files a tax return is allowed one exemption as a taxpayer, one exemption for a spouse, and one exemption for each dependent. Extra exemptions are allowed to taxpayers and their spouses who are 65 or over or blind. $1,080 is allowed for each exemption in 1986.

	See ¶
Exemptions for spouse, age, blindness	
Claiming your spouse as an exemption	1.51
An extra exemption if you or your spouse is 65 or over	1.52
Extra exemption test for blindness or partial sight	1.53
Exemptions for children and other dependents	
The dependent's relationship to you	1.54
Unrelated and distantly related dependents who are members of your household	1.541
Support provided the dependent	1.55
How to value lodging and allocate food costs and Social Security benefits	1.551

	See ¶
Examples of how support is allocated	1.552
Multiple support agreements	1.553
Children living with a divorced or separated parent	1.554
Gross income earned by your dependent	1.56
Children who are under 19 or full-time students	1.561
The dependent is a citizen or resident	1.57
The dependent does not file a joint return	1.58
Medical expenses for dependents	17.06
Child care credit for dependents	24.20

Exemptions for Spouse, Age, Blindness

¶1.51 • CLAIMING YOUR SPOUSE AS AN EXEMPTION

Your spouse is not your dependent for tax purposes. An exemption for a wife or husband is based on the marital relationship, not support.

On a joint return, each spouse receives an exemption as a taxpayer.

On a separate return, you may claim your spouse as an exemption if he or she has no gross income and is not the dependent of another taxpayer. You may not claim an exemption for your spouse who has income, *unless you file a joint return which includes that income*. For example, if a wife files a separate return, her husband may not claim her as an exemption, even if she filed the return merely for a refund of taxes withheld on her wages.

You are divorced or legally separated. You may not claim your spouse as an exemption if you are divorced or legally separated under a *final* decree of divorce or separate maintenance, even though you support your spouse and do not deduct alimony. However, an interlocutory decree does not bar you from claiming your spouse as an exemption.

Example—
An interlocutory decree of divorce is entered in 1986; a final decree in 1987. For 1986, the couple may file a joint return on which exemptions for both are claimed. A marriage is not dissolved until a final decree is entered, which here is in 1987.

Your spouse died during the year. If you did not remarry and your deceased spouse had no gross income, you may claim an exemption for the deceased on a joint return or on a separate return if the deceased was not a dependent of another taxpayer. If the deceased had gross income, to claim the exemption, you must file a joint return that includes the deceased's income.

Example—
Mrs. Smith dies on June 27. Mr. Smith files a joint return and claims her as an exemption. They were married as of the date of Mrs. Smith's death. The joint return includes all of Mr. Smith's income for the year, but only that part of Mrs. Smith's income earned up to June 27 (*see* ¶1.02).

If you remarry before the end of the year in which your spouse died, you may not claim an exemption for your deceased spouse. If a widow remarries, she may be an exemption on her deceased husband's separate return and on her present husband's joint return or separate return, provided she had no income and was not a dependent of another taxpayer.

If a spouse dies in the year of his or her 65th birthday, the survivor may claim the extra exemption for age if the deceased died after reaching the age of 65. The extra exemption is not allowed if death occurred before the 65th birthday.

If your spouse is a nonresident alien, *see* ¶1.03.

¶1.52 • EXTRA EXEMPTION—AGE 65 OR OVER (1986)

When you are 65 or over, you claim one exemption as a taxpayer plus another exemption for your age. If your spouse is also 65 or over, you may claim an extra exemption for his or her age. You are entitled to claim the extra exemption in the year you turn 65. Thus, if your birthday is December 31, you may claim the exemption for the year in which you celebrate your 65th birthday.

If your 65th birthday is on January 1, 1987, you may claim the extra exemption on your 1986 tax return. You are considered to be 65 on December 31, 1986.

Federal law changes affecting retirement age have no effect on the extra exemption.

A U.S. citizen in a U.S. possession who is entitled to treat income from sources within the possession as nontaxable may *not* claim an extra exemption.

¶1.53 • EXTRA EXEMPTION FOR BLINDNESS (1986)

A taxpayer who is blind may claim an additional exemption. Similarly, if your spouse is blind, you claim an extra exemption for his or her blindness. The condition of blindness must exist on the last day of the year.

To support the extra exemption for a blind person, attach to his return a written statement that he is blind.

Partial sight. A visually impaired person claims the additional exemption by attaching to his return a certificate from a doctor or a registered optometrist that his central visual acuity does not exceed 20/200 in the better eye with correcting lenses; or, where visual acuity is greater than 20/200, it is accompanied by a limitation in the field of vision such that the widest diameter of the visual field subtends an angle no greater than 20 degrees.

The certificate of blindness need not be filed each year if an eye specialist certifies that, in his opinion, the taxpayer's sight will not improve beyond the above minimum standards. A copy of this statement is attached to the return for the year in which the examination is made. In the following years, statements referring to the certificate must be attached to the returns.

Correcting lenses are those which are ordinarily worn. Contact lenses that are generally usable for short periods and that may not be medically advisable are not required for the above test.

A U.S. citizen in a U.S. possession who is entitled to treat income from sources within the possession as nontaxable may *not* claim an extra exemption.

Exemptions for Children and Other Dependents

¶1.54 • TESTS FOR CLAIMING DEPENDENTS

1. Relationship or member of household test (¶1.541)

A relative—Child, stepchild, adopted child, grandchild, great grandchild, son- or daughter-in-law, father- or mother-in-law, brother- or sister-in-law, parent, brother, sister, grandparent, stepparent, stepbrother or sister, half-brother or sister, uncle, aunt, niece or nephew by blood. A foster child qualifies if, for the entire year, he made your home his principal home and is a member of your household.

Or—any person, whether or not related, who for the entire year made your home his principal home and is a member of your household (except if the relationship between you and such person is in violation of state law.)

2. Support test (¶1.55)

You either contribute more than half the dependent's support or contribute more than 10%, and together with others contribute more than half.

Total the dollar amount of support spent on a dependent by you, by others, and by the dependent. If your contribution is:

More than 50% of the total spent—you claim the exemption.

More than 10% of the total spent and together with what you and the other contributors gave is more than 50% of the total spent—you or one of the others who also contributed more than 10% may claim the exemption. You and the others must decide who is to claim the exemption. If you take it, you must attach to your return a Form 2120, Multiple Support Declaration, signed by each person who contributed more than 10%.

Less than 50%, either alone or with the contribution to his own support—neither you nor the other contributors may claim the exemption for the dependent.

3. Gross income test (¶1.56)

Your dependent had less than $1,080 of gross income for the year.

Or—your dependent is your child, who is under 19 or a full-time student, in which case the amount of the dependent's gross income is not considered and may be $1,080 or over.

4. Citizenship or resident test (¶1.57)

Your dependent is a United States citizen or national, or a resident of the United States, Canada or Mexico.

5. Joint return test (¶1.58)

Your married dependent does not file a joint return with his or her spouse.

¶1.541 • TEST 1. THE DEPENDENT'S RELATIONSHIP

Your dependent must be related to you (*see* above for a list of qualifying relatives). That he is an adult, healthy, and capable of self-support does not bar you from claiming him as an exemption—provided all the other tests are met.

The following rules apply to these relationships:

Infants. A child born during the year is a dependent. For example, you may claim an exemption for the year for a child born on December 31.

A stillborn child may not be claimed as an exemption. The exemption is allowed for a child who was born alive even if the infant lived for only a moment.

Adopted children. A legally adopted child is considered your child. A child is legally adopted when a court decree is entered. In states allowing interlocutory decrees, you may claim the exemption in the year the interlocutory decree is entered. If a court decree has not been entered, a child may be your dependent provided he was placed with you for adoption by an authorized adoption agency and was a member of your household. If he has not been placed with you for adoption by an agency, you may claim him as a dependent *only if* he was a member of your household for the entire tax year (*see* ¶1.541).

Foster child. A foster child is considered to be your child if your home is his principal residence and he is a member of your household for the entire year.

Death during the year. If a dependent died during 1986 but while he was alive you supported him and you meet the other tests listed in this chapter, you may claim an exemption for him.
Example—
On January 21, 1986, your father died. Until that date, you contributed all of his support. You may claim him as an exemption for 1986. The full deduction is taken. Exemptions are not prorated.

Nephew, niece, uncle, and aunt. They must be your blood relatives to qualify as your dependents. For example, the brother or sister of your father or mother qualifies as your relative; their spouses do not. You may not claim your spouse's nephews, nieces, uncles, or aunts unless you file a joint return.
Example—
You contribute more than half of the support of the sister of your wife's mother (your wife's aunt). If you and your wife file a joint return, her aunt is allowed as an exemption on your joint return. But even on a joint return, you may not claim an exemption for supporting your wife's aunt's husband. He is not related by blood to you or your wife.

In-laws. Brother-in-law, sister-in-law, father-in-law, mother-in-law, son-in-law, and daughter-in-law are relatives by marriage. You may claim them as exemptions if you meet the other tests in this chapter.

You may claim an exemption for a dependent who was related to you by marriage and whom you continue to support after divorce or death of your spouse.
Example—
Allen has contributed all the support of his father-in-law since he

was married. His wife died in 1985. He continued as sole support of his wife's father in 1986. He may claim him as an exemption.

Stepchild's husband or wife or child. Your stepchild's spouse does not meet the relationship test. Nor may you claim an exemption for a stepgrandchild if you file a separate return. They are not on the list of relatives for whose support you may claim an exemption. (*See* ¶1.54.) But you may claim them as exemptions on a joint return. On a joint return, it is not necessary that the close relationship exist between the dependent and the spouse who furnishes the chief support. It is sufficient that the relationship exists with either spouse.

¶1.542 • UNRELATED OR DISTANTLY RELATED DEPENDENT MEMBERS OF YOUR HOUSEHOLD

A friend, foster child (not legally adopted), and a relative not listed in ¶1.54—such as a cousin who lives with you can be your dependent. You may claim an unrelated or distantly related person as a dependent if:

1. He is a member of your household, and

2. Your home is his principal home for the entire year, except for absences when attending school, vacationing, or being confined to a hospital.

Examples—

1. You support a friend who lives in your house all year. You can claim him as a dependent member of your household.

2. You provide a home for an orphan for seven months. You cannot claim him as a dependent. He did not live in your home for an entire year. However, if the child had been placed in your home for adoption by an authorized adoption agency, you may claim him as a dependent although he was not a member of your household for the entire year (*see* adopted children rule at ¶1.54).

3. You support a cousin who lives in a house you own. However, you live elsewhere. You may not claim him as a dependent. You do not live in the same house.

You may not claim a friend as an exemption when you live in his house even though you support him. You are living in his household, not your own. Also, you cannot claim an exemption for a friend who lives in your house and renders you services in return for your care.

The following are not considered dependents, even if they technically meet the above two rules:

Your spouse. Under the tax law, one spouse is not considered a dependent of the other (*see* ¶1.51).

A boarder in your house.

Housekeeper, servant, or maid.

An exemption for an unmarried mate depends on local law. Where the relationship violates local law, no exemption may be claimed.

Example—

Ensminger lived in North Carolina with a woman whom he supported. When he claimed an exemption for her, the IRS disallowed the exemption, claiming that under North Carolina law, it is a misdemeanor for an unmarried man and woman to live together. When the Tax Court supported the IRS position, Ensminger appealed, arguing that the North Carolina law was an unconstitutional invasion of his right to privacy. The appeals court held that constitutionality was not an issue for the IRS and Tax Court to decide. The states are responsible for regulating domestic affairs. Federal tax law merely follows the direction of state law. If Ensminger lived in a state that did not hold his relationship illegal, he could claim the exemption.

In a similar case, a dependency exemption was allowed where the court ruled cohabitation did not violate Missouri law.

¶1.55 • TEST 2. SUPPORT PROVIDED THE DEPENDENT

If your dependent has no financial means and you are the only person contributing to his support during the year, you can skip the following discussion on support. You meet the support test. You contribute 100% of the dependent's support. If, however, the dependent or other persons or organizations contribute to his support, you have to determine whether your contribution meets the support test.

Divorced or separated parents contributing to support of their

children may have to figure support under special rules. *See* ¶1.554.

Follow these steps to figure support: (1) Total the value of the support contributed by you, by the dependent himself, and by others. (2) Determine your share of the total. If your share is more than 50% of the dependent's total support, you meet the support test. If the dependent or some other person or organization contributed 50% or more to his support, you may not take the exemption. If the dependent or someone else did not contribute 50% or more to his support, and you contributed more than 10% of the total support, you may be able to claim the exemption under the multiple support agreement rule of ¶1.553.

You do not consider the number of days or months in which you or anyone else paid his support. You claim the exemption in the year you furnish the support, not the year you pay any debts you incurred in providing the support. Furnishing support requires more than a promise or unfulfilled duty or obligation to pay. There must be an unconditional obligation to pay for the items of support.

Example—

Your son's college tuition is due in September, 1986. His school has allowed you to postpone payment until 1987. You include that part of the tuition covering the school months in 1986 as support contributions.

You now have a general outline of how to compare support contributions. To fill in the details, you need to know what are and what are not support items. For this purpose, see the check lists of includable and nonincludable support items. Following the check lists, you will find a discussion of how to value and allocate lodging and food items and further examples of figuring support.

These Are Support Items:

Lodging, food, and clothing

Social Security benefits

Education—tuition payments and cost of books and supplies

Tax-free income, such as life insurance proceeds and tax-exempt interest, used to pay maintenance expenses, is counted as support.

Examples—

1. Your father uses his Social Security benefits for his support. You must count these amounts to find the total he uses for support.

2. Social Security benefits paid to children of deceased workers *which are used for their support* are treated as the children's contribution to their own support. Follow this rule even though benefits are paid to you as the child's parent or custodian, *and you use them for the child's support.* If the Social Security benefits used for a child's support are more than half of his total support, no one may claim him as a dependent.

Medical and dental care, including premiums paid for medical care insurance policies. Federal basic Medicare benefits under Part A and supplementary benefits under Part B are not treated as a dependent's contribution to his own support. According to the IRS, Medicaid payments are considered support in the nature of welfare payments, furnished by the dependent for his own support. A Tax Court decision rejects the IRS view.

Recreation and entertainment—including summer camp costs

Transportation

Singing and dancing lessons and cost of musical instruments

Wedding clothes and reception for a child

Purchase of auto and certain appliances (*see* discussion below)

Dependent care payments (baby sitter fees, nursery school costs)

Care provided a relative in an institution, orphanage, or old-age home supported by a state, a religious, or a fraternal organization

Example—

In 1986, your father was a patient in a state hospital. The state required you to pay part of his expenses and you paid the state $1,600. In the state budget report for 1986, the average cost of maintaining an individual in the hospital was listed at $3,000. As you contributed over half of your father's support, you may claim him as a dependent. If he required special care, such as private nursing or a major operation, the actual cost to the state agency for maintaining him during the year, rather than the average cost, would be used to measure his total support.

Educational benefits received by a student from the government as subsidy allowances under the GI Bill, U.S. Naval Educational Assistance scholarships, and Armed Forces Academies such as West Point. (However, note that courts have ruled that payments received under the Naval R.O.T.C. Program are scholarship payments that are not treated as items of support.) War Orphans Educational Assistance Act payments are not counted as support.

Student loans. If your child has obtained a loan to pay educational costs and is the primary obligor, the loan proceeds are treated as his contribution to support. That a parent is a guarantor does not change the rule.

State welfare payments. These are considered to have been furnished by the dependent for his own support, unless evidence is shown that he has used these payments for others or for nonsupport items, such as life insurance premiums.

Foster care payments by a child-placing agency to foster parents are support furnished by the agency and not the parent. A parent's unreimbursed expenses are deductible either as a charitable contribution or as a business expense (if payments in addition to reimbursements are received).

Tax-free payments by a state social service to adoptive parents to help finance the adopted child's care. This is support contributed by the state. To claim an exemption for the child, the parents must prove they contributed more to the child's support than the state.

> **Lump-sum contribution covering a dependent's stay in an old-age home. The lump sum is prorated over the dependent's life expectancy.**
> **Example—**
> A son secures his father's placement in a religious home for a lump-sum payment of $9,600. The payment was determined on the basis of $1,200 a year over the father's life expectancy of eight years. The home makes no refund if the father dies within eight years. The son counts $1,200 as an annual contribution to his father's support. If this is more than half of his father's yearly support costs, the son may claim the exemption. If the father fails to reach his life expectancy, the son may not deduct any unused part of the $9,600 as a charitable deduction.

Armed Forces support of a dependent who joined or left the Armed Forces during 1986. In determining his support, you must include the value of the board, lodging, clothing, etc., he received while in service, and any pay that he used for his support. If he has been in service for the entire year, you may not claim him as an exemption.

Armed Forces dependency allotments. Both the part of a dependency allotment contributed by the government, as well as the part withheld from a serviceman's pay, are considered as support being furnished by the serviceman. If the allotment is used to support dependents other than those for whom the allotment is authorized, an exemption may be claimed for those other dependents if they otherwise qualify as the serviceman's dependents.

Example—
You are in the Armed Forces and authorize a dependency allotment for your widowed mother. She uses the payment to support herself and your younger brother. You provide no other funds for their support. If more than half of their support is provided by your allotment, you claim exemptions for both your mother and your brother, even though the allotment was authorized only for your mother.

Serviceman's allowance for quarters paid to or on behalf of a specified dependent. If an allowance is actually used by the dependent, the serviceman is considered to have furnished the allowance. He may include it in figuring whether he contributed more than half the dependent's support.

Auto and appliances may be support items. The purchase price of an auto may be treated as a support cost item.

Example—
A dependent child buys a car for $4,500. In the same year, his parent contributes $4,000 to his support. The automobile bought by the child is treated as the child's own support contribution in the year of purchase. As the $4,000 of support furnished by the parent for the youth is less than half of the total support of $8,500, the parent may not claim him as an exemption. If the parent had purchased the automobile as a gift for the child and registered title in the child's name, the parent would have provided all the child's support.

What if a parent buys a car, registers it in his own name, but allows his dependent child to use it? The automobile itself is not a support item. However, the out-of-pocket expenses of operating the automobile for the benefit of the dependent child are support items.

A power lawn mower purchased by a parent for a child who is made responsible for keeping the lawn trimmed is not a support item even if the mower was supplied to make mowing more palatable to the child.

A TV receiver bought as a gift by a *noncustodial* parent for his child and placed in the child's bedroom was held to be a support item. If the set is bought on credit, it is a support item in the year of the gift, even though no payment for the set may have been made in the year of the gift.

These Items Are Not Counted as Support:
Life insurance premiums
Federal, state, and local income taxes and Social Security taxes paid by the dependent from his own income
Funeral expenses
Value of personal services you perform for a dependent, such as nursing
Scholarships received by your child (or stepchild or legally adopted child) who is a full-time student for at least each of five calendar months during the year. Scholarship aid is counted as support contributed by the child if he is not a full-time student during each of five calendar months of the year. Note also the exceptions above for certain government educational benefits.

> **Example—**
> Your child attends college on a $5,000 scholarship. She has no income of her own. You contribute $4,000 to her support. You may claim her as a dependent. The scholarship is not counted in figuring whether you give more than half her support.

Value of food and lodging furnished student nurses by an accredited nursing school.
Value of education, room, and board provided a handicapped child by a state agency. The state aid is treated as a scholarship.
Medical care benefits paid by an insurance company to a dependent under a policy paid by you or similar payments in compensation of medical expenses paid by a person who caused an accident resulting in injuries to the dependent.
Federal Medicare benefits paid under the supplementary medical care insurance program (Part B) or basic benefits (Part A).
Medical care provided a dependent by the federal government under the Dependents' Medical Care Act of 1956.

¶1.551 • HOW TO VALUE LODGING AND ALLOCATE FOOD COSTS AND SOCIAL SECURITY BENEFITS

You count as support *the fair rental value* of a room, apartment, or house in which the dependent lives. In your estimate, you include a reasonable allowance for the rental value of furnishing and for heat and other utilities. You do not add payments of rent, taxes, interest, depreciation, paint, insurance, and utilities. These are presumed to be accounted for in the fair rental estimate. The fair rental value of lodging you furnish a dependent is the amount you could reasonably expect to receive from a stranger for the lodging.

If the dependent lives in his own home, he contributes the total fair rental value of his home to his own support. If you help him maintain his home by giving him cash to pay, or you directly pay, such expenses as the mortgage, real estate taxes, fire insurance premiums, and repairs, you reduce the total fair rental value of his home by the amount you contributed.

Example—
You contribute $1,500 as support to your father who lives in his own home which has a fair rental value of $4,500 a year. He uses $200 of the money you give him to pay real estate taxes on the property. His total support is computed as follows:

Cash contributed by you	$1,500
Fair rental value of house ($4,500 less $200 for taxes)	4,300
Father's total support	$5,800

If you lived with your dependent rent free in his home, the fair rental value of lodging furnished to you must be offset against the amounts you spent for your dependent in determining the net amount of your contribution to his support.

Food and other similar household expenses. If the dependent lives with you, you divide your total food expenses equally among all the members of your household, unless you have records showing the exact amount spent on the dependent. If he does not live with you, you count the actual amount of food expenses spent by or for the dependent.

Allocating Social Security benefits. Where a couple receives Social Security benefit checks made out in joint names, half of the payment is considered to have been used for the support of each, unless a different use of the money is proved.

Example—
Your father and mother received $7,500 during the year as joint Social Security benefits. Although under the Social Security Act two-thirds of these benefits belong to your father and one-third to your mother, one-half of the benefits, or $3,750, is considered to have been used by your father and $3,750 by your mother.

¶1.552 • EXAMPLES OF HOW SUPPORT IS ALLOCATED

1. Your father lives with you, your spouse and three children. He receives Social Security benefits of $2,700, which he sepnds for his own needs. You spend $4,200 for food during the year. You also paid his dental bill of $200. You estimate the fair rental value of the room furnished him is $2,000. Your father's total support is:

Social Security	$2,700
Share of food costs (⅙ of $4,200)	700
Dental bill paid by you	200
Rental value of room	2,000
	$5,600

You claim him as a dependent. You contributed more than half his total support, or $2,900 ($2,000 lodging, $200 dental, $700 food).

2. Your parents live with you, your spouse and two children in a house you rent. The fair rental value of their room is $2,000. Your father receives a pension of $4,200, all of which he spent equally for your mother and himself for clothing and recreation. Your total expense in providing food for the household is $6,000. You pay heat and utility bills of $1,200. You paid your mother's medical expenses of $600. You figure the total support of your parents as follows:

	Father	Mother
Fair rental value of room	$1,000	$1,000
Pension used for their support	2,100	2,100
Share of food costs (⅙ of $6,000)	1,000	1,000
Medical expense for mother		600
	$4,100	$4,700

The support you furnish your father, $2,000 (lodging, $1,000; food, $1,000), is not over half of his total support of $4,100. The support you furnish your mother, $2,600 (lodging, $1,000; food, $1,000; medical, $600), is over half of her total support of $4,700. You claim an exemption for your mother but not your father. You do not consider the cost of heat and utilities. It is presumed to be in the rental estimate.

3. Your parents live in an apartment which they furnish with their own belongings. You pay rent of $4,800 for the apartment. The fair market value of the apartment with furnishings is $5,800. Your father receives a pension of $5,000 which he uses for his and your mother's personal needs. Their total support is:

	Father	Mother
Fair rental value of furnished apartment	$2,900	$2,900
Pension used for support	2,500	2,500
	$5,400	$5,400

You may not claim either parent as an exemption. Your payment of rent for an unfurnished apartment of $2,400 for each is less than half of their total support. If you had provided the furniture, the amount of their support would be over half for each, or $2,900. You would then have gotten both exemptions.

Earmarking support to one dependent in a household. If you are contributing funds to a household consisting of several persons and the amount you contribute does not exceed 50% of the total support cost of the household, you may be able to claim an exemption for at least one dependent by earmarking your support to his or her use, if your contribution will exceed 50% of their support costs. You may do this by marking your checks for the bene-

fit of the dependent, or by having a statement of your support arrangement at the time you start your payments. The IRS says its agents will generally accept such evidence of your arrangement. If you do not designate for whom you are providing support, your contribution is allocated equally among all members of a household (*see* example 1).

Examples—

1. A husband who lives apart from his family without a divorce or legal separation sends his wife $3,240 to meet household expenses. A son and daughter live with her. The wife contributes from her own funds $6,480; an uncle sends her $1,080. The total amount going to meet household expenses from all sources is $10,800. On a separate return, the husband may not claim any exemptions for his children; his contributions are less than 50% of their total support. As he has not earmarked who is to get his contributions, his payments are allocated equally among the three members of the household. Each is considered to have received $1,080 from him. His contribution of $1,080 is less than half of the total support of $3,600 allocated to each child.

Contributed by:		Allocated to:		
	Wife	Son	Daughter	Total
Wife	$2,160	$2,160	$2,160	$ 6,480
Husband	1,080	1,080	1,080	3,240
Uncle	360	360	360	1,080
Total	$3,600	$3,600	$3,600	$10,800

2. Same facts as above except that the husband notes on his monthly checks of $270 that $180 is for his son; $90 for his daughter. He may claim his son as an exemption on a separate return; he has contributed more than half of the son's support. As total household costs of $10,800 are allocated equally among the three household members, the wife's contribution is reallocated to make up for the difference created by the husband's increased support to the son. Here, the wife is considered to have contributed $3,240 to her own support.

Contributed by:		Allocated to:		
	Wife	Son	Daughter	Total
Wife	$3,240	$1,080	$2,160	$ 6,480
Husband		2,160	1,080	3,240
Uncle	360	360	360	1,080
Total	$3,600	$3,600	$3,600	$10,800

3. Assume in the above example the mother contributed only $6,240 and her son contributed $240. There would be no change in tax consequences; however, the allocation of support contributions would differ. The son's contribution is added to the total household costs which are allocated equally among the family members to find how much applies to each person's support. However, in determining support contributions, the son is treated as contributing $240 to his own support.

Contributed by:		Allocated to:		
	Wife	Son	Daughter	Total
Wife	$3,240	$ 840	$2,160	$ 6,240
Son		240		240
Husband		2,160	1,080	3,240
Uncle	360	360	360	1,080
Total	$3,600	$3,600	$3,600	$10,800

¶1.553 • MULTIPLE SUPPORT AGREEMENTS

Are you and others sharing the support of one person, but with no one individual providing more than half his total support? You may claim the dependent as an exemption if:

1. You gave more than 10% of the support;

2. The amount contributed by you and others to the dependent's support equals more than half the support;

3. Each contributor could have claimed the exemption—except that he gave less than half support; *and*

4. Each contributor who gave more than 10% agrees to let you take the exemption. Each signs a Form 2120, Multiple Support Agreement. You then attach the forms to your return.

Examples—

1. You and your two brothers contribute $2,000 each toward the support of your mother. She contributes $1,000 of her own to support herself. Your two sisters contribute $500 each. Thus, the total support comes to $8,000. Of this, each brother gave 25% ($2,000/$8,000) for a total of 75%. Each sister gave less than 10%, 6¼% ($500/$8,000). You or one of your brothers may claim the exemption. The total of your contributions is more than half of your mother's support. Each

of you contributed more than 10%. Among yourselves, you must decide who is to claim the exemption. If you claim the exemption, your brothers must sign Forms 2120 which you attach to your return. If one of your brothers claims the exemption, you sign a Form 2120 which is attached to the return of the brother who claims the exemption. Since neither of your sisters furnished more than 10%, neither can claim the exemption. Consequently, they need not sign Forms 2120.

2. You and your sister each furnished $1,000 to your mother's support. Her two cousins who did not live with her each contributed $1,500. No one may claim her as an exemption. Half of her support of $5,000 was not furnished by persons, such as you and your sister, who, but for the support test, could claim an exemption for her. A cousin does not meet the relationship or member of household test.

3. Your mother's support totals $6,000; you contribute $1,800, your brother $1,200, your father $600, and your mother from her savings contributes $2,400. Assume your father does not file a tax return claiming your mother as an exemption. You and your brother cannot use your father's contribution to meet the more-than-50% test required by rule 2 above. Your father may not join in a multiple support agreement because your mother is not his dependent for tax purposes although an exemption may be claimed for a wife on the basis of the marital relationship; see ¶1.51.

4. Same facts as in (3) above, but another brother contributed $200. Then you and your brothers may join in a multiple support agreement; your contributions exceeded 50% of the support costs.

¶1.554 • DIVORCED OR SEPARATED PARENTS FOLLOW SPECIAL RULES FOR FIGURING SUPPORT OF CHILDREN

Divorced or separated parents have to apply special custodial rules to determine which parent has met the support test for a dependent child.

If you had custody of the child for more than half the year, the exemption is generally yours if these tests are met:

Marital status: You are divorced or legally separated under a decree of divorce or separate maintenance, or separated under a written agreement, or live apart at all times during the last six months of 1986.

Support: In 1986, over half of the child's total support is from you and your former or separated spouse.

Custody: The child is in the custody of one or both parents for more than half of 1986. If you had custody for a greater portion of 1986, you claim the exemption unless you waive it or the noncustodial parent may claim it under a pre-1986 agreement.

Custodial parent's waiver. You may waive the exemption by signing a written declaration on Form 8332. On the form, you indicate whether you are waiving the exemption for 1986 only or for future years as well. The noncustodial parent attaches the declaration to his or her 1986 return and claims the exemption for the child.

Pre-1985 agreement specifying noncustodial parent. If a pre-1985 agreement gives you, as noncustodial parent, the exemption, you must provide at least $600 for the support of the child in 1986. The exemption must be specifically allocated to you in a decree of divorce or separate maintenance or a written agreement executed before January 1, 1985. Attach a copy of the agreement to your return.

Do relatives or friends have custody of the children? If the children are not in the custody of either or both parents for more than half of 1986 the exemption is claimed by the person who contributed more than 50% of the child's support.

Do persons other than the parents contribute to the children's support? The above rules for custodial and noncustodial parents do not apply, and thus neither parent may claim the exemption, unless the parents together give more than 50% of the child's support. If a parent remarries, support contributions made by the new spouse are treated as contributions of the parent. They are not treated as contributions of a third person.

The above custodial rules also do not apply if the parties contributing support enter into a multiple support agreement under which one of them claims the exemption under the rules at ¶1.553.

¶1.56 • TEST 3. GROSS INCOME EARNED BY YOUR DEPENDENT

The gross income test does not apply to your dependent child who is under 19 or a full-time student. He may earn any amount, and you may claim him as an exemption, provided you support him.

The gross income test applies only to—

Dependents who are not your children—such as parents, in-laws, sisters, brothers, uncles, aunts, and members of your household; *and*

Children who are 19 or over and not full-time students.

The gross income test requires your dependent to have a gross income of less than $1,080 in 1986. If he earns $1,080 or more, you may not claim him as an exemption, even if you fully support him.

Gross income here means income items included in the dependent's tax return. It does not include nontaxed items such as gifts and dividends excluded by the exclusion. *See* ¶40.00 for a list of tax-free receipts. When computing a dependent's income, figure long-term capital gains at 100%. Gross income for a service-type business is gross receipts without deductions of expenses and for a manufacturing or merchandising business is total sales less cost of goods sold. Partner's share of partnership gross income, not his share of net income, is treated as part of his gross income.

Social Security benefits are treated as gross income only to the extent they are taxable under the rules of ¶34.11.

Examples—

1. Allan gave his aunt $2,000 for her support. She had no other income except for a long-term gain of $1,100 realized on the sale of securities. The $1,100 is her gross income, even though 40% or $440 is subject to tax (*see* ¶6.001). Allan may not claim her as his dependent.

2. Jones gives $1,500 a year for his father's support. The father owns a two-family house. He lives in one apartment and rents the other for $100 a month, giving him a gross annual income of $1,200. After deducting interest and taxes, his net income is $700. Nevertheless, Jones may not take his father as a dependent as his gross income is $1,200.

3. Your son, age 25 and *not* a full-time student, received $1,300 for disabilities incurred while a member of the Armed Forces. You contributed $3,000 for his support. You get the exemption although his income exceeded the $1,080 test. Tax-free income is not considered gross income.

4. Your father received $2,400 in Social Security benefits. The benefits were not subject to tax. He used this amount to support himself. You contributed $2,600 to his support. You may claim him as an exemption. The Social Security benefits are not considered gross income. However, if you contributed $2,400 or less to his support, you could not take the exemption because you did not meet the support test at ¶1.55.

¶1.561 • CHILDREN WHO ARE UNDER 19 OR FULL-TIME STUDENTS

There is no gross income test for—

1. Your children *regardless of age* who are full-time students at an educational institution, *and*

2. Your children under 19.

This rule applies to your child, stepchild, and adopted child. It also applies to a foster child who, for the entire year, has made your home his principal home and is a member of your household. It does not apply to a grandchild, or a son- or daughter-in-law, or brother or sister who is a full-time student.

Example—

Your son is 19 on December 8, 1986. He does not attend school and has earned $1,200 during the year. You may not claim him as an exemption because he reached 19 during the year and his earnings exceeded the $1,080 limit. You may not prorate the exemption for the time he was under 19.

A full-time student is one who attends school full time during at least five calendar months in the tax year. For example: Attendance from February through some part of June—or from February through May and then from September through December—qualifies. The five months do not have to run consecutively.

Examples—

1. Your child who is 22 was a June graduate. The gross income test does not apply to his earnings in 1986.

2. Your child who is 19 worked during the first half of the year and then starts college in September. You may not claim him as an exemption if he earned $1,080 or more. Although he is a full-time student, he did not attend school for at least five months during the year.

Attending night classes. Your child who attends night school is considered a full-time student only if he is enrolled for the number of hours or classes that is considered full-time attendance at a similar day-time school.

A child taking a full-time course of institutional on-farm training is a full-time student if the training is supervised by an official agent of an educational institution or of a state or other government agency in a state.

A "co-op" job that is part of a child's prescribed course of classroom study at a vocational high school qualifies. But do not confuse a "co-op" job with "on-the-job" training. "On-the-job" training is generally not part of a prescribed study course supervised by a school and does not qualify a child as a full-time student.

An educational institution is one with a regular faculty, established courses, and an organized student body. It does not include correspondence schools, job training schools, night schools, or a hospital which trains interns. An intern is not a student but an employee of the hospital.

Where your child has income of his own that may be used for his support, be prepared to show that he does not use it for support or that your contributions exceed his.

The filing of tax returns for children is discussed at ¶1.12.

¶1.57 • TEST 4. THE DEPENDENT IS A CITIZEN OR RESIDENT

To claim an exemption for a dependent, the dependent must have at some time during 1986 qualified as:

Citizen or resident of the United States, or

United States national (one who owes permanent allegiance to the U.S.; principally, a person born in American Samoa who has not become a naturalized American citizen), or

Resident of Canada or Mexico.

Dependents in Puerto Rico. A U.S. citizen or resident may take as an exemption a dependent who is living in Puerto Rico and is a citizen of Puerto Rico, provided he is not a citizen of a foreign country. Most citizens of Puerto Rico are also citizens of the United States. All persons born in Puerto Rico on or after

April 11, 1899, and prior to January 13, 1941 (and who resided in Puerto Rico or other territory over which the United States exercised rights on January 13, 1941) are citizens of the U.S. So are all persons born in Puerto Rico on or after January 13, 1941, and who are subject to the jurisdiction of the United States.

A child born in a foreign country whose one parent is a non-resident alien and whose other parent is a U.S. citizen qualifies as a dependent. If you are a U.S. citizen living abroad, you may claim as a dependent a legally adopted child who is not a U.S. citizen or resident if for the entire year your home was the child's principal residence and he is a member of your household.

Resident status is discussed at ¶37.01.

If you treat income from a U.S. possession as tax-free income, you may not claim exemptions for your spouse, dependents, for being 65 or over, or for blindness. You are allowed only one personal exemption. *See* ¶36.08.

¶1.58 • TEST 5. THE DEPENDENT DOES NOT FILE A JOINT RETURN

You may not claim an exemption for a dependent who files a joint return with another. For example, you meet all of the four tests entitling you to an exemption for your married daughter as your dependent. She files a joint return with her husband. You may not claim her as your dependent on your tax return.

The loss of the exemption may cost a parent more than the joint return saves the couple. In such a case, it may be advisable for the couple to file separate returns so that the parent may benefit from the larger tax saving.

If the couple files a joint return and decides to revoke their election to file jointly and then file separate returns in order to preserve the exemption for a parent, they must do so before the filing date for the return. Once a joint return is filed, the couple may not, after the filing deadline, file separate returns for the same year.

The IRS allows a limited opportunity for avoiding the rule that no exemption may be claimed for a dependent filing a joint return where the income of each spouse is under the income limit required for filing a return and the couple files a return merely to obtain a refund of withheld taxes. Under these circumstances, their return is considered a refund claim, and a dependency exemption may be claimed.

Tax Credit for Dependent Care Expenses

	See ¶
Overall view of the care credit	1.61
Earned income test	1.62
Household and dependent tests	1.63

	See ¶
Expenses qualifying for the credit	1.64
Rules for separated couples	1.65

Did you hire a sitter or maid to care for your children or other dependents while you work? If so, you may qualify for a tax credit for the expenses. You may claim the credit even if you work part time. The credit is generally available to the extent you have earnings from employment.

The credit is claimed on Form 2441.

The size of the credit depends on the amount of care expenses and income. Depending on your income, the credit is 20% to 30% of up to $2,400 of care expenses for one dependent and up to $4,800 of expenses for two or more dependents.

To qualify for the credit, you must:

1. Incur the care expenses in order to earn income. In the case of a married couple, this requires both spouses to work either at full- or part-time positions. An exception to the earned income

rule is made for a spouse who is a full-time student or incapacitated.

2. Maintain a household for the dependent.

3. File a joint return if you are married, unless you are separated under the rules of ¶1.65.

4. Hire someone other than your child under age 19 or a person you can claim as a dependent (¶1.64).

Withholding tax for housekeeper. Note that where you employ help to care for your dependent, you are liable for FICA taxes if you pay wages of $50 or more in a calendar quarter. As an employer, you pay FICA at the rate of 7.15% of wages (up to $42,000) in 1986. For example, you pay a housekeeper $125 a week ($6,500 for the year). You must pay $464.75 in FICA as well as withholding the same amount from the housekeeper's wages. If you do not withhold, you are liable for the full amount. You report and pay this tax on a quarterly Form 942. Under an exception, you do not have to withhold FICA tax from wages paid to your spouse, or to a son or daughter under 21 who cares for a dependent in your home. Further, FICA generally does not apply to wages paid to your father or mother unless you are divorced or widowed and have a disabled child living at home. If your housekeeper wants income tax to be withheld and you agree, he or she must fill out a Form W-4 (withholding allowances) and you include the withholdings on quarterly Form 942. You are also liable for FUTA (unemployment) taxes which you report annually on Form 940. Withholding is required if you paid wages of $1,000 or more in any calendar quarter during 1986 or 1985. Wages paid to a spouse, your parents, or children under 21 are exempt. Obtain Form 940 for details. You must indicate on Form 2441 whether you have made the appropriate FICA and FUTA payments and include your employer identification number. These taxes are not separately deductible but are included with your other dependent care expenses. The amount of these taxes may more than offset your dependent care credit.

¶1.61 • OVERALL VIEW OF THE CARE CREDIT

The credit is a percentage of expenses paid for the care of a dependent to allow you to work and earn income. The credit percentage depends on your income. For families with adjusted gross income of $10,000 or less, a 30% credit may be claimed on care expenses of up to $2,400 for one dependent; $4,800 for two or more dependents. For adjusted gross income over $10,000, the 30% credit is reduced by 1% for each $2,000 of adjusted gross income or fraction of $2,000 over $10,000, but not below 20%. The 20% credit applies to adjusted gross incomes exceeding $28,000.

The applicable credit percentage applies to a credit base of dependent care expenses which may not exceed $2,400 for one qualifying dependent or $4,800 for two or more qualifying dependents. This is true, even if expenses exceed $2,400 or $4,800. Further, a credit base may be less than the maximum if your earned income is less (see ¶1.62).

Example—
You paid care expenses of $4,000 for two qualifying dependents but had earned income of $3,000 from a job. Your credit base is limited to $3,000. If you had earned income of at least $4,000, you then could have figured the credit on the base of $4,000.

The dependent care credit is added to the credits for the elderly, mortgage credit certificates and political contributions. The total credit is allowed up to your tax liability, figured without regard to alternative minimum tax, self-employment tax and certain penalty taxes.

If adjusted gross income is	Credit percentage	Your maximum credit for One dependent	Two or more dependents
$10,000 or less	30	$720	$1,440
10,001–12,000	29	696	1,392
12,001–14,000	28	672	1,344
14,001–16,000	27	648	1,296
16,001–18,000	26	624	1,248
18,001–20,000	25	600	1,200
20,001–22,000	24	576	1,152
22,001–24,000	23	552	1,104
24,001–26,000	22	528	1,056
26,001–28,000	21	504	1,008
28,001 and over	20	480	960

¶1.62 • EARNED INCOME TEST

You must earn wage, salary or self-employment income figured without regard to community property laws.

Earned income rule for married couples. Generally, both spouses must work at least part time, unless one is incapable of self-care or is a full-time student. The income limitation for the credit base is figured, not on combined joint income, but on the smaller income earned by either you or your spouse.

Example—
John and Mary are married. John earns $23,500. Mary earns $1,500. They incur care costs of $3,000 for their two children, ages 5 and 7. Their adjusted gross income is $25,000; their credit percentage is 22%. The child care credit base is limited to Mary's lower income of $1,500. They may claim a credit of $330 ($1,500 × 22%).

Expenses for dependent care incurred while looking for a job may be included. However, you must have earnings during the year to claim the credit.

An incapacitated spouse or a spouse who is a full-time student is considered to have earned income of $200 a month if expenses are incurred for one dependent; $400 a month for two or more such dependents.

Example—
Same facts as in the example above except Mary was a full-time student for nine months and earned no income for the year. The credit base is limited to $1,800 ($200 × 9).

A full-time student is one who attends school full time during each of five calendar months during the year.

If both husband and wife are full-time students and neither works, they may not claim the credit for dependent care costs. While one spouse may be considered to have earned income of $200 (or $400) each month, the other spouse's earned income is zero. Care costs are limited to the lesser amount of earned income, which in this case is zero.

¶1.63 • HOUSEHOLD AND DEPENDENT TESTS

You must maintain as your principal home a household for at least one of the following dependents who lives with you:

1. A dependent child under the age of 15 for whom you are entitled to deduct a dependency exemption. If you are divorced or separated, you do not have to be entitled to claim an exemption if you have custody for a greater part of the year than your former spouse (the child's other parent) (see ¶1.65).

2. Your spouse, if physically or mentally incapable of caring for himself or herself.

3. A dependent, regardless of age, who is physically or mentally incapable of caring for himself. A dependent who cannot dress himself or provide for his hygiene or nutritional needs, or who needs constant attention to avoid hurting himself or others is incapable of self-care. Relatives who qualify, if disabled, are listed at ¶1.54. A nonrelative may qualify if he made your home his principal home for the entire year and is a member of your household.

That a disabled dependent has gross income of $1,080 or more, so that you may not claim an exemption, does not bar you from claiming a credit for his care costs.

If your child becomes 15 during the year, you take into account expenses incurred for his care prior to the birthday. However, you do not prorate the $2,400 limitation. For example, if your child becomes 15 on May 1 and you incurred $2,400 in care expenses between January 1 and April 30, the entire $2,400 qualifies for the credit.

The costs of caring for a child under the age of 15 outside the home may be counted. The costs of caring for other dependents outside the home are taken into account only if the dependent regularly spends at least eight hours per day in your home. Expenses at dependent care centers qualify only if the centers are in compliance with state and local law.

Examples—
1. You live with your mother who is physically incapable of caring for herself. You hire a practical nurse to care for her in the home while you are at work. Payments to the nurse qualify as care costs. However, if you placed her in a nursing home, the cost of the nursing home would not qualify as dependent care costs; but see ¶17.10 for possible medical expense deduction.

2. You have a dependent child, 10 years old, who has been attending public school. You are offered a job which you can accept only if the child is placed in a boarding school. You take the position, and enroll the child in a boarding school. The expenses paid to the school are allocated between those covering the child's care and those covering tuition. Expenses for care qualify as dependent care costs; the tuition costs do not.

Maintaining a household. You are considered to have maintained a household if you (or you and your spouse) provided more than half the maintenance costs in 1986. You also qualify if you paid more than half the costs during a lesser period in which you had care cost expenses. Rent, mortgage interest, property tax and insurance, utility bills, upkeep, repairs, and groceries are considered maintenance expenses. Costs of clothing, education, medical expenses, vacations, life insurance, mortgage principal and capital inprovements are not.

In determining costs of maintaining a household for a care period of less than a year, the annual household costs are prorated over the number of calendar months within the period care costs were incurred. A period of less than a calendar month is treated as a calendar month.

Example—

The annual cost of maintaining a household is $6,600, and the period during which child care costs qualified for the deduction is from June 20 to December 31. To meet the household test, you must furnish more than $1,925 in maintaining the household from June 1 to December 31. The allocation covers seven months (June 1 to December 31).

$$\frac{7}{12} \text{ of } \$6,600 \qquad \$3,850$$
$$50\% \text{ of } \$3,850 \qquad \$1,925$$

Household of two or more families. If two or more families occupy common living quarters, each family is treated as a separate household.

Example—

Two unrelated women, each with children, occupy common living quarters; each pays more than one-half of her share of household costs incurred by both families; each is treated as maintaining her separate household.

¶1.64 • EXPENSES QUALIFYING FOR THE CREDIT

1. Care expenses of your child, incapacitated spouse, or incapacitated dependent in your home. If you pay FICA or FUTA taxes on your housekeeper's wages, you may include your share of the tax (employer) as part of the wages when figuring the credit.

2. Ordinary domestic services in your home, such as laundry, cleaning, and cooking (but not payments to a gardener or chauffeur). Expenses for the dependent's food, clothing or entertainment do not qualify. Food costs for a housekeeper who eats in your home may be added to qualifying expenses.

3. Outside-the-home care costs for a child under 15, as in a day care center, day camp, nursery school, or in the home of a baby sitter.

The IRS has agreed to follow a Tax Court decision allowing a working parent to include the costs of sleep-away camp. It held that summer camp was a reasonable way to provide care for a child of a working parent. The full amount you pay to a day care center or nursery school is also counted, even if it covers such incidental benefits as lunch. Tuition for a child in first grade or higher is not taken into account. The cost of transportation between home and a day care facility is not included in care expenses. Outside-the-home care for other qualified dependents qualifies where the dependent regularly spends at least eight hours per day in your home. Expenses of outside-the-home care are treated the same as expenses for care in the home. Up to $2,400 (or $4,800) a year of outside-the-home care expenses may be taken into account in figuring the credit.

The manner of care need not be the least expensive alternative. For example, where a grandparent resides with you and may provide adequate care for your child to enable you to work, the cost of hiring someone to care for the child is still eligible for the credit.

If a portion of expenses is for other than dependent care or household services, only the portion allocable to dependent care or household services qualifies. No allocation is required if the nondependent care services are minimal.

Examples—

1. A person accepts a full-time position and sends his 12-year-old child to boarding school. The expenses paid to the school must be allocated; the part representing care of the child qualifies; the part representing tuition does not.

2. A full-time housekeeper is hired to care for two children, ages 9 and 12. In addition, the housekeeper drives the mother to and from work each day. The driving is no more than thirty minutes. No allocation is required because the nondependent care services of chauffeuring are minimal.

Payments to relatives. No credit may be claimed for payments made to relatives for whom a dependency exemption is allowable (see ¶1.50) or to your child who is under 19 years at the close of the tax year. Thus, if you pay your mother to care for your child and you cannot claim your mother as a dependent, such payments qualify for the credit.

Care costs which also qualify as medical expenses. Care costs, such as a nurse's wages, may also qualify as medical expenses, but you may not claim both the dependent care credit and the medical expense deduction. If your care costs exceed the amount allowed as dependent care costs, the excess, to the extent it qualifies as a medical expense, may be added to your other deductible medical costs.

Example—

You pay $6,000 for care of your child in your home. The expenses also qualify as medical expenses. Assume your adjusted gross income is $17,000. Your dependent care costs are limited to $2,400 and you may claim a credit of $624 ($2,400 × 26%). The balance of $3,600 is deductible as medical expenses. If you had no other medical costs, your medical deduction would be $2,750 after deducting the 5% limitation on medical costs ($3,600 − $850 or 5% of $17,000).

Allocating expenses when employed less than entire year. When an expense covers a period part of which you were gainfully employed or in active search of gainful employment and part of which you were not employed or seeking employment, you must allocate expenses on a daily basis.

Example—

You are employed for only two months and 10 days. Monthly care expenses are $300. Eligible care expenses amount to $700 ($300 × 2 months, plus ⅓ of $300).

¶1.65 • RULES FOR SEPARATED COUPLES

Where you are living apart from your spouse, you may claim the credit on a separate return if you are treated as unmarried and you meet these tests:

1. You maintain as your home a household which is the principal place of abode of your dependent for more than half the year;

2. You furnish over half the cost of maintaining the household for the entire year;

3. Your spouse was not a member of the household during *the last six months* of the year; and

4. You file a separate return.

If you qualify as unmarried under this rule, you do not have to take your spouse's income into account or show that he or she is employed in order to claim a credit.

If you are legally divorced or separated, separated under a written agreement, or you live apart from your spouse during the last six months of 1986 and you are the custodial parent (have custody longer than the other parent), this favorable rule applies. You may claim the credit for care of a dependent child who is under 15 or physically or mentally incapable of caring for himself even if you waive the dependency exemption for the child or may not claim the exemption under a pre-1985 divorce or separation agreement. The child must be in your custody or the custody of yourself and the other parent for more than half of 1986.

¶ 1.70

Alimony

¶1.70 • DUAL TAX CONSEQUENCES OF ALIMONY PAYMENTS

The same rules determine whether alimony is deductible and taxable. For example, if a husband makes deductible alimony payments to his ex-wife, the payments are taxable to her. He may not deduct payments that are not taxable to her.

> The deductible and taxable portion of alimony is determined by two different sets of rules, depending on whether the payments are made under decrees and agreements entered into:
>
> *Before 1985.* These rules are discussed in ¶1.73–¶1.737.
>
> *After 1984.* These rules are discussed in ¶1.74–¶1.79
>
> A test common to both sets of rules is that the alimony must be paid under a decree of written separation agreement, *see* ¶1.72.
>
> Child support payments are neither deductible nor taxable; *see* ¶1.73 for pre-1985 rules and ¶1.79 for post-1984 rules.

How to report alimony deduction or income. On Form 1040, you deduct alimony in the year of payment. You claim the deduction whether or not you have excess itemized deductions. Payment of arrears is also deductible in the year of payment. A third party who pays alimony for you may not claim a deduction for his payment.

On Form 1040, you must enter the Social Security number and last name (if different from yours) of your ex-spouse. Otherwise, your deduction may be disallowed, and you may have to pay a $50 penalty. Your ex-spouse is required to give you the Social Security number and is subject to a $50 penalty for failure to do so.

Trust payments. To meet your alimony obligations, you may transfer income-producing property to a trust that is to pay the income to your spouse. You may not deduct payments made by the trust. You are not taxable on the income earned by the trust even though it pays your alimony obligations. This tax treatment is the equivalent of receiving a tax deduction for paying alimony. Your spouse reports the payments as trust income on Schedule E. You may deduct out-of-pocket payments that make up a shortage in the trust payments.

Funds for payments of alimony may be provided through the purchase of an annuity or endowment policy. You may not deduct payments made under the policies assigned or purchased for your spouse.

Examples—

1. To meet an alimony obligation of $500 a month, H purchases or assigns for the benefit of W a commercial annuity contract. The full $500 a month received by W is includible in her income. No part of these payments is deductible by H.

2. H transfers property to a trust which pays $1,000 a year to W as alimony. The annual $1,000 received by W, whether or not it is principal, is to be reported by W. H gets no deduction.

The IRS requires a payer of alimony to give to the IRS the Social Security number of his spouse who is also required to give him her number for this payment. A $50 penalty for failure of either spouse to do so may be imposed.

When deductible. You deduct alimony in the year of payment. You claim the deduction whether or not you have excess itemized deductions. Payment of arrears is also deductible in the year of payment, *see* ¶1.733. A third party who pays alimony for you may not claim a deduction for his payment.

Court decisions have held that payment of tax-exempt interest is not taxable. The IRS, however, claims that the payment is taxable regardless of its source.

Alimony to nonresident alien. If you pay alimony payments to a nonresident alien, and you are a U.S. citizen or resident, you must withhold 30% (or at a lower treaty rate) on each payment for income tax purposes. *See* IRS Publication 515 for more information.

Tax refund diversion for delinquent child support. The IRS can give your tax refund to a state which is paying support to your child if you fail to make support payments. The IRS has the authority to make the diversion where the delinquency is $150 or more and is overdue for at least three months. The IRS will not notify you of the diversion until it is made to the state. However, a federal court has held that a state must provide notice to all those whose refunds may be intercepted, specifying possible defenses and how to challenge the diversion before it is made; judicial review of the state's administrative decision must also be available.

¶1.701 • PLANNING ALIMONY PAYMENTS

Planning the after-tax consequences of alimony is difficult. The first problem is convincing the couple that they may have a common financial interest; the second is projecting future tax consequences.

If tax planning is approached from the viewpoint of only one spouse, the tax deduction is an advantage for the husband; tax-free income is an advantage for the wife. However, both advantages cannot be achieved, and the couple must face the reality of the tax law. They must compromise and approach the setting of amounts and tax consequences by balancing their interests. One equitable approach is to view both spouses as a single economic tax unit. If this is done and the husband is in a higher tax bracket than the wife, an agreement should generally provide for taxable and deductible alimony. The tax savings provided by the deduction can conserve more of the husband's assets while providing funds required by the wife. The final amount of alimony to be paid depends on the spouse's tax brackets. Where there is no favorable difference in tax brackets, there may be no advantage in tailoring an agreement for taxable and deductible alimony when viewing the positions of the two parties as a unit.

Examples—

Charles and Jane are planning a divorce. Jane needs $30,000 annually. Her other income equals her deductions and Charles has a taxable income of $100,000 before paying alimony and taxes.

1. *If alimony is made tax free and not deductible.* Assume the tax on Charles' taxable income of $100,000 is $36,981. After paying Jane $30,000 alimony, he is left with $33,019.

Taxable income		$100,000
Less: Alimony	$30,000	
Tax on $100,000	36,981	66,981
Net to Charles		$ 33,019

2. *If alimony of $30,000 is made taxable and deductible.* Assume Charles' tax on taxable income of $70,000 is $22,346 and Jane pays tax of $5,833 on $30,000. Jane is left with $24,167 and Charles nets $47,654.

Taxable income ($100,000—$30,000)		$70,000
Less: Alimony	$30,000	
Tax on $70,000	22,346	52,346
Net to Charles		$47,654

This result is not satisfactory to Jane; she has less after-tax income.

3. *Increase deductible alimony to $38,900.* Jane gets $30,000 after paying tax of $8,900. Charles pays a tax of $18,074 and has a net of $43,026, which is greater by $10,007 than he would realize if he paid $30,000 and received no deduction as in (1) above where his net was $33,019.

Taxable income		$100,000
Less: Alimony	$38,900	
Tax on $61,100	18,074	56,974
Net to Charles		$ 43,026

Note: Future changes in income, tax rates or filing status will upset the assumptions made in the above calculations, but risks have to be assumed in making an agreement that is to extend over many years. Depending on the circumstances of the parties, an agreement can be modified to meet new conditions.

¶1.71 • DEDUCTING LEGAL FEES IN MARITAL ACTIONS

Wife's payment of legal fees. If you are receiving taxed alimony, you may deduct part of your legal fees. Ask your attorney to divide his fees into charges for arranging:

1. The divorce or separation; *and*
2. Details of the alimony payments.

You may deduct the legal fees allocated to (2), but you may not deduct the fee attributed to the divorce or separation negotiation. If alimony is not taxed to you, you may not deduct any part of the fee. However, part of a fee allocated to a property settlement may be added to the basis of the property obtained in the settlement.

Husband's payment of legal fees. You may not deduct legal fees paid for arranging a divorce or for resisting your wife's demands for alimony. Furthermore, you may not deduct legal fees incurred in resisting your wife's claims to income-producing property, the loss of which would affect your earnings. However, these rules do not bar a husband from deducting that part of his legal fee that is identified as being paid for tax advice. The type of proof that may support a deduction is as follows:

1. The fee is charged by a firm that limits its practice to state and federal tax matters and is engaged to advise on the tax consequences of a property settlement involving the transfer of property in exchange for other property and the release of the wife's marital rights in the husband's property.
2. The fee is charged by a firm engaged in general practice which assigns tax problems, such as the tax consequences of creating an alimony trust, to its special tax department. On the bill, an allocation is made for tax advice based on time, complexity of the case, and the amount of tax involved.
3. An attorney handles the divorce for a fixed fee and also gives advice on the right to claim exemptions for the children following the divorce. The bill allocated part of the fee to the tax advice, based on time, results obtained by his negotiations, and fees customarily charged in the locality for similar services.

You may not deduct your payment of your wife's legal fees. Such payments are not for the support of your wife.

¶1.72 • DECREE OR AGREEMENT REQUIRED

Alimony, to be deductible and taxable, must be required by one of the following: (1) a decree of divorce or legal separation, (2) a written separation agreement, or (3) a decree of support. This rule applies to both pre-1985 and post-1984 decrees and agreements. Voluntary payments are not deductible.

Divorced or legally separated. The obligation to pay alimony must be imposed by the decree of divorce or separate maintenance or a written agreement incident to the divorce or separation.

Alimony paid under a Mexican divorce decree qualifies. Payments under a Mexican or state decree declared invalid by another jurisdiction do not qualify according to present IRS policy. Two appeals courts reject the IRS position.

Support payments ordered by a court in a wife's home state qualify as alimony, even though not provided for by an *ex parte* divorce decree obtained by the husband in another state. Similarly, payments qualified when a state court increased support originally ordered before the husband obtained an uncontested Mexican divorce.

Payments made under a separation approved by a Roman Catholic ecclesiastical board do not qualify.

When the decree fails to mention alimony, payments qualify as long as they are made under a written agreement considered "incident to" the divorce or separated status of the couple.

Payments made under an agreement *amended* after a divorce or legal separation may also qualify, if the amendment is considered "incident" to the divorce or separation. For example, the IRS agrees that a *written* amendment changing the amount of alimony payments is incident to the divorce where the legal obligation to support under the original agreement survived the divorce. However, payments under an amended agreement did not qualify where the original agreement settled all rights between the husband and wife and made no provision for future support. The legal obligation to support the wife did not survive the divorce and could not be revived by the new agreement.

Annulments. Payments made under an annulment decree qualify as deductible (and taxable) alimony.

Where a couple is separated and living apart, alimony is deductible by the husband and taxable to the wife if paid under either a written separation agreement or decree of support. A written separation agreement made before August 17, 1954 does not qualify unless materially modified after August 16, 1954.

Oral changes agreed to by the parties will not be recognized for tax purposes unless they are incorporated into the written separation agreement.

A decree of support. Any court decree or order requiring support payments qualifies, including alimony *pendente lite* (temporary alimony while the action is pending), and an interlocutory (not final) divorce decree.

In certain community property states, payments under a decree of alimony *pendente lite* which do not exceed the wife's interest in community income are not deductible by the husband nor taxable to the wife; payments exceeding the wife's interest are taxable to her and deductible by the husband.

Alimony Paid Under Pre-1985 Decrees and Agreements

Under a pre-1985 decree or agreement, a husband may deduct alimony payments and the wife must report the alimony as income, if these four rules are met:

1. Payments must be required by a decree of divorce or legal separation, a written separation agreement, or a decree of support, see ¶1.71.

2. There must be an obligation to support, see ¶1.73.

3. The payments must be periodic, see ¶1.733.

4. The payments must not be specifically designated for child support, see ¶1.737.

If the amount or terms of payment under a pre-1985 arrangement are changed after 1984 by a new decree or agreement, the rules for post-1984 instruments will apply; see ¶1.74.

¶1.73 • SUPPORT OBLIGATION—PRE-1985

Alimony, to be deductible (and taxable), must be paid because of the marital obligation to support the spouse. Payment of any other obligation does not qualify. These are examples of nondeductible (and nontaxable) payments:

Repayment of a bona fide loan.

Example—

During their marriage, a husband borrowed $10,000 from his wife. The divorce decree now provides that he return the $10,000 in installments over a period of 12 years. He may not deduct these payments.

Payments to settle property rights, including payment of a spouse's share of community property.

Voluntary payments in excess of required alimony. This is true even if the wife reports them as income or a court order denies temporary alimony on condition that the voluntary payments continue. Payments made in excess of the amount required by a decree or separation agreement are considered to be voluntary. Amending the decree retroactively to cover an increase does not qualify the increase as deductible and taxable alimony. The increase has to be approved by the court before the increased payments are made.

Payments to spouse who remarries. The tax deduction allowed for alimony payments made under a pre-1985 decree or agreement hinges on the obligation to support. Once the spouse receiving alimony remarries, the obligation to support generally ends under state law. In these states, any payment after remarriage is not considered alimony and is not deductible. The payments made after remarriage are considered tax-free gifts if the former husband knows of the remarriage and that he is no longer obligated to pay. If she does not inform him of her remarriage, his payments are taxable to her but are not deductible by him.

Voluntary alimony payments may also be subject to gift tax.

The decree or agreement may combine payments for support and nonmarital obligations. If the decree or agreement does not separately identify the two types of payments, the amounts paid for support may not be deductible by the husband and are not taxable to the wife.

Where an estranged couple continues to share the same home, courts disagree over the tax status of alimony paid under pre-1985 decrees or agreements. An appeals court holds that a couple does not have to live in separate quarters to be considered separated for tax purposes, as long as the evidence indicates the couple is in fact living separately. On the other hand, the Tax Court does not treat a couple living under the same roof as separated for tax purposes.

¶1.733 • PERIODIC PAYMENTS—PRE-1985

To be deductible (and taxable), alimony payments must meet a "periodic" test. The term "periodic" as used in the law is misleading. The ordinary meaning of "periodic" implies payments at regular intervals. However, Treasury regulations state that there is no requirement to pay at regular intervals. "Periodic" is then what the law and regulations have labeled as "periodic." Not periodic are noncontingent payments of a fixed sum over a period of 10 years or less. These types of payments are considered periodic:

1. *Payments over an indefinite period of time.* For example, a husband agrees to pay $500 a month to his wife for as long as she lives or remains unmarried.

2. *A fixed sum payable in installments over a period of more than 10 years.* However, each year only 10% of the fixed amount is considered a periodic payment. Thus, to the extent that payments in one year exceed 10%, the excess is not deductible by the husband or taxable to the wife. The 10% limit does not apply to payments in arrears.

3. *Fixed payments over a period of 10 years or less, subject to one or more of these contingencies:* Death of either spouse, wife's remarriage, a change of economic status of either spouse, or the court's power to modify, alter or amend. Even if the agreement does not have such a provision, the alimony may still be deductible if state law subjects the alimony to similar contingencies. For example, in your state, a court may modify the alimony agreement for the benefit of children, and by statute, the obligation to pay alimony ends at the death of either spouse. Such contingencies imposed by state law qualify the payments as periodic.

4. *Payments of an indefinite amount, such as payments based on a percentage of annual income which fluctuates.* For example, a husband agreed to pay 20% of his yearly income. Here, even if the alimony period is 10 years or less, the payments qualify.

Example—

After deductions, you have an income of roughly $40,000 a year. If you agreed to pay your spouse $50,000 in five annual payments of $10,000, you get no deductions. But if you agreed to pay 25% of your income for five years, the payments are fully deductible by you and taxable to your spouse.

Lump-sum payments. Even if provided for in the decree or written separation agreement, a lump-sum payment is not deductible because it is not a periodic payment.

If a husband has been making periodic payments and agrees to a lump-sum settlement, the lump sum is not deductible by him nor taxable to his wife except to the extent that it includes arrears of periodic alimony. To avoid loss of the deduction for the arrears, the part of your payment representing arrears should be specifically designated as such.

Example—

H has been paying W $3,600 a year in alimony. H and W agree on a $20,000 lump-sum settlement. If H pays the entire $20,000 with no mention of arrears, he gets no deduction. Had the payment been made in two checks for $16,400 and $3,600 or had $3,600 been specifically designated as being for arrears, H would get a $3,600 alimony deduction.

Alimony in arrears. Alimony in arrears is deductible by the husband and taxable to his wife in the year paid, even if paid in a lump sum. The 10% limitation on a fixed sum paid in installments over a period of more than 10 years does not apply to arrears.

¶1.734 • RENT-FREE HOME AS ALIMONY—PRE-1985

A portion of an alimony award may be allocated to the payment of expenses on a residence, such as mortgage interest and principal, taxes, and insurance. The tax consequences of the payments depends upon how the residence is owned.

Tenancy with right of survivorship (tenancy by the entirety or joint tenancy). If you and your spouse are jointly liable on the mortgage, you may deduct as alimony one-half of each principal and interest payment. You may deduct as interest the other half of your interest payments. You may not deduct the other half of principal payments as they are nondeductible personal expenses. Your spouse must include as income one-half of each interest and principal payment, but she may deduct her one-half share of interest if she itemizes deductions.

If your spouse is not personally liable on the mortgage, your payments are not deductible alimony. However, you may deduct your payments of interest and taxes as itemized deductions.

Tenants in common. Each of you owns one-half of the home; there is no right of survivorship. You may deduct as alimony amounts you pay for mortgage principal and interest, taxes, and insurance on your spouse's one-half of the home. You may separately deduct the other one-half of interest and taxes. Principal and insurance payments on your half of the property are nondeductible personal expenses.

Your spouse must include in income the payments on her half of the property, but she may deduct interest and taxes as itemized deductions.

Your spouse is sole owner of the house. If you pay real estate taxes, mortgage payments, and insurance premiums on the home your spouse owns, you may deduct your payments as alimony. Your spouse must include the payments, but may deduct taxes and interest as itemized deductions.

You are the sole owner of the house. You may agree to allow your spouse to live rent free in a house you own. You may not deduct your mortgage payments. Nor may you deduct the fair rental value of the home. You may, however, deduct interest and taxes as itemized deductions.

Rent-free use of cooperative apartment. In one case, a husband's payments of leasing charges on his co-op apartment in which his estranged wife lived were treated as deductible alimony. However, not all co-op payments are alimony. Rent payments to a co-op apartment corporation on behalf of an ex-spouse are alimony except for the portion allocable to mortgage interest, real estate taxes, and principal amortization. The payment of mortgage principal and interest and real estate taxes directly and primarily benefits the owner of the co-op stock.

Paying utilities. Regardless of the way title is held, your payments for utilities are considered periodic payments, deductible as alimony by you and taxable to your spouse.

A court held that a husband's payment of rent for a house owned by his corporation and occupied by his divorced wife was deductible as alimony and taxable to his wife.

¶1.735 • PAYMENT OF SPOUSE'S MEDICAL OR OTHER EXPENSES—PRE-1985

If you pay your spouse's medical expenses as part of your alimony obligation, the payments are deductible as alimony, provided they are considered to be periodic. If she is required to report such payments as income, she may deduct them as medical expenses under the rules of ¶17.00.

Tuition payments and support payments for a wife's relatives may be deductible alimony.

Examples—
1. Christiansen agreed to pay the cost of educating his former wife's nephew and niece. He deducted the expense as alimony. The IRS disallowed the deduction because his wife did not actually receive the payments. The Tax Court allowed the deduction. Mrs. Christiansen felt obligated to educate the children. Her husband's payments discharged that obligation, giving her an economic benefit. Whether her obligation was moral rather than legal does not matter.
2. Under a divorce settlement, a husband had to pay his former wife $20,000 a year and his former mother-in-law $5,000 a year. This arrangement was made because the wife was her mother's sole support. The $5,000 received by the mother is considered part of the taxable alimony paid to the wife.

¶1.736 • INSURANCE PREMIUMS AS ALIMONY— PRE-1985

As part of your alimony obligation, you may pay premiums on insurance assigned to your spouse. You may deduct the premium payments if the policy is assigned to her absolutely and she is irrevocably named as beneficiary. This is true even though, under the decree or agreement, your obligation to pay the premiums will cease on the death or remarriage of your spouse. Your spouse reports as income the full amount of the premium, not the smaller amount by which the premium increases the cash surrender value of the policy. If she has only a contingent interest in the policy, the deduction is lost and the premium is not taxable. Contingent interests that have barred deductions are:

The policy comes back to the husband if the wife dies first, even if the wife had the right to get the cash surrender value or borrow on the policy during her life.

Wife loses her interest in the policy if she remarries (*but see* case below).

Husband keeps rights to surrender the policy or to make a loan against it, even though the wife has power to veto his action.

If the wife's rights to the policy do not vest under the divorce decree, the premiums are not deductible, even if she later becomes absolute owner of the policy after the later assignment. The decree may require only a limited transfer, for example, to prevent you from borrowing against the policy. If, under these circumstances, you assign the policy absolutely, you may not deduct your premium payments. Your assignment is voluntary.

Premiums paid on a decreasing term policy which has no loan or cash surrender value are not deductible alimony.

You may not deduct as alimony a lump-sum payment for a policy purchased for your spouse or the cash surrender value of a policy assigned to her.

¶1.737 • CHILD SUPPORT PAYMENTS—PRE-1985

Payments specifically designated for support of a minor child of the husband are neither deductible by the husband nor taxable to the wife. Where periodic payments are not specifically earmarked for child support, the entire amount paid is taxable alimony to the wife, even where it appears child support was intended. Payments for the support of the wife's child who is not a child of the husband are not child support payments. They are deductible alimony payments if they qualify as periodic and are taxable to the wife.

Example—
Under a decree of divorce, H is ordered to pay $50 for W's support and $100 for the support of his minor children. Only $50 is taxable to W and deductible by H.

The tax law does not state at what age a child ceases to be a minor. The Tax Court has held that for tax purposes a minor is anyone under the age of 21, regardless of the age fixed by state law.

The Supreme Court holds that an allocation between taxable (deductible) alimony and child support may be made only if the agreement specifically fixes an amount as child support. Without a specific child support provision, all payments made under an agreement are alimony, although the children benefit from them. Merely stating that child support payments are fixed "for tax purposes" is not a specific designation. Amendments to the original decree to specifically fix the amount for child support do not have retroactive effect unless the amendment corrects an error by the court in the original decree.

The Supreme Court rule does not apply to support payments under post-1984 agreements, *see* ¶1.78.

Assume your spouse remarries and you continue alimony payments under an agreement that does not fix child support payments. You may deduct the alimony although you intend it for your children's support. Until a court changes the terms of the alimony agreement and provides for child support, the payments are deductible by you and taxable to your spouse. This is true, even if the court order is retroactive to the date of your spouse's remarriage. Of course, payments of child support after the court order are not deductible.

When you fail to pay the entire amount under a decree or agreement requiring both alimony and child support, the amount actually paid is applied first to child support.

Example—

Under a divorce decree, H is to pay $200 a month, $100 for support of W and $100 for support of his minor children. During 1984, H pays only $150 a month. $100 for each monthly payment in 1984 is considered support of the children. Only $50 of each month's payment is included in W's return and is deducted by H.

Paid vacation expenses for wife and children were not treated as nondeductible support payments, although payments were contingent on the children accompanying the wife. No specific amount could be allocated to the children.

While the husband may not deduct child support payments, they count in determining if he is entitled to the dependency exemption for the child. *See* ¶1.554.

Alimony Paid Under Post-1984 Decrees and Agreements

Tax legislation may modify rules 3 and 5 of ¶1.74 and the discussion in ¶1.76, ¶1.77, and ¶1.78. See the tax legislation guide in the front of the book and the Supplement for further details.

¶1.74 • PLANNING POINTERS FOR POST-1984 ALIMONY AGREEMENTS

1. The parties may specifically state in the decree or separation agreement that the alimony is neither taxable to the payee-spouse (under IRC Section 71) nor deductible by the payer-spouse (under IRC Section 215). Such a statement effectively disqualifies payments that otherwise would be taxable to the payee-spouse and deductible by the payer-spouse. The payee-spouse must attach a copy of the agreement that includes the statement to the tax return for the years in which it applies.

2. If the parties agree to deductible and taxable alimony, they must provide for cash payments. *See* ¶1.75.

3. The decree or agreement must state that the alimony is to end on the death of the payee-spouse. Failure to have this statement disqualifies the alimony as a taxable and deductible item. *See* ¶1.78.

4. There is no need to set a minimum payout period for annual alimony payments of $10,000 or less. One payment of $10,000 can qualify as deductible and taxable alimony.

5. There must be a minimum payout period of at least six years for annual alimony payments exceeding $10,000. The period can of course be longer. The minimum period is six consecutive taxable years. *See* ¶1.76.

6. In providing for the support of children, a specific allocation to their support or the setting of certain contingencies disqualifies payments as deductible and taxable alimony. *See* ¶1.78.

7. Divorced or legally separated parties may not live in the same household. If they live in the same household alimony payments are not deductible or taxable. However, there are these exceptions: A spouse who makes payments while preparing to leave the common residence may deduct payments made within one month before the departure. Also, where you are separated under a written agreement but not legally separated under a decree of divorce or separate maintenance, you may deduct alimony payments even if you both are members of the same household.

To avoid recapture of deductions of alimony exceeding $10,000, carefully plan or avoid schedules of declining payments. Recapture may occur where annual payments of over $10,000 are scheduled and paid, but in a later year a reduced payment is made and the reduction is $10,000 or more. *See* ¶1.77.

Effective date. The post-1984 rules apply generally to divorce or separation instruments made after December 31, 1984. A decree made after December 31, 1984 that incorporates or adopts without change the terms of alimony or separate maintenance payments under a divorce or separation instrument made before January 1, 1985 is treated as made before January 1, 1985.

Example—

In November 1984, a couple execute a written separation agreement. In February 1985, a decree of divorce is entered and incorporates the written separation agreement without change. The divorce decree is treated as executed before January 1, 1985. If the amount or the time period of the alimony or separate maintenance payments are not fixed in the pre-1985 separation agreement, the post-1984 decree will *not* be treated as executed before January 1, 1985. Thus, the post-1984 rules apply to the payments. Similarly, a decree that changes the amount or terms of payment of a pre-1985 arrangement or that adds or removes any conditions relating to such payments, is subject to the post-1984 rules.

Further, the parties may modify a pre-1985 divorce or separation instrument to specifically provide that the new post-1984 rules are to apply. In such a case, the post-1984 rules apply to payments made after the date of modification.

¶1.75 • CASH PAYMENTS REQUIRED—POST-1984

Only payments of cash, checks, and money orders payable on demand qualify as taxable and deductible alimony.

Providing services or transferring or providing property do not qualify. For example, you may not deduct as alimony your note, the assignment of a third-party note, or an annuity contract.

Your cash payment to a third party for a spouse qualifies if made under the terms of a divorce decree or separation instrument. For example, you pay the rent, mortgage, tax, or tuition liabilities of your former spouse. The payments qualify if made under the terms of the divorce or separation instrument. However, you may not deduct payments to maintain property owned by you but used by your spouse. For example, you pay the mortgage expenses, real estate taxes, and insurance premiums for a house which you own and in which your former spouse lives. You may not deduct those payments, even if required by a decree or agreement.

You may deduct payments made to a third party at the written request of the payee-spouse. For example, your former spouse asks you to make a cash donation to a charitable organization instead of paying alimony installments to her. Her request must be in writing and state that both she and you intend the payment to be treated as an alimony. You must receive the written request before the date of filing your return of tax for the taxable year in which the payment was made.

Premiums paid for term or whole life insurance on your life made under the terms of the divorce or separation instrument qualify as deductible alimony to the extent your former spouse owns the policy.

¶1.76 • SIX-YEAR PAYMENT PERIOD FOR ALIMONY OF OVER $10,000—POST-1984

A minimum payout period of at least six consecutive years applies if a decree or agreement requires annual payments exceeding $10,000. The minimum period does not apply to payments required by a temporary support decree.

Examples—

1. Under a divorce decree, a husband is to make a single $15,000 payment; only $10,000 of the payment qualifies as taxable and deductible alimony.

2. Under a divorce decree, Brown is to make alimony payments of $20,000 in each of the five calendar years 1985 through 1989. He is to make no payment in 1990. Only $10,000 qualifies as an alimony payment in each of the five calendar years 1985 through 1989. However, if the divorce decree had required a payment of at least $1 in 1990, the six-year rule would have been met, and each annual $20,000 payment would qualify as alimony. However, the recapture rule would apply to the reduced payment in 1990, *see* ¶1.77.

For purposes of determining whether alimony is paid in any year, the possible termination of a payment upon the happening of a contingency other than the passage of time that has not yet occurred is ignored unless the contingency may cause all or a portion of the payment to be treated as a child support payment. For example, a statement that the payments are to end on death does not affect the validity of the payout period.

The six consecutive calendar years begin with the first calendar year in which you pay deductible alimony under a decree of divorce or separate maintenance, or written separation agreement. The six-year period need not begin with the year of divorce or separation if no qualifying payments are made in that year.

If you have been making payments under a temporary support decree, the six-year period does not begin until the first calendar year in which alimony is made under a regular divorce or separation decree or agreement.

If qualifying payments begin under a written separation agreement that is later incorporated into a final decree, the period in which payments are made under the agreement is treated as part of the six-year period.

¶1.77 • RECAPTURE RULES FOR DECLINE OF PAYMENTS OF OVER $10,000—POST-1984

The recapture rules are designed to prevent the "so called" front loading of money due for property settlements rather than for alimony support. Recapture applies only when during the six-year payout period (¶1.76) an alimony payment decreases by more than $10,000 from payments made and deducted in a prior year or years in the six-year period. You must figure the recapture amount, which is usually the decrease less $10,000, and report the amount as income as illustrated in the following examples. Your former spouse may claim a deduction for the amount you recapture.

Examples—

1. Under a 1985 decree, Ross pays and deducts alimony payments of $25,000. In 1986, he pays only $12,000. As there has been a decrease of more than $10,000, recapture applies. The recaptured amount of $3,000 is the $13,000 decrease less $10,000. He reports $3,000 as income. His former spouse may also claim a $3,000 deduction.

1985 deduction		$25,000
Less:		
Payment in 1986	$12,000	
Plus $10,000	10,000	22,000
Recaptured in 1986		$ 3,000

2. Same facts as in (1) but in 1987 Ross pays only $1,000; the excess amount recaptured in 1987 is $12,000.

1985 deduction after recapture		$22,000
Less:		
Payment in 1987	$ 1,000	
Plus $10,000	10,000	11,000
Excess (1)		11,000
1986 deduction		12,000
Less:		
Payment in 1987	1,000	
Plus $10,000	10,000	11,000
Excess (2)		1,000
Recaptured in 1987		
(Total of 1 and 2)		$12,000

Recapture does not apply to payments:
Received under temporary support orders,
Made pursuant to a continuing liability over the period to pay a fixed portion of income from a business or property or from wages or self-employment. For example, John agrees to pay his former wife 50% of royalties from a patent for six years. A decline in payments by more than $10,000 does not trigger recapture.
That end because of the death of the payer or payee or the remarriage of the payee before the close of the year.

Example—

Under a 1985 divorce decree, Davis is to pay $30,000 in each of the calendar years 1985 through 1990. In 1985, he pays $30,000; in 1986, after paying $15,000, his former spouse remarries, and he stops paying alimony. The recapture rule does not apply for 1986 or any later year.

Recapture applies if alimony payments decline or stop because of a failure to pay on time or the divorce or separation instrument

is modified, or the support needs of the payee or the ability of the payer to provide support change.

The use of a trust to pay alimony may avoid recapture rules.

¶1.78 • PAYMENTS MUST STOP AT DEATH— POST-1984

If a post-1984 agreement or decree fails to require that payments stop on the death of the payee-spouse, none of the payments, whether made before or after the payee's death, qualify as taxable or deductible alimony.

Examples—

1. Jones is to pay $10,000 each year for 10 years. The decree does not state that the payments will end upon the death of his former spouse. None of the payments qualify as taxable and deductible alimony.

2. Same facts as in (1) except the decree states that the payments will end upon the death of his former spouse. Jones or his estate is also to make additional annual payments of $20,000 for 10 years. As the $20,000 payments do not end on the death of the former Mrs. Jones, they do not qualify as alimony. The separate $10,000 annual payments do qualify.

To the extent that one or more payments are to begin, increase in amount, or accelerate after the death of the payee-spouse, such payments may be treated as a substitute for the continuation of payments terminating on the death of the payee-spouse.

Examples—

1. Under the terms of a divorce decree, Smith is obligated to make annual alimony payments of $30,000, terminating on the earlier of the end of six years or the death of Mrs. Smith. She also is to keep custody of their two minor children. The decree also provides that if on her death the children are still minors, Jones is to pay annually $10,000 to a trust each year. The trust income and corpus are to be used for the children until the youngest child reaches the age of majority. Under these facts, Smith's possible liability to make annual $10,000 payments to the trust is treated as a substitute for $10,000 of the $30,000 annual payments. $10,000 of each of the $30,000 annual payments does not qualify as alimony.

2. Same facts as in (1) but the alimony is to end on the earlier of the expiration of 15 years or the death of Mrs. Smith. Further if Mrs. Smith dies before the end of the 15-year period, Smith will pay her estate the difference between the total amount that he would have paid had she survived less the amount actually paid. For example, if she dies at the end of the tenth year, he will pay her estate $150,000 ($450,000 − $300,000). Under these facts, his liability to make a lump-sum payment to the estate is a substitute for the full amount of each of the annual $30,000 payments. Accordingly, none of the annual $30,000 payments qualifies as alimony.

¶1.79 • CHILD SUPPORT PAYMENTS ARE NOT ALIMONY—POST-1984

A payment is fixed as payable for the support of your child if the divorce or separation instrument specifically fixes an amount payable for support.

Even in the absence of a support allocation, a payment will be treated as payable for support if it is to be reduced on the happening of a contingency relating to the child or at a time clearly associated with such a contingency. Reducing payments for the following events falls within this rule: The child reaches a specified age or income level, dies, marries, leaves school, leaves the parent's household, or begins to work.

Example—

On July 1, 1985, a couple is divorced when their children John (born July 15, 1970) and Jane (born September 23, 1972) are 14 and 12. Under the divorce decree, the husband is to make monthly alimony payments of $2,000. The monthly payments are to be reduced to $1,500 on January 1, 1991 and to $1,000 on January 1, 1995. On January 1, 1991, the date of the first reduction, John will be almost 20 and a half years old. On January 1, 1995, the date of the second reduction, Jane will be over 22 years old. As each reduction is to occur not more than one year before or after a child reaches the age of 21 years, the IRS will presume that the reductions are associated with the happening of a contingency relating to the children. The two reductions total $1,000 per month and are treated as the amount fixed for the support of the children. $1,000 of the $2,000 monthly payment does not qualify as alimony. The husband must prove that the reductions were not related to the support of the children.

If both alimony and child support are specified and a payment is less than the total of the two amounts, then the payment is first allocated to child support.

¶2.00

Taxable Pay and Tax-Free Pay Benefits

Illustrations of entering wage and salary income on a tax return may be found in the Supplement to YOUR INCOME TAX. Mail the card at the front of this book for your FREE Supplement, which includes filled-in returns and last-minute information.

Tax-Free Pay Benefits

¶2.01 • EMPLOYER-FURNISHED MEALS OR LODGING

The value of employer-financed food or lodging is not taxable if furnished on your employer's business premises for his convenience. The value of lodgings is not taxable if you must accept the lodging as a condition of your employment. The key words here are: "Business premises," "convenience of the employer," and "condition of employment." For meals, you must satisfy the "business premises" and "convenience of employer" tests. For lodging, you must satisfy these two tests plus the "condition of employment" test.

Business premises. The IRS generally defines "business premises" as the place of employment, such as a company cafeteria in a factory or an employer's home for a domestic. The Tax Court has a liberal view, extending the area of "business premises" beyond the actual place of business in these cases:

A house provided a hotel manager, although located across the street from the hotel. The IRS has agreed to the decision.

A house provided a motel manager, two blocks from the motel. However, a court of appeals reversed the decision and held in the IRS's favor.

A rented hotel suite used daily by executives for a luncheon conference.

Convenience of employer. This requires proof that an employer provides the free meals or lodging for a business purpose other than providing extra pay. However, that the board and lodging are described in a contract or state statute as extra pay does not bar tax-free treatment provided they are *also* furnished for other substantial, noncompensatory business reasons, for example, you are required to be on call 24 hours a day.

Generally, the value of meals furnished before or after working hours or on nonworking days is not treated as tax-free income, but see examples (1) and (3).

Examples—

1. A waitress who works from 7 A.M. to 4 P.M. is furnished two meals a day without charge. Her employer encourages her to have her breakfast at the restaurant before working, but she is required to have her lunch there. The value of her breakfast and lunch is not income because it is furnished during her work period or immediately before or after the period. But say she is also allowed to have free meals on her days off and a free supper on the days she works. The value of these meals is taxable income because they are not furnished during or immediately before or after her work period.

2. A hospital maintains a cafeteria on its premises where all of its employees may eat during their working hours. No charge is made for these meals. The hospital furnishes meals to have the employees available for emergencies. The employees are not required to eat there. Since the hospital furnishes the meals in order to have employees available for emergency call during meal periods, the meals are not income to any of the hospital employees who obtain their meals at the hospital cafeteria.

3. You are required to occupy living quarters on your employer's business premises as a condition of employment. The value of *any* meal furnished you without charge on your employer's premises is not taxable income.

Meal charges. Your company may charge for meals on company premises and give you an option to accept or decline the meals. The IRS may not point to this option as evidence that the meals are not furnished for the convenience of your employer.

Where you must incur a fixed charge for your meals (furnished for your employer's convenience) on a periodic basis, you may claim an exclusion for the meal costs, provided you incur the meal charge whether or not you accept the meals.

Condition of employment. This test requires evidence that the lodging is needed for you to perform your job properly. For example, you are required to be available for duty at all times. If you are given the choice of free lodging at your place of employment or a cash allowance, the lodging is not considered as a "condition of employment," and its value is taxable, if elected.

"Lodging" includes heat, electricity, gas, water, sewerage, and other utilities. Where these services are furnished by the employer and their value is deducted from your salary, the amount deducted is also not included as part of your wage income. But if you pay for the utilities yourself, you may not exclude their cost from your income.

Example—

Jones is employed at a construction project at a remote job site. His pay is $200 a week. Because there are no accessible places near the site for food and lodging, the employer furnishes meals and lodging for which it charges $40 a week, which is taken out of Jones's pay. Jones reports only the net amount he receives, $160. The value of the meals and lodging is a tax-free benefit.

An employer may furnish unprepared food, such as groceries, rather than prepared meals. Courts are divided on whether the value of the groceries is excludable from income. One court allowed an exclusion for the value of nonfood items, such as napkins and soap, as well as for groceries, furnished to a doctor who ate at his home on hospital grounds so he would be available for emergencies.

The IRS does not consider partners or self-employed persons as employees and so does not allow them an exclusion under the rules of this section. The IRS also does not allow a partnership to deduct the cost of meals and lodging provided a partner-manager of a hotel. Courts split on this issue.

Cash allowances. A cash allowance for meals and lodging is taxable. Only meals furnished in kind are permitted tax-free treatment.

Example—

A hotel manager's wife bought groceries, the cost of which was reimbursed by the hotel. Milk was delivered to their apartment and paid for by the hotel. The reimbursement of the grocery bills was taxable because the groceries were not "furnished in kind" by the hotel. However, the cost of the milk was not taxable because the delivery to the apartment and the payment of the bill by the hotel was considered "furnishing in kind."

Peace Corps and VISTA volunteers. Peace Corps volunteers working overseas may exclude subsistence allowances from income under a specific Code provision. The law does not provide a similar exclusion for the small living expense allowances received by VISTA volunteers.

ARE YOUR BOARD AND LODGING TAX FREE?

Yes	No
A state civil service employee works at a state institution. His job requires him to live at the institution and eat there so he may be available for duty at any time. Under state law, the value of his meals and lodgings are considered part of his pay.	Your employer gives you a cash allowance for your meals or lodgings. He supplies neither.
Hotel executives, managers, housekeepers, and auditors who are required to live at the hotel.	You have a choice of accepting cash or getting the meals or lodgings. For example, under a union contract you get meals, but you may refuse to take them and get an automatic pay increase.
The following employees usually meet the above tests: Domestics, farm laborers, fishermen, canners, seamen, servicemen, building superintendents, hospital and sanitarium employees.	A state hospital employee is given a choice: He may live at the institution rent free or live elsewhere and get an extra $30 a month. Whether he stays at the institution or lives outside, the $30 a month is included in his income.
Restaurant and other food service employees for meals furnished during or immediately before or after working hours.	A waitress, on her days off, is allowed to eat free meals at the restaurant where she works.
Employees who must be available during meal periods for emergencies.	You may buy lunch in the company's cafeteria or bring your own. There are no other eating facilities near the company's premises.
Employees who, because of the nature of the business, are given short meal periods.	
Workers who have no alternative but to use company-supplied facilities in remote areas.	
Park employees who voluntarily live in rent-free apartments provided by a park department in order to protect the park from vandalism.	

¶2.02 • Tax-Free Fringe Benefits

The tax law specifically exempts the following types of fringe benefits from tax:

Group hospitalization premiums paid by an employer or former employer, if you are retired. If you retire and have the option of receiving continued coverage under the medical plan or a lump-sum payment covering unused accumulated sick leave instead of coverage, the lump sum amount is reported as income at the time you have the option to receive it. If you elect continued coverage, the amount reported in income may be deductible as medical insurance. Medical coverage provided to the family of a deceased employee is tax free since it is treated as a continuation of the employee's fringe-benefit package.

Child or dependent care services provided by an employer under a written, nondiscriminatory plan. However, the value of services excluded from an employee's gross income may not exceed $5,000 .

Group-term life insurance premiums paid by your employer, provided the policy does not exceed $50,000. *See* ¶2.021.

Medicare premiums paid by your employer for voluntary hospital coverage (Part B).

Qualified group legal services plan contributions paid by your employer for prepaid personal legal services for you and your family. The value of legal services provided are also tax free.

Employer contributions to a qualified pension or profit-sharing plan.

Transportation in a commuter van seating eight or more adult passengers, provided the service is provided under a written plan that does not discriminate in favor of officers, shareholders, or highly compensated employees. Travel in company cars is not covered by this tax exclusion.

Employer's payment of education costs under a nondiscriminatory plan. The annual tax-free benefit may not exceed $5,250 per employee for tuition, books, fees, supplies and equipment for any courses. Courses do not have to be job related, provided they do not involve sports, games, or hobbies.

Employer-provided services that are sold to the public and offered to employees at no additional cost to the employer.

Not taxable are free or low-cost flights provided by an airline to its employees, free or discount lodging for employees of a hotel, and telephone service provided to employees of telephone companies. These tax-free fringes also may be provided to the employee's spouse and dependent children; retired employees, including employees retired on disability; and widows or widowers of deceased or retired employees. Benefits received by officers, owners and highly compensated employees are subject to nondiscrimination rules. Benefits provided by another company under a reciprocal arrangement, such as standby tickets on another airline, also qualify.

If a company has two lines of business, such as an airline and a hotel, an employee of the airline may not receive tax-free benefits provided by the hotel. There are exceptions. An employee who provides services to both business lines may receive benefits from both business lines. Benefits may also be available under a special election made by the company. Your employer should notify you of this tax benefit.

Qualified employee discounts on company goods and services. The tax-free exclusion for merchandise discounts may not exceed your employer's gross profit percentage. For example, if a company's profit percentage is 40%, the maximum tax-free employee discount for merchandise is 40% of the regular selling price; the employer has a choice of methods for figuring profit percentage. Discounts on services provided by the employer also qualify, with the maximum exclusion limited to 20% of the selling price charged customers. An insurance policy is treated as a service. Thus, insurance company employees are not taxed on a discount of up to 20% of the policy's price.

Some company products do not qualify for exclusion. Discounts on real estate and investment property such as securities, commodities, currency or bullion are taxable. Interest-free or low-interest loans given by banks or other financial institutions to employees are not excludable. The loan is subject to tax under the rules of ¶4.10.

The same line of business limitation discussed above for no-additional-cost services also applies to qualified employee discounts. Thus, if a company operates an airline and a hotel, employees who work for the airlines may generally not receive tax-free hotel room discounts. However, by making a special election the company may allow its employees to receive tax-free benefits from any line of business.

Owners and key employees are subject to the nondiscrimination rules discussed below.

Working condition fringes. The value of a company car or airplane is tax free to the extent that you use it for business, *see* ¶2.021.

Employer paid subscriptions to business periodicals are a tax-free working condition fringe, as are employer reimbursements for membership dues in a professional association.

Free or reduced-rate parking provided to employees on or near the business premises is a tax-free working condition fringe benefit.

A limited product testing exclusion applies to company manufactured goods used by employees away from company premises in order to test and evaluate the product.

De minimis fringes. There are small benefits that are administratively impractical to tax, such as typing of a personal letter by a company secretary, personal use of the company copy machine, occasional supper money or company cocktail party or picnic, and occasional theater or sporting event tickets.

The operation of an eating facility for employees is a tax-free *de minimis* fringe if it is located on or near the business premises, and the cost of the meals to employees equals or exceeds the company's operating costs. Do not confuse this type of meal benefit with employer-supplied meals for employees who must be on call on an employer's premises; these are tax free under ¶2.01. Executive dining room meals do not qualify as a *de minimis* fringe although the meals may be tax free under rules of ¶2.01 if meals must be taken on company premises.

Tuition reductions. Employees and retired employees of educational institutions, their spouses and dependent children are not taxed on tuition reductions for courses below the graduate level furnished after June 30, 1985. Widows or widowers of deceased employees or of former employees also qualify. Officers and highly paid employees may claim the exclusion only if the employer plan does not discriminate on their behalf. The exclusion applies to tuition for education at any educational institution, not only the employer's school.

Athletic facilities. The fair market value of athletic facilities, such as gyms, swimming pools, golf courses and tennis courts is tax free if the facilities are on the employer's property (not necessarily the main business premises) and substantially all of the use of the facilities is by employees, their spouses, and dependent children. Such facilities must be open to all employees on a nondiscriminatory basis in order for the company to deduct related expenses.

Nondiscrimination rules. Qualified employee discounts, no-additional-cost services, and eating facility services received by officers, owners, and highly compensated employees are tax free only if the same benefits are available to other employees on a nondiscriminatory basis. The nondiscrimination rule does not apply to working condition fringes or *de minimis* fringes other than eating facilities. A highly compensated employee is any employee who has compensation greater than the compensation of 90 percent of all employees employed by the employer. There are two exceptions to the 90 percent test: (1) any employee who has compensation of $50,000 or more during a calendar year is a highly compensated employee for that year, regardless of the 90% test and (2) any employee who has compensation of $20,000 or less during a year is not a highly compensated employee for that year, unless no employee of the employer has compensation in excess of $35,000.

Interest-free and low-interest loans. Interest-free loans received from your employer may be taxed. *See* ¶4.10.

¶2.021 • COMPANY CARS AS FRINGE BENEFITS

The use of a company car is tax free under the working condition fringe rule, provided you use the car for business. If you use the car for personal driving, you may be taxed on the value of such personal use. Your company has the responsibility of calculating taxable income based on Treasury tables that specify the value of various priced cars. For certain cars, a flat mileage allowance may be used to measure personal use. You are also required to keep for your employer a mileage log or similar record to substantiate your business use and these mileage log requirements are discussed at ¶3.05. Your employer should tell you the type of records that are required. Similarly, employees who use a company airplane for personal trips are taxable on the value of the flights, as determined by the employer using Treasury tables.

Regardless of personal use, you are not subject to tax for a company vehicle that the IRS considers to be of limited personal value. These are ambulances or hearses, flatbed trucks, dump, garbage or refrigerated trucks, one passenger delivery trucks (including truck with folding jump seat), tractors, combines, other farm equipment, or forklifts. Also not taxable is use of school buses, passenger buses (seating at least 20), moving vans where personal use is restricted, police or fire vehicles, or an unmarked law enforcement vehicle, where personal use is authorized by a government agency.

The value of a demonstration car used by a full-time auto salesperson is tax free as a working condition fringe if the use of the car facilitates job performance, and there are substantial personal-use restrictions, including a prohibition on use by family members and for vacation trips. Further, total mileage outside of normal working hours must be limited and personal driving must generally be restricted to a 75-mile radius around the dealer's sales office.

Reporting taxable automobile benefits. Social Security tax must be withheld. Income tax withholding is not required, but your employer may choose to withhold income tax. You must be notified by your employer that he is not withholding income tax so that you may consider the taxable benefits when determining your estimated tax; *see* ¶26.00. Whether or not withholdings are taken, the taxable value of the benefits is entered on your Form W-2 along with other compensation or on a separate Form W-2 for fringe benefits. A special IRS rule allows your employer to include on Form W-2 100% of the value of using the car, even if you used the car primarily for business. In this case, you must report the 100% value as income and then deduct expenses attributable to business driving on Form 2106. On Form 2106, you must claim actual expenses; the flat IRS mileage allowance (¶2.30) may not be used since you are not the owner.

Your employer may also decide to treat fringe benefits provided during the last two months of the calendar year as if paid during the following year. For example, if this election is made for a company car in 1986, only the value of personal use from January through October is taxable in 1986; personal use in November and December is taxable in 1987. If your employer has elected this special year-end rule, you should be notified near the end of the year or when you receive Form W-2.

Group Insurance, Death and Other Benefits

¶2.022 • GROUP-TERM LIFE INSURANCE PREMIUMS

You are not taxed on your employer's payments of premiums on a policy of up to $50,000 on your life. You are taxed only on his cost of premiums for coverage of over $50,000 as determined by the Treasury rates listed below. Your employer will give you a written statement of the amount of income you must report for coverage on policies exceeding $50,000. The taxable amount is not subject to withholding tax. You may not avoid tax by assigning the policy to another person.

> If you pay for a part of the insurance, reduce the amount includable as income by the payments.

If two or more employers provide you with group-term insurance coverage, the amount of taxable income is computed on the basis of only one exclusion of $50,000.

Retirees. If you retired before 1984 at normal retirement age or on disability and are still covered by a company group-term life insurance policy, you are not taxed on premium payments made by your employer even if coverage is over $50,000. If you retired after 1983 because of disability and remain covered by your company's plan, you are not taxed even if coverage exceeds $50,000. Further, if you retired after 1983 and are not disabled, you may still qualify for tax-free coverage over $50,000 if the following tests are met: the insurance is provided under a plan existing on January 1, 1984, or under a comparable successor plan, you were employed during 1983 by the company having the plan, and you were age 55 or over on January 1, 1984.

The $50,000 exclusion is not available to "key employees," generally officers and certain employees with ownership interests, unless the group plan meets nondiscrimination tests. If the plan discriminates, a key employee's taxable benefit is based on the actual cost of coverage and not the table below. The nondiscrimination rules also apply to retired "key employees."

Rates for coverage over $50,000

Age	Monthly premium per $1,000 of coverage above $50,000
Under 30	$ .08
30–34	.09
35–39	.11
40–44	.17
45–49	.29
50–54	.48
55–59	.75
60 and over	1.17

Based on the above table, a 50-year-old executive provided with $200,000 of group-term coverage has income of $864 (150 × .48 premium × 12 months).

Permanent life insurance. If your employer pays premiums on your behalf for permanent nonforfeitable life insurance, you report the cost of the benefit as taxable wages. A permanent benefit is an economic value that extends beyond one year and includes paid-up insurance or cash surrender value, but does not include, for example, the right to convert or continue life insurance coverage after group coverage is terminated. Where permanent benefits are combined with term insurance, the permanent benefits are taxed under formulas found in Treasury regulations.

¶2.03 • GIFTS FROM EMPLOYERS

A payment may be called a gift but still be taxable income. Any payment made in recognition of past services or in anticipation of future services or benefits is taxable even if the employer is not obligated to make the payment. *See also* ¶12.02. To prove a gift is tax free, you must show that the employer acted with pure and unselfish motives of affection, admiration, or charity. This is difficult to do, given the employer-employee relationship.

A gift of stock by majority stockholders to key employees has been held to be taxable income.

¶2.04 • EMPLOYEES' DEATH BENEFITS MAY BE TAX FREE UP TO $5,000

An employer's payment to his deceased employee's beneficiary is tax free up to $5,000 if: (1) Paid solely because of the employee's death; *and* (2) the employee did not have a nonforfeitable right to the payment while he was alive. An employee had a nonforfeitable right if he could have received the amount on demand or when he left his job. Where benefits were payable under an annuity contract, ask the company paying the benefits what part of the payments, if any, qualify for the $5,000 exclusion. The nonforfeitable requirement does not apply to payments that qualify as a lump-sum distribution from a qualified pension or profit-sharing plan (¶7.04) or qualified annuity plan for employees of tax-exempt schools and charities (¶7.11).

Beneficiaries of retired employees who retired on disability before reaching mandatory retirement age under Federal Civil Service laws or the Retired Servicemen's Family Protection Plan may claim the $5,000 exclusion.

Payments received from a qualified Keogh plan by beneficiaries of self-employed individuals also qualify (*see* ¶7.04).

Examples—

1. Products Co. pays Brown's widow a $5,000 bonus due Brown. The bonus is fully taxable. Brown had a right to the payment while he was alive. Similarly, payments for unused leave and uncollected salary are not tax free up to $5,000.

2. When an employee dies, Grand Co. pays the deceased's widow or other family beneficiary a death benefit of $1,000. The amount is tax free. It is paid because of the death of an employee who had no right to the amount while alive.

The death benefit exclusion may not exceed $5,000 regardless of the number of employers making payment or beneficiaries receiving payments. The $5,000 exclusion is divided among all the beneficiaries. Each claims a part of the exclusion in the same ratio as his share bears to the total benefit paid. Interest paid on tax-free death benefits is taxed.

Where benefits are paid over several years, the $5,000 exclusion must be applied to the first payments.

> **Voluntary payments as gifts.** The IRS holds that if a death benefit exceeds $5,000, the excess is taxable even if the payment was voluntarily made by the employer. Some federal district courts have allowed tax-free gift treatment for amounts over $5,000; the Tax Court has supported the IRS position.
>
> As a practical matter, a tax law provision usually forces an employer who wants to deduct amounts over $5,000 as compensation to decide whether the payment is a gift or pay. If he calls the payment a gift, he may not deduct more than $25 of the payment that exceeds $5,000. For the full deduction, he must treat it as compensation.

¶2.05 • RENTAL VALUE OF A PARSONAGE IS NOT INCOME

A duly ordained minister of the gospel pays no tax on the rental value of a home provided as part of his pay. If he is not provided a home but is paid a rental allowance, he pays no tax on the allowance if he uses the entire amount to pay his rent (including the rent of a furnished or unfurnished apartment or house and garage and utilities). Where a minister buys or owns his own home, he pays no tax on the allowance used as a down payment on the house, mortgage installments, or for utilities, interest, tax and repair expenses of the house. Any part of the allowance not used for these housing purposes is taxed. For example, that part of an allowance used to pay rent on business or farm property or for food or the services of a maid is taxed.

The IRS has generally barred an exclusion to ordained ministers working as executives of non-religious organizations even where services or religious functions are performed as part of the job. The Tax Court has focused on the duties performed; exclusions have been allowed in some cases and not in others.

Exclusion for Parsonage Allowance

Allowed to:	Not allowed to:
A teacher or executive director or administrator who is a minister of the gospel if he teaches in a school, college, or theological seminary which is part of a church organization and his position requires the services of a minister of the gospel. Cantor Ordained ministers in interdenominational organizations, if they serve in the exercise of their ministry. A traveling evangelist who is ordained and receives rental allowances from out-of-town churches, if the allowances are used to maintain his permanent home. More than one minister of the gospel for the same congregation, if the allowances are authorized by the church or congregation. A retired minister, if the allowance is furnished in recognition of past services.	Church officers who are not ordained, such as ministers of music or education. Theological students Civilian chaplains at VA hospitals. Minister-administrator of an old-age home which is not under the authority of a church. Rabbi employed by service organization as director of interreligious affairs. He was not assigned to his job by a religious body or employed as a minister to lead religious worship but performed public relations services for his employer. Minister directing anticommunist drive. An ordained priest living as a layman while he teaches college and receiving pay directly from the college, rather than from his order.

Allowance must be authorized by church or congregation. To qualify rental allowances for tax-free treatment, official church action by the local congregation designating the allowance must be made in advance of the payments. Official action may be shown by an employment contract, minutes, a resolution, or a budget allowance. The local congregation must officially designate the part of the clergyman's compensation that is a rental allowance.

Allowance subject to self-employment tax. Although parsonage allowances are not taxed income, they are reported as self-employment income for Social Security purposes (see ¶5.60). If you do not receive a cash allowance, report the rental value of the parsonage as self-employment income. Rental value is usually equal to what you would pay for similar quarters in your locality. Also include as self-employment income the value of house furnishings, utilities, appurtenances supplied, such as a garage, and the value of meals furnished that meet the rules at ¶2.01.

A minister who rents his home while abroad on church business may exclude his rental allowance only up to amounts used for capital improvements. These amounts are treated as expenses of keeping up his regular home. The balance of his rental allowance is taxable compensation even though he had expenses for maintenance, interest, taxes, repairs, and utilities during the rental period. The expenses may be deducted from rental income.

¶2.06 • CAFETERIA PAY PLANS

"Cafeteria plans" is a nickname for plans that give an employee a choice of selecting tax-free fringe benefits or taxable benefits. You are generally not taxed when you elect non-taxable benefits.

A qualified cafeteria plan must be written and not discriminate in favor of highly compensated employees and stockholders. If the plan provides for health benefits, a special rule applies to determine whether the plan is discriminatory.

Employees with three years of employment must be eligible to participate in the plan. If a plan is held discriminatory, the highly compensated participants are taxed to the extent they could have elected taxable benefits.

The law restricts the types of benefits that a cafeteria plan may offer and bars cash refunds for unused benefits. Your employer should tell you the tax status of the benefits you select.

When Is Your Pay Taxed?

¶2.07 • REPORTING WAGES

The cash basis and the accrual basis are the two usual methods of reporting income. Most individuals use the cash basis to report all income items in the year they are actually received and deduct expenses in the year they are actually paid. Under the accrual basis, income is reported when earned, even though not received. The accrual basis is used primarily to report business income. The right to use the accrual basis is conditioned on accurate bookkeeping accounts which are generally unnecessary and burdensome for personal income (see ¶5.01).

As a cash-basis taxpayer, you are subject to the "constructive receipt rule." The rule requires you to report income not actually received but which has been credited to your account, subject to your control, or put aside for you.

Examples of Taxed Wages—

Salaries, wages, expense allowances, honoraria, commissions, tips, bonuses, severance pay, dismissal pay, back pay, sick pay, vacation pay, and cash payment received upon the exercise of stock appreciation rights (SARs).

Withholdings from your wages for taxes (income, Social Security, unemployment insurance, etc.), hospitalization and life insurance premiums, savings bond payments, union dues, your pension fund contributions.

Wages garnisheed by creditors. If your wages are attached and your employer pays part of them to your creditor, you report your entire pay.

Wages received by your agent for your account.

You must pay tax on a paycheck received before the end of the year even though you do not cash or deposit it to your account. If your employer does not have funds in the bank and asks you to hold the check before depositing it, you do not have taxed income until the check is cashed. Where an employee was not at home to take delivery of a year-end check, the Tax Court held the funds were taxable in the year following the year of receipt.

Sick pay. Sick pay is generally taxable as wages unless it qualifies as worker's compensation under the rules of ¶2.17. Further, payments received under accident or health plans are tax free if you paid the premiums or your employer provides benefits for certain serious physical injuries, as explained at ¶2.19.

Assigning your pay. You may not avoid tax on income earned by you by assigning the right to payment to another person. For example, you report earnings donated by you but paid directly by your employer to a charity. You may claim a contribution deduction for the donation (*see* ¶14.00). The IRS allowed an exception for doctors working in a clinic. They were required to assign to a foundation all fees derived from treating patients with limited income (teaching cases). The fees were not taxable.

Withholdings for retirement plans. Amounts withheld as your contribution to your pension or profit-sharing account are generally taxable. Courts have held that amounts withheld from the pay of both U.S. Civil Service employees and city and county civil service employees are taxable to the employees.

Wages withheld for compulsory forfeitable contributions to a nonqualified pension plan are not taxable if these conditions exist: (1) The contribution is forfeited if employment is terminated prior to death or retirement. (2) The plan does not provide for a refund of employee contributions and, in the administration of the plan, no refund will be made. Where only part of the contribution is subject to forfeiture, the amount of withheld contribution not subject to forfeiture is taxable income.

Check with your employer to determine the status of your contributions.

Deferring tax on pay. Under certain conditions, you may contract with your employer to defer the taxable receipt of current compensation to future years. To defer pay to a future period, you must take some risk. You cannot have any control over your deferred pay account. If you are not confident of your employer's ability to pay in the future, you should not enter into a deferred pay plan.

An employee of a state or local government which has established a nonqualified deferred pay plan may defer the lesser of $7,500 or 25% of his or her pay, reduced by amounts deferred under tax-shelter annuity programs. The deferred pay is not taxed until it is paid or made available to you.

An employee is not taxed on employer contributions to a qualified cash or deferred arrangement (401 (K) plan) even though the employee had the option to take the cash. *See* ¶32.011.

Salary advances. Salary paid in advance for services to be rendered in the future is generally taxable in the year received if it is subject to your free and unrestricted use.

Barter transactions. The value of the trades by members of a barter club is subject to income tax. For example, an attorney and a housepainter, both members of a barter club, arrange for the housepainter to paint the attorney's home in exchange for legal services. The fair market value of the services received by the attorney and the housepainter are taxable. Even where no goods or services are received, a club member is taxable on the value of "credit units" credited during the year.

If you exchanged services or goods through a barter exchange during 1986, you should receive Form 1099-B from the exchange by January 31, 1987, showing the value received during the year. The IRS also gets a copy of Form 1099-B.

Child's wages. A parent is not taxed on wages paid for a child's services even if payment is made to the parent. However, a parent is taxed on income from work contracted for by the parent even if the child assists in the labor. For example, a parent whose children helped her with part-time work at home claimed that the children should be taxed on 70% of the income since they did 70% of the work. The IRS claimed that the parent was taxable on all the income because she, not the children, was the true earner, and the Tax Court agreed. Although the company knew that the children were doing part of the work, it had no agreement with them.

¶2.08 • PAY RECEIVED IN PROPERTY IS TAXED

Your employer may pay you with property instead of cash. You report the fair market value of the property as wages.
Example—
For services rendered, you receive a check for $1,000 and property having a fair market value of $500. You report $1,500 as wages.

If you receive your company's stock as payment for your services, you include the value of the stock as pay in the year you receive it. However, if the stock is nontransferrable and subject to substantial risk of forfeiture, you do not have to include its value as pay. *See* ¶32.04.

If you receive your employer's note which has a fair market value, you are taxed on the value of the note, less what it would cost you to discount it. If the note bears interest, report the full face value. But do not report income if the note has no fair market value. Report income on the note only when payments are made on it.

A debt cancelled by an employer is taxable income.

A salesman employed by a dealer has taxable income on receipt of "prize points" redeemable for merchandise from a distributor.

¶2.09 • WHEN COMMISSIONS ARE TAXED

Earned commissions. Earned commissions are taxable in the year they are credited to your account and subject to your drawing, whether or not you actually draw them.

On your 1986 tax return, you do not report commissions which were earned in 1986 but which cannot be computed or collected until a later year.
Example—
You earn commissions based on a percentage of the profits. In 1986, you draw $10,000 from your account. However, at the end of 1986 the full amount of your commissions is not known because profits for the year have not been figured. In January, 1987, your 1986 commissions are computed to be $15,000, and the $5,000 balance is paid to you. The $5,000 is taxable in 1987 even though earned in 1986.

You may not postpone tax on earned commissions credited to your account in 1986 by not drawing them until 1987 or a later year. However, where a portion of earned commissions is not withdrawn because your employer is holding it to cover future expenses, you are not taxed on the amount withheld.

Advances against unearned commissions. Under standard insurance industry practice, an agent who sells a policy does not earn his commission until premiums are received by the insurance company. However, the company may issue a cash advance on the commissions before the premiums are received. Agents have claimed that they may defer reporting the income until the year the premiums are earned. The IRS, recognizing that in practice companies rarely demand repayment, requires that advances be included in income in the year received if the agent has full control over the advanced funds. A repayment of unearned commissions in a later year is deducted as an itemized deduction.

Some courts have recognized that an advance may constitute a loan if there is an unconditional personal obligation to repay the advanced amount. Factors to be considered: A note or other evidence of indebtedness, a repayment schedule, how the advance is carried on the books of the company, and an attempt on the part of the company to collect advances.

Salesmen have been taxed on commissions received on property bought for their personal use. In one case, an insurance agent was taxed on commissions paid to him on his purchase of an insurance policy. In another case, a real estate agent was taxed on commissions he received on his purchase of land. A salesman was also taxed for commissions waived on policies he sold to friends, relatives, and employees.

An insurance agent's kickback of his commission is taxable where agents may not under local law give rebates or kickbacks of premiums to their clients.

¶2.10 • UNEMPLOYMENT BENEFITS MAY BE TAXABLE

The tax treatment of 1986 unemployment benefits generally depends on the amount of your adjusted gross income. The benefits are not taxable if the total of (1) your adjusted gross income and (2) the benefits is—
$12,000 or less if you are single, or
$18,000 or less if you are married and file a joint return.
If the amount of your adjusted gross income plus the unemploy-

ment benefits exceeds the $12,000 or $18,000 limit, your benefits are subject to tax.

Adjusted gross income is explained at ¶13.04. However, for purposes of this section, adjusted gross income does not include the amount of the unemployment benefit.

Figuring taxable benefits. If adjusted gross income increased by the amount of the benefit exceeds $12,000 or $18,000 (whichever limit applies to you), you report as taxable income the lesser of either (1) the unemployment benefit or (2) 50% of the excess of adjusted gross income and the benefit over $12,000, if you are single or over $18,000 if you are married and file a joint return. If you are married and do not file a joint return and do not live apart from your spouse at all times during 1986, you may not use the base amount of $18,000 to determine the taxability of your benefits. You are not allowed any floor. If you receive unemployment benefits, you report as taxable income the lower of either (1) the benefit or (2) 50% of the total of adjusted gross income and the benefit.

Benefits subject to tax are those paid by state agencies or by the federal government to federal employees, and those paid under the Railroad Unemployment Insurance Act, the Airline Deregulation Benefits and Allowance Programs, and the Disaster Unemployment Assistance Program. Trade readjustment allowances under the 1974 Trade Act are also treated as unemployment compensation subject to tax.

Workmen's Compensation, supplemental unemployment benefits received from company-financed funds, and union strike and lockout benefits are not subject to tax under the above rules (*see* also ¶2.101 and ¶2.17).

If your benefits are $10 or more, you will receive a statement of benefits from the agency paying you the benefit.

Examples—

1. You receive unemployment benefits totaling $950. You are married. Adjusted gross income of $15,000 is reported on the joint return of you and your spouse; all of your benefit is tax free.

2. Same facts as in example (1) but you do not file a joint return and do not live apart from your spouse. All of the benefit of $950 is taxed.

3. Same facts as in example (1) above but adjusted gross income reported on a joint return is $26,000. Your adjusted gross income plus the benefit of $950 exceeds the $18,000 limit for joint returns. The benefit of $950 is subject to tax. (The excess of the benefit plus adjusted gross income over $18,000 is $8,950—50% of this amount is $4,475. Therefore, the lower benefit of $950 is subject to tax.)

If you had to repay supplemental unemployment benefits because of receipt of Trade Readjustment Assistance payments, *see* ¶2.11.

¶2.101 • SUPPLEMENTAL UNEMPLOYMENT STRIKE BENEFIT PAYMENTS AND STRIKE PAY PENALTIES

Supplemental unemployment benefits paid from company-financed funds are fully taxable. Such benefits are usually paid under guaranteed annual wage plans made between unions and employers. Unemployment benefits from a private or union fund to which you contribute dues are taxable only to the extent the benefits exceed your contributions to the fund. Your contributions to the fund are not deductible.

Pay penalty charged striking teachers not deductible. State law may prohibit public school teachers from striking and charge a penalty equal to one day's pay for each day on strike if they do strike. For example, when striking teachers returned to work after a one-week strike, a penalty of one week's salary was deducted from their pay. Although they did not actually receive pay for the week they worked after the strike, they

earned taxable wages. Further, the penalty is not deductible. No deduction is allowed for a fine or penalty paid to a government for the violation of a law.

Strike benefits paid by a union are taxable unless you can show they are in the nature of "gifts" or "charity." Evidence tending to show that strike benefits are gifts: Payments are based on individual need; they are paid to both union and nonunion members; and no conditions are imposed on the strikers who receive benefits. If you receive benefits under conditions by which you are to participate in the strike and the payments are tied to your scale of wages, the benefits are taxable.

¶2.11 • DID YOU HAVE TO RETURN INCOME RECEIVED IN AN EARLIER YEAR?

When you return income, such as salary or commissions, which you reported in a prior taxable year, a deduction in the year of repayment may be allowed under a special statute (Section 1341), if in the year you received the income "it appeared you had an unrestricted right to the income." Further, if the repayment qualifies under Section 1341 and exceeds $3,000, you have an alternative: Instead of claiming the deduction from 1986 income, you may recompute your tax for the prior year by claiming a credit for the amount of tax overpaid in the prior year on your 1986 tax return. Choose the alternative which gives you the larger tax reduction. See Treasury regulations for how tax computations are made under Section 1341.

Section 1341 does not apply to the refund of income arising from the sale of inventory items.

Repayment of disallowed salary or T & E expenses. If a "hedge" agreement between you and your company requires you to repay salary or T & E expenses if they are disallowed to the company by the IRS, you may claim a deduction in the year of repayment. According to the IRS, you may not recalculate your tax for the prior year and claim a tax credit under the rules of Section 1341. An appeals court has rejected the IRS position and allowed a tax recomputation under Section 1341 to an executive who returned part of a disallowed salary under the terms of a corporate by-law.

Repayment of supplemental unemployment benefits. Where repayment is required because of the receipt in an earlier year of trade readjustment allowances, you may deduct the repayment from gross income. If repayment is $3,000 or more, you have the choice of a deduction or claiming a credit against your 1986 tax by recomputing your tax for the year supplemental unemployment benefits were received, as explained above.

¶2.111 • WAIVER OF EXECUTOR'S AND TRUSTEE'S COMMISSIONS

Commissions received by an executor are taxable as compensation.

An executor may waive commissions without income or gift tax consequences by giving a principal legatee or devisee a formal waiver of his right to commissions within six months after his initial appointment or by not claiming commissions at the time of filing the usual accountings.

The waiver may not be recognized if he takes any action that is inconsistent with the waiver. An example of an inconsistent action would be the claiming of an executor's fee as a deduction on an estate, inheritance, or income tax return.

A bequest to an executor is tax free.

Disability Pensions, Accident and Health Benefits, Workmen's Compensation

¶2.12 • DISABILITY PENSION EXCLUSION REPEALED

Disability pensions financed by your employer are reported as wage income unless they are tax free under the rules of ¶2.19. Turn to ¶34.02 to see if you may claim a tax credit for the receipt of a disability pension. A credit, subject to income limitations, is allowed for disability payments received while you are under the age of 65 and permanently and totally disabled.

¶2.16 • HEALTH AND ACCIDENT INSURANCE BENEFITS

You pay no tax on benefits received from a health or accident insurance policy on which you paid all of the premiums. However, if a payment reimburses a medical expense which you deducted in a prior year, you may have to report all or part of the payment. See ¶17.08.

If you and your employer each pay part of the premiums for accident and health insurance, you have, for tax purposes, two plans: One financed by you; the other financed by your employer. For treatment of benefits from a plan financed by your employer, see ¶2.19.

¶2.17 • WORKER'S COMPENSATION PAYMENTS ARE TAX FREE

You do not pay tax on worker's compensation payments for job-related injuries or illness. However, your employer might continue paying your regular salary but require you to turn over to him your worker's compensation payments. Then you may be taxed on the difference between what he paid you and what you returned to him.

Example—

You are injured while at work and are out of work for two months. Your company continues your salary of $175. You also receive workmen's compensation of $35 a week which you give to your employer. The $35 is tax free. The balance of $140 a week is considered taxable wages.

A teacher, injured while working, received full salary during a two-year sick leave. She argued that the payments were similar to worker's compensation and thus were tax free. The IRS disagreed on the grounds that the payments were not paid under a worker's compensation statute. The Tax Court supported the teacher. The payments were like worker's compensation; they were paid because of injuries sustained in the line of duty. Although not made under a worker's compensation statute, they were authorized by board of education regulations which have the force of law.

Not all payments for job related illness or injury qualify as tax-free worker's compensation. For example, payments to a government employee under the Civil Service Retirement Act are not in the nature of worker's compensation because the payments are made regardless of whether disability is caused by on-the-job injuries. Payments are taxable even if a particular employee's payments are in fact based on job related injuries.

In one case, a disabled New York City policeman argued that sick leave payments under a union labor contract were tax-free worker's compensation because his disability was work related. However, the IRS, Tax Court and an appeals court disagreed. The payments were made under a labor contract and not a worker's compensation statute or pursuant to government regulations. Further, even if authorized by a statute or regulations, the officer's sick leave would be taxable since under the labor contract, officers received sick pay whether or not their injury or illness was work related. To be considered worker's compensation, payments under the statute or regulations must be restricted to work-related disabilities. That this officer's injuries were in fact job related does not make his benefits tax free when he could have received benefits in any event.

¶2.18 • DISABILITY PENSION RULES FOR MEMBERS OF THE MILITARY, PUBLIC HEALTH SERVICE AND FOREIGN SERVICE

Tax-free treatment of disability pensions for members of the military, the Public Health Service, and Foreign Service are not available generally to individuals who joined these government services after September 24, 1975. Under prior law, tax-free treatment covered pensions or similar allowances for personal injuries or sickness resulting from active service in the Armed Forces of any country, as well as similar amounts received by disabled members of the National Oceanic and Atmospheric Administration (NOAA, formerly called the Coast and Geodetic Survey), the Public Health Service, or the Foreign Service. Also, a portion of a disability pension based on years of active service could be treated as tax-free sick pay by a disabled retiree before he reached retirement age. Finally, benefits paid by the Veterans Administration were fully exempt from tax.

Under current law, the above prior tax-exempt rules (except for the abolished sick pay exclusion) continue to apply to your disability payments if:

1. On or before September 24, 1975, you were entitled to receive disability payments, or
2. On September 24, 1975, you were a member of one of the above services (or reserve component) or under a binding written commitment to become a member.

If you do not meet either rule (1) or (2), the following tax-free benefits are available to members of the military:

Veterans Administration disability payments or an amount equivalent to benefits a member would be entitled to receive from the V.A.

Pension based on combat-related injuries. A combat-related injury or sickness which is incurred as a result of any one of the following activities: (1) as a direct result of armed conflict; (2) while engaged in extra-hazardous service, even if not directly engaged in combat; (3) under conditions simulating war, including maneuvers or training; or (4) which is caused by an instrumentality of war, such as weapons.

Tax-free treatment applies to a disability pension paid to a civilian U.S. employee for injuries incurred as a direct result of a violent attack which the Secretary of State determines to be a terrorist attack and which occurred while the employee was working for the United States in the performance of his official duties outside the United States.

Disability pensions meeting the rules of this section generally are fully tax free.

¶2.19 • TAX-FREE BENEFITS FROM ACCIDENT AND HEALTH PLANS FINANCED BY EMPLOYER

You are not taxed on contributions your employer makes for your benefit to a health or accident plan. Also, you are not taxed on benefits received under the plan if:

1. They are specific reimbursements of medical expenses (not amounts you would have received anyway) you had for yourself, your spouse, or any of your dependents. If the reimbursement is for medical expenses you deducted in a previous year, the reimbursement may be taxed income to you. (See ¶17.08 for the rules on how reimbursements affect the medical deduction.) Payment does not have to come directly to you; it may go directly to those to whom you owe money for medical expenses. A special rule applies to discriminatory self-insured reimbursed plans; see below.

2. They are for the permanent loss or loss of use of part of the body or for permanent disfigurement of yourself, your spouse, or a dependent. The payments are based on the kind of injury and have no relation to the length of time you are out of work. These payments are not for medical expenses and are tax free. In addition,

you may also deduct any medical expenses you have in connection with these injuries. An appeals court held that severe hypertension does not involve loss of a bodily part or function.

Benefits not coming within the above two categories are fully taxable if (1) your employer paid all the premiums, and (2) you were not required to report his premium payments as taxable income. If you and your employer each paid part of the premiums and you were not taxable on your employer's payment, the part of the proceeds allocated to the employer's contribution is taxed to you. Assume the annual premium is $240; you pay $80, your employer, $160. Two-thirds of your health and accident insurance proceeds is taxable. Ask your employer for the allocation ratio.

Discriminatory medical reimbursement plans. Reimbursements from an employer plan for medical expenses of an employee, his or her spouse, and dependents are generally tax free. However, the exclusion does not apply to certain highly compensated employees and stockholders if the plan is self-insured and it discriminates on their behalf. These rules apply to employees owning more than 10% of the employer's stock, the highest paid 25% of all employees (other than employees who do not have to be covered under the law) and the five highest paid officers. If the plan discriminates on their behalf, they are taxed on the amount of the discriminatory benefit not received by other employees. A plan is self-insured if reimbursement is not provided by an unrelated insurance company. If coverage is provided by an unrelated insurer, these discriminatory restrictions do not apply.

Taxable reimbursements are considered received in the taxable year of the employee in which the plan year ends. The particular plan year to which reimbursements relate is determined under plan provisions. If there are no provisions, reimbursements are attributed to the year of payment.

¶2.20

Travel and Entertainment Expenses

Illustrations of reporting travel and entertainment expenses may be found in the Supplement of YOUR INCOME TAX. Mail the card at the front of this book for your FREE Supplement which includes filled-in returns and last-minute information.

¶2.21 • Deducting Transportation Expenses

You may deduct the cost of transportation:

Required by your job. For example, you travel to see customers or clients or to deliver merchandise.

Between two work locations for the same employer. You deduct the expenses of traveling from one location to the other. If, for personal reasons such as the choice of a place to eat lunch, you do not go directly to the second location, you deduct only the expenses of what a direct trip would have cost. If your employer has several locations in the same city but you do not move from one location to another in the same day and you spend the entire day in one place, you may not deduct transportation expenses between your home and the various locations even if you report to a different location each day.

To a second job. You may deduct the transportation expenses of getting from one job to another within the same working day. If, for personal reasons you do not go directly to the second location, you deduct only the cost of the direct trip between the two job locations.

To school after work. If you are taking courses the costs of which are deductible under the rules at ¶21.02, you may deduct travel costs under the rules at ¶21.08.

To reserve meetings. See ¶35.02.

Automobile expenses. If you use your automobile for business travel, you may want to figure your travel expense deduction by using the IRS mileage allowance. The allowance may be used instead of your actual operating costs and depreciation on your car. Details of the IRS mileage allowance may be found at ¶3.01.

¶2.211 • COMMUTING EXPENSES: GENERALLY NOT DEDUCTIBLE BUT THERE ARE EXCEPTIONS

The cost of travel between your home and place of work is generally not deductible, even if the work location is in a remote area not serviced by public transportation. Nor can you justify the deduction by showing you need a car for faster trips to work or for emergency trips. Travel from union hall to assigned job is also considered commuting. If you join a car pool, you may not deduct expenses of gasoline, repairs or other costs of driving you and your passengers to work.

Exceptions. The IRS allows these exceptions to its blanket ban on commuting expense deductions.

If you are on a business trip out-of-town, you may deduct taxi fares or other transportation costs from your hotel to the first business call of the day and all other transportation costs between business calls.

If you use your car to carry tools to work, a deduction is allowed where you can prove that transportation costs were incurred in addition to the ordinary, nondeductible commuting expenses. The deduction will be allowed even if you would use a car in any event to commute.

Examples—

1. Jones commuted to and from work by public transportation before he had to carry tools. Public transportation cost $2 per day to commute to and from work. When he had to use the car to carry the tools, the cost of driving was $3 a day and $5 a day to rent a trailer to carry the tools. Jones may deduct only the cost of renting the trailer. The IRS does not allow a deduction for the additional $1 a day cost of operating the car. It is not considered related to the carrying of the tools. It is treated as part of the cost of commuting which is not deductible.

2. Same facts as above but Jones does not rent a trailer. He uses the car trunk to store his tools. He may not claim a deduction because he incurs no additional cost for carrying the tools.

3. Smith uses his car regardless of the need to transport tools. He rents a trailer for $5 a day to carry tools. He may deduct $5 a day under the "additional-cost" rule.

If you have your regular office in your home, you may deduct travel costs beginning with your first business call of the day. However, you may not deduct the cost of commuting from your regular place of employment to your home because you work at home at a second job.

Examples—

1. Dr. St. John practiced industrial medicine; his patients were employees of his industrial clients. He was on call 24 hours a day and maintained a home office with complete records. His working day began at home where he planned his rounds by telephoning his clients and his outside office. Therefore, when he started on his rounds he was traveling on business, not commuting. The cost of these trips is deductible.

2. An IRS agent argued that he could deduct his evening commuting expenses from an IRS office to his home. He claimed that he had a second place of employment at home where he kept an office to transact business as treasurer of a credit union. Therefore, he was traveling between two places of employment. The deduction was disallowed. He would have gone home evenings even if he did not transact credit union business there.

3. A self-employed home repairman deducted the cost of travel from his home, which served as his business headquarters, to the homes of customers where he actually did the repairs. The IRS disallowed the deduction, claiming that his principal place of business was the various job sites. The Tax Court disagreed. He contacted clients at home, listed his home phone as his place of business in newspaper advertisements, and kept tools and supplies there. Since his home was the sole fixed location of his business, the cost of travel from home to the job sites is deductible.

4. Wicker, a self-employed nurse and anesthetist worked at a hospital as the head of the department of anesthesiology. She deducted her driving costs from home to the hospital. She claimed the expenses were deductible because she maintained a home office as her principal place of business. Although she was the only full-time anesthetist at the hospital, she was not given hospital office space. Her only office was at home where she kept medical reference materials, patient files, billing and tax records, and where she prepared lectures that she was required to give at the hospital one day a month. She also used her home office to write the hospital manual for anesthesia procedure as well as quarterly reports to state authorities covering treatments of patients.

The IRS argued that although Wicker was self-employed, the hospital was her principal place of business; there she assisted in operations and earned all her fees. In her home office, she saw no patients, charged no fees, and performed only incidental duties.

The Tax Court allows the travel cost deductions. Wicker had to use a home office for keeping records and preparing reports and hospital procedures, particularly since the hospital refused to provide her with an office. That no specific income can be traced to her work in the office does not mean that the office is not her principal place of business. Her position is similar to that of a self-employed physician who operates at a hospital or a trial attorney who spends most of his time in court. In these cases, the principal place of business is not the operating room or courtroom but the professional's regular office. They may deduct their transportation costs from that office to the place where they perform their services. The same rule applies here.

When you commute to a temporary job location outside the general area of your principal place of work, the IRS has followed a policy of allowing a deduction for such commutation costs. It can reverse this policy at will (*see* the Supplement for further developments, if any).

¶2.22 • OVERNIGHT-SLEEP TEST LIMITS DEDUCTION OF MEAL COSTS ON ONE-DAY BUSINESS TRIPS

The overnight-sleep rule prevents the deduction of meal costs on one-day business trips. To be deductible, meal costs must be incurred on a business trip that lasts longer than a regular working day (but not necessarily 24 hours) and requires time off to sleep (not just to eat or rest) before returning home. Taking a nap in a parked car off the road does not meet the overnight sleep test.

Examples—

1. A New Yorker flies to Washington, D.C., which is about 250 miles away, to see a client. He arrives at noon, eats lunch, and then visits the client. He flies back to New York. He may deduct the cost of the plane fare, but not the cost of the lunch. He was not away overnight nor was he required to take time out to sleep before returning home.

2. Same facts as above except he sleeps overnight in a Washington hotel. He eats breakfast there, and then sees another client and returns home to New York in the afternoon. He may deduct not only the cost of the plane fare but also the cost of the meals while on the trip and the cost of the hotel. He was away overnight.

3. A trucker's run is from Seattle to Portland and return. He leaves at about 2:00 A.M. and returns to Seattle the same day, getting in at about 6:00 P.M. While in Portland, he is released from duty for about four hours layover time to get necessary sleep before returning to Seattle. He may deduct the cost of meals because he is released at the turn-around point to obtain necessary sleep. Official release from duty is not a prerequisite to satisfying the sleep or rest test.

4. A conductor living in Atlanta works for a railroad. His run begins around 7:00 A.M. and the round trip takes about 15 hours. He spends two hours at the turn-around point and eats lunch there. He may not deduct the cost of lunch. The two-hour interval between runs may have been sufficient time to eat, but not to obtain substantial sleep or rest so as to satisfy the sleep or rest rule necessary to deduct the cost of meals on a one-day trip.

Several courts held that the IRS rule was unreasonable and outdated in the world of supersonic travel, and they would have allowed the New Yorker on the one-day trip to Washington, D.C. to deduct the cost of his lunch. The Supreme Court disagreed and upheld the IRS rule as a fair administrative approach.

Meal costs during overtime. Such costs are not deductible if you are not away from your place of business. Thus, for example,

a resident physician could not deduct the cost of meals and sleeping quarters at the hospital during overnight or weekend duty.

¶2.221 • IRS MEAL ALLOWANCE

The IRS allows an optional meal allowance for overnight business travel. The allowance is designed for salesmen, long-haul truckers, and others who do not charge their meals through credit cards or keep records of cash outlays while on the road. It is $14 per day for business travel of less than 30 days in one general locality and $9 per day for travel of 30 days or more in one locality. In determining whether you are away at one general locality for at least 30 days, weekend trips home do not reduce the number of days you are considered away. If the allowance is elected, it applies to all meal expenses for the year.

The allowance is allocated for the first and last day of a trip. The day is divided into four six-hour periods, starting at midnight. For each six-hour period that you are away, you are entitled to one quarter of the allowance. If you start your business trip between midnight and 6 a.m., you are considered to be away for the entire day and may claim the full $14 or $9 a day allowance for the first day. If you start between 6 a.m. and noon, you claim 75% of the allowance for the first day; if you start between noon and 6 p.m., you claim 50% of the allowance for the first day; 25% if you leave between 6 p.m. and midnight.

> If you claim the allowance, you must be ready to support your deduction with a record of the time, place and business purpose of the trip.

The $14/$9 rate has been criticized as too low, but the IRS says it is designed to ease record-keeping burdens for relatively small amounts.

¶2.23 • Deducting Travel Expenses Away from Home

The following expenses of a business trip away from home are deductible:

Plane, railroad, taxi, and other transportation fares.

Meals, lodging, and hotel expenses.

Tips, telephone, and telegraph costs.

Laundry and cleaning expenses.

Baggage charges (including insurance).

Cab fares or other costs of transportation to and from the airport or station and hotel; cab fares or other transportation costs, beginning with your first business call of the day, of getting from one customer to another or from one place of business to another.

Keep records to support your deduction of the above expenses, *see* ¶2.35.

Travel costs to find a new job are deductible, *see* ¶19.05.

Entertainment expenses incurred while traveling away from home are deductible under the rules at ¶2.31.

How to report. If you are an employee, use Form 2106 to claim deductible travel and entertainment expenses. *See* a sample Form 2106 in the Supplement to this book.

If you are self-employed, deductible travel and entertainment expenses are claimed in Part II of Schedule C; *see* sample schedule at ¶5.03.

¶2.24 • WHEN ARE YOU AWAY FROM HOME?

You have to meet the "away from home" test to deduct the cost of meals and lodgings while traveling.

> *Tax meaning of home.* For travel expense purposes, your *home* is your place of business, employment, or post of duty, regardless of where you maintain your family residence. This *tax home* includes the entire city or general area of your business premises or place of employment. The area of your *residence* may be your tax home if your job requires you to work at widely-scattered locations, you have no fixed place of work, and your residence is in a location economically suited to your work.

Examples—

1. Your residence is in a suburb within commuting distance of New York City where you work full time. Your personal home and tax home are the same, that is, within the metropolitan area of New York City. You are away from home when you leave this area, say for Philadelphia. But as you will learn from the rules discussed below, you may be unable to deduct certain travel expenses unless you meet the overnight-sleep test or the temporary assignment test.

2. Your residence is in New York City but you work in Baltimore. Your tax home is Baltimore; you may not deduct living expenses there. But you may deduct travel expenses on a temporary assignment to New York City even while living at your home there.

3. A construction worker works for a utility company on construction sites in a 12-state area. Assignments are sent from his employer's regional office; he is not required to report to the office. The IRS ruled that his residence, which is in a city in the 12-state area, is his tax home.

The above definition of tax home, which is generally applied by the IRS and courts, has been rejected by an appeals court.

The IRS disallowed Ethel Merman's deduction of living expenses in New York while appearing in a Broadway show. A court agreed with her claim that her home was in Colorado where she maintained a residence. Since her home was in Colorado, the deduction of her New York living expenses turns on whether her role in the play was temporary. If so, she could deduct "away from home" business expenses. If "indefinite," the deduction was correctly disallowed, not because she acquired a "tax home" in New York, but because her decision to maintain a residence in Colorado was dictated by personal convenience.

No tax home. A worker who is constantly on the road may be considered by an IRS agent to have no tax home. Similarly an unmarried person who does not keep a permanent residence in one area may also face this charge. According to an IRS ruling, in reviewing a single person's away from home expense deduction, agents will look for the following type of data: (1) He does some of his work in the vicinity of his residence, house, apartment, or room and lives there while performing services in the area. (2) He pays rent for the residence even while he is away on the road. (3) The residence is in an area where he was raised or lived for a long time, or a member of his immediate family such as a parent or child lives there or he frequently lives there.

Permanent duty station of serviceman. The Supreme Court held that a member of the Armed Forces is not away from home when he is at a permanent duty station. This is true whether or not it is feasible or even permissible for his family to live with him.

¶2.25 • FIXING A TAX HOME IF YOU WORK IN DIFFERENT LOCATIONS

If you regularly work in two or more separate areas, your tax home is the area of your principal place of business or employment. You are away from home when you are away from the area of your principal place of business or employment. Therefore, you may deduct your transportation costs to and from your minor place of business and your living costs there.

A principal place of business or employment is determined by comparing: (1) The time ordinarily spent working in each area, (2) the degree of your business activity in each area, and (3) the amount of your income from each area.

The relative importance of each fact will vary, depending on the facts of a particular case. For example, where there are no substantial differences between incomes earned in two places of employment, your tax home is probably the area in which you spend more of your time. Where there are substantial income differences, your tax home is probably the area in which you earn more of your income.

Examples—

1. Sherman lived in Worcester, Mass. where he managed a factory. He opened his own sales agency in New York. He continued to manage the factory and spent considerable time in Worcester. The larger part of his income came from the New York business. However, he was allowed to treat New York as his minor place of business and to deduct his travel expenses to New York and his living expenses there. The reason: He spent most of his time in Worcester and his income there was substantial.

2. Benson, a consulting engineer, maintained a combination residence-business office in a home he owned in New York. He also taught four days a week at a Technological Institute in West Virginia under a temporary nine-month appointment. He spent three-day weekends, holidays, and part of the summer at his New York address. At the Institute, he rented a room in the student union building. The IRS disallowed transportation expenses between New York and West Virginia and meals and lodging there as not incurred while away from home. The Tax Court disagreed. A taxpayer may have more than one occupation in more than one city. When his occupations require him to spend a substantial amount of time in each place, he may deduct his travel expenses, including meals and lodging, at the place away from his permanent residence. That Benson's teaching salary happened to exceed his income from his private practice does not change the result.

3. For many years, Markey, a G.M. engineer, worked near and lived in Lewisburg, Ohio. He also owned rental property, farms, and a machine shop in Lewisburg and was an officer of a bank. When he retired from G.M., it rehired him as a consultant and reassigned him to Warren, Michigan, 250 miles away. He spent five days a week in

Warren, returning to Lewisburg every weekend. He claimed Lewisburg as his tax home. The IRS disallowed his away-from-home deduction and allowed a deduction only for the cost of a dozen trips from Warren to Lewisburg as an expense of managing his investments. It treated Warren as Markey's tax home on the grounds that he earned $12,000 a year there while his Lewisburg investments returned less than $1,500. The Tax Court sided with Markey. It reasoned that he considered his business and investment activities at Lewisburg more important than his job even though they generated little income. An appeals court reversed, supporting the IRS position. That Markey attached importance to his interests in Lewisburg was not relevant. Warren was his tax home because he spent more time and earned far more money there.

Professional sports players, coaches, and managers. When the only business of such persons is the professional sport, their home is the "club town." But if they are in another business in addition to their professional playing, the above rules determine whether their club's home town or the place of their off-season business is their tax home. If it is the club's home town, they deduct travel and living expenses while away from that town—including the time they are where the second business is. (If the second place is where their families also live, they may not deduct the families' expenses there.) If the town where the other business is located is the tax home, then expenses in the club's home town may be deducted.

¶2.26 • TAX HOME OF MARRIED COUPLE WORKING IN DIFFERENT CITIES

When a husband and wife work and live in different cities during the week, one of them may seek to deduct travel expenses away from home. Such deductions have generally been disallowed, although courts have allowed some exceptions. Although for common law purposes the domicile of the husband may be the domicile of the wife, for tax purposes when each spouse works in a different city, each may have a separate tax home.

Examples—

1. Robert worked in Wilmington, Delaware; his wife, Margaret, in New York City. During the weekend, she traveled to Wilmington and deducted, as travel expenses away from home, her living costs in New York and weekend travel expenses to Wilmington. She argued that because she and her husband filed a joint return, they were a single taxable unit, and the tax home of this unit was Wilmington—where her husband lived. The deduction was disallowed. That a couple can file a joint return does not give them deductions that are not otherwise available to them as individuals. Margaret's tax home was New York—where she worked. Therefore, her expenses there are not deductible. And, as the weekend trips to Wilmington had no relationship to her job, they, too, are not deductible.

2. Hundt and his wife worked in Washington, D.C. and lived in nearby Arlington, Va. for many years. In 1952, he became a free-lance writer and director of industrial motion pictures. He directed and did research for films in various parts of the country from New York to California. He wrote the film scripts at his Arlington home or on location. However, most of his business came from New York City, where he lived in hotels. In 1956, he spent 175 days in New York City on business and rented an apartment for $1,200 because it was cheaper than a hotel. He deducted half the annual rent for the New York apartment, the costs of traveling between Arlington and New York, and the cost of meals in New York. The IRS disallowed the expenses, finding New York to be his tax home. The court disagreed, holding Arlington was his tax home because (1) part of his income came from his creative writing in Arlington and (2) his travel to other parts of the country was temporary. In this case the fact that most of his income came from New York did not make New York his tax home.

3. Leyland worked for the census bureau and his wife as a consultant to IBM in New Haven, Connecticut. At the request of the bureau, he enrolled for a year's in-service training at the Harvard Business School in Boston. When he moved there, the couple decided to give up their apartment in New Haven, and Mrs. Leyland took a room at a club. When Leyland visited New Haven on business, he lived at the club with her. During the period, she also traveled to Boston on behalf of IBM. On their tax return, the couple claimed New Haven as their tax home and deducted living expenses in Boston. The IRS claimed that New Haven was not Leyland's home as he gave up his apartment there to live in Boston. His expenses were disallowed. However, it agreed that his wife remained a resident of New Haven; she did not change her job and was in Boston only on assignment with IBM. Therefore, she could deduct expenses in Boston. The Tax Court agreed. Although Leyland's assignment in Boston was temporary, he chose to make Boston his home for the period. He moved his furniture there. As for Mrs. Leyland, her

Boston expenses were deductible; she went there on business. Each spouse had a separate tax home: Mrs. Leyland in New Haven, Mr. Leyland in Boston.

¶2.27 • DEDUCTING LIVING COSTS ON TEMPORARY JOB ASSIGNMENT AWAY FROM HOME

A business trip or job assignment away from home may last a few days, weeks, or months. If your assignment is considered temporary, you deduct living costs away from home. If it is viewed as indefinite, you may not deduct your living costs there. An indefinite assignment shifts your tax home to the area of your work. So, you may not claim for tax purposes that you are away from home, even though you keep a permanent residence elsewhere.

What costs are deductible? While you are on a temporary job assignment, you may deduct the cost of meals and lodging at the place of your assignment, even for your days off. If you return home, say for weekends, your living expenses at home are not deductible. You may deduct travel expenses, meals, and lodging en route between your home and your job assignment provided they do not exceed your living expenses had you stayed at the job assignment.

What is a temporary assignment? The law does not define what is meant by a temporary assignment. Before 1983, the IRS adopted an administrative rule which generally treated an anticipated or actual stay of less than one year as temporary; a stay of a year or more as indefinite. In response to judicial rejection of the one-year test, the IRS now recognizes stays of up to two years as temporary if certain tests are met. It will treat an anticipated or actual employment of two years or more as indefinite regardless of circumstances. The IRS two-year test as applied to construction workers is illustrated at ¶2.271.

When you take your family with you to a temporary job location, an IRS agent may argue that this is evidence that you considered the assignment to be indefinite. In the following case, however, such a move was not considered detrimental to a deduction of living expenses at the job location.
Example—
Michaels, a cost analyst for Boeing, lived in Seattle. He traveled for Boeing, but was generally not away from home for more than five weeks. Michaels agreed to go to Los Angeles for a year to service Boeing's suppliers in that area. He rented his Seattle house and brought his family with him to Los Angeles. Ten months later, Boeing opened a permanent office in Los Angeles and asked Michaels to remain there permanently. Michaels argued that his expenses for food and lodging during the ten-month period were deductible as "away from home" expenses. The IRS contended that the Los Angeles assignment was for an indefinite period.
The Tax Court disagreed with the IRS. Michaels was told that the stay was for a year only. He leased his Seattle house to a tenant for one year, planning to return to it. He regarded his work in Los Angeles as temporary until Boeing changed its plans. The one-year period justified his taking the family but did not alter the temporary nature of the assignment.

A recurrent summer job was not considered "temporary work."
Example—
A race track manager lived and worked in Arizona. During the summer, he also managed his employer's Florida track. When he lost his job, he was offered similar work by a Florida trackowner, but only for the summer season. He worked at the job for four consecutive seasons, returning to Arizona each fall. He deducted his transportation to Florida and food and lodging there as an "away from home" business expense. He argued the job was temporary. The IRS disallowed the deduction; the Tax Court agreed. His summer job was not temporary but was recurrent seasonal employment. He knew at the end of each season that he would be rehired for the next. He had no permanent job in Arizona during this time. His decision to live in Arizona and work in Florida was a personal decision and not dictated by business reasons. Accordingly, his transportation and living expenses in Florida were not deductible.

If the manager in the above example had a seasonal position in Arizona during the balance of the year, the travel expenses to

Florida would have been deductible under the rules explained at ¶2.25.

That you do not have regular employment where you live may prevent a deduction of living costs at a temporary job in another city. The IRS will disallow the deduction on the grounds that the expenses are not incurred while away from home; the temporary job site is the tax home. The Tax Court has allowed the deduction. An appeals court has agreed with the IRS.

Examples—
1. An elderly stenographer who retired to Florida needed temporary work to supplement her Social Security. She traveled to New York and placed newspaper advertisements which brought her jobs substituting for vacationing secretaries. She earned over $3,000 in seven months and returned to Florida. The IRS disallowed her deduction of advertising costs, train fare, and hotel rent while in New York, apparently taking the position that her tax home was in New York while she worked there. The Tax Court allowed the deduction as travel expenses while away from home. Florida was her tax home even though she had no employment there. She lived, voted, and maintained all her permanent ties in Florida. When she could not find work locally, she went to New York for temporary jobs. She intended to return to Florida in a short time and did so. She could not be expected to move her permanent home for jobs lasting one to 11 weeks.
2. A Harvard law student, who took a summer job with a New York law firm, deducted the cost of food and lodging while in New York and the cost of transportation to and from Boston where she lived with her husband. The Tax Court allowed the deduction and held that her tax home was Boston; it would have been unreasonable for her to have moved to New York for a 10-week job. An appeals court reversed. The Boston home was her home for personal reasons, not for business. As she was not required by business to keep two homes, her tax home was New York, even though the job was temporary.

¶2.271 • CONSTRUCTION WORKER AT DIFFERENT PROJECTS

As explained at ¶2.27, you deduct travel expenses away from home if your assignment at the project is considered temporary. If your employment is expected to and does last for one year or more but less than two years, you must be prepared to prove:
1. You expect your employment to last less than two years and to return to the location which you claim as your tax home, *and*
2. Your residence at this location is your regular place of abode. To prove this point, you should meet the following three IRS tests: (a) You used the residence while working in the vicinity immediately prior to the current position and you continue to look for a position there, (b) you incur living expenses for the residence, and (c) your family, spouse and children, continue to live there or you use it frequently as a lodging such as on weekends. If you meet all three tests for your residence, the IRS says it will recognize that you are temporarily away from home. If you meet only two, you may still be able to convince the IRS of the temporary nature of the job, but if you meet only one, the IRS will rule that stay is indefinite. The IRS approach favors married workers who provide homes for their families in one place. Bachelors will find it difficult to get the deduction because they often do not keep permanent residences. The same applies if you live in a trailer which you move from project to project and you have no other established home. Each location becomes your principal place of business and, therefore, you are not "away from home."
Examples—
1. Adams, a construction worker and union member regularly employed in Newark, N.J., takes a job in Baltimore, Md., about 200 miles away. The project is scheduled to be completed in 16 months at which time Adams plans to return to Newark. His wife and children continue to stay in the family-owned home in Newark. While in Baltimore, Adams lives in a trailer and returns most weekends to Newark to be with his family and to check on employment opportunities there. Adams satisfies the three tests that Newark is his regular place of abode. His stay is considered temporary and his living expenses in Baltimore are deductible.
2. Same facts as in (1) except that Adams sells his house and moves to Baltimore. His stay is not considered temporary. He did not incur duplicate living costs and his family did not remain in Newark. His living costs in Baltimore are not deductible.

¶2.28 • Deducting Expenses of a Business-Vacation Trip

¶2.281 • BUSINESS-VACATION TRIPS WITHIN THE UNITED STATES

On a business trip to a resort area, you may also spend time vacationing. If the *primary purpose* of the trip is to transact business and is within the United States (50 states and District of Columbia) you may deduct all of the costs of your transportation to and from the area (including meals and lodging costs en route) even if you do spend time vacationing. If the main purpose of the trip was personal, you may not deduct any part of your travel costs to and from the area. The amount of time spent on business as opposed to sightseeing or personal visits is the most important issue in determining your primary purpose. Regardless of the primary purpose of your trip, you are allowed to deduct expenses related to the business you transacted while in the area.

> If your return is examined, proving business purpose depends on presenting evidence to convince an examining agent that the trip, despite your vacationing, was planned primarily to transact business.

If your trip is primarily for business and while at the business destination you extend your stay for a few days to visit relatives or take a nonbusiness sidetrip, you deduct travel expenses to and from the business destination.

Example—

You work in Atlanta and make a business trip to New Orleans. You stay in New Orleans for six days and your total costs, including roundtrip transportation to and from New Orleans, meals and lodging, is $400, which you may deduct. If on your way home, you spend three days in Mobile visiting relatives and incur an additional $100 in travel costs, your deduction is limited to the $400 you would have spent had you gone home from New Orleans.

¶2.282 • BUSINESS-VACATION TRIPS OUTSIDE THE UNITED STATES

On a business trip abroad, you may deduct all your travel expenses, even though you take time out to vacation, provided you can prove: (1) The primary business purpose of the trip; (2) You did not have control over the assignment of the trip.

If the IRS determines that you were primarily on vacation, it will disallow all travel costs except for costs directly related to your business in the area, such as registration fees at a foreign business convention.

Fixing the date of the trip does not mean that you had control over the assignment. Treasury regulations assume that when you travel for your company under a reimbursement or allowance arrangement, you do not control the trip arrangements, provided also that you are not: (1) A managing executive of the company; or (2) related to your employer or have 10% or more interest in the company. You are considered a managing executive if you are authorized without effective veto procedures to decide on the necessity of the trip.

Rule for managing executives and self-employed persons. If you are a managing executive, self-employed, or related to your employer or have a 10% or more interest, you may deduct all transportation costs if:

1. In planning the trip you did not place a major emphasis on taking a vacation; *or*
2. The trip outside the United States took a week or less, not counting the day you leave the U.S. but counting the day you return, *or*
3. If the trip abroad lasted more than a week, you spent less than 25% of your time, counting the days your trip began and ended, on vacation or other personal activities.

If the vacationing and other personal activities took up 25% or more of your time on a trip lasting more than one week, and you cannot prove that the vacation was a minor consideration in planning the trip, you must allocate travel expenses between the time spent on business and on personal affairs. The part allocated to business is deductible; the balance is not. To allocate, count the number of days spent on the trip outside of the United States. Count days spent on business and on vacationing or other personal activities. Divide the travel costs between the days spent on vacationing and business. You deduct the costs allocated to the days spent on business.

If you vacation near or beyond the city in which you do business, the expense subject to allocation is the cost of travel from the place of departure to the business destination and back. For example, you travel from New York to London on business and then vacation in Paris before returning to New York. The expense subject to allocation is the cost of traveling from New York to London and back.

Examples—

1. You fly from New York to Paris to attend a business meeting for one day. You spend the next two days sightseeing and then fly back to New York. The entire trip, including two days for travel en route, took five days. The plane fare is deductible. The trip did not exceed one week.

2. You fly from Chicago to New York where you spend six days on business. You then fly to London where you conduct business for two days. You then fly to Paris for a five-day vacation after which you fly back to Chicago. You would not have made the trip except for the business that you had to transact in London. The nine days of travel outside the United States away from home, including two days for travel en route, exceeded a week, and the five days devoted to vacationing were not less than 25% of the total travel time outside of the U.S. The two days spent traveling between Chicago and New York, and the six days spent in New York are not counted in determining whether the travel outside the United States exceeded a week and whether the time devoted to personal activities was less than 25%.

Assume you are unable to prove either that you did not have substantial control over the arrangements of the trip or that an opportunity for taking a personal vacation was not a major consideration in your decision to take the trip. Thus, ⅝ths of the plane fare from New York to London and from London to New York is not deductible.

Weekends, holidays, and business standby days. If you have business meetings scheduled before and after a weekend or holiday, the days in between the meetings are treated as days spent on business for purposes of the 25% business test discussed above. This is true although you spend the days for sightseeing or other personal travel. A similar rule applies if you have business meetings on Friday and the next scheduled meeting is the following Tuesday; Saturday through Monday are treated as business days.

¶2.29 • DEDUCTING EXPENSES OF CONVENTION TRIPS

Conventions at resort areas usually combine business with pleasure. Therefore, the IRS scrutinizes deductions claimed for attending a business convention where opportunities exist for vacationing. Especially questioned are trips where you are accompanied by your spouse and other members of your family.

In claiming deductions for convention expenses, be prepared to show that the convention was connected with your business. Cases and IRS rulings have upheld deductions for doctors, lawyers, and dentists attending professional conventions. One case allowed a deduction to a legal secretary for her costs at a secretaries' convention. If you are a delegate to a business convention, make sure you prove you attended to serve primarily your own business interests, not those of the association. However, it is not necessary for you to show that the convention dealt specifically with your job. It is sufficient that attendance at the convention may advance or benefit your position. If you fail to prove business purpose, the IRS will allocate your expenses between the time spent on your business and the time spent as a delegate. You then deduct only the expenses attributed to your business activities.

Keep a copy of the convention program and a record of the business sessions you attend. If the convention provides a sign-in book, sign it. In addition, keep a record of all of your expenses as explained in ¶2.35.

Examples—

1. An attorney practicing general law was interested in international law and relations. He was appointed a delegate to represent the American branch of the International Law Association at a convention in Yugoslavia. The attorney deducted the cost of the trip and convention costs as business expenses which the IRS and a court disallowed. He failed to prove that attending the conference on international law helped his general practice. He did not get any business referrals as a result of his attendance at the convention. Nor did he prove the chance of getting potential business from the conference.

2. An insurance agent doing business in Texas attended his company's convention in New York. One morning of the six-day convention was devoted to a business meeting and luncheon; the rest of the time was spent in sightseeing and entertainment. The company paid for the cost of the trip. The IRS added the reimbursement to the agent's pay and would not let him deduct the amount. The convention in New York served no business purpose. It was merely a method of entertaining company personnel. If there was any valid business to be transacted, the company could have called a meeting in Texas, the area of his home office.

You may not deduct expenses at conventions held by fraternal organizations such as the American Legion, Shriners, etc.—even though some incidental business was carried on. However, delegates to fraternal conventions may in some instances deduct their expenses as charitable contributions (see ¶14.14).

What expenses are deductible? If the convention trip is primarily for business, you may deduct travel costs both to and from the convention, food costs, tips, display expenses (such as sample room costs), and hotel bills. If you entertain business clients or customers, you may deduct these amounts too.

Keep records of your payments identifying expenses directly connected with your business dealings at the convention and those which are part of your personal activity, such as sightseeing, social visiting, and entertaining. Recreation costs are not deductible even though a part of your overall convention costs.

Example—

You attend a business convention held in a coastal resort city primarily for business reasons. During the convention period, you do some local sightseeing, social entertaining, and visiting—all unrelated to your business. You may deduct your traveling expenses to and from the resort, your living expenses at the resort, and other expenses such as business entertaining, sample displays, etc. But you may not deduct the cost of sightseeing, personal entertaining, social visiting, etc.

Foreign convention limitations are discussed at ¶2.292.

¶2.291 • DEDUCTING YOUR SPOUSE'S TRAVEL EXPENSES ON A BUSINESS OR CONVENTION TRIP

IRS agents generally disallow deductions claimed for a spouse's travel expenses. They assume, for example, that a wife's presence on her husband's business trip is for personal reasons. A spouse's secretarial services such as typing notes of the convention may not be accepted as evidence of business purpose. In one case, a taxpayer could not claim his wife's expenses even though she was the proprietor of the business, signed business checks, and spent some time in the business. In another case, a husband could not deduct his wife's expenses at a convention even though her presence at the convention was required by his company.

However, you may deduct the cost of your spouse's participation in the entertainment of business clients at convention or business trips if the trip or entertainment meets the tests at ¶2.323. Generally, you may deduct the cost of goodwill entertaining of associates immediately before or after convention business meetings. A convention meeting qualifies as a bona fide business meeting.

Courts have allowed the travel expenses of spouses in the following cases:

Examples—

1. A court allowed the travel expenses of a wife who nursed her diabetic husband on a business trip. Facts favorable to her case were: (1) The cities visited were not cities usually associated with tourist travel; (2) her expenses were reasonable when compared to the business developed on the trip and her nursing aid; (3) a doctor advised her care; (4) she was trained to nurse her husband's condition. But a court in another case disallowed the travel costs of a wife who attended her husband who was suffering from a heart condition.

2. A manufacturer's sales representative ran his business through a corporation. His wife occasionally helped in the office and was personally acquainted with many of his business clients whom she entertained at home and at conventions. At one meeting, she also set up large selling displays. On the basis of this evidence, the Tax Court allowed the corporation to deduct part of her salary and her expenses at the conventions. It said that her contacts and the entertainment contributed to the successful operation of the company which required the solicitation of supplies and selling to customers.

3. Roy Disney, president of Walt Disney Productions, traveled regularly to supervise and expand foreign operations. On one round-the-world trip, the company authorized his wife to accompany him. The IRS argued that her travels were primarily for vacation and not business. The court disagreed. It was company policy to enhance the Disney image as purveyor of family entertainment, so that wives were encouraged to accompany its executives on business trips. Mrs. Disney's presence helped her husband to more effectively entertain foreign businessmen. She toured production facilities, attended dinners, film screenings, and press gatherings, and incidentally performed clerical functions, such as receiving phone calls.

Where your spouse accompanies you, your bills will probably show costs for both of you. These usually are less than twice the cost for a single person. To find what you may deduct, do not divide the bill in half. Figure what it would have cost you alone for similar accommodations and transportation. Only the excess over the single person's costs is not deductible.

Example—

You and your spouse travel by car to a convention. You pay $110 a day for a double room. A single room would have cost $100 a day. Your spouse's presence at the convention was for social reasons. You may deduct the total cost of operating your car to and from the convention city. You may deduct $100 a day for your room. If you traveled by plane or railroad, you would deduct only your own fare.

For restrictions on deducting foreign convention expenses, *see* ¶2.292 below.

¶2.292 • RESTRICTIONS ON DEDUCTING FOREIGN CONVENTION AND CRUISE EXPENSES

You may not deduct expenses at a foreign convention outside the North American area, unless you can show the convention is directly related to your business and it was as reasonable for the meeting to be held outside the North American area as within it.

Apart from the United States, the North American area includes Puerto Rico, the Trust Territory of the Pacific Islands including American Samoa, U.S. Virgin Islands, Guam, Jamaica, Mexico, and Canada.

Conventions may also be held in eligible Caribbean countries which agree to exchange certain data with the U.S. and do not discriminate against conventions held in the U.S. Barbados has qualified and is considered to be within the North American area.

Check with the convention operator if the country in which your convention is being held has qualified.

Limited cruise ship deduction. Up to $2,000 a year is allowed for attending cruise ship conventions if all the ports of call are in the U.S. or U.S. possessions and if the ship is registered in the United States. Special reporting requirements must be met by the individual attending the convention as well as the sponsoring organization.

¶2.31 • Entertainment Expenses

Entertainment expense restrictions are designed to reduce deductions for goodwill entertainment and entertainment at such places as country clubs, nightclubs, and sporting events. The restrictions do not apply to day-by-day type of business entertainment in restaurants and other dining places. As long as you can show that you dined with business associates for a business purpose, you may deduct the cost of the meals. This important exception applies also to the cost of home entertainment. *See* ¶2.32 and ¶2.321. Finally, even if your expenses qualify as deductible, you need records in the event your return is examined. *See* ¶2.35.

¶2.311 • THE RESTRICTIVE TESTS

In addition to having to show that an entertainment expense is ordinary and necessary to your business, it must also be:

1. Directly related to the active conduct of your business, *or*
2. Directly preceding or following a substantial and bona fide business discussion on a subject associated with the active conduct of your business. This test applies to entertainment in which you seek new business or to goodwill entertainment to encourage the continuation of an existing business relationship. Under it, you may entertain business associates in nonbusiness settings such as theaters, sports arenas and nightclubs, provided the entertainment directly precedes or follows the business discussion. *See* ¶2.313.

Business associates are: Established or prospective customers, clients, suppliers, employees, agents, partners, or professional advisers, whether established or prospective.

Not considered as entertainment expenses are the costs of supper money provided by an employer to an employee working overtime, a hotel room maintained by an employer for lodging his employees while on a business trip, and an automobile used in business even though used for routine personal purposes, such as commuting to and from work. However, a hotel room or car provided an employee on vacation is an entertainment expense.

¶2.312 • DIRECTLY-RELATED ENTERTAINMENT

In 1986, the directly-related test limits the deduction of entertainment costs at night clubs, on yachts, at sporting events, on hunting trips and during social events. If such entertainment fails to meet the following tests, it may qualify under the rules discussed in ¶2.313, which require the holding of a business meeting before or after the entertainment.

Entertainment may meet the directly-related rules in one of three ways: (1) Under the generally-related test; (2) as entertainment expenses incurred in a clear business setting; or (3) as entertainment expenses incurred for services performed.

Generally-related test. Under this test, you must show a business motive for the entertainment and business activity during the entertainment. You must show that you had a general expectation of getting future income or other specific business benefit (other than goodwill). Although you do not have to prove that income or other business benefit actually resulted from the expense, such evidence will help support your claim. What type of business activity will an IRS agent look for? The agent will seek proof that a business meeting, negotiation, or discussion took place during the period of entertainment. It is not necessary that more time be devoted to business than to entertainment. What if you did not talk business? You must prove that you would have done so except for reasons beyond your control.

The IRS presumes entertainment during a hunting or fishing trip or on a yacht is not conducive to business discussion or activity. You must prove otherwise.

Entertainment must be in a clear business setting. Entertainment expenses incurred in a clear business setting meet the directly-related test provided also that you had no significant motive for incurring the expenses other than to further your business. Entertainment of people with whom you have no personal or social relationship is usually considered to have occurred in a clear business setting. For example, entertainment of business representatives and civic leaders at the opening of a new hotel or theatrical production to obtain business publicity rather than goodwill is considered to be entertainment in a clear business setting. Also, entertainment which involves a price rebate is considered to have occurred in a clear business setting, as, for example, when a hotel owner provides occasional free dinners at the hotel for a customer who patronizes the hotel.

Costs of a hospitality room displaying company products at a convention are also a directly-related expense.

Entertainment occurring under the following circumstances or in the following places is generally not considered as directly related:

You are not present during the entertainment.

The distractions are substantial, as at night clubs, sporting events, or during a social gathering such as a cocktail party.

You meet with a group which includes persons other than business associates at cocktail lounges, country clubs, golf and athletic clubs, or at vacation resorts.

Entertainment for services performed. An expense is directly related if it was directly or indirectly made for the benefit of an individual (other than an employee) either as taxable compensation for services he rendered or as a taxable prize or award. The amount of the expense must be reported on an information form, 1099 (unless the amount is less than $600).

Example—

A manufacturer of products provides a vacation trip for retailers of his products who exceed sales quotas. The value of the vacation is a taxable prize. The vacation cost is a directly-related entertainment expense.

¶2.313 • GOODWILL ENTERTAINMENT

Goodwill entertaining may qualify as deductible entertainment in one of two ways:

1. Under the quiet business meal rule of ¶2.32 *or*
2. Under the restrictive rule that allows the deduction of the entertainment costs that follow or directly precede a substantial and bona fide business discussion.

The business discussion generally must take place the same day as the entertainment. If not, and your deduction is questioned, you must give an acceptable reason for the interval between the discussion and the entertainment. Treasury regulations recognize that a day may separate a business meeting and the entertainment of an out-of-town customer. He may come to your office to have a business discussion one day and you may entertain him the next day; or you may entertain him during his first day in town and discuss business the day after.

The IRS does not estimate how long a business discussion should last. But it does warn that a meeting must involve a discussion or negotiation to obtain income or business benefits. It does not require that more time be devoted to the meeting than to the entertainment.

A meeting at a convention is considered a bona fide business discussion if it is officially scheduled as part of a convention program and (1) the expenses necessary for your attendance at the convention are ordinary and necessary business expenses, and

(2) a scheduled program of business activity is the principal activity of the convention.

Examples—

1. During the day, you negotiate with a group of business associates. In the evening, you entertain the group and their spouses at a theater and night club. The cost of the entertainment is deductible, even though arranged to promote goodwill.

2. In the evening after a business meeting at a convention, you entertain associates or prospective customers and their spouses. You may deduct the entertainment costs.

¶2.32 • QUIET BUSINESS MEALS

You may deduct the cost of wining and dining business associates in restaurants, hotels, and other places which have settings conducive to business discussions. That business was not actually discussed will not disqualify the deduction. Coming within this rule are drinks taken at a bar or cocktail lounge, provided no floor show or other entertainment was offered to distract your attention.

To support the deduction of such meals, you need records (and receipts when the bill exceeds $25, see ¶2.351) which show the cost of the meals, the names of the associates entertained, and the business purpose of the meeting. Although the restrictive tests do not apply, you must still prove that meal costs are an ordinary and necessary expense of your business or job.

¶2.321 • HOME ENTERTAINING

The cost of "quiet business meals" served to business customers or clients at home is deductible. When you claim such a deduction, be ready to prove that your motive for dining with them was commercial rather than social. Have a record of the entertainment costs, names of the guests and their business affiliation.

¶2.322 • YOUR PERSONAL SHARE OF ENTERTAINMENT COSTS

If the entertaining occurred while on a business trip away from home, you deduct the meal cost as travel expenses away from home. If the entertaining occurred within the locality of your regular place of business, whether you will be allowed a deduction for this cost will depend on the agent examining your return. The IRS said in a ruling that an agent will not disallow your deduction of your own part of the meal cost unless he finds that you are claiming a substantial amount that includes personal living expenses. In such a case, the agent will follow the stricter Tax Court rule (sometimes referred to as the "Sutter" rule) and allow only that part of the meal cost that exceeds what you would usually spend on yourself when alone.

¶2.323 • DEDUCTING THE ENTERTAINMENT COSTS OF SPOUSES

A deduction is allowed for the spouses' share of the entertainment costs if they were present during entertainment that qualified as directly-related entertainment under the general rule discussed in ¶2.312. For goodwill entertainment, the cost of entertainment of the spouses is deductible if your share and the business associate's share of the entertainment is deductible. The IRS recognizes that when an out-of-town customer is accompanied by his or her spouse, it may be impracticable to entertain the customer without your spouse. Under such circumstances, the cost of the spouse's entertainment is deductible if the customer's entertainment costs are also deductible. Furthermore, if your spouse joined the party because the customer's spouse was present, the expenses of your spouse are also deductible.

¶2.33 • COSTS OF MAINTAINING AND OPERATING ENTERTAINMENT FACILITIES ARE NOT DEDUCTIBLE

You may not deduct the expenses of maintaining and operating facilities used to entertain. By law, entertainment facilities are not considered business assets. Examples of entertainment facilities are yachts, hunting lodges, fishing camps, automobiles, airplanes, apartments, hotel suites or homes in a vacation area. A season box seat or pass at a sporting event or theater is not considered an entertainment facility.

The above disallowance rule applies also to depreciation and the investment credit but not to such expenses as interest, taxes and casualty losses which are deductible without having to show business purpose. Country club and other club dues are deductible under the rules of ¶2.331.

Entertainment expenses (such as the cost of food and drinks) incurred at an entertainment facility are deductible if they meet the rules of ¶2.311 to ¶2.321.

Dues paid to a business luncheon club are not within the limitation of entertainment facility rules as a luncheon club is not considered an entertainment facility under Treasury regulations.

¶2.331 • CLUB DUES

To deduct dues for a country club or any other social, athletic, or sporting club, you first have to show that you used the club more than 50% of the time during the year to further your business. (Business or personal use is figured on a day-by-day basis, see ¶2.332.) But this percentage of use does not give you the measure of the deduction of club dues. You must also show how much of the use of the club was for entertainment directly related to the active conduct of your business. This percentage of directly-related entertainment fixes the amount of your club dues deduction. This means that goodwill entertainment may be counted in determining if you may deduct any club dues at all. But the actual amount of dues to be deducted is based on entertainment directly related to your business.

In making this allocation, you include the cost of your own meals as part of the cost of directly-related entertainment.

The amount of direct business use is increased by entertainment of business associates at quiet business meals at the club. The costs of these meals at the club are considered directly-related business expenses. As such, the costs are deductible and the amount of time spent during the quiet business meals counts toward the time the club is used for direct business purposes.

Examples—

1. Your dues at a club cost $1,000 a year and you use the club 75% of the time for the furtherance of your business: 35% of the time for goodwill entertainment and 40% for entertainment directly related to your business. Since more than 50% of the use of the club was for business entertainment, you are entitled to a deduction, but you may deduct only 40% of your club dues or $400, the part related to direct business entertainment. If you had used the club 45% for business entertaining, no deduction would be allowed even if all of such use was directly related to the active conduct of your business.

2. You use your club 20% of the time for quiet business meals, 40% for directly-related entertainment, and 20% for goodwill entertaining. You have used the club for business purposes 80% of the time. But you may deduct only 60% of club dues attributed to quiet business meals and directly-related business entertainment.

In reviewing your deduction of club dues, an IRS agent will usually consider the nature of each use, the frequency and duration of your business use as compared with your personal use, and the amount of costs incurred for business use as compared with the amount of personal costs. If your membership entitles your family to use a club, their use will also be considered in determining whether or not business use exceeds personal use.

The key to deducting club dues is having records of your use of the club (see below). Even with records, you may find you are entitled to a small deduction of club fees or to none at all. But remember: Whether or not you can take a deduction for club dues, the actual cost of bona fide business entertainment at the club is deductible. That is, actual entertainment costs, for example, food and beverages, will be deductible under the rules applied to entertainment expenses without regard to the tax treatment of club dues.

¶2.332 • RECORD KEEPING FOR CLUB USE

To prove you have used a club to further your business, under the more than 50% test, you must have records of (1) when and how the club is used, (2) the cost of the club, and (3) the number of persons entertained. If you do not have these records, the IRS will presume that the club was used for personal purposes. A club is considered to be used primarily for business during a day on which a substantial and bona fide business discussion took place even if it was used for personal or family use during the same day. Days when the club is not used are not counted. For example, if, during the year you used a country club for only 60 days, the 50% test is met if you used the club for business purposes for 31 days.

¶2.333 • EXCEPTIONS TO THE RESTRICTIVE TESTS

The restrictive tests of ¶2.311 do not apply to the following items. Their deductibility is determined under the "ordinary and necessary business expense" rule.

1. Meals served during a business discussion in surroundings conducive to a business discussion (see ¶2.32).

2. Reimbursement of employees' expenses treated as pay and from which income tax is withheld.

3. Expenses paid or incurred by you for your employer or a client where you are reimbursed by the employer or client. To come within this exception, a nonemployee such as an attorney or similar independent contractor, must fully account to his client for entertainment expenses incurred on his behalf. In such an accounting, you must keep records in a diary and receipts as required in ¶2.351. You also must report the client's reimbursements as income. After accounting to your client for entertainment expenses, make sure you retain records of these expenses to substantiate your deduction.

Note: The client does not have to obtain records from you to substantiate his reimbursements for travel and gift expenses unless you have accounted to him for the expenses.

¶2.34 • BUSINESS GIFT DEDUCTIONS ARE LIMITED

Deductions for gifts to business customers and clients in 1986 are restricted. Your deduction for business gifts is limited to $25 a person. You and your spouse are treated as one person in figuring this limitation even if you do not file a joint return and even if you have separate business connections with the recipient. The $25 limitation also applies to partnerships; thus a gift by the partnership to one person may not exceed $25, regardless of the number of partners.

In figuring the $25 limitation to each business associate, do not include the following items:

1. A gift of a specialty advertising item which costs $4 or less on which your name is clearly and permanently imprinted. This exception saves you the trouble of having to keep records of such items as pens, desk sets, plastic bags and cases on which you have your name imprinted for business promotion.

2. Signs, displays, racks, or other promotional material which is used on business premises by the person to whom you gave the material.

3. Employee awards of tangible personal property such as watches and pens, costing not more than $100 and given for length of service or safety achievement.

4. Incidental costs of wrapping, insuring, mailing or delivering the gift. However, the cost of an ornamental basket or container must be included if it has a substantial value in relation to the goods it contains.

If you made a gift to the spouse of a business associate, the gift is considered as made to the associate. If the spouse has an independent bona fide business connection with you the gift is not considered as made to the associate unless it is intended for the associate's eventual use.

If you made a gift to a corporation or other business group intended for the personal use of an employee, stockholder, or other owner of the corporation, the gift generally is considered as made to that individual.

Theater or sporting event tickets given to business associates are entertainment, not gift, expenses if you accompanied them. If you do not accompany them, you may elect to treat the tickets either as gifts, which are subject to the $25 limitation, or as entertainment expenses of an unlimited amount, subject to the entertainment expense rules such as the requirement to show a business conference before or after the entertainment. You may change your election at any time within the period allowed for tax assessment (see ¶38.03).

Packaged food or drink given to a business associate is a gift, if it is to be consumed at a later time.

Gifts not coming within the $25 limit are: (1) Scholarships that are tax free under the rules of ¶12.10; (2) prizes and awards that are tax free under the rule of ¶12.03; (3) gifts to employees, discussed below; (4) death benefit payments coming within the $5,000 exclusion of ¶2.04. If a death benefit exceeds $5,000 and is treated as a tax-free gift, the deduction for the excess over $5,000 is limited to $25.

Employee bonuses should not be labeled as gifts. An IRS agent examining your records may, with this description, limit the deduction to $25 unless you can prove the excess over $25 was pay. By describing the payment as a gift, you are inviting an IRS disallowance of the excess over $25. This was the experience of an attorney who gave his secretary $200 at Christmas. The IRS disallowed $175 of his deduction. The Tax Court refused to reverse the IRS. The attorney could not prove that the payment was for services.

Gifts to employees. You may deduct the cost of gifts, up to $400, given to an employee in recognition of length of service, productivity, or safety achievement. A gift certificate does not qualify. In addition, if employees may choose among several gifts, the choice must be limited to no more than four different items. Giving the right to choose among five or more different items will limit the employer's deduction to the general $25 per person ceiling. The four-item restriction applies to different items. For example, an employee may choose between more than four television sets, but a diamond ring and a diamond pin are considered different items.

You may also establish a nondiscriminatory qualified awards plan and deduct your costs as long as the average cost of gifts under the plan does not exceed $400. A gift is not treated as a qualified award to the extent it exceeds $1,600.

¶2.35 • Travel and Entertainment Records

Your testimony—even if accepted by an agent or judge as truthful—is not sufficient to support a deduction of travel and entertainment expenses. By law, your personal claim must be supported by other evidence, such as records or witnesses. The most direct and acceptable way is to have records that meet IRS rules discussed in the following pages. Failure to have adequate records will generally result in a disallowance of your travel and entertainment expense deductions on an examination of your return. Only in unusual circumstances will evidence other than records provide all of the required details of proof.

The record-keeping rules are directed to one event, the possibility that an IRS agent may examine your return and question your travel and entertainment expenses. Your expense account arrangement with your company will determine the type of evidence the agent will ask for.

1. *Are your travel and entertainment expenses fully reimbursed by your company?* The agent will then inquire whether you have submitted expense account statements to your employer. If you

answer yes, he will not ask to see your expense account records. *See* ¶2.36. Nor will he dispute your travel and entertainment expense arrangement. But note this important point: He or another agent may then review your company's records to determine if you have adequately substantiated your expenses to it by means of a diary and other records. The chances of a current examination of your company's practices are increased if you are an employee of a closely-held corporation. In addition, even though you have a reimbursement arrangement, you may have to present your records if you are a stockholder-employee who owns more than 10% of the company stock.

2. *Have you claimed a deduction for travel and entertainment expenses on your return?* That is, your expenses are not reimbursed by your company, or its reimbursements did not cover all of your expenses—or you are self-employed. The agent will then ask for your diary or other account book which lists the amount of these expenses, the time they were incurred, the place they were incurred, and their business purpose. In addition, if the amount of a particular expense is over $25, he will ask to see a receipted bill for the expense. If you do not have the receipts, *your deduction will be disallowed* even though the item is recorded in the diary.

To sum up: Whether or not you have a reimbursement arrangement, you must have records, a diary, or other type of account book, and generally retain receipted bills for costs over $25. But if you have a reimbursement arrangement, your records are primarily for your company which then has the responsibility of seeing that your records are adequate and of paying you for only bona fide business expenses. If this has been done and your return is examined, you generally do not have to show your records to the agent.

The requirement for a business mileage record is discussed at ¶3.05.

Warning: If you claim expense deductions and fail to keep records of the expenses, you may not only lose the deductions but also be subject to penalties, *see* ¶38.06.

¶2.351 • YOU NEED A DIARY AND, GENERALLY, RECEIPTS

Treasury regulations require two types of records:

1. A diary, account book, or similar record to list the background and details of your travel and entertainment expenses.

2. Receipts, itemized paid bills, or similar statements for lodging regardless of amount and for other expenses when they exceed $25. But note these exceptions:

A receipt for travel expenses exceeding $25 is required only when it is readily obtainable, for example, for air travel where receipts are usually provided.

A canceled check by itself is not an acceptable voucher. If you cannot produce a bill or voucher, you may have to present other evidence such as a statement in writing from witnesses.

Record-keeping rules for attorneys and other independent contractors are discussed (*see* ¶2.333).

A receipted bill or voucher must show (1) the amount of the expense, (2) the date the expense was incurred, (3) where the expense was incurred, and (4) the nature of the expense.

A hotel bill must show the name, location, date and separate amounts for charges such as lodgings, meals and telephone calls. A receipt for lodging is not needed if its cost is covered by a per diem allowance (*see* ¶2.37).

A restaurant bill must show the name and location of the restaurant, the date and amount of the expense, and if a charge is made for items other than meals or beverages, a description of the charge.

Your diary does not have to duplicate data recorded on a receipt, provided that a notation in the diary is connected to the receipt. You are also not required to record amounts your company pays directly for any ticket or fare. Credit card charges should be recorded.

Your records must also show: (1) the names of those you entertained, (2) the business purpose served by the entertainment, (3) the business relationship between you and your guests, and

(4) the place of entertainment. Inattention to these details of substantiation can cost you the deduction. For example, an executive's company treasurer verified that the executive was required to incur entertainment expenses beyond reimbursed amounts. He also kept a cash diary in which he made contemporaneous notes of the amounts he spent. But he failed to note place, purpose, and business relationship. Consequently, there was no record that tied the expenses to his employment and the deduction was disallowed.

You should keep your diary and supporting records for at least three years after the due date for the return which the records support. However, you may not have to keep these records if the information from them is submitted to your company under the rules applied to reimbursed expenses and allowances described below.

Excuses for inadequate records:

Substantial compliance: If you have made a "good faith" effort to comply with the Treasury regulations, you will not be penalized if your records do not satisfy every requirement. For example, you would not automatically be denied a deduction merely because you did not keep a receipt.

Accidental destruction: If receipts or records are lost through circumstances beyond your control, you may substantiate deductions by reasonable reconstruction of your expenditures.

Examples—

1. Bryan's 1966 records were lost by a moving company. He claimed a T & E deduction of $15,301.87. The IRS estimated his T & E and other business expenses as $8,669 on the basis of his 1971 expense records. The Tax Court affirmed the IRS's approach. True, Bryan's loss of records made his burden of proof difficult, but he had to provide a reasonable reconstruction of his records to support his claimed deduction. His testimony of what he incurred in 1966 was not sufficient. A more accurate method was the IRS's use of his 1971 records and receipts.

2. Jackson claimed the IRS lost his records. He left his records with the IRS when he was audited, and the records were never returned. The Tax Court held that was a good excuse for not producing his records and allowed a deduction on the basis of reconstructed records. Evidence that the IRS lost his records: It turned up Jackson's worksheet a year after the initial audit interview.

3. Gizzi claimed his records were lost when he moved out of his home due to marital problems. They were inadvertently thrown out. The Tax Court held this was not a good excuse and disallowed his deduction. Marital problems, no matter how seemingly independent of one's will, do not sufficiently resemble a fire or flood to be considered a casualty. Furthermore, even if marital problems were considered an excuse, the deduction may not be allowed; Gizzi did not provide a reconstruction of his records.

4. Murray claimed he lost his records when he was evicted from his apartment for failure to pay rent for a month. The Tax Court accepted his excuse on proof that he had kept records before they were lost. The eviction was beyond his control. However, if the records had been lost during a voluntary move, the loss would not have been excused, as in example 1.

5. Canfield testified that his estranged wife destroyed his records. The Court considers the loss beyond his control. Canfield did not move out of his home voluntarily and leave his records; he was under a court order not to enter his former home. His wife either burned or destroyed his records during the time he had no access to his home because of the court order.

Exceptional circumstances: If, by reason of the "inherent nature of the situation," you are unable to keep adequate records, you may substantially comply by presenting the next best evidence. A supporting memorandum from your files and a statement from the persons entertained may be an adequate substitute. Treasury regulations do not explain the meaning of "inherent nature of the situation."

¶2.36 • HOW TO TREAT REIMBURSED EXPENSES AND ALLOWANCES

If the reimbursement or allowance equals your deductible expenses and you adequately account to your employer:

1. You do not report on your tax return the reimbursement or allowance and the expense payments.

2. You do not have to keep your records for possible IRS audit. That is, you do not have to substantiate your expense account arrangement for the agent. You have already done so with your employer. To deduct his payment to you, your employer must retain the records and receipts submitted by you.

What is an adequate accounting to your employer? You are required to keep for your employer a diary together with supporting paid vouchers and bills according to the record-keeping requirements explained on the previous pages. These records provide a basis for submitting account statements to your employer. In addition, your company must provide internal control over your account statements. A responsible company employee other than yourself must verify and approve your expense account. If your company does not provide such a check, you will have to keep your records for a possible IRS audit.

If your employer's reimbursements exceed your expenses, you report the excess as additional compensation income and file Form 2106 listing the expenses and reimbursement. You must hold on to your records for a possible audit if your expenses exceed your employer's reimbursements and you deduct the excess amount.

If you want to avoid detailing your expenses and reimbursements, and retaining your records, do not deduct the excess expenses. Treat your reimbursements as if they equaled your expenses.

Examples—

1. You charge your business expenses, such as transportation fares, hotel lodgings, meals, and entertainment, through credit accounts paid by your company. At regular intervals, you submit expense account statements to your company explaining the business nature and amounts of these expenses. None of the expenses covered personal items. You do not have to file Form 2106 to report the reimbursement and expenses.

2. You receive a company expense allowance of $1,000 for travel. Your employer requires you to give him a statement showing the business nature and amount of expenses paid with this allowance. As you accounted for your expenses, the company does not report the reimbursement on your Form W-2. During the year, the allowance was inadequate and you incurred authorized out-of-pocket traveling expenses of $500. To deduct this amount, you file Form 2106 on which you report the travel expenses. As the reimbursement was not treated as taxable pay on Form W-2, you also enter the amount of the reimbursement on Form 2106 as a reduction of the travel expenses. The $500 of unreimbursed expenses are then claimed on Form 1040 in the section for "Adjustments to Income." *See* the Supplement for a sample Form 2106.

Also *see* ¶2.38 for partially reimbursed expenses.

Are you reimbursed for incidental expenses—such as for running local errands? You do not have to report these or make a statement about them on your return.

¶2.361 • CREDIT CARDS

Credit card charge statements for traveling and entertainment expenses may meet the IRS tests provided the business purpose of the expense is also shown. Credit card statements provide space for inserting the names of people entertained, their business relationship, the business purpose of the expense, the portion of the expense to be allocated to business and personal purposes. These statements generally meet the IRS requirements of accounting, provided a responsible company official reviews them.

¶2.362 • EMPLOYEE-STOCKHOLDERS

The IRS's promise that its agent will not ask you to substantiate your expenses if you account to your company does not apply if you are an employee-stockholder who owns more than 10% of the company's stock. You will have to hold on to your records for a possible IRS audit. Further, you may not take advantage of the per diem allowance discussed in ¶2.37. The same rule applies if you work for a brother, sister, spouse, parent, or child. However, regardless of this rule, you may take advantage of the 21¢ mileage allowance test below as a means of substantiating your travel expenses.

¶2.37 • FIXED REIMBURSEMENT ALLOWANCES

The requirements for an adequate *accounting to your employer* are eased if your allowance meets the following limits:

For a fixed mileage allowance for transportation costs away from home: Where your company pays you a fixed mileage allowance of not over 21¢ a mile and you substantiate to your company the time, place and business purpose of the travel, you are considered to have substantiated the amount of the travel costs.

Your employer may give an additional allowance for parking fees and tolls. There is no dollar limit on this additional allowance.

For travel expenses away from home (exclusive of transportation costs): If your company reimburses you for such travel expenses in an amount not exceeding $44 per day, or provides you with a per diem allowance of not over $44, you are considered to have substantiated your expenses if also:

1. Your company reasonably limits the allowance or reimbursement to travel costs which are considered ordinary and necessary in its business. In deciding if your company has set reasonable limits, an IRS agent will check if your expense account is verified and approved by a responsible company employee other than yourself.

2. Where you are paid a per diem allowance, an agent will review company records to determine whether the allowance is based on a reasonably accurate estimate of travel costs.

Rates exceeding $44 per day. More than $44 per day may be paid for travel in areas in which U.S. Government employees are paid allowances exceeding $44 per day. A rate exceeding $44 per day may not generally exceed the Government rate paid in the area.

These travel costs are included in the *per diem* allowance: Lodging, meals, incidental transportation and all other travel expenses. It does not cover entertainment and general transportation expenses. Car rental costs for a traveling salesman going from town to town would not be included in the *per diem* limit. Nor would airplane or train fares or the taxi fare from the airport or railroad station. But taxi fares within the city must be included in the $44 limit.

Do not confuse the above allowance rules with the flat mileage allowance for auto costs (*see* ¶3.01).

IMPORTANT: Check the supplement to see if the above rates have been revised since the publication of this book.

¶2.38 • HOW TO TREAT PARTIALLY REIMBURSED JOB EXPENSES

As a salaried employee (not an outside salesman), you must distinguish between job expenses deductible in 1986 as itemized deductions and job expenses deductible from 1986 gross income even if itemized deductions are not claimed.

You may deduct from gross income unreimbursed travel expenses away from home, transportation expenses, and deductible moving expenses to a new job location. You file Form 2106 showing the expenses and any reimbursement not included in your pay. On Form 1040, the unreimbursed expenses are claimed in the section titled "Adjustments to Income." You may also deduct from gross income reimbursed expenses where the reimbursement was included as pay on your Form W-2 (see below). Other unreimbursed job costs like entertainment expenses, club dues, and union dues may be deducted only if you itemize deductions on Schedule A. If you receive a reimbursement covering both types of deductible expenses, the IRS requires you to allocate the reimbursement between each type.

Example—

An executive received a reimbursement allowance of $1,500 from his company which did not specify which of his expenses were reimbursed by the allowance. Expenses totaled $2,000; $1,200 for travel away from home and $800 for entertainment. The $1,200 travel expense is 60% of the total expense of $2,000; the $800 entertainment cost is 40%. Thus, the $1,500 reimbursement allowance is allocated between them on a 60%-40% basis as follows:

			Reimburse-	
	Expenses	*%*	*ment*	*Deductible*
Adjustment to income	$1,200	60%	$900	$300
Itemized deduction	800	40%	600	200
	$2,000		$1,500	$500

On Form 2106, you are required to report all reimbursed employee expenses such as travel and entertainment expenses. Form 2106 generally does not provide for the type of allocation illustrated here; therefore, make the allocation before filling in the form.

> Make sure you receive your reimbursement from your employer. Failure to be reimbursed may prevent you from deducting your out-of-pocket expenses.

Example—

To maintain good relations with his district and store managers, a shoe company supervisor entertained them and their families and also distributed gifts among them. This cost him $2,500 which he could have had his company reimburse, but he made no claim. Consequently, the court disallowed it as a deduction on his return. The expense was the company's; any goodwill he created benefited it. Because he failed to seek reimbursement, he may not now convert company expenses into his own.

Reimbursement reported as pay. A reimbursement arrangement may provide an advantage in this situation: An employee with a reimbursement arrangement may deduct from gross income expenses usually deductible as itemized deductions if the reimbursement is reported as extra pay on his Form W-2.

Examples—

1. Jones gets a straight salary of $15,000. His entertainment costs total $500. His adjusted gross income is $15,000. He may deduct the $500 only if he itemizes deductions.

2. Smith earns $14,500 but he receives $500 to pay his entertainment costs. His adjusted gross income is $14,500—his salary of $14,500 plus $500 for entertainment less the $500 for actual entertainment costs. He may deduct those costs even if his itemized deductions do not exceed the zero bracket amount.

¶2.39 • DOES AN EMPLOYER HAVE TO REPORT YOUR REIMBURSEMENTS?

An employer does not have to file an information return (Forms 1096 and 1099) reporting reimbursements or advances to employees if they submit expense account statements. However, an employer lists on its tax return its top-paid employees, their salaries, and the expenses paid on their behalf. In addition, it also states if it has taken expense deductions in connection with (1) an entertainment facility; (2) living accommodations; (3) employees' families at conventions or meetings; or (4) employee or family vacations. When examining an executive's return, the IRS may confront him with this company information. If he cannot prove the expenses were bona fide business costs, he will be charged with additional compensation.

¶ 2.40 • Deducting Moving Expenses to a New Job Location

¶2.41 • THE 35-MILE DISTANCE TEST

The distance between your new job location and your former home must be at least 35 miles more than the distance between your old job location and your former home. For this purpose, your home may be a house, apartment, trailer, or even a houseboat, but not a seasonal residence such as a summer cottage. If you had no previous job or you return to full-time work after a long period of unemployment or part-time work, the new job location must be at least 35 miles from your former home. The 35-mile test applies to the self-employed and employees.

> Find the shortest of most commonly traveled routes in measuring the distances under the 35-mile test. The following worksheet may be used as an aid.
>
> | **Distance between** | **In miles** |
> |---------------------|--------------|
> | 1. Old residence and new job location | _____ |
> | 2. Old residence and old job location | _____ |
> | 3. Difference (Must be at least 35 miles) | _____ |

The location of your new residence is not considered in applying the 35-mile test. However, if the distance between your new residence and the new job location is more than the distance between your old residence and new job location, your moving expenses may be disallowed unless you can show (1) you are required to live there as a condition of employment, or (2) an actual decrease in commuting time or expense results.

Examples—

1. Your company's office is in the center of a metropolitan area. You live 18 miles from your office. You are transferred to a new office. To deduct moving costs, you must show that the location of the new office is at least 53 miles from your previous residence.

2. Your old job was four miles from your former residence and your new job is 40 miles from your former residence. You move to a house that is less than 35 miles from your old house. Nevertheless, you have met the 35 mile test since your new job is 36 miles further from your former home than your old job was.

If you worked for more than one employer, you find the shortest of the most commonly traveled routes from your old residence to your former principal place of employment.

Your job location is where you spend most of your working time. If you work at various locations, the job location is where you report to work. If you work for several employers on a short-term basis and get jobs through a union hall system, the union hall is considered your job location.

Moving overseas. A member of the Armed Services may deduct the cost of moving his family to an overseas post.

For deducting expenses of moving overseas where you have foreign earned income, *see* ¶36.00.

Alien moving to the U.S. The deduction is not limited to U.S. citizens and residents. An alien may deduct the cost of travel here to work at a full-time position.

¶2.42 • 39-WEEK TEST FOR EMPLOYEES

In addition to meeting the 35-mile distance test, you must remain in the new locality as a full-time employee for at least 39 weeks during the 12-month period immediately following your arrival at the new job location. You do not need to have a job prior to your arrival at the new location. Your family does not have to arrive with you nor must you set up a new household. The 39 weeks of work need not be consecutive or with the same employer. You may change jobs provided you remain in the same locality for 39 weeks.

Example—
You accept a position with a company 600 miles from your former position. You move to the new location. After you have worked in the new position 14 weeks, you resign and take another job with a nearby company. You may add the 14 weeks of work with the first company to 25 weeks with the second company to meet the 39-week requirement.

If you lose your job for reasons other than your willful misconduct, the 39-week requirement is waived. Should you resign or lose your job for willful misconduct, a part-time job will not satisfy the 39-week test. The 39-week period is also waived if you are transferred from your new job for your employer's benefit or are disabled or die. However, it must be shown that you could have satisfied the 39-week test except for the termination, transfer, disablement, or death. The time test is not waived because you reach mandatory retirement age first, where this retirement was anticipated.

If you are temporarily absent from work through no fault of your own, due to illness, strikes, shutouts, layoffs, or natural disasters, your temporary absence is counted in the 39 weeks.

Full-time status. This is determined by the customary practices of your occupation in the area. If work is seasonal, off-season weeks count as work weeks if the off-season period is less than six months and you have an employment agreement covering the off season.

Joint returns. On a joint return, either spouse may meet the time test. But the work time of one spouse may not be added to the time of the other spouse.

Example—
Smith moves from New York to a new job at Denver. After working full time for 30 weeks, he resigns from his job and cannot find another position during the rest of the 12-month period. He may not deduct his moving expenses. But assume that Mrs. Smith also finds a job in Denver at the same time as her husband and continues to work for at least 39 weeks. Since she has met the 39-week test, the moving expenses from New York to Denver paid by her husband are deductible, provided they file a joint return. However, if Mrs. Smith had worked for only nine weeks, her work period could not be added to her husband's to meet the 39-week test.

¶2.43 • 78-WEEK TEST FOR THE SELF-EMPLOYED AND PARTNERS

In addition to meeting the 35-mile distance test, you must work full time for at least 78 weeks during the 24 months immediately following your arrival, of which at least 39 weeks occur in the first 52 weeks. The test is waived if death or disability prevents compliance. The full-time work requirement may prevent the semi-retired hobbyists, students, or others who work only a few hours a week in self-employed trades or occupations from claiming the deduction.

You are considered to have obtained employment at a new principal place of work when you have made substantial arrangements to begin such work. You may not deduct expenses for house-hunting or temporary quarters unless you have already made substantial arrangements to begin work at the new location.

Change of employee or self-employed status. If you start work at a new location as an employee and then become self-employed before meeting the 39-week employee time test, you must meet the 78-week test. Time spent as an employee is counted along with the time spent self-employed in meeting the test.

If, during the first 12 months, you change from working as a self-employed person to working as an employee, you may qualify under the 39-week employee time test provided you have 39 weeks of work as an *employee*. If you do not have 39 weeks as an *employee* in the first 12 months, you must meet the 78-week test.

Joint returns. Where you file a joint return, you deduct moving expenses if either you or your spouse can satisfy the time test based on individual work records.

¶2.44 • CLAIMING THE DEDUCTION BEFORE SATISFYING THE TIME TEST

Where the time for filing your 1985 tax return occurs before you can satisfy the applicable time test, you may nevertheless deduct moving expenses. If you file your return without taking the deduction, you may file an amended return or a refund claim after meeting the time test. No matter which option you choose, any reimbursement must be reported in the year received. *See* ¶2.46.—

Example—
You move to a new location on November 1, 1986. At the end of the year, you have worked in your new position only nine weeks. You deduct your moving expenses on your 1986 tax return even though you did not complete the 39- or 78-weeks of work. But if, after you file the return on which you deducted moving expenses, you move from the location before completing the applicable work period, you must, on your 1987 return, report as income the amount of moving expenses deducted in 1986. As an alternative, you may file an amended 1986 return on which you eliminate the deduction and recompute your tax.

¶2.45 • MOVING EXPENSES YOU MAY DEDUCT

The law distinguishes between two types of deductible moving expense:
1. Direct expenses of moving, which are fully deductible.
2. Indirect expenses involving the disposition of your old residence and the acquisition of a new residence. These expenses are limited by ceilings discussed below.

Direct expenses: You may deduct in full these directly related moving expenses:

1. **Traveling costs of yourself and members of your household en route from your old to the new locality.** Here, you include the costs of transportation, meals and lodging along the direct route by conventional transportation for yourself and family; food and lodging before departure for one day after the old residence is unusable; food and lodging for the day of arrival at the new locality. If you use your own car, you may either deduct your actual costs of gas, oil, and repairs (but not depreciation) during the trip or take a deduction based on the rate of 9¢ a mile. Also add parking fees and tolls. See Supplement for rate changes, if any.

2. **The actual cost of moving your personal effects and household goods.** This includes the cost of packing, crating, and transporting furniture and household belongings, in-transit storage up to 30 consecutive days, insurance costs for the goods, and the cost of moving a pet or shipping an automobile to your new residence. You may also deduct expenses of moving your effects from a place other than your former home, but only up to the estimated cost of such a move from your former home. Also deduct the cost of connecting or disconnecting utilities when moving household appliances. The cost of connecting a telephone in your new home is not deductible.

It is not necessary for you and members of your household to travel together or at the same time to claim the deduction for the expenses incurred by each member.

Indirect expenses: You may deduct, within certain limits, these indirectly related expenses of moving:

1. **The cost of pre-move house-hunting trips.** This includes the expenses of transportation, meals and lodging incurred by you and members of your household in traveling from your former home to the general area of your new job location and returning.

You must obtain employment before the trip begins and the trip must be for the principal purpose of finding a place to live.

You may deduct the expenses of more than one house-hunting trip taken by you or a member of your household. Moreover, the trip need not result in your finding a residence.

2. **Temporary living quarters at your new job location.** This includes meals and lodging for yourself and members of your household while waiting to move into permanent quarters, or while looking for a new residence. You may deduct expenses incurred within any 30 consecutive days after obtaining employment. You do not have to incur these expenses during the first 30 days after starting to work in order to claim the deduction.

3. **Expenses of selling, purchasing, or leasing a residence.** Selling expenses include real estate agents' commissions, attorneys' fees, escrow fees, and similar costs necessary to effect the sale or

exchange of your residence. But do not deduct fix-up expenses (*see* ¶29.23).

Purchasing expenses include attorney's fees, escrow fees, appraisal fees, title costs, loan placement charges (which do not represent interest), and similar expenses. Do not include real estate taxes, interest, or any part of the purchase price of your house in your moving expense deduction. A residence includes a house, apartment, cooperative, or condominium unit, or similar dwelling.

Leasing expenses include reasonable expenses in settling an unexpired lease on an old residence or acquiring a lease on a new residence, such as attorney's fees, real estate commissions, consideration paid to lessor to obtain a release, or other similar expenses. You may not deduct security deposits or payments of rent. However, you may deduct a security deposit for your old lease which you forfeit because certain terms of the lease are broken as a result of the move.

$3,000 ceiling on indirect expenses. An overall limit of $3,000 is applied to deductions for indirectly-related moving expenses (house-hunting expenses, temporary living quarters, and costs related to sale and purchase or lease of your residence). Of this amount, only $1,500 incurred for temporary living expenses during a 30-day period and for house-hunting trips is deductible.

You may not use selling expenses which you have deducted as moving expenses to reduce the amount realized on the sale of your house for purposes of determining gain. Similarly, purchase expenses which you deduct are not added to the cost basis of your new residence for purposes of determining gain. However, selling or purchasing expenses which exceed the deduction limitation here may be used to reduce your gain on sale of your old house or increase your basis on your new house. See ¶29.23.

Married couples filing separate returns. Where a married couple files separate returns and each spouse paid and deducts moving expenses, the above ceiling on each return for indirect expenses is $1,500 ($750 for house-hunting and temporary quarters).

If one spouse did not incur deductible expenses, the other spouse may deduct up to $3,000 of indirect moving expenses on a separate return.

Separated spouses may each deduct up to $3,000 for indirect expenses on separate returns under these conditions: (1) The couple did not reside together in the same residence at the new location and does not plan to within a determinable time. (2) Both incurred expenses in moving to new places of work. (3) Both spouses satisfy the time and distance tests.

Under the same conditions, a separated couple filing a joint return may deduct up to $6,000 for the indirect expenses of moving to new places of work (including $3,000 for house-hunting and temporary quarters). Both spouses must satisfy the time and distance tests.

Delay in moving to new job location. You may delay moving to the area of a new job location. A delay of less than one year does not jeopardize a deduction for moving expenses. Further, if you move to the new job area within one year, your family may stay in the old residence for a longer period. Their later moving expenses will generally be deductible, even though incurred after one year. For example, the IRS allowed a moving expense deduction to a husband who immediately moved to a new job location, although his wife and children did not join him until 30 months after he began the new job. They delayed so the children could complete their education. The IRS held that since part of the moving expenses was incurred within one year, the moving expenses incurred later were also deductible.

Nondeductible expenses. You may not deduct the cost of travel incurred for a maid, nurse, chauffeur or similar domestic help (unless the person is also your dependent), the cost of moving a boat, expenses of refitting rugs and drapes, forfeited tuition, car tags or driver's license for the state you move to, losses on disposing of memberships in clubs, mortgage penalties, expenses for trips to sell your old house or loss on the sale of the house. Furthermore, when your employer reimburses you for such costs, you realize taxable income for the amount of the reimbursement.

You may not deduct the cost of transporting furniture which you purchased en route from your old home.

¶2.46 • YOU MUST REPORT REIMBURSEMENTS

Include all moving expense reimbursements received in 1986 on your return as part of your salary or wage income whether or not it is reflected on your W-2.

You must report as income such items as payments made by your employer directly to a moving company. Your employer will show these payments on Form 4782. Use your copy of the form to figure reimbursements and expenses. You then deduct your actual costs to the extent they qualify as deductible moving expenses.

Reimbursements and the payment of the expenses generally occur in the same year. If, however, you are reimbursed in a year other than the year you pay the expenses, you may elect to deduct the expenses in the year of reimbursement, provided (1) you paid the expenses in a prior year or (2) you pay the expenses in the year following the year of reimbursement but before the due date for filing the return (including extensions).

Examples—
1. You moved and paid expenses in December, 1985. Your employer reimburses you in January, 1986. You may deduct your expenses on your 1986 return rather than your 1985 return.
2. In 1986, your employer gave you the cash for your move, but you moved in 1987 and paid the expenses in 1987. You may elect to deduct the expense on your 1986 return if you paid the expense before the due date of the 1986 return (including extensions). If you filed the 1986 return before deducting expenses, you may file a refund claim or an amended return.

Reimbursements by employers of deductible moving expenses are not subject to withholding tax.

Reimbursements on sale of home. To encourage or facilitate an employee's move, an employer may reimburse the employee for a loss he incurred on the sale of his house. The IRS taxes such reimbursements as pay.

Servicemen on active duty. A member of the Armed Forces on active duty moving pursuant to a military order and incident to a permanent change of station does not account for or report any in-kind moving and storage expense services he received from the military or any cash reimbursement or allowances to the extent expenses were actually paid. Further, if the Service moves the member and his family to separate locations, in-kind expenses, reimbursements and allowances are generally not taxable. The "distance" test and the "time" test do not apply to either the serviceman or his spouse.

Moving expenses. Payments received under the Uniform Relocation Assistance and Real Property Acquisition Policies Act of 1970 by persons displaced from their homes, farms, or businesses by federal projects are not included in income.

¶3.00

Deducting Automobile Expenses

Costs of driving on business trips are deductible under rules hedged with restrictions that:

Bar deductions of expenses allocated to driving for personal trips.

Place a ceiling on the top annual depreciation deduction. In 1986, the maximum depreciation deduction for a car purchased in 1986 may not exceed $3,200, even if the car is used only for business travel.

Allow ACRS depreciation only for autos used for business driving exceeding 50%. Where business driving is less, straight line depreciation must be used.

Recapture ACRS depreciation deductions and the investment credit claimed in prior years if business use declines below certain levels.

Give you an election to avoid accounting for actual auto expenses and depreciation by claiming an IRS mileage allowance. Whatever choice you make, keep a record of mileage of business trips.

Tax the value of personal driving with a company car.

Where to claim auto expense deductions.

Employees. You claim actual auto expenses or the IRS allowance on Form 2106. Form 2106 requires you to list mileage for business, commuting and other personal trips. If you claim actual costs you may include on Form 2106 interest and sales tax paid on a car purchase allocated to business use. The balance of the taxes and interest may be claimed as itemized deductions on Schedule A.

Self-employed. You deduct business auto costs on Schedule C; depreciation details are shown on Form 4562.

Claiming IRS Auto Allowance

¶3.01 • IRS AUTOMOBILE ALLOWANCE

You have a choice of either deducting the actual operating costs of your car during business trips or deducting a flat IRS allowance based on the business mileage traveled during the year. The flat mileage allowance takes the place of fixed operating costs such as: Gasoline (including state and local taxes), oil, repairs, license tags, insurance and depreciation. You may not take the allowance and deduct your actual outlays for these expenses. Parking fees and tolls during business trips are allowed in addition to the mileage allowance. You may deduct any interest and sales taxes paid with the purchase of the auto and still use the IRS auto allowance.

The mileage rate may apply also to business trips in pick-up or panel trucks.

The rate may not be used to deduct the costs of an automobile used for nonbusiness income-producing activities such as looking after investment property.

Use the IRS allowance in the year you place the car in service if it gives you a larger deduction than the total of the actual operating costs of the car plus depreciation or the ACRS deduction. Deductions based on actual outlays for gas, oil, repairs, and insurance plus the deduction for depreciation or ACRS may exceed the IRS allowance.

Your election also affects later tax years. Once you elect to deduct actual costs and ACRS or elect straight-line recovery under

¶3.06, you may not use the IRS auto allowance for *that car* in a later year. Similarly, claiming the IRS allowance in the first year you put a car in service forfeits your privilege to use ACRS. Therefore before claiming the IRS allowance or actual costs plus ACRS, project your auto deductions over the years you expect to use the car. Compare the total allowable under the IRS allowance for the period and your estimate of costs plus ACRS. Choose the option giving the overall larger deductions for the period.

If before 1981, you deducted actual expenses and straight line depreciation for your car, you may switch to the allowance in 1986 but if your car is considered fully depreciated (*see* below) you may only claim the lower mileage rate for business travel over 15,000 miles.

You may decide to use the allowance if you do not keep accurate records of operating costs. However, you must keep a record of your business trips, dates, customers or clients visited, business purpose of the trips, your total mileage during the year and the number of miles traveled on business. An IRS agent may attempt to verify mileage by asking for repair bills near the beginning and end of the year if the bills note mileage readings.

The IRS will not disallow a deduction based on the allowance even though it exceeds your actual car costs.

You may not claim the allowance if:

1. You first used your car for business after 1980 and deducted

actual operating costs in that first year. Similarly, you may not use the allowance if you claim ACRS for your car.

2. You have depreciated your car using a depreciation method other than the straight line method.

3. You have claimed an extra first-year depreciation deduction on your car before 1981.

4. You claim ACRS deductions or first-year expensing for the car.

5. You use in your business two or more cars simultaneously, such as in a fleet operation.

6. You use your car for hire. That is, you use it as a taxicab, in carrying passengers for a fare.

7. You lease the car.

Allowance rate. At the time this book went to press, the IRS allowance was 21¢ per mile for the first 15,000 miles of business travel and 11¢ per mile for business travel over 15,000 miles. *Check the Supplement for rate changes, if any.*
Example—
You drive your car on business trips. You keep a record of your business mileage. You traveled 20,000 miles on business. You may deduct $3,700 (15,000 × 21¢, or $3,150 plus 5,000 × 11¢, or $550).

If you have fully depreciated your car, you may not use the top IRS rate; you are limited to the rate applied to travel of over 15,000 miles (*see* ¶3.03 and ¶3.04 for depreciation rules).

If you use more than one automobile in your business travel and elect the allowance, total the business mileage traveled in both cars.
Example—
You use one car primarily for business and occasionally your spouse's car for business trips. During the taxable year, on business trips, you drove your car 10,000 miles, your spouse's car, 2,000 miles. Total business mileage is 12,000 miles.

If you replace your car during the year and both cars qualify for the allowance, you total the business mileage of both cars for the year. If you did not use the allowance rate for one of the cars, the following examples illustrate how to total the mileage:
Example—
1. *Old car does not qualify for allowance; new car does.* During the taxable year, you drove a total of 21,000 business miles, 4,000 miles in a car owned from January until May and 17,000 miles in a new car bought in May. You did not use the allowance for the old car because it was depreciated on the declining balance method. You elect to use the allowance for the new car. Although the allowance does not apply to the old car, you consider the 4,000 miles the old car was driven. As a result you may apply the allowance rate fixed for the first 15,000 miles to only 11,000 business miles. That rate applies to the *first* 15,000 business miles, including the 4,000 miles driven in the old car. You may deduct the actual expenses of operating the old car.

2. *Old car qualifies; new car does not.* Same figures as in Example 1, except the old car qualified for the allowance, but you depreciate the new car using ACRS so that you may not use the allowance for the new car. You apply the first 15,000 mile rate to the 4,000 miles driven in the old car and deduct the actual operating costs of the new car.

Where a husband and wife own separate businesses, but use a jointly owned car for individual business trips, business mileages are combined whether they file jointly or separately. The first 15,000 mile rate is applied to the first 15,000 miles of their combined business mileage. Each spouse may not treat his or her travel separately so as to apply the rate to the first 15,000 miles of their individual trips. However, if you and your spouse have separate businesses and you each drive separately owned cars, you do not have to combine mileages; you may compute separate allowances based on your individual travel.

IRS allowance includes depreciation. When you use the IRS allowance, you may not claim a separate depreciation deduction. The IRS mileage allowance includes an estimate for depreciation. After your car reaches the end of its useful life (*see* below), your car is considered fully depreciated and you may no longer use the maximum mileage allowance set for the first 15,000 miles.

If your employer reimburses your auto costs at a rate lower than the IRS allowance, you may use the IRS rate to deduct the excess over your employer's reimbursement. For example, the IRS allowance provides a deduction of $3,000. If your employer reimbursed $1,000 of your auto expenses, you may deduct $2,000 under the IRS allowance. To deduct the excess, the IRS sets these conditions: (1) The amount of your employer's reimbursement must be reported on Form 2106 attached to your return. (2) You must list all the expenses reimbursed by your employer. (3) You must meet the expense-keeping rules of accounting to your employer at ¶2.36.

Assumed depreciation based on mileage. If you have always used the IRS mileage allowance for a car bought after 1979, the IRS measures the useful life of the car by mileage. The car is considered fully depreciated after 60,000 business miles, but for this purpose, only the first 15,000 miles of annual mileage is counted.
Example—
In 1982, 1983, 1984, and 1985, you drove 20,000 miles a year for business. At the end of 1985, your car is considered fully depreciated (60,000 assumed mileage); in 1986, if you use the same car, you may not use the top rate set for the first 15,000 miles. You must use the lower rate set for mileage over 15,000 miles. If in 1986 you switch to the actual cost deduction method, you may not deduct depreciation.

Switching to allowance. If you used a rapid method of depreciation or an ACRS deduction in 1981, 1982, 1983, 1984, or 1985 you may not switch to the IRS mileage allowance in 1986. If before 1981 you deducted actual operating costs, including straight line depreciation, and in 1986, you want to use the IRS allowance, your car is considered fully depreciated at the end of the useful life used to figure the straight line depreciation. Thus, unless you figured straight-line recovery using a useful life greater than six years, you may only use the lower allowance rate for mileage over 15,000 miles in 1986.
Example—
On January 3, 1980, you bought a new car for your business. For 1980, 1981, 1982, 1983, 1984 and 1985 you deducted the actual expenses of your car. You figured depreciation using the straight line method based on a six-year useful life. In 1986, you decide to change to the standard mileage rate. You may not use the top rate for the first 15,000 business miles. Your car was fully depreciated at the beginning of 1986, and the IRS rate is limited to the lower rate for mileage over 15,000 miles.

Basis adjustment. Where you use the IRS mileage allowance, you reduce the basis of the car for depreciation estimated in the allowance. Basis is reduced by 7¢ per mile in 1980 and 1981; 7.5¢ per mile in 1982 and 8¢ per mile in 1983, 1984 and 1985. For this purpose, only the first 15,000 miles of business travel each year is taken into account. Depending on the cost of your car, these basis reductions may not in your case reduce the cost basis of your auto to zero, although after 60,000 miles of business travel (at the maximum mileage rate), your car is considered fully depreciated under the IRS rules. Further, after 60,000 business miles, you may not depreciate the remaining basis by electing to deduct your actual auto costs.

Deducting Depreciation and Actual Costs

¶3.02 • AUTO EXPENSE ALLOCATION RULES

If you do not claim the IRS mileage allowance, you may deduct car expenses on business trips such as the cost of gas and oil (including state and local taxes), repairs, parking, tolls, and garage.

If you use your car exclusively for business, all of your operating expenses are deductible.

Apportioning car expense between business and personal use. For a car used for business and personal purposes, deduct only the depreciation and expenses allocated to your business use of the car. Depreciation is discussed at ¶3.03 and ¶3.04.

If you claim itemized deductions, you may deduct only that part of the interest and taxes (other than state and local gasoline taxes) not claimed as business expenses. You may not deduct as itemized deductions the nonbusiness part of depreciation, operator's permit and license fees (no part of which is considered as a personal property tax) and state and local gasoline taxes.

The business portion of car expenses is determined by the percentage of mileage driven on business trips during the year.
Example—
A salesman drove his car 15,000 miles during the year. Of this, 12,000 miles was on business trips. The percentage of business use is 80%:

$$\frac{\text{Business mileage}}{\text{Total mileage}} = \frac{12,000}{15,000} = 80\%$$

His car expenses (gas, oil, repairs, etc.) for the year were $1,000 of which $800 ($1,000 × 80%) is deductible as a business expense.

If you lease a car for business use, you deduct the rental fee plus other costs of operating the car. If the car is also used for personal driving, the rental fee must be allocated between business and personal mileage. See also ¶3.08.

¶3.03 • DEPRECIATING A CAR PLACED IN SERVICE BEFORE JUNE 19, 1984

If you use your car for business, and you do not claim the IRS allowance, you deduct depreciation. Under ACRS, cars placed in service after 1980 and used in business are depreciated over three years. For a car placed in service in 1984 but before June 19, 1984, the 1986 rate is 37%. For a car placed in service in 1984 but after June 18, 1984, the 1986 rate is also 37% but the deductible amount is limited to $6,000; see ¶3.041.

If, in 1986, you no longer use your car for business or dispose of it, you may not claim an ACRS deduction in 1986.

Converting a pleasure car to business use. The basis for depreciation is the lower of the market value of the car at the time of conversion or its original cost. In most cases, the value of the car will be lower than cost and thus value will be your depreciable basis. If the car was bought after 1980, the ACRS rate may be applied to basis allocated to business travel. If you convert a personal automobile to business use in a year after the year of acquisition, no investment credit is allowed.

ACRS after end of recovery period. At the end of a three-year recovery period, you may continue to take ACRS deductions if the percentage of business use (and investment use) exceeds the average business (and investment) use in the prior three years. If you show such an increase, the car is treated as placed in service at the start of the taxable year in which the increased use occurs. The first-year ACRS rate is applied, but the deduction is limited by the percentage of increased business use. Basis for this new period is the lower of fair market value at the beginning of the new recovery period or the unadjusted cost basis of the car.
Example—
In 1983, you bought a car for $10,000. During 1983-1985, you claimed ACRS deductions based on 60% business use. Depreciation for the three years was $6,000. In 1986, after the end of the regular three-year ACRS period, business use increased to 70%. In 1986 you may claim an additional ACRS deduction because 70% business use exceeds the 60% average for the first three years. Assuming that fair market value at the beginning of 1986 was $7,500, basis for depreciation purposes is

$7,500, the lower of fair market value or $10,000 unadjusted basis. Your 1986 deduction is $187.50: $7,500 basis × .25 (first-year ACRS percentage) × .10 (increase in 1986 business use, or 70%, over 60% average business use during 1983-1985).

¶3.04 • DEPRECIATING A CAR PLACED IN SERVICE AFTER JUNE 18, 1984

All autos placed in service after June 18, 1984 are subject to a business use test, recapture rules, and annual ceilings on depreciation and the investment credit. Ceilings on depreciation and the investment credit are discussed at ¶3.041 and ¶3.0411. These restrictions and the business use requirement do not apply for autos acquired under contracts binding on June 18, 1984 that were placed in service before 1985; for such cars, the rules of ¶3.03 apply.

If in 1986, you disposed of a car or stopped using it for business, you may not deduct any depreciation on the car in 1986.

More than 50% business use test. Whether you are an employee or are self employed, you may claim ACRS, first-year expensing, and the investment credit for a car bought after June 18, 1984 only if you use it more than 50% of the time for business in the year you place it in service.

If business use is 50% or less in the year it is placed in service, ACRS is barred; the auto is depreciable over a six-year period under the straight line method. Technically, the recovery period is five years but the period is extended to six years because in the first year, a half year convention rule limits the deductible percentage to 10%. See rate table at ¶3.06. The straight line method must be used in future years, even though business use later exceeds 50%.

If a car is used for both business and investment purposes, only business use is considered under the more than 50% business use test to determine the right to claim ACRS and the investment credit, and/or first-year expensing. However, in allocating depreciation deductions, investment use is added to business use.
Example—
On December 1, 1986, Brown buys an automobile for $30,000 and places it in service. He uses it 40% for business and 20% for investment activity. Because he does not use his car more than 50 percent in his business, he may not claim ACRS. He figures depreciation using the straight-line method over a five-year period. The business use allocation rate for depreciation is 60% (40% for business use plus 20% investment use). His 1986 deduction is $1,800 ($30,000 × 10% straight line rate for first year × 60% business use).

Recapture of ACRS and investment credit if business use falls below 51%. If you meet the more than 50% test in the year the car is placed in service but business falls to 50% or less in a later year, the recapture rules discussed at ¶3.07 apply.

The basis rule for converting a pleasure car to business use is at ¶3.03.

Employer convenience test. If you are an employee and use your own car for work, you must be ready to prove that you use a car for the convenience of your employer who requires you to use it in your job. If you do not meet this employer convenience test, you may not use ACRS or straight line depreciation, or claim first-year expensing or the investment credit. A letter from your employer stating you need the car for business will not be enough to meet this test.

The facts and circumstances of your use of the car may show that it is a condition of employment. For example, an inspector for a construction company uses his automobile to visit construction sites over a scattered area. The company reimburses him for his expenses. According to the IRS, the inspector's use of the car is for the convenience of the company and is a condition of the job. However, if a company car were available to the inspector, the use of his own car would not meet the condition of employment and convenience of the employer tests.

Employee use of company car. In certain cases, an employer who provides a company car to employees as part of their compensation may be unable to count the employee's use as qualified business use, thereby preventing the employer from meeting the more than 50% business test for claiming ACRS and the investment credit. An employer is allowed to treat the employee's use as qualified business use only if: (1) the employee is not a relative and does not own more than 5% of the business, and (2) the employer treats the fair market value of the employee's personal use of the car as wage income and withholds tax on that amount. If such income is reported, all of the employee's use, including personal use may be counted by an employer as qualified business use.

If an employee owning more than a 5% interest is allowed use of a company car as part of his compensation, the employer may not count that use as qualified business use, even if the personal use is reported as income. The same strict rule applies if the car is provided to a person who is related to the employer.

Restrictions on vehicles other than cars. The investment credit limits and the depreciation ceilings discussed at ¶3.041 and ¶3.0411 apply only to "passenger automobiles." For this purpose, a passenger automobile is considered to be any four-wheeled vehicle that is manufactured primarily for use on public streets, roads, and highways and that is rated at 6,000 pounds unloaded gross vehicle weight or less. It does not include: (1) an ambulance, hearse, or combination ambulance-hearse used directly in a business, (2) a vehicle such as a taxicab used directly in the business of transporting persons or property for compensation or hire, and (3) commuter highway vehicles such as vans or buses that an employer uses to transport employees to and from work.

The more than 50% business use test applies generally to vehicles other than automobiles, such as trucks, vans, boats, motorcycles, airplanes, and buses. However, buses and other vehicles that are exempt from recordkeeping requirements under ¶3.05, such as a school bus, a dump truck, specialty business truck or farm tractors are not subject to the more than 50% test or recapture rule. A vehicle not listed at ¶3.05 is subject to the more than 50% test for claiming ACRS depreciation, first-year expensing or an investment credit. If you do not satisfy the more than 50% test, you must apply the straight line recovery rates shown at ¶3.06.

¶3.041 • ANNUAL CEILING ON ACRS DEDUCTIONS FOR AUTOMOBILES

Under ACRS, in the first year, the recovery percentage for a car is 25%; the second year percentage 38% and the third-year percentage 37%. The percentage is applied to the cost basis of the car. Thus if the cost basis of a car purchased in 1986 is $10,000, the ACRS deduction is $2,500 (25% of $10,000). However, deductions may be reduced by percentage of business use and the following restrictions. For a car placed in service after June 18, 1984, the depreciation deductions are limited as follows. For cars placed in service—

Before April 3, 1985, the deduction in the first year is limited to $4,000; in the second year and third year the deduction may not exceed $6,000 each year. If in the first three years business use is 100%, then any remaining basis that could not be deducted because of the $4,000 and $6,000 ceilings may be depreciated at a rate of up to $6,000 a year until basis is written off.

After April 2, 1985 and before 1987, the deduction in the first year is limited to $3,200; in the second year and third year the deduction may not exceed $4,800 each year. If in the first three years business use is 100%, then any remaining basis that could not be deducted because of the $3,200 and $4,800 ceilings may be depreciated at a rate of up to $4,800 a year until basis is written off.

First-year expensing. The $3,200 limit applies also to the first year expensing deduction. Thus the first-year expense deduction in 1986 may not exceed $3,200. If your expensing deduction is up to $3,200, no ACRS deduction may be claimed in 1986. First-year expensing is discussed at ¶5.38.

Personal use. Where a deduction is limited by the ceiling and the car is also used for personal driving, the business use percentage is applied to the ceiling. For example, in 1986 you buy a car costing $40,000. ACRS is limited by the $3,200 ceiling. You use the car 80% for business travel. The ACRS deduction is limited to $2,560 ($3,200 × 80%).

The more than 50% test and the ceilings do not apply to taxi cabs and other vehicles used to transport persons for hire.

After 1988, the above ceiling limits may be adjusted to reflect inflation.

Buyer of diesel vehicle must offset basis by one-time credit for increased diesel fuel tax. A tax credit is allowed in the year a diesel-powered car or truck weighing 10,000 pounds or less is purchased for a use other than resale. You must be the original purchaser. For a car purchased in 1986, the credit is $102; $198 for a truck or van. The credit is claimed on Form 4136, which is attached to Form 1040. For depreciation and investment credit purposes, basis must be reduced by the credit. Thus, if you buy a $16,000 diesel car in 1986, basis is reduced by the $102 credit to $15,898. *See also* ¶24.83.

Capital improvements. A capital improvement to a business auto is depreciable under ACRS in the year the improvement is made. The ACRS deductions for the improvement and auto are considered as a unit for applying the limits on the annual ACRS deduction.

¶3.0411 • INVESTMENT CREDIT FOR AUTOMOBILES

Qualification tests for claiming the investment credit depend on the tax legislation discussed in the front of this book. If a purchase qualifies, the following rules apply.

The 6% credit may not exceed $675, regardless of the cost of the car. The maximum $675 credit assumes 100% business use. If you elect to claim a reduced 4% credit to avoid a reduction in depreciable basis, the maximum credit for 100% business use is $450. (For cars placed in service from June 19, 1984 through April 2, 1985, the maximum credit was $1,000, or $667 if the reduced credit was elected.)

The investment credit is computed on Form 3468 that must be attached to your return. If you elect first-year expensing (¶5.38), you reduce the basis of the property by the first-year deduction before computing the 6% or 4% credit.

The $675 (or $450) ceiling is also reduced for personal use. For example, if business use is 80%, the maximum credit is $540 (80% of $675) or $360 (80% of $450). Keep in mind that *no* credit is allowed unless you use the car more than 50% for business; if you meet this business use test, you may then add driving for investment purposes to business driving and compute the credit on the combined business-investment percentage.

If you claim the full 6% investment credit (subject to the $675 maximum), you must reduce depreciable business by 50% of the credit before computing depreciation. The basis reduction does not apply if you elect the reduced credit of 4%.

Claiming the credit if you use the mileage allowance. If you use the IRS mileage allowance in the year you place the car in service, and you meet the more than 50% business use test, you may figure a 10% investment credit based on your estimate of the useful life for the car. If the useful life is less than three years, no credit is allowed.

Useful life is—	Qualifying % of cost is—
3 years but less than 5 years	33⅓
5 years but less than 7 years	66⅔
7 or more years	100

Choosing a useful life exceeding five years may not give you a larger credit because of the maximum $675 credit ceiling. Further, with a longer useful life, the recapture period is also increased. *See* ¶3.07.

¶3.05 • KEEPING RECORDS OF BUSINESS USE

Keep a log or diary or similar record of the business use of a car. Record the purpose of the business trips and mileage covered for business travel. In the record book, also note the odometer reading for the beginning and end of the taxable year. You need this data to prove business use.

The 1984 Act had required the keeping of "contemporaneous" records. Although this requirement has been repealed, it is advisable to keep accurate records. If you do not have a written record of business mileage and your return is examined, you will have to convince an IRS agent of your business mileage through oral testimony. Without written evidence, you may be unable to convince an IRS agent that you use the car for business travel or that you meet the business use tests for claiming ACRS and the investment credit. You may also be subject to general negligence penalties for claiming deductions that you cannot prove you incurred.

Mileage records are not required for vehicles that are unlikely to be used for personal purposes, such as, delivery trucks with seating only for the driver or with a folding jump seat, flat bed trucks, dump trucks, garbage trucks, passenger buses (capacity of at least 20), school buses, ambulances or hearses, tractors and other specialized farm vehicles, combines, marked policy or fire vehicles, unmarked law enforcement vehicles that are officially authorized for use, and moving vans if personal use is limited by the employer to travel from an employee's home to a move site.

Employees using company cars are not required to keep mileage records if (1) a written company policy allows them to use the car for commuting and no other personal driving other than personal errands while commuting home or (2) a written company policy bars all personal driving except for minor stops for lunch between business travel.

¶3.06 • STRAIGHT LINE RATE REQUIRED FOR BUSINESS USE OF 50% OR LESS

You may not use ACRS if your business use of your car is 50% or less. The following chart lists mandatory straight line recovery rates for business use of 50% or less. The first year percentage of 10% reflects a half-year convention, regardless of the date you place the car in service. Because of the half-year convention, the straight-line recovery period is extended from five to six years.

The depreciation ceilings of ¶3.041 apply.

Year	Rate
First	10%*
2nd	20
3rd	20
4th	20
5th	20
6th	10*

* The first and last year reflect a half-year convention.

Straight line election for car if business use exceeds 50%. If business use of your car exceeds 50%, you may elect to write off your cost under the straight line method instead of using ACRS, subject to the annual ceilings discussed at ¶3.041. You may elect a straight line recovery period of three, five, or twelve years. If you make the election, the actual recovery period is actually one year longer than the elected period because the writeoff percentage for the first year is reduced by 50% to reflect a half-year convention. Thus, the three-year recovery period is actually four years (17% in first year, 33% in second and third years and 17% in fourth year). If you elect five-year straight line recovery, your deductions will be spread over six years; a 12-year elected period is extended to 13 years.

By electing straight line depreciation, you avoid the recapture of excess ACRS deductions if business use drops to 50% or less in a later year. *See* ¶3.07.

¶3.061 • TRADE-IN OF BUSINESS AUTO

In the year an auto is traded for another auto, no depreciation may be claimed for the old auto. You claim depreciation on the new auto in the year it is placed in service. No gain or loss is recognized on a trade-in of business auto. Generally, the basis of the new auto is the adjusted basis of the old auto plus any additional payment. However, if you trade in an auto acquired after June 18, 1984, basis for figuring ACRS for the new auto is subject to a reduction if it was not used solely for business. To find the basis of the new car, you start with the basis of the car that was traded in, add any cash paid on the trade-in and reduce the total by the excess, if any, of (1) the total ACRS that would have been allowable if the old auto had been used solely for business or investment and (2) the total of the depreciation actually allowed. The same reduction rule applies to involuntary conversion of an auto.

Examples—

1. In January, 1984, you paid $20,000 for an auto used solely for business. In 1984, you claimed depreciation of $5,000 (25% of $20,000); in 1985 $7,600 (38% of $20,000). In March 1986, you trade in the car, paying also cash of $10,600. In 1986, no depreciation is allowed for the old car. Also, part of the investment credit claimed in 1984 is recaptured. The basis of the new car is $18,000: $7,400 adjusted basis of the old car plus $10,600 cash.

2. On December 1, 1985, Jones buys an auto for $30,000 and uses it for business 80% of the time. He claims a reduced investment credit of $360 ($450 × 80%). Thus, basis of the car is not reduced. The unadjusted basis of the car is $30,000. Depreciation for 1985 is $2,560 (80% of $3,200 limit). In 1986, the auto is stolen and Jones receives insurance of $28,500. He has a gain of $1,060, $28,500 less basis of $27,440 ($30,000 original basis less first-year depreciation of $2,560). He buys a new auto for $30,000. No gain is recognized under the rules of ¶18.20. The 1985 investment credit is recaptured as 1986 income. *See* ¶3.07. His basis for the new auto is $28,300, the cost of $30,000 less (1) gain of $1,060 not recognized on the theft and $640. The $640 reduction of basis represents the difference between $3,200, the depreciation deduction that would have been allowed in 1985 if the auto had been used 100% for business, and $2,560, the deduction actually allowed for 80% business use.

Recapture of Depreciation and Investment Credit

¶3.07 • RECAPTURE OF ACRS DEDUCTIONS ON BUSINESS AUTO

If you use your car more than 50% for business in the year you place it in service, you may use ACRS. If business use drops to 50% or less in the second, third, fourth, fifth or sixth year, earlier ACRS deductions must be recaptured and reported as ordinary income. In the year in which business use drops to 50% or less, you must recapture excess depreciation for all prior years. Excess depreciation is the difference between (1) the amount of ACRS deductions allowed in previous years, including the first-year expensing deduction, if any, and (2) the amount of depreciation that would have been allowed if you claimed straight line depreciation based on a six-year recovery period. *See* ¶3.06 for straight line rates.

Recapture is computed on Form 4797 which must be attached to Form 1040. The 50% business use test and recapture rule applies only to cars, trucks, and airplanes placed in service after June 18, 1984. There is an exception for trucks and other specialty vehicles listed at ¶3.05. If you did not use ACRS but instead elected straight line recovery over three, five, or 12 years, the recapture rules do not apply.

Recapture applies where business use is 50% or less in any of the first six years. This means that even if the entire cost of your vehicle has been written off under ACRS within three years, recapture may occur (*see* example below).

Any recaptured amount increases the basis of the property. To compute depreciation for the year in which business use drops to 50% or less, and for later years within the six-year straight line recovery period, you apply the straight line rates shown at ¶2.306.

Examples—

1. During July 1984, you buy for $18,000 a van weighing 8,000 pounds for business. The van is subject to the more than 50% test but because it weighs over 6,000 pounds, the $4,000/$6,000 depreciation limits (¶3.041) do not apply. Under ACRS, you completely write off its cost over its three-year recovery period (1984, 1985, 1986). During 1987, you use the van 50% for business and 50% for personal purposes. In 1987, you must recapture excess depreciation for 1984–1986 as follows:

Total ACRS depreciation claimed in prior years		$18,000
Allowable straight line rate over 5-year period (*see* ¶3.06)		
1984—10% of $18,000	$1,800	
1985—20% of $18,000	3,600	
1986—20% of $18,000	3,600	9,000
Excess recaptured (ACRS less straight line)		$9,000

In 1987, $9,000 is reported as income and the unrecovered basis of the van treated as $9,000. In 1987, straight line depreciation is $1,800 (original unadjusted basis of $18,000 × 20% fourth-year straight line percent × 50% business use in 1987).

2. Same facts as in example (1) except that in 1988 and 1989, the truck is used exclusively in business. The 1988 depreciation deduction is $3,600 (20% fifth-year straight line rate × $18,000). In 1989, depreciation is $1,800 (10% sixth-year percentage × $18,000).

¶3.071 • RECAPTURE OF INVESTMENT CREDIT ON BUSINESS AUTOMOBILES

Recapture is triggered if during the recovery period: (1) the percentage of business-investment use drops below the percentage used for the year in which the car was placed in service; or (2) you dispose of the car before the end of the recovery period. A gift, exchange, trade-in, theft or destruction of a car is treated as a disposition. Further, for a car placed in service after June 18, 1984, a drop in business-investment use to 50% or less is treated as a complete disposition of the car as of January 1 of that year. There are different recapture periods and percentages: (1) for cars on which ACRS is claimed and (2) for cars on which the mileage allowance was originally claimed. The recapture period for ACRS cars is three years starting from the first day of the month the car was placed in service. For IRS mileage allowance cars, it is the useful life elected for the car. The recapture percentage for a complete disposition is based on the number of *full years* that have passed between the first day of the month you placed the car in service and the date of disposition. For a drop in business-investment use, the recapture percentage is based on the number of *full years* between the first day of the month the car was placed in service and January 1 of the year the drop in business-investment use occurs.

Recapture percentage—ACRS cars*

If number of full years is	Recapture percentage is:
0	100%
1	66
2	33
3 or more	0

* Where IRS mileage allowance is claimed, see Form 4255 for recapture percentage.

Example—

In July 1985, you bought a car for $20,000. You used the car 70% for business and 10% for investment purposes in 1985. You claimed ACRS and an investment credit of $540 ($675 × 80%). In October 1986, you sell the car. On your 1986 return, $356 of the credit is recaptured and reported as income. The recapture percentage is 66%: $540 × 66% is $356.

Drop in business use. A decline in business-investment use may require a full or partial recapture of the investment credit.

1. Find the percentage of the decline of business-investment use.

Example—

You claim an investment credit of $400 when initial business use was 80% ($500 × 80%). Business use declines to 60%. The percentage decline is 25% (20/80).

2. Apply the percentage decline to the credit claimed. The resulting figure is subject to recapture.

Example—

Same facts as above. $100 (400 × 25%) is subject to recapture.

3. Apply the regular recapture percentage to the amount in step 2. Assume the recapture percentage is 66% from the above table. The recaptured amount is $66 (100 × 66%).

Examples—

1. On July 2, 1985 you bought a car for $20,000 and used it 80% for business. In 1985, you claim ACRS depreciation and an investment credit of $540 ($675 × 80%). In 1986, you used the car 60% for business. There was a 25% decline in business use (20/80), 25% of the credit or $135 is subject to recapture ($540 × 25%). The recapture percentage from the table is 100% because less than one full year passed between July 2, 1985 and January 1, 1986. Thus, you report the $135 as income for 1986. You increase the unadjusted basis of the car by $68 (50% of the recaptured $135) before figuring your 1986 depreciation deduction.

2. Same facts as in example 1 except that business use falls from 80% in 1985 to 40% in 1986. Because business use fell to 50% or less, you are considered to have sold the car as of January 1, 1986. The recapture percentage from the table is 100%. On your 1986 return, the entire credit of $540 is recaptured. Basis is increased by $270, half of the recaptured credit before figuring 1986 depreciation.

3. Same facts as example 1 except that business use drops from 60% in 1986 to 40% in 1987. Because business use fell to 50% or less, you figure recapture for 1987 as if the car was sold on January 1, 1987. The recapture percentage is 66%; you held the car more than one full year but less than two. Thus, in 1987 you recapture $267, 66% of the unrecaptured credit of $405 ($540 credit − $135 recaptured in 1986).

Leased Autos

¶3.08 · LEASED BUSINESS AUTOS: DEDUCTIONS AND INCOME

If you lease rather than purchase a car for business use, you may deduct the lease charges as a business expense deduction if you use the car exclusively for business. If you use the car also for personal driving, you may deduct only the lease payments allocated to business travel, *see* ¶3.301. You should also keep a record of business use, *see* ¶3.305.

Added income. If you leased the car after June 18, 1984, for at least 30 days, you also have to report an amount as income. Income is imposed to limit your deduction of lease payments to the approximate depreciation ceiling levels placed on deductions for purchased autos. The added income should not exceed your lease deductions. If you do not use the car exclusively for business, reportable income is allocated for business use. Further, if business use is 50% or less a second additional income amount is imposed as explained below.

Income percentages for cars leased after June 18, 1984, and before April 3, 1985. For the first three years, the income percentage is 7.5% of the excess market value of the auto over $16,500; in the fourth year, 6% of the excess (if any) of fair market value over $22,500; in the fifth year, 6% of the excess (if any) of market value over $28,500; in the sixth year, 6% of the excess (if any) of market value over $34,500; for the seventh and later years, 6% of the excess (if any) of market value over the sum of $16,500 and $6,000 multiplied by the number of tax years exceeding three. The amount determined under these formulas is multiplied by the percentage of business and investment use and prorated for the number of days the car is leased during the year.

Example—

On January 1, 1985, you lease and place in service a passenger automobile with a fair market value of $55,000. The lease period is four years. During 1985 and 1986, you use the automobile exclusively in your business. In 1985 and 1986, you deduct your lease payments *and* also include in income $2,887.50.

1. Fair market value	$55,000	
Less base:	16,500	
	$38,500	
2.	× .075	
3. Income reported	$ 2,887.50	

Added income for business use 50% or less. In addition to the income reported above, you must also report a second amount of added income if business use is 50% or less. You follow these rules to figure the added income.

If the fair market value of the automobile on the first day of the lease term exceeds $16,500, multiply the average of business and investment use by the dollar amount from the following table. Average business-investment use is the average of the business-investment use for the first tax year in which the *business* use is 50% or less and for all prior tax years of the lease.

Table 1

Tax year of lease	Lease term in years			
	1	2	3	4 or more
First year	$350	$700	$1,350	$1,850
Second year	—	—	650	1,250
Third year	—	—	—	650

If the fair market value is $16,500 or less, additional income is determined by multiplying the fair market value of the auto, the average business and investment use, and a percentage from the following table.

Table 2

Tax year of lease	Lease term in years			
	1	2	3	4 or more
First year	3%	6%	10.2%	13.2%
Second year	—	1.25%	6.2%	10.4%
Third year	—	—	2.25%	6.5%
Fourth year	—	—	—	1.7%
Fifth year	—	—	—	0.5%

Examples—

1. On September 1, 1984, you leased for four years an auto with a fair market value of $55,000. You use the auto exclusively in your business in 1984 and 1985. For each year, you reported $965.14 or 122/365 × $2,887.50 (7.5 × $38,500 ($55,000 value − $16,500 base)).

2. In 1986, you use the automobile 40% in your business. For 1986, you report income of $1,155 (7.5% × 40% × $38,500). You also report additional income of $520 ($650 × 80%). The $650 is taken from table 1 for the third tax year of a four-year lease. 80% is the average business and investment use for 1984, 1985, and 1986 (240% ÷ 3).

The above rules do not apply to automobiles leased under a contract binding on June 18, 1984, and at all times thereafter, provided that the automobile is placed in service before 1985.

Income percentages for cars leased after April 2, 1985. If a car is leased for at least 30 days after April 2, 1985, and it is valued at more than $11,250 and no more than $50,000, the amount you must add to income in 1986 is taken from an IRS table. The table amount is based on the fair market value of the car on the first day of the lease, and the calendar quarter during which your leasing use began. You prorate this amount for the number of days of the lease term included in your tax year and then multiply this result by the percentage of business and investment use of the car.

If the lease term is less than one year, income is allocated by a fraction of the number of days in the lease term over 365.

An excerpt of an IRS table for cars valued between $11,251 and $20,500 is on the next page. No amount is added to income if the leased car is valued at $11,250 or less. The full IRS table for values up to $50,000 is in IRS Publication 463.

Example—

On July 15, 1986, you lease and place in service a car with a fair market value of $19,700. The lease is for a period of five years. You use the car exclusively in your business. Days of use in 1986 are 170. You include $355 in gross income for 1986. From the table below, the dollar amount for the third quarter is $763. This is allocated by the fraction of lease days, or 170/365, to give $355. If your business use in 1986 was 60%, the income would be $213 ($355 × 60%).

If fair market value is more than $50,000, the income amount for 1986 equals a "dollar amount," prorated for the number of days of the lease during 1986 and multiplied by the percentage of business and investment use. The "dollar amount" depends on whether you leased the car for the whole year:

If the car is first used under the lease in the first quarter of 1986, the dollar amount is the sum of:

1. $90, and

2. 8% of the excess of the car's fair market value over $13,200.

If the car is first used under the lease in the second quarter of 1986, the dollar amount is the sum of:

1. $100, and

2. 9% of the excess of the car's fair market value over $13,200.

If the car is first used under the lease in the third quarter of 1986 the dollar amount is the sum of:

1. $110, and
2. 10% of the excess of the car's fair market value over $13,200.

If the car is first used under the lease in the fourth quarter of 1986, the dollar amount is the sum of:

1. $124, and
2. 11% of the excess of fair market value over $13,200.

Business use 50% or less. If a car is leased after April 2, 1985 and is not used more than 50% for business during a tax year, you must include in gross income an additional amount. The additional amount is included only in the first year that business use is 50% or less. A special rule applies for leases beginning nine months before the end of the year; *see* below.

If the fair market value of the car, as determined on the first day of the lease term or from the lease agreement, is more than $11,250, the additional income amount is determined by multiplying the average business and investment use by the dollar amount from Table 3. The average business and investment use is the average of the business and investment use of the car for the first tax year in which the business use percentage is 50% or less and all prior tax years in which the car is leased.

If the fair market value of the car is $11,250 or less, the additional inclusion amount is determined by multiplying the fair market value of the car by the average business and investment use and by the applicable percentage from Table 2 for leases before April 3, 1985.

Table 3

Tax year of lease	Lease term in years			
	1	2	3	4 or more
First year	$350	$700	$1,150	$1,500
Second year	—	150	700	1,200
Third year	—	—	250	750

Lease terms beginning within nine months before end of year. Where a lease begins within nine months before the close of a taxable year and business use is 50% or less, no additional income is reported for business use of 50% or less in the first lease year; the additional amount is reported in the following year. In the second year, multiply the average business and investment use for both years by the amount under Table 3 above for the first year of the lease; if the value of the car is $11,250 or less, use the percentage from Table 2 for leases before April 3, 1985.

50% business use test. If an employer leases a car to a related person or to a person who owns more than a 5% interest in the business, the lessee's use is not treated as qualified business use by the employer for purposes of applying the 50% business use test.

DOLLAR AMOUNTS FOR YEARS 1-3 CARS LEASED AFTER APRIL 2, 1985

Fair Market Value		Quarter of the Tax Year			
Over	Not Over	4th	3rd	2nd	1st
$11,250	$11,500	$ 8	$ 7	$ 6	$ 6
11,500	11,750	24	21	19	17
11,750	12,000	40	35	32	29
12,000	12,250	56	49	44	40
12,250	12,500	72	64	57	52
12,500	12,750	88	78	70	63
12,750	13,000	104	92	83	75
13,000	13,250	120	106	95	86
13,250	13,500	144	128	115	104
13,500	13,750	172	153	137	124
13,750	14,000	200	177	159	145
14,000	14,250	228	202	182	165
14,250	14,500	256	227	204	185
14,500	14,750	284	252	226	206
14,750	15,000	312	277	249	226
15,000	15,250	340	302	271	246
15,250	15,500	369	327	293	266
15,500	15,750	397	352	316	287
15,750	16,000	425	377	338	307
16,000	16,250	453	402	360	327
16,250	16,500	481	426	383	348
16,500	16,750	509	451	405	368
16,750	17,000	537	476	428	388
17,000	17,500	579	514	461	419
17,500	18,000	635	563	506	459
18,000	18,500	691	613	550	500
18,500	19,000	748	663	595	541
19,000	19,500	804	713	640	581
19,500	20,000	860	763	685	622
20,000	20,500	916	812	729	662

¶4.00

Interest Income

Illustrations of reporting interest income may be found in the Supplement to YOUR INCOME TAX. Mail the card at the front of this book for your FREE Supplement, which includes filled-in returns and last-minute information.

Quick Guide to Interest Income Rules

Item	Pointer	Item	Pointer
Form 1099	Information returns, Forms 1099-INT, sent by payers of interest income, simplify the reporting of interest income. The forms give you the amount of interest to enter on your tax return. Although they are generally correct, you should check for mistakes and notify payers of any error and request a form marked "corrected." If tax was withheld (¶25.10), claim this tax as a payment on your tax return. The IRS will check interest reported on your return against the Forms 1099-INT sent by banks and other payers.	U.S. Savings Bonds, Series "E," "EE"	The increase in redemption value is interest income. You do not have to report the annual increase in value until the year in which you cash the bond or the year in which the bond finally matures, whichever is earlier.
		U.S. Savings Bonds, Series "H," "HH"	Semi-annual interest is taxable when received.
Deposits in savings account	Interest credited to your savings account for 1986 is taxable even though you do not present your passbook to have the interest entered. Dividends on deposits or accounts in the following institutions are reported as interest income: Mutual savings banks, cooperative banks, domestic building and loan associations, domestic and federal savings and loan associations.	U.S. Treasury bills	You report as interest the difference between the cost and amount received on a sale or redemption of the bills at maturity in 1986. It is possible to sustain a capital loss on the sale of Treasury bills before maturity.
Savings certificates, deferred interest or bonus plan	The interest element on certificates of deposit and similar plans of more than one year is treated as original issue discount (OID) and is taxable on an annual basis. The bank notifies you of the taxable OID amount on Form 1099 OID. If you discontinue a savings plan before maturity, you may have a loss deduction for forfeited interest, which is listed on Form 1099-INT or Form 1099-OID. Tax on interest can be deferred on a savings certificate with a term of one year or less. Interest is taxable in the year it is available for withdrawal without substantial penalty. Where you invest in a six-month certificate before July 1, the entire amount of interest is paid six months later and is taxable in the year of payment. However, when you invest in a six-month certificate after June 30, only interest actually paid or made available for withdrawal is taxable in the year of issuance. The balance is taxable in the year of maturity. You can defer interest to a later year by investing in a six-month certificate after June 30, provided the payment of interest is specifically deferred to the year of maturity by the terms of the certificate.	Bearer or coupon bonds	Interest coupons due and payable in 1986 are taxable on your 1986 return regardless of when they were presented for collection. For example, a coupon due January 1986 and presented for payment in 1985 is taxable in 1986. Similarly, a coupon due December 1986 but presented for payment in 1987 is taxable in 1986.
		Corporate obligations in registered form	You report interest when received or made available to you. *See* ¶4.03 on how to treat interest when you buy or sell bonds between interest dates.
		Interest on state and local government obligations	Although you may receive a Form 1099-INT for interest on state or municipal bonds, you do not pay federal tax on the interest. If you are required to fill out the interest schedule on Form 1040 or Form 1040A, you must list the tax-exempt interest on the schedule although it is not taxable. The interest may be subject to state income tax.
		Borrow to meet minimum deposit requirements for savings certificates	Interest expenses are deductible as itemized deductions. Report the full amount of interest income listed on Form 1099-INT even if you do not take interest deductions.
		Insurance proceeds	You report interest paid on insurance proceeds left with an insurance company or included in installment payments (under options modes of payment). Exception: Up to $1,000 a year of interest included in installment payments to a surviving spouse is not taxed.

Quick Guide to Interest Income Rules (cont.)

Item	Pointer	Item	Pointer
Interest on pre-paid premium	Taxable interest is reported by insurance company on Form 1099-INT.		withdrawn only on the anniversary date of the policy (or some other specified date), then you report the interest in the year in which the anniversary date of the policy (or some other specified date) falls.
Interest on tax refunds	Interest on tax refunds is fully taxable.		Interest on GI insurance dividends on deposit with the VA is taxable, although the dividends were not taxable.
Bank gifts	The value of gifts is taxable. To attract new deposits, banks and thrifts offer cash, televisions, toasters, and the like, as inducements. The gifts are taxable as interest and reported on Form 1099-INT.	Interest on funds invested abroad	Interest must be reported in U.S. dollars. If foreign tax has been paid, you may be entitled to a deduction or credit, see ¶36.15. See also ¶36.13 for blocked currency reporting rules.
Interest on un-withdrawn life insurance dividends	If you can withdraw the interest annually, you report the interest in the year it is credited to your account. However, if, under the terms of the insurance policy, the interest can be		

¶4.01 • FORFEITURE OF INTEREST ON PREMATURE WITHDRAWAL OF TIME SAVINGS ACCOUNT

A bank may pay a fixed interest rate on a savings account, provided principal is not withdrawn during a specified period. If you prematurely withdraw funds in order to switch to higher paying investments or for any other reason, you may forfeit part of the interest earned and even the principal. In some cases, the penalty may exceed the interest earned so that principal is forfeited to make up the difference. You report the full amount of interest credited to your account; the principal as well as interest forfeited is deductible. The deductible amount is shown on the information return sent to you. You may claim the deduction even if you do not claim excess itemized deductions. On Form 1040, the line for deducting forfeited interest is included in the section "Adjustments to Income" as "penalty on early withdrawal of savings."

Loss on redemption before maturity. If you redeem a long-term savings certificate for a price less than the stated redemption price at maturity, you are allowed a loss deduction for the amount of original issue discount reported as income but not received. The amount of the loss is the excess of (1) the original issue discount reported as income for the period you held the certificate over (2) the excess of the amount received upon the redemption over the issue price. Do not include in the computation any amount based on a fixed rate of simple or compound interest which is actually payable or is treated as constructively received at fixed periodic intervals of one year or less. Basis of the obligation is reduced by the amount of the deductible loss.

Example—

In 1983, you buy a four-year savings certificate from a building and loan corporation for $4,000 redeemable on December 31, 1987, for $5,000. The original issue discount is $1,000 of which $250 is reported each year. In 1986, when you redeem the certificate, you receive $4,660. In 1983, 1984 and 1985, you reported $250 of original issue discount for a total of $750. As the excess of $660 received on redemption is less than the original issue discount of $750 which was reported as income, the difference of $90 is a deductible loss claimed on Form 1040 on the line for entry "Penalty on early withdrawal of savings."

Partial redemption. Under the terms of a plan, you may be allowed to withdraw principal but not interest. In such a case,

when you withdraw principal, you may be entitled to deduct a loss based on part of the previously reported interest. Ask your bank for a computation of your tax and investment position or check Treasury regulations for details of the computation.

¶4.02 • INTEREST INCOME ON DEBTS OWED YOU

You report interest earned on money which you loan to another person. If you are on the cash basis, you report interest in the year you actually receive it or when it is considered received under the "constructive receipt rule," see ¶5.01. If you are on the accrual basis, you report interest when it is earned, whether or not you have received it.

See ¶4.10 for minimum interest rates required for loans and ¶4.03 when OID rules apply.

Where partial payment is being made on a debt or a debt is being compromised, the parties may agree in advance what part of the payment covers interest and principal. If a payment is not identified as either principal or interest, the payment is first applied against interest due and reported as interest income to the extent of the interest due.

Interest income is not realized when a debtor gives a new note for an old note including the interest due on the old note. The new note is not considered a payment of the interest.

If you give away obligations, you report as income collectible interest due at the date of the gift. To avoid tax on the interest, the obligations must be transferred before interest becomes due.

¶4.03 • REPORTING INTEREST ON BONDS BOUGHT OR SOLD DURING THE YEAR

Where you buy or sell bonds between interest dates, interest is included in the price of the bonds. The purchaser does not report as income interest accrued before he owned the bond. (The purchaser reduces the basis of the bond by the accrued interest reported by the seller.) The seller reports the accrued amount. The following examples illustrate these rules.

Examples—

1. *Purchase.* On April 30, you buy a $5,000 corporate bond bearing interest at 12% per year, payable January 1 and July 1. The purchase price of the bond included accrued interest of $200.

Interest received 7/1	$300
Less: Accrued interest	200
Taxable interest	$100

Form 1099 sent to you includes accrued interest. On Schedule B, you report the total amount of interest of $300 and also subtract the accrued interest of $200 paid to the seller with the note "Accrued Interest."

2. *Sale.* On April 30, you sell for $3,125 a $5,000 3% bond with interest payable January 1 and July 1. You receive $3,175.

Sales price of the bond	$3,125
Accrued interest from Jan. 1 to Apr. 30	50
You receive	$3,175

You report interest of $50.

On a redemption, interest received in excess of the amount due at that time is not treated as interest income.
Example—
You hold a $5,000 9% bond with interest payable January 1 and July 1. The company can call the bonds for redemption on any interest date. In May 1986, the company announces it will redeem the bonds on July 1. But you may present the bond for redemption beginning with June 1 and it will be redeemed with interest to July 1. On June 1 you present the bond and receive $5,225: $5,000 principal, $187.50 interest to June 1, and $37.50 extra interest to July 1. The $37.50 is treated as a capital gain, not interest income. The $187.50 is interest.

Taxable interest may continue on bonds after the issuer becomes bankrupt if a guarantor continues to pay the interest when due. The loss on the bonds will occur only when they mature and are not redeemed or when they are sold below your cost. In the meantime, the interest received from the guarantor is taxed.

Bondholders exchanging their bonds for stock, securities, or other property in a tax-free reorganization, including a reorganization in bankruptcy, have interest income to the extent the property received is attributable to accrued but unpaid interest. See the Bankruptcy Tax Act of 1980 for further details.

Bonds selling at a flat price. When you buy bonds with defaulted interest at a "flat" price, a later payment of the defaulted interest is not taxed. It is a tax-free return of capital that reduces your cost of the bond. This rule applies only to interest in default at the time the bond is purchased. Interest that accrues after the date of your purchase is taxed as ordinary income.

The above rules also apply to contingent interest attributed to a period before you owned the bond. The payment of such interest is considered a return of capital; however, the payment of contingent interest covering a period during which you owned the bond is fully taxable.

Treatment of original issue discount on corporate and government obligations is discussed at ¶4.032 and ¶6.031.

¶4.031 • AMORTIZATION OF BOND PREMIUM

Bond premium is the extra amount paid for a bond in excess of its principal or face amount. You may elect to amortize bond premium and reduce basis or leave the basis of the bond unchanged. If you do not amortize the premium, you will realize a capital loss when the bond is redeemed at par or you sell it for less than you paid for it.
Examples—
1. On July 11, 1986 you pay $1,200 for a $1,000 bond which matures on July 1, 1996. You elect to amortize the premium. Amortization is allowed for the months you held the bond. You include the month of acquisition (July) since you held the bond for more than half of that month. Here, the number of months from acquisition to maturity is 120 months, which gives you a monthly amortization writeoff of $1.67 a month. In 1986, you may deduct amortization of $10: $167 × 6 months. Basis of the bond at the end of 1986 is $1,190 ($1,200 cost less $10 amortization).

If you hold the bond for all of 1987 you may claim a 1987 amortization deduction of $20: $1.67 × 12 months. The basis of the bond at the end of 1987 is $1,170 ($1,200 cost less $30 amortized in 1986 and 1987).

2. Several years ago, you bought a $1,000 corporate bond for $1,300. You did not amortize the premium of $300. The bond is redeemed at par. You realize a long-term loss of $300. The premium is treated as part of the basis of the bond.

Redemption proceeds	$1,000
Cost basis	1,300
Loss	($300)

If you choose to amortize, the election applies to all bonds owned by you at the beginning of the first year you make the choice, and to all bonds acquired thereafter. You make an election to amortize by taking the deduction on your tax return in the first year you decide to amortize the bond premium. If you file your return without claiming the deduction, you may not change your mind and make the election by filing an amended return or refund claim.

Amortizing the premium annually is usually the preferred method because it gives a current deduction against ordinary income, provided you claim itemized deductions. You deduct amortized bond premium as a miscellaneous deduction. You also reduce the cost basis of the bond by the amount of the premium taken as a deduction. If you hold the bond to maturity, the entire premium is amortized and you have neither gain nor loss on redemption of the bond. If you sell the bond at a gain (selling price exceeds your basis for the bond), you realize long-term capital gain if you hold the bond long term. A sale of the bond for less than its adjusted basis gives a capital loss.

Callable bonds. On fully taxable bonds bought after 1957, amortization is based on either the maturity or earlier call date, depending on which date gives a smaller yearly deduction. This rule applies regardless of the issue date of the bond. If the bond is called before maturity, you may deduct as an ordinary loss the unamortized bond premium in the year the bond is redeemed.
Examples—
1. On January 1, 1981, you pay $1,200 for a $1,000 bond which matures on December 31, 2000. The bond is callable on January 1, 1986 at $1,165. The premium computed with reference to the maturity date is $200 ($1,200 − $1,000). The premium computed with reference to the earlier call date is $35 ($1,200 − $1,165). The premium of $200 gives a yearly deduction ($200 divided by 20 years). The premium of $35 gives a yearly deduction of $7 ($35 divided by 5 years). You amortize to the earlier call date because that gives a lower yearly deduction until 1986. If the bond is not called by then, the deduction for each taxable year from 1986 to the end of 2000 will be $11 ($165 divided by 15 years).
2. Use the same figures as in Example 1, but say the earlier call date is January 1, 1985. You amortize the premium based on the maturity date. This gives you a lower deduction than if you used the period of the earlier call date.

If you paid a premium for a convertible bond, the premium allocated to the conversion feature may not be amortized.

Tax-exempt bonds. You may not take a deduction for the amortization of premium paid on a tax-exempt bond. When you dispose of the bond, you amortize the premium for the period you held the bond and reduce the basis of the bond by the amortized amount.

If the bond has call dates, the IRS may require the premium to be amortized to the earliest call date.
Example—
In 1977, a tax-exempt bond par $1,000 is bought for $1,055. Between January 1, 1978, and December 31, 1979, it is callable at $105; between January 1, 1980, and December 31, 1981, at $104; between January 1, 1982, and December 31, 1987, at $103; it matures on January 1, 1988, at par. Amortization is figured as follows:

1. $5 is amortizable in 1977.
2. $10 is amortizable over 1978 and 1979.
3. $10 is amortizable over 1980 and 1981.
4. $30 is amortizable over 1982 through 1987.

If the bond were sold on December 31, 1986, the basis of the bond would be reduced by $50 to $1,005.

Premium paid on bonds with original issue discount. The premium may be amortized on the straight line method over the remaining term of a bond bought on or before July 18, 1984. For bonds bought after July 18, 1984, the premium is amortized by reducing original issue discount by a fraction. The numerator of the fraction is the premium; the denominator is the amount of OID still remaining on the bond at the time of purchase.

¶4.032 • Discount on Bonds and Other Obligations

There are two types of bond discounts:

Original issue discount (OID). OID arises when a bond is issued for a price less than its face or principal amount. OID is the difference between the principal amount and the issue price. For publicly offered obligations, the issue price is the initial offering price to the public at which a substantial amount of such obligations was sold. All obligations that pay no interest before maturity, such as zero coupon bonds, are considered to be issued at a discount. For example, a bond with a face amount of $1,000 is issued at an offering price of $900. The $100 difference is OID. Depending on the issue date of the bond, you may have to report a portion of the OID as interest income each year. OID is explained at ¶4.0321 for publicly offered corporate and government bonds and ¶4.033 for private obligations.

Market discount. Market discount arises when the price of a bond declines because its interest rate is less than the current interest rate. For example, a bond originally issued at its face amount of $1,000 declines in value to $900 because the interest payable on the bond is less than the current interest rate. The difference of $100 is called market discount. The tax treatment of market discount is explained in ¶4.034.

Form 1099-OID. For bonds with a term of more than one year, the issuer of the bond will send you Form 1099-OID, reporting the amount of OID which is taxable as interest for the year. Discount on obligations with a term of one year or less is reported as interest on Form 1099-INT. In some cases, the amount on Form 1099-OID may have to be reduced to avoid reporting too much income, for example, if you do not own the bond for the entire period covered by the reported OID, see ¶4.0321. If you

are reporting less OID than shown on Form 1099-OID, first include in the interest schedule the full amount of OID listed on the Form 1099-OID; then subtract from the total the OID you are not required to report.

If you do not receive a Form 1099-OID for 1986, contact the issuer to obtain the amount or check IRS Publication 1212, which lists OID amounts for publicly offered OID instruments as well as rules for figuring OID.

Original discount bond bought at premium. If you pay more than face amount for a bond originally issued at a discount, you do not report OID as ordinary income. When you dispose of a bond bought at a premium, the difference between the sale or redemption price and your basis is a capital gain or loss, *see ¶4.031.*

Exceptions to OID. OID rules do not apply to: (1) Obligations with a term of one year or less; (2) tax-exempt obligations; (3) U.S. savings bonds; (4) an obligation issued by an individual before March 2, 1984, and (5) loans of $10,000 or less from individuals that come within the rules of ¶4.033.

You may disregard OID that is less than one fourth of one percent of the principal amount multiplied by the number of full years from the rate of original issue to maturity. On most long-term bonds, the OID will exceed this amount and will have to be reported.

Examples—

1. A 10-year bond with face amount of $1,000 is issued at $980. One fourth of one percent of $1,000 times 10 is $25. As the $20 OID is less than $25, it may be ignored for tax purposes.

2. Same facts as in (1) except that the bond is issued at $950. As OID of $50 is more than the $25, OID must be reported under the rules explained at ¶4.032.

¶4.033 • REPORTING ORIGINAL ISSUE DISCOUNT (OID) ON PUBLICLY OFFERED OBLIGATIONS

Rule for—	Example—
Corporate obligations issued after 1954 but before May 28, 1969 and government obligations issued before July 2, 1982 You pay no tax on the OID until the year the obligation is disposed of. If a gain results and the obligation is a capital asset, part of the OID is taxed as ordinary income, part capital gain. If there is a loss on the disposition, the entire loss is capital loss; no OID is taxed. The amount of gain treated as ordinary income is figured as follows: $$\frac{\text{Number of full months you held the bond}}{\text{Number of full months from date of original issue to date of maturity}} \times \text{OID} = \text{Ordinary Income}$$	1. On the original issue date of February 1, 1966, you purchased a 30-year 5% bond for $910, a $90 discount from the face amount of $1,000. You sell the bond on February 20, 1986 for $950. You have held the bond for 240 full months; the additional days amounting to less than a full month are not counted. The number of complete months from date of issue to date of maturity is 360 (30 years). Multiplying the fraction 240/360 by the discount of $90 gives $60, the OID attributable to your holding period. Therefore, on the sale in 1986 the entire gain of $40 is ordinary income since it is less than the allocable $60 OID. 2. Same facts as in (1) except that you sell the bond for $980. Here $60 of the $70 gain is ordinary income, the balance of $10 is long-term capital gain. 3. Same facts as in (1) except you sold for $800. You have a long-term capital loss of $110. 4. Same facts as in (1) except that the bond is bought by Jones on February 1, 1986 for $800. He keeps it to the maturity date (February 1, 1986) when it is redeemed for $1,000. Jones held the bond for 120 full months and on redemption, has $30 ordinary income (⅓ of $90) and $170 long-term capital gain.

(continued next page)

¶4.033 • REPORTING OID ON PUBLICLY OFFERED OBLIGATIONS

Rule for—	Example—

Corporate obligations issued after May 27, 1969 and before July 2, 1982

If you held the bond as a capital asset, you report OID as income and increase the basis of the bond by the amount of OID reported. For each year you hold the bond, you report the ratable monthly portion of OID.

If you bought the bond at OID and held it for all of 1986 or the part of 1986 they were outstanding, report the total OID from Form 1099-OID. If you bought it at issue and it was outstanding for all of 1986 but you did not hold it for all of 1986 figure taxable OID by dividing the total OID by 12 and multiplying the result by the number of complete and partial months you held it in 1986.

If you bought it after original issue, the OID shown on Form 1099-OID may not be the correct amount for you to report. For example, your purchase price exceeded the original issue price (but less than redemption price) and included the amount of accumulated OID from the date of issue. Here, the excess (called acquisition premium) reduces the amount of OID you report. In this case, you must recalculate OID. *Step 1:* Divide the OID by 12 to figure the ratable monthly portion. *Step 2:* Subtract from your cost the issue price and the amount of accumulated OID from the date of issue. If the result is zero or less, do not reduce the ratable monthly portion. *Step 3:* Divide (2) by the number of complete months and any part of a month from the date of your purchase to the stated maturity date. *Step 4:* Subtract (3) from (1). The amount you report as income each month is (1) or (4), whichever is less.

If you buy or sell an obligation on any day other than the day of the month that is the same as the date of original issue, you divide the ratable monthly portion of OID between you and the seller or the buyer, according to the number of days each of you held the obligation. Your holding period begins the day you acquired the obligation and ends the day before you dispose of it.

1. On June 1, 1982, 10-year bonds at 95% of principal amount were issued. On February 1, 1986, you bought for $9,683 a $10,000 bond. Form 1099-OID lists OID of $50. Here you bought the bonds for an amount equal to the original issue price plus accumulated OID. In 1986, $45.87 is taxed ($4.17 monthly OID times 11 months). In the interest schedule, you report $50 and then reduce the amount by $4.17.

2. Same facts as in (1) except that you buy the bonds for $9,450. You report $45.87, even though you paid less than the original issue price.

3. Same facts as in (1) except that you pay more than $9,683. Here the premium may reduce the amount of the OID following the steps outlined in the left column.

4. On June 1, 1982, a bond was issued for $9,040, redeemable in four years at a stated redemption price of $10,000. OID is $960, the monthly OID is $20 ($960 ÷ 40). You buy the bond on September 16, 1985 for $9,830 ($9,040 issue price plus $740 accumulated OID from the date of issue). You sell it on March 15, 1986. OID included in 1985 was as follows:

September (half)	$10
Three months (Oct., Nov., Dec.)	60
	$70

The OID in 1986 is as follows:

Jan., Feb. ($20 × 2 months)	$40
March (half)	10
	$50

You increase basis by OID reported. Basis of bond at the time of sale is $9,950 ($9,830 cost plus $120 OID).

Corporate and government obligations issued after July 1, 1982, and before January 1, 1985

The amount of the reportable OID is based on the daily portion of the increase in the adjusted price of the bond. If you held the bond as a capital asset for all of 1986, or it was outstanding for only part of 1986 and you held it for the entire period, report the total OID from Form 1099-OID. If the obligation was outstanding for all of 1986 but you did not hold it for the entire year, figure taxable OID by dividing the total OID by 365 and multiplying the result by the number of days you held it in 1986.

If you bought the obligation after its original issue, the amount of OID on Form 1099-OID may not be the correct amount for you. For figuring OID in such a case, see IRS Publication 1212.

Basis in the bond is increased by the OID reported on income. The daily portion of OID for the initial accrual period is computed by applying the following formula:

$$\frac{\text{(Issue Price} \times \text{Yield to Maturity)} - \text{Stated Interest}}{\text{Number of Days in the Accrual Period}}$$

The daily portion of OID for later accrual periods is computed in the same manner except that the issue price is increased by OID reported in earlier years.

1. On January 1, 1985, you bought a 20-year 13% bond for $90,000 at original issue. The redemption price of the bond is $100,000. The bond has a yield to maturity of 15%. The daily portion of OID for the first accrual period (January 1, 1985 through December 31, 1985) is figured as follows:

$$\frac{(90,000 \times 15\%) - \$13,000}{366} = \frac{500}{366} = \$1.3661$$

For 1985, you should have reported as income $1.3661 for each day you held the bond during 1985. If you held the bond for all of 1985, you reported $500 in income. In 1986 the daily portion of OID is figured on the bond's basis of $90,500:

$$\frac{(\$90,500 \times 15\%) - \$13,000}{365} = \frac{575}{365} = \$1.5753$$

If you hold the bond for all of 1986, you report $575 in income ($1.5753 × 365).

Corporate and government obligations issue after December 31, 1984

OID is reported without regard to whether you hold the obligation as a capital asset. Further, OID is computed for six-month accrual periods that generally correspond to the maturity date of the obligation and to the date which is six months before such maturity date (or the shorter period from date of issue). For example, if a bond issued April 1, 1985 matures January 1, 1987, the first six-month period for which OID must be computed is April 1, 1985 to June 30, 1985; the second is July 1, 1985 to December 31, 1985; the third January 1, 1986 to June 30, 1986 and the fourth July 1, 1986 to December 31, 1986.

See IRS Publication 1212.

¶4.034 • REPORTING INCOME ON MARKET DISCOUNT BONDS

Market discount arises where the price of a bond declines below its face amount because it carries an interest rate that is below the current rate of interest. The treatment of market discount depends on the issue date of the bond.

Bonds issued before July 19, 1984. Gain attributable to the market discount on the sale of the bond *issued* before July 19, 1984 is generally treated as capital gain. However, you may have ordinary income if you borrow money to purchase or carry a market discount bond acquired after July 18, 1984. Under a restrictive rule discussed below, your interest deduction on the loan is limited. In the year you dispose of the bond, you may claim an interest deduction for any interest expense that could not be deducted in prior years under the restrictive rule. To the extent of this deduction, gain on the disposition is ordinary income; the balance is capital gain.

Example—

In 1983, you paid $910 for a bond that had been originally issued at its face amount of $1,000. The difference of $90 is market discount. In 1986, you sell the bond for $980. The $70 profit is long-term capital gain.

Bonds issued after July 18, 1984. Gain on a bond *issued* after July 18, 1984 is taxed as ordinary interest income to the extent of the market discount accrued to the date of sale. The daily accrual is figured by dividing market discount by the number of days in the period from the date you bought the bond until the date of maturity. This method of computing the daily accrual is called the ratable accrual method.

Example—

Market discount on a bond issued after July 18, 1984 is $200, and there are 1,000 days between the date of your purchase and maturity date. The daily accrual rate is twenty cents. You hold the bond for 600 days before selling it for a price exceeding what you paid for the bond. Under the ratable accrual method, up to $120 of your profit is market discount taxable as interest income (600 × $.20).

Exceptions to ordinary income rules. The following bonds are not subject to the ordinary income rules for market discount bonds: (1) bonds acquired after July 18, 1984 that were issued on or before that date; (2) bonds maturing within one year of issuance; (3) tax-exempt obligations; (4) installment obligations; and (4) U.S. Savings Bonds. Further, you may treat as zero any market discount that is less than one-fourth of one percent of the redemption price multiplied by the number of full years after you acquire the bond to maturity. Such minimal discount will not affect capital gain on a sale.

Instead of using the ratable accrual method to compute accrual of market discount, you may elect to figure the accrued discount under the constant rate method. If you make the election, you may not change the election. The complex constant rate method is explained in IRS Publication 1212.

Electing to report market discount rate currently. Rather than report market discount in the year you sell the bond, you may elect to report market discount currently as interest income. You may use either the ratable accrual method or the constant interest rate method explained in IRS Publication 1212.

Example—

The same figures as in the above example. During a taxable year, you held the bond for 300 days. You elect to report the market discount currently. Under the ratable accrual method, you report $60 as interest income (300 × $20).

Your election to report currently applies to all market discount bonds issued after July 18, 1984 that you later acquire. You may not revoke the election without the IRS consent.

Market discount on a bond originally issued at a discount. A bond issued at original issue discount may later be acquired at a market discount because of an increase in interest rates. If you acquire at market discount an OID bond issued after July 18, 1984, the market discount is the difference between what you paid for the bond and the sum of the issue price of the bond and the total original issue discount includible in the gross income of all prior holders of the bond.

Interest deduction limited if you borrow to buy market discount bonds after July 18, 1984. If you took such a loan, your interest expense deduction is generally limited to the excess of the interest expense over the interest income earned on the bond for the year (including OID income, if any) *less* any market discount allocated to the days you held the bond during the year. The limitation on the interest deduction applies to bonds you acquire after July 18, 1984 regardless of the issue date of the bond. The allocation of market discount follows the rules explained above.

Example—

In 1986, you borrowed to buy a market discount bond. During 1986, your interest expense is $1,000. Income from the bond is $900 and ratable market discount allocated to the annual holding period is $75. You may deduct interest of $25 ($1,000 − $975) on your 1986 return.

In the year the bond is disposed of, you may deduct any interest expense disallowed in prior years because of the limitation. However, in a year in which you have net interest income from the bond, you may choose to deduct disallowed interest in expense before the year of disposition. Net interest income is interest income for the year less the interest expense incurred during the year. This election lets you deduct any disallowed interest expense to the extent it does not exceed the net interest income of that year. The balance of the disallowed interest expense is deductible in the year of disposition.

Exception. If you elect to report ratably market discount on bonds issued after July 18, 1984, the above limitations on the interest deduction do not apply.

¶4.035 • DISCOUNT ON SHORT-TERM OBLIGATIONS

Short-term obligations (maturity of a year or less) may be purchased at a discount from face. If you are on the cash basis, interest income is realized when the obligation is paid. The interest is reported on Form 1099-INT.

Example—

In May 1985, you paid $920 for a short-term note with a face amount of $1,000. In January 1986, you receive payment of $1,000 on the net. On your 1986 tax return, you report $80 as interest.

Accrual basis taxpayers report as income that part of the discount allocated to the period the note was held during the taxable year. For short-term obligations acquired after July 18, 1984, accrual basis taxpayers accrue the discount following the daily ratable accrual method explained in ¶4.03 above. The accrual rule also applies to short-term discount on an obligation held primarily for sale to customers in the ordinary course of your trade or business, by a bank, regulated investment company, or common trust fund, by certain pass through entities, or identified as part of a hedging transaction.

¶4.036 • STRIPPED COUPON BONDS

To create tax losses, investors holding coupon bonds separated or stripped the coupons from the bonds and sold either the bonds or coupons. A law bars a deduction for such losses on bonds bought or sold after July 1, 1982. However, for certain investment purposes, brokers continue to offer stripped bonds and coupons for sale.

If you buy a stripped bond or coupon, the spread between the lower cost of the bond or coupon and its face amount is treated as original issue discount. This means that you annually report a part of the spread as explained in ¶4.032. For a stripped bond, the amount of the original issue discount is the difference between the stated redemption price of the bond at maturity and the cost of the bond. For a stripped coupon, the amount of the discount is the difference between the amount payable on the due date of the coupon and the cost of the coupon.

If you strip a coupon bond, interest accrual and allocation rules prevent you from creating a tax loss. You are required to report interest accrued up to the date of the sale and also add the amount to the basis of the bond. You then allocate this basis between the bond and the coupons. The allocation is based on the relative fair market values of the bond and coupons at the date of sale. Gain or loss on the sale is the difference between the sales price of the stripped item (bond or coupons) and its allocated basis. Furthermore, the original issue discount rules apply to the stripped item which you keep (bond or coupon). Original issue discount for this purpose is the difference between the basis allo-cated to the retained item and the redemption price of the bond (if retained) or the amount payable on the coupons (if retained). You annually report a ratable portion of the discount under the rules of ¶4.032.

Tax-Free Interest on State and Local Government Bonds and Obligations

¶4.04 • EXEMPT CITY AND STATE INTEREST

You pay no tax on interest on these types of obligations—

Bonds or notes of states, cities, counties, the District of Columbia, a possession of the United States.

Bonds or notes of port authorities, toll road commissions, utility services authorities and other similar bodies created to perform public functions.

Written agreement of purchase and sale to a political subdivision of a state under which deferred payments with interest were made.

Public improvement bonds, even though general funds or the credit of the city are not to be used in payment if the city is directly liable to pay out of special assessments.

Temporary loan notes of local housing authorities created under state law.

State reclamation district bonds—even if you own considerable land in the district. It makes no difference that the deductible taxes you pay the district are used to pay the interest on the bonds, but there must be a substantial number of bonds owned by others.

Proceeds of sale before maturity of certificates of indebtedness received in lieu of interest in connection with a refunding of a city's obligations.

Interest on industrial development bonds issued by localities may or may not be tax exempt depending on the date of issue and other facts. Check with the issuer about the tax status of the interest. Interest on such bonds issued before May 1, 1968, is generally tax free.

The IRS requires tax-exempt interest to be listed in the interest schedule on your return if a Form 1099-INT is received for the interest. An offsetting reduction must also be claimed on the schedule so that the listed interest is not subject to tax. *See* the Supplement to this book.

Bonds issued after June 30, 1983 must be in registered form to qualify to pay tax-exempt interest.

¶4.05 • CITY AND STATE INTEREST NOT EXEMPT

You pay tax on this interest—

Proceeds from sale of coupons detached from tax-exempt bonds.

Interest paid on open accounts for purchases by the communities without specific agreements.

Interest paid on notes issued by volunteer fire companies.

Tax sale certificates.

Proceeds of a municipal bond bought in the open market (not from issuing city) at a discount. The difference between the purchase price and the maturity price is capital gain.

Mortgage subsidy bonds. Interest on bonds issued by a state or local government after April 24, 1979, may not be tax exempt if funds raised by the bonds are used for home mortgages. There are exceptions for certain qualified mortgage bonds and veterans' bonds and for certain issues. Check on the tax-exempt status of mortgage bonds with the issuing authority.

¶4.06 • TAX-EXEMPT BONDS BOUGHT AT A DISCOUNT

Gain attributed to original issue discount is tax-exempt; gain attributed to market discount is taxable income.

Market discount. This arises when a bond originally issued at not less than par is bought at below par. If you sell a tax-exempt bond purchased at a market discount for a price exceeding your purchase price, the excess is taxable gain. If the bond was held long term, the gain is long term. A redemption of the bond at a price exceeding your purchase price is similarly treated. The market discount rules of ¶4.034 do not apply to tax exempts.

Original issue discount. This arises when a bond is issued for a price less than the face amount of the bond. The discount is considered tax-exempt interest. Thus, if you are the original buyer and hold the bond to maturity, the entire amount of the discount is tax free. If you sell the bond before maturity, the amount of tax-free discount is based on the period of your holding compared to the period from issue date to maturity date. A succeeding holder of the bond may treat as tax-free income the remaining discount allocated up to the time he disposes of the bond. Depending on the issue and acquisition date, the allocation of OID may be on the straight line or economic constant interest method. The economic constant interest method applies to obligations issued after September 3, 1982 and acquired after March 1, 1984. Under this method, less discount accrues in the early years than under the straight line method.

Example—

In 1980, you bought a 10-year $1,000 state bond issued at $950. In 1986, you sell it for $985. Under the straight line method, you treat 60% (6/10) of the $50 discount or $30 as tax-free income. You also have a long-term gain of $5.

Amount realized on sale	$985
Less: Tax-free original issue discount	30
	$955
Cost basis	950
Taxable gain	$ 5

When bonds are redeemed before maturity, the same rule applies: That portion of original issue discount earned to the date of redemption is tax-free interest; the balance is capital gain. Bonds issued with an intention to redeem before maturity are not subject to this rule: All interest is tax exempt.

Amortization of premiums is discussed at ¶4.031.

¶4.07 • Interest on U.S. Obligations

Interest on securities issued by the federal government is fully taxable on your federal return. However, interest on federal obligations is not subject to state income taxes. Interest on Treasury bills, notes and bonds is reported on Form 1099-INT.

Treasury bonds and notes. You report the fixed or coupon interest as interest income in the year the coupon becomes due and payable. Treasury bonds and notes are capital assets; gain or loss on their sale, exchange, or redemption is reported as capital gain or loss in Schedule D (*see* ¶6.00). If you purchased a federal obligation below par (at a discount) after July 1, 1982, *see* ¶4.032 for the rules on reporting original issue discount. If you purchased a Treasury bond or note above par (at a premium), you may elect to amortize the premium (*see* ¶4.031). If you do not elect to amortize and you hold the bond or note to maturity, you have a capital loss.

Treasury bills. These are short-term U.S. obligations issued at a discount with maturities of three, six, or twelve months. Treasury bills are capital assets and a loss on the disposition is taxed as a capital loss. If there is a gain on a sale or exchange, ordinary income is realized up to the amount of the ratable share of the discount received when you bought the obligation. This amount is treated as interest income and is figured as follows:

$$\frac{\text{Days T-bill was held}}{\begin{array}{c}\text{Days from acquisition}\\\text{to maturity}\end{array}} \times \begin{array}{c}\text{T-bill's value at}\\\text{maturity minus your}\\\text{cost}\end{array}$$

Any gain over this amount is capital gain. Thus, if a six-month Treasury bill is held for four months and sold at a gain two months before maturity, the gain is taxed as ordinary income to the extent of two-thirds of the discount. Any excess gain is short-term capital gain.

On a bill held to maturity, you report as interest the difference between the discounted price and the amount you receive on a redemption of the bills at maturity.

You may postpone the receipt of interest income this year by selecting a Treasury bill maturing next year. Income is not recognized until the date on which the Treasury bill is paid at maturity, unless it has been sold or otherwise disposed of earlier.

Accrual basis taxpayers are required to report ratably the acquisition discount element on Treasury bills acquired after July 18, 1984 using the ratable accrual method explained in ¶4.034. An irrevocable election to accrue under a special accrual formula is also available.

Interest incurred on loans used to buy Treasury bills after July 18, 1984 is deductible by a cash basis investor only to the extent that interest expenses exceed the acquisition discount for each day during the year that the bill is held. The deferred interest expense is deductible in the year the bill is disposed of. If an election is made to report ratably acquisition discount, the expense may also be deducted ratably. The election applies to all future acquisitions.

¶4.08 • HOW U.S. SAVINGS BOND INTEREST IS TAXED

Series E and EE. These bonds may be cashed for what you paid for them plus an increase in their value over stated periods of time. The increase in redemption value is taxed as interest. You do not have to report the annual increase in value. You may defer the interest income until the year in which you cash the bond or the year in which the bond finally matures, whichever is earlier. But if you want, you may report the annual increase by merely including it on your tax return. If you own bonds which have increased in value in prior years and make an election to report annual increases this year, make sure you report the total of all these increases in value. But next year, report only the increases accruing then, plus increases accruing on bonds newly purchased. That is, once you make the election you must continue reporting annual increases unless you get IRS permission to change your method of reporting. If you use the accrual method of reporting, you must include the interest each year as it accrues.

Suppose you do not include the annual increase on your return and later change your mind. If the due date of the return has passed, it is too late to make the election. You may not file an amended return reporting the increase in value for that year. You have to wait until next year's return to make the election.

E Bonds may be held for additional periods of maturity after their initial maturity dates. Bonds held for additional periods increase in value and may be cashed in at any time. If you chose to postpone paying tax on accumulated interest, you may continue to postpone the tax during the extended period. You would then report the entire accumulated interest at the final maturity date or in the year you redeem the bond, whichever occurs earlier. If you have reported the increase in value each year, you must continue to do that during the extended maturity periods. However, E-Bondholders may not indefinitely defer the tax on interest. E Bonds will cease earning interest once the bonds reach their final maturity date. For example, bonds issued during 1946 cease earning interest in 1986, 40 years from the date of issuance. On your

1986 return, you must pay tax on all the accumulated interest unless the bonds are traded for new HH Bonds in multiples of $500. Exchanging E Bonds for HH Bonds will continue the tax deferral on interest. *See* ¶30.07 for a listing of final maturity dates.

Bonds for child. Interest on savings bonds bought in the name of a child is taxed to the child, even if the parent paid for the bonds and is named as beneficiary. *See* ¶30.07.

If you redeem an E or EE bond you will receive a Form 1099-INT. The amount listed on the form reports the difference between the cost of the bond and the redemption price. This amount may not be correct if you or a prior owner reported interest in prior years. List the gross amount and then subtract the prior interest reported and describe the subtraction as "U.S. Saving Bond interest previously reported."

Series EE bonds will not earn interest beyond maturity. *See* ¶30.07.

Changing the form of registration. Changing the form of registration of an E or EE Bond may result in tax. Assume a father uses his own funds to purchase a bond issued in his name, payable on his death to his son. Later, at the father's request, a new bond is issued in the son's name only. The increased value of the original bond up to the date it was redeemed and reissued in the son's name is taxed as interest to the father.

The following changes in registration do not result in an immediate tax.
Examples—
1. Jones buys an E Bond and has it registered in his name and in the name of his son as co-owner. Jones has the bonds reissued solely in his own name; he is not required to report the accrued interest at that time.
2. You and your spouse each contributed an equal amount toward the purchase of a $1,000 E Bond which was issued to you as co-owners. You later have the bond reissued as two $500 bonds, one in your name and one in your spouse's name. Neither of you has to report the interest earned to the date of reissue.
3. You add another person's name as co-owner to facilitate a transfer of the bond on death. The change in registration does not result in a tax.

Co-owners of E and EE Bonds follow these rules:
1. You paid for the entire bond: Either you or the co-owner may redeem it. You are taxed on all the interest, even though the co-owner cashes the bond and you receive no proceeds.
2. You paid for only part of the bond: Either of you may redeem it. You are taxed on that part of the interest which is in proportion to your share of the purchase price. This is so even though you do not receive the proceeds.
3. You paid for part of the bond, and then had it reissued in another's name. You pay tax only on the interest accrued while you held the bond. The new co-owner picks up his share of the interest accruing afterwards.
4. You and another person were named co-owners on a bond bought as a gift by a third party. You are taxed on 50% of the interest income; your co-owner on the remaining half.

Transfer of an E or EE Bond because of owner's death. The death of the original owner does not result in a taxable event for income tax purposes if that owner did not report the interest annually. The income tax liability on the interest accumulated during the deceased's lifetime passes to the survivor unless an election is made to report the accrued interest in the decedent's final income tax return (*see* ¶1.14). If the election is made on the decedent's final return, the new owner is taxable on interest earned after the date of death.

Where an estate tax has been incurred, the new bondholder may claim a deduction for estate tax paid on the accrued interest included in the estate when he reports interest accumulated during the decedent's lifetime (*see* ¶11.03).

Transfer to a trust. If you transfer U.S. Savings Bonds to a trust giving up all rights of ownership, you are taxed on the interest to date of transfer. If, however, you are considered to be the owner of the trust and the interest earned before and after the transfer is taxable to you, you may continue to defer reporting the interest.

Transfer to a charity. Tax on the accumulated E or EE bond interest is not avoided by having the bonds reissued to a philanthropy. Further, tax may not be deferred by first converting E bonds to HH bonds and then reissuing the HH bonds in the philanthropy's name. The IRS held that by having the bonds reissued in the philanthropy's name, the owner realized taxable income on the accumulated bond interest.

Interest on U.S. Savings bonds transferred by spouses in a divorce or settlement is not subject to tax because of the transfer. *See* ¶6.245.

Treasury regulations on transferring E or EE Bonds. Assume you have bought E or EE Bonds and had them registered in joint names of yourself and your daughter. The law of your state provides that jointly-owned property may effectively be transferred to a co-owner by delivery or possession. You deliver the bonds to your daughter and tell her they now belong to her alone. According to Treasury regulations, this is not a valid gift of the bonds. The bonds must be surrendered and reissued in your daughter's name.

If you do not have the bonds reissued and you die, the bonds are taxable in your estate. Ownership of the bonds is a matter of contract between the United States and the purchaser of the bonds. The bonds are nontransferrable. A valid gift cannot be accomplished by manual delivery to a donee unless the bonds also are surrendered and reissued in the name of the donee in accordance with Treasury regulations.

Reporting interest on Freedom shares must be the same as the method used for reporting E Bonds.

Series H. These bonds were available before 1980. They were bought at face value and pay semi-annual interest that is taxable when received. Do you own Series H Bonds purchased through the exchange of Series E or J Bonds, interest on which you did not report annually? You do not have to report the interest due on the old bonds until the H Bonds are redeemed or mature, whichever occurs first. Interest earned on Series H Bonds is taxable in the year received.

If you receive cash when exchanging E Bonds for H Bonds, you report the cash received as interest income to the extent of the interest earned on the bonds exchanged.

H bonds purchased before July, 1959 will cease earning interest when they mature between February, 1982 and May, 1989. Final maturity dates are listed at ¶30.07. These matured bonds may not be traded but must be cashed in. You report the accumulated interest in the year the bond matures.

Series HH. These bonds are issued at face value and pay semi-annual interest that is taxable when received.

Form 1099-INT for U.S. Savings Bonds interest. When you cash in an E or EE bond, you receive Form 1099-INT that lists as interest the difference between the amount received and the amount paid for the bond. The form may show more taxable interest than you are required to report because you have regularly reported the interest or a prior owner reported the interest. Report the full amount shown on Form 1099-INT on the interest schedule of your return and then, on the same schedule, reduce the amount by the interest previously reported and identify the reduction as "previously reported interest."

U.S. SAVINGS BONDS. SERIES EE—REDEMPTION VALUES BY DENOMINATION—DEC. 1986

ISSUE YEAR	ISSUE MONTHS	$50	$75	$100	$200	$500	$1,000	$5,000	$10,000
1986	July thru Dec.	NOT ELIGIBLE FOR PAYMENT							
	June	25.52	38.28	51.04	102.08	255.20	510.40	2,552.00	5,104.00
	May	25.64	38.46	51.28	102.56	256.40	512.80	2,564.00	5,128.00
	Apr.	25.78	38.67	51.56	103.12	257.80	515.60	2,578.00	5,156.00
	Mar.	25.94	38.91	51.88	103.76	259.40	518.80	2,594.00	5,188.00
	Feb.	26.08	39.12	52.16	104.32	260.80	521.60	2,608.00	5,216.00
	Jan.	26.24	39.36	52.48	104.96	262.40	524.80	2,624.00	5,248.00
1985	Dec.	26.40	39.60	52.80	105.60	264.00	528.00	2,640.00	5,280.00
	Nov.	26.54	39.81	53.08	106.16	265.40	530.80	2,654.00	5,308.00
	Oct.	26.68	40.02	53.36	106.72	266.80	533.60	2,668.00	5,336.00
	Sep.	26.80	40.20	53.60	107.20	268.00	536.00	2,680.00	5,360.00
	Aug.	26.94	40.41	53.88	107.76	269.40	538.80	2,694.00	5,388.00
	July	27.08	40.62	54.16	108.32	270.80	541.60	2,708.00	5,416.00
	Jan. thru June	27.22	40.83	54.44	108.88	272.20	544.40	2,722.00	5,444.00
1984	July thru Dec.	28.14	42.21	56.28	112.56	281.40	562.80	2,814.00	5,628.00
	Jan. thru June	29.16	43.74	58.32	116.64	291.60	583.20	2,916.00	5,832.00
1983	July thru Dec.	30.30	45.45	60.60	121.20	303.00	606.00	3,030.00	6,060.00
	Jan. thru June	31.54	47.31	63.08	126.16	315.40	630.80	3,154.00	6,308.00
1982	Nov. thru Dec.	32.94	49.41	65.88	131.76	329.40	658.80	3,294.00	6,588.00
	July thru Oct.	34.22	51.33	68.44	136.88	342.20	684.40	3,422.00	6,844.00
	Jan. thru June	35.96	53.94	71.92	143.84	359.60	719.20	3,596.00	7,192.00
1981	July thru Dec.	37.90	56.85	75.80	151.60	379.00	758.00	3,790.00	7,580.00
	May thru June	39.72	59.58	79.44	158.88	397.20	794.40	3,972.00	7,944.00
	Jan. thru Apr.	39.48	59.22	78.96	157.92	394.80	789.60	3,948.00	7,896.00
1980	Nov. thru Dec.	41.36	62.04	82.72	165.44	413.60	827.20	4,136.00	8,272.00
	July thru Oct.	40.98	61.47	81.96	163.92	409.80	819.60	4,098.00	8,196.00
	May thru June	42.92	64.38	85.84	171.68	429.20	858.40	4,292.00	8,584.00
	Jan. thru Apr.	42.50	63.75	85.00	170.00	425.00	850.00	4,250.00	8,500.00

U.S. SAVINGS BONDS, SERIES E—REDEMPTION VALUES BY DENOMINATION—DEC. 1986

ISSUE YEAR	ISSUE MONTHS	$10	$25	$50	$75	$100	$200	$500	$1,000
1980	May thru June		31.29	62.58	93.87	125.16	250.32	625.80	1,251.60
	Jan. thru Apr.		30.98	61.96	92.94	123.92	247.84	619.60	1,239.20
1979	Nov. thru Dec.		32.14	64.28	96.42	128.56	257.12	642.80	1,285.60
	July thru Oct.		31.84	63.68	95.52	127.36	254.72	636.80	1,273.60
	June		33.03	66.06	99.09	132.12	264.24	660.60	1,321.20
	May		32.96	65.92	98.88	131.84	263.68	659.20	1,318.40
	Jan. thru Apr.		32.64	65.28	97.92	130.56	261.12	652.80	1,305.60
1978	Dec.		33.86	67.72	101.58	135.44	270.88	677.20	1,354.40
	Nov.		33.77	67.54	101.31	135.08	270.16	675.40	1,350.80
	July thru Oct.		33.45	66.90	100.35	133.80	267.60	669.00	1,338.00
	June		34.70	69.40	104.10	138.80	277.60	694.00	1,388.00
	May		34.61	69.22	103.83	138.44	276.88	692.20	1,384.40
	Jan. thru Apr.		34.29	68.58	102.87	137.16	274.32	685.80	1,371.60
1977	Dec.		35.58	71.16	106.74	142.32	284.64	711.60	1,423.20
	Nov.		35.48	70.96	106.44	141.92	283.84	709.60	1,419.20
	July thru Oct.		36.54	73.08	109.62	146.16	292.32	730.80	1,461.60
	June		38.09	76.18	114.27	152.36	304.72	761.80	1,523.60
	May		37.99	75.98	113.97	151.96	303.92	759.80	1,519.60
	Jan. thru Apr.		37.63	75.26	112.89	150.52	301.04	752.60	1,505.20
1976	Dec.		39.22	78.44	117.66	156.88	313.76	784.40	1,568.80
	Nov.		39.12	78.24	117.36	156.48	312.96	782.40	1,564.80
	July thru Oct.		38.76	77.52	116.28	155.04	310.08	775.20	1,550.40
	June		40.40	80.80	121.20	161.60	323.20	808.00	1,616.00
	May		40.31	80.62	120.93	161.24	322.48	806.20	1,612.40
	Jan. thru Apr.		39.92	79.84	119.76	159.68	319.36	798.40	1,596.80
1975	Dec.		41.61	83.22	124.83	166.44	332.88	832.20	1,664.40
	Nov.		41.53	83.06	124.59	166.12	332.24	830.60	1,661.20
	July thru Oct.		41.13	82.26	123.39	164.52	329.04	822.60	1,645.20
	June		42.87	85.74	128.61	171.48	342.96	857.40	1,714.80
	May		42.76	85.52	128.28	171.04	342.08	855.20	1,710.40
	Jan. thru Apr.		42.36	84.72	127.08	169.44	338.88	847.20	1,694.40
1974	Dec.		44.16	88.32	132.48	176.64	353.28	883.20	1,766.40
	Nov.		44.05	88.10	132.15	176.20	352.40	881.00	1,762.00
	July thru Oct.		43.63	87.26	130.89	174.52	349.04	872.60	1,745.20
	June		45.48	90.96	136.44	181.92	363.84	909.60	1,819.20
	May		45.38	90.76	136.14	181.52	363.04	907.60	1,815.20
	Jan. thru Apr.		44.95	89.90	134.85	179.80	359.60	899.00	1,798.00
1973	Dec.		46.85	93.70	140.55	187.40	374.80	937.00	1,874.00
	Sep. thru Nov.		45.71	91.42	137.13	182.84	365.68	914.20	1,828.40
	Aug.		47.65	95.30	142.95	190.60	381.20	953.00	1,906.00
	July		47.54	95.08	142.62	190.16	380.32	950.80	1,901.60
	June		47.08	94.16	141.24	188.32	376.64	941.60	1,883.20
	Mar. thru May		46.97	93.94	140.91	187.88	375.76	939.40	1,878.80
	Feb.		48.97	97.94	146.91	195.88	391.76	979.40	1,958.80
	Jan.		48.85	97.70	146.55	195.40	390.80	977.00	1,954.00
1972	Dec.		48.38	96.76	145.14	193.52	387.04	967.60	1,935.20
	Sep. thru Nov.		48.28	96.56	144.84	193.12	386.24	965.60	1,931.20
	Aug.		50.32	100.64	150.96	201.28	402.56	1,006.40	2,012.80
	July		50.21	100.42	150.63	200.84	401.68	1,004.20	2,008.40
	June		49.72	99.44	149.16	198.88	397.76	994.40	1,988.80
	Mar. thru May		49.60	99.20	148.80	198.40	396.80	992.00	1,984.00
	Feb.		51.69	103.38	155.07	206.76	413.52	1,033.80	2,067.60
	Jan.		51.58	103.16	154.74	206.32	412.64	1,031.60	2,063.20
1971	Dec.		51.08	102.16	153.24	204.32	408.64	1,021.60	2,043.20
	Sep. thru Nov.		50.95	101.90	152.85	203.80	407.60	1,019.00	2,038.00
	Aug.		53.13	106.26	159.39	212.52	425.04	1,062.60	2,125.20
	July		53.00	106.00	159.00	212.00	424.00	1,060.00	2,120.00
	June		52.49	104.98	157.47	209.96	419.92	1,049.80	2,099.60
	Mar. thru May		52.34	104.68	157.02	209.36	418.72	1,046.80	2,093.60
	Feb.		54.56	109.12	163.68	218.24	436.48	1,091.20	2,182.40
	Jan.		54.44	108.88	163.32	217.76	435.52	1,088.80	2,177.60
1970	Dec.		53.92	107.84	161.76	215.68	431.36	1,078.40	2,156.80
	Sep. thru Nov.		53.80	107.60	161.40	215.20	430.40	1,076.00	2,152.00
	Aug.		55.82	111.64	167.46	223.28	446.56	1,116.40	2,232.80
	July		55.68	111.36	167.04	222.72	445.44	1,113.60	2,227.20
	June		55.14	110.28	165.42	220.56	441.12	1,102.80	2,205.60
	Apr. thru May		54.88	109.76	164.64	219.52	439.04	1,097.60	2,195.20
	Feb.		56.94	113.88	170.82	227.76	455.52	1,138.80	2,277.60
	Jan.		56.80	113.60	170.40	227.20	454.40	1,136.00	2,272.00

U.S. SAVINGS BONDS, SERIES E—REDEMPTION VALUES BY DENOMINATION—DEC. 1986

ISSUE YEAR	ISSUE MONTHS	$10	$25	$50	$75	$100	$200	$500	$1,000
1969	Dec.		56.26	112.52	168.78	225.04	450.08	1,125.20	2,250.40
	Sep. thru Nov.		55.97	111.94	167.91	223.88	447.76	1,119.40	2,238.80
	Aug.		58.07	116.14	174.21	232.28	464.56	1,161.40	2,322.80
	July		57.94	115.88	173.82	231.76	463.52	1,158.80	2,317.60
	June		58.01	116.02	174.03	232.04	464.08	1,160.20	2,320.40
	Apr. thru May		57.45	114.90	172.35	229.80	459.60	1,149.00	2,298.00
1968	Dec.		59.60	119.20	178.80	238.40	476.80	1,192.00	2,384.00
	Nov.		58.80	117.60	176.40	235.20	470.40	1,176.00	2,352.00
	July thru Oct.		58.24	116.48	174.72	232.96	465.92	1,164.80	2,329.60
	June		60.43	120.86	181.29	241.72	483.44	1,208.60	2,417.20
	May		59.71	119.42	179.13	238.84	477.68	1,194.20	2,388.40
	Jan. thru Apr.		59.13	118.26	177.39	236.52	473.04	1,182.60	2,365.20
1967	Dec.		60.62	121.24	181.86	242.48	484.96	1,212.40	2,424.80
	Nov.		60.03	120.06	180.09	240.12	480.24	1,200.60	2,401.20
	July thru Oct.		60.24	120.48	180.72	240.96	481.92	1,204.80	2,409.60
	June		62.28	124.56	186.84	249.12	498.24	1,245.60	2,491.20
	May		61.61	123.22	184.83	246.44	492.88	1,232.20	2,464.40
	Jan. thru Apr.		61.02	122.04	183.06	244.08	488.16	1,220.40	2,440.80
1966	Dec.		63.31	126.62	189.93	253.24	506.48	1,266.20	2,532.40
	Nov.		62.61	125.22	187.83	250.44	500.88	1,252.20	2,504.40
	July thru Oct.		62.01	124.02	186.03	248.04	496.08	1,240.20	2,480.40
	June		64.34	128.68	193.02	257.36	514.72	1,286.80	2,573.60
	May		63.68	127.36	191.04	254.72	509.44	1,273.60	2,547.20
	Jan. thru Apr.		63.07	126.14	189.21	252.28	504.56	1,261.40	2,522.80
1965	Dec.		65.43	130.86	196.29	261.72	523.44	1,308.60	2,617.20
	Oct. thru Nov.		63.17	126.34	189.51	252.68	505.36	1,263.40	2,526.80
	Sep.		65.54	131.08	196.62	262.16	524.32	1,310.80	2,621.60
	June thru Aug.		64.58	129.16	193.74	258.32	516.64	1,291.60	2,583.20
	Apr. thru May		65.21	130.42	195.63	260.84	521.68	1,304.20	2,608.40
	Mar.		66.32	132.64	198.96	265.28	530.56	1,326.40	2,652.80
	Feb.		66.64	133.28	199.92	266.56	533.12	1,332.80	2,665.60
	Jan.		65.65	131.30	196.95	262.60	525.20	1,313.00	2,626.00
1964	Dec.		68.26	136.52	204.78	273.04	546.08	1,365.20	2,730.40
	Oct. thru Nov.		67.83	135.66	203.49	271.32	542.64	1,356.60	2,713.20
	Sep.		70.71	141.42	212.13	282.84	565.68	1,414.20	2,828.40
	Aug.		70.36	140.72	211.08	281.44	562.88	1,407.20	2,814.40
	June thru July		69.69	139.38	209.07	278.76	557.52	1,393.80	2,787.60
	Apr. thru May		69.24	138.48	207.72	276.96	553.92	1,384.80	2,769.60
	Mar.		72.19	144.38	216.57	288.76	577.52	1,443.80	2,887.60
	Feb.		71.84	143.68	215.52	287.36	574.72	1,436.80	2,873.60
	Jan.		71.16	142.32	213.48	284.64	569.28	1,423.20	2,846.40
1963	Dec.		71.16	142.32	213.48	284.64	569.28	1,423.20	2,846.40
	Oct. thru Nov.		70.70	141.40	212.10	282.80	565.60	1,414.00	2,828.00
	Sep.		73.86	147.72	221.58	295.44	590.88	1,477.20	2,954.40
	Aug.		73.36	146.72	220.08	293.44	586.88	1,467.20	2,934.40
	June thru July		72.66	145.32	217.98	290.64	581.28	1,453.20	2,906.40
	Apr. thru May		72.19	144.38	216.57	288.76	577.52	1,443.80	2,887.60
	Mar.		75.18	150.36	225.54	300.72	601.44	1,503.60	3,007.20
	Feb.		74.83	149.66	224.49	299.32	598.64	1,496.60	2,993.20
	Jan.		74.12	148.24	222.36	296.48	592.96	1,482.40	2,964.80
1962	Dec.		74.12	148.24	222.36	296.48	592.96	1,482.40	2,964.80
	Oct. thru Nov.		73.80	147.60	221.40	295.20	590.40	1,476.00	2,952.00
	Sep.		76.94	153.88	230.82	307.76	615.52	1,538.80	3,077.60
	Aug.		76.40	152.80	229.20	305.60	611.20	1,528.00	3,056.00
	June thru July		75.66	151.32	226.98	302.64	605.28	1,513.20	3,026.40
	Apr. thru May		75.18	150.36	225.54	300.72	601.44	1,503.60	3,007.20
	Mar.		78.68	157.36	236.04	314.72	629.44	1,573.60	3,147.20
	Feb.		78.12	156.24	234.36	312.48	624.96	1,562.40	3,124.80
	Jan.		77.38	154.76	232.14	309.52	619.04	1,547.60	3,095.20
1961	Dec.		77.38	154.76	232.14	309.52	619.04	1,547.60	3,095.20
	Oct. thru Nov.		77.16	154.32	231.48	308.64	617.28	1,543.20	3,086.40
	Sep.		80.43	160.86	241.29	321.72	643.44	1,608.60	3,217.20
	Aug.		79.55	159.10	238.65	318.20	636.40	1,591.00	3,182.00
	June thru July		78.79	157.58	236.37	315.16	630.32	1,575.80	3,151.60
	Apr. thru May		78.56	157.12	235.68	314.24	628.48	1,571.20	3,142.40
	Mar.		81.89	163.78	245.67	327.56	655.12	1,637.80	3,275.60
	Feb.		80.97	161.94	242.91	323.88	647.76	1,619.40	3,238.80
	Jan.		80.19	160.38	240.57	320.76	641.52	1,603.80	3,207.60

U.S. SAVINGS BONDS, SERIES E—REDEMPTION VALUES BY DENOMINATION—DEC. 1986

ISSUE YEAR	ISSUE MONTHS	$10	$25	$50	$75	$100	$200	$500	$1,000
1960	Dec.		80.19	160.38		320.76	641.52	1,603.80	3,207.60
	Oct. thru Nov.		80.04	160.08		320.16	640.32	1,600.80	3,201.60
	Sep.		83.44	166.88		333.76	667.52	1,668.80	3,337.60
	Aug.		82.49	164.98		329.96	659.92	1,649.80	3,299.60
	June thru July		81.69	163.38		326.76	653.52	1,633.80	3,267.60
	Apr. thru May		81.55	163.10		326.20	652.40	1,631.00	3,262.00
	Mar.		85.02	170.04		340.08	680.16	1,700.40	3,400.80
	Feb.		84.06	168.12		336.24	672.48	1,681.20	3,362.40
	Jan.		83.26	166.52		333.04	666.08	1,665.20	3,330.40
1959	Dec.		86.59	173.18		346.36	692.72	1,731.80	3,463.60
	Oct. thru Nov.		85.62	171.24		342.48	684.96	1,712.40	3,424.80
	Sep.		84.80	169.60		339.20	678.40	1,696.00	3,392.00
	Aug.		85.04	170.08		340.16	680.32	1,700.80	3,401.60
	June thru July		88.67	177.34		354.68	709.36	1,773.40	3,546.80
	Feb. thru May		87.63	175.26		350.52	701.04	1,752.60	3,505.20
	Jan.		86.42	172.84		345.68	691.36	1,728.40	3,456.80
1958	Dec.		90.09	180.18		360.36	720.72	1,801.80	3,603.60
	Aug. thru Nov.		89.06	178.12		356.24	712.48	1,781.20	3,562.40
	July		87.82	175.64		351.28	702.56	1,756.40	3,512.80
	June		90.48	180.96		361.92	723.84	1,809.60	3,619.20
	Feb. thru May		89.46	178.92		357.84	715.68	1,789.20	3,578.40
	Jan.		88.97	177.94		355.88	711.76	1,779.40	3,558.80
1957	Dec.		89.46	178.92		357.84	715.68	1,789.20	3,578.40
	Aug. thru Nov.		88.92	177.84		355.68	711.36	1,778.40	3,556.80
	July		88.97	177.94		355.88	711.76	1,779.40	3,558.80
	June		91.00	182.00		364.00	728.00	1,820.00	3,640.00
	Feb. thru May		90.13	180.26		360.52	721.04	1,802.60	3,605.20
	Jan.		89.89	179.78		359.56	719.12	1,797.80	3,595.60
1956	Dec.		89.46	178.92		357.84	715.68	1,789.20	3,578.40
	Nov.		88.92	177.84		355.68	711.36	1,778.40	3,556.80
	Oct.		90.13	180.26		360.52	721.04	1,802.60	3,605.20
	Sep.		92.02	184.04		368.08	736.16	1,840.40	3,680.80
	June thru Aug.		91.14	182.28		364.56	729.12	1,822.80	3,645.60
	May		90.89	181.78		363.56	727.12	1,817.80	3,635.60
	Apr.		94.30	188.60		377.20	754.40	1,886.00	3,772.00
	Jan. thru Feb.		93.11	186.22		372.44	744.88	1,862.20	3,724.40
1955	Dec.		90.13	180.26		360.52	721.04	1,802.60	3,605.20
	Nov.		89.89	179.78		359.56	719.12	1,797.80	3,595.60
	Oct.		93.26	186.52		373.04	746.08	1,865.20	3,730.40
	Sep.		92.02	184.04		368.08	736.16	1,840.40	3,680.80
	June thru Aug.		91.25	182.50		365.00	730.00	1,825.00	3,650.00
	May		90.37	180.74		361.48	722.96	1,807.40	3,614.80
	Apr.		93.05	186.10		372.20	744.40	1,861.00	3,722.00
	Jan. thru Feb.		91.14	182.28		364.56	729.12	1,822.80	3,645.60
1954	Dec.		92.21	184.42		368.84	737.68	1,844.20	3,688.40
	Nov.		92.02	184.04		368.08	736.16	1,840.40	3,680.80
	Oct.		95.47	190.94		381.88	763.76	1,909.40	3,818.80
	Sep.		94.20	188.40		376.80	753.60	1,884.00	3,768.00
	June thru Aug.		93.28	186.56		373.12	746.24	1,865.60	3,731.20
	May		93.05	186.10		372.20	744.40	1,861.00	3,722.00
	Apr.		96.54	193.08		386.16	772.32	1,930.80	3,861.60
	Mar.		95.32	190.64		381.28	762.56	1,906.40	3,812.80
	Jan. thru Feb.		93.11	186.22		372.44	744.88	1,862.20	3,724.40
1953	Dec.		94.40	188.80		377.60	755.20	1,888.00	3,776.00
	Nov.		94.16	188.32		376.64	753.28	1,883.20	3,766.40
	Oct.		97.69	195.38		390.76	781.52	1,953.80	3,907.60
	Sep.		96.48	192.96		385.92	771.84	1,929.60	3,859.20
	June thru Aug.		95.55	191.10		382.20	764.40	1,911.00	3,822.00
	May		95.31	190.62		381.24	762.48	1,906.20	3,812.40
	Apr.		98.89	197.78		395.56	791.12	1,977.80	3,955.60
	Jan. thru Feb.		97.68	195.36		390.72	781.44	1,953.60	3,907.20
1952	Dec.		100.55	201.10		402.20	804.40	2,011.00	4,022.00
	Nov.		100.28	200.56		401.12	802.24	2,005.60	4,011.20
	Oct.		104.54	209.08		418.16	836.32	2,090.40	4,181.60
	Sep.		103.25	206.50		413.00	826.00	2,065.00	4,130.00
	June thru Aug.		102.26	204.52		409.04	818.08	2,045.20	4,090.40
	May		102.03	204.06		408.12	816.24	2,040.60	4,081.20
	Jan. thru Apr.		102.42	204.84		409.68	819.36	2,048.40	4,096.80

U.S. SAVINGS BONDS, SERIES E—REDEMPTION VALUES BY DENOMINATION—DEC. 1986

YEAR ISSUE	ISSUE MONTHS	$10	$25	$50	$75	$100	$200	$500	$1,000
1951	Dec.		106.77	213.54		427.08	854.16	2,135.40	4,270.80
	Nov.		105.24	210.48		420.96	841.92	2,104.80	4,209.60
	July thru Oct.		104.24	208.48		416.96	833.92	2,084.80	4,169.60
	June		107.09	214.18		428.36	856.72	2,141.80	4,283.60
	May		106.06	212.12		424.24	848.48	2,121.20	4,242.40
	Jan. thru Apr.		109.89	219.78		439.56	879.12	2,197.80	4,395.60
1950	Dec.		110.57	221.14		442.28	884.56	2,211.40	4,422.80
	Nov.		109.94	219.88		439.76	879.52	2,198.80	4,397.60
	July thru Oct.		108.69	217.38		434.76	869.52	2,173.80	4,347.60
	June		107.89	215.78		431.56	863.12	2,157.80	4,315.60
	May		112.48	224.96		449.92	899.84	2,249.60	4,499.20
	Jan. thru Apr.		110.96	221.92		443.84	887.68	2,219.20	4,438.40
1949	Dec.		114.56	229.12		458.24	916.48	2,291.20	4,582.40
	Nov.		113.13	226.26		452.52	905.04	2,262.60	4,525.20
	July thru Oct.		112.05	224.10		448.20	896.40	2,241.00	4,482.00
	June		116.81	233.62		467.24	934.48	2,336.20	4,672.40
	May		115.72	231.44		462.88	925.76	2,314.40	4,628.80
	Jan. thru Apr.		114.59	229.18		458.36	916.72	2,291.80	4,583.60
1948	Dec.		115.72	231.44		462.88	925.76	2,314.40	4,628.80
	Nov.		113.88	227.76		455.52	911.04	2,277.60	4,555.20
	June thru Oct.		112.78	225.56		451.12	902.24	2,255.60	4,511.20
	May		116.46	232.92		465.84	931.68	2,329.20	4,658.40
	Jan. thru Apr.		117.58	235.16		470.32	940.64	2,351.60	4,703.20
1947	Dec.		119.45	238.90		477.80	955.60	2,389.00	4,778.00
	Nov.		117.04	234.08		468.16	936.32	2,340.80	4,681.60
	June thru Oct.		118.41	236.82		473.64	947.28	2,368.20	4,736.40
	May		116.46	232.92		465.84	931.68	2,329.20	4,658.40
	Jan. thru Apr.		121.41	242.82		485.64	971.28	2,428.20	4,856.40
1946	Dec. a.		123.38	246.76		493.52	987.04	2,467.60	4,935.20
	Nov.		121.42	242.84		485.68	971.36	2,428.40	4,856.80
	June thru Oct. a.		120.25	240.50		481.00	962.00	2,405.00	4,810.00
	May a.		116.46	232.92		465.84	931.68	2,329.20	4,658.40
	Jan. thru Apr.		118.35	236.70		473.40	946.80	2,367.00	4,734.00
1945	Nov. a. b.		117.28	234.56		469.12	938.24	2,345.60	4,691.20
	June thru Oct. a.		114.43	228.86		457.72	915.44	2,288.60	4,577.20
	May a.		113.33	226.66		453.32	906.64	2,266.60	4,533.20
	Jan. thru Apr. a. b.		118.35	236.70		473.40	946.80	2,367.00	4,734.00
1944	Dec. a. b.		110.47	220.94		441.88	883.76	2,209.40	4,418.80
	Nov. a. b.		108.75	217.50		435.00	870.00	2,175.00	4,350.00
	June thru Oct. a. b.		107.70	215.40		430.80	861.60	2,154.00	4,308.00
	May a. b.		111.54	223.08		446.16	892.32	2,230.80	4,461.60
	Jan. thru Apr. a. b.		110.09	220.18		440.36	880.72	2,201.80	4,403.60
1943	Dec. a. b.		105.09	210.18		420.36	840.72	2,101.80	4,203.60
	Nov. a. b.		105.09	210.18		420.36	840.72	2,101.80	4,203.60
	June thru Oct. a. b.		103.48	206.96		413.92	827.84	2,069.60	4,139.20
	May a. b.		102.48	204.96		409.92	819.84	2,049.60	4,099.20
	Jan. thru Apr. a. b.		105.09	210.18		420.36	840.72	2,101.80	4,203.60
1942	Dec. a. b.		99.95	199.90		399.80	799.60	1,999.00	3,998.00
	Nov. a. b.		98.40	196.80		393.60	787.20	1,968.00	3,936.00
	June thru Oct. a. b.		97.45	194.90		389.80	779.60	1,949.00	3,898.00
	May a. b.		96.00	192.00		384.00	768.00	1,920.00	3,840.00
	Jan. thru Apr. a. b.		100.91	201.82		403.64	807.28	2,018.20	4,036.40
1941	Dec. a. b.		90.59	181.18		362.36	724.72	1,811.80	3,623.60
	Nov. a. b.		91.96	183.92		367.84	735.68	1,839.20	3,678.40
	June thru Oct. a. b.		92.86	185.72		371.44	742.88	1,857.20	3,714.40
	May a. b.		94.35	188.70		377.40	754.80	1,887.00	3,774.00

a. Bonds with these issue dates have reached final maturity and will earn no additional interest.

b. Bonds with issue dates of November 1945 and prior are not eligible for exchange to Series HH bonds.

Minimum Interest for Loans and Seller-Financed Debt

The law requires minimum interest on loan transactions unless a specific exception covers the transaction. Where minimum interest is not charged, the law imputes interest as if the parties agreed to the charge.

The rules are complicated and have been subject to several revisions. There are different minimum interest rates and reporting rules depending on the nature of transaction. The following discussion provides the important details for understanding the rules. For specific cases and computations, we suggest that you consult Treasury regulations for details not covered in this book.

There are two broad classes of transactions:

Loans. These are generally covered by Internal Revenue Code Section 7872. Below-market or low rate interest loans are discussed at ¶4.10.

Seller-financed sales of property. These are covered by either Internal Revenue Code Section 1274 or Section 483. Seller-financed sales are discussed at ¶4.11. Under prior law, there was a rate differential between the minimum interest rate and the imputed rate that was applied if the minimum rate was not charged. Under current law, the minimum rate is the same as the imputed rate. Thus, if parties fail to charge the minimum rates, the same minimum rate is imputed by law.

¶4.10 • INTEREST-FREE OR BELOW MARKET INTEREST LOANS

For many years, the IRS tried to tax interest-free or below-market interest loans. However, court decisions supported taxpayers who argued that such loans did not result in taxable income or gifts. To reverse these decisions, the IRS convinced Congress to pass a law imposing tax on interest-free or low-interest loans made by individuals and businesses. You may no longer make interest-free or low-interest loans to a relative who uses the loan for investment purposes without adverse tax consequences unless the exception for $10,000 or $100,000 loans applies; *see* next column.

The law generally treats a loan as two transactions:

1. The law assumes that the lender has transferred to the borrower an amount equal to the foregone interest element of the loan. In the case of a loan between individuals, such as a parent and child, the parent is subject to gift tax on this element; in the case of a stockholder borrowing from a company, the element is a taxable dividend; in the case of a loan made to an employee, taxable pay. For gift tax purposes, a term loan is treated as if the lender gave to the borrower the excess of the amount of the loan over the present value of all payments due during the loan term. Demand loans are treated as if the lender gave to the borrower annually the amount of the foregone interest.

2. The law assumes that imputed interest is paid by the borrower to the lender. The lender must report the imputed interest as income; the borrower claims an interest deduction if excess itemized deductions are claimed.

A husband and wife are treated as one person for purposes of imputing interest.

No tax withholding is required on interest imputed by the rules of the section.

There are two general classes of loans:

1. Gift loans, whether term or demand, and nongift demand loans.

2. Nongift term loans.

The distinction is important for figuring and reporting imputed interest. For example, in the case of nongift term loans, the imputed interest element is treated as original issue discount.

A demand loan is any loan payable in full at any time on the demand of the lender. This includes any nontransferable loan on which the interest arrangement is conditioned on future performance of substantial services by an individual. A term loan is any type of loan that is not a demand loan.

A demand loan is subject to the rules of this section if no interest is payable or the interest rate is less than the applicable federal rate. A term loan is subject to the rules if the amount of loan exceeds the present value of all payments due under the loan. In case of a demand note, the lender is treated as giving the borrower an amount equal to the foregone interest on an annual basis.

The amount of imputed interest is generally the excess of the amount of interest which would have been payable on the loan for the period at the applicable federal rate and any interest payable on the loan.

Refer to Treasury regulations for calculating taxable amounts.

Applicable federal rate. In the case of a term loan, the applicable federal rate is the one in effect as of the day on which the loan was made, compounded semiannually.

Loan	Federal Rate
Not more than three years	Short-term rate
Over three years but not over nine	Mid-term rate
Over nine years	Long-term rate

A demand loan is considered as a series of one-day term loans and interest on such a loan is computed on a daily basis using the federal short-term rate.

To avoid interest imputation, set the interest at the applicable federal rate at the time of the loan or modification of the loan. *See* Treasury regulations for examples of interest terms which may require compound interest values. The applicable federal rates (AFR) are released in IRS Bulletins and may be available at your local IRS office.

$10,000 exception. In the case of a gift loan, no interest is imputed to any day on which the aggregate outstanding amount of the loan is not over $10,000, provided the loan is not attributed to the purchase or carrying of income-producing assets.

The $10,000 exception also applies for compensation-related and corporate-shareholder loans, provided the principal purpose of the loan is not tax avoidance. Certain low-interest loans given to employees by their employers to purchase a new residence in connection with a move to a new job location are exempt from the imputed interest requirements.

Limitation on imputed interest for loans up to $100,000. Interest is not imputed to the lender for any day if (1) the borrower's net investment income for the year in which the day falls does not exceed $1,000, and (2) the aggregate outstanding balance on all loans from the lender to the borrower on such day does not exceed $100,000 (taking into account all loans by the lender to the borrower regardless of the rate of interest). If net investment income is over $1,000, imputed interest is limited to the borrower's net income provided the maximum aggregate amount owed for any day during a year does not exceed $100,000. Net investment income is the excess of investment income over investment expenses.

You may still be able to give an interest-free loan to a relative provided the loan comes within these exceptions. For example, you give a child an interest-free loan of $100,000 or less to finance a purchase of a home and the child's investment income is less than $1,000.

The net investment income limitations do not apply if a principal purpose of a loan is the avoidance of federal taxes.

Reporting rules. Imputed interest is generally treated as transferred by the lender to the borrower and retransferred by the borrower to the lender on December 31 in the calendar year of imputation and is reported under the regular accounting method of the borrower and lender.

Example—

On January 1, 1986, Jones Company makes a $200,000 interest-free demand loan to Frank, an employee. The loan remains outstanding for the entire 1986 calendar year. Jones Company has a taxable year ending September 30. Frank is a calendar year taxpayer. For 1986, the imputed compensation payment and the imputed interest payment is treated as made on December 31, 1986.

With gift loans between individuals, interest computed during the borrower's taxable year is treated for both the lender and the borrower as earned on the last day of the borrower's taxable year. Treasury regulations to Section 7872 provide rules for figuring "foregone" interest. Where a demand loan is in effect for the entire calendar year, an "annual blended rate" issued by the IRS to simplify reporting may be used to compute the imputed interest. The blended rate is not available if the loan was not outstanding for the entire year or if the loan balance fluctuated; computations provided by Treasury regulations must be used.

If a borrower dies, or a business entity is liquidated any imputed interest imputed during the final taxable year is treated for both the lender and the borrower as occurring on the last day of the borrower's final taxable year. If a below-market loan is repaid, any interest imputed during the borrower's taxable year which includes the date of repayment is treated for both the lender and the borrower as occurring on the day the loan is repaid.

Tax return statement requirements. Both a lender and borrower must attach statements to their income tax returns reporting the interest, how it was calculated, and the name of the parties and their tax identification numbers.

Some private debts are subject to OID reporting rules of Section 1272 (not discussed in this book) which provides the following exception for loans between individuals: (1) The loan is not made in the course of a trade or business of the lender; (2) the loan does not exceed $10,000; (3) the loan does not have a principal purpose of tax avoidance. For purposes of this exception a husband and wife are treated as one person.

Effective date. The law applies to term loans made after June 6, 1984 and demand loans outstanding after June 6, 1984. The law does not apply to any demand loan that was outstanding on June 6, 1984 and which was repaid before September 17, 1984. Further, the law does not apply to a loan made before June 6, 1984 to a continuing care facility by a resident of such facility, the loan being contingent on continued residence at such facility.

¶4.11 • MINIMUM INTEREST AND REPORTING RULES FOR SELLER FINANCING

The law requires minimum interest charges for seller-financed sales. If the minimum rate is not charged, the IRS imputes interest at the minimum applicable rate. For example, property is sold on the installment basis for $100,000 and the parties fail to charge adequate interest. Assume the IRS imputes interest of $5,000. For tax purposes, $95,000 is allocated to the sale of the property and the principal amount of the debt; the balance is imputed interest of $5,000, taxable to the seller and deductible by the buyer. However, when the property is *personal use* property, such as a residence to be used by the buyer, imputed interest rules do not apply to the buyer. Thus, the buyer may not deduct the imputed interest. His deduction is limited to his payment of interest stated in the contract.

Two statute classes. The minimum or imputed interest rules are covered by two Internal Revenue Code statutes: Sections 1274 and 483. Under both, the same minimum interest rates apply. Section 483 applies to any payment due more than six months after the date of sale under a contract which calls for some or all payments more than one year after the date of sale. Section 1274 applies where some or all payments are due more than six months after the date of sale. Section 483 does not apply if the sales price is $3,000 or less. Transactions within Section 483 are sales or exchanges of: (1) personal residences, (2) any property if total consideration received by the seller is $250,000 or less, (3) farms if

the total price is $1 million or less and (4) sales of land between family members to the extent the sales price does not exceed $500,000. All other transactions involving nonpublicly traded debt instruments for nonpublicly traded property are within Section 1274. Interest is generally figured in the same manner under both statutes.

One important practical difference between the two statutes involves the timing of the reporting and deducting of interest.

Under Section 483, a seller and buyer use their regular reporting method for imputed interest. For a cash-basis seller, interest is taxed when received; a cash-basis buyer deducts interest when paid. However, if too much interest is allocated to a payment period, the excess interest is treated as prepaid interest, and the deduction is postponed to the year or years interest is earned. Section 483 also describes imputed interest as *unstated interest.*

Under Section 1274, the interest element is generally reported by both buyer and seller ratably according to the OID accrual rules, even if they otherwise report on the cash basis. Where the sales price is $2 million or less, the parties can elect the cash method to report the interest regardless of the OID and accrual rules if: (1) the seller-lender is on a cash basis method and is not a dealer of the property sold, (2) the seller and buyer jointly elect to use the cash method; and (3) the property is not eligible for the investment credit. The cash basis election binds any cash basis successor of the buyer or seller. If the lender transfers his interest to an accrual basis taxpayer, the election no longer applies; interest is thereafter taxed under the accrual method rules. The OID rules also do not apply to a cash-basis buyer of *personal use* property; here, the cash-basis debtor deducts only payments of interest required by the contract.

Rates. The following are rates for seller-financed sales:

General rate. If seller financing is $2.8 million or less, the minimum required interest is the lower of 9% compounded semi-annually or the applicable federal rate (AFR). The amount of seller financing is the stated principal amount under the contract. If the seller-financed amount exceeds $2.8 million, the minimum interest rate is 100% of the AFR. After 1989, the $2.8 million threshold will be indexed for inflation.

The IRS has authority to write regulations allowing the parties to use an interest rate lower than the AFR if it is shown that the borrower could obtain a loan on an arm's length basis at lower interest.

Investment credit property. A rate of 100% of the AFR applies to sales of new property eligible for the investment credit.

Seller-financed sale-leaseback transactions. Interest equal to 110% of AFR must be charged.

Sales of land between family members. To the extent that sales price does not exceed $500,000 during a calendar year, the minimum interest rate is 6%, compounded semiannually. To prevent multiple sales from being used to avoid the $500,000 limit, the $500,000 ceiling applies to all land sales between family members during the same year. To the extent that the $500,000 sales price limit is exceeded, the general 9% or 100% of AFR rules apply.

Figuring AFR. Monthly, the IRS determines the AFR rate applying to the following month. The rates are listed in the Internal Revenue Bulletin. There are three AFR rates depending on the length of the contract.

Short-term AFR—a term of three years or less

Mid-term—a term of over three years but not over nine years;

Long-term—a term of over nine years.

The parties may choose the lowest AFR for the three-month period ending with the month in which a binding written sales contract is entered into. Thus, if the AFR for either of the prior two months is lower than the AFR for the month of contract, the lowest of the three AFRs applies.

The total unstated interest is allocated ratably to payments under an OID computation.

Where the contract provides adequate interest and the amount of principal and interest payments do not exceed $250,000, the

IRS will recognize the parties allocation of interest and principal payments, even if it does not match the actual interest accruing during the period.

Examples—

1. On July 1, 1986, Jones sells rental property to Smith for $100,000. Smith is required to make two installment payments of $64,857.18: one on June 30, 1988, the second on June 30, 1990. Each payment includes $50,000 principal and $14,857.18 interest. The loan provides for adequate stated interest. But Jones and Smith have allocated less interest to the first installment than the amount accruing as of that date. The interest accruing as of that date is $19,246.40: $9,200 in the first year ($100,000 × .092) $10,046.40 in the second year ($109,200 × .092). However, as the total amount payable under the contract is less than $250,000, the IRS will accept the allocation.

2. Same facts as in example (1), except that the first installment includes principal of $35,142.82 and $29,714.36 interest; the second installment is entirely principal. The parties have allocated more interest than has accrued. The excess is $10,467.96 ($29,714.36 − $19,246.40). In 1988, Jones reports the full amount of interest paid when received. In 1988, Smith may deduct only that part of the paid interest accruing up to the end of 1988. The excess is deductible in later years as it is considered to have been earned.

Assumptions of loans. The imputed interest rules of Sections 1274 and 483 do not generally apply to debt instruments assumed as part of a sale or exchange, or if the property is taken subject to the debt, provided that neither the terms of the debt instrument nor the nature of the transactions are changed.

Congressional Committee reports indicate that "wraparound" debts should *not* be exempted from the imputed interest rules unless the Treasury in final regulations determines that a wraparound debt is to be treated as an assumption under the installment sale rules.

Prior interest rates. The rates discussed here apply to transactions after June 30, 1985. For prior rates, see Treasury regulations.

A change in payment terms may require an adjustment of interest to come within the minimum rate.

If a contract provides for carrying charges, then buyer is not subject to imputed interest.

Imputed interest rules do not apply to sales of patents coming within the rules of ¶6.036.

Safe harbor for points. Under proposed regulations in cases of seller-financed residence sales, generally one-sixth of a point per year of amortization will not be counted as OID.

Important: In planning deferred or installment sales, review Treasury regulations to Section 483 and 1275 for further examples and details.

¶4.50

Dividend Income

Illustrations of reporting dividend income may be found in the Supplement to YOUR INCOME TAX. Mail the card at the front of this book for your FREE Supplement, which includes filled-in returns and last-minute information.

¶4.501 • THE DIVIDEND EXCLUSION

The first $100 ($200 on a joint return) of dividends income is not taxed.

Examples—

1. You earn dividends of $300. You are taxed on $200 as follows:

Dividends	$300
Less: Exclusion	100
Taxable amount	$200

2. Same as above except you are married and file a joint return; your spouse earns no dividends. You are taxed on $100:

Dividends	$300
Less: Exclusion	200
Taxable amount	$100

Dividends qualifying for the exclusion must be paid by domestic corporations out of earnings and profits. Also qualifying for the exclusion are ordinary dividends from nonexempt cooperatives, building and loan companies on their capital stock (but not on deposits), the Federal National Mortgage Association, taxable insurance companies on stock (not on your policy).

¶4.51 • REPORTING DIVIDEND INCOME

Dividends paid out of current or accumulated earnings of a corporation are subject to tax. Most dividends fall into this class, except for stock dividends and stock rights on common which are generally not taxed. See ¶4.56.

Dividends paid to you during 1986 are reported to the IRS by the company on Form 1099-DIV. The IRS uses this information as a check on your reporting of dividends. You receive a copy of Form 1099-DIV. Do not attach it to your tax return.

Publicly-held corporations generally inform stockholders of the tax consequences of stock dividends and other distributions. Keep such letters with your tax records. You may also want to consult investment publications such as Moody's or Standard and Poor's annual dividend record books for details of dividend distributions and their tax treatment.

¶4.52 • DIVIDENDS FROM A PARTNERSHIP, S CORPORATION, ESTATE, OR TRUST

You report dividend income you receive as a member of a partnership or as a beneficiary of an estate or trust. The fiduciary of the estate or trust should advise you of the dividend income to be reported on your return. The amount of dividends a partner reports is listed in Schedule K of the partnership tax return, Form 1065. Partners and trust and estate beneficiaries may claim the exclusion for dividends from a partnership, trust, and estate.

No dividend exclusion may be allowed for dividends distributed by a trust in its last taxable year if its deductions exceed gross income.

Distributions from S corporations. Distributions of an S corporation (*see* ¶10.05) are generally not treated as dividends. You report your pro rata share of each item of income, loss, deduction, or credit in a special schedule of your return. Allocated long-term capital gains are reported in Schedule D.

Distributions from S corporation may qualify for the exclusion if the distribution is out of accumulated earnings realized by the corporation before the election. Also your share of qualifying dividends received by the corporation on investments in other domestic companies qualifies for the exclusion.

¶4.53 • HOW MUTUAL FUND DIVIDENDS ARE TAXED

Mutual funds (open-end regulated investment companies) pay their shareholders five kinds of dividends:

1. Ordinary dividends—income from the mutual fund's investments in corporate stock and other securities, including bonds.
2. Capital gain dividends—proceeds from the mutual fund's long-term profits on its sale of securities.
3. Exempt-interest dividends—proceeds from the fund's interest income from tax-exempt bonds is tax exempt to investors.
4. Return of capital—proceeds from the receipt by the mutual fund of corporation distributions which were not out of earnings.
5. Dividends from foreign corporations—income from the fund's investments in foreign corporations.

Whether the dividend is received by you or reinvested by the fund, you must report it on your return. The fund on an information return, Form 1099-DIV (or a similar written form), gives you a breakdown of the type of dividends paid during the taxable year. Each identified part of the dividend is treated as follows:

Dividends qualifying for the exclusion. The amount of dividends qualifying for the exclusion as identified in Form 1099-DIV is added to your qualifying dividends from other sources to determine the amount of your exclusion.

Capital gain dividends. You report the capital gain dividend as a long-term capital gain regardless of how long you have held your mutual fund shares. The Supplement to Your Income Tax illustrates the reporting of mutual fund dividends.

A few mutual funds retain their long-term capital gains and pay capital gains tax on those amounts. Even though not actually received by you, you include as a capital gain dividend on your return the amount of the undistributed capital gain dividend allocated to you by the fund. If the mutual fund paid a tax on the undistributed capital gain, you are entitled to a credit (¶24.86).

A loss on the sale of mutual fund shares held for six months or less is treated as a long-term capital loss to the extent of the capital gain dividend received before the sale. This restriction does not apply to dispositions under periodic redemption plans.

Nontaxable distributions. The mutual fund designates amounts representing return of capital as nontaxable distributions. They reduce the cost basis of the mutual fund shares. A return of capital is not taxed unless the distribution (when added to other such distributions received in the past) exceeds your investment in the fund. *See* ¶4.61.

Exempt-interest dividends are also nontaxable. They do not reduce your basis in the mutual fund shares.

Deferred annuity plans. Certain deferred annuity plans invest in high yielding investments, such as money market funds. Earnings may or may not be taxed currently depending on the terms of the plan.

Tax deferral is allowed where the insurance company manages a mutual fund which is available only to policyholders. Check with an insurance company for the tax status of the plan.

Money market funds. Dividends from money market funds do not qualify for the dividend exclusion because money market income is from interest rather than dividends. Distributions from mutual funds which are not exclusively money funds may qualify for the exclusion. The fund will inform you of the nature of the dividend.

¶4.54 • HOW REAL ESTATE INVESTMENT TRUST DIVIDENDS ARE TAXED

Dividends from a real estate investment trust do not qualify for the dividend exclusion. Ordinary dividends are fully taxable. Dividends designated by the trust as capital gain dividends are reported as long-term capital gains regardless of how long you have held your trust shares.

The rule for losses incurred within six months discussed above for mutual funds applies also to sales of REIT shares.

¶4.55 • DIVIDENDS ARE TAXED WHEN CORPORATION HAS EARNINGS AND PROFITS

You pay tax on dividends only when the corporation distributing the dividends has earnings and profits. Publicly-held corporations will tell you whether or not their distributions are taxable.

If you hold stock in a close corporation, you may have to determine the tax status of its distribution. You need to know earnings and profits at two different periods:

1. Current earnings and profits as of the *end of the current taxable year.* A dividend is considered to have been made from earnings most recently accumulated.
2. Accumulated earnings and profits as of the *beginning of the current year.* However, when current earnings and profits are large enough to meet the dividend, you do not have to make this computation. It is only when the dividends *exceed* current earnings (or there are no current earnings) that you match accumulated earnings against the dividend. The tax term "accumulated earnings and profits" is similar in meaning to the accounting term "retained earnings." Both stand for the net profits of the company after deducting distributions to stockholders. However, "tax" earnings may differ from "retained earnings" for the following reasons: Surplus accounts, the additions to which are not deductible from income for income tax purposes, are ordinarily included as tax earnings.

Examples—
1. During 1986, Corporation A paid dividends of $25,000. At the beginning of 1986 it had accumulated earnings of $50,000. It lost $25,000 during 1986. You are fully taxed on your dividend income in 1986, because the corporation's net accumulated surplus exceeds its dividends.
2. At the end of 1985, Corporation B had a deficit of $200,000. Earnings for 1986 were $100,000. In 1986 it paid stockholders $25,000. The dividends are taxed; earnings exceeded the dividends.

¶4.56 • STOCK DIVIDENDS ON COMMON STOCK

If you own common stock in a company and receive a dividend of stock in the same company, the dividend is generally not taxable. See ¶6.25 and ¶6.26 for the method of computing cost basis of stock dividends and rights and sales of such stock.

Exceptions to tax-free rule. A stock dividend on common is taxable when you may elect to take either stock or cash; there are different classes of common, one class receiving cash dividends and another class receiving stock; or the dividend is of convertible preferred. See ¶4.58 below for further details of taxable stock dividends.

Fractional shares. When a stock dividend is declared, you may be entitled to a fractional share redeemable for cash. The fractional share is not taxable if a full share would be considered a tax-free stock dividend. Gain or loss on the sale of the fractional share is handled like any other sale of stock and is long or short term depending on the holding period of the original stock.

Where you receive cash or redeemable scrip instead of a fractional share without any option to take a fractional share, the cash or scrip is taxed as a cash dividend, unless the company paid the cash in order to save trouble and expense and not to change stockholder interests.

Stock rights. The rules that apply to stock dividends also apply to distributions of stock rights. If you, as a common stockholder, receive rights to subscribe to additional common, the receipt of the rights is not taxable provided the terms of the distribution do not fall within the taxable distribution rules of ¶4.58.

Stock splits. Stock splits resemble the receipt of stock dividends, but they are not dividends. They do not represent a distribution of surplus as in the case of stock dividends. The receipt of stock under a split-up is not taxable. The purpose of a split-up is generally to reduce the value of individual shares in order to increase the marketability of the shares. The basis of the old holding is divided among the new shares in order to find the basis for the new shares (*see* ¶6.25).

¶4.57 • DIVIDENDS PAID IN PROPERTY

A dividend may be paid in property such as securities of another corporation or merchandise. You report as income the fair market value of the property. A dividend paid in property is sometimes called a dividend in kind.
Example—
You receive one share of X corporation stock as a dividend from the G company of which you are a stockholder. You receive the X stock when it had a market value of $25. You report $25, the value of the property received.

Corporate benefits. On audit, the IRS may charge that a benefit given to a shareholder-employee is a taxable dividend.

¶4.58 • TAXABLE STOCK DIVIDENDS

Stock dividends paid to holders of preferred stock. However, no taxable income is realized where the conversion ratio of convertible preferred stock is increased only to take account of a stock dividend or split involving the stock into which the convertible stock is convertible.

Stock dividend elected by a shareholder of common stock who had the choice of taking stock, property or cash. (A distribution of stock that was immediately redeemable for cash at the stockholder's option was treated as a taxable dividend.)

Stock dividend paid in a distribution where some shareholders receive property or cash and other shareholders' proportionate interests in the assets or earnings and profits of the corporation are increased.

Distributions of preferred stock to some common shareholders and common stock to other common shareholders.

Distributions of convertible preferred stock to holders of common stock, unless it can be shown that the distribution will not result in the creation of disproportionate stock interests.

Dividend reinvestment plan in company stock. Some companies provide plans whereby stockholders may elect to take either cash dividends or automatically reinvest the dividends in company stock at a discount price. If you elect the stock plan, the amount of the taxable dividend is the fair market value of the stock at the time of dividend distribution plus the service fee charged for the acquisition. The basis of the stock is also fair market value at the time of dividend distribution; the service charge may be claimed as an itemized deduction. If at the same time you also have the option to buy additional stock at a discount and you exercise the option, you have additional dividend income for the difference between the fair market value of the optional shares and the amount paid for the shares.

Constructive stock dividends. You may not actually receive a stock dividend but under Treasury regulations you may be treated as having received a taxable distribution. This may happen when a company increases the ratio.

¶4.59 • WHO REPORTS THE DIVIDEND?

Stock held by broker in street name. If your broker holds stock for you in a street name, dividends earned on this stock are received by the broker and credited to your account. You report all dividends credited to your account in 1986. The broker is required to file an information return on all such dividends.

If your statement shows only a gross amount of dividends, check with your broker if any of the dividends represented nontaxable returns of capital.

Dividends on stock sold or bought between ex-dividend date and record date. Record date is the date set by a company on which you must be listed as a stockholder on its records to receive the dividend. However, in the case of publicly traded stock, an ex-dividend date, which usually precedes the record date by several days, is fixed by the exchange to determine who is entitled to the dividend.

If you buy stock before the ex-dividend date, the dividend belongs to you and is reported by you. If you buy on or after the ex-dividend date, the dividend belongs to the seller.

If you sell stock before the ex-dividend date, you do not have a right to the dividend. If you sell on or after the ex-dividend date, you receive the dividend and report it as income.

The dividend declaration date and date of payment do not determine who receives the dividend.

Stock sold short. For a discussion of how to treat a payment to a broker for dividends paid on stock sold short, *see* ¶6.261.

¶4.60 • YEAR DIVIDENDS ARE REPORTED

Dividend income is usually reported on the tax return for the year in which the dividend is unqualifiedly credited to your account or when you receive the dividend check.
Examples—
1. A corporation declares a dividend payable on December 31, 1986. It follows a practice of paying dividends by checks which are mailed so that stockholders do not receive them until January, 1987. You report this dividend in your 1987 return.
2. On December 31, 1986, a dividend is credited to a stockholder's account. The dividend is taxable in 1986, as the crediting is considered constructive receipt in 1986, even though the dividend is not paid until 1987 or a later year.

Dividends received in a year after the one in which they were declared, when you held the stock on the record date, are taxed in the year they are received.
Example—
You own stock in a corporation. In April, 1984 the corporation declared a dividend. But it provided that the dividend will be paid when it gets the cash. It finally pays the dividend in September, 1986. The dividend is taxable in 1986.

Back dividends on preferred stock accumulated before you bought the stock but paid after you acquired it are taxed in the year you receive them.

¶4.61 • DISTRIBUTIONS NOT OUT OF EARNINGS: RETURN OF CAPITAL

A return of capital or "nontaxable distribution" reduces the cost basis of the stock. If the cost basis is reduced to zero, further distributions of capital are taxed as capital gains. Whether short or long term depends on the length of time you have held the stock. The company paying the dividend will usually inform you of the tax treatment of the payment.

Dividends on insurance policies are not true dividends. They are returns of premiums previously paid. They reduce the cost of the policy and are not subject to tax until they exceed the net premiums paid for the contract. Interest paid or credited on dividends left with the insurance company is taxable. Dividends on VA insurance are tax free. Where insurance premiums are deducted as a business expense in prior years, receipts of insurance dividends are either included in income or taken as a reduction of the insurance expense deduction of the current year. Dividends on capital stock of an insurance company are taxable dividends.

¶5.00

Income or Loss From Your Business or Profession

A sample Schedule C may be found in the Supplement to YOUR INCOME TAX.
Mail the card at the front of this book for your FREE Supplement, which includes
filled-in returns and last-minute information.

¶5.01 • WHAT ACCOUNTING BASIS CAN YOU USE?

Your business income is reported on either the accrual or cash basis. You may figure your business income on the accrual basis even if you report your nonbusiness income on the cash basis. If you have more than one business, you may have a different accounting method for each business. If you have inventories, you must use the accrual basis in your business.

Cash basis. You report income items in the taxable year in which they are received; you deduct all expenses in the taxable year in which they are paid. Income is also reported under the cash basis if it is "constructively" received. You have "constructively" received income when an amount is credited to your account, subject to your control, or set apart for you and may be drawn by you at any time. For example, in 1986 you receive a pay check, but you do not cash it until 1987. You have constructively received the wage income in 1986, and it is taxable in 1986.

In general, you deduct expenses in the year of payment. Expenses paid by credit card are deducted in the year they are charged. Expenses paid through a "pay by phone" account with a bank are deducted in the year the bank sends the check. This date is reported by the bank on its monthly statement.

Advance payments. You may not deduct advance rent payments covering charges of a later tax year. The IRS applies a similar rule to advance payments of insurance premiums; however, an appeals court has allowed an immediate deduction.

> The cash basis has this advantage over other accounting methods: You may defer reporting income by postponing the receipt of income. For example, if 1986 is a high income year, you might extend the date of payment of some of your customers' bills until 1987. But make certain that you avoid the constructive receipt rule. You may also postpone the payment of presently-due expenses to a year in which the deduction gives you a greater tax saving.

Accrual basis. You report income that has been earned whether or not received, unless a substantial contingency affects your right to collect the income. The treatment of expenses is subject to more rigid rules. Under prior law, accrual basis taxpayers could deduct accrued expenses that were not payable for several years. You were allowed to deduct an accrued expense if liability was fixed and the amount could be determined with reasonable accuracy. The IRS believed that this so-called "all events" test gave a premature tax savings where performance was delayed beyond the taxable year.

Under current law a deduction may not be claimed until economic performance has occurred. Economic performance occurs for:

Rent—as the property is used.
Services—when they are performed.
Goods—when they are delivered.
Work of subcontractor hired by the taxpayer—when the subcontractor performs services.

Example—
You are a calendar-year taxpayer using the accrual method. In December 1986, you buy office supplies. You receive the supplies and are billed for them before the end of the year but make payment in 1987. You may deduct the cost of supplies in 1986. You meet the all events test as liability was fixed in 1986; economic performance also occurred in 1986 with the delivery.

Even if delivery were delayed until 1987, the supplies could qualify as a recurring expense as explained below, thereby allowing a 1986 deduction.

Exceptions to the economic performance rule are allowed for recurring expenses accrued in normal business practice which meet all of these tests:

1. The item meets the general "all events" test and economic performance occurs within a reasonable period after the end of the taxable year for which the expense is accrued, but not exceeding eight and a half months.
2. The item is recurring in nature and the taxpayer consistently from year to year treats such items as accrued in the year the all events test is satisfied.
3. The item is not a material item, or the accrual in the year before economic performance results in a better matching against income than accrual in the year of economic performance. For example, under the matching exception, where income from shipping goods is recognized in 1986 but the goods are not shipped until 1987, the shipping costs are more properly matched in 1986, the year of sale, than in 1987 when the goods are shipped.

Workmen's Compensation and tort liability do not qualify under the above exceptions. Such liabilities are deductible only when paid.

Contested liability. Under prior law, a deduction for a contested liability was allowed if the amount of the liability was paid into a trust. Under the new law, a deduction may be claimed only if the economic performance test is met, even though payment is made to a trust. Further, if economic performance itself is the actual payment of the liability, payment to a trust is not treated as economic performance.

The above restrictions do not affect the deduction of items that are covered by specific tax law provisions, such as vacation pay, bad debts, and employee-benefits plans.

A 10-year carryback period for losses arising from deferred deductions related to state or federal statutory liability or from tort liability is allowed by statute.

Deductions for lease expenses under deferred rental agreements are subject to the accrual rules of ¶9.12.

> The accrual basis has this advantage over the cash basis: It generally gives a more even and balanced financial report.

Although the accrual method and cash method of accounting are the most common methods of reporting, other methods are allowed if they clearly reflect your income. Special accounting methods include the installment method for dealers in personal property and the percentage of completion or completed contract method for construction contractors. The details of these methods are described in Treasury regulations.

Methods of valuing inventory are detailed in Treasury regulations.

> **Changing your accounting method.** Generally, you must obtain the consent of the Internal Revenue Service prior to any change in accounting method. Apply for consent by filing Form 3115 with the Commissioner of Internal Revenue, Washington, D.C. 20224, within 180 days after the beginning of the tax year in which you wish to make the change. Thus, if you are on the calendar-year basis and want to change methods for 1987, file by June 30, 1987.

¶5.02 • TAX REPORTING FOR SELF-EMPLOYED

Your taxable year must be the same for both your business and nonbusiness income. If you report your business income on a fiscal year basis, you must also report your nonbusiness income on a fiscal year basis.

Generally, you report the tax consequences of transactions that have occurred during a 12-month period. If the period ends on December 31, it is called a calendar year. If it ends on the last day of any month other than December, it is called a fiscal year. A reporting period, technically called a taxable year, can never be longer than 12 months unless you report on a 52-53 week fiscal year basis (details of which can be found in Treasury regulations). A reporting period may be less than 12 months whenever you start or end your business in the middle of your regular taxable year, or change your taxable year.

A change of reporting periods requires the consent of the IRS. Form 1128 must be filed with the Commissioner of Internal Revenue, Washington, D.C. 20224, prior to any change.

¶5.021 • REPORTING BUSINESS CASH RECEIPTS TO THE IRS

Did you receive in the course of business, cash of more than $10,000 in one transaction or two or more related transactions? If you did, you must file an infomation return, Form 8300, with the IRS for each transaction. There are penalties for failure to file.

File Form 8300 with the IRS within 15 days of the transaction. Only cash payments are reported; do not report funds received by bank check or wire transfer where cash was not physically transferred. Foreign currency is considered cash. If multiple payments from a single payer (or a payer's agent) are received within a 24-hour period, the payments are aggregated, and the total must be reported if over $10,000.

The reporting requirement applies to individuals, corporations, partnerships, trusts, and estates, except for certain financial institutions that are already required to report cash transactions to the Treasury. Cash received in transactions occurring entirely outside the U.S. does not have to be reported.

The filing requirement applies to cash received for providing goods or services. Thus, an attorney, doctor, or other professional must report cash payments of over $10,000 from a client. Further, cash received for setting up a trust of more than $10,000 for a client must be reported.

On an installment sale of business property you generally report each payment exceeding $10,000 within 15 days of receipt. If the initial installment is $10,000 or less, you must aggregate all payments received within one year of the initial payment and report the total after it exceeds $10,000.

> The IRS warns that the reporting requirement may not be avoided by splitting up a single transaction into separate transactions. Thus, a sale of property for $36,000 may not be broken down into four separate sales of $9,000 to avoid reporting. Similarly, an attorney who represents a client in a case must aggregate all cash payments by the client, although payments may be spread over several months; if the total exceeds $10,000 it must be reported.

There is an exception to the reporting requirement for persons who act as agents if they receive cash of over $10,000 from their principal and use it within 15 days in a cash transaction, provided they identify the principal to the payee in the cash transaction.

On Form 8300, you provide the payer's home address and tax identification number to the IRS. You also must provide the payer with a copy of the form or a similar statement by January 31 of the following year.

A $50 penalty may be imposed for each failure to file Form 8300 or provide the payer with a statement, unless reasonable cause is shown. The maximum penalty is $50,000 per calendar year for each type of statement. If failure to file is intentional, the penalty increases to $100 per failure, with no annual limitation; criminal penalties could also be imposed.

You must keep a copy of each Form 8300 you file with the IRS for five years from the date of filing.

Reporting Income and Expenses on Schedule C

¶5.03 • REPORTING INCOME AND EXPENSES ON SCHEDULE C

The following explanations of reporting income and expenses on Schedule C are keyed to a sample schedule on page 93. A 1986 filled-in Schedule C may be found in the Supplement.

Gross receipts or sales. The sample schedule illustrates the reporting of gross receipts by a service business operated by a self-employed person. A sample Schedule C in the supplement illustrates the reporting of retail business selling merchandise and thus is required to determine cost of goods sold in a special section of Schedule C (*see* Part III of the sample schedule). If you do not produce or sell goods but provide only services, you do not determine cost of goods sold and report only your receipts from services on line 1.

Do not report as receipts on Schedule C the following items:

Gains or losses on the sale of property used in your business or profession. These transactions are reported on Schedule D and Form 4797.

Dividends from stock held in the ordinary course of your business. These are reported as dividends from stocks held for investment.

Deductions. Deductible business expenses are claimed in Part II; the descriptive breakdown of items is generally self-explanatory. However, note these points:

Bad debts (line 7): If you are on the accrual basis and use the reserve method of charging bad debts, the addition to the reserve should be an estimate of what will probably be uncollectible based on past experience. If you do not use the reserve method, a bad debt deduction must follow the rules of ¶6.28. You may not use the reserve method if you are on the cash basis.

Depreciation (line 12): Enter here the amount of your annual depreciation deduction. A complete discussion of depreciation may be found in ¶5.30 and following. Form 4562, which is used for figuring depreciation and ACRS deductions, may be found in the Supplement.

Employee benefit programs (line 14): Enter your cost for the following programs you provide for your employees: wage continuation, accident or health plans, self-insured medical reimbursement plans; educational assistance programs; supplemental unemployment benefits; and prepaid legal expenses. Retirement plans are reported separately, as discussed below. Employee benefits supported by insurance premiums, such as group hospitalization and medical plans, are deducted as insurance, line 16.

Insurance (line 16): Premiums on insurance policies written for the protection of your business are deductible, such as accident, burglary, embezzlement, marine risks, plate glass, public liability, workmen's compensation, fire, storm, or theft and indemnity bonds upon employees. State unemployment insurance payments are deducted here or as taxes if they are considered taxes under state law.

Premiums paid on an insurance policy on the life of an employee or one financially interested in a business, for the purpose of protecting you from loss in the event of the death of the insured, are not deductible.

Prepaid insurance premiums are deducted ratably over the term covered by the policy, whether you are on the cash or accrual basis. However, an appeals court allowed a cash basis taxpayer to take an immediate deduction for premiums paid on a policy covering more than a year.

Premiums for disability insurance to cover loss of earnings when out ill or injured are nondeductible personal expenses. But you may deduct premiums in policies covering business overhead expenses.

A self-employed doctor may deduct the premium costs of malpractice insurance. However, a doctor who is not self-employed but employed by someone else, say a hospital, may deduct the premium costs only as an itemized deduction. Whether malpractice premiums paid to a physician-owned carrier are deductible depends on how the carrier is organized. If there is a sufficient number of policyholders who are not economically related and none of them owns a controlling interest in the insuring company, a deduction is allowed provided the premiums are reasonable and are based on sound actuarial principles. In one case, physicians set up a physician-owned carrier which was required by state insurance authorities to set up a surplus fund. The physicians contributed to the fund and received nontransferrable certificates that were redeemable only if they retired, moved out of the state or died. The IRS and Tax Court held the contributions to the fund were nondeductible capital expenses. In another case, a professional corporation of anesthesiologists set up a trust to pay malpractice claims, up to specified limits. The IRS and Tax Court disallowed deductions for the trust contributions on the grounds that the PC remained potentially liable. Malpractice claims wthin the policy limits might exceed trust funds and the PC would be liable for the difference. Since risk of loss was not shifted to the trust, the trust was not a true insurance arrangement.

Pension and profit-sharing plans (line 21): Keogh plan contributions made for your employees are entered here; contributions made for your account are entered directly on Form 1040 as an "Adjustment to Income." In addition, you must file an information return by the last day of the seventh month following the end of the plan year.

Rent on business property (line 22): Rent paid for the use of lofts, buildings, trucks, and other equipment is deductible. However, you may not deduct the entire amount of an advance rental in the year of its payment. This is true even if you are on the cash basis. You deduct only that portion of the payment attributed to the use of the property in the taxable year. For example, you sign a 10-year lease calling for yearly rental payments of $2,000. You pay the first year's rent on July 1. In your tax return for the calendar year, you may deduct only $1,000 (⁶⁄₁₂ of $2,000). However, an appeals court allowed a calendar year cash basis lessee to deduct advance rentals where the rental payments covered a period of a year or less. For example, on December 1, 1986, the lessee pays the entire rental due for the lease ending November 30, 1987. While the IRS would allow only ¹⁄₁₂ of the payment to be deductible in 1986, the appeals court would allow a deduction for the entire payment. The court believes this approach is within the spirit of the cash basis rule. In the case of a long-term lease where advance rental payments cover no more than a year beyond the year of payment, the IRS proration rule sacrifices the simplicity of the cash basis method without a meaningful change in the timing of deductions. *See also* ¶9.12.

Taxes on leased property that you pay to the lessor are deductible as additional rent.

Repairs (*line 23*): The cost of repairs is deductible provided they do not materially add to the value of the property or appreciably prolong its life. Expenses of replacements that arrest deterioration and appreciably increase the value of the property are capitalized and their cost recovered through depreciation.

Taxes (*line 25*): Federal import duties, excise and stamp taxes normally not deductible as itemized deductions are deductible as business taxes if incurred by the business. However, the IRS holds that you may not deduct state income taxes on business income as a business expense. Its reasoning: Income taxes are personal taxes even when paid on business income. As such, you may deduct state income tax only as an itemized deduction.

The Tax Court supports the IRS rule on the grounds that it reflects Congressional intent toward the treatment of state income taxes in figuring taxable income. However, the Tax Court's position is inconsistent. In somewhat similar cases, it has allowed business expense deductions from gross income for interest paid on state and federal income tax deficiencies and legal fees incurred on tax audits of business income.

For purposes of computing a net operating loss, state income tax on business income is treated as a business deduction.

Taxes on business property, such as an *ad valorem* tax, must be deducted here; they are not to be treated as itemized deductions.

Wages (*line 28*): You do not deduct your drawings. You may deduct reasonable wages paid to family members who work for you. If you have an employee who works in your office and also in your home, such as a domestic, you deduct that part of the salary allocated to the work in your office. If you take a targeted jobs credit (¶5.78), the credit offsets the wage deduction.

¶5.04 • DEDUCTIONS FOR PROFESSIONALS

　　Dues to professional societies
　　Operating expenses and repairs of car used on professional calls
　　Supplies
　　Subscriptions to professional journals
　　Rent for office space
　　Cost of fuel, light, water, telephone used in office
　　Salaries of assistants
　　Malpractice insurance (*see* ¶5.03)
　　Cost of books, professional instruments, and equipment with a useful life of a year or less.
　　Professional libraries are depreciable. Depreciation (ACRS) rules are discussed at ¶5.30.

The cost of preparing for a profession. You may *not* deduct the cost of a professional education and the cost of establishing a professional reputation.

The IRS does not allow a deduction for the cost of a license to practice. However, courts have allowed an attorney to amortize the cost of a bar admission over his life expectancy.

The costs of courses taken to keep abreast of professional developments are usually deductible (*see* ¶21.00).

A doctor may depreciate part of the purchase price of a medical practice, if he can show he bought a wasting asset, such as patients' records, the useful life and value of which can be estimated. The IRS on an audit may disallow the deduction. However, there is a court authority which has allowed the deduction. *See* ¶5.301. Similarly, a doctor may be able to deduct payment for the right to practice in a hospital over his life expectancy.

SAMPLE SCHEDULE

Part I Income

1a Gross receipts or sales	1a	120,000	
b Less: Returns and allowances	1b		
c Subtract line 1b from line 1a and enter the balance here	1c	120,000	
2 Cost of goods sold and/or operations (from Part III, line 8)	2		
3 Subtract line 2 from line 1c and enter the **gross profit** here	3	120,000	
4a Windfall profit tax credit or refund received in 1986 (see Instructions)	4a		
b Other income	4b		
5 Add lines 3, 4a, and 4b. This is the **gross income** ▶	5	120,000	

Part II Deductions

6 Advertising	500	20 Office expense	200	
7 Bad debts from sales or services (Cash method taxpayers, see Instructions.)	625	21 Pension and profit-sharing plans	2,000	
8 Bank service charges	3,500	22 Rent on business property	6,000	
9 Car and truck expenses		23 Repairs	300	
10 Commissions		24 Supplies (not included in Part III below)	800	
11 Depletion		25 Taxes (Do not include Windfall Profit Tax here. See line 29.)	1,510	
12 Depreciation and section 179 deduction from Form 4562 (not included in Part III below)	4,200	26 Travel and entertainment	2,500	
13 Dues and publications	800	27 Utilities and telephone	4,700	
14 Employee benefit programs	700	28a Wages　20,000		
15 Freight (not included in Part III below)		b Jobs credit		
16 Insurance	1,200	c Subtract line 28b from 28a	20,000	
17 Interest:		29 Windfall profit tax withheld in 1986		
a Mortgage (paid to financial institutions)		30 Other expenses (specify):		
b Other		a Postage	400	
18 Laundry and cleaning		b		
19 Legal and professional services	1,875	c		
		d		
31 Add amounts in columns for lines 6 through 30d. These are the **total deductions** ▶	31	51,810		
32 Net profit or (loss). Subtract line 31 from line 5 and enter the result. If a profit, enter on Form 1040, line 12, and on Schedule SE, Part I, line 2 (or Form 1041, line 5). If a loss, you **MUST** go on to line 33	32	68,190		

Payment of clients' expenses. An attorney may follow a practice of paying his clients' expenses in pending cases. He may not deduct the payments as the expenses are those of his clients. Nor are they bad debts if reimbursement is doubtful. For a bad debt deduction, it must be shown that the claim is worthless (*see* ¶6.30).

An attorney might deduct a payment to his client reimbursing the client for a bad investment recommended by the attorney. A court upheld the deduction on the grounds that the reimbursement was required to protect the reputation of an established law practice. However, no deduction is allowed when malpractice insurance reimbursement is available but the attorney fails to make a claim.

Professionals who are not in their own practice may not deduct professional expenses on Schedule C. A salaried professional may deduct his professional expenses only as itemized nonbusiness expenses.

Extracurricular teaching costs. The IRS does not allow teachers a deduction for school supplies. Some courts have been lenient and have allowed teachers to deduct out-of-pocket outlays. In one case, however, a teacher could not convince a court that his deduction for the cost of paper, pens, glue, and other supplies was a business expense. He could not support his claim that the school did not supply enough equipment.

Daily business lunches with associates have been held to back business purpose. Courts agree with the IRS that professionals do not need to have lunch together every day to talk shop. The cost of the meals are therefore not deductible.
Examples—
1. A law partnership deducted the meal costs of the staff attorneys who lunched every day at the same restaurant to discuss cases and court assignments. The deductions were disallowed as personal expenses. A court agreed with the IRS that daily lunches are not necessary. Co-workers generally do not need luncheons to provide social lubrication for business talk as is true with clients.
2. A physician held luncheon meetings three or four times a week with other physicians. He argued that the purpose of the luncheons was to generate referrals. A court held that such frequent luncheons became a routine personal event not tied to specific business. The cost of the meals was not deductible.

¶5.05 • NONDEDUCTIBLE EXPENSE ITEMS
Capital expenditures may not be deducted. Generally, the cost of acquiring an asset or of prolonging its life is a capital expenditure.
Example—
A new roof is installed on your office building. If the roof increases the life of the building, its cost is a capital expenditure recovered by depreciation deductions. The cost of repairing a leak in the roof is a deductible operating expense. A deduction was allowed for the cost of a major roof renovation on evidence that the work was not designed to increase the value of the building but to correct the defect.

If the useful life of an item is less than a year, its cost is deductible. Otherwise, you may recover your cost only through depreciation except to the extent first-year expensing applies (¶5.38).

Expenses while you are not in business. You are not allowed to deduct business expenses incurred during the time you are not engaged in your business or profession.
Example—
A lawyer continued to maintain his office while he was employed by the government. During that time he did no private law work. He only kept the office to have it ready at such time as he quit the government job and returned to practice. His costs of keeping up his office while he was working for the government were not deductible.

Payments of fines. You may not deduct the payment of a fine even though your violation was unintentional.

Bribes, kickbacks. Bribes and kickbacks are not deductible if they are illegal under a federal or a generally enforced state law which subjects the payor to a criminal penalty or provides for the loss of license or privilege to engage in business. A kickback, even if not illegal, is not deductible by a physician or other person who has furnished items or services that are payable under the Social Security Act (including state programs). A kickback includes payments for referral of a client, patient, or customer. In one case, the IRS, with support from the Tax Court and a federal appeals

court, disallowed a deduction for legal kickbacks paid by a subcontractor. The courts held that the kickbacks were not a "necessary" business expense because the contractor had obtained nearly all of its other contracts, without paying kickbacks, including contracts from the same general contractor bribed here.

¶5.051 • COSTS OF WRITING A BOOK AMORTIZED OVER INCOME PERIOD
A law (IRC § 280) designed to curb tax shelters by requiring matching of income with expenses applies also to authors. *See* ¶9.21. The costs of writing a book must be capitalized and deducted over the period during which the author reasonably expects to receive income from the book. For years within this income period, the allowable deductions must be based on a percentage formed by dividing income of the current year by estimated total income.
Example—
An author argued that the law applies only to tax shelters, not to authors. The Tax Court disagreed. True, the primary intent of the law is to limit tax shelter deductions to the period of income production, but the language of the law applies as well to authors writing books. Thus an author while working on an unpublished book may not deduct current expenses for depreciation, office supplies, rental, and typing. They must be capitalized; deductions are deferred until the book begins to produce income.

¶5.06 • DEDUCTING EXPENSES OF A SIDELINE BUSINESS OR HOBBY
There is a one-way tax rule for hobbies: Income from a hobby is taxable; losses are not deductible. The losses are considered nondeductible personal losses.

A profitable sale of a hobby collection held long term is taxable at capital gain rates; losses are not deductible (*see* ¶6.02).

The question of whether an activity, such as dog breeding or collecting and selling coins and stamps, is a hobby or sideline business arises when losses are incurred. As long as you show a profit, you may deduct the expenses of the activity. But when expenses exceed income and your return is examined, an agent may allow expenses only up to the amount of your income and disallow the remaining expenses that make up your loss. At this point, to claim the loss deduction, you may be able to take advantage of a "presumption" explained below, or you may have to prove that you are engaged in the activity to make a profit.

Allowance and disallowance of expenses. If an activity is held not to be engaged in for profit, expenses are deductible up to the extent of income from the activity; a deduction for expenses exceeding the income is disallowed. A special sequence is followed in determining which expenses are deductible from income. Deducted first are amounts allowable without regard to whether the activity is a business engaged in for profit, such as interest, state and local taxes and bad debts. If any income remains, "business" expense such as repairs, maintenance, and depreciation may be deducted to the extent of remaining income. The order and allocation of deductible items are detailed in Treasury regulations.

Presumption of profit-seeking. If you show a profit in two or more years during a period of five consecutive years, the law presumes that you are in an activity for profit. If the activity is horse breeding, training, racing or showing, the profit presumption applies if you show profits in two of seven consecutive years. The presumption does not necessarily mean that losses will automatically be allowed; the IRS may rebut the presumption (*see* below).

Election postpones determination of profit presumption. If you have losses in the first few years of an activity, and the IRS tries to disallow them as hobby losses, you have this option: You may make an election on Form 5213 to postpone the determination of whether the above profit presumption applies. The postponement is until after the end of the fourth taxable year following the first year of the activity. For example, if you enter a farming activity in 1986, you can elect to postpone the profit motive determination until after 1990. Then, if you have realized profits in at least two of the five years (1986–1990), the profit presumption applies. When you make the election on Form 5213, you agree to waive the statute of limitations for all activity-related items in the taxable years involved. The waiver generally gives the IRS an additional two years after the filing due date for the last year in the presumption period to issue deficiencies related to the activity.

To make the election, you must file Form 5213 within three years of the due date of the return for the year you started the activity. Thus, if you started your activity during 1986, you have until April 15, 1990 to make the election. If before the end of this three-year period you receive a deficiency notice from the IRS disallowing a loss from the activity and you have not yet made the election, you can still do so within 60 days of receiving the notice.

These election rules apply to individuals, partnerships and S corporations. An election by a partnership or S corporation is binding on all partners or S corporation shareholders holding interests during the presumption period.

¶5.07 · DEDUCTING EXPENSES OF LOOKING FOR A NEW BUSINESS

When you are planning to invest in a business, you may incur preliminary expenses for traveling to look at the property and for legal or accounting advice. Expenses incurred during a general search or preliminary investigation of a business are not deductible, including expenses related to the decision whether or not to enter a transaction. However, when you go beyond a general search and focus on acquiring a particular business, you may deduct the start-up expenses. The timing of the deduction depends on whether or not you actually go into the business.

Amortization election when you go into business. If you go into the business, you may elect to amortize over at least a 60-month period the costs of investigating, such as expenses of surveying potential markets, products, labor supply, transportation facilities; travel and other expenses incurred in lining up prospective distributors, suppliers, or customers; salaries or fees paid to consultants and similar professional services. The amortization period starts when you begin or acquire a going business. You make the election on the return for the year the business begins.

You may not amortize expenses incurred in acquiring or selling securities or partnership interests, such as securities registration expenses, or underwriters' commissions. You may not amortize costs of acquiring property to be held for sale or property which may be depreciated or amortized, including expenses incident to a lease and leasehold improvements.

Amortizable expenses are restricted to expenses incurred in investigating an active business; expenses of looking for investment property may not be amortized. For rental activities to qualify as an active business, there must be significant furnishing of services incident to the rentals. For example, the operation of an apartment complex, an office building, or a shopping center would generally be considered an active business.

You may not claim any deduction for start-up expenses if you do not elect to amortize. For example, if you incur expenses prior to completion of a building to be used in an active rental business, such as rental payments for leasing the land on which the building is to be constructed, you must elect to amortize the expenses or you will lose a deduction. If you do not elect to amortize, you treat expenses as follows: Costs connected with the acquisition of capital assets are capitalized and depreciated; costs related to assets with unlimited or indeterminable useful lives are recovered only on the future sale or liquidation of the business.

If the acquisition fails. Where you have gone beyond a general search and have focused on the acquisition of a particular business, but the acquisition falls through, you may deduct the expenses as a loss incurred in a transaction entered into for profit.

Examples—

1. In search of a business, you place newspaper advertisements and travel to investigate various prospective ventures. You pay for audits to evaluate the potential of some of the ventures. You then decide to purchase a specific business and hire a law firm to draft necessary documents. However, you change your mind and later abandon your plan to acquire the business. According to the IRS, you may not deduct the expenses for advertisements, travel, and audits. These are considered investigatory. You may deduct the expense of hiring the law firm.

2. Domenie left his job to invest in a business. He advertised and was contacted by a party who wished to sell. He agreed to buy, hired an attorney, transferred funds to finance the business, and worked a month with the company manager to familiarize himself with the business. Discovering misrepresentations, he refused to buy the company and deducted over $5,000 for expenses, including travel and legal fees. The IRS disallowed the deduction as incurred in a business search. The Tax Court disagreed. Domenie thought he had found a business and acted as such in transferring funds and drawing legal papers for a takeover.

Investigating and looking for a new business is treated as a business activity if you are a promoter of new businesses.

For deducting the expenses of looking for a new job, *see* ¶19.05.

Business Use of a Home

¶5.10 · EXCLUSIVE AND REGULAR USE OF HOME OFFICE

You may operate your business from your home, using a room or other space as an office or area to assemble or prepare items for sale. To deduct home expenses allocated to this activity, you, as a self-employed person, must be able to prove that you use the home area *exclusively* and on a *regular basis* either as:

A place of business to meet or deal with patients, clients, or customers in the normal course of your business. In one case, the Tax Court held that telephoning clients at home met this requirement, but an appeals court reversed, holding that the physical presence in the office of clients or customers is required.

Your principal place of business. Your home office will qualify as your principal place of business if you spend most of your

working time there and most of your business income is attributable to your activities there. In one case, the Tax Court disallowed a deduction where a road stand was operated a mile from a home where items were prepared for sale at the stand. Although the home space was used for a business purpose, the deduction was barred because the home was not the principal place of business; the road stand was.

In another case, an appeals court allowed an owner of a laundromat to deduct the costs of a home office where there was no space in the laundromat for an office, and more time was spent in the home office than at the laundromat.

Employees. Employees who use a home office must also meet the above tests. Because of the conditions of employment, most employees may be unable to prove that the office is the principal place of business. The IRS and the Tax Court generally hold that an employee's home office is not the principal place of his or her business. For example, the IRS and Tax Court did not allow an employed orchestral musician to deduct his home studio costs even though it was his only place to practice. An appeals court allowed the deduction. Home practice was the focal point of his position as concert musician. Rehearsals and performances at the opera house were made possible by the solo practice at home. Since the opera company did not provide space to its musicians for solo practice, maintaining a practice room at home was a business necessity, not a personal convenience.

The appeals court also allowed a professor to deduct the costs of a home office where his school office was inadequate. The professor showed that he spent most of his work week in his home office doing research. The appeals court held that where employer-provided space is unsuitable to do substantial work, the home office may be treated as a principal place of business. The IRS does not follow this approach.

Home office expenses of employees are discussed further at ¶5.145 and ¶19.052.

Exclusive use and regular basis tests. If you use a room, such as a den, both for business and family purposes, you must be prepared to show that a specific section of the den is used exclusively as office space. A partition or other physical separation of the office area is helpful but not required.

Under the regular basis test, expenses attributable to incidental or occasional trade or business use are not deductible even if the room is used for no other purpose but business.

The above tests will generally not present problems in deducting home expenses where the home area is the principal place of business or professional activity. For example, you are a doctor and see most of your patients at an office set aside in your home. Problems may arise where you have a principal office elsewhere and use a part of your home for occasional work. If your deduction is questioned, you must prove that the area is used regularly and exclusively to receive customers, clients, or patients. For example, evidence that you have actual office facilities is important. Furnish the room as an office with a desk, files, and a phone used only for business calls. Also keep a record of work done and business visitors.

Separate structure. If in your business you use a separate structure not attached to your home, such as a studio adjacent but unattached to your home, the expenses are generally deductible if you satisfy the exclusive use and regular basis tests discussed above. A separate structure does not have to qualify as your principal place of business or a place for meeting patients, clients or customers. However, the gross income limitation discussed at ¶5.13 applies.

In one case, a taxpayer argued that an office located in a separate building in his backyard was not subject to the exclusive and regular business use tests and the gross income limitation. However, the IRS and Tax Court held that it was. The office building was "appurtenant" to the home and thus part of it, based on these facts: The office building was 12 feet away from the house and within the same fenced-in residential area; it did not have a separate address; it was included in the same title and subject to the same mortgage as the house, and all taxes, utilities and insurance were paid as a unit for both buildings.

Day care services. The exclusive use test does not apply to business use of a home to provide day care service for children and handicapped or elderly persons, provided certain state licensing requirements are met. When day care services are provided, the allocation of expenses is made on the basis of space used for such services and then multiplied by a fraction representing the hours such space is used for business purposes. Specifically, the amount of expenses allocated to business space is then multiplied by a fraction the numerator of which is the *time* the space was used for day care services over the total time available for use.

Storage space and inventory. If your home is the only location of a business selling products, expenses allocated to space regu-larly used for inventory storage is deductible if the space is separately identifiable and suitable for storage.

¶5.11 · DEDUCTIBLE EXPENSES OF A HOME AREA USED FOR BUSINESS

A deduction for home business use may include real estate taxes, mortgage interest, operating expenses (e.g., home insurance premiums, utility costs), and depreciation allocated to the area used for business. Household expenses and repairs that do not benefit that space are not deductible. For example, the cost of painting and repairs to rooms other than the one used as a business office is not deductible. However, a pro rata share of the cost of painting the outside of a house or repairing a roof may be deductible. Costs of lawn care and landscaping are not deductible.

Figuring depreciation. For depreciation purposes, the cost basis of the house is the lower of the fair market value of the entire house at the time you started to use a part of it for business, or its adjusted basis (exclusive of the land). Only that part of the cost basis allocated to the office is depreciable.

How to claim the deduction. There is no specific form for deducting home office expenses. If you are self-employed, you deduct your business expenses for real estate taxes, mortgage interest, insurance, utilities, and repairs on the appropriate lines of Schedule C. Depreciation is computed on Form 4562 and then entered in Schedule C. On Schedule C, you must also answer a question regarding home office expenses in the affirmative.

Employees who qualify for a home office deduction claim the deduction on Schedule A as a miscellaneous itemized deduction (*see* ¶19.052).

¶5.12 · ALLOCATING EXPENSES TO BUSINESS USE

You may allocate expenses as follows: Compare the number of square feet of space used for business to the total number of square feet in the home and then apply the resulting fraction or percentage to the total deductible expenses.

If all rooms in your home are approximately the same size, you may base the allocation on a comparison of the number of rooms used as an office to the total number of rooms.

Example—

A doctor rents a 10-room apartment using three rooms for his office and seven rooms for his residence. Applying a percentage based on the ratio of rooms used as an office to the total rooms in the apartment, he deducts 30% (³⁄₁₀) of the following expenses.

	Total	Office	Residence
Rent	$ 7,200	$2,160	$5,040
Light	600	180	420
Heat	1,000	300	700
Wages of domestic	2,000	600	1,400
	$10,800	$3,240	$7,560

$3,240 is deductible as professional expenses.

¶5.13 · BUSINESS INCOME MAY LIMIT EXPENSE DEDUCTIONS

Deductible expenses allocated to the business use of an area in your home may not exceed gross income derived from that use. If you do not realize income during the year, the deduction is not allowed. For example, you are a full-time writer and use an office in your home. You do not sell any of your work this year or receive any advances or royalties. You may not claim a home office deduction for this year. If you do receive income, you follow this order in deducting expenses:

1. You deduct allocable taxes, interest (and casualty losses, if any) up to the extent of income.
2. From the balance of income, if any, you deduct operating expenses allocable to the office.
3. If a balance still remains, you deduct allocable depreciation to the amount of remaining business income.

The amount of taxes, interest, or casualty losses not allocable to the home office may be claimed as itemized deductions.

Restrictive gross income test. For purposes of limiting the deduction for business area expenses, the IRS defines gross income as gross receipts reduced by those business expenses that are not allocable to the use of the home area itself, such as salary paid to an assistant or office supplies. This rule bars a deduction if business related expenses such as salaries equal or exceed the gross receipts for the business (*see* Example 3 below).

The Tax Court has rejected the IRS definition of gross income. It holds that gross income means gross receipts with no reduction for business expenses. Legislation would specifically support the IRS rules in years after 1986.

Examples—

1. Your home office meets the exclusive and regular business test. You use 20% of your home for office space, and income attributable to business generated by the office is $1,000. You incur the following expenses allocable to your office.

	Total	20% Business
Taxes	$2,000	$400
Interest	1,000	200
Utility and maintenance	2,500	500
Depreciation	1,500	300

The allowable deduction for business use is computed as follows:

Business Income		$1,000
Less: Taxes	$400	
Interest	200	600
Balance		400
Less: Operating expenses		$400

The allocable utility and maintenance expenses are claimed before deducting depreciation. Therefore, here only $400 of operating expenses of $500 are deductible, and no deduction for depreciation is allowed. The remaining interest and taxes are deductible if excess itemized deductions are claimed.

2. A teacher uses a home office as the principal place of a sideline retail business. He also uses the office to correct student papers. The home office deductions are limited to gross income from the retail business. Teaching-related income is not counted towards the home office expenses since the home office is not the principal place of his teaching job.

3. Smith does sideline business consulting from a home office. His gross income from consulting services is $1,900. He paid an office secretary salary of $500, office telephone expenses of $150 and office supply costs of $200.

In addition, he allocated 10% of his home costs to the business space, as follows:

	Total	10% allocation
Mortgage interest	$5,000	$ 500
Real estate taxes	2,000	200
Insurance	600	60
Utilities	900	90
Depreciation	3,200	320

According to the IRS restrictive definition of gross income, the allocable deduction for business use is computed as follows:

Gross income from consulting		$1,900
Less: Secretary's salary	500	
Business phone	150	
Office supplies	200	850
Income from office		$1,050
Less: Interest	500	
Taxes	200	700
Balance		$ 350
Less: Insurance	60	
Utilities	90	150
Balance		200
Less: Depreciation		200

According to the IRS, only $200 of the allocable depreciation of $320 is deductible. The balance of interest and taxes is deductible if excess itemized deductions are claimed.

Under the Tax Court's view, deductions could be claimed against the $1,900 of gross income from consulting, rather than the reduced figure of $1,050.

¶5.14 • AN OFFICE IN A HOME FOR SIDELINE BUSINESS

You may have an occupation and also manage rental property or run a sideline business from an office in your home. The home office expenses are deductible if it is a principal place of operating the rental or sideline business.

Example—

A doctor is employed full time by a hospital. He also owns six rental properties which he personally manages. He uses one bedroom in his two-bedroom home exclusively as an office to manage the properties. The room is furnished with a desk, bookcase, filing cabinet, calculators, and answering service; furnishings and other materials for preparing rental units for tenants are stored there. He may deduct expenses allocable to the home office.

In claiming home office expenses of a sideline business, it is important to be ready to prove that you are actually in business. (*see* ¶5.06). A court has held that activities in seeking new tenants, supplying furnishings, and cleaning and preparing units for tenants are sufficiently systematic and continuous to put a person in the business of real estate rental. In some cases, the rental of even a single piece of real property may be a business.

Investors managing their securities portfolio may find it difficult to convince a court that investment management is a business activity. According to Congressional committee reports, a home office deduction should be denied to an investor who uses a home office to read financial periodicals and reports, clip bond coupons, and perform similar activities. In one case, the Claims Court allowed a deduction to Moller who spent about 40 hours a week at a home office managing a substantial stock portfolio. The Claims Court held these activities amounted to a business. However, an appeals court reversed. According to the appeals court, the test is whether or not a person is a trader. A trader is in a business; an investor is not. A trader buys and sells frequently to catch daily market swings. An investor buys securities for capital appreciation and income without regard to daily market developments. Therefore, to be a trader, one's activities must be directed to short-term trading, not the long-term holding of investments; here, Moller was an investor. He was primarily interested in the long-term growth potential of stock. He did not earn his income from the short-term turnovers of stocks. He had no significant trading profits. His interest and dividend income was 98% of his income.

Note that the IRS' restrictive definition of gross income (¶5.13) would effectively bar or severely limit any home office deduction for a home-based rental business where there are substantial writeoffs for depreciation, taxes, interest and maintenance expenses. However, the Tax Court rejects the IRS position.

¶5.15 • DEPRECIATION ON A COOPERATIVE APARTMENT USED AS AN OFFICE

If your home office meets the tests of ¶5.10, you may deduct depreciation on your stock interest in the cooperative. The basis for depreciation may be the cooperative corporation's basis for the building or an amount computed from the price you paid for the stock. The method you use depends on whether you are the first or a later owner of the stock.

You are the first owner. In figuring your depreciation, you start with the basis of the building to the cooperative in which you own stock. You then take your share of depreciation according to the percentage of stock interest you own.

If space in the building is rented to commercial tenants who do not have stock interests in the corporation, the total allowable depreciation is reduced by the amount allocated to the space used by the commercial tenants.

You are a later owner of the cooperative's stock. When you buy stock from a prior owner, the basis of depreciation is determined from the price of the stock and the outstanding mortgage on the property at the time you bought the stock.

The IRS has not ruled whether or not ACRS may be taken for cooperative interests acquired after 1980.

Figuring Net Operating Losses for Refund of Prior Taxes

¶5.20 • NET OPERATING LOSSES FOR REFUND OF PRIOR TAXES

A loss incurred in your profession or unincorporated business is deducted from other income reported on Form 1040. If the loss (plus any casualty loss) exceeds income, the excess may be first carried back to 1983, 1984, and 1985 and *then* forward 15 years to 1987 through 2001 until it is used up. A loss carried back to a prior year reduces income of that year and entitles you to a refund. A loss applied to a later year reduces income for that year.

You may elect to carry forward your loss for 15 years, foregoing the three-year carryback (*see* ¶5.24).

The rules below apply not only to self-employed individuals, farmers, and professionals but also to individuals whose casualty losses exceed income, stockholders in S corporations, and partners whose partnerships have suffered losses. Each partner claims his share of the partnership loss.

The following example shows you how a 1986 loss would be carried back and forward:

Example—
You have a 1986 operating loss of $650.

Year	Income	Loss	Loss carried back or forward to income
1983	$ 50		($ 50)
1984	80		(80)
1985	60		(60)
1986		($650)	
1987	20		(20)
1988	40		(40)
1989	50		(50)
1990	100		(100)
1991	100		(100)
1992	125		(125)
1993	150		(25)

Net operating losses from product liability may be carried back ten years for taxable years beginning after September 19, 1979. Product liability losses do not include liabilities under a warranty or resulting from services (e.g., legal or medical malpractice).

Carryover of loss from prior year to 1986. If you had a net operating loss in an earlier year which is being carried forward to 1986, the loss carryover is reported as a minus figure in the miscellaneous income section of your 1986 return. You must attach a detailed statement showing how you figured the carryover.

Restrictions on loss after accounting method change. You may realize a net operating loss for a short taxable year created by the accounting change. As a condition of allowing the accounting method change, the IRS may require you to forego the right to a loss carryback and agree to a six-year carryforward period.

Example—
You want to change from a calendar year to a fiscal year ending April 30. Assume further that May through October is your peak selling period. Thus, you may have a net operating loss for the short taxable year January 1–April 30 because of slack business. According to the IRS, if the net operating loss is $10,000 or less, you may apply the regular net operating loss rules that allow you to carryback the loss three years and then forward 15 years. But if the net operating loss exceeds $10,000 and the short period is less than nine months, the operating loss must be deducted ratably over a six-year period starting with the first tax year after the short period.

¶5.21 • YOUR NET OPERATING LOSS

A net operating loss is generally the excess of deductible business expenses over business income. The net operating loss may also include the following losses and deductions:

Casualty and theft losses, even if the property was used for personal purposes (*see* ¶18.00)

Deductible expenses of moving to a new job location (*see* ¶2.40)

Deductible job expenses, such as travel expenses, work clothes, costs and union dues.

Your share of an operating loss from a partnership or an S corporation

Loss incurred in sale of Small Business Investment Company stock (*see* ¶6.032)

Loss incurred in stock coming within the rules of Section 1244 (*see* ¶6.0321)

Loss on the sale of business real estate or rental property.

An operating loss may not include:

Net operating loss carryback or carryover from any year

Capital losses that exceed capital gain

Excess of nonbusiness deductions over nonbusiness income plus nonbusiness net capital gain

Deductions for personal exemptions

A self-employed's contribution to a Keogh plan

An IRA deduction

Income from other sources may eliminate or reduce your operating loss.

Example—
You are self-employed and incur a business loss of $10,000. Your spouse earns a salary of $10,000. When you file a joint return, your business loss will be eliminated by your spouse's salary. Similarly, if you also had salary from another position, the salary would reduce your business loss.

¶5.22 • FIGURING A NET OPERATING LOSS

Form 1045 has a schedule for computing your net operating loss deduction. On the schedule, you start with adjusted gross income and personal deductions shown on your tax return. As these figures include items not allowed for net operating loss purposes, you follow the line by line steps of Form 1045 to eliminate them. That is, you reduce the loss by the nonallowed items, such as deductions for personal exemptions, the capital gain deduction, net capital loss, and nonbusiness deductions exceeding nonbusiness income. On the schedule, the reductions are described as adjustments. The example below illustrates the steps in the schedule.

Adjustment for nonbusiness deductions. Nonbusiness expenses that exceed nonbusiness income may not be included in a net operating loss deduction. Nonbusiness deductions include deductions for IRA and Keogh plans, the married couple deduction, if applicable, and itemized deductions such as charitable contributions, interest expenses, state taxes, and medical expenses. Do not include in this nonallowed group deductible casualty and theft losses, which for net operating loss purposes are treated as business losses. If you do not claim itemized deductions in the year of the loss, you treat the zero bracket amount as a nonbusiness deduction.

Nonbusiness income is income that is *not* from a trade or business such as dividends, interest, and annuity income. The excess of nonbusiness capital gains over nonbusiness capital losses is also treated as part of nonbusiness income.

Example—

Income from dividends and interest is $6,000 and nonbusiness deductions are $6,500. The excess deduction of $500 is an adjustment that reduces your loss on Form 1045.

Adjustment for capital losses. A net nonbusiness capital loss may not be included in a net operating loss. If nonbusiness capital losses exceed nonbusiness capital gains, the excess is an adjustment that reduces your loss on Form 1045. In figuring your loss, you may take into account business capital losses only up to the total of business capital gains plus any nonbusiness capital gains remaining after the nonbusiness deduction adjustment discussed above.

Example—

In 1985, you have a salary of $2,000, interest of $1,000, a net business loss of $10,000 (income $50,000 and expenses of $60,000); itemized deductions of $4,000, IRA deduction of $2,000 and a net nonbusiness capital gain of $1,000. Your net operating loss is $8,000. The following computation approximates the steps of the Form 1045 computation schedule starting from the line showing adjusted gross income of $8,600.

Salary		$2,000
Interest		1,000
Capital gain (40% of $1,000)		400
Business loss		(10,000)
IRA deduction		(2,000)
Adjusted gross income		(8,600)
Add: Exemption and itemized deductions		(5,080)
		(13,680)
Adjustments:		
Exemptions	$1,080	
Capital gain deduction (60%)	600	
Excess nonbusiness deduction*	4,000	5,680
Net operating loss		8,000

* The excess nonbusiness expenses deduction was figured as follows:

IRA	$2,000	
Itemized deductions	4,000	$6,000
Net capital gain income	$1,000	
Interest	1,000	2,000
Excess		4,000

At risk loss limitations. The loss used to figure your net operating loss deduction is subject to the at risk rules discussed at ¶28.04. If part of your investment is in nonrecourse loans or is otherwise not at risk, you must compute your deductible loss on Form 6198 which you attach to Form 1040. The deductible loss from Form 6198 is reflected in the income and deduction figures you enter in the Form 1045 schedule to compute your net operating loss deduction.

¶5.23 • HOW TO CLAIM YOUR NET OPERATING LOSS DEDUCTION

1983 is the first year to which you may carry back your 1986 net operating loss. When you carryback the loss to 1983, you recompute your 1983 tax on Form 1045 by deducting the 1986 net operating loss. The net operating loss is deducted from the amount of your original 1983 adjusted gross income. Because of the reduction to adjusted gross income, you have to increase any 1983

medical expense and casualty loss deduction when recomputing 1983 income. You do not have to change the amount of your 1983 charitable deduction. *See* the instructions to Form 1045 and also Publication 334 for details of the recomputation calculation.

After recomputing the 1983 tax on Form 1045, your refund is the difference between the tax originally paid for 1983 and the lower tax figured after deducting the net operating loss deduction.

Use Form 1045 as a "quick refund" claim. The IRS will usually allow or reject your claim within 90 days from the time you file Form 1045. Do not attach Form 1045 to your 1986 Form 1040. File Form 1045 separately, together with a copy of your return. You may file Form 1045 within 12 months after the end of your tax year. Thus, if you are a calendar year taxpayer, you have until December 31, 1987 to carryback a 1986 loss to 1983 on Form 1045. If the IRS allows the refund, it may still determine later that the refund was excessive and assess additional tax.

Although using Form 1045 is the quickest way to obtain the refund, you may instead file an amended return on Form 1040X to claim the refund. You have three years after the due date (including extensions) of your 1986 tax return to file Form 1040X. Thus, to claim a refund on Form 1040X for 1983 because of a net operating loss carried back from 1986, you have until April 15, 1990 to file. On Form 1040X, you must attach a statement detailing how the loss carryback was figured; the schedule from Form 1045 for computing the loss may be used.

Operating losses from more than one year. If you have more than one year net operating loss to be carried to the same taxable year, you apply the loss from the earliest year first.

Example—

You had net operating losses in both 1985 and 1986 of $6,000 and $10,000 respectively. Your taxable income in 1983 was $5,000. You carried the $6,000 loss from 1985 to 1982, leaving an unused portion of $1,000 to be carried to 1983. Therefore, you have two losses to be applied against 1983 income, the unused portion of the 1985 loss and the 1986 loss. First apply the unused portion of the 1985 loss and then apply the 1986 loss.

On Form 1045 or Form 1040X you must attach a detailed schedule showing how the net operating loss for each year was computed.

Any part of the loss that may not be deducted in 1983 is carried to 1984. *See* the instructions to Form 1045 and also IRS Publication 334 for details of this computation.

¶5.24 • ELECTION TO RELINQUISH THE CARRYBACK

The discussion above is based on the general carryback and carryforward rules. You may elect to forego the carryback. Instead, you just carry forward losses. The carryforward period is still 15 years under the election. The election is irrevocable.

> You will generally make the election if you expect greater tax savings by carrying forward the loss rather than first carrying it back. You might also make the election if you are concerned you might be audited for earlier years if you carry back a loss for a refund. You make the election by attaching a statement to this effect to your return for the year of the loss, which must be filed by the due date plus extensions. The IRS refused to allow a late election and received court approval for its position.

Claiming Depreciation Deductions

¶5.30 • RAPID DEPRECIATION ENCOURAGED BY THE TAX LAW

Depreciation is an expense deduction that allows you to charge off your capital investments in equipment, machines, fixtures, autos, trucks, and buildings used in your business, profession, or rental or other income-producing activities.

For 1986, the law encourages accelerated writeoffs over short periods of time through one of the following methods or a combination of both:

Accelerated Cost Recovery System (ACRS). ACRS lets you write off the cost of autos and light trucks over a three-year period and almost all other business equipment over a five-year period. Buildings are depreciable over a 19-year period. These periods are fixed by law and have no relationship to the actual useful life of your property. Under ACRS, you simply take the rate fixed for the asset class, apply it to the basis of the asset, and the result is the depreciation deduction for the year.

First-year expensing. This one-shot deduction of up to $5,000 allows you to deduct all or part of the cost of business equipment bought in 1986 instead of depreciating the asset over the applicable three- or five-year ACRS period. First-year expensing does not apply to buildings or property used in the production of income. Whether you should elect first-year expensing is discussed at ¶5.38.

ACRS, introduced in 1981, does not apply to assets placed in service before 1981. (Prior depreciation rules are not discussed in this book.) The objective of ACRS is to provide rapid depreciation for most asset purchases and to eliminate disputes over useful life, salvage value, and depreciation methods. Useful life and depreciation methods are fixed by ACRS; salvage value is not considered. If you do not want to use the rates fixed by ACRS, you may elect a longer writeoff period with the straight line method. See ¶5.34.

ACRS applies to new and used property. It does not apply to amortizable expenses, such as leasehold improvements or low-income housing rehabilitation expenses, or intangible property such as patents or covenants not to compete. Except for certain railroad property not discussed in this book, the ACRS rules do not apply to property for which an election is made to claim depreciation under a method not expressed in terms of years, such as the unit-of-production or income forecast methods. If you may not use ACRS, use prior law rules.

¶5.301 • WHAT PROPERTY MAY BE DEPRECIATED?

Depreciation may be claimed only on property used in your business or other income-producing activity.

Examples—

1. An anesthesiologist suspended his practice indefinitely because of malpractice premium rate increases. He continued to maintain his professional competence by taking courses and keeping up his equipment. The IRS ruled that he could not take depreciation on his equip-ment. Since he is no longer practicing, the depreciation does not relate to a current trade or business.

2. An electrician spent $1,325 on a trailer to carry his tools and protective clothing. Based on a useful life of three years less salvage value of $25, annual depreciation deductions came to $433. However, the IRS claimed that he could not claim depreciation during the months he was unemployed and the trailer was not used. The Tax Court disagrees. Depreciation is allowed as long as the asset is held for use in a trade or business, even though the asset is idle or its use is temporarily suspended due to business conditions.

Depreciation may not be claimed on property held for personal purposes, such as a personal residence or pleasure car. If property, such as a car, is used both for business and pleasure, only the business portion may be depreciated (see ¶2.301, 2.302, 2.303 and ¶29.40).

Property bought for income-producing purposes, although yielding no current income, may still be depreciated.

Not all assets used in your business or for the production of income may be depreciable. Property having no determinable useful life (property that will never be used up or become obsolete), such as treasured art works or good will, may not be depreciated. Although land is not depreciable, the cost of landscaping business property may be depreciated. While good will is not depreciable, a restrictive covenant (a covenant not to compete), if separately bargained and paid for, may be "amortized," that is, deducted in equal amounts over the term of the covenant. If a business is purchased and its former owners agree not to compete for a specified period of time, be sure that the covenant is segregated and severable from good will, which may also have been purchased at the same time, in order to be able to amortize the cost of the covenant. See ¶5.461. Similarly, customer lists or records, if segregated from good will, may also be amortized.

Property held primarily for sale to customers or property includible in inventory is not depreciable, regardless of its useful life.

Farm property. Farm land is not depreciable; farm machinery and buildings are depreciable. Livestock acquired for work, breeding, or dairy purposes and not included in inventory may also be depreciated. For a detailed explanation of the highly technical rules for depreciating farm property and livestock, see IRS Publication No. 225, Farmer's Tax Guide.

For depreciation of rental residences, see ¶29.41.

For depreciation of a sublet cooperative apartment or one used in business, see ¶5.15.

Depreciation is deducted annually. Even though the deduction may give you no tax benefit in a particular year because your other deductions already exceed your income, you may not choose to forego the depreciation deduction and, instead, accumulate it for high income years. Similarly, incorrect deductions claimed in prior years may not be corrected by an adjustment to your present depreciation deduction. If the year in which the error was made is not yet closed by the statute of limitations, you may file an amended return to adjust the depreciation deduction for that year. See also ¶6.12 for other adjustments of incorrect depreciation taken in prior years.

¶5.31 • FULL INVESTMENT CREDIT REDUCES DEPRECIATION

You must reduce the depreciable basis of property on which the full investment credit is claimed. The amount of reduction is one-half of the investment credit. Thus, where the 10% credit is claimed for five-year property, the reduction amounts to 5% of basis. The basis reduction is 3% of basis for the 6% credit claimed for three-year property.

Example—

You buy equipment for $5,000 and claim the full investment credit of $500 (10% of $5,000). The depreciable basis is $4,750.

Cost	$5,000
Less 50% of $500	250
	$4,750

Over the five-year recovery period, depreciation of $4,750 will be deducted; $250 of cost is not depreciable because you claimed the full credit.

The basis reduction does not apply to assets placed in service before 1983.

Reduced credit election. You may avoid reducing basis by electing a reduced investment credit. For three-year property, the reduced credit is 4%; 8% for five-year property. It may be advisable to elect the reduced credit if you are in a high tax bracket.

Rehabilitation expense credits. Basis is reduced for claiming the 25% credit on certified historic buildings; basis is reduced by one-half of the credit. For claiming the 15% or 20% credit on certain old buildings (¶9.11), basis is reduced by the full credit.

¶5.32 • RECOVERY PERIODS FOR BUSINESS ASSETS IN 1986

Assets fall within one of the following classes:

Three-year property. This class includes automobiles, taxis, light duty trucks (actual unloaded weight of less than 13,000 pounds) and equipment used for research and experimentation. The following animals also qualify as three-year property: hogs used for breeding, race horses more than two years old, and any other horse more than twelve years old when placed in service.

The recovery rate for three-year property is:

First year	25%
Second year	38
Third year	37

However, in the case of automobiles, the full 25%, 38%, or 37% deduction may not be allowed. See ¶3.00.

Five-year property. All tangible personal property has a five-year recovery period unless specifically included in the three-year or ten-year class. Thus, most equipment and other business assets qualify for a five-year writeoff, including office furniture, typewriters, computers, calculators, copiers, and general purpose tools such as drills. Further, single purpose agricultural and horticultural structures and facilities used for the storage of petroleum and its primary products fall within the five-year class. Single purpose agricultural and horticultural structures are the same structures which are eligible for the investment credit under ¶5.70. Horses not included in the three-year class are five-year property. Public utility property with an ADR class life of 18 years or less as of January 1, 1981, is also five-year property.

The recovery rate for five-year property is:

First year	15%
Second year	22
Third year	21
Fourth year	21
Fifth year	21

Ten-year property. This is a limited category covering assets used in theme and amusement parks, residential mobile homes, railroad tank cars, public utility equipment with an ADR class life of more than 18 but not more than 25 years (except research and experimentation equipment included in the three-year class) and public utility equipment used in coal conversions.

A special 15-year period applies to public utility property with an ADR class life exceeding 25 years as of January 1, 1981. These rules are not discussed further in this book.

Special tools whose ADR class life as of January 1, 1981 was four years or less are also placed in the three-year class; this group includes special tools (not general purpose tools such as wrenches or drills) used in manufacturing motor vehicles, fabricated metal products, rubber products, glass products, and finished plaster products. Specialized containers and other handling devices used in manufacturing food and beverages also qualify as three-year property.

Real estate is discussed at ¶5.35.

If you prefer, you may choose straight line depreciation instead of using the above rates. See ¶5.34.

¶5.33 • FIGURING ACRS ON BUSINESS EQUIPMENT IN 1986

To figure depreciation for assets placed in service in 1986, follow these steps:

Step 1. Start with the depreciable basis of the asset. This is usually the cost of the asset. If you acquired the asset other than by purchase, see ¶6.10.

Step 2. Reduce basis by 50% of the full investment credit claimed as explained in ¶5.31. Do not reduce basis if you elect the reduced credit. If you elect first-year expensing, reduce basis by the amount of the first-year deduction (see ¶5.38).

Step 3. Apply the first-year rate for the asset class to the basis as adjusted in Step 2. The first-year rate for three-year property is 25%; 15% for five-year property. The result is the first-year depreciation deduction, regardless of the time of year you bought the asset. Depreciation is not prorated in the year of acquisition or year of sale except in the case of real estate. Pay special attention to this rule. This means that in the year you acquire depreciable personal property, you claim the entire depreciation allowed by law for the first year, regardless of when during the year the asset was purchased. However, in the year of disposal, no depreciation whatsoever is allowed, even if the asset is sold on the last day of the taxable year. This rule requires planning asset dispositions to save depreciation deductions. In the year real estate is acquired or sold, depreciation may be claimed for the months it was in service. See ¶5.35.

If you are claiming depreciation for a short taxable year, see ¶5.39.

Autos. Depreciation rules and business use limitation for autos are discussed at ¶3.00.

Home computers. To claim ACRS on a home computer placed in service after June 18, 1984 an employee must show that his employer required the unit for the employer's convenience and that the unit is used more than 50% for business. If the computer is not used more than 50% for business, ACRS may not be claimed, and straight line depreciation is claimed over a 12-year period. The 12-year recovery period is actually 13 years, because a half-year convention reduces the first-year deduction. Self-employed persons must also meet the more than 50% test to use ACRS. Investors who use home computers for managing portfolios must use a 12-year useful life, unless the more than 50% business-use test can be met. The mandatory straight line rate over 13 years for home computers that do not meet the more than 50% test is as follows:

Year	Rate
First year	4%
2nd through 5th year	9%
6th through 12th year	8%
13th year	4%

The more than 50% test does not apply to computers used in a business establishment. A home office qualifying under the rules of ¶5.10 is treated as a business establishment. See also ¶38.20 for discussion of home computers.

The 50% use limitations apply also to property used for entertainment and recreation, such as a boat or plane.

Example—

In October 1985, you bought equipment for $5,000. It is in the five-year class; you claimed the full investment credit of $500 (10% of $5,000). Depreciation for 1985 was $713.

Cost	$5,000
Less 50% of credit	250
Depreciable basis	$4,750
First-year rate	15%
Depreciation	$ 713

Depreciation deductions over the next four years are as follows:

Year	Rate	Deduction
1986	22%	$1,045
1987	21	998
1988	21	997
1989	21	997

¶5.34 • ELECTING STRAIGHT LINE DEPRECIATION AND LONGER RECOVERY PERIODS FOR PERSONAL PROPERTY

You may not want rapid depreciation provided by ACRS. You may prefer to write off an asset over a longer period or at an even rate using the straight line method.

Shorter useful lives and the accelerated rates of ACRS do not give any greater depreciation than your investment in an asset. They merely give you an opportunity to advance the time of taking your deduction. This may be a decided advantage where the immediate increased annual deductions will provide you with cash for working capital or for investments in other income-producing sources. That is, by taking increased deductions over a shorter period, you defer the payment of taxes that would be due if you claimed smaller depreciation deductions, using more conservative estimates of depreciation. The tax deferral lasts until the rapid method provides less depreciation deductions than would the more conservative method. Your ability to receive the benefits of ACRS generally is more feasible in a going business. If you are starting a new business in which you expect losses or low income at the start, ACRS may waste depreciation deductions that could be used in later years when your income increases. Therefore, before deciding to use the faster writeoffs of ACRS, consider your own income prospects and allocate your deduction accordingly.

You may elect the straight line method and longer useful lives, as follows:

Class of Personal Property	Elect Straight Line Period of
Three-year property	Three, five, or 12 years
Five-year property	Five, 12, or 25 years
Ten-year property	Ten, 25, or 35 years

The straight line percentages are: For three years, 33.333% annually; for five years 20%; for 10 years 10%; for 12 years 8.333%; for 25 years 4%; for 35 years 2.857%. Because of the half-year convention, only 50% of the above percentages are allowed in the year the property is placed in service. If the property is held for the entire elected recovery period, another half-year of depreciation is allowed for the year following the end of the recovery period. If property is disposed of prior to the end of the recovery period, no cost recovery is allowable in the year of disposition.

Example—

In 1985, you placed in service business equipment (five-year property) for $5,000 and elected the straight line method over five years. In 1985, you claimed a half-year's cost recovery, a full year of cost recovery in the next four years and a half-year in the sixth year.

Year	Rate	Amount of Deduction
1985	10%	$ 500
1986	20	1,000
1987	20	1,000
1988	20	1,000
1989	20	1,000
1990	10	500

Making the election. Weigh the relative merits of ACRS and straight-line depreciation and decide before filing a return for the year the property is placed in service. You may not get a second chance on an amended return after the due date. The election is made on Form 4562 by indicating that you are using straight-line rates.

Example—

The purchaser of residential real estate claimed ACRS depreciation. After the due date of the return, he filed an amended return switching to the straight-line method. The IRS refused the election for straight-line recovery on an amended return.

Under proposed regulations, the straight line election must be made on the original return for the year you place the property in service. The election may be made on an original return even if it is filed after the due date, including extensions. The election may be made on an amended return only if it is filed no later than the due date, including extensions. However, IRS Publication 534 conflicts with the regulation and requires the election to be made on a timely filed return (including extensions) although the regulation would allow the election on an original return filed late.

¶5.35 • DEPRECIATING REAL ESTATE

The ACRS recovery period of a building that is not low-income housing depends on the year the building was placed in service. For buildings placed in service after May 8, 1985 the period is 19 years. The recovery period is 15 years for buildings placed in service before March 16, 1984 and for all low-income housing; 18 years for buildings placed in service after March 15, 1984 and before May 9, 1985. Mobile homes and theme parks are in a 10-year class and agricultural, horticultural and petroleum storage structures are in the five-year class.

Under transitional rules, some 19-year buildings may be depreciated over 18 years, and some 18-year buildings over 15 years, if placed in service before 1987. Specifically, recovery over 18 years is allowed for a building placed in service after May 8, 1985 provided that *before* May 9, 1985 (1) you began construction or had a binding contract to buy the building and (2) you placed the building in service before the end of 1986. The 18-year period also applies if construction was begun, or a contract entered into by a person who transferred the rights to you and you placed the building in service before 1987. Recovery over 15 years is allowed for a building that you (or a prior owner who transferred the rights to you) began constructing or contracted for before March 16, 1984, provided you placed it in service before the end of 1986.

Election to use straight line depreciation. You may elect to use the straight line method over the regular recovery period: 19 years for 19-year property, 18 years for 18-year property, 15 years for 15-year property. Further, for any building, you may elect a longer recovery period of either 35 or 45 years. An election of the straight line method for real property may be made on a property-by-property basis. The election must be made by the return due date, plus extensions, for the year the property is placed in service.

Although ACRS writeoffs are larger in the early years, electing straight line depreciation has this advantage: If you sell real property (held long term) at a gain, the entire gain qualifies for capital gain treatment subject to the netting rules for Section 1231 assets (*see* ¶5.45). On the other hand, if you use the accelerated 15-year ACRS rates, gain will be partly or wholly taxed as ordinary income under the depreciation recapture rules. See ¶5.41.

Rate of recovery. The rate of recovery is listed in Treasury tables which are available in IRS Publication 534. Also see Form 4562. The specific rates are adjusted according to the month in the first year in which a building or improvement is placed in service.

If you elect the straight line method, the deduction for the year of acquisition and disposition also depends on the number of months the property is in service. Tables found in IRS Publication 534 provide straight line rates over the statutory life and longer optional periods.

¶5.351 • COMPONENTS AND SUBSTANTIAL IMPROVEMENTS TO BUILDING

Components of a building, such as plumbing, wiring, and storm windows, are depreciated in the same way as the building. The recovery period for a component begins when the building is placed in service or the date the component is placed in service, whichever is later.

Example—

In August 1986, you buy and place in service a building. In November 1986 you replace the roof. You decide to use the regular ACRS rate for the building; you also apply the ACRS rate for the roof as of the month of installation.

For a building you placed in service before 1981, the first component of the building placed in service after 1980 is treated as a separate building whether or not it is a substantial improvement. The component is depreciated under ACRS even though the building, itself is not.

Example—

You own a building placed in service in 1978. You place a component in service on February 1, 1986. The component is treated as a separate building placed in service on February 1, 1986. Any later component must be depreciated under the same method as used for the component placed in service on February 1, 1986.

Substantial improvement. A substantial improvement to a building is treated as a separate building rather than as one of the components of the building. You may use ACRS rates for a substantial improvement even if you elected straight line depreciation for the building, or vice versa. An improvement qualifies as a substantial improvement if: (1) The amounts added to the capital account for the building and its components during any 24-month period are at least 25% of the adjusted basis of the building (disregarding adjustments to basis for depreciation and amortization) as of the first day of the 24-month period, and (2) the improvement is made at least three years after the building was placed in service.

¶5.36 · WHEN ACRS RECOVERY MAY NOT BE USED

You may not claim cost recovery on assets which you, a family member, or other related person owned in 1980. For purposes of this rule, property is not treated as owned until it is placed in service. A deduction under ACRS is also barred if you lease back personal property to a person that owned or used it during 1980 or to a person related to such a 1980 owner or user. The "user" restriction applies to lessors of equipment which was used during 1980 so that ACRS deductions are allowed only if the user as well as the owner has changed. Thus, lessors of equipment who in 1983 exchanged equipment used during 1980 may not claim ACRS deductions unless the lessees (the users) of the property have changed.

If ACRS deductions are barred under these rules, depreciation under prior law is allowed. You are considered related to the previous owner or user if at the time you acquire the property, the previous owner or user was a family member listed at ¶33.12, a 10% controlled corporation or partnership, a fiduciary of a trust in which you are the grantor (or vice versa), or a tax-exempt organization which you or family members control. Corporations which are part of a controlled group (50% owned by a corporation) and unincorporated business which are under common control are considered related persons. Partnerships which are 10% owned (directly or indirectly) by the same persons are considered related persons. Corporations which are 10% owned (directly or indirectly) by the same individual are related persons if either corporation was a personal holding company in the taxable year preceding the sale. Certain subsidiary corporations are excluded from the category of related persons. See Treasury regulations for details of who is considered a related party.

ACRS deductions are also barred where personal or real property used by a transferor or distributor before 1981 is transferred to a corporation or partnership in certain nontaxable transactions. The transferee must generally use the same depreciation period and method used by the transferor before 1981.

If you acquire real property in 1984 which you or a related person owned during 1980, or if you lease back real property to its 1980 owner or a person related to the 1980 owner, then you may not claim ACRS deductions. Further, if you acquire real property in a like-kind exchange for property which you or a related party owned during 1980, then you may claim a cost recovery deduction only if you paid boot (cash or other property)

as part of the exchange. Your basis of the acquired property for purposes of computing the ACRS deduction includes only the amount you paid as boot; you may not include the basis of the property you gave up as part of the basis of the new property for purposes of claiming cost recovery. The same rule applies to real property acquired in the following nontaxable transactions: involuntary conversions or repossessions, and reinvestment of proceeds from sales of qualified low-income housing projects.

Examples—

1. Your son owned a rental building bought in 1980. In 1986, you buy the building from him. You may not use ACRS depreciation because your son, a related person, owned the building in 1980.

2. In 1986, you exchange a building bought before 1981 for another building. The basis of the old building was $20,000. The fair market value of the new property is $80,000. In addition to the exchanged building, you also paid $50,000. Your basis in the new building is $70,000 (basis of old building, $20,000 and cash of $50,000). You may apply ACRS to $50,000 of the basis. That part of the basis related to the old property ($20,000) must be depreciated under a method allowed under prior law.

You may not use ACRS if you use the IRS mileage rate for business travel. Business use of 50% or less also bars ACRS for autos and home computers placed in service after June 18, 1984.

¶5.361 · WHEN ACRS DEDUCTIONS ARE BASED ON TRANSFEROR'S METHOD

If you incorporate your business or otherwise transfer business property to a controlled (80% ownership) corporation, or form a partnership, the corporation or partnership must continue to use the same cost recovery period and method that you did for assets placed in service after 1980. This rule applies until the transferee has recovered the portion of its basis in the property which equals the substituted basis it took from you in the exchange. For example, if in 1985 you elect to use straight line depreciation over 12 years for equipment in the five-year class and then transfer the equipment to a controlled corporation after five years, the corporation must depreciate the equipment using the straight line method over the remaining seven years.

In the following transactions, a transferee must also use the transferor's recovery period and method in writing off basis equal to the transferor's basis: (1) acquisitions from a family member or other related person listed at ¶5.36; (2) property which is leased back to the person from whom it was acquired; (3) property distributed by a partnership to a partner, and corporate property acquired in certain subsidiary liquidations, corporate reorganizations, bankruptcy or receivership reorganizations.

Further, if you dispose of recovery property and then reacquire it, ACRS deductions must be computed as if you had never disposed of it, under rules to be provided by Treasury regulations.

¶5.362 · DEPRECIATION DEDUCTION IN YEAR OF SALE

ACRS may not be claimed on personal property such as an auto or equipment in the year the property is sold or otherwise no longer used for business or investment purposes. The rule is different for realty. If you dispose of 15-year real property, the ACRS deduction for the year of disposition is based on the number of full months in use. No deduction is allowed for the month of disposition whether or not you use the regular ACRS method or an alternate ACRS method.

Example—

On March 2, 1984, you purchase and place in service a building. The cost of the building is $98,000. On June 1, 1987, you sell the building. The ACRS deduction for 1987 is first figured for the full year; the amount is then prorated for the months of use. The full 1987 ACRS deduction is 8% of $98,000 or $7,840. This amount is then prorated to the five months of full use in 1987. The ACRS deduction is $3,267 (7,840 × 5/12).

If you dispose of 18-year or 19-year real property, the ACRS deduction for the year of disposition is based on the number of months in use; the number of months in use is determined under a mid-month convention. Under the mid-month convention, real property disposed of any time during a month is treated as disposed of in the middle of that month. You count the month of disposition as one half of a month of use.

Example—

On July 2, 1984, you buy a building; cost allocated to it is $100,000.

On September 25, 1987, you sell it. The ACRS deduction for 1987 is figured for the months of use. The full ACRS deduction for 1987 is 8% of $100,000 or $8,000. This is prorated for the 8½ months of use in 1985. The ACRS deduction for 1987 is $5,667 ($8,000 × 8.5⁄12).

See ¶5.41 for recapture rules on the sale of ACRS property.

¶5.37 • DEPRECIATING PROPERTY USED OUTSIDE THE UNITED STATES

Special cost recovery rules apply to property used predominantly outside the United States. For personal property, the recovery period is the ADR class life of the asset on January 1, 1981, or 12 years if it had no ADR class life. In proposed regulations, the Treasury has a table providing the annual percentage rate deductions over this recovery period.

No cost recovery deduction is allowed in the year the foreign personal property is disposed of.

Instead of using the prescribed accelerated recovery, straight line depreciation may be claimed for personal property used outside the United States. Straight line depreciation may be elected for three-year, five-year, and ten-year property over its ADR class life as of January 1, 1981, or, if longer, over the optional periods for each class of property described at ¶5.34.

The cost of real property used outside the United States is recovered over 35 years. In proposed regulations, there is a table providing the annual percentage rate deduction, based upon the 150% declining balance method for the early recovery years, switching later to straight line depreciation. Instead of using this prescribed accelerated method for realty, straight line depreciation may be claimed over 35 or 45 years.

¶5.38 • FIRST-YEAR EXPENSING

You may elect to deduct up to $5,000 of the cost of business equipment. Under the election, all or part of your cost for personal property used in a business may be written off in the year of acquisition instead of depreciating the cost under the ACRS rules (¶5.33). The election is limited to personal property bought for use in a business. It is not available for realty or property held merely for the production of income. The portion of cost not eligible for first-year expensing is recovered under the regular ACRS rules.

The election must be made on your original return for the year in which the property is acquired. You may not revoke the election without the consent of the IRS.

The investment credit, if available, may not be claimed to the extent first-year expensing is deducted.

In 1986, you may deduct up to $5,000 of cost ($2,500 in the case of a married individual filing a separate return).

For property bought by a partnership or an S corporation, the dollar limits apply to the business as well as the owners as individual taxpayers.

Example—

In 1986, you buy equipment for $8,000. You may deduct up to $5,000 of the cost as an expense and depreciate $3,000 over the five-year recovery period.

> You may claim the full $5,000 deduction in 1986, even if the equipment was placed in service on the last day of the taxable year.

Property does not qualify for the expense election if: (1) it is acquired from a person whose relationship to you would result in a disallowance of loss on a transaction between the taxpayers. See ¶33.12. For purposes of the expense election, a corporation is controlled by you and thus subject to the loss disallowance rule of ¶33.12 if 50% or more of the stock is owned by you, your spouse, your ancestors or descendants; (2) the property is acquired by a member of a controlled group from another member of the same group (using a 50% control test) or (3) the basis of the property is determined in whole or in part (a) by reference to the adjusted basis of the property of the person from whom you acquired it, or (b) under the stepped-up basis rules for property acquired from a decedent.

The cost of property eligible for expensing does not include that part of the basis of such property determined by the basis of property traded in.

Restriction on autos and home computers. To claim the first-year expensing deduction for an auto or computer placed in service in 1986, you must show business use of more than 50%. Further in the case of an auto placed in service in 1986 the first-year deduction may not exceed $3,200, see ¶2.303. The 50% test does not apply to a computer used exclusively at a regular business establishment. A home office qualifying under the rules of ¶5.10 may qualify as a business establishment. The 50% test may also apply to other property such as a plane or boat.

Recapture of expensing deduction. The amount expensed is treated as depreciation taken for purposes of the recapture rules. See ¶5.411. Gain recognized on disposition of the property is treated as ordinary income to the extent of expense deductions and depreciation taken. Further, if the more than 50% business use test is not met for an automobile or computer in a year after the year it is placed in service, the expensing deduction as well as prior ACRS deductions are subject to recapture. See ¶3.07 for recapture details.

¶5.39 • SHORT TAXABLE YEAR

If you place assets in service during a taxable year lasting less than 12 months, you may not claim the full ACRS deduction allowed by the tables at ¶5.33 and ¶5.35.

For personal property, the deduction from the table at ¶5.33 is reduced by this fraction: Number of months in short taxable year divided by 12.

For real property, the first-year deduction is based on the number of months it is in service during the short year. The full-year deduction provided by the table at ¶5.35 is reduced by this fraction: Number of months property in service divided by number of months in short taxable year.

Example—

On June 1, 1986, you buy property that gives an annual ACRS deduction of $2,500 during a nine-month short taxable year ending September 30, 1985. The deduction for the short taxable year is reduced to $1,875 ($2,500 × 9/12).

The deduction for the balance of the asset's recovery period follows regular rules. To compensate for the reduced first-year deduction, an extra deduction is allowed in the taxable year following the last year in the recovery period.

Sales of Business Assets and Property

The following checklist summarizes how sales of assets and property used in business are taxed.

Sales of—	Tax treatment—
Merchandise, stock in trade, etc.	Profits are taxable as ordinary income; losses are fully deductible. Sales of merchandise are reported in Schedule C if you are self-employed.
Machinery, buildings, office equipment, fixtures, van, truck, and other business property subject to depreciation	Gain is taxable as ordinary income if depreciation recapture rules of ¶5.40 or ¶5.41 apply. Capital gain may apply, if sale comes within rules of ¶5.45. Losses may be deductible as ordinary losses or capital losses under the rules of ¶5.45. Sales are reported on Form 4797.
Land	If used in your business, capital gain or ordinary income may be realized under the rules of Section 1231. If held as investment, gain or loss is subject to capital gain treatment. Sales of capital assets are reported on Schedule D.

Further details are discussed in the following sections:

¶5.40 • PROFITABLE SALES OF DEPRECIABLE PROPERTY PLACED IN SERVICE BEFORE 1981

Taxable gain may be realized on the sale of depreciable property when depreciation reduces the basis of the asset to an amount below its current selling price. The gain resulting from depreciation is generally taxable as ordinary income under the rules explained in this section.

Example—
Assume a truck cost $4,000; depreciation claimed was $3,000. It was sold for $1,200.

Sale proceeds		$1,200
Cost	$4,000	
Less: Depreciation	3,000	1,000
Profit		$ 200

The profit of $200 is attributed to depreciation that reduced the cost basis of $4,000 to $1,000. The profit is taxed as ordinary income.

Recapture rules are not uniform. Different calculations apply to types of property as follows:

Depreciable business equipment (Section 1245 assets). Profit on sale of depreciable business equipment is taxed as ordinary income to the extent of depreciation taken on the property after 1961 (see ¶5.401). Intangibles, such as patents and copyrights and elevators and escalators, may be treated as Section 1245 assets. Recapture rules for sports franchise contracts are not discussed in this book.

Livestock (Section 1245 assets). Profit on sale of livestock is ordinary income to the extent of depreciation claimed after December 31, 1969.

Depreciable real property (Section 1250 assets). Complex rules apply to realty. Depending on the type of realty held, the method of depreciation and the period held, all, part, or none of the depreciation may be subject to recapture. See ¶5.402.

There is no recapture of depreciation for real property held for more than one year and depreciated on the straight line method. After a holding period of a year, recapture applies, under varying formulas, to buildings depreciated under a rapid method of depreciation (such as the 150% or double declining method or the sum of years-digits method). If you sell depreciable realty at a profit within a year after you acquired it, that part of your gain attributed to depreciation is subject to ordinary income tax, regardless of the depreciation method you use.

¶5.401 • RECAPTURE ON BUSINESS EQUIPMENT PLACED IN SERVICE BEFORE 1981

Profit attributed to depreciation claimed after 1961 is taxable as ordinary income. If the actual gain is less than the depreciation subject to recapture, only the gain is taxed as ordinary income. If the gain exceeds the amount of depreciation subject to recapture, the portion of the gain attributable to recapture is ordinary income while the excess may be capital gain under Section 1231 (see ¶5.45).

Example—
You sell equipment for $5,000 when its adjusted basis is $4,000. The gain is $1,000. If the amount of depreciation taken on the equipment is $1,000 or more—all of the gain is taxable as ordinary income. If the depreciation is $600, the $600 is taxable as ordinary income and the balance of the gain of $400 may be capital gain.

Generally, the depreciation deduction taken into account for each year is the amount allowed or allowable, whichever is greater. For purposes of assigning ordinary income (but not for purposes of figuring gain or loss), the depreciation deductions taken into account for any year will be the amount "allowed" rather than the amount "allowable," if the allowed deduction is smaller and you can prove its amount.

Exchanges of property (¶5.47 and ¶6.20), involuntary conversions (¶18.20), and corporate distributions may result in recapture of depreciation. For distributions which are not sales, exchanges, or involuntary conversions, the amount of recapture is all depreciation claimed after 1961, but not in excess of the difference between fair market value at disposition or original cost, whichever is less, and adjusted basis.

¶5.402 • RECAPTURE ON DEPRECIABLE REALTY PLACED IN SERVICE BEFORE 1981

Real property for recapture purposes (Section 1250) includes buildings and structural components, *except* for elevators and escalators or other tangible property used as an integral part of manufacturing, production or extraction, or of furnishing transportation and communications. Property may initially be Section 1250 property and then, on a change of use, become Section 1245 property. Such property may not be reconverted to Section 1250 property.

Example—

A company builds a parking lot for its employees. Five years later, it converts the lot into a loading area for its trucks. The parking lot, which was originally Section 1250 property, is now Section 1245 property.

General recapture pattern. The amount of recapture depends on the rate of depreciation claimed, the length of time you held the property, and the type of realty. If the realty was held for less than one year, all depreciation taken is subject to recapture. If the realty was held for more than one year, only rapid depreciation claimed after 1969 in *excess* of the amount allowed under the straight line method is subject to recapture. The amount actually recaptured will vary, depending upon whether the property is residential or nonresidential realty, low-income housing, or rehabilitation expenditures. The special rules relating to low-income housing and rehabilitation expenditures are not discussed in this book (*see* Treasury regulations).

Depreciation claimed on realty during the years 1964 through 1969. Depreciation claimed during this period is not recaptured.

Depreciation claimed after 1969. 100% of the excess depreciation claimed after 1969 is subject to recapture, but not in excess of the actual gain. For residential realty, this percentage is reduced, depending on the holding period, for depreciation claimed from 1970 through 1975. For this period, the amount subject to recapture on residential property is reduced 1% per month for each month the property is held beyond 100 months. Only full months are counted (*see* table below).

Real property is considered residential realty for periods after 1975 if 85% or more of gross income is from dwelling units. For periods before 1976, the gross income test was 80% or more.

1970–1975 percentage reductions for residential realty:

Held	%	Held	%
Up to 100 months	100	156 months (13 years)	44
108 months (9 years)	92	168 months (14 years)	32
120 months (10 years)	80	180 months (15 years)	20
132 months (11 years)	68	192 months (16 years)	8
144 months (12 years)	56	200 months (16 years, 8 months) or longer	0

Examples—

1. Starting in January 1969, you depreciate on the declining balance method a newly constructed office building with a cost of $100,000 (exclusive of land). You take double declining depreciation using a 40-year useful life. After holding the building 16 years, in January 1986, you sell for $90,000. At that time, the adjusted basis of the building is $41,812 ($100,000 less depreciation of $58,183). If straight line depreciation has been taken, the total depreciation would have been $42,500 ($2,500 × 17 years) if salvage value is zero.

    A. Profit on the sale is $48,188 ($90,000 − $41,812)

    B. Additional depreciation:

Year	Claimed	Str. Line	Excess
1969	$5,000	$2,500	$2,500
1970	4,750	2,500	2,250
1971	4,513	2,500	2,013
1972	4,287	2,500	1,787
1973	4,072	2,500	1,572
1974	3,869	2,500	1,369
1975	3,675	2,500	1,175
1976	3,492	2,500	992
1977	3,317	2,500	817
1978	3,151	2,500	651
1979	2,994	2,500	494
1980	2,844	2,500	344
1981	2,702	2,500	202
1982	2,567	2,500	67
1983	2,438	2,500	(62)
1984	2,316	2,500	(184)
1985	2,201	2,500	(299)

    C. Post-1969 excess at 100% ($53,188 − $40,000) $13,188

    D. Pre-1970 excess of $2,500 not recaptured   0

    Amount subject to recapture (ordinary income) $13,188

    Amount subject to Section 1231 ($48,188 − $13,188) $35,000

2. Same as above except the building was residential realty

    A. Profit on the sale $48,188

    B. Additional depreciation—*see* chart above

    C. Post-1975 excess at 100% ($28,022 − $25,000) $ 3,022

Excess from 1970 through 1975 not subject to recapture (building held for more than 16 years, 8 months)

    Amount subject to recapture (ordinary income) $ 3,022

    Amount subject to Section 1231 $45,166

The useful life and salvage value for determining depreciation on the straight line method is the same as that used under the rapid depreciation method.

Change in method of depreciation. Where you initially used a rapid method of depreciation but switched to the straight line, *see* Treasury regulations for how to compute depreciation subject to recapture.

Special recapture rules not discussed here apply to property under certain financial arrangements sponsored by the National Housing Act or similar state or local laws.

Special recapture rules not discussed here also apply to separate elements of improvements.

¶5.41 • RECAPTURE OF ACRS DEDUCTIONS

Profitable dispositions of assets depreciable under ACRS are subject to recapture as ordinary income. To figure gain or loss, you subtract ACRS deductions from original cost to determine the adjusted basis of the asset.

Form 4797 is used to figure gain or loss on depreciable property, including the recapture of cost recovery deductions.

Personal property. Adjusted basis of personal property, such as business equipment and machinery, is fixed as of the beginning of the year of disposition because no ACRS deductions are allowed in the year of disposition.

Example—

In 1984, you bought for $10,000 a truck for your business. In 1984, ACRS deductions were $2,500 and $3,800 in 1985. In November 1986 you sell the truck for $4,000. In 1986, no ACRS deduction is allowed and basis of the truck is $3,700. Gain on the sale is $300 ($4,000 − $3,700) and taxable as ordinary income.

Real property. For real property subjected to ACRS, adjusted basis for computing gain or loss is the adjusted basis at the beginning of the year reduced by the ACRS deduction allowed for the number of months the realty is in service in the year of disposition (*see* ¶5.362).

All gain on the disposition of property held for less than one year is ordinary income. If held more than one year, gain may be taxed as ordinary income due to the recapture of prior cost recovery deductions, according to the following rules:

Personal property and real property not in the ACRS recovery period (Section 1245 assets). Gain on the disposition of personal property is ordinary income to the extent of prior ACRS deductions and the first-year expensing deduction. Further, basis adjustment required on investment credit property placed in service after 1982 will affect recapture in later years. *See* Form 4797.

These recapture rules also apply to gain on the disposition of theme park structures, single purpose agricultural and horticultural structures, and petroleum storage facilities. Gain in excess of prior cost recovery deductions is capital gain subject to the netting rules for Section 1231 assets (*see* ¶5.45). These recapture rules follow the pre-1981 recapture rules for personal property (*see* ¶5.401).

Nonresidential ACRS recovery period building. If the prescribed accelerated method is used to recover the most of nonresidential property, all gain on the disposition of the realty is recaptured as ordinary income to the extent of recovery allowances perviously taken. Thus, nonresidential realty will be treated the same as personal property for purposes of recapture if the accelerated recovery allowance is claimed. If the straight line method is elected, there is no recapture; all gain is capital gain subject to the netting rules of Section 1231 (¶5.45).

If accelerated cost recovery is used for a nonresidential building and straight line depreciation is used for a substantial improvement to that building which you are allowed to depreciate separately (*see* ¶5.35), all gain on a disposition of the entire building is treated as ordinary income to the extent of the accelerated cost recovery claimed; remaining gain is capital gain taxed under the rules for Section 1231 assets.

Residential ACRS recovery period building. Gain is ordinary income to the extent the recovery allowed under the prescribed accelerated method exceeds the recovery that would have been allowable if the straight line method over ACRS recovery period had been used. Thus, recapture for residential realty essentially follows the pre-1981 recapture rules discussed at ¶5.40. If the straight line method is elected, there is no recapture; all gain is capital gain, subject to Section 1231 netting (¶5.45).

15-year low-income rental housing. The same rule as for residential realty applies except that recapture is phased out at the rate of one percentage point per month for property held at least 100 months, so that there is no recapture of cost recovery deductions for property held at least 200 months (16 years, 8 months).

Sale of partnership interest. If a partner sells his interest in a partnership which holds business assets subject to ACRS, gain on the sale is subject to recapture. *See* Treasury regulations.

Mass asset account elections. If mass asset accounts are maintained, computation of gain or loss on account assets may be avoided by making an election to recognize gain to the extent of the proceeds received upon the asset's disposition. The asset's cost basis is fully written off under ACRS and then removed from the account. Check Treasury regulations for details.

Recapture of first-year expensing is discussed at ¶5.411.

Recapture of ACRS deductions claimed on an auto because of business use of 50% or less is discussed at ¶3.07.

¶5.411 • RECAPTURE OF FIRST-YEAR EXPENSING

The first-year expensing deduction under ¶5.38 is treated as depreciation for purposes of recapture. When expensed property is sold or exchanged, gain is ordinary income to the extent of the first year expense deduction plus ACRS deductions, if any. *See* ¶5.41. When expensed property is no longer used in a business before the close of the second taxable year following the year it is placed in service, the expensed amount is also subject to recapture to the extent of the tax benefit derived from the expensing deduction.

Automobiles and computers. If the more than 50% business use test for a business automobile (¶3.04) or a computer (¶5.33) is not met in a year after the auto is placed in service, any first-year expensing deduction is subject to recapture on Form 4797.

Installment sale. If you sell property on the installment basis, the first-year expensing deduction claimed for the property in a prior year is recaptured in the year of sale. An installment sale does not defer recapture of the first-year deduction.

¶5.412 • ADDITIONAL AMORTIZATION REALIZED ON LEASEHOLD IMPROVEMENTS

If an improvement or cost of acquiring a lease is amortized over the life of the lease including all renewal periods (or the life of the improvement, if that period is shorter), gain on the sale of the lease or leasehold improvement is not subject to ordinary income treatment. However, an amount called excess or additional amortization is subject to ordinary income treatment. Excess or additional amortization is the excess of the actual amortization taken over the amortization of depreciation that would have been taken over the lesser period of (1) the original term of the lease plus all renewal periods, or (2) 166⅔% (⅝) of the period of which actual amortization was taken.

If, as a lessee, you depreciate an improvement over a useful life that is less than the remaining term of the lease, you follow the rules applying to depreciable property.

¶5.42 • GIFTS AND INHERITANCES OF DEPRECIABLE PROPERTY

Gifts and charitable donations of depreciable property may be affected by the recapture rules. On the gift of depreciable property, the ordinary income potential of the depreciation carries over into the hands of the donee. When he later sells the property at a profit he will realize ordinary income to the extent described in ¶5.40 or ¶5.41. For purposes of the applicable percentage, the person receiving the gift includes in his holding period the period for which the donor held the property.

On the donation of depreciable property, the amount of the contribution deduction is reduced by the amount which would be taxed as ordinary income if the donor sold the equipment at its fair market value.

On the death of a decedent, the transfer of depreciable property to an heir through inheritance is not a taxable event for recapture purposes. The ordinary income potential does not carry over to the heir because his basis is usually fixed as of the date of the decedent's death.

Important: A gift of depreciable property subject to a mortgage may be taxed to the extent that the liability exceeds the basis of the property. *See* ¶14.05 and ¶28.02.

¶5.43 • INVOLUNTARY CONVERSIONS AND TAX-FREE EXCHANGES OF DEPRECIABLE PROPERTY

Involuntary conversions: Gain may be taxed as ordinary income in either of these two cases: (1) You do not buy a qualified replacement; or (2) you buy a qualified replacement, but the cost of the replacement is less than the amount realized on the conversion. The amount taxable as ordinary income may not exceed the amount of gain that is normally taxed under involuntary conversion rules when the replacement cost is less than the amount realized on the conversion. Also, the amount of ordinary income is increased by the value of any nondepreciable property which is bought as a qualified replacement property, for example, the purchase of 80% or more of stock in a company that owns property similar to the converted property.

Further details may be found in Treasury regulations.

Tax-free exchanges: Ordinary income generally is not realized on a tax-free exchange or trade-in (unless some gain is taxed because the exchange is accompanied by "boot" such as money). The ordinary income potential is assumed in the basis of the new property.

Distributions by a partnership to a partner: A distribution of depreciable property by a partnership to a partner does not result in ordinary income to the distributee at the time of the distribution. But the partner assumes the ordinary income potential of the depreciation deduction taken by the partnership on the property. When he later disposes of the property, he may realize ordinary income.

¶5.44 • INSTALLMENT SALE OF DEPRECIABLE PROPERTY

If you report on an installment basis a profitable sale of depreciable property made before June 7, 1984, "recaptured" ordinary income is reported before any of the capital gain is reported. You do not allocate the profit element of each installment payment between ordinary income and capital gain. As installments are received, you report all of the ordinary income until that amount is exhausted. For a sale after June 6, 1984, all recaptured ordinary income is fully taxable in the year of sale, without regard to the time of payment. However, this rule does not apply to installment sales made under a contract binding on March 22, 1984 and all times thereafter.

Recapture is figured on Form 4797.

¶5.45 • PROPERTY USED IN A BUSINESS (SECTION 1231 ASSETS)

The following properties used in a business are considered "Section 1231 assets:"

Depreciable assets such as buildings, machinery, and other equipment held long term.

Land (including growing crops and water rights underlying farm land) held long term.

Timber, coal or domestic iron ore subject to special capital gain treatment.

An unharvested crop on farm lands, if the crop and land are sold, exchanged or involuntarily converted at the same time and to the same person and the land has been held long term. Such property is not included here if you retain an option to reacquire the land.

Dairy, breeding, or draft animals acquired before 1970 and held for at least 12 months.

Cattle and horses acquired after 1969 and held for draft, breeding, dairy or sporting purposes, and held for at least 24 months.

Livestock (other than cattle and horses) acquired after 1969 and held for draft, breeding, dairy or sporting purposes and held for at least 12 months. Poultry is not treated as livestock for purposes of Section 1231.

Long-term holding period. The long-term holding period for property is more than six months.

Capital gain or ordinary loss. Sales and involuntary conversions of Section 1231 property are subject to a rule that allows profit to be taxed as capital gain (except for profits on equipment and real estate allocated to depreciation, *see* ¶5.40 and ¶5.41) and loss to be deducted as ordinary loss. The exact tax result depends on the net profit and loss realized for all sales of such property made during the tax year. The net result of these sales determines the tax treatment of each individual sale. In making the computation on Form 4797, you must consider also losses and gains from casualty, theft, and other involuntary conversions involving business and investment property held long term.

Recapture of net ordinary losses. Starting in taxable years beginning after December 31, 1984, net Section 1231 gain is not treated as capital gain but as ordinary income to the extent of net Section 1231 losses realized in the five most recent prior taxable years beginning after December 31, 1981. Losses are recaptured in chronological order on Form 4797.

Section 1231 netting. Add all losses and gains (except gains allocated to depreciation recapture) from:

Sale of Section 1231 assets (listed above).

The involuntary conversion of such assets and capital assets held long term for business or investment purposes. You include casualty and theft losses incurred on business or investment property held long term, whether or not insured. *See exception below if losses exceed gains from involuntary conversion in one taxable year.*

Involuntary conversions of capital assets held for personal purposes are not subject to a Section 1231 computation but are subject to a separate computation, *see* ¶18.27.

A net gain is taxed as a long-term capital gain. A net loss is fully deductible and is included as an ordinary asset transaction.

Examples—

1. You realize these gains and losses:

	Gain	Loss
Gain on sale of rental property held six years (no part attributed to rapid depreciation)	$5,000	
Loss on sale of business assets held four years		$3,000
	$5,000	$3,000
Net gain treated as long-term capital gain	$2,000	

As your gain exceeded the loss, each sale is treated as a sale of a capital asset held for more than one year. The net gain is included in Schedule D along with your other long-term gains and losses, if any. The effect of this treatment is to give you a long-term capital gain of $2,000, unless you realized a net Section 1231 loss in 1982, 1983, 1984 or 1985.

2. Assume the same facts as above but that your gain on the sale of rental property was $2,500. Since the gain does not exceed the loss and a net loss of $500 was realized, all of the transactions are treated as dispositions of noncapital assets. The net result is an ordinary loss of $500.

Involuntary conversion losses exceed involuntary conversion gains from casualties or thefts. You must compute the net financial result from all involuntary conversions arising from fire, storm, shipwreck, or other casualty or theft of assets used in your business and capital assets held for business or income-producing purposes and held long term. The purpose of the computation is to determine whether these involuntary conversions enter into the above Section 1231 computation. If the net result is a gain, all of the assets enter into the Section 1231 computation. If the net result is a loss, then these assets do not enter into the computation; the losses are deducted separately as casualty losses, the gains reported separately as ordinary income. If you incur only losses, the losses similarly do not enter into the Section 1231 computation.

Example—

You suffer an uninsured fire loss of $2,000 on equipment used in your business and a gain of $1,000 on other insured investment property damaged by a storm. All of the property was held long term. Because loss exceeds gain, neither transaction enters into a Section 1231 computation. The gain is reported as ordinary income and the loss is deducted as an ordinary loss. The effect is a net $1,000 loss deduction. If the figures were reversed, that is, if the gain was $2,000 and the loss $1,000, both assets would enter into the Section 1231 computation. If they are the only two transactions in the year, the net effect may be a net capital gain of $1,000. If only the fire loss had occurred, the loss would be treated as a casualty loss and would not enter into the Section 1231 computation.

Installment sale. Gain realized on the installment sale of business or income-producing property held long term may be long-term gain one year and ordinary gain another year. Actual treatment in each year depends on the net result of all sales including installment payments received in that year. *See also* ¶5.44.

If one spouse has a long-term capital gain and the other has the above type of fully deductible loss, separate returns might be filed to preserve the capital gain treatment and the fully deductible loss.

For an explanation of the ordinary income treatment of gain attributed to depreciation, *see* ¶5.40, ¶5.41.

Reporting Section 1231 transactions. Form 4797 (Supplementary Schedule of Gains and Losses) is used to report Section 1231 transactions and dispositions of property subject to ordinary income recapture. A sample Form 4797 is in the Supplement to this book.

¶5.46 • SALE OF A BUSINESS

Proprietorship. The sale of a sole proprietorship is *not* considered as the sale of a business unit but as sales of individual business assets. Each sale is reported separately on your tax return.

	Capital Asset	
Assets Held Over One Year	Yes	No
Customers' accounts		x
Inventory and supplies and stock in trade		x
Stocks and bonds held as investments	x	
Machinery, building, and other equipment used in your business	x*	
Land used in business	x	
Good will and nondepreciable franchises	x	
Depreciable franchises		x
Copyrights by a playwright of dramatic works		x
Literary manuscripts, etc., of a playwright		x
Assignable liquor license	x	
Noncompete contract (officer or employee)		x
Life insurance policy	x	

* *See* ¶5.45 for the rule. It is possible to get a full deduction for a net loss on a sale or treat net gain as long-term capital gain; but gain allocated to depreciation may be taxed as ordinary income (*see* ¶5.40, ¶5.41).

If the business was sold for a bulk price, you apportion the selling price among the assets sold, according to the relative fair market values of the assets. Whether you have an ordinary gain or loss, or a capital gain or loss depends on the tax classification of each asset sold. (A new law would change the method of allocation.)

Partnership. A sale of a partnership interest generally gives capital gain. But you have ordinary income to the extent the sales price covers unrealized partnership receivables, appreciated inventory items, and depreciation "recapture" on assets held by the partnership.

Unrealized receivables include any partnership rights to payment for goods delivered or services rendered that have not yet been included in the partnership income under its regular accounting method. Appreciated inventory items are those whose value is more than 120% of the partnership's basis for them; *and* more than 10% of the fair market value of all the partnership's property (except cash).

To compute the amount of ordinary income when you sell out, part of the basis of your partnership interest must be allocated to the interest in the receivables, inventory, and depreciation recapture items. You must attach a statement to your return showing the allocation of basis to receivables and inventory. Further, you must notify the partnership within 30 days of transferring a partnership interest that includes unrealized receivables or appreciated inventory. The partnership in turn notifies the IRS. See ¶10.00 for these reporting rules.

Poor timing of the sale of your partnership interest may be costly if the partnership reports on a fiscal year basis. In the year of sale, you may bunch more than a year of partnership income. The sale of a partnership interest closes the partnership year for the selling partner. Thus, in the year that you sell out, you must report your share of earnings up to the time of sale, in addition to the earnings from the regular partnership fiscal year.

In the liquidation of a retiring partner's or deceased partner's interest, ordinary income is realized on the amount of the distribution attributed to the partner's distributive share of income or guaranteed salaries or interest. Capital gain treatment is extended only to the value attributed to his partnership interest. And for this purpose, the partnership interest does not include payments for unrealized receivables which, if present, will be reflected as ordinary income. However, good will may be included as part of the partnership interest if the partnership agreement provides for such payment. It may not exceed the reasonable value of the distributee's share of the partnership good will. If the distribution includes appreciated inventory, ordinary income may also be realized.

A sale of only a part interest does not close your partnership tax year.

¶5.461 • COVENANTS NOT TO COMPETE AND SALE OF GOOD WILL

Payments for the sale of the good will of a business are subject to capital gain treatment. If, along with the sale of good will, a covenant not to compete is also given, the amount allocated to the covenant is subject to capital gain treatment provided the covenant is given to protect the transferred good will. If the covenant is not tied to good will, the payments received for the covenant are taxed as ordinary income. Payments for a noncompete covenant are treated as a form of compensation, that is, compensation not to perform services.

For a buyer of a business, a covenant not to compete gives not only legal protection but also tax advantages. He may deduct the amount paid for the covenant over the duration of the covenant. On the other hand, the seller must report the payment as ordinary income. For the sole purpose of deducting the amount allocated to the covenant, a buyer may demand a covenant although there is no danger of the seller's competition. A seller ignorant of the tax consequences to himself may agree to the demand or, if he is aware of the negative tax consequences, he may hope to get capital gain on the payment by arguing, if his return is examined, that the covenant was without substance. An appeals court and the Court of Claims would prevent a seller from proving that the covenant had no value. The terms of the contract would not be disregarded unless there was proof of mistake, undue influence, fraud, or duress. The Tax Court, however, rejects this approach and will review the terms of a contract to see if a covenant was bargained for and had business reality, but "strong proof" is required to upset the amount allowed to the covenant in the contract.

Professionals (lawyers, accountants, engineers, consultants, etc.) have good will in their firm names, which they can sell and have taxed at capital gain rates. The IRS will allow capital gain if the seller remains a member of the firm after the sale, provided good will is shown and the incoming partner has paid for part of it.

For effect of covenants not to compete on self-employment tax, see ¶5.60.

¶5.462 • SALE OF SECURITIES PURCHASED TO PROTECT BUSINESS INTERESTS

To protect a business interest, you may purchase securities of a company, or you may make the purchase of the securities to guarantee the supply of merchandise produced by the company. Under such circumstances, you may argue that your securities are not capital assets. You might take this position when you sell the securities at a loss or when they become worthless. The loss would be fully deductible as an ordinary loss rather than a capital loss. In some cases, courts have allowed such treatment. However, the IRS and Tax Court refuse to allow an ordinary loss deduction

where there was an investment motive mixed with a business reason for buying stock. To deduct an ordinary loss, be prepared to show that you had no expectation of making a profit on a rise in value of the shares. In one case, an executive claimed that when he joined a new firm, he was pressured into buying stock by the company's president. The Tax Court and an appeals court allowed only a capital loss. Although he may have felt pressured, his employment contract did not require him to buy the stock as a condition of getting or keeping his job. His investment motive was evidenced by these facts: (1) He admitted at trial that he thought he would eventually realize a profit on sale of the stock; (2) the contract he signed when buying the stock stated that the stock was being bought as an investment. The court rejected his argument that the contract language was necessary to avoid stock registration problems with the SEC.

If you are selling at a gain, your business motives in buying the stock might be used by the IRS as a reason for barring capital gain treatment. However, according to the Tax Court, you may get capital gain treatment even if you had a business motive provided some investment considerations also motivated your decision. The IRS has adopted the Tax Court approach.

Sale of partnership interest bought for business reasons. A purchase of a partnership interest for business reasons does not support ordinary loss deduction on later sale of the interest.

Example—

Pollack had invested in a limited partnership expecting the partnership to provide him with substantial consulting work. When prospects for consulting work declined, he sold his interest at a $27,100 loss which he deducted as an ordinary business loss; he claimed that the partnership interest did not qualify as a capital asset because he bought it for business rather than investment reasons. The IRS argued that the law specifically treats gain or loss from the sale of a partnership interest as a capital gain or loss (except for the portion of the sale proceeds attributable to unrealized receivables or substantially appreciated inventory). The Tax Court agreed. Pollack's loss was a capital loss, regardless of his motive for acquiring the partnership interest.

¶5.47 • SALE OF PROPERTY USED FOR BUSINESS AND PERSONAL PURPOSES

One sale will be reported as two separate sales for tax purposes when you sell a car or any other equipment used for business and personal purposes, or a house used partly as a residence and partly as a place of business or to produce rent income.

You allocate the sales price and the basis of the property between the business portion and the personal portion. The allocation is based on use. For example, with a car, the allocation is based on mileage used in business and personal driving.

Example—

Two partners bought an airplane for about $54,000. They used approximately 75% of its flying time for personal flights and 25% for business flights. After using the plane for eight years, they sold it for about $35,000. Depreciation taken on the business part of the plane amounted to $13,000. The partners figured they incurred a loss of $6,000 on the sale. The IRS, allocating the proceeds and basis between business and personal use, claimed they realized a profit of $8,250 on the business part of the plane and a nondeductible loss of $14,250 on the personal part. The allocation was as follows:

	Partners' claim	IRS Business (25%)	IRS Personal (75%)
Original cost	$54,000	$13,500	$40,500
Depreciation	13,000	13,000	
Adjusted basis	41,000	500	40,500
Selling price	35,000	8,750	26,250
Gain (Nondeductible loss)	($ 6,000)	$ 8,250	($14,250)

The partners argued that the IRS could not split the sale into two separate sales. They sold only one airplane and therefore there was only one sale. A federal district court and appeals court disagreed and held that the IRS method of allocation is practical and fair.

Other references: Allocation of a partly rented residence, see ¶29.40. Trade-in of car, see ¶3.061. Recapture of depreciation, see ¶5.40 and ¶5.41.

¶5.48 · TAX-FREE TRADES OF INVESTMENT OR BUSINESS PROPERTY

You may defer tax on gain realized on the "like-kind" exchange of business or investment property. If a loss is incurred on a like-kind exchange, the loss is not deductible (see ¶5.49).

Examples—

1. Jones, a real estate investor, purchased a parcel for investment in 1944 for $5,000. In 1982, he exchanged it for another parcel, Parcel B, which had a fair market value of $50,000. The gain of $45,000 is not taxed in 1982.

2. Same facts as above except that in 1986 Jones sells Parcel B for $50,000. His taxable gain is $45,000. The "tax-free" rules have the effect of deferring tax on appreciation. Tax is finally imposed when the exchanged item is sold.

3. Same facts as in example 1 but the value of Parcel B was $3,000. Jones may not deduct the loss. The basis of the parcel is $5,000. If Jones sells Parcel B in 1986 for $3,000, he may deduct a loss of $2,000.

For tax-free exchanges, the term "like-kind" refers to the character of the property; that is, whether real estate is traded for real estate, or whether business equipment is traded for business equipment. The term does not refer to the grade, quality or use of the property; that is, whether the property is new or used or whether a building is traded for land. Here are examples of approved like-kind trades:

An apartment house for an office building
Farmland for city lots
A building for a lot
Used business truck for a new business truck
Business machine for a business truck
Used business automobile for a new business automobile
Business automobile for a business truck
A leasehold interest of 30 years or more for an outright ownership in realty

However, trading a machine for a building would *not* be a like-kind exchange.

Whether you are holding property as an investment or as a dealer is an issue of fact (see ¶31.05).

Receipt of cash or other property. If, in addition to the exchanged property, you receive cash or other property, gain is taxable up to the amount of the cash or other property. The additional cash or other property is called "boot."

Example—

You received cash of $4,500 in addition to property you exchanged. $4,500 of the gain is subject to immediate tax, provided the gain realized on the exchange was $4,500 or more.

If a loss was incurred on the exchange, the receipt of boot does not permit you to deduct the loss.

Adjustments to basis for unrecognized gain or loss are discussed at ¶6.10.

If you give cash or other property in addition to the property exchanged, you add the amount of the boot to the basis of the property received.

If you trade mortgaged property, the amount of the mortgage is part of your boot.

Example—

A has an office building costing $30,000. It is subject to a $20,000 mortgage. He exchanges this for B's building (having a $35,000 cost) and $5,000 in cash. B takes A's building subject to the mortgage. The $5,000 in cash and B's taking subject to the $20,000 mortgage are both boot. The gain is computed this way:

Received by A:	
Cash received from B	$ 5,000
Building received from B	35,000
Mortgage on building traded to B	20,000
Total	$60,000
Less: Tax cost of building traded to B	30,000
Gain on sale	$30,000
Gain recognized (up to amount of boot)	$25,000

If depreciable property is exchanged, ordinary income may be realized if cash or other boot is taken (see ¶5.43).

Property not within the tax-free trade rules:

Property used for personal purposes (except for exchanges of personal residences; see ¶29.23)
Property held for sale
Inventory or stock-in-trade
Securities (see ¶6.21 for exception)
Notes
Partnership interests, see below

See also ¶31.021 for tax-free exchange of realty.

Exchange of partnership interests. Exchanges of partnership interests in different partnerships are not within tax-free exchange rules, if made after July 18, 1984 in taxable years ending after July 18, 1984. Prior tax-free exchange rules will apply to: (1) an exchange of partnership interests made under a binding contract effective on March 1, 1984 and at all times afterwards; (2) an exchange of a general partnership interest following a plan of reorganization of ownership interests under a contract taking effect on March 29, 1984, provided that all of the exchanges under the plan are completed on or before December 31, 1984.

Time limits for deferred exchanges. One of the parties to an exchange may not have at the time of contract property which he has promised to exchange. Under prior law, a delay in closing the exchange was not fatal to tax-free treatment. Under current law, the exchange must generally be completed within an 180-day period. The qualifying period may even be shorter than 180 days.

Property will *not* be treated as like-kind property if received after (1) 180 days after the date you relinquished property, or (2) the due date of your return for the year in which you made the transfer, *whichever date is earlier.* Further, the property to be received must be identified within 45 days after the date on which you transferred property. According to committee reports, the 45-day test may be met by describing the property in the contract or by listing a limited number of properties that may be transferred, provided the particular property to be transferred depends on contingencies beyond the control of both parties. For example, you transfer real estate for Smith's promise to transfer property X if zoning changes are approved or property Z if they are not. The exchange will qualify provided the contract covers these points and is made within the time limit. The 45/180-day rules apply to transfers after July 18, 1984 and to transfers on or before that date if the property to be received in exchange is not received before January 1, 1987. For transfers on or before July 18, 1984, the assessment period for a deficiency attributed to the new rule will not expire before January 1, 1988.

The rules do not apply if the property to be received in an exchange is identified in a binding contract in effect on June 13, 1984, and at all times after the transfer, and the property is received before January 1, 1989. The assessment period for these transfers will not expire before January 1, 1990.

¶5.49 · SHOULD YOU TRADE IN BUSINESS EQUIPMENT?

The purchase of new business equipment is often partially financed by trading in old equipment. For tax purposes, a trade-in may not be a good decision. If the market value of the equipment is below its adjusted basis, it may be preferable to sell the equipment to realize an immediate deductible loss. You may not deduct a loss on a trade-in. However, if you do trade, the potential deduction reflected in the cost basis of the old equipment is not forfeited. The undepreciated basis of the old property becomes part of the basis of the new property and may be depreciated. Therefore, in deciding whether to trade or sell where a loss may be realized, determine whether you will get a greater tax reduction by taking an immediate loss on a sale or by claiming larger depreciation deductions.

If the fair market value of the old equipment exceeds its adjusted basis, you have a potential gain. To defer tax on this gain, you may want to trade the equipment in for new equipment. Your decision to sell or trade will generally be based on a comparison between (1) tax imposed on an immediate sale and larger depreciation deductions taken on the cost basis of the new property; and (2) the tax consequences of a trade-in in which the tax is deferred but reduced depreciation deductions are taken on a lower cost basis of the property. In making this comparison, you will have to estimate your future income and tax rates. Also pay attention to the possibility that gain on the sale may be taxed as ordinary income under the depreciation recapture rules. *See* ¶5.40 and ¶5.41.

The tax consequences of a trade-in may not be avoided by first selling the used property to the dealer who sells you the new property. The IRS will disregard the sale made to the same

dealer from whom you purchase the new equipment. The two transactions will be treated as one trade-in.

When you trade in a car used partly for business and partly for pleasure, treat the deal as if you had exchanged and received two different types of assets: A personal asset and a business asset. Allocate part of the costs of the old and new car to your business use and part to your personal use. Figure the results on each part. Trade-in rules for a business auto are discussed at ¶2.305.

Self-Employment Tax

	See ¶
Self-employment tax	5.60
Partners pay self-employment tax	5.61

	See ¶
What is self-employment income?	5.62

¶5.60 • SELF-EMPLOYMENT TAX

You are liable for self-employment tax if you make a profit of $400 or more from operating a business or profession as sole proprietor, in partnership with others, or as an independent contractor.

For 1986, you pay 12.3% tax on net self-employment income of up to $42,000 ($5,166 maximum) when you pay your income tax. The self-employment tax provides funds for Social Security and Medicare benefits.

If you have more than one self-employed operation, your net earnings from all the operations are combined. A loss in one self-employed business will reduce the income from another business.

You continue to pay self-employment tax on self-employment income regardless of age and even if you receive Social Security benefits.

If you also received wages, *see* ¶5.62.

You must include the self-employment tax on your estimated tax declaration. Self-employment tax is added to your income tax liability. The two taxes are paid as one amount. Tax changes for 1987 self-employment tax are in the Supplement.

Self-employment tax rules for these positions or activities:

Clergy. An ordained minister, priest or rabbi (other than a member of a religious order who has taken a vow of poverty) is subject to self-employment tax, unless he elects not to be covered on the grounds of conscientious or religious objection to Social Security benefits. Before 1968, a minister had to elect Social Security coverage.

An application for exemption from Social Security coverage must be filed on or before the due date of a minister's income tax return for the second taxable year for which he has net earnings from his services as a clergyman of $400 or more (Form 4361).

An exemption, once granted, is generally irrevocable. However, a law did allow revocation of the exemption for 1977 or 1978. An exemption will not be granted to a minister who elected coverage under prior law.

Consultant. The IRS generally takes the position that income earned by a consultant is subject to self-employment tax. The IRS has also held that a retired executive hired as a consultant by his former firm received self-employment income, even though he was subject to an agreement prohibiting him from giving advice to competing companies. According to the IRS, consulting for one firm is a business; it makes no difference that he acts as a consultant only with his former company. The IRS has also imposed self-employment tax on fees although no services were performed for them.

The courts have generally approved the IRS position.

Director of a company. You are taxed as a self-employed person if you are not an employee of the company. Fees for attendance at meetings are self-employment income.

Employees of foreign governments or international organizations. If you are a U.S. citizen and you work in the United States, you pay tax as a self-employed worker although you are an employee of a foreign government or its wholly-owned instru-

mentality, or of an international organization given privileges, exemptions, and immunities by the International Organizations Immunities Act.

Executor. As a professional fiduciary, you will always be treated as having self-employment income, regardless of the assets held by the estate. But if you serve as a nonprofessional executor or administrator for the estate of a deceased friend or relative, you will not be treated as having self-employment income unless all of the following tests are met: (1) The estate includes a business. (2) You actively participate in the operation of the business. (3) All or part of your fee is related to your operation of the business.

Public officials and employees of a state or political subdivision. You may be subject to self-employment tax if you are compensated solely by fees. However, you do not have to pay self-employment tax on your fees if your services are covered by a state Social Security coverage agreement, or you elected exemption. (The election must have been made in 1968 and is irrevocable.)

Farmers. Cash or a payment-in-kind under the Payment-in-Kind program is considered earned income subject to self-employment tax.

Lecturer. You are not taxed as a self-employed person if you give only occasional lectures. If, however, you seek lecture engagements and get them with reasonable regularity, your lecture fees are treated as self-employment income.

Writer. Royalties from writing books are self-employment income to a writer. Royalties on books by a professor employed by a university may also be self-employment income despite employment as a professor.

Nurse. A registered nurse or a licensed practical nurse, when hired for private nursing services, is considered self-employed. He or she is an employee when hired by a hospital or a private physician in his practice and works for a salary following a strict routine during fixed hours.

Nurses' aides, domestics, and other unlicensed individuals who classify themselves as practical nurses are employees. They do not pay self-employment tax. This is true regardless of whether they work for a medical institution, a private physician, or a private household.

Babysitters. Where you perform services in your own home and determine the nature and manner of the services to be performed, you are considered to have self-employment income. However, where services are performed in the parent's home according to instructions by the parents, you are an employee of the parents and do not have earnings subject to self-employment tax.

Nonresident alien. You do not pay Social Security tax on your self-employment income derived from a trade, business, or profession. This is so even though you pay income tax. Your exemption from self-employment tax is not influenced by the fact that your business in the United States is carried on by an agent, employee, or partnership of which you are a member. However, if you live in Puerto Rico, the Virgin Islands, American Samoa, or Guam, you are not considered a nonresident alien and are subject to self-employment tax.

Dealers in commodities and options. Registered options dealers and commodities dealers are subject to self-employment tax on net gains from trading in Section 1256 contracts, which include regulated futures contracts, foreign currency contracts, dealer equity options and nonequity options. Self-employment tax also applies to net gains from trading property related to such contracts, such as stock used to hedge options. Long-term gains are considered in full without regard to the capital gains deduction.

Real estate agents and door-to-door salespersons. Licensed real estate agents are considered self-employed if they have a contract specifying that they are not to be treated as employees and if substantially all of their pay is related to sales rather than number of hours worked.

The same rule also applies to door-to door salesmen with similar contracts who work on a commission basis selling products in homes or other non-retail establishments.

¶5.61 • PARTNERS PAY SELF-EMPLOYMENT TAX

A partner includes his share of partnership income or loss in his net earnings from self-employment, including guaranteed payments. If your personal tax year is different from the partnership's tax year, you include your share of partnership income or loss for the partnership tax year which ends within 1986.

Example—
You file your return on the calendar year basis and your partnership uses the fiscal year ending March 31. You include your distributive share of partnership earnings and your guaranteed payments for the fiscal year ending March 31, 1986, in your 1986 return.

If a partner dies within the partnership's tax year, his self-employment income includes his distributive share of the income earned by the partnership through the end of the month in which his death occurs. This is true even though his estate succeeds to his partnership rights. For this purpose, partnership income for the year is considered to be earned ratably each month.

Retirement payments you receive from your partnership are not subject to self-employment tax if the following conditions are met:

1. The payments are made under a qualified written plan providing for periodic payments on retirement of partners with payments to continue at least until death.
2. You rendered no service in any business conducted by the partnership during the tax year of the partnership ending within or with your tax year.
3. By the end of the partnership's tax year, your share in the partnership's capital has been paid to you in full, and there is no obligation from the other partners to you other than with respect to the retirement payments under the plan.

Example—
Under a written plan, a retired partner was to receive monthly payments based upon a projection of partnership earnings; at the end of the partnership's year an adjustment was made to conform the retirement payments to the partnership's actual earnings. The retired partner received $24,000 in 1979. His actual share of partnership earnings turned out to be $30,000 and the excess $6,000 was paid to him in 1980, shortly after the end of the partnership's taxable year. The IRS ruled that the $6,000 was a retirement payment because the additional payment was made in accordance with the retirement plan. No self-employment tax was due on it.

A limited partner is not subject to self-employment tax on his share of partnership income.

¶5.62 • WHAT IS SELF-EMPLOYMENT INCOME?

Your self-employment income is generally your net profit from your business or profession whether you participate in its activities full or part time. However, according to the Tax Court, business interruption insurance proceeds are not subject to self-employment tax. Even though the proceeds are a substitute for lost profits, they do not arise from some actual income-producing activity, but rather, from the lack of such activity.

The following types of income or items are *not* included as self-employment income:

1. Rent from real estate is not self-employment income—*unless* it is the business income of a real estate dealer or income in a business where some services are rendered the occupant as in the leasing of—

Rooms in a hotel or in a boardinghouse.

Apartments (extra services).

Cabins or cabanas in tourist camps where you provide maid services, linens, utensils, and swimming, boating, fishing and other facilities, for which you do not charge separately.

Rents from the leasing of farm land in which the landlord materially participates in the actual production of the farm or in the management of production is considered self-employment income. For purposes of "material participation," the activities of a landlord's agent are not counted; only the landlord's actual participation.

The owner of one office building, who holds it for investment (rather than sale in the ordinary course of business), is not a real estate dealer. His rent income is not self-employment income. Furnishing heat, light, water, and trash and garbage collection to tenants is not services producing self-employment income.

2. Dividends and interest are not self-employment income. However, dividends earned by a dealer in securities and interest on accounts receivable are treated as self-employment income. A dealer is one who buys stock as inventory to sell to customers.

Income reported under an S election is not subject to self-employment tax.

3. Capital gains are not self-employment income. Similarly not treated as self-employment income are gains from the sale of property which is not inventory or held for sale to customers in the ordinary course of business. See exception for dealers in commodities and options in ¶5.60.

Net operating loss deduction. A loss carryover from past years does not reduce business income for self-employment tax purposes. Similarly, the personal exemption may not be used to reduce self-employment income.

Where you and your spouse *each* have self-employment income, each spouse must figure separate self-employment income on separate schedules. Each pays the tax on the separate self-employment income. Both schedules are attached to the joint return.

If you live in a community property state, business income is not treated as community property for self-employment tax purposes. The spouse who is actually carrying on the business is subject to self-employment tax on the earnings.

In 1986, you do not pay self-employment tax on more than $42,000. If your net earnings from self-employment are over $42,000, you pay $5,166 (12.3% of $42,000).

In 1986, if you also had wages of $42,000 or more as an employee in covered employment, you do not pay self-employment tax on your net earnings from self-employment. If you had wages of less than $42,000, you pay on the difference between your wages and $42,000. If that difference is more than your net earnings from self-employment, you pay on your net earnings.

Example—
In 1986, you have $42,000 net earnings from self-employment and $2,000 of wages subject to Social Security (F.I.C.A.) tax. Only $40,000 earned from your business ($42,000 − $2,000) is subject to the self-employment tax. If your net earnings from self-employment had been $5,000, then $5,000 would be subject to the self-employment tax.

When net self-employment earnings are less than $400, you pay no self-employment tax.

Optional self-employment income base. If your net self-employment income is less than $1,600, you may be allowed to pay self-employment tax on an increased base of up to $1,600. This option may allow you to increase your Social Security benefit base. If you are regularly self-employed, an optional method may be elected if your net earnings from non-farm self-employment are (1) less than $1,600 and (2) less than two-thirds of gross income and (3) you had net earnings of $400 or more from self-employment (both farm and non-farm) for two out of these three years: 1983, 1984, 1985. See the instructions to Form SE for further details.

¶ 6.00

Capital Gains and Losses on Sales of Property

Sample illustrations of reporting gains and losses on the sale of property may be found at ¶6.32. Also mail the card at the front of this book for a FREE Supplement with sample filled-in returns, including the separate Schedule D, and last-minute information.

How sales are taxed. Your gains and losses from sales and exchanges of property are not treated equally under the tax law. The varying tax effects on your sale depend generally on your purpose in holding the property.

WHAT KIND OF GAIN OR LOSS DO YOU HAVE?

Sale of Property Held for	Your Gain Is—	Your Loss Is—
Investment (stock, bonds, land, etc.) See ¶6.01.	Capital	Capital
Personal use (home, car, jewelry, etc.) See ¶6.012.	Capital	Nondeductible
Sale to customers (merchandise, etc.) See ¶5.03.	Ordinary income	Ordinary
Use in your business (Section 1231 property, such as depreciable buildings, trucks, machines, and equipment) See ¶5.45.	Capital or ordinary income	Capital or ordinary

Having your gain taxed as a capital gain has tax advantages. For capital gain treatment, you generally have to show:

1. *You have a capital asset or the kind of asset the gain on which qualifies as capital gain.* For example, securities which you hold for investment are capital assets. Other capital assets are described at ¶6.01.

Major subjects discussed in this chapter:

2. *You sold or exchanged the property or your transaction was the kind that is treated as a sale or exchange.* This test is automatically met when you sell property, for example, securities, real estate, etc. Nonsale dispositions that may qualify for capital gain treatment are discussed at ¶6.03.

3. *You have held the asset long term.* Capital gains and losses are either short term or long term, according to the length of time the asset has been held. This is an important distinction. Net short-term capital gains are fully taxable at ordinary income rates. Net long-term capital gains are subject to lower tax rates than the rates on ordinary income. This occurs by including in income only 40% of net long-term gains (as explained at ¶6.001). Part of your long-term capital gains may also be subject to the alternative minimum tax (see ¶23.10). A short-term gain results from the sale or exchange of property held for six months or less; long-term gain after a holding period of more than six months.

You may be able to spread the tax on gain. If the sale qualifies as an installment sale, you do not pay all the tax in one year, but over several years. See ¶6.17.

You may be able to defer tax. Tax may be deferred on certain sales or exchanges. The gain on the sale of your personal residence is not taxed when you use the proceeds to buy or build another (¶29.00). You also defer tax when you exchange investment real estate (¶6.20 and ¶31.021). If your property is destroyed or appropriated by government action and with the indemnity proceeds you buy other property, you may also defer tax (see ¶18.21).

¶6.001 • How Capital Gains and Losses Are Reported

Long-term capital gains are subject to less tax than ordinary income. Although the tax on capital gains is often spoken of as a separate tax, you do not figure it apart from your regular tax. You get the benefit of the capital gains tax by including in taxable income only 40% of net capital gains (net long-term gains less net short-term losses, if any). On Schedule D, this taxable amount is figured by subtracting the capital gain deduction of 60% of net capital gain.

The effective rate of tax on long-term capital gains will vary with your income tax bracket. For example, in the 33% income tax bracket, the effective rate of tax on capital gains is 13.2% (33% × 40%).

Schedule D is designed so that it incorporates the capital gain deduction. Therefore, for practical purposes, by following the line by line instructions of Schedule D, you figure the deduction and the balance of capital gain, which is reported on Form 1040 and is subject to tax along with your other income.

Form 1099-B. You should receive a statement from your broker, Form 1099-B (or equivalent), reporting your total sales of stocks and bonds during 1986. Income from a bartering exchange is also reported on Form 1099-B. The IRS may compare the amounts reported on Form 1099-B with the amounts reported on your return. There is a section on Schedule D for reconciling your return with Form 1099-B. For example, you may receive a Form 1099-B for a transaction that is not reportable as a sale, such as a distribution that is a tax-free return of capital; you would enter the amount in the reconciliation section and attach a statement noting that no gain or loss was realized. You may not receive a Form 1099-B for a 1986 sale which you are reporting on Schedule D, such as a year-end sale which your broker reported on a 1987 Form 1099-B instead of a 1986 form. You would indicate the year-end sale in the reconciliation section of Schedule D.

¶6.002 • FIGURING CAPITAL GAINS AND LOSSES

You segregate 1986 transactions into two groups: (1) Sales of property held long term; (2) sales of property held short term. A short-term gain or loss results from the sale or exchange of property held for six months or less; long-term gain or loss after a holding period of more than six months. In each group, offset gains and losses. In the long-term group, offset long-term gains and losses from each other. In the short-term group, offset short-term gains and losses from each other. Depending upon all your transactions in 1986, you will have one of these results:

(1) Net long-term gain. Your net long-term gain is reduced by the capital gain deduction; the balance of your gain is added to your other income reported on Form 1040.
Example—
You sell four lots of securities for long-term profit of $12,000. You list each transaction in your Schedule D. $4,800 of the $12,000 is added to your other income on Form 1040.

(2) Net long-term loss. You may deduct 50% of your long-term loss from other income, up to a maximum deduction of $3,000. You need $2 of long-term loss to deduct $1 from ordinary income. Thus, to deduct $3,000 from other income, your net long-term loss must be at least $6,000. You may carry over that part of the net long-term loss that exceeds the amount used to support a deduction from ordinary income. The computation of the carryover is discussed at ¶6.003.
Example—
Your only capital asset transaction is a sale of securities held long term. You realize a loss of $7,000. Your other income from salary, dividends, and interest is $28,000. You deduct $3,000 from your other income of $28,000. As $6,000 of your long-term loss was used to support the $3,000 deduction from ordinary income, you have a carryover loss of $1,000 to 1987 and later years.

(3) Net short-term gain. Add the full amount of it to your other income on Form 1040. Short-term gain is fully taxed as ordinary income.
Example—
Your only capital asset transaction is a sale of stock held for five months. You realize a profit of $8,000, which is shown on Schedule D, and then added to your ordinary income on Form 1040.

(4) Net short-term loss. You deduct this loss from your other income up to $3,000. If the loss exceeds your ordinary income or is over $3,000, the unused loss is carried over as a short-term loss to 1987 and later years.
Example—
Your only capital asset transaction is a sale of stock held for four months. You realize a loss of $800. You have ordinary income of $20,000 from salary. You deduct the $800 from your ordinary income on Form 1040. If the loss were $3,200, only $3,000 of the loss would be deducted from your ordinary income. The remaining $200 is carried over as a short-term loss to 1987.

(5) Net long-term gain and net short-term gain. 40% of the net long-term gain and 100% of the net short-term gain is added to your other income on Form 1040.
Example—
You sell one lot of securities held for two years at a profit of $6,000. You sell another lot held for two months at a profit of $4,000. $6,400 is added to your other income on Form 1040 (40% of the $6,000 long-term profit, or $2,400, plus all of the short-term profit of $4,000).

(6) Net long-term gain and net short-term loss. Deduct the net short-term loss from the net long-term gain. If the net short-term

loss exceeds the net long-term gain, the remaining loss is deductible from other income up to $3,000. After this deduction from ordinary income, any remaining loss is carried over to later years as a short-term loss. If the long-term gain exceeds the short-term loss, 40% of the remaining long-term gain is added to other income.
Example—
You sell two lots of securities held for two years at a profit of $9,000. You also sell a lot of securities held for three months at a loss of $10,000. Combining both the loss and the gain leaves a short-term capital loss of $1,000, which may be deducted from ordinary income. If the short-term loss were $4,000, a net long-term capital gain of $5,000 ($9,000 — $4,000) would have resulted. Of this, $2,000 would be added to your other income.

(7) Net short-term gain and net long-term loss. Deduct the long-term loss from the short-term gain. If the gain exceeds the loss, add the full amount of the remaining gain to your other income. If the loss exceeds the gain, the remaining long-term loss is deductible under the limitations explained above in (2).
Example—
You realize a net short-term gain of $3,000 and net long-term loss of $4,000. By combining both figures, you get a net loss of $1,000. $500 of this amount is deductible from ordinary income on Form 1040. There is no carryover. If the long-term loss were $2,500, net gain of $500 would be added to your ordinary income.

(8) Net long-term loss and net short-term loss. The losses reduce up to $3,000 of ordinary income in this order: First apply the short-term loss, then the long-term loss under the limitations explained above in (2). Carryovers of short-term and long-term losses keep their identity in later years as short-term or long-term losses.

If taxable income reduced by the zero bracket amount is less than $3,000, the deduction of excess capital losses may not exceed the reduced amount of taxable income. Taxable income, for purposes of figuring the capital loss limitation, does not include capital gain or loss and is not reduced by personal exemptions.

¶6.003 • CAPITAL LOSS CARRYOVERS

You have a capital loss carryover when the ordinary income ceiling of up to $3,000 prevents you from deducting the full amount of your net capital loss. You have an unlimited period of time to deduct the loss from future gains, but you do not have the option to defer claiming the deduction in a year in which the deduction provides no tax benefit.
Example—
In 1973, Smith had a long-term capital loss and no income. In 1974, he had a small adjusted gross income which was almost offset by itemized deductions and exemptions. He decided not to deduct any part of his carryover loss in 1974 so that he could deduct it in later years when his income would be larger. The IRS ruled he had no choice but to reduce the loss carried over to 1975 by the amount deductible from his 1974 gross income.

The following chart illustrates how the 50% reduction limits the deduction and carryover of long-term losses.

Net long-term loss is	Deductible from ordinary income	Carryover
$3,000	$1,500	0
4,000	2,000	0
5,000	2,500	0
6,000	3,000	0
7,000	3,000	1,000
8,000	3,000	2,000

On Schedule D, you compute the carryover for both long- and short-term losses, which keep their character over the carryover period. If the original loss is short term, the carryover is short term; if long term, the carryover is long term.
Examples—
1. From 1985, you have a long-term capital loss carryover of $2,000. In 1986, you have ordinary income of $15,000, a long-term gain of $2,000, and short-term gain of $3,000. The long-term capital loss carryover is applied to and offsets the long-term capital gain.
2. From 1985, you have a short-term capital loss carryover of $5,000. In 1986, you have ordinary income of $15,000, a short-term gain of $1,000 and a long-term gain of $1,000. The carryover is first applied to the short-term gain which is eliminated. The remaining loss of $4,000 is then applied to the long-term gain which is eliminated. The remaining

$3,000 of loss is deducted from ordinary income. The carryover has been eliminated.

3. Assume the same facts as in example (2) except that the carryover loss of $5,000 was realized in a long-term transaction in 1985. The loss is first applied to the long-term gain, then to the short-term gain; $1,500 of the loss is deducted from ordinary income. The carryover has been eliminated.

Nonresident aliens who are not in business in the United States are not allowed a carryover.

Unused carryovers of a deceased person may not be used by his estate.

Pre-1970 losses. A long-term capital loss carryover from pre-1970 years is not reduced by 50% before it is deducted from ordinary income. Where you have both a carryover of pre-1970 losses and current net long-term losses, the pre-1970 loss is deducted first.

If a pre-1970 carryover is deductible on Schedule D, you may use Form 4798 for computing the carryover. *See* Treasury regulations for details in figuring the pre-1970 carryover.

Special loss treatment for pre-1970 losses will stop after 1986.

¶6.004 • CAPITAL LOSSES OF MARRIED COUPLES

On a joint return, the capital asset transactions of both spouses are combined in one Schedule D. A carryover loss of one spouse may be applied to capital gains of the other spouse. Where both spouses incur net capital losses, only one capital loss deduction of up to $3,000 is allowed. This rule may not be avoided by filing separate returns. If you file separately, the deduction limit for each return is $1,500.

Example—

You and your spouse individually incurred capital losses of $5,000 and $4,000. If you file separate returns, the maximum amount deductible from ordinary income on each return is $1,500.

Death of spouse. The IRS holds that if a capital loss is incurred by a spouse on his or her own property and that spouse dies, the surviving spouse may not claim any unused loss carryover on a separate return.

Example—

In 1983, Smith realized a substantial long-term capital loss on separately owned property which was reported on his 1983 joint return. Part of the excess loss was carried over to the couple's 1984 joint return and in 1985, before the carryover loss was used up, Smith died. His widow could claim the unused carryover, up to the $3,000 limit, on a joint return filed for 1985, the year of death. However, any remaining loss carryover to 1986 or later years is lost. Although the loss was originally reported on a joint return, the widow may only claim her allocable share of the loss on her separate returns. Since the loss property was owned solely by the deceased husband, no loss is allocable to the widow's separate returns.

Capital Asset Transactions

¶6.01 • WHAT ARE CAPITAL ASSETS?

Generally, all properties that you own are capital assets if you are not in a business or other income-producing activity. This means that gains and losses on sales of these assets are subject to capital gain treatment as explained at ¶6.001. There is, however, one important limitation applied to losses on sales of property used for personal purposes: The losses are not deductible. *See* ¶6.012.

If you are in a business or other income-producing activity, your property may be capital assets, Section 1231 assets, or inventory or stock-in-trade type assets. Tax treatment of Section 1231 assets is discussed at ¶5.45. Profit from the sale of inventory or stock-in-trade assets is taxable at ordinary income tax rates; loss is generally fully deductible.

The following are not capital assets:

(1) Inventory items
(2) Stock in trade
(3) Property held primarily for sale to customers in the ordinary course of business, for example, subdivided lots held by a real estate dealer.
(4) Depreciable property or real estate used in a trade or business (but *see* ¶5.45).
(5) Copyrights, literary, musical, or artistic compositions, a letter or memorandum or similar property held by the creator of the property or other persons who obtained the property from the creator in a tax-free exchange or as a gift. A letter or memorandum that was prepared or produced for you is also not a capital asset.
(6) Accounts or notes receivable acquired in the ordinary

course of business from the sale of inventory or property held primarily for sale to customers, or for services rendered as an employee.

¶6.011 • EXAMPLES OF CAPITAL ASSETS

All assets that fit into any of the following categories (provided you are not a dealer in those assets and they are not your regular stock in trade)—

Stocks, bonds, and other securities.
Land, buildings, and other property not used in your business.
Warehouse receipts in which you trade or speculate.
Notes you purchased and did not hold for sale to customers in the ordinary course of your business.
Commodity and other futures bought or sold when you are speculating. You realize ordinary income or loss when you hedge with futures. For example, a cotton merchant before or at the time of contract to sell and deliver cotton at a future date also contracts to buy cotton for future delivery. He is insuring himself against price fluctuations. His activity is considered a true hedge. *See also* ¶6.0352.
Expiration records sold by insurance agent. An insurance agent generally owns the expiration records of fire and casualty insurance sold by him. These records show the beginning and expiration dates and types of policies sold. With this information, the agent can obtain renewals from clients when their policies are about to expire.
Patents, royalty interests, etc., not used in your business.
Literary properties bought for investment, for example, stories bought by a radio commentator and a motion picture director

for a hoped-for resale to the movies. These are isolated dealings, not part of their business.

Trademarks.

Obligations of state or federal governmental bodies. *See* ¶4.07 for special ordinary income rules for Treasury Bills.

Dealers: Property you own may be treated as a capital asset even though you sell similar property in your business. For example, not all securities held by a dealer in securities are stock-in-trade assets. Securities held for investment or speculation, not as stock in trade, are capital assets. Real estate dealers, *see* ¶31.05.

¶6.012 • PROPERTY USED FOR PERSONAL PURPOSES

Your residence, personal automobile, jewelry, home equipment, furniture, antiques, clothing, and similar property used for personal purposes are capital assets.

Profits from the sale of personal assets are subject to capital gains treatment. Losses are not deductible unless the properties are acquired in a transaction entered into for profit (*see* ¶6.02).

Some assets may be held both for personal and business purposes, such as an automobile used by a salesman in his work and used on weekends for pleasure. As explained in ¶5.47, the asset is treated as two separate assets for purposes of figuring gain or loss from its sale.

¶6.02 • CAN YOU DEDUCT LOSSES ON SALE OF THESE PERSONAL ASSETS?

Pleasure auto, yacht, or other vehicle

YES . . .

If acquired for the purpose of making a profit on resale and used for pleasure purposes to a slight degree.

If acquired and used for business purposes except for an occasional pleasure trip.

If used solely to demonstrate to prospective purchasers.

If sold by an executor for an estate. All transactions of an executor for an estate are assumed to be profit-seeking. The estate may claim a loss on the sale of a personal asset for less than its fair market value, even though the decedent could not if he had sold it.

NO . . .

If acquired for pleasure use—only incidentally with the hope of making a profit on resale.

Jewelry, furs, and other personal effects

YES . . .

If acquired for the purpose of making a profit on resale even if worn incidentally for ornamentation.

NO . . .

If acquired for personal adornment—even though believed to be a safer investment than stocks, bonds, or real estate.

Paintings and works of art

YES . . .

If acquired for the purpose of making a profit on resale. You indicate a profit motive when, for example, you employ an artist to clean and prepare a painting for sale, or place it with an art gallery for sale.

NO . . .

If acquired for personal use and enjoyment and held for many years without attempting to make a profit from it.

Coins, postage stamps, or autograph collections

YES . . .

If acquired primarily for financial gain even though you derive some incidental pleasure from the collection.

If you bought a collection, you do not have to wait until you sell all of it before you may take your loss. You may allocate a portion of your cost to each part. Then find your gain or loss when each unit is sold. If an apportionment is impracticable, you may wait until you sell the entire collection before taking the loss.

NO . . .

If acquired mainly for personal pleasure.

Residences—*see* ¶29.28.

Sublease of apartment. Instead of breaking a lease, a tenant who finds that he must move decides to sublet his apartment but finds he can rent it only at a rental lower than he pays. According to the IRS, he may not deduct his loss, the difference between his rent and the rent he collects.

¶6.03 • SALE OR EXCHANGE USUALLY REQUIRED FOR CAPITAL ASSET TREATMENT

Capital asset treatment generally requires a sale or exchange of a capital asset.

Exchanges treated as tax-free transactions are discussed at ¶6.20, ¶12.33, ¶29.20, ¶31.021.

A forced or involuntary sale, such as a foreclosure sale of mortgaged property, a condemnation of property, or the sale of property pledged as collateral, is treated as a sale. The IRS and some courts also consider a voluntary conveyance of mortgaged property to the mortgagee as a sale, whether or not the mortgagor is personally liable on the debt. The IRS Tax Court and some appeals courts also treat an abandonment of mortgaged property as a sale.

A debtor who gives property to his creditor in satisfaction of a debt transacts a sale or exchange. Gain or loss is the difference between adjusted basis of the property and the amount of debt. Similarly, an executor who transfers property to an heir in satisfaction of a cash bequest transacts a taxable sale for the estate.

A property settlement accompanying a divorce is treated as a tax-free transfer, *see* ¶6.245.

The IRS and most courts treat a gift of mortgaged property as a sale if the amount of the mortgage exceeds the donor's basis; the excess is taxable gain to the donor.

Capital asset treatment applies to the following transactions even though a sale or exchange has not occurred:

A nonbusiness bad debt becomes worthless. The loss is a short-term capital loss (*see* ¶6.28).

Cancellation of lease. Payments received by the tenant on the cancellation of a business lease held long term are treated as proceeds received in a Section 1231 transaction, *see* ¶5.45. Payments received by the tenant on cancellation of a lease on a personal residence or apartment are treated as proceeds of a capital asset transaction. Gain is long-term capital gain if the lease was held long term; losses are not deductible.

Cancellation of a distributor's agreement if you made a substantial capital investment in the distributorship. For example, you own facilities for storage, transporting, processing, or dealing with the physical product covered by the franchise. You do not get capital gain if you have an office mainly for clerical work, or where you handle just a small part of the goods covered by the franchise.

Pension and profit-sharing trust distributions to employees may be long-term capital gain (*see* ¶7.01).

Timber. Capital gain treatment is applied to sales and other dispositions of timber. If you own timber long term, you may treat the cutting of timber as a sale. For details, see the IRS's *Farmer's Tax Guide,* Publication 225.

¶6.031 • SALE OR RETIREMENT OF BONDS AND NOTES

Retirement of an obligation issued by an individual debtor. Capital gain treatment does not apply to retirement of a debt by an individual. Capital gain treatment, however, may apply if you sell the obligation to a third party and the obligation is a capital asset (*see* ¶6.01). A note acquired by you in your business for services rendered or for the sale of merchandise is not a capital asset. The treatment of periodic payments made on obligations purchased at a discount is discussed at ¶31.063.

Example—

You bought for $6,000 a second trust note of $10,000 of an individual. You receive payments totaling $4,000. 60% ($6,000/$10,000) of the $4,000 is treated as a return of your investment; the balance as discount or interest income. You sell the note for $3,800. To determine your profit or loss, you reduce your cost by $2,400 ($4,000 × 60%). Your capital gain is $200.

Selling price of note		$3,800
Less: Cost of note	$6,000	
Return on investment	2,400	
Adjusted basis of note		3,600
Capital gain		$ 200

Retirement of bonds. Gain or loss on the retirement of debt obligations issued by a government or corporation is generally capital gain or loss. If the bond was issued before 1955, there is capital gain or loss only if the obligation was issued with interest coupons or in registered form on or before March 1, 1954.

Corporate bonds with OID issued before May 28, 1969 and government bonds with OID issued before July 2, 1982. If the bonds were originally issued at a discount (OID), you report the OID element as ordinary income when the bonds are sold or redeemed; any gain exceeding OID is reported as capital gain. A loss is a capital loss. The method of figuring the taxable OID element is explained at ¶4.032.

Corporate bonds with OID issued after May 27, 1969 and government bonds with OID issued after July 1, 1982. The ratable amount of OID is reported annually as ordinary income and added to basis, *see* ¶4.032. If the bonds are sold or redeemed before maturity, you realize capital gain for the amount over the adjusted basis of the bond, provided there was no intention to call the bond before maturity. If there was an intention to call the obligation before maturity, the unearned discount is taxable as ordinary income; the balance is capital gain.

Market discount on bonds issued after July 18, 1984 is taxable under the rules explained at ¶4.034.

Discount on tax-exempt bonds is discussed at ¶4.06.

¶6.032 • WORTHLESS SECURITIES

You may deduct as a capital loss the cost basis of securities that have become worthless in 1986. A loss of worthless securities is deductible only in the year the securities become completely worthless. The loss cannot be deducted in any other year.

To support a deduction for 1986 you must show:

1. The stock had some value in 1985. That is, you must be ready to show that the stock did not become worthless in a year prior to 1986.

2. The stock became worthless in 1986. You must be able to present facts fixing the time of loss during this year. For example, the company went bankrupt, stopped doing business, and is insolvent. Despite evidence of worthlessness, such as insolvency, the stock may be considered to have some value if the company continues to do business, or there are plans to reorganize the company.

If a company is in financial trouble but you are not sure whether its condition is hopeless, it is advisable to claim the deduction in 1986 to protect your claim. This advice was given by a court: "The taxpayer is at times in a very difficult position in determining in what year to claim a loss. The only safe practice, we think, is to claim a loss for the earliest year when it may possibly be allowed and to renew the claim in subsequent years if there is a reasonable chance of its being applicable for those years."

Sometimes you can avoid the problem of proving worthlessness. If there is still a market for the security, you can sell. For example, the company is on the verge of bankruptcy, but in 1986 there is some doubt about the complete worthlessness of its securities. You might sell the securities for whatever you can get for them and claim the loss on the sale. However, if the security became worthless in a prior year, say in 1984, a sale in 1986 will not give you a deduction in 1986.

If you are making payments on a negotiable note you used to buy the stock which became worthless and you are on the cash basis method, your payments are deductible losses in the years the payments are made, rather than in the year the stock became worthless.

If the security is a bond, note, certificate or other evidence of a debt incurred by a corporation, the loss is deducted as a capital loss, provided the obligation is in registered form or has attached interest coupons. A loss on a worthless corporate obligation is always deemed to have been sustained on the last day of the year, regardless of when the company failed during the year. No deduction may be claimed for a partially worthless corporate bond.

If the obligation is not issued with interest coupons or in registered form or if it is issued by an individual, the loss is treated as a bad debt. If you received the obligation in a business transaction, the loss is fully deductible. You may also make a claim for a partially worthless business bad debt. If it is a nonbusiness debt, the loss is a capital loss and no claim may be made for partial worthlessness. *See* ¶6.28.

Stock which becomes worthless is deducted as a capital loss unless it fits within the rules of ¶6.0321. A sale is presumed to have occurred at the end of the year, regardless of when worthlessness actually occurred during the year. You may not claim a loss for partially worthless stock.

Example—
You buy 100 shares of Z Co. stock on June 1, 1960. On March 17, 1986, the stock is considered wholly worthless. The loss is deemed to have been incurred on December 31, 1986. The loss is deducted as a long-term capital loss; the holding period is from June 1, 1960, to December 31, 1986.

Claim for refund. You have seven years from the due date of your return to claim a refund based on a deduction of a bad debt or worthless security. *See* ¶27.01.

Example—
You have held securities which you learn became worthless in 1979. You still have until April 15, 1987 to file for a refund of 1979 taxes by claiming a deduction for the worthless securities.

Small Business Investment Company stock losses. Investors in such stock may take ordinary loss deductions for losses on the worthlessness or sale of such stock. The loss may also be treated as a business loss for net operating loss purposes. However, a loss realized on a short sale of SBIC stock is deductible as a capital loss. A Small Business Investment Company is a company authorized to provide small businesses with equity capital. Do not confuse investments in these companies with investments in small business stock (Section 1244 stock) discussed at ¶6.0321.

Bad debts of political parties are generally not deductible.

S corporation stock. If an S corporation's stock becomes worthless during the taxable year, the basis in the stock is adjusted for the stockholder's share of corporate items of income, loss, and deductions before a deduction for worthlessness is claimed.

¶6.0321 • SECTION 1244 STOCK (SMALL BUSINESS STOCK)

A law (Internal Revenue Code Section 1244) allows an ordinary loss deduction on Section 1244 stock losses, subject to the limits stated below. You may have your company plan a special issue of stock (voting or nonvoting) that will be treated as Section 1244 stock if certain tests are met.

An ordinary loss of up to $50,000 ($100,000 on a joint return) may be claimed on Section 1244 stock. Losses in excess of these limits are deductible as capital losses.

An ordinary loss may be claimed only by the original owner of the stock. If a partnership sells Section 1244 stock at a loss, an ordinary loss deduction may be claimed by individuals who were partners when the stock was issued. If a partnership distributes the Section 1244 stock to the partners, the partners may not claim an ordinary loss on their disposition of the stock.

To qualify as Section 1244 stock:

1. The corporation's equity may not exceed $1,000,000 at the time the stock is issued but including amounts received for the stock to be issued. Thus, if the corporation already has $600,000 equity from stock previously issued, it may not issue more than $400,000 worth of Section 1244 stock.

Preferred stock issued after July 18, 1984 may also qualify for Section 1244 loss treatment.

2. The stock must be issued for money or property (other than stock and securities).

3. The corporation for the five years preceding your loss must generally have derived more than half of its gross receipts from business operations and not from passive income such as rents, royalties, dividends, interest, annuities or gains from the sales or exchanges of stock or securities. This requirement is waived if the corporation's deductions (other than for dividends received or net operating losses) exceed gross income. If the corporation has not been in existence for the five years before your loss, then generally the period for which the corporation has been in existence is examined for the gross receipts test.

¶6.033 • CORPORATE LIQUIDATION

Liquidation of a corporation and distribution of its assets for your stock is generally subject to capital gain or loss treatment. For example, on a corporate liquidation, you receive property worth $10,000 from the corporation. Assume the basis of your shares, which you have held long term, is $6,000. You have realized a long-term gain of $4,000.

The corporation may distribute contracts or other assets whose value cannot be figured at the time you receive them. Later, when you receive money for these assets, treat the money as if received from a liquidation. You thus get a capital gain instead of ordinary income. It makes no difference that the corporation would have had ordinary income realized on the assets if it had not liquidated.

If you incur legal expenses in pressing payment of a claim, you treat the fee as a capital expense according to the IRS. The Tax Court and an appeals court hold that the fee is deductible from ordinary income as an expense incurred to earn income.

If you recover a judgment against the liquidator of a corporation for misuse of corporate funds, the judgment is considered part of the amount you received on liquidation and gives you capital gain, not ordinary income.

If you paid a corporate debt after liquidation, the payment reduces the gain realized on the corporate liquidation in the earlier year; thus, in effect, it is a capital loss.

If the corporation distributes liquidating payments over a period of years, gain is not reported until the distributions exceed the adjusted basis of your stock (*see* ¶3.08).

¶6.035 • SALE OF AN OPTION

The tax treatment of the sale of an option depends on the tax classification of the property to which the option relates.

If the option is for the purchase of property that will be a capital asset in your hands, you realize capital gain or loss on the sale of the option. Whether the gain or loss is long term or short term depends on your holding period.

Examples—
1. You pay $500 for an option to purchase a house. After holding the option for five months, you sell the option for $750. Your profit of $250 is short-term capital gain.

2. The same facts as in (1) above, except that you sell the option for $300. The loss is not deductible because the option is related to a sale of a personal residence (*see* ¶6.02).

If the option is for a "Section 1231 asset" (*see* ¶5.45), gain or loss on the sale of the option is combined with other Section 1231 asset transactions to determine if there is capital gain or ordinary loss.

If the option relates to an ordinary asset in your hands, then gain or loss would be ordinary income or loss.

If you fail to exercise an option and allow it to lapse, the option is considered to have been sold on the expiration date. Gain or loss is computed according to the rules explained above.

The party granting the option realizes ordinary income on its expiration, regardless of the nature of the underlying property. If the option is exercised, the option payment is added to the selling price of the property.

¶6.0351 • CALLS OR OPTION TRANSACTIONS ON OPTION EXCHANGES

Option exchanges, such as the Chicago Board of Option Exchange (CBOE) and Amex market, provide a market for standardized options on a specific number of listed stocks, eliminating any relationship between option seller and buyer. The details and risk of these options are more fully discussed in ¶30.02. The following paragraphs give the tax consequences of call options transacted by investors on option exchanges, such as CBOE and Amex.

Buyers of options. If you buy an option, the treatment of your investment in the option depends on what you do with it.

1. If you sell it, you realize short-term or long-term capital gain or loss, depending upon how long you held the option.

2. If you allow the option to expire without exercise, you incur a short-term or long-term capital loss, depending on the holding period of the option. The expiration date is treated as the date the option is disposed of.

3. If you exercise the option and buy the stock, you add the cost of the option to the basis of the stock.

Grantors of options. If you write an option through the exchange, you do not treat the premium received for writing the option as income at the time of receipt. You do not realize profit or loss until the option transaction is closed. This may occur when the option expires or is exercised or when you "buy in" on the exchange an option similar to the one you gave to end your obligation to deliver the stock. Here are the rules for these events:

1. If the option is not exercised, you report the premium as short-term capital gain in the year the option expires.

2. If the option is exercised, you add the premium to the sales proceeds of the stock to determine gain or loss on the sale of the stock. Gain or loss is short-term or long-term depending upon the holding period of the stock.

3. If you "buy in" an equivalent option in a closing transaction, you realize profit or loss for the difference between the premium of the option you sold and the cost of the closing option. The profit or loss is treated as short-term capital gain or loss. However, a loss on a covered call that has a stated price below the stock price may be long-term capital loss if at the time of the loss, long-term gain would be realized on the sale of the stock. Further, the holding period of such stock is suspended during the period in which the option is open. Finally, year-end losses from covered call options are not deductible, unless the stock is held uncovered for more than thirty days following the date on which the option is closed.

Index options. Nonequity options and dealer equity options, which include options based on regulated stock indexes and interest rate futures, are taxed like regulated futures contracts. This means that they are reported annually under the mark-to-market accounting system. You treat all such options held at the end of the year as if they were disposed of at year-end for a price equal to fair market value. Any gain or loss is arbitrarily taxed as if it were 60-percent long-term and 40-percent short-term, which gives a maximum tax rate of 32%. It is advisable to ask your broker whether the specific options which you hold come within this special rule.

¶6.0352 • STRADDLE LOSSES AND DEDUCTIONS RESTRICTIONS

Straddles are tax shelter devices to spot losses in one year and gains in another year and to convert ordinary income into capital gain. These maneuvers are now effectively barred by tax accounting rules. Straddle rules apply to commodities and actively traded stock and to stock options used in straddle positions. Straddle positions include any stock that is part of a straddle in which at least one of the offsetting positions is (1) an option tied to the stock or to substantially identical stock or securities or (2) a position in substantially similar or related property other than stock. For example, there is a straddle of stock and substantially similar or related property if offsetting positions of stock and convertible debentures of the same corporation are held and price movements of the two positions are related. Straddle rules apply also to stock of a corporation formed or used to take positions in personal property that offset positions taken by any shareholder. True hedging transactions are not subject to the straddle tax rules. Also, a call option is not treated as part of a straddle position if it is considered a qualified covered call option. A qualified covered call option is an option that a stockholder, who is not a dealer, grants on stock traded on a national securities exchange. Further, the option must be granted more than 30 days before its expiration date and must not be "deep-in-the-money." A covered call option will not qualify if gain on the sale of the stock to be purchased by the option is reported in a year after the year in which the option is closed or if the stock is not held for more than 30 days after the date on which the option is closed. In such a case, the option is subject to the straddle loss deferral rules.

Loss on a qualified covered call option with a strike price less than its applicable stock price is treated as long-term capital loss if loss realized on the sale of the stock would be long term. The holding period for stock subject to the option does not include any period during which the taxpayer is the grantor of the option.

A "deep-in-the-money option" is an option with a strike or exercise price that is below the lowest qualified bench mark. The technical rules for determining these values are not discussed in this book.

Tax rules for straddles. The following is an overview of the subject and if you have transacted straddles, we suggest that you consult with an experienced practitioner.

Realized straddle losses are deductible at the close of a taxable year only if they exceed unrealized gains in an offsetting position. Thus, an investor may not deduct losses incurred in 1985 to the extent that he has an unrealized gain position in the open end of the straddle. Form 6781 is used for straddle reporting.

Straddle positions of related persons (such as spouse or child) or controlled flow-through entities (such as a partnership or an S corporation) are considered in determining whether offsetting positions are held.

Realized losses that are not deductible at the end of the year are carried forward and become deductible when there is no unrealized appreciation in an offsetting position bought before the disposition of the loss position. This loss deferral rule may be avoided by identifying straddles before the close of the day of acquisition or at an earlier time that the IRS may set. Gain or loss in identified positions is generally netted; that is, a loss is recognized when the offsetting gain position has been closed.

If you are in a straddle arrangement you must disclose all positions of unrealized gains at the close of a tax year or you may be subject to a negligence penalty unless failure to disclose is due to a reasonable cause.

The loss deferral rule does not apply to positions in a regulated futures contract or other Section 1256 contract subject to the "mark-to-market" system explained below.

The loss deferral rule also does not apply to businesses that must hedge in order to protect their supplies of inventory or financial capital. Hedging transactions are subject to ordinary income or loss treatment. Hedging transactions entered into by syndicates do not qualify for the exception and are subject to the loss deferral rule if more than 35% of losses for a taxable year are allocable to limited partners or entrepreneurs. Further, hedging losses of limited partners or limited entrepreneurs are generally limited to their taxable income from the business in which the hedging transaction was entered into.

Regulated futures contracts and other Section 1256 contracts. Gain or loss on regulated futures contracts is reported annually under the mark-to-market accounting system of regulated commodity exchanges. To settle margin requirements, regulated exchanges determine a party's account for futures contracts on a daily basis. Each regulated futures contract is treated as if sold at fair market value on the last day of the taxable year. Any capital gain or loss is arbitrarily allocated: 40% is short term and 60% is long term.

Under the law, a regulated futures contract is considered a Section 1256 contract. Other Section 1256 contracts subject to the mark-to-market rules are foreign currency contracts and also non-equity listed options and dealer equity options for positions established after July 18, 1984.

The mark-to-market rules do not apply to true hedging transactions executed in the normal course of business to reduce risks and which result in ordinary income or loss. Syndicates may generally not take advantage of this hedging exception if more than

35% of their losses during a taxable year are allocable to limited partners or entrepreneurs. Furthermore, the ability of limited partners or entrepreneurs to deduct losses from hedging transactions is generally limited to taxable income from the business to which the hedging transaction relates.

You may elect to avoid the mark-to-market rules for contracts that are part of a mixed straddle. The election is irrevocable unless the Treasury allows a revocation. Further, in temporary regulations, the Treasury allows an election to offset gains and losses from positions that are part of mixed straddles if you separately identify each mixed straddle or establish mixed straddle accounts for a class of activities for which gain and loss will be recognized and offset on a periodic basis.

Capital losses realized on regulated futures contracts or other Section 1256 contracts may be carried back three years. The carryback applies to positions established after June 23, 1981 and to taxable years ending after that date. Thus, losses may not be carried back to 1980 and earlier years. Estates and trusts are not allowed the carryback. To claim the carryback, file an amended Form 6781 for the prior year together with an amended return (Form 1040X).

Contract cancellations. Investors buying forward contracts for currency or securities may not realize ordinary loss by canceling the unprofitable contract of the hedge transaction. Loss realized on a cancellation of the contract is treated as a capital loss.

Cash and carry transactions. Carrying costs for any period during which the commodity or stock or option is part of a balanced position are not deductible. The costs must be capitalized and added to basis. The rule does not apply to hedging. For positions established after July 18, 1984, capitalized items are reduced by dividends on stock included in a straddle, market discounts and acquisition discounts. This reduction, however, is limited to so much of the dividends and discounts as is included in income.

¶6.036 • SALES OF PATENTS AND COPYRIGHTS

A special law allows long-term capital gain to sales of patents by inventors and their backers. There are advantages to qualifying under this law: Long-term gain is not dependent on any "holding period." The invention can be transferred even before an application for the patent is made. The imputed interest rules do not apply (see ¶6.191). The sale can be in the form of an outright sale, exclusive license, assignment, or royalty agreement.

Capital gain rules for an inventor. You must transfer all *substantial rights* to the patent to a party who is not your employer and not any of the following related persons:

1. Member of your immediate family, such as your husband or wife, ancestors, and lineal descendants, but not brothers and sisters.

2. A corporation of which 25% or more in value of the outstanding stock is owned, directly or indirectly, by or for you. Stock owned by your brother or sister is not considered indirectly owned by you.

3. Certain beneficiaries, trusts, and grantors (see ¶33.12).

The following are *not* considered substantial rights and may be retained: Right to prohibit sublicensing or subassignment of rights; the retention of a security interest such as a lien; and the reservation of rights providing for forfeiture for nonperformance.

The retention of rights that limit the period or duration of the patent to a period less than the remaining life of the patent will bar capital gain treatment. Capital gain is also not allowed where the patent license limits use to a particular industry. For example, an inventor restricted production of his patented clutch to marine use only. The clutch could have been used in other industries. An appeals court agreed with the IRS that the inventor retained a substantial right. Treasury regulations also bar capital gain treatment where the license is restricted to a geographic area and the inventor keeps the right to exploit the patent elsewhere. The Tax Court holds that it is a question of fact whether geographic restrictions affect the transfer of substantial rights. Previously, it held that capital gain treatment automatically applied to a transfer limited to an exclusive geographic area.

If you are a financial backer, you must buy all of the substantial rights to the patent before the invention is reduced to practice. You will not get capital gain under the special rules if, at the time you bought your interest, you were the employer of the inventor or one of the related parties listed above.

If you cannot meet the special rules, for example, you bought the patent after it was put into operation, you may be able to get capital gain if your interest meets the general capital gain tests: You hold the patent as a capital asset or as a "Section 1231" asset, and you dispose of it in a transaction that is considered a sale or exchange after a long-term holding period. However, one court has said you may not get capital gain unless you do meet the special rules, regardless of whether you meet the general capital gain tests.

Copyrights. If you are the creator of the property covered by the copyright, you may not get capital gain on its sale. This rule applies to literary, musical, artistic compositions, letters, and memoranda, as well as to theatrical productions, radio programs, and newspaper cartoon strips. Ordinary income treatment also applies if you obtained the copyright from its creator by gift or in a tax-free exchange. If a copyright is purchased, however, it may later be sold for capital gain treatment. In such a case, capital gain treatment applies to amounts received for granting the exclusive use or right to exploit the copyrighted work throughout the life of the copyright. This is true whether the payment is measured by a fixed amount or a percentage of the receipts from the sale, performance, exhibition, or publication of the copyrighted work, or by the number of copies sold, performances given, or exhibitions.

¶6.037 • GRANTING OF AN EASEMENT

Granting an easement presents a practical problem of determining whether all or part of the basis of the property is allocable to the easement proceeds. This requires an opinion of whether the easement affects the entire property or just a part of the property. There is no hard and fast rule to determine whether an easement affects all or part of the property. The issue is factual. For example, an easement for electric lines will generally affect only the area over which the lines are suspended and for which the right of way is granted. In such a case, an allocation may be required (see example 1 below). If the entire property is affected, no allocation is required and the proceeds reduce the basis of the property. If only part of the property is affected, then the proceeds are applied to the cost allocated to the area affected by the easement. If the proceeds exceed the amount allocated to basis, a gain is realized. Capital gain treatment generally applies to grants of easements. The granting of a perpetual easement which requires you to give up all or substantially all of a beneficial use of the area affected by the easement is treated as a sale. The contribution to a government body of a scenic easement in perpetuity is a charitable contribution, not a sale.

In reviewing an easement, the IRS will generally try to find grounds for making an allocation, especially where the allocation will result in a taxable gain. In opposition, a property owner will generally argue that the easement affects the entire property or that it is impossible to make an allocation because of the nature of the easement or the particular nature of the property. If he can sustain his argument, the proceeds for granting the easement reduce the basis of the entire property.

Examples—

1. The owner of a 600 acre farm was paid $5,000 by a power company for the right to put up poles and power lines. The right of way covered 20 acres along one boundary which the owner continued to farm. The cost basis of the farm was $60,000 or $100 an acre. The IRS ruled that he had to allocate basis. At $100 an acre, the allocated basis for the 20 acres was $2,000. Thus, a gain of $3,000 was realized ($5,000 — $2,000).

2. The owner of a tract of unimproved land gave a state highway department a perpetual easement affecting only part of the land. He wanted to treat the payment as reduction of the basis of the entire tract and so report no gain. The IRS ruled that he had to allocate basis to the portion affected by the road.

3. The owner of farmland gave a transmission company a 50-foot right of way for an underground pipeline which did not interfere with farming. During construction, the right of way was 150 feet. The owner received payments for damages covering loss of rental income during construction and for the 50-foot permanent right of way. The IRS ruled that the damage payment was taxable as ordinary income; the payment for the right of way was a taxable gain to the extent that it exceeded the basis allocated to the acreage within the 50-foot strip.

If you realize a gain on a grant of an easement under a condemnation or threat, you may defer tax by investing in replacement property.

Example—

Under threat of condemnation, a farmer in a flood control area gave the government the right to flood his farm. This was expected to occur every six years and did not interfere with farming in the intervening periods. The award exceeded basis. The IRS ruled that the farmer could defer tax by reinvesting in other farmland to keep up crop production. That he retained use of the farm was no bar to the election to defer tax.

¶6.038 • RELEASE OF RESTRICTIVE COVENANT

A payment received for a release of a restrictive covenant is treated as capital gain.

Example—

You sell several acres of land to a construction company subject to a covenant that restricts construction to residential dwellings. Later, the company wants to erect structures other than individual homes and pays you for the release of the restrictive covenant in the deed. You realize capital gain on receipt of the payment. The restrictive covenant is a property interest and a capital asset in your hands.

¶6.039 • SALE OF SAND OR GRAVEL

For capital gain treatment on the sale of sand or gravel, you must sell the deposit. Even where you draft the terms of the transaction as a sale, the IRS may hold you made a lease giving the buyer only the right to extract minerals so that his payments to you are taxable as ordinary income. In disputes over the tax treatment of sales of hard material, courts have developed an "economic interest" doctrine. Under this approach, a seller who keeps an "economic interest" in the material realizes ordinary income. A seller is treated as having an "economic interest" where payments depend on extraction or production. A provision for minimum payments not based on extraction or production may not be sufficient evidence that a sale was intended. Courts generally consider such minimum payments as advance royalties (*see* ¶9.16).

Example—

Wood's contract for the removal of sand and gravel provided for payment of a fixed amount per cubic yard of mineral removed. The contract referred to the parties as vendor and vendee. Payments were called "sales price." Wood also disclaimed retention of any economic interest in the sand and gravel. A court held that payments to Wood were ordinary income. Notwithstanding the contract language, Wood retained an economic interest in the minerals: Payments were dependent on the amount of sand and gravel removed.

Where the buyer is to pay whether or not he removes minerals, payments may be treated as capital gain. In one case capital gain treatment was allowed where a mineral deposit was transferred in "fee simple," the purchase price was paid at the time of the conveyance, and payment was not based on the amount of mineral extracted or set at a percentage of the mineral's retail value. The seller kept no interest in the mineral deposits and did not look to their extraction for an investment return.

¶6.04 • Transactions Not Subject to Capital Gain or Loss

Accounts or notes receivable sold by you and you originally received them for merchandise or services. Receivables are usually discounted or sold at a loss which is fully deductible. If you make a profit (you reported a note at less than face and later sold it for a higher amount), you realize ordinary income.

Abandonment of property. Taxpayers have argued that abandonment of property is not subject to capital asset treatment. The IRS disagrees and has succeeded in getting court support for its position in treating an abandonment of mortgaged property as a sale. *See* ¶6.03.

The holder of property under a land sale contract may not abandon the property for tax purposes if the seller has the right to sue for specific performance of the contract.

Annuity contract surrendered for its cash value.

Damages received in suit for breach of contract even if contract was for sale of a capital asset.

Employment contract canceled. Lump-sum payment received on cancellation is taxed compensation.

Endowment policy paid off on maturity. *See* ¶7.07 on your choices before maturity.

Estate's collection on a claim in excess of estate's basis.

Forfeited deposit on agreement to sell property. Seller has ordinary income and buyer has ordinary loss if the breached contract was for property to be used in a business. A deposit forfeited for the purchase of property used for personal purposes, such as residence, is not deductible by the buyer but is income to seller. However, where the seller breaches the contract and fails to repay because of bankruptcy, the lost deposit may be deductible as a bad debt (*see* ¶6.28). Where a contractor absconds with a deposit, the loss may be deducted as a theft loss (*see* ¶18.03).

Franchises. A transfer of a franchise, trademark, or trade name is not a sale or exchange of a capital asset if the grantor retains a significant power, right, or interest in it such as the right to: Disapprove further assignment of all or part of the franchise; set quality standards for products, services, equipment, or facilities; require that only his products or services be sold or advertised; require that substantially all supplies or equipment be purchased from him and to receive payments contingent on use of the franchise, if such payments are a substantial element of the agreement. In addition, if the grantor has an operational control over the franchise, payment may be treated as ordinary income. Operational control includes the right to: Periodic reports, approve business methods, prevent removal of equipment from the territory, withdraw the franchise if the territory is not developed.

To receive capital gain treatment on the sale of a franchise, the grantor must avoid the retention of any of the specified powers of operational control and, in addition, he must meet the general tests for capital gains, such as not dealing in franchises.

Insurance policy sold to a third party.

Insurance renewal commission assigned by insurance agent to insurance company in return for annuity income.

Investment in notes written off as worthless. Later disposal at a bankruptcy sale gives ordinary income.

Liquidated damages on the breach of a contract to sell.
Example—
You agree to sell property for $60,000, payable $12,000 on the signing of the contract, the balance on the delivery of the deed. The contract calls for liquidated damages of $12,000. After paying $12,000 on the contract, the buyer defaults and you keep the down payment as liquidated damages. Several months later, you sell the property for $55,000 to another party. You cannot bunch the liquidated damages of $12,000 with the sales proceeds of $55,000 and get capital gain for the total. The liquidated damages are treated separately from the later sale and taxed as ordinary income.

Mortgaging property.

Note payment received after getting judgment on the note.

Property received in settlement of suit for its recovery. But if cash is received, you have a sale.

Payments under a contract right to share profits which you bought for a definite sum. The receipts are ordinary income.

Realization of full face value of land contracts purchased at a discount and held to maturity. In Michigan, land contracts require a down payment and the balance in installments over a period of years. They are somewhat similar to mortgages. Contracts bought at less than their unpaid balances and held to maturity give ordinary income for the difference between the purchase price and the amount realized.

Release of debt to the other party of a contract giving you rights to future income. Your receipt is ordinary income. You have merely released a debt.

Release of employment contract.

Release of rights to a pension.

Release of a right to receive profits from sale of gas.

Return of property to you by borrower.

Sale of right to receive income—salary, dividends, or interest. Proceeds are ordinary income.

Satisfaction of a judgment for more than you paid for it gives ordinary income. Suppose you buy a $75,000 court judgment for $11,000. Later you collect $21,000 in satisfaction of the entire judgment. You have $10,000 ordinary income. Satisfaction of a judgment is not a sale or exchange.

Termination of insurance agency contract to solicit business and receive commissions. Termination does not involve the transfer of a capital asset but the relinquishment of a right to render personal services for commissions.

Topsoil. Sale of topsoil gives ordinary income. *See also* ¶6.039. You may be entitled to depletion (*see* ¶9.17).

¶6.05 • Counting the Holding Period

The period of time you own a capital asset before its sale or exchange determines whether gain or loss is short term or long term.

The short-term holding period is six months or less; a long-term period is more than six months. For futures transactions in any commodity subject to the rules of a board of trade or commodity exchange, the same six-month rule applies regardless of the time of acquisition. For a capital asset acquired before June 23, 1984, the short-term holding period was one year or less; the long-term period was more than a year.

Rules for counting the holding period:

1. A holding period is figured in months and fractions of months.

2. The beginning date of a holding month is generally the day after the asset was acquired. The same numerical date of each following month starts a new holding month regardless of the number of days in the preceding month.

3. The last day of the holding period is the day on which the asset is sold.

As a rule of thumb, use the numerical date on which you acquired the asset as the numerical date ending a holding month in each following month. However, if you acquire an asset on the last day of a month, a holding month ends on the last day of a following calendar month, regardless of the number of days in each month.

Examples—

1. On March 12, you buy stock. Holding months begin on March 13, April 13, May 13, June 13, and end on April 12, May 12, June 12, etc.

2. You buy stock on February 28. A holding month ends on March 31, April 30, etc. To realize long-term gain on the sale of these securities, you must hold them at least one day longer than the short-term holding period.

3. You buy stock on November 30. A holding month as in example 2 ends on December 31, January 31, February 28 (or 29 in a leap year), etc.

¶6.051 • SECURITIES TRANSACTIONS

Stock sold on a public exchange. The holding period starts on the day after your purchase order is executed (trading date). The day your sale order is executed (trade date) is the last day of the holding period even if delivery and payment are not made until several days after the actual sale (settlement date). This rule applies even where a gain on a year-end sale is not reported until the next year in which the proceeds are received.

Examples—

1. On June 2, you sell a stock at a profit. Your holding period ends on June 2 although proceeds are not received until June 7.

2. You sell stock at a gain on December 31, 1986. The holding period ends on December 31, although the sale is reported in 1987 when the proceeds are received. A sale at a loss is reported in 1986. (See ¶30.00 for strategy in planning year-end sales.) Note that the December 31 gain transaction can be reported in 1986 by making an election to "elect out" of installment reporting (see ¶ 6.171).

Stock subscriptions. If you are bound by your subscription but the corporation is not, the holding period begins the day after the date on which the stock is issued. If both you and the company are bound, the acceptance of the subscription by the corporation is the date of acquisition, and your holding period begins the day after.

Tax-free stock rights. When you exercise rights to acquire corporate stock from the issuing corporation, your holding period for the stock begins on the day of exercise, *not* on the day after. You are deemed to exercise stock rights when you assent to the terms of the rights in the manner requested or authorized by the corporation. An option to acquire stock is not a stock right.

Stock sold from different lots. If you purchased shares of the same stock on different dates and cannot determine which shares you are selling, the shares purchased at the earliest time are considered the stock sold first (*see also* ¶30.01).

Example—

You purchased 10 shares of ABC stock on May 3, 1975, 10 shares of ABC stock on May 1, 1977, and 10 shares of ABC stock on September 2, 1978. In 1986, you sell 25 shares of ABC stock, and are unable to determine when those particular shares were bought. Using the "first-in, first-out" method, 10 shares are from May 3, 1975, 10 shares from May 1, 1977, and five shares from September 2, 1978.

Commodities. If you acquired a commodity futures contract, the holding period of a commodity accepted in satisfaction of the contract includes your holding period of the contract, unless you are a dealer in commodities.

Employee stock options. When an employee exercises a stock option, the holding period of the acquired stock begins on the day after the option is exercised. If an employee option plan allows the exercise of an option by giving notes, the terms of the plan should be reviewed to determine when ownership rights to the stock are transferred. The terms may affect the start of the holding period for the stock.

Example—

In April 1964, Arnold exercised a stock option by giving a note. He had to pay up by June 1965, at which time he received his stock certificate. In October 1965, he sold the shares, realizing a profit of $20,000 which he reported as a long-term gain. The IRS taxed the profit as short-term gain, claiming that he owned the stock for only four months, that is, from the time he paid the note. Arnold argued that he acquired the stock when he gave the note.

The Tax Court agreed with the IRS. The plan called for cash payment by a deadline date as a condition of issuing the stock. The note was not intended as a substitute for cash and did not entitle Arnold to delivery of shares. He did not own the optioned stock until he paid the notes.

Other references: Stock dividends, *see* ¶6.25; short sales, *see* ¶6.261; wash sales, *see* ¶6.27; convertible securities, *see* ¶6.271.

¶6.052 • REAL ESTATE TRANSACTIONS

The date of acquisition is the earlier of these two dates: (1) The date title passes to you, or (2) the date you take possession and you assume the burdens and privileges of ownership.

If your purchase of a new residence qualifies under the rules discussed at ¶29.20, the holding period for the new home includes the holding period of the former residence. If you convert a residence to rental property and later sell the house, the holding period includes the time you held the house for personal purposes.

Holding period of a newly constructed house. When you sell a newly constructed house after its completion, you may have long-term capital gain on the underlying land and both long-term and short-term capital gain on the house. The holding periods of the land and building are figured separately. The holding period of the land begins from the date of the purchase of the land (which you may have held long term before the sale). The holding period of the building follows this peculiar rule: You get long-term capital gain for that portion of the gain allocable to the cost of the building erected in the applicable long-term period before the sale. You realize short-term capital gain on the balance.

To avoid the allocation and short-term capital gain, hold the house long term after its completion. But if you have to sell before then, make sure you have records on which to base an allocation so at least part of your gain is long term.

In disputes involving the starting and closing dates of a holding period, you may have to refer to the state law that applies to your sale or purchase agreement. State law determines when title to property passes.

¶6.053 • GIFT, INHERITED, OR PARTNERSHIP PROPERTY OR INVOLUNTARY CONVERSIONS

Gift property. If, in figuring a gain or loss, your basis for the property is the same as the donor's basis, you add the donor's holding period to the period you held the property. If you sell the property at a loss for which you use as your basis the fair market value at the date of the gift, your holding period begins the day after the date of the gift (*see* ¶6.10).

Inherited property. The holding period for inherited property begins on the day after the date of decedent's death, rather than the date you receive the property from the estate. You do not use the alternate valuation date elected by an executor to fix values for estate tax purposes. Further, the law gives an automatic long-term holding period for inherited property, regardless of the actual length of time you held the property.

Where property is purchased by the executor or trustee and distributed to you, your holding period begins the day after the date on which the property was purchased.

Partnership property. When you receive property as a distribution in kind from your partnership, the period your partnership held the property is added to your holding period. But there is no adding on of holding periods if the partnership property distributed was inventory and was sold by you within five years of distribution.

Involuntary conversions. When you have an involuntary conversion and elect to defer tax on gain, the holding period for the qualified replacement property generally includes the period you held the converted property. A new holding period begins for new property if you do not make an election.

¶6.06 • COMPUTING FRACTIONS OF MONTHS

Figuring fractions of months is required in computing the holding period of stock purchased after a wash sale (*see* ¶6.27).

To figure a fraction of a holding month, follow two rules:

When a fraction falls in one calendar month, take the number of days from the end of your last holding month to the date of sale and put it over the number of days in the calendar month of sale.

Example—
You bought stock January 15 and sold it March 28. On March 15 you have two holding months. From March 15 to March 28 (the date of sale), you have 13 days. Your fraction is $^{13}/_{31}$—March has 31 days. Your holding period is $2^{13}/_{31}$ months.

When a fraction falls in two calendar months, figure the number of days from the end of your last holding month. You place this figure over the number of days in the first of the two calendar months over which the fraction extends.

Example—
You bought stock on January 21 and sold it March 7. On February 21 you have one holding month. From February 21 to March 7 (date of sale), you have 14 days. Since the fraction extends over two calendar months—February and March—you put that figure over the number of days in the first of those two months (February). Your holding period is $1^{14}/_{28}$ or $1^{1}/_{2}$ months.

After a wash sale, the holding period of a new stock includes the holding period of the old lots. If you had more than one old lot in wash sales, you add the holding periods of all the old lots to the holding period of the new lot. You do this even if your holding periods overlapped because you bought another lot before you sold the first. You do not count the periods between sale and purchase when you have no stock.

Example—
You buy and sell 100 shares of the same stock as follows:

	Date bought	Date sold at loss	"Months" held
Lot 1	Feb. 12	April 2	1 21/31
Lot 2	Mar. 12	May 12	2
Lot 3	June 10	Aug. 4	1 25/31
Holding period of Lot 3	(Total)		5 15/31

¶6.07 • Figuring Your Profit or Loss

In most cases, you know if you have realized an economic profit or loss on the sale or exchange of property. You know your cost and selling price. The difference between the two is your profit or loss. The tax computation of gain or loss is similarly figured, except that the rules explained below may require you to increase or decrease your cost or selling price. As a result, your gain or loss for tax purposes may differ from your initial calculation.

GUIDE TO FIGURING GAIN OR LOSS

1. Selling price (*see* ¶6.08) $_____
2.   Less: Selling expenses (*see* ¶6.08)   _____
3. Amount realized (*see* ¶6.08) $_____
4. Cost or unadjusted basis of property (*see* ¶6.09, ¶6.10) $_____
5.   Add: Improvements, commissions (*see* ¶6.12)   _____
6.   Less: Depreciation, losses (*see* ¶6.12) $_____
7. Less: Adjusted basis (4 plus 5 less 6) $_____
8. Net gain or loss (3 less 7) $_____

Example—
You sell property to a buyer who pays you cash of $50,000. You bought the property for $30,000. Selling expenses were $2,000. Your gain on the sale is figured as follows:

1. Selling Price		$50,000
2. Less: Selling Expenses		2,000
3. Amount Realized		48,000
4. Less: Cost		30,000
5. Net Gain		$18,000

Note: The columns in Schedule D may not follow the above order and may include step 2 *selling expenses* with step 4 cost in order to save space. See ¶6.32. If so, on Schedule D, you report the gross selling price of $50,000 in column (d) "gross sales price"; in column (e) the cost of $30,000 plus selling expenses of $2,000. The final result is the same, a net gain of $18,000 ($50,000 — $32,000). In some years, the IRS has required selling expenses to be deducted from gross sales in column (d). The 1986 Schedule D is included in the Supplement to this book.

¶6.08 • SELLING PRICE AND AMOUNT REALIZED

Selling price is cash plus the fair market value of any additional property received. The buyer's note is included in the selling price at fair market value. This is generally the discounted amount that a bank or other party will pay for the note.

Sale of mortgaged property. The selling price includes the amount of the unpaid mortgage, whether or not you are personally liable on the debt or the buyer assumes the mortgage. The full amount of the unpaid mortgage is included, even where the value of the property is less than the unpaid mortgage.

Examples—
1. You sell property subject to a mortgage of $60,000. The seller pays you cash of $30,000 and takes the property subject to the mortgage. The sales price is $90,000.
2. A partnership receives a nonrecourse mortgage of $1,851,500 from a bank to build an apartment project. Several years later, the partnership sells the project for the buyer's agreement to assume the unpaid mortgage. At the time, the value of the project is $1,400,000 and the partnership basis in the project is $1,455,740. The partnership figures a loss of $55,740, the difference between basis and the value of the project. The IRS figures a gain of $395,760, the difference between the unpaid mortgage and basis. The partnership claims the selling price is limited to the lower fair market value and is supported by an appeals court. The Supreme Court reverses, supporting the IRS position. That the value of property is less than the amount of the mortgage has no effect on the rule requiring the unpaid mortgage to be part of the selling price. A

mortgagor realizes value to the extent that his obligation to repay is relieved by a third party's assumption of the mortgage debt.

If at the time of the sale, the buyer pays off the existing mortgage or your other liabilities, you include his payment as part of the sales proceeds.

Amount realized. This is the tax term for net selling price. To figure amount realized, you reduce the selling price by commissions, legal fees, transfer taxes, advertising costs and other selling expenses.
Example—
Same facts as in example 1 above except that on the sale of the property you paid broker fees of $1,000, attorney fees of $350, and advertising cost of $50. The amount realized is $28,600 ($30,000 less $1,400).

¶6.09 • FINDING YOUR COST
In figuring gain or loss, you need the "unadjusted basis" of the property sold. This term refers to the original cost of your property, if you purchased it. If you received it by gift, inheritance, or other means, you can determine unadjusted basis in the checklist below at ¶6.10. Keep in mind that you have to adjust this figure for improvements to the property, depreciation, or losses. These adjustments are explained at ¶6.12.

¶6.10 • Unadjusted Basis of Your Property

In the following order, you will find the unadjusted basis of property acquired by—

Your cash or obligations
Rendering services
Taxable exchange of property
"Tax-free" exchange of property
Gift after December 31, 1920
Sale of old residence and you acquired new residence
Sale of residence converted to rental
Gift or transfer in trust before January 1, 1921
Life estate or remainder interest in property created by will or gift
Inheritance from a deceased person
Survivor of joint tenancy or tenancy by the entirety
Distribution from a trust to a beneficiary
Compulsory or involuntary conversion
Prenuptial agreement
Nondeductible "wash sale"
Any method—property purchased prior to March 1, 1913
Distribution on orders of the Securities and Exchange Commission
Dividends in property
Bonus on stock owned
Complete liquidation of a corporation
Settlement of debt owed to you
When, as, and if issued contract to buy securities

Your cash or obligations. Basis is your cash cost, where purchased after February 28, 1913. If you assumed a mortgage or bought property subject to a mortgage, the amount of the mortgage is part of your unadjusted basis.
Example—
You bought a building for $20,000 in cash and a purchase money mortgage of $60,000. The unadjusted basis of the building is $80,000.

Rendering services. The value of the property, when you receive it as taxable income, is your unadjusted basis.

Taxable exchange of property. Technically, your unadjusted basis is the fair market value at the time of exchange of the property surrendered. In practice, however, the basis usually is equal to the fair market value of the property received. (But note the exception below under "tax-free" exchanges.)
Example—
You acquire real estate in 1950 for $5,000. When the property has a fair market value of $10,000, you exchange it for machinery also worth $10,000. You have a gain of $5,000, and the basis of the machinery is $10,000.

"Tax-free" exchange of property—within the rules explained at ¶5.48 and ¶6.20. Your basis is that of the property which you exchanged, decreased by any cash received and increased by any taxed gain or decreased by recognized loss. Gain is taxed to the extent cash is also received, see ¶5.48 for discussion on boot.
Examples—
1. You exchange real estate, which cost you $20,000, for other real estate. You pay no tax on the exchange. The unadjusted basis of the new property received in the exchange is $20,000.

2. Same facts as in (1) but you receive real estate worth $30,000 and cash of $5,000. On this transaction, you realize gain of $15,000 (of which $5,000 is taxed to the extent of the cash). Your basis for the new property is $20,000 figured this way:

Basis of old property	$20,000
Less: Cash received	5,000
	15,000
Plus: Gain recognized	5,000
Basis of new property	$20,000

Sale of property received by gift after December 31, 1920. If you have a gain from the sale of property received as a gift, your basis is the original cost to the person who made the gift. If a loss results to you, you use the donor's cost or market value (whichever is lower) at the date of the gift. This rule applies also to gifts transferred in trust after 1920.
Example—
Assume that in 1955 you received a gift from your father which you sold in 1986. His cost was $1,000. Then—

If value of the gift at receipt was	And you sold it for	Your basis is	Your taxed gain is	Your loss is
$3,000	$2,000	$1,000	$1,000	
700	500	700		$200
300	500	*	none	none
1,500	500	1,000		500

* In the third example, there is neither gain nor loss. To compute gain, cost is used ($1,000). Thus, there is no gain. But there is no loss because the property was sold for more than its value at the time of gift. To compute loss, you must use market value, which in this case is lower than donor's cost.

If a gift tax is paid on the gift of property, the basis of the property is increased under these rules: (1) For property received after December 31, 1976, the basis is increased for the gift tax paid by an amount which bears the same ratio to the amount of tax paid as the net appreciation in the value of the gift bears to the amount of the gift. The increase may not exceed the tax paid. Net appreciation in the value of any gift is the amount by which the fair market value of the gift exceeds the donor's adjusted basis immediately before the gift. (2) For property received after September 1, 1958 but before 1977, basis is increased by the gift tax paid on the property but not above the market value of the property at the time of the gift. (3) For property received before September 2, 1958, basis is increased by the gift tax paid. But this increase may not be more than the excess of the market value of the property at the time of the gift over the basis of the property in the donor's hands. Ask the donor or his advisor for these amounts.
Examples—
1. In 1975, your father gave you rental property with a market value of $78,000. The basis of the property in his hands was $60,000. He paid a gift tax of $15,000 on the gift. The basis of the property in your hands is $75,000 ($60,000 + $15,000).
2. In 1977, your father gave you rental property with a market

value of $78,000. His basis in the property was $60,000. He paid a gift tax of $15,000 on the gift. The basis of the property in your hands is your father's basis increased by the gift tax attributable to the appreciation. Gift tax attributable to the appreciation is:

$$\frac{\text{Appreciation}}{\text{Market value}} \times \text{gift tax paid}; \quad \frac{\$18,000}{\$78,000} \times \$15,000 = \$3,462$$

Your basis for figuring gain or loss or depreciation is $63,462.

If you received a gift of property which was used by the donor or by someone before him as depreciable business property, *see* ¶5.42. You may have to adjust the basis for depreciation taken on the property, and if you sell the property at a gain, you may realize ordinary income.

Sale of old residence, and you acquired the new residence— under the tax deferral rules of ¶29.20. Your basis is what you paid for the new residence less any gain that was not taxed on the sale of the old residence. See also example of basis computation at the end of ¶29.20.

Sale of residence converted to rental. *See* ¶29.43.

Gift or transfer in trust before January 1, 1921. Your basis is the fair market value at the time the gift or transfer was made.
Example—
No matter what the gift cost the donor, if its fair market value at the time he made the gift prior to 1921 was $1,000, your cost basis in a sale is $1,000.

Life estate or remainder interest in property created by will or gift. Your basis is constantly changing. The life tenant's basis is found by applying a formula based on an "annuity" factor taken from a table in the Treasury's regulations. It varies with age of the life tenant at the time of sale. The person who owns the remainder interest makes a similar computation using a "reversion" factor from the same table. If both sell their interests together, the adjusted basis of the property must be apportioned ratably between the life tenant and the remainderman (*see* Treasury regulations).

If only the life tenant sells his interest, he is considered to have a zero basis so that the entire amount received on the sale is taxable. This zero-basis rule applies also to sales of interests in property for a term of years and income interests in trusts. The zero-basis rule does not apply where both the life tenant and remainderman sell their interests. It also does not apply to sales made on or before October 9, 1969.

Inheritance of property. Basis is generally the value of the property at date of the death of the decedent, regardless of when you acquire the property. If decedent died after October 21, 1942, and the executor elected to use an *alternate valuation date* after the death, your basis is the alternate value at that date. The same rule applies to property:

1. Placed in trust by the deceased to pay the income to him, or at his direction, if he had the right at all times before his death to get back the property.

2. Placed in trust by the deceased to pay the income to him, or at his direction, if he had the right at all times before his death to alter, amend or end the trust, and he died after December 31, 1951.

3. Passing under a general power of appointment.

4. Acquired from deceased before he died if it was subjected to estate tax at his death and he died after December 31, 1953. (You have to reduce the basis for depreciation which you claimed for the property before the deceased's death.)

If the property is subject to a mortgage, though you did not assume the mortgage, your cost is still the value of the property, and not its equity at the date of death. If the property is subject to a lease under which no income is to be received for years, the basis is the value of the property—not the equity.

You might be given the right to buy the deceased person's property under his will. This is not the same as inheriting that property. Your basis is what you pay—not what the property is worth on the date of the deceased's death.

If property was inherited from a decedent dying after 1976 and before November 7, 1978 and the executor elected to apply carry-

over basis to all estate property, your basis is figured with reference to the decedent's basis. The executor must inform you of the basis of such property.

Survivor of joint tenancy, see ¶6.101.

Distribution from a trust to a beneficiary. Generally, you take the same basis the trust had for the property. But if the distribution is made to settle a claim you had against the trust, your basis for the property is the amount of the settled claim.

If you receive a distribution in kind for your share of trust income, the basis of the distribution before June 2, 1984 is generally the value of the property to the extent allocated to distributable net income. For distributions in kind after June 1, 1984 in taxable years ending after June 1, 1984, your basis is the basis of the property in the hands of the trust. If the trust elects to treat the distribution as a taxable sale, your basis is generally fair market value.

See above rules covering inheritance when decedent retained powers over trust he created.

Involuntary conversion. If the property was acquired as a result of an involuntary conversion before 1951, basis is the cost of the property converted. You adjust basis this way: Decrease it by money received not expended for replacement of the converted property and increase it for gain or decrease it for the loss recognized upon the conversion.

If the conversion occurred after 1950, basis is the cost of the new property decreased by gain not reported. If the replacement property consists of more than one piece of property, basis is allocated to each piece in proportion to its respective cost.
Example—
A building with an adjusted basis of $100,000 is destroyed by fire. The owner receives an insurance award of $200,000, realizing a gain of $100,000. He buys a building as a replacement for $150,000. Thus, $50,000 of his gain is taxable, and the remaining $50,000 is not taxable. The basis of the new building is $100,000.

Cost of the new building	$150,000
Less: Unrecognized gain	50,000
Basis	$100,000

Prenuptial agreement in release of dower and marital rights. The basis of property received under the agreement is its value when acquired if the transfer took place before July 19, 1984.
Example—
Jones bought stock for $50,000. Under a prenuptial agreement, he later gave this stock to his prospective wife in release of her dower and marital rights. The fair market value at the time she acquired the stock was $150,000. Her basis is $150,000. She is considered to have acquired the stock by purchase not by gift.

Where transfers between spouses takes place after July 18, 1984, the transfer is treated as a tax-free exchange and the transferee takes a carryover basis, *see* ¶6.245. In the above example, the carryover basis to the wife would be $50,000.

Nondeductible "wash sale." If you transact a "wash sale," your basis is the cost of the new stock plus the loss not allowed. *See* ¶6.27.

Any method—property purchased prior to March 1, 1913. Your basis is the cost or the fair market value at March 1, 1913, whichever is greater, if a gain results. However, if you sustain a loss, your basis is the cost.

Distribution on orders of the Securities and Exchange Commission. Your basis is the same as that of the property exchanged.
Example—
Securities of a utility company cost you $1,000. The company is dissolved on order of the Securities and Exchange Commission, and you receive four classes of stock of subsidiaries owned by the utility at the time of its dissolution. You must prorate your $1,000 cost over the four new stocks on the basis of their market values at the time you received them.

Dividends in property (except stock of the issuing corporation). Fair market value at date of distribution is basis.

Bonus on stock owned. If you received common stock as a bonus upon the acquisition of preferred stock or bonds, cost of the preferred stock or bonds should be apportioned between such securities and the common stock. If this is not practicable, you do not realize any taxed profit from the sale of any of the stock or bonds until you first recover your entire cost.

Example—

You bought 100 shares of preferred stock and received 100 shares of common stock as a bonus. If there was a market for both, you could easily allocate your cost. If the common did not have a market, you are first permitted to recover your cost before a profit is determined on the sale.

Accumulated value of variable annuities on death of contract owner. Decedent's cost.

Complete liquidation of a corporation to an individual. Your basis is generally the fair market value of the property at the time of the liquidation.

Example—

If you receive securities having a market value of $1,000 in a liquidation, that is your cost when you sell them. Report gain or loss due to the liquidation at the time it occurs.

Settlement of debt owed to you. Your cost of the obligation or any value you and your debtor agree upon is your basis.

When, as, and if issued contract to buy securities. If the contract has cost you nothing, your basis is zero in computing gain or loss on the sale of the contract before its performance.

¶6.101 • JOINT TENANCY BASIS RULES FOR SURVIVING TENANTS

For deaths occurring after 1981, the law provides different basis rules for joint tenancies between husbands and wives than for tenancies between persons who are not married to each other.

For a joint tenancy by the entirety between a husband and wife, the rule for deaths occurring after 1981 is as follows: The surviving spouse's basis includes one-half of the decedent's interest fixed at fair market value used for estate tax purposes. This is generally fair market value at date of death or six months later if an estate tax return is filed and the optional valuation date is elected. The 50% decedent share applies regardless of the actual amount contributed by the decedent to the property.

Example—

Jones and his wife jointly own a house which cost them $50,000 in 1970. In 1986, Jones dies when the house is worth $200,000; $100,000 is included in his estate. For income tax purposes, Mrs. Jones's basis for the house is $125,000.

Her original basis	$ 25,000
Basis for inherited portion	100,000
New basis	$125,000

On a sale of the home for $200,000, Mrs. Jones would realize a $75,000 long-term capital gain ($200,000 − $125,000).

The following rules apply to joint tenancies between—
Persons who are not married to each other, and
A husband and wife where one spouse died before 1982.

Basis to the survivor for the entire property is your basis for your share before the joint owner died plus the fair market value of the decedent's interest at death (or on the alternate valuation date if the estate uses the alternate date). The decedent's interest does not have to be included on an estate tax return (as where the estate is too small to be taxable) for you to use the date-of-death value. If no estate tax return is required, you may not use the alternative valuation date basis.

Examples—

1. You and your sister bought a home for $10,000. She paid $6,000 and you $4,000. Title to the house was held by both of you as joint tenants. In 1986, when she died, the house was worth $30,000. Since she paid 60% of the cost of the house, 60% of the value at her death, $18,000, is included in an estate tax return (or would be included if an estate tax return was due). Basis for the house now becomes $22,000—the $4,000 you originally paid plus the $18,000 fair market value of your sister's share at her death.

2. Husband and wife owned rental property as tenants by the entirety which they purchased for $30,000. The husband furnished two-thirds of the purchase price ($20,000) and the wife furnished one-third ($10,000). Depreciation deductions taken before the husband's death were $12,000. On the date of his death in 1979, the property had a fair market value of $60,000. Under the law of the state in which the property is located, as tenants by the entirety, each had a half interest in the property. The wife's basis in the property at the date of her husband's death is computed as follows:

Interest acquired with her own funds	$10,000	
Interest acquired from husband (⅔ of $60,000)	40,000	$50,000
Less: Depreciation of ½ interest not acquired by reason of death (½ of $12,000)		6,000
Basis at date of husband's death		$44,000

If she had not contributed any part of the purchase price, her basis at the date of her husband's death would be $54,000 ($60,000 fair market value less $6,000 depreciation).

Where property was held in joint tenancy and one of the tenants died before January 1, 1954, no part of the interest of the surviving tenant is treated, for purposes of determining the basis of the property, as property transmitted at death.

Qualified joint interest. Where, after 1976, a deceased dying before 1982 elected to treat realty as a "qualified joint interest" subject to gift tax, such joint property included in his estate is treated as owned fifty-fifty by each spouse. Thus, for income tax purposes, the basis of one half of the property is the estate tax value; the other half is determined under the gift rules detailed above. Personal property is treated as a "qualified joint interest" only if it was created or deemed to have been created after 1976 by a husband and wife and was subject to gift tax.

Eligible joint interest. Where death occurred before 1982 and a surviving spouse materially participated in the operation of a farm or other business, an estate may elect to treat the farm or business property as an "eligible joint interest," which means that that part of the investment in the property may be attributed to the surviving spouse's services and is not included in the deceased spouse's estate. Where such an election is made, the survivor's basis for income tax purposes includes the estate tax value of property included in decedent's estate.

¶6.11 • WHEN TO ALLOCATE COST

Allocation of basis is generally required in these cases:

Purchase of land and building. To figure depreciation on the building, part of the purchase price must be allocated to the building. The allocation is made according to the fair market values of the building and land. The amount allocated to land is not depreciated.

Purchase of land to be divided into lots. The purchase price of the tract is allocated to each lot, so that the gain or loss from the sale of each lot may be reported in the year of its sale. Allocation is not made ratably, that is, with an equal share to each lot or parcel. It is based on the relative value of each piece of property. Comparable sales, competent appraisals, or assessed values may be used as guides.

See ¶30.01 for methods of identifying securities bought at different dates.

See ¶6.25 for allocating basis of stock dividends and stock splits; ¶6.26 for allocating the basis of stock rights.

¶6.12 • HOW TO FIND ADJUSTED BASIS

After determining the unadjusted cost basis from the checklist starting at ¶6.10, you find your "adjusted basis" in two steps—

1. Additions to basis. You add to basis the cost of all improvements and additions to the property and other capital costs, purchase commissions, legal fees such as the cost of defending or perfecting title, title insurance, legal fees for obtaining a reduction of an assessment levied against property to pay for local benefits, and similar items which were not deductible as current expenses. Note that the instructions to Schedule D may also require you to add to basis selling expenses such as commissions (*see* ¶6.07). You may elect to capitalize certain deductible taxes, interest, and other carrying charges (*see* ¶16.02).

When you buy real estate, you usually pay a portion of the

taxes paid by the seller before you took title. If you bought the property before 1954, you add such payments to basis. If you bought the property after 1953, taxes paid are not added to basis because they are immediately deductible in the year paid (*see* ¶16.07). However, if you also paid taxes attributable to the time the seller held the property, you add such taxes to basis.

If you sell land with unharvested crops, add the cost of producing the crops to the basis of the property sold.

2. Deductions from basis. You reduce cost for items such as—

Return of capital, such as dividends on stock paid out of capital or out of a depletion reserve when the company has no available earnings or surplus (*see* ¶3.08).

Losses from casualties including insurance awards and payments in settlement of damages to your property.
Example—
Your residence which cost $15,000 is damaged by fire. You deducted the uninsured loss of $1,000. Several years later, you sell the house for $16,000. To figure your profit, you reduce the original cost of the house by the loss to get an adjusted basis of $14,000. Your gain on the sale is then $2,000 ($16,000 − $14,000).

Depletion allowances.

Depreciation, ACRS deductions, amortization, and obsolescence

on property used in business or for the production of income. In some years, you may have taken more or less depreciation than was allowable. If you took more depreciation than was allowable, you may have to make the following adjustments: If you have deducted more than what was allowable, you deduct the full amount of the depreciation if you received a tax benefit from the deduction. But if the excess depreciation did not give you a tax benefit because income was eliminated by other deductions, the excess is not deducted from basis. If you claim less than what was allowable, you must deduct the allowable amount. These rules affect all tax years after 1951. However, the rule covering the treatment of excessive depreciation does not affect pre-1952 years unless you made a special election before January 1, 1955, to come within that rule. Under pre-1952 law, basis is reduced by excessive depreciation even though no tax benefit is received by the deduction. (Property held before March 1, 1913 is reduced by depreciation actually sustained prior to that date.)

No adjustment is made for any first-year expensing claimed.

If you hold bonds bought at a premium, *see* ¶4.031. If you did not pay tax on certain cancellations of debt on your business property (*see* ¶12.21), you reduce basis for the amount forgiven.

Investment credit. Where the full investment credit is claimed in 1983 or later years, basis is reduced by one-half the credit. *See* ¶5.70.

¶6.16 • Reporting an Installment Sale

If you sell property in 1986 and will receive one or more payments in a later year or years, you must report the sale as an installment sale, unless you elect otherwise. Form 6252 is used to compute installment sale income. An example of reporting an installment sale is at ¶6.321.
Examples—
1. In 1986, you sell real estate for $50,000, receiving $10,000 in 1986, 1987, and 1988, and $20,000 in 1989. You realized a profit of $25,000, giving you a profit percentage of 50%. When the buyer pays the notes, you report the following:

	You report	
In	*payment of:*	*income of:*
1986	$10,000	$ 5,000
1987	10,000	5,000
1988	10,000	5,000
1989	20,000	10,000
Total	$50,000	$25,000

In 1986 you file Form 6252 to figure your profit. You report only $5,000 as profit on Schedule D (or Form 4797 if applicable). If you do not want to use installment method, you make an election by reporting the entire gain of $25,000 on Schedule D or Form 4797. Schedule D provides a special box to check your election *out* of the installment method.

2. On December 20, 1986, you sell property for $50,000, realizing a profit of $25,000. You take a note payable in January 1987. You report the gain in 1987. Receiving a lump-sum payment in a taxable year after the year of sale is considered an installment sale.

The installment method may not be used for reporting a loss.

A farmer may use the installment method to report gain from the sale of property that does not have to be inventoried under his method of accounting. This is true, even though such property is held for regular sale.

Dealers selling personal property on the installment plan are subject to special rules not discussed in this book.

Depreciation recapture. If you make an installment sale of depreciable property after June 6, 1984, any depreciation recapture is reported as income in the year of disposition. Recaptured income increases the basis of the property for purposes of figuring the gross profit ratio for the balance of gain to be reported, if any, over the installment period, *see also* ¶5.44.

Further details are discussed in the following sections:

¶6.17 • FIGURING THE TAXABLE PART OF INSTALLMENT PAYMENTS

On the installment method, a portion of each payment represents part of your gain. The profit percentage or ratio applied to each payment is figured by dividing gross profit by contract price. What you include in the selling price, contract price, and gross profit is explained in the following paragraphs.

Selling price. Include cash, fair market value of property received from the buyer, his notes (at face value), and any existing mortgage on the property whether or not assumed by the buyer. If, under the contract of sale, the buyer pays off an existing mortgage or assumes liability for any other liens on the property or pays the sales commissions, such payments are also included in the selling price.

Interest is not included in the selling price.

Notes of a third party given to you by the buyer are valued at fair market value.

Contract price. If there is no mortgage on the property, the contract price is usually the same as the gross selling price. If there is a mortgage, the selling price is reduced by the amount of the mortgage, unless it exceeds the adjusted basis of the property. If the mortgage exceeds the adjusted basis of the property, reduce the contract price only by the amount of the mortgage equal to the amount of the adjusted basis. Do this whether or not the buyer assumes the mortgage. Wrap around mortgages are discussed below. An obligation of the seller which the buyer assumes, whether related to the sale, such as legal fees, or unrelated, such as medical bills, is not treated as part of the contract price.

Example—
You sell a building for $160,000. The property is subject to a mortgage of $60,000. The buyer will assume the mortgage and pay the $100,000 in five equal annual installments. The contract price is $100,000; the $160,000 selling price less the mortgage of $60,000.

Payments received. Payments include cash, the fair market value of property, and payments on the buyer's notes. Payments do not include receipt of the buyer's notes or other evidence of indebtedness, unless payable on demand or readily tradable. "Readily tradable" means registered bonds, bonds with coupons attached, debentures, and other evidences of indebtedness of the buyer that are readily tradable in an established securities market. This rule is directed mainly at corporate acquisitions.

Payments in the year of sale include mortgages which the buyer assumes or takes subject to only to the extent the mortgage exceeds the basis of property.

Example—
You sell a building for $160,000 subject to a mortgage of $60,000. Installments are to be paid over five years. Your basis in the property is $40,000. The buyer assumes the mortgage. In the year of the sale, you are treated as having received payment of $20,000, the amount by which the $60,000 mortgage exceeds basis of $40,000. The basis of the property is treated as being fully recovered in the year of sale. Thus, all of the installment payments received on the sale are fully taxable. The gross profit ratio is 100% (gross profit of $120,000 divided by contract price of $120,000). The contract price here is selling price less that part of the mortgage which did not exceed basis.

A third party guarantee (including a standby letter of credit) is not treated as a payment received on an installment obligation.

Gross profit. Gross profit is the selling price less the adjusted basis of the property sold. Selling expenses, such as brokers' commissions and legal fees, are added to basis for purposes of computing gross profit. If you change the selling price during the period payments are outstanding, the gross profit percentage is refigured on the basis of the new selling price. The adjusted profit ratio is then applied to payments received after the adjustment.

Example—
Jones sells real estate for $100,000 and realizes a gain of $60,000. The purchase price is to be paid in five annual installments of $20,000. Jones reported profit of $12,000 (60% of $20,000) on each installment received in 1984 and 1985. In 1986, the sales price is reduced to $85,000 and payments for 1986, 1987, and 1988 are reduced to $15,000. Jones's original profit of $60,000 is reduced to $45,000. Of this amount, $24,000 was reported in 1984 and 1985. Thus, the profit to be received is $21,000, or $7,000 each year over the three remaining installments of $15,000.

Figuring the profit percentage or ratio. The profit percentage or ratio is found by dividing gross profit by contract price. The computation may be made by following the line-by-line instructions to Form 6252.

Example—
On December 19, 1986, you sell real estate for $100,000. The property had an adjusted basis of $56,000. Selling expenses are $4,000. You are to receive installment payments of $25,000 in 1986, 1987, 1988, and 1989. The gross profit ratio is determined as follows:

Selling price (contract price)	$100,000
Less: Adjusted basis and selling expenses	60,000
Gross profit	$ 40,000

$$\frac{\text{Gross profit}}{\text{Contract price}} = \frac{\$40,000}{\$100,000} = 40\%$$

In 1986, you report a profit of $10,000 (40% of $25,000). Similarly, in each of the following three years, a profit of $10,000 is reported so that by the end of two years, the entire $40,000 profit will have been reported.

Wrap around mortgage. A wrap around mortgage is treated as if the buyer had assumed or taken the property subject to it, even though title does not pass to the buyer in the year of sale and the seller continues to make direct payments on the wrapped around mortgage. This will increase the taxable gain in the year of sale.

Example—
Seller sells real property worth $2 million, encumbered by a mort-

gage of $900,000. His basis is $700,000. The buyer pays $200,000 cash and gives an interest-bearing wrap around mortgage note for $1.8 million. The seller remains obligated to pay off the $900,000 mortgage. The $900,000 mortgage is treated as if the buyer assumed it or the property was taken subject to it. Thus, in the year of sale, the seller is treated as receiving $400,000, $200,000 cash plus $200,000 excess of the mortgages ($900,000) over basis ($700,000). Since the seller's gross profit ratio is 1 ($1,300,000 gross profit ÷ $1,300,000 contract price), the seller is taxed on the entire $400,000 in the year of sale.

Sale of depreciable property. For the effect of recapture, *see* ¶5.44.

Recapture of first-year expensing deduction. The entire recaptured amount under ¶5.411 is reported in the year of sale, even though you report the sale on the installment basis. An installment sale does not defer the reporting of the recaptured deduction. You also add the recaptured amount to the basis of the sold asset to compute the amount of the remaining gain to be reported on each installment.

¶6.171 • ELECTING NOT TO REPORT ON THE INSTALLMENT METHOD

Unless you make a timely election, an installment sale is automatically reported on the installment basis. If you want to report the entire gain in the year of sale, you must elect to do so within the time for filing your return (plus extensions) for the year of sale by reporting the entire gain on Schedule D, or Form 4797.

If you report on the cash basis and receive an obligation whose fair market value is less than face value, you report fair market value of the note. You also must show how you found your value. Fair market value of an obligation may not be set for an amount less than the fair market value of the property less other payments received on the sale. If you report on the accrual basis, you report the full face amount of the obligation.

An election not to report on the installment method may be revoked only with the consent of the IRS. A revocation will not be permitted for tax avoidance purposes. The IRS in a private ruling refused to allow a seller to use the installment method after inadvertently including the entire gain from the sale on his return. Although reporting of the entire gain was a mistake, this was treated as an election not to use the installment method. The IRS refused permission to revoke the election on the grounds that a second chance to apply the installment method would be tax avoidance.

An election after the due date must be made with IRS consent.

When to "elect out" of installment reporting. Where you have losses to offset your gain in the year of sale, installment sale reporting may not be advantageous. In such a case, you may want to elect not to report on the installment basis. There is a risk to electing out if the deduction for the losses may be disallowed. If the losses are later disallowed by an IRS audit, you may not have a second chance to use the installment method to spread the gain over the payment period. For example, a seller elected out in a year in which he planned to deduct a net operating loss carryforward from an installment sale gain. In a later year, the IRS substantially reduced the loss. The seller then asked the IRS to allow him to revoke the election to elect out of the installment method. The IRS refused, claiming that the seller had a tax avoidance purpose in asking for the revocation. The installment sale would defer gain to a later year.

¶6.18 • INSTALLMENT SALES TO RELATIVES AND OTHER RELATED PARTIES RESTRICTED

The installment sale method may not be allowed where you (1) sell to a relative who then sells the property or (2) sell depreciable property to a spouse or a controlled business.

The restrictions are primarily aimed at the following types of transactions:

1. A buyer insists on paying cash, but the seller who wants the tax deferment advantage of installment reporting arranges an installment sale with a family member who then resells the property for cash to the buyer.

2. Securities traded on the exchange cannot be sold on the exchange on the installment basis. To get installment basis reporting

an investor would sell to a related party on the installment basis, and the related party would then sell the securities on the exchange.

The tax deferral advantages of installment reporting are generally lost in the above cases when the related party sells the property to the third party; at the time of the second sale, the original seller must report income.

Example—
In 1986, Jones sells stock to his son for $25,000 realizing a profit of $10,000. The son agrees to pay in five annual installments of $5,000 starting in 1987. Later in 1986, the son sells the stock to a third party for $26,000. Jones Sr. reports his profit of $10,000 in 1986 even though he received no payment that year. Payments received by Jones Sr. from his son after 1986 are tax free because he reported the entire profit in 1986.

The amount to be reported as a result of a second sale by a related party is figured on Form 6252.

Two-year rule. If nondepreciable property other than marketable securities is sold, you are taxed on a second sale by a related party only if it occurs within two years of the initial installment sale. The two-year period is extended during any period in which the buyer's risk is lessened by a put on the property, or a short-sale or other transactions lessening the risk of loss. The two-year rule does not apply to the sale of marketable securities. Marketable securities are: (1) Securities listed on the New York Stock Exchange, the American Stock Exchange, or any city or regional exchange in which quotations appear on a daily basis, including foreign securities listed on a recognized foreign, national or regional exchange; (2) securities regularly traded in the national or regional over-the-counter market, for which published quotations are available; (3) securities locally traded for which quotations can readily be obtained from established brokerage firms; (4) units in a common trust fund; and (5) mutual fund shares for which redemption prices are published.

Related parties include a spouse, child, grandchild, parent, controlled corporation (50% or more direct or indirect ownership) and related partnerships or family trusts. There are exceptions to this related party rule. Second dispositions resulting from an involuntary conversion of the property will not be subject to the related party rule so long as the first disposition occurred before the threat or imminence of conversion. Similarly, transfers after the death of the person making the first disposition or the death of the person acquiring the property in first disposition are not treated as second dispositions. Also, a sale or exchange of stock to the issuing corporation is not treated as a first disposition. Finally, you may avoid tax on a related party's second sale by satisfying the IRS that neither the initial nor the second sale were made for tax avoidance purposes.

Where you transfer property to a related party, the IRS has two years from the date you notify it that there has been a second disposition to assess a deficiency with respect to your transfer.

Sales of depreciable property to related party. Installment reporting is not allowed for sales of depreciable property made to a controlled corporation or partnership (80% control by seller and/or spouse) and between such controlled corporations and partnerships. Installment reporting is also disallowed on a sale to a trust in which you or a spouse is a beneficiary unless your interest is considered a remote contingent interest whose actuarial value is five percent or less of the trust property's value. On these related party sales, the entire gain is reported in the year of sale, unless the seller convinces the IRS that the transfer was not motivated by tax avoidance purposes. Installment reporting may be allowed if at the time of the sale the couple were legally separated under a decree of divorce or separate maintenance, or if the sale was pursuant to a settlement in a proceeding which culminates in such a decree.

¶6.181 • CONTINGENT PAYMENT SALES

Where the final selling price or payment period of an installment sale is not fixed at the end of the taxable year of sale, you are considered to have transacted a "contingent payment sale." Special rules apply where a maximum selling price may be figured under the terms of the agreement or there is no fixed price but there is a fixed payment period, or there is neither a fixed price nor fixed payment period.

Stated maximum selling price. Under the regulations, a stated maximum selling price may be determined by assuming that all of the contingencies contemplated by the agreement are met. When the maximum amount is later reduced, the gross profit ratio is recomputed.

Example—
Smith sells stock in Acme Co. for a down payment of $100,000 plus an amount equal to 5% of the net profits of Acme for the next nine years. The contract provides that the maximum amount payable, including the $100,000 down payment but exclusive of interest, is $2,000,000. Smith's basis for the stock is $200,000; $2,000,000 is the selling price and contract price. Gross profit is $1,800,000. The gross profit ratio is 90% ($1,800,000 divided by $2,000,000). $90,000 of the first payment is reportable as gain, $10,000 as a recovery of basis.

Fixed period. When a stated maximum selling price is not determinable but the maximum payment period is fixed, basis, including selling expenses, is allocated equally to the taxable years in which payment may be received under the agreement. If in any year, no payment is received or the amount of payment received is less than the basis allocated to that taxable year, no loss is allowed unless the taxable year is the final payment year or the agreement has become worthless. When no loss is allowed in a year, the basis allocated to the taxable year is carried forward to the next succeeding taxable year.

Example—
Brown sells property for 10% of the property's gross rents over a five-year period. Brown's basis is $5,000,000. The sales price is indefinite and the maximum selling price is not fixed under the terms of the contract; basis is recovered ratably over the five-year period.

Year	Payment	Basis recovered	Gain
1986	$1,300,000	$1,000,000	$ 300,000
1987	1,500,000	1,000,000	500,000
1988	1,400,000	1,000,000	400,000
1989	1,800,000	1,000,000	800,000
1990	2,100,000	1,000,000	1,100,000

No stated maximum selling price or fixed period. If the agreement fails to specify a maximum selling price and payment period, the IRS may view the agreement as a rent or royalty income agreement. However, if the arrangement qualifies as a sale, basis (including selling expenses) is recovered in equal annual increments over a 15-year period commencing with the date of sale. If in any taxable year, no payment is received or the amount of payment received (exclusive of interest) is less than basis allocated to the year, no loss is allowed unless the agreement has become worthless. Excess basis not recovered in one year is reallocated in level amounts over the balance of the 15-year term. Any basis not recovered at the end of the 15th year is carried forward to the next succeeding year, and to the extent unrecovered, carried forward from year to year until basis has been recovered or the agreement is determined to be worthless. The rule requiring initial level allocation of basis over 15 years may not apply if you prove to the Service that a 15-year general rule will substantially and inappropriately defer recovery of basis. *See* Treasury regulations for further details.

In some cases, basis recovery under an income forecast type of method may also be allowed under Treasury regulations.

An installment sale with payments to be made in foreign currency or fungible payment units (such as bushels of wheat), is a contingent payment sale, but basis is allocated as if payment was fixed in U.S. dollars.

Example—
In 1986, Jones sells property for 10,000 English pounds. In 1987, 2,500 pounds is payable. In 1988, the balance of 7,500 pounds is payable. Basis in the property is $2,000. In 1987, 25% of the basis or $500 (25% of $2,000) is allocated to first payment. In 1988, $1,500 (75% of $2,000) is allocated to second payment.

¶6.19 • USING ESCROW AND OTHER SECURITY ARRANGEMENTS

You sell property and the sales proceeds are placed in escrow pending the possible occurrence of an event such as the approval of title or your performance of certain contractual conditions. The sale proceeds are not taxed until the year in which the escrow agent releases the funds to you.

> The escrow agreement may authorize you to receive the income it produces or it may even authorize you to control the manner in which the fund is to be invested. According to a court decision, these facts do not make the fund taxable to you before the year you actually have it. You are, of course, taxable on the income earned by the fund when it is received by you.

Example—

Anderson sold stock and mining property for almost $5 million. He agreed to place $500,000 in escrow to protect the buyer against his possible breaches of warranty and to provide security for certain liabilities. The escrow agreement called for Anderson to direct the investments of the escrow fund and receive income from the fund in excess of $500,000. The IRS claimed that in the year of sale Anderson was taxable on the $500,000 held in escrow on the grounds that Anderson's control of the fund rendered the fund taxable immediately. Anderson argued he was only taxable as the funds were released to him and the Tax Court agreed. The fund was not under his unqualified control. He might never get the fund if the liabilities materialize. Although Anderson had a free hand with investment of the money, he still lacked ultimate ownership.

If the terms of the escrow involve no genuine conditions that prevent you from demanding immediate payment, there will be immediate tax.

Example—

Rhodes sold a tract to a buyer who was willing to pay at once the entire purchase price of $157,000. But Rhodes wanted to report the sale on the installment basis over a period of years. The buyer refused to execute a purchase money mortgage on the property to allow the installment sale election (required under prior law) because he wanted clear and unencumbered title to the tract. As a solution, Rhodes asked the buyer to turn over the purchase price to a bank, as escrow agent, which would pay the sum over a five-year period. The escrow arrangement failed to support an installment sale. Rhodes was fully taxable on the entire price in the year of the sale. The buyer's payment was unconditional and irrevocable. The escrow arrangement involved no genuine conditions that could defeat Rhodes's right to payment, as the buyer could not revoke, alter, or end the arrangement.

Substitution of an escrow account for unpaid notes or deed of trust disqualifies installment reporting.

Example—

In January, an investor sold real estate for $100,000. He received $10,000 as a down payment and six notes, each for $15,000, secured by a deed of trust on the property. The notes, together with interest, were due annually over the next six years. In July, the buyer deposited the remainder of the purchase price with an escrow agent and got the seller to cancel the deed of trust. The agreement provides that the escrow agent will pay off the buyer's notes as they fall due. The buyer remains liable for the installment payments. The escrow deposit is irrevocable, and the payment schedule may not be accelerated by any party under any circumstances. According to the IRS the sale, which initially qualified as an installment sale, is disqualified by the escrow account.

> If an escrow arrangement imposes a substantial restriction, the IRS may allow installment reporting. An example of a substantial restriction: Payment of the escrow is tied to the condition that the seller refrain from entering a competing business for a period of five years. If, at any time during the escrow period, he engaged in a competing business, he forfeits all rights to the amount then held in escrow.

Use of certificates of deposit as security may prevent installment reporting.

Example—

Trivett wanted an installment sale election (as required under prior law) on the sale of a franchise but at the same time wanted to have a secure hold on the buyer's cash. Since he could not take the cash and make the election, he had the buyer give certificates of deposit as security for three promissory notes. The certificates were endorsed by the buyer to the order of Trivett and held by a bank until maturity, at which point they were paid to Trivett. He reported the sale of the franchise as an installment sale which the IRS disallowed. The promissory notes served no purpose and were not, in reality, evidences of indebtedness but merely payment for the franchise. As Trivett could have received the proceeds of the matured certificates even if the buyer was

in default, he did not rely on the promissory notes, but upon the certificates of deposit, to serve as payment for the franchise. However, the following method of using certificates of deposit was approved by the Tax Court. The seller had the buyer place certificates of deposit in an escrow account as security for his notes. When the buyer made payments on the notes, the escrow agent would then reimburse the buyer from the account. In one year, when the buyer missed a payment, the seller agreed to take it in the next year. The IRS barred installment reporting, claiming that the certificates of deposit placed in escrow were available to the seller in the year of sale. The Tax Court disagreed. The payments were treated solely as security. The buyer personally paid all installments and recovered the escrow account.

¶6.191 • MINIMUM INTEREST MAY BE REQUIRED ON DEFERRED PAYMENT SALES

The tax law requires a minimum amount of interest to be charged on deferred payment sales.

The rules for imputing interest are discussed at ¶4.11.

Imputed interest is included in the taxable income of the seller. Imputed interest is deductible by the buyer if the property is business or investment property but not if it is used substantially all the time for personal purposes.

¶6.192 • SALE OR OTHER TRANSFER OR CANCELLATION OF INSTALLMENT NOTES

A sale, a gift, or other transfer or cancellation of mortgage notes or other obligations received in an installment sale has tax consequences. If you sell or exchange the notes at other than face value, gain or loss results to the extent of the difference between the basis of the notes and the amount realized. Gain or loss is long term if the original sale was entitled to long-term capital gain treatment. This is true even if the notes were held short term. If the original sale resulted in short-term gain or ordinary income, the sale of the notes gives short-term gain or ordinary income, regardless of the holding period of the notes.

The basis of an installment note or obligation is the face value of the note less the income that would be reported if the obligation were paid in full.

Example—

You sell a lot for $2,000 which cost you $1,000. In the year of the sale, you received $500 in cash and the purchaser's notes for the remainder of the selling price, or $1,500. A year later, before the buyer makes a payment on the notes, you sell them for $1,300 cash:

Selling price of property	$2,000
Cost of property	1,000
Total profit	$1,000
(Percentage of profit, or proportion of each payment returnable as income, is 50%)	
Unpaid balance of notes	$1,500
Amount of income reportable if notes were paid in full (50% of $1,500)	750
Adjusted basis of the notes	$ 750

Your profit on the sale is $550 ($1,300 − $750). It is capital gain if the sale of the lot was taxable as capital gain.

Suppose you make an installment sale of your real estate, taking back a land contract. Later a mortgage is substituted for the unpaid balance of the land contract. The IRS has ruled that the substitution is not the same as a disposition of the unpaid installment obligations. There is no tax on the substitution.

If the installment obligations are disposed of other than by sale or exchange, gain or loss is the difference between the basis of the obligations and their fair market value at the time of the disposition. If an installment obligation is canceled or otherwise becomes unenforceable, it is subject to the same rule for determining gain or loss.

A gift of installment obligations to a person or charitable organization is treated as a taxable disposition. Gain or loss is the difference between the basis of the obligations and their fair market value at the time of the gift. If the notes are donated to a qualified charity, you may claim a contribution deduction for the fair market value of the obligations at the time of the gift.

Not all dispositions of installment obligations result in recognition of gain or loss. A transfer of installment obligations at death is not taxed. As the notes are paid, the estate or beneficiaries report income in the same proportion as the decedent would have, had he lived. A transfer of installment obligations to a revocable trust is also not taxed.

Receipt of notes in corporate liquidations. When you exchange your stock in a corporate liquidation under Section 331 and the corporation has sold some or all of its assets on the installment method and distributed notes to you and other stockholders in a Section 337 liquidation, you report your gain on the installment method as the notes are paid. Where liquidating distributions are made in more than one year, you must recompute your gain by allocating your stock basis pro rata over all payments. This may require you to file an amended return.

Installment obligations from the sale of corporate inventory qualify only if from a bulk sale of inventory.

Where the corporation makes an installment sale of depreciable property to your spouse or a corporation or partnership in which you and your spouse have 80% ownership, you may not use installment reporting; gain is recognized in the year the installment obligation is distributed, not deferred until payment is received.

¶6.193 • REPOSSESSION OF PERSONAL PROPERTY SOLD ON INSTALLMENT

When the buyer defaults and you repossess property, either through a voluntary surrender or a foreclosure, you may realize gain or loss. The method of calculating gain or loss is similar to the method used for disposition of installment notes (*see* ¶6.192 above). Gain or loss is the difference between the fair market value of the repossessed property and your basis for the installment obligations satisfied by the repossession. This rule is followed whether or not title has been kept by you or transferred to the buyer. The amount realized is reduced by costs incurred during the repossession. The basis of the obligation is face value less unreported profit.

If the property repossessed is bid in at a lawful public auction or judicial sale, the fair market value of the property is presumed to be the purchase or bid price, in the absence of proof to the contrary.

Gain or loss in the repossession is reported in the year of the repossession.
Example—
In December 1985, you sell personal property for $1,500—$300 down

and $100 a month beginning January 1986. You reported the installment sale on your 1985 tax return. The buyer defaulted after making three monthly payments. You foreclosed and repossessed the property; the fair market value was $1,400. The legal costs of foreclosure were $100. The gain on the repossession in 1986 is computed as follows:

Fair market value of property repossessed		$1,400
Basis of the buyer's notes at time of repossession:		
Selling price	$1,500	
Less: Payments made	600	
Face value of notes at repossession	$ 900	
Less: Unrealized profit (assume gross		
profit percentage of 33⅓% × $900)	300	600
Gain on repossession		$ 800
Less: Repossession costs		100
Taxable gain on repossession		$ 700

Repossession gain or loss keeps the same character as the gain or loss realized on the original sale. If the sale originally resulted in a capital gain, the repossession gain is also a capital gain.

Repossessions of real property are discussed at ¶31.06.

¶6.194 • BOOT IN A LIKE-KIND EXCHANGE PAYABLE IN INSTALLMENTS

An exchange of like-kind property is generally tax free unless boot, such as cash or notes, is received. The boot is taxable, and if payable in installments, the following rules apply. Contract price is reduced by like-kind property received. Gross profit is reduced by gain not recognized. "Payment" does not include like-kind property.
Example—
Property with a basis of $400,000 is exchanged for like-kind property worth $200,000 plus installment obligations of $800,000 of which $100,000 is payable in the year of sale. The contract price is $800,000 ($1 million less $200,000 like-kind property received); the gross profit is $600,000 ($200,000 basis attributed to notes). The gross profit ratio is 75% (gross profit of $600,000 ÷ contract price of $800,000); like-kind property is not treated as a payment received in the year of sale.

The same treatment applies to certain tax-free reorganizations which are not treated as dividends, and to exchanges of certain insurance policies, exchanges of the stock of the same corporation, and exchanges of United States obligations.

¶6.20 • Tax-Free Exchanges

	See ¶
Gain may not be recognized when—	
You trade in business equipment or machinery	5.48
You exchange stock for stock	6.21
You exchange joint ownership interests	6.22
You transfer property to a corporation you control in exchange for stock	6.23

	See ¶
You transfer property to your spouse	6.245
You exchange insurance policies	12.33
Your property is condemned or destroyed and you buy other property as a replacement	18.21
You sell your personal residence and buy another	29.20
You exchange real estate held for investment	31.021

The term "gain is not recognized" means that the gain is not taxed in the year it is realized. Gain may be taxed at a later disposition of the property because the basis of the property received in the exchange is usually the same as the basis of the property surrendered in the exchange. Thus, if you make a tax-free exchange of property with a tax basis of $10,000 for property worth $50,000, the basis of the property received in exchange is fixed at $10,000, even though its fair market value is $50,000. The gain of $40,000 ($50,000 — $10,000) is not recognized. If you later sell the property for $50,000, you realize taxable gain of $40,000 ($50,000 — $10,000).

Where property received in a tax-free exchange is held until death, the nonrecognized gain escapes tax forever because basis of the property in the hands of an heir is generally the value of the property at the death of the decedent. *See* ¶6.10.

A tax-free exchange may also involve the transfer of boot such as cash or other property. Gain on the exchange is taxable to the extent of the value of boot.

Example—
You make a tax-free exchange of property. The tax basis of the property you exchanged was $30,000; the value of the new property is $60,000. You also received cash of $20,000. Gain on the exchange is $50,000 ($80,000 — $30,000). Of this amount, $20,000 is taxed in the year of the exchange.

Tax-free exchange rules for certain corporate reorganizations are not discussed in this book.

See ¶5.48 for restrictions on deferred exchanges and exchanges of partnership interests.

¶6.21 • TAX-FREE EXCHANGES OF STOCK

Gain on the exchange of common stock for other common stock (or preferred for other preferred) of the same company is not taxable. Similarly, loss realized on such an exchange is not deductible. The exchange may take place between the stockholder and the company or between two stockholders.

An exchange of preferred stock for common, or common for preferred in the same company is generally not tax free, unless the exchange is part of a tax-free recapitalization. In such exchanges, the company should inform you of the tax consequences.

Convertible securities. Conversion of securities under a conversion privilege is tax free under the rules discussed at ¶6.271.

¶6.22 • EXCHANGES OF JOINT OWNERSHIP INTERESTS

The change to a tenancy in common from a joint tenancy is tax free. You may convert a joint tenancy in corporate stock to a tenancy in common without income tax consequences. The transfer is tax free even though survivorship rights are eliminated. Similarly, a partition and issuance of separate certificates in the names of each joint tenant is also tax free.

A joint tenancy and a tenancy in common differ in this respect. On the death of a joint tenant, his ownership passes to the surviving joint tenant or tenants. But on the death of a tenant holding property in common, his ownership passes to his heirs, not to the other tenant or tenants who held the property with him.

A tenancy by the entirety is a form of joint ownership recognized in some states and can be only between a husband and wife.

A division of properties held as tenants in common may qualify as tax-free exchanges.
Example—
Three men owned three pieces of real estate as tenants in common. Each man wanted to be the sole owner of one of the pieces of property. They disentangled themselves by exchanging interests in a three-way exchange. No money or property other than the three pieces of real estate changed hands, and none of the men assumed any liability of the others. The transactions qualified as tax-free exchanges and no gain or loss was recognized.

Receipt of boot. Exchanges of jointly owned property are tax free as long as no "boot" such as cash or other property passes between the parties. Boot may not be offset by an assumption of the other party's liabilities.
Example—
Two farmers, A and B, each owned one-half interests in two parcels of land used in their farming businesses. Each parcel cost $10,000, and had a fair market value of $200,000. One parcel was subject to a $100,000 mortgage on which they were jointly liable. They decided to exchange interests in the properties so that each owned 100% of one of the parcels: B received the nonmortgaged property; A, the mortgaged property, plus B's note of $50,000 to compensate him for taking the property subject to the mortgage.

The IRS holds that there was a tax-free exchange, but, at the same time, A received taxable boot of $50,000 in the form of B's note. Further, he may not offset this amount from his assumption of the additional mortgage liability. B did not realize any taxable boot. A's assumption of B's liability on the mortgage may be offset by the $50,000 note he gave to A.

¶6.23 • TAX-FREE TRANSFERS ALLOWED IN SETTING UP A CLOSELY-HELD CORPORATION

Tax-free exchange rules facilitate the organization of a corporation. When you transfer property to a corporation which you control solely in exchange for corporate stock or securities, no gain or loss is recognized on the transfer. For control, you alone or together with other transferors (such as partners, where a partnership is being incorporated) must own at least 80% of the combined voting power of the corporation and 80% of all other classes of stock immediately after the transfer to the corporation.

The corporation takes your basis in the property, and your basis in the stock received in the exchange is the same as your basis in the property. Thus, gain not recognized on the organization of the corporation may be taxed when you sell your stock, or the corporation disposes of the property.
Example—
You transfer a building worth $100,000, which cost you $20,000, to your newly organized corporation in exchange for all of its outstanding stock. You realize an $80,000 gain ($100,000 — $20,000) which is not recognized. Your basis in the stock is $20,000; the corporation's basis in the building is $20,000. The following year, you sell all your stock to a third party for $100,000. The $80,000 gain is now recognized.

Transfer of liabilities. When assets subject to liabilities are transferred to the corporation, the liability assumed by the corporation is not treated as a taxable "boot," but your stock basis

is reduced by the amount of liability. The transfer of liabilities may be taxable when the transfer is part of a tax avoidance scheme, or the liabilities exceed the basis of the property transferred to the corporation.

Consult an accountant or an attorney before undertaking a tax-free transfer to a closely-held corporation to determine the tax consequences of intended transfers. Also, it may not be to your advantage to fall within the tax-free exchange rules. This is so when you have property with potential losses or you wish the corporation to take a stepped-up basis for property.

¶6.24 • EXCHANGES OF COINS AND BULLION

An exchange of "gold for gold" coins or "silver for silver" coins may qualify as tax-free exchange of like-kind investment property. An exchange is tax free if both coins represent the same type of underlying investment. An exchange of bullion-type coins for bullion-type coins is a tax-free like-kind exchange. For example, the exchange of Mexican pesos for Austrian coronas has been held to be a tax-free exchange as both are bullion-type coins. However, an exchange of silver bullion for gold bullion is not tax free. Silver and gold bullion represent different types of property. Silver is an industrial commodity, whereas gold is primarily an investment in itself. Similarly, an exchange of U.S. gold collector's coins for South African Krugerrands is taxable. Krugerrands are bullion-type coins whose value is determined solely by metal content, whereas the U.S. gold coins are numismatic coins whose value depends on age, condition, number minted, and artistic merit, as well as metal content. Although both coins appear to be similar because of gold content, each represents a different type of investment.

¶6.245 • PROPERTY TRANSFERS BETWEEN SPOUSES

Tax-free exchange rules apply to all transfers between spouses—those during marriage as well as to those incident to divorce. A transfer "incident to a divorce," must either occur within one year after the date the marriage ceases or if later, be related to the cessation of the marriage, such as a transfer authorized by a divorce decree. Under temporary regulations, any transfer pursuant to a divorce or separation agreement occurring within six years of the end of the marriage is considered "incident to a divorce." Later transfers qualify only if a transfer within the six-year period was hampered by legal or business disputes, such as a fight over the property value.

Nonresident alien. The tax-free exchange rule does not apply to transfers to a nonresident alien spouse. But it does apply to a transfer to a former spouse who is a nonresident alien, provided that the "incident to a divorce" test is met.

Basis. The basis of the property to the transferee-spouse is the same as the basis of the property to the transferor-spouse. Thus, the transferee bears the tax consequences of a later sale. In a marital settlement, he or she can lessen the tax burden by negotiating for assets that have little or no unrealized appreciation.
Example—
In a property settlement accompanying a divorce, a husband plans to transfer to his wife stock worth $250,000 that cost him $50,000. In deciding whether to agree to the transfer, the wife should be aware that her basis for the stock will be $50,000; if she sells the stock, she will have to pay tax on the $200,000 gain. She should consider this tax cost in arriving at the settlement.

The tax-free rules apply to all property transfers between spouses. Under temporary IRS regulations, even a sale of business property by a sole proprietor to a spouse is a nontaxable transaction. The buyer-spouse assumes a carryover basis even if fair market value is paid. The transferor is not required to recapture previously claimed deductions or investment credits. However, the transferee is subject to the recapture rules on a premature disposition of the property or if the property is not used for business purposes.

The Tax-free rules generally apply to transfers made after July 18, 1984. Transfers made under agreements in effect before July 19, 1984 are subject to the tax-free rule only if both spouses make an election to have the tax-free rule apply.

Sales of Stock Dividends and Rights, Short Sales, and Wash Sales

¶6.25 • SALE OF STOCK RECEIVED AS DIVIDEND AND IN A STOCK SPLIT

A sale of stock originally received as a dividend is treated as any other sale of stock. The holding period of a taxable stock dividend begins on the day after the date of distribution. The holding period of a tax-free stock dividend or stock received in a split starts from the time you acquired the original stock.

Example—
You bought 100 shares of X Co. stock on December 3, 1985. On August 13, 1986, you receive 10 shares of X Co. stock as a tax-free stock dividend. On December 10, 1986, you sell the 10 shares at a profit. You report the sale as long-term capital gain because the holding period of the 10 shares goes back to your original purchase date of December 3, 1985, not August 13, 1986.

Basis of tax-free dividend in the same class of stock. Assume you receive common on common. You divide original cost by the total number of old shares and new shares to find the new basis per share.

Example—
You bought 100 shares of common stock for $1,000, so that each share has a basis of $10. You receive 100 shares of common as a tax-free stock dividend. The basis of your 200 shares remains $1,000. The new costs basis of each share is now $5 ($1,000 ÷ 200 shares). You sell 50 shares for $560. Your profit is $310 ($560 — $250).

Basis of tax-free dividend in a different class of stock. Assume you receive preferred on common. You divide the basis of the old shares over the two classes in ratio to their values at the time the stock dividend was distributed.

Basis of taxable stock dividend. Your basis is the fair market value of the stock on the date of distribution. The basis of the old stock remains unchanged.

Example—
You bought 100 shares of common for $1,000. You receive a tax-free dividend of 10 shares of preferred. On the date of distribution, the market value of the common is $9 a share; the preferred, $30. That makes the market value of your common stock $900 and your preferred $300. So you allocate ⁹⁄₁₂ of your $1,000 original cost (or $750) to your common and ³⁄₁₂ (or $250) to the preferred.

The basis of a taxable stock dividend is its fair market value at the time of the distribution. Its holding period begins on the date of distribution. The basis of the old stock remains unchanged.

Example—
You bought 1,000 shares of stock for $10,000. The company gives you a choice of a dividend in cash or in stock (1 share for every 100 held). You elect the stock. On the date of the distribution, its market value was $15 a share. The basis of the new stock is $150 (10 × $15). The basis of the old stock remains $10,000.

The tax treatment of the receipt of stock as a dividend and in a split is discussed at ¶3.05.

For the sale of stock received from a public utility dividend reinvestment plan, *see* ¶3.052.

Basis of public utility stock received under dividend reinvestment plan. For several years before 1986, an exclusion was allowed for stock dividends received from public utility companies if the dividends were reinvested in stock. If you claimed the exclusion, the stock takes a zero basis. When you sell the stock, the entire sales proceeds of the stock is reported as income. Long-term capital gain applies if:

1. You hold the shares for more than a year; and
2. You do not sell any other common stock in the utility during the period beginning with the record date of the dividend stock and ending one year after the stock dividend is distributed. If you sell other common stock, all or part of the gain may be taxable as ordinary income because you are considered to have sold your dividend stock.

Example—
You are married and elected a qualified stock dividend valued at $1,000 from Electrical Utility Company on October 1, 1985; the record date of the dividend was September 15, 1985. You exclude $1,000 on your 1985 joint return. If you sell the dividend stock any time after October 1, 1986, the sale proceeds will be taxed as long-term capital gain, provided you do not sell any other common stock of the utility before October 2, 1986.

If you sell common stock other than the dividend stock between September 15, 1985 and October 1, 1986, the sale is treated as a sale of the dividend stock to the extent of the number of dividend shares you still hold. See Treasury regulations for details.

¶6.26 • SALE, EXERCISE, OR EXPIRATION OF STOCK RIGHTS

The tax consequences of the receipt of stock rights is discussed at ¶3.05. The following is an explanation of how to treat the sale, exercise, or expiration of nontaxable stock rights.

Expiration of nontaxable distributed stock rights. When you allow nontaxable rights to expire, you do not realize a deductible loss.

Sale of nontaxable distributed stock rights. If you sell stock rights distributed on your stock, you treat the sale as the sale of a capital asset. The holding period begins from the date you acquired the original stock on which the rights were distributed.

Purchased rights. If you buy stock rights, your holding period starts the day after the date of the purchase. Your basis for the rights is the price paid; this basis is used in computing your capital gain or loss on their sale.

If you allow purchased rights to expire without sale or exercise, you realize a capital loss. The rights are treated as having been sold on the day of expiration. When purchased rights become worthless during the year prior to the year they lapse, you have a capital loss which is treated as having occurred on the last day of the year in which they became worthless.

Exercise of stock rights. You realize no taxable income on the exercise of stock rights. Capital gain or loss on the new stock is recognized when you later sell the stock. The holding period of the new stock begins on the date you exercised the rights. Your basis for the new stock is the subscription price you paid plus your basis for the rights exercised.

Figuring the basis of nontaxable stock rights. The basis of purchased stock rights is cost.

Whether rights received by you as a stockholder have a basis depends on their fair market value when distributed. If the market value of rights is less than 15% of the market value of your old stock, the basis of your rights is zero, unless you elect to allocate the basis over the rights and your original stock. You make the election on your tax return for the year in which the rights are received. The statement of election is made on a separate sheet of paper which you attach to your tax return. Keep a copy of the election and return.

If the market value of the rights is 15% or more of the market value of your old stock, you spread the tax cost of the stock between the old stock and the rights according to their respective values on the date of distribution.

Example—
You own 100 shares of M Co. which cost $10 a share. On September 15, there is a distribution of stock rights allowing for the purchase of one additional share of common for each 10 rights held at a price of $13 a share. The common is now worth $15 (ex-rights). The rights have a market value of 20¢ each. This is less than 15% of the market value of the stock. You can either:

a. Choose not to spread the tax cost of the stock between the old stock and the rights; *or*
b. Elect to spread the tax cost as follows:

Cost of your old stock 100 shares at $10, or $1,000.
Fair market value of old stock 100 shares at $15, or $1,500.
Market value of 100 rights at 20¢, or $20.
Market value of both old stock and rights, $1,520.
Apportionment of old stock:

$$\frac{\$1,500}{\$1,520} \times \$1,000 \text{ or } \$986.84.$$

Your new basis of old stock is $986.84 for 100 shares, or $9.87 a share.
    Tax cost of rights:

$$\frac{\$20}{\$1,520} \times \$1,000 \text{ or } \$13.16.$$

Basis of the rights is $13.16 for 100 rights.
When you exercise your rights and 10 shares are bought, your basis for the new stock is $130 plus the cost of the rights of $13.16 or $143.16.
If the option of allocation is not exercised, the rights have a basis of zero and the basis of the new stock is $130. Basis of the old stock remains $1,000.

No basis adjustment is required for stock rights which become worthless during the year of issue.

Example—
A corporation issued nontaxable stock rights to its common shareholders. The rights were worth more than 15% of the fair market value of the common stock. Shortly after issue, the stock market values fell and the price of common stock fell below the subscription offer. As the rights were valueless, the company decided to refund subscriptions to shareholders who exercised the option and paid the subscription price. Although the stock rights were originally 15% or more of value of stock, the IRS held that the stockholders receiving the refunds did not have to allocate basis. The allocation is not necessary as the subscription price was returned in the same taxable year in which the rights were issued.

The basis of taxable rights is their fair market value at the time of distribution.

¶6.261 • HOW TO TREAT SHORT SALES

You sell short when you sell borrowed securities. You usually borrow the securities from your broker. When you sell short, you may (1) own the identical securities but do not want to sell them just now, or (2) not own the securities. You *close* the short sale when you deliver to the broker the identical securities you have been holding or identical securities you have bought after the short sale.

Some objectives of selling short: You may want to profit from a declining market on the hope you can buy the replacement stock at lower prices, or freeze paper profits in an uncertain market, or postpone gain to another year.

Examples—
1. In December, 1986, you want to freeze your profit in Z stock, but you want to report the sale in 1987. You sell Z short on December 10, 1986. On January 3, 1987, you close the short sale by delivering your Z stock. The short sale is reported as gain on your 1987 return. You report a short sale in the year in which you close the short sale.
2. You sell short 100 shares of Steel Co. for $5,000. You borrowed the stock from your broker. The market declines. Five months later, you buy 100 shares of Steel Co. stock for $3,000, which you deliver to your broker to close the short sale. Your profit of $2,000 is taxed as short-term capital gain. Your profit would be short term regardless of how long you kept the sale open (see below).

One objective of the short sale tax rules is to prevent you from converting short-term gains into long-term gains on transactions of substantially identical securities. Another objective is to prevent you from realizing short-term losses on securities that are substantially identical to securities you are holding long term.

When analyzing short sale transactions, ask yourself these two questions:
1. When you sold short, did you or your spouse hold short-term securities substantially identical to the securities sold short? (Substantially identical securities are described at ¶6.27.)
2. After the short sale, did you or your spouse acquire sub-stantially identical securities on or before the date of the closing of the short sale?

If you answered "yes" to either or both of these questions, apply the following two rules:
1. *Gains realized on the closing of the short sale.* The gain is short term regardless of the period of time you have held the securities by the time you close the short sale.
2. *The beginning date of the holding period of substantially identical stock is suspended.* The holding period of substantially identical securities owned or bought under the facts of questions (1) or (2) above does not begin until the date of the closing of the short sale (or the date of the sale, gift, or other disposition of the securities, whichever date occurs first). But note this rule applies only to the number of securities that do not exceed the quantity sold short.

Examples—
1. *Short-term gain on closing short sale (Rule 1 above)*
Feb. 1: You buy 100 shares of Steel Co. at $10 a share.
July 1: You sell short 100 shares of Steel Co., at $16 a share.
Aug. 1: You close the short sale by delivering the stock bought on Feb. 1.
Result: You have a short-term gain of $600. On the date of the short sale (July 1), you held 100 shares of Steel Co. stock short term, as they were not held for more than six months. That more than six months elapsed between the purchase and closing date is immaterial.
2. *Holding period suspended (Rule 2 above)*
Feb. 1: You buy 100 shares of Steel Co. at $10 a share.
July 1: You sell short 100 shares of Steel Co. at $16 a share.
Aug. 1: You close the short sale with 100 shares you buy today at $18.
Aug. 2: You sell at $18 a share the lot bought on Feb. 1.
Result: (a) You have a short-term loss of $200 on the closing of the short sale:

Sales price	$1,600
Cost	1,800
Loss	($ 200)

(b) You have a short-term gain of $800 on the sale of the Feb. 1 lot ($1,800 − $1,000). Gain is short term although you held the lot for more than six months. The Aug. 1 lot was substantially identical stock held short term at the time of the short sale on July 1. Under the special holding period rule, the holding period of the Feb. 1 lot did not begin until the closing of the short sale on Aug. 1.

The effect of the holding period rule is to give the same tax result that would have been realized if you had sold the Feb. 1 lot on July 1, instead of making a short sale on that date. On July 1 a sale would have given you a short-term gain of $600.

The acquisition of a *put* (an option to sell) is treated as a short sale if you hold substantially identical securities short term at the time you buy the *put*. The exercise or failure to exercise the *put* is treated as the closing of the short sale. However, the short sale rules do not apply if on the same day you buy a *put* and stock which is identified as covered by the *put*. If you do not exercise the *put* which is identified with the stock, add its cost to the basis of the stock.

Losses on short sales. You may not realize a short-term loss on the closing of a short sale if you held substantially identical securities long term on the date of the short sale. The loss is long term. This rule prevents you from creating short-term losses when you held the covering stock long term. Loss deductions on short sales may be disallowed under the wash sale rules of ¶6.27.

A loss on a short sale is not deductible until shares closing the short sale are delivered to the broker.

Example—
Feb. 1: You buy 100 shares of Oil stock at $10 a share
Sept. 1: You sell short 100 shares of Oil stock at $16 a share.
Oct. 1: You sell 100 shares bought Feb. 1 for $18 a share. You also close the short sale by buying 100 shares at $18 and delivering them to the broker.
Result: You have a long-term gain of $800 on the sale of the Feb. 1 lot. This sale is not affected by the short sale rules because at the time of the short sale the stock was held for more than six months. However, the special lose rule applies:

The loss of $200 incurred on the closing of the short sale is long term, not short term. You held substantially identical securities for more than six months when you made the short sale. The effect of the rule is to give the same tax result you would have realized if you closed the short sale with the Feb. 1 lot instead of buying stock. That is, your net long-term gain is $600 ($800 − $200).

Expenses of short sales. Before you buy stock to close out a short sale, you pay the broker for dividends paid on stock you have sold short. For an investor, the payment of an ordinary cash dividend is deductible as a nonbusiness expense if the short sale is held open at least 46 days or more than a year in the case of extraordinary dividends. If not, the payment is not deductible and is added to basis; in counting the short sale period, do not count any period during which you have an option to buy or are obligated to buy substantially identical securities or are protected from the risk of loss from the short sale by a substantially similar position. An extraordinary dividend is generally a dividend that exceeds in value 10% of the adjusted basis of the stock or 5% in case of a preferred stock. For purposes of this test, dividends on stock received within an 85-day period are aggregated; a one-year aggregation period applies if dividends exceed 20% of the adjusted basis in the stock.

Arbitrage transactions. Special holding period rules apply to short sales involved in identified arbitrage transactions in convertible securities and stock into which the securities are convertible. These rules can be found in Treasury regulations.

¶6.27 • SECURITY LOSSES FROM WASH SALES

The objective of the wash-sale rule is to disallow a loss deduction where you recover your market position in a security within a short period of time from the sale. Under the wash-sale rule, your loss deduction is barred if you purchase, or buy an option to purchase, *substantially identical* stock or securities within 30 days of the sale. The wash-sale period is 61 days—30 days before and 30 days after the date of sale. The end of a taxable year during this 61-day period does not affect the wash-sale rule. The loss is still denied. If you sell at a loss and your spouse buys substantially identical stock, the loss is also barred.

The wash-sale rule does not apply to gains or to acquisitions by gift, inheritance, or tax-free exchange.

The wash-sale rule applies to investors and traders. It does not apply to dealers.

What is substantially identical stock or securities? Buying and selling General Motors stock is dealing in an *identical* security. Selling General Motors and buying Chrysler stock is not dealing in an identical security.

Bonds of the same obligor are substantially identical if they carry the same rate of interest; that they have different issue dates and interest payment dates will not remove them from the wash-sale provisions. Different maturity dates will have no effect, unless the difference is economically significant. Where there is a long time span between the purchase date and the maturity date, a difference of several years between maturity dates may be considered insignificant. A difference of three years between maturity dates was held to be insignificant where the maturity dates of the bonds, measured from the time of purchase, was 45 and 48 years away. There was no significant difference where the maturity dates differed by less than one year, and the remaining life, measured from the time of purchase, was more than 15 years. The wash-sale rules do not apply if you buy bonds of the same company with substantially different interest rates or buy bonds of a different company or buy substantially identical bonds outside of the wash-sale period.

A warrant falls within the wash-sale rule if it is an option to buy substantially identical stock. Consequently, a loss on the sale of common stocks of a corporation is disallowed when warrants for the common of the same corporation are bought within the period 30 days before or after the sale. But if the timing is reversed, that is, you sell warrants at a loss and simultaneously buy common of the same corporation, the wash-sale rules may or may not apply depending on whether the warrants are substantially identical to the purchased stock. This is determined by comparing the relative values of the stock and warrants. The wash-sale rule will apply only if the relative values and price changes are so similar that the warrants become fully convertible securities.

The wash-sale rule applies to an oral sale-repurchase agreement between business associates.
Example—
An investor wanted to offset a substantial capital gain with a loss on stock he wanted to retain. An investment counselor suggested that he and his wife sell stock on which they had a substantial paper loss to a business associate with the understanding that they would rebuy the stock after a 30-day period. The agreement was oral. The investor also loaned his associate funds to buy the stock. The stock, which was traded over the market, was sold at market price, and the couple claimed a loss of almost $190,000, which was used to offset their capital gain. Within 34 days, they bought back the stock. The IRS disallowed the loss claiming that the sale was a sham and also came within the wash-sale rules. The Tax Court agrees that the sale was a sham, and even if not a sham, fell within the wash-sale rules although the repurchase occurred more than 30 days after the sale. The wash-sale provision was triggered by the oral agreement to repurchase which was made *within* the 30-day period. The law does not require a written contract. It requires only that there be an agreement to buy substantially identical securities.

Although the loss deduction is barred if the wash-sale rule applies, the economic loss is not forfeited for tax purposes. Because of the following basis rules, the loss may be realized at a later date when the repurchased stock is sold. After the disallowance of the loss, the cost basis of the new lot is fixed as the basis of the old lot and adjusted (up or down) for the difference between the selling price of the old stock and the purchase price of the new stock.
Examples—
1. You bought common stock of Appliance Co. for $10,000 in 1980. On June 30, 1984 you sold the stock for $8,000, incurring a $2,000 loss. A week later, you repurchased the same number of shares of Appliance stock for $9,000. Your loss of $2,000 on the sale is disallowed because of the wash-sale rule. The basis of the new lot becomes $11,000. The basis of the old shares ($10,000) is increased by $1,000 which is the excess of the purchase price of the new shares ($9,000) over the selling price of the old shares ($8,000).
2. Assume the same facts as in Example 1 except that you repurchase the stock for $7,000. The basis of the new lot is $9,000. The basis of the old shares ($10,000) is decreased by $1,000, which is the excess of the selling price of the old shares ($8,000) over the purchase price of the new shares ($7,000).
3. Assume that in February, 1986, you sell the stock acquired in Example 1 above for $9,000 and do not run afoul of the wash-sale rule. On the sale, you realize a loss of $2,000 ($11,000 − $9,000).

The number of shares of stock reacquired in a wash sale may be less than the amount sold. Then only a proportionate part of the loss is disallowed.
Example—
You bought 100 shares of A stock for $10,000. On December 19, 1986, you sell the lot for $8,000, incurring a loss of $2,000. On January 6, 1987, you repurchase 75 shares of A stock for $6,000. Three quarters (75/100) of your loss is disallowed or $1,500 (¾ of $2,000). You deduct the remaining loss of $500 on your return for 1987. The basis of the new shares is $7,500.

After a wash sale, the holding period of the new stock includes the holding period of the old lots. If you sold more than one old lot in wash sales, you add the holding periods of all the old lots to the holding period of the new lot. You do this even if your holding periods overlapped because you bought another lot before you sold the first. You do not count the periods between sale and purchase when you have no stock.

Losses incurred on short sales are subject to the wash-sale rules. A loss on the closing of a short sale is denied if you sell the stock or enter into a second short sale within the period beginning 30 days before and ending 30 days after the closing of the short sale. Under prior law applying to sales before July 19, 1984, a loss on a short sale was treated as incurred on the day the short sale was transacted, not on the day it was closed. Consequently, the loss was disallowed as incurred on the same day as the purchase of identical stock.

Loss on sale of part of a stock lot bought less than 30 days before the sale is deductible.

Example—

You buy 200 shares of stock. Within 30 days, you sell 100 shares at a loss. The loss is not disallowed by the wash-sale rule. The wash-sale rule does not apply to a loss sustained in a bona fide sale made to reduce your market position. It does apply when you sustain a loss for tax purposes with the intent of recovering your position in the security within a few days. Thus, if after selling the 100 shares, you repurchase 100 shares of the same stock within 30 days after the sale, the loss is disallowed.

Sometimes the wash-sale rule can work to your advantage. Assume that during December, you are negotiating a sale that will bring you a large capital gain. You want to offset a part of that gain by selling certain securities at a loss. You are unsure just when the gain transaction will go through. It may be on the last day of the year. Then it may be too late to sell the loss securities before the end of the year. You can do this: Sell the loss securities during the last week of December. If the profitable deal goes through before the end of the year, you need not do anything further. If it does not, buy back the loss securities early in January. The December sale will be a wash sale and the loss disallowed. When the profitable sale occurs next year, you can sell the loss securities again. This time the loss will be allowed and offsets the gain.

¶6.271 · CONVERTIBLE STOCKS AND BONDS

You realize no gain or loss when you convert a bond into stock or preferred stock into a common stock of the same corporation if the conversion privilege was allowed by the bond or preferred stock certificate.

Holding period. Stock acquired through the conversion of bonds or preferred stock takes the same holding period as the securities exchanged. However, where the new stock is acquired partly for cash and partly by tax-free exchange, each new share of stock has a split holding period. The portion of each new share allocable to the ownership of the converted bonds (or preferred stock) includes the holding period of the bonds (or preferred stock). The portion of the new stock allocable to the cash purchase takes a holding period beginning with the day after acquisition of the stock.

Basis. Securities acquired through the conversion of bonds or preferred stock into common take the same basis as the securities exchanged. Where there is a partial cash payment, the basis of the portion of the stock attributable to the cash is the amount of cash paid.

Examples—

1. On January 4, you paid $100 for the debenture of A Co. Your holding period for the debenture begins on January 5 (*see* ¶6.05). The debenture provides that the holder may receive one share of A Co. common stock upon surrender of one debenture and the payment of $50. On October 19, you convert the debenture to stock on payment of $50. For tax purposes, you realize no gain or loss upon the conversion regardless of whether the fair market value of the stock is more or less than $150 on the date of the conversion. The basis and holding period for the stock is as follows: $100 for the portion attributed to the ownership of the debenture with a holding period beginning January 5; $50 attributed to the cash payment, and the holding period for this portion begins October 20.

2. Same as above but you acquired the debenture on January 4 through the exercise of rights on that date. Since the holding period for the debenture includes the date of exercise of the rights (*see* ¶6.26), the portion of the stock allocable to the debenture takes a holding period beginning on January 4.

If you paid a premium for a convertible bond, you may not amortize the amount of the premium attributable to the conversion feature.

¶6.28 · Bad Debt Deductions

When you lend money or sell on credit and your debtor does not repay, you may deduct your loss. The type of deduction depends on whether the debt was incurred in a business or personal transaction. This distinction is important because business bad debts receive favored tax treatment.

Business bad debt is fully deductible from gross income. In addition, you may deduct partially worthless business debts.

Examples of business debt transactions:

1. You sell merchandise on credit and later the buyer becomes insolvent and does not pay.

2. You are in the business of making loans and a loan goes bad.

3. You sell your business, but retain some accounts receivable. Later, some of these become worthless.

4. You liquidate your business and are unable to collect its outstanding accounts.

5. You operate as a promoter of corporations.

6. You finance your lessees, customers, or suppliers to help your business.

7. You lend money to protect your professional and business reputation.

8. You lend money to insure delivery of merchandise from a supplier.

9. You make a loan to your employer to keep your job.

Nonbusiness bad debt is deducted as a short-term capital loss on Schedule D. This is a limited deduction. In 1986, you deduct it from capital gains, if any, and $3,000 of other income. Any excess is deductible as a carryover in 1987 and later years (*see* ¶6.003). You may not deduct partially worthless nonbusiness bad debts.

Examples of nonbusiness bad debts:

1. You enter into a deal for profit which is not connected with your business—for example, debts arising from investments are nonbusiness bad debts.

2. You make casual personal advances with a reasonable hope of recovery and are not in the business of making loans.

3. You are assigned a debt that arose in the assignor's business. That he could have deducted it as a business bad debt does not make it your business debt. A business debt must arise in your business.

4. You pay liens filed against your property by mechanics or suppliers who have not been paid by your builder or contractor. Your payment is considered a deductible bad debt when there is no possibility of recovering reimbursement from the contractor and a judgment obtained against him is uncollectible.

5. You lose a deposit on a house when the contractor becomes insolvent.

6. You had an uninsured savings account in a savings association which went into default.

¶6.29 · PROVING A BAD DEBT DEDUCTION

To determine whether you have a bad debt deduction in 1986, read the four rules explained below. Pay close attention to the fourth rule which requires proof that the debt became worthless in the year the deduction is claimed. Your belief that your debt is bad, or the mere refusal of the debtor to pay, is not sufficient evidence. There must be an event, such as the debtor's bankruptcy, to fix the debt as worthless.

¶6.30 · FOUR RULES FOR BAD DEBT DEDUCTIONS

Rule 1. You must have a valid debt. You have no loss if your right to repayment is not fixed or depends upon some event which may not happen. Thus, advances to a corporation already insolvent are not valid debts. Nor are advances that are to be repaid only if the corporation has a profit. Voluntary payment of another's debt is also nondeductible. If usurious interest was charged on a worthless debt, and under state law the debt was void or voidable, the debt is not deductible as a bad debt. However, where the lender was in the business of lending money, a court allowed him to deduct the unpaid amounts as business losses.

Rule 2. A debtor-creditor relationship must exist at the time the debt arose. You have a loss if there was a promise to repay at the time the debt was created and you had the right to enforce it. If the advance was a gift and you did not expect to be repaid, you may not take a deduction. Loans to members of your family, to a controlled corporation or trust may be treated as gifts or contributions to capital.

Rule 3. The funds providing the loan or credit were previously reported as income or part of your capital. If you are on the cash basis, you may not deduct unpaid salary, rent, or fees. On the cash basis, you do not include these items in income until you are paid.

Rule 4. You must show that the debt became worthless during 1986. That is—

The debt had some value at the end of 1985. To prove the debt became worthless in 1986, you must show it had some value at the end of the previous year, that there was a reasonable hope and expectation of recovering something on the debt. Your personal belief unsupported by other facts is not enough. Would a businessman have placed some value on the debt on December 31, 1985?

An identifiable event occurred in 1986 which caused you to conclude that the debt was worthless, such as a bankruptcy proceeding. You do not have to go to court to try to collect the debt if you can show that a court judgment would be uncollectable, but reasonable collection steps were taken.

> You do not have to wait until the debt is due in order to prove worthlessness.

That you cancel a debt does not make it worthless. You must still show that the debt was worthless when you canceled it.

There is no hope the debt may have some value in a later year. You are not required to prove that there is no possibility of ever receiving some payment on your debt. You are not expected to be an extreme optimist.

Effect of statute of limitations. A debt is not deductible merely because a statute of limitations has run against the debt. Although the debtor has a legal defense against your demand for payment, he may still recognize his obligation to pay. A debt is deductible only in the year it becomes worthless. This event, for example, the debtor's insolvency, may have occurred even before the statute became effective.

What if your debtor recognized his moral obligation to pay in spite of the expiration of the statute of limitations, but died before paying? His executor defeats your claim by raising the statute of limitations. You have a bad debt deduction in the year you made the claim against the estate.

Guarantor or endorsement losses as business bad debts. Loss on a guarantee made after December 31, 1975 is deductible as a business bad debt deduction (ordinary loss deduction) only if the guarantee arose out of the guarantor's business of guarantying, endorsing, or indemnifying debts. If a loss arose out of a guarantee made before December 31, 1975, the loss is a business bad debt under these conditions: The borrower was not a corporation, the proceeds of the guaranteed loan were used in the borrower's trade or business, and at the time the guarantor made the payment, the borrower's obligation was worthless.

A loss on a guarantee may be a nonbusiness bad debt if the guarantee was made under circumstances that would have given rise to a nonbusiness bad debt deduction if a direct loan had been made by the guarantor.

¶6.31 • LOANS BY STOCKHOLDERS

It is a common practice for stockholders to make loans to their corporations or to guarantee loans made by banks or other lenders. If the corporation fails and the stockholder is not repaid or has to make good on the guarantee, he is generally left with a nonbusiness bad debt unless he can prove he made a business

loan. To prove a business loan, the stockholder usually has to show one of these facts: (1) He is in the business of making loans and the loan was made in that capacity, or he is in the business of promoting corporations for a fee or for profits on their sale; (2) he made the loan to safeguard his business; or (3) he wanted to protect his job with the company. The Supreme Court has ruled that a stockholder who claims he made the loan to protect his job must show that protection of his job was the *primary and dominant* motive of the loan.

Example—

To determine an executive's motive for making a loan, the Supreme Court reviewed his salary, outside income, investment in the company, and the size of his loan. His pay was $12,000 ($7,000 after tax), his outside income, $30,000. He had a $38,900 investment in the company and loaned it $165,000. On the basis of these figures, the Court concluded he could not have advanced $165,000 to protect an after-tax salary of $7,000.

The Tax Court followed this approach to determine the motive for a stockholder-employee's guarantee of company loans which went bad. His salary was $12,000 ($11,000 after tax); he had little outside income. His stock investment in the company was $22,100, and he guaranteed $13,000 of corporate debt. He claimed he hoped that his salary would increase to $20,000 if the company was successful. If it was not, he would lose his job. The Court accepted his explanation. An advance of $13,000 to protect an after-tax salary of $11,000 was not unreasonable, particularly since he expected pay increases. Also, his stock investment in the corporation was modest in relation to his salary.

A loan by a stockholder to key employees was held to be a business bad debt in the following case.

Example—

Carter, the president and majority owner of two corporations, loaned money to two key employees to buy stock in the corporations. He wanted to guarantee their future participation in the company. Both corporations went bankrupt, and the employees defaulted on the loans. Carter deducted both loans as business bad debts contending he was protecting his job; the IRS argued he had a nonbusiness bad debt; he was merely protecting his investment as a stockholder. The Tax Court disagreed. He made the loans to encourage the future of a business which would provide him salary income rather than dividends or appreciation on his stock.

When liquidation proceeds are insufficient to repay a stockholder loan and redeem his stock, the proceeds are first applied to the loan and then to the stock.

¶6.311 • FAMILY BAD DEBTS

The IRS views loans to relatives, especially to children and parents, as gifts, so that it is rather difficult to deduct family bad debts.

> To overcome the presumption of a gift when you advance money to a relative, take the same steps you would in making a business loan. Take a note, set a definite payment date, and require interest and collateral. If the relative fails to pay, make an attempt to collect. Failure to enforce collection of a family debt is viewed by the courts as evidence of a gift, despite the taking of notes and interest.

Husband's default on child support—a basis for wife's deductible bad debt? A wife who supports her children when her husband defaults on court-ordered support payments may consider claiming her expenses as a nonbusiness bad debt deduction, arguing that her position is similar to a guarantor who pays a creditor when the principal debtor defaults. The IRS does not agree to the grounds of such a claim and will disallow the deduction; its position is supported by the Tax Court. However, an appeals court left open the possibility that such a claim may have merit if a wife can show: (1) What she spent on the children and (2) her husband's obligation to support was worthless in the year the deduction is claimed. The appeals court barred a bad debt deduction to the wife who could not prove these points but refused to back the Tax Court position that defaulted support payments may never be treated as a bad debt. The Tax Court has subsequently reiterated its position that defaulted child support payments are no basis for a bad debt deduction.

¶6.32 • How to Show Transactions on Schedule D

You report many different types of transactions in separate Schedule D: Sales of securities, worthless personal loans, sales of stock rights and warrants, and sale of a personal residence. This section illustrates the treatment of transactions on Schedule D. The form has been altered to show more transactions than can be entered on an actual Schedule D. A filled-in sample Schedule D for 1986 may be found in the Supplement.

The number of each transaction is keyed to the schedule below.

1. Sale of stock (long-term gain)—You bought 100 shares of Acme Steel stock on October 1, 1960, for $5,000. On March 3, 1986, you sell the 100 shares for $6,000.

(In this and other applicable examples, broker's commissions are added to the cost of the stock. It is assumed that state transfer taxes, if any, are deducted as itemized deductions.)

2. Sale of stock (short-term gain)—You bought 200 shares of Buma Rubber stock on July 19, 1986 for $400. On October 10, 1986, you sell the 200 shares for $600.

3. Sale of stock received as a gift (long-term gain)—Your father gave you a gift of 100 shares of Crown Auto stock on March 15, 1986, which he had bought in 1960 for $4,000. The fair market value of the stock at the time of the gift was $5,900. On March 21, 1986, you sell the stock for $6,000. (No gift tax was due on the gift, *see* ¶6.10 and ¶6.053.)

4. Sale of stock received as a gift (short-term loss)—Same facts as above but the value of the stock at the time of the gift is $3,000. You sell the stock on March 28, 1986 for $2,500. This sale is short term because, when stock received as a gift is sold at a loss and its value at time of gift is less than cost, the holding period begins at the date of gift (*see* ¶6.10 and ¶6.053).

5. Sale of stock received as inheritance (long-term gain)—You inherited 300 shares of Davis Textile preferred stock from your father who died on January 2, 1975. He had bought them in 1941 for $1,500. When he died, they were selling on the exchange for $15,000, at which value they were reported for estate tax purposes. You received the stock on February 23, 1980, when they were selling at $16,500. You sold the stock for $18,000 on June 4, 1986 (*see* ¶6.10).

6. Sale of stock including stock dividends—You bought 100 shares of Box Co. stock for $1,000 on June 20, 1968. Last year, you received a stock dividend of 10 shares; this year, a stock dividend of 40 shares. On March 20, 1986, you sell the 150 shares for $3,000 (*see* ¶6.25).

7. Sale of stock dividend—You bought 100 shares of Bale Co. stock for $1,200 on January 5, 1978. You receive a stock dividend for 20 shares on April 19, 1982. You sell the 20 shares received as a stock dividend on June 5, 1986 for $300 (*see* ¶6.25).

8. Sale of stock rights—You bought 100 shares of Tel. Co. stock for $5,000 on January 30, 1962. On January 3, 1986, you receive stock rights to subscribe to 10 shares at $53 a share. The stock is worth $55 a share (ex-rights). You sell the rights for $20 on February 6, 1986 (*see* ¶6.26).

9. Worthless bond—On August 10, 1950, you bought two $1,000 bonds of Rail Co. at par. These bonds became completely worthless during 1986 (*see* ¶6.032).

10. Worthless personal loan—You loaned $500 to a person on May 1, 1981. He was adjudged bankrupt on March 5, 1986 (*see* ¶6.28).

The IRS requires that you explain the deduction in a statement attached to your return. It should show: (1) The nature of the debt, (2) the name of the debtor and his business or family relationship, if any, to you, (3) when debt was due, (4) how you tried to collect it, (5) how you determined it was worthless.

11. Short sale—You sold "short" 100 shares of Fast Co. on September 4, 1986 for $9,000. You covered this sale on October 22, 1986 by buying 100 shares for $8,500 and delivering them to your broker (*see* ¶6.261).

Short-term Capital Gains and Losses

a. Description of property (Example, 100 shares of "Z" Co.)	b. Date acquired (mo., day, yr.)	c. Date sold (mo., day, yr.)	d. Gross sales price	e. Cost or other basis plus expense of sale	f. Loss	g. Gain
2. 200 sh Buma Rubber	7/19/86	10/10/86	600	400		200
4. 100 sh Crown Auto	3/15/86	3/28/86	2,500	3,000	(500)	
10. Worthless loan (See attached)	5/1/81		Worthless	500	(500)	
11. 100 sh Fast Co.	10/22/86	9/4/86	9,000	8,500		500
12. Call Sand Co.	6/4/86	Expired		500		(500)

Long-term Capital Gains and Losses

a. Description of property (Example, 100 shares of "Z" Co.)	b. Date acquired (mo., day, yr.)	c. Date sold (mo., day, yr.)	d. Gross sales price	e. Cost or other basis plus expense of sale	f. Loss	g. Gain
1. 100 sh Acme Steel	10/1/60	3/3/86	6,000	5,000		1,000
3. 100 sh Crown Auto	1960	3/21/86	6,000	4,000		2,000
5. 300 sh Davis Textile	1/2/75	6/4/86	18,000	15,000		3,000
6. 150 sh Box Co.	6/20/68	3/20/86	3,000	1,000		2,000
7. 20 sh Bale Co.	1/5/78	6/5/86	300	200		100
8. 100 rights Tel. Co.	1/30/62	2/6/86	20			20
9. 2 bonds Rail Co.	8/10/50	12/31/86	Worthless	2,000	(2,000)	
13. 25 sh Filmco, Inc.	5/3/66	6/25/86	500	300		200
14. 5 sh Derby Corp.	1/6/61	8/6/86	150	200	(50)	
15. Lump-sum distribution from Form 4972						15,000
16. 100 sh Long Co.	1961	6/4/86	12,000	7,200		4,800

12. Call—On June 4, 1986, you bought a 60 day call on 100 shares of Sand Corp. for $500. You did not exercise it (see ¶6.0351).

13. Capital distribution—On June 25, 1986, you receive a return of capital distribution of $500 from Filmco, Inc. You purchased 25 shares on May 3, 1966, for $700 and had received a return of capital dividend for $400 in a previous year which reduced your cost basis to $300. You report that part of the return of capital distribution that exceeds your cost basis (see ¶3.08).

A return of capital distribution that results in neither gain nor loss is not reported in Schedule D.

14. Liquidating dividends—On August 6, 1986, you receive, in redemption of your stock, a final distribution of $150 in complete liquidation from Derby Corp. You purchased this stock on January 6, 1961, for $250 and had received a liquidating distribution of $50 in a prior year which reduced your cost to $200 (see ¶3.08).

15. Lump-sum profit or pension payment (pre-1974 participation)—On Form 1099 R, your employer will generally give you a breakdown of the amounts reported as capital gain and as ordinary income. The method of computing these figures is also explained at ¶7.01. On Schedule D, you report only the amount subject to capital gain treatment. Assume in 1986 on retirement, you receive a lump-sum payment of $100,000, of which $15,000 is

allocated as capital gain because of your participation in the plan before 1974. You report $15,000 on Schedule D. The tax on the ordinary income element is figured on Form 4972 (see ¶7.01). If the capital gain element of your pension is the only item you are reporting on Schedule D, you need not use Schedule D. Instead you may report 40 percent of the gain on Form 1040 in the space provided for a single capital gain item. (See *Supplement to Your Income Tax* for the exact number of the line.)

> Caution: If the effective tax rate of 10-year averaging is less than the effective capital gain rate and you qualify for 10-year averaging (see ¶7.02), do not report the item as capital gain. Compute the tax under both methods, reporting the capital gain separately or treating the entire distribution as ordinary income. Choose the method giving the lower tax. The election to treat the entire sum as ordinary income is made on Form 4972 by simply entering the entire distribution as ordinary income.

16. Bargain sale of appreciated property to charity. On June 4, 1986, you sell to a charity 100 shares of Long Co. stock for your cost of $12,000. You acquired the stock in 1961. The present value is $20,000. You allocate 60% ($12,000/$20,000) of your cost to the "sold" portion; 60% of your cost of $12,000 is $7,200. You report long-term gain of $4,800 ($12,000−$7,200). You may claim a charitable deduction for $8,000 in the itemized deduction schedule.

¶6.321 · Supplemental Schedules for Residence Sales and Installment Sale

The IRS provides special forms for reporting a profitable sale of a principal residence and an installment sale. Form 2119 is for reporting sales and exchanges of principal residences; Form 6252 for installment sales. The final result of a computation is generally transferred to Schedule D or Form 4797.

The following sample transactions are followed by a filled-in section of Form 2119 or 6252. Only the relevant sections are shown and in some cases have been altered to simplify the illustration.

1. Sale of personal residence (gain taxed)—On December 10, 1986, you sell your home for $70,000. The house originally cost you $10,000 in 1941. During the years, you added such improvements as an extra room, porch, and terrace—total cost $6,000. In

selling the house, you paid a broker's commission and legal fees of $2,500. You are under 55 and do not plan to buy a new house. You move to an apartment.

Gain of $51,500 is also entered on Schedule D.

Part I   **Computation of Gain**

4 Selling price of residence less expense of sale. (Do not include personal property items.)	**4**	67,500
5 Basis of residence sold	**5**	16,000
6 Gain on sale (subtract line 5 from line 4). If zero or less, enter zero and do not complete the rest of form. Enter the gain from this line on Schedule D, line 2 or 10*, unless you bought another principal residence or checked "Yes" to 3d. Then continue with this form	**6**	51,500

If you haven't replaced your residence, do you plan to do so within the replacement period? . . . . ☐ Yes ☒ No
(If "Yes" see instruction B.)

2. Sale of personal residence (plan to buy new house). Same facts as in example above except you plan to buy a new home in the spring of 1987 after you return from a winter vacation.

If you make a timely replacement of your residence after filing your 1986 return and the residence costs you at least as much as the adjusted sales price of the old residence, notify the IRS in writing of the replacement and attach another Form 2119 for the year of

sale, filling in both Parts I and II (see below).

If the new residence costs less than the adjusted sales price of your old residence, or if you do not buy or start construction of your new residence within the replacement period, you must file Form 1040X with attached Schedule D and Form 2119 showing the amount of the taxable gain. Interest is charged on the additional tax due.

Part I   Computation of Gain

4 Selling price of residence less expense of sale. (Do not include personal property items.)	**4**	67,500
5 Basis of residence sold	**5**	16,000
6 Gain on sale (subtract line 5 from line 4). If zero or less, enter zero and do not complete the rest of form. Enter the gain from this line on Schedule D, line 2 or 10*, unless you bought another principal residence or checked "Yes" to 3d. Then continue with this form	**6**	51,500

If you haven't replaced your residence, do you plan to do so within the replacement period? . . . . ☒ Yes ☐ No
(If "Yes" see instruction B.)

3. Sale of personal residence (new house bought). Same facts as in example above except you buy a new house on December 17, 1986. Before selling the old house, during the month of November, you had it spruced up and paid fix-up expenses of $1,000 for inside and outside painting. The price of the new house is $65,000, $15,000 cash plus a mortgage of $50,000.

In buying the new house, you paid title search and legal fees of $600. You defer tax on $50,600 of your gain by attaching Form 2119 computations to your return and showing the following computations:

Part I   Computation of Gain

4 Selling price of residence less expense of sale. (Do not include personal property items.)	**4**	67,500
5 Basis of residence sold	**5**	16,000
6 Gain on sale (subtract line 5 from line 4). If zero or less, enter zero and do not complete the rest of form. Enter the gain from this line on Schedule D, line 2 or 10*, unless you bought another principal residence or checked "Yes" to 3d. Then continue with this form	**6**	51,500

If you haven't replaced your residence, do you plan to do so within the replacement period? . . . . ☐ Yes ☐ No
(If "Yes" see instruction B.)

Part III   Gain To Be Postponed and Adjusted Basis of New Residence

Complete this part if you bought another principal residence.

9 Fixing-up expenses (see instructions for time limits)	**9**	1,000
10 Adjusted sales price (subtract line 9 from line 4)	**10**	66,500
11 Cost of new residence	**11**	65,600
12 Gain taxable this year (subtract line 11 plus line 7 (if applicable) from line 10). If result is zero or less, enter zero. Do not enter more than line 6 or line 8 (if applicable). Enter the gain from this line on Schedule D, line 2 or 10*.	**12**	900
13 Gain to be postponed (subtract line 12 from line 6. However, if Part II applies, subtract line 12 from line 8)	**13**	50,600
14 Adjusted basis of new residence (subtract line 13 from line 11)	**14**	15,000

*Caution: If you completed Form 6252 for the residence in 1a, do not enter your taxable gain from Form 2119 on Schedule D.

4. Sale of personal residence by owner 55 or over. In 1957, you bought your home for $28,000. Capital additions and improvements came to $3,500. You are over the age of 55. You sell your home for $101,000, incurring attorney's fees of $600 and broker's commission of $5,500. You do not buy a new home. To your return, you attach Form 2119 and elect the home sale exclusion, thereby avoiding tax on your gain.

Part I   Computation of Gain

4 Selling price of residence less expense of sale. (Do not include personal property items.)	**4**	94,900
5 Basis of residence sold	**5**	31,500
6 Gain on sale (subtract line 5 from line 4). If zero or less, enter zero and do not complete the rest of form. Enter the gain from this line on Schedule D, line 2 or 10*, unless you bought another principal residence or checked "Yes" to 3d. Then continue with this form	**6**	63,400

If you haven't replaced your residence, do you plan to do so within the replacement period? . . . . ☐ Yes ☒ No
(If "Yes" see instruction B.)

Do not include expenses that you deduct as moving expenses.

1 a Date former residence sold ▶   December 10, 1986

   b Enter the face amount of any mortgage, note (for example, second trust), or other financial instrument on which you will receive periodic payments of principal or interest from this sale ▶

		Yes	No
2 a	If you bought or built a new residence, enter date you occupied it; otherwise enter "None" ▶ None		
b	Are any rooms in either residence rented out or used for business for which a deduction is allowed? (If "Yes," see instructions)		x
3 a	Were you 55 or over on date of sale?	x	
b	Was your spouse 55 or over on date of sale? If you answered "No" to 3a and 3b, do not complete 3c through 3f and Part II.	x	
c	Did the person who answered "Yes" to 3a or 3b own and use the property sold as his or her principal residence for a total of at least 3 years (except for short absences) of the 5-year period before the sale?	x	
d	If you answered "Yes" to 3c, do you elect to take the once in a lifetime exclusion of the gain on the sale?	x	

   e At time of sale, was the residence owned by: ☐ you, ☐ your spouse, ☒ both of you?

   f Social security number of spouse, at time of sale, if different from number on Form 1040 ▶ (Enter "None" if you were not married at time of sale.)

Part II Age 55 or Over One-Time Exclusion

Complete this part only if you checked "yes" to 3(d) to elect the once in a lifetime exclusion; otherwise, skip to Part III.

7 Enter the smaller of line 6 or $125,000 ($62,500, if married filing separate return)	**7**	63,400
8 Gain (subtract line 7 from line 6). If zero, do not complete rest of form. Enter the gain from this line on Schedule D, line 10*, unless you bought another principal residence. Then continue with this form	**8**	0

5. Installment sale. On February 1, 1986, you sold your stock (100 shares) in a close corporation, Corp. A, for $60,000. It originally cost you $6,000 in 1950. On the same day, the buyer gave you $1,500 in cash and 20 notes, each in the amount of $2,925, payable monthly—the first note, payable January 1, 1987. Interest is due on all outstanding notes. You report your gain on the installment basis by attaching Form 6252.

A Description of property ▶ Stock

B Date acquired (month, day, and year) ▶ 10-1-50   **C** Date sold (month, day, and year) ▶ 2-1-86

D Was property sold to a related party after May 14, 1980? (See instructions) ☐ Yes ☒ No

E If the answer to D is "Yes," was the property a marketable security? ☐ Yes ☐ No

If you checked "Yes" to question E, complete Part III.
If you checked "No" to question E, complete Part III for the year of sale and for 2 years after the year of sale.

Part I Computation of Gross Profit and Contract Price *(Complete this part for the year of sale only.)*

1 Selling price including mortgages and other indebtedness (Do not include stated or unstated interest)			**1**	60,000
2 Mortgages and other indebtedness buyer assumes or takes property subject to. (Do not include new mortgages from a bank or other source.)	**2**	0		
3 Subtract line 2 from line 1	**3**	60,000		
4 Cost or other basis of property sold	**4**	6,000		
5 Depreciation allowed or allowable	**5**	0		
6 Adjusted basis (subtract line 5 from line 4)	**6**	6,000		
7 Commissions and other expenses of sale	**7**	0		
8 Income recapture from Form 4797, Part III (See instructions.)	**8**			
9 Add lines 6, 7, and 8			**9**	6,000
10 Subtract line 9 from line 1. If zero or less, do not complete rest of form			**10**	54,000
11 If question A is a principal residence, enter the sum of Form 2119, lines 7 and 13			**11**	
12 Gross profit (subtract line 11 from line 10)			**12**	54,000
13 Subtract line 9 from line 2. If line 9 is more than line 2, enter zero			**13**	0
14 Contract price (add line 3 and line 13)			**14**	60,000

Part II Computation of Taxable Part of Installment Sale
(Complete this part for the year of sale and any year you receive a payment.)

15 Gross profit ratio (divide line 12 by line 14) (for years after the year of sale, see instructions)		**15**	90%
16 For year of sale only—enter amount from line 13 above; otherwise enter zero		**16**	0
17 Payments received during year. (Do not include stated or unstated interest.)		**17**	1,500
18 Add lines 16 and 17		**18**	1,500
19 Payments received in prior years. (Do not include stated or unstated interest.)	**19**		
20 Taxable part of installment sale (multiply line 18 by line 15)		**20**	1,350
21 Part of line 20 that is ordinary income under recapture rules (See instructions.)		**21**	0
22 Subtract line 21 from line 20. Enter on Schedule D or Form 4797		**22**	1,350

¶7.00

Retirement and Annuity Income

Illustrations of reporting annuity and pension income on Form 1040 may be found in the Supplement to YOUR INCOME TAX. Mail the card at the front of this book for your FREE Supplement, including filled-in returns and last-minute information.

Roundup of Tax-Favored Retirement Plans

There are several tax-favored retirement plans. If you are an employee, you are bound to the plan provided by your employer. If you are self-employed, you may set up a Keogh plan, but, at the same time, your plan must generally also cover your employees. Finally, everyone who has earned income, whether employed or self-employed, has the opportunity to invest in IRAs. The following is a table highlighting the major features of these retirement plans.

What You Should Know About Tax-Favored Retirement Plans

Type	General Tax Considerations	Tax Treatment on 1986 Distributions
Company qualified plan	A company qualified pension or profit-sharing plan offers these benefits: (1) You do not realize current income on your employer's contributions to the plan on your behalf. (2) Income earned on funds contributed to your account compound tax free. (3) Your employer may allow you to make voluntary contributions. Although these contributions may not be deducted, income earned on the voluntary contributions is not taxed until withdrawn.	If you receive a lump sum, tax on employer contributions may be reduced by a special averaging rule, *see* ¶7.01. If you receive a lump-sum distribution in company securities, unrealized appreciation on those securities is not taxed until you finally sell the stock, *see* ¶7.06. Rather than pay an immediate tax, you may elect to rollover a lump-sum payment to an IRA account, *see* ¶7.05. If you decide to collect your retirement benefits over a period of years, *see* ¶7.09.
Keogh or self-employed plans *See* ¶7.30	You may set up a self-employed retirement plan called a Keogh plan if you earn self-employment income through your performance of personal services. You may deduct contributions up to limits discussed at ¶7.33; income earned on assets held by the plan are not taxed. You must include employees under rules explained at ¶7.30.	As a self-employed person, you may generally not withdraw funds until age 59½ unless you are disabled. Premature withdrawals are subject to a 10% penalty. Qualified distributions to a self-employed person or to their beneficiaries at death may qualify for favored lump-sum treatment under the rules of ¶7.01. Employees of Keogh plans follow rules of ¶7.01 applied to qualified plans.
IRA *See* ¶7.16	For 1986, anyone who has earned income may contribute and deduct contributions to IRAs. IRAs offer the following benefits: (1) You may deduct contributions to an IRA of up to $2,000 of earned income. Married couples who work may contribute up to $4,000. If your earned income is less than $2,000, your contribution is limited to the amount earned. If you set up IRAs for yourself and your nonworking spouse, you may contribute and deduct up to $2,250. (2) Income earned on IRA accounts is not taxed until the funds are withdrawn.	You may not withdraw funds without penalty until you are 59½ or disabled. Premature withdrawals are subject to a 10% penalty. If you delay withdrawals, you must begin to take money out of the account at age 70½, *see* ¶7.20. Distributions are fully taxable as ordinary income. *See* ¶7.19. Special averaging is not allowed.
SEP *See* ¶7.22	A simplified employee pension plan set up by your employer allows the employer to contribute to an IRA more than you can under regular IRA rules. You must include in 1986 income any employer contributions for your account. You then claim an offsetting deduction for the contribution. If you are over age 70½, you may deduct employer contributions to your account.	Withdrawals are taxable under rules explained above for IRAs.
Deferred salary or 401(K) plans *See* ¶32.011	If your company has a profit-sharing or stock bonus plan, the tax law allows the company to add a cash or deferred pay plan which can operate in one of two ways: (1) Your employer contributes an amount for your benefit to your trust account. You are not taxed on your employer's contribution. (2) You agree to take a salary reduction or to forgo a salary increase. The reduction is placed in a trust account for your benefit. The reduction is treated as your employer's contribution. Income earned on the trust account accumulates tax free until it is withdrawn.	Withdrawals are penalized unless you have reached age 59½, are separated from service, become disabled, or show financial hardship. At the time of withdrawal, the tax on the proceeds may be computed under rules of ¶7.01.

Distributions from Qualified Retirement Plans

¶7.01 • LUMP-SUM DISTRIBUTIONS RECEIVED IN 1986

The following tax elections may apply to qualified lump-sum distributions from a company retirement plan or Keogh plan.

Special averaging for the taxable amount, *see* ¶7.02, or

Capital gain treatment for gains realized for plan members before 1974 and special averaging for the taxable balance of the distribution, *see* ¶7.011, or

Tax-free rollover to an IRA or another qualified company plan, *see* ¶7.05

You choose the election that gives you the greatest after-tax return.

Distributions from an IRA or redemptions of retirement bonds do not qualify for capital gain treatment or special averaging. They may qualify for regular income averaging at ¶23.00.

To qualify as a lump-sum distribution, these tests must be met:

1. Payment must be from a qualified pension or profit-sharing plan. A qualified plan is one approved by the IRS. A civil service retirement system that has a trust fund may be treated as a qualified plan. Ask your retirement plan administrator whether the plan qualifies.

2. You must receive all that is due you under the plan. A distribution of only part of your account is not a lump-sum distribution. If your employer's plan uses more than one trust, you must receive a distribution of all that is due you from each trust. However, lump-sum treatment is not lost by receipt of a payment in a later year for your last year of work. The later payment is reported as ordinary income; it is not part of the lump sum.

3. The payment or payments must be made within one of your taxable years (usually a calendar year). For example, you retired on October 31, 1986, and start receiving monthly annuity payments under your company's plan on November 1, 1986. On February 4, 1987, you take the balance to your credit in lieu of any future annuity payments. The payments do not qualify as a lump sum; you did not receive them within one taxable year. However, if you had taken the balance of your account on or before December 31, 1986, all the payments would have qualified.

4. If you are an employee, the distribution must be made because you are separated from service, reach the age of 59½, or die. If you are self-employed, the lump-sum distribution from your Keogh plan must be made after you reach age 59½, become disabled, or die. See ¶7.03 for "separation-from-service" if you are an employee.

5. For special averaging, you must also have been a plan participant for five years or more before the year of distribution. This rule does not apply to payments made because of death. See ¶7.04.

Important: If you are married, you must generally obtain your spouse's consent to elect a lump-sum distribution. *See* ¶7.061.

Distributions after 1986. Tax rules for lump-sum distributions made after 1986 are discussed in the new law guide in the front of the book.

Should you pay tax using averaging or make a rollover? When you receive a qualified lump-sum distribution, you have only 60 days to decide whether to postpone tax by making a rollover to an IRA or pay tax using the favorable averaging method. After 60 days, a rollover may not be made. Also if you elect the rollover, you cannot change your mind and cancel the IRA account and apply special averaging. The rollover election is irrevocable, according to the IRS (*see below* for limited 1986 exception). If you need the funds immediately, take the distribution and pay the tax. Similarly, if you think you may have to withdraw the entire account in a few years, a rollover may be unwise because a distribution of the rolled-over account will be taxed as ordinary income; special averaging is not allowed for an IRA distribution. If you qualify for special averaging but do not plan to use the funds until retirement, estimate whether you will build a larger retirement fund by rolling over the distribution and letting earnings accumulate tax free, or by using special averaging and investing the funds to give you the greatest after-tax return. This is not an easy projection. You must consider the number of years to retirement, your expected tax bracket at retirement, and the estimated yield you can earn on your funds. Generally speaking, a younger person who is not planning to retire for many years may get a greater after-tax return by making a rollover and investing at peak rates, and then taking withdrawals over his life expectancy at retirement. However, if you make the rollover to an IRA and later decide to withdraw funds before age 59½, you will be subject to a penalty unless you are disabled; *see* ¶7.20.

There is a limited exception to the IRS rule that a rollover election is irrevocable. If you rolled over a 1986 distribution before March 21, 1986, you have until the filing date for your 1986 return to revoke the rollover; on your 1986 return, you may elect to pay tax using ten-year averaging. *See* ¶7.02. If you exclude the rolled over amount from income on your return, this will be considered an irrevocable election of rollover treatment.

Disqualification of retirement plan. If you receive a lump-sum distribution from a plan which loses its exempt status, the IRS may argue that the distribution does not qualify for lump-sum treatment. Under the IRS position, you may not roll over the distribution to an IRA or elect special averaging. The Tax Court holds that if the plan qualified when contributions were made, an allocable portion of the distribution is a qualified lump sum. However, the majority of appeals courts that have reviewed Tax Court decisions on this issue have supported the IRS position.

¶7.011 • CAPITAL GAIN TREATMENT FOR PRE-1974 PARTICIPATION

If you received a qualifying lump sum distribution in 1986, long-term capital gain treatment is available for participation in a

qualified plan before 1974. On Form 1099-R, the company paying the sum lists the capital gain and ordinary income parts of the distribution. If you are an employee, capital gain treatment is available, even if you do not qualify for ten-year averaging.

Ordinary income election. You may elect to treat the entire 1986 lump-sum distribution as ordinary income. You will make this election if the effective tax rate of ten-year averaging is less than the effective capital gain rate. This may be verified by computing the tax under both methods. The election may be advisable where you will be subject to alternative minimum tax on the capital gains portion (*see* ¶23.10). The election to treat the entire sum as ordinary income is made on Form 4972 by entering the entire distribution as ordinary income.

The election is irrevocable. Once made, all later lump-sum distributions from other qualified plans are also treated as ordinary income. Also, you may not make this election if, after 1975, you received a lump-sum distribution and treated part as capital gain.

If you do not make the ordinary income election, enter the capital gain portion in Schedule D, part II as a long-term capital gain. Identify it as a "Lump-sum distribution." If you do not report any other gains or losses on Schedule D, you may enter 40% of the gain directly on Form 1040 on the line provided for reporting a single capital gain item (*see* the Supplement for the exact line for 1986). A sample Schedule D entry is shown at ¶6.32(15).

Distributions after 1986. For a discussion of rules for distributions after 1986, *see* new law guide in the front of the book.

¶7.02 • SPECIAL AVERAGING ON FORM 4972

You use Form 4972 to figure the 1986 tax under the ten-year averaging method. On the form, the ordinary income part of the distribution is taxed as if it had been received evenly over ten years. The tax is taken from the unmarried individuals' tax rate schedule (single) even if you use joint return or head of household rates for your other income. The separate tax figured under ten-year averaging is added to your regular tax which is computed on your other income reported on Form 1040. Use of ten-year averaging does not bar you from applying the regular averaging rules (¶23.00) to your other income and capital gain.

For ten-year averaging, you must have been a participant in the plan for five or more years before the taxable year of the lump-sum distribution. If you receive lump-sum distributions from more than one qualified plan, you may use the ten-year averaging method only once after you reach age 59½. Before age 59½, there is no limit on the number of times you may use ten-year averaging.

The taxable portion of a lump-sum distribution does not include your contributions to the plan and net unrealized appreciation on a distribution of securities of the employer. *See* also ¶7.06.

Example—
In 1986, you receive a lump-sum distribution of $65,000, including stock of your employer. The stock had a basis of $10,000 when put in the plan; it is valued at $25,000 when distributed. You did not contribute to the plan. The taxable portion of the distribution is $50,000 ($65,000 − $15,000, the unrealized appreciation). The $50,000 is then allocated between the capital gain and ordinary income portions.

Community property. Only the spouse who has earned the lump sum may use ten-year averaging. Community property laws are disregarded for this purpose. If a couple files separate returns and one spouse elects ten-year averaging, the other spouse is not taxable on the amount subject to the computation.

Example—
A husband in a community property state receives a lump-sum distribution of which the ordinary income portion is $10,000. He and his wife file separate returns. If ten-year averaging is not elected, $5,000, or one-half, is taxable in the husband's return and the other $5,000 in his wife's return. However, if he elects the ten-year averaging method, only he reports the $10,000 on Form 4972.

"Look-back" rule for annuity contracts or receipt of more than one lump sum during a six-year period. A "look-back" provision requires that the lump-sum distributions for the taxable year be aggregated with all lump-sum distributions made during the five

previous tax years. This increases the bracket at which the ordinary income portion of the current year's lump-sum distribution is taxed. You do not aggregate lump sums which were not subject to the ten-year averaging rule. *See* Treasury regulations for examples of computing ten-year averaging under the "look-back" rule.

A "look-back" rule is also applied to the distribution of an annuity contract, although its total value is not taxable when distributed. The current actuarial value is included in the six-year aggregation computation to determine the tax bracket of the ordinary income portion of a current lump-sum distribution. An example of computing tax when a distribution includes an annuity contract is in the instructions accompanying Form 4972.

Distributions after 1986. *See* the guide to the new law in the front of the book.

¶7.03 • SEPARATION-FROM-SERVICE TEST FOR EMPLOYEES UNDER 59½

Employees who have not reached the age of 59½ must be "separated-from-service" to apply the 1986 lump-sum distribution rules of ¶7.01 and ¶7.02.

The separation-from-service test requires that you have retired, resigned, or have been discharged. If a plan is terminated but you continue on the job, distributions are not entitled to special lump-sum treatment if you have not reached age 59½. Under the law, you do not have to be separated from service after you reach age 59½. However, in rulings, the IRS has held that if you receive a lump-sum distribution from a pension plan (not a profit-sharing plan) after age 59½ but continue to work for the company, you also must reach the normal retirement age as fixed in the company plan to get lump-sum treatment unless the plan was terminated.

The separation-from-service test generally prevents lump-sum treatment when a qualified plan is terminated following a reorganization or merger of a company. According to the IRS, an employee under age 59½ who remains with a successor corporation and who receives a lump-sum distribution following reorganization, liquidation, or merger may not claim lump-sum treatment.

Recent court decisions follow the IRS position. However, the Tax Court has held that an executive working for a successor firm was "separated-from-service" on evidence of substantial changes in staff, duties, and company business. Finally, the IRS, in a private letter ruling, eased its position and allowed 20 employees of a merged company lump-sum tax benefits. They were given new jobs or took on additional responsibilities. The manager of engineering and maintenance of the old company became responsible for energy conservation and security; the former personnel manager was rehired as the purchasing and planning manager. Further, the new company reduced salaries and employee benefits and eliminated the former profit-sharing plan. Given these changes in job positions and pay benefits, employees were considered "separated from service."

A lump sum paid on account of termination of a plan may be rolled over tax free to an IRA (*see* ¶7.05).

Partnership plans. Lump-sum payments paid on the termination of a plan when a partnership dissolves do not qualify for special lump-sum treatment when the employees continue to work for the successor partnership. Similarly, an employee of a partnership, who becomes a partner and has to quit the firm's employee profit-sharing plan, may not treat his payment as a lump sum. He is still serving the firm.

¶7.04 • LUMP-SUM PAYMENTS RECEIVED BY DECEASED EMPLOYEE'S BENEFICIARY

A beneficiary of a deceased employee may apply the lump-sum rules of ¶7.01 to a 1986 payment received because of the employee's death. In addition, the $5,000 death benefit exclusion may also be claimed (*see* ¶7.103). If the payment qualifies, Form 4972 is used to compute tax under the ten-year averaging method. Any federal estate tax attributable to the distribution is deductible.

A lump sum paid because of an employee's death may qualify

for capital gain and ten-year averaging treatment, although the employee received annuity payments before he died.

The $5,000 death benefit exclusion also applies to payments received by Keogh plan beneficiaries following the death of a self-employed person after December 31, 1983.

An estate or trust receiving a lump-sum payment may also apply the lump-sum rules.

A beneficiary may elect ten-year averaging, even though the deceased employee was under 59½ or in the plan for less than five years. However, where the deceased was over 59½, you may elect ten-year averaging only once for distributions received as the beneficiary of the deceased.

A beneficiary who elects to report the capital gain as ordinary income must report all later lump sums received as beneficiary of the deceased as ordinary income. If the beneficiary does not elect to treat the capital gain as ordinary income, he may not make the ordinary income election for other lump sums received as beneficiary of the deceased.

Payment received by a second beneficiary (after the death of the first beneficiary) is not entitled to lump-sum treatment or the death benefit exclusion.

Examples—

1. Gunnison's father was covered by a company benefit plan. The father died as did Gunnison's mother before benefits were fully paid out. Gunnison received a substantial lump sum. He argued that he collected benefits on account of his father's death. The IRS disagreed. The Tax Court and an appeals court sided with the IRS. Gunnison was entitled to the payment following his mother's death, not his father's death. For special lump-sum treatment, the payout must arise solely on account of the death of the covered employee.

2. Robert's employer announced the termination of its pension plan. Before benefits were distributed, Robert died. His widow received a lump-sum distribution as his beneficiary. After subtracting the amount attributable to Robert's contributions, she excluded $5,000 as a death benefit and treated the balance as a lump-sum distribution. The IRS claimed she received the distribution on the termination of the plan, not because of Robert's death. The Tax Court agreed. Distribution was made to her under the termination provision, not the provisions for withdrawal due to separation-from-service or death. She could not take a death benefit exclusion, and the entire distribution (less Robert's contributions) could not be treated as a lump-sum distribution.

Lump-sum distribution to more than one beneficiary. A lump-sum distribution to two or more individuals may qualify for capital gain treatment and the ten-year averaging method. The distribution is first treated as made to one recipient to determine whether it is a lump sum and what portion is taxable as capital gain (*see* ¶7.011). Each beneficiary may separately elect the ten-year averaging method for the ordinary income portion, even though other beneficiaries do not so elect.

Distribution to trust or estate. If a 1986 lump sum is paid to a trust or estate, the employee, or his personal representative if he is deceased, may elect ten-year averaging. This is true, even though the ordinary income portion is distributed to the beneficiaries in the year the lump sum was received. If the fiduciary makes the election, the ordinary income is taxable to the trust or estate, even if a distribution is made to the beneficiary. However, the capital gain portion, if distributed to the beneficiaries in the year received by the trust or estate, is taxable to the beneficiaries as long-term capital gain, not to the trust. If the distribution is to the beneficiaries of a self-employed person, the beneficiaries may not treat the capital gain portion as capital gain unless the trust or estate also makes an election to use the ten-year averaging method.

¶7.05 • TAX-FREE ROLLOVER OF LUMP SUM

You can defer tax on a lump-sum distribution from a qualified company plan by transferring it within 60 days to a qualified plan of your new employer or to an individual IRA account (*see* ¶7.21). Lump-sum distributions from a key employee's Keogh plan may be rolled over to an IRA but not to a company plan.

The amount you roll over may not include your contributions to the qualified plan.

You may not claim a deduction for your rollover contribution to an IRA.

For a tax-free rollover, the lump-sum distribution must meet these tests:

1. The distribution must be all that is due you under the plan. If the employer plan uses more than one trust, you must receive a distribution of all that is due you from each trust.

2. The payment or payments must be made within one of your taxable years.

3. The distribution must be made because you are separated from service, reached age 59½, or the plan has been terminated.

You do not have to roll over the entire distribution; you may make a partial rollover. While the amount rolled over is not taxed, the part not rolled over is taxable and you may not apply capital gain treatment or special averaging to the distribution.

A surviving spouse may roll over to an IRA a lump-sum distribution paid on the death of a spouse or upon termination of a qualified retirement plan. The distribution may not be rolled over to a qualified plan of the surviving spouse's current employer.

Before making a rollover, figure what the current tax would be on the lump-sum distribution under the special averaging method. Compare it with an estimate of tax payable on a later distribution of the rolled-over account. Consider further that if you make a rollover to an IRA and not to a new employer's qualified plan, you lose the right to apply the special averaging method to the sum. Special averaging applies only to a lump-sum distribution from a qualified plan. It does not apply to a withdrawal from an IRA account. If you are under the age of 59½, also consider that a rollover to an IRA locks in your funds. If you withdraw from the IRA, you may be subject to a penalty, *see* ¶7.20. Other points to consider in deciding whether to make a rollover are discussed at ¶7.01.

Rollover of partial distributions. If a distribution made after July 18, 1984, equals at least 50% of your plan account balance, you may elect to roll it over to an IRA provided it is not one of a series of periodic payments. The rollover must be made within 60 days. Under the 50% test, you may disregard amounts credited to you under other qualified plans maintained by the same employer. A surviving spouse of a deceased employee may elect to rollover a qualifying partial distribution. If you elect rollover treatment, a later distribution of your entire account balance will not qualify for special averaging or capital gain treatment (¶7.01).

Figuring the 60-day period for more than one payment. The IRS held in a private letter ruling that if you receive several payments, the 60-day period starts from the date of the last payment, provided all of the payments are made within one taxable year. For example, you retired in July, 1986 and received a partial distribution from your company plan. You were told that you would receive the balance by December, 1986. Provided all payments are received before the end of 1986, the payments received in July and December are considered a lump-sum distribution eligible for rollover. You have 60 days from the date of the final December payment to complete the rollover.

Rollover to new employer's plan. An IRA may be used as a conduit between two company plans. The funds in the IRA may be transferred to another qualified plan of a company which employs you, provided the plan of your new employer accepts rollovers. The IRA must consist of only the assets (or proceeds from the sale of such assets) distributed from the first qualified plan and income earned on the account. You may not contribute to the account set up as a conduit. You may set up another IRA to which you make annual contributions. In such a case, you will have two accounts; one consisting of the assets (or proceeds from the sale of such assets) of the plan of your prior employer and the other of your own contributions.

Example—

You leave your employer and receive a lump-sum distribution of $5,000 from his qualified plan to which you did not contribute. You place the amount in an IRA. Four years later, you start work for another company that has a qualified plan. The new plan permits you to transfer the assets of the IRA to the plan. You must make the transfer within 60 days after closing the account (*see* ¶7.21).

Distribution includes life insurance policy. Your employer's retirement plan may invest in a limited amount of life insurance which is then distributed to you as part of a lump-sum retirement distribution. You may be able to roll over the life insurance contract to the qualified plan of your new employer but not to an IRA. The law specifically bars investment of IRA funds in life insurance contracts.

Diversification. You may wish to diversify a distribution in different investments. There is no limit on the number of rollover accounts you may have. A lump-sum distribution may be rolled over to several IRAs or retirement annuities.

Rollover of annuities for employees of tax-exempt groups and schools. If you participate in a tax-sheltered annuity program described in ¶7.11, you may roll over a distribution to an IRA.

On your return, you report a rollover only for information purposes. *See* the Supplement for the line for reporting 1986 rollovers.

¶7.051 • ROLLOVER OF PROCEEDS FROM SALE OF PROPERTY RECEIVED IN LUMP-SUM DISTRIBUTION

A lump-sum distribution from a qualified plan may include property, such as stock. If you plan to roll over the distribution, you may find a bank may not want to take the property. If you sell the property, you may roll over the sale proceeds to an IRA as long as the sale and rollover occur within 60 days of receipt of the distribution. If you roll over all of the proceeds, neither gain nor loss is recognized. The proceeds are treated as part of the distribution. If you make a partial rollover, you incur tax on the retained proceeds, and in reporting the taxable amount, you allocate between ordinary income and capital gain elements. *See* Treasury regulations for how to make the allocation.

If you receive cash and property, and you sell the property but make a partial rollover, you must designate how much of the cash is to be treated as part of the rollover. The designation must be made by the time for filing your return (plus any extensions) and is irrevocable. If you do not make a timely designation, the allocation between cash and proceeds is made on a ratable basis.

If you contributed to the plan, you may not rollover to an IRA the portion of the distribution equal to your contributions. *See* Treasury regulations for the effect of employee contributions on an allocation.

¶7.06 • SECURITIES OF EMPLOYER COMPANY RECEIVED AS PART OF A DISTRIBUTION

When a plan distributes securities of your company, the value of the securities may or may not be subject to tax at the time of the distribution. The amount reported as income depends on the value of the securities, the amount contributed by the company toward their purchase, and whether or not the distribution qualifies as a total lump-sum payment.

Lump-sum payments. If the distribution is of appreciated securities and is part of a lump-sum payment meeting the tests of ¶7.01, the unrealized appreciation is not subject to tax at the time of distribution. Only the amount of the employer's contribution is subject to tax. Tax on the appreciation is delayed until the shares are later sold by you at a price exceeding cost basis. If, when distributed, the shares are valued at below the cost contribution of the employer, the fair market value of the shares is subject to tax. If you contributed to the purchase of the shares and their value is less than your contribution, you do not realize a loss deduction on the distribution. You realize a loss only when the stock is sold or becomes worthless at a later date. If a plan distributes worthless stock, you may deduct your contributions to the stock as an ordinary loss if you itemize deductions.

Examples—

1. *Shares valued below your cost contribution.* You contributed $500 and your employer contributed $300 to buy ten shares of company stock having at the time a fair market value of $80 per share. When you retire, the fair market value of the stock is $40 per share, or a total of $400. You do not realize income on the distribution, and you do not have a deductible loss for the difference between your cost contribution and the lower fair market value. Your contribution to the stock is its basis. This is $50 per share. If you sell the stock for $40 per share,

you have a capital loss of $10 per share. However, if you sell the stock for $60 per share, you have gain of $10 per share.

2. *Appreciated shares.* You receive ten shares of company stock to which only the employer contributed toward their purchase. Your employer's cost was $50 a share. At the time of distribution, the shares are valued at $80 a share. Your employer's contribution of $50 a share or $500 is included as part of your taxable distribution. The appreciation of $300 is not included. The cost basis of the shares in your hands is $500 (the amount currently taxable to you). The holding period of the stock starts from the date of distribution. However, if you sell the shares for any amount exceeding $500 and up to $800, your profit is long-term gain even if the sale is within one year from the date of the distribution. If you sell for more than $800, the gain exceeding the original unrealized appreciation of $300 is subject to long-term capital gain treatment only if the sale is long term from the date of distribution. Thus, if within a month of the distribution, you sold the shares for $900, $300 would be long-term gain; $100 would be short-term gain.

Other than lump-sum payments. If you receive **appreciated** securities in a distribution that does not meet the lump-sum tests of ¶7.01, you report as ordinary income the amount of the employer's contribution to the purchase of the shares and the appreciation allocated to his cost contribution. You do not report the amount of appreciation allocated to your contribution to the purchase.

Example—

A qualified plan distributes ten shares of company stock with an average cost of $100, of which the employee contributed $60 and the employer, $40. At the date of distribution, the stock had fair market value of $180. The portion of the unrealized appreciation attributable to the employee's contribution is $48 (60% of $80); the employer's is $32 (40% of $80). The employee reports $72 as income; the employer's cost of $40 and share of appreciation of $32. The basis of each share is $132 which includes employee contribution of $60 and the $72 reported as taxable income. Net unrealized appreciation and cost contributions must be supplied by the company distributing the stock.

¶7.061 • SURVIVOR ANNUITY BENEFITS GENERALLY REQUIRED FOR SURVIVING SPOUSE

If you have been married for at least a year, the law generally requires that payments be in a specific annuity form to protect your surviving spouse. In plan years beginning after 1984, all defined benefit and money purchase plans must provide benefits in the form of a qualified joint and survivor annuity unless you, with the written consent of your spouse, elect a different form of benefit. A qualified joint and survivor annuity must also be provided by profit-sharing or stock bonus plans, unless you do not elect a life annuity payment and the plan provides that your non-forfeitable benefit is payable in full upon your death to your surviving spouse, or to another beneficiary if the spouse consents or there is no surviving spouse.

Under a qualified joint and survivor annuity, you receive an annuity for your life and your surviving spouse receives an annuity for his or her life that is no less than 50% of the amount payable during your joint lives. Unless you obtain spousal consent, you must take this type of annuity; you may not take a lump-sum distribution or a single life annuity ending when you die. A single life annuity pays higher monthly benefits during your lifetime than the qualified joint and survivor annuity.

The law also requires that a pre-retirement survivor's annuity be paid to your surviving spouse if you die before receiving any vested benefits. For example, under a defined contribution plan such as a profit sharing plan, the pre-retirement annuity payments must be equal to those under a single life annuity valued at 50% or more of your account balance. The pre-retirement annuity is automatic unless you, with your spouse's consent, agree to a different benefit.

Your spouse must consent in writing to any waiver and the selection of a different type of distribution. A spouse's consent must be witnessed by a plan representative or notary public. An election to waive the qualified joint and survivor annuity may be made during the 90-day period ending on the annuity starting date. An election to waive the qualified pre-retirement survivor annuity may be made from the first day of the plan year in which you reach age 35 up until your date of death. A waiver is revocable during the time permitted to make the election.

These survivor annuity requirements generally do not apply to couples who have been married for less than one year as of the participant's annuity starting date or, if earlier, the date of the participant's death.

Your plan should provide you with a written explanation of these annuity rules within a reasonable period before the annuity starting date as well as the rules for electing to waive the joint and survivor annuity benefit and the pre-retirement survivor annuity.

Cash-out of annuity. If the present value of the qualified joint and survivor annuity is $3,500 or less, your employer may "cash-out" your interest without your consent by making a lump sum distribution of the present value of the annuity before the annuity starting date. After the annuity starting date, you and your spouse must consent to a cash out. Written consent is required for a cash-out if the present value of the annuity exceeds $3,500. Similar cash-out rules apply to pre-retirement surviving annuities.

¶7.065 · WHEN RETIREMENT BENEFITS MUST BEGIN

Employees who do not have ownership interests must start to receive distributions by April 1 of the year following the *later* of the calendar year they reach age 70½ or the calendar year of retirement. Thus, if you reach age 70½ during 1986 but will continue working through 1987, you may defer the start of retirement benefits until April 1, 1988.

However, if you reached age 70½ during 1986 and in the plan year ending during 1986, you were an employee or self-employed and had more than a 5% ownership interest, you must start to receive distributions by April 1, 1987. This is true even if you continue to work after 1986.

Pre-1984 designations. Individuals who made a special election before 1984 to receive distributions under pre-1984 rules are not subject to the age 70½ rule or the beneficiary distribution methods discussed below.

Premature distributions to self-employed persons and employee-owners. A distribution made before age 59½ to a person who has an ownership interest of more than 5% is subject to 10% penalty. The penalty applies only to the extent the distribution is attributable to contributions made while holding an interest of more than 5%. It does not apply to distributions made on account of disability or death. The penalty applies whether or not the plan is top heavy.

See the guide to the new law in the front of the book for changes affecting 1987 distributions.

Distribution methods for employees and self-employed. All qualified retirement plans, including Keogh plans for the self-employed, are subject to the same distribution rules in plan years beginning after 1984.

When you retire, you may spread payments over your life, over the joint lives of yourself and any designated beneficiary, or over a specific period that does not exceed your life expectancy or the joint life expectancies of yourself and any designated beneficiary. In figuring the payout schedule, your life expectancy may be recalculated annually. If payments are made over the joint life expectancies of you and your spouse, your spouse's life expectancy may also be recalculated annually.

Basing payments on the joint life expectations of yourself and a younger beneficiary will extend the withdrawal period, but the law imposes a limit. Generally, the present value of the projected payments to you must exceed 50% of the present value of the total projected payments to you and your beneficiaries. This requirement does not affect payments required for spouses under the qualified joint and survivor annuity rule of ¶7.061. As discussed at ¶7.061, your plan must automatically provide annuity benefits in the form of a qualified joint and survivor annuity if you are married, unless you and your spouse elect otherwise.

Payout period for beneficiaries. Where an employee or self-employed individual dies after benefits have begun, beneficiaries must continue to take distributions at least as rapidly as the participant did during his or her lifetime. For example, if an employee had elected to receive benefits in equal annual installments over his 20-year life expectancy, but died after 10 years, the beneficiary would have to receive equal annual installments over the remaining 10 years but could elect to accelerate payments over a shorter period.

A surviving spouse receiving an annuity under the survivor benefit rules of ¶7.061 receives payments over his or her lifetime, starting at the participant's death.

If an employee or self-employed person dies before receiving benefits, distribution rules depend on who is the beneficiary. A surviving spouse who is not receiving annuity payments under the rules of ¶7.061 may delay distributions until the date on which the deceased spouse would have reached age 70½, or if later, one year after the decedent's death. Starting on that date, the surviving spouse must receive distributions over his or her life expectancy. If someone other than a surviving spouse is beneficiary, payments generally have to be completed within five years of the decedent's death, but there is an important exception. If the beneficiary was designated by the employee, distributions may be spread over the beneficiary's life or life expectancy provided that distributions began no later than one year after the employee's death. The IRS may extend the one-year limit if circumstances warrant delay.

These distribution rules do not apply to government retirement plans until plan years starting after 1986. For collectively-bargained plans ratified on or before July 18, 1984, the rules generally do not apply until the earlier of January 1, 1988, or the date on which the bargaining agreement terminates (without regard to extensions after July 18, 1984).

Commercial Annuities

¶7.07 • REPORTING COMMERCIAL ANNUITIES

That part of the annuity payment allocated to your cost investment is treated as a nontaxable return of the cost; the balance is taxable income earned on the investment. You may find the taxable part of your annuity payment by following the six steps below:

1. *Figure your investment in the annuity contract.*

If your annuity is	*Your cost is*
Single premium annuity contract	The single premium paid
Deferred annuity contract	The total premiums paid
A gift	Your donor's cost
An employee annuity	The total of your contributions to the plan plus your employer's contributions which you were required to report as income. *See* ¶7.09, ¶7.10, ¶7.101, ¶7.102, and ¶7.103.
With a refund feature	What was paid for the annuity, less the value of the refund feature

If you have no investment in the contract, annuity income is fully taxable; ignore steps 2 through 6 below.

From cost, you subtract the following items:

Any premiums refunded, rebates, or dividends received on or before the annuity starting date.

Additional premiums for double indemnity or disability benefits.

Amounts received under the contract before the annuity starting date to the extent these amounts were not taxed.

Value of refund feature (*see* ¶7.071).

Amounts received before the annuity starting date which are allocable to investments made before August 14, 1982 reduce the cost of the annuity contract. If they exceed your cost, the excess is subject to tax. The same rule applies if payment is made to a beneficiary where the annuitant dies before annuity payments begin. Generally, these payments will not be more than the cost—unless they are lump-sum payments to cancel the contract. The reduced cost, where the contract continues, is the investment in the contract. For investments after August 13, 1982, *see* withdrawal rules in the next column.

Dividends received on or after the date annuity payments begin (and the annuity payments continue) are fully taxed.

2. *Find your expected return.* This is the total of all the payments you are to receive. If the payments are to be made to you for life, your expected return is figured by multiplying the amount of the annual payment by a multiple based on your life expectancy as of the annuity starting date. These multiples are listed in tables published by the Treasury. You can get the tables from your local District Director, or you can write to your insurance company, requesting the amount of your expected return.

If the payments are for a fixed number of years (as in an endowment contract), find your expected return by multiplying your annual payments by the number of years you are to receive them. (Variable annuities are discussed at ¶7.074.)

3. *Divide the investment in contract (step 1) by the expected return (step 2).* This will give you a percentage. This percentage of your yearly annuity payments is tax free. The percentage remains the same for the remaining years of the annuity.

4. *Find your total annuity receipts for the year.* (For example, you received ten monthly payments as your annuity began in March. Your total is the monthly payment multiplied by ten.)

5. *Multiply the percentage in step 3 by the total in step 4.* The result is the nontaxable portion (or excludable amount) of your annuity payments.

6. *Subtract the amount in step 5 from the amount in step 4.* This is the part of your annuity for the year which is subject to tax.

Examples of reporting annuities may be found at ¶7.073.

Types of Annuity Contracts

Annuity	*Description*
One annuitant annuity	You receive payments for the rest of your life. For an example of how to find the expected return of this type of annuity, *see* ¶7.072 and ¶7.073.
Temporary annuity	You receive payment until death or until the end of a specified limited period, whichever occurs earlier. To get your expected return, you find your multiple in Treasury Table IV.
Uniform joint and survivor annuity	You receive payments for the rest of your life, and after your death the same amount is paid to the other annuitant. The expected return is based on the combined life expectancies of both of you. You use Treasury Table II to get a multiple based on joint lives. The exclusion ratio remains the same for both you and the survivor.
One annuitant stepped up annuity	You receive smaller payments at first and when you reach a certain age, usually on retiring, you receive larger payments. This contract is treated as a combination of a one annuitant contract for the larger amount minus a temporary annuity for the difference between the larger and smaller amounts. To get your expected return, you find your multiple in Treasury Tables I and IV.
One annuitant stepped down annuity	You receive larger payments at first and then, when you reach a certain age, smaller payments, usually on reaching age 65. This contract is treated as a combination of a one annuitant contract for the smaller amount plus a temporary annuity for the difference between the larger and smaller amounts. To get your expected return, you find your multiple in Treasury Tables I and IV.
Variable payment joint and survivor annuity with lesser annuity to survivor	You receive payments while both are alive and on the death of one of you, a lesser amount is paid to the survivor—regardless of which annuitant dies first. To get your expected return, you use Treasury Tables II and IIA.
Variable payment joint and survivor annuity with first and second annuitants specified	You receive payments of a certain amount, and on your death the other annuitant gets a lesser amount. To get your expected return, you use Treasury Tables I and II. The exclusion ratio remains the same for both you and the survivor.

Withdrawals from deferred annuities. Cash withdrawals before the annuity starting date may be taxable to the extent that the cash value of the contract exceeds your investment in the contract. Withdrawals are taxable if attributed to investments made after August 13, 1982, even if the contract was purchased before August 14, 1982. Loans under the contract or pledges are treated as cash withdrawals. Withdrawals from contracts bought by qualified retirement plans are not taxable.

Premature withdrawals are also subject to a penalty of 5%. A withdrawal in 1986 from an annuity contract is penalized unless: (1) the policyholder has reached age 59½ or has become disabled, (2) the distribution is a payment under an annuity for life or over a period extending at least 60 months after the annuity starting date, (3) the payment is received by a beneficiary (or state) after the policyholder's death, (4) payment is from a qualified retirement plan, or (5) payment is allocable to investments made before August 14, 1982. The amount of the penalty is 5% of the amount includable in income; for annuity contracts issued before January 19, 1985, the penalty applies only to investments made within ten years of receipt.

Note: The exception for 60-month annuities may no longer be allowed after 1986; *see* new law guide in front of this book.

¶7.071 · COST OF ANNUITY WITH A REFUND FEATURE

If your annuity has a refund feature, your investment in the contract is the cost of your annuity less the value of the refund feature.

Your annuity has a refund feature when these three requirements are present:

1. The refund under the contract depends, even in part, on the life expectancy of at least one person.

2. The contract provides for payments to a beneficiary or the annuitant's estate after the annuitant's death.

3. The payments to estate or beneficiary are in the nature of a refund of the amount paid for the annuity.

Where an employer paid part of the cost, the refund is figured on only the part paid by the employee.

The amount of the reduction for the refund feature is figured by using a multiple in Treasury Table III which your local District Director will give you at your request, or the company which has issued your contract will give you this net investment figure.

The surviving beneficiary receiving the balance of guaranteed payment does not include any amount as taxed income until the payments, when added to that portion of the payments excluded by the first annuitant, equal the investment in the contract. All later payments are taxed in full.

¶7.072 · FINDING YOUR EXPECTED RETURN

Payments for fixed number of years. If you receive payments for a fixed number of years, multiply the amount of the annual payment by the number of years you are to receive payments. The result is your expected return. For example, if you are to receive $1,000 a year for ten years, your expected return is $10,000. Assuming you paid $7,500 for the policy, the nontaxable portion of your annuity each year is $750 $\left(\dfrac{7,500}{10,000}\right)$ or 75% of $1,000; the taxable portion is $250 ($1,000 − $750).

Payments for life. The expected return is reached by multiplying the annual annuity income by the life expectancy multiple found in the Treasury table for your particular kind of annuity.

Before using the table, you must know two things:

1. Your annuity starting date. The annuity starting date is the first day of the first period for which an annuity payment is received. For example, on January 1 you complete payment under an annuity contract providing for monthly payments starting on July 1 for the period beginning June 1. The annuity starting date is

June 1. Use that date in computing your investment in the contract and your expected return. (Those who were collecting annuities before 1954 use January 1, 1954 as the annuity starting date.)

2. Adjustments to the life expectancy multiple. Adjustments are required when your annuity income is received quarterly, semi-annually, or annually.

Example—

You receive quarterly annuity payments. Your first payment comes on January 15, covering the first quarter of the year. Since the period between the starting date—January 1—and the payment date—January 15—is less than one month, you adjust the multiple according to the table below by adding .1.

When your annuity payments come to you more frequently than quarterly (for example, monthly), the multiple is not adjusted.

Increases in annuity payments are taxable in full. The excluded amount attributed to your cost remains the same as before the increase.

¶7.073 · COMPUTING THE EXPECTED RETURN OF A ONE-ANNUITANT ANNUITY

The payments go to one individual for life; on death, the payments stop. To find the multiple here, use Table 1 below.

Note: When this book went to press, the IRS was considering new tables for annuity investments after June 30, 1986. *See* the Supplement for the status of the proposed tables.

TABLE 1

Male	Female	Multi-ples	Male	Female	Multi-ples	Male	Female	Multi-ples
6	11	65.0	41	46	33.0	76	81	9.1
7	12	64.1	42	47	32.1	77	82	8.7
8	13	63.2	43	48	31.2	78	83	8.3
9	14	62.3	44	49	30.4	79	84	7.8
10	15	61.4	45	50	29.6	80	85	7.5
11	16	60.4	46	51	28.7	81	86	7.1
12	17	59.5	47	52	27.9	82	87	6.7
13	18	58.6	48	53	27.1	83	88	6.3
14	19	57.7	49	54	26.3	84	89	6.0
15	20	56.7	50	55	25.5	85	90	5.7
16	21	55.8	51	56	24.7	86	91	5.4
17	22	54.9	52	57	24.0	87	92	5.1
18	23	53.9	53	58	23.2	88	93	4.8
19	24	53.0	54	59	22.4	89	94	4.5
20	25	52.1	55	60	21.7	90	95	4.2
21	26	51.1	56	61	21.0	91	96	4.0
22	27	50.2	57	62	20.3	92	97	3.7
23	28	49.3	58	63	19.6	93	98	3.5
24	29	48.3	59	64	18.9	94	99	3.3
25	30	47.4	60	65	18.2	95	100	3.1
26	31	46.5	61	66	17.5	96	101	2.9
27	32	45.6	62	67	16.9	97	102	2.7
28	33	44.6	63	68	16.2	98	103	2.5
29	34	43.7	64	69	15.6	99	104	2.3
30	35	42.8	65	70	15.0	100	105	2.1
31	36	41.9	66	71	14.4	101	106	1.9
32	37	41.0	67	72	13.8	102	107	1.7
33	38	40.0	68	73	13.2	103	108	1.5
34	39	39.1	69	74	12.6	104	109	1.3
35	40	38.2	70	75	12.1	105	110	1.2
36	41	37.3	71	76	11.6	106	111	1.0
37	42	36.5	72	77	11.0	107	112	.8
38	43	35.6	73	78	10.5	108	113	.7
39	44	34.7	74	79	10.1	109	114	.6
40	45	33.8	75	80	9.6	110	115	.5
						111	116	0

Find your age at the nearest birthday to your annuity starting date in the proper column—"Male" or "Female." Then look opposite your age to find the proper multiple. (This multiple may have to be adjusted. *See* ¶7.072.) You then multiply this number by the total annuity payments you are to receive in one full year.

MULTIPLE ADJUSTMENT TABLE

If the number of whole months from the annuity starting date to the first payment date is—	0–1	2	3	4	5	6	7	8	9	10	11	12
And payments under the contract are to be made:												
Annually	+.5	+.4	+.3	+.2	+.1	0	0	−.1	−.2	−.3	−.4	−.5
Semiannually	+.2	+.1	0	0	−.1	−.2						
Quarterly	+.1	0	−.1									

If you have a monthly annuity, you multiply it by 12 times the monthly payments. The product is your expected return.

Example—

Jones was 66 years old on March 14, 1986. On April 1, he received his first monthly annuity check of $100. This covered his annuity payment for March. His annuity starting date is March 1, 1986. Looking at Table 1 under "Male" at age 66, Jones finds the multiple 14.4. (Jones does not have to adjust that multiple according to the rules explained in ¶7.072 because the payments are monthly.) Jones multiplies the 14.4 by $1,200 ($100 a month for a year) to find his expected return of $17,280. Say the annuity cost Jones $12,960. He divides his expected return into the investment in the contract (the cost) and gets his exclusion percentage of 75%. Thereafter, in every year for the rest of his life, Jones receives tax free 75% of his annuity payments and is taxable on 25%. For 1986 Jones reports his annuity income as follows:

Amount received	$900
Amount excludable	675
Taxable portion	$225

For 1987 and later years, Jones will receive annuity payments for the full year. The amount received will be $1,200; amount excludable, $900, and taxable portion, $300.

¶7.074 • VARIABLE ANNUITIES

Variable annuity policies pay different benefits depending on cost-of-living indices, profits earned by the annuity fund, or similar fluctuating standards.

You figure the tax due by considering your investment in the contract (adjusted for the refund feature, if any), and the number of periodic payments you expect to receive under the contract. If the annuity is for a definite period, the number of payments is determined by multiplying the number of payments to be made each year by the number of years you will receive payments.

If the annuity is for life, you divide the amount you invested in the contract by a multiple obtained from an appropriate actuarial table (see ¶7.07.) The figure you obtain is the amount of annual annuity income which is not taxed.

Example—

Your total investment in the contract was $12,000. Your annuity is to start at age 65 and will be paid starting January 1, 1986 in varying annual installments for your life. The amount of each payment excluded from tax is:

Investment in the contract	$12,000
Multiple (from actuarial table)	15.0
Amount of each payment excluded from tax ($12,000 ÷ 15)	$ 800

If your first payment is $920, $120 ($920 — $800) is included in your 1986 income.

If you receive a payment which is less than the nontaxable amount, you may elect when you receive the next payment to recalculate the nontaxable portion. The amount by which the periodic nontaxable portion exceeded the payment you received is divided by the number of payments you expect as of the time of the next payment. The result is added to the previously calculated periodic nontaxable portion. The sum is the amount of each future payment to be excluded from tax.

Example—

Using the facts of the example above, assume that after your 1986 payment you receive $700 in 1987 and $1,200 in 1988. None of the 1987 payment is taxed; you exclude $800 for each annual annuity payment. Also you may elect to recompute your annual exclusion when you receive your payment in 1988. You elect to recompute your exclusion as follows:

Amount excludable in 1987	$800
Amount received in 1987	700
Difference	$100
Multiple as of 1/1/88 (see actuarial table)	13.8
Amount added to previously determined annual exclusion ($100 ÷ 13.8)	$ 7.25
Revised annual exclusion for 1987 and later years ($800 + $7.25)	$807.25
Amount taxable in 1988 ($1,200 — $807.25)	$392.75

¶7.08 • WHEN YOU CONVERT YOUR MATURED ENDOWMENT POLICY

When an endowment policy matures, you may elect to receive a lump sum, an annuity, an interest option, or a paid-up life insurance policy. If you elect—

A lump sum. You report the difference between your cost (premium payments less dividends) and what you receive.

The payment may qualify for income averaging, see ¶23.00.

An annuity before the policy matures or within 60 days after maturity. You report income in the years you receive your annuity. (See ¶7.07 for how to report annuity income.) Use as your investment in the annuity contract the cost of the endowment policy less premiums paid for other benefits, such as double indemnity or disability income. If you elect the annuity option more than 60 days after maturity, you report income on the matured policy as if you received the lump sum (see above rule). The lump sum is treated as the cost investment in the annuity contract.

An interest option before the policy matures. You report no income on the matured policy as long as you do not have the right to withdraw the proceeds of the policy. If you make the election after maturity or have the right to withdraw proceeds, you report income as if you received a lump sum. The interest is taxed in the years received.

Paid-up insurance. You report the difference between the present value of the paid-up life insurance policy and the premium paid for the endowment policy. In figuring the value of the insurance policy, you do not use its cash surrender value, but the amount you would have to pay for a similar policy with the company at the date of exchange. Your insurance company can give you this figure. The difference is taxed at ordinary income tax rates.

Tax-free exchange rules apply to the policy exchanges listed at ¶12.33.

Sales of endowment, annuity, or life insurance policies are taxable as ordinary income, not as capital gains.

The proceeds of a veteran's endowment policy paid before the death of the veteran are not taxable.

Employee Annuities

¶7.09 • REPORTING EMPLOYEE ANNUITIES

Retirement benefits paid as annuities are generally taxed in the same manner as commercial annuities. That part of the annuity payment allocated to your cost investment is treated as a nontaxable return of cost; the balance is treated as taxable income.

If your pension was completely financed by your employer and you did not report your employer's premium contributions, you report all payments as ordinary income. You have no cost investment in the annuity contract. To determine if you have a cost investment, see the next paragraph, ¶7.10.

¶7.10 • COST OF EMPLOYEE ANNUITY

Cost includes the following items:

Premiums paid by you or by withholdings from your pay.

Payments made by your employer and reported as additional pay. Premiums paid by an employer in a nonapproved plan for your benefit give you immediate income if you have nonforfeitable rights to the policy.

Premiums paid by your employer, which, if the amounts had been paid to you directly, would have been tax free to you because you were working abroad (*see* ¶36.00).

Pre-1939 contributions by a city or state to its employees' pension fund. (Before 1939, salary payments to state and city employees were tax free for federal income tax purposes.)

If you are a beneficiary collecting because of the death of an employee, cost may include all or part of the death benefit exclusion up to $5,000 (*see* ¶7.103).

¶7.101 • THREE-YEAR RECOVERY OF COST

If, within three years of the first payment, payments under the contract will equal or exceed your cost investment, payments are not taxable as income until after they equal your cost investment. This rule may not apply to certain pensions starting after June 30, 1986; *see* the new law guide in the front of this book.

Examples—

1. Starting July 1, 1985, you receive a pension annuity of $300 a month for the rest of your life. You contributed $9,000 to the policy; your company paid the balance. Because payments will equal or exceed your cost within three years, payments received before January 1, 1988 are not taxable income.

Payments in	Total
1985 (six months)	$1,800
1986	3,600
1987	3,600
	$9,000

2. Same facts as above except you contributed only $6,000 to the policy.

Payments in	Total
1985 (six months)	$1,800
1986	3,600
1987 (two months)	600
	$6,000

Taxable payments (ten months) reported in 1987 total $3,000.

After you have received payments equaling your investment, all future payments are ordinary income.

If you will not recover your cost within three years after your pension starts, follow the regular annuity rules at ¶7.07.

An increase in the amount of payments during the three-year period does not permit use of the three-year rule if you could not have used it initially.

An employee is taxed on the full value of a nonforfeitable annuity contract which his employer buys him if the employer does not have a qualified pension plan. Tax is imposed in the year the policy is purchased. A qualified plan is one approved by the IRS for special tax benefits.

You may receive benefits from more than one program under a single trust or plan of an employer or from several trusts or plans. Check with your former employer if you are covered by more than one pension or annuity contract. If so, you have to account for each contract separately even though benefits are included in one check.

Variable annuity. The three-year cost rules apply to periodic payments under a variable annuity contract financed by you and your employer. To determine whether you will recover your cost within three years, multiply the amount of the first periodic payment by the number of periodic payments to be made within the three years beginning on the date of its receipt.

¶7.102 • CIVIL SERVICE RETIREMENT

Almost all U.S. Civil Service retirees use the three-year cost recovery rule, since they usually receive annuity benefits sufficient to recover their cost within three years after they retire.

While you worked for the federal government, contributions

to the Civil Service retirement fund were withheld from your pay. These contributions represent your cost. Also, if you repaid to the retirement fund amounts that you previously had withdrawn, or paid into the fund to receive full credit for certain uncovered service, the entire amount you paid, including that designated as interest, is part of your cost. You may not claim an interest deduction for any amount designated as interest.

The annuity statement you received when your annuity was approved shows your "total contributions" to the retirement fund (your cost) and the "monthly rate" of your annuity benefit. The monthly rate is the rate before adjustment for health benefits coverage and life insurance, if any. To determine whether you will recover your cost within three years, multiply your initial monthly rate by 36. If the result equals or exceeds your cost, you must use the three-year rule. If you will not recover your cost within the three-year period, you report your annuity by following the rules at ¶7.07.

An increase in the monthly rate of your annuity resulting from a cost-of-living increase does not affect the method of reporting your annuity on your tax return. If you determine that you must use the three-year rule, your entire annuity, including the increase, is fully taxable after you have received payments equaling your cost. If, at the time you received your first annuity payment, you determined that you may not use the three-year rule, a later increase in your monthly rate thereafter will not enable you to use it; you must use the general rules at ¶7.07. A future increase in a civil service pension to the retiree or his survivor is not treated as annuity income but is reported in full as miscellaneous income and is not reduced by the exclusion ratio. However, an increase effective on or before a survivor's civil service annuity commences must be taken into account in computing the expected return or in determining the aggregate amount receivable under the annuity.

If you retired during the past year and filed your application for retirement late or are entitled to accrued payments because your application was processed late, you may receive a lump-sum payment representing the unpaid accrued monthly installments for the period before your regular monthly payments begin. If the lump sum is less than your cost of the annuity, you determine whether the three-year rule applies as explained above. Disregarding the lump sum, multiply the monthly rate of your annuity by 36; and if that amount plus the lump sum equals or exceeds your cost, you must use the three-year rule. In determining your tax for the year under the three-year rule, the lump sum is treated as a tax-free recovery of part of your cost. If the lump sum exceeds your cost of the annuity, the excess is fully taxable. Also, all the regular monthly annuity payments you receive thereafter are fully taxable.

A lump-sum payment for accrued annual leave received upon retirement is not part of your annuity. It is treated as a salary payment and is taxable as ordinary income.

If you made voluntary contributions to the retirement fund, you report the portion of your annuity attributable to the voluntary contributions as a separate annuity, taxable under the rules at ¶7.07. If you made voluntary contributions, an information return which you receive each year will state the portion of your monthly payments attributable to your voluntary contributions.

¶7.103 • $5,000 DEATH BENEFIT EXCLUSION ADDED TO THE COST OF AN ANNUITY

A pension annuity paid to you as the beneficiary of a deceased employee may qualify for a death benefit exclusion, up to $5,000. The amount of the exclusion is added to the cost of the annuity in calculating the investment in the contract as of the annuity starting date. Thus, if the employee's contribution plus the death benefit exclusion will be recovered within three years of the annuity starting date, you report the annuity payments under the three-year rule at ¶7.101.

Example—

An employee paid in $9,000. When he died, his widow was entitled to $3,000 a year and his two children to $1,000 a year each. In the first three years, they will receive a total of $15,000. Of this amount, $14,000 is considered a tax-free recovery of the employee's cost (cost of $9,000 plus $5,000 death benefit). In the first two years, the widow and the children exclude the full amount of their pension benefits ($10,000). In the third year, the remaining $4,000 to be received tax free is allocated according to the ratio of benefits received by each person; the widow receives $2,400 tax free (⅗ of the remaining $4,000), and each child receives $800 tax free (⅕ of $4,000).

The $5,000 exclusion may not be added to the investment if the deceased had received any payment under a joint and survivor contract after reaching his retirement age.

If, after taking the $5,000 exclusion into account in computing the investment in the contract, the three-year rule is not applicable (because the contract investment exceeds the return of the first three years), the beneficiary follows the regular annuity rules to compute taxable income (see ¶7.07). If the annuity is payable over the lifetime of the beneficiary, actuarial tables are used to determine the expected return on the contract. Ask the company paying the annuity to give you these amounts. The maximum amount of the death benefit exclusion is fixed at $5,000 without regard to the number of beneficiaries or the number of employers funding pension payments.

The death benefit exclusion may also be available to beneficiaries of a self-employed person who died after December 31, 1983.

¶7.11 • ANNUITIES FOR EMPLOYEES OF TAX-EXEMPT GROUPS AND SCHOOLS

If you are employed by a tax-exempt religious, charitable, or educational organization, or are on the civilian staff or faculty of the Uniformed Services University of the Health Services (Department of Defense), you may be able to arrange for the purchase of nonforfeitable tax deferred retirement annuities. The purchase is generally made through a reduction of salary which is used to pay for the contract. The amount of the salary reduction used to buy the contract is not taxable if it comes within these rules: The tax sheltered contribution is generally 20% of your pay multiplied by the number of years of service with your employer *less* tax-free contributions made in prior years by your employer to any qualified plan; salary reductions count as tax-free employer contributions. Under this formula, you may not be allowed to exclude any part of the current year's salary reduction because of employer contributions in prior years. An exclusion allowed under the 20%—years of service rule may not exceed the lower of 25% of your pay or $30,000.

Example—
A public school teacher earning $10,000 agrees to a $1,000 salary reduction to be used to purchase an annuity contract. The employer also contributes $1,800 per year to a pension trust for the teacher's account. In the first year, the entire salary reduction contribution is tax free as it is within the 20% exclusion of $1,800 (20% of the reduced salary of $9,000 × one year service). In the second and third year, there is a taxable amount.

Second year
20% of pay	$1,800	
Years of service	× 2	$3,600
Less prior tax-free contributions		2,800
Tax-free exclusion		$ 800

Third year
20% of pay	$1,800	
Years of service	× 3	5,400
Less prior tax-free contributions		5,400
No exclusion		–0–

The entire $1,000 salary reduction in the third year is taxable to the teacher.

An employee may under alternative tests be allowed a tax sheltered contribution exceeding that allowed under the 25% limitation. He may elect a limitation equal to the lower of (1) the general 20% of pay exclusion, (2) 25% of pay plus $4,000, or (3) $15,000. Once an election is made, it is irrevocable.

A special alternative test applies to a church employee whose adjusted gross income is $17,000 or less. A church employee is allowed an exclusion allowance equal to the lesser of $3,000 or his or her includable compensation. Church employees may make a special election which allows contributions to be made on their behalf in excess of the generally applicable defined contribution ceiling. Church employees include duly ordained, commissioned, or licensed ministers and lay employees of the church.

As the annuity contribution rules have been stated in general terms and are also subject to temporary Treasury regulations, we suggest that you rely on the amount computed by your employer or the issuer of the contract.

A tax-deferred plan may also be funded in mutual fund shares.

You may make a rollover of a distribution to an IRA account (see ¶7.05), but may not use the special ten-year averaging method to report the distribution.

¶7.12 • RETIRED MILITARY PERSONNEL ALLOWED TAX EXCLUSION ON ANNUITY ELECTION

If, when you retire from the military, you elect to receive reduced retirement pay to provide an annuity for your spouse or certain child beneficiaries, you do not report that part of your retirement pay used to fund the annuity.

Example—
You are eligible to receive retirement pay of $500 a month. You elect to receive $400 a month to obtain an annuity of $200 a month for your spouse on your death. You report $400 a month for tax purposes during your lifetime, rather than the $500. On your death, your spouse generally will report the full $200 a month received as income.

If you received retirement pay before 1966 and elected reduced benefits, you reported more retirement pay than you actually received. In this case, amounts attributed to the reduction in retirement pay reported in prior years offset retirement pay received in 1966 and later years.

If you elected to receive veteran's benefits instead of some or all of your retirement pay, you may have been required to deposit with the U.S. Treasury an amount equal to the reduction for the annuity. If so, you do not report retirement pay until it equals the amount deposited.

If all of the retired person's consideration for the contract (previously taxed reductions) has not been offset against retirement income at the time of death, the beneficiary excludes all payments under the contract until the exclusions equal the remaining consideration for the contract not previously excluded by the deceased. As soon as this amount is excluded, the beneficiary reports all later payments as income.

The $5,000 death benefit exclusion is treated as a cost investment to be added to the spouse's annuity contract if the deceased serviceman retired because of disability and dies before reaching retirement age.

¶7.13 • WITHHOLDING ON PENSIONS AND ANNUITIES

Income tax is automatically withheld from your pension or annuity payments unless you elect otherwise. See ¶25.09.

¶7.14 • NONTAXABLE RETIREMENT PAY OR PENSIONS

Social Security and certain Railroad Retirement benefits, provided your income does not exceed the limits explained at ¶34.11.

Amount standing to the credit of a deceased Civil Service employee in the Civil Service Retirement and Disability Fund. This amount is paid to his survivors in a lump sum when the credit is not large enough to entitle them to an annuity.

Payments for physical disability under workmen's compensation acts, health and disability insurance policies, and employers' self-insurance plans.

State unemployment insurance if your income is below certain levels (see ¶2.10), and disability insurance payments.

Veterans' pensions and other payments that are not taxed are discussed at ¶35.011.

Public assistance payments from a general welfare fund.

Pension granted by municipality under state law to widow of volunteer fireman killed on duty.

Social Security benefits paid by a foreign country are taxable, unless they are specifically made tax exempt by a tax treaty. The IRS has ruled that Social Security benefits paid by the United Kingdom are taxable and the payments may be offset by any cost contributions made by the recipient following the usual annuity tax rules explained in ¶7.07.

Disability benefits are discussed in ¶2.12 and ¶2.16.

Individual Retirement Accounts (IRAs)

¶7.16 • RETIREMENT SAVINGS THROUGH IRAs

Contributing to an IRA for 1986 offers the following benefits:

Immediate tax savings. For 1986, you may make deductible contributions to an IRA of up to $2,000 of earned income. Married couples who work may contribute up to $4,000. If you are in the 33% tax bracket, a $2,000 contribution reduces your tax by $660. If you earn less than $2,000, your contribution is limited to the amount you earned. If you set up IRAs for yourself and your nonworking spouse, you may contribute and deduct up to $2,250 (*see* ¶7.181).

Tax-free income accumulations. Income earned on funds in the account is not taxed until the funds are withdrawn. Tax-free interest compounding can produce the following funds for retirement:

$2,000 invested annually	*With interest compounded daily*		
	8%	10% *gives you—*	12%
5 years	$12,794	$13,633	$14,540
10 years	31,879	36,109	41,030
15 years	60,349	73,164	89,294
20 years	102,820	134,252	177,227
25 years	166,176	234,962	337,437
30 years	260,688	400,993	629,329

Weigh the above benefits against these restrictions: You may not freely withdraw IRA funds until the year you reach 59½ or become disabled. If you take money out or even borrow using the account as collateral before that time, you are subject to a penalty. In the year you reach 70½, you may no longer make IRA contributions, and you must start to withdraw from the account. All IRA withdrawals are fully taxable; special averaging for lump-sum distribution does not apply. Finally, unauthorized contributions and distributions are penalized.

For IRA rules applying in 1987 *see* the new law discussion in the front of this book.

¶7.17 • LIMITS ON DEDUCTIBLE CONTRIBUTIONS FOR 1986

For 1986, you may contribute and deduct up to $2,000. If both you and your spouse work, you may each contribute up to $2,000.

You may set up an IRA for a nonworking spouse and deduct contributions of up to $2,250 on a joint return. *See* ¶7.181. If you earn less than $2,000, your contribution may not exceed the amount of your pay. You may deduct the contribution whether or not you have excess itemized deductions in 1986.

To claim the deduction, you must make the contribution no later than the due date for filing your return. Thus, your contribution for 1986 must be made no later than April 15, 1987.

You may not deduct contributions made in the year you reach age 70½. Thus persons born in June 1916 or earlier may not contribute to an IRA for 1986 and later years. However, if your employer makes a contribution to your account under a Simplified Employee Pension Plan as discussed in ¶7.22, you may claim a deduction.

Your deductible contribution must be based on payments received for rendering personal services such as salary, wages, commissions, tips, fees, bonuses, or net earnings from self-employment (less Keogh plan contributions on behalf of the self-employed). Compensation does *not* include: (1) income earned abroad for which the foreign earned income exclusion is claimed; (2) deferred compensation, pensions, or annuities; or (3) investment income such as interest, dividends, or profits from sales of property.

Example—

A trader, whose sole income was derived from stock dividends and gains in buying and selling stocks, contributed to an IRA. The IRS disallowed the deduction on the grounds that his income was not earned income. The trader argued that compensation is a broad term which should include his profits from investments. His trading activities were more than those of a mere investor. He had his own desk at a national brokerage house, spent full time at his investment activities, and traded over $3 million during the year. Despite his substantial investment activities, the Tax Court sides with the IRS. His profits came from property holdings and are not considered earned income.

If you live in a community property state, the fact that one-half of your spouse's income is considered your income does not entitle you to make contributions to an IRA. The contribution must be based on pay earned through your services.

Only cash contributions are deductible; contributions paid by check are considered cash for this purpose.

If you have more than one self-employed activity, you must aggregate profits and losses from all of your self-employed businesses to determine if you have net income on which to base an IRA contribution. For example, if one self-employed business produces a net profit of $15,000 but another a net loss of $20,000, you may not make an IRA contribution based on the net profit of $15,000. This netting rule does not apply to salary or wage income. If you are an employee who also has an unprofitable business, you may make an IRA contribution based on your salary.

Endowment contracts. You may set up an IRA with an endowment contract. The maximum premiums for the contract may not exceed $2,000. However, no deduction is allowed for contributions to the extent allocated to the cost of life insurance. The company providing the contract will allocate the deductible and nondeductible amounts. You may set up another IRA and contribute to it the difference between your maximum allowable deduction and the amount allocable to retirement savings under the contract.

Trustees' or custodians' fees. Payments to set up or manage an IRA are not considered IRA contributions if separately paid. They are investment expenses which may be deducted as a miscellaneous itemized deduction.

¶7.18 • SETTING UP AN IRA

Banks, brokerage firms, insurance companies, and credit unions offering IRA investment plans provide all of the necessary forms for setting up your IRA. You do not have to file any forms with your tax return when you set up or make contributions to your IRA. Form 5498 listing your contribution will be filed with the IRS by the company with which you set up your IRA.

You may set up an IRA as:

1. *An individual retirement account* with a bank, savings and loan association, federally insured credit union, or other qualified

person as trustee or custodian. An individual retirement account is technically a trust or custodial account. Your contribution may be invested in vehicles such as certificates of deposit, mutual funds, and certain limited partnerships.

If you wish to take a more active role in managing your IRA investments, you may set up a "self-directed" IRA using a Treasury model form. The model trust (Form 5305) and the model custodial account agreement (Form 5305A) meet the requirements of an exempt individual retirement account and so do not require a ruling or determination letter approving the exemption of the account and the deductibility of contributions made to the account. If you use this method, you still have to find a bank or other institution or trustee to handle your account or investment. If you have a self-directed IRA, you may not invest in collectibles, such as coins, stamps, antiques, rugs, metals, or guns. Assets used to acquire a collectible are treated as distributions and are taxed.

2. *An individual retirement annuity,* by purchasing an annuity contract (including a joint and survivor contract for the benefit of you and your spouse) or an endowment contract issued by an insurance company. No trustee or custodian is required. The contract, endorsed to meet the terms of an IRA, is all that is required. In the case of an endowment contract, however, no deduction is permitted for the portion of the premium allocable to life insurance. This nondeductible amount is generally called a P.S. 58 cost. As borrowing or pledging of the contract is not allowed under an IRA, the contracts will not contain loan provisions.

Annuity and endowment contracts may not have fixed premiums nor annual premiums exceeding $2,000. Further, a refund of premiums must be applied toward the payment of future premiums or to purchase additional benefits. If you contracted for a fixed premium contract before November 7, 1978, you may continue with the contract or exchange it. Tax-free exchanges were allowed prior to January 1, 1981. However, this change in the tax law does not govern the terms of the contract between you and the insurance company. Thus, you may suffer substantial nondeductible losses in the exchange of contracts because of fees and other charges by the insurance company.

Broker's restriction on transferring IRA accounts. Before you invest in an IRA carefully review the terms of the agreement for restrictions. One investor, who put his IRA in a brokerage account, was not allowed by the trustee to transfer from one account to another. Further, the trustee reserved some of the IRA funds to cover broker fees and other transfer costs. The investor asked the IRS if these restrictions violated the tax law. The IRS, in a private letter ruling, said there was no violation. An IRA is a contractual agreement between the IRA trustee and the participant. Although the tax laws do not place limitations on direct IRA-to-IRA transfers, the trustees of a particular account may restrict such transfers.

In the past, there was a third IRA alternative: Special U.S. Retirement bonds, which the Treasury stopped issuing in 1982.

Instead of setting up your own IRA, you may choose to make deductible contributions to your employer's qualified plan, provided the plan is designed to accept such contributions. *See* ¶7.183.

Similarly, employers, labor unions, and other trade or employee associations and professional associations may establish IRAs for employees or members and their beneficiaries. Separate accounting is required for the interest of each account. The assets of the accounts may be held in a common trust fund, common investment fund, or common fund. Amounts contributed directly by your employer for your benefit are taxable to you as wages. You may claim a deduction for the amount. Income tax withholdings are not required on the contribution; however the contribution is subject to other payroll taxes (FICA and FUTA). If your employer's contribution is less than the maximum allowed, you may make contributions up to the limit or set up another IRA account for the balance. In any event, your deduction may not exceed $2,000 unless you contribute on behalf of your nonworking spouse, in which case your deduction may not exceed $2,250.

Contributions after the end of the taxable year. You have until the due date for filing your 1986 return, April 15, 1987, to make an IRA contribution for 1986. If you are short of cash, you may borrow the funds without jeopardizing the deduction. If an IRA deduction would entitle you to a refund, you can file your return early, claim the IRA deduction, and use the refund to make an IRA contribution before the due date.

To be deductible for 1986, a contribution must be made by the April 15, 1987 due date, even if you get an extension to file your return.

Diversifying your investments. You may set up one type of IRA one year and choose another form the next year. You may also split your contribution between two or more investment vehicles. For example, you are eligible to contribute $2,000. You may choose to put $1,000 into an individual retirement annuity and $1,000 into an individual retirement account with your local bank.

¶7.181 • IRAs FOR MARRIED COUPLES

Both spouses have compensation. If both spouses have compensation and each is eligible to set up an IRA account, each may contribute to his or her separate IRA account up to $2,000.
Examples—
1. You earn a salary of $20,000; your spouse earns $10,000 and both of you are eligible to set up IRA plans. On a joint return, the maximum deduction may be up to $4,000. If only one of you works and qualifies to set up an IRA, the maximum deduction is $2,000, unless an account for a nonworking spouse is set up.
2. You live in a community property state. You earn a salary of $20,000. Your spouse does not work. The maximum deduction for an IRA is $2,000, even though, under the community property laws, your spouse is considered to have earned half of your salary. You may set up an IRA for your nonworking spouse. In that case, your maximum deduction may not exceed $2,250.

Account for nonworking spouse. If you are working, you may make a 1986 deductible contribution on behalf of your nonworking spouse provided you file a joint return. You may have two separate IRAs, one for you and one for your spouse, or a single IRA which has a subaccount for you and another subaccount for your spouse. A joint account is not allowed. However, each spouse may have a right of survivorship in the subaccount of the other. The maximum contribution is $2,250 and may be allocated between spouses in any way as long as no spouse receives a contribution exceeding $2,000. A working spouse who is over age 70½ may contribute to an IRA for a nonworking spouse who is under age 70½, but the maximum contribution is $2,000 and the entire contribution must be allocated to the nonworking spouse; no contribution may be made for the spouse over age 70½.

If the working spouse makes deductible voluntary contributions to an employer plan, that spouse may still make a contribution to an IRA for the nonworking spouse, subject to the maximum contribution limit above.

Generally, you may set up an account (or subaccount) for your spouse only if your spouse received no compensation, including tax-exempt foreign earned income, for the year. However, new legislation may let you claim the maximum $2,250 contribution deduction for 1986 if your spouse had compensation of less than $250; your spouse is treated as if he or she had no compensation. *See* the new law guide in the front of this book. You may set up a spousal account regardless of the amount of your spouse's unearned income, such as interest, dividends or Social Security benefits.

A spouse may start withdrawing from his or her spousal account (or subaccount) on reaching age 59½ and must start withdrawing on reaching age 70½.

If you are divorced, you may not maintain a spousal account for your former spouse. If you contributed to an account on behalf of your nonworking spouse and divorce later in the year, the contribution is an excess contribution. IRAs based on alimony are discussed at ¶7.182.

An amount distributed to one spouse may not be rolled over to an IRA account of the other spouse, except in the case of divorce (*see* ¶7.21).

If you already have an IRA for yourself and you want to make contributions on behalf of your nonworking spouse, you may do so by merely opening a new IRA for your spouse and continue your present IRA for yourself. However, if you have an annuity or endowment contract, check with your insurance agent about any contract restrictions on reducing your premium payments. Before setting up a single IRA with subaccounts for you and your spouse, check Treasury regulations covering their use.

¶7.182 • IRAs FOR DIVORCEES

A divorced spouse with little or no earnings in 1986 may treat taxable alimony as compensation, giving a basis for deductible IRA contributions. A divorced spouse may make an IRA contribution equal to 100% of taxable alimony up to $2,000. Taxable alimony is alimony paid under a decree of divorce or legal separation or a written agreement incident to such a decree, *see* ¶1.70. It does not include alimony payments made under a written agreement that is not incident to such a decree.

¶7.183 • IRA CONTRIBUTION TO EMPLOYER PLAN

For 1986, an employer's qualified retirement plan or governmental plan may be qualified to receive from employees qualified voluntary contributions, which are treated as IRA contributions. An advantage to making qualified voluntary contributions: The funds are invested by the plan's trustees.

The rules for IRA contributions to employer-sponsored plans are generally the same as for personal IRAs. Distributions will not qualify for ten-year averaging. Withdrawals of deductible contributions before age 59½ are subject to the 10% IRA penalty (*see* ¶7.20) unless you are disabled. Rollovers from the employer plan may be made to an IRA without incurring any withdrawal penalty, subject to the rule which limits rollovers to one per year.

Distributions from employer-sponsored plans generally do not have to start at age 70½ as they must with IRAs; however, employees who own more than a 5% interest in the business and highly compensated employees (*see* ¶33.00) have to begin taking distributions from the plan by April 1 following the calendar year they reach age 70½.

Although a plan may allow you to make voluntary payments to its fund, you need not count it as an IRA contribution. However, you must specifically designate the contribution as nondeductible if you do not want it treated as an IRA contribution. Check with the plan administrator for the proper designation procedure. Failure to make a designation automatically results in the treatment of voluntary contributions as deductible IRA contributions, thereby limiting the amount of the IRA contributions that you may make outside the plan. For example, your employer's plan allows you to make a voluntary contribution of $750. In 1986, you contribute $750 but do not designate the payment as nondeductible. You may contribute up to $1,250 ($2,000 − $750) to an IRA set up outside of the company plan. Your total deduction is $2,000. If you do designate the $750 as nondeductible, you may contribute and deduct up to $2,000 to your own IRA.

Your employer's plan may be amended to permit both deductible and nondeductible voluntary contributions.

> Check with your employer's plan to determine when voluntary contributions must be made to avoid losing out on a contribution deduction. While you have until April 15, 1987 to make an IRA contribution for 1986, your employer is allowed, but not required, to treat contributions made in 1987 as 1987 contributions.

For rules applying in 1987, *see* new law guide in the front of the book.

¶7.19 • IRA DISTRIBUTIONS

Payments from an IRA are reported as ordinary income in the year received. If you have an individual retirement annuity, your investment in the contract is treated as zero so all payments are fully taxable. Distributions from an endowment policy because of death are taxed as ordinary income to the extent allocable to retirement savings; to the extent allocable to life insurance, they are considered insurance proceeds. The tax on 1986 distributions may be lessened if you qualify to use income averaging as in ¶23.00.

Proceeds from U.S. retirement bonds are taxable in the year the bonds are redeemed. However, you must report the full proceeds in the year you reach age 70½ even if you do not redeem the bonds.

Your entire interest in an IRA must be, or begin to be, distributed not later than the April 1 following the end of the taxable year during which you reach age 70½. For example, if you reach age 70½ during 1986, you must start taking IRA distributions no later than April 1, 1987. *See* ¶7.20 for figuring minimum distributions to avoid a penalty.

Withdrawals from an IRA may be subject to bank interest penalties for premature withdrawals, even if no tax penalty is imposed under the rules at ¶7.20.

Distributions from an IRA are subject to withholding unless you file for exemption. See ¶25.09.

After the death of an IRA owner, distributions to beneficiaries may be spread over the same periods discussed above for pension and profit-sharing plans at ¶7.065.

Rules for IRA distributions after 1986 are discussed in the new law guide in the front of the book.

¶7.20 • PENALTIES FOR PREMATURE DISTRIBUTIONS, EXCESS CONTRIBUTIONS, INSUFFICIENT WITHDRAWALS

You must file Form 5329 with your 1986 return if you are liable for any of the penalties below. Failure to file Form 5329 may result in an additional penalty of $10 per day (up to a maximum of $5,000).

Premature distributions. If you receive a distribution in 1986 before age 59½ and are not disabled, you will be subject to a penalty tax of 10% on the premature distribution. This 10% tax is in addition to the tax that will be incurred when you include the distribution as ordinary income with your other income.
Example—
An unmarried person, age 40, withdraws $3,000 from his IRA plan. Assume his regular tax on his income (after including in income the $3,000 distribution) is $5,100. To this amount, he must add 10% of $3,000 or $300. His total tax is $5,400.

Redemption of U.S. retirement bonds before age 59½ is considered a premature distribution.

If you borrow from your IRA plan, you are considered to have received your entire interest. Borrowing will subject the account or the fair market value of the contract to tax at ordinary income rates as of the first day of the taxable year of the borrowing. Your IRA account loses its tax-exempt status. If you use the account or part of it as security for a loan, the pledged portion is treated as a distribution.

You will not be liable for a premature distribution if you are correcting an excess contribution that did not exceed $2,250.

For penalty rules after 1986 for premature distributions, *see* the new law guide in the front of the book.

Insufficient distributions. If you do not start receiving distributions by the April 1 following the year you reach age 70½ or you receive an insufficient distribution after this date, a penalty tax of 50% applies to the difference between the amount you should have received and the amount you did receive.
Example—
You receive $500 from your IRA plan. The minimum amount required to be paid to you was $700. You pay a penalty tax of $100 (50% of $200).

The first required installment amount is generally fixed by the amount of the account at age 70½ and your life expectancy. If you are married, you may figure the minimum distribution using joint lives which will result in a smaller minimum distribution requirement than the one life table.

If you have an individual retirement annuity, your insurance company should gear your payments to meet minimum distribution requirements.

Payouts at 70½. If you were born any time between July 1, 1915 and June 30, 1916, you must begin distributions by April 1, 1987; if between July 1916 and through June 1917, distributions must start by April 1, 1988.

Minimum payouts. The minimum distributable amount each year is found by dividing the amount of all of your IRA accounts as of the beginning of the taxable year by your life expectancy.

If you are married, you may elect to use the joint and last survivor expectancy of you and your spouse. Each year, you may redetermine your life expectancy and refigure the minimum distribution for that year. You may find that such a recomputation may allow you to take a smaller minimum distribution. IRS guidelines for refiguring life expectancy and computing the minimum distribution were not released at the time of publication of this book; *see* the Supplement for further details.

The IRS may waive the penalty for insufficient withdrawals if due to reasonable error and steps are being taken to remedy the situation. You must submit evidence to account for shortfalls in withdrawals and how you are rectifying the situation. The IRS has indicated that examples of acceptable reasons for insufficient withdrawals include erroneous advice from the sponsoring organization or other pension advisors or that your own good faith efforts to apply the required withdrawal formula produced a miscalculation or misunderstanding of the formula. You should attach your letter of explanation to Form 5329. You must pay the penalty; if the IRS grants a waiver, it will refund the penalty.

Excess contributions. If you contribute more than the allowable deductible amount, the excess contribution may be subject to a penalty tax of 6%. The penalty tax is cumulative. That is, unless you correct the excess, you will be subject to another penalty on the excess contribution in the following year. The penalty tax is not deductible.

The penalty tax on excess contributions may be avoided as follows: (1) An excess contribution, if not in excess of $2,250 and a deduction for the excess was not allowed, may be withdrawn at any time and the distribution may be treated as if it were never contributed (contributions in excess of $2,250 must be withdrawn prior to the due date for filing your return in order to avoid a penalty); (2) where an excess rollover contribution was made because of reliance on erroneous information, the $2,250 limitation is increased to the extent of the excess contribution attributable to the erroneous information; (3) excess contributions which are not withdrawn may be deducted in later years in which there is an unused deduction limitation.

Example—
In 1985, you contributed $1,500, but you were only entitled to contribute $1,200. If you are entitled to deduct $2,000 in 1986, you may correct your excess 1985 contribution by undercontributing $300. Your deduction for 1985 is $1,200. Your deduction for 1986 is $2,000 (the $1,700 contributed in 1986 plus the carryover of the excess contribution from 1985).

¶7.21 • ROLLOVERS OF IRAs; TRANSFERS INCIDENT TO DIVORCE
You may transfer assets tax free from one IRA to another or from a qualified corporate plan to an IRA. Such transfers are treated as a distribution of the assets from your old plan to you. To avoid tax on the transfer, these tests must be met: (1) The amount you receive from your old plan must be transferred to the new plan within 60 days of your receiving it. (2) A tax-free rollover may occur only once in a one-year period. If a second rollover occurs within the same one-year period, you are taxed on the plan assets.

A direct transfer of funds from one bank to another is not considered a rollover subject to the one-year restriction.
Example—
Smith sets up an IRA at Bank A. In January 1985, he instructs Bank A to transfer the funds to Bank B. The transfer from Bank A to Bank B is not subject to the one-year restriction on rollovers because there was no payment or distribution of the funds to Smith.

A person over age 70½ may roll over a lump-sum distribution from a company plan to an IRA, although contributions to an IRA are specifically barred to him. The rollover must be made within 60 days of the distribution and, in the year of the rollover, the individual must receive a minimum distribution from the IRA (*see* ¶7.20).

Rollover contributions are not deductible.
For transfers of a lump-sum distribution of a tax-qualified plan to an IRA (*see* ¶7.05).

Tax-free transfer of IRAs because of divorce. A spouse may transfer tax free his IRA account to his former spouse as long as the transfer is made under a valid divorce decree or written agreement incident to the divorce. The transferred account, policy, or bond must be maintained in the name of the spouse who receives it.

Surviving spouse may make tax-free rollover of inherited account. A surviving spouse who receives an IRA account upon the death of his or her spouse may make a tax-free rollover to an IRA. Beneficiaries other than surviving spouses may not make a rollover; the payout rules are similar to those for pension and profit-sharing plan beneficiaries. See ¶7.065.

¶7.22 • SIMPLIFIED EMPLOYEE PENSION PLANS
A simplified employee pension plan set up by an employer allows the employer to contribute and deduct to an employee's IRA account more money than allowable under regular IRA rules. For 1986, your employer may contribute up to 15% of your compensation or $30,000, whichever is less. An employee may also add his own IRA contribution subject to IRA contribution limits. An employee includes in income employer contributions to his account as shown on Form W-2 and claims an offsetting deduction for the contribution. On your return, the deduction is reported on the line provided for IRA deductions.

If you make a personal IRA contribution in addition to your employer's SEP contribution, your total 1986 deduction equals your employer's contribution plus your personal contribution.

An employee over age 70½ may still participate in an employer SEP plan but may not make his own personal IRA contribution.

Example—
Your salary in 1986 is $40,000. Your company pays $6,000 (15% of salary) to your SEP-IRA. On your 1986 return, you increase income by the $6,000 contribution and then claim an offsetting $6,000 deduction. You may also deduct your own IRA contribution of up to $2,000.

New law. New SEP rules effective after 1986 are discussed in the new law guide in the front of the book.

Tax Retirement Plans for Self-Employed

The advantages of setting up a self-employed retirement plan (Keogh plan) flow from: (1) Tax deductions allowed for contributions made to the plan (a form of forced savings); (2) accumulations of tax-free income earned on assets held by the plan; and (3) special averaging provisions for benefits paid on retirement.

The following discussion assumes that you are a self-employed person in your own business or profession or are a partner in a business. Most self-employed persons are considered key employees and may be subject to the restrictions on top-heavy plans discussed at ¶7.32.

Further details on Keogh plans are discussed in the following sections:

Distributions from Keogh plans are subject to the rules explained at ¶7.01 to ¶7.051.

¶7.30 • WHO MAY SET UP A PLAN

You may set up a self-employed retirement plan called a Keogh plan if you earn self-employment income from personal services. For purposes of a Keogh plan, this income is called earned income and is your net profit (gross business or professional income less allowable business deductions). Income earned abroad and excluded from federal income tax is not considered earned income for purposes of the plan. If you are an inactive owner, such as a limited partner, you may not qualify for a Keogh plan.

If you control more than one business (own more than 50% of the capital or profits interest in a partnership or the entire share of an unincorporated business): (1) You must set up pension or profit-sharing plans for all businesses under your control. These may be incorporated in one plan or remain separate. (2) Any additional plans must also conform to all regulations governing the original plan. (3) The additional plans must make contributions in an equal ratio and provide equal benefits.

The above rules prevent you from increasing your deductible contribution for your own benefit by contributing to more than one retirement plan. However, if you are an employee-member of a company retirement plan, you may set up a Keogh plan if you carry on a self-employed enterprise or profession on the side. For example, you are an attorney employed by a company that has a qualified pension plan in which you are a member. At the same time, you have an outside practice. You may set up a Keogh plan based on your self-employed earnings. Each plan is independent of the other.

A plan may not discriminate in favor of officers or other highly-compensated personnel. Benefits must be for the employees and their beneficiaries, and their plan rights may not be subject to forfeiture. A plan may not allow any of its funds to be diverted for purposes other than pension benefits. Contributions made on your behalf may not exceed the ratio of contributions made on behalf of employees.

An individual partner or partners, although self-employed, may not set up a Keogh plan. The plan must be established by the partnership.

You must formally set up your plan in writing on or before the end of the taxable year in which you want the plan to be effective. For example, if you want to make a contribution for 1986, your plan must be set up on or before December 31, 1986 if you report on a calendar-year basis; see ¶7.35.

Including employees in your plan. For plan years starting after 1984, you must include in your plan all employees who have reached age 21 with at least one year of service. If your plan provides for full and immediate vesting of benefits, an employee may be required to complete three years of service before participating. You are not required to cover seasonal or part-time employees who work less than 1000 hours during a 12-month period. If you set up a defined benefit plan, you may exclude an employee who is within five years of normal retirement age (which may not be later than age 65) when his or her period of service begins.

¶7.31 • CHOOSING A PLAN

There are two general types of Keogh plans: defined-benefit plans and defined-contribution plans. A defined-benefit plan provides in advance for a specific retirement benefit funded by contributions based on an IRS formula and actuarial assumptions. A defined-contribution plan does not fix a specific retirement benefit but rather sets the amount of annual contributions so that the amount of retirement benefits depends on contributions and income earned on those contributions. If contributions are geared to profits, the plan is a profit-sharing plan. A plan that requires fixed contributions regardless of profits is a money-purchase plan.

A defined-benefit plan may prove costly if you have older employees who also must be provided with proportionate defined benefits. Further, a defined-benefit plan requires you to contribute to their accounts even if you do not have profits. The maximum annual retirement benefit for basing annual contributions may not exceed $90,000. You may not adopt a defined-benefit plan unless it provides benefits for all your employees without taking into account benefits under Social Security. All plans of a controlled group of businesses are aggregated for purposes of the limitations applied to defined benefits.

If you are interested in following an aggressive investment policy for funds in your Keogh plan, you will set up a trust to receive Keogh contributions. You may name yourself or an independent trustee to oversee the plan.

As an owner-employee (owning more than 10% of the business), your dealings with the trust are subject to restrictions. You are subject to penalties if you borrow funds from the trust; buy property from or sell property to the trust; charge any fees for services you render to the trust. These restrictions also apply to any member of your immediate family and any corporation in which you own more than half the voting stock, directly or indirectly.

If you are considering an investment in savings certificates, you need not set up a trust; you may use a custodial account with the bank.

If you use funds to buy nontransferable annuity contracts from an insurance company, no trust may be necessary. Premium payments are made directly to the insurance company. The annuity contract may pay a fixed monthly income for life, or for a fixed period of years, or may be a variable annuity contract.

¶7.32 • TOP-HEAVY PLAN RESTRICTIONS

"Top-heavy" plan rules, which apply to corporate plans favoring "key employees," may also apply to a Keogh plan of a self-employed person. The top-heavy rules apply if more than 60% of the account balances or accrued benefits are for key employees; *see* below for definition of key employees. Even if your Keogh plan is not currently considered top heavy, your plan may be disqualified unless it includes provisions that would automatically take effect if the plan becomes top heavy.

Vesting. A top-heavy plan must provide for faster vesting of your employees' benefits. The plan must provide either 100% vesting after three years of service, or graded vesting at the rate of at least 20% after two years of service, 40% after three years of service, 60% after four years of service, 80% after five years of service, and 100% after six years of service.

There may be an advantage in electing three-year vesting if you have a high turnover of employees. Further, under three-year vesting, a plan may ignore some years of service if the employee has a break in service.

$200,000 pay limit. Under the top-heavy plan rules, only the first $200,000 of a self-employed person's earned income may be considered in determining contributions.

Distributions before age 59½. For 1986, the 10% penalty for distributions to more than 5% owners before age 59½ (¶7.065) applies whether or not the plan is top heavy. The penalty does not apply to distributions made because you are disabled.

The IRS has ruled that a tax-free rollover may be made where the Keogh plan is terminated. A timely rollover will avoid the 10% penalty on premature distributions if the recipient is under 59½.

Retirement plan bonds. If you invested Keogh plan funds in Treasury Department Retirement Plan Bonds before May 1, 1982, you may redeem them at any time, even if you are under age 59½. To avoid immediate tax, a rollover may be made within 60 days to an IRA or qualified pension or profit-sharing plan.

Who are key employees? The above top-heavy restrictions apply if more than 60% of a defined-contributions plan account balances or more than 60% of the accrued benefits of a defined-benefit plan are for key employees. Key employees are employees who at any time during the plan year or in any of the four preceding plan years own (1) one of the ten largest ownership interests and have compensation exceeding $30,000; (2) more than a 5% interest; or (3) more than a 1% interest and also earn compensation of more than $150,000. Officers of corporations are also considered key employees if they have compensation exceeding $45,000.

¶7.33 • HOW MUCH YOU MAY CONTRIBUTE AND DEDUCT

You may contribute up to the lower of 25% of earned income or $30,000 to a defined contribution plan, such as a money purchase pension plan or a profit-sharing plan. However, for purposes of figuring contributions, earned income is net earnings from self-employment *less* the deductible Keogh contribution. Because net earnings must be reduced by the deductible contribution, your maximum contribution to a money-purchase plan is reduced from 25% to 20% of net earnings (before Keogh deduction is considered). The entire 20% contribution is deductible.

However, if you have a profit-sharing plan, you may not claim a 20% deduction. The maximum deductible profit-sharing contribution is technically 15% of earned income but because net earnings must be reduced, your maximum deductible contribution is reduced from 15% to 13.0435% of your net earnings (before Keogh deduction is considered). To maximize your deductible contributions, you may establish a separate money purchase plan to supplement a profit-sharing plan. A bank or other Keogh plan trustee can help you set up separate plans and stay within the overall contribution limit of 25% of earned income.

The IRS has not yet released details for computing contributions and deduction limits. The IRS method, if available, will be in the Supplement to this book.

Only the first $200,000 of a self-employed person's earned income may be considered for purposes of computing contributions if the plan is top heavy.

No minimum contribution is permitted. Prior to 1984, if your adjusted gross income did not exceed $15,000 and your self-employment income was $750 to $5,000, you could make a minimum contribution of up to $750.

Contributions for your employees. The above earned income rule does not affect contributions for employees. You continue to make contributions for your employees at the rate specified in your plan, based upon their compensation. You deduct contributions for employees when figuring your net earnings from self-employment on Schedule C.

Contributions after age 70½. You may continue to make contributions as long as you have self-employment income. At the same time, if your ownership interest exceeds 5%, you must receive at least a minimum distribution from the plan no later than the April 1 following the year you reach age 70½. *See* ¶7.065. A penalty may be imposed if the minimum distribution is not received. The minimum distribution must be based on your life expectancy. If you are married, withdrawals may be spread over the joint lives of you and your spouse. If available, life expectancy data will be in the Supplement to this book.

Carryover of excess contributions. Contributions to a profit-sharing plan exceeding the 15% deduction ceiling (13.0435% after reduction) may be carried over and deducted in later years subject to the 15% ceiling for those years. If contributions exceed the lesser of $30,000 or 25% of net earnings (after reduction by deductible contribution), your plan may be disqualified.

¶7.34 • HOW TO CLAIM THE DEDUCTION

Contributions made for your account as a self-employed person are deducted from gross income to find your adjusted gross income. However, a deduction for a contribution made for your benefit may not be part of a net operating loss.

Contributions for your employees are entered as deductions on Schedule C for purposes of computing profit or loss from your business. Trustees' fees not provided for by contributions are deductible in addition to the maximum contribution deduction.

Deductible contributions may generally be made at any time up to the due date of your return, including any extension of time. However, the plan itself must be set up before the close of the taxable year for which the deduction is sought. If you miss the December 31 deadline for setting up a Keogh plan, you still have up to April 15, 1987 to set up an SEP (*see* ¶7.22) for 1986.

¶7.35 • HOW TO QUALIFY A PLAN

You may set up your plan and contribute to it without advance approval. But, since advance approval is advisable, you may, in a determination letter, ask your local District Director to review your plan. Approval requirements depend on whether you set up your own administered plan or join a master plan administered by a bank, insurance company, mutual fund, or a prototype plan sponsored by a trade or professional association. If you start your own individually designed plan, you apply for a determination letter on Form 5300 for a defined benefit plan or Form 5301 for a defined contribution plan; Schedule T must be filed with the appropriate form to comply with new law requirements.

If you join a master or prototype plan, the sponsoring organization applies to the IRS for approval of its plan. You should be given a copy of the approved plan and copies of any subsequent amendments.

¶7.355 • ANNUAL INFORMATION RETURNS

You must file an annual information return with the IRS. The return must be filed by the last day of the seventh month after the end of the plan year. Thus, if you have a calendar year Keogh plan, you must file your 1986 plan year return by July 31, 1987. The filing requirement applies even if you have no employees.

You must file either Form 5500-C or Form 5500-R. Form 5500-R is a shorter form which may be used for your 1986 plan year if you are the only participant. For plans with more than one and less than 100 participants, Form 5500-R may be used for 1986 if it was not your first plan year or final plan year and if you filed a Form 5500-C for your 1984 or 1985 plan year. Otherwise, you must file the more extensive Form 5500-C.

The form instructions warn that a penalty of $25 per day will be imposed for late or incomplete filing unless you attach an explanation showing reasonable cause for the improper filing.

¶7.36 • RESTRICTIONS ON LOANS

Keogh plan loans to an owner-employee (more than 10% ownership) are subject to prohibited transaction penalties. There are two penalties: (1) A 5% penalty and (2) a 100% penalty.

The 5% penalty applies in the year of the loan and in later years until the loan is repaid with interest. The penalty is figured on a fair market interest factor which is explained in the instructions to Form 5330. You are required to report loans to the IRS on Form 5330 and pay the 5% penalty when you file the form. Form 5330 must be filed within seven months after the end of the taxable year; extensions may be granted by the IRS if you apply in writing before the due date.

The 100% penalty is imposed if the loan is not repaid. The penalty may be avoided by repaying the loan within 90 days after the IRS sends a deficiency notice for the 100% tax. The 90-day period may be extended by the IRS to allow a reasonable time for repayment.

Self-employed individuals are taxable on loans from their plan under the same rules applied to regular employees, as discussed below.

Loans to employees. Employees who take loans from the plan are not subject to the 5% or 100% penalty. An employee is not taxed on the loan if it is repayable within five years and when added to other outstanding loans from the plan, does not exceed the lower of (1) $50,000 or (2) one-half of the present value of vested benefits or $10,000, whichever is greater. Further, if a loan is used to buy, build, or rehabilitate a principal residence (or relative's residence), a loan within the $50,000/$10,000 limitation is not treated as a taxable distribution, even if repayable over a period of more than five years.

The loan must specifically require payment within five years or less. If not, the loan is a taxable distribution, even if repaid within five years.

Loans from deductible IRA contributions to a company plan (¶7.183) are treated as taxable distributions regardless of the amount of the loan. Further, in figuring the present value of vested benefits under the $50,000/$10,000 rule, benefits attributable to deductible IRA contributions are disregarded.

¶8.00

Reporting Farm Income or Loss

¶8.01 • WHO IS A FARMER?

The term "farmer" includes all individuals, partnerships, syndicates and corporations that cultivate, operate or manage a farm for profit or gain, either as owners or tenants. Thus, partners in a partnership which operates a farm are considered farmers.

The term "farm" includes stock, dairy, poultry, fruit and truck farms, plantations, ranches and all land used for farming operations. A fish farm where fish are specially fed and raised, and not just caught, is a farm. Animal breeding farms, such as mink, fox, and chinchilla farms, are also considered farms.

Gentleman farming. To be treated as farmers, individuals must be engaged in farming for gain or profit. Farm losses of part-time or "gentlemen" farmers may be disallowed on the grounds that the farm is not operated to make a profit but is a hobby. The hobby rules explained at ¶5.06 apply in determining the existence of a profit motive in farming operations. Favorable evidence of an intention to make a profit are: You do not use your farm just for recreation. You have tried to cut losses by switching from unsuccessful products to other types of farming. Losses are decreasing. Losses were caused by unexpected events. You have a bookkeeping system. You consult experts. You devote personal attention to the farm.

Farm loss deductions may also be restricted by a law which limits loss deductions from most farming operations to "risk capital." The discussion of this limitation is at ¶28.04.

If your farm losses exceed your other income, *see* ¶5.20.

A guide to reporting farm income and loss may be obtained at your local Internal Revenue office or from your County Farm Agent. It is called Farmer's Tax Guide (Publication No. 225).

¶8.02 • ACCOUNTING FOR FARM INCOME

Farmers may choose between the cash method (*see* ¶2.07 and ¶5.01) or the accrual method (*see* ¶2.07 and ¶5.01). However, farming corporations (except S corporations and certain single- and multi-family corporations) or farming partnerships in which a corporation is a partner must use the accrual method if they have gross annual receipts in excess of one million dollars. Farmers, nurserymen and florists on the accrual method and who are not required to capitalize preproductive period expenses need not inventory growing crops. The term "growing crop" does not include trees grown for lumber, pulp, or other nonlife purposes.

Deferring income. Cash basis farmers who use middlemen, such as a cooperative, grain elevator, or cotton gin to sell their crops should check the middleman's status where planning to defer tax on the sale. If the middleman receives payment in the year of sale and is considered the agent of the farmer, the proceeds are taxable in the year of sale, even if the middleman does not turn over the proceeds until the following year.

A court allowed a cash basis farmer to defer income under a deferred payment contract with a cattle dealer until the sales proceeds were received in a later year. The IRS announced it will not follow the decision. Instead, it will tax sales proceeds in the year of sale.

A farmer's gross income does not include the value of produce consumed by the farmer and his family. However, expenses relating to such produce are not deductible.

Payments received under certain federal or state cost-sharing conservation programs are not taxed. However, no deduction, depreciation, amortization, or investment credit can be claimed for any expenditure made with cost-sharing funds. Also, the basis of any property acquired with cost-sharing payments may not include such payments. When property that was acquired or improved with cost-sharing payments is sold, part or all of the gain is ordinary income, depending on the holding period of the property. *See* Treasury regulations for further details.

Prepaid expenses. Individual cash basis farmers may generally deduct prepaid feed expenses in the year of payment if the payment has a business purpose, is not a refundable deposit, and the deduction does not materially distort income.

Farm syndicates are subject to stricter deduction limitations. *See* ¶8.09. Further, according to Congressional committee reports, individuals whose farming activities are operated for tax avoidance purposes are subject to the syndicate restrictions, as explained at ¶8.09.

A cash basis tax shelter generally may not deduct an expense any earlier than the time that an accrual basis taxpayer may deduct the expense under the economic performance test. *See* ¶5.01. Thus, a cash basis shelter may not deduct a prepaid expense unless economic performance has occurred. However, expenses may be deductible in the taxable year of prepayment provided economic performance occurs within 90 days after the close of the year. Further, the 90-day exception applies only if the prepayment has a business purpose, is not a deposit and does not materially distort income. The deduction for prepaid expenses under this 90-day exception is generally limited to a taxpayer's cash investment in the tax shelter plus loans that are not secured by the shelter investment and loans not arranged by the organizer or promoter. Finally, these accounting rules are applied after the farm syndicate rules. *See* ¶8.09 for details.

¶8.03 • FORMS FARMERS FILE

Use Schedule F to report income from a farm you operate as an individual. The profit or loss computed on Schedule F is then included in Form 1040. Schedule F is also used as a basis for figuring self-employment tax on Schedule SE, which must also be filed with Form 1040. Sales of farm equipment and dairy or breeding livestock are reported on Form 4797.

If you operate through a partnership, the details of your farm operation are shown on Schedule F and Form 1065. Your share of the partnership net income or loss is included in Form 1040.

Individual farmers on a calendar year basis (ending December 31) may file a 1986 declaration of estimated tax by January 15, 1987 if at least two-thirds of 1986 estimated gross income is from farming, or if at least two-thirds of 1985 total gross income was from farming. A final return is required by April 15, 1987. However, you may file your final return by March 1, 1987 instead of filing a 1986 declaration of estimated tax in January.

If you are on a fiscal year (any year not ending on December 31), ask your District Director for filing rules.

¶8.04 • FARMERS' SOCIAL SECURITY

Farmers follow special rules for figuring their self-employment income and tax. If your gross income from farming is not more than $2,400, you may figure your self-employment income in either of two ways:

You may reduce your self-employment income by your allowable deductions (as any other self-employed person would do), and pay the self-employment tax on the difference; or

You may consider your net self-employment income from farming to be two-thirds of your gross farming income.

If your gross income from farming is more than $2,400 but your net self-employment income (figuring it in the usual manner by reducing gross income by the farm's expenses) is less than $1,600, you may take the net amount or $1,600 as self-employment income.

Self-employment tax on farm income is figured on Schedule SE. See also ¶5.62.

Treasury regulations and IRS Publication 225 should be consulted for the computation of self-employment income of share-farmers and landlords.

¶8.06 • DEDUCTION OF LAND DEVELOPMENT COSTS AND RECAPTURE

A farmer may elect to deduct certain capital expenses such as land clearing and soil and water conservation costs. (The details of the election may be found in the "Farmers Tax Guide.") Where this election is made and the land is sold within a ten-year period, all or part of the expense deductions are recaptured as ordinary income. That is, gain on the sale of the land is treated as ordinary income up to the amount of expenses deducted after 1969 according to these percentages:

Land disposed of was held for:	Costs recaptured:
5 or less years	100%
6	80
7	60
8	40
9	20
10	0

There is no recapture on the sale of land held for ten years or more.

For further details of how the recapture is computed, see your local District Director or Treasury regulations.

¶8.07 • CITRUS, ALMOND GROVE DEVELOPMENT COSTS

You must capitalize amounts spent for planting, cultivation, maintenance, or development of any citrus grove within the period of four taxable years beginning with the tax year in which the trees are planted. The rule does not apply to costs of replanting a grove damaged or destroyed by a casualty. Similar rules apply to development costs of almond groves.

For the treatment of development costs incurred by syndicates, see ¶8.09.

The IRS has ruled that the cost of an irrigation system installed after April 17, 1983 for the development of a citrus grove may not be depreciated until the year the grove first produces crops.

¶8.08 • CROP INSURANCE PROCEEDS

Where a farmer on the cash basis receives insurance proceeds in compensation for damaged crops, he may elect to report the proceeds as income in the year after the year of damage. To make the election, he must show that the income from the crops would normally have been reported in the following year. A statement, attached to the return, must identify the crops damaged, the cause and date of the damage, the name of the insurer and amount of insurance paid, and a declaration that income from the crops would normally have been reported in the following year. An election of a farmer who merely noted on his return that insurance proceeds were "deferred" was invalid until he filed a timely amended return providing the statement.

Crop disaster payments. An election may be made for crop disaster payments provided they were made as a result of: (1) destruction or damage to crops caused by drought, flood or other natural disaster, or (2) the inability to plant crops because of a natural disaster.

¶8.085 • SALES OF LIVESTOCK

Sale of livestock because of drought. If drought conditions force a cash basis farmer whose principal business is farming to sell more livestock than he normally would have, he may elect to postpone reporting proceeds from the excess sales until the year after the year of sale. A special rule applies to drought sales of draft, breeding or dairy livestock; *see* below. Deferral is limited to the income from sales that exceed the number of livestock that would have been sold had the farmer followed his usual business practice. The excess sales must have been due to the drought and the drought area must have been designated as eligible for federal assistance. To make the election, a statement must be attached to the return for the year of sale which provides evidence of the drought condition and which indicates sales for the previous three years, the sales that would have been made absent the drought and the actual sales. A separate explanation must be made for each class of livestock for which an election is made, such as cattle or hogs.

If because of drought more sales of draft, breeding, or dairy livestock are made than under usual business practice, gain on the excess sales may be deferred under the rules of involuntary exchanges at ¶18.21. By purchasing new livestock within a two-year period, part or all of the gain on the excess sales may be postponed. To postpone gain, a statement must be attached to the return for the year of sale which provides evidence of the drought conditions and indicates how many fewer livestock would have been sold absent the drought.

Pregnant livestock. To create a line of purebred cattle some companies purchase purebred cows and have them artificially inseminated by purebred bulls. The embryos are surgically removed and implanted in non-purebred cows, which are then sold to farmers interested in obtaining the purebred offspring.

A farmer who purchases an implanted cow pays mostly for the value of the embryo calf. For example, a pregnant cow costing $2,500 might be worth only $800 without the implant. To figure gain or loss on the sale of the cows and calves, an allocation of cost must be made. One farmer allocated his entire cost to the cows in order to deduct a loss on their sale. He purchased 10 cows at $2,500 each and after birth sold them for $800 each. He deducted a $17,000 ordinary loss ($25,000 − $8,000). The IRS barred the loss by allocating the $25,000 cost for the pregnant cows between the cows and the embryo calves. Based on fair market value, an $8,000 cost was allocated to the cows. Thus, on the resale of or $8,000 there was no gain or loss. The 10 calves have a cost basis of $17,000 or $1,700 each.

¶8.09 • LIMITATIONS ON PREPAYMENT DEDUCTIONS FROM FARMING SYNDICATES AND FARM TAX SHELTERS

To discourage farm syndicates from offering tax shelter packages featuring large deductions for prepaid expenses and other costs, these general rules apply: (1) Farming syndicates must deduct expenses for feed, seed, fertilizer, and other farm supplies only when used or consumed, not when paid; (2) they must capitalize the costs of poultry; and (3) they must capitalize the costs of planting, cultivating, maintaining and developing a grove, orchard, or vineyard which are incurred before the year the grove, orchard, or vineyard becomes productive.

A farming syndicate includes a partnership or any other enterprise (other than a corporation which has not elected S corporation treatment) engaged in the business of farming if:

1. At any time interests in the organization have been offered for sale in an offering required to be registered with any federal or state agency having authority to regulate the offering of securities for sale, *or*

2. More than 35% of the losses during any period are allocable to limited partners or limited entrepreneurs. In general, a limited entrepreneur is a person who has an interest in an enter-

prise other than a partnership and who does not actively participate in the management of the enterprise.

Whether a person actively participates in the operation or management of a farm is an issue of fact.

Special rules (not discussed in this book) may except a person from being treated as a limited partner or entrepreneur when he has been active in farming for five years or more.

As explained in ¶8.02, a cash basis tax shelter may generally not deduct prepaid expenses any earlier than the year in which economic performance occurs. A deduction is allowed in the year of prepayment if economic performance occurs within 90 days after the end of the year. However, if a deduction for prepaid expenses is barred under the above farm syndicate rules, the 90-day exception to the economic performance test may not be taken advantage of. For example, a calendar year farm syndicate prepays feed expenses in December 1986; the feed is consumed in February 1987. Although the feed is consumed within 90 days of the end of 1986, and is within the exception to the economic performance test (¶8.02), the deduction may not be taken until 1987

because the farm syndicate rules take priority. However, if the farming tax shelter had prepaid rent in December 1986 for the first three months of 1987, the deduction would be allowed in 1986; the farm syndicate rules do not apply to prepaid rent and thus the 90-day exception applies.

Individual farm tax shelters. According to Congressional committee reports, the above deduction rules may apply to certain individual farming operations as well as to syndicates. If an individual's farming activities are considered to be a tax shelter with a principal purpose of tax avoidance, the prepayment restrictions apply. The committee reports state that the restrictions should apply where a farmer does not actively participate in the management of a farm and where the farming activity is conducted under a marketed arrangement that promotes tax benefits. In a marketed arrangement, common managerial or administrative services are provided to individual farmers. If they prepay a substantial part of their expenses with borrowed funds, their operation may be considered to have a principal purpose of tax avoidance.

¶9.00

Income from Rents and Royalties

Illustrations of reporting rental income and expenses may be found in the Supplement to YOUR INCOME TAX. Mail the card at the front of this book for your FREE Supplement, which includes filled-in returns and last-minute information.

Rental Income and Deductions

¶9.01 • REPORTING RENT INCOME

On the cash basis, you report rent income on your tax return for the year in which you receive payment.

On the accrual basis, you report income on your tax return for the year in which you are entitled to receive payment. You do not report accrued income if the financial condition of the tenant makes collection doubtful. If you sue for payment, you do not report income until you win a collectible judgment.

Advance rentals. Advance rentals or bonuses are reported in the year received, whether you are on the cash or accrual basis.

Payment of landlord's expenses. The tenant's payment of your taxes, interest, insurance, mortgage amortization (even if you are not personally liable on the mortgage), repairs, or other charges is considered additional rental income to you.

Insurance proceeds for loss of rental income because of fire or other casualty are ordinary income.

A tenant's payment for canceling a lease or modifying its terms

is ordinary income when received. You may deduct expenses incurred because of the cancellation and any unamortized balance of expenses paid in negotiating the lease.

Security deposits. Distinguish advance rentals, which are income, from security deposits, which are not. Security deposits are amounts deposited with you solely as security for the tenant's performance of the terms of his lease, and as such are usually not taxed, particularly where local law treats security deposits as trust funds. If the tenant breaches the lease, you are entitled to apply the sum as rent, at which time you report it as income.

Improvements by tenants. You do not realize taxable income when your tenant improves the leased premises, provided the improvements are not substitute rent payments. Furthermore, when you take possession of the improvements at the time the lease ends, you do not realize income. However, you may not depreciate the value of the improvements as the basis to you is considered zero.

Where to report rent income. Rental income and expenses are reported on Schedule E (*see* Supplement to Your Income Tax). You also file Form 4562 to claim ACRS deductions. If you are in the real estate business, rental income and expenses are reported on Schedule C. You are in the real estate business when you provide additional services for the convenience of the tenants, such as maid service. Payments received for the use and occupancy of rooms or other areas in a boarding house, apartment, tourist home, motel, or trailer court where services are provided primarily for the occupant are also reported on Schedule C.

See ¶9.12 for the treatment of deferred rental agreements.

¶9.02 • CHECKLIST OF DEDUCTIONS FROM RENT INCOME

Real estate taxes. But special assessments for paving, sewer or other local improvements are not deductible; they are added to the cost of the land. *See* ¶16.05 through ¶16.08 for real estate tax deductions.

Depreciation. *See* ¶5.35.

Management expenses.

Maintenance expenses: Heating, repairs, lighting, water, electricity, gas, telephone, coal, and other service costs.

Salaries and wages paid to superintendents, janitors, elevator operators, service and maintenance personnel.

Traveling expenses to look after the properties.

Legal expenses for dispossessing tenants. But expenses of long-term leases are capital expenditures deductible over the term of the lease.

Interest on mortgages and other indebtedness. But expenses and fees for securing loans are capital expenditures.

Commissions paid to collect rentals. But commissions paid to secure long-term rentals must be deducted over the life of the lease. Commissions paid to acquire the property are capitalized.

Premiums for fire, liability, plate glass insurance. If payment is made in one year for insurance covering a period longer than one year, you amortize and deduct the premium over the life of the policy, even though you are on a cash basis.

Premium paid to secure a release from a mortgage in order to get a new loan.

Construction period interest and taxes may have to be amortized, *see* ¶16.02.

If expenses exceed income, the net loss reduces your income from other sources. If the loss exceeds other income, *see* ¶5.20.

If you rent your property to a friend or relative for less than the fair rental value, you may deduct expenses and depreciation only to the extent of the rent income (*see* ¶29.42).

Deduction limitations on rental expenses of vacation home and partly rented residence, *see* ¶29.40 and ¶29.42.

Co-tenants. One of two tenants in common may deduct only half of the maintenance expenses although he pays the entire bill. A tenant in common who pays all of the expenses of the common property is entitled to reimbursement from the other co-tenant. So one-half of the bill is not his ordinary and necessary expense. Each co-tenant owns a separate property interest in the common property which produces separate income for each. Each tenant's deductible expense is that portion of the entire expense which each separate interest bears to the whole, and no more.

The Tax Court rejected the above rule for co-tenants in a case involving the deduction of real estate taxes. According to the court, the deductibility test for real estate taxes is whether the payment satisfies a personal liability or protects a beneficial interest in the property. In the case of co-tenants, nonpayment of taxes by the other co-tenants could result in the property being lost or foreclosed. To prevent this, a co-tenant who pays the tax is protecting his beneficial interest and so is entitled to deduct the payment of the full tax.

Costs of canceling lease. A landlord may pay the tenant to cancel an unfavorable lease. The way the payment is treated depends on the reason for the cancellation. If the purpose of the cancellation is to enable the landlord to construct a new building in place of the old, the cancellation payment is added to the basis of the new building. If the purpose is to sell the property, the payment is added to the cost of the property. If the landlord wants the premises for his own use, the payment is deducted over the remaining term of the old lease. If the landlord gets a new tenant to replace the old one, the cancellation payment is also generally deductible over the remaining term of the old lease.

Example—

Handlery Hotels, Inc. had to pay its lessee $85,000 to terminate a lease on a building three years before the lease term expired. Handlery entered into a new 20-year lease at more favorable terms with another lessee. Handlery amortized the $85,000 cancellation payment over the three-year unexpired term of the old lease. The IRS claimed that the payment had to be amortized over the 20-year term of the new lease because it was part of the cost of obtaining the new lease. A federal district court agreed with the IRS, but an appeals court sides with Handlery. Since the unexpired lease term is the major factor in determining the amount of the cancellation payment, the cost of cancellation should be amortized over that unexpired term.

¶9.021 • DISTINGUISH BETWEEN A REPAIR AND AN IMPROVEMENT

Maintenance and repair expenses are not treated the same as expenses for improvements and replacements. Only maintenance and incidental repair costs are deductible against rental income. Repairs that add to the value or prolong the life of the property are capital improvements. They may not be deducted but may be added to the basis of the property.

Example—

The costs of painting the outside of a building used for business purposes and the costs of papering and painting the inside are repair costs and may be deducted. The replacement of a roof or a change in the plumbing system is a nondeductible capital expenditure which may be added to the basis of the property.

Repairs may not be separated from capital expenditures when part of an improvement program.

Example—

Jones buys a dilapidated business building and has the building renovated and repaired. The total cost comes to about $13,000, of which $7,800 is deducted as repairs. But the repair deduction is disallowed because it is a capital expenditure. When a general improvement program is undertaken, you may not separate repairs from improvements. They become an integral part of the overall betterment and a capital investment, although they could be characterized as repairs when viewed independently.

What if the repairs and improvements are unconnected and not part of an overall improvement program? Assume you repair the floors of one story and improve another story by cutting new windows. You may probably deduct the cost of repairing the floors provided you have separate bills for the jobs. To safeguard the deduction, schedule the work at separate times so that the two jobs are not lumped together as an overall improvement program.

¶9.03 • SALE OF A LEASE

A profit realized on the assignment of a lease to a third party is taxed at capital gain rates. If your landlord pays you a bonus to cancel your lease, your profits are similarly taxable at capital gain rates. *See also* ¶6.03.

¶9.04 • DEDUCTING COST OF DEMOLISHING A BUILDING

When you buy improved property, the purchase price is allocated between the land and the building; only the building may be depreciated; the land may not (*see* ¶5.31). If you later demolish the building you may not deduct the cost of the demolition or the undepreciated basis of the building as a loss in the year of demolition. In taxable years beginning after 1983, expenses or losses in connection with the demolition of any structure, including certified historic structures, are not deductible. They must be capitalized and added to the basis of the land on which the structure is located.

In taxable years beginning before 1984, whether a demolition loss was allowed generally depended on whether you bought the property with the intention of demolishing the building. If you purchased with the intent to demolish the building, the entire purchase price was attributed to the land and no part to the building. Since the building was given no basis, there was no loss when it was demolished. The costs of demolition were added to the basis of the new property.

¶9.05 · DEDUCTING THE COST OF A BUSINESS LEASE

The cost of buying a business lease is amortized over the term of the lease. If you have an option to renew, you may have to add the renewed term to the original term in amortizing your cost. This means that your annual deduction will be smaller because the cost is spread over additional years. Unless you can prove you will probably not renew the lease, you must add the renewal term to the original term if less than 75% of the cost of the lease is attributed to the original term of the lease. For example, you pay $10,000 for a 20-year lease with two renewal options of five years each. You add the renewal term if the cost attributed to the 20-year period is less than $7,500. However, even when 75% or more of the cost of the lease is attributed to the original term, the IRS may add in the renewal period by showing there is a reasonable certainty of your renewal. If you are related to the landlord, the IRS will probably charge there is a reasonable certainty of renewal.

Allocating costs under the percentage test. The 75% test requires allocating leasehold costs to the original term and the renewal terms. Check Treasury regulations for further details.

¶9.06 · HOW LESSEES DEDUCT FOR LEASEHOLD IMPROVEMENTS

Each year, you write off a part of the cost of an improvement which you have constructed on leased business property. As a general rule, you deduct the cost of your improvements over the *shorter* of the following periods:

The useful life of the improvement (in this case, you recover cost by depreciation); *or*

The remaining term of the lease (in this case, you recover cost by amortization).

> The distinction between amortization and depreciation is important for this reason: When amortizing, you may use only the straight line method. When depreciating, you may be able to use an accelerated method of depreciation.

If you have an option to renew the lease, you may have to add the renewal period to the remaining term of the lease to make the above comparison with the useful life of the improvement. But you do this only when the useful life of the improvement exceeds the original term of the lease. If the useful life is less than the original term, it is not necessary to determine if the renewal period is to be added. The improvement is depreciable over its useful life because, in any event, the useful life will be less than the original term or the original term plus the renewal period. If the useful life of the improvement exceeds the original term of the lease but is less than the original term plus the renewal period, the improvement is depreciated over its useful life. If the useful life exceeds the original term plus the renewal period, the improvement is amortized over the period of the original and renewal term of the lease. A percentage test is used to determine whether a renewal is intended. You include a renewal period if the remaining term of the original lease at the completion of an improvement is less than 60% of the useful life of the improvement.

¶9.11 · INVESTMENT CREDIT FOR REHABILITATING OLD AND HISTORICAL BUILDINGS

An investment credit may be claimed for the expenses of rehabilitating old nonresidential buildings and certified historic structures. The amount of the credit is as follows:

If structure is—	Credit, based on rehabilitation costs, is—
30 to 39 years old	15%
40 years old or older	20
A certified historic structure	25

Buildings must be used for nonresidential purposes to qualify for the 15% or 20% credit. Certified historic structures eligible for the 25% credit may be residential or nonresidential.

The rehabilitation must be substantial, which means that expenditures of the present and prior tax years must exceed the greater of $5,000 or the adjusted basis of the building.

The Secretary of the Interior must approve rehabilitation of certified historic structures before the credit may be claimed.

The credit may be claimed only if an election is made to use the straight line method instead of the accelerated cost recovery deduction. For further details, *see* Treasury regulations.

Basis reduction. The basis of property for which the 15% or 20% credit is claimed is reduced by 100% of the credit. If the 25% credit is claimed, basis is reduced by one-half the credit.

¶9.12 · DEFERRED OR STEPPED-UP RENTAL AGREEMENTS

Cash basis lessors and accrual basis lessees through the use of deferred rental or stepped-up rental leases were able to coordinate tax savings benefits. Stepped-up rentals are rent payments that substantially increase during the later period of a lease. In effect, rent for the early years is deferred and repaid with interest in the later years. Through such an arrangement, a cash basis lessor did not report rent income until the year of payment while the accrual basis tenant deducted the rent by accruals to the rental period.

To prevent this type of planning, a law imposes uniform reporting for both the lessor and lessee regardless of their accounting basis if the rental agreement is within the terms of a new Code Section 467. A Section 467 rental agreement is any agreement which provides for stepped-up rents or defers rent for use of the property until after the close of the year following the year of rental use. Section 467 does not apply if the total rental payments are $250,000 or less. It also does not apply to agreements entered into before June 9, 1984 or to later agreements pursuant to a binding written contract made on or before June 8, 1984.

The lessor and lessee of a "Section 467 rental agreement" must report rental income or expense under the accrual basis and report imputed interest based on the deferred rent. The calculation of imputed interest is similar to the 110% rule of ¶4.11.

> If the rental agreement allocates rent, rent accruals may be based on the agreement. However, rents payable after the end of the rental period are accounted for according to their present value.

Stricter accrual rules apply: (1) if the agreement does not allocate rents; (2) the lease term exceeds 75% of the ACRS recovery period for such property; or (3) the agreement is considered a disqualified leaseback. In these cases, rents are "leveled" under a constant accrual method.

There is also a recapture provision preventing capital gain treatment when a sale is made by a lessor who has made certain leasebacks or long-term rental agreements.

A special rent reporting rule applies where there was a firm plan as of March 15, 1984 to enter into a lease and construction of the property began before March 16, 1984.

Royalty Income and Deductions

¶9.15 • REPORTING ROYALTY INCOME

Royalties are payment for use of patents or copyrights or for the use and exhaustion of mineral properties; royalties are taxable as ordinary income and are reported in Schedule E (Form 1040). If you own an operating oil, gas, or mineral interest, or are a self-employed writer, investor, or artist, you report royalty income and expenses in Schedule C.

Examples of royalty income—

License fees received for use, manufacture, or sale of patented article. *See* ¶6.036 for capital gain opportunities.

Renting fees received from patents, copyrights and depletable assets (such as oil wells).

Authors' royalties including advance royalties if not a loan.

Royalties for musical compositions, works of art, etc.

Proceeds of sale of part of your rights in an artistic composition or book—for example, sale of motion picture or television rights.

Royalties from oil, gas, or other similar interests (*see* ¶9.16).

Lessee's payment of taxes on mineral property.

If you give up all your rights in the property from which you earn royalty income, the amounts received are reported as payments from the sale of property, not as royalty income.

¶9.16 • HOW OIL AND GAS ROYALTIES ARE TAXED

In the development of oil and gas wells, complex arrangements are usually made among several parties. The following paragraphs provide a general outline of arrangements which require the advice and review of a tax practitioner experienced in oil and gas taxation.

Generally, an owner of property on which oil is deposited leases his property for a one-eighth royalty interest in the production of oil from his tract. The royalty, called an underlying royalty, may be measured by either a percentage of production or a stated sum per unit extracted or sold. It is taxed to the owner of the property as ordinary income and is entitled to a depletion deduction (*see* ¶9.17 and ¶9.171). If the lease payments are not tied to oil and gas extraction, no royalty has been created.

Bonus or advance royalty. Sometimes, in addition to the royalty payment, a lump-sum payment or bonus may be paid. This amount is also taxed as an ordinary royalty payment subject to depletion even though the transaction may be described as a sale or viewed as such under local law. Before production begins, percentage depletion may be claimed on advance royalties and bonuses. If the lease term expires without production, previously claimed depletion deductions must be reported as taxable income in the year the lease ends.

Do not confuse an advance royalty payment with a delayed rental payment which is paid for the privilege of postponing the development of the property. Delayed rentals not geared to production are not subject to depletion. A delayed rental is usually paid for deferring the development of the property for a period of not more than a year.

The lessee (or assignee) who has undertaken to pay the one-eighth royalty interest in the production to the owner may, in turn, carve out additional interests from his interest, such as an overriding royalty or an oil payment or a carried interest or a net profits interest.

An overriding royalty is taxed as an ordinary royalty entitled to depletion. The lessee, in receiving an overriding royalty, is in a position similar to that of the owner-lessor. If he, too, receives an advance cash payment in addition to the overriding royalty, this payment is also treated as a royalty, not as a sale.

Oil payments or production payments are royalties limited to a set amount. The limit may be based on a number of barrels of oil or a sum of money to be paid out of a part of the oil produced. A distinction must be made between royalty and oil payment

agreements. When an advance cash payment is made with an oil payment, the cash payment is treated as a sale and entitled to capital gain treatment. Gain is computed by allocating the basis of the leasehold between the part sold (cash payment) and the part retained (oil payment), according to their fair market values. Capital gain treatment on the advance cash payment will be questioned by the IRS.

To prove a sale of an oil payment rather than an overriding royalty, you have to show engineering estimates that reveal there will be a substantial reserve left after the payment for your interest. If the assignment involves both an oil payment and an overriding royalty, then the entire deal is viewed as an overriding royalty. Thus, any advance cash payment is taxed as ordinary income rather than capital gain.

An oil or production payment may be either a carved-out payment or a retained payment. A carved-out payment is created when an owner of oil property sells a part of his future production. A retained payment is created when an owner sells his working interest but reserves a production payment for himself. Generally, the retained production payment is sold to a bank. The creation of oil or production payments is treated as a mortgage loan transaction. This rule has the following effect: A seller of a carved-out payment may not treat the proceeds in payment for the interest as income in order to create his income base on which to compute percentage depletion if such depletion is applicable (*see* ¶9.171). However, an exception is made where the oil payment is carved out for exploration or development provided income is not realized by the creator of the interest on the transaction. In the case of a retained payment, the payments made by the owner of mineral interests are treated as payments on a mortgage debt and therefore are not considered as deductions from income. Also, the receipt of payments by the holder of the production payment is not considered income on which percentage depletion, if applicable, may be claimed. A production payment that is retained by a lessor is treated by the lessee as a bonus. The lessee capitalizes the bonus which is recovered through depletion. The lessor may treat the production payment as income subject to percentage depletion.

Net profits payments are based on fixed percentage of net profits from operations. The lessee tranfers his entire interest to an operator. The lessee reserves a share of net profits realized by the operator who agrees to develop the well and pay all operating expenses. This arrangement has been subject to conflicting tax opinions of whether it gives rise to a sale or is a royalty deal involving a sublease. Current tax authorities approach the arrangement as a sublease so that net profit interest is subject to depletion.

Similar to a net profits arrangement is a carried interest agreement between two co-lessees. In practice, though carried interest agreements may vary in form and detail, they usually follow this pattern: Co-lessee A has sufficient funds with which to drill and develop a well. Co-lessee B does not. So, A agrees to pay all the costs. In return, he will recover B's share of the costs from B's share of the oil if produced. A is called the carrying party and B the carried party. There is a conflict over how these interests should be taxed. The decisions say that the carried party (B) should report his share of the income. The IRS, however, holds that the carrying party (A) should report all the income until his advances are repaid.

"At risk" limitation rules may also apply to the above investments. *See* ¶28.04.

¶9.161 • INTANGIBLE DRILLING COSTS

Deducting intangible drilling costs. Intangible drilling and development costs may be deducted as current expenses or treated as capital expenditures. They include wages, fuel, repairs, hauling and supplies incident to and necessary for the drilling of wells and the preparation of wells for the production of oil or gas and geothermal wells.

The election applies only to costs of drilling and developing items, exclusive of depreciable items that do not have a salvage value. You must make this election in your income tax return for the first tax year in which you pay or incur the costs.

Tax shelter investors may deduct prepayments of drilling expenses made after March 31, 1984 only if the well is "spudded" within 90 days after the close of the taxable year in which the prepayment is made. The prepayment must also have a business purpose, not be a deposit and not materially distort income. The investor's deduction is limited to his cash investment in the tax shelter. For purposes of this limitation, an investor's cash investment includes loans that are not secured by his shelter interest or the shelter's assets and loans that are not arranged by the organizer or promoter. If the above tests are not met, a deduction may be claimed only as actual drilling services are provided.

Recapture of intangible drilling costs for oil, gas, or geothermal property. Deductions previously claimed for intangible drilling expenses and development costs on productive wells are subject to ordinary income treatment upon disposition of a working or operating interest in oil and gas property. The amounts are treated as ordinary income to the extent that the deduction exceeded what would have been allowed if the intangible costs had been capitalized and deducted through cost depletion. In no event may the amount recaptured exceed the gain upon the disposition of the property. The recapture rule for geothermal property applies only to wells commenced after September 30, 1978.

Special allocation rules apply when you dispose of less than your entire interest.

Proposed Treasury regulations explain how the recapture provisions apply to sales of partnership interests and stock in S corporations. The regulations exempt certain dispositions from the recapture provisions, such as gifts, transfers at death, and transfers in certain tax-free incorporations and reorganization.

Certain intangible drilling costs are also treated as tax preference items subject to alternative minimum tax. *See* ¶23.10.

¶9.17 • DEPLETION DEDUCTION

Properties subject to depletion deductions are mines, oil and gas wells, timber, and exhaustible natural deposits.

You claim depletion deductions if you are an operating owner or an owner of an economic interest in mineral deposits in place or standing timber. You have an economic interest when your return of capital depends on income received from the extraction of minerals or the cutting of timber (*see* ¶9.16 above).

Two methods of computing depletion are: (1) Cost depletion, and (2) percentage depletion. If you are allowed to compute under either method, you must use the one that produces the larger deduction. In most cases, this will be percentage depletion.

Cost depletion. Cost depletion of minerals is computed as follows: (1) Divide the total number of units (tons, barrels, etc.) remaining in the deposit to be mined into the adjusted basis of the property. (2) Multiply the unit rate found in step 1 by the number of units for which payment is received during the taxable year if you are on the cash basis.

Adjusted basis is the original cost of the property, less depletion allowed, whether computed on the percentage or cost depletion method. It does not include nonmineral property such as mining equipment. Adjusted basis may not be less than zero.

Timber depletion is based on the cost of timber (or other basis in the owner's hands) and does not include any part of the cost of land. Depletion takes place when standing timber is cut. Depletion must be computed by the cost method, not by the percentage method. For further details, *see* Treasury regulations.

Percentage depletion. Percentage depletion is based on a certain percentage rate applied to annual gross income derived from the resource, with certain limitations discussed below. A deduction for percentage depletion is allowed even if the basis of the property

is already fully recovered by prior depletion deductions. However, the excess of depletion deductions over the basis at the end of the year (without regard to the current year's deduction) is an item of tax preference (*see* ¶23.10). The percentage to be applied depends upon the mineral involved; the range is from 5% up to 22%.

Restrictions on the application of percentage depletion for gas and oil property are discussed at ¶9.171.

In figuring percentage depletion, rents and royalties paid for the property are not included in gross income. If you are a lessee, gross income distributed to the lessor is also excluded from your gross income. Gross income from oil and gas property is the amount received from the sale of oil or gas in the immediate vicinity of the well. If you manufacture or convert the oil or gas into a refined product for sale or transport it before sale, gross income is the market price or field price of the oil or gas at the wellhead as of the date of sale, before the conversion or transportation. The percentage depletion deduction may not exceed 50% of taxable income from the property computed without the depletion deduction. In computing the 50% limitation, a net operating loss deduction is not deducted from gross income.

¶9.171 • PERCENTAGE DEPLETION EXEMPTIONS FOR GAS AND OIL PRODUCERS

Percentage depletion for oil and gas wells was repealed as of January 1, 1975, except for exemptions allowed (1) small independent producers and royalty owners, and (2) for gas well production. The independent owner exemption is not generally available to transfers of proven oil and gas interests made after 1974. Advanced royalties received by independent producers are eligible for percentage depletion. The following discussion covers only the general pattern of the restrictions on percentage depletion.

Small independent producers and royalty owner exemption. A 15% rate applies to the extent that average daily production does not exceed certain daily rate exemptions fixed by the law. The daily rate production (called depletable oil quantity exemption) is fixed at 1,000 barrels of oil a day and 6,000,000 cubic feet of gas a day. Your total production is averaged over the entire year to reach the daily rate regardless of when production actually occurred. Where you have both oil and natural gas production, the exemption is allocated between the oil and natural gas production.

Average daily production of oil is found by dividing your aggregate production during the taxable year by the number of days in the taxable year. If you hold a partial interest in the production (including a partnership interest), production rate is found by multiplying total production of such property by your income percentage participation in such property.

The depletable natural gas quantity depends on an election made annually by independent producers or royalty owners to have crude oil treated as natural gas. The depletable quantity of natural gas is 6,000 cubic feet times the barrels of depletable oil for which an election has been made. The election is made on an original or amended return or on a claim for credit or refund. The election applies to secondary or tertiary production, subject to a limitation found in Treasury regulations.

65% taxable income test limit. Percentage depletion may not exceed 50% of the taxable income from the property. Further, the depletion deduction for a small producer or royalty owner is subject to this additional limitation. The deduction attributable to the application of the exemption may not exceed 65% of your taxable income computed without regard to depletion deduction allowed under the small producer's exemption and net operating loss carryback. Trusts may compute the 65% of taxable income limitation without regard to any deduction for distributions to beneficiaries.

If your average daily production exceeds the above exemption limit, the exemption must be allocated among all the properties in which you have an interest.

Secondary or tertiary production. There is no longer a distinction between primary and secondary or tertiary production. The 15% depletion rate applies to up to 1,000 barrels of all production.

However, percentage depletion may not be claimed for secondary or tertiary production from proven properties transferred after 1974 unless one of the exceptions discussed below applies.

Limitations where family members or related businesses own interests. The daily depletable oil quantity rate is allocated among members of the same family in proportion to their respective production of oil. Similar allocation is required where business entities are under common control. This affects interests owned by you, your spouse and minor children; by corporations, estates and trusts in which 50% of the beneficial interest is owned by the same or related persons; and by a corporation which is a member of the same controlled group.

Transfers of oil or gas property after 1974. No depletion exemption is allowed for a transfer (including the subleasing of a lease) after December 31, 1974, of an interest (including an interest in a partnership or trust) in any proven oil or gas property. A property is treated as a proven oil or gas property if, at the time of the transfer, the principal value of the property has been demonstrated by prospecting or exploration or discovery work. This limitation does not apply to a transfer of property at death, or certain tax-free transfers between an individual and his corporation under Section 351 of the Internal Revenue Code. For taxable years beginning after December 31, 1974, oil or natural gas property is not treated as "transferred" property because of changes in beneficiaries of a trust provided the changes occur because of birth, adoption, or death involving a single family.

The small producer exemption is not allowed to any producer who owns or controls a retail outlet for the sale of oil or natural gas or petroleum products. It is also not allowed to a refiner who refines more than 50,000 barrels of oil on any one day of the taxable year. A taxpayer is not treated as a retailer where gross sales of oil and gas products are less than $5 million in any one year or if all sales of oil or natural gas products occur outside the United States, and none of the taxpayer's domestic production is exported. Bulk sales of oil or natural gas to industrial or utility customers are not to be treated as retail sales.

Gas well exemptions. The 22% depletion allowance is allowed for the following two classes: (1) domestic natural gas sold under a fixed contract in effect on February 1, 1975, (2) domestic "regulated natural gas" produced and sold before July 1, 1976.

Windfall profit tax. Holders of oil and gas interests may be subject to a windfall profit tax. Any windfall profit tax paid is deductible on Schedule E.

For 1986, up to three barrels of oil a day is exempt from the windfall profit tax. To claim the three-barrel-a-day exclusion, Form 6783 is filed with the party that withholds the tax from royalty payments. This excise tax and an exemption for oil from stripper wells are not discussed further in YOUR INCOME TAX.

¶9.18 • HOW COAL AND TIMBER ROYALTIES ARE TAXED

Royalties are usually taxed at ordinary income tax rates. However, royalties from coal and timber operations may get capital gain treatment if—

Coal royalties are received by a lessor or sublessor on coal owned long term before it was mined. Gain is the difference between the payments received and the basis of the coal sold. However, percentage depletion may not be deducted; only cost

depletion may be deducted. Capital gains are not applied to royalties received through a joint venture or partnership.

Timber royalties are received by a lessor or sublessor on timber owned long term before it was disposed of. This date of disposal is usually the date the timber was cut. However, if payment under a contract is made before this time, the date of payment may be treated as the date of disposal. Gain is the difference between the payments received and the basis of the timber sold.

¶9.19 • DO YOU HAVE A ROYALTY OR AN OUTRIGHT SALE?

Problems arise when leasing arrangements combine elements of a sale and royalty. To have a royalty, you must retain an economic interest in the minerals deposited in the land. You usually have a royalty when payments are based on the amount of minerals produced. However, if you are paid regardless of the minerals produced, you have a sale which is taxed at capital gain rates if the proceeds exceed the basis of the transferred property interest (*see also* ¶9.16).

See ¶6.039 for discussion of sales of sand or gravel.

¶9.20 • DEDUCTING THE COST OF PATENTS OR COPYRIGHTS

You may deduct costs incurred to license the property or to improve it.

Deduct depreciation over the life of the patent or copyright. Basis for depreciation includes all expenses which you are required to capitalize in connection with creating the work, such as the cost of drawings and experimental models, stationery and supplies, travel expenses to obtain material for a book, fees to counsel; government charges for patent or copyright; litigation costs in protecting or perfecting title.

If you purchased the patent or artistic creation, depreciate your cost over the remaining life of the patent or copyright.

If you inherited the patent or rights to an artistic creation, your cost is the fair market value either at the time of death of the person from whom you inherited it or the alternate valuation date if elected by the executor. You get this cost basis even if the decedent paid nothing for it. Figure your depreciation by dividing the fair market value by the number of years of remaining life.

If your patent or copyright becomes valueless, you may deduct your unrecovered cost or other basis in the year it became worthless. Abnormal obsolescence does not give rise to a loss deduction. You may, however, adjust the useful life depreciation rate to reflect such obsolescence.

¶9.21 • AMORTIZATION OF PRODUCTION COSTS

The cost of producing motion pictures, books, records, and other similar property must be amortized and deducted over the period you reasonably expect to receive substantially all of the income from the particular film, book, or record. The rate of deduction is based on the ratio of income received in the year over total income expected to be received. The rule applies to amounts paid or incurred after December 31, 1975, for properties the principal production of which begins after December 31, 1975. The rule does not apply to distribution costs.

S corporations, personal holding companies and foreign personal holding companies are subject to these rules.

"At risk" rules are discussed at ¶28.04.

¶10.00
Reporting Income from Partnerships and S Corporations

Partnership Income

¶10.01 • HOW PARTNERS REPORT PARTNERSHIP PROFIT AND LOSS

A partnership files Form 1065 which informs the IRS of partnership profit or loss and each partner's share. The partnership pays no tax on partnership income; each partner reports his or her share of partnership net profit or loss and special deductions and credits, whether or not distributions are received from the partnership. Income that is not distributed or withdrawn increases the basis of a partner's partnership interest.

Your share is generally based on your proportionate capital interest in the partnership, unless the partnership agreement provides for another allocation. The following types of items are reported by partners on their personal tax return:

Net profit or loss from the partnership activity. This is listed on Schedule E.

Dividends and interest earned on partnership investments. These are reported on Schedule B.

A partner's share of tax-exempt interest keeps its tax free status.

Capital gains and losses from the sale and exchange of partnership assets. These are listed in Schedule D.

Charitable contributions made by the partnership. These are claimed on Schedule A, if excess itemized deductions are taken.

Tax preference items (see ¶23.10).

Investment or job credit.

Credit or deduction for taxes paid to foreign countries or U.S. possessions.

Partnership elections. The partnership, not the individual partners, makes elections affecting the computation of partnership income, such as the election to defer involuntary conversion gains, to amortize organization and rehabilitation costs, and to modify ACRS depreciation. An election to claim a foreign tax credit is made by the partners.

Guaranteed salary and interest. A guaranteed salary which is fixed without regard to partnership income is reported as salary income. If you receive a percentage of the partnership income with a stipulated minimum payment, the guaranteed payment is the amount by which the minimum guarantee exceeds your share of the partnership income before taking into account the minimum guarantee.

Interest on capital is reported as interest income.

Self-employment tax. You pay self-employment tax on up to $42,000 of your partnership profits, including a guaranteed salary and other guaranteed payments. Limited partners do not pay self-employment tax. *See* ¶5.61.

Special allocations. Partners may agree to special allocations of gain, income, loss, deductions or credits disproportionate to their capital contributions. The allocation should have a substantial economic effect to avoid an IRS disallowance. The IRS will not issue an advance ruling on whether an allocation has a substantial economic effect. If the allocation is rejected, a partner's share is determined by his or her partnership interest.

To have substantial economic effect, a special allocation must be reflected by adjustments to the partner's capital account; liquidation proceeds must be distributed in accordance with the partners' capital accounts, and following a liquidating distribution, the partners must be liable to the partnership to restore any deficit in their capital.

If there is a change of partnership interests during the year, items are allocated to a partner for that part of the year he or she is a member of the partnership. Thus, a partner who acquires an interest late in the year is barred from deducting partnership expenses incurred prior to his entry into the partnership. If the partners agree to give an incoming partner a disproportionate share of partnership losses for the period after he becomes a member, the allocation must meet the substantial economic effect test to avoid IRS disallowance. *See* Treasury regulations and IRS Publication 541 for further details.

Organization expenses. The costs of organizing a partnership may be deducted ratably over a period of not less than 60 months. Organizational expenses include legal fees for the negotiation and preparation of the partnership agreement, accounting fees for establishing the partnership accounting system, and necessary filing fees. If the partnership is liquidated before the end of the 60-month period, the balance can be deducted as a loss. A partnership must make an election to amortize organization expenses on a statement attached to the partnership return for the first year of business, filed by the due date, plus extensions.

Syndication expenses are not deductible. These are the costs of issuing and marketing interests in a partnership, such as brokerage commissions, legal and accounting fees relating to tax and securities law disclosures in the offering materials, and printing costs of the prospectus and other promotional materials. Such syndication costs are nondeductible capital expenses.

Reporting transfers of interest to IRS. If you transfer a partnership interest that includes an interest in partnership receivables and appreciated inventory, you must report the disposition to the partnership within 30 days. The partnership in turn files a report with the IRS on Form 8308. You must also attach a statement to your income tax return describing the transaction and allocating basis to the receivables and inventory items. The IRS wants to keep track of such dispositions because partners have to pay ordinary income tax on the portion of profit attributable to the receivables and inventory.

Within 30 days of your transfer, provide the partnership with a statement that includes the date of the exchange and that identifies the transferee (include Social Security number of known). You can be penalized $50 for failure to notify the partnership. You and your transferee should receive a copy of the Form 8308 which the partnership will send to the IRS along with its Form 1065.

Generally, the partnership must file a separate Form 8308 for each transfer but the IRS may allow a composite Form 8308 for the calendar year if there were at least 25 reportable transfers.

¶10.02 • WHEN A PARTNER REPORTS INCOME OR LOSS

You report your share of the partnership gain or loss for the partnership year which ends in your tax reporting year. If you and the partnership are on a calendar year basis, you report your share of the 1986 partnership income on your 1986 income tax return. If the partnership is on a fiscal year ending March 31, for example, a partner (in a calendar year) reports on his 1986 return his share of the partnership income for the whole year ending March 31, 1986.

¶10.03 • PARTNERSHIP LOSS LIMITATIONS

Your share of partnership losses may not exceed the adjusted basis of your partnership interest. If the loss exceeds basis, the excess loss may not be deducted until you have partnership earnings to cover the loss or contribute capital to cover the loss. The basis of your partnership interest is generally the amount paid for the interest (either through contribution or purchase), less withdrawals plus accumulated taxed earnings that have not been withdrawn.

Partners, except those whose partnership's principal activity is real estate, are subject to the "at risk" loss limitation rules. These rules limit the amount of loss that may be deducted to the amount each partner personally has at stake in the partnership,

such as contributions of property and loans for which the partner is personally liable. *See* ¶28.04 for a discussion of the "at risk" rules.

Further, if the IRS determines that a tax shelter partnership is not operated to make a profit, deductions may be disallowed even where there is an "at risk" investment. *See* ¶28.00.

¶10.04 • UNIFIED TAX AUDITS OF PARTNERSHIPS WITH MORE THAN TEN PARTNERS

For partnership taxable years beginning after September 3, 1982, tax audits of both a partnership of more than ten partners and its partners must be at the partnership level. To challenge the partnership treatment of an item, the IRS must generally audit the partnership, not the individual partners. To avoid a personal audit of a partnership item, a partner should report partnership items as shown on the partnership return or identify any inconsistent treatment on his or her return. Otherwise the IRS may assess a deficiency without auditing the partnership.

For a partnership level audit, the partnership names a "tax matters partner" (TMP) to receive notice of the audit. If one is not named, the IRS will treat as a TMP the general partner having the largest interest in partnership profits at the end of the taxable year involved in the audit. Notice of the audit must also be given to the other partners at least 120 days before the IRS mails the TMP notice of its final determination. All partners may participate in the partnership audit. If the IRS settles with some partners, similar settlement terms must be offered to the other partners.

Within 90 days after the IRS mails its final determination, the TMP may appeal to the Tax Court; individual partners have an additional 60 days to file a court petition if the TMP does not do so. An appeal may also be filed in a federal district court or the Claims Court if the petitioning partner first deposits with the IRS an amount equal to the tax that would be owed if the IRS determination were sustained. A Tax Court petition takes precedence over petitions filed in other courts. The first Tax Court petition filed is heard; if other partners have also filed petitions, their cases will be dismissed. If no Tax Court petitions are filed, the first petition filed in federal district court or the Claims Court takes precedence. Regardless of which petition takes precedence, all partners who hold an interest during the taxable year involved will be bound by the decision (unless the statute of limitations with respect to that partner has run).

Partnerships with ten or fewer partners may elect to come within the unified audit procedures provided all of the partners are individuals or estates.

Important: The above discussion covers only the general features of partnership tax reporting. It also does not cover new law changes in other partnership areas, such as contributions of property. Specific partnership rules are complex and their implementation requires the services of an experienced tax practitioner. IRS Publication 541 has further information on partnership reporting.

S CORPORATION ELECTION

An S corporation election allows an incorporated business to avoid paying a corporate income tax, thus eliminating the double tax feature of corporate operations while retaining limited liability and other advantages of doing business as a corporation.

The S corporation files a return on Form 1120S, informing the IRS of corporate net earnings and losses and the stockholders' shares of income or loss items which they report on their personal tax returns. This tax reporting procedure is similar to that of partnerships.

An election is not advisable for an existing company which has an operating loss carryover. The loss may not be used by the corporation after the election and it may not be passed through to the stockholders. The loss may be revived if the election is

terminated. Each year the election is in force counts as a year in figuring the carryover period even though the loss has not been used.

You will generally make an S election when your personal tax rates do not exceed the corporate tax rates, when you cannot take sufficient money out of a corporation without subjecting some or all of it to the double tax, or when a special advantage is offered by an S election. For example, in the early years of the corporation's existence, substantial losses are expected. The S election allows the pass-through of operating losses to stockholders who may have substantial income from other sources to offset these losses.

Important: The following sections discuss general features of the election, the implementation and review of which require the services of an experienced tax accountant or attorney. A detailed discussion of these issues along with the particular objectives of an election may be found in tax services dealing with corporate tax problems and in IRS Publication 589.

¶10.05 • STOCKHOLDER REPORTING OF S CORPORATION INCOME AND LOSS

S corporations are subject to tax reporting rules similar to those applied to partnerships. However, shareholders who work for the corporation are treated as employees for FICA purposes. They do not pay self-employment tax on their salary income or other receipts from the corporation.

Each stockholder reports his or her share of corporate items of income and loss, deductions, and credits, as shown on Schedule K-1 of Form 1120S.

The allocation of items is based on the proportion of stock held in the corporation. If your interest changed during the year, the pro rata share must also consider on a daily basis the time you held the stock.

The following items are allocated to and pass through to the stockholders:

Gains and losses from the sale and exchange of capital assets and Section 1231 property. Each stockholder reports his or her share of capital gains and aggregates Section 1231 transactions with his or her other Section 1231 transactions, if any.

Interest and dividends on corporate investments and losses. Investment interest expenses subject to the rules of ¶15.06 also pass through.

Tax-exempt interest. Tax-exempt interest remains tax free in the hands of the stockholders but increases the basis of their stock. Dividends from other companies may qualify for the exclusion.

First-year expense deduction.

Charitable contributions made by the corporation.

Foreign income or loss.

Foreign taxes paid by the corporation. Each stockholder elects whether to claim these as a credit or deduction.

Tax preference items.

Recovery of bad debts and prior taxes.

Investment credit property. The basis of property is allocated among the stockholders who claim the credit on their personal tax returns. Each stockholder is also liable for investment credit recaptures.

If the corporation reports on a fiscal year, the stockholders report their shares of corporate items on their tax returns for the year in which the corporate tax year ends.

Basis limits loss deductions. Deductible losses may not exceed your basis in corporate stock and loans to the corporation. If losses exceed basis, the excess loss is carried over and becomes deductible when you invest or lend an equivalent amount of money to the corporation. This rule may allow for timing a loss deduction. In a year in which you want to deduct the loss, you may contribute capital to the corporation. If a carryover loss exists when an S election terminates, a limited loss deduction may be allowed.

Family corporations. The IRS has the authority to change the amounts of items passed through to stockholders to properly reflect the value of services rendered or capital contributed by family members of one or more S corporation shareholders. If you are the member of a family of an S corporation shareholder and perform services or furnish capital to the corporation without receiving reasonable compensation, the IRS may reallocate salary or interest income to you from the other shareholders to reflect the value of your services or capital. The term "family" includes only a spouse, parents, ancestors, children, and any trusts for the benefit of such relatives.

Basis adjustments. Because of the nature of S corporation reporting, the basis of each stockholder's stock is subject to change. Basis is *increased* by the passthrough of income items and *reduced* by the passthrough of loss items and the receipt of distributions.

Because income and loss items pass through to stockholders, an S corporation has no current earnings and profits. An income item will not increase basis unless you actually report the amount on your tax return. The specific details and order of basis adjustments are listed in Treasury Publication 589.

Expenses owed to shareholders. An S corporation is deemed to be on the cash method of accounting for purposes of deducting business expenses and interest owed to cash basis shareholders who own at least 2% of the corporate stock. Therefore expenses accruing to such stockholders are deductible only when paid to the stockholders.

Example—

In 1985, a calendar-year S corporation accrues $5,000 of salary to an employee-stockholder. It does not pay the salary until February 1986. In 1986, the $5,000 is deductible by the corporation and reported by the employee-shareholder as income.

An S corporation recognizes taxable gain if it distributes to a stockholder corporate property which has appreciated in value, except in the case of a complete liquidation of the corporation. Gain is also not recognized on distribution of stock in a reorganization to the extent that the receipt of stock is tax free under Sections 354, 355, or 356.

Allocating income and loss for changes in stock ownership during the year. In a year stock ownership changes, income and loss items are either allocated on a daily basis or all persons who were stockholders during the entire taxable year may elect to allocate income and loss items as if there were two short taxable years, the first year ending on the date the shareholder's interest ended. The allocation of items for each short taxable year is determined according to corporate records and workpapers. The following examples illustrate how the allocation on a daily basis is made.

Examples—

1. A calendar year corporation incurs a loss of $10,000. Smith and Jones each own 50% of the stock. On May 1, Smith sells all of his stock to Harris. For the year, Smith was a shareholder for 120 days, Jones for 365 days, and Harris for 245 days. The loss is allocated on a daily basis; the daily basis of the loss is $27.3973 ($10,000 divided by 365 days). The allocation is as follows:

Smith: $1,644 ($27.3973 × 120 days × 50% interest)
Jones: $5,000 ($27.3973 × 365 days × 50% interest)
Harris: $3,356 ($27.3973 × 245 days × 50% interest)

2. Same facts as in example 1 except that on May 1, Smith sells only 50% of his stock to Harris. The allocation for Smith accounts for his 50% interest for 120 days and his 25% interest for the remainder of the year.

Smith: $3,322 ($27.3973 × 120 days × 50% plus $27.3973 × 245 days × 25%)
Jones: $5,000 (as above)
Harris: $1,678 ($27.3973 × 245 days × 25%)

In a year in which stock ownership changes, determine tax consequences both ways: using the daily allocation method and the two short-period method. Choose the method providing the best overall tax consequences for the shareholders. Different tax results will occur, especially if substantial loss items were incurred in one short year and income items in the other short year. The daily allocation method will average the items between the two years. The short-period method basis will place the items in the period they were incurred.

¶10.06 • QUALIFYING TESTS FOR AN S ELECTION

The election may be made for a domestic corporation which is not a member of an affiliated group and which has—

1. No more than 35 stockholders, all of whom must agree to the election. For purposes of the stockholder test, a husband and wife (and their estates) are counted as one shareholder, regardless of how they hold the stock. However, when consenting to S corporation status, each spouse must separately consent. When spouses divorce, each spouse is treated as a separate stockholder, even though they own stock jointly.

For purposes of the stockholder test, each beneficiary of a voting trust is counted as a stockholder.

Each minor owning stock held by a custodian is counted. The minor, his legal or natural guardian, or custodian who is also his guardian must consent to the election. The same rule applies to incompetents.

2. Stockholders who are either U.S. citizens or residents, estates, or certain trusts. You may not make the election if a nonapproved trust, partnership, or another corporation owns stock in your company. The following trusts may be electing shareholders: (1) A trust all of which is treated for tax purposes as owned by an individual who is a U.S. citizen or resident. The trust may continue as a shareholder for a 60-day period following the death of the owner; if the entire corpus is includible in the deemed owner's gross estate, the trust may continue as a shareholder for a two-year period following the date of death. (2) A voting trust. (3) A testamentary trust which receives the stock under the terms of a will, but only for a 60-day period beginning on the day on which such stock is transferred to it. The creation of a bankruptcy estate by filing a petition for bankruptcy does not result in a nonqualified stockholding. (4) A qualified Subchapter S trust. A qualified trust is one in which all of the income is distributed currently to a beneficiary who is a U.S. citizen or resident and who has elected to have the trust qualify. There may be only one income beneficiary at any one time and a new election must be made for each successive income interest. Where the trust terminates during the life of the income beneficiary, all the assets must be distributed to that beneficiary.

3. One class of stock. You may not make the election if your company has common and preferred stock. Differences in voting rights will not cause one class of stock to be treated as two classes. Only outstanding stock is counted in determining whether there is one class of stock. Treasury stock or unissued preferred stock of a different class does not disqualify the election.

The issuance of options and warrants to acquire its stock and convertible debentures does not disqualify the election.

Straight debt instruments are not treated as a second class of stock. Shareholder loans are treated as straight debt provided: (1) the loan is a written unconditional promise by the corporation to pay a specified sum on demand or on a set date; (2) the interest rate and payment date are not contingent on corporate profits or on the discretion of the corporation; and (3) the debt is not convertible into stock.

A corporation with an inactive subsidiary may make the election as long as the subsidiary has no gross income.

¶10.07 · FILING AN S ELECTION

The corporation makes an election by filing Form 2553 with the Internal Revenue officer designated in the instructions to the form. All shareholders must sign written consents to the election in the space provided on Form 2553 or in an attached statement. If the election is made after the start of the first year for which the election is to be effective, consents must be filed by all shareholders who held interests *before* the date of election, even if they have sold their interests.

An election may be filed during the entire taxable year before the year in which the election is to be effective and before the 16th day of the third month of the current taxable year. An election which is ineffective because of late filing is automatically effective in the following year. Even if the election is filed on time within the first two months and 15 days of the current year, the election will not take effect until the following year unless all those with shareholders interests before the filing date consent to the election.

Examples—

1. A calendar year corporation wants to elect S corporation status for 1987. It may file an election on Form 2553 any time during 1986 upon or before March 16, 1987.

If Form 2553 were filed after March 16, 1987, the election would take effect in 1988.

2. A Form 2553 filed on March 10, 1987 does not contain the written consent of a shareholder who sold his interest in February 1987. The election will not take effect until 1988.

Once a valid election is made, it is effective for all following tax years unless revoked or terminated under the rules of ¶10.08.

A valid election may not be filed before a corporation is formally incorporated. The first day of a tax year of a new corporation does not begin until one of these events occurs: It has shareholders, acquires assets, or begins doing business. However, if, under state law, corporate existence begins with filing articles of incorporation, even though the corporation has no assets and does not begin doing business until a later date, the first day of the tax year begins on the date of such filing.

Newly organized corporation. Usually, the first tax year of a newly organized corporation will be for a period less than 12 months. An election may be made for this short tax year as long as it is made before the 16th day of the third month of the corporation's first taxable year. If the first taxable year of a new corporation is for a period of less than 2½ months, the election may be made for that year within 2½ months from the beginning of the taxable year. The first taxable year begins when the corporation has shareholders, acquires assets, or begins doing business, whichever occurs first.

New stockholders. A new shareholder does not have to file any consent nor can he terminate the election. However, a majority stockholder may revoke the election; *see* ¶10.08.

¶10.08 · REVOCATION OR TERMINATION OF AN S ELECTION

An election may be revoked or may automatically terminate because the corporation no longer qualifies as an S corporation.

Revocation. Shareholders owning a majority of stock may agree to revoke the election by filing a statement of revocation. They may specify the future effective date of the revocation. If they do not fix a date, the revocation is effective on the first day of the taxable year in which the revocation is filed if filed on or before the 15th day of the third month of that year; if filed later in the year, the effective date is the first day of the following taxable year.

Termination. An election terminates when a company no longer qualifies under the rules of ¶10.06. A termination is effective as of the date the corporation no longer qualifies as an S corporation. The last day of the S corporation's short taxable year is the day before termination is effective; the day that termination is effective starts a short taxable year as a C corporation. The corporation's items of income and loss are allocated to the two short taxable years on a daily basis unless a unanimous election to have items assigned to the two short years under normal accounting rules is made by all of the persons who are shareholders in the corporation at any time during the S short taxable year and all persons who are shareholders on the first day of the (C) short year. For purposes of computing the corporate tax, the taxable income for the (C) short year must be annualized. This is true regardless of the method of allocation used for allocating income and loss items.

The pro rata allocation requirement does not apply if there is a sale or exchange of 50% or more of stock during the year of termination.

It is important to determine tax consequences under the daily allocation method and the normal accounting method. Choose the method providing the best overall tax consequences for the shareholders reporting their shares for the first short year and for the corporation reporting as a C corporation for the second short year. Different tax results will occur especially if substantial loss items were incurred in one short year and income items in the other short year. The daily allocation basis will average these between the two years. The actual allocation basis will place the items in the period they were incurred.

Election following termination. When the election is revoked or terminated, you may not make another election until the fifth year following the year in which the election was revoked or terminated, unless the IRS gives its consent. The five-year rule does not apply to terminations and revocations under prior law. An exception to the five-year rule also applies to inadvertent terminations (see below). Based on prior law (pre-1983 Subchapter S rules), the

IRS will not consent to an election before the end of the five-year period if the termination is considered reasonably within the control of the corporation or controlling shareholders.

Inadvertent termination. If the IRS decides that the termination was inadvertent and steps are taken by the corporation to reestablish its qualified status within a reasonable time after discovering the disqualifying event, then the corporation is treated as an S corporation. The corporation and each shareholder must agree to adjustments required by the IRS.

¶10.081 • TAX ON FRINGE BENEFITS RECEIVED BY STOCKHOLDERS

For S elections made after September 28, 1982, owners of more than 2% of the stock will realize taxable income for receiving fringe benefit coverage such as in employee group insurance and accident and health plans. This tax rule does not apply until 1988 to shareholders of an S corporation existing as of September 28, 1982, provided the corporation does not have passive income of more than 20% of gross receipts or does not have a change of majority stockholders after 1982.

¶10.082 • PASSIVE INVESTMENT INCOME

The receipt of passive investment income does not disqualify an S election as long as the corporation does not have accumulated earnings from taxable years prior to the election. Passive investment income includes dividends, interest, rents, royalties, and securities sale gains.

If a corporation does have accumulated earnings and passive investment income exceeding 25% of gross receipts, a portion of the excess passive income is subject to tax. A worksheet included in the instructions to Form 1120S is used to compute the tax.

The IRS has authority to waive this tax where the corporation proves that it had determined in good faith that it did not have accumulated earnings and profits at the close of the taxable year, and the earnings and profits were distributed within a reasonable period of time after the corporation determined that it did have accumulated earnings and profits.

Further, the election may be lost if for three consecutive years (beginning after 1981) the company has prior accumulated earnings and passive investment income exceeding 25% of gross receipts.

¶10.083 • CORPORATE FISCAL YEAR RESTRICTIONS

A corporation filing an S election on Form 2553 may select a fiscal tax year only if certain requirements are met. The corporate officer signing Form 2553 must certify, under penalty of perjury, that the selected fiscal year either:

    Is the corporation's natural business year, or
    Results in no more than a three-month deferral of income for shareholders owning more than 50% of the stock, or
    Coincides with the tax year of the shareholders holding more than 50% of the stock.

A gross receipts test must be met to qualify a fiscal year as the corporation's natural business year. If a fiscal year is based on the three-month income deferral test and the first tax year is less than 12 months, the corporation must make adjustments to taxable income for the first year and the following nine years.

A corporation which elected S status before October 20, 1982 may continue to use the fiscal year as long as at least 50% of the stock ownership does not change after December 31, 1982. Stock acquired after 1982 because of a shareholder's death or as a gift from certain relatives is not considered an ownership change. If a more than 50% ownership shift occurs after 1982, the corporation must switch to a calendar year or obtain IRS permission for a fiscal year.

¶10.084 • TAX ON "ONE-SHOT" CAPITAL GAINS

To prevent the use of an S election for the passthrough of substantial capital gains, a tax is imposed. A special tax applies if taxable income for the year exceeds $25,000 and the net capital gains exceed $25,000 and 50% of taxable income.

The tax does not apply to a corporation that has been an S corporation for the three preceding taxable years or to a new corporation that has been in existence for less than four years and has been an S corporation for that entire period.

¶10.085 • AUDITS OF S CORPORATIONS AND SHAREHOLDERS

S corporations and shareholders are subject to the new audit rules for partnerships discussed in ¶10.031. These rules require the tax treatment of disputed items to be determined in a unified administrative proceeding at the corporate level rather than in separate proceedings with the individual shareholders. Under these rules, the IRS will examine returns in a corporate-level administrative proceeding in taxable years starting after 1982. S corporation shareholders are generally required to report income and deductions as they appear on the S corporation's return. The IRS must give all shareholders notice of their right to participate in any corporate-level administrative proceeding.

¶11.00

Income From a Trust or Estate

¶11.01 • HOW BENEFICIARIES REPORT ESTATE OR TRUST INCOME

Tax accounting for trust or estate income is complicated. As a beneficiary, you are not required to understand the rules governing the taxing of trusts and estates. That is the trustee's or executor's responsibility. After he or she has computed trust or estate income, the fiduciary should inform you of your share of taxable income and its source. The fiduciary should also tell you whether the distribution is out of current income or accumulated income. If it is out of accumulated income, *see* ¶11.02.

Trust or estate income is treated as if you had received the income directly from the original source instead of from the estate or trust. This means capital gain remains capital gain, ordinary income is fully taxed, and tax-exempt income remains tax free. Dividends received from the trust qualify for the dividend exclusion. Tax preference items of a trust or estate are apportioned between the estate or trust and beneficiaries according to allocation of income (*see* ¶23.10).

Following these rules and the allocation of income provided by the fiduciary, you report trust or estate income as follows:

Dividend income. The dividends are added to your other dividend income. They may be fully or partially offset by the dividend exclusion.

Example—
According to the trustee, $400 of the trust income paid to you is from dividends received by the trust. You are single and have dividend income of $25 from your own investments. Total dividend income is $425. You deduct the $100 dividend exclusion from the $425 total and are taxed on $325. The exclusion may not be claimed for dividends distributed in a year in which deductions of a trust exceed its gross income.

Capital gains. Report these in Schedule D. Report short-term capital gain in the regular short-term section. Report long-term capital gains with your other long-term capital gains.

Tax-exempt income. This income is not taxable.

Example—
The trustee paid you $1,500 during the year; $700 was interest received from municipal bonds, $800 interest from bank deposits. Since municipal bond interest is tax free, the $700 is tax free in your hands.

Foreign income. Check with the trustee for how to report items from a foreign trust. New law changes not discussed in this book may affect the trust income reporting.

Depreciation and depletion. Income beneficiaries and the trustee share depreciation and depletion deductions in proportions provided by the trust agreement. If directions are omitted, the deduction is apportioned on the basis of trust income allocated to each.

Losses. A trust or estate takes a deduction for losses; not the beneficiaries. Unused capital loss carryovers, net operating loss carryovers, or deductions in excess of gross income in the final year of the trust or estate are passed on to the beneficiaries who receive the trust property.

Tax preference items. You report your share of tax preference items.

Employee benefit payments, see ¶7.04.

Reporting rule for revocable grantor trusts. A grantor who sets up a revocable trust or keeps certain powers over trust income or corpus must report all of the trust income, deductions, and credits. If a grantor is also a trustee, filing Form 1041 is not necessary.

The grantor simply reports the trust income, deductions, and credits on Form 1040.

This reporting rule is optional for revocable trusts created before 1981. Grantors of such trusts who want to report trust income on their own returns without having to file Form 1041 must file a final Form 1041 for the current tax year with a notation on the form alerting the IRS that in later years they will report trust income on their own returns.

Distributions of property. The trustee should give you the basis of distributed property. *See* ¶6.10 for basis rules.

Multiple trusts. If two or more trusts have the same grantor and substantially the same beneficiaries, the IRS may treat the trusts as one trust if tax avoidance is the principal purpose for setting them up.

¶11.02 • DISTRIBUTIONS OF ACCUMULATED TRUST INCOME

Where you are the beneficiary of an accumulation trust, the trust accumulates income on which it pays tax. When the trust distributes income to you, the trustee tells you what part of the distribution is attributable to current income and what part is attributable to accumulations of prior income. Distributions of current income are reported according to the rules of ¶11.01.

Distributions of accumulated income are subject to tax, provided the accumulation exceeds the accounting income of the trust for the year. However, only that portion of the accumulation distribution that would have been included in the beneficiary's income had it been distributed when earned is currently taxed. Thus, tax-exempt interest is never taxed. Taxes imposed on the trust on an accumulation distribution are considered an additional distribution. Taxes imposed on the trust are the gross federal income taxes before credits.

Although a beneficiary pays a tax in the year of receiving the accumulation distribution, tax is computed as if the accumulated income were actually distributed in the years in which it was earned. The tax is the sum of: (1) A tax on taxable income exclusive of the accumulation distribution, (2) a tax, computed by a shortcut method, on the accumulation distribution, and (3) an interest charge in the case of a foreign trust.

In preparing your return, the tax on your regular taxable income is computed on Form 1040; the tax on the distribution is computed on Form 4970 and added to the tax on Form 1040.

Where a trust has already been subject to estate tax or the generation-skipping transfer tax, the partial tax on a distribution is reduced by the estate or generation-skipping tax attributable to the accumulated income. The reduction is limited by a special statutory formula for determining the pre-death portions. Consult Treasury regulations for more details. The reduction is only for estate tax from a decedent dying after 1979 or for generation-skipping transfer taxes after June 11, 1976.

Where the beneficiary receives an accumulation distribution from more than two trusts for the same year, tax for the distributions from the third trust is computed under the method described above except that no credit is given for any taxes previously paid by the trust with respect to the accumulation distribution. A *de minimis* rule provides that accumulation distributions are not subject to the multiple trust rule unless the distribution equals or exceeds $1,000.

Income accumulated prior to the beneficiary's attaining the

age of 21 and the years before a beneficiary was born are not subject to the throwback rule unless distributions are made under the multiple trust rule.

No refunds or credits are made to any beneficiary or trust, even though the taxes paid by the trust exceed the accumulation distributions.

If you receive a distribution of accumulated income from a trust, contact the trustee or an experienced tax practitioner for advice in computing your tax on the accumulation.

Sale of capital gain property by trust within two years of transfer. Capital gain is not subject to the throwback rules. However, if the trust sells property within two years of receiving it by gift or bargain sale, gain is taxed at the same rate that the grantor would have paid if the grantor sold the property. This rule for taxing gain does not apply if the grantor dies within the two-year period.

Trust for the benefit of a spouse. Where a spouse creates a trust for the benefit of the other spouse after October 9, 1969, income of the trust is taxed to the spouse who created the trust as income is earned.

There are special rules for foreign trusts. *See* Treasury regulations.

¶11.03 • DEDUCTIONS FOR INCOME SUBJECT TO ESTATE TAX

If you receive income which was earned by, but not paid to, a decedent before death, you are said to have "income in respect of a decedent." You report the income, and if an estate has paid a federal estate tax on the income, you may deduct part of the estate tax allocated to the income. No deduction is allowed for state death taxes. Ask the executor of the estate for data in computing the deduction.

Example—

When your uncle died, he was owed a fee of $1,000. He also had not collected accrued bond interest of $500. You, as the sole heir, will collect both items and pay income tax on them. These items are called income in respect of a decedent. Assume that an estate tax of $390 was paid on the $1,500. You collect the $1,000, which you report on your income tax return. You may deduct $260, computed as follows:

$$\frac{\$1,000}{\$1,500} \times \$390, \text{ or } \$260$$

When you collect the $500, you will deduct the balance, or $130 ($390 − $260).

The deduction is generally claimed as an itemized deduction. However, if you receive long-term capital gain income, such as an installment payment on a sale transacted before decedent's death, the estate tax attributed to the capital gain item is not claimed as a miscellaneous deduction. The deduction is treated as if it was an expense of sale and thus reduces the amount of gain before the computation of the capital gain deduction. This rule applies to capital gain received because of a decedent dying after November 6, 1978.

Lump-sum distributions from qualified retirement plans. When a beneficiary receiving a lump-sum distribution because of an employee's death reports the distribution using the special ten-year averaging method and capital gain treatment, the distribution is subject to estate tax. However, beneficiaries of decedents dying after April 1, 1980 may reduce the taxable amount of the distribution by the deduction for estate taxes attributable to the distribution. For beneficiaries of decedents dying before April 2, 1980 but after November 6, 1978, only the capital gain element is reduced by estate taxes.

¶12.00

Prizes, Scholarships, Damages, Life Insurance and Other Income

Illustrations of reporting other income on Form 1040 are in the Supplement to YOUR INCOME TAX. Mail the card at the front of this book for your FREE Supplement, which includes filled-in returns and last-minute information.

Gifts and Inheritances, Bargain Purchases, Prizes and Awards, and Gambling Winnings

¶12.01 · GIFTS AND INHERITANCES

Gifts and inheritances are not taxable. Income earned from gift or inherited property after you receive it is taxable.

Describing a payment as a gift or inheritance will not necessarily shield it from tax, if it is, in fact, a payment for services.
Examples—

1. An employee is promised by his employer that he will be remembered in his will if he continues to work for him. The employer dies but fails to mention the employee in his will. The employee sues the estate which settles his claim. The settlement is taxable.

2. A nephew left his uncle a bequest of $200,000. In another clause of the will, the uncle was appointed executor, and the bequest of the $200,000 was described as being made in lieu of all commissions to which he would otherwise be entitled as executor. The bequest is considered tax-free income. It was not conditioned upon the uncle performing as executor. If the will had made the bequest contingent upon the uncle acting as executor, the $200,000 would have been taxed.

3. An attorney performed services for a friend without expectation of pay. The friend died and in his will left the attorney a bequest in appreciation for his services. The payment was considered a tax-free bequest. The amount was not bargained for.

4. A lawyer agreed to handle a client's legal affairs without charge; she promised to leave him securities. Twenty years later, under her will, he inherited the securities. The IRS taxed the bequest as pay. Both he and the client expected that he would be paid for legal services. If she meant to make a bequest apart from their agreement, she could have said so in her will.

A sale of an expected inheritance from a living person is taxable as ordinary income.

Campaign contributions. Campaign contributions are not taxable income to a political candidate if the funds are used for political campaign expenses or some similar purposes. Detailed records of receipts and disbursements are advisable to avoid tax on the political funds. Also nontaxable are contributions which are intended for the candidate's unrestricted personal use and qualify as gifts.

Treatment of gifts to employees is at ¶2.03.

¶12.02 · BARGAIN PURCHASES

Whether a bargain purchase is taxable depends on the relationship of the parties. When you make a bargain purchase from your employer, the difference between what you pay and the value of the property may be taxable as compensation. If you are a stockholder purchasing from your corporation, the difference may be taxable as a dividend.
Example—
A corporation takes out an insurance policy on the life of a key executive, pays the premiums, and names itself as beneficiary. Several years later, the executive buys the policy from the company for its cash surrender value so he can name his own beneficiary. He has taxable income on the bargain purchase from his company. The true value of the policy to him is not its cash surrender value but what it would cost him to buy such a policy at his present age.

Courtesy discounts are discussed at ¶2.02.

¶12.03 · PRIZES AND AWARDS

Prizes and awards are, with limited exceptions, taxable income.

Tax-free awards and prizes. A prize or award must meet these tests for tax-free treatment: (1) It is in recognition of past accomplishments in religious, charitable, scientific, educational, artistic, literary, or civic fields. (2) You did not enter the contest or proceeding. That is, you were selected as a recipient without any action on your part. (3) You are not required as a condition of receiving the prize to perform substantial future services.
Example—
Mary Green, a federal civil service employee, receives an award under the Rockefeller Public Service Program. The selection is made

primarily in recognition of Green's past accomplishments. This award is tax free.

Other awards that qualify as tax free under the above tests are the Nobel Prize and the Pulitzer Prize.

A government award substituting for royalties is taxable.

The following are examples of prizes and awards that are taxable:

A door prize
An essay contest prize
Prizes won in charity bazaars
Awards to salesmen, including scrip redeemable in merchandise
Athletic awards, even though there is no direct competition. For example, Paul Hornung was taxed on the value of a car received for being elected the most outstanding player in a National Football League championship game.
Prizes from radio or television contests. You are taxed even if you do nothing to get the prize. You may report prizes of list-priced goods at their fair market value rather than the higher list prices.
Noncash awards to employees for length of service or contributions to safety or productivity are generally considered taxable pay. See ¶2.03.

A prize of merchandise is taxed at fair market value. For example, where a prize of first-class steamship tickets was exchanged for tourist class tickets for the winner's family, the taxable value of the prize was the price of the tourist tickets. The taxable value of an automobile won as a prize is its immediate trade-in value, not its list price.

A prize you refuse to accept is not taxable.

¶12.04 · SWEEPSTAKE AND LOTTERY WINNINGS

Sweepstake, lottery and raffle winnings are taxable. You may deduct the price of the ticket from the winnings. If you do not win, you may not deduct the cost of the ticket. If you frequently buy state lottery chances and win a drawing, you may also deduct the cost of your prior losing tickets bought in 1986 up to the amount of your winnings.

To split income, potential sweepstakes winnings may be divided among family members or others before the prize is won. You might buy the sweepstakes or lottery ticket in your name and the names of others. The prize is shared and each portion separately taxed. Income-splitting is generally not possible after the prize is won if you bought the ticket.

Where a minor wins a state lottery and the prize is held by his parents as custodians under the Uniform Gifts to Minors Act, the prize is taxed to the minor in the year the prize is won.

Winnings may be averaged (see ¶23.00).

¶12.05 · GAMBLING WINNINGS AND LOSSES

Gambling winnings are taxable. Losses from gambling are deductible only up to the gains from gambling. You may not deduct a net gambling loss even though a particular state says gambling is legal. Nor does it matter that your business is gambling. You may not deduct the loss.

If you are not a professional gambler, gambling income is included on your tax return with your other income. Gambling losses (but not exceeding the amount of the gains) are deductible under "Miscellaneous deductions" on Schedule A. According to the IRS, professional gamblers who bet only for their own account are not in a business and must deduct losses (up to gains) as itemized deductions. The Tax Court allows full-time gamblers to deduct losses as business expenses. An appeals court sides with the IRS.

To prove your losses in the event your return is questioned, you must retain evidence of losses.

Scholarships, Fellowships, and Grants

Tax legislation may apply new limits to scholarships granted after August 1986; see the new law discussion in the front of this book.

¶12.10 • AWARDS TO DEGREE CANDIDATES

If you are a degree candidate, the following amounts paid under a grant are tax free: Tuition, matriculation fees, room, board, laundry and other services, and family allowances.

Studies leading to your certification to practice a profession, such as psychiatric nurse, are not equivalent to being a candidate for a degree.

Work-study programs. Tuition and work payments are tax free if your college requires all its students to take part in the work-study program. Payments for services not required by the program are taxable.

Travel and other expenses. You are not taxed on allowances specifically designated for expenses incident to the grant, such as for travel (including meals and lodging while traveling and family travel allowance), research, clerical help, and equipment. You are taxable to the extent the allowance is not spent for these purposes.

Payments for teaching or research. Where the primary purpose of teaching or research is to further your own training and education, payment for such services is tax free if the services are required of all degree candidates. Where the primary purpose is to pay you for services, the payments are taxable, even if teaching or research is required for the degree. Where you are paid for services not required of all degree candidates, a portion of the grant attributable to the services is taxed according to the going rate paid for similar services.

Examples—

1. You are studying for a bachelor's degree in education. Teaching certain classes is a degree requirement. You do not report any part of your grant as income.

2. You are a candidate for a masters degree in education for which internship teaching is required. You are taxable on payments paid to you by a municipal school system where you assume full classroom responsibilities and receive a salary in accordance with the pay scale for all teachers. The payments are considered compensation for services.

3. You are earning a degree in mathematics. You do not need teaching experience for your degree. You receive a university grant requiring you to instruct certain classes. You report as income that part of the grant attributed to your teaching services. The taxed portion is found by multiplying the number of hours worked by the going hourly rate of pay for similar work. If you taught for 100 hours and the going hourly rate is $20, $2,000 of your grant is taxable income and the remaining portion is tax free.

4. For a bachelor of science degree, a university required students of medical technology to complete a year of study at a hospital laboratory. Apart from regular lecture and study hours in the training year, they spent 35 hours a week at the hospital, three quarters of the time in supervised on-the-job training, and one quarter on independent work projects. The hospital paid them $250 a month, the same amount paid to employees doing similar work. The IRS treats these stipends as taxable pay. Even though they had to work at the hospital to get the university degree, the students were paid for services.

¶12.11 • AWARDS TO NONDEGREE CANDIDATES

If you are not working for a degree, your scholarship or fellowship grant is tax free up to $300 a month for each month during the year in which you receive payments under the grant. You may claim the $300 a month exclusion for only 36 months during your lifetime. The months do not have to run consecutively. A grant does not qualify for this tax-free exclusion if it represents payment for services or for research or studies primarily for the grantor's benefit.

After you exclude income for 36 months, all further grants are taxable.

Examples—

1. In March, 1986, Smith is awarded a post-doctoral fellowship to start in September and to end on June 1, 1987. The fellowship grant is for $4,500. He receives this in monthly installments of $500. During 1986, he receives $2,000 for the four months of September through December. He excludes $1,200 ($300 per month × 4) from gross income. He reports the remaining $800 on his 1985 return.

2. Under a fellowship grant, Brown receives $200 a month for 40 months. Only $7,200 ($200 per month × 36 months) is tax free. The remaining $800 ($200 per month × 4 months) is taxable—even though he could not, in any of the 36 months, make use of the full $300 exclusion.

If you receive two or more grants during the year, total all payments to figure the tax-free exclusion. If the payments are received during the same month or months, each month counts only once for the purpose of determining the number of months for which you are paid.

Keep records to show whether your grants are taxable or tax free. Months in which you could have excluded payment under a grant may be counted in the 36 months, even if you did not claim the exclusion. It is up to you to show that you could *not* have excluded the payment.

The $300-a-month exclusion is the maximum set by law. There is no authority to increase it because of particular circumstances. For example, the IRS refused a request to allow a larger exclusion for a researcher who had a family to support.

Travel and other expense allowances. In addition to the $300 monthly exclusion, allowances specifically designated for expenses incident to the grant, such as for travel (including meals and lodgings while traveling and family travel allowance) research, clerical help, and equipment are not taxable to the extent spent for such expenses.

Example—

An executive of a state agency, who received a grant to travel and study foreign rehabilitation programs, was allowed to exclude $300 a month but not amounts exceeding $300 a month for travel expenses. His entire grant was intended to cover travel expenses, but he was not required to use it for travel; in fact, there were no restrictions on how he used the money. Therefore, tax-free treatment was limited to payments to $300 a month; no part of the excess was allowed for travel expenses. To come within the expense exclusion, the allowance had to be specifically restricted to travel costs.

Who makes the grant. To qualify for the 36-month exclusion, the grant must be received from one of the following sources:

The United States, or any agency or instrumentality of the United States.

A state, territory, or possession of the United States, or any of their subdivisions, or the District of Columbia.

A tax-exempt nonprofit organization operated exclusively for religious, charitable, scientific, literary, testing for public safety, prevention of cruelty to children or animals, or educational purposes.

A foreign government.

An organization under the Mutual Educational and Cultural Exchange Act of 1961.

¶12.12 • FELLOWSHIPS FOR INTERNS AND RESIDENT PHYSICIANS

According to the IRS, payments received from hospitals are generally taxable as compensation for services performed even though training and experience are gained while working. Most court decisions follow this IRS position.

Examples—

1. Three psychiatric residents received grants from a state hospital. A university medical school ran the residency program, but the doctors were trained in a state hospital. The Tax Court stressed their contractual obligation to work for the health department after completing the training. The grants were paid to qualify them for employment by the state and are taxable.

2. A district court allowed a fellowship exclusion to an intern at a university hospital. An appeals court disagreed. Although he interned at a teaching hospital, his duties were similar to those of interns at general hospitals. He was paid for services to patients.

3. Dr. Moll accepted an Air Force commission in his last year of medical school, agreeing to three years additional military service after

his internship. He interned at the Air Force Medical Center, receiving an officer's active duty pay. He was not allowed a fellowship exclusion. The doctor made a "package deal" with the Air Force. He received military pay while completing his medical education in return for his commitment to serve three years in the Air Force.

4. Adams received a stipend and a housing allowance while working as an intern at an osteopathic hospital. He claimed that his stipend was a tax-free fellowship because he had the option of selecting assignments on the basis of what he determined to be most educational. But the Tax Court held the stipend to be a taxable "quid pro quo" for performing emergency room services, examining patients and assisting in surgery. Further, he was treated as an employee by the hospital; income tax and FICA taxes were withheld, and he received fringe benefits available to employees.

Courts have sometimes treated residents' grants as tax-free fellowships.
Examples—
1. A doctor, who had been a public health officer for two years, entered a medical school research program designed to prepare physicians for careers in academic medicine. The school was under contract to provide medical services to a hospital and the doctor spent approximately 25% of his time on hospital clinical work. The school withheld taxes from his stipend and paid his malpractice insurance. The doctor joined the staff when he finished the research program. The IRS taxed the doctor claiming that he was paid for his work at the hospital and that he was expected to join the staff. The Tax Court rejected both arguments. The doctor did not take care of patients and was not a resident. He did not take calls or keep regular hospital hours and spent most of his clinical time in conferences. His research was of interest to the academic community, but of no special advantage to the medical school. He did not have to work on projects the school was committed to. While the school may have hoped he would join the staff, its purpose was to educate him in a specialty, not to train him as an employee.
2. Two residents, an orthopedist and a pathologist, received stipends from a university medical center; the pathologist also had a VA grant. They convinced a district court jury and an appeals court that they were paid to further their medical training, not as compensation for services to the medical center. The medical center was a teaching institution with a full time faculty to supervise the residents. Patients were not billed for services from the residents. Residents were not required to work for the center after training. These facts offset evidence that they were treated as employees for purposes of fringe benefits and payroll deductions. The pathologist's VA grant was also a fellowship. He spent only three months at the VA hospital as part of his residency at the medical center.

3. A doctor was accepted in a cardio-renal training program at a hospital. Although he went on rounds, the doctor argued that he performed no useful service to the hospital. He was there to learn from the leading experts in his field of study. The IRS, in taxing his stipend, noted that not only did he see patients on rounds but he also accepted a staff position when he finished training. The Tax Court held that the doctor received a tax-free fellowship. He was developing diagnostic skills on diagnostic rounds, not helping senior staff. The hospital did not pay the grant in the expectation that he would later join their staff, and he was not obliged to do so. Finally, the amount of his grant was geared to his personal financial needs, not to his length or quality of service to the hospital.

4. Grants to 15 residents at a state university medical center qualified for the $300 per month exclusion. The grants were designed to defray living expenses during training and were not conditioned on job performance or treatment of patients; the residents were not required to work for the state upon completion of the residency program. Further, fees were not charged for work performed by residents and the residents were always supervised by medical school faculty when seeing hospital patients. An appeals court held that given these facts, a jury verdict in favor of the residents should not be overruled, despite evidence that the residents were treated as employees for purposes of fringe benefits and annual increases.

For a list of nontaxed grants, *see* ¶12.16.

¶12.13 • AWARDS TO NURSES AND HOSPITAL PERSONNEL

Nurses. A stipend received while in training as a specialist may be taxable income or a tax-free scholarship depending on whether the nurse is being paid for services to the hospital. For example, an annual stipend was a tax-free scholarship where close supervision of the trainee actually reduced the efficiency of the regular staff.

The value of room and board given to student nurses by a school of nursing is not taxed.

Payments were taxable income where the nurses were active members of the staff doing work geared to the operational needs of the hospital.

Government stipends to employees training to be nurses are taxable pay.

Public Health Service awards made by the Surgeon General to professional nurses for advanced courses of training are not taxed.

VA hospital administration and training. The VA pays stipends to interns serving as staff assistants in VA hospitals. The IRS considers the amounts as taxable pay, even though internship is a requirement for a graduate degree. Court decisions have allowed tax-free treatment.

Payments made to students of medical technology while training in a general hospital were treated as tax-free grants where the training was credited to a B.S. degree at an affiliated college. But in another case where medical technology students were paid the same amount as hospital employees doing similar work, the payments were treated as taxable pay.

¶12.14 • EMPLOYER GRANTS

The IRS generally treats as taxable pay the value of scholarships or grants provided by employers or prospective employers. However, if you receive a grant under a federal program that requires you to work for the government, you may exclude from income amounts used for tuition, books, supplies and equipment related to the courses. If your employer pays for your tuition or similar fees under an educational assistance plan meeting the rules at ¶2.02, the payments are not taxable. Where your employer's payment of tuition or similar fees is not pursuant to such an educational assistance plan (¶2.02), the payments are not taxable to you if the studies are job related, provided that the courses are not taken to meet the minimum education requirements of your job and do not qualify you for a new profession. If your employer reimburses your tuition expenses for such job related studies, the reimbursement is not taxable if you do not deduct the expenses. On your return, you state that the reimbursement does not exceed your deductible expenses.

¶12.15 • CHECKLIST OF TAXABLE GRANTS

Grants provided to a teacher by his school are taxed because of the employer-employee relationship which exists between them. However, a faculty member may receive a tax-free grant to continue his studies if the award is made by a qualified tax-exempt organization legally distinct from the school.

Grants to student interns who perform routine office work and other assignments for state legislatures and political leaders are taxable.

Employee's education grant given in return for promise to work for employer in the future is taxable. Employee's education grant was held to be taxable even where there was no promise to return the work.
Example—
An insurance company paid the living expenses of employees enrolled in a graduate school for actuaries. Although they were not required to return to work for the company after completing the course, the grants were taxed. The employees were induced to continue work as better qualified actuaries for the benefit of the employer. According to an appeals court, "Hearts may be won as well as coerced."

Amounts paid under grants made by an educational institution to journalism students working as regular staff members of newspapers (which financed the grants) are taxable.

Stipends for post-doctoral research during temporary assignment to the National Bureau of Standards are taxed as compensation for services.

Payments received by social service agency interns are taxable compensation.

A grant provided a social worker by his department for educational leave is taxable when he continues to be treated as an employee by the department and is required to return to his office after the completion of the courses.

Armed Forces Health Professions Scholarships. Before 1985, grants received by those entering the program before 1981 were allowed tax-free treatment.

Payments to National Teacher Corps teacher-interns during training and in-service periods do not qualify as fellowships.

Domestic Volunteer Service Act stipends are taxable income.

The Tax Court may be more flexible than the IRS and permit the fellowship exclusion, although there are facts pointing to an employment relationship.

Example—

Vaccaro was a research associate at a university doing post-doctoral research as an educator. The IRS taxed his stipend as wages. It was paid out of HEW funds earmarked for salaries. He had full faculty privileges, was on the payroll as an employee, received employee fringe benefits, and the year counted towards tenure. Nevertheless, the Tax Court allowed the fellowship exclusion. There was one underlying reason for his grant. It provided him with financial support while he developed his professional skills. He studied, read and worked independently. His activities were of no special benefit to the university. He was on the payroll on account of the university's government contract, not because he gave services to the university.

If you win a scholarship prize in a contest and are not required to use the award for educational purposes, the prize is taxable. This is true even if you do use it for an educational purpose.

¶12.16 • CHECKLIST OF NONTAXABLE GRANTS

Educational assistance allowances paid by the Veterans' Administration.

Educational benefits received under the War Orphans' Educational Assistance Act of 1956.

National Science Foundation stipends, and National Institute of Public Affairs grants to government employees for an academic year of study.

National Institute of Health grants are generally tax free but may be considered taxable where you are selected on the basis of your experience and the NIH reserves patent and copyright rights arising from your research. NIH grants under the Visiting Fellows Programs to residents of the following countries are exempt under tax conventions: Belgium, Finland, France, Iceland, Japan, the Netherlands, Norway, Poland, Romania and Trinidad and Tobago.

National Defense Education Act of 1958 Title IV grants to graduate students to help them prepare for careers as college teachers.

Research fellowships by the American Heart Association. However, "established investigatorship" awards to conduct independent research in the cardiovascular field are taxable.

Free or partially free tuition for undergraduate studies provided to faculty member by his own school. Tuition is also tax free in this case: A faculty member of one school attends another school, and both schools have a plan under which the child's tuition is forgiven. However, such tuition benefits after June 30, 1985 may be taxable to officers or highly compensated employees if the tuition plan discriminates in their favor. In addition to current employees, tax-free tuition benefits may be provided to a spouse, dependent child, former employee who retired or left on disability, widow or widower of an individual who died while employed by the school or a widow or widower of a retired or disabled employee. If both parents have died and one of the parents qualified as an employee, the fact that the child is a dependent of another person does not affect tax-free treatment of tuition benefits.

Grants provided by a private person are not eligible for the tax-free exclusion. However, such grants may be tax-free gifts if they have been motivated by philanthropic reasons. Tax-free treatment applies if the grant is turned over to a university which then pays the grant to you.

National Research Service Award.

Interest on student loans paid by the Department of Education under the Higher Education Act are not taxable to the student.

¶12.17 • FULBRIGHT AWARDS

How your Fulbright award is taxed depends on the purpose of the award. If you receive the award to—

Teach or lecture—the entire amount of the award is taxed as compensation for services, including any supplemental grant you receive under the Smith-Mundt Act. However, provided you are not a U.S. government employee, you may claim the foreign earned income exclusion to avoid tax on the grant (*see* ¶36.00). If you do not qualify for the exclusion and if your overseas stay is temporary and you intend to return to your regular teaching position in the United States, you may deduct the cost of your travel, meals, and lodgings overseas.

Further your education as a student or research grantee— all or part of your award is tax free depending on whether or not you are a candidate for a degree. To figure how much of your award is tax free, follow the rules discussed in ¶12.10 and ¶12.11.

Tax Refunds, Debt Cancellations, and Court Awards

¶12.20 • TAX REFUNDS AND OTHER RECOVERIES OF PREVIOUSLY DEDUCTED ITEMS

You may realize taxable income when you receive a:

Refund of state or local taxes which you deducted in a prior year. (A refund of federal income tax is not taxable.)

Payment from a debtor of a debt you deducted as a bad debt in a prior year,

A return of donated property for which you claimed a charitable contribution deduction in a prior year, or

Reimbursement for a loss which you claimed as a casualty loss in a prior year.

Example—

The Browns file a joint return. In 1985, their adjusted gross income was $30,000, state income tax deduction was $2,000 and other itemized deductions were $5,000. They claimed three exemptions. In 1986, they

received a refund of $1,000 of their 1985 state income tax.

	1985 income		1985 income without state tax deduction
Adjusted gross income		$30,000	$30,000
Itemized deductions	$7,000		$5,000
Zero bracket amount	(3,540)		(3,540)
Excess itemized deductions		(3,460)	(1,460)
Exemptions		(3,120)	(3,120)
Taxable income		$23,420	$25,420
Income without state tax deduction		$25,420	
Income actually reported		23,420	
Tax benefit from deduction		$2,000	

Since the entire $2,000 state income tax deduction reduced the 1985 tax, the $1,000 refund is taxable in 1986.

If you did not itemize deductions for the year in which the state income tax was paid, no amount of a later refund of that tax is taxable in the year the refund is received.

In figuring whether you have a tax-free recovery of an item deducted in a prior year now closed by the statute of limitations, count only deductions taken on the return. Deductions you could have claimed but did not are ignored. *See* ¶27.00 for statute of limitations.

If a casualty loss deduction is claimed in one year and in a later year the loss is reimbursed, the reimbursement is taxable income. However, in the case of a personal casualty loss, the reimbursement is not taxable to the extent that the $100 floor reduced the deduction.

For treatment of reimbursed medical costs, *see* ¶17.04.

Recovery of previously deducted items used to figure carryover. A deductible expense may not reduce your tax because you have an overall loss. If in a later year the expense is repaid or the obligation giving rise to the expense is cancelled, the deduction of that expense will be treated as having produced a tax reduction if it increased a carryover that has not expired by the beginning of the taxable year in which the forgiveness occurs. For example, you are on the accrual basis and deducted, but did not pay, rent in 1985. The rent obligation is forgiven in 1986. The 1985 rent deduction is treated as having produced a reduction in tax even if it resulted in no tax saving in 1985, if it figured in the calculation of a net operating loss that has not expired or been used by the beginning of 1986, the year of forgiveness. The same rule applies to other carryovers, such as the investment credit carryover.

Price rebate on energy credit equipment. If you claim a home energy credit (¶24.30) and in a later year receive a manufacturer's rebate for the product on which the credit was based, the tax benefit rule applies and taxable income may be realized. The amount of income equals the portion of the credit attributable to the rebate. For example, in 1985, you buy solar-energy equipment costing $5,000 and claim a $2,000 credit (40% of $5,000). In 1986, you receive a price rebate of $500 on the item. You must recapture $200 of the credit (40% of $500). You add the recaptured $200 to your 1986 tax.

This recapture rule for price rebates does not apply to the investment tax credit, the business energy credit, the rehabilitation credit, the employer-plan credit or the foreign tax credit.

¶12.21 • CANCELLATION OF DEBTS YOU OWE

If your creditor cancels a debt you owe, you may realize taxable income. For example, a prepayment of a home mortgage at a discount is taxable.
Example—
A bank allows a homeowner to prepay a low-interest mortgage of $20,000 for $18,000. The discount of $2,000 is taxable as ordinary income.

You are not taxed if you can prove that your creditor intended a gift or you meet the following rules of the 1980 Bankruptcy Act.

Cancellation of student loans. A student loan canceled after 1982 is taxable income with this exception: If a loan by a government agency or a qualified hospital organization is canceled because you worked for a period of time in certain geographical areas (such as practice medicine in rural areas) or because you worked for certain employers (such as an inner city school), then the canceled amount is not taxable.

Debts discharged in bankruptcy or insolvency. A discharge of a debt in a Title 11 bankruptcy case is not taxable, but is used to reduce specified "tax attributes" in this order: (1) Net operating losses and carryovers dollar for dollar of debt discharge; (2) carryovers of investment tax credit (other than ESOP credit), WIN credit, jobs credit, and credit for alcohol used as fuel—50 cents for each dollar of debt cancellation; (3) capital losses and carryovers dollar for dollar; (4) basis of depreciable and nondepreciable assets dollar for dollar (but not below the amount of your total undischarged liabilities); (5) foreign tax credit carryovers—50 cents for each dollar of debt cancellation. After these reduc-

tions, any remaining balance of the debt discharge is disregarded. On Form 982, you may make a special election to first reduce the basis of any depreciable assets and realty held as inventory or for sale to customers before reducing other tax attributes in the order shown above. The election allows a bankrupt or insolvent debtor to maximize the advantages of a net operating loss or other carryovers by first reducing basis of depreciable assets or realty held as inventory.

In a Title II case, the tax attribute reductions are made to the attributes in the bankruptcy estate. Reductions are not made to attributes of an individual debtor that come into existence after the bankruptcy case begins or that are treated as exempt property under bankruptcy rules. Basis reduction does apply to property transferred by the bankruptcy estate to the individual.

Similar rules apply to a debt discharged outside of bankruptcy while you are insolvent. Insolvency means that liabilities exceed the value of your assets immediately before the discharge. The discharged debt is not taxed to the extent of your insolvency (liabilities in excess of assets) and is applied to the reduction of tax attributes in the same manner as a bankrupt individual. Any remaining balance of the canceled debt is treated as if it were a debt cancellation of a solvent person, as discussed below.

The above rules for bankrupt and insolvent individuals apply for debt discharges occurring, or court proceedings beginning on or after January 1, 1982. For debt discharges occurring after December 31, 1980 and before January 1, 1982, or in a court proceeding commencing before 1982, a bankrupt or insolvent taxpayer applies the discharged amount to reduce the basis of all depreciable and nondepreciable assets, but not below the property's fair market value on the date of the discharge.

Discharge of a solvent person's debts related to business property. If you are solvent and outside bankruptcy when the debt is discharged, the discharged amount is taxable unless the following rules for business related property are met. If you purchased business property on credit and the seller reduces or cancels your debt arising out of the purchase while you are solvent (and not in a Title 11 bankruptcy proceeding), the reduction is generally treated as a price adjustment having no tax consequences to you. This favorable price adjustment rule does not apply if you have transferred the property to a third party, or if the seller has transferred the debt to a third party, such as where the seller sells your installment contract to another company. The price adjustment rule also does not apply if your debt on the purchase becomes unenforceable because the statute of limitations for collecting the debt has run out.

If a debt relating to business property is held by a third party (other than the seller) who cancels it, you will realize income unless you elect to reduce the basis of your depreciable assets or of real estate held as inventory for sale to customers. Treasury regulations for basis reductions have not yet been issued, but are expected to apply the debt first to the property subject to the debt and then to other depreciable property. The basis reduction election applies to depreciable property held at the beginning of the taxable year following the taxable year in which the discharge occurs. You make the basis reduction election on Form 982.

Basis reduction rules applicable to dealers in real property are not discussed here.

The repurchase of your debt obligation at a discount is treated in the same way as a debt discharge.

You may decide to report the debt discharge as income instead of electing to reduce basis where you have a loss which can offset the income. If you do not elect to reduce basis, or if you make the election and a portion of the discharged debt discharge remains after the basis reduction, the excess is taxable income.

Partnership debts. When a partnership's debt is discharged, the discharged amount is allocated among the partners. A bankrupt or insolvent partner applies the allocated amount to reduce tax attributes, as discussed above; a solvent partner must elect to reduce basis in depreciable assets (and realty held as inventory) to avoid tax.

Effect of basis reduction on later disposition of property. Where a solvent, insolvent, or bankrupt debtor reduces basis under the above rules, the reduction is treated as a depreciation deduction.

The effect of this rule is that when the asset is later sold at a gain, the gain may be taxed as ordinary income under the recapture rules of Section 1245, regardless of the nature of the asset. *See* ¶5.40.

Effect of basis reduction on investment credit. Where you reduce the basis of your property under the above rules, the basis reduction is not treated as a disposition of the property triggering recapture of a previously claimed investment credit. *See* ¶5.75.

¶12.22 • RECEIPTS IN COURT ACTIONS FOR DAMAGES

Tax-free damages. You do not report damages received from suits for personal injuries, slander or libel of personal reputation, breach of promise to marry, alienation of affection, annulment of marriage, or amounts received for child support. Alimony may be taxed. *See* ¶20.00.

Taxable damages. According to the IRS and Tax Court, you report as taxable income damages collected for injuries to business reputation or for loss of profits (*see* defamation below). Damages received for patent or copyright infringement or breach of contract are considered to be for loss of profits and thus are taxable. Courts reason that payments for loss of profits are taxable because the profits themselves would have been taxable if realized.

> When a payment compensates for loss of profits and good will or capital, make sure to have evidence for allocating the award between profits and good will or capital assets. Otherwise, the entire amount may be taxed as a recovery of profits. Be certain that your complaint is drawn so that it clearly demands a recovery both for loss of profits *and* injury to property. Seek to have any lump-sum award divided between the two in any judgment. If your action is settled, make sure the settlement agreement specifically earmarks the nature of the payments. To support a claim that good will was damaged, have evidence of the specific customers lost.

When damages compensate for the loss of property, you have taxable gain if the damages exceed adjusted basis of the property. A deductible loss will generally be allowed when the recovery is less than adjusted basis. The nature of the gain or loss takes on the same character (that is, capital gain or loss or ordinary income gain or loss) as the property lost.

Payments compensating for an anticipated invasion of the right of privacy are taxable in the absence of proof that actual damage has been suffered.

Punitive damages are taxable. The IRS will impose tax on punitive damages received for personal injuries or wrongful death. Under an exception, damages will not be taxed if received in consideration of a release from liability signed before July 16, 1984 under a wrongful death statute that provides exclusively for punitive damages.

An award from the National Labor Relations Board as a result of a discharge in violation of the National Labor Relations Act is taxable income.

Awards received in arbitration and amounts received in settlement of a dispute are treated according to the above rules.

Employment contracts. A settlement of an employment contract is generally taxable, unless a part of the settlement is allocated to personal injury claim.

Example—
A corporate executive refused to leave when he was fired. The company sued, and the incident was widely reported in newspapers. The executive threatened a countersuit. He settled for a year's salary of $60,000 plus $45,000 for personal embarrassment. He argued that $45,000 was a tax-free payment for personal injuries. The Tax Court agreed. His "embarrassment" was part of a personal injury claim.

Defamation. Where a libelous statement damages both personal and business reputation, damages compensating for personal injury are tax free; damages for business reputation are taxable. If the award does not specify the character of the damages the IRS may tax all of the payments as a replacement of lost earnings due to injury to business reputation. The Tax Court will support this IRS position if there is evidence that business reputation was damaged. An appeals court disagrees with the IRS and the Tax Court approach. According to the appeals court, tax consequences should depend on how state law treats defamations. If state law treats defamation as a personal injury, the award is tax free, even if business reputation has been damaged.

Legal fees. The rules for deducting legal fees closely follow the above rules. If the damages are tax free, you may not deduct your litigation costs. If your damages are fully taxed, you deduct all of your litigation costs. If your damages are only partially taxed, then you deduct only that portion of your litigation costs attributed to the taxed damages.

When your attorney receives payment of taxable damages and then turns over the money after deducting his fee, you are taxed in the year you receive your share.

Life Insurance and Other Insurance Proceeds

¶12.30 • HOW LIFE INSURANCE PROCEEDS ARE TAXED TO BENEFICIARY

Life insurance proceeds received because of the death of the insured are generally tax free. However, insurance proceeds may be subject to estate tax so that the beneficiary actually receives a reduced amount (*see* ¶38.10). Interest paid on proceeds left with the insurer is taxable except in this case: A surviving spouse who elects to receive installments rather than a lump sum does not pay tax on the first $1,000 of interest received each year. (The interest and dividend exclusion may increase the tax-free amount of interest.) Read the following checklist to find how your insurance receipts are taxed—

A lump-sum payment of the full face value of a life insurance policy: The proceeds are generally tax free.

The tax-free exclusion also covers death benefit payments under endowment contracts, workmen's compensation insurance contracts, employers' group insurance plans, or accident and health insurance contracts. The exclusion does not apply to a policy combined with a nonrefund life annuity contract where a single premium equal to the face value of the insurance is paid.

Insurance proceeds may be taxable where the policy was transferred for valuable consideration. Exceptions to this rule are made for transfers among partners and corporations and their stockholders and officers.

Installment payments spread over your life under a policy that could have been paid in a lump sum: Part of each installment attributed to interest may be taxed. Divide the face amount of the policy by the number of years the installments are to be paid. The result is the amount which is received tax free each year.

> If you are the surviving spouse of the insured, up to $1,000 of interest paid with the annual installment is also tax free. You are still treated as a spouse if separated from the insured at the date of his death, but not if divorced. (If you receive payments under a policy with a "family income rider," *see* ¶12.31.)

Example—
Alice is the wife and beneficiary under her husband John's life insurance policy. On his death, she can get $100,000 (the face or principal amount of the policy) in one lump sum. Instead, she elects to take installment payments for the rest of her life. Alice's life expectancy is 20 years. $5,000 ($100,000 ÷ 20) is the principal amount spread to each year. The first $6,000 received each year ($5,000 principal plus $1,000 of the spouse's special interest exclusion) is exempt from tax. If Alice lives more than 20 years, she may continue to treat up to $6,000 of annual payments as tax-free receipts.

If the policy guarantees payments to a secondary beneficiary if you should die before receiving a specified number of payments, the tax-free amount is reduced by the present value of the secondary beneficiary's interest in the policy. The insurance company can give you this figure.

Installment payments for a fixed number of years under a policy which could have been paid in a lump sum: Divide the full face amount of the policy by the number of years you are to receive the installments. The result is the amount which is received tax free each year.

Example—

Same facts as in example above, but Alice elects to take installment payments for 10 years. $10,000 ($100,000 divided by 10) is the principal amount received tax free. So, up to $11,000 per year may be received tax free by Alice, $10,000 of principal sum plus up to $1,000 of interest, under the surviving spouse's interest exclusion.

Installment payments when there is no lump-sum option in the policy: You must find the discounted value of the policy at the date of the insured's death and use that as the principal amount. The insurance company can give you that figure. After you find the discounted value, you divide it (as above) by the number of years you are to receive installments. The result is the amount that is tax free. The remainder is taxed.

Examples—

1. Under an insurance policy, the surviving wife is entitled to $5,000 a year for life. Her life expectancy is 20 years. There is no lump sum stated in the policy. Say the discounted value of the wife's rights is $60,000. The principal amount spread to each year for the wife is $3,000 ($60,000 divided by 20). In addition she gets a $1,000 interest exclusion. Subtracting this $4,000 from each annual $5,000 payment gives her taxed income of $1,000.

2. Under the same insurance policy, a surviving daughter gets $5,000 a year for 10 years. Say the discounted value of her rights is $35,000. The principal amount spread to each of the 10 years is $3,500 ($35,000 divided by 10). Subtracting this $3,500 from each annual $5,000 payment gives her taxed income of $1,500.

Payments to you along with other beneficiaries under the same policy, by lump-sum or varying installments.

Example—

Under one life insurance policy, a surviving wife, daughter, and nephew of the insured are all beneficiaries. The wife is entitled to a lump sum of $60,000. The daughter and the nephew are each entitled to a lump sum of $35,000. Under the installment options, the wife chooses to receive $5,000 a year for the rest of her life. (She has a 20-year life expectancy.) The daughter and the nephew each chooses yearly payment of $5,000 for 10 years. This is how each yearly installment is taxed:

WIFE: The principal amount spread to each year is $3,000. In addition, she gets a $1,000 interest exclusion. Subtracting this $4,000 from the yearly $5,000 payment gives the wife taxed income of $1,000.

DAUGHTER AND NEPHEW (both are taxed the same way): The principal amount spread to each of the 10 years is $3,500. Subtracting this $3,500 from the yearly $5,000 installment gives the daughter and the nephew each taxed income of $1,500.

Interest, when proceeds are left on deposit under the "interest only" option, is fully taxed; the lump sum is not taxed. A surviving spouse may not exclude $1,000 interest under the "interest only" option. However, if the surviving spouse later elects to receive proceeds from the policy in installments, the interest exclusion applies from the time of the election.

Universal life policy. A universal life policy allows a policyholder to apply premium payments to cash value instead of to death benefits. Death benefits may be tax free if the policies meet certain technical tests. These tests must be determined by the insurance company. Therefore you must check with company paying the proceeds whether the payments qualify as tax-free life insurance proceeds.

Other names applied to universal life may be "flexible premium" or "adjustable life premium" policies.

¶12.31 • A POLICY WITH A FAMILY INCOME RIDER

Payments received under a family income rider are taxed under a special rule. A family income rider provides additional term insurance coverage for a fixed number of years from the date of the basic policy. Under the terms of a rider, if the insured dies at any time during the term period, his beneficiary receives monthly payments during the balance of the term period, and then at the end of term period, he receives the lump-sum proceeds of the basic policy. If the insured dies after the end of the term period, the beneficiary receives only the lump sum from the basic policy.

When the insured dies during the term period, part of each monthly payment received during the term period includes interest on the lump-sum proceeds of the basic policy (which is held by the company until the end of the term period). That interest is fully taxed. The balance of the monthly payment consists of an installment (principal plus interest) of the proceeds from the term insurance purchased under the family income rider. You may exclude from this balance: (1) A prorated portion of the present value of the lump sum under the basic policy, and (2) an additional amount of up to $1,000 attributable to interest if you are a surviving spouse. The lump sum under the basic policy is tax free when you eventually receive it.

The rules here also apply to an integrated family income policy and to family maintenance policies, whether integrated or with an attached rider.

In figuring your taxable portions, ask the insurance company for its interest rate and the present value of term payments.

¶12.32 • HOW OTHER INSURANCE PROCEEDS ARE TAXED

Dividends paid by the insurance company as reduction of premiums (taken in cash, left as interest with the company or used to accelerate the maturity of the policy) are not taxable. They serve to reduce the cost basis of your policy, thus increasing gain sometimes computed upon maturity of some policies. (But interest on these "dividends" is taxed even if the policy is issued by the Veterans Administration, *see* ¶4.02.)

Matured endowment policies. Gain is taxable, *see* ¶7.08. The payment on an endowment contract because of the insured's death is treated as the payment of tax-free life insurance proceeds provided the policy meets certain technical definitions not discussed in this book.

Sale of an endowment contract before maturity. Taxed as ordinary income. *See* ¶7.08.

Proceeds received from a health, accident, or disability policy other than at death. *See* the rules at ¶2.15, ¶2.16, and ¶2.19.

Surrender of policy for cash. Taxed as ordinary income (not capital gain), if the cash received exceeds the premiums paid, less dividends received. If you take, instead, a paid-up policy, you may avoid tax. *See* ¶12.33. You get no deduction if there is a loss on the surrender of a policy.

Collection of proceeds on policy purchased by or assigned to you on life of someone else. Where a policy is transferred for a valuable consideration, only the amount paid and the premiums paid after the transfer are tax free when collected; the balance is taxed. There is no tax on life insurance proceeds paid under contracts which have been transferred to a partner or to a corporation in which the insured was a shareholder or officer.

Proceeds received under an annuity or pension, retirement payments, Federal Old Age Benefits, state unemployment insurance, or a combination death benefit and annuity. *See* ¶2.10, ¶7.14.

¶12.33 • TAX-FREE EXCHANGES OF INSURANCE POLICIES

These exchanges are tax free—

Life insurance policy for another life insurance policy, endowment policy, or an annuity contract.

Endowment policy for another endowment policy which provides for regular payments beginning no later than the date payments would have started under the old policy, or for an annuity contract.

Annuity contract for another annuity contract with identical annuitants.

These exchanges are not tax free—

Endowment policy for a life insurance policy, or an endowment policy which provides for payments beginning at a date later than payments would have started under the old policy.

Annuity contract for a life insurance or an endowment policy.

¶13.00

Claiming Itemized Deductions

What You Should Know About Itemized Deductions and Zero Bracket Amount

Item	Explanation	Limitation
Zero bracket amount	The law gives a standard deduction called zero bracket amount. You do not have to calculate the zero bracket amount as it is incorporated into the tax rate schedules and tax tables and thus automatically reduces your income subject to tax. The zero bracket amount depends on your filing status. Certain individuals, such as dependent children with unearned income, may be unable to claim the full zero bracket amount, see ¶13.01.	The zero bracket amount in 1986 is: $3,670 if you are married, filing jointly, or a surviving spouse. $2,480, if you are unmarried (including head of household). $1,835 if you are married, filing separately.
Itemized deductions	You get greater tax savings by claiming itemized deductions which exceed the zero bracket amount for your filing status. Itemized deductions are charitable contributions, interest expenses, local and state taxes, medical and dental costs, casualty and theft losses, job and investment expenses, and educational costs.	There is no dollar limit on the amount of excess itemized deductions. But individual itemized deductions are subject to limitations explained below. **Example—** *Joint* *Single* Itemized deductions $15,000 $15,000 Less: Zero bracket amount 3,670 2,480 Excess itemized deductions $11,380 $12,520
Charitable contributions	You may deduct donations to religious, charitable, educational, and other philanthropic organizations that have been approved to receive deductible contributions. See ¶14.13. If you do not itemize deductions, you may deduct 100% of your contributions.	The contribution deduction is generally limited to 50% of adjusted gross income. Lower ceilings apply to property donations and contributions to foundations. See ¶14.15 for further details.
Interest expenses	You may deduct interest on loans and other debts. A list of common interest payments is at ¶15.01. You deduct the interest on the tax return of the year in which you paid the interest, unless you are on the accrual basis. Prepaid interest is deductible over the period of the loan, see ¶15.021.	No dollar limit on interest on business loans. But there is a limit on interest on loans to carry investments. Such interest may not exceed $10,000 plus your net investment income. Excess interest may be carried over. See ¶15.06.
Taxes	You may deduct payments of state, local, and foreign real property and income taxes as well as state and local personal property taxes and general sales and use taxes. You claim your deduction on the tax return of the year in which you paid the taxes unless you report on the accrual basis. See ¶16.05.	No dollar limitation.
Medical expenses	You may deduct payments of medical expenses for yourself and dependents. A checklist of over one hundred deductible medical items is at ¶17.01. Deductible drug costs are limited to drugs prescribed by a licensed professional.	Only expenses in excess of 5% of adjusted gross income are deductible.
Casualty and theft losses	You may deduct property losses caused by storms, fires, and other natural events and as the result of theft. See ¶18.00.	Each individual casualty loss must exceed $100 and the total of all losses during the year must exceed 10% of adjusted gross income.
Job expenses	You may deduct the cost of union dues, work clothes, entertainment, and looking for a new job. See ¶19.00.	No dollar limitation.
Investment expenses	You may deduct investment expenses and other expenses of producing and collecting income, expenses of maintaining income-producing property, expenses of tax return preparation, refunds and audits. See ¶19.14.	No dollar limitation.
Educational costs	You may deduct the cost of courses to maintain or improve your job skills, or those required by your employer or by law to keep your present salary or position. See ¶21.00.	No dollar limitation.

ZERO BRACKET AMOUNT

¶13.01 • COMPUTING THE UNUSED ZERO BRACKET AMOUNT

Certain taxpayers may not be entitled to the full zero bracket amount. They must compute "unused zero bracket amount" which is simply that part of the zero bracket amount not allowed to them. The "unused zero bracket amount" is added to adjusted gross income. As a result, the individual pays tax at a higher rate than would apply if the zero bracket amount had not been reduced.

The "unused zero bracket amount" is generally the zero bracket amount less itemized deductions. If the total of itemized deductions equals or exceeds the zero bracket amount, there is no "unused zero bracket amount," and the amount exceeding the zero bracket amount is claimed as excess itemized deductions.

The following taxpayers must compute the "unused zero bracket amount":

A married person filing a separate return whose spouse claims excess itemized deductions. See ¶13.02.

A child for whom parents may claim a dependency exemption and who has unearned income. See ¶13.03.

A nonresident alien.

A U.S. citizen who makes a tax election on income from sources within U.S. possessions.

¶13.02 • HUSBANDS AND WIVES FILING SEPARATE RETURNS

If you file separate returns, you and your spouse must first decide whether each of you will claim itemized deductions or limit yourselves to the zero bracket amount of $1,835 each. You must elect the same method. That is, if one spouse has itemized deductions exceeding $1,835 (zero bracket amount) and elects to itemize, the other spouse must also itemize, even if his or her itemized deductions are less than $1,835. In such a case, the spouse with itemized deductions of less than $1,835 computes the unused zero bracket amount, which increases taxable income. The purpose of this computation is to prevent a married person filing a separate return from claiming the zero bracket amount to the extent that itemized deductions are less than the zero bracket amount.

Example—

The Smiths decide to file separate returns. Mrs. Smith has wages of $10,000 and itemized deductions of $600. Mr. Smith itemizes his deductions, which exceed $1,835. Mrs. Smith must compute the unused zero bracket amount, which she adds to her adjusted gross income.

Adjusted gross income		$10,000
Add: Unused zero bracket amount:		
Zero bracket amount	$1,835	
Less: Itemized deductions	600	1,235
Taxable income before exemptions		$11,235

Choose the method that gives the lowest combined tax: Itemizing deductions or restricting yourselves to the $1,835 zero bracket amount each. Note, however, you may not itemize unless at least one spouse has itemized deductions exceeding $1,835, or is otherwise required to itemize deductions (see ¶13.03).

On a separate return, each spouse may deduct only those itemized expenses for which he or she is liable. This is true even if one spouse pays expenses for the other. For example, if property is owned by the wife, then the interest and taxes imposed on the property are her deductions, not her husband's. If he pays them, neither one may deduct them on separate returns. The husband may not because they were not his liability. The wife may not because she did not pay them. This is true also of interest on a personal loan and casualty or theft losses.

Claiming excess itemized deductions when you are living apart from your spouse. When a husband and wife are separated under a decree of divorce or separate maintenance, they are free to compute their tax as they see fit, without reference to the return of the other spouse. If one spouse has excess itemized deductions, that spouse may elect to claim them, and the other spouse is not required to itemize. The zero bracket amount is not limited to $1,835. They are treated as single.

If a husband and wife are separated but do not have such a decree, both must either itemize or limit the zero bracket amount for each of them to $1,835. There is an exception if you are married and live apart from your spouse and meet the following conditions:

Your spouse was not a member of your household during the last six months of 1986;

You maintained as your home a household which was the principal place of abode for your child, adopted child, foster child, or stepchild for more than half of 1986;

You are entitled to claim the child as a dependent (¶1.541) or the child's other parent has the right to the exemption under the rules of ¶1.554.

You provide over half the cost of supporting the household.

If you satisfy these conditions and file a separate return, you may compute your tax as though you were single. That is, your zero bracket amount is $2,480 and you may elect to itemize without regard to whether your spouse itemizes or not. You may use head of household rates if you meet the rules at ¶1.05.

¶13.03 • UNUSED ZERO BRACKET AMOUNT FOR DEPENDENT CHILD WITH UNEARNED INCOME

A dependent unmarried child with unearned income of less than $1,080 generally does not have to file a 1986 return, unless his gross income is $3,560 or more. A married child claimed as a dependent must file if gross income is $1,080 or more and must follow the rules of ¶13.02 if separate returns are filed.

In 1986, the zero bracket amount for a child for whom you are allowed a dependency exemption (whether or not you claim it) is generally $2,480. In the case of a married child filing separately, the zero bracket amount is $1,835.

A dependent child is required to itemize whatever deductions he has on Schedule A and to compute the unused zero bracket amount if *unearned* income is $1,080 or more and *earned* income is less than $2,480 or $1,835 if married filing separately (see Example 1). The unused zero bracket amount is then added to the child's adjusted gross income for purposes of determining tax liability. If a dependent child has *earned* income of at least $2,480 ($1,835 if married filing separately), there is no unused zero bracket amount and deductions do not have to be itemized on Schedule A (see Example 2). If the child's *earned* income is less than the zero bracket amount of $2,480 or $1,835, but exceeds itemized deductions, the unused zero bracket amount must be figured, but itemized deductions are ignored and need not be listed on Schedule A (see Example 3 below).

Examples—

1. The Smiths may claim their daughter Ellen as a dependent. Ellen's income is $1,200 of interest and wages of $300 and itemized

deductions of $500 (including sales tax from the optional sales tax table). Her taxable income before subtracting her personal exemption is figured as follows:

Adjusted gross income		$1,500
Zero bracket amount	$2,480	
Less: Itemized deductions from Schedule A	500	
Add: Unused zero bracket amount		1,980
Taxable income before exemption		$3,480

2. Same as above except Ellen earned $2,500. She does not have an unused zero bracket amount; her earned income of $2,500 exceeds the zero bracket amount of $2,480. Her taxable income before the deduction of the exemption is $3,700.

3. Same as Example 1 except that she earned $1,000. Since her earned income is less than her zero bracket amount but more than itemized deductions of $500, she does not itemize deductions on Schedule A but computes her unused zero bracket amount as follows:

Adjusted gross income		$2,200
Zero bracket amount	$2,480	
Less: Earned income	1,000	
Add: Unused zero bracket amount		1,480
Taxable income before exemption		$3,680

¶13.04 • ADJUSTED GROSS INCOME

Adjusted gross income is a technical term used in the tax law. It is the amount used in figuring the 5% floor for the medical expense deductions, the 10% floor for personal casualty and theft losses, and the charitable contribution limitation. If you follow the instructions and order of the tax return, you will arrive at adjusted gross income without having to know or understand the following steps of finding adjusted gross income. But if you are planning the tax consequences of a transaction in advance of preparing your return, this is how to figure adjusted gross income.

Adjusted gross income is the difference between gross income (Step 1) and deductions listed in Step 2 below. If you do not have any of these deductions, adjusted gross income is the same as gross income.

Step 1: Figure gross income. This is all income received by you from any source, such as wages, salary, gross business income, income from sales and exchanges, interest and dividends (less the exclusion), rents, royalties, annuities, pensions, etc. But gross income does not include such items as tax-free interest from state or local bonds, tax-free parsonage allowance, tax-free insurance proceeds, gifts and inheritances, Social Security benefits which are not subject to tax under the rules of ¶34.11, tax-free scholarship grants, tax-free board and lodging allowance, and the first $5,000 of death benefits.

Step 2: Deduct from gross income only the following items:
Deduction for two-earner married couples if applicable.

Trade or business expenses. These items are listed on Schedule C.

Certain travel expenses of employees. Expenses in this category include local transportation expenses, travel expenses away from home, outside salesperson expenses and reimbursed job expenses.

Moving expenses.

Capital gain deduction for net capital gains. This deduction is figured on Schedule D.

Capital loss deduction. Where capital losses exceed capital gains, capital loss deduction up to $3,000 may be deducted from gross income. Schedule D is used to figure this loss deduction.

Net operating losses.

Certain deductions of life tenants and income beneficiaries of property.

Contributions to a Keogh plan. The deduction for the contribution on your behalf is taken on Form 1040; contributions for your employees on Schedule C.

Contributions to IRAs.

Contributions to pension plans of S corporations.

Certain portion of lump-sum pension distributions.

Alimony payments.

Forfeit penalties because of a premature withdrawal of funds from time savings accounts or deposits.

Expenses to produce rent and royalty income.

Repayment of supplemental unemployment benefits required because of receipt of trade readjustment allowances.

Reforestation expenses.

Step 3: The difference between Steps 1 and 2 is adjusted gross income.

¶14.00
Charitable Contribution Deduction

Illustrations of deducing charitable contributions may be found in the Supplement to YOUR INCOME TAX. Mail the card at the front of this book to receive the FREE Supplement, which includes filled-in returns and last-minute information.

¶14.01 • DEDUCTIBLE CONTRIBUTIONS

You may deduct donations to religious, charitable, educational, and other philanthropic organizations which have been approved by the IRS to receive deductible contributions (*see* ¶14.13). If you are unsure of the tax status of a philanthropy, ask the organization about its status, or check the IRS list of tax-exempt organizations (IRS Publication No. 78). Donations to federal, state, and local governmental bodies are also deductible.

Generally, charitable contributions are deductible only as itemized deductions. However, a deduction is allowed in 1986 to those who do not itemize deductions. See ¶14.011.

Timing your contributions. You deduct donations on the tax return filed for the year in which you paid them in cash or property. A contribution by check is deductible in the year you give the check, even if it is cashed in the following year. A check mailed and dated on the last day of 1986 is deductible in 1986. A postdated check with a 1987 date is not deductible until 1987. A pledge or a note is not deductible until paid. Donations made through a credit card are deductible in the year the charge is made. Donations made through a pay-by-phone bank account are not deductible until the payment date shown on the bank statement. Keep a record of canceled checks or receipts from charities.

If you are planning to donate appreciated securities near the end of the year, make sure that you consider these delivery rules in timing the donation. If you unconditionally deliver or mail a properly endorsed stock certificate to the donee or its agent, the gift is considered completed on the date of delivery or mailing, provided it is received in the ordinary course of the mails. If you deliver the certificate to your bank or broker as your agent, or to the issuing corporation or its agent, your gift is not complete until the stock is transferred to the donee's name on the corporation's books. This transfer may take several weeks, so if possible, make the delivery at least three weeks before the end of the year to assure a current deduction.

Limits on deduction. In general, the amount of your charitable deduction is limited to 50% of adjusted gross income. A 30% ceiling applies to deductions for donations of certain types of appreciated property (*see* ¶14.15). Where donations in one year exceed the statutory limit, a five-year carryover of the excess may be allowed (*see* ¶14.16).

Debts. You may assign to a charity a debt payable to you. A contribution deduction may be claimed in the year your debtor pays the charity.

Dues. Dues paid to a tax-exempt organization may be deductible if you receive no benefits or privileges from the organization for the dues, such as monthly bulletins or journals, use of a library, or the right to attend luncheons and lectures.

If dues are paid to a social club with the understanding that a specified part goes to a named charity, you may claim a charitable deduction for dues earmarked for the charity. If the treasurer of your club is actually the agent of the charity, you take the deduction in the year you give him the money. If the treasurer is merely your agent, you may take the deduction only in the year the money is turned over to the charity.

¶14.011 • CONTRIBUTION DEDUCTION FOR NONITEMIZERS

You may deduct 100% of your charitable contributions on your 1986 return even if you do not claim itemized deductions. The maximum deduction is subject to the percentage ceilings explained at ¶14.15.

You may save taxes by claiming this nonitemized charitable deduction rather than itemizing deductions. This will occur if your deductible charitable contributions exceed your *excess* itemized deductions, including the charitable contributions.

Example—
Your 1986 itemized deductions are $4,500, including charitable donations of $2,500. You file a joint return. You would save by not itemizing. If you itemized, your deductible excess itemized deductions would be $830 ($4,500 less zero bracket amount of $3,670). If you do not itemize but claim the 100% charitable deduction, you deduct $2,500.

¶14.02 • BENEFIT TICKETS, BAZAARS, AND BINGO

Tickets to theater events, tours, concerts, and other entertainments are often sold by charitable organizations at prices higher than the regular admission charge. The difference between the regular admission and the higher amount you pay is deductible as a charitable contribution. If you decline to accept the ticket or return it to the charity for resale, your deduction is the price you paid.

If the benefit ticket price is the same or less than the regular admission price, you have no deduction unless you refuse to accept the ticket or you return the ticket to the charity for resale. If you purchase season tickets to a charity-sponsored series of programs and your average cost per program equals or is less than the cost for individual performances, your deduction for a returned ticket depends upon how long you held the tickets. Generally, you may deduct only your cost. However, if you have held the ticket for more than a year, you may deduct the fair market value, the price the charity will charge on resale of the ticket.

You may not deduct the cost of raffle tickets, bingo games, or other types of lotteries organized by charities.

Donations tied to football season tickets. To encourage donations to athletic scholarship programs, universities allow donors who contribute a specific amount to buy a season ticket for football games in preferred seating locations. A deduction is allowed to the extent that the donation exceeds the value of the right to buy the season ticket.
Examples—
1. An alumnus pays $300 for the right to buy a season ticket in a designated location before season tickets are offered to noncontributors. There are comparable seats that he could have purchased even if he had not made the contribution. $300 is deductible. The right to get tickets early and to sit with other contributors is not a substantial benefit.
2. $300 must be paid for the right to buy a season ticket in a specific section. The university brochure states that the fair market value of the right to buy the ticket is $120 and that $180 is the contribution. $180 is deductible unless the IRS claims that the seating privilege is worth more than $120.

¶14.03 • UNREIMBURSED EXPENSES OF VOLUNTEER WORKERS

If you work without pay for an organization listed at ¶14.13, you may deduct as charitable contributions your unreimbursed travel expenses, including commutation expenses to and from its place of operations, and meals and lodging on a trip away from home for the organization. To qualify for the deduction, the expenses must be incurred for a domestic organization which authorizes your travel.

You may not deduct the value of your donated services.

You may deduct either the actual operating costs of your car in volunteer work, or a flat mileage rate of 12¢ a mile allowed by the IRS. Parking fees and tolls are deductible under both methods.
Example—
You are a volunteer worker for a philanthropy. In the course of

your volunteer work, you drove the car approximately 1,000 miles. You may claim a contribution deduction of $120 plus tolls and parking.

The 12¢ a mile deduction rate is not mandatory. If your out-of-pocket expenses are greater, you may deduct your actual costs of operating the automobile exclusively for charitable work, such as gas and oil, in addition to tolls and parking fees.

Also deductible as charitable contributions are:

Uniform costs required in serving the organization.

Cost of telephone calls, and cost of materials and supplies furnished (stamps, stationery).

Convention expenses of official delegates to conventions of church, charitable, veteran, or other similar organizations. Members who are not delegates get no such deduction. However, they may deduct expenses paid for the benefit of their organization at the convention.

Expenses incurred by volunteers in operating their equipment. No deduction, however, is allowed for the rental value of such equipment, depreciation, and premiums paid on liability or property damage insurance.

Expenses of unsalaried city and town officials.

The IRS does not allow a deduction for "baby-sitting" expenses of charity volunteer workers. Although incurred to make the volunteer work possible, baby-sitting costs are a nondeductible personal expense. Further, the expense is not a dependent care cost; it is not related to a paying job.

¶14.04 • SUPPORT OF A STUDENT IN YOUR HOME

A limited charitable deduction is allowed for support of an elementary or high school student in your home under an educational program arranged by a charitable organization. If the student is not a relative, you may deduct as a charitable contribution your support payments up to $50 for each month the student stays in your home. For this purpose, 15 days or more of a calendar month is considered a full month. You may not deduct any payments received from the charitable organization in reimbursement for the student's maintenance.

To support the deduction, be prepared to show a written agreement between you and the organization relating to the support arrangement. Keep records of amounts spent for such items as food, clothing, medical and dental care, tuition, books, and recreation in order to substantiate your deduction. No deduction is allowed for depreciation on your house.

Property Donations

¶14.05 • APPRECIATED PROPERTY DONATIONS

Donations of property (securities, houses, collectibles, automobiles, paintings, manufactured goods, etc.) are deductible. Whether the full amount of the fair market value of the property is deductible depends on the type of property donated, the holding period, the nature of the philanthropy, and the use to which the property is put. You may have to attach an appraisal summary to your return; see ¶14.101.

Intangible personal property (such as securities) and real estate held long term. Fair market value is deductible where such property is given to a publicly supported charity or to a private foundation which distributes donations to publicly supported charities within 2½ months after the end of the tax year in which it receives the donations. Deductions for such appreciated property are limited to 30% of adjusted gross income, with a five-year carryover for the excess. Carryovers are discussed at ¶14.16. If the donation exceeds the 30% ceiling you may consider a special election which allows you to apply the 50% ceiling. See ¶14.17.

Tax advantage of donating securities or realty held long term. You may claim a deduction for the fair market value of the property and also avoid tax on the appreciation in value of the property. The amount of tax you avoid further reduces the cost of your donation.

You may figure the reduced cost of such a donation of appreciated property by following these two steps:
1. Figure the tax reduction resulting from the deduction of the fair market value of the property. For example, you donate appreciated stock which is selling at $1,000. Your top tax bracket is 38%. The deduction for the donation reduces your taxes by $380.
2. Estimate how much tax you would have paid on a sale of the stock. Assume you would have to pay tax of $108 on a sale of the stock at $1,000. The total tax savings from your donation is $488 ($380 + $108). The cost of your contribution is $512 ($1,000 − 488).

The IRS ruled that you may not claim a deduction on donated stock if you retain the voting rights, even though the charity has the right to receive dividends and sell the stock. The right to vote is considered a substantial interest and is crucial in protecting a stockholder's financial interest.

Ordinary income property. This is property which, if sold by you at its fair market value, would *not* result in long-term capital gain. The deduction for donations of this kind of property is restricted to your cost for the property. Examples of ordinary income property are: Stock held short term, inventory items donated by business, farm crops, Section 306 stock (preferred stock received as a tax-free stock dividend, usually in a closely-held corporation), and works of art, books, letters, and memoranda donated by the person who prepared or created them.

Examples—

1. You hold short-term stock which cost you $1,000. It is now worth $1,500. If you donate it to a philanthropy, your deduction would be limited to $1,000. You would get no tax benefit for the appreciation of $500. On the other hand, if the stock were held long term, you could claim a deduction for the full market value of the stock on its donation.

2. A former Congressman claimed a charitable deduction for the donation of his papers. His deduction was disallowed. His papers were ordinary income property and, since his cost basis in the papers was zero, he could claim no deduction.

Tangible personal property held long term. Items such as furniture, books, equipment, fixtures (severed from realty), jewelry and art objects are tangible personal property. When held long term, deductions for donations of this type of asset may be subject to restrictions. If the philanthropy to which you donate the property does not put it to a use that is related to its charitable function, you have to reduce the deduction by 40% of appreciation reflected in the property's fair market value. If the charity must sell your gift to obtain cash for its exempt purposes, your deduction is also reduced by 40% of appreciation. Where a donation of property is subject to a reduction as a nonrelated gift, the reduced gift is then subject to the 50% annual ceiling. If the gift is related to the organization's charitable purposes, you may deduct the property's fair market value subject to the 30% ceiling, or you may elect to deduct up to 50% of adjusted gross income by reducing the deduction by 40% of the appreciation. See ¶14.17.

Donating capital gain property to private nonoperating foundations. Generally, you may not deduct the full fair market value of gifts of capital gain property to private nonoperating foundations that are subject to the 20% deduction ceiling discussed at ¶14.15. The deduction must be reduced by 40% of the appreciation reflected in fair market value. Capital gain property is property which, if sold by you at fair market value would result in long-term capital gain. However, you may deduct the full value, without reduction, of contributed stock for which there is a readily available market quotation on an established securities market on the date of contribution. If you or family members contribute more than 10% of any corporation's stock, the full deduction may be claimed only for the first 10%.

> *Donation of mortgaged property may be taxable.* Before you give mortgaged property to a charity, have an attorney review the transaction. You may deduct the excess of fair market value over the amount of the outstanding mortgage. However, you may realize a taxable gain. The IRS and Tax Court treat the transferred mortgage debt as cash received in a part-gift, part-sale subject to the bargain-sale rules discussed at ¶14.07. This is true even if the charity does not assume the mortgage. You will realize a taxable gain if the transferred mortgage exceeds the portion of basis allocated to the sale part of the transaction.

Example—

You donate to a college land held long term which is worth $250,000 and subject to a $100,000 mortgage. Your basis for the land is $150,000. As a charitable contribution, you may deduct $150,000 ($250,000 − $100,000). You also are considered to have made a bargain sale for $100,000 on which you realized $40,000 long-term capital gain.

40% of the transaction is treated as a bargain sale.

$100,000 (amount of mortgage)
$250,000 (fair market value) = 40%

Basis allocated to sale: 40% of $150,000 or $60,000

Amount realized	$100,000
Allocated basis	60,000
Gain	$ 40,000

Figuring value. When donating securities listed on a public exchange, fair market value is readily ascertainable from newspaper listings of stock prices. It is the average of the high and low sales price on the date of the donation.

To value other property, such as real estate or works of art, you will need the services of an experienced appraiser. Fees paid to an appraiser are not deductible as a contribution, but rather as a miscellaneous itemized deduction.

U.S. Saving Bonds. You may not donate U.S. Saving Bonds, such as E Bonds, because you may not transfer them. They are nonnegotiable. You must first cash the bonds and then give the proceeds to the charity, or surrender the bonds and have new ones registered in the donee's name. When you do this, you have to report the accrued interest on your tax return. Of course, you will get a charitable deduction for the cash gift.

Gift of installment obligations. You may deduct your donation of installment notes to a qualified philanthropy. However, if you received them on your sale of property which you reported on the installment basis, you may realize gain or loss on the gift of the notes (see ¶6.192). The amount of the contribution is the fair market value of the obligation, not the face amount of the notes.

Tax return requirements. Save records to support the market value and cost of donated property. Get a receipt or letter from the charitable organization acknowledging and describing the gift. Lack of substantiation may disqualify an otherwise valid deduction. If the total claimed value of your property donations exceeds $500, you must report the donation on Form 8283, which you attach to Schedule A, Form 1040. See also ¶14.101 for when you need an appraisal of the value of the property.

¶14.06 • PROPERTY THAT HAS DECLINED BELOW COST

Unless the charity needs the property for its own use, you should not donate business or investment property whose value has declined below your cost. You may not claim a deductible loss when you make a gift. When the property is held for investment or business purposes, you may get the loss deduction by first selling the property and then a charitable deduction by donating the cash proceeds of the sale.

Example—

You own securities which cost $20,000 several years ago but which have declined in value to $5,000. A donation of these securities gives a charitable contribution of $5,000. But selling the securities for $5,000 to make a cash donation provides a long-term capital loss of $15,000.

If property is a personal asset (clothing, automobile) you may not deduct a loss on the sale (see ¶6.02). It makes no difference whether you sell and donate the sales proceeds or give the property directly to the charity.

¶14.07 • BARGAIN SALES OF APPRECIATED PROPERTY

A sale of appreciated property to a philanthropy for less than fair market value allows you to claim a charitable deduction for the donated appreciation while receiving proceeds from the sale. However, you must pay a tax on part of the gain attributed to the sale. That is, the transaction is broken down into two parts: (1) The sale and (2) the gift.

To compute gain on the sale, you allocate the adjusted basis of the property between the sale and the gift.

1. Find the percentage of the sales proceeds over fair market value of the property.
2. Apply the percentage to the adjusted basis of the property.
3. Deduct the resulting basis of step (2) from the sales proceeds to find the gain.

Example—

You sell to a university for $12,000 stock held long term. The adjusted basis of the stock is $12,000 and the fair market value $20,000. On the sale, you have recouped your investment and donated appreciation of $8,000, but at the same time, you have realized taxable gain of $4,800 computed as follows:

1. Percentage of basis applied to the sale:

(sales proceeds)	$12,000	or 60%.
(fair market value)	$20,000	

2. Basis allocated to sale: 60% of adjusted basis of $12,000 or $7,200.
3. Gain on sale:

Sales proceeds	$12,000
Allocated basis	7,200
Gain	$ 4,800

In the case of stock where individual shares may be sold, it will make no practical difference whether you bargain-sell all of your shares to a charity, or you sell some of the shares on the open market for a price that equals your cost and make a donation of the balance of the shares. However, the bargain sale may provide an overall tax benefit if you want to recover part or all of the cost on donating a piece of property that may not be divided for sale.

The above discussion applies to bargain sales of (1) intangible personal property such as securities (including exchanges for an unassigned gift annuity); (2) real estate; and (3) tangible personal property that can be used by the charity. *See* ¶14.05. The bargain sale allocation rules apply whether or not the taxable gain realized is long- or short-term gain or ordinary income. But the allocation rules apply only where a deduction is allowable.

Examples—

1. You sell to your church ordinary income property worth $10,000 for your adjusted basis of $4,000. The gift of $6,000 must be reduced by the ordinary gain element of $6,000. The contribution deduction is reduced to zero. Consequently, no allocation of basis is required. You have no taxable gain. ($4,000 sale proceeds − $4,000 adjusted basis).

2. You sell securities held short term to your college for $6,000. Your adjusted basis is $4,000. Fair market value is $10,000. Your charitable contribution of $4,000 is reduced to zero because the gift is reduced by the $6,000 ordinary income element ($4,000 − $6,000). Since no charitable deduction is allowable under the sale, the allocation rules do not apply. Your taxable gain is $2,000 ($6,000 − $4,000).

3. You sell to a church for $2,000 stock held short term which has an adjusted basis of $4,000 and a fair market value of $10,000. Without allocation of basis, a charitable deduction of $2,000 would be allowed (the gift of $8,000 less the ordinary gain element of $6,000). Since a deduction would be allowed, the bargain sale allocation formula is applied. Thus 20% of basis

$$\frac{\$2,000 \text{ proceeds}}{\$10,000 \text{ market value}} \times \$4,000 \text{ adjusted basis}$$

or $800 is the allocated basis of the "sold" property. You have realized a taxable short-term gain of $1,200 ($2,000 less $800). However, your charitable contribution deduction is $3,200 (80% of basis of $4,000).

Where the property is subject to a debt, the amount of the debt is included as part of the amount realized for tax purposes.

The bargain sale computations are more complicated if you sell tangible personal property subject to the percentage reduction explained at ¶14.05, or if you bargain-sell property to a private foundation subject to the 20% ceiling. Basis must be allocated to both the gift portion and the sale portion of the transaction. To determine the allowable deduction, the gift is reduced by 40% of the appreciation in the allocated gift portion. *See* Publication 526 and Treasury regulations for details.

¶14.08 • ART OBJECTS

You may claim a charitable deduction for a painting or other art object donated to a charity. The amount of the deduction depends on (1) whether you were the artist; (2) if you are not the artist, how long you owned it; (3) the type of organization receiving the gift.

If you are the artist, your deduction is limited to cost regardless of how long you held the art work or to what use the charity puts it. In the case of a painting, the deduction would be the lower of cost for canvas and paints or the fair market value.

If you owned the art work short term, your deduction is limited to cost, under the rules applying to donations of ordinary income property at ¶14.05.

If you held the art object long term, your deduction depends upon how the charity uses it. If the charity uses it for its exempt purposes, you may deduct the fair market value. However, if the charity uses it for unrelated purposes, your deduction is reduced by 40% of the appreciation. A donation of art work to a general fund raising agency would be reduced because the agency would have no direct use for it. It would have to sell the art work and use the cash for its exempt purposes.

Examples—

1. You give your college a painting which you have owned for many years. Its cost was $100 but is now worth $1,000. The school displays the painting in its library for study by students. This use is related to the school's educational purposes. Your donation is deductible at fair market value. If, however, the school proposed to sell the painting and use the proceeds for general education purposes, its use would not be considered related. Your deduction would be reduced by $360 (40% of the $900 appreciation) to $640. That the school sells the painting does not necessarily reduce the donation if you show that, when you made the gift, it was reasonable to anticipate that your gift would not be put to such unrelated use.

2. You donate to the Community Fund a collection of first edition books held for many years and worth $5,000. Your cost is $1,000. Since the charity is a general fund raising organization, its use of your gift is not related. Your deduction would be $3,400 ($5,000 less 40% of $4,000 appreciation).

3. You contribute to a charity antique furnishings you owned for years. The antiques cost you $500 and are now worth $5,000. The charity uses the furnishings in its office in the course of carrying on its functions. This is a related use. Your contribution deduction is $5,000.

A sale by the charity of an insubstantial part of a collection does not result in reduction of the contribution deduction.

Be prepared to support your deduction with detailed proof of cost, the date of acquisition, and how value was appraised. The appraisal fee is deductible as an itemized "miscellaneous" expense.

The IRS has its own art advisory panel to assess whether the fair market value of art works is reasonable.

¶14.09 • INTERESTS IN REAL ESTATE

No deduction is allowable for the fair rental value of property you allow a charity to use without charge even in direct furtherance of its charitable functions as, for example, for a thrift shop.

If you donate an undivided fractional part of your entire interest, a deduction will be allowed for the fair market value of the proportionate interest donated.

A donation of an option is not deductible until the year the option to buy the property is exercised.

Remainder interest in a home or farm. You may claim a charitable deduction for a gift of the remainder value of a residence or farm donated to a charity, even though you reserve the use of the property for yourself and your spouse for a term of years or life. Remainder gifts generally must be made in trust. However, where a residence or farm is donated the remainder interest must be conveyed outright, not in trust. A remainder interest in a vacation home or in a "hobby" farm is also deductible. There is no requirement that the home be your principal residence or that the farm be profit making.

Contribution of real property for conservation purposes. A deduction may be claimed for the contribution of certain partial interests in real property to government agencies or publicly supported charities for exclusively conservation purposes. Deductible contributions include: (1) Your entire interest in real property other than retained rights to subsurface oil, gas, or other minerals, (2) a remainder interest, or (3) an easement, restrictive covenant, or similar property restriction granted in perpetuity. The contribution must be in perpetuity and further at least one of these "conservation purposes": Preservation of land areas for outdoor recreation, education, or scenic enjoyment; preservation of historically important land areas or structures; the protection of plant, fish, and wildlife habitats or similar natural ecosystems. To obtain the deduction, there must be legally enforceable restrictions that prevent you from using your retained interest in the property in a way contrary to the intended conservation purpose. The donee organization must be prohibited from transferring the contributed interest except to other organizations that will hold the property for exclusively conservation purposes. If you retain an interest in subsurface oil, gas, or minerals, surface mining must generally be specifically prohibited. However, there is a limited exception where the mineral rights and surface interests have been separately owned since June 12, 1976. A deduction will be allowed if the probability of surface mining is too remote to be considered negligible. The exception does not apply if you are related to the owner of the surface interest or if you received the mineral interest (directly or indirectly) from the surface owner.

¶14.10 • LIFE INSURANCE

You may deduct the value of a life insurance policy if the charity is irrevocably named as beneficiary and you make both a legal assignment and a complete delivery of the policy. You should reserve no right to change the beneficiary.

The amount of your deduction generally depends on the type of policy donated. Your insurance company can furnish you with the information necessary to calculate your deduction. In addition, you may deduct premiums you pay after you assign the policy.

¶14.101 • APPRAISALS NEEDED FOR PROPERTY DONATIONS

If the total value of your property donations exceeds $500, you must provide details for each donation on Form 8283. Further, if you donate property other than publicly traded securities valued at more than $5,000, you must get a written appraisal to support your deduction. An appraisal is also required if several similar items such as coins or paintings with an aggregate value exceeding $5,000 are donated, even if the donees are different. For nonpublicly traded securities valued at more than $5,000 but not more than $10,000, an appraisal is not required but the gift must be reported on Form 8283.

An appraisal must be made by an unrelated professional appraiser no earlier than 60 days before your gift, and you must receive it by the due date, including extensions, of your return.

Keep the appraisal for your records. You do not have to attach the appraisal to your return, but you must complete an appraisal summary on Form 8283. The appraisal summary must be signed by an authorized representative of the donee organization, acknowledging receipt of the property. Further, your appraiser must certify the appraised value and his or her qualifications on the form.

If you do not complete a required appraisal summary on Form 8283, the IRS may disallow the deduction, or it may give you 90 days to provide the information. If you comply, the deduction will be allowed unless the IRS concludes that the original failure was not a good faith omission.

A professional appraiser is subject to a $1,000 penalty if he knowingly overvalues charitable contribution property; $10,000 for corporate returns. If you rely on the appraisal of a disqualified appraiser, you may avoid penalties for claiming an overvalued deduction by showing that you were not aware of the appraiser's overvaluation. Penalties for overvaluation of property values are discussed at ¶38.06.

A fee paid an appraiser is deductible as a "miscellaneous" expense.

Charity reports transfers within two years. If the charity sells or otherwise disposes of the appraised property within two years after your gift, it must notify the IRS on Form 8282 and send you a copy. The IRS could compare the selling price received by the charity with the value you claimed on Form 8283.

¶14.11 • BUSINESS OR FARM INVENTORY

Business owners and accrual basis farmers generally may not deduct more than cost for donations of inventory. Costs incurred in a year prior to the donation must be removed from inventory if a charitable deduction is claimed. No contribution deduction is allowed for a gift of merchandise which was produced or acquired in the year donated. Instead, the cost is deducted as a business expense or added to the cost of goods sold. A business expense deduction is not subject to the percentage limitation applied to donations.

A cash basis farmer may not claim a charitable deduction for a donation of inventory products. This is because the fair market value of his donated property must be reduced under the ordinary income rule to zero.

¶14.12 • DONATING INCOME AND REMAINDER INTERESTS THROUGH TRUSTS

Outright gifts are not the only way to make deductible gifts to charities. You may transfer property to a charitable income trust or a charitable remainder trust to provide funds for charity.

A charitable income trust involves your transfer of property to a trust directed to pay income to a charity you name, for the term of the trust, and then to return the property to you or to someone else.

A charitable remainder trust is one which provides income for you or another beneficiary for life, after which the property passes to a charity.

Trust arrangements require the services of an experienced attorney who will draft the trust in appropriate form and advise you of the tax consequences.

Deductions for gifts of income interests in trust. Current law is designed to prevent a donor from claiming an immediate deduction for the present value of trust income payable to a charity for a term of years. In limited situations, a donor may claim a deduction if either: (1) He gives away all his interests in the property. For example, he puts his property in trust, giving an income interest for 20 years to a church and the remainder to a college. A deduction is allowed for the value of the property. (2) He creates a unitrust or annuity trust, and he is taxable on the income. A unitrust for this purpose provides that a fixed percentage of trust assets is payable to the charitable income beneficiary each year. An annuity trust provides for payment of a guaranteed dollar amount to the charitable income beneficiary each year. A deduction is allowed for the present value of the unitrust or annuity trust interest.

Alternative (2) will probably not be chosen, unless the income of the trust is from tax-exempt securities. A tax may be due if the donor dies before the trust ends or is no longer the taxable owner of trust income. The law provides for a recapture of a proportion of the tax deduction, even where the income was tax exempt (*see* Treasury regulations).

Charitable remainder trusts. A charitable deduction is allowable for transfers of property to charitable remainder trusts only if the trust meets these requirements: The income payable for a noncharitable income beneficiary's life or a term of up to 20 years must be guaranteed under a unitrust or annuity trust. If a donor gives all of his interests in the property to the charities, the annuity or unitrust requirements need not be satisfied. The value of the charitable deduction allowable for a gift in trust is determined by Treasury tables.

Life income plans. A philanthropy may offer a life income plan (pooled income fund) to which you transfer property or money in return for a guaranteed income for life. After your death, the philanthropy has full control over the property. If you enter such a plan, ask the philanthropy for the amount of the deduction that you may claim for the value of your gift.

Limitations Placed on Donations

¶14.13 • ORGANIZATIONS QUALIFIED TO RECEIVE DEDUCTIBLE DONATIONS

The following types of organizations may qualify to receive deductible contributions:

1. The United States, a possession or political subdivision, a state, city, or town. The gift must be for public purposes. The gift may be directed to a government unit, or it may be to a government agency, such as a state university, a fire department, a civil defense group, or a committee to raise funds to develop land into a public park. Donations may be made to the Social Security system (Federal Old Age and Survivors Insurance trust fund). Donations may be made to the federal government to help reduce the national debt; checks should be made payable to "Bureau of the Public Debt."

A donation to an American Indian tribe is not deductible. An Indian tribe is not a political subdivision of the United States, any state, or territory.

2. A domestic nonprofit organization, trust, community chest, fund or foundation operated exclusively for one of the following purposes—

Religious. Payments for pew rents, assessments, and dues to churches and synagogues are deductible.

Charitable. In this class are organizations such as Boy Scouts, Girl Scouts, American Red Cross, Community Funds, Cancer Societies, CARE, Salvation Army, Y.M.C.A., Y.W.C.A., etc.

Scientific, literary and educational. Included in this group are hospitals, research organizations, colleges, universities, and other schools that do not maintain racially discriminatory policies; leagues or associations set up for education or to combat crime, improve public morals, and aid public welfare.

Prevention of cruelty to children or animals.

Fostering amateur sports competition. However, the organization's activities may not provide athletic facilities or equipment.

3. Domestic nonprofit veteran organizations or auxiliary units.

4. A domestic fraternal group operating under the lodge system, only if contributions are to be used exclusively for religious, charitable, scientific, literary or educational purposes, or for the prevention of cruelty to children or animals.

5. Nonprofit cemetery and burial companies, where the voluntary contribution benefits the whole cemetery, not your plot.

6. Legal services corporation established under the Legal Services Corporation Act which provides legal assistance to financially needy people in noncriminal proceedings.

Foreign charities. You may deduct donations to domestic organizations which distribute funds to charities in foreign countries, as long as the American organization controls the distribution of the funds overseas. An outright contribution to a foreign charitable organization may not be deducted. Some exceptions to this ban are provided by international treaties. A limited exception applies to contributions to certain Canadian organizations if you have income from Canadian sources. For further details, write IRS, Foreign Operations District, Washington, D.C. 20225.

¶14.14 • NONDEDUCTIBLE CONTRIBUTIONS

1. Payments to an organization that devotes a substantial part of its activities to lobbying, trying to influence legislation, or carrying on propaganda or whose lobbying activities exceed certain limits set by the law causing the organization to lose its tax-exempt status. The IRS has disallowed contributions to a civic group opposing saloons, nightclubs, and gambling places, although the group also aided libraries, churches, and other public programs.

2. Gifts to needy or worthy individuals, scholarships for specific students or gifts to organizations to benefit only certain groups. However, the IRS in private rulings has allowed deductions for scholarship funds which are limited to members of a particular religion, so long as that religion is open to all on a racially nondiscriminatory basis, and to scholarship funds open only to male students.

3. Gifts to organizations such as—

Fraternal groups—except when they set up special organizations exclusively devoted to charitable, educational, or other approved purposes.

Professional groups—such as those organized by accountants, lawyers, and physicians—except when they are specially created for exclusive charitable, educational, or other philanthropic purposes. The IRS will disallow unrestricted gifts made to state bar associations, although such organizations may have some public purposes. Courts have allowed donations to bar associations on the ground that their activities benefit the general public.

Clubs for social purposes—fraternities and sororities are generally in this class.

4. Donations to civic leagues, communist or communist-front organizations, chambers of commerce, business leagues, or labor unions.

5. Contributions to a hospital or school operated for profit.

6. Purchase price of church building bond. To claim a deduction, you must donate the bond to the church. The amount of the deduction is the fair market value of the bond when you make the donation. Interest on the bond is income each year, under the original issue discount rules of ¶4.01, where no interest will be paid until the bond matures.

7. Donations of blood to the Red Cross or other blood banks.

8. Contributions to foreign charitable organizations or directly to foreign governments. Thus, a contribution to the State of Israel was disallowed. Similarly, contributions to international charitable organizations are nondeductible.

9. Donations which provide you with goods or services. You may not deduct tuition payments to a parochial or other church-sponsored school for the education of your children. Payments exceeding the usual tuition charge are deductible.

You may not deduct fees paid to a tax-exempt rest home in which you live, or to a hospital for the care of a particular patient. A gift to a retirement home, over and above monthly fees, is not deductible if the size or type of your quarters depends on the gift.

Unless you contribute to an organization exclusively operated for a charitable, religious, or other approved purpose, you may not deduct your contribution, even though your funds are used for a charitable or religious purpose.

Donation of services. You may not deduct the value of volunteer work you perform for charities. But see ¶14.03 for the deductions allowed for unreimbursed expenses incurred during such work.

Free use of property. You may not deduct the rental value of property you allow a charity to use without charge. That is, if you allow a charity rent-free use of an office in your building, you may not deduct the fair rental value. You also have no deduction when you lend money to a charity without charging interest.

Political contributions to campaigns are discussed at ¶24.60.

¶14.15 • CEILING ON CHARITABLE DEDUCTIONS

Depending on the type of contribution and the organization to which the donation is made, an annual ceiling of 20%, 30%, or 50% may be placed on the amount of contributions allowed as a deduction. The ceiling is based on a technical term called "contribution base." For most purposes, "contribution base" is adjusted gross income (see ¶13.04). "Contribution base" is adjusted gross income computed without regard to a net operating loss carryback.

For most individuals, the 50% limit will apply, except where they contribute appreciated securities or other intangible personal property and real estate held long term. Such contributions are subject to the 30% ceiling if made to organizations qualifying for the 50% ceiling. A 20% limit generally applies to contributions of capital gain property to organizations that do not qualify for the 50% ceiling, such as nonoperating private foundations and charities that do not receive substantial support from the general public. However, for contributions of cash and ordinary income property to such organizations, a 30% ceiling applies. A 30% ceiling also applies to gifts, such as gifts in trust, which are considered to be "for the use of," rather than directly "to" a qualified charity.

A husband and wife filing a joint return figure the ceiling on their total joint adjusted gross income.

50% ceiling. Contributions of cash and noncapital gain property generally are subject to the 50% ceiling if *made to* the following types of charitable organizations:

Churches, synagogues and other religious organizations.

Schools, colleges and other educational organizations that normally have regular faculties and student bodies in attendance.

Hospitals and medical research organizations.

Foundations for state colleges.

Publicly supported organizations that receive a substantial part of their financial support from the general public or a government unit. Libraries, museums, drama, opera, ballet and orchestral societies, community funds, the American Red Cross, Heart Fund and other groups providing research and aid in treatment of disease are generally in this category.

Private operating foundations.

Private foundations that distribute their income annually to qualified charities within the time prescribed by law.

Private foundations that pool donations, allow donors to designate the charities to receive their gifts, and pay out all funds received within times stated by IRS rules.

Donations made merely *for the use of* an organization do not qualify for the 50% ceiling. This restriction affects certain trust dispositions (*see* Treasury regulations).

30% limit for certain capital gain property. The 30% limit generally applies to donations of appreciated intangible personal property (like securities) and real estate held long term where the gift is to a publicly supported charity or a foundation that qualifies for the 50% ceiling; *see* list above. This 30% limit also applies to donations of appreciated tangible personal property held long term (like a boat, furnishings, art work, etc.) where the charitable organization's use of your gift is directly related to its charitable purposes. However, the 50% ceiling applies to gifts of tangible personal property held long term where the organization's use of the gift is not directly related to its charitable purposes and the deduction is reduced for appreciation (*see* ¶14.05). The 50% ceiling may also apply to appreciated intangible personal property under an election providing for a percentage reduction explained in ¶14.17.

30% limit for gifts to nonoperating private foundations and certain other organizations. Gifts of cash or ordinary income property are subject to a 30% limit if made to nonoperating private foundations and other charities that are not in the above list of corporations qualifying for the 50% ceiling. For example, a gift of cash or ordinary income property to a veteran's organization, fraternal society or nonprofit cemetery is subject to the 30% ceiling.

Such gifts are deductible only to the extent of the lower of: (1) 30% of your adjusted gross income, or (2) 50% of your adjusted gross income, less donations to publicly supported charities or foundations qualifying for the 50% ceiling (including donations of capital gain property which are subject to the 30% ceiling.)

Contributions that cannot be deducted due to the 30% ceiling may be carried forward for five years; *see* ¶14.16.

20% limit for capital gain property. Gifts of capital gain property to private nonoperating foundations and other organizations not eligible for the 50% ceiling (see list above) are deductible only to the extent of the lower of: (1) 20% of your adjusted gross income or (2) 30% of adjusted gross income less donations of capital gain property which qualify for the 30% ceiling (contributed to organizations qualifying for the 50% ceiling).

Contributions not deductible due to the 20% limitation may be carried over for five years; *see* ¶14.16.

Applying the ceiling. To figure your deduction follow this order in applying the various income limitations: (1) Gifts qualifying for the 50% ceiling; (2) gifts of cash and ordinary income property to nonoperating private foundations and other organizations that qualify for the 30% ceiling; (3) gifts of capital gain property to organizations qualifying for the 50% ceiling that are subject to the 30% of income deduction limit; (4) gifts of capital gain property to nonoperating private foundations and other organizations not qualifying under the 50% ceiling.

Example—

Smith has an adjusted gross income of $100,000. He makes charitable contributions of $40,000 in 30% capital gain property to a college and $30,000 in cash to a nonoperating private foundation subject to the 30% ceiling. The 30% limitation for cash gifts to nonoperating private foundations is applied before the 30% limitation applicable to gifts of capital gain property to public charities. The deduction for the cash gift is reduced to $10,000 ([50% of $100,000] — $40,000). The amount of the contribution of 30% capital gain property is limited to $30,000 (30% of $100,000). Accordingly, Smith's charitable contributions deduction is $40,000 ($10,000 + $30,000). Smith is allowed to carry over $10,000 ($40,000 — $30,000) from his contributions of 30% capital gain property. He is also allowed to carry over the nondeductible $20,000 cash donation ($30,000 — $10,000).

¶14.16 • FIVE-YEAR CARRYOVER FOR EXCESS DONATIONS EXCEEDING STATUTORY CEILING

If your donations to charities which qualify for the 50% ceiling total more than 50% of your adjusted gross income, you may carry over the excess over the next five years.

Where contributions of appreciated long-term intangible personal property and real estate (or tangible personal property put to a related use by the charity) exceed the 30% ceiling, the excess over 30% also may be carried over for five years. The excess is subject to the 30% ceiling in the carryover years. A five-year carryover applies also to excess contributions to nonoperating private foundations and other organizations qualifying for the 30% or 20% ceiling.

When planning substantial donations that may exceed the annual ceiling, make a projection of your income for at least five years. Although the carryover period of five years will probably absorb most excess donations, it is possible that the excess may be so large that it will not be completely absorbed during the year of the contribution and the five-year carryover period. It is also possible that your income may drop in the future so that you cannot adequately take advantage of the excess.

If a donor dies during the carryover period, the excess carryover for the years after his death is not deductible.

If in any taxable year a deduction is claimed for part or all of a carryover, you attach a statement showing the contribution year or years, and the excess carried over for each year. *See* Treasury regulations for further details and for the effect of a net operating loss carryback.

¶14.17 • ELECTION TO REDUCE APPRECIATION OF CERTAIN PROPERTY GIFTS

Although the 30% ceiling generally applies to long-term intangible property (such as securities) and real estate, you may elect the 50% ceiling, provided you reduce the deduction by 40% of the appreciation on all donations during the year of long-term intangible property and real estate and tangible personal property related in use to the organization's charitable function. In most cases, this election will be made only where the amount of appreciation is negligible. Where there is substantial appreciation, the increase in the deduction may not make up or exceed the required 40% reduction. If the election is made in a year in which there are carryovers of capital gain property subject to the 30% ceiling, the carryovers are subject to reduction (*see* Treasury regulations for the adjustment).

The election is made by attaching a statement to your original return or amended return filed by the original due date.

¶15.00

Deductions for Interest You Pay

Illustrations of claiming deductions of interest may be found in the Supplement to YOUR INCOME TAX. Mail the card at the front of this book to receive your FREE Supplement, which includes filled-in returns and last-minute information.

¶15.01 • DEDUCTIBLE INTEREST

You may deduct interest paid on:

Home mortgage loans (*see* also ¶15.011)
Personal loans
Bank loans
Margin accounts (*see* also ¶15.02)
Tax deficiencies
Judgments
Installment purchases
Retail revolving credit accounts (*see* also ¶15.03)
Oil company credit card accounts (*see* also ¶15.03)
Bank credit card plans (*see* also ¶15.03)
Tuition contracts (*see* also ¶15.03)
Scholarship loans
Insurance loans (*see* also ¶15.02)
Usurious loans
Business loans (*see* below)
Redeemable ground rents

You may deduct interest on debts for which you are legally liable. You may not deduct interest due on another person's debt. Other restrictions are discussed at ¶15.04.

Check your payment of personal judgments, loans, and other debts for full interest charges. If you make a late payment of taxes or mortgage payment, or you pay a deficiency at a later date, part of the amount will include deductible interest. A penalty charge may or may not be deductible as additional interest. A penalty for late payment which is merely a service charge is not deductible. A fixed charge having no relationship to the amount borrowed or the time given to pay suggests that the charge is a service charge and not interest.

Some utility companies charge an additional percentage if a bill is not paid within 20 days of the due date. The IRS says that the late-payment charge is deductible as interest if it is not connected to any service provided by the utility but is assessed solely on the basis of late payment.

Imputed interest deductions. Interest imputed under the rules for interest-free loans (¶4.10) and unstated interest within the OID and deferred payment rules (¶4.11) are deductible.

Interest on loans to buy market discount bonds and Treasury bills. Limits apply to the deduction for interest on loans used to buy or carry market discount bonds (*see* ¶4.034) and Treasury bills (*see* ¶4.07) acquired after July 18, 1984.

Business loans. Distinguish between interest paid for personal purposes and interest paid for rental or business purposes. Interest on debts incurred for nonbusiness purposes is deductible only if you have excess itemized deductions. Interest paid on a debt connected with rental property or a business is deducted from rent or business income, even if you do not claim excess itemized deductions.

Whether interest is a business or a personal expense depends upon the use made of the money borrowed, not on the kind of property used to secure the loan. Interest on a business loan is deductible from business income, even though the loan is secured by a mortgage on nonbusiness assets. Interest on personal loans, even though secured by a business asset, is deductible only if you have excess itemized deductions. If you rent part of your personal residence and you borrow money for the purchase or repair of the house, part of the interest payment allocable to the rented portion is deducted from rent income. The balance is an itemized deduction. Interest on an income tax deficiency is personal interest, even though the deficiency is related to your business.

A creditor may hold a debtor's stock as collateral. If the creditor receives and applies the dividends to the interest, the debtor may claim an interest deduction for such amounts.

Loan fees. Whether a loan fee is deductible as interest in a lump sum in the year of payment or must be amortized over the life of the loan depends on how you structure the initial transfer of funds. To get the immediate deduction, first obtain the full amount of the loan and then pay the fee to the lender. The deduction is allowed even if the prepayment is an integral part of the loan agreement, and the lender would not have made the loan without charging the fee. Where the lender gives you only the net proceeds of the loan, you must amortize the fee over the life of the loan.

Interest on loan obtained by dummy corporation. You may be forced to set up a dummy corporation to obtain loans that would otherwise violate state usury laws. According to the IRS, you may not deduct interest paid on the loan; the interest is deductible only by the corporation although it is a shell. Courts are split on this issue.

¶15.011 • MORTGAGE INTEREST

Payments to the bank or lending institution holding your mortgage may include interest, principal payments, taxes, and fire insurance premiums. Deduct only the payments of interest and taxes. You may not deduct the payments of mortgage principal and insurance premiums.

Banks and other lending institutions report mortgage interest payments of $600 or more to the IRS on Form 1098. You should receive a copy of Form 1098 or similar statement by February 2, 1987, showing your mortgage payments in 1986. The form does not include payment of points.

In the year you sell your home, check your settlement papers for interest charged up to the date of sale; this amount is deductible.

Mortgage credit. If you qualify for the special tax credit for interest on qualified home mortgage certificates, you only deduct interest in excess of the allowable credit. *See* ¶24.87.

Jointly owned property. When mortgaged property is jointly owned, a joint owner who pays the entire interest charge may deduct the amount of the entire payment.

Example—
Barbara and John owned the family house jointly. During one year, Barbara paid the mortgage, including interest of $638, with money supplied by John. She paid taxes of $532 with funds from a joint account. They filed separate returns. Barbara deducted one-half of the mortgage interest and taxes while John deducted all, arguing he supplied all the funds. The court allowed John to deduct all of the interest because he supplied the cash for its payment. But, since he could not prove he supplied all of the cash for the tax payment (the money having come from a joint account), he had to split the deduction with Barbara.

Prepayment penalty. A penalty for prepayment of a mortgage is usually deductible as interest.

Mortgage assistance payments. You may not deduct interest paid on your behalf under Section 235 of the National Housing Act.

Interest reduction payments under Section 237 of the National Housing Act. Payments made to sponsors of low-income rental apartments must be reported as income; the full amount of HUD interest payments are deductible.

Graduated payment mortgages. Monthly payments are initially smaller than under the standard mortgage on the same amount of principal, but payments increase each year over the first five- or ten-year period and continue at the increased monthly amount for the balance of the mortgage term. As a cash basis taxpayer, you deduct the amount of interest actually paid even though, during the early years of the mortgage, payments are less than the interest owed on the loan. The unpaid interest is added to the loan principal, and future interest is figured on the increased unpaid mortgage loan balance. The bank, in a year-end statement, will identify the amount of interest actually paid. (An accrual basis taxpayer may deduct the accrued interest each year.)

Reverse mortgage loan. Homeowners who own their homes outright may in certain states cash in on their equity by taking a "reverse mortgage loan." Typically, 80% of the value of the house is paid by a bank to a homeowner in a lump sum or in installments. Principal is due when the home is sold or the homeowner dies; interest is added to the loan and is payable when the principal is paid. The IRS rules that no interest deduction may be claimed by a cash basis homeowner when the interest is added to the outstanding loan balance.

Zero interest mortgage. Under this type of loan, a buyer makes a cash down payment and then pays off the balance of the purchase price in equal monthly installments over a mortgage term which is generally five years. Although no interest is charged, a portion of each monthly payment may be treated as deductible interest under the imputed interest rule of ¶6.191. The exact amount is determined by Treasury tables. However, no interest deduction may be claimed for payments in the first six months. Cost basis in the house is reduced by the total interest amount allocated during the term of the note.

Shared appreciation mortgage. Under a shared appreciation mortgage (SAM) for a personal residence, the lender agrees to charge a lower rate of interest than the prevailing market rate.

In return, the homeowner promises to pay a percentage of the appreciation on the property at a later date to make up the difference. For example, a homeowner agrees to pay interest of 12% plus 40% of the appreciation in the value of the property within 10 years or earlier if he sells the house or pays off the mortgage. If, at the end of ten years, the residence is not sold or the loan repaid, the owner may refinance at the prevailing rate the outstanding balance plus the interest based on the appreciation. If he refinances with the same lender, he may not claim an immediate deduction for the extra interest. The execution of a note is not considered payment. The amount covering the extra interest is deducted ratably over the period of the new loan. If he refinances with another lender and uses the funds to pay off the old loan plus the extra interest, the extra interest is deductible in the year of payment.

¶15.012 • "POINTS"

Lenders charge "points" above the regular interest rate to get around state limits on interest when the cost of money climbs and pushes interest rates above state maximums. Whether points are deductible as interest depends on what the charge covers. As a borrower, you may deduct points if your payment is solely for your use of the money and is not for specific services performed by the lender which are separately charged. Whether a payment is called "points" or "loan processing fee" does not affect its deductibility if it is actually a charge for the use of money. The purpose of the charge, that is, for the use of the money or the services rendered, will be controlling.

Points treated as prepaid interest. Points are treated as prepaid interest and must be deducted over the period of the loan unless they are charged on a loan to buy or improve your principal residence. In this case, points are deductible in the year paid, provided: (1) The loan is secured by your principal residence; (2) the charging of points is an established business practice in the geographic area in which the loan is made; and (3) the points charged do not exceed the points generally charged in the area. For deducting prepaid interest, *see* ¶15.021.

Example—
To obtain a $40,000 mortgage to buy a home, you agree to pay the lender, in addition to 10% stated annual interest, a loan processing fee of $800 prior to receiving the loan proceeds. The fee is not paid with funds originally obtained from the lender, nor is it for any specific services under the loan agreement. You pay separately charges made for services, such as title reports, escrow fees, and drawing of deed and other papers. You may deduct as interest the $800 as points. The points are deductible in the year paid.

Points paid on refinancing. The IRS does not allow a current deduction for points on a refinanced mortgage. The points must be deducted over the loan period. Thus, if you pay points of $2,400 when financing a 20-year loan, you may deduct only $10 a month, $120 each full year. The points are not currently deductible because they are incurred for repaying the existing mortgage debt, not buying a home or financing home improvements.

Points withheld from loan principal are not immediately deductible. To deduct loan fees, you should obtain the full amount of the loan and then pay the fee to the lender. If fees are withheld and you receive only the net proceeds, the fees are amortized over the life of the loan.

A seller who assumes the buyer's payment of points may not claim the points paid as an interest deduction. The payment is subtracted from the amount realized on the sale.

Example—
Smith sells his home for $42,000 and takes a $2,000 down payment from the buyer. To assist the buyer in obtaining a $40,000 F.H.A. mortgage loan, Smith accepts $39,000 in full satisfaction of the balance of $40,000, thereby assuming payment of points of $1,000. He may not deduct this as interest; the loan was not his obligation. However, Smith reduces the amount realized on the sale from $42,000 to $41,000.

¶15.02 • YEAR TO CLAIM AN INTEREST DEDUCTION

As a cash basis taxpayer, you deduct interest in the year in which it is paid. Limitation on deductions of prepayments of interest is discussed at ¶15.021. An accrual basis taxpayer generally deducts interest in the year in which the interest expense accrues.

Giving a promissory note is not considered payment. Increasing the amount of a loan by interest owed, as with insurance loans, is also not considered payment and will not support a deduction (*see* below). If a person pays your interest obligation with the understanding you will repay him, you take the deduction in the year he pays the interest, not when you repay him.

The following paragraphs illustrate how a cash basis taxpayer treats interest in the following situations:

On a life insurance loan, you claim a deduction in the year in which the interest is paid. You may not claim a deduction when the insurance company adds the interest to your debt. You may not deduct your payment of interest on an insurance loan after you assign the policy.

Example—
You borrow $500 at 5% interest from your insurance company against your life insurance policy. This year, instead of paying the interest ($25), you execute a new note to the company for $525 to replace the old note plus the interest due. This is not payment of interest, and no deduction is permitted. If you allow the interest to accumulate on the loan by executing new notes each year until the cash surrender value of the policy is about equal to the loan plus all the accumulated interest, you might then surrender your policy. This is the same as repayment of the loan and interest, and you claim your interest deduction at that time.

See ¶15.04 below discussing when interest is not deductible on certain insurance purchase plans.

On a margin account with a broker, you claim a deduction in the year in which the interest is paid or your account is credited after the interest has been charged. But a mere interest charge to your account is not payment if you do not pay it in cash or the broker has not collected dividends, interest, or security sales proceeds which he may apply against the interest due him.

For partial payment of loan, you claim a deduction in the year the payment is credited against interest due. When a loan has no provision for allocating payments between principal and income, the law presumes that a partial payment is applied first to interest and then to principal, unless you agree otherwise. Where the payment is in full settlement of the debt, the payment is applied first to principal, unless you agree otherwise. Where there is an involuntary payment, such as that following a foreclosure sale of collateral, sales proceeds are applied first to principal, unless you agree to the contrary.

Examples—
1. Assume you owe $1,000 on a note, plus interest of $120. If you should pay $800 on account, the law presumes that $120 of the $800 represents a payment of interest for which you may claim a deduction.

2. Same as above but the payment is accepted in full settlement of the debt. The law presumes that the $800 represents a payment of principal for which no deduction is allowed.

Using borrowed funds to pay interest. To get an interest deduction you must pay the interest; you may not claim a deduction by having the creditor add the interest to the debt. If you do not have funds to pay the interest, you may borrow money to pay the interest. Borrow the funds from a different creditor. The IRS disallows deductions where a debtor borrows from the same creditor to make interest payments on an earlier loan; the second loan is considered merely a device for getting an interest expense deduction without actually making payments. Courts tend to side with the IRS.

Note renewed. You may not deduct interest by merely giving a new note. You claim a deduction in the year the renewed note is paid. The giving of a new note or increasing the amount due is not payment. The same is true when past due interest is deducted from the proceeds of a new loan. This is not deemed payment of the interest.

¶15.021 • PREPAID INTEREST ALLOCATED OVER TERM OF LOAN

Prepaid interest must be deducted over the period of the loan, whether you are a cash basis or accrual taxpayer. In the year of prepayment, you may not deduct a prepayment of interest allocable to any period falling in a later taxable year.

Treatment of interest included in a level payment schedule. Where payments of principal and interest are equal, a large amount of interest allocated to the payments made in early years of a loan will generally not be considered prepaid interest. However, if the loan calls for a variable interest rate, the IRS may treat interest payments as consisting partly of interest, computed under an average level effective rate, and partly of prepaid interest allocable to later years of the loan. An interest rate which varies with the "prime rate" does not necessarily involve a prepaid interest element.

¶15.022 • INTEREST ON DISCOUNT LOANS

When you borrow money and give a note to the lender, the amount of your loan proceeds may be less than the face value of the note. The difference between the proceeds and the face amount is interest discount. For loans that do not fall within the OID rules of ¶4.032, such as loans of a year or less, you deduct interest in the year you make payment if you are on the cash basis. If you use the accrual basis, you deduct the interest as it accrues.

Example—
In February 1985, you borrow $1,000 and receive $900 in return for your $1,000 note. You repay the full loan in January 1986. You are on the cash basis. You do not deduct the interest of $10 when the note is given. The $10 interest is deductible when the loan is paid in 1986.

For loans that fall within OID rules, your lender should provide a statement showing the interest element and the tax treatment of the interest.

¶15.023 • RULE OF 78'S

When payments of a loan are made in installments, the lender may charge interest under the "rule of 78's." Under the "rule of 78's," more interest is charged to the earlier installments of the loan. If you are on the accrual basis, you must deduct interest under the regular accrual basis; you may not claim a deduction based on the "rule of 78's."

If you are on the cash basis, the IRS will allow interest deductions based on the "rule of 78's" only for interest paid on a short-term consumer loan covering a period of five years or less. If you have borrowed under terms requiring a computation of interest under the "rule of 78's," ask the lender for the amount of deductible interest. For loans other than qualifying short-term consumer loans, the deductible amount must be based on the accrual method even if you are on the cash basis.

According to the IRS, a short-term consumer loan qualifying for the "rule of 78's" is a self-amortizing loan that requires level payments at regular intervals at least annually, over a period of five years or less (with no balloon payment at the end of the loan term). The loan agreement must also provide for the calculation of interest under the "rule of 78's" method.

The "rule of 78's" method is based on the sum of the months' digits. Seventy-eight is the sum of digits for a loan requiring 12 installments. Under the method, interest due for the loan period is allocated by a fraction to determine the amount of interest due for the installment. The denominator of the fraction always remains the same and is the sum of the digits for the number of installment payments of the loan. The denominator of a 12-installment loan is 78 $(12 + 11 + 10 \ldots + 1 = 78)$; the denominator of a 10-installment loan is 55 $(10 + 9 \ldots + 1 = 55)$. The denominator of a 60-installment loan is 1,830 $(60 + 59 + 58 \ldots + 1 = 1,830)$. The numerator of the fraction changes from installment to installment and is the number of installments remaining on the note. Thus the fraction for figuring the interest due for the second installment of a 12-installment loan is 11/78.

Loans that are not short-term consumer loans. If you claimed deductions based on the rule of 78's on a loan made before 1984 and the loan is not a short-term consumer loan as defined above, special interest deduction rules apply. If the loan was for $50,000 or less and was used to buy personal items (not for investment or business purposes) you may generally figure your interest deductions using a formula and table included in IRS Publication 545 and Revenue Procedure 84-29, Internal Revenue Bulletin 1984-14. If you cannot use this method, you must get IRS consent to change to the accrual method by filing Form 3115. When you make the change, you may have to report income for the excess deductions previously claimed. This income may be spread ratably over a period of years depending on the number of years the "rule of 78's" was used and the year for which Form 3115 is filed. *See* IRS Revenue Procedures 84-27 and 84-28, Internal Revenue Bulletin 1984-14, and IRS Publication 545 for details.

¶15.03 • FINANCE CHARGES

You may deduct as interest finance charges paid on credit purchases through:

Credit cards. The finance charge of a bank, gasoline company or department store credit card plan is generally deductible as interest.

Revolving credit accounts. Finance charges on a revolving credit account in a retail store are deductible as interest.

Installment contract where the charge is separately stated as a percentage of the unpaid balance. A prepayment penalty, sometimes called an acquisition charge or minimum fee, may also be incurred and is deductible as interest.

Educational service contract for tuition and lodgings. The separately stated finance charge on the unpaid balance is deductible as interest.

In addition to monthly finance charges, also deductible is a one-time charge for each new cash advance and each new check and overdraft advance added to your balance, provided it is not a service charge, loan fee, credit investigation fee, or other similar fee.

Fixed fee on installment purchase contract may require averaging. If a fixed or flat fee is charged on an installment contract to buy personal property or educational services provided by educational institutions, the deduction may be limited as follows: If the interest rate is given, then that part of the fee allocated to the interest is deductible. If the interest rate is not given, the deduction is based on 6% of the average balance figured according to Treasury regulations.

Interest paid on deferred tuition plan. Students of some universities are allowed to defer tuition payments until they graduate and earn income. Each student joins a group that is obligated to pay the tuition over a period up to 35 years. The IRS says a participant may not deduct any part of a payment as interest until he has paid up his total tuition and the insurance premiums. Further payments are then deductible as interest.

¶15.04 • NONDEDUCTIBLE INTEREST

A checklist at ¶42.00 lists nondeductible interest charges, some of which are detailed below.

Interest paid on another person's debts if you are not legally obligated to make the payment. However, a father was allowed to deduct interest on a mortgage on property owned by a family trust; under state law, he was still liable on the mortgage.
Example—
You pay interest on behalf of a relative to avoid the foreclosure of a mortgage. This would not be deductible unless you were liable for the interest under terms of the loan (as comaker or as endorser). In the absence of a legal obligation, these payments are in the nature of a gift to the person liable for the loan.

Interest on minimum deposit life insurance plans. If, after August 6, 1963, you bought life insurance policies under a plan whereby loans on the cash value of the policy pay for part of the premiums, you may not deduct the interest paid on the loans, unless you meet *one* of these conditions: (1) The interest paid during the year is not over $100. (2) During the first seven years of the policy, you paid at least four of the annual premiums without having to borrow under the plan. (3) You borrowed because of an unforeseen substantial loss of income or increase in financial obligations. (4) You incurred the debt in your business. For further details, see Treasury regulations.

Interest on debts incurred or continued to purchase or carry a single premium life insurance, endowment, or annuity contract

if substantially all the premiums are paid within four years (or deposited with the company within that time).

Interest on debts to carry tax-exempt obligations. See ¶15.041.

Interest on debts to purchase or carry straddles unless the straddle is a hedging transaction. See ¶6.0352.

Construction period interest with respect to real property held for business or investment purposes. See ¶16.02.

Interest where no real debt exists. If there is no recourse against you personally, you have not incurred a real liability. Loans between family members are particularly vulnerable to attack as being mere gifts.

Interest incurred on loans to finance the purchase of securities in tax avoidance schemes. However, one court allowed the deduction where an actual bank loan was made to finance the purchase of short-term U.S. Treasury notes. In another case, the deduction was disallowed where the loans and interest were merely reflected in "bookkeeping entries."

Interest charged for reinstating GI insurance is not deductible. Lapsed GI insurance may be reinstated on the payment of the back premiums plus interest charged on these premiums. The interest charge is not deductible. It is not real interest because no debt is outstanding between the parties. It is merely a charge for reinstating the policy.

Handling charges, loan commitment fees, insurance, financing charges, and other costs computed without reference to the period of the loan are not deductible as interest. Such charges are added to the basis of the asset financed by the loan. If you want an interest deduction, insist that these charges be called interest if they are the price you have to pay to postpone full payment. Under the "Truth in Lending Act," finance charges on consumer loans must be stated separately. The IRS has ruled that the extra charge by an insurance company against policyholders who choose to pay premiums on other than an annual basis is not interest. The Tax Court held that bank service charges on a checking account are not deductible as interest.

A voluntary payment of additional interest, or a retroactive increase in interest without additional consideration, is not deductible. For example, a loan calls for 7% interest and you voluntarily pay 8%. You may deduct only 7%.

Interest beyond the limitations of the "at risk" rules at ¶28.04.

¶15.041 • INTEREST ON DEBTS TO CARRY TAX-EXEMPT OBLIGATIONS AND SHORT SALES

When you borrow money in order to buy or carry tax-exempt bonds, you may not deduct any interest paid on your loan. Application of this disallowance rule is clear where there is actual evidence that loan proceeds were used to buy tax exempts or that tax exempts were used as collateral. But sometimes the relationship between a loan and the purchase of tax exempts is less obvious, as where you hold tax exempts and borrow to carry other securities or investments. IRS guidelines explain when a direct relationship between the debt and an investment in tax exempts will be inferred so that no interest deduction is allowed. The IRS will *not* infer a direct relationship between a debt and an investment in tax exempts in these cases:

1. The investment in tax exempts is not substantial. That is, it is not more than 2% of the adjusted basis of the investment portfolio and any assets held in an actively conducted business.

2. The debt is incurred for a personal purpose. For example, an investor may take out a home mortgage instead of selling his tax exempts and using the proceeds to finance the home purchase. Interest on the mortgage is deductible.

3. The debt is incurred in connection with the active conduct of a business and does not exceed business needs. But, if a person reasonably could have foreseen when he purchased the tax exempts that he would have to borrow to meet ordinary and recurrent business needs, his interest expenses are not deductible.

The guidelines infer a direct relationship between the debt and an investment in tax exempts in this type of case: An investor in tax exempts has outstanding debts not directly related to personal expenses or to his business. The interest will be disallowed even if the debt appears to have been incurred to purchase other portfolio investments. Portfolio investments include transactions entered into for profit, including investments in real estate, which are not connected with the active conduct of a business.

Example—

An investor owning $360,000 in tax-exempt bonds purchased real estate in a joint venture, giving a purchase money mortgage and cash for the price. He deducted interest on the mortgage. The IRS disallowed the deduction, claiming the debt was incurred to carry tax exempts. A court allowed the deduction. A mortgage is the customary manner of financing such a purchase. Furthermore, since the purchase was part of a joint venture, the other parties' desires in the manner of financing had to be considered.

Note: If you receive exempt-interest dividends from a mutual fund during the year, you may not deduct interest on a loan used to buy or carry the mutual fund shares.

Short sale expenses. Expenses incurred to carry personal property used in a short sale occurring after July 18, 1984 are generally treated as interest incurred to carry tax-exempts and thus not deductible. This disallowance rule applies to payments to a broker in lieu of dividends which do not have to be capitalized under the rules discussed at ¶6.261. However, a deduction is not barred for short sale expenses if you provide cash as collateral for a short sale and do not receive a material return on the deposited cash.

¶15.05 • DEDUCTIONS FOR OWNERS OF COOPERATIVE AND CONDOMINIUM APARTMENTS

Cooperative apartments. If you are a tenant-stockholder of a cooperative apartment, you may deduct your portion of:

Interest paid by the cooperative on its debts. This includes your pro rata share of the permanent financing expense (points) of the cooperative on its mortgage covering the housing project.

Taxes paid by the cooperative. (However, if the cooperative does not own the land and building but merely leases them and is required to pay real estate taxes under the terms of the lease, you may not deduct your share of the tax payment.)

In some localities, such as New York City, rent control rules allow tenants of a building converted to cooperatives to remain in their apartments even if they do not buy into the co-op. A holdover tenant may prevent some co-op purchasers from occupying an apartment. The IRS rules that the fact that a holdover tenant stays in the apartment will not bar the owner from deducting his share of the co-op's interest and taxes.

Condominiums. If you own an apartment or unit in a condominium, you have a direct ownership interest in the property and are treated, for tax purposes, just as any other property owner. You may deduct your payments of real estate taxes and mortgage interest. You may also deduct taxes and interest paid on the mortgage debt of the project allocable to your share of the property. If you use your condominium apartment for business, a profession, or for the production of income, or if you rent it to others, you may deduct expenses of maintenance and repairs and claim depreciation deductions subject to rules of ¶29.42.

¶15.06 • INTEREST ON INVESTMENT LOANS MAY BE PARTIALLY DISALLOWED

Part of the interest paid on loans to carry investments may be disallowed in the year of payment. The disallowance rule applies mainly to interest that exceeds investment income. The law attempts to discourage the payment of interest solely for the purpose of offsetting income from noninvestment sources.

You may deduct investment interest which is equal to the total of the following items:

1. *$10,000 allowance.* You may deduct without restriction investment interest of up to $10,000 ($5,000 if you are married and file separately).

2. *Net investment income.* In addition to the $10,000 allowance, you may deduct interest that does not exceed net investment income. Net investment income is the difference between (1) income from dividends, interest, rents, royalties, net short-term capital gain from sale of investment property and depreciation recapture gains, and (2) investment expenses. Mutual fund capital gain dividends are not considered investment income. Investment expenses, to the extent directly related to the production of investment income, include depreciation (to the extent allowable under the straight line method), real and personal property taxes, bad debts, depletion (as if the cost method was used), and amortizable bond premium.

Investment interest which exceeds the sum of (1) and (2) above is not deductible in the current year. The disallowed amount is carried over to the next year and treated as investment interest paid or accrued in that year and is again subject to the above limitation: Any amount not deductible in that year is carried over until it becomes deductible by not coming within the limitations of that particular year. You may continue to carry forward any investment interest until fully deducted.

You compute and report the allowable amount of investment interest on Form 4952—Investment Interest Expense Deduction.

Example—

In 1985, you pay interest of $70,000 on loans to carry investments. You have interest and dividend income of $50,000. Your interest deduction is computed as follows:

Interest paid		$70,000
Allowable items:		
Allowance	$10,000	
Net investment income	50,000	
Total allowable deduction		$60,000
Excess carried over to 1986		$10,000

Special $15,000 allowance. A special allowance of up to $15,000 per year (up to $7,500 on a separate return filed by a married person) is permitted for interest paid on debts incurred to acquire the stock in a corporation or a partnership interest, where you, your spouse, and children have or acquired at least 50% of the stock or capital interest in the enterprise.

What is investment interest expense? Interest subject to disallowance is interest paid or accrued on debts incurred or continued to purchase or to carry property held for investment.

Examples—

1. You obtain an unsecured loan of $100,000 and on the same day buy securities for $120,000. The IRS will hold that the entire loan was incurred for the purpose of buying the securities.

2. You own substantial amounts of business property and investment property with a value of $150,000. You obtain an unsecured loan of $150,000. If you are unable to show that the loan was for business or personal purposes, as opposed to investment use, the IRS will hold that the loan was for buying or carrying investment property.

Deductible expenses of short sales after July 18, 1984 are considered investment interest.

What is investment property? Whether property is held for investment is a factual determination. Property is held for investment if it is held for the production or collection of passive income, such as interest, rent, dividends, royalties, or capital gain. Generally, stock in a corporation other than an S corporation is investment property. Stock in an S corporation or a partnership interest is investment property to the extent that the assets of the corporation or partnership are held for investment.

Rental real estate is generally considered business property. However, property subject to a net lease is generally passive rental income property (*see* below). If you have interest subject to a disallowance because of insufficient investment income, you may want to argue that rental income is investment income. This may reduce or eliminate interest subject to the disallowance. When this book went to press, the Treasury had not released rules on how to determine when rental income is passive for purposes of the interest deduction.

Property subject to a net lease. Property is considered to be subject to a net lease if the lessor has in any manner, formal or informal, an assurance by the lessee or a related party that he will receive a specified return as a result of the lease, or will not suffer a loss as a result of the lease. The return test is not based on a year-by-year analysis but on an analysis of the leasing arrangement as a whole. Property is also considered subject to a net lease and thus treated as held for investment if business expenses are less than 15% of rental income (*see* Treasury regulations).

¶16.00

Deductions for Taxes

Illustrations of deducting taxes may be found in the Supplement to YOUR IN-COME TAX. Mail the card at the front of this book to receive your FREE Supplement, which includes filled-in returns and last-minute information.

¶16.001 • GENERAL RULES FOR DEDUCTING TAXES

You may deduct as itemized deductions your payments of state, local and foreign real property and income taxes as well as state and local personal property taxes and general sales and use taxes. Stock transfer taxes paid on the sale of securities may be claimed as an itemized deduction if you are an investor.

Claim the deduction on the tax return for the year in which you paid the taxes, unless you report on the accrual basis, *see* ¶16.05.

The following table lists whether a particular type of tax may be claimed as an itemized deduction in 1986.

Type of tax	Deductible as itemized deduction
Admission	No
Alcoholic beverage	No
Assessments for local benefits	No
Automobile license fees not qualifying as personal property tax	No
Cigarette	No
Customs duties	No
Driver's license	No
Estate—federal or state (except *see* ¶11.03)	No
Excise—federal or state, for example, on telephone service	No
Gasoline—federal	No
Gasoline and other motor fuel—state and local	No
Gift taxes—federal and state	No
Income—federal (including minimum tax)	No
Income—state or local or foreign	Yes
Inheritance tax	No
Mortgage tax	No
Personal property—state or local	Yes
Poll	No
Real estate (state, local or foreign)	Yes
Regulatory license fees—(dog licenses, parking meter fees, hunting and fishing licenses)	No
Sales and use	Yes
Social Security	No
Tolls	No
Transfer tax on securities and income-producing realty—state and local	Yes
Utility taxes imposed under state or local law if rate is the same as general sales tax	Yes

Other state, local, and foreign taxes are deductible if paid in a business, for the production or collection of income, or the maintenance, management, or conservation of property held for the production of income. See ¶16.10.

State and local taxes on gasoline used for personal purposes are not deductible, but are deductible as part of the cost of gasoline used for business travel. See ¶2.30.

Windfall profit tax. The tax is deductible in the year withheld from payments received by crude oil purchasers. The tax is deductible from royalty income reported on Schedule E.

¶16.01 • DEDUCTING STATE INCOME TAXES

You may deduct on your 1986 return state and local income taxes withheld and estimated taxes paid in 1986. If you pay in 1987 additional state income tax on your 1986 income, you deduct the payment on your 1987 tax return.

To increase your itemized deductions on your 1986 return, consider prepaying state income taxes before the end of 1986. The prepayment is deductible provided the state tax authority accepts prepayments and state law recognizes them as tax payments. The IRS has ruled, however, that prepayments are not deductible if you do not reasonably believe that you owe additional state tax. Do not make prepayments if you may be subject to alternative minimum tax. See ¶23.10.

If you report on the accrual basis and you contest a tax liability, *see* Treasury regulations for how to treat the item.

State and local income taxes allocable to interest income that is exempt from federal but not state and local income tax are deductible. However, state and local taxes allocated to other federal exempt income are not deductible. For example, state income tax allocated to a cost-of-living allowance exempt from federal income tax is not deductible.

State income taxes may be claimed only as itemized deductions, even if attributed solely to business income. That is, state income taxes may not be deducted as business expenses from gross income (see ¶5.05).

Mandatory employee contributions to the following state disability insurance funds are deductible as state income taxes: California Nonoccupational Disability Benefit Fund; New Jersey Nonoccupational Disability Benefit Fund; New York Nonoccupational Disability Benefit Fund; and Rhode Island Temporary Disability Benefit Fund. However, employee contributions to a private or voluntary disability plan in California, New Jersey or New York are not deductible.

Mandatory employee contributions to a state unemployment fund are deductible.

Note: A refund of state income taxes claimed as an itemized deduction may have to be reported as income. See ¶12.20.

¶16.02 • TAXES AND OTHER CARRYING CHARGES YOU CAPITALIZE OR DEDUCT

For certain property, you may elect to capitalize certain deductible taxes and other carrying charges, such as interest, by adding these amounts to the basis of the property. This may be to your advantage if you do not need the immediate deduction because you have little or no income to offset, or because you do not have excess itemized deductions or expect a greater tax benefit by adding the taxes to the basis.

An election to capitalize applies not only to taxes but also to interest and other deductible carrying charges incurred during your ownership of the property. The election is limited to—

Unimproved and nonproductive real property.

Real property being improved or developed. You may elect to capitalize costs up to the time the development or construction work has been completed. These costs include interest on loans to furnish funds for this work, taxes on pay to your employees, and taxes on the materials used and other expenses incurred in the development. *See* ¶16.021 for mandatory amortization of certain construction period interest and taxes.

Personal property up to the time of its installation or actual use (whichever is later).

Examples—

1. Jones, in 1985 and 1986, pays taxes and interest on a mortgage on vacant and nonproductive property. In 1986, he operates the property as a parking lot. Jones may capitalize the taxes and mortgage interest paid in 1985, but not the tax and interest paid in 1986.

2. Smith began in April, 1986 to erect a building for himself. In 1986, he paid $6,000 in employer Social Security taxes in erecting the building. On his 1986 return, he elected to capitalize these taxes. He must continue to capitalize them until the building is finished.

To make the election, indicate your choice on your tax return. IRS permission is not required. The election, once made, may not be revoked when made for personal property or real property being improved or developed. With unimproved and nonproductive realty, the election may be made in any year, regardless of how the items were treated in a prior year.

¶16.021 • AMORTIZATION OF CONSTRUCTION PERIOD INTEREST AND TAXES

For realty held for business or investment purposes, construction period interest and real estate taxes *must* be capitalized in the year paid or incurred and amortized generally over a 10-year period.

Transitional amortization period. The rate of amortization during the 10-year period depends on whether the property is residential realty (apartment house, etc.) or nonresidential realty (office building, etc.).

Nonresidential realty. Construction period interest and taxes must be capitalized over a 10-year period. For construction begun before 1982, the length of the amortization period varied according to a phase-in schedule (*see* Treasury regulations).

Residential realty. The capitalization and amortization rule first applied to residential realty in taxable years beginning after December 31, 1977, and the amortization period began its phase-in from four years in 1978 to 10 years in 1984. Thus, expenses paid or incurred in 1986 must be amortized over 10 years at a rate of 10% a year.

The rules of this section do not apply to any interest and taxes that are capitalized under a carrying charge election made under the rules of ¶16.02 and to interest and taxes paid during the construction of your personal residence.

The rules of this section do not apply to interest and taxes incurred for the construction of low-income housing.

"Construction period" is the period beginning on the date construction of the building or other improvement begins. It ends on the date the property is ready to be placed in service or is ready to be held for sale.

General rule for claiming the deduction. The taxable years in which an amortization deduction may be claimed are:

1. The taxable year in which the expense is paid or incurred, and
2. The taxable years following the year in (1) or, if later, the taxable year in which the property is ready to be placed in service or held for sale, and in the following taxable years until the full amount is deducted or the property is sold or exchanged.

Example—

In 1984, construction of residential realty starts and $120,000 of interest and taxes is paid or accrued; the property is ready to be placed in service in 1986. Construction period interest and taxes of $120,000 is amortized as follows: In 1984, the $120,000 is treated as a capital expense; the 1984 amortization rate of 11⅑% gives an amortization deduction of $13,333 (11⅑% of $120,000). Starting in 1986, the remaining $106,667 (8/9 of the total) is deducted ratably over an eight-year period. 1986 is the year in which the property is ready to be placed in service. Thus, $13,333 is deducted in 1986 and in each of the next seven years.

When the property is sold or exchanged, a proportionate part of the percentage allowable for the year of sale is deductible. Regulations are to explain the method of allocation in the year of sale. The remaining unamortized balance of the construction period interest and taxes is added to the basis of the property. In the case of a nontaxable transfer, for example, a gift, the transferor continues to deduct the amortization allowable over the amortization period remaining after the transfer. The deduction is considered to be the personal expense of the one who originally paid or incurred the interest and taxes.

¶16.03 • DEDUCTING RETAIL SALES TAX IN 1986

In 1986, you may deduct general sales taxes imposed on you as the consumer of the property or services. Those levied upon the retailer are deductible by you as the consumer if they are collected or charged as separate items.

Sales tax on cars. Retail sales taxes on motor vehicles are deductible. However, if the rate charged on the car exceeds the general sales tax rate, you may deduct only that part of the tax that would have been charged at the lower general sales tax rate.

Example—

In your state, the general sales tax is 5%. The sales tax on cars is 6%. You purchase a car for $4,000, paying a sales tax of $240. You may deduct only $200 ($4,000 × 5%).

Sales tax on materials in home construction. Generally, if you acted as your own contractor, purchased and paid for the materials, you deduct the sales taxes.

Example—

Graham, who had experience in planning and supervising government construction projects, took an active role in constructing his home. He helped the architect complete plans for the house and draw up specifications for each phase of construction. He hired a builder who agreed to get his prior approval for subcontractors and to keep a separate account of all sales taxes, for which he was reimbursed by Graham.

Graham deducted $6,050 in sales taxes for which he had reimbursed the builder. The IRS disallowed the deduction claiming the builder was the contractor and that the taxes he paid were included in the cost of the house. Graham argued that he was the general contractor; the builder his agent. He testified that he was daily at the building site and dealt directly with the subcontractors and suppliers.

The Tax Court sided with Graham. He had the expertise and experience to act as his own contractor and did so. He helped design the construction specifications and actively supervised the construction, right down to the type of nails used in the house.

If you contract with a builder to construct the house at a fixed price or on a cost-plus basis, the sales tax the builder pays on materials is reflected in the price and so passed on to you. You may not claim a sales tax deduction for materials he buys; he is considered the purchaser. However, if you have an agreement with the contractor under which he acts as your agent, you may deduct the sales tax.

Examples—

1. A building contractor's final statement for a house built on a cost-plus contract included a $480 item for sales taxes he paid. The Tax Court agreed with the IRS in disallowing the homeowner a deduction. The contractor purchased the material and paid the tax even though it was passed on to the homeowner. On the other hand, the IRS did not challenge a homeowner's deduction for sales taxes paid on materials where the homeowner paid the dealer directly for the materials, but the materials had been purchased in the name of the contractor.

2. New Mexico imposed a 3.75% gross receipts tax on the sale of personal property and the performance of services. A builder included in the price of a home the taxes attributable to improvements constructed on the property. The buyer was not allowed a deduction. He was treated as buying real estate, not materials or services.

3. Same as in example (2) but under an agency agreement, the builder bought the construction materials and billed them directly to the buyer. The buyer was allowed to deduct the gross receipts tax on the materials if under the agreement the buyer was liable for the builder's negligence during construction. A deduction was allowable for separately stated gross receipts tax paid to the builder for his services, provided the agency relationship was complete and not limited to the purpose of acquiring building materials while the builder was otherwise free to act independently.

Compensating use taxes may be deductible as a general sales tax. A compensating use tax is generally imposed on the use or consumption of an item brought in from another taxing jurisdiction. It is deductible if imposed at the same rate as the general sales tax and if complementary to a general sales tax which is also deductible under the above rules.

Deductible sales taxes are listed at ¶16.12. Sales tax tables are discussed at ¶16.04. The Supplement lists rate changes, if any.

Sales tax paid on business property purchases. Whether you may deduct the sales tax charged on the purchase of business equipment, such as a computer or business auto, depends on the state law imposing the tax. If state law imposes the sales tax on the ultimate consumer, you may deduct the tax, or, if the property is depreciable, you may elect to add the tax to the cost of the equipment that is then written off through annual depreciation deductions.

If state law imposes the sales tax on the seller who passes it on to the consumer, you may *not* deduct the sales tax if the property is a depreciable business asset or an inventory item. In this case, you *must* add the sales tax to the depreciable cost of the property.

¶16.04 • SALES TAX TABLES

You may use Treasury sales tax tables to figure your deduction. The tables are in the instruction booklet accompanying your returns. They may also be found in the Supplement to YOUR INCOME TAX, provided they are available at the time of its publication.

> The tables do not limit what you may deduct. You may deduct more than the suggested Treasury figure if your actual sales tax payments are more, but be prepared to support your deduction with records if your return is questioned.

The Treasury tables may be helpful not only in preparing your return but also in defending your deduction from an IRS disallowance. The IRS may be unable to convince a court that your deduction should be lower than that fixed by the table.
Example—
Porterfield, a CPA practicing in California, claimed a tax deduction of $200. The IRS cut it to $105, even though its sales tax table for California allowed a deduction of $131 to Porterfield's income bracket. The Tax Court increased the deduction to $155. Considering the Treasury's table and Porterfield's purchases in other states, the Court believed $155 a reasonable estimate of his sales tax deduction.

You may find the tables inadequate. The table for your state may be incomplete because—

1. It may not include city and local sales taxes. If so, these should be estimated and added to your state sales tax. In some states this problem is reversed. The table may be based on a rate which includes a tax levied by counties. If your county does not levy a tax, the estimate for your bracket in the guide should be reduced. The Treasury tables note adjustments to be made.

2. The Treasury estimate may not include purchases of expensive items, such as autos, boats, airplanes, mobile homes, and materials used to build a new home where you are your own contractor (*see* ¶16.03). If you bought such an item, the IRS says to add the sales tax paid on the item to the amount listed in the table provided the tax rate was the same as the general tax rate and the tax was stated separately from the sales price. You may not add the sales tax on purchases of any other large and unusual items, such as furniture or appliances. The IRS position is

arbitrary, but as the table is an administrative measure, the IRS has authority to fix the rules for its use. In this, the IRS has court support. The Tax Court has not allowed deductions for sales taxes paid on furniture in addition to the amounts allowed by the table.

3. The size of your family may exceed the number listed.

The term "income" used in the tables means adjusted gross income (*see* ¶13.04) increased by nontaxable income items, such as Social Security not subject to tax under ¶34.11, workmen's compensation, veterans and railroad retirement benefits, tax-exempt bond interest, the untaxed portion of unemployment compensation, public assistance payments, dividend exclusion, excludable disability benefits, the deduction for working married couples, annuity and pension receipts (cost), and nontaxable part of long-term capital gains (60% capital gain deduction).

¶16.05 • DEDUCTING REAL ESTATE TAXES

You may deduct payments of real estate tax on your property if you claim excess itemized deductions. Real estate taxes included in a mortgage payment to a bank are not deductible until paid to the taxing authority. The monthly mortgage payment to a bank generally includes amounts allocated to real estate taxes, which the bank pays to the taxing authority on their due date. You may not deduct the amounts allocated to the taxes in the year paid to the bank, unless the bank has paid them to the tax authority. Typically, banks will furnish you with a year-end statement of disbursements to taxing authorities, indicating dates of payment.

Cooperative apartments. Tenant-stockholders of a cooperative housing corporation may deduct their share of the real estate taxes paid by the corporation. However, no deduction is allowed if the corporation does not own the land and building but merely leases them and pays taxes under the lease agreement.

Assessments by homeowner's association not deductible as taxes. Assessments paid to a local homeowner's association for the purpose of maintaining the common areas of the residential project and for promoting the recreation, health, and safety of the residents are not deductible as real property taxes.

Nondeductible governmental charges. Such charges include municipal water bills (even if described as a "tax"); sewer assessments; assessments for sanitation service; title registration fees; permit to build or improve a personal residence (you add the permit fee to the cost basis of the house).

¶16.06 • TENANTS' PAYMENT OF TAXES GENERALLY NONDEDUCTIBLE

You may not generally deduct a portion of your rent as property taxes. This is so even where state or local law identifies a portion of the rent as being tied to tax increases.
Example—
A municipal rent control ordinance allowed landlords to charge real property tax increases to the tenants as a monthly "tax surcharge." The ordinance stated that the surcharge was not to be considered rent for purposes of computing cost-of-living rental increases. The IRS ruled that the tenant may not deduct the "tax surcharge" as a property tax. The tax is imposed on the landlord, not on the tenant. The city ordinance, which permitted the landlord to pass on the tax increases to a tenant, did not shift liability for the property taxes from the landlord to the tenant. For federal tax purposes, the surcharge is merely an additional rental payment by the tenant. Similarly, "rates tax" or "renters' tax" imposed on tenants was ruled to be nondeductible because the tax is imposed on the person using the property rather than on the property itself.

> Tenants have been allowed a deduction for property taxes in the following areas: In Hawaii, tenants with leases of 15 years or more may deduct the portion of the rent representing taxes. In California, tenants who have their names placed on the tax rolls and who pay the taxes directly to the taxing authority may claim a deduction.

In New York liability for tax is placed directly on the tenant and the landlord is a collecting agent for paying over the tax to the taxing authorities; the landlord also remains liable for the tax. The IRS ruled that it will not permit tenants to deduct a portion of rent as a payment of taxes.

¶16.07 • ALLOCATING TAXES WHEN YOU SELL OR BUY REALTY

When property is sold, the buyer and seller apportion the real estate taxes imposed on the property during the "real property year." A "real property year" is the period which a real estate tax covers. This allocation is provided for you in a settlement statement at the time of closing. If you want to figure your own allocations, your local tax authority can give you the "real property year" of the taxes you plan to apportion. With this information, you then make the following allocation. If *you* are the:

Seller, you deduct that portion of the tax covering the beginning of the real property year through the day before the sale.

Buyer, you deduct the part of the tax covering the date of the sale through the end of the real property year.

Example—

The real property year in East County starts April 1 and ends March 31. On July 2, 1986, you sell realty located in East County to Jones. Assume the real estate tax for the real property year ending March 31, 1987 is $365. You deduct $92 ($^{92}\!/_{365}$ of $365, since there are 92 days in the period beginning April 1 and ending July 1, 1986). Jones deducts $273 ($^{273}\!/_{365}$ of $365, since there are 273 days in the period beginning July 2, 1986 and ending March 31, 1987).

The above allocation is mandatory whether or not your contract provides for an allocation. However, you do not allocate taxes of a real property year when:

Property is sold before the real property year. This rule prevents the seller from deducting any part of the tax for that year, even though it became a personal liability or lien while he owned the property. The buyer gets the deduction because the tax covers the property year he owns the property.

Property is sold after the real property year. This rule prevents the buyer from deducting the tax even though it becomes a personal liability or lien after he takes possession of the property. The seller gets the deduction because the tax covers the property year he owns the property.

The allocation is limited to a tax covering a property year during which both the seller and the buyer own the property.

Example—

The real property tax for the calendar year in 1986 in North County becomes a lien on November 1, 1985. On November 15, 1985, you sell real property in the county to Brown. You apportion the 1985 tax between yourself and Brown. However, you may not deduct any part of the real property tax for the 1986 real property year, even though it became a lien while you owned the property on November 1, 1985. The entire real property tax for the 1986 real property tax year may be deducted by Brown when paid or accrued, depending on his method of accounting.

When to deduct allocated taxes. After you have made the allocation based on the "real property year," you then must fix the year in which you deduct your share of the allocated tax. Here you consider your method of reporting your income—cash or accrual basis—and the date on which either you or the other party became liable for the tax or paid the tax. If neither you nor the other party is liable for the tax under local law, then the party who holds the property at the time the tax became a lien on the property is considered liable. Check the following rules to determine when you deduct the apportioned tax:

*Seller on the cash basis—*If the buyer is liable for the tax, the seller may deduct the tax either in the year of the sale or, at a later time, in the year the tax is actually paid.

If a buyer is obligated to pay taxes under a land contract but fails to pay, the owner who pays the tax may deduct the payment if the tax is assessed to him.

If the seller is liable for the tax and the tax is not payable until after the date of sale, the seller may deduct the tax either in the year of sale or in the year he pays the tax.

*Buyer on the cash basis—*If the seller is liable for the tax, the buyer may deduct the tax either in the year of sale or when the tax is actually paid.

If the buyer is liable for the tax, he deducts the tax in the year he pays the tax.

*Seller on the accrual basis—*The seller accrues his share of the tax on the date of the sale, unless he has been accruing taxes ratably over the years. If this is so, his last accrual is the date of the sale.

*Buyer on the accrual basis—*If the seller is liable for the tax, the buyer accrues his share of the tax on the date of the sale, unless he accrues taxes ratably. If he accrues taxes ratably, the accrual begins with the date of sale. If he is liable for the tax, he deducts the tax in the return for the year the tax accrues unless he elects to accrue ratably from the date of sale.

Seller's deduction in excess of the allocated amount is taxed as income. If, in the year before the sale, the seller deducts an amount for taxes in excess of the amount allocated above, he reports the excess as income in the year of the sale. This may happen when seller is on the cash basis and pays the tax in the year before the sale.

Example—

A real property tax is due and payable on November 30 for the following calendar year. On November 30, 1985, Jones, who uses the cash basis and reports on a calendar year, pays the 1986 tax. On June 30, 1986, he sells the real property. Under the apportionment rule, he is allowed to deduct only $181\!/_{365}$ (January 1–June 30, 1986) of the tax for 1986 real property tax year. But he has already deducted the full amount in the 1985 return. Therefore, he reports as income that part of the tax deduction he was not entitled to under the apportionment.

Buyer's payment of seller's back taxes. A buyer may not deduct his payment of the seller's back taxes. The back taxes paid are added to the cost of the newly purchased property. The amount realized by the seller is increased by the buyer's payment of back taxes.

On the sale of a personal residence, transfer or stamp taxes imposed on and paid by the seller are not deducted as itemized deductions but reduce the sales proceeds. If imposed on and paid by the buyer, they are added to the cost basis of the house.

Seller's payment upon buyer's failure to pay. If a buyer is obligated to pay taxes under a land contract but fails to pay, the owner who pays the tax may deduct the payment if the tax is assessed to him.

Buyer of foreclosed property. If you buy realty at a tax sale, you may not be able to deduct payment of realty taxes for several years if you do not receive immediate title to the property under state law until after a redemption period.

Example—

In Illinois, an original owner had two years to reclaim the property by paying the delinquent taxes, the tax-sale purchase price, and interest. In a private letter ruling, the IRS held that the buyer's payment of taxes paid during the two-year period are treated as part of his purchase price.

¶16.08 • WHO MAY DEDUCT REAL PROPERTY TAXES

If the tax is paid by	Then it is deductible by
You, for your spouse	Neither, if your spouse has title to the property and you each file a separate return. This is true even if the mortgage requires you to pay the taxes. The tax is deductible on a joint return.
You, as owner of a condominium	You deduct real estate tax paid on your separate unit. You also deduct your share of the tax paid on the common property.
A life tenant	A court allowed the deduction to a widow required to pay the taxes under a will for the privilege of occupying the house during her life.
A tenant	The tenant of a business lease may deduct the payment of tax as additional rent, not tax. The tenant of a personal residence may not deduct the payment as either a tax or rent expense, unless he places himself on the real estate assessment rolls, so the tax is assessed directly against him.
You, as a local benefit tax to maintain, repair, or meet interest costs arising from local benefits	You deduct only that part of the tax which you can show is for maintenance, repair, or interest. If you cannot make the allocation, no deduction is allowed. If the benefit increases the value of the property, you add the nondeductible assessment to the basis of the property.

If the tax is paid by	Then it is deductible by
Your cooperative apartment or corporation	You deduct your share of real estate tax paid on the property. *See* ¶15.05. But if the organization leases the land and building and pays the tax under the terms of the lease, you may not deduct your share.
One whose property was foreclosed for failure to pay taxes	You may not deduct the taxes paid out of the proceeds of the foreclosure sale if your interest in the property ended with the foreclosure.
Tenant by the entirety or joint tenant	The tenant who is jointly and severally liable and who pays the tax. If real property is owned by husband and wife as tenants by the entirety or joint tenants, either spouse may deduct the taxes he has paid on a separate return or a joint return. When property is owned as a tenancy in common, under an IRS rule, a tenant may deduct only his share of the tax even if he has paid the entire tax. However, a court has allowed a deduction for the full amount. *See* ¶9.02.
A mortgagee	No deduction. If paid before the foreclosure, it is added to the loan. If paid after the foreclosure, it is added to the cost of property.

¶16.09 • AUTOMOBILE LICENSE FEES

You may not deduct an auto license fee based on weight, model, year, or horsepower. But you may deduct a fee based on the value of the car if these three tests are met: (1) The fee is an *ad valorem* tax, based on a percentage of value of the property. (2) It is imposed on an annual basis, even though it is collected more or less frequently. (3) It is imposed on personal property. This third test is met even though the tax is imposed on the exercise of a privilege of registering a car or for using a car on the road.

If the tax is based partly on value and partly on weight or other test, the tax attributed to the value is deductible. For example, assume a registration fee based on 1% of value, plus 40 cents per hundred-weight. The part of the tax equal to 1% of value qualifies as an *ad valorem* tax and is deductible.

The majority of state motor vehicle registration fees are not *ad valorem* taxes and so do not qualify for the deduction. Various states and localities impose *ad valorem* or personal property taxes on motor vehicles that may qualify for the deduction. If you pay fees or taxes on your auto in these states, we suggest you contact a state or local authority to verify the amount of tax qualifying: Arizona, California, Colorado, Georgia, Indiana, Iowa, Maine, Massachusetts, Mississippi, Montana, Nebraska, Nevada, Oklahoma, Washington, and Wyoming.

¶16.10 • TAXES DEDUCTIBLE AS BUSINESS OR INCOME-PRODUCING EXPENSES

That a tax is not deductible as an itemized deduction does not mean you may not deduct it elsewhere in your return. You may deduct taxes incurred as a cost of doing business or producing income. Here are some examples.

If you pay excise taxes on merchandise you sell in your business, you deduct the tax as a business expense.

If you pay Social Security taxes (FICA) on your employees' wages, you deduct the tax as a business expense on Schedule C. You may not generally deduct Social Security taxes paid on the wages of household help. But *see* ¶24.20 for dependent and child care expenses. You may not deduct self-employment tax.

If you pay state transfer taxes on the sale of securities, you deduct the tax as an "other" tax on Schedule A.

¶16.11 • FOREIGN TAXES

You may deduct your payment of foreign real property taxes and income and excess profits taxes as itemized deductions. Where you pay foreign income or excess profits tax, you have an election of either claiming the tax as a deduction or a credit. Claiming the credit may provide a larger tax savings. *See* ¶36.14.

¶16.12 • Survey of State and Local Income and Sales Taxes

The following survey contains brief descriptions of the income and sales taxes of every state and the District of Columbia. The survey does not include local sales tax rates which may be imposed in addition to the state sales tax rate listed below. Consult local taxing authorities. For more information, you may write to the appropriate addresses provided for your convenience. Also see the Supplement for changes, if any.

ALABAMA: Basic income tax rates range from 2% on the first $500 of taxable income to 5% on taxable income over $6,000. However, rates vary according to filing status. The city of Birmingham has a form of income tax.

Sales tax rate: 4%

For more information, write: Department of Revenue, Montgomery, Alabama 36102.

ALASKA: No income tax or state sales tax.

ARIZONA: Basic income tax rates range from 2% on the first $1,000 of taxable income to 8% on taxable income of $6,000 or more. These tax brackets, the optional standard deduction, exemptions and certain credits are indexed for inflation. Rates also vary according to filing status.

Sales tax rate: 5%

For more information, write: Department of Revenue, Phoenix, Arizona 85007.

ARKANSAS: Income tax rates range from 1% on the first $2,999 of net income to 7% on net income of $25,000 or over.

Sales tax rate: 4%

For more information, write: Director, Department of Finance and Administration, Little Rock, Arkansas 72203.

CALIFORNIA: Income tax rates range from 1% to 11% over brackets which are adjusted annually by an inflation adjustment factor.

San Francisco imposes an income tax in the form of a payroll expense tax.

Sales tax rate: 4¾%; local rates may be higher

For more information, write: Franchise Tax Board, Sacramento, California 95808.

COLORADO: Income tax rates range from 3% to 8% over brackets which are adjusted annually by an annual inflation factor. The tax reduction credit, standard deduction, low income allowance and exemptions are also adjusted by AIF. In addition to the normal income tax, there is a 2% surtax on dividends and interest over $15,000.

Sales tax rate: 3%

For more information, write: Department of Revenue, Denver, Colorado 80203.

CONNECTICUT: No personal income tax. There is a tax of between 1% and 12% on interest and dividends if federal adjusted gross income is $54,000 or more. And, too, there is a 7% tax on net capital gains which exceed a $100 or $200 base.

Sales tax rate: 7.5%

For more information, write: Department of Revenue Services, Hartford, Connecticut 06115.

DELAWARE: Income tax rates range from 1.2% on the first $1,000 of taxable income to 9.7% on taxable income over $40,000. There is a separate tax on lump-sum distributions from qualified pension and profit-sharing plans.

Wilmington also imposes a 1.25% tax on wages, salaries, commissions and net profits.

State sales tax: None

For more information, write: Department of Finance, Dover, Delaware 19801.

DISTRICT OF COLUMBIA: Income tax rates range from 2% on the first $1,000 of taxable income to 11% on taxable income over $25,000. In addition, there is a 9% tax on unincorporated business income and a 10% surtax.

Sales tax rate: 6%

For more information, write: Department of Finance and Revenue, Washington, D.C. 20001.

FLORIDA: No state income tax.

Sales tax rate: 5%

For more information, write: Department of Revenue, Tallahassee, Florida 32304.

GEORGIA: Income tax rates range from 1% to 6% with brackets varying for single and married persons.

Sales tax rate: 3%

For more information, write: State Revenue Commissioner, Atlanta, Georgia 30334.

HAWAII: Basic income tax rates range from 2.25% on $500 of taxable income to 11% on taxable income over $30,000. However, these rates vary according to filing status.

Sales tax rate: 4%

For more information, write: Department of Taxation, Honolulu, Hawaii 96809.

IDAHO: Income tax rates range from 2% on the first $1,000 of taxable income to 7.5% on taxable income over $5,000.

Sales tax rate: 4%; 5% after 3/31/86.

For more information, write: Department of Revenue and Taxation, Boise, Idaho 83722.

ILLINOIS: Tax of 2½% on net income.

Sales tax rate: 5%

For more information, write: Department of Revenue, Springfield, Illinois 62708.

INDIANA: Tax of 3% is imposed on adjusted gross income. Counties may impose an adjusted gross income tax at the rate of ½%, ¾%, or 1% on residents or ¼% on nonresidents and an occupational income tax of 1.5%. Check with your county officials to determine your local tax.

Sales tax rate: 5%

For more information, write: Department of Revenue, Indianapolis, Indiana 46204.

IOWA: Income tax rates range from 0.5% on the first $1,000 of taxable income to 13% on taxable income over $75,000. Tax brackets are adjusted by an inflation factor. In addition, school boards are authorized to levy income surtaxes in certain circumstances. Check with your local school district to determine if there is a local surtax.

Sales tax rate: 4%

For more information, write: Department of Revenue, Des Moines, Iowa 50319.

KANSAS: Income tax rates range from 2% on the first $2,000 of taxable income to 9% on taxable income over $25,000. An additional tax is imposed on lump-sum distributions from qualified pension and profit-sharing plans subject to federal income tax. The rate is 13% of the federal tax liability.

Sales tax rate: 3%; after 6/30/86 4%

For more information, write: Department of Revenue, Topeka, Kansas 66625.

KENTUCKY: Income tax rates range from 2% on the first $3,000 of net income to 6% on net income of $8,000 or over.

Louisville and Jefferson County also impose a form of income tax.

Sales tax rate: 5%

For more information, write: Department of Revenue, Frankfort, Kentucky 40601.

LOUISIANA: Income tax rates range from 2% on the first $10,000 of taxable income to 6% on taxable income over $50,000.

Sales tax rate: 4%

For more information, write: Department of Revenue and Taxation, Office of Tax Administration, Group I, Baton Rouge, Louisiana.

MAINE: Income tax rates range from 1% on the first $2,000 of taxable income to 10% on taxable income over $25,000. Married persons filing jointly, surviving spouses and heads of households pay less tax. In addition, there is a tax on preference items equal to 15% of the federal minimum tax and a 15% tax on lump-sum distributions from qualified pension and profit-sharing plans. Tax rates are indexed for inflation.

Sales tax rate: 5%

For more information, write: Bureau of Taxation, Augusta, Maine 04330.

MARYLAND: Income tax rates range from 2% on the first $1,000 of taxable income to 5% on taxable income over $3,000. There is also a minimum tax on most federal tax preference items.

Each county and Baltimore City also has an income tax ranging from 20% to 50% of state income tax liability. Check with your county tax authority for more details.

Sales tax rate: 5%

For more information, write: State Comptroller, Annapolis, Maryland 21401.

MASSACHUSETTS: There is a tax of 10% on interest and dividends (other than from savings accounts under $100,000) and net capital gains. There is a tax of 5% on the remainder of income. There is an additional tax of 7.5%.

Sales tax rate: 5%

For more information, write: Department of Revenue, Boston, Massachusetts 02204.

MICHIGAN: Annualized tax rate based on 4.6% effective 4/1/86 and 5.1% before that date. Detroit has an income tax of 3% and several other cities have a tax of 2% on residents (½ of 1% on nonresidents). Check with your city taxing authority.

Sales tax rate: 4%

For more information, write: Department of Treasury, Revenue Division, Lansing, Michigan 48904.

MINNESOTA: Income tax rates range from 1.5% to 14%. Rates are indexed for inflation. There is a tax based on a percentage of federal alternative minimum tax liability. There is also a tax on lump-sum distributions from qualified pension and profit-sharing plans.

Sales tax rate: 6%

For more information, write: Department of Revenue, St. Paul, Minnesota 55145.

MISSISSIPPI: Income tax rates are 3% on the first $5,000 of taxable income, 4% on next taxable income and 5% on taxable income over $10,000.

Sales tax rate: 6%

For more information, write: State Tax Commission, Jackson, Mississippi 39205.

MISSOURI: Income tax rates range from 1½% on the first $1,000 of net taxable income to 6% on net taxable income over $9,000. In addition, Kansas City and St. Louis have a tax of 1% on salaries, wages, and compensation and net profits from unincorporated businesses.

Sales tax rate: 4.225%

For more information, write: State Tax Commission, Jefferson City, Missouri 65105.

MONTANA: Income tax rates range from 2% to 11% (adjusted annually for inflation).

State sales tax: None

For more information, write: Department of Revenue, Helena, Montana 59601.

NEBRASKA: The income tax is 19% of adjusted federal income tax liability.

Sales tax rate: 3½%

For more information, write: Department of Revenue, Lincoln, Nebraska 68509.

NEVADA: No state income tax.

Sales tax rate: 5.75%

For more information, write: Tax Commission, Carson City, Nevada 89701.

NEW HAMPSHIRE: A tax of 5% is imposed on certain interest and dividends.

State sales tax: None

For more information, write: Department of Revenue Administration, Concord, New Hampshire 03301.

NEW JERSEY: The income tax rate is 2% on taxable income up to $20,000, 2.5% on next $30,000; 3.5% on taxable income over $50,000. There is a New York—New Jersey commuter tax ranging from 2% to 14%. New Jersey residents pay either the regular income tax or the commuter tax, whichever is less. Newark also imposes a payroll tax of ¾ of 1% on certain employers.

Sales tax rate: 6%

For more information, write: Department of the Treasury, Trenton, New Jersey 08646.

NEW MEXICO: Income tax rates range from 2.4% to 8.5% depending on income and filing status.

Sales tax rate: 3¾%; after 6/30/86, 4¾%

For more information, write: Taxation and Revenue Department, Santa Fe, New Mexico 87501.

NEW YORK: Income tax rates range from 2% on the first $1,000 of taxable income to 13.75% on taxable income over $26,000. There are a maximum tax of 9.5% on personal service taxable income, a minimum tax of 6% on federal tax preference items, separate additional tax on lump-sum distributions from qualified pension and profits-sharing plans.

New York City imposes an income tax with rates ranging from .9% on the first $1,000 of city taxable income to 4.3% on city taxable income over $25,000. In addition there is a surcharge of 5% on city taxable income over $15,000 and 10% on city taxable income over $20,000. There is an earnings tax on nonresidents deriving wages or self-employment income within the city of .45% on wages and .65% on net earnings from self-employment.

Sales tax rate: 4% (4¼% in the Metropolitan Commuter Transportation District; the IRS ruled that the additional ¼% tax is not deductible). New York City imposes an additional 4% sales tax; other localities also have additional sales taxes.

For more information, write: Department of Taxation and Finance, Albany, New York 12226.

NORTH CAROLINA: Income tax rates range from 3% on the first $2,000 of net income to 7% on net income over $10,000.

Sales tax rate: 3% (1% on prescription drugs and food purchased for consumption off the premises)

For more information, write: Department of Revenue, Raleigh, North Carolina 27602.

NORTH DAKOTA: Income tax rates range from 2% on the first $3,000 of taxable income to 9% on taxable income over $50,000. Optional tax in lieu of state graduated income tax: 10.5% of adjusted federal income tax liability.

Sales tax rate: 4%

For more information, write: Tax Commissioner, Bismarck, North Dakota 58501.

OHIO: Income tax rates range from 0.855% on the first $5,000 of taxable income to 8.55% on taxable income over $100,000. In addition, the following cities impose an income tax: Akron, Canton, Cincinnati, Cleveland, Columbus, Dayton, Toledo and Youngstown.

Sales tax rate: 5%

For more information, write: Department of Taxation, Columbus, Ohio 43215.

OKLAHOMA: Income tax rates range from .5% on the first $2,000 ($1,000 for married individuals filing separately and single individuals other than surviving spouses and heads of households) of taxable income to 6% on taxable income over $15,000 ($7,500 for married individuals filing separately and single individuals other than surviving spouses and heads of households).

Sales tax rate: 3¼%

For more information, write: Tax Commissioner, Oklahoma City, Oklahoma 73194.

OREGON: Income tax rates range from 4% on the first $500 of taxable income to 10% on taxable income over $5,000. Spouses filing jointly pay tax of twice the amount figured when income is divided in half. There is also a minimum tax on federal tax preference items. Multnomah County (which includes Portland) has a business income tax. The Tri-County Metropolitan Transit District and the Lane County Mass Transit District impose a payroll tax.

State sales tax: None in 1986

For more information, write: Department of Revenue, Salem, Oregon 97310.

PENNSYLVANIA: 2.2% on certain classes of taxable income. In addition, Philadelphia, Pittsburgh, and Scranton impose an income tax.

Sales tax rate: 6%

For more information, write: Department of Revenue, Harrisburg, Pennsylvania 17127.

RHODE ISLAND: Income tax is imposed at an effective rate of 22.21% of a modified federal income tax liability.

Sales tax rate: 6%

For more information, write: Department of Administration, Providence, Rhode Island 02908.

SOUTH CAROLINA: Basic income tax rates range from 2% on the first $2,000 of taxable income to 7% on taxable income over $10,000 (indexed for inflation). However, rates vary depending on filing status.

Sales tax rate: 5%

For more information, write: Tax Commission, Columbia, South Carolina 29202.

SOUTH DAKOTA: No state income tax.

Sales tax rate: 4%

For more information, write: Secretary of Revenue, Pierre, South Dakota 57501.

TENNESSEE: A tax of 6% is imposed on dividends and interest except that the rate drops to 4% on dividends from corporations having 75% of property taxable within the state.

Sales tax rate: 5½%

For more information, write: Department of Revenue, Nashville, Tennessee 37242.

TEXAS: No state income tax.

Sales tax rate: 4.125%

For more information, write: Comptroller of Public Accounts, Austin, Texas 78711.

UTAH: Basic income tax rates vary from 2.75% to 7.75% with different brackets applying to single individuals and married persons filing separately and married persons filing jointly and heads of households.

Sales tax rate: 4⅝%; after 6/30/86, 4.594%

For more information, write: Tax Commission, Salt Lake City, Utah 84114.

VERMONT: The income tax is 26.5% of regular federal income tax liability less a percentage allocated to non-Vermont income. In addition, there is a surtax of 1/24th of Vermont income tax.

Sales tax rate: 4%.

For more information, write: Commissioner of Taxes, Montpelier, Vermont 05602.

VIRGINIA: Income tax rates range from 2% on the first $3,000 of taxable income to 5.75% on taxable income over $12,000.

Sales tax rate: 4% (including 1% local tax)

For more information, write: Department of Taxation, Richmond, Virginia 23215.

WASHINGTON: There is no state income tax.

Sales tax rate: 6.5%; county rates may vary.

For more information, write: Department of Revenue, Olympia, Washington 98504.

WEST VIRGINIA: Income tax rates range from 2.1% to 13% depending on income and filing status. In addition, a partial 12% surcharge applies to certain incomes. Further, there is a minimum tax equal to 25% of federal alternative minimum tax.

Sales tax rate: 5%

For more information, write: State Tax Department, Charleston, West Virginia 25305.

WISCONSIN: Income tax rates range from 5% to 7.9% depending on income bracket and filing status.

Sales tax rate: 5%

For more information, write: Department of Revenue, Madison, Wisconsin 53702.

WYOMING: No state income tax.

Sales tax rate: 3%

For more information, write: State Board of Equalization, Cheyenne, Wyoming 82001.

¶17.00
Medical and Dental Expense Deductions

Illustrations of deducting your medical and dental expenses may be found in the Supplement to YOUR INCOME TAX. Mail the card at the front of this book to receive your FREE Supplement, which includes filled-in returns and last-minute information.

	See ¶		See ¶
Allowable medical care costs	17.01	Travel costs may be medical deductions	17.08
Nondeductible expenses	17.02	Schooling costs for the handicapped	17.09
Income limit applied to medical expense deduction	17.03	Convalescent home costs	17.10
Reimbursements of medical costs	17.04	Nurses' wages	17.11
Premiums of medical care policies	17.05	Home improvements as medical expenses	17.12
Dependents' medical costs	17.06	Costs deductible as business expenses	17.13
Decedent's medical expenses	17.07		

¶17.01 • Allowable Medical Care Costs

A deductible medical expense is any cost of diagnosis, cure, mitigation, treatment or prevention of disease, or any treatment that affects a part or function of the body. The following is a list of deductible expenses.

PROFESSIONAL SERVICES
Chiropodist
Chiropractor (lic.)
Christian Science Practitioner
Dermatologist
Dentist
Gynecologist
Neurologist
Obstetrician
Oculist
Optician
Optometrist
Orthopedist
Osteopath (lic.)
Pediatrician
Physician
Physiotherapist
Plastic Surgeon
Podiatrist
Practical or other nonprofessional nurse for medical services only; not for care of a healthy person or a small child who is not ill. Costs for medical care of elderly person, unable to get about, or person subject to spells, are deductible. *See* ¶17.11.
Psychiatrist
Psychoanalyst
Psychologist
Registered Nurse
Surgeon
Payments to an unlicensed practitioner are deductible if the type and quality of his services are not illegal.

DENTAL SERVICES
Cleaning teeth
Dental X-rays
Extracting teeth
Filling teeth
Gum treatment
Oral surgery
Straightening teeth

EQUIPMENT AND SUPPLIES
Abdominal supports
Air conditioner where necessary for relief from an allergy or for relieving difficulty in breathing. *See* ¶17.12.
Ambulance hire
Arches
Artificial teeth, eyes
Autoette (Auto device for handicapped person), but not if used to travel to job or business.
Back supports
Braces
Contact lenses
Cost of installing stair-seat elevator for person with heart condition. *See* ¶17.12.
Crutches
Elastic hosiery
Eyeglasses
Fluoridation unit in home
Hearing aids
Heating devices
Invalid chair
Iron lung
Orthopedic shoes
Reclining chair if prescribed by doctor.
Repair of special telephone equipment for the deaf
Sacroiliac belt
Special mattress and plywood bed boards for relief of arthritis of spine.
Splints
Truss
Wig advised by doctor as essential to mental health of person who lost all her hair from disease.

MEDICAL TREATMENTS
Abortion
Acupuncture
Blood transfusion
Cosmetic surgery
Diathermy
Electric shock treatments
Healing services
Hydrotherapy (water treatments)
Injections
Insulin treatments
Navajo healing ceremonies ("sings")
Nursing
Organ transplant
Pre-natal; post-natal treatments
Psychotherapy
Sterilization
Radium therapy
Ultra-violet ray treatments
Vasectomy
Whirlpool baths
X-ray treatments

MEDICINES AND DRUGS
Cost of prescriptions only

LABORATORY EXAMINATIONS AND TESTS
Blood tests
Cardiographs
Metabolism tests
Spinal fluid tests
Sputum tests
Stool examination
Urine analyses
X-ray examinations

HOSPITAL SERVICES
Anesthetist
Hospital bills
Oxygen mask, tent
Use of operating room
Vaccines
X-ray technician

PREMIUMS FOR MEDICAL CARE POLICIES
See ¶17.05 for how to deduct for:
Blue Cross and Blue Shield
Contact lens replacements
Federal voluntary Medicare (Part B)
Federal Medicare (Part A) by persons not covered by Social Security
Health insurance covering hospital, surgical, and other medical expenses

Membership in medical service cooperative

MISCELLANEOUS
Alcoholic inpatient care costs
Asylum (*see* ¶17.10).
Birth control pills or other birth control items prescribed by your doctor.
Braille books—excess cost of braille works over cost of regular editions
Clarinet lessons advised by dentist for treatment of tooth defects.
Convalescent home—for medical treatment only (*see* ¶17.10).
Drug treatment center—inpatient care costs
Face lifting operation, even if not recommended by doctor
Fees paid to health institute where the exercises, rubdowns, etc., taken there are prescribed by a physician as treatments necessary to alleviate a physical or mental defect or illness.
Hair transplant operation
Kidney donor's or possible kidney donor's expenses
Legal fees for guardianship of mentally ill spouse where commitment was necessary for medical treatment.
Nurse's board and wages, including Social Security taxes you pay on wages.
Remedial reading for child suffering from dyslexia
Sanitarium and similar institutions (*see* ¶17.10).
"Seeing-eye" dog and its maintenance.
Special school costs for physically and mentally handicapped children (*see* ¶17.09).
Wages of guide for a blind person.
Telephone-teletype costs and television adapter for closed caption service for deaf person

Medicine and drugs. To be deductible, medicines and drugs must *require* a prescription by a doctor. You may not deduct the cost of over-the-counter medicines and drugs, such as aspirin and other cold remedies. The cost of insulin is deductible.

Special foods. According to the IRS, the cost of special food or beverages is not a deductible medical expense if the food or beverages are taken as substitutes for those normally consumed.

Examples—

1. Your doctor prescribes two ounces of whiskey to be taken twice a day for relief of angina pain resulting from a coronary artery disease. The expense of the prescribed amount of whiskey is deductible as a drug expense.

2. To alleviate an ulcer, the doctor puts you on a special diet. The cost of your food and beverages is not deductible. The special diet replaces the food you normally eat.

The Tax Court has set its own standard for deducting the extra cost of special foods as medical costs. The test is to show a medical need for taking the special food and the extra cost of the health food over ordinary food. Only the extra cost is deductible.

Example—

Von Kalb suffered from hypoglycemia and her physician prescribed a special high protein diet, which required her to consume twice as much protein as an average person and exclude all processed foods and carbohydrates. She spent $3,483 for food, and deducted 30%, or $1,045, as the extra costs of her high protein diet. The IRS disallowed the deduction, claiming that the protein supplements were a substitute for foods normally consumed. The Tax Court disagreed. The high protein food did not substitute for her usual diet but helped alleviate her hypoglycemia. Thus, she may deduct its additional expense.

¶17.02 • NONDEDUCTIBLE EXPENSES

Over-the-counter medicines and drugs.
Toothpaste.
Maternity clothes.
Antiseptic diaper service.
Funeral, cremation or burial, cemetery plot, monument, mausoleum.
Illegal operations and drugs.
Your divorced spouse's medical bills—but *see* ¶17.06 and ¶20.033. You may be able to deduct them as alimony.
Special food or beverage substitutes—but excess cost of chemically uncontaminated foods over what would have ordinarily been spent on normal food was deductible for allergy patients.
Bottled water bought to avoid drinking fluoridated city water.
Health programs offered by resort hotels, health clubs, and gyms.
Domestic help—even if recommended by doctor because of spouse's illness. But part of cost attributed to any nursing duties performed by the domestic is deductible. See ¶17.11.
Deductions from your wages for sickness insurance under state law.
Premiums, in connection with life insurance policies, paid for disability, double indemnity, or for waiver of premiums in event of total and permanent disability or policies providing for reimbursement of loss of earnings or a guarantee of a specified amount in the event of hospitalization.
Athletic club expenses to keep physically fit.
Tattooing; ear piercing.

Boarding school fees paid for healthy child while parent is recuperating from illness. It makes no difference that this was done on a doctor's advice.
Tuition and travel expenses to send a problem child to a particular school for a beneficial change in environment. *See* ¶17.09.
Transportation costs of a disabled person to and from work.
Traveling costs to look for a new place to live—on doctor's advice.
Cost of trips for a "change of environment" to boost morale of ailing person. That doctor prescribed the trip is immaterial.
Travel costs to favorable climate when you can live there permanently.
Dance lessons advised by doctors as physical and mental therapy or for the alleviation of varicose veins or arthritis; however, the cost of a clarinet and lessons for the instrument were allowed as deductions when advised as therapy for a tooth defect.
Scientology fees.
Cost of divorce recommended by psychiatrist.
Cost of hotel room suggested for sex therapy.
Marriage counseling fees.
Veterinary fees for pet; pet is not a dependent.
Babysitting fees to enable you to make doctor's visits.
Weight reduction or stop smoking programs undertaken for general health, not for specific ailments.
Cost of moving away from airport noise by person suffering a nervous breakdown.

¶17.03 • INCOME LIMIT APPLIED TO MEDICAL EXPENSE DEDUCTION

A wide range of expenses, such as those listed at ¶17.01, qualify as deductible medical expenses. However, you may not be able to claim the deduction because of a percentage floor. In 1986, you may deduct only expenses exceeding 5% of your adjusted gross income. Adjusted gross income is explained at ¶13.04.

Married persons filing joint returns figure the 5% limit on combined adjusted gross income.

You include the cost of prescribed drugs and medical insurance premiums with other medical expenses subject to the 5% floor.

Example—

Your adjusted gross income in 1986 is $16,000. Your unreimbursed medical expenses were $900 for medical care, $187 for prescribed drugs and medicines, and $600 for medical insurance premiums. You deduct medical expenses of $887 figured this way:

Unreimbursed medical care	$900
Premiums	600
Drugs	187
Total	$1,687
Less: 5% of adjusted gross income (5% of $16,000)	800
Medical expense deduction	$ 887

On your 1986 return, you may deduct only expenses paid in 1986 for yourself, your spouse, or dependents. If you borrow to pay medical or dental expenses, you claim the deduction in the year you use the loan proceeds to pay the bill, not in the later year

HOW YOUR 1986 DEDUCTION IS REDUCED BY THE 5% LIMIT

If your adjusted gross income is	\$200	\$300	\$400	\$500	\$600	\$700	\$800	\$900	\$1,000	\$1,500	\$2,000	\$2,500
$ 2,000	$100	$200	$300	$400	$500	$600	$700	$800	$900	$1,400	$1,900	$2,400
3,000	50	150	250	350	450	550	650	750	850	1,350	1,850	2,350
4,000	0	100	200	300	400	500	600	700	800	1,300	1,800	2,300
5,000	0	50	150	250	350	450	550	650	750	1,250	1,750	2,250
6,000	0	0	100	200	300	400	500	600	700	1,200	1,700	2,200
7,000	0	0	50	150	250	350	450	550	650	1,150	1,650	2,150
8,000	0	0	0	100	200	300	400	500	600	1,100	1,600	2,100
9,000	0	0	0	50	150	250	350	450	550	1,050	1,550	2,050
10,000	0	0	0	0	100	200	300	400	500	1,000	1,500	2,000
11,000	0	0	0	0	50	150	250	350	450	950	1,450	1,950
12,000	0	0	0	0	0	100	200	300	400	900	1,400	1,900
13,000	0	0	0	0	0	50	150	250	350	850	1,350	1,850
14,000	0	0	0	0	0	0	100	200	300	800	1,300	1,800
15,000	0	0	0	0	0	0	50	150	250	750	1,250	1,750
18,000	0	0	0	0	0	0	0	0	100	600	1,100	1,600
20,000	0	0	0	0	0	0	0	0	0	500	1,000	1,500
25,000	0	0	0	0	0	0	0	0	0	250	750	1,250
30,000	0	0	0	0	0	0	0	0	0	0	500	1,000
40,000	0	0	0	0	0	0	0	0	0	0	0	500
50,000	0	0	0	0	0	0	0	0	0	0	0	0

Your medical expenses are / You may deduct

when you repay the loan. If you pay for medical or dental expenses by credit card, the deduction is allowed in the year of the charge.

You may not deduct the payment of expenses you are not legally obliged to pay until 1987 or some later year. You may not deduct medical expenses for which you have been reimbursed by insurance or other awards (see ¶17.04). Furthermore, reimbursement of medical expenses deducted in prior tax years may be taxable income (see ¶12.20).

¶17.04 • REIMBURSEMENTS OF MEDICAL COSTS

Insurance or other reimbursements of your medical costs reduce your medical deductions. Reimbursements for loss of earnings or damages for personal injuries and mental suffering do not.

A reimbursement first reduces the medical expense for which it is paid. The excess is then applied to your other deductible medical costs.

Example—

Premiums paid for medical insurance totaled $800. You paid doctor and hospital bills totaling $700 and prescribed drug costs of $150. Group hospitalization insurance reimbursed $300 for doctors and hospital bills and $25 for medicines and drugs. Your adjusted gross income is $8,000. Your 1986 deduction is computed as follows:

Prescribed drugs	$150
Medical care expenses	700
Premiums	800
Total	$1,650
Less Reimbursement	325
	1,325
Less 5% of $8000	400
Medical expense deduction	$ 925

Personal injury settlements or awards. Generally, a cash settlement recovered in a personal injury suit does not reduce your medical expense deduction. The settlement is not treated as reimbursement of your medical bills. But when part of the settlement is specifically earmarked by a court or by law for payment of hospital bills, the medical expense deduction is reduced.

Reimbursements in excess of your medical expenses. If you paid the entire premium of the policy, the excess payment is not taxed. If you and your employer each contributed to the policy, you may have to include in income that part of the excess reimbursement which is attributable to your employer's premium contributions and which was not included in your gross income and not paid for permanent injury, disfigurement, or as tax-free disability pension. See ¶2.19.

If your employer paid the total cost of the policy and his contributions were not taxed to you, you report as income all of your excess reimbursement, unless it covers payment for permanent injury, disfigurement or tax-free disability pension.

Examples—

1. Smith pays premiums of $240 and $120 for two personal health insurance policies. His total medical expenses are $900. He receives $700 from one insurance company and $500 from the other. The excess of $300 ($1,200 — $900) is not taxable.

2. Jones' employer paid premiums of $240 and $120 for two employee health insurance policies covering medical expenses. Jones's medical expenses in one year are $900. He receives $1,200 from the two companies. The entire $300 excess is taxable.

3. Brown's employer paid a premium of $240 for a group health policy covering Brown, and Brown himself paid $120 for a personal health policy. His medical expenses are $900; he recovers $700 under his employer's policy and $500 under his own policy. The taxable portion attributed to his employer's premium contribution is $175, computed this way:

Reimbursement allocated to Brown's policy, 5/12 × $900	$375
Reimbursement allocated to employer's policy, 7/12 × $900	525
Total	$900
Taxable excess allocated to employer's policy ($700 − $525)	$175

4. Green's employer paid $240 for a health insurance policy but contributed only $90 and deducted $150 from Green's wages. Green also paid $120 for a personal health insurance policy. His medical expenses are $900. He recovered $700 from the employer's policy and

$500 from his personal policy. The excess attributable to the employer's policy is $175 (computed as in example 3 above). However, the taxable portion is only $65.63. Both Green and his employer contributed to the cost of the employer's policy and a further allocation is necessary:

Green's contribution	$150
Employer's contribution	90
Total cost of policy	$240
Ratio of employer's contribution to annual cost of policy (90/240)	
Taxable portion—90/240 of excess reimbursement of $175	$65.63

Reimbursement in a later year. If you took a medical expense deduction in one year and are reimbursed for all or part of the expense in a later year, the reimbursement may be taxed in the year received. The reimbursement is taxable income to the extent the deduction reduced your tax in the prior year.

Examples—

1. In 1985, you had adjusted gross income of $12,000. During that year, you paid medical expenses of $1,300. You deducted $700 computed as follows:

Medical expenses	$1,300
Less: 5% of $12,000	600
Allowable deduction	$ 700

In 1986 you collect $500 insurance reimbursing part of your 1985 medical expenses. If you had collected that amount in 1985, your medical expense deduction would have been $200. The entire reimbursement of $500 is taxable in 1986. It is the amount by which the 1985 deduction of $700 exceeds the deduction of $200 that would have been allowed if the reimbursement had been received in 1985.

2. Same facts as above but you did not deduct the medical expense because you did not itemize deductions. The reimbursement is not taxable.

¶17.05 • PREMIUMS OF MEDICAL CARE POLICIES

You may deduct as medical expenses premiums paid for medical care policies covering yourself, your spouse, or dependents. Such policies include Blue Cross, Blue Shield, and Federal Voluntary Medicare insurance (Medicare Part B). Payment for coverage under Medicare (Part A) is deductible by those over age 65 who are not covered by Social Security. Deductions may be claimed for membership payments in associations furnishing cooperative or free-choice medical services, group hospitalization or clinical care policies, and medical care premiums paid to colleges as part of tuition bill, if the amount is separately stated in the bill.

Deductible premiums include amounts paid for health insurance providing reimbursements for hospital, surgical, drug costs, and other medical expenses. Also deductible are premiums paid for contact lens replacement and premiums on policies providing solely for indemnity for hospital and surgical expenses, even though benefits are paid regardless of the amount of expenses incurred.

Premiums paid before you reach age 65 for medical care insurance for protection after you reach 65 are deductible in the year paid if they are payable on a level payment basis under the contract (1) for a period of 10 years or more, or (2) until the year you reach age 65 (but in no case for a period of less than five years).

You may *not* deduct premiums for a policy guaranteeing you a specified amount each week (not to exceed a specified number of weeks) in the event you are hospitalized. Also, no deduction may be claimed for premiums paid for a policy which compensates you for loss of earnings while ill or injured, or for loss of life, limb, or sight. If your policy covers both medical care and loss of income or loss of life, limb, or sight, no part of the premium is deductible unless (1) the contract or separate statement from the insurance company states what part of the premium is allocated to medical care, and (2) the premium allocated to medical care is deductible. You may not deduct a portion of car insurance premiums that provides medical insurance coverage for persons injured by or in your car.

There is no separate deduction for health insurance premiums. All qualifying premiums are treated as medical expenses subject to the overall 5% limit.

¶17.06 • DEPENDENTS' MEDICAL EXPENSES

Spouse. You may deduct as medical expenses your payments of medical bills for your spouse. You must have been married either at the time the expenses were incurred or at the time the bills were paid. That is, you may deduct your payment of your spouse's medical bills even though you are divorced or widowed, if, at the time the expenses were incurred, you were married. Further, if your spouse incurred medical expenses before you married and you pay the bills after you marry, you may deduct the expense.

Examples—

1. Your spouse has doctor bills covering an operation performed in 1985, before you were married. You married in 1986. You pay those bills in 1986. You may claim a medical expense deduction for your payment.

2. In October 1985, your spouse had dental work done. In February 1986, you are divorced; in April 1986, you pay your former spouse's dental bills. You may deduct the payment on your 1986 tax return.

3. In 1986, you pay medical expenses for your spouse who died in 1986. You remarry in 1986. In a joint return which you file with your new spouse in 1986, you may deduct your payment of your deceased spouse's medical expenses.

Children and other dependents. You may deduct your payment of medical bills for your children or other dependents. The person must be someone you could claim as a dependent except for the fact that he earned more than $1,080 or filed a joint return. You must be able to prove you: (1) paid the medical expenses and (2) contributed more than half the support. (See ¶1.50 for a list of persons you may claim as dependents.) The close family relationship must exist either at the time the expense was incurred or at the time you paid it.

Examples—

1. You contribute more than half of your married son's support, including a payment of a medical expense of $800. Because he filed a joint return with his wife, you may not claim him as a dependent. But you may still deduct your payment of the $800 medical expense. You contributed more than half of his support.

2. Your mother underwent an operation in November, 1985. You paid for the operation in February, 1986. You may deduct the cost of the operation in 1986 if you furnished more than one-half your mother's support in either 1985 or 1986.

Divorced and separated parents. You may be able to deduct your payment of your child's medical costs, even though your ex-spouse is entitled to claim the child as a dependent. For purposes of the medical deduction, the child is considered to be the dependent of *both* parents if (1) they are divorced or legally separated under a written agreement, separated under a written agreement, or married but living apart during the last six months of 1986; (2) the child was in the custody of one or both parents for more than half of 1986, and (3) more than half of the child's 1986 support was provided by both parents.

A child may not deduct medical expenses paid with his parent's welfare payments.

Example—

A son is the legal guardian of his mother who is mentally incompetent. As guardian, he received his mother's state welfare and Social Security benefits which he deposited in his personal bank account and used to pay part of his mother's medical expenses. On his tax return, he claimed a deduction for the total medical expenses paid on behalf of his mother. The court held that he could deduct only medical expenses in excess of the amounts received as welfare and Social Security payments. The benefits, to the extent used for medical expenses, represented the mother's payments on her own behalf.

Adopted children. You may deduct medical expenses of an adopted child if you may claim the child as a dependent either when the medical services are rendered or when you pay the expenses. An adopted child may be claimed as a dependent when a court has approved the adoption. In the absence of a court decree, the child is an exemption if he is a member of your household for the entire year. However, you do not have to show that he lived in your home for the entire year if he has been placed in your custody by an authorized agency.

If you reimburse an adoption agency for medical expenses it paid under an agreement with you, you are considered to have paid the expenses. But reimbursement of expenses incurred and paid before adoption negotiations do not qualify as your medical expenses and you may not deduct them.

You may not deduct medical expenses for services rendered to the natural mother of the child you adopt.

Example—

A couple adopted a son on the day of his birth. They paid all medical expenses of the birth. They were denied a deduction because they could not show the expenses were for the child, their dependent, and not for the natural mother, a nondependent.

Multiple support agreements. You may be able to deduct your payment of a relative's medical expenses although you do not contribute more than one-half his support. You must meet the tests for a multiple support agreement. *See* ¶1.553. If your relative has gross income over $1,080, you may still deduct your payment of medical expenses provided the other tests for multiple support are met.

You may deduct only the amount you actually pay for the relative's medical expenses. If you are reimbursed by others who signed the multiple support agreement, you must reduce your deduction by the amount of reimbursement.

Example—

You and your brother and sister share equally in the support of your mother. Part of your mother's support includes medical expenses. Should the three of you share in the payment of the bills or should only one of you pay them? The answer: Payment should be made by the person who may claim her as a dependent under a multiple support agreement. Only he may deduct the payment. If you are going to claim her as an exemption, you should pay the bill. You may deduct the payment although you did not contribute more than half of her support. If your brother and sister reimburse you for part of the bill, you must reduce your medical deduction by the amount of the reimbursement. And neither your brother nor your sister may deduct this share. Thus, a deduction is lost for these amounts.

¶17.07 • DECEDENT'S MEDICAL EXPENSES

The executor or administrator of a decedent's estate may pay the decedent's medical expenses out of the estate. Where the expenses are paid within one year of death, they may be treated as paid when incurred and claimed as income tax deductions. Thus, a claim for refund or an amended return may be filed for an earlier year when the expenses were incurred but not paid until after death by the executor.

Example—

Jones incurred medical expenses of $500 in 1985 and $300 in 1986. He died June 1, 1986 without having paid these expenses. He had already filed his 1985 return before the due date. In August 1986, his executor pays the $800 in medical expenses. He may file an amended return for 1985 and claim a medical expense deduction for the $500 and get a refund for the increased deductions. He may claim the remaining $300 as a medical expense deduction on Jones's final return.

A decedent's medical expenses claimed as an income tax deduction may not again be claimed as an estate tax deduction. If the expenses may be claimed as an estate tax deduction but are claimed as an income tax deduction, the executor must file a statement with the decedent's income tax return that the expenses have not been deducted on the estate tax return and the estate waives its right to deduct them for estate tax purposes.

If medical expenses are claimed as an income tax deduction, the portion of the expenses that are below the 5% floor and, therefore, not deductible, may not be deducted on the estate tax return. Although the expenses were not actually deducted, the IRS considers them to be part of the overall income tax deduction.

¶17.08 • TRAVEL COSTS MAY BE MEDICAL DEDUCTIONS

You may deduct the cost of travel to a place where you receive medical treatment or which is prescribed as a place that will help relieve a specific chronic ailment. Trips to and from a doctor's office are the most common type of deductible travel expense.

The amount of the deduction is limited to the cost of transportation, such as the cost of operating a car or fares for public transportation. If you use your automobile, you may deduct a flat rate of 9¢ a mile and, in addition, you may deduct parking fees and tolls. If, however, auto expenses exceed this standard mileage rate, you may deduct your actual out-of-pocket costs for gas, oil, repairs, tolls, and parking fees. Do not include depreciation, general maintenance, or car insurance.

Example—

You drive your car to a doctor's office for treatment. You made 40 such round trips of 25 miles each. As the total mileage is 1,000 miles, you claim $90 (1,000 × 9¢) as medical expenses. If you incurred tolls or parking fees during the trips, you add these expenses to the deduction.

Important: The 9¢ rate was effective when this edition went to press. Any change in the rate is listed in the Supplement.

Per diem lodging allowance. A daily lodging allowance of up to $50 is allowed on trips to obtain medical care by a physician at a licensed hospital, hospital-related facility, or equivalent facility such as an outpatient clinic. The deduction is allowed only if the lodging is not considered extravagant and there is no significant vacation or recreation element to the trip. Food expenses are not deductible. A separate $50 per diem lodging deduction is also allowed to a parent who accompanies a dependent child on a qualifying trip to obtain medical care. For example, the IRS ruled that the $50 allowance could be claimed by a parent for a six-week hotel stay while her eight-year-old daughter was treated in a nearby hospital for serious injuries received in an automobile accident. The mother's presence was necessary so that she could sign release forms for surgery.

Examples of travel costs which have been allowed as medical deductions by rulings or court decisions are:

Nurse's fare if nurse is required on trip.

Parent's fare if parent is needed to accompany child who requires medical care.

Parent's fare to visit his child at an institution where the visits are prescribed by a doctor.

Trip to visit specialist in another city.

Airplane fare to a distant city in which a patient used to live to have check up by a family doctor living there. That he could have received the same examination in the city in which he presently lived did not bar his deduction.

Trip to escape a climate that is bad for your health. For example, the cost of a trip from a northern state to Florida made by a person recovering from a throat operation was ruled deductible.

Travel to an Alcoholics Anonymous Club meeting if membership in the group has been advised by a doctor.

Disabled veteran's commuting expenses where a doctor prescribed work and driving as therapy.

Wife's trip to provide nursing care for an ailing husband in a distant city. The trip was ordered by her husband's doctor as a necessity.

Driving prescribed as therapy.

Travel costs of kidney transplant donor or prospective donor.

Nondeductible costs—

Trip for the general improvement of your health.

Traveling to areas of favorable climates during the year rather than living permanently in a locality suitable for your health.

Meals while on trip for medical treatment—even if cost of transportation is a valid medical cost, but a court has allowed the deduction of the extra cost of specially prepared food.

Trip for medical treatment at a distant city when you could have been treated in your home city. For example, a trip to Florida for an appendectomy is not deductible.

Trip to get "spiritual" rather than medical aid. For example, cost of trip to the Shrine of Our Lady of Lourdes is not deductible.

Moving a family to a climate more suitable to an ill mother's condition. Only the mother's travel costs would be deductible.

Moving household furnishings to area advised by physician.

Operating an auto or special vehicle to go to work because of disabled condition. But the cost of wheel chair or autoette or special auto devices for handicapped persons is deductible.

Convalescence cruise advised by a doctor for a patient recovering from pneumonia.

Loss on sale of car bought for medical travel.

Medical seminar cruise taken by patient whose condition was reviewed by physicians taking the cruise.

¶17.09 • SCHOOLING COSTS FOR THE HANDICAPPED

You may deduct as medical expenses the costs of sending a mentally or physically handicapped person to a special school or institution to overcome or alleviate his handicap. Such costs may cover—

Teaching of braille or lip reading.

Training, caring for, supervising, and treating a mentally retarded person.

Cost of meals and lodgings, if boarding is required at the school.

Costs of regular education courses also taught at the school, provided they are incidental to the special courses and services furnished by the school.

The parent of a problem child may deduct only that part of a private school fee directly related to psychological aid given to the child.

Examples—

1. An emotionally disturbed child is sent to a private school which has a staff of three psychologists. His father deducted the school fee of $6,270 as a medical expense. IRS disallowed the amount claiming that the child, who was neither mentally retarded nor handicapped, was sent to school primarily for an education. The Tax Court allowed the father to deduct $3,000 covering the psychological treatment.

2. A boy could not understand subjects taught in public schools. He was withdrawn and enrolled at a private military academy. The deduction of tuition costs was disallowed by a court. The academy furnished no psychiatric treatment and, furthermore, enrollment in the academy was not recommended by a doctor.

3. A retarded boy with a speech defect attends a state school for therapy. On the advice of school authorities, the boy is sent to a "half-way home" in another community so that he may have major orthodontic work to reduce his speech disability. The state school has neither an orthodontist nor facilities to take the child to one. The half-way home is operated by a private couple who care for several other people, all with disabilities and placed there through a local welfare service. The cost of maintaining the boy at the private home and transportation costs incurred in taking the child from the home to his residence and back on visits are deductible.

4. A retarded boy had been excluded from several schools for the mentally handicapped because he needed close attention. The director of a military academy had extensive experience in training young boys. Although it was not the usual practice of the academy to enroll mentally handicapped children, the director accepted the boy on a day-to-day basis as a personal challenge. The Tax Court holds that the cost of both tuition and transportation to bring the boy to and from the school are deductible medical expenses. The primary purpose of the training given the boy was not ordinary education but remedial training designed to overcome his handicap. But note that in other cases, a deduction for tuition of a military school to which a child was sent in order to remove him from a tense family environment, and the cost of a blind boy's attendance at a regular private school which made a special effort to accommodate his braille equipment, were disallowed.

The fact that a particular school or camp is recommended for an emotionally disturbed child by a psychiatrist will not qualify the tuition as a deduction if the school or camp has no special program geared to the child's problem. However, you may deduct the costs of maintaining a mentally retarded person in a home specially selected to meet the standards set by his psychiatrist to aid him in his adjustment from life in a mental hospital to community living.

Payment for future medical care expenses is deductible if immediate payment is required by contract.

¶17.10 • CONVALESCENT HOME COSTS

A payment for meals and lodging to a nursing home, convalescent home, home for the aged, or sanitarium is a deductible medical expense if the patient is confined for medical treatment.

Helpful in establishing the full deductibility of payments to these institutions are facts such as these:

The patient entered the institution on the direction or suggestion of a doctor.

Attendance or treatment at the institution had a direct therapeutic effect on the condition suffered by the patient.

The attendance at the institution was for a specific ailment rather than for a "general" health condition. That the patient suffers from an ailment is not sufficient proof that he is in the home for treatment.

If you cannot prove that the patient entered the home for medical care (which would permit a deduction for meals and lodging in addition to medical costs), you may nevertheless deduct that part of the cost covering actual medical and nursing care.

Example—

A husband and wife pay $500 per month to a rest home for lifetime care. They prove, on the basis of the home's experience, that it costs the home $100 to provide them with medical care, medicines, and hospitalization. Under such circumstances, $100 of each monthly fee is a deductible medical expense.

In an unusual case, a court allowed a medical expense deduction for apartment rent of an aged parent.

Example—

A doctor recommended to Ungar that his 90-year-old mother, convalescing from a brain hemorrhage, could receive better care at less expense in accommodations away from a hospital. A two-room apartment was rented, hospital equipment installed, and nurses engaged for seven months. The rent totaled $1,400. Ungar's sister, who worked in her husband's shoe store, nursed her mother for six weeks. Ungar paid the wages of a clerk who was hired to substitute for his sister in the store. Ungar deducted both the rent and wages as medical expenses. The IRS disallowed them; a Tax Court reversed the IRS. The apartment rent was no less a medical expense than the cost of a hospital room. As for the clerk's wages, they too were deductible medical costs. The clerk was hired specifically to allow the daughter to nurse her mother, thereby avoiding the larger, though more direct, medical expense of hiring a nurse.

Payment for future lifetime care. Generally, no deduction is allowed for prepayment of medical expenses for services to be performed in a later taxable year. However, this disallowance rule does not apply where there is a current obligation to pay.

Examples—

1. A 78-year-old man entered into an agreement with a retirement home. For a lump-sum payment, the home agreed to provide lifetime care, including medical care, medicine, and hospitalization. The lifetime care fee was calculated without regard to fees received from other patients, and was not insurance. The home allocated 30% of the lump-sum payment to medical expenses based on its prior experience. The IRS holds that this part of the payment is deductible in the year paid. It holds that the legal obligation to pay the medical expenses was incurred at the time the lump-sum payment was made, even though medical services would not be performed until a future time, if at all. Should any portion of the lump-sum payment be refunded, that part attributable to the deducted amount must be reported as income (*see* ¶12.20).

2. Parents contracted with an institution to care for their handicapped child after their death. The contract provided for payments as follows: 20% on signing, 10% within 12 months, 10% within 24 months, and the balance when the child enters. Payment of specified amounts at specified intervals was a condition imposed by the institution for its agreement to accept the child for lifetime care. Since the obligation to pay was incurred at the time payments were made, they are deductible as medical expenses, although the medical services were not to be performed until a future time, if at all.

3. A couple entered a retirement home which would provide them with accommodations, meals, and medical care for life. They agreed to pay a founder's fee of $40,000 and a monthly fee of $800. If they quit the home, they may get a refund of a portion of the founder's fee. Fifteen percent of the monthly fee and 10% of the founder's fee will be used for medical care and 5% of the founder's fee will be used for construction of a health facility. On the basis of these figures, the couple may deduct as medical costs 10% of the founder's fee and 15% of the monthly fee. However, the portion of the founder's fee for the possible health facility does not qualify as a medical expense. Finally, any refund of the founder's fee received in a later year may be income to the extent medical deductions were previously claimed for the fees.

4. An entrance fee to a retirement community gave new residents not only the right to live in the development but also the right to 30 days of free care at a nearby convalescent home in the first year, with additional free days in later years of residency. The community allocated 7% of the $20,000 entrance fee, or $1,400, to the convalescent care. Smith deducted the $1,400 as a medical expense which the IRS disallowed. It claimed that the amount could not be deducted in the year of payment because most of the promised free services would not be received until future years. The Tax Court disagreed and allowed the deduction because the obligation to pay was incurred when the residency agreement was signed.

¶17.11 • NURSES' WAGES

The costs of a nurse attending an ill person are deductible. Costs include any Social Security (FICA) tax paid by you. That the nurse is not registered or licensed will not bar the deduction, provided the services are performed for the medical aid or treatment of the patient. When you use a nonprofessionally trained person, such as a practical nurse, be prepared to show that the nurse performed medical services. If the nurse also performs domestic services, deduct only that part of the pay attributed to medical aid to the patient.

Examples—

1. Dodge's wife was arthritic. His doctor advised that he have someone take care of her to prevent her from falling. He moved her to his daughter's home and paid the daughter to care for her mother. He deducted the payments to his daughter. The IRS disallowed the deduction, claiming that the daughter was not a trained nurse. The Tax Court allows that part of the deduction attributed to the nursing aid. Whether a medical service has been rendered depends on the nature of the services rendered, not on the qualifications or title of the person who renders them. Here, the daughter's services, following the doctor's advice, qualify as medical care.

2. A husband hires a domestic to care for his home so that his wife can get a complete rest as prescribed by her doctor. He may deduct only that part of the domestic's salary directly attributed to nursing aid given to the wife. No deduction is allowed for the cost of the domestic services in the home. (But *see* ¶24.20, tax credit for dependent care expenses.)

3. An attendant hired by a quadriplegic performs household duties, in addition to caring for his medical and personal needs. The quadriplegic pays him wages and also provides food and lodging. According to the IRS, a medical expense deduction is allowable only for that portion of the wages attributable to medical and personal care. The wages are apportioned on the basis of time spent performing nursing-type services and time spent performing household duties. The same allocation is used to determine the portion of the cost of the attendant's meals which are deductible as a medical expense. However, the attendant's lodging is not deductible as a medical expense unless the quadriplegic shows additional expenditures directly attributable to lodging the attendant, such as paying increased rent for an apartment with another bedroom for the attendant.

The salary of a clerk hired specifically to relieve a wife from her husband's store in order to care for her ill mother was allowed as a medical expense (*see* the example in ¶17.10).

If, in order to work, you pay a nurse to look after a physically or mentally disabled dependent, you may be able to claim a credit for all or part of the nurse's wage as a dependent care expense. You may not, however, claim both a credit and a medical expense deduction. First, you claim the nurse's wage as a dependent care cost. If not all of the wages are utilized as a care cost because of the expense limits (*see* ¶24.20), the remaining balance is deductible as a medical expense.

¶17.12 • HOME IMPROVEMENTS AS MEDICAL EXPENSES

A disease or ailment may require the construction of special equipment or facilities in a home: A heart patient may need an elevator to carry him upstairs; a polio patient, a pool; an asthmatic patient, an air cleaning system.

You may deduct the full cost of equipment installed for a medical reason if it does not increase the value of your property, as for example, the cost of a detachable window air conditioner. Where equipment increases the value of your property, you may take a medical deduction to the extent that the cost of the equipment exceeds the increase in the value of the property. Of course, if the equipment does not increase the value of the property, its entire cost is deductible, even though it is permanently fixed to the property.

Examples—

1. Gerard's daughter suffered from cystic fibrosis. While there is no known cure for the disease, doctors attempt to prolong life by preventing pulmonary infection. One approach is to maintain a constant temperature and high humidity. A doctor recommended that Gerard install a central air-conditioning unit in his home for his daughter. It cost $1,300 and increased the value of his home by $800. The balance of $500 was deductible as a medical expense.

2. After a three-year-old child had been diagnosed as having lead poisoning, health officials required removal of the lead-based paint and a refinishing of surfaces reachable by the child, or those that were in poor repair. The cost of removing the lead-based paint from surfaces reachable by the child or in poor repair qualifies as a medical expense

because of the child's history of lead poisoning and the hazardous condition of his home as certified by local authorities. Also deductible was the cost of installation of wallboard or wall paneling over such surfaces to the extent that the cost of the work exceeds the increase in the value of the house. No deduction was allowed for the cost of painting or repairing any of the surfaces which were not reachable by the child or were not in poor repair.

If swimming is prescribed as physical therapy, the cost of constructing a home swimming pool may be partly deductible as a medical expense. However, the IRS is likely to question the deductions because of the possibility that the pool may be used for recreation. If you can show that the pool is specially equipped to alleviate your condition and is not generally suited for recreation, the IRS will allow the deduction. For example, the IRS allowed a deduction for a pool constructed by an osteoarthritis patient. His physician prescribed swimming several times a day as treatment. He built an indoor lap pool with specially designed stairs and a hydrotherapy device. Given these features, and the fact that the pool did not have a diving board, the IRS concluded that the pool was specially designed to provide medical treatment and was not intended for personal recreation.

In one case the IRS tried to limit the cost of a luxury indoor pool built for therapeutic reasons to the least expensive construction. The Tax Court rejected the IRS position, holding that a medical expense is not to be limited to the cheapest form of treatment, but on appeal, the IRS position was adopted.

If, instead of building a pool, you buy a home with a pool, can you deduct the part of the purchase price allocated to the pool? The Tax Court said no. The purchase price of the house includes the fair market value of the pool. Therefore, there is no extra cost above the increase in the home's value which would support a medical expense deduction.

The operating costs of an indoor pool were allowed as a deduction to an emphysema sufferer.
Example—
Cherry was advised by his doctor to swim to relieve his severe emphysema and bronchitis. He could not swim at local health spas; they did not open early enough or stay open late enough to allow him to swim before or after work. His home was too small for a pool. He bought a lot and built a new house with an indoor pool. He used the pool several times a day, and swimming improved his condition; if he did not swim, his symptoms returned. Cherry deducted pool operating costs of $4,000 for fuel, electricity, insurance and repairs. The IRS disallowed the deductions claiming that the pool was used for personal recreation. Besides, it did not have special medical equipment. The Tax Court allowed the deduction. Cherry built the pool to swim in in order to exercise his lungs. That there was no special equipment is irrelevant; Cherry did not need special ramps, railings, a shallow floor or whirlpool. Finally, his family rarely used the pool.

No deduction is allowed where the primary purpose of the improvement is for personal convenience rather than medical necessity.
Example—
Haines broke his leg in a skiing accident and underwent various forms of physical therapy, including swimming. To aid his recovery, his physician recommended that he install a swimming pool at his home. The Tax Court agreed with the IRS that the cost of the pool was not deductible. Although swimming was beneficial to his condition, he needed special therapy for only a limited period of time, and he could have gotten it at less cost at a nearby public pool. Finally, because of

weather conditions, the pool could not be used for about half of the year.

Cost of maintaining and operating improvement. The expense of maintaining and operating equipment installed for medical reasons may be claimed as a medical expense, although the cost of the equipment and its installation is not deductible under the above rules.

¶17.13 • COSTS DEDUCTIBLE AS BUSINESS EXPENSES
The following examples illustrate cases in which expenses are deductible as business expenses rather than as medical expenses. Claiming a business deduction is preferable because the deduction is not subject to the 5% adjusted gross income limit.

Costs of a checkup required by your employer are business expenses and are not subject to the 5% limit.
Example—
An airline pilot is required by his company to take a semi-annual physical exam at his own expense. If he fails to produce a resultant certificate of good health, he is subject to discharge. The cost of such checkups certifying physical fitness for a job is an ordinary and necessary business expense. If the doctor prescribes a treatment or further examinations to maintain the pilot's physical condition, the cost of these subsequent treatments or examinations may be deducted only as medical expenses, even though needed to maintain the physical standards required by the job. Thus, a professional singer who consults a throat specialist may not deduct the fee as a business expense. The fee is a medical expense subject to the 5% limit.

The Tax Court allowed the costs of psychoanalysis by a licensed social worker working as a therapist to be deducted as an education cost.

Some expenses incurred by a physically handicapped person because of his handicap may be deductible as a business expense rather than as a medical expense. A business expense deduction may be allowed if the expense is necessary for the person to satisfactorily perform his job and is not required or used, except incidentally, for personal purposes.

Examples—
1. A blind person requires a reader to help him perform his job. The costs of the reader's services are deductible as an itemized business deduction.
2. A professor is paralyzed from the waist down and confined to a wheelchair. When he attends out-of-town professional meetings, he has his wife, a friend, or a colleague accompany him to help him with baggage, stairs, narrow doors, and to sit with him on airplanes when airlines will not allow wheelchair passengers without an attendant. While he does not pay them a salary, he does pay their travel costs. He may deduct these costs as business expenses. They are incurred solely because of his occupation.
3. An attorney uses prostheses due to bilateral amputation of his legs and takes medication several times a day for other ailments. When he must take out-of-town business trips, his wife or a neighbor accompanies him to help with his wheelchair, luggage, driving, daily removal and replacement of his prostheses, and administration of medication and to help him should he have an allergic reaction to the drugs. The attorney requires many of these services in conducting his personal and business affairs in his home town. He may deduct the out-of-town expenses incurred for his neighbor's services only as a medical expense. The services are not considered business expenses as he regularly uses them for personal purposes. When his wife accompanies him, he may deduct her transportation costs as a medical expense; her food and lodging are nondeductible ordinary living expenses.

¶18.00

Casualty and Theft Losses and Involuntary Conversion Gains

DEDUCTIBLE LOSSES MUST EXCEED 10% INCOME FLOOR

A 10% income floor limits the amount of personal casualty and theft losses deductible as itemized deductions. The 10% limit based on adjusted gross income applies to total losses incurred during 1986, after each loss is reduced by $100 (*see* ¶18.042).

Example—

In January 1986, you have an uninsured theft loss of $1,000, and in July 1986 uninsured car damage of $3,000. Your adjusted gross income is $25,000. Your deduction is $1,300 figured as follows:

Theft loss	$1,000	
Less	100	$900
Car damage	$3,000	
Less	100	2,900
Total loss		$3,800
Less 10% of $25,000		2,500
Deductible loss		$1,300

The 10% limit does not apply to losses of business or income-producing property and certain netting computations explained at ¶18.27.

¶18.01 • DEDUCTIBLE PERSONAL CASUALTY AND THEFT LOSSES

A loss of nonbusiness property must result from a sudden and destructive force. Chance or a natural phenomenon must be present. Examples include earthquakes, hurricanes, tornadoes, floods, severe storms, landslides and fires. Damage to your car from an accident is generally deductible; *see* ¶18.06. Courts have allowed deductions for other types of accidents; see example 2 below. The requirement of suddenness is designed to bar deductions for damage caused by a natural action such as erosion, corrosion, and termite infestation occurring over a period of time. The requirement of suddenness does not apply to losses of business or income-producing property.

Examples—

1. A home owner claimed a loss for water damage to wallpaper and plaster. The water entered through the frames of a window. The loss was disallowed. He gave no evidence that the damage came from a sudden or destructive force, such as a storm. The damage might have been caused by progressive deterioration.

2. Unaware that his wife had reached back into their automobile, Mr. White slammed the door on her hand. The impact loosened a large diamond in the ring she wore. In pain, she shook her hand vigorously and the diamond flew out of its loosened setting to the leaf-covered gravel driveway. It was never found. In disallowing White's deduction, the IRS contended that a casualty loss requires a cataclysmic event. The Tax Court disagreed and allowed the deduction. Whenever an accidental force is exerted against property, and its owner is powerless to prevent the damage because of the suddenness, the resulting damage is a deductible casualty loss. The IRS has agreed to accept the decision.

Personal casualty and theft losses after the floor reductions must be taken as itemized deductions. Casualty and theft losses of business and rental or royalty-producing property are deductible, even if you do not itemize deductions.

Drought damage. The IRS does not generally allow deductions for drought damage. An agent may argue that the loss resulted from progressive deterioration which does not fit the legal definition of a personal casualty loss. Courts have allowed deductions for severe drought.

Destruction of a lawn by the careless use of weed killer has been held to be a casualty.

Loss due to vandalism during riots or civil disorders is treated as a casualty loss.

Loss due to buyer resistance because of damage to surrounding property is generally not deductible. However in the following case a deduction was allowed by a federal district court and appeals court.

Example—

Floods damaged 12 homes which were razed by local authorities for safety reasons. Although Finkbohner's home suffered only minor damage, he claimed that the removal of the neighboring homes decreased the attractiveness of the neighborhood and made it more susceptible to crime. He estimated that the value of his home fell from $120,000 to $95,000 and claimed a casualty loss for the $25,000 difference. The IRS disallowed the loss on the grounds that it was not based on actual physical damage. It allowed a deduction only for the cost of repairs, about $1,200. A federal district court jury allowed a $12,500 casualty loss after being instructed by the trial judge that permanent buyer resistance after the flood damage to the neighborhood is basis for a loss deduction. An appeals court upheld the loss because permanent buyer resistance affected the value of the home. The court distinguished Finkbohner's case from that of a homeowner who after a flood and mud slide was barred from deducting a loss based on fears of future floods. In that situation, the owner was trying to claim a loss that could only be deducted, if and when a future disaster occurred, by the future owner. Here, the buyer resistance confronting Finkbohner was not based on expected future casualties, but on changes to their neighborhood that already occurred.

Termites. Termite damage is generally nondeductible since it often results from long periods of termite infestation. Proving a *sudden* action in the sense of fixing the approximate moment of the termite invasion is difficult. Some courts have allowed a deduction, but the IRS will disallow deductions for termite damage under any conditions based on a study that found that serious termite damage results only after an infestation of three to eight years. Examples of other nondeductible casualty losses are at ¶18.07.

Destruction of trees by southern pine beetles over a period of 5–10 days was held by the IRS to be a casualty. One court held similarly where destruction occurred over a 30-day period. For figuring the deduction for tree and shrub damage, *see* ¶18.061.

Failure to protect against a foreseeable casualty does not bar a deduction for the loss if it does occur.

Examples—
1. Heyn owned a hillside lot on which he contracted for the building of a home. A soil test showed a high proportion of fine-grain dense sandstone, which is unstable. His construction contract called for appropriate shoring up and support. But, because of the contractor's negligence, a landslide occurred. The IRS disallowed the loss on the grounds that it was not due to a "casualty" because the danger was known before Heyn undertook the project and because of the negligence involved. The court disagreed. The contractor's negligence is not a factor in determining whether there was a casualty. For example, an automobile collision is considered a casualty, even if caused by negligent driving. Foreseeability is not a factor. A weather report may warn property owners to take protective steps against an approaching hurricane, but losses caused by the hurricane are deductible. The IRS has agreed to accept the decision.

2. Mrs. Carpenter placed her dirty ring in a glass of ammonia beside the sink. Not knowing the contents of the glass, her husband emptied it into the sink and started the automatic garbage disposal, crushing the ring. The court allowed a full deduction for the loss which it said resulted from a destructive force. That Mr. Carpenter was negligent has no bearing on whether the event was a casualty.

The cost of preventative measures, such as burglar alarms or smoke detectors, is not deductible.

Example—
A utility company cut down trees interfering with power lines and removed branches of the remaining trees. Later, the property owner feared that the lack of branches on the remaining trees might cause them to uproot during an ice storm and damage his home. So he had all of the trees removed and claimed a $3,900 deduction for the removal. He argued that preventive measures taken to avoid casualty loss damage qualify for a casualty loss deduction. The IRS with Tax Court support disagrees. A casualty loss is allowed only if it is caused by a sudden and unexpected event, such as a storm.

Faulty construction no bar to casualty loss. A plumber stepped on a pipe which was improperly installed two years before. Resulting underground flooding caused damage of over $20,000. The IRS argued that this was caused by a construction fault and did not qualify as a casualty loss. The Tax Court disagreed. The plumber caused the damage. Improper construction was only an element in the causative chain.

¶18.011 • WHO MAY CLAIM THE LOSS DEDUCTION

The casualty and theft loss deduction may be claimed only by the owner of the property. For example, a husband filing a separate return may not deduct the loss of jewelry belonging to his wife; only she may deduct it on her separate return.

On jointly owned property, the loss is divided among the owners. If you and your spouse own the property jointly, you deduct the entire loss on a joint return. If you file separately, each owner deducts his share of the loss on each separate return.

If you have a legal life estate in the property, the loss is apportioned between yourself and those who will get the property after your death. The apportionment may be based on actuarial tables that consider your life expectancy.

You may claim a casualty loss deduction for the loss or destruction of property used by your dependent if you own the property. You may not claim a loss deduction for the destruction of property belonging to your child who has reached majority, even though your child is still your dependent.

Lessee. A person leasing property may be allowed to deduct payments to a lessor compensating him for a casualty loss. A tenant was allowed to deduct as a casualty loss payment of a judgment obtained by the landlord for fire damage to the rented premises which had to be returned in the same condition as at the start of the lease. However, the Tax Court does not allow a deduction for the cost of repairing a rented car, as the lessee has no basis in the car.

¶18.02 • PROVING A CASUALTY LOSS

If your return is audited, you will have to prove that the casualty occurred and the amount of the loss. The time to collect your evidence is as soon after the casualty as possible.

To prove	You need this information
That a casualty actually occurred	With a well-known casualty, like regional floods, you will have no difficulty proving the casualty occurred, but you must prove it affected your property. Photographs of the area, before and after and newspaper stories placing the damage in your neighborhood are helpful. If only your property is damaged, there may be a newspaper item on it. Some papers list all the fire alarms answered the previous day. Police, fire and other municipal departments may have reports on the casualty.
The cost of repairing the property	Cost of repairs is allowed as a measure of loss of value if it is not excessive and the repair merely restored your property to its condition immediately before the casualty. Save canceled checks, bills, receipts, vouchers for expenses of clearing debris and restoring the property to its condition before the casualty.
The value immediately before and after the casualty	Appraisals by a competent expert are important. Get them in writing—in the form of an affidavit, deposition, estimate, appraisal, etc. The expert—an appraiser, engineer, architect—should be qualified to judge local values. Any records of offers to buy your property either before or after the casualty, are helpful. Automobile "blue books" may be used as guides in fixing the value of a car. But an amount offered for your car as a trade-in on a new car is not usually an acceptable measure of value.
Cost of your property—the deductible loss cannot be more than that	A deed, contract, bill of sale, or other document probably shows your original cost. Bills, receipts, and canceled checks show the cost of improvements. One court refused to allow a deduction because an owner failed to prove the original cost of a destroyed house and its value before the fire. In another case, estimates were allowed where a fire destroyed records of cost. A court held that the homeowner could not be expected to prove cost by documents lost in the fire that destroyed her property. She made inventories after the fire and again at a later date. Her reliance on memory to establish cost, even though inflated, was no bar to the deduction. The court estimated the market value based on her inventories. If you acquired the property by gift or inheritance, you must establish adjusted basis in the property from records of the donor or the executor of the estate. *See* ¶6.10 and ¶6.12.

¶18.03 • THEFT LOSSES

The taking of property must be illegal under state law to support a theft loss deduction. That property is missing is not sufficient evidence to sustain a theft deduction. It may have been lost or misplaced. So, if all you can prove is that an article is missing or lost, your deduction may be disallowed. Sometimes, of course, the facts surrounding the disappearance of an article indicate that it is reasonable to assume that a theft took place.

You deduct a theft loss in the year you discover the property was stolen. If you have a reasonable chance of being reimbursed for your loss, you may not take a deduction until the year in which you learn there is no reasonable prospect of recovery.

A legal fee paid to recover stolen property has been held to be deductible as part of the theft loss.

Proving a theft. Get statements from witnesses who saw the theft or police records of a breaking into your house or car. A newspaper account of the crime might also help.

When you suspect a theft, make a report to the police. Even though your reporting does not prove that a theft was committed, it may be inferred from your failure to report that you were not sure that your property was stolen. But a theft loss was allowed where the loss of a ring was not reported to the police or an attempt made to demand its return from the suspect, a domestic. The owner feared being charged with false arrest.

Fraud by building contractors. A deduction was allowed when a building contractor ran away with a payment he received to build a residence. The would-be home owner was allowed a theft loss deduction for the difference between the money he advanced to the contractor and the value of the partially completed house. In another case, a theft deduction was allowed for payments to subcontractors. The main contractor had fraudulently claimed that he had paid them before he went bankrupt. A deduction has also been allowed for the theft of trees.

Embezzlement losses are deductible as theft losses in the year the theft is discovered. However, if you report on a cash basis, you may not take a deduction for the embezzlement of income you have not reported. For example, an agent embezzled royalties of $46,000 due an author. The author's theft deduction was disallowed. The author had not previously reported the royalties as income; therefore, she could not get the deduction.

The embezzlement must be the direct cause of the loss, not merely a contributing factor.

Example—

A depositor kept $102,000 in a bank which went bankrupt as a result of a large employee embezzlement. The Federal Deposit Insurance Corporation paid him $100,000, the maximum amount insured by law. He claimed a $1,900 theft loss ($2,000 — $100 floor) in a year prior to the 10% floor. The IRS disallowed the deduction on the grounds that the embezzlement was only an indirect factor in his loss. He was allowed to claim a nonbusiness bad debt deductible as a short-term capital loss in the year in which his account became worthless, that is, when the receiver in bankruptcy notified the depositor that payment after liquidation is doubtful.

Worthless stock purchased on the representation of false and fraudulent sales offers are deductible as theft losses in the year there is no reasonable prospect of recovery. However, the illegal sale of unregistered stock does not support a theft loss deduction.

Confiscated personal property is not deductible as a theft or casualty loss.

Seizure of a car by creditors under an invalid writ is not a deductible theft loss.

Payment of a ransom to a kidnapper is generally a deductible theft loss. However, the expenses of trying to find an abducted child is not a theft loss.

To figure the amount of a theft loss deduction, *see* ¶18.04.

¶18.031 • RIOT LOSSES ARE DEDUCTIBLE

Losses caused by fire, theft, and vandalism occurring during riots and civil disorders are deductible.

To support your claim, keep evidence of the damage suffered and the cost of repairs. Photographs taken prior to repairs or replacement, lists of damaged or missing property, and police reports would help to establish and support your loss deduction.

When a reception is canceled because of a curfew, no loss deduction is allowed for perishable food that is discarded.

¶18.04 • FIGURING YOUR LOSS

The deductible loss is usually the difference between the market value of the property before and after the casualty less (1) reimbursements received for the loss, and (2) $100, if the property was used for personal purposes. The deductible loss may not exceed the basis of the property. The total of all deductible personal casualty and theft losses incurred during 1986 is limited by the 10% adjusted gross income ceiling, *see* ¶18.00.

To figure a loss, follow these four steps:

1. Compute the loss in market value of the property. This is the difference between the market value immediately before and immediately after the casualty. You will need written appraisals to support your claim for loss of value.

2. Compute the adjusted basis of the property. This is usually the cost of the property plus the cost of improvements, less previous casualty loss deductions and depreciation if the property is used in business or for income-producing purposes. Basis of property acquired by other than purchase is explained at ¶6.10. Adjusted basis is explained at ¶6.12.

3. Take the lower amount of step (1) or (2). The lower amount, reduced by the adjustments in step (4), is your casualty loss, with one exception: Where property used for business or income-producing purposes is totally destroyed, and before the casualty its market value is less than its adjusted basis, the measure of the loss is the adjusted basis.

4. Reduce the loss in step (3) by the insurance proceeds or other compensation for the loss (*see* ¶18.0412) and $100, if the property was used for personal purposes (*see* ¶18.042).

You reduce the basis of the damaged property by (1) the casualty loss deduction claimed and (2) compensation received for the loss.

Examples—

1. Your home which cost $16,000 was damaged by a fire. The value of the house before the disaster was $67,500, afterwards $62,500. Your household furnishings were destroyed. You separately compute the loss on each item of furnishings and figure a combined loss of $2,000 on the furnishings. The insurance company reimbursed you $2,000 for your house damage and $500 for your furnishings. You figure your loss as follows:

1. Decrease in market value		
Value of house before fire	$67,500	
Value of house after fire	62,500	
Decrease in value	$ 5,000	
2. Adjusted basis	$16,000	
3. Loss sustained (lower of 1 or 2)	$ 5,000	
Less: Insurance	2,000	
Loss on house	$ 3,000	
4. Loss on furnishings	$ 2,000	
Less: Insurance	500	
Loss on furnishings	$ 1,500	
5. Total loss ($3,000 and $1,500)	$ 4,500	
Less: $100 floor	100	
Casualty loss (subject to 10% ceiling)	$ 4,400	

2. Depreciable business property with a fair market value of $1,500 and an adjusted basis of $2,000 is totally destroyed. The loss is measured by the larger adjusted basis of $2,000 because the property was used in your business. Disregard the $100 floor applied to casualty losses on personal property. If the property were used for personal purposes, the loss would have been limited to the lower market value of $1,500 less $100, leaving a casualty loss of $1,400.

For examples of auto losses, *see* ¶18.06.

You may not claim sentimental or aesthetic values or a fluctuation in property values caused by a casualty; you must deal with cost or market values of what has been lost.

Inventory losses are reflected in an adjustment to the cost of goods sold. If the loss is separately deducted, an offsetting credit must be applied either to opening or closing inventory. See IRS Publication No. 549 for further details.

The casualty must have caused damage to your property. Damage to a nearby area which lowered the value of your property does not give you a loss deduction.

Example—

You buy or lease a lot on which to build a cottage. Along with your purchase or lease, you have the privilege of using a nearby lake. The lake is later destroyed by a storm and the value of your property drops. You may not deduct the loss. The lake is not your property. You had only a privilege to use it, and this is not an ownership right which supports a casualty loss deduction.

No deduction may be claimed for estimated decline in value based on buyer resistance in an area subject to landslides. The Tax Court has allowed casualty loss deductions that were not based on market value comparisons, but on cost less depreciation.

Example—

The fair market rule applied to household items generally limits your deduction to the going price for second-hand furnishings. But one house-holder claimed that the fair market value should be original cost less depreciation. He based his figures on an inventory prepared by certified public adjusters describing each item, its cost and age. The deduction figured this way came to approximately $27,500 ($55,000 cost, less $13,000 depreciation, a $14,400 insurance recovery, and the $100 floor). The IRS estimated that the furniture was worth $15,304 before the fire and limited the deduction to $804 after setting off the insurance and the $100 floor. The Tax Court disagreed. The householder's method of valuing his furniture is consistent with methods used by insurance adjusters who have an interest in keeping values low. He is not limited to the amount his property would bring if "hawked off by a second-hand dealer or at a forced sale." However, in another case, the court refused to allow the cost less depreciation formula where the homeowner's inventory list was based on memory.

For property held partly for personal use and partly for business or income, the loss deduction is computed as if two separate pieces of property were damaged, destroyed, or stolen.

Example—
A building with two apartments, one used by the owner as his home and the other rented to a tenant, is damaged by a fire. The fair market value of the building before the fire was $69,000 and after the fire, $56,000. Its cost basis was $20,000. Depreciation taken before the fire was $4,000. The insurance company paid $2,000. The owner has adjusted gross income of $20,000. This is his only loss this year. He has a business casualty loss of $5,000 and a deductible personal casualty loss of $3,400.

	Business	Personal
1. Decrease in value of building:		
Value before fire ($69,000)	$34,500	$34,500
Value after fire ($56,000)	28,000	28,000
Decrease in value	$ 6,500	$ 6,500
2. Adjusted basis of building:	$10,000	$10,000
Less: Depreciation	4,000	
Adjusted basis	$ 6,000	$10,000
3. Loss sustained (lower of 1 or 2)	$ 6,000	$ 6,500
Less: Insurance (total $2,000)	$ 1,000	$ 1,000
4. Loss	$ 5,000	$ 5,500
Less: $100 floor and 10% of adjusted gross income		2,100
Deductible casualty loss	$ 5,000	$ 3,400

Indirect expenses. Expenses such as personal injury, temporary lights, fuel, moving or rentals for temporary living quarters, are not deductible as casualty losses.

Appraisal costs of damaged property, see ¶18.10.

¶18.0411 • REPAIRS MAY BE "MEASURE OF LOSS"
The cost of repairs may be treated as evidence of the loss of value if the amount is not excessive and the repairs do nothing more than restore the property to its condition before the casualty (see ¶18.02). An estimate for repairs will not suffice; only actual repairs may be used as a measure of loss. However, where you are not relying on repairs as a measure of loss but rather are using appraisals of value of the property before and after the casualty, repairs may be considered in arriving at a post-casualty value even though no actual repairs are made.

A casualty loss deduction is not limited to repair expense where the decline in market value is greater.

Examples—
1. Connor claimed that the market value of his house dropped $93,000 after it was extensively damaged by fire. His cash outlay ($52,000) in repairing the house was reimbursed by insurance. Connor claimed a casualty loss deduction of approximately $40,000, the uncompensated drop in market value. The IRS disallowed the deduction. The house was restored to pre-casualty condition. The cost of the repairs is a realistic measure of the loss, and, as the expense was fully compensated by insurance, Connor suffered no loss. A court disagreed. It found that the house dropped $70,000 in market value, of which $20,000 was uncompensated by insurance. The deduction is measured by the uncompensated difference in value before and after the casualty. It is not limited to the cost of repairs, even where the repair expense is less than the difference in market values. Had the repairs cost more than this difference, the IRS would not have allowed Connor a larger deduction.

2. Seven months after Hagerty bought his house for $78,000, it was severely damaged by fire. The insurance company hired a general contractor to repair the house at a cost of $33,000. Hagerty claimed a casualty loss of $20,000 on the basis of these figures:

Value before fire	$78,000
Value after fire	25,000
	$53,000
Less: Insurance	33,000
Loss	$20,000

The IRS disallowed the deduction, arguing that the loss was completely compensated by the insurance company. It paid for the repairs, which is a measure of the loss here. The Tax Court disagreed. Repairs are not a measure of the loss where they do not completely restore the residence to its pre-fire condition. Hagerty proved that the contractor of the insurance company did not do as thorough a job as contractors hired by him would have done. However, the court set the fair market value of the home after the fire at $35,000, reducing Hagerty's loss to $10,000.

¶18.0412 • INSURANCE REIMBURSEMENTS
You reduce the amount of your loss by insurance proceeds, voluntary payments received from your employer for damage to your property and cash or property received from the Red Cross. However, cash gifts from friends and relatives to help defray the cost of repairs do not reduce the loss where there are no conditions on the use of the gift. Also, gifts of food, clothing, medical supplies and other forms of subsistence do not reduce the loss deduction nor are they taxable income.

Cancellation of part of a disaster loan under the Disaster Relief Act is treated as a partial reimbursement of the loss and reduces the amount of the loss. Urban renewal agency's payments to acquire property under the Federal Relocation Act of 1970 are considered reimbursements reducing a casualty loss deduction.

Insurance payments for the cost of added living expenses because of damage to a home do not reduce a casualty loss. The payments are treated separate and apart from payments for property damage. Payments for extra living costs are generally not taxable (see ¶18.11).

Failure to make an insurance claim. If you are insured for the extent of your loss and do not file a claim because you do not want to risk cancellation of liability coverage, the IRS says you may not claim a deduction. The Tax Court and an appeals court have rejected the IRS position and allowed a loss deduction despite the failure to make an insurance claim.

¶18.042 • HOW THE $100 FLOOR IS APPLIED
The $100 floor reduces casualty and theft losses of property used for personal purposes. It does not apply to losses of business property or property held for the production of income, such as securities. If property used both in business and personal activities is damaged, the $100 offset applies only to the loss allocated to personal use.

The $100 reduction applies to a loss arising in each casualty or theft occurring during the year. For example, you are involved in five different casualties during the year. There will be a $100 offset applied to each of the five losses. But when two or more items of property are destroyed in one event, only one $100 offset is applied to the total loss. For example, a storm damages your residence and your car parked in the driveway. Only one $100 offset limits the amount of the loss stemming from storm damage to your house and car.

The $100 floor applies to the entire loss sustained from each casualty. For example, in 1986, you incur a casualty loss of $290, on which you expect a reimbursement of $250. Thus, your unreimbursed loss in 1986 is $40, but you may not deduct the amount as it does not exceed $100. Now assume that in 1987, you learn that you cannot recover the expected reimbursement of $250. In claiming a casualty loss deduction in 1987, you reduce the $250 by $60. $40 of the $100 limitation had applied to part of the same casualty loss in 1986.

The $100 limit applies separately to the loss of each individual whose property has been damaged by a single casualty, even where the damaged property is owned by two or more individuals.

Examples—

1. Two sisters own and occupy a house which sustains a casualty loss of $500. Each sister applies the $100 limit.

2. Your house is partially damaged by a fire which also damages the personal property of a house guest. You are subject to one $100 limitation and the house guest is subject to a separate $100 limitation.

Where a husband and wife own property either jointly or separately and they file a joint return, only one $100 floor applies to their joint return. If they file separate returns, each applies a $100 floor to the respective loss.

Where a single casualty results in losses to a husband and wife in two or more tax years, the rules for deductions are as follows: If a joint return was filed for the first year for which the loss was sustained, only one $100 limitation applies. If they file separate returns in the first year of the loss, each applies a separate $100 limitation to the loss deducted on the separate return. If the couple files a joint return for the first loss year and separate returns for the later years, each allocates any unused portion of the $100 limitation equally between them in the later years.

¶18.05 • WHEN TO DEDUCT YOUR CASUALTY LOSS

Generally, you deduct a casualty loss in the year the casualty occurs, regardless of when you repair or replace damaged or destroyed property. But say a casualty strikes in one year and you do not discover the damage until a later year. Or you know damage has been inflicted but you do not know the full extent of the loss because you expect reimbursement in a later year. Here is what to do:

If you reasonably expect reimbursement in a later year, deduct in the year the casualty occurred only that part of your loss for which you do not expect reimbursement. For example, if you expect a full insurance recovery next year for a 1986 loss, you would take no deduction in 1986.

If you do not expect reimbursement and deduct a loss in 1986 but you receive insurance or other reimbursement in 1987, you would then report as income in 1987 the amount of the deduction you claimed in 1986 if it gave you a tax benefit by reducing your taxable income (see ¶12.20). You may not amend your 1986 tax return.

Example—

In 1969, Hurricane Camille destroyed oceanfront real estate owned jointly by two brothers. The buildings were insured under two policies which included wind damage but not losses resulting from floods, tidal waves or water. The insurers, claiming the tidal wave had caused the destruction, denied their claim. The brothers consulted an attorney about the possibility of suit against the insurance companies, but there seemed little likelihood of recovery, so they deducted their shares of the casualty loss in 1969. However, in January, 1970, the adjusters of both companies changed their decisions, reimbursing the brothers for more than two-thirds of their loss. One of the brothers filed an amended 1969 tax return, reducing the previously reported casualty loss.

The IRS claimed that the insurance recovery is taxable in the year of receipt, 1970, to the extent that the prior deduction reduced 1969 income. The brother claimed that he made an error in claiming the deduction in 1969 because he had a reasonable prospect of reimbursement. Therefore, he was not entitled to the deduction; his amended return reducing the deduction by the reimbursement was proper.

The Tax Court disagreed. Tax liability is based on facts as they exist at the end of each year. A recovery in a later tax year does not prove that a reasonable prospect of recovery existed in the earlier year. Amendments to previously filed tax returns may be made only to correct mathematical errors or miscalculations, not to rearrange facts and readjust income for two years.

Assume you took no loss deduction in 1986 because you expected to recover your entire loss in 1987—but the insurance company refuses to pay your claim. When do you deduct your loss? You deduct your loss in the year you find that you have no reasonable prospect of recovery. For example, you sue the company in 1987, with a reasonable prospect of winning your claim. However, in 1988, a court rules against you. You deduct your loss in 1988.

If you do not discover the loss until a later year, Treasury regulations do not specifically allow the deduction of the loss in the year it is discovered, but court decisions have. In one case, an

unseasonable blizzard damaged a windbreak planted to protect a house, buildings, and livestock. The damage to the evergreens did not become apparent until the next year, when about half of the trees died and the others were of little value. The court held that the loss occurred in the later year. In another case, hurricane damage did not become apparent for two years. The Tax Court allowed the deduction in the later year.

If you, as lessee, are liable to the lessor for damage to property, you may deduct the loss in the year you pay the lessor.

¶18.051 • DISASTER LOSSES

If you suffer a loss to property from a disaster in an area declared by the President as warranting federal assistance, you may deduct the loss either on the return for the year of the loss or on the return of the prior tax year.

You may elect to claim the deduction on a prior return any time on or before the later of (1) the due date (without extensions) of the return for the year of the disaster or (2) the due date considering any extension for filing the return for the prior tax year.

Examples—

1. *1986 disaster losses.* You have generally until April 15, 1987, to amend a 1985 tax return to claim a disaster loss occurring during 1986.

2. *1987 disaster losses.* You have generally until April 15, 1988, to amend a 1986 tax return to claim a disaster loss occurring during 1987.

After making your election, you have 90 days in which to revoke it. After the 90-day period, the election becomes irrevocable. However where an early election is made, you have until the due date for filing your return for the year of the disaster to change your election.

Your revocation of an election is not effective unless you repay any credit or refund resulting from the election within the revocation period. A revocation made before you receive a refund will not be effective unless you repay the refund within 30 days after you receive it.

You make an election in a signed statement attached to your return (original or amended) or refund claim. List the date of the disaster and where the property was located (city, town, county, and state).

To amend a filed return for a prior year, use Form 1040X.

Homeowners forced to relocate. If you were forced to relocate or demolish your home in a disaster area, you may be able to claim the loss even though the damage, such as from erosion, does not meet the sudden test of ¶18.01. For example, after a severe storm, there is a danger to a group of homes from nearby mudslides. State officials order homeowners to evacuate and relocate their homes. Under prior law, a deduction could be barred if there was no actual physical damage to the home. A new law allows disaster loss treatment if these tests are met: (1) The president has determined that the area warrants federal disaster relief; (2) within 120 days of the President's order, you are ordered by the state or local government to demolish or relocate your residence, and (3) the home was rendered unsafe by the erosion or other disaster. The law applies to vacation homes and rental properties as well as to principal residences.

The loss is treated as a disaster loss so that you may elect to deduct the loss either in the year the demolition or relocation order is made or in the prior taxable year.

Fiscal year. If you are on a fiscal year, an election may be made for disaster losses occurring after the close of a fiscal year.

Example—

You are on a fiscal year ending on April 30, and suffer a disaster loss on or before April 30, 1986. You may elect to deduct the loss on your return for the year ended April 30, 1985.

Should you make an election? Consider making the election if the deduction on the return of the prior year gives a greater tax reduction than if claimed on the return for the year in which the loss occurred or you want a refund of all or part of the tax paid for the prior year.

Cancellation of part of a disaster loan under the Disaster Relief Act is treated as a reimbursement that reduces your loss.

For the treatment of crop disasters, *see* ¶8.08.

¶18.06 • DEDUCTING DAMAGE TO YOUR CAR

Damage to your car in an accident may be a deductible loss unless the damage is caused by your willful negligence, such as drunken driving.

You may not deduct legal fees and costs of a court action for damages or money paid for damages to another's property because of your negligence while driving for commuting or other personal purposes. But if at the time of the accident you were using your car on business, you may deduct as a business loss a payment of damages to the other party's car. For purposes of a business loss deduction, driving between two locations of the same business is considered business driving but driving between locations of two separate businesses is considered personal driving. Therefore, the payment of damages arising from an accident while driving between two separate businesses is not deductible.

A court has allowed deductions for damage resulting from a child pressing the starter button of a car and from flying stones while driving over a temporary road. In a private letter ruling, the IRS disallowed a loss for damage to a race car by an amateur racer on the grounds that in races, crashes are not an unusual event and so do not constitute a casualty.

If the deduction is questioned, be prepared to show the amount, if any, of your insurance recovery. A deduction is allowed only for uninsured losses. Not only must the loss be proved, but also that it was not compensated by insurance.

When you use an automobile partly for personal use and partly for business, your loss is computed as though two separate pieces of property were damaged—one business and the other personal. The $100 and 10% floors reduce only the loss on the part used for business purposes.

Towing costs are not included as part of casualty loss.

A parent may not claim a casualty loss deduction for damage to a car registered in his son's name, although the parent provided funds for the purchase of the car.

Expenses of personal injuries arising from a car accident are not a deductible casualty loss.

¶18.061 • DAMAGE TO TREES AND SHRUBS

Not all damage to trees and shrubs qualifies as a casualty loss. The damage must be occasioned by a sudden event (see ¶18.01). Destruction of trees over a period of 5–10 days by southern pine beetles is deductible. One court allowed a deduction for similar destruction over a 30-day period. However, damage by Dutch Elm disease or lethal yellowing disease has been held to be gradual destruction not qualifying as a casualty loss. The Tax Court has allowed a deduction for the cost of removing infested trees.

> If shrubbery and trees on nonbusiness property are damaged by a sudden casualty, you figure the loss on the value of the entire property before and after the casualty. You treat the buildings, land, and shrubs as one complete unit; in fixing the loss on business or income producing property, however, shrubs and trees are valued separately from the building.

Examples—

1. Smith bought an office building for $90,000. The purchase price was allocated between the land ($18,000) and the building ($72,000). Smith planted trees and ornamental shrubs on the grounds surrounding the building at a cost of $1,200. When the building had been depreciated to $66,000, a hurricane caused extensive property damage. The fair market value of the land and building immediately before the hurricane was $18,000 and $70,000; immediately afterwards, $18,000 and $52,000. The fair market value of the trees and shrubs immediately before the casualty was $2,000 and immediately afterwards, $400. Insurance of $5,000 is received to cover damage to the building. The deduction for the building is $13,000, computed as follows:

Value of property immediately before casualty	$70,000
Less: Value immediately after casualty	52,000
Value of property actually destroyed	18,000
Less: Insurance received	5,000
Deduction allowed	$13,000

The deduction for the trees and shrubs is $1,200:

Value immediately before casualty	$2,000
Less: Value of trees immediately after casualty	400
Value of property actually destroyed	$1,600*

* However, the loss cannot exceed the adjusted basis of property, $1,200.

2. Same facts as Example 1 except Smith purchases a personal residence instead of an office building. Smith's adjusted gross income is $25,000, and this is his only 1985 loss. No allocation of the purchase price is necessary for the land and house because the property is not depreciable. Likewise, no individual evaluation of the fair market values of the land, house, trees, and shrubs is necessary. The amount of the deduction for the land, house, trees, and shrubs is $12,000, computed as follows:

Value of property immediately before casualty		$90,000
Less: Value of property immediately after casualty		70,400
Value of property actually destroyed		19,600
Less: Insurance received	$5,000	
10% and $100 floors	2,600	7,600
Deduction allowed		$12,000

¶18.07 • NONDEDUCTIBLE LOSSES

Certain losses, though casualties for you, may not be deducted if they are not due to theft, fire, or from some other sudden natural phenomenon. The following losses have been held not to be deductible—

Termite damage, see ¶18.01.
Carpet beetle damage.
Dry rot damage.
Damages for personal injuries or property damage to others caused by your negligence.
Legal expenses in defending a suit for your negligent operation of your personal automobile.
Legal expenses to recover personal property wrongfully seized by the police.
Expenses of moving to and rental of temporary quarters.
Loss of personal property while in storage or in transit.
Loss of passenger's luggage put aboard a ship. The passenger missed the boat and the luggage could not be traced.
Accidental loss of a ring from your finger.
Injuries resulting from tripping over a wire.
Loss by husband of joint property taken by his wife when she left him.
Loss of a valuable dog which strayed and was not found.
Damages to a crop caused by plant diseases, insects, or fungi.
Damage to property from drought in an area where a dry spell is normal and usual.
Damage to property caused by excavations on adjoining property.
Damages from rust or corroding of understructure of house.
Moth damage.
Dry well.
Losses occasioned by water pockets, erosion, inundation at still water levels, and other natural phenomena. (There was no sudden destruction.)
Amount paid to a public library for damages to a book you borrowed.
Death of a saddle horse after eating a silk hat.
A watch or spectacles dropped on the ground.
Sudden drop in the value of securities.
Loss in earnings of a lawyer resulting from his illness.
Loss of contingent interest in property due to the unexpected death of a child.
Improper police seizure of private liquor stock.
Chinaware broken by a family pet.
Temporary fluctuation in value.
Loss of tree from Dutch Elm disease and lethal yellowing disease.
Loss of trees after horse ate bark.
Damage to property from local government construction project

Note: But some of the listed items in the prior column may be allowed to persons in business.

¶18.09 • DO YOUR CASUALTY LOSSES EXCEED YOUR INCOME?

If they do, you pay no tax in 1986. You may also carry the excess loss back to 1983 and file a refund claim for that year. Any remaining loss may be carried back to 1984 and 1985 and carried forward to 1987 through 2000 or you may just carry your loss forward 15 years until it is used up. *See* ¶5.20 on figuring your net operating loss for a refund of prior taxes.

Note that the $100/10% of adjusted gross income floors for personal casualty losses apply only in the year of loss; you do not again reduce your loss in the carryback or carryover years.

¶18.10 • HOW TO DEDUCT YOUR CASUALTY AND THEFT LOSSES

Generally, you deduct nonbusiness casualty or theft losses as itemized deductions on Schedule A. You figure the loss on Form 4684. The amount of the loss is then entered on Schedule A. If you have suffered more than one casualty or theft event, use separate Forms 4684 to figure the losses for each event. Where you have realized both gains and losses from personal casualty and theft events, see ¶18.27.

Appraisal fees and other incidental costs (photos, etc.) incurred in establishing the amount of your casualty loss do not offset your loss; they are claimed as a miscellaneous itemized deduction on Schedule A.

¶18.11 • EXCESS LIVING COSTS PAID BY INSURANCE ARE NOT TAXABLE

Your insurance contract may reimburse you for excess living costs when a casualty or a threat of casualty forces you to vacate your house. The payment is not taxable income if these tests are met:

1. Your principal residence is damaged or destroyed by fire, storm, or other casualty or you are denied use of it by a governmental order because of the occurrence or threat of the casualty.

2. You are paid under an insurance contract for living expenses resulting from the loss of occupancy or use of the residence. The living expenses must be paid by the insurance company for yourself and members of your household.

The tax-free exclusion covers only excess living costs paid by the insurance company. The excess is the difference between: (1) the actual living expenses incurred during the time you could not use or occupy your house, and (2) the normal living expenses which you would have incurred for yourself and members of your household during the period. Living expenses during the period may include the cost of renting suitable housing and extraordinary expenses for transportation, food, utilities, and miscellaneous services. The expenses must be incurred for items and services (such as laundry) needed to maintain you in the same standard of living that you enjoyed before the loss and must be covered by the policy.

Where a lump-sum settlement does not identify the amount covering living expenses, an allocation is required to determine the tax-free portion. In the case of uncontested claims, the tax-free portion is that part of the settlement which bears the same ratio to total recovery as increased living expense bears to total loss and expense. If your claim is contested, you must show the amount reasonably allocable to increased living expenses consistent with the terms of the contract, but not in excess of coverage limitations specified in the contract.

The exclusion does not cover insurance reimbursements for loss of rental income or for loss of or damage to real or personal property.

If your home is used for both residential and business purposes, the exclusion does not apply to insurance proceeds and expenses attributable to the nonresidential portion of the house. There is no exclusion for insurance recovered for expenses resulting from governmental condemnation or order unrelated to a casualty or threat of casualty.

The insurance reimbursement may cover part of your normal living expenses as well as the excess expenses due to the casualty. The part covering normal expenses is income; it does not reduce your casualty loss.

Examples—

1. On March 1, your home was damaged by fire. While it was being repaired, you and your spouse lived at a motel and took meals at restaurants. Costs are $200 at the motel, $180 for meals, and $25 for laundry services. You make the required March payment of $190 on your home mortgage. The mortgage payment has no relationship to the casualty and is not considered an actual living expense resulting from the loss of use of your residence. Your customary $40 commuting expense is $20 less for the month because the motel is closer to your work. Your usual commuting expense is therefore treated as not being incurred to the extent of the $20 decrease. Further, you do not incur your customary $150 food expense for meals at home, $75 for utilities, and $10 for laundry at home. The tax-free exclusion is limited to $150 computed in the last column.

2. Same facts as example (1) except that you rented the residence for $100 per month and the risk of loss was on the landlord. You did not pay the March rent. The excludable amount is $50 ($150 less $100 normal rent not incurred).

	Actual expenses resulting from casualty	Normal expenses not incurred	Increase (Decrease)
Housing	$200.00		$200.00
Utilities		$ 75.00	(75.00)
Meals	180.00	150.00	30.00
Transportation		20.00	(20.00)
Laundry	25.00	10.00	15.00
Total	$405.00	$255.00	$150.00

¶18.20 • Gains from Involuntary Conversions

You may realize a gain when your property is destroyed by a casualty or taken by a government authority if insurance or other compensation exceeds the adjusted basis of the property. Tax on the gain may be postponed if you elect to defer gain and invest the proceeds in replacement property, the cost of which is equal to or exceeds the net proceeds from the conversion. If you do not plan to replace the property or you plan to replace but do not want to defer tax, see ¶5.45 for the tax treatment of gains from involuntary conversions and ¶18.27. The following sections discuss the election to defer tax on gains realized from involuntary conversions.

¶18.21 • INVOLUNTARY CONVERSIONS QUALIFYING FOR TAX DEFERRAL ELECTION

For purposes of an election to defer tax, "involuntary conversion" is more broadly defined than casualty loss. You have an involuntary conversion when your property is—

Damaged or destroyed
Stolen, or
Seized, requisitioned, or condemned by a governmental authority. If you voluntarily sell land made useless to you by the condemnation of your adjacent land, the sale may also qualify as a conversion. Condemnation of property as unfit for human habitation does not qualify. Condemnation, as used by the tax law, refers to the taking of private property for public use, not to the condemnation of property for noncompliance with housing and health regulations. Similarly a tax sale to pay delinquent taxes is not an involuntary conversion.

Sold under a threat of seizure, condemnation, or requisition.

The threat must be made by an authority qualified to take property for public use. A sale following a threat of condemnation made by a government employee is a conversion if you reasonably believe he speaks with authority and could and would carry out the threat to have your property condemned. If you learn of the plan of an imminent condemnation from a newspaper or the radio, the IRS requires you to confirm the report from a government official before you act on the news.

Farmers also have involuntary conversions when—

Land is sold within an irrigation project to meet the acreage limitations of the federal reclamation laws;

Cattle are destroyed by disease or sold because of disease, *or*

Draft, breeding, or dairy livestock is sold because of drought. The election to treat the sale as a conversion is limited to livestock sold over the number which would have been sold but for the drought. In some cases, livestock may be replaced with other farm property where there has been soil or other environmental contamination.

If property subject to depreciation recapture is involuntarily converted, see ¶5.43; if an investment credit was claimed for the purchase of the property, see ¶5.75.

If your residence is condemned or destroyed, see ¶29.20.

An election gives an immediate advantage: Tax on gain is postponed and the funds that would have been spent for the payment of tax may be used for other investments.

As a condition of deferring tax, the basis of the replacement property is usually fixed at the same cost basis as the converted property. As long as the value of the replacement property does not decline, tax on the gain is finally incurred when the property is sold.

To decide whether postponement of gain at the expense of a reduced basis for property is advisable, compare the tax consequences of an election with those resulting if no election is made.

Example—
Assume a rental building is destroyed by fire and a proper replacement is made. Assume that gain on the receipt of the fire proceeds is taxable at capital gain rates. An election is generally not advisable if you have capital losses to offset the gain. However, even if you have no capital losses, you may still decide not to make the election and pay capital gain tax in order to fix, for purposes of depreciation, the basis of the new property at its purchase price, if the future depreciation deductions will offset ordinary income taxable at a higher rate than the capital gain tax. If there is little or no difference between the two rates so that a net after tax benefit from the depreciation would not arise, an election might be made solely to postpone the payment of tax.

¶18.22 · HOW TO ELECT TO DEFER TAX

You make an election by omitting the taxable gain as income on the tax return for the year in which gain is realized. However, attach to your return a statement giving details of the transaction, including computation of the gain and your plan to buy a replacement.

If the conversion is directly into similar property, no election is necessary. Postponement of tax on the gain is required. For example, the city condemns a store building and compensates the owner by giving him another store building the value of which exceeds the cost basis of the old one. Gain is not taxed.

Election to defer tax on involuntary conversion gain may be irrevocable. If you change your mind and prefer to pay tax, you may not revoke the election if you have made a qualified replacement within the time limits. Both the IRS and the Tax Court hold that the election is irrevocable once a qualified replacement has been made.

To nullify the effect of the election and to subject the conversion to tax, these options may be available: You do not make a replacement; you purchase property that does not qualify as a replacement; you invest in the replacement property less than the amount realized from the conversion; or you replace after the time limits have expired.

Partnerships. The election to defer gain must be made at the partnership level. Individual partners may not make separate elections unless the partnership has terminated, with all partnership affairs wound up. Dissolution under state law is not a termination for tax purposes.

¶18.23 · TIME PERIOD FOR BUYING REPLACEMENT PROPERTY

To defer tax, you must generally buy property similar or related in use to the converted property within two years after the end of the taxable year in which you realize any gain from the conversion. However, if investment or business [noninventory] realty has been condemned, the replacement period is three years after the end of the taxable year in which any gain was realized.
Example—
On January 10, 1986, a parcel of land is condemned; the parcel cost $1,500. On February 26, 1986 you receive a check for $10,000 from the state. You may defer the tax on the gain of $8,500 if you invest at least $10,000 in other real estate not later than December 31, 1989.

Gain is realized in the year compensation for the converted property exceeds the basis of the converted property. An advance payment of an award which exceeds the adjusted basis of the property starts the running of the replacement period.
Example—
When Stewart's property was condemned, he received an advance of $70,000 on which he realized gain. Three years later, a final payment was made after a court determined the value of the condemned property. He paid no tax on the advance, claiming that he made a qualified replacement within the allowable period after receiving the full amount of the award. The IRS argued that the advance payment began the replacement period, which ended before he bought the replacement. The Tax Court agreed. Stewart had unrestricted use of the advance. The advance payment began the period for purchase of replacement property.

This is true even though he might have had to return part of the award if the court found it exceeded the value of the condemned property.
Stewart could have deferred tax by applying for an extension of time to replace the condemned property when he realized there would be a delay in getting the final award.

An award is treated as received in the year that it is made available to you without restrictions, even if you contest the amount.

Replacement before actual condemnation. You may make a replacement after a threat of condemnation. If you buy property before the threat of condemnation, it will not qualify as a replacement even though you still own it at the time of the actual condemnation.
Example—
While condemnation proceedings are under way, you find property to replace the property being condemned. The purchase of the new parcel before the condemnation qualifies as a replacement provided you hold the new property at the time the old property is condemned.

The replacement test may be satisfied by purchasing a controlling interest (80%) in a corporation owning property that is similar or related in service to the converted property (*see* Treasury regulations for further details).

Extension of time to replace. A contract to buy replacement property within the time limits is not considered a qualified replacement. If you cannot replace property within the time required, ask your local District Director for additional time. Apply for an extension before the end of the period. If you apply for an extension within a reasonable time after the statutory period has run out, you must have a reasonable cause for the delay in asking for the extension.

Replacement by an estate. A person whose property was converted may die before he makes a replacement. According to the IRS, his estate may not reinvest the proceeds within the allowed time and postpone tax on the gain. The Tax Court rejects the IRS position and has allowed tax deferral where the replacement was made by the deceased owner's estate. However, the Tax Court agreed with the IRS that a surviving spouse's investment in land did not defer tax on gain realized by her deceased husband on an involuntary conversion of his land. She had received his property as survivor of joint tenancy and could not, in making the investment, be considered as acting for his estate.

Notice of replacement. If you have not bought replacement property by the time you file your return for the year of the involuntary conversions, but you intend to do so attach a statement to your return describing the conversion and the computation of gain and state that you intend to make a timely replacement. Then, on the return for the year of replacement, attach a statement giving the details of your replacement property. This notice starts the running of the period of limitations for any tax on the gain. Failure to give notice keeps the period open. Similarly, a failure to give notice of an intention not to replace also keeps the period open. When you do not buy replacement property after making an election to postpone tax on the gain, file an amended return for the year in which gain was realized and pay the tax (if any) on the gain.

Assume you have the involuntary conversion resulting in a gain and do not expect to reinvest the proceeds. You report the gain and pay the tax. In a later year, but within the prescribed time limits, you buy similar property. You may make an election to defer tax on the gain and file a claim for tax refund.

¶18.24 · CHARACTER OF REPLACEMENT PROPERTY

Although exact duplication is not required, the replacement must be generally similar or related in use to the converted property. Where real property held for productive use in a business or for investment is converted through a condemnation or threat of condemnation, the replacement test is more liberal. A replacement merely has to be of a *like kind* to the converted property. Under the *like kind* test, the replacement of improved property by unimproved qualifies (*see* ¶5.48). Under the *related use* test, the replacement of unimproved land for improved does not. A replacement generally must be closely related in function to the destroyed property. For example, a condemned personal residence must be replaced with another personal residence. The replacement of a house rented to a tenant with a house used as a personal residence does not qualify for tax deferral; the new house is not being used for the same purpose as the condemned one. This functional test, however, is not strictly applied to conversions of rental property. Here, the role of the owner toward the properties, rather than the functional use of the buildings, is reviewed. If an owner held both properties as investments and offered similar services and took similar business risks in both, the replacement may qualify.

You may own several parcels of property, one of which is condemned. You may want to use the condemnation award to make improvements on the other land such as drainage and grading. The IRS generally will not accept the improvements as a qualified replacement. However, an appeals court has rejected the IRS approach in one case.

If it is not feasible to reinvest the proceeds from the conversion of livestock because of soil contamination or other environmental contamination, then other property (including real property) used for farming purposes is treated as similar or related and qualifies as replacement property.

¶18.25 • INVESTMENT IN REPLACEMENT PROPERTY

To defer tax, the cost of the replacement property must be equal to or exceed the net proceeds from the conversion. If replacement cost is less than the adjusted basis of the converted property, you report the entire gain. If replacement cost is less than the amount realized on the conversion but more than the basis of the converted property, the difference between the amount realized and the cost of the replacement is reported as gain. You may elect to postpone tax on the balance of the gain reinvested (*see* example 2).
Examples—
1. The cost basis of a four-family apartment house is $75,000. It is condemned to make way for a thruway. The net award from the state is $100,000. Your gain is $25,000. If you buy a similar apartment house for $75,000 or less, you report the entire $25,000 gain.
2. Using the same figures as in example (1) except that you buy an apartment house for $85,000. Of the gain of $25,000, you report $15,000 as taxed gain ($100,000 − $85,000). You may elect to postpone the tax on the balance of the gain, or $10,000.
3. Using the same figures as in example (1) but you buy an apartment house for $100,000. You may elect to postpone tax on the entire gain because you have invested all of the award in replacement property.

Condemnation award. The award received from a state authority may be reduced by expenses of getting the award, such as legal, engineering, and appraisal fees. The treatment of special assessments and severance damages received when part of your property is condemned is explained at ¶18.26. Payments made directly by the authority to your mortgagee may not be deducted from the gross award.

Do not include as part of the award interest paid on the award for delay in its payment; you report the interest as interest income. The IRS may treat as interest part of an award paid late, even though the award does not make any allocation for interest.

Relocation payments are not treated as taxable income to the extent that they are spent for purposes of relocation.

Distinguish between insurance proceeds compensating you for loss of profits because of business interruption and those compensating you for the loss of property. Business interruption proceeds are fully taxed as ordinary income and may not be treated as proceeds of an involuntary conversion.

A single standard fire insurance policy may cover several assets. Assume a fire occurs, and in a settlement the proceeds are allocated to each destroyed item according to its fair market value before the fire. In comparing the allocated proceeds to the tax basis of each item, you find that on some items, you have realized a gain; that is, the proceeds exceed basis. On the other items, you have a loss; the proceeds are less than basis. According to the IRS, you may elect to defer tax on the gain items by buying replacement property. You do not treat the proceeds paid under the single policy as a unit, but as separate payments made for each covered item.

¶18.26 • HOW TO TREAT SPECIAL ASSESSMENTS AND SEVERANCE DAMAGES

When only part of a property parcel is condemned for a public improvement, the condemning authority may: (1) Levy a special assessment against the remaining property, claiming that it is benefited by the improvement. The authority usually deducts the assessment from the condemnation award. (2) Award severance damages for damages suffered by the remaining property because of the condemnation.

Special assessments reduce the amount of the gross condemnation award. If they exceed the award, the excess is added to the basis of the property. An assessment levied after the award is made may not be deducted from the award.
Example—
Two acres of a 10-acre tract are condemned for a new highway. The adjusted basis of the land is $30,000 or $3,000 per acre. The condemnation award is $10,000; the special assessment against the remaining eight acres is $2,500. The net gain on the condemnation is $1,500:

Condemnation award		$10,000
Less:		
Basis of two condemned acres	$6,000	
Special assessment	2,500	8,500
Net gain		$ 1,500

When both the condemnation award and severance damages are received, the condemnation is treated as two separate involuntary conversions: (1) A conversion of the condemned land. Here, the condemnation award is applied against the basis of the condemned land to determine gain or loss on its conversion. (2) A conversion of part of the remaining land in the sense that its utility has been reduced by condemnation, for which severance damages are paid.

Severance damages reduce the basis of the retained property. If the damages exceed basis, gain is realized. Tax may be deferred on the gain through the purchase of replacement property under the "similar or related in use test" at ¶18.24, such as adjacent land or restoration of the property to its original condition.

Allocating the proceeds between the condemnation award and severance damages will either reduce the gain or increase the loss realized on the condemned land. The IRS will allow such a division only when the condemnation authority specifically identifies part of the award as severance damage in the contract or in an itemized statement or closing sheet. The Tax Court, however, has allowed an allocation in the absence of earmarking where the state considered severance damages, and the value of the condemned land was small in comparison to the damages suffered by the remaining property. To avoid a dispute with the IRS, make sure the authority makes this breakdown. Without such identification, the IRS will treat the entire proceeds as consideration for the condemned property.

¶18.27 • IF YOU HAVE GAINS AND LOSSES FROM CASUALTIES AND THEFTS

Gains and losses from involuntary conversion of property used for personal purposes are netted against each other. If as a result of the netting, recognized gains exceed recognized losses, all such gains and losses are treated as capital gain transactions. The $100 floor applies to each loss before the netting. The 10% adjusted gross income floor does not apply to the losses if capital gain treatment applies. *See* Form 4684.

If recognized losses exceed recognized gains, all gains and losses are treated as ordinary asset transactions. The net loss is reduced by the 10% adjusted gross income floor. Further, if losses exceed gains, for computing adjusted gross income, the loss is treated as a deduction from gross income to the extent of the gain.
Example—
Jones has an adjusted gross income of $40,000, a personal involuntary conversion gain of $20,000, and a personal casualty loss of $5,000 after applying the $100 floor. As gains exceed losses, all of the casualty gains and losses are treated as capital gain and losses. The 10% floor does not apply to the losses.

For purposes of netting gains and losses, the 10% adjusted gross income ceiling applies to estates and trusts. Administration expenses are first deducted to compute adjusted gross income.

¶19.00

Deductible Itemized Job Expenses

Illustrations of claiming other deductible costs on your tax return may be found in the Supplement to YOUR INCOME TAX. Mail the card at the front of this book to receive your FREE Supplement which includes filled-in returns and last-minute information.

	See ¶		*See ¶*
Deductible job costs	19.01	Unusual job expenses	19.051
Unreimbursed entertainment expenses	19.02	Home office expenses of employees	19.052
Business association and union dues	19.03	Phone and telegraph costs	19.053
Expenses for uniforms and work clothes	19.04	Checklist of deductions	41.00
Small tools	19.041	Checklist of nondeductible items	42.00
Expenses of looking for a job	19.05		

¶19.01 • Deductible Job Costs

Expenses that are ordinary and necessary in performing your job are deductible in 1986. However, job expenses are not treated alike. They may be deductible from either:

1. Gross income to compute adjusted gross income. These deductions are listed on page 1 of Form 1040 as Adjustments to Income. They are travel expenses away from home, transportation expenses, reimbursed expenses, and moving expenses.
2. Adjusted gross income. These are itemized deductions which are reported on Schedule A and then deducted from adjusted gross income on page 2 of Form 1040. These ex-

penses are unreimbursed job expenses, such as entertainment, gifts, club dues, union dues, and uniform and work clothes costs.

Changes, if any, to the above page numbers on the 1986 Form 1040 are in the Supplement to this book.

Outside salesman. Outside salesmen may deduct all business expenses from gross income as described in Step 1. You are an outside salesman if you work full time soliciting business away from your employer's place of business. Outside salesman status is not affected by use of your employer's office to write up orders, send out orders, and make and receive telephone calls.

CHECKLIST OF DEDUCTIBLE JOB EXPENSES IN 1986

Agency fees for job, ¶19.05
Air fares, ¶2.23
Auto club membership, ¶2.301
Auto expenses, ¶2.301
Auto registration fees, ¶2.301
Books used in position
Business machines, ¶5.30, ¶19.041
Car insurance premiums, ¶2.301
Christmas gifts, ¶2.34
Cleaning costs, ¶19.04
Commerce association dues, ¶19.03
Commuting costs, ¶2.211
Convention trips, ¶2.29
Correspondence course, ¶21.00
Depreciation, ¶5.30
Display, samples, room costs ¶2.23
Driver's license, ¶2.301
Dues, ¶19.03
Educational expenses, ¶21.00
Employment agency fees, ¶19.05
Entertainment expenses, ¶2.31
Equipment, ¶5.30, ¶19.041
Fidelity bond costs
Foreign travel costs, ¶2.292
Furniture, ¶5.30, ¶19.051, ¶19.052

Garage rent, ¶2.301
Gasoline, ¶2.301
Gasoline taxes, ¶2.301
Gifts, ¶2.34
Helmets, safety, ¶19.04
Home office expenses, ¶19.052
Hotel costs, ¶2.23
House-hunting costs, ¶2.45
Inspection fees, ¶2.301
Instruments, ¶5.30, ¶19.041
Labor union dues, ¶19.03
Laboratory breakage fees
Laundry, ¶19.04
Legal expenses, ¶19.17
Living expenses, ¶2.23
Local transportation, ¶2.21
Lodging, ¶2.23
Magazines
Malpractice liability premiums, ¶5.03
Meals, ¶2.23
Medical examinations, ¶17.13
Membership dues and fees, ¶19.03
Motel charges, ¶2.23
Moving expenses, ¶2.40
Parking fees, ¶2.301

Passport fees for business travel
Pay turned over to employer, ¶2.11
Periodicals
Protective clothing, ¶19.04
Rail fares, ¶2.23
Reimbursed expenses, ¶2.36
Repairs
Safety shoes, ¶19.04
Salary of assistant
Secretarial convention, ¶2.29
Subscriptions
Supplies
Taxi fares, ¶2.23
Telegrams, ¶19.053
Telephone calls, ¶19.053
Tips, ¶2.35
Toll charges, ¶2.301
Tools, ¶5.30, ¶19.041
Trade association dues, ¶19.03
Transportation and travel expenses, ¶2.20
Tuition, ¶21.00
Typewriter, ¶5.30, ¶19.041
Uniforms, ¶19.04
Union dues, ¶19.03
Work clothes and uniforms, ¶19.04

¶19.02 • UNREIMBURSED ENTERTAINMENT EXPENSES

If you are an employee, you may claim as 1986 "miscellaneous" deductions your unreimbursed expenses for entertainment, country club dues, and business gifts provided your itemized deductions exceed your zero bracket amount.

The importance of reimbursement arrangements is discussed at ¶2.381. Deductible entertainment costs are discussed at ¶2.31, country club dues at ¶2.331, and business gifts at ¶2.34.

¶19.03 • BUSINESS ASSOCIATION AND UNION DUES

You may deduct as 1986 miscellaneous itemized deductions dues paid to a—

Professional society if you are a lawyer, accountant, teacher, physician, or other professional.

Trade association if it is conducted for the purpose of furthering the business interests of its members.

Stock exchange if you are a securities dealer.

Community "booster" club conducted to attract tourists and settlers to the locality where the members do business.

Chamber of Commerce if it is conducted to advance the business interest of its members.

Union costs. Union members may deduct as "miscellaneous" itemized deductions union dues and initiation fees. Similarly, non-union employees may deduct monthly service charges to a union. An assessment paid for unemployment benefits is deductible if payment is required as a condition of remaining in the union and holding a union job. However, no deduction is allowed for mandatory contributions to a union pension fund applied toward the purchase of a retirement annuity; the contributions are treated as the cost of the annuity which may be recovered tax free under the rules of ¶7.07. Further, to the extent that an assessment covers sick, accident, or death benefits payable to you or your family, it is not deductible. Similarly, an assessment for a construction fund to build union recreation centers was disallowed by the Tax Court even though the payment was required for keeping a job.

Campaign costs for running for union office are not deductible.

¶19.04 • EXPENSES FOR UNIFORMS AND WORK CLOTHES

The cost of uniforms and other apparel, including their cleaning, laundering, and repair, is deductible for 1986 *only* if they are:

1. Especially required to keep your job; *and*
2. Not adaptable to general or continued wear to the extent they replace your regular clothing.

Courts have held the cost of special work clothes that protect you from injury is deductible even if you are not required to wear them to keep your job. You may not deduct the cost of special clothing, such as aprons and overalls, which protect your regular street clothing. Nor may you deduct the cost of ordinary clothes used as work clothes on the grounds that:

They get harder use than customary garments receive.

They are soiled after a day's work and cannot be worn socially.

They were purchased for your convenience to save wear and tear on your better clothes. For example, a sanitation inspector, a machinist's helper, a carpenter, and a telephone repairman were not allowed to deduct the cost of their work clothes.

Example—

A painter may not deduct the cost of work clothing consisting of a white cap, a white shirt, white bib overalls, and standard work shoes. The clothing is not distinctive in character as a uniform would be. That his union requires him to wear such clothing does not make it a deductible expense.

An allowance paid by an employer for work clothes or a uniform must be reported as income. You may deduct the amount paid for the uniform or work clothes up to the amount of reimbursement, even if you do not claim excess itemized deductions. Any expenses over the allowance are deductible only if you itemize deductions.

An employer may be able to help your claim of a work clothes deduction if he requires you to wear a uniform.

High fashion work clothes. That your job requires you to wear expensive clothing is not, according to the IRS, a basis for deducting the cost of the clothes, if the clothing is suitable for wear off the job. In one case involving the manager of a boutique selling clothes designed by Yves St. Laurent (YSL), the Tax Court allowed a deduction upon proof that the clothes were not worn off the job and were unsuitable to the worker's lifestyle. An appeals court reversed the decision. According to the appeals court, as long as the clothing is suitable off the job, the cost is not deductible.

Deductions for costs of uniforms and work clothes have been allowed to—

Airline pilot	Police officer
Baseball player	Railroad conductor
Bus driver	Railway man
Firefighter	Reservist
Jockey	State highway patrol officer
Letter carrier	Surgeon

Bakery salesperson—for a uniform with a company label

Cement finisher's gloves, overshoes, and rubber boots

Civilian faculty members of a military school

Commercial fisherman's protective clothing, such as oil clothes, work gloves, and rubber boots

Dairy worker's rubber boots, white shirts, trousers, and cap worn only while working inside the dairy

Entertainer's theatrical clothing used solely for performances

Factory foreman's white coat bearing the word "foreman" and the name of the company

Factory worker's safety shoes

Hospital attendant's work clothes; he came in contact with patients having contagious diseases

Meat cutter's special white shoes

Musician's formal wear

Paint machine operator's high top shoes and long leather gloves

Plumber's special shoes and gloves

Railroad fireman's boots, leather gloves, short raincoat, and caps

Railway fireman's work gloves, where he handled hot steam pipes and valves

Cleaning and laundering. If you may deduct the cost of work clothes and uniforms under the rules explained above, you may also deduct the cost of cleaning and laundering them. Also, courts have allowed the cost of cleaning and laundering where—

The clothes could only be worn one day at a time because they became so dirty.

Dirty clothes were a hazard—they became baggy and might get caught in the machinery.

Clothes were only worn at work and a place for changing clothes was provided by the employer.

A meat cutter had to wear clean work clothes at all times.

Uniform costs of reservists and servicemen are discussed at ¶35.02.

¶19.041 • SMALL TOOLS

If in 1986 you furnished your own small tools used on your job, you may deduct their cost if they are expected to last for a year or less. The cost of tools with a useful life of more than a year must be recovered through depreciation or first-year expensing (*see* ¶5.30). Be prepared to substantiate your deduction with receipts showing the cost and type of tools purchased, and business necessity for the tool.

A deduction for the cost of tools is taken as a miscellaneous itemized deduction.

¶19.05 • EXPENSES OF LOOKING FOR A JOB

The IRS allows a 1986 deduction for the expenses of looking for a new job in the same line of work, whether or not a new job is found. If you are unemployed when seeking a job, the IRS may disallow the deduction if it finds a substantial lack of continuity of time between the past job and the current job search. It provides no specific guidelines for what it considers a continuity of time.

Expenses of seeking your first job are not deductible, even if a job is obtained.

The IRS may also dispute the deduction of search expenses of a previously employed professional who forms a partnership with others rather than take another position.

Example—

A CPA working for a firm decided to go out on his own. After a period of investigation, he formed a partnership with another CPA.

The IRS disallowed his deduction of search expenses claiming his expenses were incurred in a new business. As an employee he was in a different business than that of a self-employed practitioner. Thus, the expenses should be capitalized as a cost of setting up or organizing the partnership. The Tax Court disagreed, allowing the deduction. The travel expenses were incurred to seek work as a CPA, whether as a self-employed or employed CPA. Further, the expenses were not partnership organization expenses. Although a partnership was formed, the expenses were incurred to determine if he could get sufficient clients to leave his firm, regardless of the business form his new practice might take.

Travel expenses. If you travel to find a new job in the same line of work, such as an interview in a distant city, you may deduct travel expenses, including living costs. If, during the trip, you also do personal visiting, you may deduct the transportation expenses if the trip was primarily related to your job search. Time spent on personal activity is compared with time spent looking for a job to determine the primary purpose of the trip. If the transportation expenses to and from the destination are not deductible under this test, you may still deduct expenses allocated to seeking the new job.

Employment agency fee. If your employer pays the fee under an agreement with the agency, you may disregard the payment for tax purposes. However, if you pay the fee and after a certain period of employment are reimbursed by your employer, you must report the reimbursement as taxable income. This additional income may be offset by deducting the fee as an itemized deduction.

A company interested in your services may invite you to a job interview and agree to pay all of the expenses of the trip to its office, even if you are not hired. The company payment is tax free to the extent it does not exceed your actual expenses.

While trying to make a new contact after leaving your job, you continue to see and entertain your former customers. According to the IRS, you may not deduct the costs of entertainment and other business expenses during this period on the grounds that you are not in business and earning income. However, the Tax Court in the following case allowed the deduction.

Example—
Haft was a successful jewelry salesman earning as much as $60,000 a year. In the fall of one year, he left his employer and started to look for a new connection. During the following year, he continued to maintain contacts with his former customers by entertaining buyers and their representatives. He deducted the expenses of entertaining and other business costs. The IRS disallowed the deduction, claiming he was not in business. The court disagreed. His lack of business income was temporary and during a period of transition which lasted a reasonable time.

¶19.051 • UNUSUAL JOB EXPENSES

The following are not typical deductible expenses. Courts have allowed deductions in the following cases.

Shoe shine expenses of a pilot.
Example—
Company rules required a commercial airline pilot to look neat, keep his hair cut, and wear conservative black shoes, properly shined. The pilot deducted as a business expense $100 for his haircuts and $25 for shoe shines. The IRS disallowed the deductions, but the Tax Court allowed the cost of the shoe shines. The shoes were of a military type which he wore only with his pilot's uniform. The cost of keeping up a uniform is deductible. The haircuts were merely nondeductible personal expenses.

Cost of lobbying for better working conditions.

Depreciation on furnishings bought by executive for his company office.
Example—
Following a quarrel with an interior decorator, a sales manager bought his own office furniture when his firm moved to new quarters. Rather than complain or ask for reimbursement, he footed the bill and deducted depreciation. The IRS disallowed the deduction, claiming the expense was that of his company. The Tax Court allowed the deduction. The manager's action was unusual, but prudent. He did not want to cause difficulties, and at the same time had to maintain his image as a successful manager. His expenses for furniture were appropriate and helpful.

Salesman's cost of operating a private plane.

Example—
Sherman flew his own plane to visit clients in six southern states and deducted $18,000 as operating costs of the plane. The IRS disallowed the deduction, claiming there was no business reason for the plane. He could have taken commercial flights or used a company car to reach the clients. Further, his company did not reimburse him for the private airplane costs, although it would cover costs of his car and commercial air travel. Finally, the amount of airplane expenses was unreasonable compared to his salary of $25,000. Sherman convinced the Tax Court that use of a private airplane was the only reasonable way he could cover his six-state sales area. He showed that most of his clients were not near commercial airports. Although the airplane costs were large in relation to his salary, they were still reasonable and, therefore, deductible.

Executive's purchase of blazers for sales force.
Example—
Jetty, the president of an oil equipment manufacturing firm, thought that he could generate good will for the company if employees who attended industrial trade shows wore a blazer and vest set in the company colors. He personally paid and deducted $6,725 for 27 blazers and vests. The IRS disallowed the deduction on the grounds that it was a company expense and that Jetty should have sought reimbursement from the company.

The Tax Court allowed the deduction. Paying for the clothes was a legitimate business expense for Jetty since he depended on bonuses for a large portion of his pay, and as company president, he had responsibility for seeing to it that there were profits to share in. Further, the outlay was not the type of expense covered by the company's manual on expense reimbursements.

Repayment of lay-off benefits to restore pension credit.
Example—
When he was laid off, an employee received a lump-sum payment from his company based on his salary and years of service. When he was rehired a year later, he repaid the lump sum in order to restore his pension credits and other benefit rights. The IRS ruled that he may deduct the repayment as a condition of being rehired; the repayment was required to restore employee benefits.

An employee may have to pay his employer for release from an employment contract. Such a situation is rare, and there are no cases or rulings on the issue. However, tax commentators claim the employee's payment, such as liquidated damages, is deductible as an itemized deduction if the employee takes a new job with another employer. The IRS states in one of its publications that an amount paid as liquidated damages to a former employer for breach of an employment contract is a deductible employee expense. Its statement does not limit the deduction to those who take a new job.

Job dismissal insurance. Some insurance companies offer corporate executives policies to pay lost income if they are fired for reasons other than misconduct or physical disability. For example, one policy covers salary for up to two years after a job dismissal, or, if a lower paying job is obtained, the difference between the old and new salaries. In addition, the policy pays for re-employment counseling, secretarial help, and office space. The IRS has ruled that the premium covering career counseling and other re-employment services is deductible provided the executive seeks another position as a corporate executive.

Benefits paid under the policy are taxable income.

Politician's expenses. Elected officials may incur out-of-pocket expenses in excess of the allowances received from the government. They may deduct as itemized deductions their payment of office expenses such as salaries, office rent and supplies. Part-time officials may claim the deduction. The expenses are deductible even if they exceed the official's income.

¶19.052 • HOME OFFICE EXPENSES OF EMPLOYEES

The law severely limits employees from claiming deductions for home office expenses by setting conditions most employees cannot meet. To deduct 1986 office expenses, the office must be exclusively used on a regular basis as your principal place of business or as a place in which patients, clients, or customers meet or deal with you in the normal course of your profession or business. As an employee, it is only in rare situations that your home office is your principal place of business or a place for meeting patients, clients or customers. Both the Tax Court and an appeals court agree with the IRS that making and receiving telephone calls at a home office is not the equivalent of clients' visits.

An appeals court has developed a pro-taxpayer exception where an employer does not provide adequate working space. It has allowed home office expense deductions to a violinist working for the Metropolitan opera upon proof that the Met did not provide space for practice and to a professor who did substantial work at home because his school did not provide adequate office space.
Example—
An associate professor at the City University of New York taught classes three days a week, three hours per day. He had to do research and writing in his two-room home office. An office provided by the college had to be shared with three other professors and was unsafe for keeping research materials. The IRS, with Tax Court approval, disallowed his home office deduction on the grounds that the college was his principal place of business. An appeals court allows the deduction. Where employer-provided space is unsuitable to do substantial work, the home office may be considered a principal place of business. Here, the professor needed a private place to read, think and write. The college did not provide such a facility.

An anesthesiologist who used a home office for billing and recordkeeping was not allowed to claim a deduction because the focal point of his practice was the hospital where he rendered the bulk of his services.

Exclusive use means that the space used as an office must not be used for personal purposes, such as a family den. Further, you must show the office is used for the convenience of your employer. Finally, even if you meet these rules the amount of your deduction may be limited; deductible expenses may not exceed gross income derived from the office.
Example—
A married couple both teach in an elementary school. Neither can use the school facilities after 5 p.m. and so are required to work at home, preparing lessons, constructing charts and learning materials, and reading education literature. They do this in a room exclusively used for this purpose. The IRS ruled that no home office deduction is available because the room is not their principal place of business.

Office in separate structure. The restrictive tests discussed in the prior paragraphs do not apply to an office located in a separate structure that is not considered part of your home.
Examples—
1. Heineman built an office about 100 yards from his Wisconsin summer home. It had a desk, file cabinets, a telephone, a separate switchboard extension to his office, and a computer terminal connected to the company main computer.
Every August, he used the office to avoid the hot Chicago weather and the distractions of company headquarters. Over a three-year period, he deducted depreciation of $33,700 and office maintenance expenses of $16,800. The IRS stipulated that the office was not part of the home; however, it claimed that the office expenses were not necessary business expenses; Heineman could have worked in an isolated office in Chicago by ordering his staff not to interrupt him. The Tax Court allowed the deduction. The office was helpful and appropriate in his business and thus constituted a necessary business expense. The office allowed

him to review long-range plans more effectively than at company headquarters.
2. The Tax Court held that an office in a separate structure was part of a home and subject to the restrictions where (1) the office structure was 12 feet from the residence and within the same fenced-in lot; (2) the structure was under the same title and mortgage; and (3) taxes and upkeep costs were paid as a unit for both the house and structure.

Home office deductions may not be claimed by investors who use a home office to review investments and make investment decisions unless the activity constitutes a business. *See* ¶20.01.

Deductible expenses. Deductible office expenses include real estate taxes, mortgage interest, operating expenses of the office (such as utilities and home insurance premiums) and depreciation. Not deductible are family household expenses and repairs that do not benefit the space used as an office. For example, the costs of painting and repairs to rooms other than the one used as an office are not deductible. However, a pro rata share of the cost of painting the outside of a house, or repairing the roof, may be deductible. The costs of painting and repairing the office space are fully deductible, as well as the cost of an office phone. Costs of lawn care and landscaping are not deductible.

Allocating expenses. Only the expenses attributable to the home office are deductible. You may allocate expenses as follows: Compare the number of rooms or square feet of space used as an office to the total number of rooms or square feet in the home, and then apply the resulting fraction or percentage to the total deductible expenses.
Example—
One room out of a five-room apartment is used for an office; ⅕ or 20% of deductible home expenses are allocated to the use of the office.

How to claim the deduction. Home office expenses may be claimed only if you claim excess itemized deductions (*see* ¶13.04), unless you are an outside salesperson.
To support your deduction, keep records to show how you allocated the expenses, in addition to canceled checks, receipts and other evidence of the expenses paid.
You need physical evidence of an office. A bare minimum is a desk, chair, and filing cabinet.
Retain business mail directed to your home.
Keep a record of business phone calls you make, particularly charges for long distance telephone calls, and a diary of business visitors, including those who come to your home for entertainment.
The home office provisions as they apply to a self-employed person are explained at ¶5.10.

¶19.053 • PHONE AND TELEGRAPH COSTS

For business calls made outside the office or at home, keep a record or diary of business calls to support your deduction. To avoid the problem of allocating the costs of a single home phone between business and personal use, consider installing a separate home phone for business use only. For long distance business calls, you might ask the phone company to transfer the charges to your office phone.

¶20.00

Investment and Other Nonbusiness Expenses

For 1986, you may deduct investment expenses and other expenses of producing and collecting income, expenses of maintaining income-producing property, expenses of tax return preparation, refunds and audits and, in certain instances, legal expenses. You deduct such expenses as miscellaneous itemized deductions, provided your total itemized deductions exceed your zero bracket amount. These expenses are also described as "nonbusiness expenses."

Expenses of earning royalty or rental income may be deducted directly from royalty or rental income, rather than as itemized deductions deductible from adjusted gross income (see ¶9.00 and ¶13.04).

¶20.01 • CHECKLIST OF DEDUCTIBLE INVESTMENT EXPENSES IN 1986

Accounting fees for keeping record of investment income.

Fees for collecting interest and dividends. Also deductible are fees paid to a bank which acts as dividend agent in an automatic dividend reinvestment plan of a publicly-owned corporation. Costs of collecting tax-exempt interest are not deductible; expenses deducted on an estate tax return are also not deductible. Fees paid to a broker to acquire securities are not deductible but are added to the cost of the securities. Commissions and fees paid by an investor on the sale of securities reduces the selling price; a dealer, however, may deduct selling commissions as business expenses.

Fees to set up or administer an IRA. The fees must be billed and paid separately from the regular IRA contribution.

Guardian fees or fees of committee for a ward or minor incurred in producing or collecting income belonging to the ward or minor or in managing income-producing property of the ward or minor.

Investment management or counsel fees. But fees allocated to advice dealing with tax-exempt obligations are not deductible.

Legal costs, see ¶20.03.

Mutual fund custodian fees paid for his services in collecting and reinvesting dividends, keeping records, and holding the shares. However, the fees paid to the sponsor of the plan when entering the fund are *not* deductible, but are capital costs added to the cost of the shares.

Premiums and expenses on indemnity bonds for the replacement of missing securities. If part of the expenses are refunded in the year the expenses are paid, only the excess expense is deductible. A refund in a later year is taxable income to the extent the expenses were deducted and reduced your tax. See ¶12.20.

Proxy fight expenses where the dispute involves legitimate corporate policy issues, not a frivolous desire to gain membership on the board.

Safe deposit box rental fee or home safe to hold your securities, but not if it is used to hold personal effects or tax-exempt securities. A home safe is 5-year property subject to the rules at ¶5.30.

Salary of a secretary, bookkeeper or other employee hired to keep track of your investment income.

Subscriptions to investment services.

Travel costs of trip away from home to look after investments, confer with your attorney, accountant, trustee, or investment counsel about the production of income.

Expenses incurred in managing property held for income are deductible, even if the property does not currently produce income. Similarly, expenses incurred to avoid further losses or to reduce anticipated losses on such property are deductible.

Nondeductible travel costs. Investors may not deduct the cost of trips to investigate prospective rental property. Further, the IRS does not generally allow deductions for the cost of travel to stockholder meetings. However, in a private letter ruling, one stockholder was allowed a deduction. He owned substantial stockholdings which had lost value because his corporation had been issuing stock to the public at prices below book value. He went to the annual shareholder's meeting to present a resolution requesting management to stop the practice; the resolution passed. Under such circumstances, the IRS held that the trip was directly related to his stockholdings and allowed him the deduction. The IRS distinguished his case from a ruling which bars most stockholders from deducting the cost of travel to an annual meeting. Here the stockholder's purpose in getting the resolution passed was more closely related to his investment activities than if he had attended the meeting, as most stockholders do, to pick up data for future investment moves.

In one case, an investor won a travel expense deduction by linking information gathered at investment club conventions with her investment decisions.

Example—

The National Association of Investment Clubs (NAIC) holds conventions where members hear lectures from stock market experts on investment strategies and presentations from company executives. A member of a Wisconsin investment club and an officer of the NAIC attended three conventions in Holland, Cleveland, and San Diego. She deducted her travel costs for the three trips of $2,430 as an investment expense. The IRS disallowed the deduction claiming that the relationship between the travel and her investments was too weak. The Tax Court allowed the deduction. Her principal purpose in making the trips was to gather information on which she acted. After the convention in Holland, she purchased DeBeers stock; at both the Cleveland and San Diego conventions, she sold stock of the companies after discussion with their representatives. She sold shares of another company after she learned at a convention that the company was having trouble with its computers. Finally, the trip costs of $2,430 were reasonable given the size of her portfolio of $98,000.

In a private letter ruling, the IRS barred a deduction for an investor's travel expenses to a two-week seminar on investment and tax planning. He owned stocks, bonds, mutual funds, real estate, a car wash and a laundry business. The IRS held that the investor did not prove a connection between the general investment and tax strategies discussed at the seminar and his personal holdings and tax position.

Home office of an investor. An investor may not deduct the costs of an office at home unless investing constitutes a business. For example, you get no deduction for use of a home office in your residence where you read financial periodicals and reports and clip bond coupons. These activities are not considered a business.

Example—

In his home office, Moller spent 40 hours a week managing four stock portfolios worth over $13 million. However, an appeals court held he could not deduct home office expenses despite the time spent there managing his investment. To deduct home office expenses, Moller had to show he was a trader. A trader is in a business; an investor is not. A trader buys and sells frequently to catch daily market swings. An investor buys securities for capital appreciation and income without regard to daily market developments. Here, Moller was an investor. He was primarily interested in the long-term growth potential of stock. He did not earn his income from the short-term turnovers of stocks. He had no significant trading profits.

Hobby expenses. For the limitations on deducting hobby expenses, *see* ¶5.06.

¶20.02 • COSTS OF TAX RETURN PREPARATION, TAX REFUNDS, AND TAX AUDITS

You may deduct your payment in 1986 of fees charged for:

The preparation of your tax return or refund claim involving any tax, and

Representing you before any examination, trial, or other type of hearing involving any tax.

The term "any tax" covers not only income taxes but also gift, property, estate or any other tax, whether the taxing authority be federal, state or municipal.

Deductible fees for services of tax practitioners are claimed as itemized deductions. The deduction is claimed on the tax return for the year in which the fee was paid. For example, if in March 1986, you pay an accountant to prepare your 1985 return, you deduct the fee on your 1986 return. If the tax was directly imposed on your business income, the fee is deductible as a business expense. One exception to this rule is applied to the fees involving federal or state income taxes on self-employed business or professional income. The IRS insists that the expense is a nonbusiness itemized deduction. *See* ¶5.05.

There have been disputes over the deductibility of fees charged for general tax advice unconnected to the preparation of a return or a tax controversy. A deduction for fees charged for general tax advice not within these areas may be disallowed, unless the fee can be related to the production of business or investment income or the management of income-producing property. The following case distinguished between advice covering tax liabilities and advice concerning the tax consequences of a possible future transaction. According to the court, no deduction was allowed for that part of the fee covering the future transactions.

Example—

Stockholders of a closely-held corporation negotiated with a publicly-held company for a tax-free exchange of their stock. An accounting firm asked the IRS for a ruling to determine whether the exchange would be taxable or tax free. The accounting fee was $8,602. Of this, $7,602 was for the ruling and $1,000 was for fixing the basis of the new stock. The stockholders deducted the full fee, which the IRS disallowed because the fee was not charged for the preparation of a tax return or representation at a contest of a tax liability. The court disagrees in part. The fee paid for the ruling is deductible; it was connected with determining the extent of the stockholders' liability, if any, in the proposed exchange. But a deduction cannot be allowed for the $1,000 charged to determine the basis of the new stock. This was computed for the stockholders' information, not for determining tax liability. The disallowed fee could be added to the cost basis of the stock.

An accountant's fee for arranging the purchase of real estate was deductible where the purchase was part of a plan to minimize taxes.

Example—

Collins paid an accountant $4,511 for tax advice to reduce his tax on a sweepstake winning. He was advised to buy an apartment house under a contract obligation to make a large prepayment of interest (which was deductible under prior law). The accountant helped prepare contracts, escrow agreements, and other documents to implement the plan. Collins' deduction of his accountant's fee as a business expense was disallowed. The IRS held that the fee was a capital expense in acquiring the property. The Tax Court disagreed. The accountant was hired to minimize Collin's income tax through the purchase of the building and the terms of the purchase. Therefore, his fee was deductible.

The purchase of *Your Income Tax* in 1986 is deductible as an itemized deduction in 1986.

Personal checking account fees. These are nondeductible, even though the checks are used for tax records. Similarly, the per check fee on an interest-bearing NOW account is nondeductible. However, fees charged on a bank money market account may be deductible if check writing is severely limited and writing excess checks forfeits the status of the account as a money market account.

Appraisal fees. Fees to establish the amount of such tax deductions as a casualty loss or a charitable deduction are claimed as miscellaneous deductions. Appraisal fees in connection with the purchase of your principal residence are not deductible but are added to the basis of your house.

For deductibility of legal costs, *see* ¶20.03.

¶20.03 • DEDUCTING LEGAL COSTS

A legal expense is generally deductible if the dispute or issue arose in the course of your business or employment or involves income-producing property. Legal expenses for personal matters are generally not deductible. The IRS may disallow the deduction on the grounds that the legal dispute does not directly arise from the business or income activity. Thus, for example, the cost of contesting suspension of a driver's license for drunken driving is not deductible despite a business need for the license; the suspension arose out of a personal rather than a business-related activity. A deduction may also be disallowed where the dispute involves title to property. Further, the deductibility of a legal expense may depend on whether the damages received are taxable.

For the deductibility of legal fees in organizing a new business, *see* ¶5.07.

Employment suits. The following cases illustrate when legal costs for employment-related matters may be deductible.

Examples—

1. Waldheim, a corporate officer, director, and stockholder, incurred legal fees in a suit to prevent his discharge. His legal costs were deductible.

2. An Army officer was allowed to deduct the cost of successfully contesting a court martial based on charges of misrepresentations in official statements and reports. He would have lost his position had he been convicted.

3. Tellier, a securities dealer, was convicted of mail fraud and securities fraud. He was allowed to deduct legal fees as business expenses related to his securities business. That he was found guilty of the criminal charge does not affect the deductibility of the expense. The deduction of legal expenses is not disallowed on public policy grounds since a defendant has a constitutional right to an attorney.

4. In an alimony action, Gilmore was successful in preventing his wife from securing stock and taking control of corporations from which he earned practically all his income. He was not allowed to deduct his legal costs; the dispute did not arise from an income-producing activity; the fact that an adverse determination of the dispute might affect his income did not make the legal expenses deductible.

5. A doctor, who attempted to bribe a judge to suspend his sentence for tax evasion, was convicted of the bribe attempt and lost his license to practice medicine. He could not deduct his defense costs. His practice of medicine did not give rise to his need for an attorney. The fact that the conviction affected his ability to earn income was merely a consequence of personal litigation.

6. Siket, a police officer, was not allowed to deduct expenses of successfully defending a criminal charge of assault while off duty. The origin of the claim was personal, even though a conviction might have been detrimental to his position as a police officer. The arrest did not

occur within the performance of his duties; he was off duty and in a different municipality at the time of the arrest.

7. The president of Weight Watchers International, Inc., Jean Nidetch, had a dispute with her fellow directors regarding management of the company. Fearing that her position as president was in jeopardy, she planned a proxy fight, and to solidify her position replaced trustees of a family trust who sided with the other directors. Later, the dispute was settled and the proxy fight never took place. The deduction for $102,500 in legal fees incurred in replacing the trustees was disallowed by the IRS. The Tax Court allowed the deduction. Although a proxy fight never actually took place, the legal expenses of the trustee substitution were a crucial first step in an anticipated proxy contest. To deny deductibility of those expenses while allowing a deduction for actual proxy fight costs would penalize those who are able to amicably settle their disputes.

The legal costs of defending against disbarment are deductible.

Legal fees for tax advice and tax return preparation. You may deduct legal fees paid in 1986 for preparing your tax return or refund claim, or for representing you in a trial, examination, or hearing involving any tax. *See* ¶20.02. Legal fees incurred in defending against a tax imposed by a foreign country are also deductible. However, legal fees incurred in reducing an assessment on property to pay for local benefits are not deductible; the fees are capital expenses which are added to basis.

Libel suits. The IRS and Tax Court hold that compensatory damages received for injury to personal reputation are tax free; damages to business reputation are taxable (*see* ¶12.22). Thus, legal expenses allocable to an award or settlement for injury to personal reputation are not deductible.

If the libel action is for damage to business reputation, legal expenses are deductible as business expenses.
Examples—

1. A professional dancer was publicly accused of being pro-communist. He sued for libel and deducted his legal expenses as business expenses. The deduction was allowed because his suit was to reestablish his reputation and to protect his business as a public performer.

2. An attorney brought a libel suit against a newspaper. The libel suit was dismissed. However, he could deduct his legal costs as business expenses since the expenses were incurred to protect his reputation as an attorney.

Will contests and wrongful death actions. Legal costs of a will contest are generally not deductible because an inheritance is not taxable income. Similarly, legal fees incurred to collect a wrongful death award (which is tax-free income) are not deductible.
Example—
Parker, an heir who was left out of his grandmother's estate, sued to recover his inheritance. In a settlement, he received his share of his grandmother's property plus income earned on that property. The allocable portion of legal fees attributed to the income, which was taxable, was deductible; the balance of the fees were not deductible.

Title issues or disputes. Legal costs related to the acquisition of property or to the determination of title to property, whether or not such property is business or personal, are nondeductible capital expenditures. They are added to the basis of the property. For example, litigation costs to fix the value of shares of dissident shareholders were not deductible because they were related to the purchase of the stock and were part of the cost of acquisition.

Legal fees incurred to quiet title to stock were also held to be nondeductible.

Where a dispute over property does not involve title, such as

in a recovery of income-producing securities loaned as collateral, the Tax Court holds that legal fees are deductible.

Personal injury or marital actions. Where you recover taxable damages, you may deduct the legal fees; if the damages are not taxable, legal fees are not deductible (*see* ¶12.07). For legal expenses incurred in marital actions, *see* ¶1.71.

Estate tax planning fee. Not all of an attorney's fee for estate tax planning services may be deductible in 1986. Estate tax planning usually involves tax and nontax matters. To the extent that the services do not cover tax advice or income-producing property, the fee is not deductible. A bill allocating a fee between deductible and nondeductible services may help support a deduction claimed for the deductible portion of the fee.
Example—
Estate planning for a doctor involved the drawing of wills, trusts, property transfers, and gift tax returns. The doctor deducted the lawyer's fee of $2,000 in full. The IRS disallowed the deduction because the fee was not allocated between tax and nontax matters. The Tax Court viewed the IRS's position as a concession that fees are deductible to the extent allocable to tax advice in estate planning. All the doctor failed to do was to show how much of the fee was for tax advice. This the majority of the Tax Court did for him. It figured from the evidence that 20% of the attorney's time was spent on tax matters and so allowed a deduction of 20% of the bill.

Your lawyer should bill you separately or itemize fees for services connected with deductible items (collection of taxable alimony or separate maintenance payments, preparation of tax returns, tax audits, and tax litigation) and nondeductible capital items (expenses incurred in purchase of property or dispute over title).

Recovery of attorney's fees from government. See ¶38.08.

¶20.04 • QUALIFIED GROUP LEGAL SERVICES PLANS

As a tax-free fringe benefit, a company may provide employees and their dependents legal services through a qualified group legal service plan.

A qualified legal service plan must be a separate written plan established for the exclusive benefit of the employees, and their spouses and dependents; it must not discriminate in favor of officers, shareholders, or highly compensated employees. The plan may be funded by insurance or a special trust, or the company through the plan may pay the attorney providing legal services. The IRS must have notice of the plan within certain time limits.

If you are not required to include the value of legal services in your gross income, you may not claim a deduction for legal services even though you would have been entitled to one under ¶20.03 if you had paid for the legal services directly.

¶20.05 • ADOPTION COSTS OF HARD-TO-PLACE CHILDREN

Adoption expenses are generally nondeductible personal expenses. However, a limited deduction is allowed to those who adopt children receiving Social Security adoption assistance payments. You may deduct adoption fees, court costs, attorney fees and other directly related expenses. The deduction for each adopted child may not exceed $1,500.

The deduction applies only to children who, under the Social Security law, have special needs and are receiving maintenance payments. No deduction is allowed for expenses reimbursed under a federal, state, or local program.

The deduction is claimed as an itemized deduction.

¶21.00

Deductible Education Costs

¶21.01 • GENERAL RULES FOR DEDUCTING EDUCATION COSTS IN 1986

To deduct education costs, you must show:

1. You are employed or self-employed;

2. You meet the minimum requirements of your job, business, or profession; and

3. The course maintains or improves your job skills, or you are required by your employer or by law to take the course to keep your present salary or position.

The details of these requirements are explained at ¶21.02.

The cost of courses preparing you for a new profession or for meeting the minimum requirements for your job are not deductible, even if you take them to improve your skills or to meet your employer's requirements. This rule prevents the deduction of law school costs, see ¶21.03.

That courses lead to a degree will not bar a deduction provided the above three tests are met. If the courses lead to a change of position or promotion within the same occupation, the deduction for their costs will not be disallowed, if your new duties involve the same general type of work.

> Courses qualifying for the deduction may range from refresher courses to advanced academic courses. They may be correspondence school or vocational courses and even private tutoring.

¶21.02 • DEDUCTION TESTS FOR EDUCATION COSTS

Employment test. Educational costs are not deductible if you are unemployed or inactive in a business or profession. The cost of "brushup" courses taken in anticipation of resuming work are also not deductible. However, in one case, a court allowed an unemployed teacher to deduct the cost of tuition, fees, and books where the IRS conceded that the teacher, although unemployed, remained in the teaching profession while attending college classes.

You are not considered unemployed when you take courses during a vacation or temporary leave of absence. See ¶21.07.

Example—

A substitute teacher left his job to go to Norway for doctoral studies in linguistics and anthropology. The IRS disallowed his deduction for the cost of travel, room, board and books, claiming that he abandoned teaching before he went abroad. Also, the studies abroad fitted him for a new career. The Tax Court disagreed. He did not abandon his teaching profession as evidenced by these facts: He applied for work at an American school in Oslo and was available for substitute teaching, although he only taught one day. He also made arrangements to teach on his return. Furthermore, his studies were appropriate and helpful to his career as a teacher of language and social studies.

If you are practicing your profession, the cost of courses leading to a specialty within that profession are deductible.

Example—

A practicing dentist returned to school full time to study orthodontics while continuing his practice on a part-time basis. When he finished his training, he limited his work to orthodontics. The IRS ruled he may deduct the cost of his studies. His post-graduate schooling improved his professional skills as a dentist. It did not qualify him for a new profession.

Minimum standards. You may not deduct the cost of courses taken to meet the minimum requirements of your job. The minimum requirements of a position are based on a review of your employer's standards, the laws and regulations of the state you live in, and the standards of your profession or business. That you are presently employed does not in itself prove that you have met the minimum standards for your job.

Examples—

1. A full-time engineering student works part time for an engineering consulting firm with whom he expects to continue full time after completing his engineering degree. He may not deduct the cost of the courses; they are required to meet the minimum requirements of his profession.

2. An employed social worker changes jobs. The new employer requires a master's degree and she takes courses leading to such a degree. That she would have taken the courses in any event to improve her skills is irrelevant. The cost of taking courses to meet minimum job requirements of the new employer is not deductible.

3. An accountant worked for an accounting firm in Idaho and could, under Idaho law, perform the same accounting services as a CPA. However, he could not become a partner in an accounting firm. In order to do so, he took a CPA review course. The cost of the review course is not deductible as the course enabled the accountant to meet the minimum requirements of becoming a CPA, a position entitling one to become a partner in an accounting firm and to practice before the IRS.

If minimum standards change after you enter a job or profession, you are required to meet only the standards that existed when you entered.

The minimum standards for teachers are discussed at ¶21.05.

> *Maintaining or improving skills.* That you are established in your position and that persons in similar positions usually take such education indicates that the courses are taken to maintain and improve job skills. However, the IRS may not allow a deduction for a general education course that is a prerequisite for a job-related course. If, as a consequence of taking a job-related course, you receive a substantial advancement and the IRS questions the deduction of the course costs, be prepared to prove that you took the course primarily to maintain or improve job skills.

Employer's requirement. If, to retain your present job or rate of pay, your employer requires you to obtain further education, you may deduct the cost of the courses. The fact that you also qualified for a raise in pay or a substantial advancement in your position after completing the courses should not bar the deduction.

The employer's requirement must be for a bona fide business reason, not merely to benefit you. Only the minimum education necessary for the retention of your job or rate of pay is considered by the IRS as taken to meet your employer's requirement. You must show any education beyond your employer's minimum requirements is taken to maintain or improve your job skills.

College tuition. You may not deduct tuition costs of undergraduate courses in preparation for a career or employment. But in one case a minister convinced the Tax Court and an appeals court that his tuition costs were deductible. He took nine years to complete his college education because he was a working professional. He was not in school to prepare for a career. His studies were appropriate to the skills required of a minister. He did not seek a teaching certificate awarded by the college.

¶21.03 • LAW SCHOOL COSTS

The IRS does not allow deductions for law school courses because they qualify a person for a new profession. Courts generally support the IRS position.

Bar review courses. The costs of bar review courses and taking the bar exam are not deductible, even where you are seeking admission to the bar of a second state.

An attorney who practices law in one state may not deduct the later costs of getting a degree necessary to the practice of law in another state.

Additional legal education. A lawyer must practice his profession before the expenses of further legal education are deductible. Compare these cases:

Examples—
1. A young lawyer, newly admitted to the Illinois bar, could not deduct the cost of courses for a masters degree in tax law, which he started the fall after he graduated from law school. According to the Tax Court, he never stopped being a full-time student. He earned income to help defray his educational expenses; he did not incur the educational expense to improve his skills as a tax return preparer.
2. The Tax Court allowed a lawyer to deduct educational expenses to obtain an LL.M. degree where he worked for a law firm as a beginning lawyer during the summer between graduating from law school and starting work on the LL.M. degree. He was admitted to the state bar before he graduated from law school, and the work he did during the summer was normally assigned to beginning lawyers rather than to law students.

¶21.04 • COURSES TAKEN BY DOCTORS AND NURSES

The IRS allows general practitioners to deduct the cost of short refresher courses, even though the courses relate to specialized fields. These courses maintain or improve skills and do not qualify the doctor for a new profession.

A practicing psychiatrist may deduct the cost of attending an accredited psychoanalytic institute to qualify to practice psychoanalysis. A social worker has also been allowed a deduction for the cost of psychoanalysis. In one case, a psychiatrist was allowed by the Tax Court to deduct the cost of personal therapy sessions conducted through telephone conversations and tape cassettes. The court was convinced that the therapy improved his job skills by eliminating psychological blind spots that prevented him from understanding his patient's problems.

A doctor was allowed by a court to deduct the cost of law school courses. He was a forensic pathologist, and he needed the law background to help in his investigation of sudden, violent, and suspicious deaths for possible criminal prosecution.

A licensed practical nurse may not deduct the costs of a college program which qualifies her as a "physician's assistant" which is a new job. Physician's assistants and practical nurses are subject to different registration and certification requirements under state law, and, more importantly, the physician's assistant may perform duties, such as physical examinations and minor surgery, which go beyond practical nursing duties.

¶21.05 • COURSES TAKEN BY TEACHERS

You must meet the minimum level of education for your present position as set down by law or regulations before you may deduct the cost of courses. The educational requirements are those that existed when you were hired. If your employer set no tests fixing a minimum educational level, you meet the minimum requirements when you become a member of the faculty. Whether you are a faculty member depends on the custom of your employer. You are ordinarily considered a faculty member if (1) you have tenure, or your service is counted toward tenure, (2) the institution is contributing toward a retirement plan based on your employment (other than Social Security or similar program), or (3) you have a vote in faculty affairs.

Examples—
1. A state requires a bachelor's degree for beginning high school teachers including 30 credit hours of education courses. To retain his position, a teacher must complete a fifth year of preparation within 10 years after beginning employment. If enough teachers with these minimum requirements cannot be found, individuals may be hired if they have completed a minimum of 90 semester hours of college work. However, to remain as a teacher, such an individual must get his bachelor's degree and complete the required education courses within three years. Under these facts, a bachelor's degree is considered to be the minimum educational requirement for qualification as a school teacher in the state. The IRS says that an individual with a bachelor's degree has met the minimum educational requirements, although he has not completed 30 credit hours of education courses. Costs of taking education courses are deductible.
2. Because of a shortage of applicants meeting the requirements stated above, Smith is employed as a high school teacher, although he has only 90 semester hours of college work toward his bachelor's degree. After his employment, he takes courses leading to a bachelor's degree. These courses (including any courses in professional education) constitute education required to meet the minimum educational requirements. The costs for such education are not deductible.
3. Same facts as above but, after Smith is employed and gets his B.A. degree, the state changes its minimum requirements for beginning teachers to five years of college preparation. As the requirements were changed after he began employment, they do not affect Smith, and he may deduct the cost of his fifth year's courses.
4. Brown, who holds a bachelor's degree, is hired as a temporary instructor at a university. At the same time, he takes courses toward his graduate degree. To become a faculty member, he must earn his graduate degree, and his present position is contingent on making satisfactory progress toward the degree. Costs are not deductible.

Elementary and secondary school teachers may deduct the cost of courses taken to make any of the following job changes: (1) Elementary to secondary school classroom teacher; (2) classroom teacher in one subject (such as mathematics) to a classroom teacher in another subject (such as art); (3) classroom teacher to guidance counselor; (4) classroom teacher to principal.

The IRS held that a "discussion leader" in a college adult education program could not deduct the costs of a master's degree program that led to certification as a high school guidance counselor because this was a new business. The Tax Court disagreed, holding that the responsibilities of discussion leader are similar to the responsibilities of a school counselor. The court distinguished an earlier decision in which a classroom paraprofessional assistant was not allowed to deduct education costs that qualified her as a classroom teacher. The court considered this as a change in professions. A paraprofessional does not have the same control and responsibilities for classroom work as a classroom teacher.

Employed teacher taking courses for teaching certificate. That you are already employed as a teacher, with all the responsibilities of a teacher, may not establish that you have met the minimum educational requirements. A school system which requires a bachelor's degree before granting a permanent teaching certificate may grant temporary or provisional certificates after a person has completed a number of college credits. Renewal of the provisional certificate may be conditioned on the teacher's continuing education for a bachelor's degree. In this case, the IRS will disallow a deduction for the educational costs. The minimum requirements are not met until the teacher has the degree. Current Tax Court decisions follow the IRS position, although in the past the court took a contrary view.

The IRS has allowed a teacher with a provisional certificate to deduct educational costs under these circumstances: She was a fully qualified teacher with a permanent certificate. She moved to another state where the educational requirements for a permanent certificate were greater. The IRS said she was merely fulfilling her new employer's requirements.

¶21.06 • PROFESSOR'S RESEARCH EXPENSES

Research costs incurred by a college professor are deductible under this condition: He or she is appointed to lecture and teach with the understanding that research in the field will be carried on with the goal of incorporating the findings in teaching and writing. If this test is met, the IRS is satisfied that the research is an express requirement of the teaching position and that research expenses are deductible job expenses.

Deductible research costs include traveling expenses and stenographic and other costs of preparing a manuscript. If income is later realized from the research in the form of lecture or royalty fees, the previously deducted research costs may not again be deducted in determining the income realized from the research.

Expenses of a research project undertaken for a scholarly publication are not deductible if the research is not linked to an income-producing activity or job requirement.

Research expenses incurred in writing a textbook for profit are not deductible but are added to the cost of writing the book.

¶21.07 • LEAVE OF ABSENCE TO TAKE COURSES

The IRS will allow a deduction for full-time graduate courses taken by a teacher during a leave of absence if these conditions are met: (1) the absence must not be for more than one year and; (2) upon completion of the education courses, the same type of employment must be resumed, although you may take a job with a new employer. You may also have to show that you had more than a vague intention to go back to your employment, for example, that you were actually negotiating for a new teaching position and that, in fact, you did obtain a position soon after finishing the graduate courses.

The IRS has also applied the one-year test to those who leave jobs to pursue MBA degrees.

The Tax Court considers the IRS "one year" absence rule too narrow and inflexible and has allowed a school principal who resigned his position to deduct the cost of full-time courses taken over a three-year period. Similarly, a manager who quit his job to pursue a two-year MBA course was allowed to deduct the cost of his courses. In one case, the IRS did not object to a teacher's two-year absence from the job.

¶21.08 • HOW TO DEDUCT EDUCATION COSTS IN 1986

For 1986, if your courses meet the requirements explained in ¶21.02, you may deduct:

1. Tuition, textbooks, fees, equipment and other aids required by the courses.
2. Certain transportation costs described below.
3. Travel to and from a school away from home.
4. Living expenses (food and lodging) while at the school away from home. The IRS will not disallow traveling expenses to attend a school away from home or in a foreign country merely because you could have taken the course in a local school. But it may disallow your board and lodging expenses at the school if your stay lasts longer than a year.

Transportation expenses. On days you work and attend courses which qualify for an education expense deduction, if your place of employment and school are located within the same general area, you may deduct the cost of travel between your office and school. If you stop off at home on your way to school, you may deduct the cost of travel from your home to the school to the extent it does not exceed the cost you would have incurred in going directly from work to school. If your school is located beyond the general area of your principal place of business, you may deduct your round-trip transportation expenses. The cost of traveling between your home and school on a nonworking day is not deductible.

Examples—
1. After work, you attend classes in the same city in which your office is located. You deduct the costs of going from your office to school, provided you go directly to school.
2. You work in Newark, New Jersey and attend night classes in New York City. You may deduct your round-trip transportation expenses.

Transportation expenses include tolls and parking fees.

Travel and living expenses away from home. "Away from home" as explained at ¶2.23 has a special tax meaning. You are not away from home unless you are away overnight.

Examples—
1. You attend a summer course at a college which is 50 miles from your home. You drive to classes and return home each day. You may not deduct the expenses of your trip as transportation expenses because they are incurred on a nonwork day. Nor may you deduct them as travel expenses because you are not away from home.
2. You live in Akron, Ohio and travel to New York to attend courses. Your hotel room is several miles from the college. You may deduct travel costs to and from New York and your living expenses there. You may not, however, deduct the commuting costs between the hotel and school.

Expenses of sightseeing, social visiting, and entertaining while taking the courses are not deductible. If your main purpose in going to the vicinity of the school is to take a vacation or for other personal reasons, you may deduct only the cost of the courses and your living expenses while attending school. You may not deduct any part of your travel costs.

To determine the purpose of your trip, an IRS agent will pay close attention to the amount of time devoted to personal activities relative to the time devoted to the courses.

Examples—
1. You are a tax attorney practicing in Cleveland. You take a one-week refresher course in taxation in New York City. You make a side trip to spend one day visiting in Philadelphia and while you are in New York you take sightseeing trips and entertain friends at your hotel. Your transportation expenses to New York and return to your home are deductible, but your transportation expenses to Philadelphia are not deductible. Your expenses for meals and lodging while away from home will be allocated between your courses and your personal activities. Those expenses which are entirely personal, such as sightseeing and entertaining friends, are not deductible.
2. The facts are the same as in example 1, except that your primary purpose in going to New York is to take a vacation. This is evidenced by the fact that you spend only one week attending the tax course and devote five weeks entirely to personal activities. None of your transportation expenses are deductible, and your expenses for meals and lodging while away from home are not deductible to the extent attributable to personal activities. Your expenses for meals and lodging allocable to the week you attend the tax course are, however, deductible.
3. A high school mathematics teacher in New York City travels to California in the summer to take a single three-hour mathematics course at a university; the course tuition and other expenses qualify for deduction. A full course of study for the summer session is 12 hours. Since he takes only one-fourth of a full course of study and the remainder of his time is devoted to personal activities, the trip is considered as taken primarily for personal reasons unless he can show a substantial nonpersonal reason for taking the course in California. The cost of traveling from New York City to California and back is not deductible. However, one-fourth of the cost of meals and lodging while attending the university in California is deductible.

The way you deduct educational expenses depends on your occupational status. If you are:

An employee—You may deduct certain educational expenses from gross income whether or not you claim excess itemized deductions. These are unreimbursed travel and living expenses away from home and transportation costs plus parking and tolls if you drive directly from your job to your courses. List the expenses on Form 2106 (or a similar statement) to your return. The deduction from gross income is claimed on Form 1040 as an employee business expense.

Other unreimbursed costs, such as tuition, books, fees and equipment are deductible only if you claim excess itemized deductions exceeding your zero bracket amount (¶13.00). They are claimed as miscellaneous itemized deductions on Schedule A.

If your educational expenses are reimbursed by your employer and the reimbursement was included as pay on your Form W-2, you may claim an offsetting deduction from gross income. Use Form 2106 to report the expenses and claim the deduction. Reimbursements that are not reported on Form W-2 do not have to be reported as income if the expenses equal or exceed the reimbursement and you do not deduct the expenses. If your employer pays the tuition directly to the institution, you are not required to report the payment in any way on your return.

Example—
Miss Green, a teacher, was required to take a summer course. Tuition and books cost $160; travel, meals and lodging away from home

cost her $320. None of her expenses were reimbursed. Miss Green may deduct the $320 spent for travel, meals and lodging away from home whether or not she itemizes deductions. The $160 for tuition and books may be deducted as a "miscellaneous deduction," if Miss Green claims excess itemized deductions.

An outside salesperson—you deduct all of your education costs from your gross income, whether or not you claim excess itemized deductions.

A self-employed businessowner or professional—you deduct all of your education costs on Schedule C. You also attach a statement to your return explaining your deduction and the relationship of the education to your position. Form 2106 gives the details which the IRS requires to support these expenses. (You are not required to file this form. Its use is optional.)

A veteran receiving educational benefits from the V.A.—According to the IRS, educational expenses reimbursed by the V.A. are not deductible. This does not apply to a living stipend paid without regard to amounts spent for education.

Payments for substitute teachers. Where a school system has a policy of paying teachers full salary during sabbatical leaves, a teacher on sabbatical may be required to pay a fixed percentage of salary into a fund to pay substitute teachers. A teacher reports the full amount of the salary paid during the sabbatical but may claim as an itemized deduction payments to the fund.

¶21.09 • TRIP TAKEN FOR EDUCATIONAL PURPOSES

Sabbatical travel expenses *directly related* to the duties of a teacher's position are deductible. The following facts do *not* conclusively prove that there is a direct relationship between a teacher's duties and his travel: (1) It is customary for teachers to travel while on sabbatical leave; (2) the travel program of a teacher has been approved by his school; or (3) the school has accepted the sabbatical travel as meeting a salary or status requirement.

An IRS ruling gives one specific example of when expenses of sabbatical travel might be deductible as educational expenses: A teacher of French who, on a sabbatical leave for purposes of travel, journeys through France to improve his knowledge of the French language. His travel expenses are deductible as education expenses if he can show that his itinerary was chosen, and the major part of his activities was undertaken, for the primary purpose of improving his skill in the use and teaching of the French language.

The IRS distinguishes between sabbatical travel and travel taken for study or research in one location. Travel costs to do research or to study are deductible if the study or research is undertaken as a job requirement or to maintain or improve teaching skills. A teacher on sabbatical is not required to and generally does not engage in study or research in a fixed location, but rather travels from one locality to another according to an itinerary usually approved in advance by the school board. The above rules apply as well to individuals other than teachers whose educational travel is directly related to income-producing activities.

Examples—

1. An elementary school teacher was allowed to deduct the costs of a European trip. Facts influencing the court's decision were: Her school board approved the trip as an alternative to taking courses; she turned in a trip report to the school board; she visited museums which the court held was helpful in teaching art to her pupils.

2. A first grade teacher deducted travel costs of $1,700 to Europe. The Tax Court allowed a deduction for 80% of her expenses based on these facts: Her schedule did not allow time for recreation. Her school superintendent certified she completed the program for which she was granted leave and traveled for the improvement of her teaching skills. An appeals court reversed. She did not show that her trip resulted in some specific improvement of her teaching skills. Following the trip, she merely introduced into her classes dolls, games and pictures from the trip, and adopted one teaching technique learned abroad (a slate and abacus at each child's desk).

3. A high school teacher had to earn six credits within three years to be eligible for salary increases. She took a two-week trip to Mexico sponsored and directed by the University of Indiana, and earned two and one-half credits by keeping a diary of the trip. The credits were accepted as partially meeting the requirement for an increase. She deducted the expense of the trip. The IRS disallowed it, arguing that the requirement was for a salary increase. The Tax Court allowed the deduction. It held that she took the trip to preserve her existing salary rights, which included rights to salary advances that would otherwise be lost.

4. An assistant high school principal in charge of racial relations in the school and the community was allowed to deduct the cost of travel to 44 countries during an approved sabbatical. The IRS argued that the travel was too general to be directly related to her job. The Tax Court, in allowing the deduction, noted that the travel was primarily to improve her skills as an administrator in a multi-racial community. What she learned from the sabbatical was translated into innovative classroom techniques and was shared with other educators and students during seminars following the sabbatical.

The Tax Court has held that a high school teacher could deduct the cost of a summer trip that had been approved by his school. The travel qualified for special credits necessary for his salary advancement. Failure to obtain such credits would adversely affect his salary.

¶22.00

Figuring Your Tax Liability

There are two ways to figure your 1986 tax liability: By using the tax tables which begin on page 313 or by using the tax schedules below and on the next page. You will not have to compute your tax mathematically if you use the tax tables. You use the tables if your taxable income is less than $50,000.

To use the tables, you first figure your taxable income. Then turn to your income bracket and look for the tax liability listed in the column for your filing status. Filing status (single, married, head of household) is discussed at page 2.

You may *not* use the tax tables and must use the schedules if you income average (¶23.00), claim the foreign income exclusion (¶36.10), or file for a short period due to change of accounting period.

Estates and trusts may not use the tax tables.

The amount of your tax liability may be reduced by credits. *See* ¶24.00.

Figuring taxable income. By following the line-by-line steps of your tax return, you reach taxable income. If you do not claim excess itemized deductions, taxable income is adjusted gross income reduced by the nonitemized charitable contribution deduction and exemptions.

If you do claim excess itemized deductions, taxable income is adjusted gross income reduced by excess itemized deductions and exemptions. If you must compute an unused zero bracket amount (*see* ¶13.03), taxable income is adjusted gross income increased by the unused zero bracket amount and then decreased by exemptions.

Examples—

1. You have adjusted gross income of $15,000, no excess itemized deductions, a $100 nonitemized charitable contribution deduction and two exemptions.

Adjusted gross income		$15,000
Less: Contribution deduction	$ 100	
Exemptions (2)	2,160	2,260
Taxable income		$12,740

2. A married couple has adjusted gross income of $25,000, excess itemized deductions of $7,000 and four exemptions.

Adjusted gross income		$25,000
Less: Excess itemized deductions	$7,000	
Exemptions (4)	4,320	11,320
Taxable income		$13,680

3. A dependent who must compute the unused zero bracket amount has adjusted gross income of $6,000, an unused zero bracket amount of $1,100 and one exemption.

Adjusted gross income	$6,000	
Unused zero bracket amount	1,100	$7,100
Less: Exemption		1,080
Taxable income		$6,020

Using the Tax Rate Schedules

You compute your 1986 tax using tax rate schedules below if you fit into any one of these cases:

Your taxable income is $50,000 or more,

You income average (¶23.00),

You claim the foreign income exclusion (¶36.00), or

You file for a short period due to change of accounting period.

Example—

A head of household has taxable income of $51,500. Schedule Z shows taxable income falls between $48,240 and $65,390

Tax on first $48,240	$11,543.50
Tax on excess, $3,260 at 42%	1,369.20
Tax	$12,912.70

1986 Tax Rate Schedules

SINGLE (Schedule X)

If taxable income— not over $2,480

Over—	but not over—	Tax is —0— Plus following percentage		of the amount over
$ 2,480	$ 3,670		11%	$ 2,480
3,670	4,750	$ 130.90	12	3,670
4,750	7,010	260.50	14	4,750
7,010	9,170	576.90	15	7,010
9,170	11,650	900.90	16	9,170
11,650	13,920	1,297.70	18	11,650
13,920	16,190	1,706.30	20	13,920
16,190	19,640	2,160.30	23	16,190
19,640	25,360	2,953.80	26	19,640
25,360	31,080	4,441.00	30	25,360
31,080	36,800	6,157.00	34	31,080
36,800	44,780	8,101.80	38	36,800
44,780	59,670	11,134.20	42	44,780
59,670	88,270	17,388.00	48	59,670
88,270		31,116.00	50	88,270

JOINT RETURN (Schedule Y)

If taxable income— not over $3,670

Over—	but not over—	Tax is —0— Plus following percentage		of the amount over
$ 3,670	$ 5,940		11%	$ 3,670
5,940	8,200	$ 249.70	12	5,940
8,200	12,840	520.90	14	8,200
12,840	17,270	1,170.50	16	12,840
17,270	21,800	1,879.30	18	17,270
21,800	26,550	2,694.70	22	21,800
26,550	32,270	3,739.70	25	26,550
32,270	37,980	5,169.70	28	32,270
37,980	49,420	6,768.50	33	37,980
49,420	64,750	10,543.70	38	49,420
64,750	92,370	16,369.10	42	64,750
92,370	118,050	27,969.50	45	92,370
118,050	175,250	39,525.50	49	118,050
175,250		67,553.50	50	175,250

HEAD OF HOUSEHOLD (Schedule Z)

If taxable income is— not over $2,480

Over—	but not over—	Tax is —0— Plus following percentage		of the amount over
$ 2,480	$ 4,750		11%	$ 2,480
4,750	7,010	$ 249.70	12	4,750
7,010	9,390	520.90	14	7,010
9,390	12,730	854.10	17	9,390
12,730	16,190	1,421.90	18	12,730
16,190	19,640	2,044.70	20	16,190
19,640	25,360	2,734.70	24	19,640
25,360	31,080	4,107.50	28	25,360
31,080	36,800	5,709.10	32	31,080
36,800	48,240	7,539.50	35	36,800
48,240	65,390	11,543.50	42	48,240
65,390	88,270	18,746.50	45	65,390
88,270	116,870	29,042.50	48	88,270
116,870		42,770.50	50	116,870

MARRIED FILING SEPARATELY (Schedule Y)

If taxable income is— not over $1,835

Over—	but not over—	Tax is —0— Plus following percentage		of the amount over
$ 1,835	$ 2,970		11%	$ 1,835
2,970	4,100	$ 124.85	12	2,970
4,100	6,420	260.45	14	4,100
6,420	8,635	585.25	16	6,420
8,635	10,900	939.65	18	8,635
10,900	13,275	1,347.35	22	10,900
13,275	16,135	1,869.85	25	13,275
16,135	18,990	2,584.85	28	16,135
18,990	24,710	3,384.25	33	18,990
24,710	32,375	5,271.85	38	24,710
32,375	46,185	8,184.55	42	32,375
46,185	59,025	13,984.75	45	46,185
59,025	87,625	19,762.75	49	59,025
87,625		33,776.75	50	87,625

¶23.00

Income Averaging

A copy of Schedule G for income averaging may be found in the Supplement to YOUR INCOME TAX. Mail the card at the front of this book for your FREE Supplement, which includes filled-in returns and last-minute information.

	See ¶		See ¶
Averaging for income increases	23.01	File Schedule G to average	23.04
Rules for recent graduates and aliens	23.02	Change in marital status or type of return filed during	
Adjustment of community property income if separate		1982–1985 requires income adjustments	23.05
return is filed in 1986	23.03	You must elect to average	23.06
Adjustments for premature retirement distributions			
and trust accumulation distributions	23.031		

¶23.01 • AVERAGING IF INCOME INCREASED IN 1986

You may income average on Schedule G if your 1986 income increased over a certain level. To income average, you do not need a dramatic increase in income. You may qualify if your income has increased steadily or if you are married and your spouse has started to work.

By following the steps in the chart below, you may determine if you qualify. The purpose of the steps is to find your average income for the three years preceding 1986; 1986 income exceeding this average, increased by 25%, is treated as if it were earned over a four-year period and subject to lower tax rates. Averaging

is not permitted unless your 1986 taxable income exceeds by more than $3,000 an amount equal to 140% of the average of your taxable income in the three prior years.

Averaging is not permitted to nonresident aliens and recent graduates (*see* ¶23.02). Averaging is not available to trusts, estates, or corporations. If you income average, you may not exclude income earned abroad.

Dollar limitations for joint returns. When a joint return is filed, the $3,000 floor for averageable income applies to the total of the couple's income.

TO FIND IF YOU CAN INCOME AVERAGE

DO THIS

1. *Start with your 1986 taxable income.* First, figure your 1986 income and deductions as if you were not averaging. Your taxable income equals adjusted gross income minus excess itemized deductions or the nonitemized charitable contribution deduction, if any, and the deduction for personal exemptions. If you have an unused zero bracket amount (*see* ¶13.03), it must be added to adjusted gross income to calculate taxable income.

If you earned tax-free foreign income in 1986 under the rules of ¶36.00 and you elect to income average, you must report that income on Form 1040. If, in a later year, your election to average is disqualified, for example, because of a net operating loss carryback, you may then exclude your foreign pay as tax-free income and recompute your tax in the regular way.

2. *Take out your tax returns for 1983, 1984, and 1985,* and total taxable incomes for those years. You take taxable income directly from your tax return. Add to taxable income any tax-free foreign income. Reduce foreign income by expenses incurred to earn that income even though the expenses were not deductible because the income was tax free. This adjustment does not affect prior tax-free treatment of the income. Also reduce taxable income in any of the years 1983–1985 in which you received certain trust distributions of accumulated income.

If your marital status changed during the years 1983–1985 or if you are married but file a separate return in 1986, *see* ¶23.05.

3. *Divide the total of the taxable income for the three-year period by 3.* The result is average base period income. Divide by the number three, even if you do not have taxable income in all of the three years.

4. *Multiply the average by 140%.* To qualify for averaging, your 1986 taxable income must exceed, by more than $3,000, 140% of average base period income. The excess is called averageable income.

EXAMPLE

1. In 1986, Jones, a married person has:

Salary and bonus	$55,500	
Long-term gain (40%)	5,000	
Adjusted gross income		$60,500
Less:		
Excess itemized deductions	940	
Personal exemptions	4,320	5,260
Taxable income		$55,240

2. Jones had the following taxable incomes in:

1983	$13,000
1984	14,000
1985	12,000
Total base period income	$39,000

3. $39,000 ÷ 3 = $13,000. This is average base period income.

4. 140% of $13,000 = $18,200. Jones may average. His 1986 taxable income of $55,240 (*see* step 1) exceeds $18,200 (140% of average base period income) by more than $3,000.

1986 taxable income	$55,240
Less	18,200
Averageable income	$37,040

¶23.02 • RULES FOR RECENT GRADUATES AND ALIENS

Citizenship or resident. In addition to the income tests listed in ¶23.01, you must be a citizen or resident of the United States throughout 1986 and must not have been a nonresident alien during any of the years 1983–1985. If you file a joint return and want to income average, both you and your spouse must meet the citizen or resident test.

Example—

You are a U.S. citizen. In 1983, when living abroad, you married an alien. On December 31, 1984, you returned with your spouse to live in the United States. You and your spouse may not average if you file a joint return for 1986, since your spouse was a nonresident alien for the years 1983, 1984, and 1985. You, however, may average if you file a separate return.

Support and student restrictions. The law generally bars averaging to (1) students, (2) recent graduates, and (3) persons who recently started to work and were supported by others. The law sets down a general rule and then allows exceptions.

General rule. You cannot average if during any base period year (1983, 1984, 1985), you were a full-time student or furnished less than 50% of your support. A full-time student is one who attends school for at least five calendar months.

Exceptions. The student ban does not apply to a joint return where one spouse was a student in 1983, 1984, or 1985 but that spouse's share of 1986 joint adjusted gross income is 25% or less. This exception allows averaging to a person whose share of joint adjusted gross income is 75% or more and who married a student.

The support ban rule does not apply to you if more than 50% of your 1986 income substantially comes from work performed by you in at least two base period years. The support ban rule also does not apply to a joint return where the nonsupporting spouse's share of joint adjusted gross income is 25% or less. This exception allows averaging to a person whose share of joint adjusted gross income is 75% or more and who married a person who was not self supporting in a base period year.

Examples—

1. In 1986, Jones, who is 20 years old and has always been supported by his parents, sells a novel which he wrote during 1984–1985. He may elect to average although he was previously supported by his parents. The proceeds for the sale of his novel, which took two years to write, will exceed 50% of his taxable 1986 income.

2. John and Mary Smith were married in August, 1986. Mary's parents furnished more than 50% of her support prior to her marriage. For 1986, John and Mary file a joint return showing adjusted gross income of $16,000. John's earnings are $12,500 and Mary's $3,500. If they otherwise qualify, they may elect income averaging for 1986, even though Mary has never supported herself. Less than 25% of their joint adjusted gross income is attributable to Mary.

For purposes of figuring support, the Tax Court ruled you must count scholarships. This rule prevented an athlete from income averaging. In his first year after graduation, he made $50,000, but he and his wife could not satisfy the support test for prior years because of an athletic scholarship. The exception for scholarships in determining dependency exemptions (¶1.55) does not extend to income averaging.

The Tax Court also held that a student could not count as his own support contribution Social Security and Veterans Administration survivor benefits he received while at college. This prevented him from meeting the more than 50% support test and barred him from income averaging earnings from his first full-time job after graduation.

¶23.03 • ADJUSTMENT OF COMMUNITY PROPERTY INCOME IF SEPARATE RETURN IS FILED IN 1986

If you live in a community property state (*see* ¶1.04) and file a separate return in 1986, the amount of earned income used in determining your taxable income for averaging purposes is the lower of (1) your share of the community earned income under community property law, or (2) your earned income without regard to community property law.

Earned income is compensation for personal services, such as wages, salaries, and fees. If you earn income from a business in which capital, as well as personal services, is a material income-producing factor, a reasonable amount of your net profit (not more than 30% of your share of profits) is considered earned income. Earned income does not include interest, dividends, pensions, annuities, or capital gains. Rental income is earned income only if personal services are rendered.

Example—

You earn a salary of $20,000, your spouse, $10,000. You file separate returns and each reports a gross income of $15,000 (50% of $30,000) as his respective share of community income. You elect to income average. You do not adjust the salary income reported on your return as $15,000 is the lower of (1) your share of the community income of $30,000 or (2) your earned income determined without applying community property law ($20,000). If your spouse elects income averaging, her income of $15,000 for purposes of income averaging is reduced to $10,000. This is the lesser of her share of community income ($15,000) or her earned income computed without applying community property law, or $10,000. (On Schedule G, your spouse shows $15,000 as her income, $5,000 as excess community income, and adjusted income of $10,000.)

¶23.031 • ADJUSTMENTS FOR PREMATURE RETIREMENT DISTRIBUTIONS AND FOR TRUST ACCUMULATION DISTRIBUTIONS

Two adjustment items are made to determine whether you may average your income and, if so, the amount subject to averaging.

Premature retirement plan distributions. A corporate executive or self-employed individual with more than a 5% interest may not average a premature retirement plan distribution subject to the penalty rules of ¶7.065. On Schedule G, reduce your 1986 taxable income by the amount of the premature distribution. Similarly, if before age 59½ you withdraw deductible IRA contributions made to your employer's plan, the penalized distribution (¶7.183) reduces taxable income on Schedule G. No corresponding adjustment is made in the base period. Finally, on Schedule G you must reduce 1986 taxable income by premature annuity distribution (¶7.07).

Trust accumulation distributions. A trust beneficiary may not average an accumulation distribution subject to the throwback rules. Taxable income, for purposes of averaging, is reduced by the amount of such accumulation distribution included in income. This adjustment applies in the computation year and base period years.

In a base period year, you may have had losses and no taxable income; you may not reduce taxable income of another base year by that loss for purposes of averaging.

¶23.04 • FILE SCHEDULE G TO AVERAGE

When you have averageable income exceeding $3,000, you calculate your tax on Schedule G. By following the steps on Schedule G, you determine a tax on averageable income that is four times the increase in tax resulting from adding 25% of averageable income to 140% of average base period income. A sample Schedule G illustrating the tax calculation is in the Supplement to this book.

That you have averageable income of over $3,000 does not mean income averaging will reduce your taxes. Averaging reduces your tax only if the amount of averageable income falls within a bracket that is lower than the top bracket in which your income would be taxed without averaging.

¶23.05 • CHANGE IN MARITAL STATUS OR TYPE OF RETURN FILED DURING 1983–1986 REQUIRES BASE PERIOD INCOME ADJUSTMENTS

You need not be concerned with the following discussion if you have been married to and have filed joint returns with your present spouse during the base period years 1983–1985, and will file jointly in 1986. However, if you married, were divorced, or remarried during 1983–1986, you have to refigure taxable income during the base period years. Even if you did not change your marital status, you may have to do some refiguring if you changed your method of filing your tax return during the period. For example, you are married but filed a separate return in one or all of the base period years, or plan to file a separate return in 1986. The purpose of the adjustments is to refigure your base period income for each base period year in a manner consistent with the type of return you file in 1986. The following examples illustrate the complicated problems arising in this area.

Examples—

1. You have been married to the same spouse during the years 1983–1986. In 1986, you file a separate return, although in all of the prior years you have filed joint returns. Your right to average will depend on the relationship between the income reported on your separate return in 1986 and *your share of income* reported on the joint returns in the years 1983–1985. The law provides special rules on how to determine your share. (*See* below.)

2. In 1986, you married and will file a joint return. In previous years, both you and your spouse were single. Your right to average will depend on the relationship between the income reported in the prior years not only by you when you were single but also by your spouse. In computing taxable income for each of the base period years 1983–1985, you combine the taxable income reported by each of you on your separate returns.

3. You and your spouse have been married and filing joint returns since 1943, except for 1983 when you filed separate returns. In computing base period taxable income for 1983, you combine the taxable incomes reported by both you and your spouse on the separate returns.

4. During 1983 you were married and filed a joint return with Jane. In 1984, you were divorced and filed a separate return. In 1985, you married Doris and filed a joint return with her. In 1986, you will also file a joint return with her. Your right to average will depend on income reported on the 1986 joint return and the income attributed to you and your present wife during the years 1983 through 1985. To find your income during this period, you must figure your share of the income reported with your former wife before you can combine it with your present wife's income. (*See* below.)

Surviving spouses. If you file as a surviving spouse in 1986, your base period income for each of the years 1983 to 1985 is the sum of your base period income and that of your deceased spouse for each such year.

Figuring your separate share of taxable income reported on a joint return during a base period year. Start with your income earned from services, investments, or other sources. From this amount, subtract deductions you claimed for expenses deductible from gross income. Examples of such expenses are local transportation, travel away from home, IRA contributions, and business expenses (*see* ¶13.04). As for itemized deductions (contributions, casualty losses, medical expenses, etc.), and exemptions, you take a proportionate part of your deductions for exemptions and itemized deductions. Your share is determined by multiplying the total amount of these deductions on the joint return by a fraction whose numerator is your separate adjusted gross income and whose denominator is the combined adjusted gross income for you and your spouse in that year. However, if you earned 85% or more of the combined adjusted gross income, you may claim all of the deductions.

Examples—

1. You are married but file a separate return for 1986. In 1983, you filed a joint return in which combined adjusted gross income was $10,000. Of this, $8,000 was from your salary. Deductions from adjusted gross income totaled $2,200 ($200 excess itemized deductions and $2,000 exemptions). The amount of your separate deductions in 1983 is $1,760 ($8,000/$10,000 × $2,200). For purposes of figuring base period income, your separate taxable income in 1983 is $6,240 ($8,000 less $1,760).

2. Assume the same facts in the example above except that your salary was $9,000. You claim all of the $2,200 deductions. Your portion of the combined adjusted gross income was 85% or more of the total ($9,000/$10,000 or 90%). Your separate taxable income is $6,800 ($9,000 less $2,200).

Limitations applied to your separate share of income. Your share of income during a base period year may be subject to the following type of adjustment. For example, if you are married and file a joint return with your present spouse in 1986, but had a different spouse for a base period year, your separate base period income for the year in question is the larger of:

1. The amount of your separate income and deductions for the base period year.

2. 50% of the total amount of base period income resulting from adding your separate income and deductions to the separate income and deductions of your former spouse for the base period year.

If you and your spouse file separate returns for 1986, a third computation is necessary. Your separate base period income is the largest of the amounts figured under (1) and (2) above and:

3. 50% of the total amount of the base period income resulting from adding your separate income and deductions to the separate income and deductions of your present spouse for that base period year.

Under methods (2) and (3) above, you may not decrease your income by a loss incurred by the spouse with whom you are combining your income unless you filed a joint return with him or her in the base period year in question. For example, you filed a separate return in 1983 and had net long-term capital gain of $20,000. Your spouse had a net long-term capital loss of $5,000. Your net capital gain income is $8,000 ($20,000 × 40%). If you had filed a joint return, your combined net capital gain income would have been $6,000 ($15,000 × 40%).

In computing separate base period income, community property rules are generally not considered in apportioning income from services. In figuring your separate income and deductions for the base period year under methods (1) and (3) above, earned income attributable to services is adjusted. You must take into account the greater of all the earned income attributable to you without regard to the community property laws, or your share of the community earned income.

See Treasury regulations for examples of the above computations.

¶23.06 • YOU MUST ELECT TO AVERAGE

You make the election on your tax return by computing your tax on Schedule G. If you fail to elect to average on your 1986 return by April 15, 1987, you have until April 15, 1990, in which to make your election on an amended return or on a refund claim.

If you average your income, you must include earned income from abroad and U.S. possessions which is otherwise tax free.

Effect of net operating loss carryback on averaging. Net operating loss carrybacks affect income averaging. Assume that in a later year you incur a net operating loss that is carried back to the year in which you elected to average. If the carryback reduces your averageable income to $3,000 or less, you lose the right to average. In any event, a carryback will require you to recompute your tax for that year. On the other hand, a carryback to a year before the year in which you elect to average may increase the amount of income to be averaged by reducing the amount of income in a base period year. A carryback to a base period year may even entitle you to average by reducing the base period income to a point where income averaging is permissible in a later year previously not within the averaging rules.

Correct taxable income of "closed" base year. If you have averaged income and the IRS audits your return, an agent may review the returns filed for the four prior years. Depending on when the audit takes place, at least one or more of those years may be closed for tax deficiencies. If an error which increases taxable income is found on a return for a closed year, the IRS may adjust income for averaging purposes, but not to assess a tax deficiency.

¶23.10

Alternative Minimum Tax

The alternative minimum tax (AMT) is designed to recoup tax benefits that have reduced or eliminated your regular income tax. AMT is imposed if it exceeds your regular income tax or you have no tax liability after claiming certain tax deductions or credits. In 1986, you may incur an AMT if you have—

Substantial long-term capital gains which are your major or only source of income in 1986,

Deductions for accelerated and ACRS depreciation, percentage depletion, and intangible drilling and development costs, and/or

A substantial investment credit, if available.

Even when you do not have the above preference items, you may incur an AMT if you have substantial itemized deductions that are not deductible for AMT purposes. For AMT purposes, state and local income taxes are not deductible, and there is a limited interest deduction.

In 1986, the AMT rate is 20% after deducting an exemption of $30,000 if single; $40,000 if married and filing jointly.

The following example illustrates how AMT is incurred in the case of substantial long-term capital gains.

Example—

Jones, who is single and in the 50% income tax bracket, has a net long-term capital gain of $250,000. His other income is offset by itemized deductions and exemptions.

His regular tax is $36,981, his additional liability due to AMT is $7,019 ($44,000 AMT—$36,981 regular tax).

	Regular tax	AMT
Long-term capital gain	$100,000	$250,000
Less AMT exemption		30,000
Taxable income	$100,000	$220,000
Tax	$ 36,981	$ 44,000

In computing AMT, the capital gain deduction of $150,000 (60% of $250,000), which is considered a tax preference item, is added back to Jones's income. Thus part of the tax benefit of realizing long-term gain has been recovered by the AMT.

The details of computing AMT are discussed in the following sections:

¶23.11 • PATTERN OF AMT TAXATION

You compute your AMT after you have figured your regular tax on Form 1040. You figure AMT liability on Form 6251, which is attached to Form 1040.

The starting point for computing AMT is adjusted gross income. See the Supplement for the line of adjusted gross income on Form 1040. Also see ¶13.04 for an explanation of adjusted gross income.

On Form 6251, adjusted gross income is *increased* by tax preference items listed in ¶23.12 and *reduced* by certain itemized deductions. State and local taxes are not deductible for AMT purposes.

AMT deductions are listed at ¶ 23.13. If you have a net operating loss, the loss for AMT purposes is not included in adjusted gross income. The loss is reduced under the rules of ¶23.14 before it is deductible from AMT income.

The AMT tax rate is a flat 20% applied to AMT taxable income after claiming the following exemption for your tax status.

Filing status	1986 Exemption
Married filing jointly	$40,000
Surviving spouse	40,000
Unmarried individual	30,000
Head of household	30,000
Married filing separately	20,000
Trust or estate	20,000

The resulting AMT is imposed to the extent it exceeds **regular** taxes which are all income taxes *except* the penalty tax on a premature distribution to a more than 5% owner (¶7.37), the separate tax on lump-sum distributions (¶7.02), the penalty tax on a premature distribution from an IRA or retirement bond (¶7.20), the penalty tax on early redemptions from annuity contracts (¶7.07), and the tax on accumulation distributions from trusts (¶11.02).

Example—

You are married filing jointly. You have an adjusted gross income of $48,000. AMT itemized deductions total $10,000. You have a tax preference item for capital gains of $60,000. Your regular tax is $6,170. Your AMT is $11,600 requiring an additional tax payment of $5,430.

Adjusted gross income	$ 48,000
Tax preference item	60,000
	$108,000
Less: AMT deductions	10,000
	98,000
Less: AMT exemption	40,000
AMT taxable income	58,000
AMT at 20%	11,600
Less: regular tax	6,170
Additional tax	$ 5,430

AMT liability must be considered in estimated tax payments.

¶23.12 • TAX PREFERENCE ITEMS SUBJECT TO TAX

The following items are tax preference items subject to AMT in 1986. Certain expense preference items may escape AMT under an election discussed at ¶23.16.

Dividend exclusion. The amount of the dividend exclusion claimed (up to $100 or $200 on a joint return) is a tax preference item. The exclusion for dividends from public utility dividend reinvestment plans is not an AMT preference item.

Capital gain deduction. 60% of the amount by which the net long-term capital gain exceeds net short-term capital loss is a preference item. However, capital gain from the sale of a principal residence is not included as a preference item. See ¶29.21 for definition of principal residence.

Incentive stock options. Exercise of an incentive stock option produces a preference item. The amount is the excess of the fair market value of a share at the time of exercise over the option price. No preference is created if there is an early disposition of stock acquired through the exercise of the option which results in immediate income tax. For the meaning of "early disposition," *see* ¶32.04, requirement 1.

Accelerated depreciation and amortization. For property placed in service before 1981, the difference between the depreciation that would have been allowable if the straight line method had been used and accelerated depreciation claimed on real property during the taxable year is a tax preference item. The excess is computed for each asset depreciated through an accelerated method. This rule also applies to accelerated depreciation, including additional depreciation from the use of ADR system, taken on personal property subject to a lease. Five-year amortization of certified pollution control facilities and child care facilities is a preference item to the extent that the claimed deduction exceeds *allowable* depreciation. In the year a building is sold, you do not treat accelerated depreciation as a preference item to the extent that depreciation is recaptured as ordinary income.

The basis of an asset is *not* adjusted for the depreciation element taxed as a preference item.

For property placed in service after 1980, different rules apply. For ACRS recovery property, a tax preference item is the difference between ACRS depreciation and depreciation that would have been allowable if the straight line method (without regard to salvage value) had been used. The excess is computed for each recovery property. In the case of personal property subject to a lease for which an ACRS deduction was claimed, the difference between depreciation that would have been allowable using the straight line method and the following recovery periods (with a half-year convention, but without regard to salvage value) and accelerated cost recovery claimed for the property is an item of tax preference. For three-year property, the recovery period is five years; for five-year property, the period is eight years, and for 10-year property, 15 years.

Depletion. The difference between claimed percentage depletion and the adjusted basis of the property at the end of the year (without regard to current depletion) is a preference item. You figure the amount separately for each property for which you claim a depletion allowance. No tax preference occurs until the total depletion claimed over a period of years exceeds the cost basis of the property.

Intangible drilling costs. The preference item is the excess of intangible drilling costs over net income from oil and gas properties for the taxable year. Excess intangible drilling costs are those expenses in excess of the amount which could have been deducted had the expenses been capitalized and either deducted ratably over ten years or deducted over the life of the well as cost depletion. Net income from oil and gas properties is gross income (excluding rent or royalties paid to another for use of the property) reduced by deductions other than excess intangible drilling costs. Deductions attributable to properties with no gross income are not to be taken into account. Costs incurred in drilling a nonproductive well are not counted as a tax preference.

The preference rule does not apply if you elected to capitalize intangible drilling costs. It does not apply to nonproductive wells. A nonproductive well is one which is plugged and abandoned without having produced oil and gas in commercial quantities for any substantial period of time. According to committee reports, a well which has been plugged and abandoned may have produced some relatively small amount of oil and still be considered a nonproductive well, depending on the amount of oil produced in relation to the costs of drilling. In some cases, it may not be possible to determine whether a well is in fact nonproductive until after the close of the taxable year. In these cases, no preference is included in the minimum tax base to any wells which are later determined to be nonproductive. If a well is proved to be nonproductive after the end of the taxable year but before the tax return for the year in question is filed, that well can be treated as nonproductive on that return. If a well is not determined to be nonproductive by the time the return for the year in question is filed, the intangible expenses related to that well are subject to the minimum tax. However, you may file an amended return and claim a credit or refund for the amount of any minimum tax paid on expenses related to that well if the well later proves to be nonproductive.

Other preference items. Not discussed in this book are tax preference items for certain mining and development costs and for circulation and research and experimental expenditures.

Tax benefit rule. If you have incurred a loss, determine whether tax preference items entered into the loss computation. If you would have incurred the loss without the preference items, the items may not be subject to minimum tax. Tax preference items which provide no tax benefit are not subject to minimum tax. To determine whether preference items produced a tax benefit, follow these steps. Reduce income first by nontax preference items and then by tax preference items. The amount of preference items used to reduce your income to zero is the actual tax benefit from the items and the amount subject to tax.

¶23.13 • AMT ITEMIZED DEDUCTIONS
AMT income is reduced by the following deductions in 1986.
    Charitable contributions
    Medical expenses exceeding 10% of adjusted gross income
       Do not confuse this limit with the 5% limit for regular tax purposes.
    Casualty and theft losses exceeding 10% of adjusted gross income
    Wagering losses
    Estate tax deductions for income in respect of a decedent
    Home mortgage interest and other interest deductible to extent of net investment income

State and local taxes are not deductible for AMT purposes.

Home mortgage interest. This is interest paid on a debt incurred to buy, construct, or substantially rehabilitate your principal residence or other dwelling. The residence must be used by you or a member of your family (spouse, parent, child, grandchild, or brother or sister). The residence may be a house, apartment, condominium, or mobile home not used on a transient basis. Interest on a mortgage debt incurred before July 1, 1982 for any purpose qualifies as an AMT deduction if the mortgage is secured by your principal residence or other dwelling in which you or your family reside.

Other interest. Other interest is deductible to the extent of net investment income (investment income minus investment expenses). Investment income is the sum of (1) gross income from interest, dividends, rents, and royalties; (2) 100% of net capital gain income from sales of investment property; (3) the dividend exclusion; and (4) net income from a limited partnership interest or shareholder income from an S corporation (if the shareholder is not active in management). Investment expenses are those taken directly from gross income (not as itemized deductions) and which are not items of tax preference. Interest incurred to acquire a limited partnership or interest as an S corporation shareholder is not treated as a qualified investment expense. *See* instructions to Form 6251 for further details.

If you did not claim itemized deductions on Form 1040, you may not claim the zero bracket amount as an AMT deduction in lieu of itemized deductions.

¶23.14 • AMT NET OPERATING LOSS DEDUCTION
A 1986 net operating loss deductible for AMT purposes is generally the amount of the regular net operating loss with these exceptions: (1) The loss must be reduced by any deductions which are considered tax preference items (*see* ¶23.12). (2) In figuring the nonbusiness income adjustment, only AMT itemized deductions may be taken. Under the rules of ¶5.21, the nonbusiness income adjustment is reduced by itemized deductions, but for AMT purposes, state and local taxes and certain interest may not reduce nonbusiness income before it is applied to the net operating loss.

The above rules require you to keep a separate accounting of net operating losses for regular and AMT purposes. In some cases, a net operating loss will eliminate your regular tax liability but not the AMT because the loss for AMT purposes is reduced by the disallowance of substantial tax preference deductions and state and local taxes.

¶23.15 • CLAIMING TAX CREDITS FROM ALTERNATIVE MINIMUM TAX

The amount of tax credits which may be applied to reduce your alternative minimum tax is subject to restrictions. The law distinguishes between refundable and nonrefundable credits. A refundable credit is a credit which entitles you to a refund if the credit exceeds your tax liability. A nonrefundable credit cannot exceed your tax liability. For example, you have regular tax of $10,000 and have a credit for withholding tax of $11,000. You get a refund of $1,000. However, if the credit had been an investment credit, you would not receive a refund of $1,000. The investment credit reduces your tax liability to zero and the excess of $1,000 may be carried to a later year. Nonrefundable credits are the investment credit, if available, dependent care credit, credit for the elderly, foreign tax credit, campaign contribution credit, targeted jobs credit, and the credit for tax paid by a mutual fund on undistributed gains.

Refundable credits (credit for overwithholding of taxes, earned income credit, and credit for special fuels) are fully deductible for alternative minimum tax purposes. The foreign tax credit is also deductible (after certain adjustments) even though it is a nonrefundable credit. The foreign tax credit adjustments are explained on Form 6251.

Nonrefundable credits such as the investment credit may not be claimed against the alternative maximum tax. However, certain nonrefundable credits that are not allowed against the alternative minimum tax may be carried back or forward to other years. This rule applies to the credit for interest on certified home mortgage certificates, the investment credit, targeted jobs credit, alcohol fuels credit and research credit.

Example—

Your regular tax before claiming an investment tax credit is $10,000. The investment credit is $5,000 and reduces your regular tax to $5,000.

If your AMT is $8,000, you must pay an additional tax of $3,000 over your regular tax. In effect, the AMT has prevented you from taking a tax benefit from the credit to the extent of $3,000. However, $3,000 of the credit may be carried over to next year.

Recaptured investment tax credit. For AMT purposes, a recaptured investment tax credit is not considered part of the regular tax liability. Thus, the recaptured credit does not have the effect of reducing AMT liability.

¶23.16 • ELECTION FOR 10-YEAR WRITE-OFF OF PREFERENCES

You may avoid AMT on certain expenditures by electing to deduct them ratably over a 10-year period beginning with the year in which the expenditure was made. Expenditures qualifying for this election are intangible drilling costs, mining and development costs, circulation expenditures, and research and experimental expenditures.

Taxable year	Percent of write-off
1	15%
2	22
3	21
4	21
5	21

The election is made under rules to be prescribed by the IRS. Revocation of the election is allowed only with IRS consent. Partners may make separate elections.

For intangible drilling costs for wells located in the United States, a partnership which is not a limited partnership may make a special five-year election.

¶24.00

Tax Credits

A credit reduces your tax liability dollar-for-dollar. The following chart lists credits that reduce income tax liability.

Credit for	For	Rate
Campaign contributions (¶24.60)	Contributions to political campaigns or newsletter funds	50% of contribution. Top credit $50 ($100 on joint return)
Dependent care (¶1.60)	Care of child under the age of 15 or disabled dependent to enable you to work	20% to 30% (depending on income) of expenses up to $2,400 for one dependent or $4,800 for two or more dependents. Top credit for those with adjusted gross income over $28,000 is $480 for one dependent; $960 for two or more dependents
Elderly (¶34.02)	Persons 65 or older or under age 65 who are permanently and totally disabled and receive disability income	Top credit $1,125; limits may reduce or eliminate credit
Earned income (¶24.50)	Certain low-income wage earners	Top credit $500 subject to reductions for income over $6,000
Federal gasoline and fuels tax (¶24.82)	Gasoline and fuels used for other than highway or aviation vehicles, such as tractors, for a qualified business use	9¢ per gallon of gas
Foreign taxes (¶36.14)	Income taxes paid to a foreign country or U.S. possession	Amount of foreign tax not to exceed U.S. tax multiplied by the ratio of foreign taxable income over total taxable income (less zero bracket amount)
Investment in business equipment (¶24.10)	Machinery and equipment with a recovery period of at least three years used in your business. Special coverage for farm units. Availability of the credit depends on tax legislation discussed in the front of this book.	10% if recovery period is 5 or 10 years; 6% if recovery period is 3 years. Special limits apply to business autos placed in service after June 18, 1984, *see* ¶3.00
Targeted jobs (¶24.20)	Employment of disadvantaged persons	50% of first $6,000 of first-year wages and 25% of first $6,000 of second-year wages per employee (maximum credit, $3,000 per employee up to 90% of employer's tax liability)
Diesel vehicles (¶24.83)	To account for increased fuel tax	$102 per car, $198 for van or light truck
Tax paid by mutual fund on undistributed gains (¶24.86)	Tax paid by mutual fund on capital gains earned by fund and retained	Amount of tax paid by fund on retained capital gains which are reported in your income
Interest on qualified home mortgage certificates (¶24.87)	Interest on home mortgages authorized by special state and local programs	Depends on interest paid and credit rate under certificate

Business Credits

	See ¶		See ¶
Investment credit	24.10	General business credit	24.30
Targeted jobs credit and other business credits	24.20		

¶24.10 • INVESTMENT CREDIT

Qualification tests for claiming the investment credit depend on the tax legislation discussed in the front of this book. Other business credits include the targeted jobs credit, alcohol fuels credit, and ESOP credit.

You compute each credit separately. If you claim only one credit, that credit is considered your *general business credit* for 1986 and is entered as such on Form 1040. If you claim more than one credit, the credits are combined into one general business credit on Form 3800 and subject to an overall limitation discussed at ¶24.30.

Business energy credits for investments in solar, wind, geothermal and other alternative energy sources are allowed to qualified investments in 1986.

An allowable investment credit is figured on Form 3468 which you attach to your regular income tax return. The credit for business energy property is figured on separate Schedule B of Form 3468. The full investment credit of 10% applies only to assets with a recovery period of five years or more. For three-year recovery property, the 10% rate applies to 60% of cost basis, giving an effective credit of 6% of basis. A limitation may prevent you from claiming the full investment credit. The credit may not exceed the first $25,000 of your tax liability plus 75% of your tax liability over $25,000. If you also claim a targeted job credit, carryforwards of the WIN credit, alcohol fuels credit or an employee stock ownership plan credit, the $25,000/75% limit applies to the total of the credits, as explained in ¶24.75.

The depreciable basis of an asset in 1986 is reduced by one-half of the credit claimed, unless you elect a lower credit of 8% for property with a recovery period of five or more years or a 4% credit for three-year recovery property. The lower investment credit may be elected in a special section on Form 3468.

The credit applies also to annual purchases of used property of up to $125,000. No dollar investment limit is placed on purchases of new property.

Where property is used partly in business and partly for personal use, the credit is taken on only that part of the property attributed to business use and on which depreciation is claimed.

No investment credit may be claimed to the extent that invested amounts are not at risk (*see* ¶28.13).

Recapture of credit. If you dispose of the property before the end of the recovery period, part of the credit is recaptured. The recaptured amount is added to your tax liability. Recapture is figured on Form 4255.

Business autos. If available, the investment credit for a passenger auto may not exceed $675. Further, to claim the investment credit, an employee must show that the car was required by his employer for the convenience of the employer and is used for business more than 50%. To claim the credit on a business auto, a self-employed person must also meet the more than 50% use test. The more than 50% test also applies to a home computer or any other property used for entertainment, recreation, or amusement, placed in service after June 18, 1984. If the test is not met, the credit is not allowed. The more than 50% test does not apply to a computer used in a business establishment or home office meeting the rules of ¶5.10.

¶24.20 • TARGETED JOBS CREDIT AND OTHER BUSINESS CREDITS

The targeted jobs credit, WIN credit carryforwards, the alcohol fuels credit, and the employee stock ownership plan credit are added to the investment credit for purposes of applying the overall general business credit limitation; *see* ¶24.30.

Targeted jobs credit. This credit is designed to encourage business employment of the hard-to-hire. The credit, computed on Form 5884, is based on a percentage of wages. An eligible employee is one who is a member of one of the following targeted groups: A vocational rehabilitation referral, an economically disadvantaged youth (age 18 through 24), an economically disadvantaged Vietnam-era veteran, an SSI recipient, a general assistance recipient, a youth (age 16 through 19) participating in a cooperative education program, or an economically disadvantaged ex-convict. Special rules apply to summer employment of certain disadvantaged youths. Wages paid to related employees do not qualify. Further, an employee must be certified by a designated local agency as qualifying as a member of a targeted group.

The credit is generally 50% of the first $6,000 of first-year wages of an eligible employee. See Form 5884 for details.

Work incentive expense (WIN) credit. This credit may not be claimed for wages paid or incurred in taxable years after December 31, 1981. However, unused credits may still be used up through carrybacks and carryovers under the general business credit and the credit carryback and carryover provisions of ¶24.75.

Alcohol fuels credit. On Form 6478, you compute the credit for sale or use of alcohol fuels and certain alcohol mixture. Different credits apply depending on the type of fuel.

Employee Stock Ownership Credit (ESOP). Corporations may claim a credit on Form 8007 for the value of employer securities transferred to an employee stock ownership plan.

Other business credits. A 25% tax credit is allowed for incremental increases in certain research and development. A credit is allowed for ½% of aggregate compensation under employee stock ownership plans. A credit is allowed for 50% of certain clinical testing of so-called orphan drugs. These credits are not discussed further in this book. The federal gasoline and oil tax credit is discussed in ¶24.82.

¶24.30 • GENERAL BUSINESS CREDIT

Form 3800 is used to figure the general business credit when you claim two or more of the following credits: investment credit, targeted jobs credit (or WIN credit carryovers), alcohol fuel credit and employer stock ownership credit. Form 3800 must be attached to your return.

Each credit is first computed separately and then listed on Form 3800. The combined credit is allowed in full if your income tax liability is $25,000 or less. If liability exceeds $25,000, the maximum credit is $25,000 plus 75% of your tax liability over $25,000. The allowable credit is considered your 1986 general business credit and entered on Form 1040. If the limitation bars a portion of the credit, credit carrybacks and carryforwards are allowed (see below).

For purposes of the limitation, tax liability is generally the income tax liability shown on your return less personal tax credits (dependent care credit, credit for elderly and disabled and political contributions credit) and the foreign tax credit. Do not count self-employment tax as income tax liability for purposes of the limitation. Further, disregard the penalty taxes for premature distributions from IRAs, Keogh or company retirement plans, and annuity contracts.

Carryback and carryforward of unused credits. If your full 1986 general business credit may not be claimed because of the $25,000/75% tax liability limitation, you may carry back the excess three years, starting with the earliest year. After the carryback, any remaining credit may be carried forward 15 years until used up. The carrybacks and carryforwards are listed on Form 3800.

If in 1985 you have carryforwards from more than one type of unused credit (investment credit, jobs credit and WIN credit carryovers, alcohol fuel credit and ESOP credit) you report the total carryforward on Form 3800. You do not have to file Form 3800 if you only have one type of carryforward and in 1986 you claim only one type of credit. In that case, you file only the form used to compute the particular credit.

Earned Income Credit for Low Income Householders

A special tax credit for low income workers with families may provide a refund or subsidy of up to $550 in 1986. An "earned income credit" is available only to low income workers who have dependent children and maintain a household.

The credit is designed to encourage low income wage earners to file income tax returns. The credit is a form of negative income tax. Even if no tax withholding has been taken from your wages and you do not have to file a return because you do not meet the gross income filing requirements, you may receive a payment from the federal government. If you have a tax liability, the credit will be first applied against your tax liability. Any excess credit is refunded to you. Alternatively, you may elect to have your credit figured into your withholding to receive advanced payment of the credit throughout the year.

The credit is based only on "earned income," wages, salaries and other employee compensation, plus earnings from self-employment. For 1986, the maximum credit is $550 or 11% of your first $5,000 of earned income. If you have income over $5,000, the credit is reduced by 12⅔% for the excess over $6,500. Thus, the credit is eliminated when your income reaches $11,000. You do not figure the credit; you find your credit in special tables included in the Government's instructions to the 1986 tax forms.

The credit will affect benefits under federal assistance programs.

¶24.50 • ARE YOU ELIGIBLE FOR THE CREDIT?
You are eligible if you are:

(1) Married and entitled to a dependency exemption for a child;
(2) A surviving spouse; or
(3) Head of household (an unmarried child in your household need not be your dependent, but a married child must be your dependent).

A special rule applies if you are divorced or legally separated, separated under a written agreement, or you live apart from your spouse for the last six months of 1986 and you have custody of your child during a greater portion of the year than the other parent. You may claim the credit even though you waive the dependency exemption for the child or you may not claim the exemption under a pre-1985 divorce or separation agreement. For this rule to apply, the child must be in your custody, or the custody of you and the other parent for more than half of 1986.

You are not eligible if you are entitled to exclude tax-free income from sources outside the United States or within the possessions of the United States (see ¶36.00).

Under the household test, you must provide over half of the cost of maintaining a household that is your principal place of abode in the United States. You may qualify whether you are

married or single. A single person is considered to be maintaining a household if he provides over half of the cost of maintaining the household. A married person is considered to be maintaining a household if both spouses together furnish over one-half of the cost of maintaining the household. The cost of maintaining a household includes such costs as property taxes, mortgage interest, rent, utility charges, upkeep and repairs, property insurance, and food.

Household costs do not include costs of clothing, education, medical treatment, vacations, life insurance, mortgage principal, and permanent improvements to the premises.

Welfare payments under a state Aid to Families with Dependent Children (AFDC) program for which the recipient is accountable to the state for spending payments for the well-being of the children are treated as not furnished by the recipient. To the extent that AFDC payments are used for household costs, they are counted in the total cost of maintaining the household.

If you maintain a household for a foster child, the child must reside with you for the entire year. In the case of an adopted child or stepchild, your home must be the child's principal place of abode only during the portion of the year the child became your child.

A married person must file a joint return to claim the credit. However, a married individual who is treated as not married may claim the credit as a single person who maintains a household and claims a child as a dependent.

¶24.51 • WHAT IS EARNED INCOME?
Earned income includes all wages, salaries, tips, and other compensation, plus net earnings from self-employment and pro rata share of partnership income. Net self-employment income of less than $400 qualifies as earned income even though not subject to the self-employment tax. Losses from self-employment reduce earned income. Where there is a net loss from self-employment but you elect to have $1,600 deemed as net earnings from self-employment on Schedule SE, the $1,600 is treated as earned income.

Disability payments, a parsonage allowance, and the value of meals and lodging excluded from gross income qualify as earned income. The IRS has ruled that strike benefits paid by a union to members who may or may not perform strike-related duties is treated as earned income.

Earned income is computed without regard to community property laws. Therefore, you may claim a credit based on the full amount of your own earnings, even though, under community property laws, half of the earnings is treated as gross income of your spouse.

What is not earned income. Pensions and annuity payments are not earned income for purposes of this credit. Income received by nonresident aliens not connected with a U.S. trade or business is not earned income. Interest, dividends, income from an estate or trust, and capital gains are not earned income. Rents will generally not qualify as earned income, except where you render services to tenants or materially help in the production of farm crops grown on rented land. Unemployment benefits and Workmen's Compensation are not earned income.

¶24.52 • HOW TO FIGURE THE CREDIT

The earned income tax credit for 1986 is 11% of the first $5,000 of earned income. Thus, the maximum credit is $550.

Example—

You earned $3,000. Your earned income tax credit is $330 ($3,000 × 11%).

Reduction of credit. The maximum credit must be reduced (but not below zero) by an amount equal to 12⅚% of adjusted gross income which exceeds $6,500 ($1.222 for every $10 over $6,500). If earned income exceeds adjusted gross income, the 12⅚% reduction is based on the larger amount of earned income. Generally the reduction will be based on adjusted gross income if you have income from sources other than wages or self-employment such as interest or dividends. The reduction will be based on earned income if you have incurred losses deductible from gross income, tax-free disability benefits, moving expenses and travel expenses. *See* ¶13.04 which lists deductions to find adjusted gross income.

Special tables provided by the Government list the credit and reduction adjustments. They are not reproduced in this book.

¶24.53 • ADVANCE PAYMENT OF THE CREDIT

If you believe you are entitled to an earned income credit, you may file a certificate, Form W-5, with your employer to have a portion of the credit added to your paycheck throughout the year.

If you receive any advance payments, you must file an income tax return, even though you owe no tax. If you receive payments in excess of the amount you are entitled to, as figured at the end of the year, you are liable for the excess. But if you receive less than the amount you are entitled to, you claim the balance on the tax return.

Other Tax Credits

¶24.60 • CREDIT FOR CONTRIBUTIONS TO POLITICAL CAMPAIGNS IN 1986

You may claim a tax credit on your 1986 return for contributions to a political campaign, political party, or a political newsletter fund. The credit is one-half of all your political contributions during the year up to $100 on a joint return, $50 on a single return. Only monetary contributions qualify.

Donations to committee or candidate. Your contribution may be to a candidate for nomination or election to a public office, a campaign committee, or a national, state, or local committee of a national political party. A candidate remains a candidate until enough money has been raised to pay debts incurred in a previous campaign for public office.

Contributions to permanent campaign committees, such as the Congressional campaign committees, will not be disqualified, although they are organized for the purpose of influencing future as well as present candidacies. However, contributions to a permanent campaign committee will be eligible for a credit only if the committee uses the contributions for announced candidates. Where a candidate runs for an office other than the one for which the contribution was made, the entire activity will be treated as one.

You may claim a credit for contributions to a fund or division of a labor union or business league which operates exclusively to further the nomination or election of individual candidates for public office, provided the fund or division is, in fact, operated separately.

Purpose of contributions. Your contribution must be used to further the nomination or election of a candidate for public office. To claim the credit in 1986 for your contributions during 1986, the candidate must publicly announce his candidacy on or before December 31, 1987.

If you buy a ticket to a political dinner or other political function, you may claim a credit for the cost only if the function is "clearly in the context of a campaign" for a candidate and the affair is primarily devoted to political speeches or discussions. If the primary purpose of the affair is a meal and entertainment, and political speeches or discussions are merely incidental, only the excess of the amount paid for the ticket over the fair market value of the meal and entertainment qualifies as a political contribution. If the ticket is paid for but refused, its full cost is a political contribution. If you keep the ticket but do not attend, your credit is subject to the same test applied to a person who does attend.

Similarly, if you buy a ticket in a raffle used to raise funds for a political candidate, no part of the cost of the ticket qualifies for a credit. However, if you refuse to accept the ticket, its cost qualifies as a credit.

Political check-off. On your return each year, you may instruct the Treasury to turn over $1 ($2 on a joint return) of your tax to the Presidential election fund. This is in addition to the credit discussed above. The check-off does not affect your tax liability in any way.

¶24.82 • FEDERAL GASOLINE AND FUEL TAX CREDIT

For a qualified business use, a refundable credit of 9¢ per gallon of gasoline or special motor fuel may be claimed for fuel used in nonhighway vehicles (other than motorboats); 15¢ per gallon for diesel fuel. The 9¢ and 15¢ credits also apply for a qualified farm use. Examples of nonhighway vehicles include generators, compressors, forklift trucks, and bulldozers. A credit may also be claimed for aviation fuel used for farming or commercial aviation.

You must claim the credit on a timely filed income tax return, including extensions. You compute the credit on Form 4136, which you attach to Form 1040. If you do not claim the credit on your tax return, you may do so on a timely-filed refund claim or amended return for that year. If the credit exceeds $1,000 during any of the first three quarters of the taxable year, you may file a refund claim on a quarterly basis. A quarterly refund claim must be filed on Form 843 on or before the last day of the quarter following the quarter for which the refund is claimed.

For further explanation, *see* Publication 378; farmers *see* Publication 225.

If the cost of the gasoline and special fuel is deducted as a business expense, the credit claimed on these items is reported as income. If you use the cash basis method of reporting, you report the credit as income in the year in which you file a tax return on which the credit is claimed. If you are on the accrual basis, you report the credit in the year the fuel is used.

¶24.83 • CREDIT FOR DIESEL VEHICLE FUEL

If in 1986, you bought a diesel-powered car or truck weighing 10,000 pounds or less, you may claim a one-time credit for the diesel fuel tax. You must be the original purchaser, that is, the first purchaser for use other than resale. The credit for an auto is $102; for a truck or van, $198. The credit is claimed on Form 4136.

For depreciation and investment credit purposes, basis is reduced by the credit. Thus, if a new diesel-powered car is purchased, basis is reduced by the $102 credit to $15,898.

¶24.86 • CREDIT FOR TAX PAID BY MUTUAL FUND ON UNDISTRIBUTED GAINS

A mutual fund that does not distribute all of its capital gains earned during the year pays a tax on the undistributed gain. The law treats this tax payment as made on your behalf. The company will notify you of the amount of tax paid which is the amount of your credit.

To claim a tax credit, you do the following:

1. Report on Schedule D as 1986 long-term capital gain your share of the undistributed capital gain. Your company sends you Form 2439 which lists your share of the undistributed gain and the amount of tax paid on it.

2. You enter your share of the tax the company paid on this gain on Form 1040 on the line reading "Credit from a Regulated Investment Company (attach Form 2439)." Attach Copy B of Form 2439 to your return to support your tax credit.

3. Increase the basis of your stock by the difference between the undistributed capital gain and the amount of tax paid by the mutual fund, as reported on Form 2439.

¶24.87 • INTEREST ON QUALIFIED HOME MORTGAGE CERTIFICATES

Homebuyers who qualify under special state and local programs may obtain "mortgage credit certificates" to finance the purchase of a principal residence or to borrow funds for certain home improvements. Under the program, a tax credit for interest paid on the mortgage may be claimed. The tax credit equals the interest paid multiplied by the certificate rate set by the governmental authority. The credit rate must be at least 10%, and if it exceeds 20%, the maximum annual credit is $2,000. Interest not qualifying for the credit may be deducted as an itemized deduction.

The credit is computed on Form 8396, which must be attached to Form 1040.

Example—

You pay $5,000 interest on a mortgage issued under a qualifying mortgage credit certificate. Under its terms, you are allowed a tax credit of $750. You may claim the balance of interest or $4,250 ($5,000 − $750) as an itemized deduction.

If the allowable credit exceeds tax liability, a three-year carryover is allowed.

Generally, a qualifying principal residence may not cost more than 110% of the average area purchase price; 120% in certain targeted areas.

¶24.90 • RESIDENTIAL ENERGY CREDIT EXPIRED

You may no longer claim a credit for the cost of home insulation or other energy savings expenditures, such as storm windows or solar energy systems. The residential energy credits expired at the end of 1985.

If you claimed an energy credit before 1986 that exceeded your tax liability for that year reduced by the credit for dependent care costs, the credit for the elderly and disabled, and the credit for political contributions, the excess credit may be carried forward and claimed in 1986.

¶25.00

Tax Withholdings

¶25.01 • WHEN INCOME TAXES ARE WITHHELD ON WAGES

The amount of income tax withheld for your wage bracket depends on your marital status and the number of exemptions you claim. Exemptions for withholding correspond with the exemptions allowed on your tax return (see ¶1.50). You file a withholding certificate, Form W-4, with your employer, indicating your status and exemptions. Without the certificate, your employer must withhold tax as if you are a single person with no exemptions.

If you do not expect withholdings to meet your final tax liability, ask your employer to withhold a greater amount of tax (see ¶25.02). On the other hand, if the withholding rate applied to your wages results in overwithholding, you may claim extra withholding allowances to reduce withholding during the year (see ¶25.04 and ¶25.041).

INCOME TAXES ARE WITHHELD ON:

Payments to employees as salaries, wages, fees, bonuses, commissions, pensions, retirement pay, vacation allowances, dismissal pay, etc. (whether paid in cash or goods). See ¶25.09 for avoiding withholding on pensions and annuities.

Pay to members of the U.S. Armed Forces.

Prize awarded to a salesman in a contest run by his employer.

Retroactive pay and overtime under Fair Labor Standards Act.

Taxable supplemental unemployment compensation benefits.

Back pay under National Labor Relations Board order and settlements under the Civil Rights Act of 1964 for job applicants refused employment on discriminatory grounds.

Payments to Canadians and Mexicans who cross borders frequently and who are not working in transportation service.

INCOME TAXES ARE NOT WITHHELD ON:

Payments to domestic servants, agricultural workers, college domestics, ministers of the gospel (except chaplains in the Armed Forces), casual workers, nonresident aliens, public officials who receive fees directly from the public—notaries public, jurors, witnesses, precinct workers, etc. (but see voluntary withholding agreements, ¶25.02).

Pay for newspaper home delivery by children under age 18.

Advances for traveling expenses if kept separate from wages.

Value of tax-free board and lodging furnished by an employer.

Fringe benefits not subject to tax.

Reimbursements for deductible moving expenses or medical care benefits under a self-insured medical reimbursement plan.

Tuition, fees, and supplies paid by employer under ¶2.041.

Death benefit payments to beneficiary of employee; wages due but unpaid at employee's death and paid to estate or beneficiary.

Pay for U.S. citizen working abroad or in U.S. possessions to the extent that the pay is tax free (see ¶36.00 for rules).

Lump-sum settlement of employment contract.

Employer contributions to SEPs (see ¶7.22).

Withholding does not apply to earnings of self-employed persons. They pay their income taxes currently through estimated tax.

Form W-2. By the end of January, your employer must give you duplicate copies of Form W-2, which is a record of your pay and the withheld income and Social Security taxes. If you leave your job during the year, you may ask your employer for a W-2 by making a written request within 30 days of leaving the job.

If you have worked for more than one employer during the year, attach all Copies B of Form W-2 to your return. Check to see that a total of no more than $3,003 of Social Security (FICA) taxes was withheld. If too much was withheld, claim the excess as a credit on the line on your return "Excess F.I.C.A. tax withheld."

Employees covered by the Railroad Retirement Tax Act receive Form W-2 (RR) which lists total wages paid and withholdings of income and Railroad Retirement taxes.

If your employer makes a withholding error, you do not have to wait until filing your return to get a refund; request the refund directly from your employer.

¶25.02 • INCREASING WITHHOLDING ON YOUR PAY

For withholding tax purposes, you do not have to claim all your exemptions. This will increase the amount withheld and help reduce the final tax payment on filing your tax return. It may also relieve you of making quarterly estimated tax payments, provided the withholdings are sufficient to meet your estimated tax liability. A waiver of exemptions for withholding taxes does not prevent you from claiming the "waived" exemptions on your final tax return. The waiver is merely a bookkeeping aid to your company's payroll department. If you find that even a waiver of exemptions does not cover all of the tax you want withheld, you may ask your employer to withhold additional amounts. See the instructions to Form W-4 for details.

A domestic or farm worker whose pay is not generally subject to withholding may make a withholding agreement. You may ask your employer to withhold taxes on pay not ordinarily subject to withholding. Your written request should include your name, address, and Social Security number and your employer's name and address. You also give your employer a Form W-4. The employer must agree to this arrangement. Either of you may end the agreement by written notice.

¶25.03 • AVOIDING WITHHOLDING ON YOUR PAY

If you had no income tax liability in 1986 and expect none for 1987, you may be exempt from income tax withholdings on your 1987 wages. By claiming this special exemption, students working for the summer, retired persons, and other part-time workers do not have to wait for a refund of withheld taxes they do not owe. *See* ¶1.00 for income levels at which you would owe no tax.

To claim exemption, you file withholding exemption certificate, Form W-4, with your employer. The form may be obtained from an IRS district office or from your employer. If you will file a joint return for 1987, do not file an exemption on Form W-4 if the joint return will show a tax.

Social Security taxes are withheld, even though you are exempt from income tax withholding.

¶25.04 • WITHHOLDING ALLOWANCES FOR TAX REDUCTION ITEMS

Too much may be withheld from your pay if you have tax reduction items. The overpayment will be refunded when you file your return, but you lose the use of your money during the year. By filing Form W-4 with your employer, you may avoid this and reduce withholding taxes by claiming additional withholding allowances based on: (1) estimated itemized deductions, (2) IRA contribution deductions, (3) moving expense deduction, (4) alimony deduction, (5) tax credits.

Working couples filing jointly figure withholding allowances on combined wage income and may allocate them between employers. On separate returns, the allowances must be figured separately.

If you work for two or more employers at the same time, you may claim withholding allowances from only one employer.

File a new Form W-4 each year for withholding allowances based on itemized deductions and credits. Further, you may have to file a new Form W-4 if your spouse starts work during the year and you have been claiming additional withholding allowances.

A civil penalty of $500 may be imposed if, for purposes of claiming tax withholding allowances, you overstate your itemized deductions and credits or understate your wages without a reasonable basis. There is also a criminal penalty of $1,000 plus a jail sentence for willfully supplying false information.

¶25.041 • SPECIAL WITHHOLDING ALLOWANCE

A special withholding allowance designed to eliminate overwithholding may be claimed on Form W-4 by certain employees. The withholding allowance, like an exemption, frees wage income from withholding. An unmarried person may claim this special withholding allowance, provided he is not working for more than one employer. A married person may claim the allowance, provided he also works for only one employer and his spouse does not work. This special allowance is only for withholding purposes. You may not claim it on your tax return.

¶25.05 • WHEN TO FILE NEW WITHHOLDING EXEMPTION CERTIFICATE, FORM W-4

You may file a new certificate any time the number of your exemptions increases. For example: A child is born or adopted; you marry; you or your spouse will be 65 during the year.

Your employer may make the new certificate effective with the next payment of wages. However, he may by law postpone the new withholding rate until the payment of wages on or after a date called the first status determination date. This may be January 1, May 1, July 1, or October 1, as the case may be, provided there is at least a 30-day interval between the date of the new certificate and the determination date.

> You do not have to wait until your 65th birthday to file a new withholding certificate to reduce withholding because of your age. If you will be 65 by the end of the year, you are allowed to reduce your withholdings for that entire year.

You must file a new certificate within 10 days if the number of exemptions previously claimed by you decreases because: You divorce or legally separate; you stop supporting a dependent; a dependent for whom you claimed an exemption will receive $1,040 or more income (except your child who is a student or under 19 years of age).

The death of a spouse or a dependent in a current year does not affect your withholding until the next year, but requires the filing of a new certificate, if possible, by December 1. However, a widow or widower entitled to joint return rates as a surviving spouse (*see* ¶1.00) need not file a new withholding certificate.

When you file on or before December 1, your employer must reduce your withholding as of January 1 of the next year.

¶25.06 • WHEN AND HOW TIPS ARE SUBJECT TO INCOME TAX AND FICA WITHHOLDINGS

Tips are subject to income tax and FICA (Social Security) withholding. If you receive cash tips amounting to $20 or more in a month, you must report the total amount of tips received during the month to your employer on Form 4070 (or a similar written report). You make the report on or before the 10th day after the end of the month in which the tips are received. (If the 10th day is a Saturday, Sunday, or legal holiday, you report by the next day that is not a Saturday, Sunday, or legal holiday.) For example, tips amounting to $20 or more and received during January are reported by February 10. Your employer may require more frequent reporting.

You include cash tips paid to you on your own behalf. If you "split" or share tips with others, you include in your report only your share. You do not include tips received in the form of merchandise or your share of service charges turned over to you by your employer.

Your employer withholds the Social Security and income tax due on the tips from your wages or from funds you give him for withholding purposes. If he cannot collect the taxes due on the tips, either from your wages or from voluntary contributions, by the 10th day after the end of the month in which tips are reported, you have to pay the tax when you file your income tax return.

Your employer is required to pay Social Security taxes on the wages he pays you, but not on the tips.

Where wages are insufficient to meet all of the withholding liability, the wages are applied first to Social Security tax.

If your employer is unable to collect enough money from your wages during the year to cover the Social Security tax on the tips reported to him, the uncollected amount is shown on your W-2 Form as "Uncollected Employee Tax on Tips." You compute your Social Security tax on unreported tips on Form 4137. You must file Form 1040 and include the amount of unreported tips from Form 4137 as wage income on Form 1040 and enter any uncollected employee Social Security tax on tips as shown on your W-2. Attach Form 4137 to your Form 1040.

Failure to report tip income of $20 or more received during the month to your employer may subject you to a penalty of 50% of the tax due on the unreported tips, unless your failure was due to reasonable cause rather than to willful neglect.

Tips of less than $20 per month are taxable, but are not subject to withholding.

You are considered to have income from tips when you make your report to your employer. However, if you do not report your tips to your employer, you are considered to have tip income when you receive the tips. For example, if you received tips of $75 during December 1986 and reported the tips to your employer on January 6, 1987; the tips are considered paid to you in January 1987 and the $75 is included in your 1987 income tax return. On the other hand, if your tips during December 1986 totaled only $18, you are not required to report the amount to your employer. The tips are considered paid to you in 1986 and must be included in your 1986 income tax return.

Tip allocation reporting. To help the IRS audit the reporting of tip income, restaurants employing at least 10 people must make a special report of income and allocate tips based on gross receipts. For purposes of the allocation, the law assumes tip income of at least 8%. If you voluntarily report tips equal to your allocable share of 8% of the restaurant's gross receipts, no allocation will be made to you. However, if the total tips reported by all employees is less than 8% of gross receipts and you do not report your share of the 8%, your employer must make an allocation based on the difference between the amount you reported and your share of the 8% amount. The allocated amount is shown on W-2. However, taxes are not withheld on the allocated amount. Taxes are withheld only on amounts actually reported by employees. An employer or majority of employees may ask the IRS to apply a tip percentage of less than 6%, but no lower than 2%.

¶25.07 • WITHHOLDING ON GAMBLING WINNINGS

Your winnings from gambling may be subject to withholding at the rate of 20%. Winnings subject to withholding include wagering proceeds exceeding: (1) $5,000 from a state-conducted lottery; (2) $1,000 from sweepstakes and wagering pools (whether or not state-conducted) and other lotteries. Wagering pools include all parimutuel betting pools and on- and off-track racing pools; (3) $1,000 from other wagering transactions, if the proceeds are at least 300 times as large as the amount wagered; and (4) gambling proceeds of $1,000 or more from a parimutuel pool on horse races, dog races, or jai alai, if the proceeds are at least 300 times as large as the amount wagered.

Treasury regulations require you to tell the payers of gambling winnings if you are also receiving winnings from identical wagers; winnings from identical wagers must be added together to determine if withholding is required.

Winnings from bingo, keno, and slot machines, however, are not subject to withholding.

Wagering proceeds means winnings less the amount of the wager.

¶25.08 • FICA WITHHOLDINGS

FICA (Federal Insurance Contributions Act) withholdings are employee contributions for Social Security coverage. Your employer is liable for the tax if he fails to make proper withholdings. The amount withheld is figured on your wages and is not affected by your marital status or number of exemptions. As long as you have wages, you pay FICA, even though you may be over 65 or 72 and are collecting Social Security.

For 1986, the FICA withholding rate was 7.15% on wages up to $42,000. The maximum employee contribution was $3,003. If more than this amount was withheld from your wages, *see* ¶25.01. For the 1987 rate and base, *see* the Supplement.

Subject to FICA tax are your regular salary, bonuses, commissions, vacation pay, Christmas bonuses, lump-sum settlements of wage disputes, and contributions to cash or deferred pay plans. Not subject to tax are the value of tax-free meals and lodgings under ¶2.01, reimbursements for travel or entertainment expenses or for moving expenses, educational assistance under ¶2.041, and prepaid legal services under ¶2.02. The first six months of sick pay are subject to FICA withholding; thereafter, sick pay is generally not subject to FICA tax. *See* Treasury regulations for further details on FICA tax on sick pay.

¶25.09 • WITHHOLDING ON PENSIONS AND ANNUITIES

Generally, withholding on pensions, IRA distributions, and annuity payments is automatic unless an election to avoid withholding is made either on Form W-4P or a substitute form furnished by the payor.

No withholding is required if a distribution consists solely of your company's securities and cash of $200 or less in lieu of fractional shares.

Withholdings on periodic payments are figured according to wage withholding tables as if you were married and claiming three withholding exemptions. No tax is withheld from pension or annuity payments of $450 a month or less ($5,400 annually).

Withholding allowances may be claimed for estimated itemized deductions, alimony payments, business losses, and tax credits.

You may also request the payor to withhold additional amounts of tax.

Nonperiodic payments are subject to withholding at a flat 10% rate unless the payment is considered a total distribution or you elect to avoid withholding on Form W-4P (or substitute form). IRA distributions that are payable upon demand are considered nonperiodic and thus subject to the 10% withholding rule.

The flat 10% rate does not apply to lump-sum distributions from a qualified pension or profit-sharing plan, stock bonus, or annuity plan. The rate on such distributions approximates the tax that would be due under the averaging method, whether or not you are eligible to elect averaging.

¶25.10 • BACKUP WITHHOLDING

Backup withholding is designed primarily to pressure taxpayers to report interest and dividend income. You may be subject to backup withholding if you do not give your taxpayer identification number to parties paying you interest or dividend income or if you give an incorrect number. The backup withholding rate is 20%. Each failure to give your number to a payer may also be subject to a $50 penalty. Failure to report interest and dividends is also subject to a 5% penalty based on the deficiency attributed to the failure to report such income.

¶ 26.00
Estimated Tax Payments

Income taxes are collected on a pay-as-you-go basis through withholding on wages and pensions as well as estimated tax payments on other income. Where all or most of your income is from wages, pensions, and annuities, you will generally not have to pay estimated tax because your estimated tax liability has been satisfied by withholding. But do not assume you are not required to pay simply because taxes have been withheld from your wages. Always check your estimated tax liability. Withholding may not cover your tax; the withholding tax rate may be below your actual tax rate when considering other income such as interest, dividends, business income and capital gains.

If you are self-employed, include the self-employment tax. Your estimate may be based on projected income averaging if you believe you will qualify. Alternative minimum tax liability is also subject to the estimated tax rules.

Failure to pay estimated tax may be subject to a penalty, *see* ¶26.02. Make your estimated tax payment accompanied by the appropriate 1040ES voucher.

You do not have to make estimated tax payments if your estimated tax is less than $500.

Farmers file only one declaration by January 15 of the following year. For example, the 1986 declaration must be filed by January 15, 1987. Or farmers may file a final return by March 2, 1987 instead of making a declaration. To qualify under these rules, a farmer must have two-thirds of his gross income from farming.

Fishermen who expect to receive at least two-thirds of their gross income from fishing pay estimated taxes as farmers do.

Nonresident aliens do not pay estimated tax unless they are residents of Mexico or Canada who enter the United States frequently, but not as employees of a transportation company, *or* they are residents of Puerto Rico during the entire taxable year.

The four installment dates for 1987 estimated tax are April 15, 1987, June 15, 1987, September 15, 1987, and January 15, 1988.

¶26.01 • WHO MUST PAY ESTIMATED TAX?

Estimate your income (including income subject to withholding), deductions, and exemptions for 1987 and compute the tax using 1987 tax rates, which may be found in the Supplement to this book. Include in your estimate self-employment tax and alternative minimum tax, if any. If you receive Social Security benefits that may be taxable under the rules of ¶34.11, estimate the taxable portion as part of your projected income. Reduce the estimated tax by tax credits and withholdings from wages, pensions, and annuities.

If your estimated tax liability is $500 or more, you must pay the balance in installments unless withholdings from income will cover your estimated 1987 liability or 100% of your 1986 liability. *See* ¶26.03.

If your estimate changes during the year, you may revise it, *see* ¶26.06.

You may use the worksheet included in Form 1040-ES to figure your estimated tax liability.

If you are due a refund when you file your 1986 return, you may credit the refund to your 1987 estimated tax by making an election on your 1986 return. The IRS will credit the refund to the April installment of 1987 estimated tax unless you attach a statement to your return instructing the IRS to apply the refund to later installments.

Members of a partnership declare their estimated taxes in their **individual capacities. Each partner's estimate must include his share of the partnership income, whether actually paid to him or not.**

The estimated tax may be paid in full with your estimated tax voucher or in four equal installments. This estimate, at your election, may be revised up or down with corresponding changes in your income and exemptions during the year.
Example—
You estimate a tax of $6,000 on April 15, 1987 for the year 1987. An installment of $1,500 is paid at that time. On June 15, 1987, you amend your estimate showing a tax of $3,000 instead of $6,000. Your next three installments will each be $500.

¶26.02 • PENALTY FOR UNDERESTIMATES—TAX YEARS BEFORE 1987

You are not subject to a penalty if your estimated tax payments for 1986, including withholdings, equal at least 80% of the tax shown on your final return (66⅔% if you are a farmer). Alternatively, if your estimated payments, including withholdings, equal at least 100% of the prior year's final tax, no penalty is imposed even though this is less than 80% of the 1986 liability. The 100% exception applies only if you filed a return for 1985 covering a full 12 months. These are the two basic exceptions to the penalty for underestimating. If your income fluctuates throughout the year, you may be able to avoid a penalty based on an annualized income exception. See ¶26.03 for details.

A penalty is charged if you underpay any installment of estimated tax. In 1986, the penalty rate was 10% for the first half of the year; 9% for the second half. The rate for the first half of 1987 is listed in the Supplement to this book.

Withholding payments are treated as if they were payments of estimated tax. They reduce the amount of your underestimate. In applying them, the total withholdings of the year are divided equally to each quarterly installment date unless you want to show the actual payment dates. Then they are applied in the quarter they are actually withheld.

The penalty is figured separately for each installment date. This means that if after taking into account withholdings, you underpay an early installment, you may owe a penalty for that period even though you overpay later installments to make up the difference. The penalty for each period runs until the amount is paid or until the filing date for the final tax return, whichever is earlier.

Figuring the penalty for 1986. Form 2210 is used to determine any penalty. You do not have to fill out Form 2210 or pay any penalty if for 1986 you qualify for the exceptions at ¶26.03.

On Form 2210, the penalty is based on the *lower* of 80% of the 1986 tax or 100% of the 1985 tax (if your return covered 12 months). One fourth of the lower amount is the payment required for each installment period. That is, the penalty for *each* 1986 installment quarter is applied to the difference between your payments for the quarter, if any, and the *lower* of (1) 20% of the 1986 tax, or (2) 25% of the 1985 tax (if your return covered 12 months). A special computation applies if you qualify for the annualized income exception.

Withholdings are considered paid in four equal installments unless you elect otherwise.

If you underpaid for any quarter, the amount of the underpayment reduces the payment made in the following quarter. That is, an underpayment of one quarter is carried over to succeeding quarters. If you overpaid in any quarter, the excess carries over to the next quarter. The excess cannot be used to make up an underpayment of the prior quarter. These rules do not apply to withholdings that are allocated equally over the year.

¶26.03 • AVOIDING THE PENALTY FOR 1987

Exception 1. You avoid any penalty for 1987 if your estimated payments, including withholdings, equal at least 90% of the tax shown on your 1987 return and at least 22.5% of your 1987 tax (25% × 90%) is paid by each installment date. *See* the tax legislation discussion in the front of the book for any changes to this percentage.

Exception 2. You avoid the penalty and guesswork by figuring and paying as your 1987 estimated tax an amount that equals or exceeds the tax shown on your 1986 tax return. Pay 25% of your 1986 tax for each installment period. Include 1986 self-employment tax if you are self-employed. To come within this exception, you must have filed a 1986 return covering a period of 12 months.

Exception 3. You may avoid the penalty on an estimated tax installment based on income which was earned in the months ending before the due date of the installment and which was annualized for purposes of computing the estimated tax. This exception may apply if you do not earn income evenly throughout the year, such as where you operate a seasonal business. Form 2210 includes a worksheet for figuring the annualized income exception.

Exception 4. No penalty will be imposed for 1987 if you did not have a 1986 liability, your 1986 taxable year included 12 months, and you were a citizen or resident of the United States throughout 1986.

Exception 5. No penalty is imposed if your estimated tax liability, after taking into account withholdings, is less than $500.

Form 2210. File Form 2210 with your tax return to show that your underestimate of tax liability is within one of the first three exceptions. You do not have to file Form 2210 if you qualify under Exception 4 or 5. If your underestimate is not within one of the exceptions and is subject to a penalty, you may use Form 2210 to figure the penalty. If you owe a penalty and attach Form 2210 to your return, the penalty decreases any refund due or increases any tax balance due. No penalty attaches for failure to file Form 2210.

Waiver of penalty for hardship, retirement or disability. The IRS may waive the penalty if you can show you failed to pay the estimated tax because of casualty, disaster, or other unusual circumstances. The IRS may also waive a penalty for a 1986 underpayment if in 1986 or 1985 you retired after reaching age 62 or became disabled and you failed to make a payment due to reasonable cause and not due to willful neglect. This rule would apply to a 1987 underpayment if you became disabled or retired (after age 62) in 1986 or 1987. To apply for the waiver, attach an explanation on Form 2210.

Withholdings from pay. Tax withheld from your pay may help you avoid the penalty for underpayment of estimated tax. You have a choice in allocating your withholdings over the year: (1) You may treat your entire year's withholdings as having been withheld in equal amounts for each quarter; or (2) you may allocate to each quarter the actual withholdings that were taken out of your pay for that quarter. If, toward the end of the year, you find that you have underestimated for an earlier quarter, ask your employer to withhold an extra amount which may be allocated equally over the four quarters. This way you may eliminate the underestimate for the earlier quarters.

¶26.04 • FINAL PAYMENT

That you paid an estimated tax for 1986 does not excuse you from filing a tax return on or before April 15, 1987. You must file a final return and pay the difference between the total of your withholding plus your estimated tax payments and your final tax. If the tax is less than your withholdings and payments, you get a refund or credit on the 1987 estimated tax. You may also split up the amount due you. You may take part of the overpayment

as a refund. The other part may be credited to your next year's estimate. You may get interest only on the part refunded.

Check your mathematics before you apply an overpayment as a credit on your next year's estimate. If you apply too much— even through an unintentional mathematical error—you must pay interest if there is a tax deficiency for that year.

¶26.05 • IF YOU USE A FISCAL YEAR

A fiscal year is any year other than the calendar year. If you file using a fiscal year, your first estimate installment is due on or before the 15th day of the fourth month of your fiscal year. Amendments may be made on the 15th day of the sixth and ninth months of your year with the final amendment on the 15th day of the first month of your next fiscal year. Your installments are also due then.

¶26.06 • AMENDING YOUR ESTIMATE

During the year, income, expense, or exemption changes may require you to amend your estimated tax.

If you amend, you merely refigure your estimated tax. You enter the new estimated tax on the currently due voucher and sign the amended voucher. You adjust your payment schedule as explained in ¶26.01.

You do not have to file the January voucher providing you file your final return and pay in full the balance of tax due on or before January 31. For 1986, you do not have to file the January 15, 1987 voucher if you file a final return and pay the balance of tax by February 2, 1987.

If taxes paid in the previous installments total more than your revised estimate, you cannot obtain a refund at that time. You must wait until you file your final return showing that a refund is due.

WHEN TO AMEND 1987 ESTIMATES

If you want to make a change	You amend on
After April 1 and before June 2.	Voucher 2 by June 15, 1987
After June 1 and before September 2.	Voucher 3 by September 15, 1987
After September 1 and before January 1.	Voucher 4 by January 15, 1988

¶26.07 • TAX ESTIMATES BY HUSBAND AND WIFE

A married couple may pay joint or separate estimated taxes. The nature of the estimated tax does not control the kind of final return you file.

Where a joint estimated tax is paid but the final tax is reported on separate returns, the estimated tax may be treated as the estimate of either the husband or the wife, or divided between them in any proportion. If the couple does not agree, the estimated tax payments are apportioned on the basis of each spouse's tax liability as compared with their total liability.

If separate taxes are paid, overpayment by one spouse is not applied against an underpayment by the other when separate final returns are filed.

A joint estimated tax may be made by husband and wife only if they are both citizens or residents of the United States. Both must have the same taxable year. A joint estimate may not be made by a couple that is divorced or legally separated under a decree.

Responsibility for paying estimated tax rests upon each spouse individually. Each must pay if individually required by the rules.

If a joint estimated tax is made and one spouse dies, the estate does not continue to make installment payments. The surviving spouse is required to pay the remaining installments unless he or she amends. *See* ¶1.14. Amounts paid on the joint estimate may be divided as agreed upon by the spouse and the estate of the deceased. If they do not agree, an apportionment is based on the amount of each spouse's tax liability compared with the total liability.

¶27.00

Filing Refund Claims, Amended Returns, and Extensions

¶27.001 • FILING FOR A REFUND ON FORM 1040X

File a refund claim on Form 1040X if you have overpaid your tax because you failed to take allowable deductions or credits, overstated income, or want to take advantage of a retroactive change in the law. *See* sample Form 1040X on page 249.

File in time. The time limits discussed at ¶27.01 must be strictly observed; otherwise, a valid refund claim will be denied because of late filing.

If you file your 1986 return early and discover an error before April 15, 1987, you may file a corrected return before that date; a corrected return filed before its due date is treated as a regular return, not as an amended return. A corrected return filed after the due date of the return is treated as an amended return and acts as a refund claim.

> Before filing a refund claim for a prior year, carefully review the return of that year for accuracy. A refund claim may subject the return to an examination in which the IRS may find errors that reduce or completely eliminate the refund claim, or may even lead to the assessment of a deficiency.

Income tax overwithholding. You do not have to file a refund claim if you have overpaid your tax due to excessive withholding of taxes on your wages or salary, or if you have overestimated your estimated tax. You get a refund on these overpayments by filing your tax return requesting a refund for these amounts. You may not recover an overpayment of estimated tax until you file your final return.

If you are entitled to a refund due to the earned income credit for certain low income wage earners (¶24.50), you must file your tax return to get your refund, even though your income and filing status would not otherwise require that a return be filed.

Married persons. If a joint return was filed for a year in which a refund is due, both spouses are entitled to recover jointly and both must file a joint refund claim. Where separate returns were filed, each spouse is a separate taxpayer and may not file a claim to recover a refund based on the other spouse's return, except if that spouse becomes fiduciary when one spouse becomes incompetent or dies. If you are divorced and incur a net operating loss or credit that may be carried back to a year in which you were married, you may file a refund claim with your signature alone and the refund check will be made out only to you.

¶27.01 • WHEN TO FILE A REFUND CLAIM

You may file a claim for refund within three years from the time your return was filed, or within two years from the time you paid your tax, whichever is later. A return filed before its due date is treated as having been filed on the due date.

Failure to file a timely refund claim is fatal, regardless of its merits. Even if you expect that your claim will have to be pursued in court, you must still file a timely refund claim.

The time for filing refund claims based on carrybacks of net operating losses or credits is figured with reference to the return (including extensions) for the year the loss or credit arose.

If you filed an agreement giving the IRS an extended period of time in which to assess a tax against you, you are allowed an additional period in which to file a claim for refund. The claim, up to certain amounts, may be filed through the extension period and for six months afterwards.

If you have failed to take a bad debt deduction or take a loss for worthless securities, you have seven years (instead of three years) in which to file a claim. Refunds based on items from federally registered partnerships may be filed within four years.

Armed Forces servicemen and veterans. In determining the time limits within which a refund claim may be filed, you disregard intervening periods of service in a combat zone, plus periods of continuous hospitalization outside the United States as a result of combat zone injury, and the next 180 days thereafter. You may also disregard a postponement period if you were missing in action (see ¶35.00). Servicemen and civilian government employees who were taxed on pay while in "missing" status also have additional time to file refund claims.

¶27.02 • HOW TO FILE FOR A REFUND

File your claim with the Internal Revenue Service center for the district or region where you filed your return in which the overpayment was made. It should be made on an amended return, Form 1040X, unless you are entitled to file a quick refund on Form 1045. If you made an overpayment of Social Security taxes and you are not required to file a return (see ¶1.00), you file your refund claim on Form 843.

> *What a refund claim must contain.* The most important part of a refund claim is a statement of the "reasons" for the refund. A general claim simply noting an overpayment, without supporting facts and grounds, is not sufficient. If a claim is denied by the IRS, it may become the basis of a court suit. If you have not stated all the grounds, you may not be allowed to argue them in court. The courts have limited taxpayers to the exact claim shown on the form. You must make a full claim showing all the:
>
> Facts that support the claim. If you need more space than is on the form, the statement and supporting exhibits must be on letter-sized sheets (8½ × 11).
> Grounds for the claim. If you are uncertain about the exact grounds, alternate and even inconsistent grounds may be given. For example: "The loss was incurred from an embezzlement; if not, from a bad debt."
>
> To protect against your understating the amount of your claim, you might preface the claim with this phrase: "The following or such greater amounts, as may be legally refunded."

¶27.03 • QUICK REFUND CLAIMS

Form 1045 may be used for filing refunds due to carrybacks from net operating losses, investment credit, and WIN credit. This form must be filed within 12 months after the loss year. The IRS must act on the claim within 90 days. Payment of quick refund claims is not a final settlement of your return; the IRS may still audit and then disallow the refund claim. This refund process may also be used for certain claim of right adjustments not discussed here. Note that the filing of a quick refund, if rejected, may not be the basis of a suit for refund; a regular refund claim must be filed.

File a separate claim for each year you claim a refund.

The IRS may withhold payment of a quick refund claim if it determines that you have invested in a tax shelter that has misrepresented tax benefits. *See* ¶28.03.

¶27.04 • INTEREST PAID ON REFUND CLAIMS

Interest is not paid on refunds made within 45 days of the day the tax was due (without regard to extensions of time). For example, you file your return on April 1, claiming an overpayment due to overwithholding on your wages. Interest does not begin to run until May 30, which is 45 days after April 15, the day the tax was due. If the overpayment is not refunded within 45 days, interest is paid from the date the tax was overpaid to a date 30 days or less preceding the date of the refund check.

The IRS does not have to pay interest on overpayments resulting from net operating loss carrybacks, net capital loss carrybacks, or carrybacks of investment credit or WIN credit if a refund is paid within 45 days of the filing of the refund claim.

If a refund claim based on a loss or credit carryback is filed and subsequently a quick refund claim is filed on Form 1045 for the same refund, the 45-day period starts to run on the date Form 1045 is filed.

Overpayments resulting in retroactive law changes are generally not entitled to interest as Congress usually puts such stipulation in the retroactive law change.

Interest rates applied to amounts outstanding as follows:

Amounts outstanding between—	Rate—
2/1/78–1/31/80	6%
2/1/80–1/31/82	12
2/1/82–12/31/82	20
1/1/83–6/30/83	16
7/1/83–12/31/84	11
1/1/85–6/30/85	13
7/1/85–12/31/85	11
1/1/86–6/30/86	10
7/1/86–12/31/86	9
1/1/87–6/30/87	*See* Supplement

¶27.05 • APPLY FOR EXTENSION IF YOU CANNOT FILE ON TIME

If you cannot file your return on time, apply before the due date to the Internal Revenue Service office with which you file your return for an extension of time to file.

Automatic extension. You may get an extension without waiting for the IRS to act on your request. You receive an automatic four-month extension if you file Form 4868 by April 15 and pay the full amount of tax you estimate that you owe. If you were abroad on April 15 so that your return is not due until June 15, you may receive an additional two-month extension if you file Form 4868 and pay the taxes due by June 15.

Form 4868 must be filed by the date on which the return would otherwise be due. This extension of time for filing does not extend the time for payment of tax. If, on filing Form 4868, you pay less than the final tax you owe, you will be charged interest on the unpaid amount. If the tax paid is less than 90% of the amount due, you may also be subject to a late-payment penalty.

When you file your return within the extension period, you attach a duplicate of Form 4868 and include the balance of the unpaid tax, if any.

While the extension is automatically obtained by a proper filing on Form 4868 (including payment of tax), the IRS may terminate the extension on ten days notice to you.

A general extension of time to file outside of the automatic extension rules above may be granted. You must make a request on Form 2688. An extension of up to six months may be granted if a full explanation showing reasonable cause is shown. The IRS has warned that if the explanation is found to be false or misleading, it will void the extension and apply late filing penalties.

¶27.06 • GETTING AN EXTENSION OF TIME TO PAY TAX

Do not allow your inability to pay the tax stop you from filing a return. Inability to pay the tax is not a reason for receiving an extension to file. If you cannot pay your tax, file your return and apply for an extension of time to pay your tax. You request an extension on Form 1127.

With Form 1127, you must show that you do not have cash above necessary working capital, liquid assets, or the financial ability to get a loan to meet the tax liability. If you have other assets, such as a house, you must also show that a sale of the asset would be at a sacrifice price and cause you undue financial hardship. You attach to Form 1127 a list of receipts and disbursements for the three months before the due date and also a statement of assets and liabilities as of the end of the month preceding your application.

If the extension is allowed, you are usually given six months from the date the tax was due. An additional six months may be allowed if you are abroad. You may also be required to put up property you own as collateral. Collateral is not required if you do not own property.

Receiving an extension does not stop the running of interest on the tax.

¶27.07 • AMENDED RETURNS

If, after filing your return, you find that an error has been made, you should file an amended return. Form 1040X may be used to correct a return for 1986 or a return from a prior year. You may also file an amended return on Form 1040. According to the IRS, Form 1040X is processed more rapidly than amended Form 1040. File Form 1040X with the Service Center serving the region or district in which the tax was paid. *See also* ¶27.001.

Form 1040X (page 1)

Form 1040X (Rev. October 1985)

Department of the Treasury—Internal Revenue Service

Amended U.S. Individual Income Tax Return

OMB No. 1545-0091
Expires 4-30-88

This return is for calendar year ▶ 19 85 , OR fiscal year ended ▶ .... , 19 .....

Your first name and initial (if joint return, also give spouse's name and initial) — Daniel & Sarah

Last name — Frame

Your social security number — 1X0 : XX : X1X1

Present home address (number and street, including apartment number, or rural route) — 16 Emory Avenue

Spouse's social security number — X01 : XX : 1XX1

City, town or post office, state, and ZIP code — City, State XXXXX

Telephone number (optional) — ( )

Enter below name and address as shown on original return (if same as above, write "Same"). If changing from separate to joint return, enter names and addresses used on original returns. (**Note:** *You cannot change from joint to separate returns after the due date has passed.*)

"Same"

a Service center where original return was filed — City, State

b Has original return for the year being changed been audited? ☐ Yes ☑ No
If "No," have you been notified that it will be? ☐ Yes ☑ No
If "Yes," identify IRS office

c Are you amending your return to include any item (loss, credit, deduction, other tax benefit, or income) relating to a tax shelter required to be registered? ☐ Yes ☑ No
If "Yes," you **MUST** attach Form 8271, Investor Reporting of Tax Shelter Registration Number.

d Filing status claimed. (**Note:** *You cannot change from joint to separate returns after the due date has passed.*)
On original return ▶ ☐ Single ☑ Married filing joint return ☐ Married filing separate return ☐ Head of household ☐ Qualifying widow(er)
On this return ▶ ☐ Single ☑ Married filing joint return ☐ Married filing separate return ☐ Head of household ☐ Qualifying widow(er)

Income and Deductions

		A. As originally reported or as adjusted (see instructions)	B. Net change—increase or (Decrease)—explain on page 2	C. Correct amount
1	Total income (see instructions)	39,400		39,400
2	Adjustments to income (see instructions)	4,500		4,500
3	Adjusted gross income (subtract line 2 from line 1)	34,900		34,900
4	Deductions (see instructions)	1,225	1,050	2,275
5	Subtract line 4 from line 3	33,675		32,625
6	Exemptions (see instructions)	2,080		2,080
7	Taxable income (subtract line 6 from line 5)	31,595		30,545

Tax Liability

8	Tax (see instructions). (Method used in col. C ..Tax Tables..)	5,113	(276)	4,837
9	Credits (see instructions)			
10	Subtract line 9 from line 8. Enter the result, but not less than zero	5,113	(276)	4,837
11	Other taxes (such as self-employment tax, alternative minimum tax)			
12	Total tax liability (add line 10 and line 11)	5,113	(276)	4,837

Payments

13	Federal income tax withheld and excess FICA and RRTA tax withheld	5,400		5,400
14	Estimated tax payments			
15	Earned income credit			
16	Credits for Federal tax on gasoline and special fuels, regulated investment company, etc.			
17	Amount paid with Form 4868, Form 2688, or Form 2350 (application for extension of time to file)		17	
18	Amount paid with original return, plus additional tax paid after it was filed		18	
19	Total of lines 13 through 18, column C		19	5,400

Refund or Amount You Owe

20	Overpayment, if any, as shown on original return (or as previously adjusted by IRS)		20	287
21	Subtract line 20 from line 19 (see instructions)		21	5,113
22	**AMOUNT YOU OWE.** If line 12, col. C, is more than line 21, enter difference. Please pay in full with this return		22	
23	**REFUND** to be received. If line 12, column C, is less than line 21, enter difference.		23	276

Please Sign Here
Under penalties of perjury, I declare that I have filed an original return and that I have examined this amended return, including accompanying schedules and statements, and to the best of my knowledge and belief this amended return is true, correct, and complete. Declaration of preparer (other than taxpayer) is based on all information of which the preparer has any knowledge.

Your signature ▲ Daniel Frame — Date June 10, 1986
Spouse's signature (if filing jointly, BOTH must sign) ▲ Sarah Frame

Paid Preparer's Use Only
Preparer's signature ▶ — Date — Check if self-employed ☐ — Preparer's social security no.
Firm's name (or yours, if self-employed) and address ▶ — E.I. No. — ZIP code

For Paperwork Reduction Act Notice, see page 1 of separate instructions. — **BE SURE TO COMPLETE PAGE 2**

Form 1040X (Rev. 10-85) — Page 2

Part I Exemptions (see Form 1040 or Form 1040A instructions)
If claiming more exemptions, complete lines 1—9.
If claiming fewer exemptions, complete lines 1—6.

		A. Number originally reported	B. Net change	C. Correct number
1	Exemptions—yourself and spouse, 65 or over, blind	2		2
2	Your dependent children who lived with you			
3	If amending your 1985 return, your dependent children who did not live with you			
4	Other dependents			
5	Total exemptions (add lines 1 through 4)	2		2
6	Multiply $1,040 ($1,000, for tax years beginning before 1985) by the total number of exemptions claimed on line 5. Enter this amount here and on page 1, line 6	2,080		2,080

7 First names of your dependent children who lived with you and were not claimed on original return: .... Enter number ▶ ☐

8 If amending your 1985 return, first names of your dependent children who did not live with you and were not claimed on original return (see instructions). (If pre-1985 agreement, check here ☐) .... Enter number ▶ ☐

9 Other dependents not claimed on original return:

(a) Name	(b) Relationship	(c) Number of months lived in your home	(d) Did dependent have income of $1,040 ($1,000) for tax years beginning before 1985) or more?	(e) Did you provide more than one-half of dependent's support?

Enter number ▶ ☐

Part II Explanation of Changes to Income, Deductions, and Credits

Enter the line number from page 1 for each item you are changing and give the reason for each change. Attach all supporting forms and schedules for items changed. Be sure to include your name and social security no. on any attachments.

If the change pertains to a net operating loss carryback, a general business credit carryback, or a research credit carryback, attach the schedule or form that shows the year in which the loss or credit occurred. See the instructions. Also, check here .... ▶ ☐

Line 4: On original 1985 return, we failed to add to the sales tax allowed by the IRS table sales tax of $1,050 paid on the purchase of a personal automobile on June 20, 1985 from Acme Auto Center, City, State, xxxxx.

Part III Presidential Election Campaign Fund
Checking below will not increase your tax or reduce your refund.

If you did not previously want to have $1 go to the fund, but now want to .... Check here ▶ ☐
If joint return and if spouse did not previously want to have $1 go to the fund, but now wants to .... Check here ▶ ☐

¶27.08 • OFFICES OF DISTRICT DIRECTORS*

ALABAMA—Birmingham, 35203.
ALASKA—Anchorage, 99501.
ARIZONA—Phoenix, 85025.
ARKANSAS—Little Rock, 72203.
CALIFORNIA—Los Angeles, 90012; San Francisco, 94102.
COLORADO—Denver, 80202.
CONNECTICUT—Hartford, 06103.
DELAWARE—Wilmington, 19801.
DISTRICT OF COLUMBIA—Baltimore, 21202.
FLORIDA—Jacksonville, 32202.
GEORGIA—Atlanta, 30303.
HAWAII—Honolulu, 96813.
IDAHO—Boise, 83707.
ILLINOIS—Chicago, 60602; Springfield, 62704.
INDIANA—Indianapolis, 46204.
IOWA—Des Moines, 50309.
KANSAS—Wichita, 67202.
KENTUCKY—Louisville, 40202.
LOUISIANA—New Orleans, 70130.
MAINE—Augusta, 04330.
MARYLAND—Baltimore, 21201.
MASSACHUSETTS—Boston, 02203.
MICHIGAN—Detroit, 48226.
MINNESOTA—St. Paul, 55101.
MISSISSIPPI—Jackson, 39202.
MISSOURI—St. Louis, 63101.
MONTANA—Helena, 59601.
NEBRASKA—Omaha, 68102.

NEVADA—Reno, 89502.
NEW HAMPSHIRE—Portsmouth, 03810.
NEW JERSEY—Newark, 07102.
NEW MEXICO—Albuquerque, 87101.
NEW YORK—Brooklyn, 11201; 120 Church Street, New York, 10007; Albany, 12210; Buffalo, 14202.
NORTH CAROLINA—Greensboro, 27401.
NORTH DAKOTA—Fargo, 58102.
OHIO—Cincinnati, 45202; Cleveland, 44199.
OKLAHOMA—Oklahoma City, 73102.
OREGON—Portland, 97204.
PENNSYLVANIA—Philadelphia, 19106; Pittsburgh, 15222.
RHODE ISLAND—Providence, 02903.
SOUTH CAROLINA—Columbia, 29201.
SOUTH DAKOTA—Aberdeen, 57401.
TENNESSEE—Nashville, 37203.
TEXAS—Austin, 78701; Dallas, 75201.
UTAH—Salt Lake City, 84110.
VERMONT—Burlington, 05401.
VIRGINIA—Richmond, 23240.
WASHINGTON—Seattle, 98121.
WEST VIRGINIA—Parkersburg, 26101.
WISCONSIN—Milwaukee, 53202.
WYOMING—Cheyenne, 82001.

* This list gives the location of the main office of each district. There are additional branch offices in principal cities. You can get the address of the nearest branch office by consulting your local post office.

¶27.09 • WHERE TO SEND YOUR RETURN—SERVICE CENTERS

Address the envelope containing your return to the Internal Revenue Service Center for the place where you live. No street address is needed. Write -2222 after the five digit ZIP Code listed below for your state, for example Ogden, UT 84201-2222.

ALABAMA—Atlanta, GA 31101
ALASKA—Ogden, UT 84201
ARIZONA—Ogden, UT 84201
ARKANSAS—Austin, TX 73301
CALIFORNIA—File with the IRS Service Center at Ogden, UT 84201, if you live in the counties of Alpine, Amador, Butte, Calaveras, Colusa, Contra Costa, Del Norte, El Dorado, Glenn, Humboldt, Lake, Lassen, Marin, Mendocino, Modoc, Napa, Nevada, Placer, Plumas, Sacramento, San Joaquin, Shasta, Sierra, Siskiyou, Solano, Sonoma, Sutter, Tehama, Trinity, Yolo, and Yuba.
    All other California residents file at Fresco, CA 93888.
COLORADO—Ogden, UT 84201
CONNECTICUT—Andover, MA 05501
DELAWARE—Philadelphia, PA 19255
DISTRICT OF COLUMBIA—Philadelphia, PA 19255
FLORIDA—Atlanta, GA 31101
GEORGIA—Atlanta, GA 31101
HAWAII—Fresno, CA 93888
IDAHO—Ogden, UT 84201
ILLINOIS—Kansas City, MO 64999
INDIANA—Memphis, TN 37501
IOWA—Kansas City, MO 64999
KANSAS—Austin, TX 73301
KENTUCKY—Cincinnati, OH 45999
LOUISIANA—Austin, TX 73301
MAINE—Andover, MA 05501
MARYLAND—Philadelphia, PA 19255
MASSACHUSETTS—Andover, MA 05501
MICHIGAN—Cincinnati, OH 45999
MINNESOTA—Andover, MA 05501
MISSISSIPPI—Atlanta, GA 31101
MISSOURI—Kansas City, MO 64999
MONTANA—Ogden, UT 84201
NEBRASKA—Ogden, UT 84201
NEVADA—Ogden, UT 84201

NEW HAMPSHIRE—Andover, MA 05501
NEW JERSEY—Holtsville, NY 00501
NEW MEXICO—Austin, TX 73301
NEW YORK—*New York City and Counties of Nassau, Rockland, Suffolk and Westchester*—Holtsville, NY 00501
   All Other Counties—
   Andover, MA 05501
NORTH CAROLINA—Memphis, TN 37501
NORTH DAKOTA—Ogden, UT 84201
OHIO—Cincinnati, OH 45999
OKLAHOMA—Austin, TX 73301
OREGON—Ogden, UT 84201
PENNSYLVANIA—Philadelphia, PA 19255
RHODE ISLAND—Andover, MA 05501
SOUTH CAROLINA—Atlanta, GA 31101
SOUTH DAKOTA—Ogden, UT 84201
TENNESSEE—Memphis, TN 37501
TEXAS—Austin, TX 73301
UTAH—Ogden, UT 84201
VERMONT—Andover, MA 05501
VIRGINIA—Memphis, TN 37501
WASHINGTON—Ogden, UT 84201
WEST VIRGINIA—Cincinnati, OH 45999
WISCONSIN—Kansas City, MO 64999
WYOMING—Ogden, UT 84201
AMERICAN SAMOA—Philadelphia, PA 19255
GUAM—Commissioner of Revenue and Taxation, Agana, GU 96910
PUERTO RICO (*or if excluding foreign income under section 933*)— Philadelphia, PA 19255
VIRGIN ISLANDS: NON-PERMANENT RESIDENTS— Philadelphia, PA 19255
VIRGIN ISLANDS: PERMANENT—Bureau of Internal Revenue, P.O. Box 3186, St. Thomas, VI 00801
FOREIGN COUNTRY: *U.S. citizens and those filing Form 2555 or Form 4563, even if you have an A.P.O. or F.P.O. address*— Philadelphia, PA 19255
A.P.O. OR F.P.O. address of: Miami—Atlanta, GA 31101
   New York—Holtsville, NY 00501
   San Francisco—Fresno, CA 93888
   Seattle—Ogden, UT 84201

¶27.10 • LIST OF SUPPLEMENTAL FORMS

In addition to Form 1040 and its accompanying schedules, the IRS provides other forms for claiming tax credits, for supporting deductions and exemptions, for requests for extensions of time, etc. These forms, as well as others not listed below, may be obtained from any Internal Revenue Service office. The use of many of these forms is optional; a statement may suffice. Supplemental forms include the following:

Form 1040X—Amended U.S. Individual Income Tax Return

Form 1045—Quick Refund for Carryback Adjustments (*see* ¶27.03)

Form 1116—Foreign Tax Credit (*see* ¶36.14)

Form 1127—Application for Extension of Time for Payment of Tax

Form 1128—Application for Change in Accounting Period

Form 1310—Statement of Claimant to Refund Due Deceased Taxpayer (*see* ¶1.14)

Form 2106—Statement of Employee Business Expenses (*see* ¶2.20)

Form 2119—Statement Concerning Sale or Exchange of Personal Residence (*see* ¶29.15)

Form 2120—Multiple Support Declaration (*see* ¶1.553)

Form 2210—Statement Relating to Underpayment of Estimated Tax (*see* ¶26.05). Form 2210F (for farmers and fishermen)

Form 2350—Application for Extension of Time for Filing Tax Return (for U.S. citizens abroad who expect to receive exempt earned income) (*see* ¶36.06)

Form 2439—Notice to Shareholder of Undistributed Long-Term Capital Gains (*see* ¶24.86)

Form 2441—Credit for Dependent Care Expenses (*see* ¶24.20)

Form 2553—Election by Corporation as to Taxable Status Under Subchapter S

Form 2555—Exclusion for Income Earned Abroad (for U.S. citizens abroad; file with Form 1040) (*see* ¶36.00)

Form 2688—Application for Extension of Time to File Tax Return (*see also*, Form 4868 below)

Form 2848—Power of Attorney

Form 3115—Application for Change in Accounting Method

Form 3468—Computation of Investment Credit

Form 3621—Net Operating Loss Computation

Form 3621-A—Computation of Net Operating Loss Deduction

Form 3903—Moving Expense Adjustment (*see* ¶2.40)

Form 4070—Employee Tip Income Reported

Form 4070A—Daily Record of Tips

Form 4136—Computation of Credit for Federal Tax on Gasoline and Lubricating Oil (for claiming credit for diesel vehicles, *see* ¶24.82)

Form 4137—Computation of Social Security Tax on Unreported Tip Income

Form 4255—Tax From Recomputing a Prior Year Investment Credit (*see* ¶5.75)

Form 4469—Computation of Excess Hospital Insurance Benefits Tax

Form 4506—Request for Copy of Tax Return

Form 4562—Depreciation (*see* ¶5.30)

Form 4563—Exclusion of Income from Sources in U.S. Possession

Form 4684—Casualties and Thefts (*see* ¶18.00)

Form 4782—Employee Moving Expense Information (*see* ¶2.40)

Form 4797—Supplementary Schedule of Gains and Losses (*see* ¶5.45)

Form 4798—Capital Loss Carryover (*see* ¶6.003)

Form 4835—Farm Rental Income and Expenses (*see* ¶8.00)

Form 4868—Application for Automatic Extension of Time to File Return (*see* ¶1.22)

Form 4952—Investment Interest Deduction (*see* ¶15.06)

Form 4972—Ten-Year Averaging Method for Lump-Sum Distributions (*see* ¶7.02)

Form 5213—Election to Postpone Determination on Presumption That an Activity Is Engaged in for Profit (*see* ¶5.06)

Form 5329—Return for Individual Retirement Savings (*see* ¶7.16)

Form 5500—Annual Return/Report of Employee Benefit Plan (100 or more participants)

Form 5500-C—Annual Return/Report of Employee Benefit Plan (less than 100 participants; filed once every three years)

Form 5500-R—Report of Employee Benefit Plan (to be filed in years Form 5500-C is not filed)

Form 5884—Jobs Credit (*see* ¶5.78)

Form 6251—Alternative Minimum Tax (*see* ¶23.20)

Form 6252—Computation of Installment Sale Income (*see* ¶6.16)

Form 6781—Regulated Futures Contracts and Straddles (*see* ¶6.0352)

Form 8271—Investor Reporting of Tax Shelter Registration Number (¶28.00)

Form 8283—Noncash Charitable Contributions (¶14.101).

Form 8300—Report of Cash Payments Over $10,000 Received in a Trade or Business (¶5.021)

Form 8332—Release of Claim to Exemption for Child of Divorced or Separated Parents (¶1.554)

Form 8396—Mortgage Interest Credit (¶24.87)

Tax-Saving Ideas and Planning

¶28.00 • Tax Shelter Investments

¶28.01 • TAX SHELTER LOSSES IN 1986

In 1986, losses from tax shelter investments are deductible from other income as long as the venture is bona fide and your loss is not limited by the at risk rules of ¶28.04. For the treatment of 1987 tax shelter losses, *see* the tax legislation discussion in the front of this book.

See also ¶23.10 for possible alternative tax liability because of tax preference items.

¶28.02 • PRE-FILING WARNINGS TO TAX SHELTER INVESTORS

The IRS tries to investigate tax shelter offerings as soon as they are publicized. In each IRS district, the IRS gathers information on the marketing of tax shelter plans in its area. It examines the prospectus for details of the financial organization, the promised tax writeoffs, and the promoter's past record.

If the reviewers determine that the promoter may have misrepresented the tax benefits, the promoter receives a letter stating that he may be subject to possible penalties for promoting an abusive tax shelter. He is asked for documents, records, and names of investors. He must make them available within 10 days. If he does not provide the data, the IRS will go to court to have a summons enforced. If after an examination of these records, and the IRS decides to act against the offering, the promoter is given an opportunity at a conference to defend his position. If he fails to attend the meeting or provide requested information, the IRS may impose penalties, seek a court injunction barring the promotions, and issue pre-filing notices to investors who have entered the plan. The pre-filing notices to investors state that purported tax benefits in the promotion are not allowable and that investors may be penalized if they claim the benefits. The district making the investigation also forwards a list of the investors to IRS service centers for possible examinations of the investors' tax returns. The IRS will examine the returns of investors who claim tax shelter benefits after receiving a pre-filing notice or who receive an IRS notice after filing their return but do not amend their return. The IRS will freeze refund claims of investors who have received pre-filing notices, pending an examination of their returns. *See* ¶28.031.

¶28.03 • REPORT TAX SHELTER REGISTRATION NUMBER TO IRS

Most new tax shelter offerings are required to register with the IRS. If registration is required, the IRS assigns the tax shelter an identification number that must be furnished to investors. As an investor, you must report the registration number on Form 8271. Form 8271 must be attached to your tax return if you report any income or claim any deductions or credits from the shelter.

On Form 8271, the tax shelter must be identified, and you must list from the shelter the gross income, deductions, credits and gains and losses reported on your return; you must identify the forms or schedules on which the income or deductions are reported, such as Schedule D or Schedule E.

A penalty may be imposed if you fail to include the tax shelter registration number on your return.

Promoters of registered tax shelters and any other tax shelter arrangements which the IRS considers as potentially abusive must also keep a list of investors for seven years and provide the list to the IRS upon request. Further, an investor who sells his interest in such a tax shelter to another investor must keep records identifying the buyer.

¶28.031 • TAX SHELTER REFUNDS WITHHELD BY IRS

The IRS may withhold refunds based on questionable tax shelter claims. In each IRS service center, returns of tax shelter investors are screened to determine if the tax shelter has fraudulently misrepresented tax benefits or grossly overvalued assets or services. If the tax shelter is considered to be abusive and if claimed deductions or tax credits are not allowable, refunds attributable to the tax shelter items will not be paid. The balance of your refund claim will be paid.

A refund will also be frozen under the above rules if you file your return after receiving a pre-filing notification letter from the IRS warning you not to claim certain tax shelter writeoffs. *See* ¶28.031.

The above rules apply to original tax returns showing a refund due as well as to refund claims. Further, if you file a quick refund claim on Form 1045 (¶27.03), and the IRS determines it is likely that excessive tax shelter benefits have been claimed, the IRS will offset the quick refund claim by a deficiency attributable to the tax shelter items. You will receive the balance and receive a notice of the tax shelter deficiency.

Tax shelter partnerships. The IRS will freeze refunds of investors in tax shelter partnerships if it determines that it is highly likely that the partnership has fraudulently misrepresented tax benefits or grossly overvalued property or services, leading to excessive tax writeoffs by the partners. The refund freeze will continue until completion of the partnership level audit. *See* ¶10.04 for partnership audits.

¶28.04 • AT RISK LIMITS

Prior tax accounting rules made it possible to claim loss deductions exceeding actual cash investments by allowing investors to include nonrecourse liabilities as part of the tax basis of their investments. In 1986, the at risk rules bar this advantage for all ventures except real estate.

Example—

You invest cash of $1,000 in a venture and sign a nonrecourse note for $8,000. In 1986, your share of the venture's loss is $1,200. The at risk rules limit your deduction to $1,000, the amount of your cash investment; as you are not personally liable on the note, the amount of the liability is not included as part of your basis for loss purposes.

If you have amounts that are not at risk, you must file Form 6198. A separate form must be filed for each activity. Further, if you have an interest in a partnership or S corporation that has more than one investment in any of the following five activities, check the instructions to Form 6198 to see if you must file a separate Form 6198 for each investment.

1. Holding, producing, or distributing motion picture films or video tapes;

2. Leasing business equipment subject to depreciation recapture;

3. Exploring for, or exploiting, oil and gas resources; or

4. Exploring for, or exploiting, geothermal deposits (for wells commenced on or after October 1, 1978); and

5. Farming. For this purpose, farming is defined as the cultivation of land, raising or harvesting of any agricultural or horticultural commodity including raising, shearing, breeding, caring for or management of animals. Forestry and timber activities are not included, but orchards bearing fruits and nuts are within the definition of farming. Certain activities carried on within the physical boundaries of the farm may not necessarily be treated as farming.

For 1986, the IRS also has authority to apply the at-risk rules to business or income-producing activities which have tax shelter characteristics, except for real estate.

Exempted from the at-risk rules are C corporations which meet active business tests and are not in the equipment leasing business or any business involving master sound recording, films, video tapes or other artistic, literary or musical property. The active business tests are not discussed in this book.

The at risk limitation applies only to tax losses produced by expense deductions which are not disallowed by reason of another provision of the law. For example, if a prepaid interest expense is deferred under the prepaid interest limitation (¶15.021), the interest will not be included in the loss subject to the at risk limitation. When the interest accrues and becomes deductible, the expense may be considered within the at risk provision. Similarly, if a deduction is deferred because of farming syndicate rules (¶8.09), that deduction will enter into the computation of the tax loss subject to the risk limitation only when it becomes deductible under the farming syndicate rules.

In determining deductions allowed under the at risk rules, long-term capital gains from an at risk activity are considered in full, even though for reporting purposes, they may be reduced by the capital gain deduction.

¶28.05 • WHAT IS AT RISK

Amounts considered at risk are:
Cash,
Adjusted basis of property which you contribute, and
Borrowed funds for which you are personally liable to pay.

Pledges of other property as security. If you pledge personally owned real estate to secure a nonrecourse debt and invest the proceeds in an at risk activity, the proceeds may be considered part of your risk investment. The proceeds included in basis are limited by the fair market value of the property used as collateral (determined as of the date the property is pledged as security) less any prior (or superior) claims to which the collateral is subject.

Personal liability alone does not assure that the borrowed funds are considered at risk. The lender must have no interest in the venture other than as creditor.

Example—

An investor pays a promoter of a book purchase plan $45,000 for a limited partnership interest. The promoter is the general partner. The investor pays $30,000 cash and gives a note for $15,000 on which he is personally liable. His amount at risk is $30,000; the $15,000 personal liability note is not counted because it is owed to the general partner.

Basis, limiting losses, is figured at the end of a taxable year.

Examples—

1. On January 1, 1983, an investor contributes $5,000 cash to a farming venture. He also borrows $3,000 from a bank for which he is personally liable. By the end of 1983, he pays off $750 of the loan. The venture has no income or losses in 1983. The investor's at risk basis as of December 31, 1983 is $7,250, determined as follows:

Contributions	$5,000	
Recourse financing	3,000	$8,000
Less: Partial loan repayment		750
Amount at risk as of 12/31/83		$7,250

2. Same as example 1 but on February 1, 1984, he borrows $10,000 on a nonrecourse basis. He pays off $1,000 on the personal liability loan and $500 on the nonrecourse loan. The venture earns $3,000 and distributes $2,000 to him. The at risk basis as of December 31, 1984 is $7,250, determined as follows:

Amount at risk as of 1/1/84		$7,250
Plus: Income		3,000
		$10,250
Less: Repayment of personal liability loan	$1,000	
Distribution	2,000	3,000
Amount at risk as of 12/31/84		$7,250

Payment on the nonrecourse loan with funds or other nonrecourse loans from only the activity does not affect the amount at risk.

3. Same as example 2 but on March 1, 1985, the investor contributes $2,500 and pays off the personal liability loan. The venture has losses of $10,500 for 1985. As of December 31, 1985, the investor's amount at risk is $8,500, determined as follows:

Amount at risk as of 1/1/85	$7,250
Plus: Contribution	2,500
	9,750
Less: Payment of personal liability loan	1,250
Amount at risk as of 12/31/85	$8,500

The investor's loss deduction is limited to the amount at risk of $8,500; the $2,000 loss disallowed is carried over to 1986.

The above adjustments of basis are only for at risk purposes. Basis for depreciation and computing gain or loss on a sale is controlled by the adjusted basis rules at ¶6.10.

Activities begun before 1976. A special rule determines the amount at risk as of the first day of the first tax year after 1975. Again, you start with the amounts considered at risk. Losses incurred and deducted in taxable years before 1976 first reduce the basis allocated to amounts considered not at risk, such as nonrecourse loans. If the losses exceed the amount not at risk, the excess reduces the at risk investment. Distributions reduce at risk amounts. If records are insufficient to establish the amount at risk, the amount at risk is your basis in the activity reduced (but not below zero) by your share of nonrecourse or other similar financing or loans from interested persons.

If a loss is partly disallowed, deductible items are claimed in the following order: (1) All capital losses; (2) Section 1231 losses; (3) losses from deductions other than tax preference items (such as taxes, interest, etc.); (4) all tax preference items.

¶28.06 • AMOUNTS NOT AT RISK

The following may not be treated as part of basis for at risk purposes:

Liabilities for which you have no personal liability.

Liabilities for which you have personal liability, but the lender also has a capital or profit-sharing interest in the venture.

Example—

An investor purchases cattle from a rancher for $10,000 cash and a $30,000 note payable to the rancher. The investor is personally liable on the note. In a separate agreement, the rancher agrees to care for the cattle for 6% of the investor's net profits from the cattle activity. The investor is considered at risk to $10,000; he may not increase the amount at risk by the $30,000 borrowed from the rancher.

Recourse liabilities convertible to a nonrecourse basis.

Example—

A tax shelter promoter offered an equipment leasing deal which required $25,000 cash and an investor's recourse note of $250,000 subject to 10% annual interest. The equipment had a seven-year useful life (under pre-1981 law). In the first seven years, the note was payable in annual installments of $25,000. Payments were first applied to unpaid interest. Principal would be reduced if certain excess rentals were made. At the end of seven years, the investor could extend the note for another term or convert the balance of the note to nonrecourse liability by paying $10,000. The promoter claimed the investor was at risk for the full purchase price so that he could deduct depreciation based on a $275,000 investment. The IRS disagreed, ruling that the investor's basis is only $35,000 ($25,000 cash plus $10,000 to be paid after seven years). The liability of $250,000 may not be considered part of basis, although the note on its face entailed personal liability. The way the plan was structured, annual payments covered only interest and at the end of seven years, the investor, by paying $10,000, could avoid personal liability on the balance. The seven-year term over which the investor was personally liable was arranged solely for the depreciation deduction and served no business purpose.

Money borrowed from a relative listed at ¶33.12, who has an interest in the venture, other than as a creditor, or from a partnership in which you own more than a 10% interest.

Funds borrowed from a person whose recourse is either your interest in the activity or property used in the activity.

Amounts for which your economic loss is limited by nonrecourse financing guarantee, stop-loss agreement, or other similar arrangement.

Investments protected by insurance or loss reimbursement agreement between you and another person. If you are personally liable on a mortgage but you separately obtain insurance to compensate you for any mortgage payments, you are at risk only to the extent of the uninsured portion of the personal liability. You may, however, include as at risk any amount of premium paid from your personal assets. Taking out casualty insurance or insurance protecting you against tort liability is not considered within the at risk provisions, and such insurance does not affect your investment basis.

Potential cash call. The IRS and Tax Court held that a limited partner was not at risk with respect to a partnership note where under the terms of the partnership agreement, he could be required to make additional capital contributions if the general partners did not pay off the note at maturity. The possibility of such a potential cash call was too uncertain; the partnership might earn profits to pay off the note and even if there were losses, the general partners might not demand additional contributions from the limited partners.

Examples—

1. Some commercial feedlots in livestock feeding operations may reimburse investors against any loss sustained on sales of the livestock above a stated dollar amount per head. Under such "stop loss" orders, an investor is at risk only to the extent of the portion of his capital against which he is not entitled to reimbursement. Where a limited partnership agrees with a limited partner that, at the partner's election, his partnership interest will be bought at a stated minimum dollar amount (usually less than the investor's original capital contribution), the partner is considered at risk only to the extent of his investment exceeding the guaranteed repurchase price.

2. A promoter of TV films sold one-half hour programs in a TV series to individual investors. Each investor gave a cash down payment and a note for which he was personally liable for the balance. Each investor's note, which was identical in face amount, terms and maturity date, was payable out of the distribution proceeds from the film. Each investor also bought from the promoter the right to the unpaid balance on another investor's note. The promoter arranged the distribution of the films as a unit and was to apportion the sales proceeds equally among the investors. The IRS held that each investor is not at risk on the investment evidenced by the note. Upon maturity, each may receive a payment from another investor equal to the one that he owes.

3. A gold mine investment offered tax write-offs of four times the cash invested. For $10,000 cash, an investor buys from a foreign mining company a seven-year mineral claim lease to a gold reserve. Under the lease, he can develop and extract all of the gold in the reserve. At the same time, he agrees to spend $40,000 to develop the lease before the end of the year. To fund this commitment, the investor authorizes the promoter to sell an option for $30,000 to a third party who is to buy all the gold to be extracted. The $30,000 along with the $10,000 down payment is to be used to develop the reserve. The promoter advises the investor that he may claim a $40,000 deduction for certain development costs. The IRS ruled that $30,000 is not deductible because the amount is not "risk capital." The investor gets $30,000 by selling an option that can be exercised only if gold is found. If no gold is found, he is under no obligation to the option holder. His risk position for the $30,000 is substantially the same as if he had borrowed from the option holder on a nonrecourse basis repayable only from his interest in the activity. The Tax Court struck down a similar plan on different grounds. Without deciding the question of what was at risk, the court held that the option was only a right of first refusal. Thus, $30,000 was taxable income to the investor in the year of the arranged sale.

According to proposed regulations, a partner is treated as at risk to the extent that his basis in the partnership is increased by his share of partnership income. That partnership income is then used to reduce the partnership's nonrecourse indebtedness will have no effect on a partner's amount at risk. If the partnership makes actual distributions of the income in the taxable year, the amount distributed reduces the partner's amount at risk. A buy-sell agreement, effective at a partner's death or retirement, is not considered for at risk purposes.

¶28.07 • INVESTMENT IN SEVERAL ACTIVITIES

If you invest in several activities, each is generally treated separately when applying the at risk limitation on Form 6198; you may not aggregate basis, gains and losses from the activities for purposes of at risk limitations. Thus, income from one activity may not be offset by losses from another; the income from one must be reported while the losses from the other may be nondeductible because of at risk limitations.

The law allows partnerships and S corporations to treat as a single activity all Section 1245 properties (*see* ¶5.40) which are leased or held for lease.

The IRS also has authority to set guidelines for aggregating or separating the other activities listed at ¶28.04. *See* Form 6198 instructions.

The at risk rules are not applied at the corporate level to S corporations.

¶28.08 • ALLOCATING REAL PROPERTY LOSSES

Losses are allocated between the real estate and nonreal estate portions of the business; losses attributable to real estate are not subject to at risk limits in 1986. Allocation is not allowed for the five activities listed at ¶28.04. For example, real estate used in farming is not a separate activity requiring an allocation of losses.

Personal property and services provided by a motel or in the renting of furnished apartments is treated as real estate activity; health care and meals furnished in nursing homes are not considered part of real estate activity.

To allocate losses, begin by dividing income between the real and nonreal property portions of the activity according to the ratio of real property to nonreal property deductions.

Example—

In 1986, a restaurant operated at a loss of $100,000; its gross income was $500,000; expenses totaled $600,000 of which $150,000 was attributed to the building which houses the restaurant. In this case, $125,000 or 25% of the income is allocated to the building because the $150,000 real property expenses were 25% of the total expenses of $600,000. As a result of the allocation, the building for purposes of the at risk rules is treated as having incurred a loss of $25,000 ($125,000–$150,000); the restaurant, a loss of $75,000 ($375,000–$450,000). Only the restaurant loss is subject to the at risk limitation.

Alternative method of allocation. If the fair rental value of the property can be established, you may elect to treat the fair rental value of the real property as the amount of income allocable to that property. In the example above, if you could show that the annual fair rental value was $100,000, that amount (as opposed to the $125,000 figured under the allocation formula) would be treated as the income allocable to the real property and would produce a greater loss deduction not subject to the at risk limitations. In this example, use of the alternative method results in a deductible loss of $50,000 ($100,000–$150,000). The loss attributable to the restaurant (and subject to the at risk limitations) is $50,000 ($400,000–$450,000). Use the alternative method if it produces a greater loss deduction allocable to real property.

¶28.09 • CARRYOVER OF DISALLOWED LOSSES

A loss disallowed in a current year by the at risk limitation may be carried over and deducted in the next taxable year provided it does not fall within the at risk limits in that year. The loss is subject to an unlimited carryover period until there is an at risk basis to support the deduction. This may occur when additional contributions are made to the business or when the activity has income which has not been distributed.

Gain from the disposition of property used in an at risk activity is treated as income from the activity. In general, the reporting of gain will allow a deduction for losses disallowed in previous years to be claimed in the year of disposition.

¶28.10 • RECAPTURE OF LOSSES WHERE AT RISK LESS THAN ZERO

To prevent manipulation of at risk basis after a loss is claimed, there is a special recapture rule. If the amount at risk is reduced to below zero because of a distribution or a change in the status of an indebtedness from recourse to nonrecourse, income may be realized to the extent at risk basis is below zero. The taxable amount may not exceed the amount of losses previously deducted.

The recaptured amount is not treated as income from the activity for purposes of determining whether current or suspended losses are allowable.

¶28.13 • THE INVESTMENT CREDIT AND AT RISK RULES

If you finance the purchase of equipment eligible for the investment credit (see ¶24.10) you may have to reduce the basis of the property by the amount of any nonrecourse loans. However, you may avoid at risk reductions of basis where (1) you buy property from an unrelated seller and (2) pay at least 20% of the cost with your own funds or with loans on which you are personally liable. In such a case, basis of the property for investment credit purposes may include nonrecourse qualified commercial financing, which is financing from any nonrelated lender. The following are considered related lenders: family members, corporations or partnerships in which you have at least a 10% interest, a person from whom you acquired the property, and a promoter to whom you paid a fee on making the investment.

Nonrecourse financing is tested at the end of the tax year in which the property is placed in service. If the amount of nonqualified nonrecourse financing decreases after the year the property is placed in service, an additional credit may be claimed in the later year. If the amount of nonqualified nonrecourse financing increases after the year the property is placed in service, you must recapture part of the credit originally claimed.

Partners and S corporation shareholders. Where property is purchased by a partnership, financing is tested at the level of the individual partners. A special rule allows an allocable share of recourse financing provided to an S corporation to be treated by a shareholder as recourse even if the shareholder is not personally liable for repayment. The financing must be recourse at the corporate level and must be for property used in an active business. The business must have at least three full time employees other than owner-employees and one full time manager. This rule does not apply to master sound recordings or any literary artistic or musical properties.

Energy property. A less strict at risk rule, not discussed in this book, applies to seller-financing of energy property such as solar or wind property. *See* IRS Publication 572.

The above rules for qualified commercial financing apply to property placed in service after July 18, 1984. Further, an election may be made to apply the rules for all assets placed in service after February 18, 1981; *see* Temporary Treasury regulations.

¶29.00 · Tax Savings for Homeowners

¶29.10 · TAX CONSEQUENCES OF SELLING YOUR HOME

Tax on all or a part of a profit from the sale of your home may be avoided or deferred depending on your age.

If you are 55 or over, you may elect to avoid tax on gain of up to $125,000. *See* ¶29.30.

If you are under 55 or are 55 or over and do not want to elect to avoid tax, you may defer tax by buying or building another residence within the rules of ¶29.20. Tax deferment is not elective but mandatory if the tests are met. If you do not meet the deferment tests, your profit is taxed. In 1986, if you held the house long term, the profit is taxable as long-term capital gain. Installment sale reporting may be used to defer tax as explained below.

If you sold at a loss, you may not deduct the loss. Losses on the sale of property devoted to personal use are nondeductible (*see* ¶6.02). However, *see* ¶29.28 which explains under what conditions you may claim a loss deduction for a residence which you rent out or inherit.

Reporting a sale. Report the details of a 1986 sale on Form 2119, which must be attached to Form 1040. On Form 2119, you compute gain on the sale and the basis of a new residence and may make the election to exclude gain if over age 55. Sample filled-in portions of Form 2119 are at ¶6.321. If you do not qualify for tax deferral or the exclusion, taxable gain from Form 2119 is entered on Schedule D.

The IRS may tax you on the unreported gain from the sale of your residence during a three-year period that starts when you notify the IRS of the cost of your new residence or your intention not to buy one, or your failure to acquire one before the required time limit. In the absence of notice, the IRS may assess the tax on unreported taxable gain at any time.

Installment sale reporting. Where some or all of the sales proceeds will be received after the year of sale and you do not qualify for deferral or elect the exclusion, your gain must be reported on the installment basis, unless you elect to report the entire gain in the year of sale. For installment sale rules, *see* ¶6.16.

¶29.20 · DEFERRING TAX ON THE SALE OF A RESIDENCE

You defer tax on the gain realized on the sale of your house if you meet the following three tests—

Principal residence test—requires that you have used your old house as your principal residence and now use or intend to use your new house as a principal residence.

Time test—requires you to buy or build your new house and use it within two years before or after you sell your old house.

Investment test—requires you to buy or build a house at a cost at least equal to the amount you received from the sale of the old house. If the replacement property costs less, part or all of the gain is taxed.

If you come within the above three tests, tax deferment is mandatory.

Exchanging houses. When you exchange residences, the trade is considered to be a sale of your old house and a purchase of a new house. If you make an even exchange or pay additional cash, there is no tax on the exchange. If you receive cash in addition to the new house, you generally realize taxable gain.
Examples—
1. Your old house cost $58,000. You exchange it for a new house worth $61,000. You also receive $1,000 in cash. Your gain is $4,000 ($62,000 less your $58,000 cost). As you reinvested $61,000 in the new house, taxable gain is $1,000. Cost basis of the new house is $58,000 ($61,000 purchase price less the $3,000 nontaxed gain).
2. Your old house cost $58,000. You exchanged it for a new house worth $60,000, and pay an additional $2,000. You have no taxed gain. The cost of your new house is $60,000 (the cost of your old house, $58,000, plus the $2,000 cash).

Condemnations. When a residence is condemned by a government authority, a homeowner may elect to treat the condemnation as a sale rather than as an involuntary conversion. Under current law, there is no advantage in making this election, although the involuntary conversion rules (*see* ¶18.21) allow more time to replace the residence than the rules for deferral.

How to claim deferral. You must report a 1986 sale on Form 2119. If by the time you file your return you have already purchased a new home, details of the purchase are shown on Form 2119. You qualify for deferral if the cost of the new home equals or exceeds the adjusted sale price of the old home. If you plan to buy a new home within the two-year replacement period but have not yet done so when you file your 1986 return, you indicate your intention on Form 2119; you do not have to report the gain from the sale on your 1986 return. If you later make a timely replacement that qualifies for full deferral (purchase price exceeds adjusted sales price of old home), you should notify the IRS and attach a new Form 2119 for 1986. If the purchase price of a replacement home does not at least equal the adjusted sales price of the old home, or if you do not make a timely replacement, you must file an amended return on Form 1040X to report taxable gain for 1986 and attach a new Form 2119 and Schedule D; you will also owe interest on the tax due. You may also file an amended return to claim a refund if you paid tax on a 1986 gain and later buy a new home within the two-year replacement period.

¶29.21 · PRINCIPAL RESIDENCE TEST

You may have only one principal residence for the purpose of deferring tax. You may not defer tax on the profitable sale of a second house, such as a summer cottage. Nor may you defer tax on the sale of a principal residence by buying a summer home.

If you own two houses, only one is considered a principal residence at one time. Assume you sell the unit which you consider your principal residence and decide to use the second house as a principal residence. The cost basis of the second house is not considered in figuring tax deferral unless it was bought during the replacement time period.
Example—
The Shaws sold their house and immediately moved into a house bought 10 years earlier. They did not report gain from the sale, claiming that the cost basis of the new residence exceeded the sales price of the

old house. They treated as cost the market value of the house as of the date they began using it as a principal residence. They argued that, although they owned it for 10 years, they did not acquire it for purposes of tax deferral until they began using it as a principal residence. The IRS and Tax Court held that only reconstruction expenses paid within the replacement period could be considered costs of purchasing a new residence.

Tax deferment is not restricted to one-family houses. You may defer tax on the sale and purchase of a mobile home, trailer, houseboat, cooperative apartment (tied to stock ownership) and condominium apartment, which you use as a principal residence. For example, in a private letter ruling, the IRS allowed deferral of gain recognized on the conversion of a co-op apartment to a condominium. An investment in a retirement home project does not qualify if you do not receive equity in the property.

Tax deferment applies also to your sale of a multifamily building in which you have an apartment. You may defer tax on gain allocated to your apartment (*see* ¶29.27). Similarly, where you actively use part of your house for business purposes, such as in operating a farm or a store while living in an apartment in the same building, an allocation is required. If part of your home was used as an office for which no deduction was allowed, no allocation is required.

If you sell your old house to one buyer and adjacent land to another buyer, the land sale may be treated as part of the sale of your principal residence, and tax on gain is deferred if the other tests are met. However, if the tract of land is substantial, the IRS may attempt to treat the sales as separate transactions. To avoid this possibility where you want to avoid or defer tax on the sale, try to arrange for the sale of the entire property to one buyer who, in turn, may sell the part he does not want to the other buyer.

If you sell only part of a lot on which your residence stands, the gain on the sale may not be postponed by reinvesting in a similar lot or by purchasing a residence. Similarly, if you sell the lot and move your house to a new lot, you may not defer gain on the sale of the old lot. The sale is not of the personal residence.

The location of the principal residences is not relevant. Tax deferment may apply to residences in a foreign country.

Title to both the old and new home must be in your name. If you place title to the new home in someone else's name, the new home does not qualify you for deferral. An exception exists for a married couple who files a consent form. See ¶29.25.

Delay in sale of old residence after you move. When you cannot find a buyer and must move, you may face a problem in deferring tax on a later sale of the house. If you have bought a new house, there is the possibility that the sale of the old house may not occur within the time limits. If you delay the purchase of a new house until the sale of the old one, you may face this problem: The IRS may charge that, at the time of the sale, you no longer considered the house as your principal residence.

Temporary rentals. You may defer tax if you move into a new home and temporarily rent out your old home while trying to sell it. See ¶29.42.

You may also defer tax in this case: You buy a new house and rent it before selling your old house in which you continue to live. You later sell your old house and move into the new house.

Example—

An executive left his residence in suburban New York to live in a New York City apartment near his office; he made no efforts to sell his old home for two years, until just before he purchased a new home in Virginia. The Tax Court held that he had abandoned the old home as a principal residence. He timed the sale merely to take advantage of the tax deferral. In another case, a serviceman rented his residence over a six-year period until he could sell at a profit. He had refused earlier offers which would have given him a loss. The Tax Court held that he had abandoned his home as a residence.

In later decisions, the Tax Court commented that these two cases should not be interpreted as laying down a rule of law that an intention not to return to a home is, by itself, an abandonment of the home as a principal residence. Whether a homeowner has abandoned his residence is a question of fact. The absence of an intention to return is only one fact to be considered.

Separated couples. If you and your spouse agree to live apart, sell your jointly owned home and buy and live in separate new homes, you may each be able to defer tax. You each report the sale on Form 2119 as if two separate homes were sold. For example, assume that under state law, each of you is entitled to half the proceeds. On Form 2119, you each report half of the sales price. If the cost of your new home exceeds your respective half of the old home's adjusted sales price, you defer tax on your half of the gain. The same deferral test applies to your spouse.

¶29.22 • TIME TEST

If you buy or build a new home, you must do so and begin to use it within two years before or after you sell your old one. The time test is strictly applied; failure to comply will not be excused for any reason.

A contract to purchase a new home is not sufficient to satisfy the time test. A sale is considered to occur at the earlier of the passage of title or the assumption of the benefits and burdens of ownership.

When you build, you must complete and occupy the house within the two-year period.

Examples—

1. Bayley sold his house at a profit, started construction on a new house and elected to defer tax. The new house was not completed before the end of the required time period. A day before the end of the period, Bayley moved some of his furniture into the house but could not live there. The house had no water or sewage connections. He finally moved in two months later. The IRS taxed the gain because the house had not been timely occupied. The Tax Court agreed. Bayley had made the necessary investment but failed to meet the requirement of occupying the house.

2. The Lokans bought land to farm and build a new residence. Several months later, they sold their old house at a profit. During construction, they set up a trailer on the property. When one bedroom and a bath in the new house was completed, three children slept in the house; they and one other child slept in the trailer. The house was not fully completed until three years after the sale. The IRS and the Tax Court held that the Lokans did not reside in the new house; the trailer was their principal residence.

Deferment for workers abroad. If your tax home (¶2.24) is outside the United States, the replacement period is suspended while you are abroad. The suspension applies only if your stay abroad began before the end of the replacement period and lasts until you return from abroad or until four years after the sale, whichever occurs first. Your spouse is also protected by the suspension provided that you both used the old home and new home as your principal residence.

Deferment on entering the Armed Forces. If you go on active duty for more than 90 days, the two-year replacement period is suspended while you are in the Service. The suspension applies only if your service began before the end of the two-year replacement period. The suspension generally lasts until your discharge, when the two-year replacement period starts to run again, but regardless of the length of service, the replacement period ends four years after the date of sale. Thus, even if you remain in the Service, you must buy and live in a replacement no more than four years after you sell your home. For a sale after July 18, 1984, if you are stationed outside of the U.S. on extended duty or have to live in government quarters at a remote site after returning from a tour of duty outside the U.S., the replacement period may extend beyond the four-year period. The replacement period is suspended while you are at the foreign or remote site. However, the replacement period may not exceed eight years after the sale. If your spouse is in the armed forces and you are not, you are also protected by the suspension if you owned the old home and both you and your spouse used the old home and new home as principal residences. If you divorce or separate during the suspension period, your replacement period starts to run again the day after the divorce or separation.

¶29.23 • INVESTMENT TEST

To defer tax on the full amount of gain, you must buy another principal residence, and your investment must generally equal or exceed the selling price of your old home.

To arrive at your actual gain on the sale and the gain that is not taxed, you have to figure the *amount realized* on the sale, the *adjusted sales price,* and the cost of the new residence. If the cost of the new residence equals or exceeds the adjusted sales price of the old residence, no part of the actual gain is taxed in the year of sale.

If you reinvest proceeds in two homes, one for summer and one for winter, you may not figure the investment in both houses. You consider the investment in the house used as your principal residence.

Amount realized. This is the selling price of your old house less selling expenses for commissions, advertising, preparing the deed, and other legal and title services. "Points" paid by you as the seller also reduce the selling price.

The selling price includes the amount of the mortgages on the old house, whether the buyer has assumed or bought the property subject to them. If immediately after the sale, you discount notes received on a deferred payment contract, include the discounted value of the notes, not the face amounts.

Do not include amounts received for furnishings, such as rugs and furniture, sold with the house. Sale of furnishings is reported separately if sold at a gain. Sales at a loss are not deductible.

Your actual gain is the difference between the amount realized and the cost of the old house. The cost basis of the old house is explained at ¶6.12.

Adjusted sales price. This is the amount realized less fix-up costs spent to make your old house salable, like papering, painting, and other similar repairs. Include costs for work done only within the 90-day period ending on the day on which the contract to sell is entered into and paid for within 30 days after the sale.

If you do not buy or build a house within the rules explained in this section, you may not deduct fix-up costs from the amount realized. Nor may you deduct them separately on your tax return. Furthermore, fix-up costs do not include costs of permanent improvements spent to clinch a sale, for example, installing a new roof or furnace. They are capital expenditures added to the cost basis of the old house.

Cost of the new house. You are not required to reinvest the cash proceeds of the sale of your old house. You may buy the new house with a small cash payment plus a large mortgage loan. The cost of the new house includes not only cash payments but also any mortgages you assume or take subject to. You also include broker's commissions and lawyer's fees. The treatment of "points" is explained at ¶15.012.

The present value of future land lease payments may not be added to the cost of your new house.

When you build a house, include all costs paid in the construction of the house during the two years prior to the sale and two years after the sale. Costs paid after the two-year period are not included even if you have incurred liability for them before the end of the two-year period. However, these costs do become a part of the cost of the new house to figure gain or loss if you later sell it. Gifts and inheritances of all or part of a new home do not count as part of your purchase price in figuring whether you have reinvested your gain on the sale of your old residence. However, you may include costs of reconstructing an inherited house to make it habitable.

Compare the *adjusted sales price* with the *cost of the new house.* If the cost of the new house is the same or greater than the adjusted sales price of the old house, then none of the actual gain is taxed. But if the cost of the new house is less than the adjusted sales price, you are taxed on the difference—but not on more than your actual gain. Basis of the new home is reduced by nontaxed gain.

Cost basis of a cooperative apartment. Include the price for the stock in the cooperative and part of the mortgage to which the cooperative is subject, if these three tests are met: (1) The mortgage is properly allocated to your apartment. (The IRS will accept a mortgage allocation based on the same ratio as your stock interest bears to the total value of all the stock in the corporation.) (2) The corporation retains your stock as a pledge for payment of

your annual charges, such as interest and principal payments on the mortgage. (3) Your share of corporate assets will be reduced by the unpaid balance of your proportionate share of the mortgage if the corporation is liquidated.

Examples—

1. You are under 55. You plan to sell your house, which has a basis of $30,000. To make it more attractive to buyers, you paint the outside at a cost of $300 in April, 1986. You pay for the painting when the work is finished. In May, 1986, you sell the house for $71,000. Broker's commissions and other selling expenses are $2,000. In October, 1986 you buy a new house for $68,000. This is how you compute the amount realized, the adjusted sales price, gain taxable on your 1986 return and your basis in the replacement property:

Selling price	$71,000
Less: Selling expenses	2,000
Amount realized	69,000
Less: Basis of old house	30,000
Actual gain	$39,000
Amount realized	$69,000
Less: Fix-up costs	300
Adjusted sales price	68,700
Less: Cost of new house	68,000
Taxable gain	$ 700

Of the $39,000 gain $700 is taxable in 1986, the balance, $38,300 is not taxable. The cost basis of the new house is $29,700 ($68,000 — $38,300).

2. Same facts as above except that in 1987 you sell the new house for $68,000 and move to an apartment. Taxed gain is $38,300:

Selling price	$68,000
Less: Cost basis	29,700
Taxed gain	$38,300

The exact amount of additional gain would have been taxed on the sale of your old house if you had not bought the second house. In other words, you merely deferred tax on the sale of your first house until you sold the new house without a further replacement.

Remodeling a vacation home as a permanent residence. A couple, planning to sell their principal home and remodel their vacation home into a permanent residence, asked the IRS if the remodeling costs could be considered as a purchase of a new residence. They planned to add 35% more living space by converting storage space to living areas, put in a new roof, heating and air conditioning systems and expand the basement. The IRS answered that the remodeling qualified because of the substantial structural alterations. Further, the remodeling costs were to be paid within the qualifying replacement period discussed in ¶29.22.

The IRS warned that merely adding a tennis court, pool, or new roof would not have qualified for tax deferral. However, once the major alterations are made, all improvements, such as the construction of a pool, could be considered part of the total cost of the renovation.

¶29.24 • REVIEWING PURCHASE AND SALES RECORDS FOR TAX REPORTING

Arrange your records into three groups: (1) records of the purchase of the old house and improvements; (2) records of the sale of your old house; (3) records of the new purchase.

Energy conserving capital improvements do not increase your basis to the extent of an energy credit claimed. The basis of your old house is the total costs shown by these records. If you deduct a casualty loss for damage incurred to your house, the basis of the house should be reduced by the amount deducted.

Sale of old house. Here you should have: (1) the sales contract showing the sales price of the old house; (2) a statement showing settlement costs at the closing and allocating taxes and fire insurance; (3) the bill and record of payment of legal fees; (4) record of payment of broker's fees, if any; (5) a closing statement from the bank holding the mortgage on your old house showing final interest charges up to the date of transfer of title and prepayment penalties, if any; (6) if you incurred fix-up costs, records of when the work was done and when payment was made; (7) a record of payments for advertising the sale of the house, if any.

You reduce the selling price of the house by payments for

broker's commissions, legal fees, and advertising expenses. The allocated property taxes are deducted according to the rules at ¶16.05. The bank interest and the prepayment penalty are deductible as interest if you itemize deductions. You may not deduct fire insurance premium payments. The treatment of fix-up costs is explained at ¶29.23 above. The paying off of the principal balance of the mortgage to the bank does not enter into the tax computation.

Purchase of and improvements to the old house. Your records here should show the purchase price of the old house plus title insurance fees, recording fees, transfer taxes, and attorney's fees. Also, bills or other records detailing capital improvements made to the house for additional rooms, equipment, landscaping and similar capital items (*see* ¶9.021). In one case, an accountant forgot to keep adequate records. He bought his house for $5,000 and later sold it for $11,000. In figuring his taxable gain, he claimed he had spent $5,000 for improvements; the IRS allowed him only $2,750. A court permitted him to increase his cost by $4,000. While his proof was not adequate, he was able to show that the house was in dilapidated condition when he bought it. The court estimated that he spent at least $4,000 to make the house habitable.

Purchase of the new residence. Here you should have: (1) your contract showing the cost of the new house plus any additional improvements; (2) the closing statement showing title insurance fees, adjustment of taxes, mortgage fees, and recording fees.

The cost basis of your new house includes the purchase price (even though all or part is covered by a mortgage), attorney's fees, mortgage fees, title insurance fees, and recording fees less the gain not taxed on the sale of your old home. You deduct taxes according to the allocation rules at ¶16.05. The payment of fire insurance premiums on the house is not deductible. The treatment of "points" is discussed at ¶15.012.

¶29.25 • A MARRIED COUPLE MAY HAVE TO AGREE TO TAX DEFERMENT

When title to your new house differs from title to your old house, you and your spouse must file consent statements to defer tax. This happens when you or your spouse held title to the old house and now you both hold title jointly to the new house, or title to the old house was in your joint names and now only one of you holds title to the new house. Form 2119 may be used for consent.

Examples—

1. Smith holds title to a condominium which he sells for $40,000. Its cost basis was $30,000, and he realizes a $10,000 gain. However, within the year, he and his wife contribute $20,000 each to buy a new house for $40,000 in their joint names. Smith pays no tax on the gain if he and his wife file consent statements in which they agree to allocate the basis of the new house between them. They file the consent on Form 2119 or on an attached statement in the year gain on the sale is realized. The basis of the new house is $15,000 to Smith and $15,000 to his wife.

2. Same facts as in the above example except the condominium was owned jointly by Smith and his wife, and the new house is bought by Mrs. Smith and placed in her name. Tax on the gain is deferred if both file consent statements. The basis of the new house to Mrs. Smith is $30,000.

Consents are ineffective to defer tax unless the old and new houses were principal residences of the couple.

If a husband and wife separate and sell their common home and each receives one-half the sales proceeds, each may defer tax on the gain by reinvesting his or her share in a new home.

Where a husband and wife each sell separate homes owned before marriage, tax on the gain is postponed if the total proceeds of the two sales is reinvested in a new home within the time limit and each contributes one-half the purchase price and takes joint title to the new home. No consent statement is required.

¶29.26 • SALE OF MORE THAN ONE RESIDENCE WITHIN TWO YEARS

Tax may not be deferred if, within two years before the sale, you deferred tax on a profitable sale of another principal residence. However, this rule does not apply if you moved to a new job location and your moving expenses qualify under the rules of ¶2.40.

Examples—

1. In August, 1985, you sell your house at a profit and buy a new principal residence with the sale proceeds in the same month. In July, 1986, you sell the new residence at a profit and buy another principal residence in September, 1986. You may not defer tax on the July, 1986 sale because it was within two years of the August, 1985 sale. The house purchased in September, 1986 is treated as a new principal residence for purposes of postponing tax on the gain on the August, 1985 sale.

2. Same facts as in 1 but you had to sell your house in July, 1986 because of a job relocation to a new city 500 miles away from your prior area of work and residence. Your moving expenses also meet the other tests of ¶2.40. You may defer tax on the sale made in August, 1985 and the sale made in July, 1986. For deferring tax on the August, 1985 sale, you compare the cost of the residence bought in August, 1985 with the adjusted sales price of the residence sold in August, 1985. For deferring tax on the July, 1986 sale, you compare the cost of the new residence bought in September, 1986, with the adjusted sales price of the house sold in July, 1986.

When you buy a new residence before the sale of the old house and then sell the new house, you may not defer tax on a subsequent sale of the original house, even if all sales and purchases fall within two years. To defer tax on the sale of the original house, you must own the new house at the time of the sale of the old house.

Example—

You own a house which cost $20,000. In January, you buy another house for $30,000. In July, you sell the house you bought in January for $32,000. In October, you sell your original house for $40,000. You have a $20,000 taxed gain on the October sale. Even though you bought another residence within two years before the October sale, you sold that new residence before you sold the original residence. So you may not avoid tax. You also have a $2,000 gain on the July sale.

¶29.27 • SALE OF HOUSE USED PARTLY FOR BUSINESS

When you use part of your residence for business or rental to tenants, you treat the sale as if you sold two separate pieces of property. You apportion the sales price and basis of the house between the rented portion and the residential portion. You deduct depreciation from only the rented part.

You do not pay tax on gain allocated to your personal use of the house if your reinvestment in a new residence is at least equal to the selling price of the portion of the old house allocated to your personal use. Similarly, if only part of the new property is used as your personal residence, only the cost allocated to that use is considered as reinvested for purposes of deferring tax on gain.

Examples—

1. You sell for $97,000 a three-family house that cost you $33,000. Selling expenses (commissions and legal fees) were $7,000. You lived in one of the apartments. You rented the other two. On the rental part, you took $4,400 of straight line depreciation. You compute your gain by allocating ⅔ of the selling price and basis to the rental part and ⅓ to the personal part:

		Rental	Personal
Net sales price ($97,000 − $7,000)		$60,000	$30,000
Cost ($33,000)	$22,000		
Less: Depreciation	4,400	17,600	11,000
Net gain		$42,400	$19,000

You pay tax on the gain of $42,400. You defer tax on the gain of $19,000, if you invest at least $30,000 in a new residence under the rules at ¶29.20. You also defer tax if you buy a new multifamily house and the cost allocated to your apartment in the house is at least $30,000. If you are 55 or over, you can make an election under the rules of ¶29.30 and avoid tax on the personal profit even though you do not make a reinvestment.

2. Same facts as above except the net selling price is only $30,000. Here you have a gain of $2,400 ($20,000 − $17,600) on the rental part, and a loss of $1,000 ($10,000 − $11,000) on the residential part. You may not offset the $1,000 loss against the gain. Each is treated as a separate transaction. The loss is not deductible because it is a personal loss.

¶29.28 • CLAIMING A LOSS ON SALE OF PERSONAL RESIDENCE

Loss on the sale of a personal residence is not deductible. However, a loss may be claimed in these instances: (1) You convert the house from personal use to some profit-making purpose before the sale. (2) You sell a house acquired by gift or inheritance which you did not personally use but rather offered for rental or sale shortly after acquisition. (3) You sell stock in your cooperative apartment in which there were nonstockholder tenants when you acquired your stock.

Profit-making purposes. Renting a residence is a changeover from personal to profit-making purposes. Merely putting the house up for rent or an isolated rental of several months may not be recognized by the IRS as a conversion to rental property.

The Tax Court has approved a loss deduction where a house was rented on a 90-day lease with an option to buy. The court set down two tests for determining when a house is converted to rental property: (1) The rental charge returns a profit. (2) The lease prevents you from using or reoccupying the house during the lease period. Under the Tax Court approach, you have a conversion if you have a lease that gives possession of the house to the tenant during the lease period, and the rent, after deducting taxes, interest, insurance, repairs, depreciation and other charges, returns you a profit.

You may deduct a loss if you rented part and occupied part for your own purposes. A loss on a sale is allowable on the rented portion.

A loss deduction is also allowed where you acquired the house as an investment with the intention of selling it at a profit even though you occupied it incidentally as a residence prior to sale.
Examples—
1. An owner bought a house with the intention of selling it. He lived in it for six years, but during that period it was for sale. He was allowed to deduct the loss on its sale by proving he lived in it to protect it from vandalism and to keep it in good condition so it would be attractive to possible buyers.
2. An architect and builder built a house and offered it for sale through an agent and advertisements. He had a home and no intention to occupy the new house. On a realtor's advice, he moved into the house to make it more saleable. Ten months later, he sold the house at a loss of $4,065 and promptly moved out. The loss was allowed on proof that his main purpose in building and occupying the house was to realize a profit by a sale; the residential use was incidental.

Rental loss may be barred for temporary rental preceding sale. The IRS and Tax Court disallowed a loss deduction for rental expenses under the "profit motive rules" (¶5.06) where a residence was rented for 10 months until it could be sold. According to the Tax Court, the temporary rental did not convert the residence to rental property. Since the sales effort was primary, there was no profit motive for the rental. Thus, no loss could be claimed; rental expenses were deductible only to the extent of rental income. *See* ¶5.06. The favorable side of the Tax Court position: Since the residence was not converted to rental property, the owners could defer tax on the gain from the sale under the rules of ¶29.20 by buying a new home. An appeals court reversed the Tax Court and allowed both tax deferral and a loss deduction. The rental loss was allowed since the old home was actually rented for a fair rental price. Further, the owners had moved and could not return to the old home, which was rented almost continuously until sold.

Residence acquired by gift or inheritance. You may deduct a loss on the sale of a house which was received as an inheritance or gift if you personally did not use it and you offered it for sale or rental immediately or within a few weeks after acquisition.

If you inherit a residence in which you do not intend to live, it may be advisable to put it up for rent or sale, not for sale alone. If you merely try to sell, and you finally do so at a loss, you are limited to a capital loss. If you first try to rent but cannot, you will probably get an ordinary loss when you finally sell.

The Tax Court held that a surviving spouse realized a deductible loss on the sale of a house previously held jointly with a deceased spouse.
Example—
A couple owned a winter vacation home in Florida. When the husband died, his wife immediately put the house up for sale and never lived in it. It was sold at a loss. The IRS disallowed the capital loss deduction, claiming it was personal and nondeductible. The wife argued that her case was no different from the case of an heir inheriting and selling a home, since at the death of her husband her interest in the

property was increased. The court agreed with her reasoning and allowed the deduction.

Stock in cooperative apartment. Normally, you get no deduction for a loss on the sale of your stock in a cooperative housing corporation. It makes no difference that you occasionally sublet your apartment. It is still not considered property used in a business. But you may get a loss deduction when there were nonstockholder tenants in the cooperative housing corporation when you bought your stock. Then, you get a partial capital loss deduction if you sell your stock or if it becomes worthless. To figure your capital loss—

First find the difference between your cost and your selling price. This would ordinarily be your capital loss.

Then find the percentage of nonstockholding tenants (based on rental values) in the housing corporation when you bought your stock.

Apply this percentage to the loss you figured above. This is the capital loss you are allowed.

See ¶5.15 for when depreciation may be taken on the basis of the cooperative stock ownership.

¶29.30 • TAX-FREE RESIDENCE SALE BY HOME-OWNERS AGE 55 OR OVER

If you are 55 years of age or older and sell or exchange your home at a profit, you may avoid tax on profits up to $125,000. To claim this exclusion, you must: (1) elect to avoid tax; (2) be 55 or over before the date of sale; and (3) have owned and occupied the house as your principal residence for at least three of the five years preceding the day of sale.

The election applies to cooperative apartment ownership tied to stock ownership and to condominiums. It applies also to gain realized from an involuntary conversion of your home through fire, storm or other casualty, or condemnation. Although you avoid tax on gain, you consider the gain as gross income in determining whether you are required to file a return (*see* ¶1.00).

The election to exclude gain does not apply where only a partial interest in the home is sold. In a private letter ruling, the IRS refused to permit an exclusion to a homeowner who sold the remainder interest in her home while retaining the right to live in it for life. However, the exclusion is allowed if a homeowner gives away a remainder interest in the house and then sells the retained life interest. The exclusion may be claimed because the life interest is the owner's entire interest in the residence.

Age test. You must be 55 or over before the date of sale. It is not sufficient that you will be 55 sometime during the year in which the sale occurs. According to the IRS, you reach 55 the day before your birthday. Thus, a sale on the date of your 55th birthday qualifies.

If you receive an offer that you want to accept before your 55th birthday, contract to sell but do not give title or possession until you are 55 if you want to make the election. A sale may be considered to have occurred for tax purposes when you give the buyer possession of the house, although you have not formally passed title.

The use and ownership test. You must have owned and occupied your home as your principal residence for three of the five years preceding the date of sale. Ownership and use for 36 full months or for 1,095 days (365 × 3) qualifies. The three years need not be consecutive. Short temporary absences for vacations, although accompanied with rental of the residence, are counted as periods of use.
Examples—
1. You are over 55. You started to use a house as your principal residence in 1950. On January 1, 1985, you move to another state and rent the house. On July 1, 1986, you sell it. You may elect tax-free gain. You owned and used the house as your principal residence for three out of the five years preceding the sale.
2. You live with your son and daughter-in-law in a house owned by your son from 1972 through 1983. On January 1, 1984, you buy the house from your son. You sell it on March 31, 1986. You may not make the election in 1986. Although you used the property as your principal residence for more than three years, you did not own it for three of the five years preceding the date of the sale.
3. On January 1, 1983, a teacher, age 55, bought and moved into a house which he used as his principal residence. On February 1, 1984,

he went abroad on a one-year sabbatical and, during part of the year, leased the house. On March 1, 1985, one month after his return, he sold the house. He may not make the election. He did not use the residence for the required three years. Under Treasury regulations, his one-year leave is not considered a temporary absence that may be counted as part of the three-year occupancy period.

> **Making the election.** The tax-free election is available to you only once in your lifetime. If, at the time you sell your home, you plan to invest the money in another home of sufficient cost to completely defer tax but later change your plans, you can make the election at any time before the end of the period for making a refund claim for the year in which the sale occurred. This is generally within three years from the due date of the return filed for the year of the sale. Similarly, if you make the election and then decide to revoke it, you may do so within the same three-year period.

You make the election on Form 2119 or in a signed statement which you attach to your income tax return for the year of sale. In the statement, you write that you elect to exclude from income the gain realized on the sale. In addition, you give the following data: (1) your name, age, Social Security number, and marital status as of the date of sale; (2) the dates you bought and sold your residence; (3) the adjusted sale price and the adjusted basis of the property on the date of sale; and (4) the length of any absences during the five years preceding the sale.

If you are married at the time of the sale, your spouse must agree to the election. In revoking the election, you must also have your spouse's consent. If you are divorced after the election but then want to revoke, you must get your former spouse's consent to the revocation. If your spouse dies after the sale but before you could make an election, your deceased spouse's personal representative (administrator or executor) must join with you in making an election. Similarly, the personal representative must join in a revocation of any election previously made by you and your deceased spouse. Joint elections and revocations are required, even though the residence was separately owned, separate tax returns are filed, or the nonowning spouse does not meet the three-year residence requirement. Also see ¶29.32.

In one case, the IRS permitted an election by an executor where a sale was completed after the death of the owner under an executory contract made by the owner prior to his death.

A revocation is made in a signed statement showing: (1) your name and Social Security number; (2) the year in which the election was made and filed; and (3) the Internal Revenue office where you filed the election.

When you might not want to elect the exclusion. If you sell your principal residence at a gain which is substantially less than the exclusion, and you plan to reinvest at least all of the net proceeds from the sale in a new home, consider deferring tax under the rules at ¶29.20 rather than electing to exclude gain. You are permitted only one lifetime exclusion. For example, if you have a gain of $10,000 and elect to exclude it, you have used up your once-in-a-lifetime election; a later home sale will not be entitled to a $115,000 exclusion. If you buy a new house at a cost at least equal to the adjusted sales price of the old home (¶29.20), the entire gain from the sale of your old home is deferred. If and when you sell the new house without a further home purchase, the election to exclude gain may then be made.

Property used in part as principal residence. An election may be made for that part of the gain attributed to personal use. For example, you use a part of your home as an office for more than two years out of the last five years before the sale. The election does not apply to the gain allocable to the office.

> Rental of the house for periods during the five-year period preceding the date of sale will not disqualify the election. Where you do rent your house and you want to avail yourself of the tax-free election, make sure that a rental during the five-year period does not exceed two years. If it does, the three-year residence test will not be met.

Sale by marital trust. Property may be left to marital trust for the benefit of a surviving spouse if there is concern that the survivor may be unable to manage the property. A personal residence may be put into the trust. If the surviving spouse is entitled to all the trust income and has an unlimited power to receive trust corpus upon request or appoint the property to any other person, the surviving spouse is considered the owner of the trust for tax purposes. Thus, if the trust sells the personal residence, the surviving spouse can elect to claim the $125,000 home sale exclusion provided her or she is over age 55 on the date of sale and has (1) owned (through the trust) and used the residence as a principal residence for three of the last five years preceding the date of sale, and (2) the $125,000 exclusion was not previously elected by the surviving spouse or the deceased spouse with respect to a prior sale.

¶29.31 • COMBINING THE EXCLUSION WITH TAX DEFERRAL

If you sell your principal residence at a gain of over $125,000 and plan to purchase a new home, you may take advantage of the exclusion as well as the tax-free deferral rules of ¶29.20. Where you qualify for the exclusion, your gain up to the exclusion is tax free. You may then defer all or part of the remaining gain, depending on the amount of your investment in the new home. You may defer all of the remaining gain by making an investment at least equal to the adjusted sales price of the old house (sales price less selling expenses and fix-up costs—see ¶29.23) less the tax-free gain. If you invest less than this amount, the difference between (1) adjusted sales price of the old house less the tax-free gain, and (2) the new investment, is taxed, but not exceeding the remaining gain.

In determining whether you have to file a return, the tax-free gain realized from the sale of your house is counted as gross income, although not taxed.

Example—
You sell your home for $180,000. You incurred fix-up costs of $2,000. Basis of the house is $40,000. You make a profit of $140,000. You elect to exclude $125,000 of the profit from tax. You may still defer all or part of the remaining profit of $15,000 of gain by investing in a new home which costs at least $53,000.

Sales price	$180,000
Less: Fix-up costs	2,000
Adjusted sales price	$178,000
Less: Excluded gain	125,000
	$ 53,000

If you buy a new residence for $50,000, $3,000 of the gain is taxable ($53,000 − $50,000).

Selling on the installment method. Where you sell your home and take back a purchase money mortgage that will be paid off after the year of sale, you have made an installment sale. Only a portion of each payment is taxable.

Example—
Smith sold his home which cost him $140,000 for $300,000 and elects the exclusion. The buyer is unable to get outside financing so Smith agrees to take back a purchase money mortgage of $150,000, payable over 15 years. Of the $160,000 profit ($300,000 − $140,000), only $35,000 is taxable; $125,000 is tax free. The $35,000 gain is reported over the 15 years in which payment on the mortgage loan is received. To determine the amount of each payment taxable as income, the gross profit ratio is applied to each payment actually received. The gross profit ratio is figured by dividing the taxable gain by the total contract price (see ¶6.17). Here, this is $35,000 divided by $300,000, which gives a profit ratio of 11.66%. Thus, in the year of sale, $17,490 (11.66% of the $150,000 down payment) is taxable. Of each annual $10,000 installment payment received over the 15 years, $1,166 is taxable ($10,000 × 11.66%).

¶29.32 • THE EXCLUSION AND JOINTLY OWNED RESIDENCES

Where you own the house jointly with your spouse and file a joint return in the year the residence is sold, only one of you need meet the age requirement of 55 or over and the residence and ownership requirement of three out of the last five years. Marital status is determined as of the date of the sale.

Where a spouse who has died held and used the house as a personal residence for three out of the last five years and had not previously claimed a tax-free exemption election, the surviving spouse who is 55 or over and not remarried at the time of the sale may make an election.

Example—

In 1986, a woman, 56 years old, plans to marry later in the year. She also plans to sell her home at a substantial profit. Her fiance sold his home at a profit of $100,000 in August 1985 and elected on his 1985 return to avoid tax. If she sells the house before the marriage, she may claim the exclusion on her 1986 return. True, only one lifetime election of the exclusion is allowed to a married couple, but for purposes of this test, marital status is determined at the time of sale. Thus, if she sells before she marries, her right to claim the election is not affected by her spouse's prior election. However, if she sells after the marriage, she may not claim the $125,000 exclusion because of her spouse's 1985 election. Once married, the right to claim the election on a sale of her home is forfeited because of a spouse's prior election, even though the spouse's home sale may have taken place prior to her marriage.

Only one lifetime election is allowed to a married couple; you and your spouse do not each have a separate election to claim the exclusion. If either you or your spouse has previously elected the exclusion, neither of you may make another election. If spouses make an election during marriage and later divorce, no further elections are available to either of them or to either of their new spouses should they remarry. If both you and your spouse before your marriage owned and used separate residences and each elected the exclusion, there is no recapture of taxes attributable to the gain excluded on the sale of one of the residences.

What if before your marriage you and your spouse each owned and used a separate residence, and after your marriage both residences are sold? May two elections be made? No. An election may be made for a sale of either residence (but not for both residences) provided the age, ownership and use requirements are met. To take advantage of two exclusions, the sales should take place before marriage.

A husband and wife selling a jointly-owned residence are considered as one taxpayer for purposes of the exclusion limitation. But if joint owners are not married, each owner who meets the tests for age (55), use (principal residence), and holding period (three of five years), may exclude gain up to $125,000 on his interest in the residence. That one owner meets the requirements does not qualify the other for the exclusion.

A married person who files a separate return may exclude only up to $62,500 of profit.

Joint ownership with someone other than spouse. If you own the home jointly with someone other than your spouse, each owner who meets the age 55 test and the three out of five year ownership and use test may exclude their share of the gain.

¶29.40 • DEDUCTING EXPENSES OF RENTING OUT PART OF YOUR HOME

You report rent receipts and deduct expenses allocated to the rented part of the property on Schedule E (*see* Supplement to Your Income Tax). Expenses allocated to rental are deductible, whether or not you itemize deductions. You deduct interest and taxes on your personal share of the property as itemized deductions, if you itemize deductions.

Example—

You bought a three-family house in 1970. You occupy one apartment as a personal residence. The house cost you $30,000 ($27,000 for the building, $3,000 for the land). It has a useful life of 30 years. This is how you deduct expenses:

Depreciation % of building Cost—$27,000	Cost basis $18,000	Useful life 30 years	Depreciation $600

	Total	Deduct itemized deductions	Deduct in rent schedule	Not deductible
Taxes	$ 600	$200	$ 400	
Interest	390	130	260	
Repairs	300		200	$100
Depreciation	600		600	
	$1,890	$330	$1,460	$100

The expenses allocated to personal use are deductible provided you have itemized deductions in excess of your zero bracket amount. Repairs allocated to your apartment are nondeductible personal expenses.

¶29.41 • TAKING DEPRECIATION WHEN YOU RENT YOUR RESIDENCE

When you convert your residence to rental property, you can begin to take depreciation on the building. You figure depreciation on the *lower* of the building's:

Fair market value at the time you convert it to rental property, or

Adjusted basis (original cost plus or minus capital additions or reductions until time of conversion).

In 1986, you may claim ACRS if the property was acquired after 1980. If you bought your home before 1981 and converted it to rental property after 1980, ACRS is not allowed. Depreciation must be claimed under prior law rules.

Example—

In 1960, you bought a residence for $20,000 ($5,000 allocated to the land, $15,000 to the building). In 1969, you added a porch and patio at a cost of $3,000. On January 1, 1986, you rent the house, when its fair market value is $60,000. You figure depreciation on the adjusted basis of the house at the time of conversion or $18,000 ($15,000 original cost plus $3,000 capital improvement). It is lower than the fair market value of $60,000. Applying prior depreciation rules, you estimate a rate of depreciation under the straight-line method of 4%. The depreciation deduction for 1986 is $720 ($18,000 × 4%). You may not use the faster write-off allowed under ACRS because you owned the building before 1981.

If the property qualifies for ACRS, the date of conversion fixes the write-off rate in the first year. *See* ¶5.35.

Example—

In 1981, you purchased for $100,000 a house which you used as a personal residence until June, 1986 when you move out of the home and rent it for a two-year period. At that time, the fair market value of the house is $125,000. You apply ACRS rate, provided by an IRS table for placing the property in service in the sixth month. The tables may be found in Treasury regulations and in the instructions to Form 4562 (Depreciation).

TAX RESULT WHEN YOU CONVERT RESIDENCE TO RENTAL PROPERTY

Cost on Jan. 1, 1973 When Bought		Market Value When Converted, Jan. 1, 1985		Basis for Depreciation	Depreciation on Building (2 Years at 4%)	Sold Dec. 31, 1986 for	Basis for Sale	Gain or (Loss)
Land	Building	Land	Building					
$2,000	$8,000	$2,400	$9,600	$8,000 ¹	$640	$16,000	$9,360 ²	$6,640
					640	8,000	9,360 ³	(1,360)
					640	11,000	9,360 ²	1,640 ⁴
$2,000	$8,000	$1,600	$6,400	$6,400 ¹	$512	$12,000	9,488 ²	$2,512
					512	7,000	7,488 ³	(488)
					512	9,000	None	None ⁵

¹ Depreciation is taken on the lower of (1) adjusted basis at time of conversion (cost plus or minus capital additions or reductions) or (2) fair market value at time of conversion.

² Gain is always figured on adjusted basis at time of conversion, less depreciation (see column 4).

³ Loss is figured on the lower of (1) fair market value at the time of conversion less depreciation or (2) adjusted basis at time of conversion, less depreciation (see column 4).

⁴ There is taxed gain even though sales price is less than value at time of conversion.

⁵ There is neither gain nor loss. Although the property was sold for less than its adjusted basis, it was sold for more than its fair market value at the time of its conversion.

Basis to use when you sell a rented residence. If you realize a gain, you use adjusted basis at the time of the conversion, less depreciation. If you realize a loss, you use the *lower* of adjusted basis or fair market value at the time of the conversion, less depreciation. *See* the table below.

Have an appraiser estimate the fair market value of the house when it is rented. The appraisal will help support your basis for depreciation or a loss deduction on a sale if your return is examined.

Depreciation on a vacant residence. If you move from your house before it is sold, you may generally not deduct depreciation on the vacant residence while it is held for sale. The IRS will not allow the deduction, and according to a Tax Court case, a deduction is possible only if you can show that you held the house, expecting to make a profit on an increase in value over and above the value of the house when you moved from it. That is, you held the house for sale on the expectation of profiting on a future increase in value after abandoning the house as a residence.

Example—

In 1967, Lowry put his summer home up for sale. At the time, it was worth $50,000. However, he decided he would not sell the house for less than $150,000. He expected the value of his land to appreciate greatly during the next few years. He did not rent the house because he felt it would be easier to sell an empty house, and the amount of rental income would not justify the expense of equipping the house for rental. He deducted the maintenance expenses, claiming he held the property as an investment. The IRS disallowed the deduction, claiming that since he did not try to rent it, he held it for personal use.

A federal district court allowed the deduction. Lowry had sound business reasons for not renting. He intended to benefit from post-abandonment appreciation in land values. When he put the house on the market, it was worth $50,000. Six years later, he finally got his asking price of $150,000. That he immediately listed the house for sale did not negate his intention to hold the house for future appreciation.

An investor may claim depreciation on a vacant building held for resale. However, the IRS may dispute the deduction as it has withdrawn a prior acceptance of a court decision which allowed the deduction to an investor.

¶29.42 • DEDUCTING RENTAL EXPENSES OF A VACATION HOME

The law prevents most homeowners from deducting losses (expenses in excess of income) from renting a personal vacation home. Tests based on days of personal and rental use determine whether you may deduct losses. The following tests are designed to disallow losses.

1. *If you rent the vacation home for less than 15 days,* you may not deduct any expenses attributed to the rental (except for interest, real estate taxes, and casualty losses, if any). If you realize a profit on the rental, you are not taxable on the profit.

2. *If the rental of the home is for 15 days or more,* you then determine if your personal use of the home exceeds a 14-day or 10% time test. If it does, you are considered to have used the unit as a residence during the year and rental expenses are deductible only to the extent of gross rental income. This limitation on loss deductions applies if the number of days you personally *use* the vacation home during your taxable year exceeds the greater of 14 days or 10% of the number of days the home is rented at a fair rental. (The use of rental pool arrangements is discussed below.) If rental income exceeds expenses, your operating gain is fully taxable.

3. *You rent the home for 15 days or more, but the days of your personal use are less than the days fixed by the 14-day/10% test.* You are not considered to have made any personal use of the residence during the year. Therefore, expenses in excess of rental income may be deductible. However, the IRS may disallow the loss deduction if you cannot prove that you rent the residence to make a profit under the "profit-motive" tests of ¶5.06.

The Tax Court has allowed loss deductions where the owner made little personal use of the home and proved he bought the house to make a profitable resale.

Examples—

1. (*Loss allowed.*) In 1973, Clancy purchased a house and land in a coastal resort area of California. Prior to the purchase, Clancy was told by a renting agent that he could expect reasonable income and considerable appreciation from the property. Previously, he had sold similar property in the same development at a profit. After the purchase, Clancy spent $5,000 to prepare the house for rental, and gave a rental agency the exclusive right to offer the property for rent. The house was available for rent 95% of the time in 1973, and 100% of the time in 1974. However, rentals proved disappointing, totaling only $280 in 1973 and $1,244 in 1974, despite the active efforts of the agency to rent the property. However, the house did appreciate in value and was eventually sold at a profit of $14,000. In 1973 and 1974, Clancy deducted rental expenses of approximately $21,000 which the IRS disallowed. The IRS claimed that the house was not rental property used in a business. Further, as Clancy knew that he could not make a profit from the rentals, he could not be considered to hold the property for the production of income.

The Tax Court agrees that the expenses are not deductible business expenses. But this does not mean that they are not deductible as expenses of income production. Although the rental income from the property was minimal, Clancy acquired and held the property expecting to make a profit on a sale. He had previously sold similar property at a profit and was told to expect considerable rental income as well as appreciation from the new house. Where an owner holds property, as Clancy did here, because he believes that it may appreciate in value, such property is held for the production of income. Further evidence that Clancy held the property to make a profit: He rarely used it for personal purposes and an agent actively sought to rent it.

2. (*Loss allowed.*) Allen, a banking executive, built a ski lodge near a popular resort at Bromley Mountain in Vermont. The lodge was rented out as a summer or fall vacation home as well as during the ski season. He used the lodge overnight only when preparing it for a tenant. Allen claimed unfavorable weather, gasoline shortages, and a glut of competitors contributed to poor rentals. Deductions of $3,271 in 1971 and $6,500 in 1972 were disallowed by the IRS on the grounds that Allen did not intend to make a profit from the lodge.

The Tax Court disagreed. True, it might be argued that Allen had no profit motive as he had independent income sources. However, he operated the lodge in a businesslike manner, experimenting with different types of rental arrangements in an attempt to turn a profit. The substantial and repeated losses were caused by forces beyond his control: by unfavorable weather and gasoline shortages. Further, he suffered actual economic losses. Finally, he never used the lodge for his own personal enjoyment; he stayed overnight only to get the lodge in rental shape.

3. (*Loss allowed.*) Nelson bought a condominium, hired a rental agent, and even advertised the unit in the Wall Street Journal and Indianapolis Star. He also listed the unit for sale. During 1974, he was unable to rent the apartment but deducted expenses and depreciation of over $6,100 which the IRS disallowed. The IRS argued he did not buy the unit to make a profit but to tax shelter substantial income. The Tax Court disagreed. Although his efforts to rent were not successful in 1974, he was successful in later years in renting the unit. He rarely visited the apartment other than to initially furnish it. When he went on vacation, he went abroad or to other vacation spots.

4. (*Loss disallowed.*) The Lindows purchased a condominium which they rented out during the prime winter rental season. However, over an eight-year period their expenses consistently exceeded rental income. The Tax Court agreed with the IRS that expenses in excess of rental income were not deductible. Substantial, repeated losses, even after the initial years of operation, indicate that the operation was not primarily profit oriented. The rental return during the prime rental season could not return a profit. Even if the condominium was fully rented for the entire prime rental season, annual claimed expenses would exceed rent income. The couple also used the unit for several months and intended to live there on retirement. They did not consider putting the unit up for sale with an agent. Finally, that they had detailed records of income and expenses did not prove a business venture. Records, regardless of how detailed, are insufficient to permit the deduction of what are essentially personal expenses.

5. (*Loss disallowed.*) A married couple rented their Florida condominium to the husband's parents at less than fair market value. Although the couple might have hoped to realize a profit on resale of the condominium, their failure to profit by renting at the highest possible price indicated that their primary motive for holding the property was personal, rather than to make a profit.

> A "vacation home" may be a house, apartment, condominium, house trailer, mini motor home, boat, or similar property, including any environs and outbuildings such as a garage. The term does not include that portion of a dwelling unit that is used exclusively as a hotel, motel, inn, or similar establishment.

The loss limitation rules apply not only to individuals but also to trusts, estates, partnerships, and S corporations owning vacation residences.

Figuring "personal" use time for the 14-day /10% test. A vacation home is considered to have been personally used if for any part of the day the home is used by: (1) you or any other person who owns an interest in the home unless you and the co-owner have a shared equity financing agreement (*see* below); (2) your relatives or the relatives of a co-owner, such as brothers and sisters, spouse, parents, grandparents, children, or spouses of your children. However, if a relative pays a fair rental to use the home as his principal residence, this use is *not* considered personal use; (3) any person who uses the home under a reciprocal arrangement under which you use some other dwelling (whether or not a fair rental is charged); or (4) any other person who uses the vacation home during a day unless for that day the home is rented for a fair rental.

Use by a co-owner is not considered personal use if these tests are satisfied: (1) you have a shared equity financing agreement under which the co-owner pays you a fair rent for using the home as his principal residence; (2) you and your co-owner each have undivided interests for more than 50 years in the entire home and in any appurtenant land acquired with the residence.

Any use by a co-owner which does not meet the above tests is considered personal use by you if, for any part of the day, the home is used by a co-owner or a holder of any interest in the home (other than a security interest or an interest under a lease for fair rental) for personal purposes. For this purpose, any other ownership interest existing at the time you have an interest in the vacation home is counted, even if there are no immediate rights to possession and enjoyment of the vacation home under such other interest. For example, you have a life estate in the home and your friend owns the remainder interest. Use by either of you is personal use.

An owner is not considered to have personally used a vacation home used by his employee if the value of such use is not taxable under the rules of ¶2.01.

For a home owned by a partnership, trust, estate, or S corporation, the number of days of personal use is the total number of days of use by the owners or beneficiaries. Under proposed regulations, this rule would not apply to a partnership rental of a unit to a partner as his principal residence if there are no special allocations of deductions. If two or more owners or beneficiaries use a home during the same day, that day would constitute only one day of personal use.

Rental of principal residence. You are not considered to have made any personal use of a principal residence which you rent or try to rent at a fair rental for a consecutive period of 12 months or more or for a period of less than 12 months that ends with the sale or exchange of the residence. This means that deductions are not limited by the personal use tests of this section, ¶29.42. However, where the rental precedes a sale, deductions for the period have been limited under the "profit motive rules" of ¶5.06.

Example—
In July 1977, Bolaris moved into a new home after failing to find a buyer for his old home. He rented the old house for 10 months before its sale in 1978. In 1977, he reported a rental loss of $1,638 and in 1978, $4,727, which the IRS disallowed. The items making up the loss were depreciation, insurance premiums and repair expenses. The IRS did not think the residence could be considered a residence for tax deferral purposes and rental property at the same time. The Tax Court sided with the IRS. An appeals court reversed, allowing the deductions. Bolaris was also allowed to defer tax on the sale of the residence. The IRS did not question his right to do so.

Allocation of expenses to rental activity. When you personally use a vacation home on any day during the taxable year, expenses must be allocated between personal and rental use. By law, deductible expenses of renting, except for interest and taxes, are limited by this fraction:

$$\frac{\text{Days of fair rental}}{\text{Total days of rental and personal use}}$$

Days a vacation home is held out for rent but not actually rented are not counted as rental days.

The IRS has also used the above fraction for allocating interest and taxes to rental use, but the Tax Court and an appeals court disagree, as explained below.

If expenses allocated to rental exceed gross rental income and

your personal use falls within the 14-day/10% test, deduct allocated expenses in this order: First, interest and taxes allocated to rental activity are subtracted from rental income. Next, operating expenses (other than depreciation) are deducted to the extent of remaining rental income. Finally, if there is any rental income remaining, depreciation may be deducted up to the balance of income.

Example—
You rent out your vacation home receiving a rental of $2,000. Assume that, because of your personal use, you may deduct expenses only up to the amount of this income. Assume further that you may deduct two-thirds of the following expenses: Mortgage interest of $1,200; real estate taxes of $600, maintenance and utility costs of $900, and depreciation (if the house had been used only for rental purposes) of $1,200. The allocated expenses are deducted in this order:

Rent income		$2,000
Less: Interest	$800	
Taxes	400	1,200
		800
Less: Maintenance		600
		200
Less: Depreciation		200

The balance of the depreciation is not deductible.

The balance of interest and taxes is deductible as itemized deductions provided you have itemized deductions in excess of the zero bracket amount. Interest, taxes and casualty losses are deductible, regardless of whether the activity is personal or income producing.

The Tax Court disagrees with the IRS formula for allocating interest and taxes. According to the Tax Court, interest and taxes are allocated on a daily basis. Thus, if the house is rented for 61 days in the year, ⅙ of interest and taxes (61/365) is deducted first from rental income. This rule allows a larger amount of other expenses to be deducted from rental income.

Example—
The Boltons paid interest and property taxes totaling $3,475 on their vacation home. Maintenance expenses (not including depreciation) totaled $2,693. The Boltons stayed at the home 30 days and rented it for 91 days, receiving rents of $2,700. Because of the personal use for 30 days, the Boltons could deduct rental expenses only up to the gross rental income of $2,700 reduced by interest and taxes allocable to rental. In figuring the amount of interest and taxes deductible from rents, they divided the number of rental days, or 91, by 365, the number of days in the year. This gave them an allocation of 25%. After subtracting $868 for interest and taxes (25% of $3,475) from rental income, they deducted $1,832 of maintenance expenses from rental income.

The IRS argued that 75% of the Bolton's interest and tax payments had to be allocated to the rental income. The IRS used an allocation base of 121 days of personal and rental use. Thus, the IRS allocated 75% (91/121) of the interest and taxes, or $2,606, to gross rental income of $2,700. This allocation allowed only $94 maintenance expenses to be deducted ($2,700 − $2,606).

The Tax Court sided with the Boltons and an appeals court agrees. The IRS method of allocating interest and taxes to rental use is bizarre. Interest and taxes are expenses that accrue ratably over the year and are deductible even if a vacation home is not rented for a single day. Thus, the allocation to rental use should be based on a ratable portion of the annual expense by dividing the number of rental days by the number of days in a year.

Rental pool arrangements. Such arrangements have been devised to avoid the loss restriction by attempting to increase the days the home is held for a fair rental value. They have not been successful.

Examples—
1. Fine, a Florida resort condominium owner, used his home 20 days and rented it for 149 days during the year under a rental pool arrangement that made his home available for rental for 333 days. He received a small fee for the days the home was not rented; a larger sum for the days of actual rental. Under the 14-day/10% test, he could not deduct losses if he counted only the 149 days of actual rental; his 20 days of personal use exceeded 10% of the 149 rental days. However, Fine argued that the home was rented for 333 days under the pool arrangement and, therefore, personal use was less than 10% of 333 days.

The IRS argued that the management company was not a lessee, but merely Fine's agent in arranging rentals; thus, only the 149 days of actual rental could be considered. Further, even if the arrangement is considered a lease, Fine is still considered to have received a fair rental for only the 149 days; the lower pool fee received was not a fair rental value. A federal appeals court agreed that the pool fee was not a fair rental because it did not allow for a profit. Since Fine's personal use of the home for 20 days exceeded 10% of the 149 days for which the home was actually rented at a fair rental value, he may deduct only expenses up to his rental income.

2. Byers bought two condominium units in a Sarasota, Florida resort. Under an agreement, he could use his unit for up to 30 days; during the rest of the year, it was in a rental pool. He deducted losses of $27,000 which the IRS disallowed, claiming that he did not prove how many days his units were actually rented. He could not base the loss deduction on the number of days all of the units were rented from the rental pool. Although the Tax Court agreed with the IRS claims, it allowed part of Byers' deduction. It estimated actual rentals on rental pool records of average pool rentals because there was no record of rentals of individual units. The court accepted the testimony of resort officials that Byers' units were in a popular location and were rented most of the time they were available.

In proposed regulations, the IRS also holds that a rental pool is not a basis for counting fair rental days. However, the proposed regulations permit rental pool participants to elect to average the rental use of their units. The number of rental days for a unit is determined by multiplying the aggregate number of days that all units in the rental pool were rented at fair rental during the pool season by a fraction. The numerator of the fraction is the number of participation days of a particular unit; the denominator is the aggregate number of participation days of all units.

¶29.43 • REPORTING GAIN OR LOSS ON SALE OF RENTAL PROPERTY IN 1986

Depreciable property held in the business of rental is Section 1231 property. This means that profit may be subject to capital gain treatment; loss may be deductible as an ordinary loss de-

pending on the net result of all Section 1231 transactions occurring during the taxable years. *See* ¶5.45. Whether the renting out of a residence or an apartment in a residence is a business has been disputed in the courts. The IRS has agreed to follow a case which held that the rental of a residence is a business so that the sale is within Section 1231. Contrary court decisions have held that the renting of a house and the collection of rent do not constitute a business any more than an investor's buying and selling of corporate shares. Whether a rental is a business is determined by the extent of your or your agents' activities. Are they so extensive as to be treated as a business? If not, you are holding the house as income-producing property. When you sell, your profit or loss is capital gain or loss.

In cases of a loss, Section 1231 treatment generally offers the larger tax savings.

Recapture of depreciation. If you rented part of the house or used a part in your business and claimed accelerated depreciation, gain allocated to the rental or business portion may be subject to the recapture rules of ¶5.40. If, before the sale, you used the residence solely for residential purposes, there is no recapture even though it was previously used for rental or business. However, if you buy another principal residence within the rules of ¶29.20, the depreciation recapture element is carried over to the basis of the new residence.

If you are age 55 or over at the time of sale and have used the property solely as your principal residence for the past three out of five years, there is no recapture, even if all or part of the property was previously used for business or rental. This rule applies even if you do not or may not elect to avoid tax on the sale. *See* ¶29.30. On the other hand, if part or all of your home was rented or used in your business for more than two years of the five-year period, there will be recapture under ¶5.40.

¶30.00 • Tax Savings for Investors in Securities

For the effect of tax legislation on capital gains and other investment income, see *the tax legislation guide in the front of this book.*

¶30.00 • YEAR-END SALES IN 1986

If you have realized a substantial profit on which you want long-term capital gain treatment in 1986, the sale must take place in 1986.

In planning year-end sales, watch the deadline for recording sales. In the case of a regular sale of publicly-held stock, give your broker instructions no later than December 23, 1986; this assumes a five-day delivery period so that the settlement date should fall before the end of 1986. Even if payment is not received until 1987, you may elect to report your gain in 1986 under the installment sale rules. A sale ordered at the end of December 1986 for which payment is received at the beginning of January 1987 is

considered an installment sale. You have an opportunity to "elect out" of installment reporting by reporting the gain in the year of sale, 1986, rather than when payment is received in 1987. The decision to elect out of installment reporting may be made as late as the time for filing your 1986 return (plus extensions). *See* ¶6.171. Thus, if you make a year-end sale, you have several months to decide in which year to report the sale.

If you are selling at a loss, you can do so until the last business day of the year, regardless of the settlement dates. If you are on the accrual basis, you have until the last business day of the year to realize both gains and losses.

Realizing losses may pose a problem if you believe the security is due to increase in value sometime in the near future. Although the wash sale rule (*see* ¶6.27) prevents you from taking the loss if you buy 30 days before or after the sale, these possibilities are open to you—

If you believe the security will go up, but not immediately, you can sell now, realize your loss, wait 31 days, then recover your position by repurchasing before the expected rise.

You can hedge by repurchasing similar securities immediately after the sale provided they are not identical. They can be in the same industry, of the same quality, without being considered substantially identical. Check with your broker to see if you can use a loss and still maintain your position. Some brokerage firms maintain recommended "switch" lists and suggest a practice of "doubling up," that is, buying the stock of the same company and then 31 days later selling the original shares. Doubling up has disadvantages: It requires additional funds for the purchase of the second lot, exposes you to additional risks should the stock price fall, and the new shares take a new holding period.

Example—

You own 100 shares of Steel stock which cost you $10,000. In November, 1986 the stock is selling at $6,000 ($60 a share × 100 shares). You would like to realize the $4,000 loss but at the same time, you want to hold on to the investment. You buy 100 shares at market price of $60 a share (total investment $6,000) and 31 days later, sell your original 100 shares, realizing the loss of $4,000. You retain your investment in the new lot. In 1986, November 28 is the last day to buy new shares to allow a loss sale on December 31.

Postponing taxable gain to 1987. If you do not want to realize taxable gains, such as short-term gain, on a security sale in 1986, but you think that the price of your stock may decline by the time you sell in 1987, you can freeze your profit by ordering a short sale of the stock in 1986. You transact a short sale by selling shares borrowed from your broker. In January, 1987, you deliver your shares to the broker as a replacement of the borrowed shares you sold in 1986. By delivering the stock in 1987, the gain on the short sale is fixed in 1987. For tax purposes, a short sale is not completed until the covering stock is delivered.

¶30.01 • KEEP RECORDS OF YOUR STOCK PURCHASES

Keep a record of all your stock transactions, especially when you buy the stock of one company at varying prices. By keeping a record of each stock lot, you may control the amount of gain or loss on a sale of a part of your holdings.

Example—

Over a three-year period, you bought the following shares of Acme Steel stock: In 1970, 100 shares at $77 per share; in 1971, 200 shares at $84 per share; in 1972, 100 shares at $105 per share. When the stock is selling at $90, you plan to sell 100 shares. You may use the cost of your 1972 lot and get a $1,500 loss if, for example, you want to offset some gains or other income you have already earned this year. Or you may get capital gains of varying amounts by either selling the 1970 lot or part of the 1971 lot. You must clearly identify the lot you want to sell. Say you want a loss and sell the 1972 lot. Unless you identify it as the lot sold, the IRS will hold that you sold the 1970 lot under the "first-in, first-out" rule. This rule assumes that, when you have a number of identical items that you bought at different times, your sale of any of them is automatically the sale of the first you bought. So the cost of your first purchase is what you match against your selling price to find your gain or loss. Here is what to do to counteract the first-in, first-out rule: If the stock certificates are registered in your name, show that you delivered the 1972 stock certificates.

See ¶30.03 for averaging cost on the sale of mutual fund shares.

If your stock is held by your broker, the IRS considers that an adequate identification is made if you grant your broker the power to buy and sell in your name at will. He is to notify you at the time of sale, requesting instructions on which shares he should sell. Before the settlement date (usually four business days from the time of sale), you instruct him by letter which shares to deliver. He, in turn, signs and dates his confirmation, which is printed at the bottom of your letter of instruction, and returns the letter to you. In addition, he submits to you monthly statements of the transactions and your cash position and stock on hand.

HOW TO IDENTIFY SECURITIES WHEN YOU ARE SELLING

If your securities are	Identify them by
Registered in your own name	The number, your name, and any other identification which they bear.
In a margin account registered in a "street" name	A specified block or security bought on a designated day at a particular price. A mere intention to sell a particular share without informing the broker is without significance.
New certificates received for old in a recapitalization	Record the new certificate with the lowest number as being in exchange for the old certificate with the lowest number. Do this until all the new certificates are matched with all the old.
Shares exchanged for shares in a reorganization	Allocate each of the new certificates to each of the old in your records. Where the exchange involves several blocks of stock and there is no specific identification, the IRS says you must average your costs.
Shares received in a split-up	Match the new certificates with the old ones surrendered. Identification of your selling securities as the "highest cost" or "lowest cost" stock is insufficient. You have to match at the time of the split-up.
Stock dividends	The lot of stock on which you received the dividend. The new stock is part of the old lot. But, if you receive one certificate for more than one lot, you may have to apply the rule of first-in, first-out to the new stock sold.
Acquired by exercise of nontaxed stock rights	The number, or other identification of the lot you receive by exercising the rights. Each lot you so acquire is considered a separate lot received on the date of subscription.

¶30.02 • PUTS AND CALLS AND INDEX OPTIONS

You may buy options to buy and sell stock. On the stock exchange, these options are named calls and puts. A call gives you the right to require the seller of the option to sell you stock at a fixed price during the option period. A put gives you the right to require the seller of the option to buy stock you own at a fixed price during the option period.

Puts and calls allow you to speculate at the expense of a small investment—a call, for expected price rises; a put, for expected price declines. They may also be used to protect paper profits or fix the amount of your losses on securities you own.

You do not have to exercise a put or call to realize your profit. You may sell the option to realize your profit. If you exercise a call, the cost of the call is added to the cost of the stock purchased. If you exercise a put, you reduce the selling price of stock sold by the cost of the put. If you do not exercise a call or put, you realize a capital loss.

The option price depends on the value of the stock, the length of the option period, the volatility of the stock, and the demand and supply for options for the particular stock.

Puts may be treated as short sales. Be careful in using puts when you own stock covered by the put. If you have held the stock short term, the purchase of the put is a short sale. The exercise or expiration of the put will then be treated as the closing of the short sale. Short sale rules, however, do not apply (1) when you hold stock long term, and (2) when you buy a put and the related stock on the same day and identify the stock with the put (*see* ¶6.261).

Using a call as leverage. You expect a stock to appreciate in value but you do not have sufficient capital for a further investment. Instead of investing your limited amount of capital in an outright purchase, you might buy a call covering such stock. With a call, the same amount of capital allows you to speculate in many more shares than you could if you purchased stock outright. If the stock rises in value, your call also increases in value.

Exchange option trading. Option market exchanges have standardized market conditions for trading in puts and call options. The overwhelming number of options transacted are calls; the trading of puts is currently limited. Financial sections of the daily newspapers provide data on the market prices and volume of the options.

Option markets are the CBOE, Amex, the Philadelphia Stock Exchange, the Midwest Exchange, and the Pacific Stock Exchange.

Trading in options is highly speculative, attracting those who hope to make profits on minimum investments. At the same time, the market has provided investors and institutions holding large portfolios with an opportunity to earn income through the sale of options based on their holdings. Thus, it takes two to play the option game: (1) the owner of shares who sells an option on his stock, and (2) the option buyer who generally speculates that, by buying an option for a smaller price than he would have to pay for the stock, he will be able to make a profit if the price of the stock goes up. The odds generally favor the option seller.

The income tax consequences of option trading are discussed at ¶6.0351.

If you are inexperienced in the use of options, read several technical explanations of the use of options before investing. Master the technical use of options such as straddles and hedges used by professional traders, as the outright purchase of straight calls is generally too speculative. Finally, do not overlook commission costs which can cut into your profits or increase your losses.

Stock index options. Index options—fresh entries in the market, with a track record of less than three years—give you a chance to speculate on the general movement of stock. The success of the index option has tended to reduce interest in regular stock options given on individual stocks. On the other hand, index options are pegged to the price movement of the stocks that comprise the index option. Thus, with index options, you do not have to be concerned about the market fate of a particular stock. The stock group of the index option follows the general stock market movement. For example, assume that 100 stocks make up the index. The option contract represents an index multiplier of $100 times the index value of the group or basket of 100 stocks. Therefore, when a newspaper reports an index value of 170, which is also called the *strike price*, the contract is worth $17,000. However, as the option is only a right to buy or sell this particular contract, you pay an option price that is only a percentage of the contract value. The particular option price is set by the market in an open auction.

Your role is to weigh how the market will fare within the option period. Should you anticipate lower interest rates within the option period, which can be from approximately a week up to three months, you might buy an index option, betting that the stock market will advance. For example, when the index is at 165, you buy for $1,200 an option with a strike price of 170. If the stock market advances during the option period, pushing the strike price to 177, you have won your bet. At 177, you might sell your option for $7,000, thereby making a $5,800 profit.

Do not let this example encourage you to enter the index option market precipitously. If you guess wrong, you have lost your money. In the example just cited, had the index not moved above 170, you would have lost $1,200.

The S&P 100 index option is offered by the Chicago Board Options Exchange. It is based on Standard & Poor's 100 list of stocks, and it also offers an index option of 500 shares. The Philadelphia Stock Exchange trades the Value Line index option that has an index basket of more than 1,600 stocks traded on several exchanges. The New York Stock Exchange and the American Stock Exchange also offer index options.

If you are interested in playing the index option market, track the market for several months until you get used to the movement of the option. Plot hypothetical purchases and see how you would have fared. You might make a bundle—but, as at roulette, you might lose your shirt in a very short time.

¶30.03 • INVESTING IN MUTUAL FUNDS

You may buy a tax liability if you invest in a mutual fund which has already realized significant capital gains during the year. Your investment is on the basis of the current value of its portfolio. At the end of the year, the gains realized by the fund before your investment are distributed to you as a capital gain distribution.

Then you have to pay tax on the return of your own money. However, an experienced fund adviser can tell you when to make your investment. Or, you can postpone investing until the stock goes ex-dividend. By that time, your buying price is based on an asset value which is reduced by capital gain distribution.

Averaging cost for sale of mutual fund shares. A Treasury regulation sets rules for averaging the cost of purchases made at different times if only part of your holdings are sold. The election applies to open-end mutual fund shares held by an agent, usually a bank, in an account kept for the periodic acquisition or redemption of shares in the fund. Averaging avoids the difficult task of identifying the exact shares being sold where shares were bought at different prices and dates. There are two averaging methods: Single-category method and double-category method.

Single-category method. Under the single-category method, all shares in an account are totaled. The basis of each share is the total basis of all shares in the account at the time of a sale or transfer, divided by the number of shares in the account. For purposes of determining holding period, the shares sold or transferred are considered to be those shares acquired first.

Double-category method. At the time of each sale, you divide all shares in an account into two classes: Shares held long term and shares held short term. Shares are deemed transferred from each class without regard to stock certificates. You may tell the agent from which class you are selling. If you do not so specify, the long-term shares are deemed to have been sold first. If the number of shares sold exceeds the number in the long-term class, the excess shares are charged to the short-term class.

Details of these methods are provided in IRS Publication 564.

You make the election to average on your tax return for the first taxable year you want the election to apply. Note on your return which method you have chosen. Keep records to support the average basis used on your return. The election applies to all shares of the particular mutual fund in which the election is initially made.

You may not average shares of a mutual fund acquired by gift, if the adjusted basis of such shares in the hands of the donor was greater than their fair market value at the time of the gift.

¶30.04 • REDUCING THE TAX ON DIVIDEND INCOME

The tax on dividend income may be reduced by the following types of investments:

Selling stock on which a dividend has been declared but not yet paid. During the period a dividend is declared but not paid, the price of the stock includes the value of the dividend. If you plan to sell stock in this position and figure that the tax on the dividend reflected in the selling price will be less than the tax on the dividend received, transact the sale before the stock goes ex-dividend (see ¶3.07).

Investing in companies paying tax-free dividends. Some companies pay tax-free dividends. A list of companies that do may be provided by your broker. When you receive a tax-free dividend, you do not report the dividend as income as long as the dividend does not exceed your stock basis. A tax-free dividend reduces the tax cost of your stock; dividends in excess of basis produce capital gain (see ¶3.08).

Investing in companies paying stock dividends. On receipt of a stock dividend, you do not generally have taxable income.

¶30.05 • INVESTING IN SHORT-TERM PAPER, TREASURY BILLS, CD'S, TAX-EXEMPT NOTES, AND OTHER SHORT-TERM OBLIGATIONS

Short-term paper (maturity of one year or less) provides an opportunity for earning income on funds during periods of uncertainty in the stock and other investment markets. Funds which you do not wish to tie up long term and do not want to remain unproductive may be invested in Treasury bills or notes or certificates of deposit. These investments offer safety and negotiability, earning current interest rates from the day of purchase to the day of redemption, either on maturity or sale.

Treasury bills. These are direct obligations of the U.S. Treasury issued to finance budgetary needs. Bills are offered for three-month, six-month, and 12-month maturities in denominations of $10,000,

$15,000, $50,000, $100,000 and $1,000,000. Bills are sold at a discount at Treasury auctions held at the Federal Reserve Banks which serve as agents for the Treasury. They are redeemed at face value. Your return on a Treasury bill is the difference between the discount price you pay for the bill and its face value, if you hold it to maturity, or the amount you receive for it on a sale before maturity. The selling price of a Treasury bill before maturity will vary with changes of current interest rates.

You may buy Treasury bills directly without charge from any Federal Reserve Bank, which gives you a receipt indicating that a book entry has been recorded of your purchase. You may also buy or sell Treasury bills through your bank or your stockbroker who will charge you for handling the transaction.

Most investors submit noncompetitive tenders (bids) for the Treasury bills they wish to buy. To submit a *competitive* tender, you must specify the price you are willing to pay for your bill, and you run the risk of bidding too low and not getting the bills you want. Noncompetitive tenders do not have to specify a price. They are filled at a price which is the average of the accepted competitive tenders for that specific auction. Check the Federal Reserve Bank or branch in your area for auction dates on Treasury bills.

Figuring the yield on your Treasury bill. On the day of the auction, the Treasury will figure the average price bid by those who submitted acceptable competitive tenders. The difference between this average price and the full value of the Treasury bill is the *discount* at which the bill is sold. All noncompetitive tenders are filled at this price. A check for the difference between the purchase price and the face value is mailed to you by first class mail on the issue date of the bills.

Example—

Assume the accepted average bid on three-month bills is $9,700. You gave the government $10,000. To reflect the actual purchase price of $9,700, a "discount" check of $300 is mailed to you.

The equivalent annual yield on your Treasury bill is figured this way:

1. Find the yield on your investment by dividing discount by purchase price.
2. Convert this yield to the annual rate by dividing the yield by .2500 if the bill is a three-month one; .5000 if six months.

On a three-month bill your discount is $150 (cost $9,850); the equivalent annual yield is .0608:

$$\frac{\$150}{\$9,850} = .0152; \frac{.0152}{.2500} = .0608 \text{ or } 6.08\% \text{ per year}$$

Financial pages of the newspapers report the previous day's auction, including the discount rate and what this amounts to as an annual percentage yield.

Cashing bills before maturity. If you decide you need funds before the maturity date of your bill, you can sell it through a commercial bank or a securities broker. The Federal Reserve Bank and the Treasury do not handle bills which have not matured.

For bills sold before maturity, current interest rates will determine the amount you receive. The market value of Treasury bills is listed daily in the financial section of newspapers and financial periodicals.

At maturity. Redemption is automatic at maturity, unless you notify the Federal Reserve Bank that you wish to roll over matured bills into new bills. The Treasury will mail you a check for the amount of your bill. If you bought your bill through a bank, the bank will credit your account on the date the bill matures. To roll over your maturing bill, you follow the same procedures as in buying a new bill and use your matured bill as payment. A discount check for the difference between the price of the new bills and the face value of your matured bills will be mailed to you on the issue date of the new bills.

Certificates of deposit. Negotiable certificates of deposit, (CD's), are another form of short-term investment which offers a high return with safety and negotiability.

Certificates of deposit represent money lent by investors to a bank for a specified short period of time, generally 30, 60, or 90 days, although in some cases certificates of deposit for six months and a year are available.

The rate of interest banks will pay for these funds is set in advance and depends on supply and demand in the money market. The interest rate may vary with the size of your investment. For deposits of $100,000 or more, you may be able to get a "heavy duty" CD at a higher rate than offered on smaller deposits.

Purchasing CD's. Certificates of deposit are generally purchased through your bank which will have available a list of those banks interested in obtaining funds through such deposits. Banks are careful about their dealings in these instruments and will handle such orders only for known clients. In most cases, your bank will charge a small fee to arrange the transfer of your funds for the certificate of deposit of another bank.

Before investing, check with the bank for minimum investment requirements. Also check the status of the broker, insurance, and charges.

Liquidity. CD's may be sold before their maturity date through commercial banks or stockbrokers. However, they are not quite as readily sold as are Treasury bills. As is the case with Treasury bills, you may receive either more or less than you paid for them upon a resale before maturity, depending on the rise or fall of interest rates during the time you hold the certificates of deposit.

CD's may be registered in the name of the purchaser. As a rule, when the intermediary transactions are between two banks, the certificates are made out to bearer to be delivered against payment at the bank where you have deposited your money. That bank will then register the certificate in your name.

Repurchase agreements (repos). This investment offered by banks and thrifts allows you to earn high interest rates by sharing in a portion of the bank's portfolio of government securities. The bank is required to repurchase your investment from you at your request. The minimum investment is $1,000; maturities vary, on average, three months. Repos are not FDIC or FSLIC insured, and there is no interest penalty for early repurchase, as long as you hold them for a minimum of a week or more. There may be a small service charge for early repurchase.

Commercial paper. Many corporations requiring large sums of money periodically during the year to finance short-term customer receivables offer short-term promissory notes at high rates of interest. These notes are generally referred to as commercial paper. Although much of this paper is sold in units of $100,000 or more, commercial paper in denominations of $25,000 and even less is sometimes available.

Finance companies, automobile manufacturers, and large retail stores are types of businesses which typically issue commercial paper for periods ranging from one week to 270 days.

Although companies like General Motors Acceptance Company (GMAC), one of the largest issuers of commercial paper, will sell direct to a buyer, most sales of these notes are made through commercial banks or brokerage houses that can give you information about the paper available, terms and denominations offered, and can complete the sale for you.

Investments in commercial paper may not be as liquid as other short-term paper and are subject to greater risks.

Tax-exempt notes are discussed at ¶36.06.

¶30.051 • INVESTING IN MONEY MARKET FUNDS

The investor who does not have the capital needed to invest in specific money market obligations may consider a money market fund. A fund portfolio will generally include U.S. government obligations, CD's of major commercial banks, bankers acceptances, and commercial paper of prime-rated firms. Most funds have a minimum investment requirement, varying from $500 to $10,000. Money market funds charge an annual management fee, generally about ½% annually of the fund's average total assets. Investors should check each fund's charges because they differ.

Yields, which change daily, are not guaranteed. Investments are not federally insured. Some state-chartered banks, however, offer money market funds insured by a state insurance fund.

Gains and losses are generally not realized in money market funds; shares are redeemed for exactly what you paid (usually

$1 per share) plus accrued interest. Withdrawals may be requested by mail, wire, or telephone. Some funds offer limited checking privileges.

The names of funds which charge commissions may be available through your securities broker. A free list of funds which have no sales charge may be obtained from the No-Load Mutual Fund Association, Valley Forge, Pa. 19481.

Tax-free money funds. These funds invest in short-term notes of state and local governments issued in anticipation of tax receipts, bond sales, and other revenues, and in "project notes" issued by local entities and backed by the federal government. The interest paid by these funds is tax exempt. Since the yields are lower than those of taxable funds, these funds are best suited to high tax bracket investors. Minimum investments range from $1,000 to $50,000. These funds may offer check writing privileges.

A tax-free interest return may also be available through unit-investment trusts holding tax-exempt state and municipal bonds. Offered by certain brokerage houses and other companies, these trusts mature in a specified number of years or as called.

¶30.0511 • INVESTING IN SAVINGS INSTITUTIONS

Banks and savings and loan associations (S&Ls) aggressively compete for funds that would have normally entered the money market. The banking industry, favored by deregulation, offers money market funds and certificates of deposit (CD's) with different maturities and terms.

Bank money market funds are competitive with money market mutual funds. The bank money market funds guarantee for one-week or one month periods interest rates tied to the Treasury bill rate or the average money market rate. Bank funds also offer this added attraction: They are federally insured. Bank money market accounts require certain average monthly balances which the government is planning to phase out; if the account falls below the minimum, interest is reduced.

Investments in money market funds allow you to take advantage of volatile interest rates which are rising. Investments in CD's allow you to lock into the highest available interest rate for a fixed period of time if you are concerned with a decline of rates during that period.

Current banking regulations allow banks and savings institutions to pay what they please on certificates of deposit and do not require minimum balances on CD's with terms over 31 days.

Withdrawals within certain limits may be made from money market funds without penalty. Premature withdrawals from CD's are penalized.

CD investments in savings institutions allow you to lock into high interest rates only for the short term, generally up to five years. If you are concerned that rates will substantially decline in the future, you may want to invest in a currently available investment that fixes a high rate over longer periods, such as bonds with long-term maturities. Bond investments are discussed in ¶30.052.

Savings certificates versus Treasury bills. Certificates keyed to the Treasury bill rate may be purchased in fractions once you make a minimum bill rate investment. Treasury bills are only in fixed units. *See* ¶30.05. There is no fee charged for the purchase of certificates, while a fee may be charged to purchase Treasury bills unless purchased directly from the Treasury or a Federal Reserve Bank. Where you do not have the minimum to invest, some institutions may lend the difference at a lower interest rate, typically 1% to 2% over the rate earned on the certificate. Treasury bills have a tax advantage over the certificates. Interest on Treasury bills is exempt from state and local taxes; interest on saving certificates is not. Further, there are penalties for redeeming certificates before maturity. *See* ¶4.01 for taxation of interest and ¶4.011 for forfeiture of interest on premature withdrawals.

Investment options vary from bank to bank. Not all banks offer the maximum rates or compound interest in the same manner. Whether interest is compounded daily or annually will affect your rate of return. Each bank also has its own policy on procedures concerning maturity of certificates. Some banks automatically renew the CD for another term at the current rate unless notified to the contrary; some banks will not renew a matured CD without express authority from you. If you fail to act, you may find your funds switched to a day-of-deposit account on maturity.

Banking institutions can also change their rules after you have opened an account.

Deferring interest income. You may defer interest income by buying a six-month certificate after June 30. Interest is taxable in the next year when the certificate matures unless you receive interest during the current year. Your bank may offer you the choice of when to receive the interest. You may also defer interest by buying Treasury bills which come due next year.

¶30.052 • INVESTING IN CORPORATE BONDS

When you buy a corporate bond, you are lending money to the issuer of the bonds. You become a creditor of the issuing company. The corporation pledges to pay you interest on specified dates, generally twice a year, and to repay the principal on the date of maturity stated on the bond.

For investment purposes, a bond may be described according to the length of the period of maturity. Short-term bonds usually mature within one to five years; medium-term bonds in five to 20 years; long-term bonds in 20 or more years.

Where the interest is paid out on a regular schedule, the bond is called a "current income" bond. An accrual or discount bond is a bond on which interest is accumulated and paid as part of the specified maturity value (the bond having been issued at a price lower than the specified maturity value).

Figuring the yield of a bond. The investment value of bonds is generally expressed in rates of yield. There are four types of yield: The nominal or coupon yield; the actual yield; the current market yield; and the net yield to maturity.

The nominal or coupon yield is the fixed or contractual rate of interest stated on the bond. A bond paying 7% has a nominal yield of 7%.

The actual yield is the rate of return based on the price at which the bond was purchased. If bought below par, the actual yield will exceed the nominal or coupon yield. If bought at a premium (above par), the actual yield will be less than the coupon or nominal yield. For example, if you paid $850 for a $1,000 bond paying 6% interest, the actual yield is 7.06% ($60 divided by $850).

The current market yield is the rate of return on the bond if bought at the prevailing market price. It is figured in the same manner as actual yield. For example, if the 6% bond was quoted at $750, its current yield would be 8%.

Net yield to maturity represents the rate of return on the bond if it is held to maturity, plus appreciation allocated to a discount purchase or less reductions for any premium paid on a bond selling above par. If you buy a bond below par at a market discount, your annual return is proportionately increased by a part of the discount allocated to the number of years before maturity. If the discount was $50 on a bond with a five-year maturity, then your annual income return on the bond is increased by $10 ($50 divided by 5). On the other hand, if you bought at a premium, the extra cost is a reduction against your income because you paid more than can be recovered at maturity. This cost is allocated over the remaining life of the bond. Thus, if you bought a five-year bond at $50 over par, your average annual return is reduced by $10 ($50 divided by 5).

Call privileges may reduce the investment value of the bond. A call privilege gives the issuer a chance to redeem the obligation before maturity if interest rates have declined below the rate fixed by the obligation. The existence of a call is a disadvantage to an investor; it may deprive him of a favorable investment at a time he may not be able to replace it with another. To take some of the "sting" out of a call provision, the issuer may provide for the payment of a "premium" on the exercise of the call and a minimum period during which the bonds will not be called. The call premium is usually expressed as a percentage of the maturity value, for example, 105%. The amount of the premium varies with the length of the period in which the bond may be called. As the maturity date approaches, the call premium will decrease. Some bonds now carry a guarantee that they will not be called for a specified number of years, such as five or ten years.

A call privilege will generally not be exercised if the going interest rate remains about the same as, or is higher than, the interest rate of the bond. If interest rates decline below the interest rate of the bond, the bond will probably be called because the issuer can obtain the borrowed money at lower cost elsewhere.

Interest on bearer bonds issued with coupons attached is paid when a bondholder clips the coupon and deposits it for payment. A registered bond carries the name of the owner who receives his interest by mail from the issuing corporation.

Whether a bond is registered or in bearer form has no effect on its investment quality or yield. A coupon-type or bearer bond may be preferred by institutional investors because it can be transferred by hand without registration. However, this advantage must be weighed against the risks of loss through fire, theft, or casualty.

Issuing and trading bonds. New bond issues are generally placed through investment bankers who usually assist in the preparation of the issue. Often an issue may be sold directly by the issuing organization to an institutional investor. Many newly-issued bonds are purchased directly from issuers or from their investment bankers by institutional investors before the bonds are offered to individual investors. Issuers prefer this type of placement as it involves less expense than a public offering. Normally, only the new issues (or part of new issues) which cannot be marketed this way are offered to private investors.

Bonds are also traded on the open market where individuals, as well as institutional buyers, may buy or sell them at competitive, market-determined prices, through dealers or brokers.

Investment return on a bond is generally limited to the stated interest. You cannot expect any appreciation of principal as you can in a stock investment, unless you have bought bonds selling at a discount.

Bond sales and prices on the major exchanges are listed in the major financial dailies. Bond prices fluctuate in response to changes in interest rates and business conditions. In setting the daily price of a bond, the market weighs the current status, performance, and future prospects of the issuing corporation, as well as the interest rate and maturity period of the bond.

Quotations are based on 100 as equal to par, even though the basic unit for an actual bond may be in denominations of $1,000. A quote of 90½ simply means a bond with a face value of $1,000 will cost $905 at market.

Calls under sinking fund redemption. A bond may be called in at par under the terms of a sinking fund arrangement. Not all bonds are called and those that are selected are picked by lot. Redemptions for sinking fund purposes account for only a small percentage of a single bond issue. But some issues may retain the right to use a blanket sinking fund under which they may redeem bonds paying interest at their highest rate.

Put privileges. A put privilege is the flip side of a call privilege. It permits the buyer to sell the bonds at par to the issuer after a stated number of years. This feature is valuable to investors for long-term bonds. If interest rates rise, investors are not locked into low yields.

Current interest rates affect the selling price of bonds:

1. *If current interest rates increase over the interest rate of your bond, the market value of your bond will decline.* The decline in value has nothing to do with the credit rating of the issue. It simply means that other investors will buy only at terms that will give them the current higher return. If you bought a bond paying a rate of 8% at par, $1,000, and a few months later, interest rates go to 11%, another investor will not pay $1,000 for the bond for an 8% return. To match the 11% return on a dollar, the market value of the bond will drop to a level which will return 11% on the money invested, based on its actual 8% return and the period remaining before maturity. Thus, during periods of rising interest, the price of bonds issued at lower rates in prior years declines. This occurs to even top quality bonds; the highest credit rating will not protect the market value of a low-interest paying bond. When this happens there may be bond bargains available, as prices on outstanding bonds decrease.

2. *If interest rates decline below the interest rate of your bond, the value of your bond will increase,* but, at the same time, the

company, if it has an exercisable call option, may redeem the bond to rid itself of the high interest cost and attempt to raise funds at current lower rates. Thus, an early redemption of the bond could upset your long-range investment plans in that particular issue.

With these points in mind, you can understand why in recent years investors have shied away from long-term bonds when volatile interest rates ran into double digits. Investors preferred the high short-term rates. The effect of the investor flight from long-term issues hurt the ability of lenders to raise funds and forced them to devise new types of issues, such as zero coupon bonds and floating rate bonds.

Corporate zero coupon bond. A zero coupon bond is a deep discount obligation issued by companies that have found it difficult to market traditional long-term bonds. The zero coupon bond allows them to compete during periods of high interest rates. The bonds are issued at considerably less than face value and redeemed at face at a set date. No annual interest is paid. A zero coupon bond allows an investor to lock in a return. He knows how much he will receive at maturity and so avoids the problem of turning over his investments at fluctuating short-term rates. Brokers have lists of zero coupon bonds; the prices vary with the credit rating of the companies, current market rates, and maturity dates.

Zero coupon bond discount is reported annually as interest over the life of the bond, even though interest is not received. This tax cost tends to make zero coupon bonds unattractive to investors, unless the bonds can be bought for IRA and other retirement plans which defer tax on income until distributions are made.

Zero coupon bonds may also be a means of financing a child's education. A parent buys the bond for the child. The child must report the income, but as the child is probably in a low tax bracket, little or no tax may be due.

The value of zero coupon bonds fluctuates sharply with interest rate changes. Consider this fact before investing in long-term zero coupon bonds. If you sell before the maturity term, at a time when interest rates rise, you may lose part of your investment.

Floating rate or variable interest bonds. For investors unwilling to gamble on the future of interest rates, some bonds have been offered with floating interest rates. The rate is updated periodically, but there may be a floor and ceiling limiting the changes. The market price of the bond should remain near par since its interest rate moves with the market. Although this feature is a form of insurance for the investor, it may not be worth its added cost.

¶30.053 • INVESTING IN TREASURY BONDS AND NOTES AND OTHER U.S. AGENCY OBLIGATIONS

The federal government offers the following obligations for investment opportunities. They are guaranteed by the federal government and are exempt from state and local taxes.

Treasury bonds have maturity dates in excess of 10 years. The minimum denomination is $1,000. Interest is paid semiannually at a rate which varies with each issue. These bonds may be purchased through a commercial bank or directly from the Federal Reserve Bank.

Zero coupon Treasury bonds. Certain major brokerage houses have created zero coupon Treasury bonds by stripping the coupons from Treasury bonds and selling the bonds at deep discounts. They have been promoted under such names as "TIGRS," "LIONS," "COUGARS," and "CATS" as investments suitable for IRAs, retirement plan trusts, and custodian accounts for minors. The U.S. Treasury itself now offers its own version of the zero coupon bond under the name "STRIPS." STRIPS are not offered directly by the government to individual investors but are sold to banks and brokers who then sell them to the public. Because STRIPS have the direct backing of the U.S. government, they are considered to be the safest zeros and generally yield up to one tenth of one percent less than TIGRS, CATS or similar brokerage firm or bank created zeros. With all zero coupon Treasury obligations, an investor can select a particular maturity date suited to his needs, such as the year he will start taking IRA distributions or the year a child will start college. For tax reporting rules, *see* ¶30.052 on corporate zero coupon bonds.

Treasury notes are similar to Treasury bonds but have shorter maturity dates from two to 10 years. Minimum investments range from $1,000 to $5,000, depending on the issue. Interest is paid semiannually and interest varies with each issue. Notes are purchased from commercial banks or directly from the Federal Reserve Bank.

Other U.S. obligations, such as savings bonds, are discussed at ¶30.07 and Treasury bills are discussed at ¶30.05.

Certain federal agencies, like the Tennessee Valley Authority, offer their own securities. The types of securities offered vary. Such securities must be purchased through brokers or commercial banks.

Federally chartered companies, such as Government National Mortgage Association ("Ginnie Maes") and Federal National Mortgage Association ("Fannie Maes"), authorize certain firms and institutions to issue securities based on insured mortgages. While interest on these securities is generally not exempt from state and local taxes, they offer the investor a higher yield than Treasury securities. Some of these obligations carry a U.S. government full faith and credit guarantee; some have only an implied guarantee; and some no backing from the federal government, but risk is generally considered to be negligible.

Ginnie Maes are offered in minimum denominations of $25,000. Monthly payments to security holders include not only interest, but also a return of principal. Rather than buying Ginnie Maes in the open market, you may consider investing in a fund or trust which has a portfolio of such securities. Minimum investment units typically begin at $1,000.

¶30.06 • INVESTING IN TAX EXEMPTS

Interest on state and local obligations is not subject to federal income tax. It is also exempt from the tax of the state in which the obligations are issued. In comparing the interest return of a tax exempt with that of a taxable bond, you figure the taxable return that is equivalent to the tax-free yield of the tax exempt. This amount depends on your tax bracket. For example, a municipal bond of $5,000 yielding 8% is the equivalent of a taxable yield of 11.1% subject to the tax rate of 28%.

You can compare the value of tax-exempt interest to taxable interest for your tax bracket by using this formula:

Tax-exempt interest return = E
Taxable interest (to be found) = T
Your tax bracket = B

$$T = \frac{E}{1 - B}$$

Example—
You are deciding between a tax-exempt bond and a taxable bond. You want to find which will give you more income after taxes. You have a choice between a tax-exempt bond paying 6% and a taxable bond paying 8%. Your tax bracket is 28%.

Using the above formula, you find that the tax exempt is a better buy in your tax bracket as it is the equivalent of a taxable bond paying 8.3%.

$$T = \frac{.06}{1 - .28}$$
$$T = .083\%$$

Ratings of tax-exempt bonds. As in the case of commercial bonds, tax-exempt issues are rated by services such as Standard & Poor's and Moody's. In rating a bond, the services will consider the size of the issuer, the amount of its outstanding debt, its past record in paying off prior debts, whether it has competent officials and a balanced budget, its tax assessment and collection record, and whether the community is dominated by a single industry which might be subject to economic change. Generally, an issuer with a good credit rating will offer lower interest rates than one plagued with revenue deficits or similar problems. A basic test is the sufficiency of tax yields or revenues even in times of economic stress.

General obligation bonds will normally be rated higher than revenue bonds because they have the support of the taxing power of the community. Revenue bonds (backed by the revenue of the issuer) may receive high ratings once a capacity to produce earnings is shown.

Purchase and trading of tax exempts. Tax-exempt municipals are traded over-the-counter and are generally handled through a firm specializing in this field or having a department for municipals. Prices quoted represent a percentage of par. For example, a par value $5,000 bond quoted at 90 is selling for $4,500 (90% of $5,000); a par value $1,000 bond quoted at 90 is selling for $900 (90% of $1,000). It may not pay to buy tax exempts unless you intend to hold them to maturity because the additional cost of selling a small order might be as much as a year's interest.

The bid and asked prices of tax-exempt bonds are generally not quoted in the daily newspapers, although some brokerage houses which specialize in them do print such prices. As in the general bond market, an offer of unusually high interest compared with the average bond rates may be an indication that the bonds are riskier than others.

The market for tax exempts is not as large as the market for stock. This poses a risk if you ever need ready cash and are forced to sell a tax-exempt bond at a discount. If you are concerned with liquidity, restrict your investments to major general obligation bonds of state governments and revenue bonds of major authorities.

Instead of purchasing the exempts directly, you may consider investing in municipal bond funds. The funds invest in various municipal bonds and thus offer the safety of diversity. Also, an investment in the fund may be as small as $1,000 compared with the typical $5,000 municipal bond. Check on fees and other restrictions in municipal bond funds.

Tax-exempt notes. Although generally bought by banks and large corporations, short-term tax-exempt notes may sometimes be available to individuals. The majority of the notes are offered in face amounts of $25,000 and up, but sometimes in denominations of $5,000 and $10,000. They are issued by states and municipalities to tide them over until expected revenues are received or until longer-term money can be raised through an issue of long-term bonds. Where rising interest rates have made the cost of long-term issues high, a government authority may postpone a long-term offering and try to fill the gap with short-term notes. The interest rates on tax-exempt notes may be higher than on tax-exempt bonds if the authority is willing to pay the extra interest for the short term in the expectation that a future long-term offering may be placed at lower rates.

Interest on these short-term notes is exempt from federal tax. Many of the notes are from housing authorities and issued to pay construction costs on projects for which bonds will eventually be issued. Housing notes are guaranteed by the FHA and, because of their safety, yields are lower than more speculative paper.

¶30.061 • INVESTING IN UNIT INVESTMENT TRUSTS

A unit investment trust is a closed-end unmanaged portfolio of bonds marketed by investment houses. Yield is fixed for the life of the trust with interest payable semiannually or more frequently. As bonds in the portfolio mature, a unit holder receives a repayment of principal. Unit trusts provide investors with the possibility of locking into high yields for the long term. However, a trust has this disadvantage: If principal is needed before the end of the trust term, an investor may sacrifice substantial amounts of principal if interest rates rise or if the general investment market is shying away from long-term investments; even where the trust may offer a current return equal to market value, its price may be depressed because there may be few investors willing to take the risk of tying up their funds in long-term investments. Despite these drawbacks, the performance of unit trusts has been rated higher than that of similar mutual funds.

Unit trusts hold varying types of debt instruments. Tax-exempt municipal bond trusts, made up of tax-exempt obligations, are generally favored by investors in the top tax brackets. Taxable unit trusts hold investments such as corporate bonds, bank certificates of deposit, and Treasury obligations. Usually, units are offered in denominations of $1,000. An investor pays a front-end sales charge, but no management fee as there is no need for management once a unit trust is closed.

Maturities of the various trusts range as follows: The short-term, tax-exempt average is three years; intermediate, six to 12 years; and long term, 18 to 30 years. An average for corporate intermediate is six years; 25 years for long term.

¶30.07 • SAVINGS BOND PLANS

Savings bonds purchases give you an opportunity to defer tax (see ¶4.08). Series EE bonds, issued since November 1982, have maturity periods of 10 years. If held at least five years, EE bonds earn interest at a variable market rate tied to five-year Treasury securities, with a guaranteed minimum rate of 7.5%. Bonds held less than five years earn interest on a fixed graduated scale ranging between 5.5% and 7.5%, depending on the term held.

Savings bonds can be used to build up values during a lifetime without paying taxes. Heirs may continue to defer tax on the interest. When the bonds are finally cashed, the person cashing them and reporting the income gets a deduction for the estate tax paid (if any) on the income (see ¶4.08).

Savings bonds can be used in a savings program for a child's college education. Bonds can be bought in a child's name. Tax on interest may be deferred or reported annually. Choose the method that you project gives a greater after-tax return over the period. In making the election, consider the effect of tax legislation on income earned by a minor. Tax legislation is discussed in the front of this book.

E bonds issued between May 1941 and April 1952 have a 40-year term, after which no interest will accrue. Series H bonds issued between June 1952 and January 1957 have a term of 29 years, eight months. For maturity dates of other E bonds, EE bonds, and H bonds, you may obtain a schedule from the Treasury Department which also shows the interest rate on the bonds.

¶30.08 • REPORTING INCOME FROM INVESTMENT CLUBS

Investment clubs are a method of pooling funds for stock market investments. The club may be formed by any number of persons who may manage the investments of the club under an informal or a formal agreement or charter. A majority of clubs currently operating are, for tax purposes, partnerships. Some, however, are taxable as corporations or trusts. Corporate or trust status is usually evidenced by formal incorporation or the creation of a trust. However, a group may be taxed as a corporation even though it has not formally incorporated if its manner of operation gives it the characteristics of a corporation. Treasury regulations provide tests for determining when a group is a corporation. If the club is considered a corporation, it reports and pays a tax on the club's earnings. You report dividend distributions made by the club to you. The overall cost of corporate tax reporting is generally more than the tax cost of partnership reporting.

If the club is a partnership, the club files a partnership return on which it reports the tax consequences of its transactions and the shares of each member. The club does not pay a tax. You and the other members pay tax on your shares of dividends, interest, capital gain, and other income earned by the club. You report your share as if you earned the income personally. For example, you report your share of the club's capital gains and losses on your Schedule D on the line provided for partnership gains and losses; you report your share of dividends and interest in the respective dividend and interest schedules of your personal tax return. You may also deduct as itemized deductions your share of the club's investment expenses.

The following is an example of a club treated as a partnership under Treasury regulations:

Example—

Twenty-five persons each contribute $10 a month for the purpose of jointly investing in securities. They share investment income equally. Under the agreement, the club will operate until terminated by a three-quarter vote of the total membership and will not end upon the withdrawal or death of any member. However, under local law, each member has the power to dissolve the club at any time. Members meet monthly; buy or sell decisions must be voted on by a majority of the organization's membership present. Elected officers perform only ministerial functions, such as presiding at meetings and carrying out the directions of the members. Members of the club are personally liable for all debts of, or claims against, the club. No member can transfer his membership. The club does not have the corporate characteristics of limited liability, free transferability of interests, continuity of life, and centralized management. Therefore, it is treated as a partnership. See ¶10.00.

¶31.00 • Tax Savings for Investors in Real Estate

For the effect of tax legislation on real estate investments, see the tax legislation guide in the front of this book.

¶31.001 • INVESTMENTS IN REAL ESTATE VENTURES

Individuals may participate in a large real estate venture by investing in limited partnerships, corporations, trusts, or real estate investment trusts.

A limited partnership. Real estate ventures are frequently organized as limited partnerships. The limited partnership is not taxed. Tax is imposed on the individual share of income received by each partner. Little or no tax may be incurred by the investors at the start of the operations because depreciation and other expense deductions and credits are passed directly to the investors. Depreciation deductions taken on the property reduce the partners' taxable income without reducing the amount of cash available to them. This tax saving is temporary and limited by the terms and the amount of the mortgage debt on the property. Mortgage amortization payments reduce the amount of cash available to investors without an offsetting tax deduction. Thus, the amount of an investor's tax-free return depends on the extent to which depreciation deductions exceed the amortization payments.

To provide a higher return of tax-free income, at least during the early years of its operations, a venture must obtain a constant payment mortgage that provides for the payment of fixed annual amounts which are allocated to continually decreasing amounts of interest and increasing amounts of amortization payments. Consequently, in the early years, a tax-free return of income is high while the amortization payments are low, but as the amortization payments increase, nontaxable income decreases. When this tax-free return has been substantially reduced, a partnership must refinance the mortgage to reduce the amortization payments and once again increase the tax-free return.

Examples—

1. A limited partnership of 100 investors owns a building that returns an annual income of $100,000 after deduction of operating expenses, but before a depreciation deduction of $80,000. Thus, taxable income is $20,000 ($100,000 − $80,000). Assuming that there is no mortgage on the building, all of the $100,000 is available for distribution. (Since the depreciation requires no cash outlay, it does not reduce the cash available for distribution.) Each investor receives $1,000. Taxable income being $20,000, only 20% ($20,000/$100,000) of the distribution is taxable. Thus, each investor reports as income only $200 of his $1,000 distribution; $800 is tax free.

2. Same facts as above, except that the building is mortgaged, and an annual amortization payment of $40,000 is being made. Consequently, only $60,000 is available for distribution, of which $20,000 is taxable. Each investor receives $600, of which ⅓ ($20,000/$60,000) or $200 is taxed, and $400 is tax free. In other words, the $60,000 distribution is tax free to the extent that the depreciation deduction of $80,000 exceeds the amortization of $40,000—namely $40,000. If the amortization payment was increased to $50,000, only $30,000 of the distribution would be tax free ($80,000 − $50,000).

The tax-free return is based on the assumption that the building does not actually depreciate at as fast a rate as the tax depreciation rate. If the building is depreciating physically at a faster rate, the so-called tax-free return on investment does not exist. Distributions to investors (over and above current income return) which are labeled tax-free distributions are in fact, a return of the investor's own capital.

Disadvantages of limited partnerships. Although limited partnerships are organized to prevent double taxation inherent in the corporate form, there is a danger that the partnership may be taxed as a corporation if its operations resemble those of a corporation. Also, partnership operations do not provide for the diversification of investments or for the free transfer of the investor's individual interests. Investors may find it difficult to sell their interests because of transferability restrictions and a lack of an open market for the sale of their interests.

Reviewing an investment offer. Consider the following pointers in reviewing an offering.

1. If the venture is constructing a development, discount projected income which may be eroded by increasing construction costs caused by inflation, material shortages, and labor disputes. Escalating costs not accounted for in long-term construction can jeopardize the project or income prospects. Adequate cash reserves should be available for emergencies.

2. Check the market conditions. Has there been overconstruction in the area? Is the area changing socially and economically?

3. Check the fees of managers. See that they are reasonable for your area. A promoter may conceal the amount of money he is drawing from the project. He may be taking a real estate commission by having a commission paid to a company which he controls. A reliable promoter should disclose this fact and be willing to collect the commission only after the investors have recovered their capital. Also check the reasonableness of prepaid management fees and loan fees and whether or not the sale of property to the syndicate is from a corporation in which the syndicator has an interest. If there is such a sale, check its terms, price, interest rates, and whether there is any prepaid interest which may conceal a cash profit payout to the syndicator.

4. Check the experience and reliability of the manager.

Real estate investment trusts (REITs). The tax treatment of real estate investment trusts resembles that of open-end mutual funds. Distributions are taxed to the investors in the trust as ordinary income, but no dividend exclusion is allowed on such distributions. Distributed long-term capital gains are reported by the investors as long-term gains. If the trust operates at a loss, the loss may not be passed on to the investors.

A REIT may not necessarily invest in equities. It may operate for interest return by providing loans. Before investing, check the scope of the REIT's operations and current market conditions and projections.

¶31.002 • DETERMINING WHETHER A TENANCY IN COMMON IS A PARTNERSHIP

In a tenancy in common, each tenant owns an undivided share in the property. Upon the death of a co-tenant, his interest passes to his heirs, not to the other tenants as in a joint tenancy. Tenants in common may or may not be considered as holding the property in a partnership. The determination of whether they are partners affects whether a partnership return must be filed, whether the involuntary conversion election (¶18.21) and first-year expensing (¶5.38) must be made by the partnership or the co-tenants, and the deductibility of property taxes beyond a co-tenant's percentage of ownership (¶16.06).

Treasury regulations defining partnerships note that the co-ownership of property which is merely maintained, kept in repair, and rented or leased is not a partnership. If you wish to operate the property as a partnership, you may do so by forming a partnership. Even if you do not formally set up a partnership, the IRS may treat your co-ownership as a partnership if the services or other activity in holding the property is considered a business. Collecting rents or hiring agents to collect rents is not considered a business activity. In one case, tenants were held to be partners where the property had been previously owned by a corporation in which they were stockholders. On liquidation, they received interests in the property equal to their former stock interests. As they continued the business of the corporation using the same assets and the same methods of operation, they were treated as in business as a partnership.

¶31.01 • HOW INVESTORS TREAT SALES OF SUBDIVIDED REAL ESTATE IN 1986

Investors who subdivide tracts risk being treated as dealers whose gains are taxed at ordinary rates. However, special tax rules provide certainty in claiming capital gain on certain subdivisions. If you meet the rules, you can subdivide the tract into lots and even engage in advertising and other promotional activities without being taxed as a dealer. This advantage is tied to arbitrary holding period rules and similar restrictions: You may not make substantial improvements; you generally may not install water or sewer facilities unless you have held the tract for more than 10 years, and then you must show that you could not sell the land at the prevailing price for similar land in your locality without such improvements. These restrictions may prove too burdensome or impossible to meet. Read the following rules. If you come within them, you may qualify for capital gain without having to be concerned with whether your activity in selling lots may be viewed as those of a dealer. To qualify you must show that:

1. You are not a dealer in real estate and do not hold any other land primarily for sale to customers in the ordinary course of your business. If you are a dealer, you cannot avoid the "dealer" taint by transferring property to a relative.

2. You did not previously hold the subdivided land primarily for sale to customers in the ordinary course of your business.

3. You did not make any substantial improvements on the tract which increased the value of the lots sold (*see* below).

4. You owned the land for five years or inherited it.

If you meet the rules above, you get capital gains on the first five lots you sell—assuming you do not sell the sixth lot in the same year you sell any of the first five. In or after the year you sell the sixth lot in the tract, you are taxed this way: Ordinary gain on 5% of the selling price. Capital gain on the balance of the sales price.

Selling expenses on sales giving limited capital gains are also allocated. You get an ordinary deduction up to the amount of gain taxed as ordinary income. The balance of selling expenses reduces the capital gain.

Examples—
1. You sell your sixth lot for $12,000; its adjusted basis was $10,000. Selling expenses are $800. You have ordinary income of $600 (5% of $12,000); capital gain of $1,400 ($2,000 less $600). Of the $800 selling expenses, you have an ordinary deduction of $600, and the remainder of $200 reduces capital gain to $1,200 ($1,400 less $200).

2. You bought land in 1961. You subdivide it into 20 lots in 1986. You make no substantial improvements on the land. You sell the lots at a profit as follows:

HOW YOU ARE TAXED ON SUBDIVIDED REAL ESTATE

Sales by year	Report profits as
1985—5 lots	Capital gains
1986—15 lots	Ordinary income on 5% of sales price—capital gains on the balance
1985—6 lots	Ordinary income on 5% of sales price—capital gains on the balance
1986—14 lots	Same
1985—3 lots	Capital gains
1986—17 lots	Ordinary income on 5% of sales price—capital gains on the balance

¶31.02 • INVESTORS WHO CANNOT MEET THE SPECIAL CAPITAL GAIN RULES IN 1986

You may be unable to comply with one or more of the rules discussed in ¶31.01. This does not mean you cannot qualify for capital gain. In the event your return is questioned, you must prove that your subdividing and selling activities have not put you into the real estate business as a dealer. To convince an IRS agent or a court you are an investor, this type of evidence will be needed to build a strong argument for capital gains:

1. You bought the property as an investment, or to use for some personal purpose—for example, to build a residence. Or you received the property as a gift or by inheritance.

2. No substantial improvements have been added to the tract.

3. You subdivided the property to liquidate your investment.

4. You did not advertise or use agents. Sales came through unsolicited offers.

5. Sales were infrequent.

6. You have had no previous activities as a real estate dealer.

7. You are engaged in a business unrelated to real estate. (That you have another occupation, however, does not by itself mean that you cannot also be in the real estate business.)

8. Your original intention to sell was motivated by a desire to liquidate an investment.

9. You have held the property for a long period of time.

10. You invested the proceeds in investment property.

If you do not sell any additional lots from a tract for a period of five years from the last sale, the remainder of the original tract is considered a "new tract." You are then permitted to sell five more lots before the 5% rule applies (*see* ¶31.01).

You do not get capital gain treatment if you made substantial improvements. These are considered substantial improvements: The erection of a shopping center which materially increases the value of all the lots, the putting in of public utilities for the entire tract, or the laying of a hard surface road to each lot.

Improvements that are not considered substantial are: Erecting your personal residence on one of the lots, clearing operations, or the construction of minimum all-weather access roads to each lot (if climate requires it, this may be of gravel).

You may build or install water, sewer, and drainage facilities or roads in some cases, and they will not be considered substantial improvements if you held the property at least 10 years and you could not sell it at the going price for similar property without these improvements. But you must elect not to increase the basis of your property for these improvements. The rules covering elections and proving you could not sell the property at going local prices without improvement do not apply if: The property was acquired by foreclosing a lien on it, *or*, it is property adjacent to foreclosed property and 80% of the real property you own was acquired by foreclosure of liens.

Certain improvements may add substantially to the value of some lots in a tract, and not to others. If so, you get capital gain treatment only on the lots which were not materially affected in value. Even if you personally do not make the improvements, you are considered to have made them if they were made by your brother, sister (including half-blood), wife, husband, parent, grandparent, child or grandchild; a corporation which you control; a partnership of which you are a partner; a lessee—but only if the improvements give you income (see ¶9.01); or the federal, state, or local government—but only if you must add the improvement to the tax cost of the property (see ¶6.12).

You may not divide a single tract of land into two tracts to sell 10 lots instead of five at capital gains. Two or more pieces are considered a single tract if you held them at any time as one piece. Also, they are treated as one if they would be connected except for a road, street, railroad, stream, etc.

The above rule applies only to profits. The tax treatment of losses depends on the purpose for which you held the subdivided real estate. If you held it primarily for sale to customers, report the losses as ordinary losses; if as an investment, report the losses as capital losses.

¶31.021 • EXCHANGING REAL ESTATE WITHOUT TAX

You may trade real estate held for investment for other investment real estate and incur no tax. The potential tax on the gain is postponed to the time you sell the exchanged property at a price exceeding the tax basis of the property. A tax-free exchange may also defer a potential tax due on gain from depreciation recapture and might be considered where the depreciable basis of a building has been substantially written off. Here the building may be exchanged for other property which will give off larger tax deductions.

The postponement of tax is equivalent to receiving an interest-free government loan in the amount you would have owed in taxes had you sold the property. With no part of your capital depleted by tax, you can reinvest the full value of your old property.

To transact a fully tax-free exchange, you must satisfy these conditions:

1. The property traded must be solely for property of a like kind. The words "like kind" are liberally interpreted. They refer to the nature or character of the property, not its grade, quality or use. Some examples of "like kind" exchanges are: Farm or ranch for city property; unimproved land for improved real estate; rental house for a store building; fee in business property for 30-year or more leasehold in the same type of property.

2. The property exchanged must have been held for productive use in your business or for investment and traded for property to be held for productive use in business or investment. Therefore, trades of property used, or to be used, for personal purposes, such as exchanging a residence for rental property, cannot receive tax-free treatment. Special rules, however, apply when you trade your residence for another home (see ¶29.20).

3. The trade must generally occur within a 180-day period and property identification must occur within 45 days of the first transfer, see ¶5.48 for further details of this test.

A real estate dealer cannot transact a tax-free exchange of property he holds for sale to customers. Furthermore, an exchange is not tax free if the property received is held for immediate resale.

Although the tax-free exchange has this major tax attraction, there are limitations to its use. The primary problem is bringing together suitable exchange properties and investors interested in trading. This difficulty may sometimes be overcome by brokers specializing in real estate exchanges. Another serious limitation attaches to exchanges dealing with depreciable property. It is posed by the tax rule that requires you to carry over the basis of the old property to the new property. If you have property with a basis of $25,000, now valued at $50,000, which you exchanged for another property worth $50,000, your basis for depreciation for

the new property is $25,000. Further, if you acquired the original property before 1981, you are barred from using ACRS for the property acquired through the exchange.

If you sell the old property and use the proceeds to buy new property the tax basis for depreciation is $50,000, giving you larger deductions than you are getting in the exchange transaction. If increased depreciation deductions are desirable, then it may pay to sell the property and purchase new property. Tax on the sale is generally subject to capital gain treatment. Further, tax may be spread by transacting an installment sale. Project the tax consequences of both types of transactions and choose the one giving the greater overall tax benefits. You may find it preferable to sell the property and purchase new property on which ACRS may be claimed.

A tax-free exchange may be advantageous in the case of land which is not depreciable. It may be exchanged for a depreciable rental building. The exchange is tax free and depreciation or ACRS may be claimed on the building.

A tax-free exchange is not desirable if the transaction will result in a loss, since you may not deduct a loss in a tax-free exchange. To ensure the loss deduction, first sell the property, then buy new property with the proceeds.

A nonresident alien may not defer tax on an exchange of U.S. realty unless he receives realty which, if sold, is subject to U.S. tax.

Partially tax-free exchanges. Not all property exchanges are without tax. To be completely tax free, the exchange must be a property-for-property exchange. If the trade includes boot, such as cash or other property, gain is taxed up to the amount of the boot. If property is depreciated under a rapid depreciation method, boot may be subject to ordinary income tax under the rules of ¶5.40.

If you trade mortgaged property, the mortgage released is treated as boot. This holds true whether or not the other party assumes, or takes subject to, the mortgage. Therefore, if you exchange your property worth $50,000 on which there is a $10,000 mortgage, for unmortgaged land worth $45,000, a $2,000 automobile, and $3,000 cash, you would be receiving $15,000 in boot: The release of the $10,000 mortgage, plus $5,000 representing the value of the cash and the car. Whether part or all of the boot is taxed depends on whether you realize gain on the exchange. When you give boot such as cash, other property, or assume or take subject to an existing mortgage, you get no loss deduction. It is simply added to your investment, thereby increasing your basis in the new property.

When there are mortgages on both properties, the mortgages are netted. The party giving up the larger mortgage and getting the smaller mortgage treats the excess as boot.

Example—

You own a small office building with an adjusted basis of $50,000 on which there is a $30,000 mortgage. You exchange it for Low's building valued at $55,000, having a $20,000 mortgage, and for $5,000 in cash. You compute your gain in this way:

What you received

Present value of Low's property		$55,000
Cash		5,000
Mortgage on building traded		30,000
Total received		$90,000
Less:		
Adjusted basis of building traded	$50,000	
Mortgage assumed by you	20,000	70,000
Actual gain on the exchange		$20,000

However, the actual gain of $20,000 is taxed only up to the amount of boot, $15,000.

Figuring boot

Cash		$ 5,000
Mortgage on building traded	$30,000	
Less: Mortgage assumed on Low's property	20,000	10,000
Total gain taxed to you		$15,000

If the amount of boot exceeds your actual gain, your tax is limited to the amount of your gain.

Cash received as boot may not be netted against a mortgage, except in limited circumstances.
Example—
Jones exchanges property worth $55,000 but subject to a $20,000 mortgage, for Smith's property worth $65,000 but subject to a $30,000 mortgage. Jones did not receive taxable boot because he took subject to a $30,000 mortgage while being relieved of a $20,000 mortgage. But now assume because of certain contract conditions, Smith does not want to assume the $20,000 mortgage; instead he gives $20,000 cash to Jones to pay off the $20,000 mortgage. The IRS would argue that Jones has received taxable boot in the form of cash; he may not net the cash against the $30,000 mortgage which he assumed. The Tax Court would disagree. It would allow Jones to net the cash against the mortgage because the contract specifically requires him to apply the cash to the mortgage. Here, the court would not treat the cash as ordinary boot because he does not have free use of it.

¶31.03 • TIMING YOUR REAL PROPERTY SALES

Generally, a taxable transaction occurs in the year in which title or possession to property passes to the buyer. By controlling the year title and possession passes, you may select the year in which to report profit or loss. For example, you intend to sell property this year, but you estimate that reporting the sale next year will incur less in taxes. You can postpone the transfer of title and possession to next year. Alternatively, you can transact an installment sale, giving title and possession this year but delaying the receipt of all or most of the sale proceeds until next year. *See* ¶6.16.

¶31.05 • DEALER GETS CAPITAL GAIN IN 1986 BY SEPARATING INVESTMENT FROM STOCK IN TRADE

In addition to parcels for ordinary business sales, it is not unusual for a real estate dealer to hold other parcels for investment in expectation of capital gain. But the capital gain objective is not easily reached. The IRS will probably treat a 1986 sale as part of the dealer's usual selling activity. Courts have granted capital gain treatment to dealers who have succeeded in showing a clear segregation between their investment properties and those held for usual business sale. The Supreme Court ruled that courts should recognize that dealers can hold property for business as well as investment purposes.

Some dealers whose land has been condemned have argued that the condemnation converts their holdings to investment property which is entitled to capital gain treatment. The Tax Court originally agreed with the argument but now holds that a condemnation notice does not change the character of the property. Once a condemnation notice is received, there is a constructive sale to the condemning authority, with only price to be settled later. The proceeds are taxable as ordinary income.

¶31.06 • SELLER'S REPOSSESSION OF REALTY AFTER BUYER'S DEFAULT ON PURCHASE MONEY MORTGAGE DEBT

When you, as a seller, repossess realty on the buyer's default of a debt which the realty secures, you may realize gain or loss. (If the realty was a personal residence, the loss is not deductible.) A debt is secured by real property whenever you have the right to take title or possession or both in the event the buyer defaults on his obligation under the contract.

Figuring gain on the repossession. Gain on the repossession is the excess of:

1. Payments received on the original sales contract prior to and on the repossession, including payments made by the buyer for your benefit to another party; *over*

2. The amount of taxable gain previously reported prior to the repossession.

Gain computed under these two steps may not be fully taxable. Taxable gain is limited to the amount of original profit less gain on the sale already reported as income for periods prior to the repossession and less your repossession costs.

The limitation on gain does not apply if the selling price cannot be computed at the time of sale as, for example, where the selling price is stated as a percentage of the profits to be realized from the development of the property sold.
Example—
Assume you sell a house for $25,000. You take a $5,000 down payment plus a $20,000 mortgage, secured by the property, from the buyer with principal payable at the rate of $4,000 annually. The adjusted basis of the house was $20,000 and you elected to report the transaction on the installment basis. Your gross profit percentage is 20% ($5,000 profit over $25,000 selling price). In the year of sale, you include $1,000 in your income on the installment basis (20% of $5,000 down payment). The next year you reported profit of $800 (20% of $4,000 annual installment). In the third year, the buyer defaults on his payments, and you repossess the property. The amount of gain on repossession is computed as follows:

1. Compute gain.		
Amount of money received ($5,000 plus $4,000)		$9,000
Less: Amount of gain taxed in prior years ($1,000 plus $800)		1,800
Gain		$7,200
2. Compute limited gain, assuming cost of repossession is $500.		
Original profit		$5,000
Reduced by:		
Gain reported as income	$1,800	
Cost of repossession	500	2,300
Taxable gain on repossession		$2,700

The above rules do not affect the character of the gain. Thus, if you repossess property as a dealer, the gain is subject to ordinary income rates. For example, if you, as an investor, repossess in 1986 a tract originally held long term whose gain was reported on the installment method, the gain is capital gain. According to Treasury regulations, if the sale was originally reported as a deferred payment sale and title was transferred to the buyer who voluntarily reconveyed it, gain on a 1986 repossession is ordinary income. However, if the buyer's obligations are those of a corporation or governmental agency, capital gain treatment may apply.

The basis of repossessed property. It is the adjusted basis of the debt (face value of the debt less the unreported profits) secured by the property, figured as of the date of repossession, increased by (1) the taxable gain, and (2) the amount of money, costs, or other consideration paid by you on the repossession.
Example—
Same facts as in the example above. The basis of the repossessed property is computed as follows:

1. Face value of debt		$16,000
2. Less: Unreported profit (20% of above)		3,200
3. Adjusted basis at date of repossession		$12,800
4. Plus: Gain on repossession	$2,700	
Cost of repossession	500	3,200
5. Basis of repossessed property		$16,000

If you treated the debt as having become worthless or partially worthless before repossession, you are considered to receive, upon the repossession of the property securing the debt, an amount equal to the amount of the debt treated as worthless; you increase the basis of the debt by an amount equal to the amount previously treated as worthless.

If your debt is not fully discharged as a result of the repossession, the basis of the undischarged debt is zero. No loss may be claimed if the obligations subsequently become worthless. This rule applies to undischarged debts on the original obligation of the purchaser, a substituted obligation of the purchaser, a deficiency judgment entered in a court of law into which the purchaser's obligation was merged, and any other obligations arising from the transaction.

The above repossession rules do not apply if you repurchase the property by paying the buyer a sum in addition to the discharge of his debt, unless the repurchase and payment was provided for in the original sale contract, or the buyer has defaulted on his obligation, or his default is imminent.

Personal residence. The above rules do not apply to repossessions of a personal residence if (1) gain on the original sale was not taxed because you made an election to avoid tax (¶29.30) or to defer gain on the purchase of a new residence (¶29.20), and (2) within a year after the repossession you resell the property. The resale is treated as a part of the transaction comprising the original sale.

¶31.061 • FORECLOSURE BIDS BY MORTGAGEES ON MORTGAGES OTHER THAN PURCHASE MONEY MORTGAGES

If you, as a mortgagee, bid in on a foreclosure sale to pay off a mortgage that is *not a purchase money mortgage,* your actual financial loss is the difference between the unpaid mortgage debt and the value of the property. For tax purposes, however, you may realize a capital gain or loss and a bad debt loss which are reportable *in the year of the foreclosure sale.*

Your bid is treated as consisting of two distinct transactions:

1. The repayment of your loan. To determine whether this results in a bad debt, the bid price is matched against the face amount of the mortgage.

2. A taxable exchange of your mortgage note for the foreclosed property, which may result in a capital gain or loss. This is determined by matching the bid price against the fair market value of the property.

Examples—

1. *Mortgagee's bid less than market value.* You hold a $40,000 mortgage on property having a fair market value of $30,000. You bid on the property at the foreclosure sale at $28,000. The expenses of the sale are $2,000, reducing the bid price to $26,000. The mortgagor is insolvent, so you have a bad debt loss of $14,000 ($40,000 − $26,000). You also have a $4,000 capital gain (the fair market value of the property of $30,000 − $26,000).

2. *Mortgagee's bid equal to market value.* Suppose your bid was $32,000, and the expenses $2,000. The difference between the net bid price of $30,000 and the mortgage of $40,000 is $10,000. As the mortgagor is insolvent, there is a bad debt loss of $10,000. Since the net bid price equals the fair market value, there is neither capital gain nor loss.

3. *Mortgagee's bid greater than market value.* Suppose you had bid $36,000 and had $2,000 in expenses. Your bad debt deduction is $6,000 —the difference between the mortgage debt of $40,000 and the net bid price of $34,000. You also had a capital loss of $4,000 (difference between the net bid price of $34,000 and the fair market value of $30,000).

Where the bid price equals the mortgage debt plus unreported but accrued interest, you report the interest as income. But where the accrued interest has been reported, the unpaid amount is added to the collection expenses.

Preserve evidence of the property's fair market value. At a later date, the IRS may claim that the property was worth more than your bid and may tax you for the difference. Furthermore, be prepared to prove the worthlessness of the debt to support the bad debt deduction.

Voluntary conveyance. Instead of forcing you to foreclose, the mortgagor may voluntarily convey the property to you in consideration for your canceling the mortgage debt. Your loss is the amount by which the mortgage debt plus accrued interest exceeds the fair market value of the property. If, however, the fair market value exceeds the mortgage debt plus accrued interest, the difference is taxable gain. The gain or loss is reportable in the year you receive the property. Your basis in the property is its fair market value when you receive it.

¶31.062 • HOW MORTGAGEES TREAT PROCEEDS RECEIVED FROM FORECLOSURE SALE TO THIRD PARTY

When a third party buys the property in a foreclosure, the mortgagee receives the purchase price to apply against the mortgage debt. If it is less than the debt, the mortgagee may proceed against the mortgagor for the difference. Foreclosure expenses are treated as offsets against the foreclosure proceeds and increase the bad debt loss.

You deduct your loss as a bad debt. The law distinguishes between two types of bad debt deductions, business bad debts and nonbusiness bad debts. A business bad debt is fully deductible. A nonbusiness bad debt is a short-term capital loss that can be offset only against capital gains, plus a limited amount of ordinary income (*see* ¶6.28). In addition, you may deduct a partially worthless business bad debt, but you may not deduct a partially worthless nonbusiness bad debt. Remember this distinction if you are thinking of forgiving part of the mortgage debt as a settlement. If the debt is a nonbusiness bad debt, you will not be able to take a deduction until the entire debt proves to be worthless. But whether you are deducting a business or a nonbusiness bad debt, your deduction will be allowed only if you show the debt to be uncollectible—for example, because a deficiency judgment is worthless, or because the mortgagor is bankrupt or has disappeared.

Example—

You hold a $30,000 note and mortgage which are in default. You foreclose, and a third party buys the property for $20,000. Foreclosure expenses amount to $2,000. The deficiency is uncollectible. Your loss of $12,000 is figured as follows:

Unpaid mortgage debt		$30,000
Foreclosure proceeds	$20,000	
Less: Expenses	2,000	
Net proceeds		18,000
Bad debt loss		$12,000

¶31.063 • TREATMENT OF DISCOUNT ON PURCHASED MORTGAGE

According to the IRS, when you buy a mortgage note at a discount, you report each payment as a partial return of principal and discount income. For example, you buy for $10,000 a second mortgage note, the face amount of which is $15,000. If you receive a payment of $1,200, $800 (⅔ of $1,200) is a return of capital; $400 (⅓ of $1,200) is ordinary income. However, taxpayers have disputed the IRS rule which requires a current reporting of discount income and have been allowed to treat all payments as a return of cost (until their investment is fully recovered) when they have been able to convince a court that the mortgage was of a highly speculative nature.

If you decide to defer the reporting of discount income until you recover your cost, anticipate a dispute with the IRS. To support your case, you have to prove that your investment was "speculative." The Tax Court set down these tests for determining whether an obligation is speculative:

1. Is the debtor personally liable? Is there a guarantor? If a party is personally liable, what are his credit standing and resources?

2. The marketability of the note. Is it negotiable?

3. At the time the note is bought, is the debtor in substantial default on payments due?

4. What are the terms of payment? Is the debt a first, second, or other lien?

5. What is the market value of the underlying property?

Even assuming that you can prove that there is a speculative element to the obligation, the next step of proof presents difficulties because the courts are not in agreement on just what part of the note must be proved speculative. In one court, an investment is speculative if you are uncertain that the entire obligation will be paid. This is the most liberal approach. In another court, the test is whether you can expect to recover at least your cost. If you can, then you must currently report part of the discount as income. The Tax Court set down a test that straddles these two tests. The note is speculative if you are uncertain that you will recover your cost and a major portion of the discount. Furthermore, speculativeness of an obligation is to be measured by the facts known at the time of the purchase of the obligation. That the debtor is later able to meet his obligation does not negate the speculative nature of the obligation at the time of its purchase.

¶31.064 • TRANSFERRING MORTGAGED REALTY

Mortgaging realty that has appreciated in value is one way of realizing cash on the appreciation without current tax consequences. The receipt of cash by mortgaging the property is not taxed; tax will generally be imposed only when the property is sold. However, there is a possible tax where the mortgage exceeds the adjusted basis of the property and the property is given away or transferred to a controlled corporation (ownership of at least 80%).

Where the property is transferred to a controlled corporation, the excess is taxable gain. Further, if the IRS successfully charges that the transfer is part of a tax avoidance scheme, the taxable gain may be as high as the amount of the mortgage liability.

Gifts. The IRS holds that a gift of mortgaged property results in taxable income to the donor to the extent that the mortgage liability exceeds the donor's basis. The IRS position has been supported by the Tax Court and an appeals court.

Example—
Levine had owned a building for 19 years before transferring it to a trust for the grandchildren. During that period, he obtained nonrecourse loans of $672,000 of which $127,000 was repaid, $334,000 was invested in building improvements and the balance was apparently retained for personal purposes. Upon the transfer, the trust assumed nonrecourse mortgages (with accrued interest) on the building of $785,908, as well as $124,574 in building-related expenses for which Levine was personally liable. The total liabilities taken on by the trust exceeded Levine's adjusted basis by $425,000; the IRS charged that this excess was taxable gain to Levine. The Tax Court agreed and an appeals court affirmed.

Levine had argued that no gain is recognized on the making of a gift; any potential gain is preserved in the donee's basis and will eventually be taxed when the donee sells the property. The appeals court side-stepped this basis argument by noting that no Code provision specifically exempts from taxation gain on a gift of mortgaged property.

¶ 32.00 • Tax Savings for Executives

¶32.001 • GENERAL PRINCIPLES

Executive pay plans have one objective—to reduce or eliminate the tax cost of earning salary income. There are pay benefits that are not taxable, such as certain fringe benefits, disability pensions, health and accident and death benefits, and certain housing costs while working abroad. Other tax saving benefits may be developed through pension and profit-sharing plans, stock options and deferred pay plans. The objective of deferring pay is to postpone the receipt of salary income to a time when you expect to be in a lower tax bracket. However, a deferred pay plan is generally not advisable where a projection of future income shows that there probably will be no substantial income decline, and/or the tax bracket differentials will not be wide. An after-tax dollar in hand for current use is preferable to an expectation of a tax saving that may not materialize.

Fringe benefits. Fringe benefits provided executives by employers increase after-tax income by being either tax exempt or subject to special tax treatment. The tax consequences of fringe benefits and other pay benefits are discussed in the following sections:

	See ¶
Employer-furnished meals and lodgings	2.01
Tax-free fringe benefit checklist	2.02
Group-term life insurance	2.021
Gifts from employers	2.03
Death benefit exclusion	2.04
Cafeteria plans	2.06
Deferring tax on pay	2.07
Accident and health plans	2.16
Travel and entertainment expenses	2.30
Advantage of reimbursement arrangements	2.381
Moving expenses	2.40
Pension and profit-sharing payments	7.00–7.37
Reimbursement of medical costs	17.04
Tax-free income earned abroad	36.00

¶32.01 • PENSION AND PROFIT-SHARING PLANS

A company qualified pension or profit-sharing plan offers these benefits: (1) You do not realize current income on your employer's contributions to the plan on your behalf. (2) Funds contributed by both your employer and you compound tax free within the plan. (3) If you receive a lump sum, tax on employer contributions may be reduced by a special averaging rule. (4) If you receive a lump-sum distribution in company securities, unrealized appreciation on those securities is not taxed until you finally sell the stock.

Where you are allowed to choose the type of payout from a qualified plan, make sure that you compare the tax on receiving a lump-sum distribution with the projected tax cost of deferring payments over a period of years or rolling over the distribution to an IRA account. *See* ¶7.01 and ¶7.05.

¶32.011 • CASH OR DEFERRED PAY ARRANGEMENTS: 401(k) PLANS

If your company has a profit-sharing or stock bonus plan, it has the opportunity of giving you additional tax sheltered pay. The tax law allows the company to add a cash or deferred pay plan, called a 401(k) plan, which can operate in one of two ways:

1. Your employer contributes an amount for your benefit to a trust account. You are not taxed on your employer's contribution. Although there is no income tax, the contribution is subject to Social Security tax.
2. You agree to take a salary reduction or to forego a salary increase. The reduction is placed in a trust account for your benefit. The reduction is treated as your employer's contribution. In addition, your company may match part of your contribution.

Income earned on the trust account accumulates tax free until it is withdrawn. You may not withdraw funds until you reach age 59½, are separated from service, become disabled, or show financial hardship. At the time of withdrawal, the tax on the proceeds may be computed by special averaging (*see* ¶7.02).

Taking a pay reduction may be an ideal way to defer income, benefit from a tax-free buildup of income, and take advantage of averaging at the time of distribution.

¶32.02 • INSURANCE PLANS MAY BE TAX FREE

Company-financed insurance for employees is a common method of giving additional benefits at low or no tax cost.

Group life insurance. Group insurance plans may furnish not only life insurance protection but also accident and health benefits. Premium costs are low and tax deductible to the company while tax free to you unless you have nonforfeitable rights to permanent life insurance, or, in the case of group-term life insurance, your coverage exceeds $50,000 (*see* ¶2.021). Even where your coverage exceeds $50,000, the tax incurred on your employer's premium payment is generally less than what you would pay privately for similar insurance.

It may be possible to avoid estate tax on the group policy proceeds if you assign all of your ownership rights in the policy, including the right to convert the policy, and the beneficiary is other than your estate. Where the policy allows assignment of the conversion right, in addition to all other rights, and state law does not bar the assignment, you are considered to have made a complete assignment of the group insurance for estate tax purposes.

The IRS has ruled that where an employee assigns a group life policy and the value of the employee's interest in the policy cannot be ascertained, there is no taxable gift. This is so where the employer could simply have stopped making payments. However, there is a gift by the employee to the assignor to the extent of premiums paid by the employer. That gift is a present interest qualifying for the $10,000 annual exclusion.

Split-dollar insurance. Where you want more insurance than is provided by a group plan, your company may be able to help you get additional protection through a split-dollar insurance plan. Under this type of plan, your employer purchases permanent life insurance on your life. He pays the annual premium to the extent of the yearly increases in the cash surrender value of the policy, and you pay only the balance of the premium. At your death, your employer is entitled to part of the proceeds equal to the cash surrender value or any lesser amount equaling the total premiums he paid. You have the right to name a beneficiary to receive the remaining proceeds which, under most policies, is substantial compared with the employer's share.

You annually report as taxable income an amount equal to the one-year term cost of the declining life insurance protection to which you are entitled less any portion of the premium provided by you. Simplified somewhat, here is how the tax would be figured in one year. Assume the share of the proceeds payable to your beneficiary (face value less cash surrender value) from a $100,000 policy is $77,535. If the term cost of $77,535 insurance provided by the employer is $567, you pay a tax on $567, less your payment of premium. So, if you paid a premium of $209, you pay tax on $358. Assume in the fourth year, you pay no premium and the amount payable to your family is $69,625. (Under the split-dollar plan, the benefits payable to your beneficiary continuously decline; the employer's share increases annually because of the continued payment of premiums and the increase in the cash surrender value.) The term cost provided by your employer toward $69,625 is $549; you pay tax on the full $549.

Despite the tax cost, you may find the arrangement an inexpensive method of obtaining additional insurance coverage with your employer's help. For example, taking the taxable premium benefit of $549 from the above example, if you are in the 32% bracket, the cost of almost $70,000 insurance protection in that year is $175.68 ($549 × 32%).

Split-dollar insurance policies entered into before November 14, 1964 are not subject to the above tax on the employer's payment of premiums.

Qualified group legal services plan. If a qualified group legal services plan established by your employer provides prepaid legal services for personal (nonbusiness) legal matters for you, your spouse, and your dependents, you do not include in income your employer's contributions to the plan or the value of legal services or amounts paid for them under the plan. *See* ¶19.171.

¶32.03 • STOCK APPRECIATION RIGHTS (SARs)

SARs are a form of cash bonus tied to an increase in the price of employer stock. Each SAR entitles an employee to cash equal to the excess of the fair market value of one share on the date of exercise over the value on the date of the grant of the SAR.
Example—
When a stock is worth $30 a share, you get 100 SARs exercisable within five years. Two years later when the stock price increases to $50 a share, you exercise the SAR and receive $2,000. You are taxed when you receive the cash.

If the rights increase in value, keep a close watch on the expiration date. Do not let them expire before exercise. If you do, not only will you lose income but you will be taxed on income you never received. According to the IRS, an employee who does not exercise the SARs is taxed as if they had been exercised immediately before they expire. The IRS claims that an employee has constructive receipt of income immediately before they expire. At that time, the amount of gain realized from the SAR is fixed because the employee can no longer benefit from future appreciation in value.

An executive may realize taxable income when he becomes entitled to the maximum SAR benefit allowed by the company plan. For example, in 1983, when company stock is worth $30, an executive is granted 100 SARs exercisable within five years. By exercising the SARs, he may receive cash equal to the appreciation up to $20 per share. If the stock appreciates to $50 per share in 1986, the executive realizes taxable income of $2,000 ($20 per share × 100) in 1985, even if he does not exercise the SARs. The reason: Once the stock value appreciated to $50, the maximum SAR benefit of $20 was realized.

Performance shares. The company promises to make an award of stock in the future, at no cost to you, if the company's earnings reach a set level. You are taxed on the receipt of stock (unless the stock is restricted, as discussed in ¶32.04).

¶32.04 • STOCK OPTIONS AND RESTRICTED STOCK

Incentive stock options (ISOs). A corporation may provide its executives with incentive stock options to acquire its stock (or the stock of its parent or subsidiaries). ISOs are not taxed when granted or exercised. The option spread is generally taxable as capital gain in 1986 if the stock acquired by the exercise of the option is sold.

To qualify for this special tax treatment, these requirements must be met: (1) The stock must be held for two years after the date the option was granted and for one year after the exercise of the options. (2) The executive must have been an employee of the granting corporation (or its parent or subsidiary) until three months before the date of exercise. (A disabled employee may qualify if the option is exercised within 12 months of leaving employment). (3) The fair market value of stock for which an employee may be granted options may not exceed $100,000; if the $100,000 limit is not completely used, one-half of the excess may be carried forward for up to three years. (4) The option must be granted pursuant to a plan approved by the shareholders. (5) The option price is not less than the fair market value of the stock at the time it is granted. (6) The option is not exercised after 10 years from the date it was granted. (7) The option is not exercisable while other granted options are outstanding.

Fair market value of ISO stock is determined without regard to restrictions which will lapse, starting with options granted after March 24, 1984, except for options authorized before May 15, 1984 and granted before September 20, 1984.

Stock options granted after 1975 and before 1981 qualify for ISO treatment if the corporation makes an election. Stock acquired on the exercise of the ISO may be paid for with stock of the corporation granting the option. If paid for by exercising other statutory stock options, the exercise will result in ordinary income treatment, unless the transferred stock has met minimum holding period requirements. ISO treatment is available even though the employee has a right to receive cash or other property at the time of exercising the ISO as long as the cash or property is included in income. ISO may be granted in tandem with SARs as long as certain requirements are met. *See* temporary Treasury regulations.

ISOs are subject to alternative minimum tax. *See* ¶23.11.

Nonqualified stock options. If a nonqualified stock option has an ascertainable fair market value, the value of the option is taxable as ordinary income at the time of transfer. On the exercise of the option, no taxable gain is realized; gain or loss is realized on the later sale of the stock. Where the option has no ascertainable fair market value, no income is realized on the receipt of the option. Income is realized when the value of the option is ascertainable. This may occur when the option is exercised. For other details and requirements, *see* Treasury regulations.

Nonqualified stock options may be granted in addition to or in place of incentive stock options. There are no restrictions on the amount of nonqualified stock options that may be granted.

Note: For rules governing incentive stock options granted after 1986, see the new law guide at the front of this book.

When sale of stock is treated as grant of option. If company stock is purchased on the basis of the executive's promissory note and he is not personally liable, the company can recover only its stock in the event of default on the note. In terms of risk, the executive has given nothing and is somewhat in the same position as the optionee. If the stock value drops, he may walk away from the deal with no personal risk. According to Treasury regulations, the deal may be viewed as an option arrangement. Application of the Treasury regulation would give the executive ordinary taxable income when he pays for the stock if the value of the stock at the time of purchase exceeds the purchase price. For example, on July 1, 1982, a corporation sells 100 shares of its stock to an executive. The stock has a fair market value on that date of $25,000 and the executive executes a nonrecourse note secured by the stock in that amount, plus 8% annual interest. He is required by the note to make annual payment of $5,000 of principal, plus interest, beginning the following year. In 1985, he pays the interest on the note but no principal. He also collects dividends and votes the stock. In 1986, when the stock has appreciated in value to $30,000, he pays off the note. Under the Treasury regulation, the executive would realize ordinary income upon payment of the nonrecourse note to the extent of the difference between the amount paid ($25,000 in 1986) and the value of the stock ($30,000).

Restricted stock. Stock subject to restrictions is taxed as pay in the first year in which it is either transferable or not subject to a substantial risk of forfeiture. A risk of forfeiture exists where your rights are conditioned upon the future performance of substantial services. Generally, taxable income is the difference between the amount, if any, that you pay for the stock and its value at the time the risk of forfeiture is removed. The valuation at the time the forfeiture restrictions lapse is not reduced because of restrictions imposed on the right to sell the property. However, restrictions which will never lapse do affect valuation.

SEC restriction on insider trading is considered a substantial risk of forfeiture so that receipt of stock subject to such restriction is a nontaxable event. Similarly, if the stock is subject to a restriction on transfer to comply with SEC pooling-of-interests accounting rules, the stock is considered to be subject to a substantial restriction.

> You may elect to be taxed on the unrestricted (market) value of the stock at the time you receive it and to be treated as an investor. If you do, later appreciation in value is not taxed as pay. However, you may not claim a loss deduction if you later forfeit the stock. The election must generally be made not later than 30 days after the date of the transfer of the stock.
>
> The restricted stock rule is not restricted to compensation of employees; it may apply to any type of fee arrangement for services.

¶32.05 • EDUCATIONAL BENEFITS FOR EMPLOYEES' CHILDREN

Private foundations. The IRS has published guidelines under which a private foundation established by an employer may make tax-free grants to children of employees. If the guidelines are satisfied, employees are not taxable on the benefits provided their children. Advance approval of the grant program must be obtained from the IRS.

IRS guidelines require:

   Grant recipients must be selected by a scholarship committee which is independent of the employer and the foundation. Former employees of the employer or the foundation are not considered independent.

   Eligibility for the grants may be restricted to children of employees who have been employed for a minimum of up to three years, but eligibility may not be related to the employee's position, services, or duties.

   Once awarded, a grant may not be terminated if the parent leaves his job with the employer, regardless of the reason for the termination of employment. If a one-year grant is awarded or a multiyear grant is awarded subject to renewal, a child who reapplies for a later grant may not be considered ineligible because his parent no longer works for the employer.

   Grant recipients must be based solely upon objective standards unrelated to the employer's business and the parent's employment, such as prior academic performance, aptitude tests, recommendations from instructors, financial needs, and conclusions drawn from personal interviews.

   Recipients must be free to use the grants for courses which are not of particular benefit to the employer or the foundation.

   The grant program must not be used by the foundation or employer to recruit employees or induce employees to continue employment.

   There must be no requirement or suggestion that the child or parent is expected to render future employment services.

The grant program must also meet a percentage test: The number of grants awarded in a given year to children of employees must not exceed (1) 25% of the number of employees' children who were eligible, applied for the grants, and were considered by the selection committee in that year, or (2) 10% of the number of employees' children who were eligible during that year, whether or not they applied. Renewals of grants are not considered in determining the number of grants awarded.

If all guidelines other than the percentage test are satisfied, the IRS will determine whether the primary purpose of the program is to educate the children, in which case the grants will be considered tax-free scholarships or fellowships, or whether the grants are to be taxed to the parent-employee as extra compensation.

Educational benefit trusts and other plans. A medical professional corporation set up an educational benefit plan to provide the payment of college costs to the children of "key" employees. The plan defined a key employee as an employee who was salaried at over $15,000. To receive benefits, the child must have been a candidate for a degree within two years after graduating from high school. If an eligible employee quit for reasons other than death or permanent disability, his children could no longer receive benefits except for expenses actually incurred before termination. The company made annual contributions to the trust for which a bank was trustee. According to the IRS, amounts contributed to the trust are a form of pay to qualified employees, as they are contributed on the basis of employment and earnings record, rather than on the basis of competitive standards, such as need, merit or motivation. However, employees are not currently taxable. The right to have their children receive benefits is conditioned upon each employee's future performance of services. Further, there is a substantial risk of forfeiture. Tax is not incurred until a child has a vested right to receive benefits; here, vesting does not occur until a child becomes a candidate for a degree at an educational institution, has actually incurred educational expenses, and his parent is employed by the company. Once the right to receive a distribution from the plan becomes vested, the parent of the child who has incurred the expenses is taxable on the amount of the distribution. The company may then claim a deduction for the amount reported as income by the employee. The Tax Court and appeals court have upheld the IRS position in similar plans.

¶32.07 • PENALTY TAX ON EXCESS GOLDEN PARACHUTE PAYMENTS

Executives who receive substantial "golden parachute" payments as compensation following a corporate takeover may be subject to a 20% penalty tax. If the payment exceeds three times the average compensation for the preceding five years, the 20% penalty applies to payments in excess of the five-year compensation average.

The law presumes that excess parachute payments are not reasonable compensation but if it can be shown by clear evidence that the payment represented reasonable compensation, that amount reduces the excess payment subject to penalty.

Golden parachute payments are subject to income tax withholding as if they were wages; employers must also withhold the 20% penalty tax if applicable. The corporation may not deduct the penalized payment.

Any penalty is reported separately on Form W-2 and must be reported on the executive's tax return. *See* the Supplement for where to report the penalty.

¶ 33.00 • Tax Savings in Family Income Planning

Tax legislation would discourage income splitting between parents and minor children under the age of 14 and the use of short-term trusts for shifting tax on trust income from the trust grantor to income beneficiaries as follows: (1) income earned on property transferred to children under age 14 by a parent would generally be subject to tax at the parent's tax rates, (2) the short-term trust (10-year) exception for grantor trusts would no longer be available. However, income splitting opportunities would remain within the limits of the legislation. Parents could set up income transfers to children age 14 or over and to children under 14 within certain limits. Relatives other than parents could also aid family members. For example, a grandparent could set up a custodian account or a nonreversionary trust in favor of grandchildren, and the income from the account would be taxable to the child at the child's tax bracket regardless of the child's age. A grandparent could not set up a short-term reversionary trust and avoid tax on the trust income with a repeal of the short-term trust exception. For further details, *see* the guide to tax legislation in the front of this book.

¶33.00 • GIFT TAX BASICS

As family income planning generally requires the transfer of property, you must consider possible gift tax liability. The gift tax rates and credit are the same as those of the estate tax listed in ¶38.10. However, gift tax liability may be avoided by making gifts within the annual exclusion of $10,000 (or $20,000 for joint gifts). To each donee, you may give annually up to $10,000 tax free; further, if your spouse joins in the gift, you may give annually tax free to each donee up to $20,000. Thus, if you (with your spouse's consent) make annual gifts to four persons, you could give away without gift tax up to $80,000 (4 × $20,000 exclusion). Gifts over this exclusion may also avoid tax after applying the unified gift and estate tax credit listed in ¶38.10.

If you make an interest-free or low-interest loan to a family member, you may be subject to income tax as well as gift tax, *see* ¶4.10.

Each additional dollar of ordinary income you receive, such as interest, dividends, and rent, is taxed in your highest bracket. If under the tax laws you can deflect income to a lower tax bracket of a child or other dependent relative, he or she will pay a smaller tax on the income than you would pay. This tax-saving technique known as income splitting allows more after-tax income to remain within the family.

To split income, you must do more than make gifts of income. You must transfer the actual property from which the income is produced. For example, you do not avoid tax on interest by instructing your savings bank to credit interest to your children's account. Unless you actually transfer the complete ownership of the account to your children, the interest income is earned on money owned by you and must be reported by you. The same holds true with dividends, rents, and other forms of income. Un-

less you transfer the property providing the income, the income will be taxed to you.

You may not split earned income; income resulting from your services is taxed to you. You may not avoid this result by setting up trusts to receive your earned income.

¶33.01 • CUSTODIAN ACCOUNTS FOR CHILDREN

Custodian accounts set up in a bank, mutual fund, or brokerage firm can achieve income splitting; the tax consequences discussed below generally apply to such accounts. Trust accounts which are considered revocable under state law are ineffective in splitting interest income.

Purchase of securities through custodian accounts provides a practical method for making a gift of securities to a minor child, eliminating the need for a trust. The mechanics of opening a custodian account are simple. An adult opens a stock account for a minor child at a broker's office. He registers the securities in the name of a custodian for the benefit of the child. The custodian may be a parent, a child's guardian, grandparent, brother, sister, uncle or aunt. In some states, the custodian may be any adult or a bank or trust company. The custodian has the right to sell securities in the account, collect sales proceeds and investment income, and use them for the child's benefit or reinvestment.

There are limitations placed on the custodian. He may not take proceeds from the sale of an investment or income from an investment to buy additional securities on margin. While he should prudently seek reasonable income and capital preservation, he generally is not liable for losses unless they result from bad faith, intentional wrongdoing, or gross negligence.

When the minor reaches majority (depending on state law), property in the custodian account is turned over to him. No formal accounting is required. The child, now an adult, may sign a simple release freeing the custodian from any liability. But on reaching majority, the child may require a formal accounting if he has any doubts as to the propriety of the custodian's actions while acting as custodian. For this reason and also for tax record-keeping purposes, a separate bank account should be opened in which proceeds from sales of investments and investment income are deposited pending reinvestment on behalf of the child. Such an account will furnish a convenient record of sales proceeds, investment income, and reinvestment of the same.

Although custodian accounts may be opened anywhere in the United States, the rules governing the account may vary from state to state. The differences between the laws of the states generally do not affect federal tax consequences.

Income tax treatment. Income from a custodian account is taxable to the child as long as it is not used by the parent who set up the account to pay for the child's support. Tax-exempt income from a custodian account is not taxable to the parent even when used for child support. Tax legislation discussed in the front of this book would tax income from a custodian account set up by a parent at the parent's tax rate if the child is under 14. This rule would not apply to children 14 or over or to accounts set up by other relatives or benefactors.

Gift tax treatment. When setting up a custodian account, you may have to pay a gift tax. A transfer of cash or securities to a custodian account is a gift. But you are not subject to a gift tax if you properly plan the cash contributions or purchase of securities for your children's accounts. You may make gifts up to $10,000 to one person, which is shielded from gift tax by the annual exclusion. The exclusion applies each year to each person to whom you make a gift. If your spouse consents to join with you in the gift, you may give annually tax free up to $20,000 to each person.

If the custodian account is set up at the end of December, another tax-free transfer of $20,000 may be made in the first days of January of the following year. In this way, a total of $40,000 is shifted within the two-month period.

Estate tax treatment. The value of a custodian account will be taxed in your estate if you die while acting as custodian of an account before your child reaches his majority. However, you may avoid the problem by naming someone other than yourself as custodian. If you should decide to act as custodian, taking the risk that the account will be taxed in your estate, remember no estate tax is incurred if the tax on your estate is offset by the estate tax credit (*see* ¶38.10).

If you act as custodian and decide to terminate the custodianship, care should be taken to formally close the account. Otherwise, if you die while retaining power over the account, the IRS may try to tax the account in your estate.

¶33.02 • OTHER TYPES OF INVESTMENTS FOR CHILDREN

A minor generally lacks the ability to manage property. Yet, if you exercise control over the property you give to him, the gift may not be recognized for purposes of shifting income. You might appoint a fiduciary for the child, but this step may be costly. Alternatively you might select property which does not require management and which can be transferred by a minor. For example—

1. Bonds may be purchased and registered in a minor's name and coupons or the proceeds on sale or maturity of bonds may be cashed or deposited in a minor's name.

2. Insurance companies will write policies on the lives of minors and recognize their ownership of policies covering the lives of others. Depending on the age of the minor, state law, and company practice, it may be necessary to appoint a guardian for the purpose of cashing in or borrowing on insurance policies given to a minor. A gift of a life insurance policy or an annuity will usually qualify as a gift of a present interest in property for the annual gift tax exclusion.

3. Mutual fund shares, such as money market funds, may be purchased and registered in the name of a minor. The problem of management and sale for reinvestment is minimized because the investment trust itself provides continuous supervision. Changes in the underlying investments of the fund are made without reference to the minor. Most funds provide for automatic reinvestment of dividends in additional shares.

¶33.04 • HOLDING PROPERTY AS JOINT TENANTS

Owning property jointly with one's spouse seems a reasonable solution to a family estate problem. It is easy to arrange: have both names listed as owners. On the death of one, the surviving spouse becomes sole owner of the property. The property does not pass through the estate incurring probate and other costs. Further, there is no estate tax on the property. One-half the property is included in the deceased spouse's estate, but it is not taxed because of the marital deduction.

Jointly owned property, however, might pass to people whom the couple would not have named as heirs. Assume a married man with no children puts nearly all of his property in his and his wife's joint names and then the couple is in an automobile accident that is fatal to the husband. His wife survives for a few weeks. Upon her death, under local law, all the property goes to her brothers and sisters. Both the husband and wife might have wanted to assure his parents of support for their lives. Perhaps the couple might have chosen to distribute the property between both families. The survivorship feature of joint ownership is rigid and cannot be changed once one or both of the joint owners die.

The principal objection to joint ownership is that it deprives each owner of the ability to direct the transfer of ownership of his interest. He cannot specify who is ultimately to inherit it and the time and method of inheritance. The best way to control an estate is through a program of estate planning. While joint ownership offers what seems an easy solution, it involves a fixed disposition of property. Through estate planning it is possible to provide alternatives to meet unexpected events at the lowest possible tax cost.

Joint brokerage account in a street name. Setting up a joint brokerage account in a street name is not an effective transfer for gift tax purposes. Securities are held in a "street" name—that is, the name of the broker—when you have a margin account. Even when you have a cash account, securities may be held in a street name to facilitate trading. The IRS has ruled that where you, with your separate funds, have set up a joint brokerage account for yourself and another person, and the securities are registered in the name of a broker, you have not made a gift for gift tax purposes. The gift is completed only when the other party draws on the account without any obligation to account to you. The value of the gift would be the amount of money or property withdrawn. The IRS contends in a ruling that an account in a street name is like a joint bank account set up by one person. He has not given up any control over the funds in either type of account. Income tax consequences were not covered by the ruling. However, a strong inference from the ruling is that the dividends and sales and exchanges are taxable to the party who contributed the funds to the account.

¶33.05 • TRUSTS IN FAMILY PLANNING

You establish a trust by transferring legal title to property to a trustee who manages the property for one or more beneficiaries. As the one who set up the trust, you are called the grantor or settlor of the trust. The trustee may be one or more individuals or an institution such as a bank or trust company.

You can create a trust during your lifetime or by your will. A trust created during your lifetime is called an inter vivos trust; one established in your will is a testamentary trust. An inter vivos trust can be revocable or irrevocable. An irrevocable trust does not allow for changes of heart; it requires a complete surrender of property. By conveying property irrevocably to a trust, you may relieve yourself of tax on the income from the trust principal. Further, the property in trust usually is not subject to estate tax, although it may be subject to gift tax. A trust should be made irrevocable only if you are certain you will not need the trust property in a financial emergency.

In a revocable trust, you retain control over the property by reserving the right to revoke the trust. As such, it is considered an incomplete gift and offers no present income tax savings. Further, the trust property will be included as part of your estate. But a revocable trust minimizes delay in passing property to beneficiaries if you die while the trust is in force. When you transfer property to a trust, the property is generally not subject to probate, administration expenses, delays attendant on distributions of estates, or claims of creditors. The interests of trust beneficiaries are generally more secure than those of heirs under a will because a will may be denied probate if found invalid.

Under tax legislation discussed in the front of the book, you could not shift tax on income from yourself to a trust beneficiary by setting up a trust in which you will recover the trust property after a period of time.

You can shift income to trust beneficiaries by setting up an irrevocable trust in which you generally have no reversionary interest. However, under tax legislation, such income transfers may provide no income tax advantage to you as a grantor-parent if the income beneficiary is your child under the age of 14.

A special rule restricts the tax advantages of making a gift of appreciated property to a trust. In general, the trust as a separate entity pays tax at its own marginal rate unless it sells appreciated property within two years after receiving it from the grantor. In that case, the appreciation attributed to the time the grantor held the property will be taxed at the marginal rates of the grantor (including any alternative minimum tax that may be due). Appreciation recognized after the transfer is taxed at the trust's regular rates. The effect of this law is to tax the property as if the grantor had sold it, paid tax, and then transferred the net proceeds to the trust. In figuring what would have been the grantor's tax, carrybacks and loss deductions that may be carried over to another year are disregarded.

Gain subject to tax at the grantor's rate is the lesser of the gain recognized by the trust or the amount of gain that would have been realized had the property been sold immediately after the trust received it. The basis of the property includes any increases for gift taxes paid. *See* ¶6.10. Further, the character of the gain is determined by the purpose the grantor had in holding the property. For example, if the grantor held the property for sale in the ordinary course of his business, the gain is taxed as ordinary income, even though the property may be a capital asset in the hands of the trust.

An attempt to avoid the two-year rule by a short sale is ineffective since the two-year period is extended through the closing of a short sale. Similarly, use of an installment sale will not take the sale out of the two-year rule if the sale itself is within the period. Each installment is to be considered a separate sale falling within the two-year rule.

If the trustee does not know the transferor's marginal rates, regulations to be issued may allow the trustee to state his lack of information and direct the IRS to compute the tax.

The two-year rule does not apply (1) if the transferor dies before the trust has sold the property; (2) where tax is deferred under a tax-free exchange or involuntary conversion rule; or (3) if the trust is a pooled income fund or a charitable remainder annuity trust or charitable remainder unitrust.

¶33.08 • OTHER TRANSFERS THAT MAY SAVE TAXES

Making a gift of appreciated property that will eventually be sold may reduce income tax. To shift the profit and the tax, the gift must be completed before the sale or before the donor has made a binding commitment to sell. By making a gift of interests in the property to several family members, it is possible to spread the tax among a number of taxpayers in the lowest tax bracket. Note: the IRS may claim that the gift was never completed, if after sale the donor controls the sales proceeds or has the use of them.

Under tax legislation, a sale by a child under 14 years of age would not affect tax savings to the parent as the tax rate on the sale would be at the parent's top rate.

Do not make a gift of property which has decreased in value if you want a deduction for the loss. Once you give the property away, the loss deduction is gone forever. Neither you nor your donee can ever take advantage of it. The better way is to first sell the property, get a loss deduction, and then make a gift of the proceeds.

Before transferring appreciated property, consider the fact that the appreciation on property passed by inheritance will escape income tax; the heir takes a basis equal to estate tax value, usually fair market value at the date of death. Further, appreciated property encumbered by mortgage may result in income tax to the donor when a gift of the property is made.

Interest-free loans. The tax law discourages income splitting through interest-free loans by imposing gift and income tax on loans coming within the rules of ¶4.10.

¶33.09 • SPLITTING BUSINESS INCOME WITH YOUR FAMILY

Tax on your business income may be reduced if you can shift it to members of your family. You may also avoid estate tax on the value of the capital interests transferred to children. If you keep within the annual gift tax exclusion for each donee (on gifts made by husband and wife), there will be no gift tax consequences.

Business income may be shifted by forming a family partnership or by making your family stockholders in a corporation. Generally speaking, an S corporation in which stockholders elect to report income may be used more freely to split income than a partnership.

A minor child will not be recognized as a partner unless he is competent to manage his own property or control of the property is exercised by another person as fiduciary for his sole benefit. Here, a trust may be set up to hold the partnership interest. The IRS may review not only the terms of the trust and the partnership agreement but also actual operation of the trust to make certain the grantor-partner has not retained any ownership rights over the interest he transferred.

Transfers of stock to a trust for a minor terminate an S election, unless the trust is a qualified trust. For this purpose, a "Subchapter S trust" may be used. Alternatively, stock may be transferred for the minor's benefit to a custodian account in which the parent may act as custodian. Most states allow such transfers.

In order to get the income-shifting benefits from setting up a stock custodian account, there must be a bona fide transfer of stock entailing a complete surrender by you of any control over the transferred stock.

Example—

Two owners of a beer distributorship operating as an S corporation sold all of their stock to their children. They had two objectives: (1) To shift income to the children, and (2) to avoid the limitations on pension plan contributions applied to shareholder-employees of S corporations. As stockholder-employees, they could contribute only a maximum of $2,500 to the company's pension plan; as nonshareholders, up to $5,700. The plan failed because the fathers continued to run the corporation as if the stock transfers had not been made. As key employees and directors of the corporation, they retained complete control over the business. The children exercised no voice in corporate affairs. No custodian or guardian was appointed to represent the interests as stockholders of two of the children who were minors. Further, despite substantial company profits, the children received only a small amount as dividends, generally enough only to offset the inclusion of corporate income on their returns. On the other hand, the fathers continued to take sizable unsecured interest-free loans from the corporation as they had before the stock transfer.

With a partnership, shifting income may be more difficult, depending on whether capital is a material income-producing factor in the business. If it is, a gift or sale of a partnership interest to a family member is effective. But in a service partnership—real estate or insurance brokers, for example—a mere gift of a partnership interest to a family member will not shift partnership income unless the person actually performs services for the partnership. In one case, the Tax Court held that where substantially all of a family partnership's capital consists of borrowed funds guaranteed by family members, the family partnership interests may be disregarded on the grounds that the borrowed funds are not a material income-producing factor in the business.

In an S corporation, pass through items must reflect the value of services rendered or capital contributed by family members of the shareholders. If a relative of an S corporation shareholder performs services for the corporation or loans money to the corporation without receiving reasonable pay or interest, the IRS may allocate income to reflect the value of the services or capital provided. The term "family" of an individual includes only spouse, ancestors, lineal descendants, and any trusts for the primary benefit of such persons.

Important. Under tax legislation, income on property transferred by parents to children under 14 would generally be taxed at the parent's tax bracket.

¶33.10 • LIFE INSURANCE OFFERS TAX ADVANTAGES

Insurance may provide a tax-free accumulation of cash. During the time you pay premiums, the value of your contract increases at compound interest rates. The increase is not subject to income tax. In addition, when your policy is paid at death, the proceeds are not subject to income tax.

Estate tax planning. To shelter life insurance proceeds from estate tax, you must not have ownership rights. If you have an existing policy, you must assign your ownership rights, such as the right to change beneficiaries, the right to surrender or cancel the policy, the right to assign it, and the right to borrow against it. An assignment must occur more than three years before death to exclude the proceeds from your estate.

If you are buying a new policy, you must buy the policy in another's name, such as in your spouse's name, or have your spouse buy the policy. For example, a wife bought a policy on her husband's life. She paid the premiums from household funds. Although he provided household funds, she controlled their use, so there was no indirect premium payment by the husband. Proceeds of the policy were free of estate tax.

Group insurance provided by an employer may be assigned. The IRS has agreed to follow a court decision holding that the power to convert a group policy into an individual policy when you leave the company will not subject the group-term insurance proceeds to estate tax. Since the conversion privilege is exercisable only by taking an economically disadvantageous step of quitting, this right is too remote to be considered a retained ownership right in the policy. If other incidents of ownership are transferred, such as the power to name beneficiaries and fix the type of benefit payable, the transfer will remove the policy from your estate.

The substitution of a new group carrier does not jeopardize assignments under a prior carrier.

When you plan to assign a policy, review your gift tax liability on such a transfer. In the case of an assignment of a group policy, the cost of the policy is determined by actuarially apportioning the employer's total premium payment among the covered employees. This is difficult for an individual employee to do, particularly where there are many employees, so the IRS generally allows employees to value the assigned policy using the same tax tables used to determine the amount of the employee's compensation where group coverage exceeds $50,000. *See* tables at ¶2.021. Key employees may not use the table to determine gift tax liability.

Example—
An employee assigns his $80,000 group-term policy to a family trust. Several months later, when he is age 54, the employer pays the annual premium on the group policy. The value of the gift equals the annual cost of the $80,000 coverage as determined under the table at ¶2.021. Under the table, the value of the gift is $460.80. Gift tax may be avoided under the annual $10,000 gift tax exclusion.

You may want to readjust your coverage to meet new family conditions. You can exchange your policies without tax (*see* ¶12.33).

Using a trust to purchase insurance. If you create a trust to carry a policy on your life by transferring income-producing property the income of which is used to pay the premiums, you are taxable on the trust income. Similarly, if your spouse creates the trust to carry the policy on your life, he or she is taxable on the trust income. This tax rule does not apply to the trust funding of life insurance covering the life of a third party other than your spouse. For example, a grandparent transfers income-producing property to a trust to pay the premiums on a policy on the life of his son. His grandchildren are named trust beneficiaries. The grandparent is not taxed on the income earned by the trust on the transferred property because the trust purchased insurance on his son's life, not his own.

Insurance trust to receive proceeds. A trust may be used to receive insurance proceeds where there is concern that the beneficiary may be unable to manage a large insurance settlement. The trustee may be a bank or a person directed to invest the proceeds and pay income to beneficiaries according to standards provided in the trust. The trustee may be given the discretion to pay out more or less as circumstances warrant. He may be directed to terminate the trust when the beneficiaries reach a certain age, or when they demonstrate their ability to manage money. There may also be investment advantages in a trust. The trust investments

may yield a higher rate of return than that of an insurance company under a settlement option.

Insurance proceeds are not subject to income tax whether paid directly to named beneficiaries or to a trust.

Universal life insurance plans. Universal life insurance offers tax-free buildup of interest income at current high market rates and on death, tax-free receipt of insurance proceeds. A universal life insurance policy is made up of (1) life insurance protection and (2) a cash reserve on which interest income accumulates without tax.

Universal life insurance differs from regular whole life in that the interest rate of universal life is pegged to current bond market rates; whole life rates are low, currently about 5%. Further, a universal life policy lets you withdraw the cash reserve if you want to invest it elsewhere and to allocate how much of your premium payment is to cover insurance protection and how much is to go into the cash reserve.

The tax law sets limits to the amount of premiums that may be earmarked for the cash reserve. If these limits are violated, tax-free treatment for the proceeds may be lost. For these limits, check with the company issuing the policy.

Disadvantage of universal life. You must incur an upfront commission payment which may be 50% or more of the first premium. There may also be a fee for withdrawing the cash reserve. Therefore, before considering a universal plan, determine the possibility that the purchase of term insurance and an investment in money market funds or long-term bonds may be a better alternative to a universal life plan.

¶33.11 • LOSSES MAY BE DISALLOWED ON SALES TO RELATIVES

A loss on a sale to any one of the related taxpayers listed in ¶33.12 is not deductible, even though you make the sale in good faith, the sale is involuntary (for example, a member of your family forecloses a mortgage on your property), or you sell through a public stock exchange and one of the related persons buys the equivalent property.

Examples—
1. You sell 100 shares of A Co. stock to your brother for $1,000. They cost you $5,000. You may not deduct your $4,000 loss even though the sale was made in good faith.

2. A husband and wife each owned stock which had declined in value. They sought to realize the losses for tax purposes but were unwilling to sell unless they could preserve their position in the stock. To achieve this, the husband bought on the New York Stock Exchange an identical number of shares of the same stock that his wife owned; his wife bought over-the-counter an identical number of shares of the same stock that he owned. The next day each sold the stock originally owned. Their losses were disallowed. Losses incurred on indirect sales between husband and wife are not deductible. That they were incurred in the open market is immaterial.

3. The stock investments of a mother and son were managed by the same investment counselor. But neither the son nor mother had any right or control over each other's securities. The counselor followed separate and independent policies for each. Without the son's or his mother's prior approval, the counselor carried out the following transactions: (1) On the same day he sold at a loss the son's stock in four companies and bought the same stock for the mother's account. (2) He sold at a loss the son's stock in a copper company, and 28 days later bought the same stock for his mother. The losses of the first sale were disallowed, but not the losses of the copper stock sale because of the time break of 28 days. However, the court did not say how much of a minimum time break is needed to remove a sale-purchase transaction from the rule disallowing losses between related parties.

¶33.12 • LOSSES AND GAINS BETWEEN FAMILY MEMBERS AND OTHERS

Losses are not allowed in a transaction between:
1. Husband and wife.

Example—
Purchase by husband of stock pledged by his wife; loss is disallowed even though the sale is carried out by pledgee and not directly by wife.

See also ¶6.245 for new rules affecting property transfers between spouses.

2. Members of a family. Brothers or sisters (whether by the whole or half blood), spouse, ancestors and lineal descendants are the only ones included. Loss is disallowed where the sale is made to your sister-in-law, as nominee of your brother. This sale is deemed to be between you and your brother. But you may deduct the loss on sales to your spouse's relative (for example, your brother-in-law or spouse's stepparent) even if you and your spouse file a joint return. One case allowed the loss on a direct sale to a son-in-law. Other cases disallowed losses upon withdrawal from a joint venture and from a partnership conducted by members of a family. Family members have argued that losses should be allowed because the sales were motivated by family hostility. The Tax Court ruled that family hostility may not be considered; losses between proscribed family members are disallowed in all cases.

3. An individual or partnership and a controlled corporation (where that individual or partnership owns more than 50% in value of the outstanding capital stock).

Examples—

1. In calculating the stock owned, not only must the stock held in your own name be taken into account, but also that owned by your family. You also add (a) the proportionate share of any stock held by a corporation, estate, trust or partnership in which you are interested as a shareholder, beneficiary, or partner; and (b) the stock owned individually by your partner.

2. You may own 30% of the stock of a company. A trust in which you have a one-half beneficial interest owns 30%. Your partner owns 10% of the stock of the same company. You are deemed the owner of 55% of the stock of that company (30%, plus one-half of 30%, plus 10%).

3. If a father and four sons each owns 20% of the stock of a company *each* member is also deemed to own the stocks of all the others. A family includes brothers, sisters, spouses, ancestors and lineal descendants.

Losses may also be disallowed in sales between controlled companies, a trust and its creator, a trust and a beneficiary, or a tax-exempt organization and its founder. Check with your tax counselor whenever you plan to sell property at a loss to a buyer who may fit one of these descriptions.

Sometimes, the disallowed loss may be saved. Your purchaser gets the benefit of your disallowed loss if he sells at a gain. His gain up to the amount of your disallowed loss is not taxed.

Example—

Smith bought securities in 1960 which cost $10,000. In 1963, he sold them to his spouse for $8,000. The $2,000 loss is not deductible by Smith. His spouse's basis for the securities is $8,000. In 1984, she sells them for $9,000. The $1,000 gain is not taxed because it is washed out by part of the disallowed loss. If she sold securities for $11,000, then only $1,000 of the $3,000 gain is taxed.

¶34.00 • Tax Pointers for Senior Citizens

¶34.01 • TAX RULES FOR PERSONS 65 OR OVER

If you are 65 years old or over, several tax benefits and rules apply to your income tax. They are:

Filing requirements. You do not file an income tax return for 1986 unless your gross income is $4,640 or more. If you are married and entitled to file a joint return, you do not have to file a return if your combined gross income is under $6,910. If your spouse is also 65 or over, you do not file if your combined gross income is under $7,990. However, you must file a return to obtain a refund of withheld taxes on your pay, if any.

Gross income includes your total salary or wages, interest, dividends (less exclusion), gross rents before deductions for expenses, gross profit of a self-employed business or profession (before expenses), gain from the sale of your personal residence (before the $125,000 exclusion), annuity income (after deducting your cost element), certain distributions from pension or profit-sharing plans, and capital gains (before the capital gains deduction).

If you are self-employed, you must file a return and pay self-employment tax if your net earnings from self-employment are $400 or more even if you are 65 or over and you are receiving Social Security benefits.

Extra exemptions for age in 1986. When you are 65 or older, you receive one exemption as a taxpayer plus another exemption for your age. If your spouse is also 65 or over, you may claim an extra exemption for his or her age.

If you or your spouse's 65th birthday is on January 1, 1987, you claim the extra exemption on your 1986 tax return. You are considered to be 65 on December 31, 1986. The extra exemption for age may not be claimed for a dependent. *See also* ¶1.51.

Tax credit for the elderly. If you are over age 65, you may be entitled to a credit. *See* ¶34.02.

Tax-free sale of your principal residence. If you are 55 or over and sold your principal residence at a gain, you may elect to avoid tax on up to $125,000 of profit, provided you meet certain tests and file an election. *See* ¶29.30 for details.

Other sections of this book of special interest to retired persons are:

¶34.02 • TAX CREDIT FOR THE ELDERLY AND DISABLED

In 1986, the credit for the elderly is available mainly to those persons 65 or over who do not receive Social Security or Railroad Retirement benefits or persons under 65 who are permanently and totally disabled and receive disability income. For example, if you are single or married but only you are eligible, are over 65 and receive more than $417 each month from Social Security, you may not claim the credit. If you are married and both you and your spouse are over 65 and file a joint return, you may not claim the credit if you receive more than $625 each month from Social Security. The amount of the credit is 15% times the "base amount" after reductions. For a single person, the tax credit for the elderly may be as high as $750; for a married couple, $1,125.

A married couple may claim the credit only if they file a joint return. However, if a husband and wife live apart at all times during the taxable year and file separately, the credit may be claimed on a separate return.

The credit for the elderly and disabled is combined with the credits for dependent care, mortgage, credit certificates, and political contributions. The total credits may not exceed regular tax liability without the alternative minimum tax and self-employment tax and penalty taxes for premature retirement distributions. If you also claim a foreign tax credit, the credit for the elderly is deducted first from tax liability before computing the limitation on the foreign tax credit.

The credit is claimed on Schedule R; *see* the Supplement to this book.

¶34.03 • WHO QUALIFIES FOR THE CREDIT?

You may qualify for the credit if you are:

65 or over before the close of 1986, or

Under 65 and permanently and totally disabled and receiving disability income, *see* ¶34.05.

Nonresident aliens. You may not claim the credit if you are a nonresident alien at any time during 1986, unless you are married to a citizen or resident and you have elected to be treated as a resident (*see* ¶1.03).

Prior law allowed retirees from a public retirement system to claim the credit when they were under 65. This provision no longer applies to taxable years after 1983.

¶34.04 • INITIAL BASE FOR THE CREDIT

The law fixes an initial base amount for figuring the credit. This base amount is reduced by certain tax-free benefits and excess adjusted gross income (*see* ¶34.06). The credit is 15% of the base amount after reductions. You do not have to have retirement income to claim the credit.

The base amount is:

$5,000, if you are single.

$5,000, if you file a joint return and only one spouse is eligible for the credit.

$7,500, if you file a joint return and both spouses are eligible for the credit. The credit is figured solely on this base; no separate computation is made for each spouse.

$3,750, if you are married and file a separate return. The credit may be claimed on a separate return only if you and your spouse have lived apart at all times during the year.

¶34.05 • INITIAL BASE FOR DISABLED PERSONS

If you are under 65 and disabled, the base for figuring the credit is the lower of your 1986 disability income or the initial base amount for your filing status in ¶34.04.

Examples—

1. You are single, under 65, and permanently and totally disabled. You received disability income of $4,800. You figure the credit on $4,800, which is less than the base of $5,000 for single persons.

2. Same facts as above except your disability income is $7,000. You figure the credit on the initial base of $5,000 for single status.

Joint return and both spouses qualify for the credit. If one spouse is 65 or over and one spouse under 65 and receives disability income, the initial base amount is $5,000 plus the disability income of the spouse under 65 but not to exceed $7,500. If both spouses are under 65 and disabled, the initial base amount is the total of their disability income, but not to exceed $7,500.

Disability income is taxable wages or payments in lieu of wages paid while absent from work because of permanent and total disability.

You are considered permanently and totally disabled if you are unable to engage in any substantial gainful activity by reason of any medically determinable physical or mental impairment which can be expected to result in death or can be expected to last for a continuous period of not less than 12 months.

¶34.06 · REDUCTION OF BASE AMOUNT

The base amount is reduced by:

Social Security and Railroad Retirement benefits which are not taxable under rules of ¶34.11.

Tax-free pension, annuity, or disability income paid under a law administered by Veterans' Administration.

Certain tax-free pension or annuity income, and

One-half of adjusted gross income exceeding $7,500, if you are single; $10,000 if you are married filing a joint return; $5,000, if you are married and file a separate return. Applying these income floors, the credit is no longer available to a single person when his adjusted gross income reaches $17,500, $20,000 on a joint return where one spouse is age 65 or over, and $25,000, where both spouses are 65 or over.

Example—

You receive Social Security benefits of $6,000. If under the rules of ¶34.11, $1,500 of the benefits are taxable, only $4,500 of the benefits reduce the base amount.

You do not reduce the base amount for: Military disability pensions received for active service in the Armed Forces or in the Coast and Geodetic Survey or Public Health Service, certain disability annuities paid under the Foreign Service Act of 1980, and worker's compensation benefits. However, if Social Security benefits are reduced by worker's compensation benefits, the amount of worker's compensation benefits is treated as Social Security benefits that reduce the base.

Examples—

1. A single person over 65 has adjusted gross income (AGI) of $9,000 and receives Social Security benefits of $4,200 which are not taxable under ¶34.11. His credit is $7.50.

Initial base amount		$5,000
Less: Social Security		4,200
		800
Less 50% of AGI over $7,500		750
Credit base		$ 50
Credit (15%)		$7.50

2. A married couple over 65 files a joint return showing adjusted gross income of $12,000. They received tax-free Social Security benefits of $5,000.

Initial base amount		$7,500
Less: Social Security		5,000
		2,500
Less: 50% of AGI over $10,000		1,000
Credit base		$1,500
Credit (15%)		$ 225

¶34.10 · RETIRING ON SOCIAL SECURITY BENEFITS

Benefits are not paid automatically. You must register at the local Social Security office three months before your 65th birthday to allow time for your application to be processed and to locate all necessary information. Even if you do not plan to retire at age 65, you must register to insure your Medicare coverage.

If you retire before age 65, you may elect reduced Social

Security benefits. The reduction formula is based on the number of months before age 65. If you retire at the earliest age, 62, the reduction is about 20%. By electing benefits at age 62, a person receives a larger total amount of benefits than the total payable from age 65 provided he or she does not live beyond the age of 77. After age 77, the total benefits paid to those retiring at age 65 is greater than the amount paid to those retiring at age 62.

If you do not retire at age 65, your potential Social Security benefit increases for each year you delay retirement. For those born in 1916 or earlier, the increase is 1% per year for each year of delayed retirement; for those born in 1917 through 1924, the increase is 3% per year. Larger credits for delayed retirement will be available for those born after 1924.

If you are under 70, Social Security benefits are reduced by earned income (wages and self-employment income). If you were 65 or older but under 70 in 1986, you could earn $7,800 without losing benefits. If you were under 65 for the whole year, you could earn $5,760 without losing benefits. *See* the Supplement for the earnings ceilings for 1987. Once you earn more than these amounts, benefits are reduced. For each $2 you earn, you lose $1 in benefits. A special monthly rule applies in the year you reach retirement age. After 1989, you will lose $1 in benefits for each $3 you earn above the earnings ceiling.

For those age 70 or over, benefits are not reduced by earnings. You can work, earn any amount, and receive full Social Security benefits.

So long as you continue to work, you pay Social Security taxes on your earnings, regardless of your age.

Regardless of your age, you may receive any amount of income from sources other than work, for example, private pensions or investments, without affecting the amount of Social Security retirement benefits. However, benefits may be taxable if your income exceeds the limits discussed in ¶34.11.

Keep a record of credits. The Social Security Administration has been criticized for not keeping up with workers' earnings records. Do not risk a problem by ignoring your record. At least once every three years, you should mail Form SSA-7004, Request for Statement of Earnings, to the Social Security Administration, Wilkes-Barre Data Operations Center, P.O. Box 20, Wilkes-Barre, PA 18703. This form is available at your local Social Security office and the headquarters in Baltimore. You will receive a response in about six weeks.

Social Security forms state that if you wait more than three years, three months and 15 days after an error is discovered to request a correction, a change may not be possible. The agency waived the deadline in 1981 since it had fallen behind in its record keeping, but you should still try to correct any errors immediately.

If you are age 55 or older, your local Social Security office can give you an estimate of your retirement benefits.

¶34.11 · HOW SOCIAL SECURITY BENEFITS ARE TAXED

If you received or repaid Social Security benefits in 1986, you should receive Form SSA-1099 by February 2, 1987. The form will show the total of paid or repaid benefits. Amounts withheld for Medicare premiums, worker's compensation offset, or attorney's fees are itemized and included in the total benefits you received. Keep Form SSA-1099 for your records; do not attach it to your return.

The *net benefit* shown on Form SSA-1099 (benefits paid less benefits repaid) is the benefit amount used in the following computations to determine taxable benefits.

Part of your net Social Security benefits may be subject to tax if your income exceeds a base amount. The maximum taxable amount is 50% of benefits.

There are two steps in figuring the taxation of Social Security benefits: (1) Figuring whether your income exceeds a base amount for your filing status. (2) Figuring the amount of benefits subject to tax.

Step 1. Start with adjusted gross income (*see* ¶13.04). Add to it 50% of your net Social Security benefits (amount received less amount repaid, if any), tax-free interest income, excluded foreign earned income (¶36.01), excluded income from U.S. possessions (¶36.08) and Puerto Rico (¶36.10), and the marriage penalty deduction (¶1.01).

Part of your Social Security benefits are taxable if the total of adjusted gross income plus the other items in step (1) exceed $25,000 and you are single, or $32,000 and you are married filing jointly.

Examples—

1. You are married and have dividend and interest income of $28,000 and tax-exempt interest of $2,000. Your net Social Security benefits are $4,000 and you file a joint return.

Adjusted gross income		$28,000
Plus: Tax-exempt interest	$2,000	
50% of benefits	2,000	4,000
		$32,000
Less: Base amount		32,000
		0

Your benefits are not taxable.

2. Same as above except your Social Security benefits are $8,000.

Adjusted gross income		$28,000
Plus: Tax-exempt interest	$2,000	
50% of benefits	4,000	6,000
		$34,000
Less: Base amount		32,000
Excess		$ 2,000

Part of your benefits are subject to tax under the rules of Step 2.

Step 2. The amount of benefits subject to tax is 50% of the excess over the base amount or 50% of benefits, whichever is less.

Example—

In example 2 above, $1,000 of benefits are subject to tax because 50% of the excess over the base amount (50% of $2,000) is less than 50% of benefits (50% of $8,000).

Married filing separately. If you are married and file a separate return, the base amount is zero so that one half of your benefits is subject to tax regardless of their amount or the amount of your other income. However, if you live apart from your spouse at all times during the year and file separately, the $25,000 base applies.

¶34.12 · SOCIAL SECURITY BENEFITS SUBJECT TO TAX

Social Security benefits subject to tax include your monthly retirement, survivor, or disability benefits. Monthly Tier 1 Railroad Retirement benefits are treated as Social Security benefits; Tier 2 Railroad Retirement benefits are not treated as Social Security benefits subject to tax. By February 2, 1987, you should receive Form RRB-1099 from the government, showing the types and amounts of Railroad Retirement benefits you received in 1986.

Social Security benefits are not reduced by withholdings for supplementary medical insurance. Your Form SSA-1099 includes the withholdings in total benefits.

Benefits paid on behalf of child or incompetent. If a child is entitled to Social Security benefits, such as after the death of a parent, the benefit is considered to be the child's regardless of who actually receives the payment. Whether the child's benefit is subject to tax will depend on the amount of the child's income.

Workmen's compensation. If you are receiving Social Security disability payments and Workmen's Compensation for the same disability, your Social Security benefits may be reduced by the workmen's compensation. For example, you are entitled to Social Security disability benefits of $5,000 a year. After receiving a $1,000 workmen's compensation award, your disability benefits are reduced to $4,000. For purposes of the 50% of benefits rule, you treat the full $5,000 as Social Security benefits.

Repayment of benefits. If you forfeit part of your Social Security benefits because of excessive outside income, the forfeited amount reduces your benefits for purposes of the 50% inclusion rule. You make the reduction even if the forfeit relates to benefits received in a prior year. For example, your regular 1986 benefit of $5,000 is reduced by $1,000 because of earnings of the prior year. For tax purposes, your 1986 benefits are considered $4,000.

If in 1986, Social Security benefits were subject to tax and in 1987 you must repay 1986 benefits that were taxed, you first re-

duce 1987 benefits by the amount of repayment. If the repayment exceeds 1987 benefits, you may claim the excess as an itemized deduction. If the repayment exceeds $3,000, you may follow the rules of ¶2.11.

Taxable Social Security benefits may not be the basis of an IRA contribution (¶7.17), earned income credit (¶24.50), deduction for two-earner married couples (¶1.01), or foreign earned income exclusion (¶36.00).

Nonresident aliens. A special rule applies to Social Security and Tier 1 Railroad Retirement benefits received by nonresident aliens. Unless provided otherwise by tax treaty, one half of a nonresident alien's Social Security benefits will be subject to the 30% withholding tax imposed on U.S. source income that is not connected with a U.S. trade or business (¶37.03).

You will receive an information return reporting the amount of benefits received during the year.

In the following chart, the second column lists how much income (*including tax-exempt interest*) you may receive before benefits become taxable. The last column lists the levels at which 50% of benefits become taxable.

Single		
Monthly Social Security benefits	No benefits taxed unless other income exceeds—	50% of benefits taxed if other income is at least—
$ 300	$23,200	$26,800
350	22,900	27,100
400	22,600	27,400
450	22,300	27,700
500	22,000	28,000
550	21,700	28,300
600	21,400	28,600
650	21,100	28,900
700	20,800	29,200
750	20,500	29,500
800	20,200	29,800
850	19,900	30,100
900	19,600	30,400
950	19,300	30,700
1,000	19,000	31,000

Married filing jointly		
Monthly Social Security benefits	No benefits taxed unless other income exceeds—	50% of benefits taxed if other income is at least—
$ 700	$27,800	$36,200
750	27,500	36,500
800	27,200	36,800
850	26,900	37,100
900	26,600	37,400
950	26,300	37,700
1,000	26,000	38,000
1,050	25,700	38,300
1,100	25,400	38,600
1,150	25,100	38,900
1,200	24,800	39,200
1,250	24,500	39,500
1,300	24,200	39,800
1,350	23,900	40,100
1,400	23,600	40,400

¶34.13 · ELECTION FOR LUMP-SUM BENEFIT PAYMENT COVERING PRIOR YEARS

If in 1986 you receive a lump-sum payment of benefits covering prior years, you have a choice: (1) you may treat the entire payment as taxable under the rules of ¶34.11 in 1986 or (2) you may allocate the benefits over the taxable years in which they were payable. The payer will notify you of the years covered by the payments.

When you elect to allocate benefits to a prior year, you do not amend the return for that year. You compute the increase in income (if any) that would have resulted if the Social Security benefits had been received in that year. You then add that amount to the income of the current year.

Example—

In 1985, you apply for Social Security disability benefits but the Social Security office rules you are ineligible. You appeal and are awarded benefits. In 1986, you receive a lump-sum payment of $8,000 ($3,000 for 1985 and $5,000 for 1986). You may include the $8,000 benefit in 1986 to figure if Social Security benefits are taxable, or you may elect to treat $3,000 of benefits as received in 1985 and $5,000 in 1986. You make the election and figure that in 1985 the inclusion of the award would have resulted in an increase of income of $1,000. You add the $1,000 plus taxable 1986 benefits to your 1986 income. You may not revoke the election unless the IRS consents.

¶34.14 • HOW TAX ON SOCIAL SECURITY REDUCES YOUR EXTRA EARNINGS

There is an added tax cost of earning income if the earnings will subject your Social Security benefits to tax. Therefore, if your benefits are not currently exposed to tax, you have to figure *not only* the tax on the extra income *but also* the amount of Social Security benefits subjected to tax by those earnings.

Examples—

1. You are over 70 and planning to work part time. You and your spouse receive Social Security benefits of $8,000. Your adjusted gross income before adding 50% of Social Security benefits is $28,000. At this point, no part of your Social Security benefits are taxable.

Adjusted gross income	$28,000
Plus: 50% of benefits	4,000
	32,000
Less: Base	32,000
No excess	0

2. Same as above except that you plan to earn up to $8,000 from a part-time job. The $8,000 will subject $4,000 of Social Security benefits to tax.

Other income	$28,000
Part-time earnings	8,000
	$36,000
50% of benefits	4,000
	$40,000
Less: Base	32,000
Excess	$ 8,000
50% of excess taxable	$ 4,000

Thus, for every dollar or extra earnings above the $32,000 or $25,000 base, fifty cents of your Social Security benefits is taxable. Here, earnings of $8,000 subject $4,000 of Social Security benefits to tax.

If you are under 70, you must also consider that Social Security benefits may be reduced by earnings from a job or self-employment; see ¶34.10.

¶35.00 • Tax Savings for Veterans and Members of the Armed Forces

	See ¶		*See* ¶
Extension to pay your tax when entering the service	35.00	Tax abatement for military personnel killed in action	35.04
Disability retirement pay	35.01	State income tax withholding	35.05
You do not report this income	35.011	Armed Forces dependency allotments	1.55
You may deduct	35.012	Disability retirement pay	2.18
Tax information for reservists	35.02	Moving expense reimbursements	2.46
Tax-free combat pay	35.03	Deposits of pay overseas	4.01

¶35.00 • EXTENSION TO PAY YOUR TAX WHEN ENTERING THE SERVICE

If you are unable to pay your tax when you enter the Armed Forces, you may get an extension until six months after your initial period of service ends. File your return by April 15, 1987 and get a form at the office of your District Director of Internal Revenue, or write a letter to the District Director (your spouse or parent may do it for you). An extension may be given if payment involves hardship, *and* you actually apply for it.

The extension does not cover your spouse who must file a separate return and pay the tax due. But you and your spouse may file a joint return before the postponement period expires even though your spouse filed a separate return for that particular year. **No** interest is charged on this postponement of your tax.

Automatic extension of time to file your return. If you are on duty outside the U.S. or Puerto Rico on April 15, 1987, you get an automatic two-month extension to file your return. *See* ¶27.05.

¶35.01 • DISABILITY RETIREMENT PAY

Your disability retirement pay may be tax free if you are a former member of the Armed Forces of any country, the Coast Guard, National Oceanic and Atmospheric Administration or the Public Health Service. For details, *see* ¶2.18.

Tax-free treatment of disability retirement pay is retroactive to the date of the application for the benefits.

Readjustment payments to reservists are discussed at ¶35.02.

¶35.011 • YOU DO NOT REPORT THIS INCOME

Adjustments in pay to compensate for losses resulting from inflated foreign currency.

Allotments for dependents. Neither the serviceman **nor his** dependents are taxed on the government's contribution. But the serviceman may not deduct his contribution from his gross income.

Allowance to an officer for unusual expenses incurred for food and lodgings pending assignment at an overseas station.

Amounts received by former prisoners of war from the U.S. Government in compensation for inhumane treatment suffered at the hands of an enemy government.

Benefits under Servicemen's Group Life Insurance.

Bonuses paid by any state or political subdivision for military service.

Combat pay. *See* ¶35.03.

Death gratuity payments (six months' pay to beneficiaries of servicemen who died in active service).

Dividends on G.I. insurance are not taxed. Many veterans and members of the Armed Forces receive dividend checks on their National Life Insurance. This is merely a return of premiums paid. Nor are the dividends from the U.S. Government Life Insurance (World War I insurance) taxed. Interest on dividends left on deposit is taxed.

Education, training, or subsistence allowances paid under any law administered by the Veterans' Administration. However, deductible education costs must be reduced by the VA allowance.

Family separation allowance received because of overseas assignments.

Grants for homes designed for wheelchair living.

Grants for motor vehicles for veterans who lost their sight or the use of their limbs.

Government endowment policy proceeds paid before the death of the veteran.

Housing and cost-of-living allowances to cover excess cost of quarters and subsistence while on permanent duty outside U.S., whether paid by U.S. government or by government of country in which stationed.

Medical or hospital treatment provided by the United States in government hospitals.

Moving and storage expenses furnished in kind (or reimbursement or allowance for such expenses) to a member on active duty where the move is pursuant to a military order and incident to a permanent change of station.

Mustering-out pay.

Naval attaché's expense money, if used solely in connection with official duties.

Pay forfeited on order of a court martial.

Reduction in retirement benefits to provide survivor annuities.

Rental allowance where quarters are not furnished in kind.

Subsistence allowance where subsistence is not furnished in kind and per diem allowance in lieu of subsistence. (However, you are taxed on mileage and per diem subsistence allowance while in travel status or on temporary duty.)

Travel expenses while ship or squadron is away from home post or base. However, a serviceman is not considered "away from home" if he is at his *permanent* duty station or is a naval officer assigned to *permanent* duty aboard a ship. *See also* ¶2.251.

Uniform allowances of officers.

Uniforms furnished.

Veterans' Administration death benefits to families of deceased veterans.

See also the checklist beginning at ¶40.00.

¶35.012 • YOU MAY DEDUCT

Board and lodging costs over those paid you by the government while on temporary duty away from your home base.

Costs of rank insignia, collar devices, gold braid, etc. The cost of altering rank insignia when promoted or demoted is also deductible.

Cleaning costs of fatigues are deductible if: (1) The fatigues are required to be worn on duty; (2) they cannot under military regulations be worn off duty; (3) the cost and maintenance of the fatigues exceed any tax-free clothing allowance received by you.

Contributions to "Company" fund made according to Service regulations. But personal contributions made to stimulate interest and morale in a unit are not deductible.

Court martial legal expenses in successfully defending against the charge of conduct unbecoming an officer and a gentleman.

Dues to professional societies. But you cannot deduct dues for officers' and noncommissioned officers' clubs.

Expense of obtaining increased retirement pay.

Out-of-pocket moving expenses for service connected moves (without meeting either the 35-mile test or the 39-week test).

Subscriptions to professional journals.

Transportation, food and lodging expenses while in official travel status. But you are taxed on mileage and per diem subsistence allowance.

Travel expense of reserve personnel where required to be away from home overnight for authorized drill for which they are paid.

In addition, you may deduct all the expenses and losses permitted other persons. (*See* the checklist beginning at ¶41.00.)

¶35.02 • TAX INFORMATION FOR RESERVISTS

Transportation costs. If you attend prescribed drills under competent orders, you may deduct the round-trip transportation costs if the drills are held outside your city or general area in which you work.

If the drills are held within your city or in the general area in which you work on a day you work, you deduct only the one-way cost of traveling between the location of your regular job and the location of the drill even if you first go home for dinner. Do not deduct the cost of the return trip home or the cost of traveling to drill on a day you are not working.

The above transportation costs are deductible whether or not you elect to itemize deductions.

Readjustment payments. Amounts received by reservists involuntarily released from active duty as readjustment payments are taxed income. If the reservist becomes entitled to retirement pay, he is taxed on only the remainder of the retirement pay after

its required reduction by an amount equal to 75% of any readjustment payment previously received. Readjustment payments are eligible for income averaging (*see* ¶23.00).

Uniform costs. You deduct the cost and maintenance of uniforms that you wear at drills or temporary duty. If you received a tax-free uniform allowance, reduce the deduction by the amount of the allowance. Servicemen on full-time duty may not deduct their uniform costs.

¶35.03 • TAX-FREE COMBAT PAY

The combat pay exclusion applies to income earned by a serviceman in a combat zone. Military personnel below the rank of commissioned officer serving in a combat zone are not taxed on any part of their active duty pay, or on pay received while hospitalized as a result of a combat zone wound, disease or injury. The tax-free exclusion for commissioned officers' pay is limited to $500 a month.

The exclusion for a hospitalized serviceman may generally apply during a two-year period after the end of combat.

¶35.04 • TAX ABATEMENT FOR MILITARY PERSONNEL KILLED IN ACTION

If a member of the Armed Forces is killed in a combat zone or dies from wounds or disease incurred while in a combat zone, any income tax liability for the year of death is waived. In addition, his estate is entitled to a refund for income tax paid by him after he began serving in a combat zone.

If a member of the Armed Forces was a resident of a community property state and his wife reported half of his military pay on a separate return, she may get a refund of taxes paid on her share of his pay for the years he served in a combat zone.

Determination of death for MIAs. Servicemen missing in action in Vietnam are presumed dead as of December 31, 1982. This date applies for such rules as whether to file as a surviving spouse, postponing the due date for filing returns and paying taxes, and for tax liability abatement for those killed in action.

Tax abatement for civilian or military personnel killed in terroristic or military action. Tax liability is waived for civilian or military personnel killed in terroristic or military actions outside the U.S. even if the President has not designated the area a combat zone. Tax liability is waived for the period beginning with the last taxable year before the year in which the injuries were incurred and ending with the year of death. The individual must also be a U.S. employee both on the date of injury and date of death.

Example—

On January 20, 1986, a soldier is killed in a terroristic attack overseas; tax liability on the soldier's income is waived for both 1985 and 1986.

Tax abatement does not apply to a U.S. civilian or military employee who dies as a result of an accident or a training exercise. Abatement also does not apply to terroristic action within the United States. However, abatement does apply if the individual dies in the U.S. from a wound or injury incurred in a terroristic or military action outside the United States.

The rules apply to personnel dying as a result of wounds incurred after November 17, 1978.

¶35.05 • STATE INCOME TAX WITHHOLDING

A state that makes a withholding agreement with the Secretary of the Treasury may subject members of the Armed Forces regularly stationed within that state to its payroll withholding provisions. National guardsmen and reservists are not considered to be members of the Armed Forces for purposes of this section.

How to Treat Foreign Income

¶36.00 • RULES FOR REPORTING FOREIGN INCOME

In 1986, up to $80,000 of your foreign earned income may be tax free, if you satisfy a foreign residence or physical presence test. In addition, if you are an employee, you may claim an exclusion for housing expenses; if you are self-employed, you may deduct certain housing costs (*see* ¶36.02).

You must file a U.S. return if your gross income meets the filing limit at ¶1.00, even though all or part of your foreign earned income may be tax free. You claim the foreign earned income exclusion on Form 2555, which you attach to Form 1040.

A separate exclusion is allowed for the value of meals and lodging received by employees living in qualified camps (¶36.07).

If you claim the foreign earned income exclusion of $80,000, you may not:

Claim foreign taxes paid on the excluded income as a credit or deduction,

Claim business deductions allocable to the excluded income,

Make an IRA contribution based on the excluded income, or Income average.

In deciding whether to claim the exclusion, compare (1) the overall tax with the exclusion and (2) without the exclusion but with the full foreign tax credit and allocable deductions. Choose whichever gives you the lower tax.

See ¶36.01 and ¶36.05.

Years after 1986. *See* the new law guide at the front of this book for changes to the exclusion rules effective in 1987.

¶36.01 • CLAIMING THE FOREIGN EARNED INCOME EXCLUSION

You may elect the exclusion for foreign earned income only if your tax home is in a foreign country *and* you meet (1) the foreign residence test or (2) the foreign physical presence test of 330 days discussed at ¶36.04. Tax home is discussed at ¶2.24. If your tax home is in the U.S., you may not claim the exclusion but may claim the foreign tax credit and your living expenses while away from home if you meet the rules at ¶2.27.

If you are married and you and your spouse each have foreign earned income and meet the foreign residence or physical presence test, you may each claim a separate exclusion. If your permanent home is in a community property state, your earned income is not considered community property for purposes of the exclusion.

If you qualify under the foreign residence or physical presence test for only part of 1986, the exclusion is reduced on a daily basis.

Examples—

1. You were a resident of France from February 20, 1984 until June 30, 1986 when you returned to the U.S. Since your period of foreign residency included all of 1985, thereby satisfying the foreign residence test, you may claim a prorated exclusion for 1986. As you were abroad for 182 of the 365 days in 1986, you exclude earnings up to 182/365 of the maximum exclusion. If you earned $70,000 from January through June 1986, you would exclude $39,890 ($80,000 × 182/365).

2. You worked in France from June 1, 1985 through September 30, 1986. Your only days outside of France were a 15 day vacation to the U.S. in December 1985. You do not qualify for an exclusion under the foreign residence test because you were not abroad for a full taxable year; you were not abroad for either the full year of 1985 or 1986. You do qualify under the physical presence test; you were physically present abroad for at least 330 full days during a 12-month period. The 12-month period giving you the largest 1986 exclusion is the 12-month period starting October 21, 1985 and ending October 20, 1986. *See* ¶36.04 for figuring the 12-month period. Since you were abroad for at least 330 full days during that 12-month period, you may claim an exclusion. In 1986, you were abroad for 293 days within the 12-month period (January 1 to October 20, 1986 is 293 days). Thus, you exclude earnings up to 293/365 of the maximum exclusion. If your earnings in France for 1986 were $70,000, your exclusion is limited to $64,219 ($80,000 × 293/365).

> The exclusion is not automatic. You elect the exclusion on Form 2555. An election made for a prior year automatically applies in 1985 and future years unless you revoke it. IRS permission is not required for a revocation but if you do revoke without IRS consent, you may not make another election for five years unless the IRS consents to it.

Foreign earnings from a prior year. Foreign income earned in a prior year but paid in 1986 does not qualify for the 1986 exclusion. However, if the income was attributable to foreign services performed in 1985, the pay is tax free provided you did not use the full 1985 exclusion of $80,000 in 1985. If the services were performed before 1985, no exclusion is available to shelter the pay.

Income for services performed in the U.S. does not qualify for the exclusion, even though it is paid to you while you are abroad.

Foreign tax credit. Foreign taxes paid on tax-free foreign earned income do not qualify for a credit or deduction. But if your foreign pay exceeds $80,000, you may claim a foreign tax credit or deduction for the foreign taxes allocated to taxable income. The instructions to Forms 2555 and 1116 and IRS Publication 514 provide details for making the computation.

¶36.02 • HOW TO TREAT HOUSING COSTS

The housing costs of employees and self-employed persons are treated differently by the tax law. Employees get a housing exclusion; self-employed persons a deduction from *taxable* foreign earned income. If you live in a special camp provided by your employer, all housing costs are excluded (*see* ¶36.07).

Exclusion for employer-financed housing costs. If the total of your foreign wage or salary income plus the value of employer-financed housing costs in 1986 does not exceed $80,000, both parts of your pay package are tax free. Your housing costs are considered to be employer-financed as long as they are covered by salary, employer-reimbursements, a housing allowance, or if they are paid directly by your employer. If the total exceeds $80,000, a special housing exclusion will shelter part of your housing costs from tax. The housing exclusion is the difference between the employer's payment of reasonable housing expenses and a "base housing amount." The base housing amount is 16% of the salary for a U.S. government employee at the GS-14, Step 1 level as of the beginning of the year (the 1986 base amount may be found in Form 2555). If you qualify under the foreign residence or physical presence test for only part of 1986, the base housing amount is reduced on a daily basis. Follow instructions to Form 2555. The housing cost exclusion is elected on Form 2555. Employer housing payments exceeding this housing cost exclusion may also escape tax if your foreign salary is below the maximum foreign earned income exclusion (*see* Example 1). That part of the foreign earned income exclusion not applied to your salary may be applied to housing costs.

On Form 2555, you figure the housing exclusion before the foreign earned income exclusion. The earned income exclusion is limited to the excess of foreign earned income over the housing exclusion.

Examples—

1. In 1986 your salary for work abroad is $60,000 and your employer pays $10,518 for your housing. The total amount of salary and housing costs is tax free. On Form 2555, you list $70,518 (salary plus housing) as your foreign earned income. Assume that the housing cost exclusion is $3,650 (housing costs of $10,518 exceeding a base housing amount of $6,868). Your earned income exclusion is $66,868: $70,518 earned income—$3,650 housing exclusion.

2. In 1986 you earn $73,000 abroad and your employer pays $10,518 for your housing. Assume the housing cost exclusion is $3,650 (housing costs of $10,518 exceeding a base housing amount of $6,868). All of your salary plus the full amount of the housing costs avoids tax: The housing cost exclusion of $3,650 and an earned income exclusion of $79,868 ($83,518 foreign income less $3,650 housing exclusion).

3. Same as Example 2 except you earn $75,000. Foreign earned income is $85,518 ($75,000 plus $10,518) but the total amount of income not subject to tax is $83,650. The total tax-free amount is made up to the housing cost exclusion of $3,650 and the maximum foreign earned income exclusion of $80,000.

Reasonable housing expenses of your spouse and dependents living with you include rent, utilities, insurance, parking, furniture rentals, and repairs. The following expenses do not qualify: Cost of purchasing a home, furniture, or accessories, home improvements, payments of mortgage principal, domestic labor, and depreciation on a home or on improvements to leased housing. Further, interest and taxes which are otherwise deductible do not qualify for the exclusion.

You may include the costs of a separate household which you maintain outside the U.S. for your spouse and dependents because living conditions at your foreign home are adverse.

Self-employed persons. Self-employed individuals may claim a limited deduction for housing costs exceeding the base housing amount. You may claim this deduction only to the extent it offsets taxable foreign earned income.

Examples—

1. In 1986, you are self-employed and have foreign earnings of $100,000 and qualifying housing expenses of $20,000 in excess of the base amount. You may deduct the expenses of $20,000 from $20,000 of taxable foreign earned income ($100,000 less $80,000 exclusion).

2. Same as above except your earnings are $80,000. You may not deduct any housing costs. You have no taxable foreign earned income as your earnings are fully excluded.

Where you cannot deduct expenses because you do not have taxable foreign earned income, expenses may be carried forward one year and deducted in the next year to the extent of taxable foreign earned income.

The deduction may be claimed whether or not you itemize deductions.

If you are employed and self-employed during the same year. Housing expenses above the base amount are partly excludable and partly deductible. For example, if half of your foreign earned income is from services as an employee, half of the excess housing expenses are excludable. The remaining excess housing costs are deductible to the extent of taxable foreign earned income. Follow the instructions to Form 2555.

¶36.03 • WHAT IS FOREIGN EARNED INCOME?

Earned income includes salaries, wages, commissions, professional fees, and bonuses. Earned income also includes allowances from your employer for housing or other expenses, as well as the value of housing or a car provided by the employer. It may also include business profits, royalties, and rents, provided this income is tied to the performance of services. Earned income does not include pension or annuity income, payments for nonqualified employee trusts or nonqualified annuities, dividends, interest, capital gains, gambling winnings, alimony, or the value of tax-free meals or lodging under the rules at ¶2.01.

If you are an employee of the U.S. government or its agencies, you may not exclude any part of your pay from your government employer. If you are not an employee of the U.S. government or any of its agencies, your pay is excludable even if paid by a government source. You are not an employee of the U.S. if you work under a contract made between your employer and the government.

Under a special law, tax liability is waived for a civilian or military employee of the U.S. government killed in a military action overseas; *see* ¶35.04.

Foreign earned income eligible for the exclusion must be received no later than the taxable year after the year in which you perform the services. Pay is excludable in the year of receipt if you did not use the full exclusion in the year of the services.

Profits from sole proprietorship or partnership. If your business consists solely of services (no capital investment), 100% of net profits is considered earned income. If services and capital are both income-producing factors, no more than 30% of your net profit may be considered earned income.

If you do not contribute any services to a business (for example, you are a "silent partner"), your share of the net profits is *not* earned income.

Examples—

1. A U.S. citizen resides in England. He invests in an English partnership that sells manufactured goods outside the U.S. He performs no services for the business. His share of net profits does not qualify as earned income.

2. Same facts as above, except he devotes his full time to the partnership business. 30% of his share of the net profits qualifies as earned income. Thus, if his share of profits is $50,000, earned income is $15,000 (30% of $50,000).

3. You and another person are consultants, operating as a partnership in Europe. Since capital is not an income-producing element, the entire net profits of the business is earned income.

The partnership agreement generally determines the tax status of partnership income in a U.S. partnership with a foreign branch. Thus, if the partnership agreement allocates foreign earnings to partners abroad, the allocation will be recognized unless it does not have substantial economic effect.

Fringe benefits. The value of fringe benefits, such as the right to use company property and facilities, is added to your compensation when figuring the amount of your earned income.

Royalties. Royalties from articles or books may be earned income depending on your royalty agreement. If you write a book and sell the manuscript or "lease" your rights to the book, the royalties are not earned income. However, if you contract to write a book for an amount in cash plus a commission on any sales, your receipts under the contract are earned income.

Royalties from the leasing of oil and mineral lands and from patents are not earned income.

Rental income. Rental income is generally not earned income. However, if you perform personal services, such as an owner-manager of a hotel or rooming house in a foreign country, then up to 30% of your net rents may be earned income.

Reimbursement of employee expenses. Do not include reimbursement of expenses in earned income to the extent they equal expenses which you adequately accounted for to your employer. See ¶2.36. If your expenses exceed reimbursements, the excess is allocated according to the rules in ¶36.05. If reimbursements exceed expenses, the excess is treated as earned income.

Straight commission salespersons or other employees who arrange with their employers, for withholding purposes, to consider a percentage of their commissions as attributable to their expenses, treat such amounts as earned income.

Reimbursed moving expenses. Employer reimbursement of

moving expenses must be reported on your return in the year of receipt. However, for purposes of claiming the earned income exclusion, the reimbursement may be considered to have been earned in a different year. This is important because an exclusion is allowed only for the year income is earned. If the move is from the U.S. to a foreign country, the reimbursement is considered foreign earned income in the year of the move if you qualify under the foreign residence or physical presence test for at least 120 days during that tax year. Reimbursement of moving expenses from one foreign country to another is considered foreign earned income in the year of the move if you qualify under the residency or physical presence test at the new location for at least 120 days during the tax year. If you do not meet one of these tests in the year of the move, the reimbursements are earned income which must be allocated between the year of the move and the following tax year. Employer reimbursements for moves back to the U.S. are considered income from U.S. sources if you continue to work for the same employer. If you move back to the U.S. and take a job with a new employer, or if you retire and move back to the U.S. and your old employer reimburses your moving expenses, the reimbursement is considered to be for past services in the foreign country and qualifies as foreign earned income eligible for the exclusion. The reimbursement is considered earned in the year of the move if you qualified under the residency or physical presence test for at least 120 days during the tax year. Otherwise, the reimbursement is allocated between the year of the move and the year preceding the move. *See* IRS Publication 54 for details.

¶36.04 • MEETING THE FOREIGN RESIDENCE OR PHYSICAL PRESENCE TEST

To qualify for the foreign earned income exclusion, you must be either a U.S. citizen meeting the foreign residence test or a U.S. citizen or resident meeting the physical presence test in a foreign country. The following areas are not considered foreign countries: Puerto Rico, U.S. Virgin Islands, Guam, Northern Mariana Islands, any possession of the United States, or the Antarctic region.

If war or civil unrest prevented you from meeting the foreign residence or physical presence test, you may claim the exclusion for the period you actually were a resident or physically present abroad. Foreign locations and the time periods which qualify for the waiver of the residency and physical presence tests are listed in the instructions to Form 2555.

If, by the due date of your 1986 return, you have not yet satisfied the foreign residence or physical presence test, but you expect to meet either test after the filing date, you may either file on the due date and report your earnings or ask for a filing extension under the rules at ¶36.06.

Foreign residence test. You must be a bona fide resident of a foreign country for an uninterrupted period that includes one full tax year. Business or vacation trips to the U.S. or another country will not disqualify you from satisfying the foreign residence test. If you are abroad more than one year but less than two, the entire period qualifies if it includes one full tax year.

Example—
You are a bona fide foreign resident from September 30, 1985 to March 25, 1987. The period includes your entire tax year 1986. Therefore, up to $80,000 of your 1986 earnings are excludable. Your overseas earnings in 1987 will qualify for a proportionate part of the exclusion which will be available in 1987.

To prove you are a foreign resident, you must show your intention to be a resident of the foreign country. Evidence tending to confirm your intention to stay in a foreign country is: Your family accompanies you; you buy a house or rent an apartment rather than a hotel room; you participate in the foreign community activities; you can speak the foreign language; you have a permanent foreign address; you join clubs there, or you open charge accounts in stores in the foreign country.

Residence does not have the same meaning as domicile. Your domicile is a permanent place of abode; it is the place to which you eventually plan to return wherever you go. You may have a residence in a place other than your domicile. Thus, you may go, say, to Amsterdam, and take up residence there and still intend to return to your domicile in the U.S. But the fact that you leave your domicile does not, by itself, establish a bona fide residence in

a new place. You must intend to make a place your residence. For example, you may go to Amsterdam on a short business trip or a short holiday. In neither case have you established a residence. You are a mere transient.

You will not qualify if you take inconsistent positions toward your foreign residency. That is, you will not be treated as a bona fide resident of a foreign country if you have earned income from sources within that country, filed a statement with the authorities of that country that you are not a resident there, and have been held not subject to the income tax of that country. However, this rule does not prevent you from qualifying under the physical presence test.

If you cannot prove that you are a resident, check to determine if your stay qualifies under the physical presence test.

Physical presence test. To qualify under this test, you must show you were on foreign soil 330 days (about 11 months) during a 12-month period. Whether you were a resident or a transient is of no importance. You have to show you were physically present in a foreign country or countries for 330 full days during any 12-consecutive-month period. The 12-month period may begin with any day. There is no requirement that it begin with your first full day abroad. It may begin before or after arrival in a foreign country and may end before or after departure from a foreign country. A *full* day is from midnight to midnight (24 consecutive hours). You must spend each of the 330 days on foreign soil. In departing from U.S. soil to go directly to the foreign country, or in returning directly to the U.S. from a foreign country, the time you spend on or over international waters does not count toward the 330-day total.

Example—
On August 9 you fly from New York City to Paris. You arrive there at 10 A.M. of August 10. Your first qualifying day toward the 330-day period is August 11.

You may count in your 330-day period:
Time spent traveling between foreign countries.
Time spent on a vacation in foreign countries. There is no requirement that the 330 days must be spent on a job.
Time spent in a foreign country while employed by the U.S. Government counts towards the 330-day test even though pay from the government does not qualify for the earned income exclusion.
Time in foreign countries, territorial waters, or travel in the air over a foreign country. However, you will lose qualifying days if any part of such travel is on or over international waters and takes 24 hours or more, or any part of such travel is within the U.S. or its possessions.

Example—
You depart from Naples, Italy, by ship on June 10 at 6:00 P.M. and arrive at Haifa, Israel, at 7:00 A.M. on June 14. The trip exceeded 24 hours and passed through international waters. Therefore, you lose as qualifying days June 10, 11, 12, 13 and 14. Assuming you remain in Haifa, Israel, the next qualifying day is June 15.

Choosing the 12-month period. You qualify under the physical presence test if you were on foreign soil 330 days during any period of 12 consecutive months. Since there may be several 12-month periods during which you meet the 330 day test, you should choose the 12-month period allowing you the largest possible exclusion if you qualify under the physical presence test for only part of 1986.

Example—
You work in France from June 1, 1985 through September 30, 1986, when you leave the country. During this period, you leave France only for a 15 day vacation to the U.S. during December 1985. You earn $70,000 for your work in France during 1986. Your maximum 1986 exclusion is $64,219, figured as follows:
1. Start with your last full day, September 30, 1986, and count back 330 full days during which you were abroad. Not counting the vacation days, the 330th day is October 21, 1985. This is the first day of your 12-month period.
2. From October 21, 1985, count forward 12 months, to October 20, 1986, which is the last day of your 12-month period.
3. Count the number of days in 1986 which fall within the 12-month period ending October 20, 1986. Here, the number of qualifying days is 293, from January 1 through October 20, 1986.
4. The maximum 1986 exclusion is $80,000 × 293/365 or $64,219.

You may exclude $64,219, the lesser of the maximum exclusion or your actual earnings of $70,000.

¶36.05 • CLAIMING DEDUCTIONS IF YOU ELECT THE EARNED INCOME EXCLUSION

If you elect the earned income exclusion, you deduct expenses as follows:

Personal or nonbusiness deductions, such as medical expenses, mortgage interest, and real estate taxes paid on a personal residence, are deductible if you itemize deductions. Business expenses attributable to earning excludable income are not deductible. Dependency exemptions are fully deductible.

Example—

You were a resident of Denmark and elect to exclude your wages of $70,000 from income. You also incurred unreimbursed travel expenses of $2,000. You may not deduct the travel expenses, since the amount is attributable to the earning of tax-free income.

If your foreign earnings exceed the exclusion ceiling, you allocate expenses between taxable and tax-exempt income and deduct the amount allocated to taxable earned income.

Example—

In 1986, you earn $100,000 and satisfy the physical presence test. Your unreimbursed travel expenses are $5,000. If you elect the $80,000 exclusion, you may deduct 20% of the travel expenses, or $1,000 since 20% of your earnings or $20,000 are taxed.

If your job expenses are reimbursed and the rules of reporting are met (*see* ¶2.31), the reimbursements are not reported to the extent of the expenses incurred. If the reimbursement is less than expenses, the excess expenses are allocated as in the example above.

You may have to allocate state income taxes paid on your income.

If either you or your spouse elect the earned income or housing exclusion, you may not claim the special deduction for two-earner couples (¶1.01) or an IRA deduction based on excluded income.

Overseas moving expenses. These expenses are generally treated as related to your foreign earnings. Thus, if you move to a foreign country and exclude your income you may not deduct your moving expenses. If your earned income exceeds the exclusion limit, you allocate moving expenses between your tax-exempt and taxable earned income. Employer reimbursement is considered earned income in the year of receipt and is added to other earned income before taking the exclusion and making the allocation. *See* ¶36.03 for allocating reimbursements between the year of the move and the following year for purposes of claiming the exclusion. In allocating moving expenses to taxable earned income, apply the following rules for computing the moving expense deduction: (1) A deduction of up to $6,000 is allowed for the cost of temporary living arrangements at the foreign location, house hunting costs, and expenses incident to the sale of your old home and purchase of a new one at the foreign location; of this amount, up to $4,500 may be claimed for temporary living arrangements and house hunting costs. (2) You may deduct expenses for temporary living arrangements incurred within any 90 consecutive days after obtaining work abroad. (3) You may deduct in full as directly related moving expenses the cost of moving household goods and personal effects to and from storage and the cost of storing the goods or effects while your new foreign work site is your principal place of work.

If, after working in a foreign country, your employer transfers you back to the U.S. or you move back to the U.S. to take a different job, your moving expenses are deductible under the general rules at ¶2.40. If your residence and principal place of work was outside the U.S. and you retire and move back to the U.S., your moving expenses are also deductible under ¶2.40 except you do not have to meet the 39-week test for employees or the 78-week test for the self-employed and partners.

Survivors of workers abroad returning to U.S. If you are the spouse or dependent of a worker who died while his principal place of work was outside the U.S., you may deduct your moving expenses back to the U.S. For the costs to be deductible, the move must begin within six months of the worker's death. The requirements for deducting moving expenses (¶2.40) apply, except for the 78-week test for the self-employed and partners.

Compulsory home leave. Foreign service officers stationed abroad must periodically return to the U.S. to reorient themselves to American ways of life. Because the home leave is compulsory, foreign service officers may deduct their travel expenses; travel expenses of the officer's family are not deductible.

¶36.06 • WHAT TO DO IF YOUR RIGHT TO AN EXCLUSION IS NOT ESTABLISHED WHEN YOUR RETURN IS DUE

When your 1986 return is due, you may not have been abroad long enough to qualify for the exclusion. If you expect to qualify under either the residence or physical presence test after the due date for your 1986 return, you may either: (1) Ask for an extension of time for filing your return until after you qualify under either rule, or (2) file your return on the due date, reporting the foreign income in the return, pay the full tax, and then file for a refund when you qualify.

Extension of time to file. If you are abroad on April 15, 1987, you have an automatic extension to June 15, 1987. For an additional two months, file Form 4868 by June 15, 1987 and pay an estimated tax. For a longer extension, in anticipation of owing no tax on your foreign income, you may file Form 2350 either with the Internal Revenue Service, Philadelphia, Pennsylvania 19255, or with a local IRS representative. File Form 2350 before the due date for filing your 1986 return which is June 15, 1987 if you are abroad and are on a calendar year. If you cannot get Form 2350, apply for the extension on your own stationery. State the facts you rely on to justify the extension and the earliest date you expect to be in a position to determine under which rule you will qualify. You will receive an official letter and copy granting the extension. Generally, you will be granted an extension of time for a period ending 30 days after the date you expect to qualify for the foreign earned income exclusion.

If you will have tax to pay even after qualifying, for example, your earned income exceeds the exclusion, you may file for an extension to file but you will owe interest on the tax due. To avoid interest charges on the tax, you may take one of the following steps:

1. File your return on time and pay the total tax due without the application of the exclusion. When you do qualify, make sure you file a refund claim within the time limits discussed at ¶27.00; or

2. Pay estimated tax for the amount of tax you expect to owe and later ask for an extension to file. When you file your return, you apply the estimated tax against the tax due. An estimated tax for 1986 must be made by January 15, 1987 and an extension to file a final return must be made by June 15, 1987. If you fail to make a timely estimate, you cannot use this option.

3. Pay the estimated tax liability when you apply for the extension to file on Form 2350. If the extension is granted, the paid amount is applied to the tax shown on your return when you file.

¶36.07 • TAX-FREE MEALS AND LODGING FOR WORKERS IN CAMPS

If you must live in a camp provided by your employer, you may exclude from income the value of the lodging and meals furnished if the camp is (1) provided because you work in a remote area where satisfactory housing is not available; (2) located as near as practicable to the worksite; (3) a common area (enclave) not open to the public which normally accommodates at least 10 employees.

You may also qualify for the earned income exclusion under the general rules at ¶36.01.

¶36.08 • EARNINGS IN U.S. POSSESSIONS

If you are a U.S. citizen employed in one of the following places, you may be able to treat your earnings as tax-free income earned in a possession: Midway, Palmyra, Johnston Island, Kingman Reef, Wake Island, Howland Island, Baker Island, Jarvis Island, American Samoa, and other islands, cays, and reefs of the United States which are not part of one of the 50 states.

Earnings in the U.S. Virgin Islands, Puerto Rico, Guam, and

the Northern Mariana Islands do not qualify for the possession exemption.

You may elect not to pay tax on your income from a possession if, during the three-year period ending with the close of the tax year, or the applicable part of that period—

1. 80% of your gross income comes from sources in the possession. If you were not working or in business in the possession for three years, you count the lesser period you were employed or in business there.

2. During that same period, 50% or more of your gross income came from active conduct of a trade or business in the possession. This requirement is satisfied whether you have your own business or you are an employee or agent of a business.

If you meet the above tests, all types of income from sources outside the U.S., including earned income, investment income, and capital gains, qualify for tax exemption. However, if the income is received within the U.S., it is taxable. The income must not only be derived, but also be received, outside the U.S.

You may not exclude income earned in a U.S. possession if derived from working for the U.S. or its agencies. Working for the local government of a possession is considered working for an agency of the U.S.

If you claim the possession exemption, you are allowed only one personal exemption. You may not claim exemptions for your spouse, children, and other dependents, or exemptions for age or blindness. You may claim deductions only to the extent they are related to your taxable income. However, you may deduct charitable contributions and casualty losses based on property located in the U.S. If the total of these deductions is less than your zero bracket amount, you must compute the unused zero bracket amount and add it to your adjusted gross income (see ¶13.03). You may not claim a credit for income taxes paid to a foreign country or U.S. possession, or the earned income credit.

If you live in a community property state, half of your income (from the possession) is treated as earned by your spouse. Half of what your spouse earns in the U.S. is treated as earned by you. In applying the community property rules, you may find you are unable to meet the 80% and 50% gross income tests and therefore do not qualify for the possession exemption.

For further details, see *Tax Guide for U.S. Citizens Employed in U.S. Possessions,* IRS Publication 570.

¶36.09 • EARNINGS IN U.S. VIRGIN ISLANDS

If you are a U.S. citizen and are also a bona fide resident of the U.S. Virgin Islands on the last day of your 1986 taxable year, you file a tax return with the government of the Virgin Islands and pay your entire tax liability to the Virgin Islands. You do not file a U.S. tax return if you are a resident of the U.S. Virgin Islands on the last day of the year. You are a bona fide resident of the Virgin Islands if you intend to make your home there and are not a visitor or tourist.

Example—
You leave the United States on December 1, 1986 and arrive in the U.S. Virgin Islands on the same day. You intend to make your home there. You qualify as a bona fide resident of the U.S. Virgin Islands on the last day of your tax year, December 31, 1986. You file your 1986 income tax return with the government of the U.S. Virgin Islands, even though you resided in the United States for most of the year.

If you are a U.S. citizen who earns income in the U.S. Virgin Islands but are not a resident on the last day of the tax year, you file both Virgin Islands and U.S. tax returns. On your Virgin Islands return, you report only Virgin Islands source income; on your U.S. tax return, you report your income from all sources including Virgin Islands sources. You may claim a credit on your U.S. return for the income taxes paid to the Virgin Islands (see ¶36.14).

If you are a permanent resident of the U.S. Virgin Islands, tax returns are filed with the Bureau of Internal Revenue, Tax Division, Charlotte Amalie, St. Thomas, Virgin Islands, 00801.

¶36.10 • EARNINGS IN PUERTO RICO

Puerto Rican tax returns. If you are a U.S. citizen who is also a resident of Puerto Rico, you generally report all of your income on your Puerto Rican tax return. Where you report income from U.S. sources on the Puerto Rican tax return, a credit against the Puerto Rican tax may be claimed for income taxes paid to the U.S.

If you are not a resident of Puerto Rico, you report on a Puerto Rican return only income from Puerto Rican sources. Wages earned for services performed in Puerto Rico for the U.S. government or for private employers is treated as income from Puerto Rican sources.

U.S. tax return. As a U.S. citizen, you must file a U.S. tax return reporting income from all sources. But, if you are a bona fide resident of Puerto Rico for an entire tax year, you do not report on a U.S. tax return any income from Puerto Rican sources except amounts received for services performed in Puerto Rico as an employee of the U.S. government. On a U.S. tax return, you may not deduct expenses applicable to the excludable income. Personal exemptions are fully deductible.

If you are not a bona fide resident of Puerto Rico for the entire tax year, you report on your U.S. tax return all of your Puerto Rican income as well as all income from other sources. If you are required to report Puerto Rican income on your U.S. tax return, you may claim a credit for income tax paid to Puerto Rico. You figure the credit on Form 1116.

Example—
You and your spouse are bona fide residents of Puerto Rico during the entire year of 1986. You receive $15,000 in wages as an employee of the U.S. government working in Puerto Rico, a $100 dividend from a Puerto Rican corporation that does business in Puerto Rico, and a $500 dividend from a U.S. corporation that does business in the U.S. Your spouse earned $8,000 in wages from a Puerto Rican corporation for services performed in Puerto Rico. Your exempt and taxable income for U.S. federal tax purposes:

	Taxable	Exempt
Your wages	$15,000	
Your spouse's wages		$8,000
Puerto Rican corporation dividend		100
U.S. corporation dividend	500	
Totals	$15,500	$8,100

You file tax returns with both Puerto Rico and the United States. You have gross income of $15,500 for U.S. tax purposes and $23,600 for Puerto Rican tax purposes. A tax credit may be claimed on the U.S. tax return for income taxes paid to Puerto Rico and on your Puerto Rican return for income taxes paid to the United States.

Information on Puerto Rican tax returns may be requested from Oficina de Apelaciones Administrativas, Consultas y Legislación, Negociado de Contribución sobre Ingresos, Apartado S 2501, San Juan, Puerto Rico 00903.

¶36.11 • EARNINGS IN GUAM AND NORTHERN MARIANA ISLANDS

Guam. If you are a U.S. citizen and a resident of Guam on the last day of your 1986 tax year, you file a tax return with Guam and pay your entire tax on income from all sources to Guam. You do not file a U.S. tax return.

If you are a U.S. resident at the end of your tax year and have income from Guamanian sources, you file your return and pay your entire tax liability to the U.S. You do not file a Guam tax return.

If you file a joint return and the spouse with the greater adjusted gross income is a resident of Guam at the end of the tax year, the joint return is filed with Guam. If the spouse with the greater adjusted gross income is a U.S. resident at the end of the tax year, the joint return is filed with the U.S. For purposes of this income test, each spouse's income is determined without regard to community property laws.

For further information, write to the Commissioner of Revenue and Taxation, Government of Guam, Agana, Guam 96910. Also ask your local District Director for the Tax Guide for U.S. Citizens Employed in U.S. Possessions, IRS Publication 570.

Northern Mariana Islands. If you are a resident of the Northern Mariana Islands on the last day of your 1986 tax year, you file a tax return with the Northern Mariana Islands and pay your entire tax on income from all sources to the Northern Mariana Islands. You do not file a U.S. tax return.

If you are a U.S. resident at the end of your tax year, you file your return and pay your entire tax liability on income from all sources to the U.S. You do not file a tax return with the Northern Mariana Islands.

If filing a joint return, the same filing rule as discussed above for Guam determines whether the joint return is filed with the U.S. or the Northern Mariana Islands.

Tax returns to the Northern Mariana Islands are filed with, and information may be obtained from, the Division of Revenues, Saipan, Mariana Islands 96950.

¶36.12 • TAX TREATIES WITH FOREIGN COUNTRIES

Tax treaties between the United States and foreign countries modify some of the rules discussed above. The purpose of the treaties is to avoid double taxation. Consult your tax advisor about the effect of these treaties on your income.

¶36.13 • EXCHANGE RATES AND BLOCKED CURRENCY

Income reported on your federal income tax return must be stated in U.S. dollars. Where you are paid in foreign currency, you report your pay in U.S. dollars on the basis of the exchange rates prevailing at the time the income is actually or constructively received. You use the rate that most closely reflects the value of the foreign currency—the official rate, the open market rate or any other relevant rate. You may even be required to use the black market rate if that is the most accurate measure of the actual purchasing power of U.S. dollars in the foreign country. Be prepared to justify the rate you use.

Fulbright grants. If 70% of a Fulbright grant is paid in nonconvertible foreign currency, U.S. tax may be paid in the foreign currency. *See* IRS Publication 520 for details.

A citizen or resident alien may be paid in a foreign currency that cannot be converted into American dollars and removed from the foreign country. If your income is in blocked currency, you may elect to defer the reporting of that income until: (1) The currency becomes convertible into dollars. (2) You actually convert it into dollars. (3) You use it for personal expenses (for example, in the foreign country when you go there). Purchase of a business or investment in the foreign country is not the kind of use that is treated as a conversion. (4) You make a gift of it or leave it in your will. (5) You are a resident alien and you give up your U.S. residence.

If you use this method to defer the income, you may not deduct the expenses of earning it until you report it. You must continue to use this method after you choose it. You may only change with permission of the IRS.

You do not defer the reporting of capital losses incurred in a country having a blocked currency.

There may be some disadvantages in making the choice to defer the income—

1. Many years' income may accumulate and all be taxed in one year.

2. You have no control over the year in which the blocked income becomes taxable. You usually cannot control the events that cause the income to become unblocked.

You choose to defer income in blocked currency by filing a tentative tax return reporting your blocked taxable income and explain that you are deferring the payment of income tax because your income is not in dollars or in property or currency which is readily convertible into dollars. You must attach to your tentative return a regular return, reporting any unblocked taxable income received during the year or taxable income which became unblocked during the year. When the currency finally becomes unblocked or convertible into a currency or property convertible to dollars, you pay tax on the earnings at the rate prevailing in the year the currency became unblocked or convertible. On the tentative return, note at the top: "Report of Deferrable Foreign Income." File separate returns for each country from which blocked currency is received. The election must be made by the due date for filing a return for the year in which an election is sought.

¶36.131 • INFORMATION RETURNS ON FOREIGN CURRENCY

If you have a financial interest in, or signature or other authority over a foreign bank account, a foreign securities account, or any other foreign financial account, you must report this fact on Form 90-22.1, Report of Foreign Bank and Financial Accounts. The form does not have to be filed if the aggregate value of the accounts during the entire year does not exceed $5,000, or if the accounts were with a U.S. military banking facility operated by a U.S. financial institution. Taxpayers filing Form 1040 must also indicate on Schedule B whether they had an interest in a foreign account during the year. Form 90-22.1 is not filed with your income tax return. The form must be filed by June 30 of the year following the year in which you had this financial interest. Foreign accounts for 1986 must be reported by June 30, 1987 to the Department of the Treasury, Post Office Box 28309, Central Station, Washington, D.C. 20005.

Treasury regulations impose reporting and record keeping requirements for currency transactions outside the United States. Generally, transactions involving a physical transfer of funds or monetary instruments into or outside the U.S. must be reported if the amount involved exceeds $5,000 on any one occasion.

Financial institutions are also subject to record keeping requirements covering advice, requests or instructions for transfers outside the country of over $10,000 in cash, instruments, securities, or credit (*see* Treasury regulations and Form 4789 for details).

¶36.14 • FOREIGN TAX CREDIT

You must file Form 1116 to compute your credit. You may not claim a foreign tax credit or deduction for taxes paid on income not subject to U.S. tax. If all of your foreign earned income is excluded, none of the foreign taxes paid on such income may be taken as a credit or deduction on your U.S. return. If you exclude only part of your foreign pay, you determine which foreign taxes are attributable to excluded income and thus disallowed as foreign tax credits by applying the fractional computation provided in the instructions to Form 1116 and IRS Publication 514.

If you qualify for a credit or deduction, you will generally receive a larger tax reduction by claiming a tax credit rather than a deduction. A deduction is only a partial offset against your tax, whereas a credit is deducted in full from your tax. Also, taking a deduction may bar you from carrying back an excess credit from a later year. However, a deduction may give you a larger tax saving if the foreign tax is levied at a high rate and the proportion of foreign income to U.S. income is small. Compute your tax under both methods and choose the one providing the larger tax reduction.

In one tax year, you may not elect to deduct some foreign taxes and claim others as a credit. One method must be applied to all taxes paid or accrued during the tax year. If you are a cash basis taxpayer, you may claim a credit for accrued foreign taxes, but you must consistently follow this method once elected.

The credit is the amount of foreign taxes paid or accrued, not to exceed the effective U.S. tax on foreign income multiplied by a ratio of foreign taxable income over total taxable income reduced by the zero bracket amount.

The credit may not be claimed if:

You are a nonresident alien. However, under certain circumstances, an alien who is a bona fide resident for an entire taxable year in Puerto Rico may claim the credit. Also a nonresident alien engaged in a U.S. trade or business may claim a credit if he receives income *effectively connected* to that business.

You receive tax-exempt income from a U.S. possession.

Taxes qualifying for the credit. The credit is allowed only for foreign income, excess profits taxes, and similar taxes in the nature of an income tax. It is not allowed for any taxes paid to foreign countries on sales, gross receipts, production, the privilege to do business, personal property, or export of capital. But it may apply to a—

Tax like one of our own taxes on income.

Tax paid by a domestic taxpayer in lieu of the tax upon income, which would otherwise be imposed by any foreign country or by any U.S. possession.

Tax of a foreign country imposing income tax, where, for reasons growing out of the administrative difficulties of determining net income or basis within that country, the tax is measured by gross income, sales, number of units produced.

Pension, unemployment, or disability funds of a foreign country; certain foreign social security taxes do not qualify.

Reporting foreign income on your return. You report the gross amount of your foreign income in terms of United States currency. You also attach a schedule showing how you figured the foreign income in United States currency.

Example—

You earn Canadian dividends of $100 (Canadian dollars), from which $15 of Canadian taxes were withheld. When the dividends were declared, a Canadian dollar could be exchanged for $.82 of United States currency. Therefore, the dividend of $100 (in Canadian dollars) is reported on your return as $82 ($100 × .82). The tax withheld which may be taken as a credit is $12.30 ($15 × .82).

¶36.15 • COMPUTING THE FOREIGN TAX CREDIT

The credit is based on the amount of foreign taxes you paid or accrued. However, the amount of foreign taxes taken into account is limited where the foreign taxes exceed the effective U.S. tax rate on the foreign income. You compute the limitation on Form 1116. You must use the *overall* method of limitation.

The overall limitation is computed according to this formula:

$$\text{U.S. tax} \times \frac{\text{Taxable income from all foreign countries}}{\text{Taxable income from all sources—Zero bracket amount}}$$

Income which is tax free under the foreign earned income exclusion is not taken into account when figuring taxable income. Foreign taxable income, for purposes of computing the ratio, is reduced by all expenses directly related to earning the income. Itemized deductions, such as medical expenses, which are not directly related to foreign sources are allocated to foreign income according to relative gross incomes from foreign and U.S. sources. If you do not itemize deductions, you allocate the zero bracket amount and deduct the allocable portion from foreign income. You do not consider personal exemptions when figuring foreign or total taxable income. For purposes of computing the overall limitation, taxable income from all sources is reduced by the zero bracket amount, whether or not you itemize deductions.

Example—

Jones, a single individual, receives taxable income from three countries as follows:

	Taxable income	Income taxes paid
Country A	$ 2,000	$ 100
Country B	$ 4,000	$1,200
United States	$ 6,300	
Taxable income	$12,300	
Less: Zero bracket amount	2,300	
Total taxable income	$10,000	

Assume that the U.S. tax is $2,000.

Tax Credit on Overall Basis

$$\frac{\text{Taxable income from all foreign countries}}{\text{Total taxable income}} \times \text{U.S. tax}$$

	Maximum foreign tax	Actual foreign tax	Foreign tax credit allowable
Countries A and B: $\frac{\$\,6,000}{\$10,000} \times \$2,000 = \$1,200$		$1,300	$1,200

Capital gains. In figuring the overall limitation, taxable income from foreign countries (the numerator) includes gain from the sale of capital assets only to the extent of foreign source capital gain net income, which is the lower of net capital gain from foreign sources or net capital gain from all sources. Gain on the sale of personal property sold outside of the country of your residence may be treated as gain from U.S. sources, unless the gain is subject to a foreign income tax at a rate of 10% or more of the gain. *See* instructions to Form 1116. The same rule applies to personal property (other than corporate stock) sold other than in a country in which such property is used in business or in which you derived more than 50% of your gross income for the three-year period ending with the close of the taxable year preceding the year during which the sale or exchange occurred.

Examples—

1. You sell personal property at a gain in your country of residence. The gain is *not* treated as U.S. source income even if the foreign tax is under 10% of the gain.
2. You sell at a gain personal property outside of your country of residence and the foreign tax is under 10%. The gain is treated as U.S. source income.
3. You sell at a gain business property in the country in which the property is used in your business. The gain is *not* treated as U.S. source income, even if the foreign tax is under 10% of the gain.

The foreign tax credit allowable may not exceed foreign taxes actually paid or accrued. Where a joint return is filed, the limitation is applied to the aggregate taxable income of both spouses.

A limited foreign tax credit may be applied against the alternative minimum tax. *See* ¶23.14.

Recapture of foreign losses. If you sustain an "overall foreign loss" for any taxable year, a recapture provision treats part of foreign income realized in a later year as income from U.S. sources. By treating part of the later year's foreign income as U.S. income, the numerator of the fraction used to compute the overall limitation (*see* above) is reduced and this in turn reduces the maximum foreign tax credit that may be claimed in the later year. More specifically, the portion of foreign income in succeeding years which is treated as U.S. income equals the lower of (a) the amount of the loss or (b) 50% (or a larger percentage, as you may choose) of taxable income from foreign sources. An "overall foreign loss" means the amount by which the gross income for the taxable year from foreign sources for that year is exceeded by the sum of allocated deductions. For this purpose, the following deductions are not considered and so are not subject to recapture: Operating loss deductions, any uncompensated foreign expropriation or casualty loss. Special rules apply to dispositions of property if used predominantly outside the United States in a trade or business.

The limitation on a credit for tax on certain types of interest income must be computed separately using the overall basis. Interest income subject to separate computation includes all interest resulting from transactions occurring after April 2, 1962, except: (1) Interest from transactions directly related to the active conduct of foreign business; (2) interest from the conduct of a banking, financing, or similar business; (3) interest received from a corporation in which you have at least a 10% voting stock interest; (4) interest on obligations received upon a disposition of an active foreign business, or upon the disposition of stock or other obligations of a corporation in which you had at least a 10% voting stock interest.

For further details, *see* IRS Publication 514.

¶36.16 • CARRYBACK AND CARRYOVER OF EXCESS FOREIGN TAX CREDIT

Where the amount allowable as a credit under either the per-country (prior law) or overall basis is restricted, the excess may be carried back to the two preceding years and then carried forward to the five succeeding taxable years. Generally, there can be no carryover from a per-country year to an overall basis year, or vice versa. However, exceptions to this rule (not discussed in this book) may be allowed during a transitional period. The carryback or carryover will not be allowed in a year you have no income from foreign sources or the credit limitation already applies to taxes of that year.

For further details, *see* IRS Publication 514.

How Aliens Are Taxed in the United States

Tax treatment depends on: (1) Whether the alien is a resident or nonresident; (2) if a nonresident, whether he is engaged in a U.S. business; and (3) tax treaties. A treaty prevails over a less favorable tax law.

¶37.01 • RESIDENT OR NONRESIDENT?

A resident alien, like a U.S. citizen, is taxed on income from all sources.

A nonresident alien is generally taxed only on income from U.S. sources at special rates. However, capital gains from the sale of U.S. real estate are subject to tax at regular U.S. rates. See ¶37.03. Other capital gains are not taxed unless a nonresident alien has a U.S. business, or is in the U.S. for 183 days during the year. If he is doing business here, business income is taxed differently from investment income.

An alien's mere presence in the U.S. does not make him a "resident."

For taxable years starting after 1984, an alien is generally treated as a "resident" only if he is a lawful permanent resident or meets a substantial presence test. See ¶37.025.

Before 1985, intent to stay for an indefinite period generally determined resident status. A stay of one year or more raised a presumption that a person was a resident; he or she had to prove otherwise.

Dual status. An alien may be both a resident and nonresident in the same year.

Example—
On June 1, 1986, you arrive on a nonimmigrant visa and are present in the U.S. for the rest of the year. From January 1 to May 31, 1986, you are a nonresident; from June 1 to the end of the year, you are a resident. Despite "dual status," you do not file two returns. You file one return, reporting income on the basis of your status for each part of the year.

Certain restrictions apply to dual status taxpayers. For example, a joint return may not be filed, unless you and your spouse agree to be taxed as U.S. residents for the entire year. Further, you are not allowed the full benefit of the zero bracket amount; as a dual status taxpayer, you must figure the unused zero bracket amount which is added to income. See ¶13.01.

For details on filing a return for a dual status year, *see* IRS Publication 519 and the instructions to Form 1040NR.

¶37.02 • HOW A RESIDENT ALIEN IS TAXED

A resident alien is taxed like a U.S. citizen. Income earned abroad may be excluded if the foreign physical presence test is satisfied (*see* ¶36.04). A resident alien may generally claim a foreign tax credit (*see* ¶36.14). He is taxed on a pension from a foreign government. An alien working in the United States for a foreign government is not taxed on his pay if the foreign government allows a similar exemption to American citizens.

¶37.025 • WHO IS A RESIDENT ALIEN?

Starting in 1985, the following tests determine whether an alien is taxed as a U.S. resident. Intent to remain in the U.S. is not considered.

You are treated as a resident alien and taxed as a U.S. resident if you meet either of the following tests for 1986:

1. You are a lawful permanent resident of the U.S. *at any time* during the calendar year. If you hold a green card, you meet this test and are considered a U.S. resident. If you were outside of the U.S. for part of 1986 and then become a lawful permanent resident, *see* the rules below for first year of residency.

2. You meet a substantial presence test. Under this test, you are treated as a U.S. resident if you were in the U.S. for at least 31 days during the calendar year and have been in the U.S. within the last three years for 183 days. The 183 day test is complicated and there are several exceptions.

To determine if you meet the 183 day test, the following cumulative times are totaled. Each day in the U.S. during 1986 is counted as a full day. Each day in 1985 counts as ⅓ of a day; each day in 1984 counts as ⅙ of a day. However, do not count days of presence before 1985 unless you were a U.S. resident at the end of 1984 under prior law rules. If you were not a U.S. resident at the end of 1984 (under prior law) you count days of presence in 1985 and 1986 but not in 1984 toward the 183 day test.

Note that you must be physically present in the U.S. for at least 31 days in the current year. If you are not, the 183 day test does not apply.

Other exceptions to the substantial presence test are: commuting from Canada or Mexico; keeping a tax home and close contacts or connections in a foreign country; having a diplomatic, teacher, trainee or student status, or being confined in the U.S. for certain medical reasons. These are explained in the following paragraphs.

Commute from Mexico or Canada. If you regularly commute to work in the U.S. from Mexico or Canada, commuting days do not count as days of physical presence for the 183 day test.

Tax home/close connection exception. If you are in the United States for less than 183 days during 1986 and show that you had a closer connection with a foreign country than with the U.S. and a tax home there for the year, you will generally not be subject to tax as a resident under the substantial presence test. Under this exception, it is possible to have a U.S. abode and a tax home in a foreign country. A tax home is usually where a person has his principal place of business; if he has no principal place of business, it is the place of his regular abode. Proving a tax home alone is not sufficient; the closer connection relationship must also be shown.

The tax home/closer connection test does not apply to an alien who is present for 183 days or more during a year or who has applied for a green card. A relative's application is not considered as the alien's application.

Exempt-person exception. Days of presence in the U.S. are not counted if you are considered an exempt person, such as a teacher, trainee, student, or a foreign government-related person.

A foreign government-related person is any individual temporarily present in the U.S. who has (1) diplomatic status, or a visa which the Secretary of the Treasury (after consultation with the Secretary of State) determined represents full-time diplomatic or consular status; (2) is a full-time employee of an international organization; or (3) is a member of the immediate family of a diplomat or international organization employee.

A teacher or trainee is any individual other than a student who is temporarily present in the U.S. under a "J" visa (subparagraph (J) of section 101(15) of the Immigration and Nationality Act) and who substantially complies with the requirements for being so present.

A student is any individual who is temporarily present in the U.S. under either an "F" or "J" visa (subparagraph (F) of section 101(15) of the Immigration and Nationality Act or subparagraph (J) of such section 101(15)) and who substantially complies with the requirements for being so present.

The exception does not apply to teacher or trainee who has

been exempt as a teacher, trainee, or student for any part of two of the six preceding calendar years. The exception also does not apply to a student if he has been exempt as a teacher, trainee, or student for more than five calendar years, unless he shows that he does not intend to reside permanently in the U.S. and that he or she has substantially complied with the requirements of the student visa providing for temporary presence in the U.S.

Medical exception. An alien who cannot physically leave the U.S. because of a medical condition that arose in the U.S. may be treated as a nonresident even if present here for more than 182 days during the year.

Tax treaty exception. The lawful permanent residence test and the substantial physical presence test do not override tax treaty definitions of residence. Thus, you may be protected by a tax treaty from being treated as a U.S. resident even if you would be treated as a resident under either test.

First year of residency. If you first became a lawful permanent resident of the U.S. (have green card) during 1986 and were not a U.S. resident during 1985, your period of U.S. residency begins with the first day in 1986 you are present in the U.S. with the status of lawful permanent resident. Before that date, you are a nonresident alien. This means that if you become a lawful permanent resident after January 1, 1986 you have a dual status tax year. On Form 1040, you attach a separate schedule showing the income for the part of the year you are a nonresident subject to the rules of ¶37.03.

To figure tax for a dual status year, *see* IRS Publication 519 and the instruction to Form 1040NR.

You may also have a dual status year if you were not a U.S. resident in 1985 and in 1986, you are a U.S. resident under the 183 day presence test. Your period of U.S. residency starts on the first day in 1986 for which you were physically present. However, if you meet the 183 day presence test (but not the green card test) and also spent 10 days or less in the U.S. during a period in which you had a closer connection to a foreign country than to the U.S., you may disregard the 10-day period. The purpose of this exception is to allow a brief presence in the U.S. for business trips or house-hunting before the U.S. residency period starts.

Examples—
1. An alien who has never before been a U.S. resident lives in Spain until May 15, 1986. He moves to the U.S. and remains in the U.S. through the end of the year, thereby satisfying the physical presence test. On May 15, he is a U.S. resident. For the period before May 15, he is taxed as a nonresident.
2. Same facts as above but he attends a meeting in the U.S. on February 2 through 8. On May 15, he moves to the U.S. May 15, not February 2, is the starting date of the residence. During February, he had closer connection to Spain than to the U.S. Thus, his short stay in February is an exempt period.

If you were not a resident during 1984 but in 1985 you satisfy both the lawful resident (green card) test and the 183 day presence test, your residence begins on the earlier of the first day you are present in the U.S. while a lawful permanent resident of the U.S. or the first day of physical presence.

Last year of residence. An alien who does not hold a green card is not treated as a resident after the last day he was present in the U.S. provided (1) he is not treated as a resident during the next calendar year and (2) after leaving the U.S., he had a closer connection to a foreign country than to the U.S. Presence of up to 10 days in the U.S. may be disregarded if during that period you had a closer connection to a foreign country than to the U.S. If an alien who holds a green card gives up his permanent resident status in the current year and meets rules (1) and (2) above, his residency status ends after the day he was no longer a permanent resident.

In the last year of residence, the rules for dual status taxpayers apply. *See* ¶37.01.

¶37.03 • HOW A NONRESIDENT ALIEN IS TAXED IN 1986

Nonresident aliens engaged in a U.S. business (*see* ¶37.05) are taxed differently from those not so engaged, and all nonresident aliens are taxed on sales of U.S. realty (*see* below).

No U.S. business. A nonresident alien pays a flat 30% tax on periodic investment income such as dividends and certain interest from U.S. sources (*see* ¶37.04). He may not claim the dividend exclusion unless dividends are effectively connected with a U.S. business. Except for gains from disposition of U.S. realty, capital gain is not taxed unless he is in this country for 183 days, not necessarily continuous. In that case, gain is taxed at 30% and is not reduced by a capital loss carryover or the net capital gain deduction. The 30% rate is imposed on gross income without deductions or the credit for the elderly. The 30% tax does not apply to original issue discount on three-month and six-month Treasury bills. The 30% tax does not apply to portfolio interest on obligations issued after July 18, 1984 (*see* ¶37.07).

U.S. business. The income of a nonresident in a U.S. business falls into two classes: (1) Business income, and investment income "effectively connected" to business income; (2) investment income not connected to a U.S. business.

Class (1) income is taxed at graduated rates. Deductions are limited to business expenses, theft and casualty losses of property in the U.S., charitable contributions, and one personal exemption (residents of Canada and Mexico are not limited to one personal exemption). The IRS allows a deduction for state and local income taxes withheld by a U.S. employer. An alien whose status changes during the year from nonresident engaged in a U.S. business to resident alien may claim more than one exemption, but exemptions may not exceed earnings for the period in which he is a resident. Generally, if a nonresident is in any U.S. business, all income from U.S. sources (with the exception of certain investment income) is taxable at graduated rates, even if not actually connected with the business. A dual status alien may deduct travel expenses, including meals and lodging, incurred during the portion of the year that he is a nonresident because during that time he is away from his foreign tax home. On becoming a resident alien, his tax home is the location of his U.S. employment.

"Effectively connected" investment income is traceable to business assets or related to business activities, for example, interest from short-term Treasury bills purchased with surplus cash from the business in a slack season. You deduct expenses incurred in producing such income. Capital gain effectively connected with a U.S. business is taxed as it would be to a citizen without regard to the 183-day rule.

Class (2) investment income, such as interest, dividends and royalties, not "effectively connected" is taxed at 30%. However, interest on a deposit with a bank or insurance company is not taxed.

Compensation. Generally, working in the U.S. is a business and pay is taxed as Class (1) income. If you worked in 1985 but not in 1986 and received part or all of your salary in 1986, the payment is taxed as Class (2) income. If you are engaged in *any* business in 1986, even though not the same one that produced the salary payments, the payment is Class (1) income. If in 1986 you change jobs, payments from the 1985 job are taxed at graduated rates.

Sales of U.S. real property. Unless a specific treaty provision allows tax-free treatment, gain from sales of interests in U.S. real property are taxed at graduated rates as Class (1) income. There is a minimum tax imposed on nonresidents equal to 20% of the lesser of: the nonresident's alternative minimum taxable income for the taxable year, or the nonresident's net U.S. real property gain for the taxable year. See the worksheet included in the instructions to Form 1040NR.

Interests subject to tax include co-ownership, leaseholds and options in land or improvements to land, interests in U.S. wells, mines and other natural deposits, and furnishings and other personal property associated with the use of real property. The sale of a partnership, trust, or estate interest is subject to tax to the extent the proceeds are allocable to U.S. real property assets.

A nonresident alien is generally taxed on gains from the sale of stock in a U.S. corporation which held 50% or more (in terms of fair market value) of its worldwide business and real property assets in U.S. real property at any time after June 18, 1980 while he held the stock. However, gain from a sale of regularly traded stock is not taxable if he owned 5% or less of that class of stock at all times after June 18, 1980; here, a seller is treated as owning stock held by close relatives and certain controlled corporations.

Tax does not apply to sales of stock if the corporation held no U.S. real property at the time of the sale, and any gains on real property interests after June 18, 1980 were recognized by the corporation.

Foreigners holding at least $50,000 in U.S. real property interests at any time during the year may be required to file annual information returns. Check with the IRS for details.

If you sell real estate the buyer may have to withhold tax. *See* ¶37.07.

Example—

Julius, a foreign resident never in the U.S., buys goods overseas and sells here on a regular basis. He rents an office and employs two salesmen. He is engaged in a U.S. business. He invests in the stock market through a U.S. broker. In 1985, he had the following income, gains and expenses: Gross income from the business, $50,000; gain from the sale of foreign stock, $3,000; dividends, $1,000; office expense, $38,250; U.S. charitable contributions, $1,000. The dividends are not effectively connected with his business. Julius' income subject to regular graduated tax is calculated as follows:

Gross income from business		$50,000
Less: Business deductions (salaries and rent)		38,250
Adjusted gross income		11,750
Less: Total itemized deductions	$1,000	
Minus: Zero bracket amount	2,390	0
Tentative taxable income		11,750
Zero bracket amount	2,390	
Less: Itemized deduction	1,000	
Add unused zero bracket amount		1,390
Taxable income before personal exemption		$13,140

Gain from the stock sale is not taxed; Julius was not present in the U.S. for 183 days. The dividends are taxed at 30% for a tax of $300. (Nonresident aliens are not allowed the dividend exclusion unless the dividends are "effectively connected.") If the dividends had been effectively connected with Julius' business, $1,000 (less exclusion of $100 or $200 on a joint return) would have been added to the $50,000 business income.

Nonresident aliens with gross income of $1,040 or more in 1985 must file a tax return and must compute the unused zero bracket amount (*see* ¶13.00). Returns are due June 15 if no taxes are withheld from wages. If taxes are withheld from wages, the return is due April 15. Estimated tax declarations may also be required (*see* ¶26.00).

Nonresident aliens may elect to file joint returns with U.S. citizen or resident spouses reporting income from worldwide sources (*see* ¶1.03).

Certain foreign community property laws disregarded. Under prior law, a couple from a community property country could split income between themselves on the basis of the community property law. However, for tax years beginning after 1984, where either spouse is a nonresident alien, and the couple does not elect to file jointly and to report income from worldwide sources (*see* ¶1.03), certain community property rules are disregarded. Earned income such as salary that is not income from a business or partnership is treated as the income of the spouse who renders the personal services; it is not 50% taxed to the other spouse despite the community income law. Trade or business income, other than partnership income, is treated as the husband's income and taxed only to him unless the wife exercises substantially all management control over the business. Partnership income or loss is taxed to the spouse holding the partnership interest. Other types of income from one spouse's separate property (determined under applicable community property law) is treated as that spouse's income. Apart from these exceptions, all other community income rules apply.

¶37.04 • WHAT IS U.S. SOURCE INCOME?

A nonresident is taxed on U.S. source income. Except for business income and capital gain, the income must be "periodic." Most investment income is periodic, even if paid in a lump sum.

U.S. source income. (1) Pay for personal services in the U.S. (*see* ¶37.05). (2) Rents from property in the U.S. (3) Royalties from the use in the U.S. of patents, copyrights, good will, franchises, and similar property. (4) Gains from the sale of real prop-

erty located in the U.S. (5) Gains from the sale of personal property, such as stock, in the U.S. If the property was produced abroad or purchased in a U.S. possession by the alien and sold here, an allocation is made according to Treasury regulations. (6) Interest from U.S. residents or corporations but not from U.S. banks, unless effectively connected with the nonresident alien's U.S. business. Interest from a U.S. corporation if 20% or more of the corporation's gross income for the three-year period preceding the payment was from U.S. sources. Interest from a foreign corporation if 50% or more of its gross income for the three-year prior period was effectively connected with a U.S. business. Interest from an insurance company on amounts held under an agreement to pay interest but only if effectively connected with the nonresident's U.S. business. Interest from a U.S. branch bank of a foreign corporation if connected with the alien's U.S. business. Under an election, rental income from the lease of an American made ship or aircraft which qualifies as Section 38 property is U.S. source income if leased to a U.S. person and is treated like interest. The same is true for gain on the sale of the leased property. (7) Dividends from U.S. corporations, but not certain dividends where the corporation's activities take place in U.S. possessions. Dividends from foreign corporations, see *interest* above.

A nonresident alien is taxed on the following items even though they do not technically qualify as "periodic." (1) gain from the sale of certain copyrights, patents, good will, and similar items; (2) a distribution from a qualified deferred compensation plan that may be taxable to a resident as capital gain; (3) certain employee annuities that may qualify for capital gains; (4) timber, coal, or iron ore deposits that would qualify for capital gain treatment to a resident.

Original issue discount obligations. The 30% tax applies to original issue discount other than portfolio interest (*see* ¶37.07) on obligations issued after March 31, 1972, and payable more than 183 days from the date of issue, other than tax-exempt obligations. If interest is paid on the obligation, the tax applies to the original issue discount accrued since the last interest payment; the tax on the discount may not exceed the interest less the tax on the interest.

When an original issue discount obligation is sold or exchanged, gain is subject to the 30% tax up to the original issue discount that accrued while you held the bond less any discount that was taxed when interest payments were made.

Example—

Julius, a citizen and resident of a foreign country and never present in the U.S., had income as follows:

(1) $500 in dividends from X, a U.S. corporation which derived all its gross income from U.S. operations. The dividend is taxable.

(2) $400 in dividends from Y, a foreign corporation, which did no business in the U.S. This dividend is not taxed.

(3) $100 in interest from a U.S. citizen residing abroad. The interest is not from a U.S. source and is not taxed.

(4) $300 interest on savings in a New York bank. This interest is not taxable.

(5) He owned an apartment house in New York and collected $30,000 in rent. This is taxable income.

(6) He sold stock on an exchange through a broker, realizing a $500 capital gain. The gain is not taxable under the rules for sales of U.S. real property (¶37.03) and, since he was not present in the United States for 183 days, he is not taxed on capital gains.

(7) He made a $1,000 contribution to a U.S. charity, had medical expenses of $1,000, and depreciation and repairs expenses on his apartment building of $5,000. Because he is not in a U.S. business, he may not deduct any of these expenses.

His total U.S. income is:

X Co. dividends	$ 500	
Rents	30,000	
	$30,500	(taxed at 30%)

If Julius elected to treat the real estate as a U.S. business (*see* ¶37.06), he could deduct the $5,000 for depreciation and repairs, the contribution of $1,000, and a personal exemption of $1,040. His business income would be $23,000 and, after computation of the unused zero bracket amount, the tax would be figured at graduated rates. The dividends of $500 would still be taxed at the flat 30% rate.

All nonresidents file Form 1040 NR. The IRS may deny allowable deductions or credits (other than the credit for withheld taxes) if a "true and accurate return" is not filed. Presumably, this does not refer to unintentional mathematical errors, but is directed at the failure to disclose sources of income.

¶37.05 • WHAT IS A U.S. BUSINESS?

Generally, a nonresident who maintains a business office here as a "permanent establishment," or who produces goods here, is in a U.S. business. Merely sending a representative does not amount to a business unless he can accept orders.

A nonresident working here is in a U.S. business, with this exception: He works fewer than 91 days in the year for a nonresident alien, foreign partnership, or corporation not in a U.S. business and earns $3,000 or less. If compensation exceeds $3,000, the entire amount is taxable.

Trading in securities or commodities. An alien trading through a broker on an organized exchange is not in a U.S. business if he has no office here. If he has, he is in a U.S. business unless he is trading only on his own account and is not a dealer.

Partners and beneficiaries of estates and trusts. When a partnership, trust or estate is in a U.S. business, the partner or beneficiary is in that business even though he is not physically here. If a partner representing the partnership engages in activities sufficient to constitute a U.S. business, all partnership income is taxable.

¶37.06 • REAL ESTATE ELECTION FOR A NONRESIDENT ALIEN

A nonresident alien may treat income from real estate located in the U.S. as business income even where his rental property does not qualify as a business. "Business" requires more than collecting rents; usually advertising and soliciting tenants through agents must be shown. Under an election, rent less allowable deductions may be taxed at ordinary rates rather than at the flat 30% rate applied to investment income. An election applies to all income from real property not otherwise connected with your business.

The property must produce income. The IRS will not allow the election solely to create deductible losses. The election is effective until revoked with IRS consent; a new election generally will not be allowed for five years. Some treaties allow an alien to decide each year whether to make the election.

¶37.07 • WITHHOLDING ON A NONRESIDENT ALIEN'S INCOME

A 30% withholding rate applies to interest, dividends, rent, premiums, annuities, compensation, alimony, certain capital gains from qualified pension plans, gains from certain dispositions of timber, iron and coal, capital gains from certain patent transfers made prior to October 5, 1966 (*see* ¶6.036), gains from transfers after October 4, 1966 of patents, copyrights and like property (*see* ¶37.04), gains from the sale or exchange of bonds or other indebtedness where there is original issue discount (*see* ¶6.031), and generally investment income.

In the case of original issue discount obligations issued after March 31, 1972, the 30% withholding rate applies to the discount accrued since the last payment of interest; the withholding is from the next interest payment due you. Withholding on the accrued discount and on the interest payment itself may not exceed the total interest payment. On a sale or exchange of the obligation, the withholding rate applies to the extent of the accrued discount except for discount on which tax was previously withheld from interest payments.

Special exception for certain portfolio interest. The 30% withholding tax has been repealed for interest paid on portfolio obligations issued after July 18, 1984. The 30% tax still applies to interest on obligations issued before July 18, 1984. Generally, portfolio interest is interest, including original issue discount, from U.S. sources on (1) bearer obligations sold only to foreign investors, or (2) registered obligations targeted to foreign markets where interest is paid through foreign financial institutions. Further, if you file a statement with the payer that you are not a U.S. citizen or resident, portfolio interest also includes interest on registered obligations that are not targeted to foreign markets. Portfolio interest does not include interest on an obligation issued by an organization in which you own at least a 10% interest.

Withholding on 1986 real estate sales. A 10% withholding tax generally applies to sales of U.S. real property by a foreign person in 1986. The buyer must withhold the payment and pay it to the IRS with Form 8288. There are exceptions. No withholding is required for the sale of a residence costing no more than $300,000. Further, if the seller gives the buyer a written certification that he is not a foreign person together with his U.S. tax identification number, withholding is not required. *See* instructions to Form 8288.

Certain employee annuities from qualified pension plans are exempt from withholding. Certain fellowship grants are subject to a 14% rate. Salaries or wages for personal services performed within the United States are subject to regular graduated withholding rates, rather than the flat 30% rate. Certain other types of wages for services are subject to the 30% rate, while others are exempt from withholding.

A *resident* alien with dividend or interest income files Form 1078 with the withholding agent to avoid withholding.

¶37.08 • WHEN AN ALIEN LEAVES THE UNITED STATES

You must obtain a "sailing permit," technically known as a "certificate of compliance," which states that you have fulfilled your income tax obligations to the U.S. Without it, unless you are excused from obtaining one, you will be required at your point of departure to file a tax return and pay any tax due.

The sailing permit is obtained from your local District Director of Internal Revenue about two weeks, but no earlier than 30 days, before your departure. You submit all information pertaining to your income and stay in the U.S., such as passport and alien registration form, copies of U.S. tax returns for the past two years, bank records, and any profit and loss statements. You also file a Form 1040C or Form 2063.

You may avoid paying tax if you satisfactorily convince the District Director that you are returning to the United States. In other cases, you may avoid paying tax on the current year (or previous year if the filing date has not yet passed) by posting a bond for the amount of tax due.

These aliens are not required to obtain a sailing permit: Those traveling under a diplomatic passport, members of their households, and servants accompanying them; employees of foreign governments and international organizations and members of their households whose official compensation is tax exempt and who receive no other income subject to U.S. tax; certain students admitted solely on an F visa; certain industrial trainees admitted solely on an H-3 visa; and certain aliens temporarily in the U.S. who have received no U.S. taxable income, such as visitors on a B-2 visa, a C-1 visa, or similar arrangement; aliens admitted to the United States on a border-crossing identification card or for whom passports, visas, and border-crossing identification cards are not required; certain alien military trainees; and an alien resident of Canada or Mexico who frequently commutes between his country and the United States for employment purposes and whose wages are subject to withholding tax.

See IRS Publication 519 for further details.

What Happens After You File Your Return

¶38.00 • HOW THE IRS EXAMINES YOUR RETURN

Your return is first checked for arithmetic accuracy. If a mistake is found, you receive either a refund or a bill for additional tax.

Special IRS screening also spots the following errors:

1. Medical expenses without the adjusted gross income limitation.
2. Casualty and theft losses without the adjusted gross income limitation.
3. The use of auto mileage rate for business travel exceeding the allowed IRS rate.
4. Claim for household care expenses of children or disabled dependents claimed by a married person filing a separate return.
5. Dividend exclusion in excess of $100 on a separate return or $200 on a joint return.
6. Income on Form W-2 or Form 1099 incorrectly reported on tax return.
7. Fractional exemptions.

The IRS also screens returns claiming refunds from tax shelters. *See* ¶28.033.

If you make errors of this type, you will probably be advised by mail of the corrections and of additional tax due. If you disagree, you may request an interview or submit additional information. If you file early and the correction is made before April 15, 1987, interest is not charged.

If your return is selected for a more thorough review, you are notified by letter. This may not happen for a year or two.

The examination may be held at a local IRS office or at your place of business or home if your return is complex or based on many outside records. If the matter can be settled through correspondence, you may not be asked to appear in person.

You may handle the examination yourself if the issues are simple. If your return is complicated or a large amount of tax is involved, it is advisable to have an experienced tax practitioner represent you.

After the examination, the Revenue Agent may accept your return as filed. If he recommends changes that result in additional taxes and you agree, you sign Form 870. If you disagree, and the examination takes place in an IRS office, you may ask for an immediate meeting with a supervisor to argue your side of the dispute. If an agreement is not reached at this meeting or the audit is at your office or home, the agent prepares a report of his proposed adjustments. You are given the opportunity to request a conference. You may decide not to ask for a conference and await a formal notice of deficiency.

If your case began as an office audit, you do not have to prepare a written protest for a conference. If your case began as a field audit, you must file a written protest if the disputed amount exceeds $2,500. In the protest, you present your reason for disagreeing with the agent's report. At the conference, you may appear for yourself or be represented by an attorney or other agent, and you may bring witnesses.

If you cannot reach a settlement, you will receive a Notice of Deficiency, commonly called a 90-day letter. In it, you are notified that at the end of 90 days from the date it was mailed, the government will assess the additional tax.

When you receive a 90-day letter, if you are still convinced that your position is correct, you may take your case to one of three courts: You may within 90 days file a petition with the Tax Court; or you may pay the additional tax, file a refund claim for it, and after the refund claim is denied, sue for a refund in a federal district court or the U.S. Claims Court.

Generally, the decision to litigate should be considered by an experienced tax practitioner.

The Tax Court has a small tax case procedure for deficiencies of $10,000 or less. Such cases are handled expeditiously and informally. Cases may be heard by commissioners, rather than judges. A small claim case may be discontinued at any time before a decision, but the decision, when made, is final. No appeal may be taken.

TCMP audit. Your return may be selected at random for a special type of audit, a TCMP (Taxpayer Compliance Measurement Program) audit. The TCMP audit is more comprehensive than an ordinary tax examination because the IRS seeks data for setting audit guidelines for others in your tax and economic position. The IRS is protected from having to disclose the standards used in TCMP audits.

¶38.01 • AUTOMATIC DATA PROCESSING (ADP)

Computers process tax returns. They do not examine returns but facilitate examination by pinpointing returns to be examined and items to be questioned. The IRS uses an automatic formula system to select returns that indicate the "greatest audit potential." The criteria used in the automatic formula system are not made public by the IRS. However, under the Freedom of Information law, the IRS may be forced to make public the standards governing internal procedures except where the IRS determines that such disclosure would seriously impair the assessment, collection, or enforcement of the tax laws.

At regional IRS centers, data is recorded from tax returns and other documents into computers which transfer the data onto magnetic tape. The tape is sent to the National Computer Center in Martinsburg, West Virginia, for posting to the master list of taxpayers arranged by account number. Information from individual tax returns is processed. Failures to file returns, duplicate or multiple filings, and other discrepancies can be detected. Data on information returns can be matched with that reported on individual returns.

To implement ADP, you are required to put your Social Security number on your tax return (see ¶38.02). Your number also appears on information returns sent to the IRS reporting the wages, interest, dividends, royalties, etc., paid to you. Your number serves as a basis for posting and cross-referencing data to your account in the master file.

¶38.02 • SOCIAL SECURITY NUMBERS FOR TAX RETURNS

Your Social Security number must be on your tax return. It must be used on any return, statement or other document filed with the IRS, and should be noted on any check or other remittance sent to the IRS. It must also be furnished to payers of interest or dividends to avoid backup withholding. *See* ¶25.10.

Husband and wife. Your spouse needs a number if she receives dividends or interest in her own name (as distinguished from accounts in your joint names). Both your number and your spouse's number should appear on your return whether a joint or separate return is filed.

Your minor children need numbers if they receive income.

United States citizens outside the United States also need numbers.

Applying for a number. If you do not have a Social Security number, apply for one on Form SS-5 (application for Social Security number). Applications may be obtained at Social Security offices, IRS offices, and most post offices. If you lost your card and do not know your number, the Social Security Administration will send it on request.

You are also required to furnish your number to any payor who in turn must report to the government the dividends, interest or other payments made to you. The number must be given even when a tax return may not be required.

Whose Social Security number should be furnished? When a bank account is owned by two or more individuals, only one Social Security number need be furnished. As between husband and wife, give the husband's number. As between adult and minor, give the adult's number.

If the account reads "John Jones, Custodian, (Guardian or Committee) for Robert Smith, Ward (Minor or Incompetent)," give the number of the ward, minor, or incompetent.

If you are a custodian of stock for your child, give the child's number.

If the account is a valid trust, entitled "John Jones, Trustee under Trust for Robert Smith," give the trust's number.

If the account is entitled "John Jones, Trustee," without disclosing the name of the trust, give the trustee's number.

If John Jones owns stock but arranges with his broker to pay the dividends to Sarah Jones, his mother, give the number of John Jones, who is the registered owner of the stock.

If Alice Jones, a widow, and Thomas Jones, a minor, receive income from the estate of John Jones, give the numbers of both the widow and minor to the executor or administrator of the estate.

If John Jones, Howard Jones and Frank Jones support Sarah Jones, their mother, none contributing more than 50% of the support, but she is claimed by John Jones as a dependent, give the numbers of John, Howard and Frank Jones on the written declaration (Form 2120, Multiple Support Declaration) required to be filed with John Jones's tax return.

If a final income tax return is filed for a decedent, give the decedent's number. If he had no number, his representative should apply for one. In addition, an identification number must also be obtained for his estate for returns it files.

Those who do not need individual numbers are:

1. A widow drawing Social Security benefits who has no number of her own. She may use her deceased husband's number provided she was 62 or over as of January 1, 1963.

2. A nonresident alien who is not engaged in trade or business in the United States.

Penalty. You run the risk of a penalty if you fail to show your Social Security number on your return or if you do not furnish it to a payor.

¶38.03 • WHEN THE IRS CAN ASSESS ADDITIONAL TAXES

Three-year statute. The IRS has three years after the date on which your return is filed to assess additional taxes. When you file a return before the due date, however, the three-year period starts from the due date.

Where the due date of a return falls on a Saturday, Sunday, or legal holiday, the due date is postponed to the next business day.

Examples—

1. You filed your 1983 return on April 16, 1984. The last day on which the IRS can make an assessment on your 1983 return is April 16, 1987.

2. You file your 1984 return on February 4, 1985. The last day on which the IRS can make an assessment on your 1984 return is April 15, 1988.

3. You file your 1986 return on May 25, 1987. The IRS has until May 25, 1990 to assess a deficiency.

If the IRS cannot complete an audit within three years, it may request a signed agreement to an extension of time. However, where an individual was "scared" into signing such an agreement, it was held invalid.

Example—

Robertson, a plumber, won $30,000 in a sweepstakes. An IRS agent asked him to sign an extension agreement. Robertson never had any prior dealings with the IRS, did not know his return was under examination and was not in touch with the lawyer who prepared the return on which his sweepstakes winnings were averaged. Robertson wanted to see his lawyer before signing Form 872, but the agent pressed hard for the signature, phoning him and his wife at home and at work twenty times in a week. The agent did not tell him the amount of additional tax that might be involved, or explain that if he refused to sign he would have an opportunity before the IRS and the courts to contest any additional tax. Instead, the agent's comments gave him the impression that his home could be confiscated if he refused to sign. Robertson signed and the IRS later increased his tax. Robertson argued that the agreement was not valid. He signed under duress. The Tax Court agreed. He convinced the court that he really believed he could lose his house and property if he did not comply. No adequate explanation of the real consequences of refusal to sign was made, although Robertson asked. Since he signed Form 872 under duress, the IRS could not increase his tax after the three-year period.

Amended returns. If you file an amended return shortly before the three-year limitations period is about to expire and the return shows that you owe additional tax, the IRS has 60 days from the date it receives the return to assess the additional tax, even though the regular limitations period would expire before the 60-day period. This rule applies to amended returns received by the IRS after July 18, 1984.

Six-year statute. When you fail to report an item of gross income which is more than 25% of the gross income reported on your return, the IRS has six years after the return is filed to assess additional taxes.

Where a false or fraudulent return is filed with intent to evade the tax, or where no return is filed, there is no limitation on when the tax may be assessed.

¶38.04 • INTEREST ON DEFICIENCIES

Interest is charged on a deficiency at rates listed below per year. Interest begins to accrue from the due date of the return. As of January 1, 1983, interest is compounded daily except for estimated tax penalties. IRS tables on compound interest may be found in Treasury regulations. Where a taxpayer has relied on IRS assistance in preparing a return, and taxes are owed because of a mathematical or clerical error, interest does not begin to accrue until 30 days from a formal demand by the IRS for the payment of additional taxes.

Rates on amounts outstanding are:

From	To	Rate
7/1/86	12/31/86	9%
1/1/86	6/30/86	10
7/1/85	12/31/85	11
1/1/85	6/30/85	13
7/1/83	12/31/84	11
1/1/83	6/30/83	16
2/1/82	12/31/82	20
2/1/80	1/31/82	12
2/1/78	1/31/80	6
2/1/76	1/31/78	7
7/1/75	1/31/76	9

The rate beginning January 1, 1987 was not available when this book went to press; it is listed in the Supplement.

Higher rate on tax shelter deficiencies. If for any taxable year there is a deficiency of more than $1,000 attributable to a tax shelter transaction, the IRS may charge interest on that deficiency at a rate equal to 120% of the regular rate. *See* the tax legislation discussion in the front of this book for any changes to this rate. The higher rate applies to deficiencies of more than $1,000 due to: (1) disallowed losses or investment credit under the at risk rules; (2) deductions based on overvaluations of property by 150% or more; (3) tax straddles. The IRS may add other items to this list.

¶38.05 • INFORMATION RETURNS ARE IMPORTANT IRS CHECKS

The IRS matches tax returns with information returns from employers, payers of interest and dividends, brokers and others to check if income has been omitted from an individual's tax return. In 1985, the IRS questioned approximately 8 million taxpayers after finding discrepancies between their tax returns and the income reported on information returns. Here is a checklist of the information returns sent to the IRS by payers:

Employers report wage income to the IRS on Form W-2.

Dividend and interest payments of $10 or more during the calendar year are reported to the IRS on Form 1099. Each payer must furnish you by January 31, 1987, a statement showing the dividend and interest payments made in 1986.

Corporations, banks and other payers, as well as persons or firms who receive such payments for you as nominee, report annually the dividend and interest payments totaling $10 or more per person.

Dividends, for reporting purposes, include dividends paid by corporations, and "dividend equivalents" paid to you while your stock is on loan for a short sale.

Interest, for reporting purposes, includes interest on registered corporate bonds, debentures, notes and certificates; also interest on deposits with savings banks, savings and loan associations, stockbrokers and insurance companies. No returns are required for tax-free interest.

States are required to report income tax refunds of $10 or more.

Similarly, unemployment payments of $10 or more during the year are reported to the IRS on information returns, a copy of which will be furnished to unemployment benefits recipients.

Brokers are required to report to the IRS gross proceeds from sales of stocks, bonds, commodities, and regulated-futures and forward contracts. Commodity options are not covered by this reporting rule.

Information returns are required of persons who in the course of business make payments totaling $600 or more in the calendar year to persons (or partnerships) in the form of:

Compensation for personal services (including salaries, wages, commissions, professional fees) from which no tax is withheld. However, no information return is required for payments to a domestic or other household employee;

Rents (collected by real estate agent on behalf of property owner);

Royalties, pensions, annuities, and other gains and profits;

Life insurance, endowment or annuity contracts (unless payment was made by reason of insured's death or surrender or lapse of policy);

Distributions from employees' pension or annuity plan—if the total distributions plus the employee's wages equal $600 or more;

Travel or other expense allowances of employee who does not have to account to employer—if the allowance added to the employee's wages totals $600 or more;

Foreign interest or dividends collected for citizen or resident.

Payments of fees to physicians by insurance companies such as Blue Cross or by a government agency under Medicare or Medicaid;

Cooperatives must file annual information returns for patronage dividends to patrons totaling $10 or more during the calendar year. A statement showing the amount reported must be furnished to the patron by the end of January of the following year.

A partnership does not pay income taxes, but must file an annual information return (Form 1065), stating all items of income and deductions. Also included in the return are the names and addresses of all partners, and the amount of each partner's distributive share. The return is filed at the close of the partnership's tax year, whether or not it coincides with that of its partners. Failure to file the return will result in a penalty assessable against the partnership. If a partner sells or exchanges a partnership interest and payment is partly attributable to the partner's share of unrealized receivables or substantially appreciated inventory, the partnership must be notified of the transaction and the partnership must then file an information return with the IRS. The purpose of the reporting requirement is to enable the IRS to verify the income attributable to the receivables and inventory, which is taxable as ordinary income. Statements to the transferor and transferee of the partnership interest must also be provided.

Interest and dividend income information disclosed to Social Security and other agencies. To verify your eligibility for certain government benefits, agencies such as the Social Security Administration, state unemployment compensation agencies and state welfare agencies may obtain from the IRS information on the interest and dividend income shown on your tax return.

¶38.051 • REPORTING MORTGAGE INTEREST AND PROPERTY FORECLOSURES AND ABANDONMENTS

Mortgage interest. Banks, government agencies and businesses receiving mortgage interest of $600 or more for any calendar year report the interest to the IRS. The reporting requirement applies to interest on all obligations secured by real property. If you pay interest on more than one mortgage secured by the same property, the $600 floor applies separately to each obligation. Thus, interest will not be reported if the interest paid on a particular obligation is less than $600.

The lender must provide you a statement of the interest reported to the IRS for 1986 by January 31, 1987.

Foreclosures and abandonments of property. If a business or government agency lends you money and later forecloses on your property or knows that you have abandoned property secured by the loan, the lender must file a report with the IRS. A purchase of the property by a party other than the lender at a foreclosure sale is treated also as an abandonment which the lender must report to the IRS.

The reporting rule does not apply to consumer loans for personal property such as an automobile, computer or boat. However, if the lender knows that such property will be used in your business, a foreclosure or abandonment is subject to the reporting requirement.

The purpose of the reporting requirement is to help the IRS check whether you have realized income from discharge or indebtedness or gain on foreclosure, or whether you must recapture a previously claimed investment credit.

If a report to the IRS has been made, you will be sent a statement by the lender by January 31 following the year of the foreclosure or abandonment.

¶38.06 • WHAT ARE THE PENALTIES IN THE LAW?

If you are late in paying your taxes, a nondeductible monthly penalty of 0.5% (½ of 1%) is imposed on the net amount of tax due and not paid by the due date, the maximum penalty is 25% of the tax due. The penalty is in addition to the regular interest charge. A similar penalty applies for failure to pay a tax deficiency within 10 days of the date of notice and demand for payment. The penalty does not apply if you can show that the failure to pay is due to reasonable cause and not to willful neglect. The penalty does not apply to the estimated tax. Under tax legislation, the IRS may assess a 1% monthly penalty (instead of 0.5%) after you fail to pay the tax after repeated requests and the IRS notifies you that it will "levy" upon your assets to collect the tax.

If your return is filed late without reasonable cause, the IRS may impose a penalty of 5% of the net tax due for each month the return is late, with a maximum penalty of 25%. If the return is more than 60 days late, the penalty will not be less than the smaller of $100 or 100% of the tax due.

There are, in addition, penalties for willful evasion of taxes, filing false, fraudulent, or frivolous returns, willful failure to pay taxes or file the proper returns disclosing all the required information, or for willful failure to keep adequate records, file information returns or supply other data required by the IRS.

A "willful failure" generally assumes an act done without a good excuse. There must be an intent to avoid the obligation of the law. If you take an unreasonable position, or make no effort to fairly approximate your deductions, that might also be termed willful failure to observe the law. You *might* avoid penalties if you can prove that you followed the advice of reputable counsel, or you misinterpreted the law; or without request or demand, you later filed the return or you assumed your agent or employee had filed the return or paid the tax.

Overvaluation of property. If you overvalue property, such as by claiming an inflated deduction for a donation of appreciated property to charity, you may be subject to a penalty. The penalty applies if the overvaluation is 150% or more and results in an underpayment of tax of at least $1,000. It does not matter how long the property was held. For returns filed before 1985, the penalty applied only if the property was acquired within five years of the end of the year for which the overvaluation was made.

The amount of the penalty depends upon the extent of overvaluation. If the claimed overvaluation is at least 150% but not more than 200%, the penalty equals 10% of the resulting underpayment of tax. If the overvaluation is over 200% but not over 250%, the penalty is 20% of the resulting underpayment. The maximum penalty is 30% of the underpayment for overvaluations of over 250%. However, if charitable contribution property is overvalued by 150% or more on a return filed after 1984, the penalty is a flat 30% of the tax underpayment due to the overvaluation.

The IRS may generally waive the penalty upon a showing that the overvaluation was made in good faith and had a reasonable basis. However, for overvaluations of charitable contribution property on returns filed after 1984, the penalty will not be waived unless the claimed value was based on an appraisal by a qualified appraiser and, in addition, you show that you made a good faith investigation of the value.

Penalty for substantial underpayment of tax. If you understate tax liability on your return by the greater of $5,000 or 10% of the proper tax, you may be subject to a penalty. For penalty rates, see the tax legislation guide in the front of this book. The penalty may be avoided if on your return you provided the IRS with a statement of facts relating to your position, or if you can show that your position was substantially supported by statute, regulations, court decisions, or revenue rulings and procedures. However, if the understatement of tax is due to tax shelter items, you may avoid the penalty only if there is substantial authority for your position and you reasonably believed that your position was "more likely than not" correct.

This penalty does not apply to the extent that a penalty has been imposed for understating tax due to an overvaluation of property (*see* above).

Interest on certain penalties. A higher interest cost is imposed on individuals subject to the following penalties: failure to file a timely return, overvaluation of property, or substantial understatement of tax liability. Generally, for penalties imposed after July 18, 1984, interest will start to run from the due date of the return (including extensions) until the date the penalty is paid. Under prior law, interest on the penalty did not start to run until the IRS imposed the penalty.

PENALTIES FOR TAX LAW VIOLATIONS

Violation	Penalty
Unpaid tax or deficiency.	Generally .5% per month penalty (maximum 25%) and interest from the due date of tax or deficiency (*see* above).
Negligence (without intent to defraud).	5% of net amount due plus 50% of the interest due on the underpayment. For returns due (without extensions) after 1986, *see* tax legislation guide.
Attempt to depart from U.S. or conceal property.	25% of tax or deficiency plus interest.
Failure to file return within 60 days of due date plus extensions.	Minimum penalty is lesser of $100 or the taxes due (*see* above).
Bad check used to pay tax.	1% of amount of check, or, if check is under $500, the penalty is $5, or the amount of the check, whichever is less.
Fraud with intent to evade tax.	50% of the underpayment plus 50% of the interest due. For returns due (without extensions) after 1986, *see* tax legislation guide.
Willful failure to pay tax or file return.	Misdemeanor—up to $25,000 fine or one year in prison, or both.
Willful making and subscribing to false return.	Felony—up to $100,000 fine or three years in prison, or both.
Willful attempt in any manner to evade or defeat tax.	Felony—up to $100,000 fine or five years in prison, or both.
Failure to file certain information returns.	$50 for each such failure, not to exceed a total of $50,000.
Failure to file partnership return.	$50 times the number of partners for each month (or fraction of a month) not to exceed five months.
Overvaluation of property.	10% to 30% of the resulting underpayment of tax due to the overvaluation of property (*see* above).
False withholding information.	Civil penalty up to $500; criminal penalty of up to $10,000 plus up to but not more than one year in prison.
Frivolous or incomplete return.	$500, regardless of actual tax liability.
Frivolous Tax Court actions.	Up to $5,000 if taxpayer position is groundless.

¶38.08 • RECOVERING ATTORNEYS' FEES FROM THE GOVERNMENT

In a tax dispute, you may feel that the IRS has taken an unreasonable position that forced you to incur legal fees and other expenses to win your point. You may be able to recover all or part of your costs under the following rules in a civil tax case.

For cases begun on or after March 1, 1983 and before 1986, you may recover litigation expenses, including attorneys' fees, of up to $25,000 from the government. The $25,000 limit applies to attorneys' fees, fees of expert witnesses, cost of reports or studies necessary for your case, and court costs.

Whether the IRS has acted unreasonably during litigation is a factual issue which courts decide on a case by case basis. Court decisions have split on the issue of whether attorneys' fees may be awarded if the IRS concedes before trial. Some federal courts have allowed awards if the IRS conduct before trial was unreasonable. Other federal courts have held that if the IRS concedes before trial, no award is allowed even if the IRS acted unreasonably before trial.

The Tax Court has held that unreasonable IRS conduct during its administrative proceedings is not a basis for claiming a legal fee award. Only if the IRS acts unreasonably after a Tax Court petition is filed may an award be made. If the IRS concedes the case after a Tax Court petition is filed, the costs of preparing and filing the petition and later legal expenses are recoverable only if the IRS litigating position was unreasonable. The IRS position may be reasonable even though it eventually concedes the case. Expenses paid or incurred during pre-trial administrative proceedings may not be recovered. A federal appeals court disagreed with the Tax Court holding and held that unreasonable IRS conduct before litigation may support an award.

To win an award, the law requires that you "substantially prevail" in any federal court, including the Tax Court and Claims Court, prove that the IRS was unreasonable, and show that you exhausted all administrative remedies. According to proposed rules, to exhaust administrative remedies, you must ask for an Appeals Office conference before filing a refund action in court or a Tax Court petition. If the Appeals Office asks you to sign Form 872 to extend the time for assessing tax, your administrative remedies will be considered exhausted if you consent to the extension. If the IRS refuses your request for a conference, or if you file a refund claim which the IRS does not act on within six months, you are considered to have exhausted your administrative remedies. You must request an Appeals conference even though there is an IRS ruling contrary to your position and you believe a conference would be unproductive. In actions involving summonses, levies, and liens, administrative remedies will be considered exhausted if a written refund claim is filed with the District Director and it is denied or no action is taken within a reasonable period.

For cases begun after 1985. Tax legislation would allow for attorney's fees and other litigation costs if you prevail in the Tax Court or other federal court and show that you exhausted all administrative remedies. The burden of proof is then on the IRS to show that its position was substantially justified or that special circumstances would make it unfair to award you damages. An award may be based on unjustified IRS conduct during pre-trial administrative proceedings as well as on IRS conduct after litigation begins.

The maximum recovery for attorney's fees is $75 per hour, unless the court determines that a higher rate is justified. Reasonable fees for expert witnesses may not exceed the rate paid by the government for its expert witnesses. The $25,000 cap under prior law has been eliminated.

The tax legislation guide may be found in the front of this book.

¶38.09 • Income Tax Return Preparers

Who are preparers? Anyone who prepares a return or refund claim for a fee.

Where more than one person works on the return or claim, each schedule or entry is reviewed separately to determine the preparer of that schedule or item. A practitioner who gives advice directly relevant to a determination of the existence, characterization, or amount of an entry on a return is considered the preparer of that item. Regulations provide tests for determining whether a part of a return is considered substantial.

A practitioner who prepares entries on a return that affect entries on the return of another taxpayer may be considered the preparer of the other return if the entries are directly reflected on the other return and constitute a substantial portion of that return. For example, a practitioner preparing a partnership return may be considered the preparer of a partner's return if the entries picked up from the partnership return constitute a substantial portion of the partner's individual tax return.

You are not a preparer if you merely type or reproduce a return or claim or prepare a return for your employer or an officer of your employer or fellow employee.

Penalties. Preparers who understate the tax on a taxpayer's return or refund claim are subject to a $100 penalty if the understatement is due to negligence; $500 if willful. A preparer is not subject to penalty for failure to report additions to tax for an underpayment of estimated tax.

A self-employed return preparer and any person who employs people who prepare returns for others must retain a record of the name, Social Security number, and place of work of each employed preparer. The records must be kept for a three-year period following the close of the return period and the records must be made available for inspection upon request of the district director. There is a $100 penalty for each failure to keep and make available a proper record and a $5 penalty for each required item that is missing from the record. The maximum penalty for any return period is $20,000.

In lieu of the $100 or $500 per return penalty, the IRS may impose a $1,000 civil penalty for knowingly understating tax on an individual return ($10,000 on a corporate return). Only one $1,000/$10,000 civil penalty may be imposed on a preparer with respect to the same taxpayer for any taxable year, regardless of the number of returns filed on that taxpayer's behalf.

The IRS has applied the $100 negligence penalty to a preparer's failure to list interest shown on a taxpayer's 1099s which resulted in a substantial underpayment of tax. A mathematical error made in totaling interest statements was not penalized, but a penalty was applied to a preparer who incorrectly totaled the amount of itemized deductions and used the wrong tax table. Although the total understatement of tax was not substantial, the errors, taken as a whole, were considered negligence. Failure to ask a taxpayer whether he had records to support a claimed entertainment expense was penalized, but not where the preparer asked for records which the taxpayer lied that he had.

Tax preparers are subject to a $500 penalty if they endorse or negotiate a refund check issued to a taxpayer whose return they have prepared. Business managers for athletes, actors, or other professionals who prepare their clients' tax returns and handle their tax refunds may also be subject to the penalty. To avoid the penalty, the manager must act only as an agent in depositing the client's refund check.

A preparer must also meet the following requirements:

1. Furnish a completed copy of the return or claim for refund to the taxpayer not later than when it is presented for the taxpayer's signature; a $25 penalty is imposed for each failure.

2. Keep for three years and have available for inspection by the IRS a completed copy of each return or claim prepared, or a list of the names and identification numbers of taxpayers for whom returns or claims were prepared: a $50 penalty is imposed for each failure. A preparer who sells his business is not relieved of the requirement of retaining those records.

3. Sign the return and include his or her identifying number or the identifying number of his or her employer; a $25 penalty is imposed for each failure. Regulations provide that preparers must physically sign the return or refund claim; they may not use a stamped signature or signature label. However, the manual signature requirement may be satisfied by a photocopy of a manually signed copy of a return or refund claim, provided that, before it is photocopied, no one but the preparer has altered entries on the manually signed copy, except to correct arithmetical errors. The individual preparer or the employer-preparer must retain the manually signed copy, as well as a record of any corrected arithmetical errors. If unable to manually sign the return because of a temporary or permanent disability, the words "unable to sign" must be printed, typed, or stamped on the preparer's signature line, together with his name.

In addition to the penalties imposed, the IRS may also seek to enjoin fraudulent or deceptive practice or to enjoin a person from acting as an income tax return preparer. The IRS may seek an injunction against a preparer for "aiding and abetting" a taxpayer to underpay tax. The IRS publishes a list of enjoined preparers in its weekly Internal Revenue Bulletin.

For additional details regarding income tax return preparers, *see* the Professional Edition of Your Income Tax.

¶38.10 · A Guide to Estate Taxes and Planning

The estate you built up may not be entirely yours to give away. The federal government and in all probability at least one state government stand ready to claim their shares.

Do you know what will remain for your family, your favorite philanthropies, your other beneficiaries? If you do not, you cannot intelligently estimate what you can give to each. To help you make such an estimate, we offer this general guide to federal estate taxation. It will alert you to the extent of estate tax costs, and if you find that you have an estate subject to tax, to plan for estate tax savings that you may discuss with your attorney.

WHAT IS THE ESTATE TAX?

The federal estate tax is a tax on the act of transferring property at death. It is not a tax on the right of the beneficiary to receive the property; the estate and the estate alone pays the tax.

Understand what the word *estate* means in estate tax law so that you do not underestimate the value of your taxable estate. The estate includes not only your real estate (foreign and domestic), bank deposits, securities, personal property and other more obvious signs of wealth, but can also include insurance, your interest in trusts and jointly-held property, and certain interests you have in other estates.

TAKE INVENTORY

The first step in estate planning follows a simple business practice of taking inventory of everything you own.

Listing one's belongings takes thought, time, and a surprising amount of work with lists, records of purchases, fire and theft insurance inventories, bank books, brokers' statements, etc. You need to include your cash, real estate (here and abroad), securities, mortgages, rights in property, trust accounts, life insurance payable to your estate or payable to others if you have kept a certain measure of ownership, personal effects, collections and art works.

If you own property jointly with your spouse, include only one-half the value of the property.

If you have had appraisals made of unusual or specially treasured items or collections, or property of substantial value, file such appraisals with your estate papers and enter the value on your inventory.

There are some assets that you might not ordinarily consider as part of your estate. Nevertheless, include in your inventory any trust arrangements created by you in which you have (1) a life estate (the income or other use of property for life); (2) income that is to be used to pay your legal obligations (support of a child, for example; (3) the right to change the beneficiary or his interest (a power of appointment); (4) the right to revoke a trust transfer or gift; (5) a reversionary interest (possibility that the property can come back to you). Also include benefits from any of the following retirement plans which are payable to your estate: Pension plan, profit-sharing plan, Keogh plan, individual retirement account, annuity, or bonds. However, the first $100,000 of benefits payable to a beneficiary other than your estate and not payable in a lump sum *are* excluded from your estate if you were an active participant of a plan as of December 31, 1984, in pay status and before July 18, 1984, you irrevocably elected the form of your beneficiary's benefits. The exclusion does not apply to the extent of your own nondeductible contributions to the plan.

FINDING THE VALUE OF YOUR ESTATE

When you have completed your inventory, assign to each asset what you consider to be its fair market value. This may be difficult to do for some assets. Resist the tendency to overvalue articles which arouse feelings of pride or sentiment and undervalue some articles of great intrinsic worth. For purposes of your initial estimate, it is better to err on the side of overvaluation.

If you have a family business, your idea of its value and that of the IRS may vary greatly. Estate plans have been upset by the higher value placed on such a business by the IRS. You can protect your estate by anticipating and solving this problem with your business associates, accountant and legal counsel.

If your business is owned by a closely held corporation, and there is no ready or open market in which the stock can be valued, get some factual basis for a figure that will be reported on the estate tax return. One of the ways to do this is by arranging a buy-sell agreement with a potential purchaser. This agreement must fix the value of the stock. Generally, an agreement that binds both the estate and the purchaser and restricts lifetime sales of the stock will effectively fix the value of the stock for estate tax purposes. Another way would be to make a gift of some shares to a family member and have value established in gift tax proceedings. Unless there is a drastic change, the valuation thus established will have considerable weight in later estate tax proceedings.

If a substantial part of your estate is real estate used in farming or a closely held business, your executor may be able to elect, with the consent of heirs having an interest in the property, to value the property on the basis of its farming or business use, rather than its highest and best use. The special use valuation, however, may not reduce the gross estate by more than $750,000. But this may mean substantial tax savings. This savings may be recaptured from your heir if he or she stops using the property in farming or business within 10 years of your death.

You can list ordinary personal effects at nominal value.

HOW THE ESTATE TAX IS APPLIED

A single unified rate schedule applies to a decedent's estate and all his post-1976 lifetime gifts over the annual gift tax exclusion. Under the unified gift and estate tax rate, the overall tax on your property holdings is theoretically the same whether or not you make lifetime gifts. In actual cases, however, lifetime gifts may reduce the potential overall tax because of the annual gift tax exclusion.

If you make no taxable gifts during your life, calculating your estate is fairly easy. You start with the total market value of the property in the estate. This is called the gross estate. From the gross estate you subtract certain deductions. The remaining amount is your taxable estate. The unified credit is subtracted from the tax calculated on the taxable estate. Other credits, including the state death tax credit, further reduce the tax on your estate.

If you make gifts after 1976, calculating your estate tax is more complicated. The estate tax is cumulative. That is, the unified tax rate is applied to the sum of: (1) Your taxable estate at death and (2) taxable lifetime gifts made after 1976 (other than gifts included in your estate). The tax you figure on (1) and (2) is reduced by gift taxes payable on gifts made after 1976. The unified credit and other credits are then subtracted from the remaining amount.

UNIFIED TAX CREDIT

The unified tax credit is $155,800 for decedents dying in 1986. The amount of the credit is the same for gift tax and estate tax purposes. Applying it to the taxable estate, no tax would apply to estates under $500,000.

In 1987, the unified credit increases to $192,800, so that after 1986, estates up to $600,000 will be exempt from tax.

These exempt amounts assume that you did not make any taxable gifts and that the taxable estate is your gross estate less allowable deductions.

The unified tax credit replaces the $60,000 estate tax exemption and $30,000 lifetime gift tax exemption allowed prior to 1977.

Where part or all of the $30,000 lifetime gift tax exemption was used after September 8, 1976, and before January 1, 1977, the unified credit is reduced by 20% of the amount allowed as an exemption on those gifts. Thus, if you used the entire $30,000 exemption on a gift made after September 8, 1976, your unified credit is permanently reduced by $6,000 (20% of $30,000).

YOU ARE NOW READY TO ESTIMATE THE FEDERAL ESTATE TAX

Gross estate (your estimated inventory) $_____
Less:
1. Administration expenses
   (executor's commissions,
   attorney's fees, etc.;
   estimate about 5% to 10%
   of your estate) $_____
2. Debts, mortgages, liens _____
3. Funeral expenses _____
4. Marital deduction _____
5. Charitable deduction _____
Total of (1), (2), (3), (4) and (5) $_____
Your taxable estate $_____
Plus: Post-1976 taxable gifts
   (over the annual
   exclusion) $_____
Total taxable amount $_____
Tentative tax on total _____
   Less: Gift tax payable
      on post-1976 gifts $_____

   Unified credit $_____ _____

Estate tax due $_____

Example—
Assume an unmarried person, who made no taxable gifts after 1976, dies in 1986, leaving a gross estate of $600,000. Debts, administration and funeral expenses total $60,000. The decedent bequeaths $60,000 to charity.

Gross estate $600,000
Less:
   Debts, administration and funeral expenses 60,000
                                            $540,000
Less:
   Charitable deduction 60,000
Taxable estate $480,000
Tentative tax $149,000
   Less: Unified credit 155,800
Estate tax due None

Tax may be less if state tax credit not shown here is claimed.

REDUCING OR ELIMINATING A POTENTIAL ESTATE TAX

Here are general approaches to eliminating or reducing a potential estate tax: You can make direct lifetime gifts. Any appreciation on the property transferred will be removed from your estate. Furthermore, each gift, to the extent of the annual exclusion, reduces your gross estate (see ¶33.01). Life insurance can be assigned to avoid estate tax (see ¶33.10). You can provide in your will for bequests that will qualify for the marital and charitable deductions.

THE MARITAL DEDUCTION

A married person may greatly reduce or eliminate estate tax by using the marital deduction. Property passing to a spouse is generally free from estate or gift tax because of an unlimited marital deduction.

Weigh carefully the tax consequences of leaving your spouse all of your property. For maximum tax savings, you may want to reduce your taxable estate to the exemption floor (with marital deduction property). The unified credit will then eliminate tax on that amount at the time of your death. By leaving your spouse less than the maximum deductible amount, you may also reduce the tax at the time of his or her death.

To qualify for the marital deduction, the property must generally be given to the spouse outright or by other legal arrangements that are equivalent to outright ownership in law. There is an exception in the case of income interests in charitable remainder annuity or unitrusts and certain other terminable interests (QTIPs) for which the executor makes an election.

Life insurance proceeds may qualify as marital deduction property. Name your spouse unconditional beneficiary of the proceeds with unrestricted control over any unpaid proceeds. If your spouse is not given this control or general power of appointment, then proceeds remaining on your spouse's death must be payable to his or her estate. Otherwise, the insurance proceeds will not qualify for the marital deduction.

What should be done if you believe your spouse cannot manage property? You will not want to give complete and personal control. The law permits you to put the property in certain trust arrangements that are considered equivalent to complete ownership. Your attorney can explain how you can protect your spouse's interest and qualify the trust property for the marital deduction.

A FINAL WORD

You are now aware of the costs of transferring an estate and of the amount of tax that may be levied. But no estate plan is ever really final. Economic conditions and inflation constantly change values. For this reason, your plan must be reviewed periodically as changes occur in your family and business; when a birth or death occurs; when you receive a substantial increase or decrease in income; when you enter a new business venture or resign from an old one; when you sell, retire, bring new persons into business. A member of your family may no longer need any part of your estate, while others may need more. Estate or gift tax laws may be revised, or material changes may occur in the health or life expectancy of one of your beneficiaries.

A final word of caution: Estate tax planning is not a do-it-yourself activity. We suggest that you contact experienced counsel to help you.

UNIFIED GIFT AND ESTATE TAX RATES

If taxable amount is—		The tax is—		
Over	But not over	This—	Plus %	Over
$ 0	$ 10,000	$ 0	18	$ 0
10,000	20,000	1,800	20	10,000
20,000	40,000	3,800	22	20,000
40,000	60,000	8,200	24	40,000
60,000	80,000	13,000	26	60,000
80,000	100,000	18,200	28	80,000
100,000	150,000	23,800	30	100,000
150,000	250,000	38,800	32	150,000
250,000	500,000	70,800	34	250,000
500,000	750,000	155,800	37	500,000
750,000	1,000,000	248,300	39	750,000
1,000,000	1,250,000	345,800	41	1,000,000
1,250,000	1,500,000	448,300	43	1,250,000
1,500,000	2,000,000	555,800	45	1,500,000
2,000,000	2,500,000	780,800	49	2,000,000
2,500,000	3,000,000	1,025,800	53	2,500,000
3,000,000		1,290,800	55	3,000,000

Beginning in 1988 and thereafter, the top rate will drop to 50% for taxable estates over $2.5 million.

¶ 38.20 • Using a Home Computer for Tax Return Preparation and Planning

REVIEW YOUR CURRENT PRACTICES

Review the nature and number of transactions which must be recorded for tax purposes and then determine whether a computer program can reduce the time spent in assembling and organizing this data for tax planning and reporting purposes.

Appraise your current method of keeping financial records and your procedure of gathering them for tax reporting. Review your check record book; estimate the number of checks you write during the year and how many cover tax-related items. Consider the amount of time you spend at all these tasks and the degree of accuracy you maintain. After this survey, determine whether entering your data in a computer program can save you time and give you a better record for preparing your return and making tax-planning projections. Take into consideration that learning how to operate a computer program is time-consuming. Further, unless you are prepared to use a computer frequently and consistently, you may also have to spend time relearning its operating procedures each time you use the machine after a lapse of time. If you do not have many transactions during the year, your present record-keeping practice may be adequate, especially if you segregate tax-related items as they occur.

Remember, the computer is a time-saving device. Its usefulness to you is in direct proportion to the volume of work which you have for the computer to process. But a computer will not give you any more expertise than you already have. In the field of taxation, a computer program cannot make you a tax expert. Every tax program is based on the assumption that you have a working knowledge of the tax laws and how they apply to your transactions. You must also be familiar with how to fill out a tax return.

There are two important phases to tax work:

1. Keeping records of financial data and organizing the data for tax purposes.

2. Using the data for preparing a tax return and for tax planning.

Computer programs are currently available that can process data for each phase. You may decide to buy programs covering both phases, or only one.

If you already own a computer, determine your need for a program, and then shop for one that meets those needs and is compatible with *all* of your computer equipment.

If you do not have a computer but are interested in one, your decision to buy will generally be based on considerations other than taxes. Unless you are a professional tax preparer, the expense of a computer system may be too high to warrant the purchase of a system for tax purposes alone. If you plan to buy a computer for other work, such as word processing, the capacity of a computer to process tax data is a potential bonus. For whatever reason you decide to buy, do not make an investment until you first consider the programs you intend to use. If you buy a computer first, you face the possibility that the system may not have the capacity to handle the programs you need. Programs are the operating intelligence of a computer. Programs are available either on disks or tapes. Comprehensive tax programs usually require disk equipment.

SOFTWARE PROGRAMS

The following types of programs are available for tax-related work:

Tax return preparation programs. The cost of a program is directly related to the type and number of transactions the program can handle, the number of forms and schedules the program can produce and its capacity to prepare state tax returns with data entered for the federal return. Some programs also provide for "what if" tax-planning decisions. By changing figures, for example, capital gains income, the program can tell you the effect of a sale in either the current or a later taxable year.

A professional tax return program requires computer systems with large storage capacity, disk drives, and a printer which can provide copy that conforms to IRS standards. Form 1040 must be printed according to the exact format furnished by the Government Printing Office, including all the lines, boxes, cross-hatching, and notes. If you do not use preprinted forms, clear plastic overlay of an exact copy of the 1040 may be placed on the printout in a copier to produce a copy of the 1040.

In considering a program for your own use, check that it covers all the schedules you need. Further, its cost should be less than what a professional preparer would charge for doing your return.

Tax-planning programs. These are designed to help you make tax decisions with data fed into the program. They require the input of current tax data as a base. You may then project the effect of additional income, expenses or losses on your current and future tax liability. Programs can also provide depreciation schedules, the tax effect of an annuity or lump-sum retirement election, monthly mortgage payment schedules at different interest rates and the after tax cost of each loan, and the different after-tax values of taxable and tax-exempt investments. A program of this type is not as useful as a return preparation program and many of its functions may be incorporated into a spreadsheet program or performed by formulas developed on your own.

Financial record-keeping program. Keeping adequate account of tax data during the year and organizing it properly is frequently the most difficult part of tax return preparation. A financial record-keeping program can ease this burden by providing at any time a list of tax deductions and other tax data which you can use to prepare your return.

The program assumes the function of a check record book. You enter all your financial transactions, outlays and receipts into the computer, which can then process the data. For this purpose, electronic worksheet or spreadsheet programs are available. The programs can manipulate your data according to built-in formulas or those devised by you. A spreadsheet can give you reports and budgets based on current data or on "what-if" assumptions. The programs can accommodate security investment and real estate investment planning.

A spreadsheet program generally requires a system with large memory capacity.

In buying a program, make sure that it is compatible with your other programs such as a word processing program that can accept the data from the spreadsheet.

If you have substantial investment activities, a spreadsheet program can help you keep a record of your investments and provide you status reports of the performance of your holdings. Built-in formulas can give investment comparisons and projections. You can also tie your computer into an investment service with a modem device connected to your telephone. Through the modem, investment data is fed into your computer. You can get current price quotations and investment analyses, graphs and investment news.

Financial record-keeping programs coordinated with a tax program. This program combines a spreadsheet type of financial program with a tax preparation program. The data of the financial program is transferable to a compatible tax program for planning and preparation purposes. The program has an advantage over separate financial record-keeping packages: It allows the data of the financial program to be used by the tax program without the need of re-entering data, as is necessary with the use of a financial program that is not compatible with the tax program.

See the end of this book for the features of J. K. Lasser software for tax return preparation and money management.

BUYING SOFTWARE

Software programs are sold through retail and mail order firms. Begin your investigation by visiting a retail store. Present your requirements and ask for a demonstration of the suggested software. An on-the-spot view of the program will give you an insight into the scope and complexity of the program.

For operating ease, the program should provide a menu or list of directions. This feature will save you the effort of having to memorize codes for each program stage. The menu list provides you with your options and operating controls. It should also allow you to move quickly within subsections of a schedule and from one schedule to another. Transfer times vary among various software programs.

Test for how the program traps errors: By entering incorrect data, such as a number when the program requests a letter; by choosing an option that the program does not offer; by striking the "Return" key of the computer while it is operating a program.

If you find a particular program meets your expectations, you should then ask to see the manual which accompanies the program.

The manual is a key element of a software program. A poorly prepared manual may be a sign that the program itself has not been designed well; even if the program has been well designed, a poorly written manual may fail to teach you how to use the program properly.

Look for these features in the manual:

1. An introduction summarizing the main points and objectives of the program. The introduction should be clearly written and free of technical jargon.

2. An explanation of how to start the program.

3. Sample screen displays and printouts. These will give you a visual view of what the program produces as final copy.

4. A summary of each command.

5. A technical explanation of the program for users who have the technical know-how to modify the program.

6. Troubleshooting section which explains how to diagnose and solve problems. There should be a list of error messages and an explanation of how to recover the program when an error has been made.

7. Index to the subjects and sections of the manual explaining the program.

Before buying a program, especially if it is costly, ask whether the company provides a hotline for answering consumer queries. The company should provide a telephone number which you can use for help. Also inquire how the company upgrades and corrects errors in its programs. Updates are vital. A tax program must reflect the latest tax law changes and tax return forms and schedules. Changes must be supplied promptly. If you are investing in a costly tax preparation program, you should check whether the program is updated for changes or requires the purchase of a new program package. If the entire package is revised, make certain that data from the prior package may be used by the new program package without the need of re-entering data from the prior package.

DESIGNING YOUR OWN PROGRAMS

To use a computer, you must have a grasp of computer language. There are several computer languages, of which BASIC is designed for and widely used by laymen. It is not difficult to learn, and its principles may be mastered within several hours. Once you are familiar with BASIC, you can design programs that allow you to figure any tax liability, provide depreciation sched-

ules and interest calculations for investment decisions. Many programs in BASIC for financial analysis are illustrated in popular computer books and magazines.

WRITING OFF THE COST OF YOUR COMPUTER IN 1986

Computer placed in service in 1986. If you are an employee, you may claim ACRS (five-year life) and/or first-year expensing and the investment credit (if available in 1986) only if the computer was required for your job. In addition, the unit must be used more than 50% of the time for business. The more than 50% test also applies to self-employed persons. If the computer is not used more than 50% for business, ACRS, first-year expensing and the investment credit may not be claimed; you claim straight line depreciation over a 12-year period. The more than 50% test does not apply to computers used exclusively in a business establishment. A home office qualifying under the rules of ¶5.10 is treated as a business establishment.

Merely getting an employer letter stating that a computer is needed for a position does not meet the terms of the law. Even where the employer encourages use of a computer that is used for basic job requirements, a deduction may not be allowed.

Examples—

1. An electric company offers to help pay for its engineers' personal computers where they will improve productivity. Qualifying engineers receive extra pay and must buy a computer meeting company specifications, take approved computer courses, and agree to restrictions on resale of the computer. An engineer buys a computer, uses it 95% of the time for writing business memos and reports and studying business flow charts. He does not use the computer for entertainment.

2. A professor of nursing, trying to keep her temporary position, buys a personal computer, needing a word processor for independent research papers and to document her qualifications for research grants. The research and external grant support were implied University requirements for faculty appointment. She did not have access to University word-processing equipment during regular work hours and because of her classroom responsibilities, her research and grant development work had to be done on her own time. To help her pursue outside grants, the University bought her a "modem" that allowed a phone hookup with its computer system at night. The computer was used 100% for her research and grant work.

The IRS disallows depreciation and investment credit writeoffs in both examples. According to the IRS, the computer use by the engineer and the professor, although work-related and benefiting their employers, was not "inextricably related" to proper job performance. In each case, there was no evidence that employees who did not use computers were professionally disadvantaged. As for the engineer, his participation in the computer program was optional, not mandatory.

Investors who use home computers for managing portfolios must use a 12-year useful life, unless the computer is *also* used for more than 50% of the time for business. Further, they may not claim the investment credit and first-year expensing. Business and investment uses are combined for determining the allowable part of deductible depreciation.

Examples—

1. In 1986 Jane buys a computer; she uses it 50% of the time to manage her investment and 40% in a part-time research business. The business-use test is not met for claiming the investment credit and ACRS deduction. She may use straight line depreciation of which 90% is deductible.

2. Assume that Jane used the computer 60% of the time for business and 30% for investment. As business use exceeds 50%, she may claim the investment tax credit and ACRS; and the allowable deductible percentage for these items is 90%.

When you buy a computer with software and the cost of software is not separately stated, the cost of the software may be added to the cost of the computer for figuring ACRS or regular depreciation. Software which may be used for only one year, such as a program for preparing your 1986 return, may be deducted in full if purchased in 1986.

1986 Tax Table**

Based on Taxable Income
For persons with taxable incomes of less than $50,000.

Your zero bracket amount has been built into the Tax Table.

Example: Mr. and Mrs. Brown are filing a joint return. Their taxable income is $25,325. First, they find the $25,300-25,350 income line. Next, they find the column for married filing jointly and read down the column. The amount shown where the income line and filing status column meet is $3,470. This is the tax amount.

At least	But less than	Single	Married filing jointly *	Married filing separately	Head of a household
			Your tax is —		
25,200	25,250	4,406	3,448	5,468	4,075
25,250	25,300	4,419	3,459	5,487	4,087
25,300	25,350	4,432	(3,470)	5,506	4,099
25,350	25,400	4,446	3,481	5,525	4,112

If taxable income is — At least	But less than	Single	Married filing jointly *	Married filing separately	Head of house-hold
			Your tax is—		
$0	$1,850	$0	$0	$0	$0
1,850	1,875	0	0	3	0
1,875	1,900	0	0	6	0
1,900	1,925	0	0	9	0
1,925	1,950	0	0	11	0
1,950	1,975	0	0	14	0
1,975	2,000	0	0	17	0
2,000					
2,000	2,025	0	0	20	0
2,025	2,050	0	0	22	0
2,050	2,075	0	0	25	0
2,075	2,100	0	0	28	0
2,100	2,125	0	0	31	0
2,125	2,150	0	0	33	0
2,150	2,175	0	0	36	0
2,175	2,200	0	0	39	0
2,200	2,225	0	0	42	0
2,225	2,250	0	0	44	0
2,250	2,275	0	0	47	0
2,275	2,300	0	0	50	0
2,300	2,325	0	0	53	0
2,325	2,350	0	0	55	0
2,350	2,375	0	0	58	0
2,375	2,400	0	0	61	0

If taxable income is — At least	But less than	Single	Married filing jointly *	Married filing separately	Head of house-hold
			Your tax is—		
2,400	2,425	0	0	64	0
2,425	2,450	0	0	66	0
2,450	2,475	0	0	69	0
2,475	2,500	a1	0	72	a1
2,500	2,525	4	0	75	4
2,525	2,550	6	0	77	6
2,550	2,575	9	0	80	9
2,575	2,600	12	0	83	12
2,600	2,625	15	0	86	15
2,625	2,650	17	0	88	17
2,650	2,675	20	0	91	20
2,675	2,700	23	0	94	23
2,700	2,725	26	0	97	26
2,725	2,750	28	0	99	28
2,750	2,775	31	0	102	31
2,775	2,800	34	0	105	34
2,800	2,825	37	0	108	37
2,825	2,850	39	0	110	39
2,850	2,875	42	0	113	42
2,875	2,900	45	0	116	45
2,900	2,925	48	0	119	48
2,925	2,950	50	0	121	50
2,950	2,975	53	0	124	53
2,975	3,000	56	0	127	56
3,000					
3,000	3,050	60	0	131	60
3,050	3,100	65	0	137	65
3,100	3,150	71	0	143	71
3,150	3,200	76	0	149	76
3,200	3,250	82	0	155	82
3,250	3,300	87	0	161	87
3,300	3,350	93	0	167	93
3,350	3,400	98	0	173	98

If taxable income is — At least	But less than	Single	Married filing jointly *	Married filing separately	Head of house-hold
			Your tax is—		
3,400	3,450	104	0	179	104
3,450	3,500	109	0	185	109
3,500	3,550	115	0	191	115
3,550	3,600	120	0	197	120
3,600	3,650	126	0	203	126
3,650	3,700	132	b1	209	131
3,700	3,750	138	6	215	137
3,750	3,800	144	12	221	142
3,800	3,850	150	17	227	148
3,850	3,900	156	23	233	153
3,900	3,950	162	28	239	159
3,950	4,000	168	34	245	164
4,000					
4,000	4,050	174	39	251	170
4,050	4,100	180	45	257	175
4,100	4,150	186	50	264	181
4,150	4,200	192	56	271	186
4,200	4,250	198	61	278	192
4,250	4,300	204	67	285	197
4,300	4,350	210	72	292	203
4,350	4,400	216	78	299	208
4,400	4,450	222	83	306	214
4,450	4,500	228	89	313	219
4,500	4,550	234	94	320	225
4,550	4,600	240	100	327	230
4,600	4,650	246	105	334	236
4,650	4,700	252	111	341	241
4,700	4,750	258	116	348	247
4,750	4,800	264	122	355	253
4,800	4,850	271	127	362	259
4,850	4,900	278	133	369	265
4,900	4,950	285	138	376	271
4,950	5,000	292	144	383	277

*This column must also be used by a qualifying widow(er).

Continued on next page

a If your taxable income is exactly $2,480 or less, your tax is zero.

b If your taxable income is exactly $3,670 or less, your tax is zero.

**This table is based on an IRS proof sheet as of August 15, 1986 and is subject to change.

1986 Tax Tables (Continued)**

5,000 – 7,950

At least	But less than	Single	Married filing jointly*	Married filing separately	Head of household
5,000	5,050	299	149	390	283
5,050	5,100	306	155	397	289
5,100	5,150	313	160	404	295
5,150	5,200	320	166	411	301
5,200	5,250	327	171	418	307
5,250	5,300	334	177	425	313
5,300	5,350	341	182	432	319
5,350	5,400	348	188	439	325
5,400	5,450	355	193	446	331
5,450	5,500	362	199	453	337
5,500	5,550	369	204	460	343
5,550	5,600	376	210	467	349
5,600	5,650	383	215	474	355
5,650	5,700	390	221	481	361
5,700	5,750	397	226	488	367
5,750	5,800	404	232	495	373
5,800	5,850	411	237	502	379
5,850	5,900	418	243	509	385
5,900	5,950	425	248	516	391
5,950	6,000	432	254	523	397
6,000	6,050	439	260	530	403
6,050	6,100	446	266	537	409
6,100	6,150	453	272	544	415
6,150	6,200	460	278	551	421
6,200	6,250	467	284	558	427
6,250	6,300	474	290	565	433
6,300	6,350	481	296	572	439
6,350	6,400	488	302	579	445
6,400	6,450	495	308	586	451
6,450	6,500	502	314	594	457
6,500	6,550	509	320	602	463
6,550	6,600	516	326	610	469
6,600	6,650	523	332	618	475
6,650	6,700	530	338	626	481
6,700	6,750	537	344	634	487
6,750	6,800	544	350	642	493
6,800	6,850	551	356	650	499
6,850	6,900	558	362	658	505
6,900	6,950	565	368	666	511
6,950	7,000	572	374	674	517
7,000	7,050	579	380	682	523
7,050	7,100	587	386	690	530
7,100	7,150	594	392	698	537
7,150	7,200	602	398	706	544
7,200	7,250	609	404	714	551
7,250	7,300	617	410	722	558
7,300	7,350	624	416	730	565
7,350	7,400	632	422	738	572
7,400	7,450	639	428	746	579
7,450	7,500	647	434	754	586
7,500	7,550	654	440	762	593
7,550	7,600	662	446	770	600
7,600	7,650	669	452	778	607
7,650	7,700	677	458	786	614
7,700	7,750	684	464	794	621
7,750	7,800	692	470	802	628
7,800	7,850	699	476	810	635
7,850	7,900	707	482	818	642
7,900	7,950	714	488	826	649
7,950	8,000	722	494	834	656

8,000 – 10,950

At least	But less than	Single	Married filing jointly*	Married filing separately	Head of household
8,000	8,050	729	500	842	663
8,050	8,100	737	506	850	670
8,100	8,150	744	512	858	677
8,150	8,200	752	518	866	684
8,200	8,250	759	524	874	691
8,250	8,300	767	531	882	698
8,300	8,350	774	538	890	705
8,350	8,400	782	545	898	712
8,400	8,450	789	552	906	719
8,450	8,500	797	559	914	726
8,500	8,550	804	566	922	733
8,550	8,600	812	573	930	740
8,600	8,650	819	580	938	747
8,650	8,700	827	587	947	754
8,700	8,750	834	594	956	761
8,750	8,800	842	601	965	768
8,800	8,850	849	608	974	775
8,850	8,900	857	615	983	782
8,900	8,950	864	622	992	789
8,950	9,000	872	629	1,001	796
9,000	9,050	879	636	1,010	803
9,050	9,100	887	643	1,019	810
9,100	9,150	894	650	1,028	817
9,150	9,200	902	657	1,037	824
9,200	9,250	910	664	1,046	831
9,250	9,300	918	671	1,055	838
9,300	9,350	926	678	1,064	845
9,350	9,400	934	685	1,073	852
9,400	9,450	942	692	1,082	860
9,450	9,500	950	699	1,091	869
9,500	9,550	958	706	1,100	877
9,550	9,600	966	713	1,109	886
9,600	9,650	974	720	1,118	894
9,650	9,700	982	727	1,127	903
9,700	9,750	990	734	1,136	911
9,750	9,800	998	741	1,145	920
9,800	9,850	1,006	748	1,154	928
9,850	9,900	1,014	755	1,163	937
9,900	9,950	1,022	762	1,172	945
9,950	10,000	1,030	769	1,181	953
10,000	10,050	1,038	776	1,190	962
10,050	10,100	1,046	783	1,199	971
10,100	10,150	1,054	790	1,208	979
10,150	10,200	1,062	797	1,217	988
10,200	10,250	1,070	804	1,226	996
10,250	10,300	1,078	811	1,235	1,005
10,300	10,350	1,086	818	1,244	1,013
10,350	10,400	1,094	825	1,253	1,022
10,400	10,450	1,102	832	1,262	1,030
10,450	10,500	1,110	839	1,271	1,039
10,500	10,550	1,118	846	1,280	1,047
10,550	10,600	1,126	853	1,289	1,056
10,600	10,650	1,134	860	1,298	1,064
10,650	10,700	1,142	867	1,307	1,073
10,700	10,750	1,150	874	1,316	1,081
10,750	10,800	1,158	881	1,325	1,090
10,800	10,850	1,166	888	1,334	1,098
10,850	10,900	1,174	895	1,343	1,107
10,900	10,950	1,182	902	1,353	1,115
10,950	11,000	1,190	909	1,364	1,124

11,000 – 13,950

At least	But less than	Single	Married filing jointly*	Married filing separately	Head of household
11,000	11,050	1,198	916	1,375	1,132
11,050	11,100	1,206	923	1,386	1,141
11,100	11,150	1,214	930	1,397	1,149
11,150	11,200	1,222	937	1,408	1,158
11,200	11,250	1,230	944	1,419	1,166
11,250	11,300	1,238	951	1,430	1,175
11,300	11,350	1,246	958	1,441	1,183
11,350	11,400	1,254	965	1,452	1,192
11,400	11,450	1,262	972	1,463	1,200
11,450	11,500	1,270	979	1,474	1,209
11,500	11,550	1,278	986	1,485	1,217
11,550	11,600	1,286	993	1,496	1,226
11,600	11,650	1,294	1,000	1,507	1,234
11,650	11,700	1,302	1,007	1,518	1,243
11,700	11,750	1,311	1,014	1,529	1,251
11,750	11,800	1,320	1,021	1,540	1,260
11,800	11,850	1,329	1,028	1,551	1,268
11,850	11,900	1,338	1,035	1,562	1,277
11,900	11,950	1,347	1,042	1,573	1,285
11,950	12,000	1,356	1,049	1,584	1,294
12,000	12,050	1,365	1,056	1,595	1,302
12,050	12,100	1,374	1,063	1,606	1,311
12,100	12,150	1,383	1,070	1,617	1,319
12,150	12,200	1,392	1,077	1,628	1,328
12,200	12,250	1,401	1,084	1,639	1,336
12,250	12,300	1,410	1,091	1,650	1,345
12,300	12,350	1,419	1,098	1,661	1,353
12,350	12,400	1,428	1,105	1,672	1,362
12,400	12,450	1,437	1,112	1,683	1,370
12,450	12,500	1,446	1,119	1,694	1,379
12,500	12,550	1,455	1,126	1,705	1,387
12,550	12,600	1,464	1,133	1,716	1,396
12,600	12,650	1,473	1,140	1,727	1,404
12,650	12,700	1,482	1,147	1,738	1,413
12,700	12,750	1,491	1,154	1,749	1,421
12,750	12,800	1,500	1,161	1,760	1,430
12,800	12,850	1,509	1,168	1,771	1,439
12,850	12,900	1,518	1,176	1,782	1,448
12,900	12,950	1,527	1,184	1,793	1,457
12,950	13,000	1,536	1,192	1,804	1,466
13,000	13,050	1,545	1,200	1,815	1,475
13,050	13,100	1,554	1,208	1,826	1,484
13,100	13,150	1,563	1,216	1,837	1,493
13,150	13,200	1,572	1,224	1,848	1,502
13,200	13,250	1,581	1,232	1,859	1,511
13,250	13,300	1,590	1,240	1,870	1,520
13,300	13,350	1,599	1,248	1,882	1,529
13,350	13,400	1,608	1,256	1,895	1,538
13,400	13,450	1,617	1,264	1,907	1,547
13,450	13,500	1,626	1,272	1,920	1,556
13,500	13,550	1,635	1,280	1,932	1,565
13,550	13,600	1,644	1,288	1,945	1,574
13,600	13,650	1,653	1,296	1,957	1,583
13,650	13,700	1,662	1,304	1,970	1,592
13,700	13,750	1,671	1,312	1,982	1,601
13,750	13,800	1,680	1,320	1,995	1,610
13,800	13,850	1,689	1,328	2,007	1,619
13,850	13,900	1,698	1,336	2,020	1,628
13,900	13,950	1,707	1,344	2,032	1,637
13,950	14,000	1,717	1,352	2,045	1,646

*This column must also be used by a qualifying widow(er).

Continued on next page

**This table is based on an IRS proof sheet as of August 15, 1986 and is subject to change.

1986 Tax Tables (Continued)**

14,000 / 15,000 / 16,000

At least	But less than	Single	Married filing jointly *	Married filing separately	Head of household
14,000	14,050	1,727	1,360	2,057	1,655
14,050	14,100	1,737	1,368	2,070	1,664
14,100	14,150	1,747	1,376	2,082	1,673
14,150	14,200	1,757	1,384	2,095	1,682
14,200	14,250	1,767	1,392	2,107	1,691
14,250	14,300	1,777	1,400	2,120	1,700
14,300	14,350	1,787	1,408	2,132	1,709
14,350	14,400	1,797	1,416	2,145	1,718
14,400	14,450	1,807	1,424	2,157	1,727
14,450	14,500	1,817	1,432	2,170	1,736
14,500	14,550	1,827	1,440	2,182	1,745
14,550	14,600	1,837	1,448	2,195	1,754
14,600	14,650	1,847	1,456	2,207	1,763
14,650	14,700	1,857	1,464	2,220	1,772
14,700	14,750	1,867	1,472	2,232	1,781
14,750	14,800	1,877	1,480	2,245	1,790
14,800	14,850	1,887	1,488	2,257	1,799
14,850	14,900	1,897	1,496	2,270	1,808
14,900	14,950	1,907	1,504	2,282	1,817
14,950	15,000	1,917	1,512	2,295	1,826
15,000	15,050	1,927	1,520	2,307	1,835
15,050	15,100	1,937	1,528	2,320	1,844
15,100	15,150	1,947	1,536	2,332	1,853
15,150	15,200	1,957	1,544	2,345	1,862
15,200	15,250	1,967	1,552	2,357	1,871
15,250	15,300	1,977	1,560	2,370	1,880
15,300	15,350	1,987	1,568	2,382	1,889
15,350	15,400	1,997	1,576	2,395	1,898
15,400	15,450	2,007	1,584	2,407	1,907
15,450	15,500	2,017	1,592	2,420	1,916
15,500	15,550	2,027	1,600	2,432	1,925
15,550	15,600	2,037	1,608	2,445	1,934
15,600	15,650	2,047	1,616	2,457	1,943
15,650	15,700	2,057	1,624	2,470	1,952
15,700	15,750	2,067	1,632	2,482	1,961
15,750	15,800	2,077	1,640	2,495	1,970
15,800	15,850	2,087	1,648	2,507	1,979
15,850	15,900	2,097	1,656	2,520	1,988
15,900	15,950	2,107	1,664	2,532	1,997
15,950	16,000	2,117	1,672	2,545	2,006
16,000	16,050	2,127	1,680	2,557	2,015
16,050	16,100	2,137	1,688	2,570	2,024
16,100	16,150	2,147	1,696	2,582	2,033
16,150	16,200	2,157	1,704	2,596	2,042
16,200	16,250	2,168	1,712	2,610	2,052
16,250	16,300	2,180	1,720	2,624	2,062
16,300	16,350	2,191	1,728	2,638	2,072
16,350	16,400	2,203	1,736	2,652	2,082
16,400	16,450	2,214	1,744	2,666	2,092
16,450	16,500	2,226	1,752	2,680	2,102
16,500	16,550	2,237	1,760	2,694	2,112
16,550	16,600	2,249	1,768	2,708	2,122
16,600	16,650	2,260	1,776	2,722	2,132
16,650	16,700	2,272	1,784	2,736	2,142
16,700	16,750	2,283	1,792	2,750	2,152
16,750	16,800	2,295	1,800	2,764	2,162
16,800	16,850	2,306	1,808	2,778	2,172
16,850	16,900	2,318	1,816	2,792	2,182
16,900	16,950	2,329	1,824	2,806	2,192
16,950	17,000	2,341	1,832	2,820	2,202

17,000 / 18,000 / 19,000

At least	But less than	Single	Married filing jointly *	Married filing separately	Head of household
17,000	17,050	2,352	1,840	2,834	2,212
17,050	17,100	2,364	1,848	2,848	2,222
17,100	17,150	2,375	1,856	2,862	2,232
17,150	17,200	2,387	1,864	2,876	2,242
17,200	17,250	2,398	1,872	2,890	2,252
17,250	17,300	2,410	1,880	2,904	2,262
17,300	17,350	2,421	1,889	2,918	2,272
17,350	17,400	2,433	1,898	2,932	2,282
17,400	17,450	2,444	1,907	2,946	2,292
17,450	17,500	2,456	1,916	2,960	2,302
17,500	17,550	2,467	1,925	2,974	2,312
17,550	17,600	2,479	1,934	2,988	2,322
17,600	17,650	2,490	1,943	3,002	2,332
17,650	17,700	2,502	1,952	3,016	2,342
17,700	17,750	2,513	1,961	3,030	2,352
17,750	17,800	2,525	1,970	3,044	2,362
17,800	17,850	2,536	1,979	3,058	2,372
17,850	17,900	2,548	1,988	3,072	2,382
17,900	17,950	2,559	1,997	3,086	2,392
17,950	18,000	2,571	2,006	3,100	2,402
18,000	18,050	2,582	2,015	3,114	2,412
18,050	18,100	2,594	2,024	3,128	2,422
18,100	18,150	2,605	2,033	3,142	2,432
18,150	18,200	2,617	2,042	3,156	2,442
18,200	18,250	2,628	2,051	3,170	2,452
18,250	18,300	2,640	2,060	3,184	2,462
18,300	18,350	2,651	2,069	3,198	2,472
18,350	18,400	2,663	2,078	3,212	2,482
18,400	18,450	2,674	2,087	3,226	2,492
18,450	18,500	2,686	2,096	3,240	2,502
18,500	18,550	2,697	2,105	3,254	2,512
18,550	18,600	2,709	2,114	3,268	2,522
18,600	18,650	2,720	2,123	3,282	2,532
18,650	18,700	2,732	2,132	3,296	2,542
18,700	18,750	2,743	2,141	3,310	2,552
18,750	18,800	2,755	2,150	3,324	2,562
18,800	18,850	2,766	2,159	3,338	2,572
18,850	18,900	2,778	2,168	3,352	2,582
18,900	18,950	2,789	2,177	3,366	2,592
18,950	19,000	2,801	2,186	3,380	2,602
19,000	19,050	2,812	2,195	3,396	2,612
19,050	19,100	2,824	2,204	3,412	2,622
19,100	19,150	2,835	2,213	3,429	2,632
19,150	19,200	2,847	2,222	3,445	2,642
19,200	19,250	2,858	2,231	3,462	2,652
19,250	19,300	2,870	2,240	3,478	2,662
19,300	19,350	2,881	2,249	3,495	2,672
19,350	19,400	2,893	2,258	3,511	2,682
19,400	19,450	2,904	2,267	3,528	2,692
19,450	19,500	2,916	2,276	3,544	2,702
19,500	19,550	2,927	2,285	3,561	2,712
19,550	19,600	2,939	2,294	3,577	2,722
19,600	19,650	2,950	2,303	3,594	2,732
19,650	19,700	2,963	2,312	3,610	2,743
19,700	19,750	2,976	2,321	3,627	2,755
19,750	19,800	2,989	2,330	3,643	2,767
19,800	19,850	3,002	2,339	3,660	2,779
19,850	19,900	3,015	2,348	3,676	2,791
19,900	19,950	3,028	2,357	3,693	2,803
19,950	20,000	3,041	2,366	3,709	2,815

20,000 / 21,000 / 22,000

At least	But less than	Single	Married filing jointly *	Married filing separately	Head of household
20,000	20,050	3,054	2,375	3,726	2,827
20,050	20,100	3,067	2,384	3,742	2,839
20,100	20,150	3,080	2,393	3,759	2,851
20,150	20,200	3,093	2,402	3,775	2,863
20,200	20,250	3,106	2,411	3,792	2,875
20,250	20,300	3,119	2,420	3,808	2,887
20,300	20,350	3,132	2,429	3,825	2,899
20,350	20,400	3,145	2,438	3,841	2,911
20,400	20,450	3,158	2,447	3,858	2,923
20,450	20,500	3,171	2,456	3,874	2,935
20,500	20,550	3,184	2,465	3,891	2,947
20,550	20,600	3,197	2,474	3,907	2,959
20,600	20,650	3,210	2,483	3,924	2,971
20,650	20,700	3,223	2,492	3,940	2,983
20,700	20,750	3,236	2,501	3,957	2,995
20,750	20,800	3,249	2,510	3,973	3,007
20,800	20,850	3,262	2,519	3,990	3,019
20,850	20,900	3,275	2,528	4,006	3,031
20,900	20,950	3,288	2,537	4,023	3,043
20,950	21,000	3,301	2,546	4,039	3,055
21,000	21,050	3,314	2,555	4,056	3,067
21,050	21,100	3,327	2,564	4,072	3,079
21,100	21,150	3,340	2,573	4,089	3,091
21,150	21,200	3,353	2,582	4,105	3,103
21,200	21,250	3,366	2,591	4,122	3,115
21,250	21,300	3,379	2,600	4,138	3,127
21,300	21,350	3,392	2,609	4,155	3,139
21,350	21,400	3,405	2,618	4,171	3,151
21,400	21,450	3,418	2,627	4,188	3,163
21,450	21,500	3,431	2,636	4,204	3,175
21,500	21,550	3,444	2,645	4,221	3,187
21,550	21,600	3,457	2,654	4,237	3,199
21,600	21,650	3,470	2,663	4,254	3,211
21,650	21,700	3,483	2,672	4,270	3,223
21,700	21,750	3,496	2,681	4,287	3,235
21,750	21,800	3,509	2,690	4,303	3,247
21,800	21,850	3,522	2,700	4,320	3,259
21,850	21,900	3,535	2,711	4,336	3,271
21,900	21,950	3,548	2,722	4,353	3,283
21,950	22,000	3,561	2,733	4,369	3,295
22,000	22,050	3,574	2,744	4,386	3,307
22,050	22,100	3,587	2,755	4,402	3,319
22,100	22,150	3,600	2,766	4,419	3,331
22,150	22,200	3,613	2,777	4,435	3,343
22,200	22,250	3,626	2,788	4,452	3,355
22,250	22,300	3,639	2,799	4,468	3,367
22,300	22,350	3,652	2,810	4,485	3,379
22,350	22,400	3,665	2,821	4,501	3,391
22,400	22,450	3,678	2,832	4,518	3,403
22,450	22,500	3,691	2,843	4,534	3,415
22,500	22,550	3,704	2,854	4,551	3,427
22,550	22,600	3,717	2,865	4,567	3,439
22,600	22,650	3,730	2,876	4,584	3,451
22,650	22,700	3,743	2,887	4,600	3,463
22,700	22,750	3,756	2,898	4,617	3,475
22,750	22,800	3,769	2,909	4,633	3,487
22,800	22,850	3,782	2,920	4,650	3,499
22,850	22,900	3,795	2,931	4,666	3,511
22,900	22,950	3,808	2,942	4,683	3,523
22,950	23,000	3,821	2,953	4,699	3,535

*This column must also be used by a qualifying widow(er).

Continued on next page

**This table is based on an IRS proof sheet as of August 15, 1986 and is subject to change.

1986 Tax Tables *(Continued)***

If taxable income is —		And you are —				If taxable income is —		And you are —				If taxable income is —		And you are —			
At least	But less than	Single	Married filing jointly *	Married filing separately	Head of household	At least	But less than	Single	Married filing jointly *	Married filing separately	Head of household	At least	But less than	Single	Married filing jointly *	Married filing separately	Head of household
		Your tax is—						Your tax is—						Your tax is—			
23,000						**26,000**						**29,000**					
23,000	23,050	3,834	2,964	4,716	3,547	26,000	26,050	4,641	3,624	5,772	4,294	29,000	29,050	5,541	4,358	6,912	5,134
23,050	23,100	3,847	2,975	4,732	3,559	26,050	26,100	4,656	3,635	5,791	4,308	29,050	29,100	5,556	4,371	6,931	5,148
23,100	23,150	3,860	2,986	4,749	3,571	26,100	26,150	4,671	3,646	5,810	4,322	29,100	29,150	5,571	4,383	6,950	5,162
23,150	23,200	3,873	2,997	4,765	3,583	26,150	26,200	4,686	3,657	5,829	4,336	29,150	29,200	5,586	4,396	6,969	5,176
23,200	23,250	3,886	3,008	4,782	3,595	26,200	26,250	4,701	3,668	5,848	4,350	29,200	29,250	5,601	4,408	6,988	5 190
23,250	23,300	3,899	3,019	4,798	3,607	26,250	26,300	4,716	3,679	5,867	4,364	29,250	29,300	5,616	4,421	7,007	5,204
23,300	23,350	3,912	3,030	4,815	3,619	26,300	26,350	4,731	3,690	5,886	4,378	29,300	29,350	5,631	4,433	7,026	5,218
23,350	23,400	3,925	3,041	4,831	3,631	26,350	26,400	4,746	3,701	5,905	4,392	29,350	29,400	5,646	4,446	7,045	5,232
23,400	23,450	3,938	3,052	4,848	3,643	26,400	26,450	4,761	3,712	5,924	4,406	29,400	29,450	5,661	4,458	7,064	5,246
23,450	23,500	3,951	3,063	4,864	3,655	26,450	26,500	4,776	3,723	5,943	4,420	29,450	29,500	5,676	4,471	7,083	5,260
23,500	23,550	3,964	3,074	4,881	3,667	26,500	25,550	4,791	3,734	5,962	4,434	29,500	29,550	5,691	4,483	7,102	5,274
23,550	23,600	3,977	3,085	4,897	3,679	26,550	26,600	4,806	3,746	5,981	4,448	29,550	29,600	5,706	4,496	7,121	5,288
23,600	23,650	3,990	3,096	4,914	3,691	26,600	26,650	4,821	3,758	6,000	4,462	29,600	29,650	5,721	4,508	7,140	5,302
23,650	23,700	4,003	3,107	4,930	3,703	26,650	26,700	4,836	3,771	6,019	4,476	29,650	29,700	5,736	4,521	7,159	5,316
23,700	23,750	4,016	3,118	4,947	3,715	26,700	26,750	4,851	3,783	6,038	4,490	29,700	29,750	5,751	4,533	7,178	5,330
23,750	23,800	4,029	3,129	4,963	3,727	26,750	26,800	4,866	3,796	6,057	4,504	29,750	29,800	5,766	4,546	7,197	5,344
23,800	23,850	4,042	3,140	4,980	3,739	26,800	26,850	4,881	3,808	6,076	4,518	29,800	29,850	5,781	4,558	7,216	5,358
23,850	23,900	4,055	3,151	4,996	3,751	26,850	26,900	4,896	3,821	6,095	4,532	29,850	29,900	5,796	4,571	7,235	5,372
23,900	23,950	4,068	3,162	5,013	3,763	26,900	26,950	4,911	3,833	6,114	4,546	29,900	29,950	5,811	4,583	7,254	5,386
23,950	24,000	4,081	3,173	5,029	3,775	26,950	27,000	4,926	3,846	6,133	4,560	29,950	30,000	5,826	4,596	7,273	5,400
24,000						**27,000**						**30,000**					
24,000	24,050	4,094	3,184	5,046	3,787	27,000	27,050	4,941	3,858	6,152	4,574	30,000	30,050	5,841	4,608	7,292	5,414
24,050	24,100	4,107	3,195	5,062	3,799	27,050	27,100	4,956	3,871	6,171	4,588	30,050	30,100	5,856	4,621	7,311	5,428
24,100	24,150	4,120	3,206	5,079	3,811	27,100	27,150	4,971	3,883	6,190	4,602	30,100	30,150	5,871	4,633	7,330	5,442
24,150	24,200	4,133	3,217	5,095	3,823	27,150	27,200	4,986	3,896	6,209	4,616	30,150	30,200	5,886	4,646	7,349	5,456
24,200	24,250	4,146	3,228	5,112	3,835	27,200	27,250	5,001	3,908	6,228	4,630	30,200	30,250	5,901	4,658	7,368	5,470
24,250	24,300	4,159	3,239	5,128	3,847	27,250	27,300	5,016	3,921	6,247	4,644	30,250	30,300	5,916	4,671	7,387	5,484
24,300	24,350	4,172	3,250	5,145	3,859	27,300	27,350	5,031	3,933	6,266	4,658	30,300	30,350	5,931	4,683	7,406	5,498
24,350	24,400	4,185	3,261	5,161	3,871	27,350	27,400	5,046	3,946	6,285	4,672	30,350	30,400	5,946	4,696	7,425	5,512
24,400	24,450	4,198	3,272	5,178	3,883	27,400	27,450	5,061	3,958	6,304	4,686	30,400	30,450	5,961	4,708	7,444	5,526
24,450	24,500	4,211	3,283	5,194	3,895	27,450	27,500	5,076	3,971	6,323	4,700	30,450	30,500	5,976	4,721	7,463	5,540
24,500	24,550	4,224	3,294	5,211	3,907	27,500	27,550	5,091	3,983	6,342	4,714	30,500	30,550	5,991	4,733	7,482	5,554
24,550	24,600	4,237	3,305	5,227	3,919	27,550	27,600	5,106	3,996	6,361	4,728	30,550	30,600	6,006	4,746	7,501	5,568
24,600	24,650	4,250	3,316	5,244	3,931	27,600	27,650	5,121	4,008	6,380	4,742	30,600	30,650	6,021	4,758	7,520	5,582
24,650	24,700	4,263	3,327	5,260	3,943	27,650	27,700	5,136	4,021	6,399	4,756	30,650	30,700	6,036	4,771	7,539	5,596
24,700	24,750	4,276	3,338	5,278	3,955	27,700	27,750	5,151	4,033	6,418	4,770	30,700	30,750	6,051	4,783	7,558	5,610
24,750	24,800	4,289	3,349	5,297	3,967	27,750	27,800	5,166	4,046	6,437	4,784	30,750	30,800	6,066	4,796	7,577	5,624
24,800	24,850	4,302	3,360	5,316	3,979	27,800	27,850	5,181	4,058	6,456	4,798	30,800	30,850	6,081	4,808	7,596	5,638
24,850	24,900	4,315	3,371	5,336	3,991	27,850	27,900	5,196	4,071	6,475	4,812	30,850	30,900	6,096	4,821	7,615	5,652
24,900	24,950	4,328	3,382	5,354	4,003	27,900	27,950	5,211	4,083	6,494	4,826	30,900	30,950	6,111	4,833	7,634	5,666
24,950	25,000	4,341	3,393	5,378	4,015	27,950	28,000	5,226	4,096	6,513	4,840	30,950	31,000	6,126	4,846	7,653	5,680
25,000						**28,000**						**31,000**					
25,000	25,050	4,354	3,404	5,392	4,027	28,000	28,050	5,241	4,108	6,532	4,854	31,000	31,050	6,141	4,858	7,672	5,694
25,050	25,100	4,367	3,415	5,411	4,039	28,050	28,100	5,256	4,121	6,551	4,868	31,050	31,100	6,156	4,871	7,691	5,708
25,100	25,150	4,380	3,426	5,430	4,051	28,100	28,150	5,271	4,133	6,570	4,882	31,100	31,150	6,172	4,883	7,710	5,724
25,150	25,200	4,393	3,437	5,449	4,063	28,150	28,200	5,286	4,146	6,589	4,896	31,150	31,200	6,189	4,896	7,729	5,740
25,200	25,250	4,406	3,448	5,468	4,075	28,200	28,250	5,301	4,158	6,608	4,910	31,200	31,250	6,206	4,908	7,748	5,756
25,250	25,300	4,419	3,459	5,487	4,087	28,250	28,300	5,316	4,171	6,627	4,924	31,250	31,300	6,223	4,921	7,767	5,772
25,300	25,350	4,432	3,470	5,506	4,099	28,300	28,350	5,331	4,183	6,646	4,938	31,300	31,350	6,240	4,933	7,786	5,788
25,350	25,400	4,446	3,481	5,525	4,112	28,350	28,400	5,346	4,196	6,665	4,952	31,350	31,400	6,257	4,946	7,805	5,804
25,400	25,450	4,461	3,492	5,544	4,126	28,400	28,450	5,361	4,208	6,684	4,966	31,400	31,450	6,274	4,958	7,824	5,820
25,450	25,500	4,476	3,503	5,563	4,140	28,450	28,500	5,376	4,221	6,703	4,980	31,450	31,500	6,291	4,971	7,843	5,836
25,500	25,550	4,491	3,514	5,582	4,154	28,500	28,550	5,391	4,233	6,722	4,994	31,500	31,550	6,308	4,983	7,862	5,852
25,550	25,600	4,506	3,525	5,601	4,168	28,550	28,600	5,406	4,246	6,741	5,008	31,550	31,600	6,325	4,996	7,881	5,868
25,600	25,650	4,521	3,536	5,620	4,182	28,600	28,650	5,421	4,258	6,760	5,022	31,600	31,650	6,342	5,008	7,900	5,884
25,650	25,700	4,536	3,547	5,639	4,196	28,650	28,700	5,436	4,271	6,779	5,036	31,650	31,700	6,359	5,021	7,919	5,900
25,700	25,750	4,551	3,558	5,658	4,210	28,700	28,750	5,451	4,283	6,798	5,050	31,700	31,750	6,376	5,033	7,938	5,916
25,750	25,800	4,566	3,569	5,677	4,224	28,750	28,800	5,466	4,296	6,817	5,064	31,750	31,800	6,393	5,046	7,957	5,932
25,800	25,850	4,581	3,580	5,696	4,238	28,800	28,850	5,481	4,308	6,836	5,078	31,800	31,850	6,410	5,058	7,976	5,948
25,850	25,900	4,596	3,591	5,715	4,252	28,850	28,900	5,496	4,321	6,855	5,092	31,850	31,900	6,427	5,071	7,995	5,964
25,900	25,950	4,611	3,602	5,734	4,266	28,900	28,950	5,511	4,333	6,874	5,106	31,900	31,950	6,444	5,083	8,014	5,980
25,950	26,000	4,626	3,613	5,753	4,280	28,950	29,000	5,526	4,346	6,893	5,120	31,950	32,000	6,461	5,096	8,033	5,996

*This column must also be used by a qualifying widow(er).

Continued on next page

**This table is based on an IRS proof sheet as of August 15, 1986 and is subject to change.

1986 Tax Tables (Continued)**

If taxable income is — At least	But less than	Single	Married filing jointly *	Married filing separately	Head of household	If taxable income is — At least	But less than	Single	Married filing jointly *	Married filing separately	Head of household	If taxable income is — At least	But less than	Single	Married filing jointly *	Married filing separately	Head of household
32,000						**35,000**						**38,000**					
32,000	32,050	6,478	5,108	8,052	6,012	35,000	35,050	7,498	5,941	9,298	6,972	38,000	38,050	8,567	6,783	10,558	7,968
32,050	32,100	6,495	5,121	8,071	6,028	35,050	35,100	7,515	5,955	9,319	6,988	38,050	38,100	8,586	6,800	10,579	7,986
32,100	32,150	6,512	5,133	8,090	6,044	35,100	35,150	7,532	5,969	9,340	7,004	38,100	38,150	8,605	6,816	10,600	8,003
32,150	32,200	6,529	5,146	8,109	6,060	35,150	35,200	7,549	5,983	9,361	7,020	38,150	38,200	8,624	6,833	10,621	8,021
32,200	32,250	6,546	5,158	8,128	6,076	35,200	35,250	7,566	5,997	9,382	7,036	38,200	38,250	8,643	6,849	10,642	8,038
32,250	32,300	6,563	5,171	8,147	6,092	35,250	35,300	7,583	6,011	9,403	7,052	38,250	38,300	8,662	6,866	10,663	8,056
32,300	32,350	6,580	5,185	8,166	6,108	35,300	35,350	7,600	6,025	9,424	7,068	38,300	38,350	8,681	6,882	10,684	8,073
32,350	32,400	6,597	5,199	8,185	6,124	35,350	35,400	7,617	6,039	9,445	7,084	38,350	38,400	8,700	6,899	10,705	8,091
32,400	32,450	6,614	5,213	8,206	6,140	35,400	35,450	7,634	6,053	9,466	7,100	38,400	38,450	8,719	6,915	10,726	8,108
32,450	32,500	6,631	5,227	8,227	6,156	35,450	35,500	7,651	6,067	9,487	7,116	38,450	38,500	8,738	6,932	10,747	8,126
32,500	32,550	6,648	5,241	8,248	6,172	35,500	35,550	7,668	6,081	9,508	7,132	38,500	38,550	8,757	6,948	10,768	8,143
32,550	32,600	6,665	5,255	8,269	6,188	35,550	35,600	7,685	6,095	9,529	7,148	38,550	38,600	8,776	6,965	10,789	8,161
32,600	32,650	6,682	5,269	8,290	6,204	35,600	35,650	7,702	6,109	9,550	7,164	38,600	38,650	8,795	6,981	10,810	8,178
32,650	32,700	6,699	5,283	8,311	6,220	35,650	35,700	7,719	6,123	9,571	7,180	38,650	38,700	8,814	6,998	10,831	8,196
32,700	32,750	6,716	5,297	8,332	6,236	35,700	35,750	7,736	6,137	9,592	7,196	38,700	38,750	8,833	7,014	10,852	8,213
32,750	32,800	6,733	5,311	8,353	6,252	35,750	35,800	7,753	6,151	9,613	7,212	38,750	38,800	8,852	7,031	10,873	8,231
32,800	32,850	6,750	5,325	8,374	6,268	35,800	35,850	7,770	6,165	9,634	7,228	38,800	38,850	8,871	7,047	10,894	8,248
32,850	32,900	6,767	5,339	8,395	6,284	35,850	35,900	7,787	6,179	9,655	7,244	38,850	38,900	8,890	7,064	10,915	8,266
32,900	32,950	6,784	5,353	8,416	6,300	35,900	35,950	7,804	6,193	9,676	7,260	38,900	38,950	8,909	7,080	10,936	8,283
32,950	33,000	6,801	5,367	8,437	6,316	35,950	36,000	7,821	6,207	9,697	7,276	38,950	39,000	8,928	7,097	10,957	8,301
33,000						**36,000**						**39,000**					
33,000	33,050	6,818	5,381	8,458	6,332	36,000	36,050	7,838	6,221	9,718	7,292	39,000	39,050	8,947	7,113	10,978	8,318
33,050	33,100	6,835	5,395	8,479	6,348	36,050	36,100	7,855	6,235	9,739	7,308	39,050	39,100	8,966	7,130	10,999	8,336
33,100	33,150	6,852	5,409	8,500	6,364	36,100	36,150	7,872	6,249	9,760	7,324	39,100	39,150	8,985	7,146	11,020	8,353
33,150	33,200	6,869	5,423	8,521	6,380	36,150	36,200	7,889	6,263	9,781	7,340	39,150	39,200	9,004	7,163	11,041	8,371
33,200	33,250	6,886	5,437	8,542	6,396	36,200	36,250	7,906	6,277	9,802	7,356	39,200	39,250	9,023	7,179	11,062	8,388
33,250	33,300	6,903	5,451	8,563	6,412	36,250	36,300	7,923	6,291	9,823	7,372	39,250	39,300	9,042	7,196	11,083	8,406
33,300	33,350	6,920	5,465	8,584	6,428	36,300	36,350	7,940	6,305	9,844	7,388	39,300	39,350	9,061	7,212	11,104	8,423
33,350	33,400	6,937	5,479	8,605	6,444	36,350	36,400	7,957	6,319	9,865	7,404	39,350	39,400	9,080	7,229	11,125	8,441
33,400	33,450	6,954	5,493	8,626	6,460	36,400	36,450	7,974	6,333	9,886	7,420	39,400	39,450	9,099	7,245	11,146	8,458
33,450	33,500	6,971	5,507	8,647	6,476	36,450	36,500	7,991	6,347	9,907	7,436	39,450	39,500	9,118	7,262	11,167	8,476
33,500	33,550	6,988	5,521	8,668	6,492	36,500	36,550	8,008	6,361	9,928	7,452	39,500	39,550	9,137	7,278	11,188	8,493
33,550	33,600	7,005	5,535	8,689	6,508	36,550	36,600	8,025	6,375	9,949	7,468	39,550	39,600	9,156	7,295	11,209	8,511
33,600	33,650	7,022	5,549	8,710	6,524	36,600	36,650	8,042	6,389	9,970	7,484	39,600	39,650	9,175	7,311	11,230	8,528
33,650	33,700	7,039	5,563	8,731	6,540	36,650	36,700	8,059	6,403	9,991	7,500	39,650	39,700	9,194	7,328	11,251	8,546
33,700	33,750	7,056	5,577	8,752	6,556	36,700	36,750	8,076	6,417	10,012	7,516	39,700	39,750	9,213	7,344	11,272	8,563
33,750	33,800	7,073	5,591	8,773	6,572	36,750	36,800	8,093	6,431	10,033	7,532	39,750	39,800	9,232	7,361	11,293	8,581
33,800	33,850	7,090	5,605	8,794	6,588	36,800	36,850	8,111	6,445	10,054	7,548	39,800	39,850	9,251	7,377	11,314	8,598
33,850	33,900	7,107	5,619	8,815	6,604	36,850	36,900	8,130	6,459	10,075	7,566	39,850	39,900	9,270	7,394	11,335	8,616
33,900	33,950	7,124	5,633	8,836	6,620	36,900	36,950	8,149	6,473	10,096	7,583	39,900	39,950	9,289	7,410	11,356	8,633
33,950	34,000	7,141	5,647	8,857	6,636	36,950	37,000	8,168	6,487	10,117	7,601	39,950	40,000	9,308	7,427	11,377	8,651
34,000						**37,000**						**40,000**					
34,000	34,050	7,158	5,661	8,878	6,652	37,000	37,050	8,187	6,501	10,138	7,618	40,000	40,050	9,327	7,443	11,398	8,668
34,050	34,100	7,175	5,675	8,899	6,668	37,050	37,100	8,206	6,515	10,159	7,636	40,050	40,100	9,346	7,460	11,419	8,686
34,100	34,150	7,192	5,689	8,920	6,684	37,100	37,150	8,225	6,529	10,180	7,653	40,100	40,150	9,365	7,476	11,440	8,703
34,150	34,200	7,209	5,703	8,941	6,700	37,150	37,200	8,244	6,543	10,201	7,671	40,150	40,200	9,384	7,493	11,461	8,721
34,200	34,250	7,226	5,717	8,962	6,716	37,200	37,250	8,263	6,557	10,222	7,688	40,200	40,250	9,403	7,509	11,482	8,738
34,250	34,300	7,243	5,731	8,983	6,732	37,250	37,300	8,282	6,571	10,243	7,706	40,250	40,300	9,422	7,526	11,503	8,756
34,300	34,350	7,260	5,745	9,004	6,748	37,300	37,350	8,301	6,585	10,264	7,723	40,300	40,350	9,441	7,542	11,524	8,773
34,350	34,400	7,277	5,759	9,025	6,764	37,350	37,400	8,320	6,599	10,285	7,741	40,350	40,400	9,460	7,559	11,545	8,791
34,400	34,450	7,294	5,773	9,046	6,780	37,400	37,450	8,339	6,613	10,306	7,758	40,400	40,450	9,479	7,575	11,566	8,808
34,450	34,500	7,311	5,787	9,067	6,796	37,450	37,500	8,358	6,627	10,327	7,776	40,450	40,500	9,498	7,592	11,587	8,826
34,500	34,550	7,328	5,801	9,088	6,812	37,500	37,550	8,377	6,641	10,348	7,793	40,500	40,550	9,517	7,608	11,608	8,843
34,550	34,600	7,345	5,815	9,109	6,828	37,550	37,600	8,396	6,655	10,369	7,811	40,550	40,600	9,536	7,625	11,629	8,861
34,600	34,650	7,362	5,829	9,130	6,844	37,600	37,650	8,415	6,669	10,390	7,828	40,600	40,650	9,555	7,641	11,650	8,878
34,650	34,700	7,379	5,843	9,151	6,860	37,650	37,700	8,434	6,683	10,411	7,846	40,650	40,700	9,574	7,658	11,671	8,896
34,700	34,750	7,396	5,857	9,172	6,876	37,700	37,750	8,453	6,697	10,432	7,863	40,700	40,750	9,593	7,674	11,692	8,913
34,750	34,800	7,413	5,871	9,193	6,892	37,750	37,800	8,472	6,711	10,453	7,881	40,750	40,800	9,612	7,691	11,713	8,931
34,800	34,850	7,430	5,885	9,214	6,908	37,800	37,850	8,491	6,725	10,474	7,898	40,800	40,850	9,631	7,707	11,734	8,948
34,850	34,900	7,447	5,899	9,235	6,924	37,850	37,900	8,510	6,739	10,495	7,916	40,850	40,900	9,650	7,724	11,755	8,966
34,900	34,950	7,464	5,913	9,256	6,940	37,900	37,950	8,529	6,753	10,516	7,933	40,900	40,950	9,669	7,740	11,776	8,983
34,950	35,000	7,481	5,927	9,277	6,956	37,950	38,000	8,548	6,767	10,537	7,951	40,950	41,000	9,688	7,757	11,797	9,001

*This column must also be used by a qualifying widow(er).

Continued on next page

**This table is based on an IRS proof sheet as of August 15, 1986 and is subject to change.

1986 Tax Tables (Continued)**

If taxable income is — At least	But less than	Single	Married filing jointly *	Married filing separately	Head of household	If taxable income is — At least	But less than	Single	Married filing jointly *	Married filing separately	Head of household	If taxable income is — At least	But less than	Single	Married filing jointly *	Married filing separately	Head of household
41,000						**44,000**						**47,000**					
41,000	41,050	9,707	7,773	11,818	9,018	44,000	44,050	10,847	8,763	13,078	10,068	47,000	47,050	12,077	9,753	14,363	11,118
41,050	41,100	9,726	7,790	11,839	9,036	44,050	44,100	10,866	8,780	13,099	10,086	47,050	47,100	12,098	9,770	14,385	11,136
41,100	41,150	9,745	7,806	11,860	9,053	44,100	44,150	10,885	8,796	13,120	10,103	47,100	47,150	12,119	9,786	14,408	11,153
41,150	41,200	9,764	7,823	11,881	9,071	44,150	44,200	10,904	8,813	13,141	10,121	47,150	47,200	12,140	9,803	14,430	11,171
41,200	41,250	9,783	7,839	11,902	9,088	44,200	44,250	10,923	8,829	13,162	10,138	47,200	47,250	12,161	9,819	14,453	11,188
41,250	41,300	9,802	7,856	11,923	9,106	44,250	44,300	10,942	8,846	13,183	10,156	47,250	47,300	12,182	9,836	14,475	11,206
41,300	41,350	9,821	7,872	11,944	9,123	44,300	44,350	10,961	8,862	13,204	10,173	47,300	47,350	12,203	9,852	14,498	11,223
41,350	41,400	9,840	7,889	11,965	9,141	44,350	44,400	10,980	8,879	13,225	10,191	47,350	47,400	12,224	9,869	14,520	11,241
41,400	41,450	9,859	7,905	11,986	9,158	44,400	44,450	10,999	8,895	13,246	10,208	47,400	47,450	12,245	9,885	14,543	11,258
41,450	41,500	9,878	7,922	12,007	9,176	44,450	44,500	11,018	8,912	13,267	10,226	47,450	47,500	12,266	9,902	14,565	11,276
41,500	41,550	9,897	7,938	12,028	9,193	44,500	44,550	11,037	8,928	13,288	10,243	47,500	47,550	12,287	9,918	14,588	11,293
41,550	41,600	9,916	7,955	12,049	9,211	44,550	44,600	11,056	8,945	13,309	10,261	47,550	47,600	12,308	9,935	14,610	11,311
41,600	41,650	9,935	7,971	12,070	9,228	44,600	44,650	11,075	8,961	13,330	10,278	47,600	47,650	12,329	9,951	14,633	11,328
41,650	41,700	9,954	7,988	12,091	9,246	44,650	44,700	11,094	8,978	13,351	10,296	47,650	47,700	12,350	9,968	14,655	11,346
41,700	41,750	9,973	8,004	12,112	9,263	44,700	44,750	11,113	8,994	13,372	10,313	47,700	47,750	12,371	9,984	14,678	11,363
41,750	41,800	9,992	8,021	12,133	9,281	44,750	44,800	11,132	9,011	13,393	10,331	47,750	47,800	12,392	10,001	14,700	11,381
41,800	41,850	10,011	8,037	12,154	9,298	44,800	44,850	11,153	9,027	13,414	10,348	47,800	47,850	12,413	10,017	14,723	11,398
41,850	41,900	10,030	8,054	12,175	9,316	44,850	44,900	11,174	9,044	13,435	10,366	47,850	47,900	12,434	10,034	14,745	11,416
41,900	41,950	10,049	8,070	12,196	9,333	44,900	44,950	11,195	9,060	13,456	10,383	47,900	47,950	12,455	10,050	14,768	11,433
41,950	42,000	10,068	8,087	12,217	9,351	44,950	45,000	11,216	9,077	13,477	10,401	47,950	48,000	12,476	10,067	14,790	11,451
42,000						**45,000**						**48,000**					
42,000	42,050	10,087	8,103	12,238	9,368	45,000	45,050	11,237	9,093	13,498	10,418	48,000	48,050	12,497	10,083	14,813	11,468
42,050	42,100	10,106	8,120	12,259	9,386	45,050	45,100	11,258	9,110	13,519	10,436	48,050	48,100	12,518	10,100	14,835	11,486
42,100	42,150	10,125	8,136	12,280	9,403	45,100	45,150	11,279	9,126	13,540	10,453	48,100	48,150	12,539	10,116	14,858	11,503
42,150	42,200	10,144	8,153	12,301	9,421	45,150	45,200	11,300	9,143	13,561	10,471	48,150	48,200	12,560	10,133	14,880	11,521
42,200	42,250	10,163	8,169	12,322	9,438	45,200	45,250	11,321	9,159	13,582	10,488	48,200	48,250	12,581	10,149	14,903	11,538
42,250	42,300	10,182	8,186	12,343	9,456	45,250	45,300	11,342	9,176	13,603	10,506	48,250	48,300	12,602	10,166	14,925	11,558
42,300	42,350	10,201	8,202	12,364	9,473	45,300	45,350	11,363	9,192	13,624	10,523	48,300	48,350	12,623	10,182	14,948	11,579
42,350	42,400	10,220	8,219	12,385	9,491	45,350	45,400	11,384	9,209	13,645	10,541	48,350	48,400	12,644	10,199	14,970	11,600
42,400	42,450	10,239	8,235	12,406	9,508	45,400	45,450	11,405	9,225	13,666	10,558	48,400	48,450	12,665	10,215	14,993	11,621
42,450	42,500	10,258	8,252	12,427	9,526	45,450	45,500	11,426	9,242	13,687	10,576	48,450	48,500	12,686	10,232	15,015	11,642
42,500	42,550	10,277	8,268	12,448	9,543	45,500	45,550	11,447	9,258	13,708	10,593	48,500	48,550	12,707	10,248	15,038	11,663
42,550	42,600	10,296	8,285	12,469	9,561	45,550	45,600	11,468	9,275	13,729	10,611	48,550	48,600	12,728	10,265	15,060	11,684
42,600	42,650	10,315	8,301	12,490	9,578	45,600	45,650	11,489	9,291	13,750	10,628	48,600	48,650	12,749	10,281	15,083	11,705
42,650	42,700	10,334	8,318	12,511	9,596	45,650	45,700	11,510	9,308	13,771	10,646	48,650	48,700	12,770	10,298	15,105	11,726
42,700	42,750	10,353	8,334	12,532	9,613	45,700	45,750	11,531	9,324	13,792	10,663	48,700	48,750	12,791	10,314	15,128	11,747
42,750	42,800	10,372	8,351	12,583	9,631	45,750	45,800	11,552	9,341	13,813	10,681	48,750	48,800	12,812	10,331	15,150	11,768
42,800	42,850	10,391	8,367	12,574	9,648	45,800	45,850	11,573	9,357	13,834	10,698	48,800	48,850	12,833	10,347	15,173	11,789
42,850	42,900	10,410	8,384	12,595	9,666	45,850	45,900	11,594	9,374	13,855	10,716	48,850	48,900	12,854	10,364	15,195	11,810
42,900	42,950	10,429	8,400	12,616	9,683	45,900	45,950	11,615	9,390	13,876	10,733	48,900	48,950	12,875	10,380	15,218	11,831
42,950	43,000	10,448	8,417	12,637	9,701	45,950	46,000	11,636	9,407	13,897	10,751	48,950	49,000	12,896	10,397	15,240	11,852
43,000						**46,000**						**49,000**					
43,000	43,050	10,467	8,433	12,658	9,718	46,000	46,050	11,657	9,423	13,918	10,768	49,000	49,050	12,917	10,413	15,263	11,873
43,050	43,100	10,486	8,450	12,679	9,736	46,050	46,100	11,678	9,440	13,939	10,786	49,050	49,100	12,938	10,430	15,285	11,894
43,100	43,150	10,505	8,466	12,700	9,753	46,100	46,150	11,699	9,456	13,960	10,803	49,100	49,150	12,959	10,446	15,308	11,915
43,150	43,200	10,524	8,483	12,721	9,771	46,150	46,200	11,720	9,473	13,981	10,821	49,150	49,200	12,980	10,463	15,330	11,936
43,200	43,250	10,543	8,499	12,742	9,788	46,200	46,250	11,741	9,489	14,003	10,838	49,200	49,250	13,001	10,479	15,353	11,957
43,250	43,300	10,562	8,516	12,763	9,806	46,250	46,300	11,762	9,506	14,025	10,856	49,250	49,300	13,022	10,496	15,375	11,978
43,300	43,350	10,581	8,532	12,784	9,823	46,300	46,350	11,783	9,522	14,048	10,873	49,300	49,350	13,043	10,512	15,398	11,999
43,350	43,400	10,600	8,549	12,805	9,841	46,350	46,400	11,804	9,539	14,070	10,891	49,350	49,400	13,064	10,529	15,420	12,020
43,400	43,450	10,619	8,565	12,826	9,858	46,400	46,450	11,825	9,555	14,093	10,908	49,400	49,450	13,085	10,546	15,443	12,041
43,450	43,500	10,638	8,582	12,847	9,876	46,450	46,500	11,846	9,572	14,115	10,926	49,450	49,500	13,106	10,565	15,465	12,062
43,500	43,550	10,657	8,598	12,868	9,893	46,500	46,550	11,867	9,588	14,138	10,943	49,500	49,550	13,127	10,584	15,488	12,083
43,550	43,600	10,676	8,615	12,889	9,911	46,550	46,600	11,888	9,605	14,160	10,961	49,550	49,600	13,148	10,603	15,510	12,104
43,600	53,650	10,695	8,631	12,910	9,928	46,600	46,650	11,909	9,621	14,183	10,978	49,600	49,650	13,169	10,622	15,533	12,125
43,650	43,700	10,714	8,648	12,931	9,946	46,650	46,700	11,930	9,638	14,205	10,996	49,650	49,700	13,190	10,641	15,555	12,146
43,700	43,750	10,733	8,664	12,952	9,963	46,700	46,750	11,951	9,654	14,228	11,013	49,700	49,750	13,211	10,660	15,578	12,167
43,750	43,800	10,752	8,681	12,973	9,981	46,750	46,800	11,972	9,671	14,250	11,031	49,750	49,800	13,232	10,679	15,600	12,188
43,800	43,850	10,771	8,697	12,994	9,998	46,800	46,850	11,993	9,687	14,273	11,048	49,800	49,850	13,253	10,698	15,623	12,209
43,850	43,900	10,790	8,714	13,015	10,016	46,850	46,900	12,014	9,704	14,295	11,066	49,850	49,900	13,274	10,717	15,645	12,230
43,900	43,950	10,809	8,730	13,036	10,033	46,900	46,950	12,035	9,720	14,316	11,083	49,900	49,950	13,295	10,736	15,668	12,251
43,950	44,000	10,828	8,747	13,057	10,051	46,950	47,000	12,056	9,737	14,340	11,101	49,950	50,000	13,316	10,755	15,690	12,272

*This column must also be used by a qualifying widow(er).

50,000 or over—use tax rate schedules

**This table is based on an IRS proof sheet as of August 15, 1986 and is subject to change.

Convenient Check Lists to Reduce Your Tax

ITEMS YOU MUST *INCLUDE* IN YOUR GROSS INCOME   *See* ¶ 39.00

ITEMS YOU MAY *EXCLUDE* FROM YOUR GROSS INCOME   40.00

YOUR *POSSIBLE* DEDUCTIONS   41.00

ITEMS WHICH YOU MAY *NOT* DEDUCT   42.00

¶39.00 • What to Include in Gross Income

NOTE: *All references are to ¶ numbers which you will find throughout this book.*

A

Administrators' and executors' fees, *see* ¶2.111 and ¶12.01

Advance payments of income of which you have unrestricted use, such as rent and commissions, *see* ¶2.07, ¶2.09, and ¶9.01

Agents—include only your income, not that of your principal

Agreement not to compete, payments from

Aliens—*see* ¶37.00

Alimony—*see* ¶1.70, when taxable

Annuities, in part, *see* ¶7.07, 7.09

Annuity purchased by your employer, ¶7.09

Army or Navy pay—*see* Military and naval personnel

Awards—see ¶2.00, 12.03, 12.10, 12.15

Awards to employees under Title VII of the Civil Rights Act of 1964

B

Back pay

Bad debts recovered, if previously deducted. *See* ¶12.20

Bank interest, ¶4.00

Bargain purchases under the rules of ¶2.08, 12.02

Beneficiary—distributions of income to you by trusts or estates. *See* ¶11.00

Beneficiary of deceased employee—payment from deceased's employer in excess of $5,000, *see* ¶2.04

Benefits from your union while on strike, *see* ¶2.101

Board and lodging—not furnished for your employer's convenience, *see* ¶2.01

Bonds, income on retirement or sale

Bonds, tax-exempt, income from sale

Bonuses

Breeding fees

Building and Loan Association, dividends and interest received from, ¶4.01

Business overhead insurance proceeds to cover overhead costs while you are unable to work in your business due to illness or injury

Business profits, ¶5.00

C

Cancellation of a lease, receipt for, ¶9.03

Canceled debts owed by you—*see* ¶12.21

Capital gains, *see* ¶6.00

Capital gain dividends, *see* ¶4.53

Christmas bonus

Civil Service retirement payments, ¶7.102

Commissions—*see* ¶2.09

Commodity Credit Corporation loan to farmers

Community income

Compensation, *see* also ¶2.00

  Cancellation of an indebtedness by an employer in payment for services

  Compensation even when deemed "unreasonable" and disallowed by the IRS as a deduction to the employer. If you repay the disallowed portion, *see* ¶2.11

  Compensation received near end of year, though deposited following year

Compensation set apart or credited to your account on company books, which you have not received but could have withdrawn during the year, *see* ¶2.07

Cost of living allowances to federal employees (except those civilian officers or employees stationed in Alaska, Hawaii, or elsewhere outside continental U.S.)

Cost of living allowances to Red Cross members outside continental U.S.

Dismissal pay

Earned abroad, above exclusion, *see* ¶36.00

Excess drawings (on a salesman's account) which are forgiven by an employer, *see* ¶2.09

Executors' fees, *see* ¶2.111 and 12.01

Income taxes paid for you by your employer

Offerings, fees and other contributions received by a clergyman, evangelist or religious worker for funerals, marriages, baptisms, Masses, or other services rendered

Payments received for an agreement not to compete, *see* ¶5.461

Pensions, *see* ¶7.00

Personal expenses paid for you by your company

Prizes and awards, ¶12.03

Retroactive wage adjustments (for example, in settlement of labor disputes) are compensation when received

Severance pay based on the value of employee's services, responsibility, attitude, and general contribution to the company

Sick leave and disability benefits paid, *see* ¶2.12

Stipends paid to student nurses

Tips, prizes, and awards

Withholdings, *see* ¶2.07 and ¶25.00

Condemnation award to the extent of your gain —unless you reinvest in similar property, *see* ¶18.21

Condemnation award for use of your property for a limited time. This is treated as rent income

Conservation payments by Dept. of Agriculture

Contest winnings, ¶12.03

Cost of living allowances, *see* Compensation

County fair prizes, ¶12.03

Crop damage payments

Crop sales

Crop share rentals

D

Damages received in litigation, *see* ¶12.22

Debts, canceled, ¶12.21

Deferred payment sales, *see* ¶6.16

Deposits received as security from your tenant, *see* ¶9.01

Director's fees

Disability, salary payments during, *see* ¶2.12

Discount on advance payment of insurance or annuity premium

Discounts or interest received, ¶4.01

Dividends, *see* ¶4.50

Dividends from mutual funds, *see* ¶4.53

Drawings, *see* ¶2.09

E

E and EE bond interest, *see* ¶4.08

Economic Opportunity Act pay to work-training enrollees

Embezzlement proceeds, in the year of embezzlement

Employees, annuities (in part), ¶7.09

Employees, benefits, ¶2.01, 2.02

Employer's stock, *see* ¶32.04

Employment discrimination, pay for, under Title VII of the Civil Rights Act of 1964

Endowment policy, *see* ¶7.08

Estates and trusts, *see* ¶11.00

Excess drawings, forgiven by employer

Exchanges of property, *see* ¶6.20

Executors' fees

Expense allowances, *see* ¶2.31

F

Facilities and privileges received from your employer in certain cases, *see* ¶2.02

Family income, *see* ¶33.00

Family, profit on sales between members of, *see* ¶33.11

Federal savings and loan interest, *see* ¶4.00

Fellowship awards—if they do not meet rules of ¶12.10 and 12.11

Fiduciaries, income from—*see* ¶11.00

Foreign government, income from

Foreign income *but see* ¶36.00

Forfeited deposit on agreement to buy real estate, *see* ¶6.04

Forgiven debts, in many cases, ¶12.21

Fringe benefits, *see* ¶2.02

G

Gambling gains, ¶12.05

Golden parachute payments, ¶32.07

Group-term life insurance over $50,000—premiums paid by employer, *see* ¶2.021

H

H and HH bond interest, ¶4.08

Hedging gains, ¶6.011

I

Illegal business or transactions, profits of

Income tax paid for another:

  Employer for employee

  Trustee for beneficiary

Independent contractor's income

Installment obligations, sale of, *see* ¶6.192

Installment sales, profits realized, *see* ¶6.17

Insurance premiums paid for you by your employer on non-group policies, but see exception for group-term life, ¶2.021

Insurance proceeds for loss of rent income because of fire, *see* ¶9.01

Insurance proceeds—in some cases, *see* ¶12.30

Insurance, surrender value in excess of cost, *see* ¶12.32

Interest, *see* ¶4.00

Interest foregone on loan from employer, ¶4.10
Interest on deferred payment contracts, ¶6.191
Interest reduction payments under National Housing Act, ¶15.011
Involuntary conversion gain, when you do not replace the property, see ¶18.20
IRA distributions, ¶7.19

J

Joint tenant—your share of income
Joint venture income, see ¶10.00
Jury fees

K

Keogh plan distributions, ¶7.35

L

Life insurance, ¶12.30
Life insurance premiums—see ¶2.021
Liquidation of a corporation, ¶6.033
Literary work, income from
Living allowance paid civilian employee of Army
Living quarters and meals, etc., furnished by your employer in some cases, see ¶2.01
Lottery or raffle winnings, ¶12.03
Lump-sum distributions from pension and profit-sharing plans, ¶7.01

M

Merchant Marine members, pay of
Military and naval personnel, see also ¶35.00
    Allotments to dependents deducted from your pay (portion chargeable against your pay)
    Base pay
    Compensation received from the federal government for services rendered within or without the U.S.
    Drill pay
    Extra pay to work in officers' club
    Foreign duty pay (increase of base pay)
    Lump-sum payments for accrued leave
    Mileage allowance paid in cash for travel under competent orders without troops (your actual expenses may be deducted)
    National Guard pay
    Per diem allowance in lieu of subsistence paid on travel or temporary duty (your actual expenses are deductible)
    Reenlistment bonus
    Salaries received from former employers during military service
    Voluntary allotments
Mortgage liability paid by client in lieu of fee
Moving expense reimbursements, see ¶2.40
Mutual funds dividends. Part may be capital gain and part tax free, see ¶4.53

N

National Guard pay
NLRB award to employee for illegal discharge
National Teaching Fellowships
Notary public fees

O

Option other than I.S.O. to buy employer stock, see ¶32.04
Options—sums received by you when option to another is not exercised, ¶6.035
Options—sums received by you not to exercise an option you hold
Overtime pay (but not supper money)

P

Partnership, pool or syndicate income, ¶10.00
Patent, royalties, license receipts and any infringement compensation, ¶6.036
Patronage dividends
Pay even if not received in cash
Pension and profit-sharing plan income, see ¶7.01, 7.10
Pensions paid by an employer or the U.S.
Performance shares, ¶32.03
Premiums paid by employer on group-term life insurance policies over $50,000, see ¶2.021
Prizes, see ¶12.03
Proceeds on sale of life insurance policy over premiums paid, ¶7.08
Professional services, fees received for, ¶5.00
Profit-sharing income, from:
    All profit-seeking transactions, ¶5.00, 6.00
    Business operations, joint ventures, pools, syndicates, or partnerships
Profit-sharing plan income, ¶7.00
Promissory notes received from your employer, in some cases, ¶2.08
Punitive damages, see ¶12.22

R

Radio or TV contest prizes, see ¶12.03
Raffle winnings, ¶12.03
Railroad Retirement Tier 1 benefits, if income limits exceeded, ¶34.12
Receivers' compensation
Recovery of bad debts previously charged off, ¶12.20
Recovery of certain medical costs, see ¶17.04
Redemption of obligations—see ¶12.21
Redemption value of U.S. Savings Bonds, at your election, ¶4.08
Refund of taxes previously deducted, ¶12.20
Regulated investment company dividends, see Mutual funds
Reimbursement by employer in excess of actual business expenses. See ¶2.37
Reimbursement for medical expenses or casualty loss deducted in earlier year, ¶17.04, 18.05
Reimbursement of personal expense
Rents, ¶9.00
Residence sales, profit upon, if you do not buy another residence under rules of ¶29.20 or if you are not 55 or over, ¶29.30
Resident alien—same income that must be reported by a citizen, ¶37.01, 37.02
Restaurant employees' meals. See ¶2.01 when tax free
Retirement pay from Armed Forces not for service-connected injury or sickness
Retirement pay when the payments are compensation for past services
Retirement pay to U.S. Public Health Service employee
Retroactive wage payments, but see ¶2.12
Rewards, ¶12.03
Rights
    Payment in form of rights which are really compensation. Stock right dividends are usually tax free. See ¶4.58
    Sale of, ¶6.26
Royalties received by authors, musicians, inventors, lessors of property
Rural mail carriers' mileage allowance

S

Salaries—see Compensation
Sale of property, see ¶6.00
Salesperson, commissions, ¶2.09
Savings bank deposit, interest on, see ¶4.01
Securities, sales of, see ¶6.00
Separation allowances, ¶20.00
Severance pay

Social Security benefits, if income limits exceeded, ¶34.11
State and federal employees' compensation
State tax refunds if prior deduction produced tax benefit, ¶12.20
Stock appreciation rights (SARs), when exercised, ¶32.03
Stock options, nonqualified, even if given for a proprietary interest, ¶32.04
Stock, payment in form of stock which is really compensation
Strike benefits, see ¶2.101
Suggestion awards, see ¶12.03
Survivor annuity receipts, see ¶7.103
Sweepstakes, winnings, ¶12.03
Swindling proceeds
Syndicate, income from, see ¶10.00

T

Tax refund of tax previously deducted, ¶12.20
Taxes, for which you are liable, paid by another unless the payment is a gift
    Income tax of employee paid by employer
Tenant, joint or by the entirety—include income allocated in accordance with the rules in your state
Tips
Traveling expense allowances to the extent not used for travel expenses, see ¶2.31 for further details
Treasure you find
Treble damages in anti-trust actions
Trustees fees, ¶2.111
Trust income, see ¶11.00

U

Unemployment benefits paid by union or private unemployment fund; paid by public fund if income over certain limits, see ¶2.10
Union award for service
University Year for Action program stipend
U.S. Savings Bond interest, ¶4.08
U.S. Savings Bonds, deductions from salary to purchase
Use and occupancy insurance proceeds where reimbursement is for profits lost. Proceeds are taxed as ordinary income
Usurious interest

V

Vacation pay
Value of any property received as compensation
Veterans
    Damages for loss of wages paid by your employer because of failure to give you your former position
    Damages for discharge paid by an employer within one year of restoration of your position
    National Guard pay
    Retirement pay, see ¶35.011
    Terminal leave pay for service
    Wages received for on-the-job training as apprentices
Violation of civil rights, payments for, under Title VII of the Civil Rights Act of 1964 for employment discrimination
VISTA volunteer living expense allowance, ¶2.01

W

Wages
Winnings at exhibitions, fairs, in newspaper or magazine contests, sweepstakes, raffles or TV or radio shows (both money and property), ¶12.03
Withholding from salary, for U.S. Savings Bond purchases, income tax, Social Security tax
Work training program payments under Economic Opportunity Act of 1964

¶40.00 • What You May Exclude From Gross Income

NOTE: *All references are to ¶ numbers which you will find throughout this book.*

A

Accident insurance compensation, ¶12.22

Accrued interest included in purchase price of bond or note and later collected, ¶4.03

Adoptive parents' payments received from state agency

Advances drawn from your employer which are repayable (taxable to you if debt is canceled by your employer), ¶2.09

Agent—the income of your principal (taxed to principal)

Alien working for a foreign government here

Alimony, which does not meet rules of ¶20.00

Allotment paid to serviceman's dependent

Allowances

Cost-of-living to civilian officers and employees of U.S. stationed outside U.S.

To widow under applicable state law if required to be paid out of estate principal

Ambassadors or consular officers of foreign governments, compensation to

Annuities, ¶7.07, 7.09

Portion of your annuity payment that is a repayment of your cost

Railroad Retirement Act

Social Security retirement payments

Appreciation in property not yet realized by either sale or exchange

Armed Forces Health Professions Scholarships, ¶12.16

Assigned income received if source is not assigned to you

Award, ¶12.03–12.17

From a public foundation in recognition of scientific achievements and services in promoting public welfare

On a competitive basis to scientists, scholars, or students; for example, Nobel prizes, Rhodes scholarships

Scholarships, fellowships, etc.—where you work for a degree without performing services

Fellowships—not working toward a degree— up to $300 a month for 36 months, ¶12.11

B

Bad debts, recovery of, where previous deduction did not offset income, ¶12.20

Beneficiary of deceased employee—payments up to $5,000, from deceased's employer, ¶2.04

Benefit payments to veterans—*see* Veterans

Bequests and devises, ¶12.01

"Black Lung" benefits

Blocked currency income, ¶36.13

Board and lodging furnished by an employer if for convenience of employer, ¶2.01

Bond interest when received on certain obligations of the state or local governments, ¶4.04

Borrowed money returned to you

Breach of promise to marry—*see* Damages

Building superintendent—value of apartment furnished you for employer's convenience

C

Canceled debts, if forgiveness is gratuitous, ¶12.21

Capital gains of trust required to be added to trust principal are taxed to trust, not to you

Capital return to you

Car pool receipts

Cash rebates on purchase of new car or other items

Casualty insurance proceeds

Check you are holding because payor will not have funds to meet it until a later date

Check you refuse to cash because you claim a larger amount than the payor is then willing to deliver

Child care provided by employer under non-discriminating plan

Child support payments, ¶20.04

Children's income is not income to parents

Clergymen, rental value of parsonage, ¶2.05

Clergymen, retired—payments by congregation, in addition to pension, motivated by congregation's love and affection

Combat pay up to certain limits, *see* ¶35.03

Compensation—

Compensation depending on happening of certain future events

Compensation if neither computed nor made available to you

Compensation (up to certain limits) earned in a foreign country, ¶36.01, or U.S. possession, ¶36.08

Cost-of-living allowances paid to federal employees stationed outside the U.S.

D

Damages resulting from suit for: *see* ¶12.22

Breach of promise to marry

Injury to goodwill or loss of capital. Recovery for loss of profits or loss of profits and capital combined—without segregating the amounts—is fully taxed.

Libel

Loss of life

Personal injuries

Property settlements and lump-sum payments in divorce proceedings, ¶1.70

Slander

Support money for minor children

Death benefits of $50,000 payable from Law Enforcement Assistance Administration to surviving dependents of public safety officers killed in the line of duty

Debts collected which, if previously deducted, had not given you a tax benefit, ¶12.20

Devises and bequests, ¶12.01

Diplomatic and consular officers (of foreign governments), compensation of

Disaster Relief Act of 1974 grants to victims of natural disasters

Discount on tax-exempt bonds

Dividends, *see* ¶4.50

Distribution from a corporation with no current or accumulated earnings; distribution reduces the cost basis of your stock. Distributions exceeding the cost of your stock give you capital gain

Insurance dividends from mutual insurance companies. These are merely an adjustment of the premiums paid. However, when amounts received exceed the aggregate premiums or other consideration paid for a policy, then they are taxed. Same rule applies to dividends on paid-up policies whether dividends received or left with company. But interest on such dividends is taxed.

Stock dividend or stock rights under rules of ¶4.56

VA insurance dividends, ¶4.61

Dwelling furnished a clergyman—or rental allowance paid in lieu of furnishing a residence, ¶2.05

E

Education costs paid by employer under plan, *see* ¶2.041

Educational assistance allowance paid by Veteran's Administration, ¶12.16

Educational benefits received under War Orphans' Educational Assistance Act of 1956, ¶12.16

Employee death benefits, *see* ¶2.04

Endowment policies proceeds—the part covering your cost. If paid in installments follow annuity rules at ¶7.07. If paid in a lump sum, *see* ¶7.08

Energy assistance payments by state directly or indirectly to qualified persons to reduce the cost of winter energy use

Escrow, payments held in

Estate, beneficiary may not be taxed on income accumulated in estate, ¶11.02

Exchange of property, tax-free exchanges, ¶6.20

Executor's fees if waived before performance of duties, *see* ¶2.111

Executor's fees if the will provides:

The payment is a form of legacy, *see* ¶12.01

You only have to qualify as executor to receive the money

You receive the fees whether or not you act as executor

F

Facilities and privileges supplied by your employer, ¶2.01, 2.02

Farmers' income of the following type:

Gain on sale of farm residence—if you buy a new residence within two years before or after the sale. *See* rules at ¶29.20

Increase—in value of livestock not sold

Patronage rebate from cooperative for purchases made for personal use

Value of farm produce consumed by farmer and his family. (However, the farmer's expenses must be reduced by the estimated cost of raising such produce)

Federal income tax refunds

Fellowships, ¶12.10

Food benefits under the Nutrition Program for the Elderly

Foreign earned income, ¶36.01

Foreign housing costs, employer-financed, ¶36.02

Foreign income in blocked currency, ¶36.13

Foreign income from country having tax treaty with U.S. to avoid double taxation, ¶36.12

Forgiveness of some types of debts, ¶12.21

Foster parent's payments received from a child-placing agency as reimbursement for expenses of taking care of foster children. These payments are not more than the expenses. Neither the payments received nor the expenses need be shown on the foster parents' tax returns.

Fractional stock dividends under rules of ¶4.56

G

Gains not recognized on certain exchanges ¶6.20, 12.33, 29.20, 31.021

Gifts, ¶12.01

Government endowment insurance dividends

Group-term life insurance premiums for coverage under $50,000 paid by employer, *see* ¶2.02, 2.021

Guardian not taxed on ward's income

H

Health and welfare payments, *see* ¶2.16–2.19

Health insurance proceeds, ¶12.32

Home energy assistance payments under SSI or AFDC

House, sale of by owner 55 or over, within certain limits, *see* ¶29.30

I

Impounded payments of compensation

Improvement by lessees (not income to landlord)

Income assigned to you, if the property creating the income was not assigned to you

Income exempt under tax treaty, ¶36.12

Income from sources outside the United States —in certain cases, ¶36.01

Income of the following types:

Appreciation of value of property not yet realized by a sale or exchange of the property

Disputed—the dispute must be settled by litigation or otherwise before it is taxed to you

Escrow—income held by agent. It is not included until available to you but see ¶6.191

Improvements erected by tenant on your land *see* ¶9.01

Income assigned to you—if the property creating the income was not assigned to you

Income, fair value of which is not "capable of being ascertained with reasonable certainty." Thus there might be no tax where you have entered restrictive agreements that make sale or negotiation impossible or require deposit of the property with disinterested persons until clearance under the agreement, ¶6.19

Income received by you as agent for others, as—

Proceeds of your family's securities that you retained by agreement

Fees you collected as a lawyer (or physician) in behalf of an associate group of lawyers (or physicians)

Income received by you where you act as nominee for another

Gains from stock trading that is for a group of participants or for another

Recovery of a bad debt, taxes, or interest on delinquent taxes which had been deducted in a previous year when they did not reduce your taxes—usually a year in which you had a loss

Reduction of debt due on purchase of property—when it is an adjustment of purchase price

Income tax refunds from federal government

Indian grants paid by U.S. for relocation and vocational training

Inherited land, monies, and other property

Injury to goodwill, payments received for—see Damage

Insurance payment for excess living costs following casualty, ¶18.11

Insurance premium on group-term life policies under $50,000 paid by your employer

Insurance proceeds—see ¶12.30–12.33

Interest, if it is:

Interest on the tax-exempt securities listed at ¶4.04. But if you detach and sell the coupons separately from the bonds, you include the proceeds

Due, but cannot be collected (it is taxed when collected)

Received in worthless bonds or notes

Interest included in the purchase of an obligation (as a bond or note). You must first recover the amount paid for interest. Any amount in excess is taxed

Interest on bonds in default at time of purchase if coupons mature prior to the date of purchase. These are usually purchased "flat" on the open market. Interest received reduces your cost

Interest accumulated on note to date of gift

Received in property which has no fair market value

Received without any legal obligation and proven to be a gift from your creditor

Received by a surviving spouse under a life insurance policy—and payments are made in installments. Excluded interest is limited annually to $1,000. See ¶12.30

Wholly or partially exempt, on obligations of state, territory, any political subdivision thereof, or the District of Columbia

L

Legacies received in lieu of executor's commission, ¶12.01

Legal fee turned over to legal aid society by lawyer employed by the society

Legal services under qualified group legal services plan, ¶20.04

Lessee's improvements, ¶9.01

Libel damages, ¶12.22

Life insurance premiums paid by your employer, within certain limits, see ¶2.02, 2.021, 32.02

Life insurance received because of the death of the insured, generally, ¶12.30

Living quarters and subsistence received from your employer for his convenience, ¶2.01

Loans

Loss of life, compensation for, ¶12.30

Lump-sum benefits received from Social Security Board

M

Mileage allowance paid to parent for taking children to school where there is no school bus service

Military and naval personnel, see ¶35.01

Minister's dwelling or rental allowance, ¶2.05

Mortgage assistance payments under Section 235 of the National Housing Act

Moving expense payments under Uniform Relocation Assistance and Real Property Acquisition Policies Act of 1970 to persons displaced by federal projects.

Municipal bond interest, ¶4.04

Mutual funds' dividends that are returns of capital and pass through of tax-free interest, ¶4.53

Mutual insurance company dividends (but not interest thereon)

N

National Defense Education Act grants under Title IV to graduate students preparing for college teaching careers

Nominee—the income of the person for whom you act is not your income

Notes received from your employer as security for salary he owes you. (The salary has not been paid because the employer does not have the money)

Nutrition Program for the Elderly food benefits

O

Old Age and Survivors Insurance benefits under Social Security Acts, if income limits are not exceeded, ¶34.11

Options to purchase employer's stock in certain cases, ¶32.04

Option payments to you as seller until option is given up

P

Parsonage allowances, ¶2.05

Partial payments received from a debtor in liquidation are not taxable until capital has been recovered

Payments to reduce cost of winter energy consumption

Payments to union's vacation fund under certain conditions

Payments under the state unemployment laws if income below certain limits, see ¶2.10

Peace Corps allowances for living and travel expenses

Pensions paid by—

Employees' trusts out of payments by employees—see ¶7.10

Federal government to soldiers' widows

Federal pension acts enacted prior to March 20, 1933, for World War I veterans

Pension plan contributions by employer to qualified plan

Personal injuries, amounts received for, ¶12.32

Political campaign contributions used in the campaign and not for candidate's personal use

Premiums paid by employers on group-term life insurance policies under $50,000, ¶2.021

Prizes—see ¶12.03

Proceeds of certain life insurance contracts, ¶12.30

Profit on sale of house by owner 55 or over, up to certain limits, see ¶29.30

Promissory notes, renewal

Property appreciation

Property damages—see Damages

Property which you received as an inheritance, gift, bequest, or devise, ¶12.02

Public assistance payments from a general welfare fund

R

Railroad Retirement Act Benefits, if income limits are not exceeded, ¶34.11

Rebates of cash on purchase of new car or other items

Receipts in court actions, in certain cases, ¶12.22

Recoveries of certain deductions in loss years in the operation of a business, ¶12.20

Recovery of medical costs, in certain cases, ¶17.08

Reduction of debt due on purchase of property—when it is an adjustment of purchase price, ¶12.21

Refunds of federal income tax and state tax if deduction did not give you tax benefits, ¶12.20

Regulated Investment Companies' dividends—see ¶3.03

Reimbursements for out-of-pocket expenses in these volunteer programs: Retired Senior Volunteer Program (RSVP), Foster Grandparent Program, Older American Community Service Program, Senior Corps of Retired Executives (SCORE), Active Corps of Executives (ACE)

Rental allowance or value of home given to minister, see ¶2.05

Rents collected by mortgagee after taking possession after a default. The rents collected are applied against the mortgage debt

Rent security, see ¶9.00

Reorganization, certain types of property received in a, ¶6.20

Residence sales' gains—if you buy, exchange, or build a new residence under the rules of ¶29.20

Residence, sale of, by owner age 55 or over, tax free up to certain limits, see ¶29.30

Restaurant employees' meals, in some cases—see ¶2.02

Restricted, indeterminable, unavailable or disputed income. You pay tax when the income, gains or profits are fully available to you

S

Scholarship awards, ¶12.10

Security paid to landlord, ¶9.00

Separation allowances, in some cases, ¶20.00

Slander compensation—see Damage

Social Security benefits, if income limits are not exceeded, ¶34.11

State unemployment (up to certain limits) and disability payments, ¶2.10

Stock appreciation rights, ¶32.03

Stock dividends, ¶4.56

Stock option to buy employer's stock, ¶32.04

Stock rights, received, ¶4.56

Support payments for children, ¶20.04

T

Tax refunds—see Refunds—(but not interest thereon)

Tax-free trades of property

Tax-exempt interest—see Interest

Tax paid for bondholder by corporation under tax-free covenant clause, ¶24.00

Tools from your employer, needed in your work

Tenant relocation payments by federal government

Treaty exemptions, ¶36.12

U

Unemployment insurance benefits up to certain limits, ¶2.10

Uniform allowances for Armed Forces personnel

Uniform supplied by your employer, ¶2.02

Use and occupancy insurance proceeds paid on a fixed daily allowance, see ¶18.20

V

Veterans—

Allowances under Public Law 16 for disabled veterans

Automobile or allowance for automobile given to disabled veteran through Administrator of Veteran Affairs

Transportation in kind from your last station to your home

Disability pension, see ¶2.18

Free hospitalization or outpatient service in veterans' hospitals

Clothing or clothing allowance on separation

Refund of National Service Life Insurance premiums if you were hospitalized more than six months

Federal Readjustment Allowance

Various other state benefits and bonuses
Proceeds from government endowment insurance contracts of World War I
Payments to veterans of World War I under Adjusted Compensation Act, including interest
Benefits under War Risk Insurance Act
Benefits and pensions received under World War Veterans' Acts or war risk insurance acts
Bonuses paid by any state or political subdivision for military service
Gratuitous medical or hospital treatment provided by U.S. government hospitals

Money paid upon discharge to enlisted men, in place of unused clothing allowance to their credit
Mustering out pay
Prisoner of war payments under 1954 War Claims Act
Value of travel furnished in kind to discharged enlisted men
War risk insurance and government endowment policies (dividends and proceeds)
War risk insurance (dividends and proceeds)
Widows' pension paid by U.S. to soldiers' widows

W

War pensions—benefits, mustering out pay paid to veterans or widows under any Act of Congress relating to veterans
Welfare benefits
Widow of deceased employee, payments received from his employer—up to $5,000, ¶2.04
Will contest, amount received in settlement of
Winter energy assistance payments
Workmen's Compensation Acts, amount received under, ¶2.17

¶41.00 • What You May Deduct

A

Accelerated cost recovery on business equipment, ¶5.30
Accident insurance premiums in your business
Accounting and auditing expenses paid for:
    Keeping your books and accounts
    Preparation of tax returns
Accrued expenses under economic performance test, ¶5.01
Adoption expenses for hard-to-place child, ¶20.05
Advertising expenses for business
Alimony paid under the rules of, ¶20.00
Alterations and repairs on business or income-producing property
Amortization of bond premiums, ¶4.031
Amortization of construction period interest and taxes, ¶16.02
Appraisal costs for tax and business purposes
Army and Navy—see ¶35.00
Assessments paid to labor unions for "out of work" benefit payments
Assessments on worthless bank stock
Attending conventions, ¶2.29
Attorney fees related to your job or business
    Estate planning, ¶20.03
    Libel suits, business reputation, ¶20.03
    Obtaining alimony, ¶1.71
    Tax advice, ¶20.03
    See also Expenses paid for the production and collection of income
Automobile—damages to, *see* ¶18.06
Automobile expenses incurred during business trips (*see* ¶3.00), job-related moving (*see* ¶2.45), trips for charitable organizations (*see* ¶14.03), and trips for medical care (*see* ¶17.08)

B

Back pay, expenses to collect
Bad debts, *see* ¶6.28
Bad debt reserve, additions to—for businesses using reserve method
Bank deposit loss by failure of bank, *see* ¶6.28
Bank charges on business or farm accounts
Blizzard losses, *see* ¶18.00
Board and lodging given employees, *see* ¶2.01
Bonding premium (in business)
Bond premium amortization on fully or partly taxed bonds. *See* ¶4.031
Bonds, worthless, ¶6.032
Bonus to employees
Bonus payment to lessee or lessor, ¶9.01
Bookkeeping expenses (business)
Brokerage fee to obtain a mortgage loan if property is used in business. The fee is amortized over the mortgage term. In the year you sell the property and the buyer assumes the mortgage, you may deduct the unrecovered balance.
Burglary losses, *see* ¶18.00
Bus drivers' uniforms, ¶19.04
Business expense and losses ¶5.03, 5.04, 5.10
Business expenses of employees in excess of amounts received as reimbursements, ¶2.39
Business overhead insurance premiums for insurance that pays your business operating costs if you are out sick or injured
Business start-up costs, amortizable, ¶5.07

C

Cancellation of lease, payment made by tenant for (as a business expense only)

Cancellation of lease, expenses of lessor in connection with, including unamortized balance of expenses paid in negotiating the lease
Capital asset loss, ¶6.00
Capital loss carryover, ¶6.003
Carrying charges, as interest or taxes, but *see* ¶16.02
Carryover and carryback of a net operating loss, ¶5.23
Casualty losses, *see* ¶18.00
Chamber of Commerce dues (business)
Charitable contributions paid to religious, charitable, scientific, literary, educational, and other organizations (including family foundations) which operate in the manner prescribed, ¶14.01
Christmas presents and other holiday gifts to employees, customers or prospects up to $25 per person, *see* ¶2.34
Clothing—uniforms, costumes, and working clothes—cost, laundering, and cleaning if required by your job and not adaptable to general wear ¶19.04
Cleaning charges for windows, carpets, office furniture, equipment, draperies, etc., in your business
Collection of income and business debts, expenses connected with ¶20.01
Commissions to employees—for example those paid to obtain business
Commissions paid to agents (press agents, literary agents, booking agents, etc.)
Commissions paid in connection with rented property, ¶9.01
Commissions paid to brokers on sale of property is deducted from sales proceeds, *see* ¶6.08
Compensation paid employees and assistants
Compensation which you have to repay to your employer because of overpayments in former years. *See* ¶2.11
Compromises, of business debts or as a result of litigation
Condominium owners' interest and realty taxes
Conductors' uniforms, ¶19.04
Congressman's salary he returns to the government. This is deductible as a charitable contribution. He must include his entire salary in income—he cannot merely report the net amount he keeps
Contributions, *see* Charitable contributions
Contributions to IRAs, ¶7.16
Contributions to simplified employee pension plans, ¶7.22
Contributions to disability insurance funds in certain states, *see* ¶16.01
Convention expenses, *see* ¶2.29
Cooperative apartment and house owners—
    Depreciation if used in business or rented to tenant, ¶5.15
    Partial capital loss on worthlessness of stock
    Proportionate share of real estate taxes and interest, ¶15.05
Cost depletion, ¶9.17
Costumes, wigs, and make-ups (actors and entertainers)
Country club expenses, ¶2.331
Court proceedings, cost of (business only), except when guilty of a criminal offense
Covenant not to compete, ¶5.461
Credit bureau reports and service charges
Custodian fees paid to banks or investment counsel, fees incurred in the management of your investments where they produce taxable income

D

Damage to property held for personal use, as a result of a casualty such as a fire, shipwreck, storm, if above certain amounts—*see* ¶18.00
Damages paid in connection with suits concerning your business
Debts, cancellation of employees'
Debts, uncollectible, ¶6.28
Delivery and freight charges in your business
Depletion of oil and gas wells, other natural deposits, and timber, ¶9.17
Depreciation on business or income-producing property, ¶5.30
Directors' expenses
Disability insurance deductions in certain states, *see* ¶16.01
Disaster losses, ¶18.051
Disbarment proceedings, expenses in successful defense
Discounts allowed customers
Donations to charities, ¶14.01
Drugs and medicines, *see* ¶17.01
Dues to (*see also* ¶19.03)
    Clubs and associations, employer requires you to belong to hold your job
    Membership in organized labor unions
    Professional societies
    Trade associations

E

Education—tuition fees, books, traveling expenses, etc.—if required to keep your employment or professional standards, *see* ¶21.00
    Carrying charges on installment payments of tuition
Efficiency expert, fees to
Embezzlement losses, *see* ¶18.03
Employees, payments to
Employment agency fees, ¶19.05
Endorser's losses, ¶6.28
Entertainment of customers, ¶2.31
Estate tax paid on income reported by heirs, ¶11.03
Excess foreign housing costs of self-employed or not employer financed, ¶36.02
Expenses paid for the production and collection of income, and expenses to maintain, manage, and conserve property held for investment, *see* ¶19.14–19.16

F

Farm expenses, if operated for profits, *see* ¶8.00
Fees paid—
    To bank acting as dividend agent in automatic dividend reinvestment plan, ¶20.01
    To secure employment under limits of ¶19.05
    To secure admission to organized labor union
    For passports on a business trip
    To lawyers, accountants, etc. (*See* "Attorneys' Fees," and "Accounting and Auditing Expenses")
Fidelity bond—if you pay for it
Finance charges, *see* ¶15.03
Fire insurance premiums (on business or income producing property)
Fire losses—*see* Losses
Firemen's uniforms and equipment, ¶19.04
First-year expensing of depreciable property, ¶5.38
Flood losses, *see* ¶18.00
Food and drinks (for business entertainment), *see* ¶2.31

Forced sales, losses
Foreign taxes paid, ¶16.11, 36.14
Future account losses, ¶6.01

G

Gambling losses (only to extent of gambling gains), ¶12.05
General sales taxes imposed on consumer
Gifts for business purposes, *see* ¶2.34 for limitation
Gifts (*see* under Charitable contributions)
Goodwill
    Abandonment of
    Loss on sale of
    Promotion and maintenance of
Government employee's traveling expense which is necessary to do his job
Group life insurance upon employees
Guarantor's losses, ¶6.28
Guaranty against loss on sale of securities paid by securities' salesman to his customer

H

Health expenses—*see* Medical expenses
Heating (*see* under "Office maintenance")
Home office, limitations, *see* ¶5.10, 19.052
Hotel costs when on a business trip, *see* ¶2.23
Household or personal assets stolen or destroyed by fire or other casualty, *see* ¶18.00
Housing costs while working abroad if self-employed or costs not employer-financed, ¶36.02
Hurricane losses, *see* ¶18.00

I

Income tax return, fees for preparing, ¶20.02
Income tax, state or city
Individual retirement account (IRA) contributions, *see* ¶7.16
Information, cost of obtaining, including cost of standard services for business, tax, or investment use
Injury benefits to employees (not compensated by insurance)
Insurance premiums on policies written in connection with your business. Advance premium payments must be allocated, *see* ¶5.03
Interest paid or imputed, ¶15.00, ¶4.10, ¶6.191
Interest, prepaid, must be allocated over life of loan, *see* ¶15.021
Interest, although not stated, on tuition installment plans or personal property purchases, *see* ¶15.03
Interest paid in form of dividends from stock pledged for your loan
Investment counsel fees, ¶20.01
Investor's cost in short selling premiums, dividends, etc.
Involuntary conversion, loss, ¶18.00

J

Job expenses, *see* ¶2.20, 19.01
Jockey's uniforms, ¶19.04
Joint venture losses, ¶10.00

K

Keogh plan contributions, ¶7.31

L

Labor expenses
Labor union dues, ¶19.03
Lawsuit expenses—*see* Attorneys' fees
Library expenses used only for business or profession, ¶5.04
License and regulatory fees for your business paid annually
Livestock killed by authorities
Living costs on a business trip, ¶2.23
Loans, uncollectible, ¶6.28
Lodging on trips to obtain medical care, ¶17.08
Losses (except to the extent covered by insurance) arising from:
    Abandoned property
    Abandonment of worthless business machinery
    Bad debts, **¶6.28**
    Bonds sold or exchanged, **¶6.031**
    Bonds—worthless, ¶6.032
    Business operations, ¶5.00
    Capital assets, sale of, ¶6.00

Casualties such as fire, theft, storm, shipwreck, ¶18.00
Deposit to secure business lease, forfeited
Deposits in closed banks, ¶6.28
Endorser or guarantor compelled to pay for principal when transaction was entered into for profit
Forced sales, ¶18.21
Foreclosures
Forfeitures
Futures account closed by broker
Gambling to the extent of gains, ¶12.05
Goodwill—sale or abandonment
Investments—worthless, ¶6.032
Joint ventures, syndicates, pools, etc., participation in, ¶10.00
Loans not repaid, ¶6.28
Machinery abandoned
Mortgaged property sold (business or investment)
Net operating loss carried over and back, ¶5.20
Obsolescence of business asset
Partnership operations
Profit-seeking transactions, ¶5.00
Sale of capital assets, ¶6.00
Sale of inherited residence, ¶29.28
Sales and exchanges of property, ¶6.00
Securities—sale or exchange, ¶6.00
Securities—worthless, ¶6.032
Seizures by the government
Short sales, ¶6.261
Stocks—worthless, ¶6.032
Transactions entered into for profit, even though not connected with a business, ¶20.00
Worthless securities, ¶6.032

M

Magazines, technical or in waiting room of professional
Malpractice, expenses of professional in defense of suit for
"Marriage penalty" deduction, ¶1.011
Materials and supplies used in your business
Meals and lodging—*see* ¶2.23
Medical expenses in excess of 5% of adjusted gross income, ¶17.03
Membership dues—*see* ¶19.03
Messenger service (for business)
Military personnel, *see* ¶35.00
Mortgage foreclosure losses, *see* ¶31.06–31.062
Mortgage brokerage fees, *see* Brokerage fees to obtain a mortgage loan
Moving expense of business property
Moving expenses paid by lessor for prospective lessee (spread ratably over term of lease)
Moving expenses of employees, ¶2.40
Musician—cost of sheet music, arranger's fees, depreciation and repairs on instruments

N

National Defense Education Act grants under Title IV to graduate students preparing for college teaching careers, ¶12.04
Net loss in the operation of a business may be carried back and/or forward, *see* ¶5.20
Net loss resulting from a casualty may be carried back and over. *See* ¶18.09
Non-trade and non-business expense. Be sure to read the deductions allowed, ¶19.00 and ¶20.00
Nurse's expense for medical kit and drugs, ¶19.041
Nurse's uniforms, ¶19.04

O

Obsolescence, ¶5.30
Office maintenance expenses
Office rent you pay
Office stationery and supplies, including: Bills, cards or envelopes, labels and letterheads
Ordinary and necessary business expenses
Outside salesperson's deductions, ¶19.01
Overdrawn advances of employee charged off as compensation

P

Painting expense, rental property, ¶9.02
Parking meter deposits (business car or truck)
Partially worthless business bad debts, ¶6.28
Patents, ¶9.20

Cost of improvement by licensee
Depreciation
Infringement litigation settlement payment
Litigation costs
Payments to Workmen's Compensation Funds
Penalty paid for prepaying mortgage payments
Pension plan contributions to simplified employee pension plan, ¶7.22
Percentage depletion, ¶9.17
Periodicals used in your business or profession
Plane fare for business trips
Points paid for loan under certain circumstances, ¶15.012
Police officers' revolvers, cartridges, etc., paid for by them
Postage (in business)
Prepaid tax shelter expenses, if paid within 90 days, ¶8.09, ¶9.161
Premiums on business insurance. The IRS has required cash basis taxpayers to prorate the deduction of prepaid insurance premiums over the life of the insurance policy. One court, however, has allowed a full deduction
Preparation of tax returns, cost of
Professional dues (see "Dues")
Professional's expenses, including books and equipment of short life
Property damage, *see* ¶18.00
Property taxes, ¶16.05
Publicity costs in your business

R

Rebates on sales
Real estate, as charitable contributions
Real estate, expenses of rental or investment property, ¶9.02
Real estate sales losses, ¶6.00
Real estate taxes, ¶16.05
Receivers' fees for services rendered in carrying on business of a bankrupt
Refund by you to your employer of overpayment of compensation in a previous year. Note the special rule if the repayment is over $3,000. *See* ¶2.11
Religious organizations, contributions to, ¶14.01
Rents, including
    Payment to cancel a business lease
    Payments assumed to secure tenants
    Payments for the use of:
        Business property
        Safe deposit box used for business investment purposes
Repairs of business or income-producing property
Repairs to a residence or property which you rent to others, ¶9.02
Replacing business property damaged by negligence, theft, casualties, etc., when the replacement does not prolong the life of the property damaged
Research and development costs in business amortized over 60 months or more
Research expenses required for courses—the cost of which are deductible under rules of ¶21.00
Reservists' travel expenses, ¶35.02
Restaurant and night club bills for entertaining customers under rules at ¶2.31
Royalty expenses

S

Safe deposit box cost for records used in your business or for income-producing or investment property, ¶20.01
Salaries or other compensation for services paid
Sales expenses
    Discounts and rebates
    Entertainment of clients and prospects
    Promotion expenses
    Special commissions and compensation
Salespersons' expenses, ¶19.01
Sales taxes, general, city, state, ¶16.03, 16.04, 16.12
Sample rooms, cost of
Savings, investment and protection
    Loss if bank fails (only amount not recovered), ¶6.28
    Sales of securities result in a loss or they become worthless. *See* ¶6.28. (Interest on brokerage account is deductible only when paid, not when charged to the account, ¶15.01)

Worthless notes and loans to others
Life insurance loan interest deductible when paid in cash or by check, ¶15.01
Health and accident insurance premiums are considered medical expenses, ¶17.05
Scrapping of business property, losses caused by
Securities as charitable contributions, ¶14.05
Security transactions, cost of
Services of assistants
Shipwreck damages, see ¶18.00
Short sales losses, ¶6.261
Short selling costs, see ¶6.261
Simplified employee pension plan contributions, ¶7.22
Social Security taxes paid by you as employer
Soil conservation costs may be deducted currently or capitalized. See Farm deductions
Stamp taxes, if in connection with business or production of income
State income and other taxes ¶16.001
State legislators, living costs
Stationery, supplies, and printing used in business and profession
Stock—see Losses
Stock rights, worthless
Storage charges in business
Storm damage, see ¶18.00
Subscriptions to professional or trade journals
Substitutes paid by you. Payments to a substitute teacher to take your place are deductible
Supplies used in profession or business
Support of a student, unrelated to you, in your home, up to $50 per month, ¶14.04

Surgeons' uniforms
Syndicate losses, ¶10.00

T

Tax preparation fees, ¶20.02
Taxes paid (property, general sales, income), ¶16.001
Taxi fare, on business trips, see ¶2.23
Teachers' expenses of attending summer school, ¶21.00
Technical magazines used in your business
Telegrams and telephones for business
Telephone cost, where you have a telephone at home solely to be called to work (you have no regular hours), ¶19.053
Tenants—payment of real estate taxes, interest or other items for your landlord (if property is leased for income-producing purposes)
Termination expenses of lessor
Theater tickets, cost (for business), ¶2.34
Theft losses, see ¶18.00
Tips, in connection with deductible travel or entertainment expenses
Tools, tires, and other assets used in your business having a life of less than a year, ¶19.041
Trade associations' dues
Transportation costs, ¶2.22
Traveling and entertaining expenses, ¶2.23, 2.31 19.02
Traveling between two jobs
Traveling to professional convention, limits, see ¶2.29, 2.292

Traveling to get medical care, ¶17.08
Traveling to look after income producing property, ¶20.01
Trustees' expenses, certain commissions
Tuition costs, see ¶19.06 for limitations
Two-earner married couple, ¶1.01

U

Uncollectible debts, ¶6.28
Uniforms, required for your job and not generally adaptable for ordinary wear, ¶19.04
Union assessments, ¶19.03
Union dues, ¶19.03
Unreimbursed volunteer expenses for charity, ¶14.03
Unstated interest, ¶6.191, 15.01, 15.011
Upkeep, care and maintenance of real estate held for investment or rented to others, ¶9.02

W

Water damage to lake-front property, when caused by a storm—not merely action of waves during high water level periods, see ¶18.00
Windfall profits tax, ¶16.001
Worthless bonds or stocks—see ¶6.032

Y

"Your Income Tax," ¶20.02

¶42.00 • You May Not Deduct the Following

A

Accident, automobile, loss resulting from, caused by willful negligence, ¶18.06
Adoption costs
Alcoholic beverage taxes
Alimony payments (lump sum), ¶1.73
Alimony payments, if not part of decree or written separation agreement, ¶1.72
Assessments: Labor union members' payment for sickness, accident, and death benefits in some cases
Assessments, local, which benefit property, ¶16.05
Attorneys' fees
    See below, Expenses not concerned with production or collection of income
    See also Litigation expenses
Automobile expenses such as
    For personal use
    Those incurred going to office from home, ¶2.211

B

Bad debts which did not become worthless in this year—see ¶6.28
Bank fees on personal checking account, ¶20.02
Bar examination fees, ¶21.00
Betting losses which exceed winnings, see ¶12.05
Blood donations
Bribes
Brokerage fees or commissions—generally added to purchase price or deducted from sales price
Burial costs

C

Campaign expenses by a public officer or union leader
Capital expenditures
Caretaker expenses for unoccupied residence never offered for rent but merely listed for sale with broker
Carfares for traveling to and from work, ¶2.211
Casualty loss, personal, below certain limits, see ¶18.00
Casualty losses as listed at ¶18.07
Child support payments, ¶1.737
Cigarette taxes, ¶16.001
City permit to build a personal residence

Club dues, if membership is for personal convenience and pleasure, even if club is also used for entertaining visitors, ¶2.331
Commissions on sales of real estate
Commissions on purchases and sales of stocks and bonds, if investor or trader, ¶6.08, 6.12
Commutation fares, ¶2.211
Compensation to domestics
Construction costs
Contributions described in ¶14.14
Convention expenses on cruiseship, see limits in ¶2.292
Corporation's expenses paid by stockholder
Cost of earning exempt income—see Interest
Cost of proceedings to find mental competency

D

Damages resulting from suits for the following—
    Alienation of affections
    Breach of promise
    Negligence in the operation of your car when used for personal use
    Slander, libel, other defamation of character
Debts of another, voluntary payment of
Decrease in the value of property because current market values are less than cost. No loss realized until sale, exchange, or determination of worthlessness
Deductions from your salary for withholding tax, Social Security, U.S. savings bonds, etc., ¶2.00
Defamation of character—libel and slander—see Damages
Defending or clearing title to property, cost
Demolition losses, ¶9.04
Depreciation on property held for personal use (such as your home or personal auto)
Development costs for farms, orchards, and ranches. See Farm expenditures
Distribution to beneficiaries of a trust or estate taxable to the trust or estate, ¶11.02
Divorce, attorneys' fees, other expenses, ¶1.71
Dog licenses, ¶16.001
Domestics' Social Security tax paid by the employer and the employee
Dues and fees of a personal nature, unconnected with your trade or profession, such as clubs, societies, fraternities, ¶19.03

E

Educational expenses for yourself or family, see exceptions, ¶21.00
Employees' Social Security contributions, ¶2.07
Entertainment, personal
Estate administration expenditures and fees, other than for the production or collection of income, or for the management, conservation, or maintenance of property held to produce income, ¶20.01
Excise taxes, ¶16.001
Exempt income expenses
Expenditures to obtain publicity and personal popularity not directly connected with business or the production of income—see Personal expenses
Expenses
    Attorneys' fees and costs,
        To defend, protect, or perfect title to property
        To establish your right to hold a public office to which you were elected
        To get a court to allow you to reduce the interest rate you have to pay on borrowed money
        See also Litigation expenses
    Carrying on transactions which are primarily a sport, hobby, or recreation and are not prompted by the profit motive
    Commuting to your office or place of business
    Cost of improving personal appearance
    Cost of campaigning for public office or union office
    Costs in connection with property used as your personal residence. However, if you rent the residence or convert it to income-producing property, then you are entitled to these deductions
    Creditor's payments of life insurance premiums on debtor's life
    Payment to another stockholder for his proxy to give you sufficient voting power to prevent a proposed merger
    Safe deposit box rentals for personal effects
    Stockholder's travel expenses for trips on behalf of the corporation
Expenses for which you are entitled to reimbursement from your employer but fail to claim reimbursement

F

Farms conducted for pleasure, expenses of ¶8.01
Federal income, estate, excise, and gift taxes
Fines for violation of law
Fishing license and fees
Food, clothing, and personal entertainment
Foreclosure of mortgage on personal residence, owner's loss on, ¶6.02
Foreign taxes for which a tax credit has been taken, ¶36.14
Funeral costs

G

Gasoline, taxes on, for personal driving, ¶16.001
Gambling losses exceeding winnings, see ¶12.05
Gifts
Gifts to customers or their employees—where it is against the law for them to accept gifts
Gift tax

H

Health or athletic club membership to improve or maintain general good health, ¶17.02
Hobby expenses or losses, ¶5.06
Home expenses, such as—
  Allowances to your children
  Clothing for the family
  Domestics, but see ¶24.20
  Education of children
  Electric light, heating and cooking fuel, water, ice, food, liquor, flowers, cleaning
Home office expenses, unless you meet rules at ¶5.10 and 19.052
Hunting license fees, ¶16.001

I

Improvements to buildings or equipment
Income anticipated but not received
Inheritance taxes, ¶16.001
Insurance premiums which you pay on:
  Any other personal assets
  Building during construction
  Dwelling which you own and live in
  The life of any executive, employee or stockholder from whose loss by death you are protecting yourself
  Your life
Interest not actually paid, i.e., giving a note, increasing principal, reverse annuity mortgage, see ¶15.01, 15.011
Interest paid, such as that paid on: ¶15.04
  Another's note
  Mortgages on another's property
  Life insurance loans if interest is added to the loan and not paid in cash
  A note which is a gift. The interest on such a note is also considered a gift
  Debts incurred or continued to purchase or carry obligations, interest from which is wholly exempt from federal income taxes
  Interest paid or incurred to carry accounts or obligations whose interest is excludable
  Interest paid by Civil Service employees when reinstated under the Civil Service Retirement Act, in order to receive retirement benefits
  On an ordinary margin account with your broker if you do not pay it in cash and the broker has not collected dividends, interest, or proceeds from the sale of securities out of which interest due him may be applied
  Interest incurred or continued to purchase or carry single premium life insurance annuity or endowment contracts
  Interest incurred or continued to purchase or carry life insurance, annuity, or endowment contracts (other than single premium) purchased after 8/6/63 under systematic plan for borrowing against increasing cash value, see ¶15.00
  Interest payments where there is no real debt
  Interest on obligations originally owed by others but subsequently assumed by you for prior interest due. Interest for the period after you assumed the obligation is deductible
  Interest voluntarily paid
  Tax deficiencies, where compromised lump-sum payment is less than the total deficiency, penalty, and interest claimed, unless a collateral agreement permits collection of the total deficiency

L

Labor costs—your estimate of your own labor's worth
Laundry service, cost of personal
Legal fees—see Litigation
Lessee's expenses to make necessary repairs to leased property—where landlord promised to reimburse him but did not
Libel suits—see Damages
Life insurance, personal, premiums on
Life insurance premiums on client's life paid by entertainer's agent (the agent being named as beneficiary)
Light, heat, laundry, etc., for home
Litigation or legal expenses for these personal reasons:
  Breach of promise suit
  Contesting a will
  Defamation of character, by libel or slander
  Defending yourself against a criminal suit which is of a personal nature, as opposed to one connected with business
  Divorce or separation, and dower rights, but see ¶1.71
Living and family expenses
Living expenses except when traveling on business, ¶2.23
Local assessments benefiting property, ¶16.05
Losses arising from:
  Difference between the rate of exchange on date you made a loan and the date on which it was repaid (for nonbusiness loans)
  Farms operated for recreation with no intention of making profit
  Fictitious sales
  Gambling—even if it is your business, but see ¶12.05
  Gradual sinking of land
  Illegal transactions
  Reduction in value
  Sales of personal residence, car, etc., ¶6.02
  Sale to family, ¶33.11

M

Military personnel—
  Cost of uniforms
  Cleaning, repairing and laundering of uniforms and equipment
  Cost of packing, crating, freight, etc., in changing official station, of personal effects of members of officer's family
  Cost of additional clothing purchased
  Daily transportation cost between home and station
  Damage to household equipment in moving
  Depreciation in value of uniforms
  Dues to officers' clubs
  Deductions for bonds, allotments or allowances, insurance and hospital fund
  Expense of visiting home while on furlough, leave, or liberty
  Fines imposed by court-martial sentence
  Professional textbooks, school equipment, etc., purchased to secure education in military school
  Premiums paid on war risk, converted government or commercial policies, life insurance policies, and premiums paid for increased insurance to cover hazards of aviation duty
Minor's allowances—see Allowances
Missing items—where you cannot prove theft

O

Old-age home, payments to, but see ¶17.10

P

Partially worthless securities, ¶6.032
Payments of an employee (teacher, civil service) into a retirement or pension fund, ¶2.00
Penalties and fines
Penalties assessed by the IRS
Pensions, trust or profit-sharing payments, by employers unless the trust is organized in the manner provided by law
Permanent improvements, amounts paid for same, if the improvement increases the value of the property or estate, ¶6.12
Personal asset, loss on sale, ¶6.02
Personal expenses, see Home expenses
Probate expenses
Professions, expenses for admission to, ¶21.00
Propaganda contributions, ¶14.14
Pursuing a hobby, cost of, ¶5.06

R

Recreation, expenses in pursuit of
Related taxpayers, losses, between, ¶33.12
Relief fund withholdings from your pay
Rental cost of keeping a safe deposit box for assets which do not produce income
Rent, when it includes payment for option to purchase property
Repairs to personal automobile or residence
Repayment of loans which you made

S

Securing title—a capital expenditure
Selective sales and excise taxes
Self-employed Social Security tax
Separation allowances to a spouse in some cases, ¶1.70
Separation suits—see Damages
Servants, domestic, wages paid to
Sewer taxes, ¶16.001, 16.05
Shrinkage in value of property not sold, or exchanged (except inventories)
Slander and libel, damages paid for
Social Security taxes—
  Employee's tax withheld by employer
  Employer's share—paid domestics, unless part of medical expense deduction
Self-employment tax
Sports, expenses incurred in pursuit of (unless business expense)
Spouse's deductions if filing separately, ¶1.012
Stamps, except as a business expense
Stock exchange membership cost—a capital expenditure
Stock in cooperative apartment in which you live, loss for worthlessness
Stockholders' contributions to capital
Supper costs when working overtime
Support payments, ¶1.73

T

Tax penalties
Taxes on gasoline used for personal driving, ¶16.001
Termite damages, ¶18.01
Title to property, cost of defending
Trademark, payment for
Traveling
  Between home and place of work, ¶2.22
  By members of your family who accompany you on business trips, ¶2.22
  By student on a summer job away from home
  To explore general investment possibilities in an area—where there is not already an existing income-producing right or interest
  For pleasure, ¶2.20
Truck overweight fines
Tuition costs to get better position. See ¶21.00

U

Uniforms, if adaptable to general wear, ¶19.04
Union assessments—see Assessments
Unemployment insurance payments to state, except in some cases, ¶16.01
Uncollectible judgment based on breach of contract to buy a house

V

Voluntary alimony, ¶1.70

W

"Wash sales," losses in, ¶6.27
Water rents for personal residence, ¶16.001
Will contest, litigation and compromise

INDEX

Note: All references are to ¶ numbers which you will find throughout this book.

TAX WORK SHEETS FOR PREPARING YOUR 1986 TAX RETURN

Here are forms to help you organize your tax data for preparing your tax return.

RECORD OF PAYMENTS OF FEDERAL ESTIMATED TAX

(Also see ¶26.00 of YOUR INCOME TAX)

PAYMENT FOR	AMOUNT	
FIRST INSTALLMENT—APRIL 15 (include amount of overpayment credited to estimated tax)	$	
SECOND INSTALLMENT—JUNE 15		
THIRD INSTALLMENT—SEPTEMBER 15		
FOURTH INSTALLMENT—JANUARY 15		
TOTAL PAYMENTS	$	

WORK SHEET FOR DETERMINING SUPPORT

To claim an exemption for a dependent child, relative or household member, you must generally provide at least 50% of their support. Use this form to determine whether you meet the 50% support test. Other tests for claiming an exemption are at ¶1.50 of YOUR INCOME TAX.

Dependent's Income	1) Did the dependent receive any income, such as wages, interest, dividends, pensions, rents, social security, or welfare? (If yes, complete lines 2, 3, 4 and 5)	☐ Yes ☐ No	
	2) Total income received by dependent	$	
	3) Amount of dependent's income used for his or her support	$	
	4) Amount of dependent's income used for other purposes	$	
	5) Amount of dependent's income saved	$	
	(The total of lines, 3, 4, and 5 should equal line 2)		
Expenses for Entire Household (where dependent lived)	6) Lodging (Complete item a or b)		
	a) Rent paid	$	
	b) If not rented, show fair rental value of home. If dependent owns home, include this amount in line 20.	$	
	7) Food	$	
	8) Utilities (heat, light, water, etc. not included in line 6a or 6b)	$	
	9) Repairs (not included in line 6a or 6b)	$	
	10) Other. Do not include expenses of maintaining home, such as mortgage interest, real estate taxes, and insurance.	$	
	11) Total household expenses (Add lines 6 through 10)	$	
	12) Number of persons, including dependent, living in household		
Expenses for Dependent Only	13) Dependent's part of household expenses (line 11 divided by line 12)	$	
	14) Clothing	$	
	15) Education	$	
	16) Medical, dental	$	
	17) Travel, recreation	$	
	18) Other (specify)	$	
	19) Total cost of dependent's support for the year (Add lines 13 through 18)	$	
	20) Amount dependent provided for own support (line 3, plus line 6b if dependent owns home)	$	
	21) Amount others provided for dependent's support. Include amounts provided by state, local, and other welfare societies or agencies.	$	
	22) Amount you provided for dependent's support (line 19 minus lines 20 and 21)	$	
	23) 50% of line 19	$	

If line 22 is more than line 23, you meet the support test for the dependent. If the other dependency tests are met, you may claim an exemption for that person.

If line 23 is more than line 22, you may be able to claim an exemption for the dependent under a multiple support agreement. See ¶1.553 of YOUR INCOME TAX.

SALARY OR WAGE INCOME FROM FORM W-2 STATEMENTS

You should receive a W-2 from each employer for whom you worked showing your wages and the amount of income and Social Security (F.I.C.A.) taxes withheld. Record the withholdings shown on your W-2 on this page. Also record amounts withheld for other items such as medical insurance, etc.

Enter the total state and city income taxes withheld in the work sheet for deductible taxes on page 347. Enter the amount withheld for medical insurance in the work sheet for medical and dental expenses on page 345. Also keep records of other tax deductible items withheld from your pay such as union dues and contributions to a company SEP plan.

NAME OF EMPLOYER	ADDRESS	TOTAL WAGES	F.I.C.A.	FEDERAL TAX	STATE TAX	CITY TAX	MEDICAL INSURANCE	OTHER DEDUCTIONS
HUSBAND		$	$	$	$	$	$	$
TOTAL FOR HUSBAND		$	$	$	$	$	$	$
WIFE		$	$	$	$	$	$	$
TOTAL FOR WIFE		$	$	$	$	$	$	$
TOTAL WAGE INCOME		$	$	$	$	$	$	$

CAPITAL GAINS AND LOSSES

Stocks and Bonds

Use the work sheet below for keeping track of your security transactions. For sales and exchanges of property other than stocks, bonds, and your personal residence, use the work sheet on page 341. On your return, you report sales of stocks, bonds, and similar investments, and the sale of a residence on Schedule D.

NUMBER OF SHARES OR BONDS	DESCRIPTION	SOLD		BOUGHT		SHORT-TERM GAIN (LOSS)	LONG-TERM GAIN (LOSS)
		DATE	SALES PRICE*	DATE	COST**		
			$		$	$	$
				TOTAL		$	$

*Excluding state transfer tax, if any, which is claimed as itemized deduction.
**Including commissions. For bonds, add to cost basis amount of bond discount reported as interest (¶ 6.031 of YOUR INCOME TAX); deduct bond premium amortization from cost basis (see ¶ 4.031 of YOUR INCOME TAX).

SALES AND EXCHANGES OF PROPERTY

(Other than Stocks, Bonds, and Personal Residence)

Use the work sheet below for keeping records of your sales of property other than stocks, bonds, or your personal residence. On your tax return, you report on Form 4797 sales and exchanges of the following: Property used in a trade or business, real estate (other than a personal residence), and property subject to the depreciation recapture rules (see ¶5.45 of YOUR IN-COME TAX).

SHORT-TERM OR LONG-TERM	1. DESCRIPTION OF PROPERTY	2. DATE ACQUIRED	DATE SOLD	3. SALES PRICE	4. DEPRECIA-TION	5. COST (OR OTHER BASIS)	6. IMPROVE-MENTS	7. SELLING EXPENSES	GAIN OR LOSS 3 plus 4 less 5, 6, and 7	
									GAIN	LOSS
				$	$	$	$	$	$	$
TOTAL									$	$

PENSION AND ANNUITY INCOME

How you report your pension or annuity income on your tax return depends upon the kind of pension or annuity you have and whether or not you have a cost investment in the contract. Where you have a cost investment in a pension or annuity contract, your payments consist of two parts: (1) A return of your cost, which is tax free, and (2) income on your investment, which is taxable (see ¶7.07 of YOUR INCOME TAX). There is a special rule for reporting certain employee annuities where the employee's contribution will be recovered within a three-year period (see ¶7.09 of YOUR INCOME TAX). If you did not contribute to the cost of your annuity or pension (and you paid no tax on your employer's contribution), your payments are fully taxable.

Keep a record of your pension and annuity payments in the schedule below. Check these totals against the amount shown on Form W-2P which will be sent to you by the payer.

MONTH	POLICY (IDENTIFY)		POLICY (IDENTIFY)		POLICY (IDENTIFY)	
January	$		$		$	
February						
March						
April						
May						
June						
July						
August						
September						
October						
November						
December						
TOTAL	$		$		$	

WITHHOLDINGS

Taxes will be withheld from your pension unless you elect to avoid withholding on a Form W-4 which you file with the payer (see ¶25.09 of YOUR INCOME TAX). Any withholdings will be shown on Form W-2P which you will receive from the payer. Record the amount withheld on the line below.

Federal Tax Withheld, if any—Form W-2P

POLICY	POLICY	POLICY
$_____	$_____	$_____

RENTAL INCOME

You report rental income in the rental schedule of your return. If you rent out part of your house, deduct the share of expenses allocated to the rent-producing part of the house as a rental expense. The mortgage interest and taxes allocated to your personal use of the house are deductible as excess itemized deductions. A work sheet for allocating rental expenses appears on the next page.

MONTH	PROPERTY (IDENTIFY)		PROPERTY (IDENTIFY)		PROPERTY (IDENTIFY)		PROPERTY (IDENTIFY)	
January	$		$		$		$	
February								
March								
April								
May								
June								
July								
August								
September								
October								
November								
December								
TOTAL	$		$		$		$	

EXPENSE WORK SHEET FOR RENTAL PROPERTY

The form below is for listing expenses of rental property. The ___ and allocate deductible expenses. The other columns are for deduct-
first two columns are for rental property where part of the property is ___ ible expenses of rental property, no part of which is personally used
used for your personal use. These two columns allow you to earmark ___ by you.

	IF YOU USE PART OF PROPERTY		FULLY RENTED (NO PERSONAL USE)				
ITEM	(a) EXPENSES OF ENTIRE PROPERTY TO BE ALLOCATED	(b) SPECIFIC EXPENSES OF RENTAL AREA	PROPERTY (IDENTIFY)	PROPERTY (IDENTIFY)	PROPERTY (IDENTIFY)	PROPERTY (IDENTIFY)	PROPERTY (IDENTIFY)
Repairs:	$	$	$	$	$	$	$
Plumbing							
Electric							
Painting							
Roofing							
Carpentry							
Other							
Total	$	$	$	$	$	$	$

Allocate to column (b) _____ % of column (a)   **Deductible Repairs**

	(a)	(b)					
Other Expenses:	$	$	$	$	$	$	$
Heat							
Utilities							
Interest*							
Water							
Taxes*							
Insurance							
Cleaning and maintenance							
Gardening							
Professional fees							
Other							
Total	$	$					$

Allocate to column (b) _____ % of column (a)   **Other Deductible Expenses**

* The interest and taxes not allocated
to the rental area may be claimed as itemized deductions.

MEDICAL AND DENTAL EXPENSE WORK SHEET

A check list of deductible medical costs is at ¶17.01 of YOUR INCOME TAX. Keep track of your auto mileage on trips for medical care, and do not overlook medical insurance premiums deducted from your wages.

ITEM	AMOUNT
1. Medical insurance premiums	
Withheld by employer _____	$
Other _____	
TOTAL _____	$
2. Medicines and drugs	
_____	$
_____	
_____	
_____	
_____	
_____	
_____	
TOTAL _____	$
3. Payments to physicians	
_____	$
_____	
_____	
_____	
TOTAL _____	$
4. Payments to dentists	
_____	$
_____	
_____	
_____	
TOTAL _____	$

ITEM	AMOUNT

5. Hospital costs

$ _____

_____

_____

_____

TOTAL _____ $ _____

6. Other medical costs (identify)

$ _____

_____

_____

_____

_____

_____

TOTAL _____ $ _____

7. Transportation for medical care

Number of miles _____ × .09* _____ $ _____

Parking fees _____

Tolls _____

Other travel costs _____

_____

TOTAL _____ $ _____

8. Reimbursements of medical costs

$ _____

_____

_____

_____

TOTAL _____ $ _____

*Rate when this book went to press

WORK SHEET FOR DEDUCTIBLE INCOME TAXES

ITEM	AMOUNT
State income taxes (YOUR INCOME TAX ¶16.01, ¶16.12) **ESTIMATED TAX PAYMENTS**	

INSTALLMENT	DATE	AMOUNT	
		$	

TOTAL ESTIMATED TAX PAID IN YEAR _____ $

TAX PAID ON FILING TAX RETURN _____

TAX WITHHELD FROM YOUR PAY (*INCLUDE SPOUSE'S WITHHOLDING ON JOINT RETURN*) _____

TOTAL STATE INCOME TAX PAID IN YEAR _____ $

City income taxes
(YOUR INCOME TAX ¶16.01)
ESTIMATED TAX PAYMENTS

INSTALLMENT	DATE	AMOUNT	
		$	

TOTAL ESTIMATED TAX PAID IN YEAR _____ $

TAX PAID ON FILING TAX RETURN _____

TAX WITHHELD FROM YOUR PAY (*INCLUDE SPOUSE'S WITHHOLDING ON JOINT RETURN*) _____

TOTAL CITY INCOME TAX PAID IN YEAR _____ $

WORK SHEET FOR OTHER DEDUCTIBLE TAXES

ITEM	AMOUNT
Personal property taxes (YOUR INCOME TAX ¶16.001)	$
TOTAL	$
Real estate taxes (YOUR INCOME TAX ¶16.05, ¶16.07, ¶16.08) City or Town	$
School	
Other	
TOTAL	$
State stock transfer taxes	$
TOTAL	$
Sales taxes (YOUR INCOME TAX ¶16.04, and Supplement) From Treasury Sales Tax Table	$
plus sales tax paid on purchase of auto, boat, airplane, or mobile home	
If you do not use Treasury Tables, enter the total of your sales tax payments	
TOTAL	$

WORK SHEET FOR CASH CHARITABLE CONTRIBUTIONS

See ¶14.00 of YOUR INCOME TAX for a discussion of the charitable contribution deduction. Use this work sheet to keep track of your cash donations. Also keep a record of your auto mileage when using your car for volunteer charity work.

NAME OF ORGANIZATION	AMOUNT	
Place of worship	$	
College, university		
Red Cross		
United Fund, Community Chest		
Girl/Boy Scouts		
March of Dimes		
Xmas/Easter Seals		
Cancer Fund		
Heart Fund		
YM/YWCA		
Salvation Army		
Car expense for charities _____ miles × .12		
Misc. organized charities		
TOTAL	$	

RECORD OF INTEREST EXPENSES

You can find the information for this work sheet from the following sources: Mortgage statements from bank, contracts, stock brokers' statements, credit card bills, department store bills, and reports from your cooperative indicating your share of mortgage interest. See ¶15.00–¶15.06 of YOUR INCOME TAX for an explanation of the interest expense deduction. References to specific discussions in YOUR INCOME TAX are in the work sheet below.

ITEMS OF INTEREST EXPENSE	TO WHOM PAID	AMOUNT	
Interest on home mortgage		$	
Interest on cooperative apartment			
Charges on revolving charge accounts (¶15.03)			
Charges on credit cards (¶15.03)			
Interest on installment purchases (¶15.03)			
Interest on auto loan			
Margin interest			
Interest on income tax deficiency			
Other interest (specify)			
TOTAL		$	

MISCELLANEOUS DEDUCTIONS WORK SHEET

In the work sheet below is a list of items you may claim as deductions in the miscellaneous deductions section of your return. Here, you may list your miscellaneous deductions; refer to the designated sections of YOUR INCOME TAX for the rules applied to each item.

ITEM	AMOUNT	
Alimony (¶1.70) _____	$	
Union dues (¶19.03) _____		
Entertainment expenses (¶2.36 and ¶19.02) _____		
Educational expenses (¶21.00) _____		
Uniforms and work clothes (¶19.04) _____		
Dues to professional societies (¶19.03 and ¶5.04) _____		
Safe deposit box (¶20.01) _____		
Fees for preparation of tax return and tax advice (¶20.02) _____		
Investment counsel fees and services (¶20.01) _____		
Tax publications (¶20.02) _____		
Business publications (¶5.04) _____		
Professional expenses of salaried professionals (¶5.04) _____		
Employment agency fee (¶19.05) _____		
Home office expenses (¶19.052 and ¶5.10) _____		
_____		
_____		
_____		
_____		
_____		
_____		
_____		
_____		
_____		
TOTAL _____	$	

CASUALTY OR THEFT LOSS WORK SHEET

This work sheet based on IRS Form 4684 is for figuring a single casualty or theft loss of property used only for personal purposes. If you suffered more than one casualty or theft during the year, use a separate work sheet for each event entering your figures up to line 9. Then on a separate sheet of paper, total the amount of the losses from line 9 of each worksheet and reduce the total by 10% of adjusted gross income. Deductible casualty and theft losses are discussed at ¶18.01 of YOUR INCOME TAX. A guide on how to prove a casualty loss deduction is at ¶18.02 of YOUR INCOME TAX. References to specific discussions in YOUR INCOME TAX are in the body of the work sheet.

	ITEM		ITEM		ITEM		ITEM	
1. Identify property								
2. Cost or adjusted basis (¶6.12 and ¶18.04)	$		$		$		$	
Decrease in market value: Value before casualty or theft								
Less: Value after casualty or theft								
3. Decrease in value								
4. Loss *(lower of line 2 or line 3)*								
5. *Less:* Insurance recovery or other compensation								
6. Net loss	$		$		$		$	
7. Total losses shown on line 6								
8. *Less:* $100 limitation (¶18.042)								
9. Net casualty or theft loss								
10. *Less:* 10% of your adjusted gross income								
11. Deductible casualty or theft loss (¶18.00 and ¶18.04)							$	

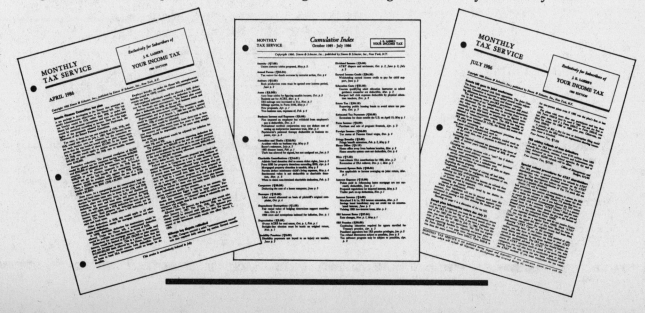

Save on Taxes

1. The Prentice-Hall Business Tax Deduction Master Guide—1987 Edition
By W. Murray Bradford, CPA, President
Tax Reduction Institute, Washington, D.C.

1987 edition
THE PRENTICE-HALL
BUSINESS
Strategies for Business
& Professional People
TAX
DEDUCTION
MASTER GUIDE
For the more than 25 million independent-business taxpayers who want to PAY LESS TAX...and be less afraid of an IRS audit
Prepared by: Tax Reduction Institute, Washington, D.C.

LEARN 1987 PLANNING STRATEGIES:

- Whether to disincorporate or not
- 9 strategies to get maximum travel deductions and combine business with pleasure
- 7 ways to get tax money to finance your child's education
- Why hiring your spouse can put $3,000 or more in your pocket each year
- 7 tax reformed ways to qualify for a
- home office deduction and 12 ways to audit-proof that deduction
- 3 techniques to double your business car deductions
- How tax reform made retirement plans a top tax-favored investment
- How to "audit-proof" your deductions with air-tight documentation

TAX PLANNING MADE EASY

Not an ordinary tax preparation book, the **Master Guide** is a tax planning guide that allows you to take advantage of every possible tax break. Designed for 1987 tax planning, it will put money in your pocket and make your tax life more comfortable, reducing fears of an IRS audit.

This fact-filled, jargon-free tax reduction book will arm you with the knowledge necessary to find more than 31 commonly overlooked tax deductions, find the right form of business, combine family with business affairs, and build audit-proof documentation.

Check #1 on order card.

AVERAGE DEDUCTION OF $5,000

The Prentice-Hall Business Tax Deduction Master Guide is written for you if you spend money to make money. You need this book if you are a small business (incorporated or not), an independent contractor, an outside salesperson ... even if you operate a part-time business. Based on actual material tested by over 40,000 business people each year, its advice has been documented as increasing tax deductions by an annual average of $5,000!

ABOUT THE AUTHOR

W. Murray Bradford has sixteen years as a practicing CPA. Called "an accountant's accountant" by his colleagues, he is the publisher and executive editor of *Write-Off*, a newsletter dedicated to the problems of small business people. He is president of the Tax Reduction Institute, a tax education company that offers seminars to thousands annually.

(0-13-108242-6) $29.95   clothbound

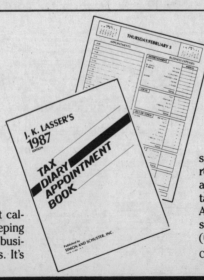

2. J.K. Lasser's 1987 Tax Diary and Appointment Book

Attractive, hardcover appointment calendar that is also perfect for keeping track of everyday, tax-deductible business expenses and appointments. It's specifically designed to meet every IRS requirement for expense record keeping and business mileage, with a guide on tax rules for travel and entertainment. Also contains a telephone and address section.

(0-13-622937-9) $16.95

Check #2 on order card.

Keep More of What You Earn

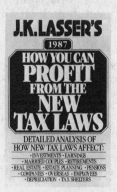

Does your paycheck seem to just slip through your fingers?

Here's an easy way to take control of the money you earn and lock-in financial security for you and your family!

Like a lot of people today you bring home a nice paycheck...but the more you earn, the more you feel your money is just slipping away.

More than 50,000 people who feel the same way have enrolled in the Personal Financial Management Seminar sponsored by Touche Ross, one of America's "Big 8" accounting firms. They come to this seminar because they feel "broke" much of the time, and they want to regain control over their hard-earned money.

Now you can get the same wealth-building techniques revealed in this seminar — *without* the expense or bother of attending. All these techniques are clearly spelled out for you in the new 1987 Edition of

The Touche Ross Guide to Personal Financial Management

Simply fill out and mail the coupon below, and we'll send you the guide to examine and use, **FREE** for 15 days, as soon as it comes off the press (early 1987).

How it Works

First the guide shows you how to set ambitious, yet realistic, goals based on your personal situation. Then it provides you with a complete set of planning forms that, when completed, show you the best and fastest way to meet your goals — whether for retirement, investment, savings, your children's education...whatever!

You'll have a complete and accurate picture of your net worth . . . a statement of your financial goals linked to a timetable . . . a plan for reducing next year's taxes to a realistic level . . . a clear grasp of your insurance needs . . . *plus* specific steps you can take right now to increase investment income and ensure a worry-free retirement.

Why it Works

Because its wealth-building plans (all developed by Touche Ross' crack financial planning team) are based on *your* income, expenditures and investments...*your* goals, objectives and lifestyle. And by following the Financial Checkup Calendar that's included, it's easy to keep your plan completely up to date. It's almost like having your own personal financial advisor.

What It Will Do for You

- It will help increase your net worth — you will be able to identify choices, foresee their consequences, and convert them into action. You will gain *full control* over your finances while improving the rate of return on your investment assets.

- It will help you save taxes — the guide shows you smart moves that can save you a bundle in taxes under the new 1986 tax law changes...tells you how to handle Estimated Taxes for maximum tax savings...shows you how to make the most of tax deductions, exemptions, credits — and much more.

- It will help you plan your estate and insurance needs — make certain your family receives maximum benefit from your estate — size-up your present life coverage and decide when to discontinue or replace old policies.

- It will help you meet the soaring costs of your children's education, showing exactly how much to invest *now* to ensure that the money is there when you need it.

Don't wait to start planning for your family's financial security. Fill out and mail the coupon below

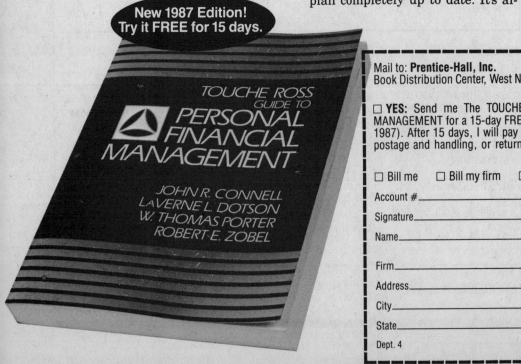

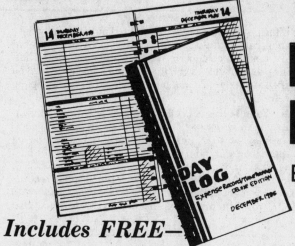

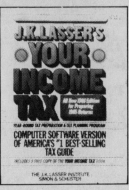

J. K. Lasser's

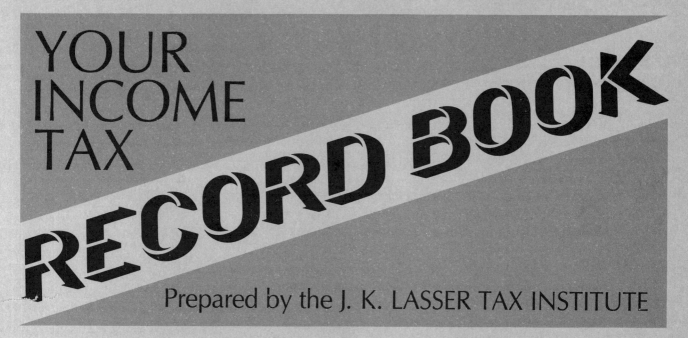

YOUR INCOME TAX

RECORD BOOK

Prepared by the J. K. LASSER TAX INSTITUTE

SIMON AND SCHUSTER
New York

SIMON AND SCHUSTER
New York

Copyright © 1970, 1971, 1972, 1973, 1984 by Simon & Schuster, Inc.
All rights reserved
including the right of reproduction
in whole or in part in any form
Published by Simon & Schuster, Inc.
Simon & Schuster Building
Rockefeller Center
1230 Avenue of the Americas
New York, New York 10020

SIMON AND SCHUSTER and colophon are registered trademarks of Simon & Schuster, Inc.
Designed by Irving Perkins
Manufactured in the United States of America

2 3 4 5 6 7 8 9 10

ISBN: 0-671-52893-9

INTRODUCTION

J. K. Lasser's YOUR INCOME TAX RECORD BOOK is designed to lighten the burden of keeping tax records which should be no more troublesome than maintaining a checking account. Since you pay the majority of your tax-deductible expenses by check, why not, at the same time, make a tax record of your payments? Your present checkbook is not designed for this purpose. But J. K. Lasser's YOUR INCOME TAX RECORD BOOK is; it lets you keep records not only of your checks and bank balance but also of your deductible items at the same time you enter your checks. Thus, when you have to prepare your tax return, you have an immediate, complete record of your deductible expenses already itemized for entry on your tax return. This is not all. YOUR INCOME TAX RECORD BOOK also gives you:

A travel and entertainment record keeper. The forms are designed to help you keep a record of these expenses and at the same time meet IRS rules.

Tax work sheets for organizing your data for your tax return.

A budget planner to develop your money management for the year.

A financial net worth statement to record changes over the year.

Forms for keeping records of IRA investments, bank accounts, and stocks.

In J. K. Lasser's YOUR INCOME TAX RECORD BOOK, you have at your finger tips a complete system for maintaining an ongoing, up-to-date record of your personal finances with the least possible time and trouble.

CONTENTS

Part IV Financial Records   153

PART I

CHECK RECORD

HOW TO USE THE CHECK RECORD

1. Beginning on page 10, you will find double pages on which you will enter your checks and deposits for each month or banking period of the year. Enter the appropriate month or period at the top of each page.

   a. On the left hand page, to the right of the words "OPENING BALANCE," enter your last balance from your previous checkbook.

   b. When you make deposits, write in the appropriate column under "RECORD OF DEPOSITS," the **date,** the **source,** and the **amount** of each item deposited.

   c. After you have listed all the items included in the particular deposit, you draw a line under the "Item" amount column. Then you enter the total for that particular deposit in the adjacent column to the right **on the same line** with the last item in the deposit. Label the source of your deposits clearly, for at the end of the month you will analyze the total amounts from each source and enter them in the SUMMARY OF YOUR DEPOSITS on page 65.

2. Follow these steps when you write a check:

   a. Under "RECORD OF CHECKS YOU DRAW," enter the check number in the first column. If your checks are prenumbered, use these numbers. In the next four columns, you write the **Date, To Whom Paid, Explanation,** and **Amount.**

   b. The remaining columns on each page under "RECORD OF CHECKS YOU DRAW" can be used to make your tax return preparation easier. As you enter each check, simply repeat the amount under the proper heading, such as **Taxes, Medical & Drugs,** etc.

   c. Then, to get the figures you need at the end of the year, carry the monthly totals from the bottom of the page over to the SUMMARY OF YOUR CHECKS on page 66.

3. To get your cash balance at any time, add your **Total Deposits** column, including your opening balance plus all deposits made to date. Subtract the subtotal of checks drawn from the figure and make note of this interim balance in the **Source of Items Deposited** column to the left. Use small

penciled figures when getting your balances, so they will not interfere with your inked record of checks and deposits, as follows:

4. Use the summary at the bottom of the "RECORD OF DEPOSITS" column to get your cash balance at the end of the month or banking period. This balance you will carry forward to the next check record page. To arrive at your cash balance, you deduct your **total** expenditures from the total of your **opening balance plus all deposits.**

5. When you receive your monthly statement from your bank, use the instructions on page 46 and the reconciliation page for that month or period to check your balance with the bank's statement.

If your volume of check writing exceeds the number of lines available in a double page for a particular period or month, carry your balance to the next double page, noting your deposits and checks there. This book provides 18 pages, sufficient for the requirements of a year of check writing.

Record of Deposits

Record of Checks You Draw

DATE	SOURCE OF ITEMS DEPOSITED	AMOUNT OF EACH DEPOSIT ITEM	AMOUNT OF TOTAL DEPOSIT	CHECK NO.	DATE	TO WHOM PAID	EXPLANATION
	OPENING BALANCE	$ 726 38					
1/3	Acme Corp.—salary	$ 210 —	$	101	1/3	Lincoln Savings Bank	Mortgage payment
	Steel Co.—dividend	30 —	240 —	102	1/3	Dr. S. Jones	Dentist
	Balance — $668.02		966 38	103	1/8	Fair Stores	Clothing
				104	1/10	Insurance Company	Life Policy #X72

Record of Deposits

Record of Checks You Draw

DATE	SOURCE OF ITEMS DEPOSITED		AMOUNT OF EACH DEPOSIT ITEM	AMOUNT OF TOTAL DEPOSIT		CHECK NO.	DATE	TO WHOM PAID	EXPLANATION
	OPENING BALANCE	$							
			$	$					
	TOTAL DEPOSITS			$					
	FIGURING MONTHLY BALANCE								
	1. OPENING BALANCE	$							
	2. TOTAL DEPOSITS	$							
	3. TOTAL OF 1 AND 2			$					
	4. LESS TOTAL MONTHLY EXPENDITURES			$					BANK CHARGES
	5. TRANSFER BALANCE TO NEXT MONTH			$					TOTAL MONTHLY EXPENDITURES

Month or Period of _____

| AMOUNT | DEDUCTIBLE EXPENSES | | | | | MORTGAGE PAYMENTS OR RENT | SAVINGS & INVEST-MENTS | HOME: UTILITIES, REPAIRS, ETC. | PERSONAL: FOOD, CLOTHING, ETC. | AUTO & TRANS-PORTATION | |
	TAXES	INTEREST	MEDICAL & DRUGS	CONTRI-BUTIONS	OTHER: JOB COSTS, TAX HELP, ETC.						
$	$	$	$	$	$	$	$	$	$	$	$
$	$	$	$	$	$	$	$	$	$	$	

NOTE: FOR TAX PURPOSES—MARK PLAINLY ANY BUSINESS EXPENDITURES FOR TRANSPORTATION, ENTERTAINMENT, ETC.

Record of Deposits

Record of Checks You Draw

DATE	SOURCE OF ITEMS DEPOSITED		AMOUNT OF EACH DEPOSIT ITEM		AMOUNT OF TOTAL DEPOSIT		CHECK NO.	DATE	TO WHOM PAID	EXPLANATION
	OPENING BALANCE	$								
			$		$					
	TOTAL DEPOSITS				$					

FIGURING MONTHLY BALANCE

1. OPENING BALANCE	$			
2. TOTAL DEPOSITS	$			
3. TOTAL OF 1 AND 2			$	
4. LESS TOTAL MONTHLY EXPENDITURES			$	
5. TRANSFER BALANCE TO NEXT MONTH			$	

BANK CHARGES

TOTAL MONTHLY EXPENDITURES

Month or Period of _____

AMOUNT	DEDUCTIBLE EXPENSES					MORTGAGE PAYMENTS OR RENT	SAVINGS & INVEST-MENTS	HOME: UTILITIES, REPAIRS, ETC.	PERSONAL: FOOD, CLOTHING, ETC.	AUTO & TRANS-PORTATION	
	TAXES	INTEREST	MEDICAL & DRUGS	CONTRI-BUTIONS	OTHER: JOB COSTS, TAX HELP, ETC.						
$	$	$	$	$	$	$	$	$	$	$	$
$	$	$	$	$	$	$	$	$	$	$	

NOTE: FOR TAX PURPOSES—MARK PLAINLY ANY BUSINESS EXPENDITURES FOR TRANSPORTATION, ENTERTAINMENT, ETC.

Record of Deposits

Record of Checks You Draw

DATE	SOURCE OF ITEMS DEPOSITED			AMOUNT OF EACH DEPOSIT ITEM	AMOUNT OF TOTAL DEPOSIT		CHECK NO.	DATE	TO WHOM PAID	EXPLANATION
	OPENING BALANCE	$		$	$					
		TOTAL DEPOSITS			$					

FIGURING MONTHLY BALANCE

1. OPENING BALANCE	$			
2. TOTAL DEPOSITS	$			
3. TOTAL OF 1 AND 2			$	
4. LESS TOTAL MONTHLY EXPENDITURES			$	BANK CHARGES
5. TRANSFER BALANCE TO NEXT MONTH			$	TOTAL MONTHLY EXPENDITURES

Month or Period of _____

AMOUNT	DEDUCTIBLE EXPENSES						MORTGAGE PAYMENTS OR RENT	SAVINGS & INVEST-MENTS	HOME: UTILITIES, REPAIRS, ETC.	PERSONAL: FOOD, CLOTHING, ETC.	AUTO & TRANS-PORTATION	
	TAXES		INTEREST	MEDICAL & DRUGS	CONTRI-BUTIONS	OTHER: JOB COSTS, TAX HELP, ETC.						
$	$		$	$	$	$	$	$	$	$	$	$
$	$		$	$	$	$	$	$	$	$	$	$

NOTE: FOR TAX PURPOSES—MARK PLAINLY ANY BUSINESS EXPENDITURES FOR TRANSPORTATION, ENTERTAINMENT, ETC.

Record of Deposits

Record of Checks You Draw

DATE	SOURCE OF ITEMS DEPOSITED	AMOUNT OF EACH DEPOSIT ITEM	AMOUNT OF TOTAL DEPOSIT	CHECK NO.	DATE	TO WHOM PAID	EXPLANATION
	OPENING BALANCE $	$	$				
	TOTAL DEPOSITS		$				
	FIGURING MONTHLY BALANCE						
	1. OPENING BALANCE	$					
	2. TOTAL DEPOSITS	$					
	3. TOTAL OF 1 AND 2		$				
	4. LESS TOTAL MONTHLY EXPENDITURES		$				BANK CHARGES
	5. TRANSFER BALANCE TO NEXT MONTH		$				TOTAL MONTHLY EXPENDITURES

Month or Period of _____

| AMOUNT | DEDUCTIBLE EXPENSES | | | | | | MORTGAGE PAYMENTS OR RENT | SAVINGS & INVEST-MENTS | HOME: UTILITIES, REPAIRS, ETC. | PERSONAL: FOOD, CLOTHING, ETC. | AUTO & TRANS-PORTATION | |
	TAXES	INTEREST	MEDICAL & DRUGS	CONTRI-BUTIONS	OTHER: JOB COSTS, TAX HELP, ETC.							
$	$	$	$	$	$		$	$	$	$	$	$
$	$	$	$	$	$		$	$	$	$	$	$

NOTE: FOR TAX PURPOSES—MARK PLAINLY ANY BUSINESS EXPENDITURES FOR TRANSPORTATION, ENTERTAINMENT, ETC.

Record of Deposits

Record of Checks You Draw

DATE	SOURCE OF ITEMS DEPOSITED		AMOUNT OF EACH DEPOSIT ITEM		AMOUNT OF TOTAL DEPOSIT		CHECK NO.	DATE	TO WHOM PAID	EXPLANATION
	OPENING BALANCE	$								
			$		$					
	TOTAL DEPOSITS				$					
	FIGURING MONTHLY BALANCE									
	1. OPENING BALANCE		$							
	2. TOTAL DEPOSITS		$							
	3. TOTAL OF 1 AND 2				$					
	4. LESS TOTAL MONTHLY EXPENDITURES				$					BANK CHARGES
	5. TRANSFER BALANCE TO NEXT MONTH				$					TOTAL MONTHLY EXPENDITURES

Month or Period of _____

AMOUNT	DEDUCTIBLE EXPENSES					MORTGAGE PAYMENTS OR RENT	SAVINGS & INVEST-MENTS	HOME: UTILITIES, REPAIRS, ETC.	PERSONAL: FOOD, CLOTHING, ETC.	AUTO & TRANS-PORTATION	
	TAXES	INTEREST	MEDICAL & DRUGS	CONTRI-BUTIONS	OTHER: JOB COSTS, TAX HELP, ETC.						
$	$	$	$	$	$	$	$	$	$	$	$
$	$	$	$	$	$	$	$	$	$	$	

NOTE: FOR TAX PURPOSES—MARK PLAINLY ANY BUSINESS EXPENDITURES FOR TRANSPORTATION, ENTERTAINMENT, ETC.

Record of Deposits

Record of Checks You Draw

DATE	SOURCE OF ITEMS DEPOSITED	AMOUNT OF EACH DEPOSIT ITEM	AMOUNT OF TOTAL DEPOSIT	CHECK NO.	DATE	TO WHOM PAID	EXPLANATION
	OPENING BALANCE $						
		$	$				
	TOTAL DEPOSITS		$				
	FIGURING MONTHLY BALANCE						
1. OPENING BALANCE		$					
2. TOTAL DEPOSITS		$					
3. TOTAL OF 1 AND 2			$				
4. LESS TOTAL MONTHLY EXPENDITURES			$				BANK CHARGES
5. TRANSFER BALANCE TO NEXT MONTH			$				TOTAL MONTHLY EXPENDITURES

20

Month or Period of _____

| AMOUNT | DEDUCTIBLE EXPENSES | | | | | | MORTGAGE PAYMENTS OR RENT | SAVINGS & INVEST-MENTS | HOME: UTILITIES, REPAIRS, ETC. | PERSONAL: FOOD, CLOTHING, ETC. | AUTO & TRANS-PORTATION | |
	TAXES	INTEREST	MEDICAL & DRUGS	CONTRI-BUTIONS	OTHER: JOB COSTS, TAX HELP, ETC.							
$	$	$	$	$	$		$	$	$	$	$	$
$	$	$	$	$	$		$	$	$	$	$	$

NOTE: FOR TAX PURPOSES—MARK PLAINLY ANY BUSINESS EXPENDITURES FOR TRANSPORTATION, ENTERTAINMENT, ETC.

Record of Deposits

Record of Checks You Draw

DATE	SOURCE OF ITEMS DEPOSITED	AMOUNT OF EACH DEPOSIT ITEM	AMOUNT OF TOTAL DEPOSIT		CHECK NO.	DATE	TO WHOM PAID	EXPLANATION
	OPENING BALANCE $							
		$	$					
	TOTAL DEPOSITS		$					
	FIGURING MONTHLY BALANCE							
	1. OPENING BALANCE	$						
	2. TOTAL DEPOSITS	$						
	3. TOTAL OF 1 AND 2		$					
	4. LESS TOTAL MONTHLY EXPENDITURES		$					BANK CHARGES
	5. TRANSFER BALANCE TO NEXT MONTH		$					TOTAL MONTHLY EXPENDITURES

Month or Period of _____

| AMOUNT | DEDUCTIBLE EXPENSES | | | | | MORTGAGE PAYMENTS OR RENT | SAVINGS & INVEST-MENTS | HOME: UTILITIES, REPAIRS, ETC. | PERSONAL: FOOD, CLOTHING, ETC. | AUTO & TRANS-PORTATION | |
	TAXES	INTEREST	MEDICAL & DRUGS	CONTRI-BUTIONS	OTHER: JOB COSTS, TAX HELP, ETC.						
$	$	$	$	$	$	$	$	$	$	$	$
$	$	$	$	$	$	$	$	$	$	$	

NOTE: FOR TAX PURPOSES—MARK PLAINLY ANY BUSINESS EXPENDITURES FOR TRANSPORTATION, ENTERTAINMENT, ETC.

Record of Deposits

Record of Checks You Draw

DATE	SOURCE OF ITEMS DEPOSITED	AMOUNT OF EACH DEPOSIT ITEM	AMOUNT OF TOTAL DEPOSIT		CHECK NO.	DATE	TO WHOM PAID	EXPLANATION
	OPENING BALANCE $							
		$	$					
	TOTAL DEPOSITS		$					
	FIGURING MONTHLY BALANCE							
	1. OPENING BALANCE	$						
	2. TOTAL DEPOSITS	$						
	3. TOTAL OF 1 AND 2		$					
	4. LESS TOTAL MONTHLY EXPENDITURES		$					BANK CHARGES
	5. TRANSFER BALANCE TO NEXT MONTH		$					TOTAL MONTHLY EXPENDITURES

Month or Period of _____

| AMOUNT | DEDUCTIBLE EXPENSES | | | | | MORTGAGE PAYMENTS OR RENT | SAVINGS & INVEST-MENTS | HOME: UTILITIES, REPAIRS, ETC. | PERSONAL: FOOD, CLOTHING, ETC. | AUTO & TRANS-PORTATION | |
	TAXES	INTEREST	MEDICAL & DRUGS	CONTRI-BUTIONS	OTHER: JOB COSTS, TAX HELP, ETC.						
$	$	$	$	$	$	$	$	$	$	$	$
$	$	$	$	$	$	$	$	$	$	$	

NOTE: FOR TAX PURPOSES—MARK PLAINLY ANY BUSINESS EXPENDITURES FOR TRANSPORTATION, ENTERTAINMENT, ETC.

Record of Deposits

Record of Checks You Draw

DATE	SOURCE OF ITEMS DEPOSITED			AMOUNT OF EACH DEPOSIT ITEM	AMOUNT OF TOTAL DEPOSIT		CHECK NO.	DATE	TO WHOM PAID	EXPLANATION
	OPENING BALANCE	$								
				$	$					
	TOTAL DEPOSITS				$					
	FIGURING MONTHLY BALANCE									
	1. OPENING BALANCE	$								
	2. TOTAL DEPOSITS	$								
	3. TOTAL OF 1 AND 2			$						
	4. LESS TOTAL MONTHLY EXPENDITURES			$						BANK CHARGES
	5. TRANSFER BALANCE TO NEXT MONTH			$						TOTAL MONTHLY EXPENDITURES

Month or Period of _____

AMOUNT	DEDUCTIBLE EXPENSES						MORTGAGE PAYMENTS OR RENT		SAVINGS & INVEST-MENTS		HOME: UTILITIES, REPAIRS, ETC.		PERSONAL: FOOD, CLOTHING, ETC.		AUTO & TRANS-PORTATION		
	TAXES		INTEREST	MEDICAL & DRUGS	CONTRI-BUTIONS	OTHER: JOB COSTS, TAX HELP, ETC.											
$	$		$	$	$	$	$		$		$		$		$		
$	$		$	$	$	$	$		$		$		$		$		$

NOTE: FOR TAX PURPOSES—MARK PLAINLY ANY BUSINESS EXPENDITURES FOR TRANSPORTATION, ENTERTAINMENT, ETC.

Record of Deposits

Record of Checks You Draw

DATE	SOURCE OF ITEMS DEPOSITED		AMOUNT OF EACH DEPOSIT ITEM	AMOUNT OF TOTAL DEPOSIT		CHECK NO.	DATE	TO WHOM PAID	EXPLANATION
	OPENING BALANCE	$							
			$	$					
	TOTAL DEPOSITS			$					
	FIGURING MONTHLY BALANCE								
1. OPENING BALANCE		$							
2. TOTAL DEPOSITS		$							
3. TOTAL OF 1 AND 2			$						
4. LESS TOTAL MONTHLY EXPENDITURES			$						BANK CHARGES
5. TRANSFER BALANCE TO NEXT MONTH			$						TOTAL MONTHLY EXPENDITURES

Month or Period of _____

| AMOUNT | DEDUCTIBLE EXPENSES | | | | | MORTGAGE PAYMENTS OR RENT | SAVINGS & INVEST-MENTS | HOME: UTILITIES, REPAIRS, ETC. | PERSONAL: FOOD, CLOTHING, ETC. | AUTO & TRANS-PORTATION | |
	TAXES	INTEREST	MEDICAL & DRUGS	CONTRI-BUTIONS	OTHER: JOB COSTS, TAX HELP, ETC.						
$	$	$	$	$	$	$	$	$	$	$	$
$	$	$	$	$	$	$	$	$	$	$	

NOTE: FOR TAX PURPOSES—MARK PLAINLY ANY BUSINESS EXPENDITURES FOR TRANSPORTATION, ENTERTAINMENT, ETC.

Record of Deposits

Record of Checks You Draw

DATE	SOURCE OF ITEMS DEPOSITED			AMOUNT OF EACH DEPOSIT ITEM		AMOUNT OF TOTAL DEPOSIT		CHECK NO.	DATE	TO WHOM PAID	EXPLANATION
	OPENING BALANCE	$									
				$		$					
	TOTAL DEPOSITS					$					
	FIGURING MONTHLY BALANCE										
	1. OPENING BALANCE	$									
	2. TOTAL DEPOSITS	$									
	3. TOTAL OF 1 AND 2			$							
	4. LESS TOTAL MONTHLY EXPENDITURES			$							BANK CHARGES
	5. TRANSFER BALANCE TO NEXT MONTH			$							TOTAL MONTHLY EXPENDITURES

30

Month or Period of _____

| AMOUNT | DEDUCTIBLE EXPENSES | | | | | MORTGAGE PAYMENTS OR RENT | SAVINGS & INVEST-MENTS | HOME: UTILITIES, REPAIRS, ETC. | PERSONAL: FOOD, CLOTHING, ETC. | AUTO & TRANS-PORTATION | |
	TAXES	INTEREST	MEDICAL & DRUGS	CONTRI-BUTIONS	OTHER: JOB COSTS, TAX HELP, ETC.						
$	$	$	$	$	$	$	$	$	$	$	$
$	$	$	$	$	$	$	$	$	$	$	$

NOTE: FOR TAX PURPOSES—MARK PLAINLY ANY BUSINESS EXPENDITURES FOR TRANSPORTATION, ENTERTAINMENT, ETC.

Record of Deposits

Record of Checks You Draw

DATE	SOURCE OF ITEMS DEPOSITED	AMOUNT OF EACH DEPOSIT ITEM	AMOUNT OF TOTAL DEPOSIT		CHECK NO.	DATE	TO WHOM PAID	EXPLANATION
	OPENING BALANCE $							
		$	$					
	TOTAL DEPOSITS		$					
	FIGURING MONTHLY BALANCE							
	1. OPENING BALANCE	$						
	2. TOTAL DEPOSITS	$						
	3. TOTAL OF 1 AND 2		$					
	4. LESS TOTAL MONTHLY EXPENDITURES		$					BANK CHARGES
	5. TRANSFER BALANCE TO NEXT MONTH		$					TOTAL MONTHLY EXPENDITURES

Month or Period of _____

| AMOUNT | DEDUCTIBLE EXPENSES | | | | | | MORTGAGE PAYMENTS OR RENT | SAVINGS & INVEST-MENTS | HOME: UTILITIES, REPAIRS, ETC. | PERSONAL: FOOD, CLOTHING, ETC. | AUTO & TRANS-PORTATION | |
	TAXES	INTEREST	MEDICAL & DRUGS	CONTRI-BUTIONS	OTHER: JOB COSTS, TAX HELP, ETC.							
$	$	$	$	$	$		$	$	$	$	$	$
$	$	$	$	$	$		$	$	$	$	$	$

NOTE: FOR TAX PURPOSES—MARK PLAINLY ANY BUSINESS EXPENDITURES FOR TRANSPORTATION, ENTERTAINMENT, ETC.

Record of Deposits

Record of Checks You Draw

DATE	SOURCE OF ITEMS DEPOSITED			AMOUNT OF EACH DEPOSIT ITEM		AMOUNT OF TOTAL DEPOSIT		CHECK NO.	DATE	TO WHOM PAID	EXPLANATION
	OPENING BALANCE	$									
				$		$					
	TOTAL DEPOSITS					$					
	FIGURING MONTHLY BALANCE										
	1. OPENING BALANCE			$							
	2. TOTAL DEPOSITS			$							
	3. TOTAL OF 1 AND 2					$					
	4. LESS TOTAL MONTHLY EXPENDITURES					$					BANK CHARGES
	5. TRANSFER BALANCE TO NEXT MONTH					$					TOTAL MONTHLY EXPENDITURES

Month or Period of _____

AMOUNT	DEDUCTIBLE EXPENSES					MORTGAGE PAYMENTS OR RENT	SAVINGS & INVEST-MENTS	HOME: UTILITIES, REPAIRS, ETC.	PERSONAL: FOOD, CLOTHING, ETC.	AUTO & TRANS-PORTATION	
	TAXES	INTEREST	MEDICAL & DRUGS	CONTRI-BUTIONS	OTHER: JOB COSTS, TAX HELP, ETC.						
$	$	$	$	$	$	$	$	$	$	$	
$	$	$	$	$	$	$	$	$	$	$	

NOTE: FOR TAX PURPOSES—MARK PLAINLY ANY BUSINESS EXPENDITURES FOR TRANSPORTATION, ENTERTAINMENT, ETC.

Record of Deposits

Record of Checks You Draw

DATE	SOURCE OF ITEMS DEPOSITED			AMOUNT OF EACH DEPOSIT ITEM		AMOUNT OF TOTAL DEPOSIT		CHECK NO.	DATE	TO WHOM PAID	EXPLANATION
	OPENING BALANCE	$									
				$		$					
	TOTAL DEPOSITS					$					
	FIGURING MONTHLY BALANCE										
	1. OPENING BALANCE			$							
	2. TOTAL DEPOSITS			$							
	3. TOTAL OF 1 AND 2					$					
	4. LESS TOTAL MONTHLY EXPENDITURES					$					BANK CHARGES
	5. TRANSFER BALANCE TO NEXT MONTH					$					TOTAL MONTHLY EXPENDITURES

36

Month or Period of _____

| AMOUNT | DEDUCTIBLE EXPENSES | | | | | MORTGAGE PAYMENTS OR RENT | SAVINGS & INVEST-MENTS | HOME: UTILITIES, REPAIRS, ETC. | PERSONAL: FOOD, CLOTHING, ETC. | AUTO & TRANS-PORTATION | |
	TAXES	INTEREST	MEDICAL & DRUGS	CONTRI-BUTIONS	OTHER: JOB COSTS, TAX HELP, ETC.						
$	$	$	$	$	$	$	$	$	$	$	$
$	$	$	$	$	$	$	$	$	$	$	

NOTE: FOR TAX PURPOSES—MARK PLAINLY ANY BUSINESS EXPENDITURES FOR TRANSPORTATION, ENTERTAINMENT, ETC.

Record of Deposits

Record of Checks You Draw

DATE	SOURCE OF ITEMS DEPOSITED			AMOUNT OF EACH DEPOSIT ITEM		AMOUNT OF TOTAL DEPOSIT		CHECK NO.	DATE	TO WHOM PAID	EXPLANATION
	OPENING BALANCE	$									
				$		$					
	TOTAL DEPOSITS					$					
	FIGURING MONTHLY BALANCE										
	1. OPENING BALANCE			$							
	2. TOTAL DEPOSITS			$							
	3. TOTAL OF 1 AND 2					$					
	4. LESS TOTAL MONTHLY EXPENDITURES					$					BANK CHARGES
	5. TRANSFER BALANCE TO NEXT MONTH					$					TOTAL MONTHLY EXPENDITURES

Month or Period of _____

AMOUNT	DEDUCTIBLE EXPENSES					MORTGAGE PAYMENTS OR RENT	SAVINGS & INVEST-MENTS	HOME: UTILITIES, REPAIRS, ETC.	PERSONAL: FOOD, CLOTHING, ETC.	AUTO & TRANS-PORTATION	
	TAXES	INTEREST	MEDICAL & DRUGS	CONTRI-BUTIONS	OTHER: JOB COSTS, TAX HELP, ETC.						
$	$	$	$	$	$	$	$	$	$	$	$
$	$	$	$	$	$	$	$	$	$	$	

NOTE: FOR TAX PURPOSES—MARK PLAINLY ANY BUSINESS EXPENDITURES FOR TRANSPORTATION, ENTERTAINMENT, ETC.

Record of Deposits

Record of Checks You Draw

DATE	SOURCE OF ITEMS DEPOSITED	AMOUNT OF EACH DEPOSIT ITEM	AMOUNT OF TOTAL DEPOSIT		CHECK NO.	DATE	TO WHOM PAID	EXPLANATION
	OPENING BALANCE $							
		$	$					
	TOTAL DEPOSITS		$					
	FIGURING MONTHLY BALANCE							
	1. OPENING BALANCE	$						
	2. TOTAL DEPOSITS	$						
	3. TOTAL OF 1 AND 2		$					
	4. LESS TOTAL MONTHLY EXPENDITURES		$					BANK CHARGES
	5. TRANSFER BALANCE TO NEXT MONTH		$					TOTAL MONTHLY EXPENDITURES

Month or Period of _____

| AMOUNT | DEDUCTIBLE EXPENSES | | | | | MORTGAGE PAYMENTS OR RENT | SAVINGS & INVEST-MENTS | HOME: UTILITIES, REPAIRS, ETC. | PERSONAL: FOOD, CLOTHING, ETC. | AUTO & TRANS-PORTATION | |
	TAXES	INTEREST	MEDICAL & DRUGS	CONTRI-BUTIONS	OTHER: JOB COSTS, TAX HELP, ETC.						
$	$	$	$	$	$	$	$	$	$	$	$
$	$	$	$	$	$	$	$	$	$	$	$

NOTE: FOR TAX PURPOSES—MARK PLAINLY ANY BUSINESS EXPENDITURES FOR TRANSPORTATION, ENTERTAINMENT, ETC.

Record of Deposits

Record of Checks You Draw

DATE	SOURCE OF ITEMS DEPOSITED	AMOUNT OF EACH DEPOSIT ITEM	AMOUNT OF TOTAL DEPOSIT	CHECK NO.	DATE	TO WHOM PAID	EXPLANATION
	OPENING BALANCE $						
		$	$				
	TOTAL DEPOSITS		$				
	FIGURING MONTHLY BALANCE						
	1. OPENING BALANCE	$					
	2. TOTAL DEPOSITS	$					
	3. TOTAL OF 1 AND 2		$				
	4. LESS TOTAL MONTHLY EXPENDITURES		$				BANK CHARGES
	5. TRANSFER BALANCE TO NEXT MONTH		$				TOTAL MONTHLY EXPENDITURES

Month or Period of _____

AMOUNT	DEDUCTIBLE EXPENSES					MORTGAGE PAYMENTS OR RENT	SAVINGS & INVEST-MENTS	HOME: UTILITIES, REPAIRS, ETC.	PERSONAL: FOOD, CLOTHING, ETC.	AUTO & TRANS-PORTATION	
	TAXES	INTEREST	MEDICAL & DRUGS	CONTRI-BUTIONS	OTHER: JOB COSTS, TAX HELP, ETC.						
$	$	$	$	$	$	$	$	$	$	$	$
$	$	$	$	$	$	$	$	$	$	$	

NOTE: FOR TAX PURPOSES—MARK PLAINLY ANY BUSINESS EXPENDITURES FOR TRANSPORTATION, ENTERTAINMENT, ETC.

Record of Deposits

Record of Checks You Draw

DATE	SOURCE OF ITEMS DEPOSITED		AMOUNT OF EACH DEPOSIT ITEM		AMOUNT OF TOTAL DEPOSIT		CHECK NO.	DATE	TO WHOM PAID	EXPLANATION
	OPENING BALANCE	$								
			$		$					
	TOTAL DEPOSITS				$					
	FIGURING MONTHLY BALANCE									
	1. OPENING BALANCE	$								
	2. TOTAL DEPOSITS	$								
	3. TOTAL OF 1 AND 2				$					
	4. LESS TOTAL MONTHLY EXPENDITURES				$					BANK CHARGES
	5. TRANSFER BALANCE TO NEXT MONTH				$					TOTAL MONTHLY EXPENDITURES

44

Month or Period of _____

| AMOUNT | | DEDUCTIBLE EXPENSES | | | | | MORTGAGE PAYMENTS OR RENT | SAVINGS & INVEST-MENTS | HOME: UTILITIES, REPAIRS, ETC. | PERSONAL: FOOD, CLOTHING, ETC. | AUTO & TRANS-PORTATION | |
		TAXES	INTEREST	MEDICAL & DRUGS	CONTRI-BUTIONS	OTHER: JOB COSTS, TAX HELP, ETC.						
$		$	$	$	$	$	$	$	$	$	$	$
$		$	$	$	$	$	$	$	$	$	$	$

NOTE: FOR TAX PURPOSES—MARK PLAINLY ANY BUSINESS EXPENDITURES FOR TRANSPORTATION, ENTERTAINMENT, ETC.

RECONCILING YOUR BANK STATEMENT WITH YOUR BOOK BALANCE

1. When you receive your bank statement and canceled checks, first arrange the checks in numerical order. Then, going down the Check Record page, place a check (√) next to each entry for which you have a canceled check. If there is a bank charge on the statement, reduce your book balance by the amount of the charge.

2. In the bank reconciliation, enter on line 1 your book balance from your Check Record.

3. Enter your Bank Statement Balance as of the end of the month or period on line 2.

4. Then note each item that you did not check. These are your outstanding checks; list them on line 3. Enter the total on line 4.

5. In your Record of Deposits, mark with a (√) each deposit that appears on the bank statement. Enter the sum of the unchecked (or outstanding) deposits on line 6.

6. Now add and subtract your figures as indicated. You should come up with the same figure on line 7 as on line 1.

Bank Reconciliation for Month or Period of _____

1. BOOK BALANCE			$	
2. BANK STATEMENT BALANCE			$	

3. LESS OUTSTANDING CHECKS:	CHECK NO.	AMOUNT		
		$		

4. TOTAL OUTSTANDING CHECKS			$	
5. BANK STATEMENT BALANCE LESS OUTSTANDING CHECKS (Line 2 less Line 4)			$	
6. ADD: SUM OF DEPOSITS NOT ON STATEMENT			$	
7. BANK STATEMENT BALANCE (Line 2) ADJUSTED TO BOOK BALANCE (Line 1)			$	

Bank Reconciliation for Month or Period of _____

1. BOOK BALANCE			$	
2. BANK STATEMENT BALANCE			$	

3. LESS OUTSTANDING CHECKS:	CHECK NO.	AMOUNT		
		$		

4. TOTAL OUTSTANDING CHECKS			$	
5. BANK STATEMENT BALANCE LESS OUTSTANDING CHECKS (Line 2 less Line 4)			$	
6. ADD: SUM OF DEPOSITS NOT ON STATEMENT			$	
7. BANK STATEMENT BALANCE (Line 2) ADJUSTED TO BOOK BALANCE (Line 1)			$	

Bank Reconciliation for Month or Period of _____

		CHECK NO.	AMOUNT		
1. BOOK BALANCE				$	
2. BANK STATEMENT BALANCE				$	
3. LESS OUTSTANDING CHECKS:			$		
4. TOTAL OUTSTANDING CHECKS				$	
5. BANK STATEMENT BALANCE LESS OUTSTANDING CHECKS (Line 2 less Line 4)				$	
6. ADD: SUM OF DEPOSITS NOT ON STATEMENT				$	
7. BANK STATEMENT BALANCE (Line 2) ADJUSTED TO BOOK BALANCE (Line 1)				$	

Bank Reconciliation for Month or Period of _____

1. BOOK BALANCE			$	
2. BANK STATEMENT BALANCE			$	

3. LESS OUTSTANDING CHECKS:	CHECK NO.	AMOUNT		
		$		

4. TOTAL OUTSTANDING CHECKS	$	
5. BANK STATEMENT BALANCE LESS OUTSTANDING CHECKS (Line 2 less Line 4)	$	
6. ADD: SUM OF DEPOSITS NOT ON STATEMENT	$	
7. BANK STATEMENT BALANCE (Line 2) ADJUSTED TO BOOK BALANCE (Line 1)	$	

Bank Reconciliation for Month or Period of _____

1. BOOK BALANCE			$	
2. BANK STATEMENT BALANCE			$	

3. LESS OUTSTANDING CHECKS:	CHECK NO.	AMOUNT		
		$		

4. TOTAL OUTSTANDING CHECKS	$	
5. BANK STATEMENT BALANCE LESS OUTSTANDING CHECKS (Line 2 less Line 4)	$	
6. ADD: SUM OF DEPOSITS NOT ON STATEMENT	$	
7. BANK STATEMENT BALANCE (Line 2) ADJUSTED TO BOOK BALANCE (Line 1)	$	

51

Bank Reconciliation for Month or Period of _____

1. BOOK BALANCE			$
2. BANK STATEMENT BALANCE			$

3. LESS OUTSTANDING CHECKS:	CHECK NO.	AMOUNT	
		$	

4. TOTAL OUTSTANDING CHECKS	$	
5. BANK STATEMENT BALANCE LESS OUTSTANDING CHECKS (Line 2 less Line 4)	$	
6. ADD: SUM OF DEPOSITS NOT ON STATEMENT	$	
7. BANK STATEMENT BALANCE (Line 2) ADJUSTED TO BOOK BALANCE (Line 1)	$	

Bank Reconciliation for Month or Period of _____

	CHECK NO.	AMOUNT		
1. BOOK BALANCE			$	
2. BANK STATEMENT BALANCE			$	
3. LESS OUTSTANDING CHECKS:		$		
4. TOTAL OUTSTANDING CHECKS			$	
5. BANK STATEMENT BALANCE LESS OUTSTANDING CHECKS (Line 2 less Line 4)			$	
6. ADD: SUM OF DEPOSITS NOT ON STATEMENT			$	
7. BANK STATEMENT BALANCE (Line 2) ADJUSTED TO BOOK BALANCE (Line 1)			$	

53

Bank Reconciliation for Month or Period of _____

1. BOOK BALANCE			$	
2. BANK STATEMENT BALANCE			$	

3. LESS OUTSTANDING CHECKS:	CHECK NO.	AMOUNT		
		$		

4. TOTAL OUTSTANDING CHECKS			$	
5. BANK STATEMENT BALANCE LESS OUTSTANDING CHECKS (Line 2 less Line 4)			$	
6. ADD: SUM OF DEPOSITS NOT ON STATEMENT			$	
7. BANK STATEMENT BALANCE (Line 2) ADJUSTED TO BOOK BALANCE (Line 1)			$	

Bank Reconciliation for Month or Period of _____

1. BOOK BALANCE			$	

2. BANK STATEMENT BALANCE			$	

3. LESS OUTSTANDING CHECKS:	CHECK NO.	AMOUNT		
		$		

4. TOTAL OUTSTANDING CHECKS			$	
5. BANK STATEMENT BALANCE LESS OUTSTANDING CHECKS (Line 2 less Line 4)			$	
6. ADD: SUM OF DEPOSITS NOT ON STATEMENT			$	
7. BANK STATEMENT BALANCE (Line 2) ADJUSTED TO BOOK BALANCE (Line 1)			$	

Bank Reconciliation for Month or Period of _____

		CHECK NO.	AMOUNT		
1. BOOK BALANCE				$	
2. BANK STATEMENT BALANCE				$	
3. LESS OUTSTANDING CHECKS:			$		
4. TOTAL OUTSTANDING CHECKS				$	
5. BANK STATEMENT BALANCE LESS OUTSTANDING CHECKS (Line 2 less Line 4)				$	
6. ADD: SUM OF DEPOSITS NOT ON STATEMENT				$	
7. BANK STATEMENT BALANCE (Line 2) ADJUSTED TO BOOK BALANCE (Line 1)				$	

Bank Reconciliation for Month or Period of _____

1. BOOK BALANCE			$	
2. BANK STATEMENT BALANCE			$	

3. LESS OUTSTANDING CHECKS:	CHECK NO.	AMOUNT		
		$		

4. TOTAL OUTSTANDING CHECKS			$	
5. BANK STATEMENT BALANCE LESS OUTSTANDING CHECKS (Line 2 less Line 4)			$	
6. ADD: SUM OF DEPOSITS NOT ON STATEMENT			$	
7. BANK STATEMENT BALANCE (Line 2) ADJUSTED TO BOOK BALANCE (Line 1)			$	

57

Bank Reconciliation for Month or Period of _____

1. BOOK BALANCE			$	
2. BANK STATEMENT BALANCE			$	

3. LESS OUTSTANDING CHECKS:	CHECK NO.	AMOUNT		
		$		

4. TOTAL OUTSTANDING CHECKS		$	
5. BANK STATEMENT BALANCE LESS OUTSTANDING CHECKS (Line 2 less Line 4)		$	
6. ADD: SUM OF DEPOSITS NOT ON STATEMENT		$	
7. BANK STATEMENT BALANCE (Line 2) ADJUSTED TO BOOK BALANCE (Line 1)		$	

Bank Reconciliation for Month or Period of _____

1. BOOK BALANCE			$	
2. BANK STATEMENT BALANCE			$	

3. LESS OUTSTANDING CHECKS:	CHECK NO.	AMOUNT		
		$		

4. TOTAL OUTSTANDING CHECKS			$	
5. BANK STATEMENT BALANCE LESS OUTSTANDING CHECKS (Line 2 less Line 4)			$	
6. ADD: SUM OF DEPOSITS NOT ON STATEMENT			$	
7. BANK STATEMENT BALANCE (Line 2) ADJUSTED TO BOOK BALANCE (Line 1)			$	

Bank Reconciliation for Month or Period of _____

1. BOOK BALANCE		$	
2. BANK STATEMENT BALANCE		$	

3. LESS OUTSTANDING CHECKS:	CHECK NO.	AMOUNT	
		$	

4. TOTAL OUTSTANDING CHECKS	$	
5. BANK STATEMENT BALANCE LESS OUTSTANDING CHECKS (Line 2 less Line 4)	$	
6. ADD: SUM OF DEPOSITS NOT ON STATEMENT	$	
7. BANK STATEMENT BALANCE (Line 2) ADJUSTED TO BOOK BALANCE (Line 1)	$	

Bank Reconciliation for Month or Period of _____

1. BOOK BALANCE			$	
2. BANK STATEMENT BALANCE			$	

3. LESS OUTSTANDING CHECKS:	CHECK NO.	AMOUNT		
		$		

4. TOTAL OUTSTANDING CHECKS	$	
5. BANK STATEMENT BALANCE LESS OUTSTANDING CHECKS (Line 2 less Line 4)	$	
6. ADD: SUM OF DEPOSITS NOT ON STATEMENT	$	
7. BANK STATEMENT BALANCE (Line 2) ADJUSTED TO BOOK BALANCE (Line 1)	$	

Bank Reconciliation for Month or Period of _____

1. BOOK BALANCE				$		
2. BANK STATEMENT BALANCE				$		

3. LESS OUTSTANDING CHECKS:	CHECK NO.	AMOUNT			
		$			

4. TOTAL OUTSTANDING CHECKS			$		
5. BANK STATEMENT BALANCE LESS OUTSTANDING CHECKS (Line 2 less Line 4)			$		
6. ADD: SUM OF DEPOSITS NOT ON STATEMENT			$		
7. BANK STATEMENT BALANCE (Line 2) ADJUSTED TO BOOK BALANCE (Line 1)			$		

Bank Reconciliation for Month or Period of _____

		CHECK NO.	AMOUNT		
1. BOOK BALANCE				$	
2. BANK STATEMENT BALANCE				$	
3. LESS OUTSTANDING CHECKS:			$		
4. TOTAL OUTSTANDING CHECKS				$	
5. BANK STATEMENT BALANCE LESS OUTSTANDING CHECKS (Line 2 less Line 4)				$	
6. ADD: SUM OF DEPOSITS NOT ON STATEMENT				$	
7. BANK STATEMENT BALANCE (Line 2) ADJUSTED TO BOOK BALANCE (Line 1)				$	

63

Bank Reconciliation for Month or Period of _____

		CHECK NO.	AMOUNT		
1. BOOK BALANCE				$	
2. BANK STATEMENT BALANCE				$	
3. LESS OUTSTANDING CHECKS:			$		
4. TOTAL OUTSTANDING CHECKS				$	
5. BANK STATEMENT BALANCE LESS OUTSTANDING CHECKS (Line 2 less Line 4)				$	
6. ADD: SUM OF DEPOSITS NOT ON STATEMENT				$	
7. BANK STATEMENT BALANCE (Line 2) ADJUSTED TO BOOK BALANCE (Line 1)				$	

Summary of Your Deposits

Year ___

	TOTAL DEPOSITS	NET SALARY	FEES & COMMIS-SIONS	INTEREST	DIVIDENDS	LOANS	SALE OF STOCKS & BONDS	SALE OF OTHER ASSETS	GIFTS	REFUNDS OF INSURANCE, TAXES ETC.			TOTAL
JAN.	$	$	$	$	$	$	$	$	$	$	$	$	$
FEB.													
MAR.													
APR.													
MAY													
JUNE													
JULY													
AUG.													
SEPT.													
OCT.													
NOV.													
DEC.													
TOTAL	$	$	$	$	$	$	$	$	$	$	$	$	$

Summary of Your Checks

Year _____

| | TOTAL | DEDUCTIBLE ON TAX RETURN | | | | MORTGAGE PAYMENTS OR RENT | SAVINGS & INVEST-MENTS | HOME: UTILITIES, REPAIRS, ETC. | PERSONAL: FOOD, CLOTHING, ETC. | AUTO & TRANS-PORTATION | |
		TAXES	INTEREST	MEDICAL & DRUGS	CONTRI-BUTIONS	OTHER: JOB COSTS, TAX HELP, ETC.						
JAN.	$	$	$	$	$	$	$	$	$	$	$	$
FEB.												
MAR.												
APR.												
MAY												
JUNE												
JULY												
AUG.												
SEPT.												
OCT.												
NOV.												
DEC.												
TOTAL	$	$	$	$	$	$	$	$	$	$	$	$

TRAVEL AND ENTERTAINMENT RECORD KEEPER

To support tax deductions for travel and entertainment expenses, you need detailed records. In this section of YOUR INCOME TAX RECORD BOOK, you will find 52 weekly worksheets for recording travel and entertainment expenses. Weekly totals may be entered on the summary sheet on page 120. This breakdown of expense information, plus a work sheet for keeping track of reimbursements from your employer, will make it easy to determine your deductible expenses when you prepare your tax return. For the tax record keeping rules, see ¶2.31 of YOUR INCOME TAX.

WEEKLY RECORD OF TRAVEL AND ENTERTAINMENT EXPENSES AND BUSINESS MILEAGE

From _____ 19 __ to _____ 19 __

	Sunday	Monday	Tuesday	Wednesday	Thursday	Friday	Saturday	Total
Travel Expenses: Airlines	$	$	$	$	$	$	$	$
Bus—Train								
Cab								
Tips								
Meals and Lodgings: Include tips Breakfast								
Lunch								
Dinner								
Hotel								Total $
Other Expenses: Postage								
Telephone								
Stationery								
Stenographer								
Sample Room								
Advertising								Total $
Car Expenses: Gas, oil, lube, wash								
Repairs, parts								
Tires, supplies								
Parking fees, tolls								
Leasing or rental costs								Total $

MILEAGE

Mileage: End							
Start							
Total							
Business Mileage							

Where:
Business Purpose:

Entertainment

Date	Place	Amount	Guests—Type—Business Purpose
		$	
Total		$	

List all car expenses; allocate business and personal car expenses at the end of the year according to business mileage. See Your Income Tax, ¶2.302. Keep all bills for lodging expenses and other expenses of $25 or more, see Your Income Tax, ¶2.351.

WEEKLY RECORD OF TRAVEL AND ENTERTAINMENT EXPENSES AND BUSINESS MILEAGE

From _____ 19 __ to _____ 19 __

	Sunday	Monday	Tuesday	Wednesday	Thursday	Friday	Saturday	Total
Travel Expenses: Airlines	$	$	$	$	$	$	$	$
Bus—Train								
Cab								
Tips								
Meals and Lodgings: Include tips Breakfast								**Total** $
Lunch								
Dinner								
Hotel								
Other Expenses: Postage								**Total** $
Telephone								
Stationery								
Stenographer								
Sample Room								
Advertising								**Total** $
Car Expenses: Gas, oil, lube, wash								
Repairs, parts								
Tires, supplies								
Parking fees, tolls								
Leasing or rental costs								**Total** $

MILEAGE

Mileage: End							
Start							
Total							
Business Mileage							

Where:

Business Purpose:

Entertainment

Date	Place	Amount	Guests—Type—Business Purpose
		$	
	Total	$	

List all car expenses; allocate business and personal car expenses at the end of the year according to business mileage. See Your Income Tax, ¶2.302. Keep all bills for lodging expenses and other expenses of $25 or more, see Your Income Tax, ¶2.351.

WEEKLY RECORD OF TRAVEL AND ENTERTAINMENT EXPENSES AND BUSINESS MILEAGE

From _____ 19___ **to** _____ 19___

	Sunday		Monday		Tuesday		Wednesday		Thursday		Friday		Saturday		Total	
Travel Expenses: Airlines	$		$		$		$		$		$		$		$	
Bus—Train																
Cab																
Tips																
Meals and Lodgings: Include tips Breakfast																
Lunch																
Dinner																
Hotel												**Total**		$	
Other Expenses: Postage																
Telephone																
Stationery																
Stenographer																
Sample Room																
Advertising												**Total**		$	
Car Expenses: Gas, oil, lube, wash																
Repairs, parts																
Tires, supplies																
Parking fees, tolls																
Leasing or rental costs												**Total**		$	

MILEAGE

Mileage: End									
Start									
Total									
Business Mileage									

Where:
Business Purpose:

Entertainment

Date	Place	Amount	Guests—Type—Business Purpose
		$	
Total		$	

List all car expenses; allocate business and personal car expenses at the end of the year according to business mileage. See Your Income Tax, ¶2.302. Keep all bills for lodging expenses and other expenses of $25 or more, see Your Income Tax, ¶2.351.

WEEKLY RECORD OF TRAVEL AND ENTERTAINMENT EXPENSES AND BUSINESS MILEAGE

From _____ 19 __ to _____ 19 __

	Sunday	Monday	Tuesday	Wednesday	Thursday	Friday	Saturday	Total
Travel Expenses: Airlines	$	$	$	$	$	$	$	$
Bus—Train								
Cab								
Tips								
Meals and Lodgings: Include tips Breakfast							Total	$
Lunch								
Dinner								
Hotel								
Other Expenses: Postage							Total	$
Telephone								
Stationery								
Stenographer								
Sample Room								
Advertising								
Car Expenses: Gas, oil, lube, wash							Total	$
Repairs, parts								
Tires, supplies								
Parking fees, tolls								
Leasing or rental costs							Total	$

MILEAGE

Mileage: End							
Start							
Total							
Business Mileage							

Where:

Business Purpose:

Entertainment

Date	Place	Amount	Guests—Type—Business Purpose
		$	
Total		$	

List all car expenses; allocate business and personal car expenses at the end of the year according to business mileage. See Your Income Tax, ¶2.302. Keep all bills for lodging expenses and other expenses of $25 or more, see Your Income Tax, ¶2.351.

WEEKLY RECORD OF TRAVEL AND ENTERTAINMENT EXPENSES AND BUSINESS MILEAGE

From _____ 19___ **to** _____ 19___

	Sunday		Monday		Tuesday		Wednesday		Thursday		Friday		Saturday		Total	
Travel Expenses: Airlines	$		$		$		$		$		$		$		$	
Bus—Train																
Cab																
Tips																
Meals and Lodgings: Include tips Breakfast														Total	$	
Lunch																
Dinner																
Hotel																
Other Expenses: Postage														Total	$	
Telephone																
Stationery																
Stenographer																
Sample Room																
Advertising																
Car Expenses: Gas, oil, lube, wash														Total	$	
Repairs, parts																
Tires, supplies																
Parking fees, tolls																
Leasing or rental costs																
														Total	$	

MILEAGE

Mileage: End								
Start								
Total								
Business Mileage								

Where:
Business Purpose:

Entertainment

Date	Place	Amount	Guests—Type—Business Purpose
		$	
	Total	$	

List all car expenses; allocate business and personal car expenses at the end of the year according to business mileage. See Your Income Tax, ¶2.302. Keep all bills for lodging expenses and other expenses of $25 or more, see Your Income Tax, ¶2.351.

WEEKLY RECORD OF TRAVEL AND ENTERTAINMENT EXPENSES AND BUSINESS MILEAGE

From _____ 19___ to _____ 19___

	Sunday	Monday	Tuesday	Wednesday	Thursday	Friday	Saturday	Total
Travel Expenses: Airlines	$	$	$	$	$	$	$	$
Bus—Train								
Cab								
Tips								
Meals and Lodgings: Include tips Breakfast							Total	$
Lunch								
Dinner								
Hotel								
Other Expenses: Postage							Total	$
Telephone								
Stationery								
Stenographer								
Sample Room								
Advertising							Total	$
Car Expenses: Gas, oil, lube, wash								
Repairs, parts								
Tires, supplies								
Parking fees, tolls								
Leasing or rental costs							Total	$

MILEAGE

Mileage: End								
Start								
Total								
Business Mileage								

Where:

Business Purpose:

Entertainment

Date	Place	Amount		Guests—Type—Business Purpose
		$		
Total		$		

List all car expenses; allocate business and personal car expenses at the end of the year according to business mileage. See Your Income Tax, ¶2.302. Keep all bills for lodging expenses and other expenses of $25 or more, see Your Income Tax, ¶2.351.

WEEKLY RECORD OF TRAVEL AND ENTERTAINMENT EXPENSES AND BUSINESS MILEAGE

From _____ 19__ **to** _____ 19__

	Sunday		Monday		Tuesday		Wednesday		Thursday		Friday		Saturday		Total	
Travel Expenses:																
Airlines	$		$		$		$		$		$		$		$	
Bus—Train																
Cab																
Tips																
Meals and Lodgings:																
Include tips Breakfast														Total	$	
Lunch																
Dinner																
Hotel																
Other Expenses:														Total	$	
Postage																
Telephone																
Stationery																
Stenographer																
Sample Room																
Advertising																
Car Expenses:														Total	$	
Gas, oil, lube, wash																
Repairs, parts																
Tires, supplies																
Parking fees, tolls																
Leasing or rental costs																
														Total	$	

MILEAGE

Mileage: End															
Start															
Total															
Business Mileage															

Where:

Business Purpose:

Entertainment

Date	Place	Amount		Guests—Type—Business Purpose
		$		
Total		$		

List all car expenses; allocate business and personal car expenses at the end of the year according to business mileage. See Your Income Tax, ¶2.302. Keep all bills for lodging expenses and other expenses of $25 or more, see Your Income Tax, ¶2.351.

WEEKLY RECORD OF TRAVEL AND ENTERTAINMENT EXPENSES AND BUSINESS MILEAGE

From _____ 19 __ to _____ 19 __

	Sunday	Monday	Tuesday	Wednesday	Thursday	Friday	Saturday	Total
Travel Expenses: Airlines	$	$	$	$	$	$	$	$
Bus—Train								
Cab								
Tips								

Meals and Lodgings: **Total** $

Meals and Lodgings: Include tips Breakfast								
Lunch								
Dinner								
Hotel								

Total $

Other Expenses: Postage								
Telephone								
Stationery								
Stenographer								
Sample Room								
Advertising								

Total $

Car Expenses: Gas, oil, lube, wash								
Repairs, parts								
Tires, supplies								
Parking fees, tolls								
Leasing or rental costs								

Total $

MILEAGE

Mileage: End								
Start								
Total								
Business Mileage								

Where:
Business Purpose:

Entertainment

Date	Place	Amount	Guests—Type—Business Purpose
		$	
Total		$	

List all car expenses; allocate business and personal car expenses at the end of the year according to business mileage. See Your Income Tax, ¶2.302. Keep all bills for lodging expenses and other expenses of $25 or more, see Your Income Tax, ¶2.351.

WEEKLY RECORD OF TRAVEL AND ENTERTAINMENT
EXPENSES AND BUSINESS MILEAGE

From _____ 19 __ **to** _____ 19 __

	Sunday		Monday		Tuesday		Wednesday		Thursday		Friday		Saturday		Total	
Travel Expenses: Airlines	$		$		$		$		$		$		$		$	
Bus—Train																
Cab																
Tips																
Meals and Lodgings: Include tips Breakfast													Total		$	
Lunch																
Dinner																
Hotel																
Other Expenses: Postage													Total		$	
Telephone																
Stationery																
Stenographer																
Sample Room																
Advertising																
Car Expenses: Gas, oil, lube, wash													Total		$	
Repairs, parts																
Tires, supplies																
Parking fees, tolls																
Leasing or rental costs																
													Total		$	

MILEAGE

Mileage: End															
Start															
Total															
Business Mileage															

Where:
Business Purpose:

Entertainment

Date	Place	Amount		Guests—Type—Business Purpose
		$		
Total		$		

List all car expenses; allocate business and personal car expenses at the end of the year according to business mileage. See Your Income Tax, ¶2.302. Keep all bills for lodging expenses and other expenses of $25 or more, see Your Income Tax, ¶2.351.

WEEKLY RECORD OF TRAVEL AND ENTERTAINMENT EXPENSES AND BUSINESS MILEAGE

From _____ 19 __ to _____ 19 __

	Sunday		Monday		Tuesday		Wednesday		Thursday		Friday		Saturday		Total	
Travel Expenses: Airlines	$		$		$		$		$		$		$		$	
Bus—Train																
Cab																
Tips																
Meals and Lodgings: Include tips Breakfast															Total	$
Lunch																
Dinner																
Hotel																
Other Expenses: Postage															Total	$
Telephone																
Stationery																
Stenographer																
Sample Room																
Advertising																
Car Expenses: Gas, oil, lube, wash															Total	$
Repairs, parts																
Tires, supplies																
Parking fees, tolls																
Leasing or rental costs															Total	$

MILEAGE

Mileage: End							
Start							
Total							
Business Mileage							

Where:

Business Purpose:

Entertainment

Date	Place	Amount		Guests—Type—Business Purpose
		$		
Total		$		

List all car expenses; allocate business and personal car expenses at the end of the year according to business mileage. See Your Income Tax, ¶2.302. Keep all bills for lodging expenses and other expenses of $25 or more, see Your Income Tax, ¶2.351.

WEEKLY RECORD OF TRAVEL AND ENTERTAINMENT
EXPENSES AND BUSINESS MILEAGE

From _____ 19__ to _____ 19__

Travel Expenses:	Sunday		Monday		Tuesday		Wednesday		Thursday		Friday		Saturday		Total	
Airlines	$		$		$		$		$		$		$		$	
Bus—Train																
Cab																
Tips																

Meals and Lodgings: Include tips														Total	$	
Breakfast																
Lunch																
Dinner																
Hotel																

Other Expenses:														Total	$	
Postage																
Telephone																
Stationery																
Stenographer																
Sample Room																
Advertising																

Car Expenses:														Total	$	
Gas, oil, lube, wash																
Repairs, parts																
Tires, supplies																
Parking fees, tolls																
Leasing or rental costs														Total	$	

MILEAGE

Mileage: End								
Start								
Total								
Business Mileage								

Where:
Business Purpose:

Entertainment

Date	Place	Amount	Guests—Type—Business Purpose
		$	
Total		$	

List all car expenses; allocate business and personal car expenses at the end of the year according to business mileage. See Your Income Tax, ¶2.302. Keep all bills for lodging expenses and other expenses of $25 or more, see Your Income Tax, ¶2.351.

WEEKLY RECORD OF TRAVEL AND ENTERTAINMENT EXPENSES AND BUSINESS MILEAGE

From _____ 19 __ to _____ 19 __

	Sunday		Monday		Tuesday		Wednesday		Thursday		Friday		Saturday		Total	
Travel Expenses: Airlines	$		$		$		$		$		$		$		$	
Bus—Train																
Cab																
Tips													Total		$	
Meals and Lodgings: Include tips Breakfast																
Lunch																
Dinner																
Hotel													Total		$	
Other Expenses: Postage																
Telephone																
Stationery																
Stenographer																
Sample Room																
Advertising													Total		$	
Car Expenses: Gas, oil, lube, wash																
Repairs, parts																
Tires, supplies																
Parking fees, tolls																
Leasing or rental costs													Total		$	

MILEAGE

Mileage: End							
Start							
Total							
Business Mileage							

Where:
Business Purpose:

Entertainment

Date	Place	Amount		Guests—Type—Business Purpose
		$		
Total		$		

List all car expenses; allocate business and personal car expenses at the end of the year according to business mileage. See Your Income Tax, ¶2.302. Keep all bills for lodging expenses and other expenses of $25 or more, see Your Income Tax, ¶2.351.

WEEKLY RECORD OF TRAVEL AND ENTERTAINMENT EXPENSES AND BUSINESS MILEAGE

From _____ 19__ to _____ 19__

	Sunday	Monday	Tuesday	Wednesday	Thursday	Friday	Saturday	Total
Travel Expenses: Airlines	$	$	$	$	$	$	$	$
Bus—Train								
Cab								
Tips								
Meals and Lodgings: Include tips Breakfast							Total	$
Lunch								
Dinner								
Hotel								
Other Expenses: Postage							Total	$
Telephone								
Stationery								
Stenographer								
Sample Room								
Advertising								
Car Expenses: Gas, oil, lube, wash							Total	$
Repairs, parts								
Tires, supplies								
Parking fees, tolls								
Leasing or rental costs								

MILEAGE

								Total	$
Mileage: End									
Start									
Total									
Business Mileage									

Where:

Business Purpose:

Entertainment

Date	Place	Amount	Guests—Type—Business Purpose
		$	
	Total	$	

List all car expenses; allocate business and personal car expenses at the end of the year according to business mileage. See Your Income Tax, ¶2.302. Keep all bills for lodging expenses and other expenses of $25 or more, see Your Income Tax, ¶2.351.

WEEKLY RECORD OF TRAVEL AND ENTERTAINMENT EXPENSES AND BUSINESS MILEAGE

From _____ 19 __ to _____ 19 __

	Sunday		Monday		Tuesday		Wednesday		Thursday		Friday		Saturday		Total	
Travel Expenses: Airlines	$		$		$		$		$		$		$		$	
Bus—Train																
Cab																
Tips																

Meals and Lodgings: Include tips
Total $

Breakfast																
Lunch																
Dinner																
Hotel																

Other Expenses:
Total $

Postage																
Telephone																
Stationery																
Stenographer																
Sample Room																
Advertising																

Car Expenses:
Total $

Gas, oil, lube, wash																
Repairs, parts																
Tires, supplies																
Parking fees, tolls																
Leasing or rental costs																

Total $

MILEAGE

Mileage: End							
Start							
Total							
Business Mileage							

Where:
Business Purpose:

Entertainment

Date	Place	Amount	Guests—Type—Business Purpose
		$	
Total		$	

List all car expenses; allocate business and personal car expenses at the end of the year according to business mileage. See Your Income Tax, ¶2.302. Keep all bills for lodging expenses and other expenses of $25 or more, see Your Income Tax, ¶2.351.

WEEKLY RECORD OF TRAVEL AND ENTERTAINMENT EXPENSES AND BUSINESS MILEAGE

From _____ 19 __ to _____ 19 __

	Sunday		Monday		Tuesday		Wednesday		Thursday		Friday		Saturday		Total	
Travel Expenses: Airlines	$		$		$		$		$		$		$		$	
Bus—Train																
Cab																
Tips																

Meals and Lodgings: Include tips Breakfast														**Total**	$	
Lunch																
Dinner																
Hotel																

Other Expenses: Postage														**Total**	$	
Telephone																
Stationery																
Stenographer																
Sample Room																
Advertising																

Car Expenses: Gas, oil, lube, wash														**Total**	$	
Repairs, parts																
Tires, supplies																
Parking fees, tolls																
Leasing or rental costs														**Total**	$	

MILEAGE

Mileage: End														
Start														
Total														
Business Mileage														

Where:

Business Purpose:

Entertainment

Date	Place	Amount	Guests—Type—Business Purpose
		$	
Total		$	

List all car expenses; allocate business and personal car expenses at the end of the year according to business mileage. See Your Income Tax, ¶2.302. Keep all bills for lodging expenses and other expenses of $25 or more, see Your Income Tax, ¶2.351.

WEEKLY RECORD OF TRAVEL AND ENTERTAINMENT EXPENSES AND BUSINESS MILEAGE

From _____ 19 __ to _____ 19 __

	Sunday		Monday		Tuesday		Wednesday		Thursday		Friday		Saturday		Total	
Travel Expenses: Airlines	$		$		$		$		$		$		$		$	
Bus—Train																
Cab																
Tips																
														Total	$	
Meals and Lodgings: Include tips Breakfast																
Lunch																
Dinner																
Hotel																
														Total	$	
Other Expenses: Postage																
Telephone																
Stationery																
Stenographer																
Sample Room																
Advertising																
														Total	$	
Car Expenses: Gas, oil, lube, wash																
Repairs, parts																
Tires, supplies																
Parking fees, tolls																
Leasing or rental costs																
														Total	$	

MILEAGE

Mileage: End								
Start								
Total								
Business Mileage								

Where:

Business Purpose:

Entertainment

Date	Place	Amount	Guests—Type—Business Purpose
		$	
	Total	$	

List all car expenses; allocate business and personal car expenses at the end of the year according to business mileage. See Your Income Tax, ¶2.302. Keep all bills for lodging expenses and other expenses of $25 or more, see Your Income Tax, ¶2.351.

83

WEEKLY RECORD OF TRAVEL AND ENTERTAINMENT EXPENSES AND BUSINESS MILEAGE

From _____ 19 __ to _____ 19 __

	Sunday	Monday	Tuesday	Wednesday	Thursday	Friday	Saturday	Total
Travel Expenses: Airlines	$	$	$	$	$	$	$	$
Bus—Train								
Cab								
Tips								
Meals and Lodgings: Include tips Breakfast							Total	$
Lunch								
Dinner								
Hotel								
Other Expenses: Postage							Total	$
Telephone								
Stationery								
Stenographer								
Sample Room								
Advertising								
Car Expenses: Gas, oil, lube, wash							Total	$
Repairs, parts								
Tires, supplies								
Parking fees, tolls								
Leasing or rental costs							Total	$

MILEAGE

Mileage: End							
Start							
Total							
Business Mileage							

Where:

Business Purpose:

Entertainment

Date	Place	Amount	Guests—Type—Business Purpose
		$	
		Total $	

List all car expenses; allocate business and personal car expenses at the end of the year according to business mileage. See Your Income Tax, ¶2.302. Keep all bills for lodging expenses and other expenses of $25 or more, see Your Income Tax, ¶2.351.

WEEKLY RECORD OF TRAVEL AND ENTERTAINMENT EXPENSES AND BUSINESS MILEAGE

From _____ 19 __ to _____ 19 __

	Sunday		Monday		Tuesday		Wednesday		Thursday		Friday		Saturday		Total	
Travel Expenses: Airlines	$		$		$		$		$		$		$		$	
Bus—Train																
Cab																
Tips																
Meals and Lodgings: Include tips Breakfast														**Total**	$	
Lunch																
Dinner																
Hotel																
														Total	$	
Other Expenses: Postage																
Telephone																
Stationery																
Stenographer																
Sample Room																
Advertising																
														Total	$	
Car Expenses: Gas, oil, lube, wash																
Repairs, parts																
Tires, supplies																
Parking fees, tolls																
Leasing or rental costs																
														Total	$	

MILEAGE

	Sunday	Monday	Tuesday	Wednesday	Thursday	Friday	Saturday	
Mileage: End								
Start								
Total								
Business Mileage								

Where:

Business Purpose:

Entertainment

Date	Place	Amount		Guests—Type—Business Purpose
		$		
Total		$		

List all car expenses; allocate business and personal car expenses at the end of the year according to business mileage. See Your Income Tax, ¶2.302. Keep all bills for lodging expenses and other expenses of $25 or more, see Your Income Tax, ¶2.351.

WEEKLY RECORD OF TRAVEL AND ENTERTAINMENT EXPENSES AND BUSINESS MILEAGE

From _____ 19 __ to _____ 19 __

Travel Expenses:	Sunday	Monday	Tuesday	Wednesday	Thursday	Friday	Saturday	Total
Airlines	$	$	$	$	$	$	$	$
Bus—Train								
Cab								
Tips								

Meals and Lodgings: Include tips								Total	$
Breakfast									
Lunch									
Dinner									
Hotel									

Other Expenses:								Total	$
Postage									
Telephone									
Stationery									
Stenographer									
Sample Room									
Advertising									

Car Expenses:								Total	$
Gas, oil, lube, wash									
Repairs, parts									
Tires, supplies									
Parking fees, tolls									
Leasing or rental costs									
								Total	$

MILEAGE

	Sunday	Monday	Tuesday	Wednesday	Thursday	Friday	Saturday	Total
Mileage: End								
Start								
Total								
Business Mileage								

Where:

Business Purpose:

Entertainment

Date	Place	Amount	Guests—Type—Business Purpose
		$	
Total		$	

List all car expenses; allocate business and personal car expenses at the end of the year according to business mileage. See Your Income Tax, ¶2.302. Keep all bills for lodging expenses and other expenses of $25 or more, see Your Income Tax, ¶2.351.

WEEKLY RECORD OF TRAVEL AND ENTERTAINMENT EXPENSES AND BUSINESS MILEAGE

From _____ 19___ **to** _____ 19___

	Sunday		Monday		Tuesday		Wednesday		Thursday		Friday		Saturday		Total	
Travel Expenses: Airlines	$		$		$		$		$		$		$		$	
Bus—Train																
Cab																
Tips																
Meals and Lodgings: Include tips Breakfast															Total	$
Lunch																
Dinner																
Hotel																
Other Expenses: Postage															Total	$
Telephone																
Stationery																
Stenographer																
Sample Room																
Advertising																
Car Expenses: Gas, oil, lube, wash															Total	$
Repairs, parts																
Tires, supplies																
Parking fees, tolls																
Leasing or rental costs															Total	$

MILEAGE

	Sunday	Monday	Tuesday	Wednesday	Thursday	Friday	Saturday	
Mileage: End								
Start								
Total								
Business Mileage								

Where:

Business Purpose:

Entertainment

Date	Place	Amount		Guests—Type—Business Purpose
		$		
Total		$		

List all car expenses; allocate business and personal car expenses at the end of the year according to business mileage. See Your Income Tax, ¶2.302. Keep all bills for lodging expenses and other expenses of $25 or more, see Your Income Tax, ¶2.351.

WEEKLY RECORD OF TRAVEL AND ENTERTAINMENT EXPENSES AND BUSINESS MILEAGE

From _____ 19 __ to _____ 19 __

	Sunday		Monday		Tuesday		Wednesday		Thursday		Friday		Saturday		Total	
Travel Expenses:																
Airlines	$		$		$		$		$		$		$		$	
Bus—Train																
Cab																
Tips																
Meals and Lodgings: Include tips														**Total**	$	
Breakfast																
Lunch																
Dinner																
Hotel																
Other Expenses:														**Total**	$	
Postage																
Telephone																
Stationery																
Stenographer																
Sample Room																
Advertising																
Car Expenses:														**Total**	$	
Gas, oil, lube, wash																
Repairs, parts																
Tires, supplies																
Parking fees, tolls																
Leasing or rental costs														**Total**	$	

MILEAGE

Mileage: End							
Start							
Total							
Business Mileage							

Where:

Business Purpose:

Entertainment

Date	Place	Amount		Guests—Type—Business Purpose
		$		
		Total	$	

List all car expenses; allocate business and personal car expenses at the end of the year according to business mileage. See Your Income Tax, ¶2.302. Keep all bills for lodging expenses and other expenses of $25 or more, see Your Income Tax, ¶2.351.

WEEKLY RECORD OF TRAVEL AND ENTERTAINMENT EXPENSES AND BUSINESS MILEAGE

From _____ 19 _ **to** _____ 19 _

	Sunday		Monday		Tuesday		Wednesday		Thursday		Friday		Saturday		Total	
Travel Expenses: Airlines	$		$		$		$		$		$		$		$	
Bus—Train																
Cab																
Tips																
Meals and Lodgings: Include tips Breakfast													Total		$	
Lunch																
Dinner																
Hotel																
Other Expenses: Postage													Total		$	
Telephone																
Stationery																
Stenographer																
Sample Room																
Advertising																
Car Expenses: Gas, oil, lube, wash													Total		$	
Repairs, parts																
Tires, supplies																
Parking fees, tolls																
Leasing or rental costs													Total		$	

MILEAGE

Mileage: End								
Start								
Total								
Business Mileage								

Where:
Business Purpose:

Entertainment

Date	Place	Amount		Guests—Type—Business Purpose
		$		
		Total $		

List all car expenses; allocate business and personal car expenses at the end of the year according to business mileage. See Your Income Tax, ¶2.302. Keep all bills for lodging expenses and other expenses of $25 or more, see Your Income Tax, ¶2.351.

WEEKLY RECORD OF TRAVEL AND ENTERTAINMENT EXPENSES AND BUSINESS MILEAGE

From _____ 19___ to _____ 19___

	Sunday		Monday		Tuesday		Wednesday		Thursday		Friday		Saturday		Total	
Travel Expenses: Airlines	$		$		$		$		$		$		$		$	
Bus—Train																
Cab																
Tips																
Meals and Lodgings: Include tips Breakfast																
Lunch																
Dinner																
Hotel														Total	$	
Other Expenses: Postage																
Telephone																
Stationery																
Stenographer																
Sample Room																
Advertising														Total	$	
Car Expenses: Gas, oil, lube, wash														Total	$	
Repairs, parts																
Tires, supplies																
Parking fees, tolls																
Leasing or rental costs																
														Total	$	

MILEAGE

Mileage: End								
Start								
Total								
Business Mileage								

Where:

Business Purpose:

Entertainment

Date	Place	Amount		Guests—Type—Business Purpose
		$		
	Total	$		

List all car expenses; allocate business and personal car expenses at the end of the year according to business mileage. See Your Income Tax, ¶2.302. Keep all bills for lodging expenses and other expenses of $25 or more, see Your Income Tax, ¶2.351.

WEEKLY RECORD OF TRAVEL AND ENTERTAINMENT EXPENSES AND BUSINESS MILEAGE

From _____ 19 __ **to** _____ 19 __

	Sunday	Monday	Tuesday	Wednesday	Thursday	Friday	Saturday	Total
Travel Expenses: Airlines	$	$	$	$	$	$	$	$
Bus—Train								
Cab								
Tips								
Meals and Lodgings: Include tips Breakfast							**Total**	$
Lunch								
Dinner								
Hotel								
							Total	$
Other Expenses: Postage								
Telephone								
Stationery								
Stenographer								
Sample Room								
Advertising								
							Total	$
Car Expenses: Gas, oil, lube, wash								
Repairs, parts								
Tires, supplies								
Parking fees, tolls								
Leasing or rental costs								
							Total	$

MILEAGE

Mileage: End								
Start								
Total								
Business Mileage								

Where:

Business Purpose:

Entertainment

Date	Place	Amount		Guests—Type—Business Purpose
		$		
Total		$		

List all car expenses; allocate business and personal car expenses at the end of the year according to business mileage. See Your Income Tax, ¶2.302. Keep all bills for lodging expenses and other expenses of $25 or more, see Your Income Tax, ¶2.351.

WEEKLY RECORD OF TRAVEL AND ENTERTAINMENT EXPENSES AND BUSINESS MILEAGE

From _____ 19 __ to _____ 19 __

	Sunday	Monday	Tuesday	Wednesday	Thursday	Friday	Saturday	Total
Travel Expenses: Airlines	$	$	$	$	$	$	$	$
Bus—Train								
Cab								
Tips								
Meals and Lodgings: Include tips Breakfast								Total $
Lunch								
Dinner								
Hotel								
Other Expenses: Postage								Total $
Telephone								
Stationery								
Stenographer								
Sample Room								
Advertising								Total $
Car Expenses: Gas, oil, lube, wash								
Repairs, parts								
Tires, supplies								
Parking fees, tolls								
Leasing or rental costs								Total $

MILEAGE

Mileage: End							
Start							
Total							
Business Mileage							

Where:
Business Purpose:

Entertainment

Date	Place	Amount	Guests—Type—Business Purpose
		$	
Total		$	

List all car expenses; allocate business and personal car expenses at the end of the year according to business mileage. See Your Income Tax, ¶2.302. Keep all bills for lodging expenses and other expenses of $25 or more, see Your Income Tax, ¶2.351.

WEEKLY RECORD OF TRAVEL AND ENTERTAINMENT
EXPENSES AND BUSINESS MILEAGE

From _____ 19__ **to** _____ 19__

	Sunday		Monday		Tuesday		Wednesday		Thursday		Friday		Saturday		Total	
Travel Expenses: Airlines	$		$		$		$		$		$		$		$	
Bus—Train																
Cab																
Tips																
Meals and Lodgings: Include tips Breakfast														Total	$	
Lunch																
Dinner																
Hotel																
Other Expenses: Postage														Total	$	
Telephone																
Stationery																
Stenographer																
Sample Room																
Advertising																
Car Expenses: Gas, oil, lube, wash														Total	$	
Repairs, parts																
Tires, supplies																
Parking fees, tolls																
Leasing or rental costs																
														Total	$	

MILEAGE

Mileage: End								
Start								
Total								
Business Mileage								

Where:
Business Purpose:

Entertainment

Date	Place	Amount		Guests—Type—Business Purpose
		$		
Total		$		

List all car expenses; allocate business and personal car expenses at the end of the year according to business mileage. See Your Income Tax, ¶2.302. Keep all bills for lodging expenses and other expenses of $25 or more, see Your Income Tax, ¶2.351.

WEEKLY RECORD OF TRAVEL AND ENTERTAINMENT EXPENSES AND BUSINESS MILEAGE

From _____ 19__ **to** _____ 19__

	Sunday	Monday	Tuesday	Wednesday	Thursday	Friday	Saturday	Total
Travel Expenses: Airlines	$	$	$	$	$	$	$	$
Bus—Train								
Cab								
Tips								
							Total	$
Meals and Lodgings: Include tips Breakfast								
Lunch								
Dinner								
Hotel								
							Total	$
Other Expenses: Postage								
Telephone								
Stationery								
Stenographer								
Sample Room								
Advertising								
							Total	$
Car Expenses: Gas, oil, lube, wash								
Repairs, parts								
Tires, supplies								
Parking fees, tolls								
Leasing or rental costs								
							Total	$

MILEAGE

Mileage: End								
Start								
Total								
Business Mileage								

Where:
Business Purpose:

Entertainment

Date	Place	Amount		Guests—Type—Business Purpose
		$		
	Total	$		

List all car expenses; allocate business and personal car expenses at the end of the year according to business mileage. See Your Income Tax, ¶2.302. Keep all bills for lodging expenses and other expenses of $25 or more, see Your Income Tax, ¶2.351.

WEEKLY RECORD OF TRAVEL AND ENTERTAINMENT EXPENSES AND BUSINESS MILEAGE

From _____ 19 __ to _____ 19 __

	Sunday		Monday		Tuesday		Wednesday		Thursday		Friday		Saturday		Total	
Travel Expenses: Airlines	$		$		$		$		$		$		$		$	
Bus—Train																
Cab																
Tips																
Meals and Lodgings: Include tips Breakfast														Total	$	
Lunch																
Dinner																
Hotel																
Other Expenses: Postage														Total	$	
Telephone																
Stationery																
Stenographer																
Sample Room																
Advertising																
Car Expenses: Gas, oil, lube, wash														Total	$	
Repairs, parts																
Tires, supplies																
Parking fees, tolls																
Leasing or rental costs														Total	$	

MILEAGE

Mileage: End								
Start								
Total								
Business Mileage								

Where:
Business Purpose:

Entertainment

Date	Place	Amount		Guests—Type—Business Purpose
		$		
Total		$		

List all car expenses; allocate business and personal car expenses at the end of the year according to business mileage. See Your Income Tax, ¶2.302. Keep all bills for lodging expenses and other expenses of $25 or more, see Your Income Tax, ¶2.351.

WEEKLY RECORD OF TRAVEL AND ENTERTAINMENT EXPENSES AND BUSINESS MILEAGE

From _____ 19 __ **to** _____ 19 __

	Sunday		Monday		Tuesday		Wednesday		Thursday		Friday		Saturday		Total	
Travel Expenses: Airlines	$		$		$		$		$		$		$		$	
Bus—Train																
Cab																
Tips																
Meals and Lodgings: Include tips Breakfast																
Lunch																
Dinner																
Hotel												**Total**		$	
Other Expenses: Postage																
Telephone																
Stationery																
Stenographer																
Sample Room																
Advertising												**Total**		$	
Car Expenses: Gas, oil, lube, wash																
Repairs, parts																
Tires, supplies																
Parking fees, tolls																
Leasing or rental costs												**Total**		$	

MILEAGE

Mileage: End														
Start														
Total														
Business Mileage														

Where:

Business Purpose:

Entertainment

Date	Place	Amount	Guests—Type—Business Purpose
		$	
	Total	$	

List all car expenses; allocate business and personal car expenses at the end of the year according to business mileage. See Your Income Tax, ¶2.302. Keep all bills for lodging expenses and other expenses of $25 or more, see Your Income Tax, ¶2.351.

WEEKLY RECORD OF TRAVEL AND ENTERTAINMENT EXPENSES AND BUSINESS MILEAGE

From _____ 19__ **to** _____ 19__

	Sunday		Monday		Tuesday		Wednesday		Thursday		Friday		Saturday		Total	
Travel Expenses: Airlines	$		$		$		$		$		$		$		$	
Bus—Train																
Cab																
Tips																
Meals and Lodgings: Include tips Breakfast														Total	$	
Lunch																
Dinner																
Hotel																
Other Expenses: Postage														Total	$	
Telephone																
Stationery																
Stenographer																
Sample Room																
Advertising																
Car Expenses: Gas, oil, lube, wash														Total	$	
Repairs, parts																
Tires, supplies																
Parking fees, tolls																
Leasing or rental costs																
														Total	$	

MILEAGE

Mileage: End							
Start							
Total							
Business Mileage							

Where:
Business Purpose:

Entertainment

Date	Place	Amount		Guests—Type—Business Purpose
		$		
Total		$		

List all car expenses; allocate business and personal car expenses at the end of the year according to business mileage. See Your Income Tax, ¶2.302. Keep all bills for lodging expenses and other expenses of $25 or more, see Your Income Tax, ¶2.351.

WEEKLY RECORD OF TRAVEL AND ENTERTAINMENT EXPENSES AND BUSINESS MILEAGE

From _____ 19__ **to** _____ 19__

	Sunday	Monday	Tuesday	Wednesday	Thursday	Friday	Saturday	Total
Travel Expenses: Airlines	$	$	$	$	$	$	$	$
Bus—Train								
Cab								
Tips								
Meals and Lodgings: Include tips Breakfast							Total	$
Lunch								
Dinner								
Hotel								
Other Expenses: Postage							Total	$
Telephone								
Stationery								
Stenographer								
Sample Room								
Advertising							Total	$
Car Expenses: Gas, oil, lube, wash								
Repairs, parts								
Tires, supplies								
Parking fees, tolls								
Leasing or rental costs							Total	$

MILEAGE

Mileage: End							
Start							
Total							
Business Mileage							

Where:
Business Purpose:

Entertainment

Date	Place	Amount	Guests—Type—Business Purpose
		$	
Total		$	

List all car expenses; allocate business and personal car expenses at the end of the year according to business mileage. See Your Income Tax, ¶2.302. Keep all bills for lodging expenses and other expenses of $25 or more, see Your Income Tax, ¶2.351.

WEEKLY RECORD OF TRAVEL AND ENTERTAINMENT EXPENSES AND BUSINESS MILEAGE

From _____ 19__ **to** _____ 19__

Travel Expenses:	Sunday		Monday		Tuesday		Wednesday		Thursday		Friday		Saturday		Total	
Airlines	$		$		$		$		$		$		$		$	
Bus—Train																
Cab																
Tips																

Meals and Lodgings: Include tips														**Total**	$	
Breakfast																
Lunch																
Dinner																
Hotel																

Other Expenses:														**Total**	$	
Postage																
Telephone																
Stationery																
Stenographer																
Sample Room																
Advertising																

Car Expenses:														**Total**	$	
Gas, oil, lube, wash																
Repairs, parts																
Tires, supplies																
Parking fees, tolls																
Leasing or rental costs																
														Total	$	

MILEAGE

Mileage: End							
Start							
Total							
Business Mileage							

Where:

Business Purpose:

Entertainment

Date	Place	Amount		Guests—Type—Business Purpose
		$		
Total		$		

List all car expenses; allocate business and personal car expenses at the end of the year according to business mileage. See Your Income Tax, ¶2.302. Keep all bills for lodging expenses and other expenses of $25 or more, see Your Income Tax, ¶2.351.

WEEKLY RECORD OF TRAVEL AND ENTERTAINMENT EXPENSES AND BUSINESS MILEAGE

From _____ 19__ **to** _____ 19__

	Sunday	Monday	Tuesday	Wednesday	Thursday	Friday	Saturday	Total
Travel Expenses: Airlines	$	$	$	$	$	$	$	$
Bus—Train								
Cab								
Tips								
Meals and Lodgings: Include tips Breakfast							**Total**	$
Lunch								
Dinner								
Hotel								
Other Expenses: Postage							**Total**	$
Telephone								
Stationery								
Stenographer								
Sample Room								
Advertising							**Total**	$
Car Expenses: Gas, oil, lube, wash								
Repairs, parts								
Tires, supplies								
Parking fees, tolls								
Leasing or rental costs							**Total**	$

MILEAGE

Mileage: End							
Start							
Total							
Business Mileage							

Where:

Business Purpose:

Entertainment

Date	Place	Amount		Guests—Type—Business Purpose
		$		
Total		$		

List all car expenses; allocate business and personal car expenses at the end of the year according to business mileage. See Your Income Tax, ¶2.302. Keep all bills for lodging expenses and other expenses of $25 or more, see Your Income Tax, ¶2.351.

WEEKLY RECORD OF TRAVEL AND ENTERTAINMENT EXPENSES AND BUSINESS MILEAGE

From _____ 19 __ to _____ 19 __

	Sunday	Monday	Tuesday	Wednesday	Thursday	Friday	Saturday	Total	
Travel Expenses: Airlines	$	$	$	$	$	$	$	$	
Bus—Train									
Cab									
Tips									
Meals and Lodgings: Include tips Breakfast								Total	$
Lunch									
Dinner									
Hotel									
Other Expenses: Postage								Total	$
Telephone									
Stationery									
Stenographer									
Sample Room									
Advertising									
Car Expenses: Gas, oil, lube, wash								Total	$
Repairs, parts									
Tires, supplies									
Parking fees, tolls									
Leasing or rental costs									
								Total	$

MILEAGE

Mileage: End								
Start								
Total								
Business Mileage								

Where:
Business Purpose:

Entertainment

Date	Place	Amount		Guests—Type—Business Purpose
		$		
Total		$		

List all car expenses; allocate business and personal car expenses at the end of the year according to business mileage. See Your Income Tax, ¶2.302. Keep all bills for lodging expenses and other expenses of $25 or more, see Your Income Tax, ¶2.351.

WEEKLY RECORD OF TRAVEL AND ENTERTAINMENT EXPENSES AND BUSINESS MILEAGE

From _____ 19__ **to** _____ 19__

	Sunday	Monday	Tuesday	Wednesday	Thursday	Friday	Saturday	Total
Travel Expenses: Airlines	$	$	$	$	$	$	$	$
Bus—Train								
Cab								
Tips								
Meals and Lodgings: Include tips Breakfast							**Total**	$
Lunch								
Dinner								
Hotel								
Other Expenses: Postage							**Total**	$
Telephone								
Stationery								
Stenographer								
Sample Room								
Advertising								
Car Expenses: Gas, oil, lube, wash							**Total**	$
Repairs, parts								
Tires, supplies								
Parking fees, tolls								
Leasing or rental costs								
							Total	$

MILEAGE

Mileage: End								
Start								
Total								
Business Mileage								

Where:

Business Purpose:

Entertainment

Date	Place	Amount		Guests—Type—Business Purpose
		$		
Total		$		

List all car expenses; allocate business and personal car expenses at the end of the year according to business mileage. See Your Income Tax, ¶2.302. Keep all bills for lodging expenses and other expenses of $25 or more, see Your Income Tax, ¶2.351.

WEEKLY RECORD OF TRAVEL AND ENTERTAINMENT EXPENSES AND BUSINESS MILEAGE

From _____ 19 __ to _____ 19 __

	Sunday		Monday		Tuesday		Wednesday		Thursday		Friday		Saturday		Total	
Travel Expenses: Airlines	$		$		$		$		$		$		$		$	
Bus—Train																
Cab																
Tips																
Meals and Lodgings: Include tips Breakfast														Total	$	
Lunch																
Dinner																
Hotel																
Other Expenses: Postage														Total	$	
Telephone																
Stationery																
Stenographer																
Sample Room																
Advertising																
Car Expenses: Gas, oil, lube, wash														Total	$	
Repairs, parts																
Tires, supplies																
Parking fees, tolls																
Leasing or rental costs														Total	$	

MILEAGE

Mileage: End							
Start							
Total							
Business Mileage							

Where:
Business Purpose:

Entertainment

Date	Place	Amount		Guests—Type—Business Purpose
		$		
Total		$		

List all car expenses; allocate business and personal car expenses at the end of the year according to business mileage. See Your Income Tax, ¶2.302. Keep all bills for lodging expenses and other expenses of $25 or more, see Your Income Tax, ¶2.351.

WEEKLY RECORD OF TRAVEL AND ENTERTAINMENT
EXPENSES AND BUSINESS MILEAGE

From _____ 19 __ **to** _____ 19 __

	Sunday		Monday		Tuesday		Wednesday		Thursday		Friday		Saturday		Total	
Travel Expenses:																
Airlines	$		$		$		$		$		$		$		$	
Bus—Train																
Cab																
Tips																
Meals and Lodgings:														**Total**	$	
Include tips Breakfast																
Lunch																
Dinner																
Hotel																
Other Expenses:														**Total**	$	
Postage																
Telephone																
Stationery																
Stenographer																
Sample Room																
Advertising														**Total**	$	
Car Expenses:																
Gas, oil, lube, wash																
Repairs, parts																
Tires, supplies																
Parking fees, tolls																
Leasing or rental costs														**Total**	$	

MILEAGE

	Sunday	Monday	Tuesday	Wednesday	Thursday	Friday	Saturday	
Mileage: End								
Start								
Total								
Business Mileage								

Where:
Business Purpose:

Entertainment

Date	Place	Amount		Guests—Type—Business Purpose
		$		
Total		$		

List all car expenses; allocate business and personal car expenses at the end of the year according to business mileage. See Your Income Tax, ¶2.302. Keep all bills for lodging expenses and other expenses of $25 or more, see Your Income Tax, ¶2.351.

WEEKLY RECORD OF TRAVEL AND ENTERTAINMENT EXPENSES AND BUSINESS MILEAGE

From _____ 19 __ to _____ 19 __

	Sunday		Monday		Tuesday		Wednesday		Thursday		Friday		Saturday		Total	
Travel Expenses: Airlines	$		$		$		$		$		$		$		$	
Bus—Train																
Cab																
Tips																
Meals and Lodgings: Include tips Breakfast														Total	$	
Lunch																
Dinner																
Hotel														Total	$	
Other Expenses: Postage																
Telephone																
Stationery																
Stenographer																
Sample Room																
Advertising														Total	$	
Car Expenses: Gas, oil, lube, wash																
Repairs, parts																
Tires, supplies																
Parking fees, tolls																
Leasing or rental costs														Total	$	

MILEAGE

Mileage: End							
Start							
Total							
Business Mileage							

Where:
Business Purpose:

Entertainment

Date	Place	Amount		Guests—Type—Business Purpose
		$		
Total		$		

List all car expenses; allocate business and personal car expenses at the end of the year according to business mileage. See Your Income Tax, ¶2.302. Keep all bills for lodging expenses and other expenses of $25 or more, see Your Income Tax, ¶2.351.

WEEKLY RECORD OF TRAVEL AND ENTERTAINMENT EXPENSES AND BUSINESS MILEAGE

From _____ 19___ **to** _____ 19___

	Sunday		Monday		Tuesday		Wednesday		Thursday		Friday		Saturday		Total	
Travel Expenses: Airlines	$		$		$		$		$		$		$		$	
Bus—Train																
Cab																
Tips																
Meals and Lodgings: Include tips Breakfast													**Total**		$	
Lunch																
Dinner																
Hotel																
Other Expenses: Postage													**Total**		$	
Telephone																
Stationery																
Stenographer																
Sample Room																
Advertising																
Car Expenses: Gas, oil, lube, wash													**Total**		$	
Repairs, parts																
Tires, supplies																
Parking fees, tolls																
Leasing or rental costs													**Total**		$	

MILEAGE

Mileage: End														
Start														
Total														
Business Mileage														

Where:
Business Purpose:

Entertainment

Date	Place	Amount		Guests—Type—Business Purpose
		$		
Total		$		

List all car expenses; allocate business and personal car expenses at the end of the year according to business mileage. See Your Income Tax, ¶2.302. Keep all bills for lodging expenses and other expenses of $25 or more, see Your Income Tax, ¶2.351.

WEEKLY RECORD OF TRAVEL AND ENTERTAINMENT EXPENSES AND BUSINESS MILEAGE

From _____ 19 __ **to** _____ 19 __

	Sunday		Monday		Tuesday		Wednesday		Thursday		Friday		Saturday		Total	
Travel Expenses: Airlines	$		$		$		$		$		$		$		$	
Bus—Train																
Cab																
Tips																
Meals and Lodgings: Include tips Breakfast															Total	$
Lunch																
Dinner																
Hotel																
Other Expenses: Postage															Total	$
Telephone																
Stationery																
Stenographer																
Sample Room																
Advertising																
Car Expenses: Gas, oil, lube, wash															Total	$
Repairs, parts																
Tires, supplies																
Parking fees, tolls																
Leasing or rental costs															Total	$

MILEAGE

Mileage: End							
Start							
Total							
Business Mileage							

Where:
Business Purpose:

Entertainment

Date	Place	Amount		Guests—Type—Business Purpose
		$		
Total		$		

List all car expenses; allocate business and personal car expenses at the end of the year according to business mileage. See Your Income Tax, ¶2.302. Keep all bills for lodging expenses and other expenses of $25 or more, see Your Income Tax, ¶2.351.

WEEKLY RECORD OF TRAVEL AND ENTERTAINMENT EXPENSES AND BUSINESS MILEAGE

From _____ 19___ **to** _____ 19___

	Sunday		Monday		Tuesday		Wednesday		Thursday		Friday		Saturday		Total	
Travel Expenses:																
Airlines	$		$		$		$		$		$		$		$	
Bus—Train																
Cab																
Tips																
Meals and Lodgings: Include tips													**Total**		$	
Breakfast																
Lunch																
Dinner																
Hotel																
Other Expenses:													**Total**		$	
Postage																
Telephone																
Stationery																
Stenographer																
Sample Room																
Advertising																
Car Expenses:													**Total**		$	
Gas, oil, lube, wash																
Repairs, parts																
Tires, supplies																
Parking fees, tolls																
Leasing or rental costs																

MILEAGE

Total $

Mileage: End								
Start								
Total								
Business Mileage								

Where:

Business Purpose:

Entertainment

Date	Place	Amount		Guests—Type—Business Purpose
		$		
Total		$		

List all car expenses; allocate business and personal car expenses at the end of the year according to business mileage. See Your Income Tax, ¶2.302. Keep all bills for lodging expenses and other expenses of $25 or more, see Your Income Tax, ¶2.351.

WEEKLY RECORD OF TRAVEL AND ENTERTAINMENT EXPENSES AND BUSINESS MILEAGE

From _____ 19 __ to _____ 19 __

	Sunday		Monday		Tuesday		Wednesday		Thursday		Friday		Saturday		Total	
Travel Expenses: Airlines	$		$		$		$		$		$		$		$	
Bus—Train																
Cab																
Tips																
Meals and Lodgings: Include tips Breakfast														Total	$	
Lunch																
Dinner																
Hotel																
Other Expenses: Postage														Total	$	
Telephone																
Stationery																
Stenographer																
Sample Room																
Advertising																
Car Expenses: Gas, oil, lube, wash														Total	$	
Repairs, parts																
Tires, supplies																
Parking fees, tolls																
Leasing or rental costs														Total	$	

MILEAGE

Mileage: End							
Start							
Total							
Business Mileage							

Where:
Business Purpose:

Entertainment

Date	Place	Amount		Guests—Type—Business Purpose
		$		
Total		$		

List all car expenses; allocate business and personal car expenses at the end of the year according to business mileage. See Your Income Tax, ¶2.302. Keep all bills for lodging expenses and other expenses of $25 or more, see Your Income Tax, ¶2.351.

WEEKLY RECORD OF TRAVEL AND ENTERTAINMENT EXPENSES AND BUSINESS MILEAGE

From _____ 19__ to _____ 19__

	Sunday		Monday		Tuesday		Wednesday		Thursday		Friday		Saturday		Total	
Travel Expenses: Airlines	$		$		$		$		$		$		$		$	
Bus—Train																
Cab																
Tips																

	Sunday		Monday		Tuesday		Wednesday		Thursday		Friday		Saturday			Total	
Meals and Lodgings: Include tips Breakfast																	$
Lunch																	
Dinner																	
Hotel																	

	Sunday		Monday		Tuesday		Wednesday		Thursday		Friday		Saturday			Total	
Other Expenses: Postage																	$
Telephone																	
Stationery																	
Stenographer																	
Sample Room																	
Advertising																	

	Sunday		Monday		Tuesday		Wednesday		Thursday		Friday		Saturday			Total	
Car Expenses: Gas, oil, lube, wash																	$
Repairs, parts																	
Tires, supplies																	
Parking fees, tolls																	
Leasing or rental costs																	

MILEAGE

Total $

	Sunday	Monday	Tuesday	Wednesday	Thursday	Friday	Saturday	
Mileage: End								
Start								
Total								
Business Mileage								

Where:

Business Purpose:

Entertainment

Date	Place	Amount	Guests—Type—Business Purpose
		$	
Total		$	

List all car expenses; allocate business and personal car expenses at the end of the year according to business mileage. See Your Income Tax, ¶2.302. Keep all bills for lodging expenses and other expenses of $25 or more, see Your Income Tax, ¶2.351.

WEEKLY RECORD OF TRAVEL AND ENTERTAINMENT EXPENSES AND BUSINESS MILEAGE

From _____ 19__ to _____ 19__

	Sunday		Monday		Tuesday		Wednesday		Thursday		Friday		Saturday		Total	
Travel Expenses: Airlines	$		$		$		$		$		$		$		$	
Bus—Train																
Cab																
Tips																

														Total	$
Meals and Lodgings: Include tips Breakfast															
Lunch															
Dinner															
Hotel															

Total $

| **Other Expenses:** Postage |
| Telephone |
| Stationery |
| Stenographer |
| Sample Room |
| Advertising |

Total $

| **Car Expenses:** Gas, oil, lube, wash |
| Repairs, parts |
| Tires, supplies |
| Parking fees, tolls |
| Leasing or rental costs |

Total $

MILEAGE

Mileage: End								
Start								
Total								
Business Mileage								

Where:
Business Purpose:

Entertainment

Date	Place	Amount		Guests—Type—Business Purpose
		$		
Total		$		

List all car expenses; allocate business and personal car expenses at the end of the year according to business mileage. See Your Income Tax, ¶2.302. Keep all bills for lodging expenses and other expenses of $25 or more, see Your Income Tax, ¶2.351.

WEEKLY RECORD OF TRAVEL AND ENTERTAINMENT EXPENSES AND BUSINESS MILEAGE

From _____ 19__ to _____ 19__

	Sunday		Monday		Tuesday		Wednesday		Thursday		Friday		Saturday		Total	
Travel Expenses: Airlines	$		$		$		$		$		$		$		$	
Bus—Train																
Cab																
Tips																

															Total	$	
Meals and Lodgings: Include tips Breakfast																	
Lunch																	
Dinner																	
Hotel																	

															Total	$	
Other Expenses: Postage																	
Telephone																	
Stationery																	
Stenographer																	
Sample Room																	
Advertising																	

															Total	$	
Car Expenses: Gas, oil, lube, wash																	
Repairs, parts																	
Tires, supplies																	
Parking fees, tolls																	
Leasing or rental costs																	

Total $

MILEAGE

Mileage: End														
Start														
Total														
Business Mileage														

Where:
Business Purpose:

Entertainment

Date	Place	Amount		Guests—Type—Business Purpose
		$		
Total		$		

List all car expenses; allocate business and personal car expenses at the end of the year according to business mileage. See Your Income Tax, ¶2.302. Keep all bills for lodging expenses and other expenses of $25 or more, see Your Income Tax, ¶2.351.

112

WEEKLY RECORD OF TRAVEL AND ENTERTAINMENT EXPENSES AND BUSINESS MILEAGE

From _____ 19__ to _____ 19__

	Sunday		Monday		Tuesday		Wednesday		Thursday		Friday		Saturday		Total	
Travel Expenses: Airlines	$		$		$		$		$		$		$		$	
Bus—Train																
Cab																
Tips																
														Total	$	
Meals and Lodgings: Include tips Breakfast																
Lunch																
Dinner																
Hotel																
														Total	$	
Other Expenses: Postage																
Telephone																
Stationery																
Stenographer																
Sample Room																
Advertising																
														Total	$	
Car Expenses: Gas, oil, lube, wash																
Repairs, parts																
Tires, supplies																
Parking fees, tolls																
Leasing or rental costs																
														Total	$	

MILEAGE

Mileage: End							
Start							
Total							
Business Mileage							

Where:
Business Purpose:

Entertainment

Date	Place	Amount	Guests—Type—Business Purpose
		$	
Total		$	

List all car expenses; allocate business and personal car expenses at the end of the year according to business mileage. See Your Income Tax, ¶2.302. Keep all bills for lodging expenses and other expenses of $25 or more, see Your Income Tax, ¶2.351.

WEEKLY RECORD OF TRAVEL AND ENTERTAINMENT EXPENSES AND BUSINESS MILEAGE

From _____ 19__ to _____ 19__

	Sunday		Monday		Tuesday		Wednesday		Thursday		Friday		Saturday		Total	
Travel Expenses:																
Airlines	$		$		$		$		$		$		$		$	
Bus—Train																
Cab																
Tips																
Meals and Lodgings:														Total	$	
Include tips Breakfast																
Lunch																
Dinner																
Hotel																
Other Expenses:														Total	$	
Postage																
Telephone																
Stationery																
Stenographer																
Sample Room																
Advertising																
Car Expenses:														Total	$	
Gas, oil, lube, wash																
Repairs, parts																
Tires, supplies																
Parking fees, tolls																
Leasing or rental costs																

MILEAGE

Total $

Mileage: End														
Start														
Total														
Business Mileage														

Where:

Business Purpose:

Entertainment

Date	Place	Amount	Guests—Type—Business Purpose
		$	
		Total $	

List all car expenses; allocate business and personal car expenses at the end of the year according to business mileage. See Your Income Tax, ¶2.302. Keep all bills for lodging expenses and other expenses of $25 or more, see Your Income Tax, ¶2.351.

WEEKLY RECORD OF TRAVEL AND ENTERTAINMENT EXPENSES AND BUSINESS MILEAGE

From _____ 19 __ to _____ 19 __

	Sunday		Monday		Tuesday		Wednesday		Thursday		Friday		Saturday		Total	
Travel Expenses: Airlines	$		$		$		$		$		$		$		$	
Bus—Train																
Cab																
Tips																

Meals and Lodgings: Total $

	Sunday		Monday		Tuesday		Wednesday		Thursday		Friday		Saturday		Total	
Include tips Breakfast																
Lunch																
Dinner																
Hotel																

Total $

Other Expenses: Postage																
Telephone																
Stationery																
Stenographer																
Sample Room																
Advertising																

Total $

Car Expenses: Gas, oil, lube, wash																
Repairs, parts																
Tires, supplies																
Parking fees, tolls																
Leasing or rental costs																

Total $

MILEAGE

Mileage: End							
Start							
Total							
Business Mileage							

Where:
Business Purpose:

Entertainment

Date	Place	Amount	Guests—Type—Business Purpose
		$	
Total		$	

List all car expenses; allocate business and personal car expenses at the end of the year according to business mileage. See Your Income Tax, ¶2.302. Keep all bills for lodging expenses and other expenses of $25 or more, see Your Income Tax, ¶2.351.

WEEKLY RECORD OF TRAVEL AND ENTERTAINMENT EXPENSES AND BUSINESS MILEAGE

From _____ 19___ to _____ 19___

	Sunday		Monday		Tuesday		Wednesday		Thursday		Friday		Saturday		Total	
Travel Expenses: Airlines	$		$		$		$		$		$		$		$	
Bus—Train																
Cab																
Tips																
Meals and Lodgings: Include tips Breakfast													**Total**	$		
Lunch																
Dinner																
Hotel																
Other Expenses: Postage													**Total**	$		
Telephone																
Stationery																
Stenographer																
Sample Room																
Advertising																
Car Expenses: Gas, oil, lube, wash													**Total**	$		
Repairs, parts																
Tires, supplies																
Parking fees, tolls																
Leasing or rental costs																
													Total	$		

MILEAGE

Mileage: End								
Start								
Total								
Business Mileage								

Where:

Business Purpose:

Entertainment

Date	Place	Amount		Guests—Type—Business Purpose
		$		
Total		$		

List all car expenses; allocate business and personal car expenses at the end of the year according to business mileage. See Your Income Tax, ¶2.302. Keep all bills for lodging expenses and other expenses of $25 or more, see Your Income Tax, ¶2.351.

116

WEEKLY RECORD OF TRAVEL AND ENTERTAINMENT EXPENSES AND BUSINESS MILEAGE

From _____ 19 __ to _____ 19 __

	Sunday		Monday		Tuesday		Wednesday		Thursday		Friday		Saturday		Total	
Travel Expenses: Airlines	$		$		$		$		$		$		$		$	
Bus—Train																
Cab																
Tips																
Meals and Lodgings: Include tips Breakfast																
Lunch																
Dinner																
Hotel													Total		$	
Other Expenses: Postage																
Telephone																
Stationery																
Stenographer																
Sample Room																
Advertising													Total		$	
Car Expenses: Gas, oil, lube, wash																
Repairs, parts																
Tires, supplies																
Parking fees, tolls																
Leasing or rental costs													Total		$	

MILEAGE

Mileage: End														
Start														
Total														
Business Mileage														

Where:
Business Purpose:

Entertainment

Date	Place	Amount		Guests—Type—Business Purpose
		$		
Total		$		

List all car expenses; allocate business and personal car expenses at the end of the year according to business mileage. See Your Income Tax, ¶2.302. Keep all bills for lodging expenses and other expenses of $25 or more, see Your Income Tax, ¶2.351.

WEEKLY RECORD OF TRAVEL AND ENTERTAINMENT EXPENSES AND BUSINESS MILEAGE

From _____ 19___ to _____ 19___

	Sunday	Monday	Tuesday	Wednesday	Thursday	Friday	Saturday	Total
Travel Expenses: Airlines	$	$	$	$	$	$	$	$
Bus—Train								
Cab								
Tips								
Meals and Lodgings: Include tips Breakfast								Total $
Lunch								
Dinner								
Hotel								
Other Expenses: Postage								Total $
Telephone								
Stationery								
Stenographer								
Sample Room								
Advertising								
Car Expenses: Gas, oil, lube, wash								Total $
Repairs, parts								
Tires, supplies								
Parking fees, tolls								
Leasing or rental costs								Total $

MILEAGE

Mileage: End								
Start								
Total								
Business Mileage								

Where:

Business Purpose:

Entertainment

Date	Place	Amount	Guests—Type—Business Purpose
		$	
Total		$	

List all car expenses; allocate business and personal car expenses at the end of the year according to business mileage. See Your Income Tax, ¶2.302. Keep all bills for lodging expenses and other expenses of $25 or more, see Your Income Tax, ¶2.351.

WEEKLY RECORD OF TRAVEL AND ENTERTAINMENT EXPENSES AND BUSINESS MILEAGE

From _____ 19 __ to _____ 19 __

	Sunday		Monday		Tuesday		Wednesday		Thursday		Friday		Saturday		Total	
Travel Expenses: Airlines	$		$		$		$		$		$		$		$	
Bus—Train																
Cab																
Tips																
Meals and Lodgings: Include tips Breakfast														Total	$	
Lunch																
Dinner																
Hotel																
Other Expenses: Postage														Total	$	
Telephone																
Stationery																
Stenographer																
Sample Room																
Advertising																
Car Expenses: Gas, oil, lube, wash														Total	$	
Repairs, parts																
Tires, supplies																
Parking fees, tolls																
Leasing or rental costs														Total	$	

MILEAGE

Mileage: End							
Start							
Total							
Business Mileage							

Where:
Business Purpose:

Entertainment

Date	Place	Amount		Guests—Type—Business Purpose
		$		
	Total	$		

List all car expenses; allocate business and personal car expenses at the end of the year according to business mileage. See Your Income Tax, ¶2.302. Keep all bills for lodging expenses and other expenses of $25 or more, see Your Income Tax, ¶2.351.

SUMMARY OF T&E EXPENSES AND BUSINESS MILEAGE

Date	Travel Expenses		Meals and Lodging		Enter-tainment		Other Expenses		Car Expenses		Miles Total	Miles Busin.
	$		$		$		$		$			
Total	$		$		$		$		$			

SUMMARY OF T&E EXPENSES AND BUSINESS MILEAGE

Date	Travel Expenses		Meals and Lodging		Enter-tainment		Other Expenses		Car Expenses		Miles	
											Total	Busin.
	$		$		$		$		$			
Total	$		$		$		$		$			

Date	Explanation	Travel Expenses		Meals and Lodging		Entertainment		Other Expenses		Car Expenses	
		$		$		$		$		$	
Total		$		$		$		$		$	

122

Date	Explanation	Travel Expenses		Meals and Lodging		Entertainment		Other Expenses		Car Expenses	
		$		$		$		$		$	
Total		$		$		$		$		$	

SUMMARY OF T&E EXPENSES AND REIMBURSEMENTS

	Travel Expenses		Meals and Lodging		Enter-tainment		Other Expenses		Car Expenses	
Total Expenses	$		$		$		$		$	
Total Reimbursements										
Net Expenses	$		$		$		$		$	

TAX RECORDS AND WORK SHEETS FOR PREPARING YOUR TAX RETURN

In this section of YOUR INCOME TAX RECORD BOOK are forms to help you organize your tax data for preparing your tax return. Some of the information will come from your checks; others from information returns, dividend report letters, brokers' statements, mortgage statements, and paid bills.

Keeping accurate tax records throughout the year will pay dividends when you prepare your return. With complete records, you will overlook no tax-saving opportunity. Your records will be in one convenient place—no last-minute frenzied search for your tax data. AND, you will prepare your return with maximum ease, minimum strain—saving yourself TIME, TROUBLE, AND MONEY.

WORKSHEET FOR DETERMINING SUPPORT

To claim an exemption for a dependent child, relative or household member, you must generally provide at least 50% of their support. Use this form to determine whether you meet the 50% support test. Other tests for claiming an exemption are at ¶1.50 of YOUR INCOME TAX.

Dependent's Income	1) Did the dependent receive any income, such as wages, interest, dividends, pensions, rents, social security, or welfare? (If yes, complete lines 2, 3, 4 and 5)	☐ Yes ☐ No	
	2) Total income received by dependent	$	
	3) Amount of dependent's income used for his or her support	$	
	4) Amount of dependent's income used for other purposes	$	
	5) Amount of dependent's income saved	$	
	(The total of lines, 3, 4, and 5 should equal line 2)		
Expenses for Entire Household (where dependent lived)	6) Lodging (Complete item a or b)		
	a) Rent paid	$	
	b) If not rented, show fair rental value of home. If dependent owns home, include this amount in line 20.	$	
	7) Food	$	
	8) Utilities (heat, light, water, etc. not included in line 6a or 6b)	$	
	9) Repairs (not included in line 6a or 6b)	$	
	10) Other. Do not include expenses of maintaining home, such as mortgage interest, real estate taxes, and insurance.	$	
	11) Total household expenses (Add lines 6 through 10)	$	
	12) Number of persons, including dependent, living in household		
Expenses for Dependent Only	13) Dependent's part of household expenses (line 11 divided by line 12)	$	
	14) Clothing	$	
	15) Education	$	
	16) Medical, dental	$	
	17) Travel, recreation	$	
	18) Other (specify)	$	
	19) Total cost of dependent's support for the year (Add lines 13 through 18)	$	
	20) Amount dependent provided for own support (line 3, plus line 6b if dependent owns home)	$	
	21) Amount others provided for dependent's support. Include amounts provided by state, local, and other welfare societies or agencies.	$	
	22) Amount you provided for dependent's support (line 19 minus lines 20 and 21)	$	
	23) 50% of line 19	$	

If line 22 is more than line 23, you meet the support test for the dependent. If the other dependency tests are met, you may claim an exemption for that person.

If line 23 is more than line 22, you may be able to claim an exemption for the dependent under a multiple support agreement. See ¶1.553 of YOUR INCOME TAX.

126

SALARY OR WAGE INCOME FROM FORM W-2 STATEMENTS

You should receive a W-2 from each employer for whom you worked showing your wages and the amount of income and Social Security (F.I.C.A.) taxes withheld. Record the withholdings shown on your W-2 on this page. Also record amounts withheld for other items such as medical insurance, etc.

Enter the total state and city income taxes withheld in the work sheet for deductible taxes on page 145. Enter the amount withheld for medical insurance in the work sheet for medical and dental expenses on page 142. Also keep records of other tax deductible items withheld from your pay such as union dues and contributions to a company SEP plan.

NAME OF EMPLOYER	ADDRESS	TOTAL WAGES	F.I.C.A.	FEDERAL TAX	STATE TAX	CITY TAX	MEDICAL INSURANCE	OTHER DEDUCTIONS
HUSBAND		$	$	$	$	$	$	$
TOTAL FOR HUSBAND		$	$	$	$	$	$	$
WIFE		$	$	$	$	$	$	$
TOTAL FOR WIFE		$	$	$	$	$	$	$
TOTAL WAGE INCOME		$	$	$	$	$	$	$

127

DIVIDEND INCOME

Generally, companies paying dividends, pay quarterly. Use this record to keep track of your dividend income. Dividends of $10.00 or more paid to you during the year are reported to the Treasury by the company on an information return. You also receive a copy of the information return, Form 1099-DIV. Check the amount reported with your own dividend records, and correct any discrepancy. Keep the information returns with your tax records. Do not attach them to your tax return.

NUMBER OF SHARES	NAME OF COMPANY	DIVIDEND RATE	1ST QUARTER	2ND QUARTER	3RD QUARTER	4TH QUARTER	TOTAL
			$	$	$	$	$
					TOTAL	$	

MUTUAL FUND DIVIDENDS

Depending on your arrangement with the fund, you receive either a dividend check or are notified of the amount reinvested in the fund and the number of additional shares purchased by the reinvested dividend. Whether received by you or reinvested in the fund, you must report the mutual fund dividend on your tax return. The mutual fund will advise you on Form 1099-DIV (or a similar written notice) how to report the dividend and give you a breakdown of the gross dividend showing the amount of dividend qualifying for the exclusion, the amount not qualifying for the exclusion, capital gain dividend, and nontaxable distribution (see ¶3.03 of YOUR INCOME TAX).

You report the capital gain dividend as a long-term capital gain on your return, regardless of how long you have held your mutual fund shares.

NAME OF MUTUAL FUND	TOTAL DIVIDENDS		QUALIFYING DIVIDENDS		NONQUALIFYING DIVIDENDS		CAPITAL GAIN DIVIDENDS		NONTAXABLE DIVIDENDS	
	$		$		$		$		$	
TOTAL	$		$		$		$		$	

INTEREST INCOME

By January 31, banks and other payers of interest notify you on an information return, Form 1099-INT, of interest of $10.00 or more paid to you during the year. Keep track of your taxable interest income which includes interest on personal loans, savings bank deposits, earnings from savings and loan associations, credit unions, and bond interest.

It is a good practice to keep a complete record of all your bank accounts in a single place. For this purpose, you can use "RECORD OF BANK ACCOUNTS" on page 158 of YOUR INCOME TAX RECORD BOOK.

PAYER OF INTEREST	ACCOUNT #	AMOUNT	
		$	
	TOTAL	$	

U. S. SAVINGS BONDS

Keep a record of the proceeds you receive when you redeem Series E or EE Savings Bonds. The proceeds represent a return of your cost plus accumulated interest. Unless you made an election to report annually the increase in value of the bonds (see ¶4.08 of YOUR INCOME TAX), you must report the accumulated E Bond or EE Bond interest in the year you cash in the bond.

REGISTERED BONDHOLDER	SERIAL NUMBER	PROCEEDS ON REDEMPTION		COST OF BOND		TAXABLE INTEREST	
		$		$		$	
		TOTAL				$	

BUSINESS OR PROFESSIONAL INCOME

If you have income from a personally-owned business or profession, you should maintain a permanent and complete set of books of account from which you can determine your business income and expenses. The work sheet below is adapted from Schedule C to determine your net profit or loss for tax purposes.

INCOME	1. Gross receipts or sales $_____ Less returns and allowances $_____ Balance	$	
	2. *Less:* Cost of goods sold (Cost of Goods Sold Schedule, line 8)		
	3. Gross Profit		
	4. Other income		
	5.　　　TOTAL income (*add lines 3 and 4*)		
DEDUCTIONS	6. Advertising		
	7. Bad debts from sales or services		
	8. Bank service charges		
	9. Car and truck expenses		
	10. Commissions		
	11. Depletion		
	12. Depreciation (from Form 4562)		
	13. Dues and publications		
	14. Employee benefit programs		
	15. Insurance		
	16. Interest on business indebtedness		
	17. Laundry and cleaning		
	18. Legal and professional services		
	19. Office supplies and postage		
	20. Pension and profit-sharing plans		
	21. Rent on business property		
	22. Repairs		
	23. Supplies (not included in cost of goods sold)		
	24. Taxes (but not Windfall Profits tax)		
	25. Travel and entertainment		
	26. Utilities and telephone		
	27. a.　　Wages		
	b.　　Jobs credit		
	c.　　Subtract line 27b from 27a		
	28. Windfall Profit tax withheld		
	29. Other expenses (specify):		
	a.	$	
	b.		
	c.		
	d.		
	e.		
	f.		
	g.		
	h.		
	i.		
	j.		
	k.		
	l.		
	m.		
	n.　　Total other business expenses [*add lines 29(a) through 29(m)*]		
	30. Total deductions (*add lines 6 through 29*)		
	31. Net profit (or loss) (*subtract line 30 from 5*)	$	
COST OF GOODS SOLD SCHEDULE	1. Inventory at beginning of year	$	
	2. Purchases $_____ *Less* cost of items withdrawn for personal use $_____ Balance		
	3. Cost of labor (*do not include salary paid to yourself*)		
	4. Materials and supplies		
	5. Other costs		
	6. Total of lines 1 through 5		
	7. *Less:* Inventory at end of year		
	8. Cost of goods sold	$	

Stocks and Bonds

Use the work sheet below for keeping track of your security transactions. For sales and exchanges of property other than stocks, bonds, and your personal residence, use the work sheet on page 134. On your return, you report sales of stocks, bonds, and similar investments, and the sale of a residence on Schedule D.

NUMBER OF SHARES OR BONDS	DESCRIPTION	SOLD		BOUGHT		SHORT-TERM GAIN (LOSS)	LONG-TERM GAIN (LOSS)
		DATE	SALES PRICE*	DATE	COST**		
			$		$	$	$
					TOTAL	$	$

*Excluding state transfer tax, if any, which is claimed as itemized deduction.
**Including commissions. For bonds, add to cost basis amount of bond discount reported as interest (¶ 6.031 of YOUR INCOME TAX); deduct bond premium amortization from cost basis (see ¶ 4.031 of YOUR INCOME TAX).

SALES AND EXCHANGES OF PROPERTY

(Other than Stocks, Bonds, and Personal Residence)

Use the work sheet below for keeping records of your sales of property other than stocks, bonds, or your personal residence. A guide for figuring your profit or loss is on page 135. On your tax return, you report on Form 4797 sales and exchanges of the following: Property used in a trade or business, real estate (other than a personal residence), and property subject to the depreciation recapture rules (see ¶5.45 of YOUR INCOME TAX).

SHORT-TERM OR LONG-TERM	DESCRIPTION OF PROPERTY	1. DATE ACQUIRED	2. DATE SOLD	3. SALES PRICE	4. DEPRECIA-TION	5. COST (OR OTHER BASIS)	6. IMPROVE-MENTS	7. SELLING EXPENSES	GAIN OR LOSS 3 plus 4 less 5, 6, and 7	
									GAIN	LOSS
				$	$	$	$	$	$	$
TOTAL									$	$

SALES OF PROPERTY—GUIDE TO FIGURING PROFIT OR LOSS

1. Selling price (¶6.07, ¶6.08 of YOUR INCOME TAX) $_____
2. Deduct selling expenses (¶6.07, ¶6.08 of YOUR INCOME TAX)   _____
3. Amount realized (line 1 less line 2)   _____
4. Cost or unadjusted basis of property (¶6.09 and ¶6.10 of
   YOUR INCOME TAX) $_____
5. Add improvements, purchase commissions (¶6.12 of
   YOUR INCOME TAX)   _____
6. Deduct depreciation, losses (¶6.12 of YOUR INCOME TAX)   _____
7. Adjusted basis (line 4 plus line 5 less line 6)   _____
8. Net profit (or loss) (line 3 less line 7) $_____

When filing Schedule D, follow the IRS instructions; the form may differ from the above guide by requiring you to include selling expenses as part of your basis instead of as a reduction from the sales price. The net profit or loss is the same whichever method is used.

GUIDE TO FIGURING GAIN ON SALE OF RESIDENCE AND BASIS OF NEW HOME

You may defer tax on some or all of the gain from the sale of your residence by buying or building a new home within two years. Use the following guide to figure your taxable gain and basis for the new home.

Gain on sale

1. Selling price of residence $_____
2. Selling expenses   _____
3. Amount realized (line 1 less line 2)   _____
4. Adjusted basis of residence (including improvements)   _____
5. Gain realized on sale (line 3 less line 4) $_____

Taxable gain

6. Amount realized (line 3 above) $_____
7. Less fix-up expenses   _____
8. Adjusted sales price (line 6 less line 7)   _____
9. Less cost of new home   _____
10. Taxable gain (line 8 less line 9) $_____

Basis of new home

11. Cost of new home (line 9 above) $_____
12. Less gain not taxed (line 5 less line 10)   _____
13. Basis of new home (line 11 less line 12) $_____

PENSION AND ANNUITY INCOME

How you report your pension or annuity income on your tax return depends upon the kind of pension or annuity you have and whether or not you have a cost investment in the contract. Where you have a cost investment in a pension or annuity contract, your payments consist of two parts: (1) A return of your cost, which is tax free, and (2) income on your investment, which is taxable (see ¶7.07 of YOUR INCOME TAX). There is a special rule for reporting certain employee annuities where the employee's contribution will be recovered within a three-year period (see ¶7.09 of YOUR INCOME TAX). If you did not contribute to the cost of your annuity or pension (and you paid no tax on your employer's contribution), your payments are fully taxable.

Keep a record of your pension and annuity payments in the schedule below. Check these totals against the amount shown on Form W-2P which will be sent to you by the payer.

MONTH	POLICY (IDENTIFY)		POLICY (IDENTIFY)		POLICY (IDENTIFY)	
January	$		$		$	
February						
March						
April						
May						
June						
July						
August						
September						
October						
November						
December						
TOTAL	$		$		$	

WITHHOLDINGS

Taxes will be withheld from your pension unless you elect to avoid withholding on a Form W-4 which you file with the payer (see ¶25.09 of YOUR INCOME TAX). Any withholdings will be shown on Form W-2P which you will receive from the payer. Record the amount withheld on the line below.

Federal Tax Withheld, if any—Form W-2P

POLICY   POLICY   POLICY

$_____ $_____ $_____

RENTAL INCOME

You report rental income in the rental schedule of your return. If you rent out part of your house, deduct the share of expenses allocated to the rent-producing part of the house as a rental expense. The mortgage interest and taxes allocated to your personal use of the house are deductible as excess itemized deductions. A work sheet for allocating rental expenses appears on the next page.

MONTH	PROPERTY (IDENTIFY)		PROPERTY (IDENTIFY)		PROPERTY (IDENTIFY)		PROPERTY (IDENTIFY)	
January	$		$		$		$	
February								
March								
April								
May								
June								
July								
August								
September								
October								
November								
December								
TOTAL	$		$		$		$	

EXPENSE WORK SHEET FOR RENTAL PROPERTY

The form below is for listing expenses of rental property. The first two columns are for rental property where part of the property is used for your personal use. These two columns allow you to earmark and allocate deductible expenses. The other columns are for deductible expenses of rental property, no part of which is personally used by you.

	IF YOU USE PART OF PROPERTY		FULLY RENTED (NO PERSONAL USE)				
ITEM	(a) EXPENSES OF ENTIRE PROPERTY TO BE ALLOCATED	(b) SPECIFIC EXPENSES OF RENTAL AREA	PROPERTY (IDENTIFY)	PROPERTY (IDENTIFY)	PROPERTY (IDENTIFY)	PROPERTY (IDENTIFY)	PROPERTY (IDENTIFY)
Repairs:	$	$	$	$	$	$	$
Plumbing							
Electric							
Painting							
Roofing							
Carpentry							
Other							
Total	$	$	$	$	$	$	$

Allocate to column (b) _____ % of column (a)

Deductible Repairs

Other Expenses:	$	$	$	$	$	$	$
Heat							
Utilities							
Interest*							
Water							
Taxes*							
Insurance							
Cleaning and maintenance							
Gardening							
Professional fees							
Other							
Total	$	$	$	$	$	$	$

Allocate to column (b) _____ % of column (a)

Other Deductible Expenses

* The interest and taxes not allocated to the rental area may be claimed as itemized deductions.

DEPRECIATION TAX RECORD OF RENTAL PROPERTY

DESCRIPTION OF PROPERTY	DATE ACQUIRED	COST OR OTHER BASIS	DEPRECIATION ALLOWED OR ALLOWABLE IN PRIOR YEARS	METHOD OF COMPUTING DEPRECIATION	LIFE OR RATE	DEPRECIATION FOR THIS YEAR
		$	$			$
					TOTAL	$

Use the following work sheet to figure cost basis of property subject to depreciation:

ITEM	PROPERTY (IDENTIFY)		PROPERTY (IDENTIFY)		PROPERTY IDENTIFY		PROPERTY IDENTIFY		PROPERTY (IDENTIFY)	
1. Cost of property	$		$		$		$		$	
2. *Less:* Land										
3. Attributed to building										
4. *Less:* Personal use___% of line 3										
5. Cost subject to depreciation	$		$		$		$		$	

Where a residence is converted to rental you may use this guide to figure cost:

1. Original cost of building (including improvements)	$	
2. Fair market value at date of conversion to rental		
3. Basis subject to depreciation: Lower of line 1 or 2 (See ¶29.41 of YOUR INCOME TAX)	$	

INCOME FROM PARTNERSHIPS, CORPORATIONS, ESTATES, AND TRUSTS

Use the work sheet below to keep track of your income from partnerships, S Corporations, estates, and trusts.

TYPE OF INCOME	NAME AND ADDRESS OF PAYER	EMPLOYER IDENTIFICA-TION NUMBER	AMOUNT	
PARTNERSHIP INCOME			$	
S CORPORATION				
ESTATE INCOME				
TRUST INCOME				
	TOTAL		$	

ALIMONY

If you pay alimony to a divorced or separated spouse, your payments are deductible. If you receive alimony, the payments are taxable. Read ¶20.00 of YOUR INCOME TAX to determine whether or not your payments are deductible or your receipt of alimony is taxable. If it is deductible or taxable, keep a record of the payments in the following work sheet.

DATE	PAYMENT	AMOUNT	
		$	
		TOTAL	$

MEDICAL AND DENTAL EXPENSE WORK SHEET

A check list of deductible medical costs is at ¶17.01 of YOUR INCOME TAX. Keep track of your auto mileage on trips for medical care, and do not overlook medical insurance premiums deducted from your wages (work sheet on page 127).

ITEM	AMOUNT
1. Medical insurance premiums	
Withheld by employer _____	$
Other _____	
TOTAL _____	$
2. Medicines and drugs	
_____	$
_____	
_____	
_____	
_____	
_____	
_____	
TOTAL _____	$
3. Payments to physicians	
_____	$
_____	
_____	
_____	
TOTAL _____	$
4. Payments to dentists	
_____	$
_____	
_____	
_____	
TOTAL _____	$

ITEM	AMOUNT

5. Hospital costs

$ ____

_____

_____

_____

_____

TOTAL _____ $ ____

6. Other medical costs (identify)

$ ____

_____

_____

_____

_____

_____

_____

TOTAL _____ $ ____

7. Transportation for medical care

Number of miles _____ × .09* _____ $ ____

Parking fees _____

Tolls _____

Other travel costs _____

_____

TOTAL _____ $ ____

8. Reimbursements of medical costs

$ ____

_____

_____

_____

_____

TOTAL _____ $ ____

*Rate when this book went to press

143

WORK SHEETS FOR DEDUCTIBLE TAXES

The following sources will provide the information for the work sheets:

Wage income record and W-2 forms, for state & local income taxes deducted from your salary. See page 127.

Your checks for income taxes, personal property taxes, and real estate taxes.

Mortgage statement, for real estate taxes if your monthly payments to bank include tax.

Advice from cooperative or condominium of your share of real estate taxes.

Tax bills and receipts.

Sales confirmation notices from stockbrokers for state transfer taxes.

Sales slips for sales taxes.

Supplement to YOUR INCOME TAX for Treasury state sales tax tables.

Refer to the guide to deducting taxes at ¶16.001 of YOUR INCOME TAX.

There are also references in the work sheets to specific paragraphs and check lists in YOUR INCOME TAX.

WORK SHEET FOR DEDUCTIBLE INCOME TAXES

ITEM	AMOUNT

State income taxes

(YOUR INCOME TAX ¶16.01, ¶16.12)

ESTIMATED TAX PAYMENTS

INSTALLMENT	DATE	AMOUNT	
		$	

TOTAL ESTIMATED TAX PAID IN YEAR _____ $

TAX PAID ON FILING TAX RETURN _____

TAX WITHHELD FROM YOUR PAY (*INCLUDE SPOUSE'S WITHHOLDING ON JOINT RETURN*) _____

TOTAL STATE INCOME TAX PAID IN YEAR _____ $

City income taxes

(YOUR INCOME TAX ¶16.01)

ESTIMATED TAX PAYMENTS

INSTALLMENT	DATE	AMOUNT	
		$	

TOTAL ESTIMATED TAX PAID IN YEAR _____ $

TAX PAID ON FILING TAX RETURN _____

TAX WITHHELD FROM YOUR PAY (*INCLUDE SPOUSE'S WITHHOLDING ON JOINT RETURN*) _____

TOTAL CITY INCOME TAX PAID IN YEAR _____ $

WORK SHEET FOR OTHER DEDUCTIBLE TAXES

ITEM	AMOUNT
Personal property taxes (YOUR INCOME TAX ¶16.001)	$
TOTAL	$
Real estate taxes (YOUR INCOME TAX ¶16.05, ¶16.07, ¶16.08) City or Town	$
School	
Other	
TOTAL	$
State stock transfer taxes	$
TOTAL	$
Sales taxes (YOUR INCOME TAX ¶16.04, and Supplement) From Treasury Sales Tax Table	$
plus sales tax paid on purchase of auto, boat, airplane, or mobile home	
If you do not use Treasury Tables, enter the total of your sales tax payments	
TOTAL	$

WORK SHEET FOR CASH CHARITABLE CONTRIBUTIONS

See ¶14.00 of YOUR INCOME TAX for a discussion of the charitable contribution deduction. Use this work sheet to keep track of your cash donations. Also keep a record of your auto mileage when using your car for volunteer charity work.

NAME OF ORGANIZATION	AMOUNT	
Place of worship	$	
College, university		
Red Cross		
United Fund, Community Chest		
Girl/Boy Scouts		
March of Dimes		
Xmas/Easter Seals		
Cancer Fund		
Heart Fund		
YM/YWCA		
Salvation Army		
Car expense for charities_____ miles × .09*		
Misc. organized charities		
TOTAL	$	

*Rate for 1984; $.12 for 1985

RECORD OF INTEREST EXPENSES

You can find the information for this work sheet from the following sources: Mortgage statements from bank, contracts, stock brokers' statements, credit card bills, department store bills, and reports from your cooperative indicating your share of mortgage interest. See ¶15.00–¶15.06 of YOUR INCOME TAX for an explanation of the interest expense deduction. References to specific discussions in YOUR INCOME TAX are in the work sheet below.

ITEMS OF INTEREST EXPENSE	TO WHOM PAID	AMOUNT	
Interest on home mortgage		$	
Interest on cooperative apartment			
Charges on revolving charge accounts (¶15.03)			
Charges on credit cards (¶15.03)			
Interest on installment purchases (¶15.03)			
Interest on auto loan			
Margin interest			
Interest on income tax deficiency			
Other interest (specify)			
TOTAL		$	

MISCELLANEOUS DEDUCTIONS WORK SHEET

In the work sheet below is a list of items you may claim as deductions in the miscellaneous deductions section of your return. Here, you may list your miscellaneous deductions; refer to the designated sections of YOUR INCOME TAX for the rules applied to each item.

ITEM	AMOUNT	
Alimony (¶20.001) _____	$	
Union dues (¶19.03) _____		
Entertainment expenses (¶2.36 and ¶19.02) _____		
Educational expenses (¶21.00) _____		
Uniforms and work clothes (¶19.04) _____		
Dues to professional societies (¶19.03 and ¶5.04) _____		
Safe deposit box (¶19.15) _____		
Fees for preparation of tax return and tax advice (¶19.16) _____		
Investment counsel fees and services (¶19.15) _____		
Tax publications (¶19.16) _____		
Business publications (¶5.04) _____		
Professional expenses of salaried professionals (¶5.04) _____		
Employment agency fee (¶19.05) _____		
Home office expenses (¶19.052 and ¶5.10) _____		
_____		
_____		
_____		
_____		
_____		
_____		
_____		
_____		
TOTAL _____	$	

CASUALTY OR THEFT LOSS WORK SHEET

This work sheet based on IRS Form 4684 is for figuring a single casualty or theft loss of property used only for personal purposes. If you suffered more than one casualty or theft during the year, use a separate work sheet for each event entering your figures up to line 9. Then on a separate sheet of paper, total the amount of the losses from line 9 of each worksheet and reduce the total by 10% of adjusted gross income. Deductible casualty and theft losses are discussed at ¶18.01 of YOUR INCOME TAX. A guide on how to prove a casualty loss deduction is at ¶18.02 of YOUR INCOME TAX. References to specific discussions in YOUR INCOME TAX are in the body of the work sheet.

	ITEM		ITEM		ITEM		ITEM	
1. Identify property								
2. Cost or adjusted basis (¶6.12 and ¶18.04)	$		$		$		$	
Decrease in market value: Value before casualty or theft								
Less: Value after casualty or theft								
3. Decrease in value								
4. Loss (lower of line 2 or line 3)								
5. Less: insurance recovery or other compensation								
6. Net loss	$		$		$		$	
7. Total losses shown on line 6								
8. Less: $100 limitation (¶18.042)								
9. Net casualty or theft loss								
10. Less: 10% of your adjusted gross income								
11. Deductible casualty or theft loss (¶18.00 and ¶18.04)							$	

WORK SHEET FOR POLITICAL CAMPAIGN CONTRIBUTIONS

If you make a cash contribution to a political candidate, a campaign committee, political party or political newsletter fund, you may claim a tax credit equal to one-half the contribution, but it may not exceed $50 if you are single or $100 if you are married and file a joint return. See ¶29.60 of YOUR INCOME TAX for a discussion of political contributions. Keep a record of your political campaign contributions in the work sheet below.

DATE	POLITICAL CANDIDATE, CAMPAIGN COMMITTEE, ETC.	AMOUNT OF DONATION	
		$	
	TOTAL	$	

RECORD OF PAYMENTS OF FEDERAL ESTIMATED TAX

(Also see ¶26.00 of YOUR INCOME TAX)

PAYMENT FOR	AMOUNT	
FIRST INSTALLMENT—APRIL 15 (include amount of overpayment credited to estimated tax)	$	
SECOND INSTALLMENT—JUNE 15		
THIRD INSTALLMENT—SEPTEMBER 15		
FOURTH INSTALLMENT—JANUARY 16		
TOTAL PAYMENTS	$	

RECORD OF PAYMENTS OF OTHER ESTIMATED TAXES

PAYMENT FOR	AMOUNT	
FIRST INSTALLMENT	$	
SECOND INSTALLMENT		
THIRD INSTALLMENT		
FOURTH INSTALLMENT		
TOTAL PAYMENTS	$	

PART **IV**

FINANCIAL RECORDS

Managing your family finances requires good records for your review. In this section of YOUR INCOME TAX RECORD BOOK, you will find a work sheet for figuring your net worth, a budget planner, a record of your IRA and bank accounts, and a stock record.

Budget Planner

Money management starts with a budget. It helps you to keep track of the money that comes in and to know where it goes. Use the budget planner on the next page to lay out a full year's picture of your fixed and foreseeable expenses and savings. The totals at the bottom of the page tell you how much cash you will need to meet your expenses each month. Spreading your fixed payments so that each month bears a share of them is wise planning.

ITEMS	JAN.		FEB.		MAR.		APR.		MAY		JUNE	
Taxes Federal	$		$		$		$		$		$	
State												
Real Estate												
School												
Home—Mortgage Payments or Rent												
Insurance Life												
Automobile												
Hospitalization												
Fire												
Debts Auto Loan												
Loans												
Installment Payments												
Savings & Investments Bank												
Government Bonds												
Mutual Funds												
Securities												
Personal Household (food, etc.)												
Clothing												
Transportation												
Tel., Heat, Gas, Electricity, etc.												
Furnishings and Equipment												
Education												
Recreation												
Medical												
Contributions												
TOTAL	$		$		$		$		$		$	

YOUR BUDGET PLANNER FOR PAYMENTS YOU WILL HAVE TO MEET THIS YEAR

JULY		AUG.		SEPT.		OCT.		NOV.		DEC.		TOTAL		LAST YEAR		Next Year Estimate	
$		$		$		$		$		$		$		$		$	
$		$		$		$		$		$		$		$		$	

NET WORTH STATEMENT

In making plans for the future, it is useful to make an annual assessment of your family's financial net worth. It serves as a guide to what is financially possible for you and the family and may help you achieve those goals.

Fill in your NET WORTH STATEMENT using the **Present** or **Opening Value** column. At the end of the year, you will enter your closing values. The last column gives you a detailed analysis of how your net worth increased or decreased during the year.

Your Net Worth and How It Changed for the Year

	PRESENT OR OPENING VALUE		CLOSING VALUE (IN 1 YEAR)		INCREASE OR DECREASE	
YOU OWN **CASH** in checking account	$		$		$	
in savings accounts						
INVESTMENTS (Market Value)						
U.S. bonds						
tax-free bonds						
other bonds						
stocks						
mutual funds						
REAL ESTATE (Market Value)						
home						
investment property						
INSURANCE						
cash surrender value plus dividend accumulations						
OTHER PERSONAL PROPERTY (Market Value)						
automobile						
jewelry						
other						
loans to others (repayment expected)						
pension and retirement funds						
TOTAL YOU OWN	$		$		$	
YOU OWE **UNPAID CURRENT BILLS**	$		$		$	
charge accounts						
credit card accounts						
taxes						
PERSONAL LOANS & INSTALLMENT DEBT						
MORTGAGE (balance)						
OTHER LIABILITIES						
TOTAL YOU OWE						
NET WORTH (Total owned less total owed)	$		$		$	

IRA INVESTMENTS

DESCRIPTION OF ACCOUNT LOCATION	MATURITY DATE	RATE	ACCOUNT BALANCE						
			1st YEAR	2nd YEAR	3rd YEAR	4th YEAR	5th YEAR	6th YEAR	7th YEAR
			$	$	$	$	$	$	$
TOTAL			$	$	$	$	$	$	$

RECORD OF BANK ACCOUNTS

TYPE OF ACCOUNT	BANK AND LOCATION	NAME OF ACCOUNT (INDIVIDUAL, JOINT, TRUST)	DESCRIPTION OF ACCOUNT, TERM OF CERTIFICATE, ETC.	ACCOUNT # OR CERTIFICATE #	INTEREST RATE	AMOUNT
SAVINGS						$
TERM						
CHECKING						
OTHER						

SAFE DEPOSIT BOX			